A
CATHOLIC DICTIONARY
OF
THEOLOGY

Volume Two

Catechism — Heaven

A
CATHOLIC DICTIONARY
OF
THEOLOGY

A WORK PROJECTED WITH THE APPROVAL OF THE CATHOLIC HIERARCHY

OF ENGLAND AND WALES

Volume Two

Catechism — Heaven

NELSON

THOMAS NELSON AND SONS LTD
36 Park Street London W1
P.O. Box 336 Apapa Lagos
P.O. Box 25012 Nairobi
77 Coffee Street San Fernando Trinidad

THOMAS NELSON (AUSTRALIA) LTD
597 Little Collins Street Melbourne

THOMAS NELSON & SONS (SOUTH AFRICA) (PROPRIETARY) LTD
P.O. Box 9881 Johannesburg

THOMAS NELSON AND SONS (CANADA) LTD
81 Curlew Drive Don Mills Ontario

THOMAS NELSON AND SONS
Copewood and Davis Streets Camden 3 N.J.

———

Nihil obstat :

HENRICUS FRANCISCUS DAVIS, DD
AIDANUS WILLIAMS, ABBAS, OSB, STD
IVO THOMAS, OP, STM
JOSEPH HUGO CREHAN, SJ, DD
Censores Deputati

Imprimatur :

PATRITIUS CASEY
Vic. Gen.
Westminasterii, die 15 Februarii 1966

Printed in Great Britain by
Thomas Nelson (Printers) Ltd, London and Edinburgh

Editorial Board

Editors' Preface

When introducing Volume I in 1962 the Editors were able to speak somewhat tentatively about the growing interest in Catholic theology displayed by the English-speaking world. That it would become a shouting-point for popular journalism, as has happened in the interim, was not within their expectations. The work of the Second Vatican Council has arrested popular attention at so many points that the demand for straightforward exposition, on a historical basis, of what Catholics believe is now unprecedented. The results of the Council have been taken into account in what is here presented. It should be borne in mind that the Council itself (in the *notificatio* of 15 November 1965) declared that in view of its pastoral purpose it was to be understood to define only those matters which the Council itself clearly declared to be defined. All other decrees were to be accepted loyally by the faithful, according to the mind of the Council, and this mind was to be gathered from the subject matter or the wording of the decrees, interpreted in the light of traditional theological principles. It will in fact be found that the Council was chary of definition but that it gave new life to many theological ideas which, in one way or another, were used to elucidate its teaching. It will be the task of theology in the years to come to take stock of these new ideas and to draw out their implications. (One might instance the notion of the prophetic office of the Church, employed here in the article FAITHFUL AS A SOURCE OF DOGMA.)

As the Council reached its last session, one of the Editors, Abbot Aidan Williams, died suddenly in Rome. It is with great regret that his three surviving colleagues record this loss and they wish to express to his religious *familia* their condolences and their great appreciation of the work he did on these two volumes.

The position already accorded to the first volume as a standard work of reference in our greater libraries encourages the Editors to think that the hope they expressed in Volume I of being able to forward theological exploration is being fulfilled, and they approach Volumes III and IV with more confidence on that account.

List of Contributors to Volume Two

A. H. A.	ARMSTRONG, Professor A. H.	M. E. H.	HILL, Rev. Edmund, OP
B. C. B.	BUTLER, Right Rev. Abbot Christopher, OSB	L. J.	JOHNSTON, Rev. Leonard
		J. P. K.	KENNY, Rev. J. P., SJ
F. C.	COURTNEY, Rev. Francis, SJ	A. K.	KERRIGAN, Rev. Alexander, OFM
J. H. C.	CREHAN, Rev. J. H., SJ	J. McD.	McDONALD, Rev. Dr Joseph
J. D. C.	CRICHTON, Rev. J. D.	B. McG.	McGUINNESS, B. F., Esq.
G. C.	CULKIN, Rev. Gerard (ob.)	R. A. M.	MARKUS, Dr R. A.
H. F. D.	DAVIS, Very Rev. Mgr. H. F., DD	R. M.	MOLONEY, Rev. Robert, SJ
P. DE L.	DE LETTER, Rev. P., SJ	F. X. M.	MURPHY, Rev. F. X., CSSR
G. S. D.	DOLAN, Rev. G. S., SJ	J. M.	MURRAY, Rev. J., SJ
G. E.	ELLARD, Rev. G., SJ (ob.)	R. P. M.	MURRAY, Rev. Robert, SJ
P. F.	FLANAGAN, Right Rev. Mgr. Philip, DD	P. O'C.	O'CONNELL, Rev. Patrick, SJ
		E. O'C.	O'CONNOR, Rev. Edward, CSC
K. F.	FOSTER, Rev. Kenelm, OP	A. R.	REGAN, Rev. A., CSSR
P. G. F.	FOTHERGILL, Professor P. G.	G. R.	REIDY, Rev. Gabriel, OFM (ob.)
J. G.	GILL, Rev. J., SJ	J. L. R.	RUSSELL, Rev. John, SJ
E. H.	HARDWICK, Rev. Dr E.	E. A. S.	SILLEM, Rev. Dr Edward A. (ob.)
P. F. H.	HARRIS, Rev. Peter	R. F. S.	SMITH, Rev. R. F., SJ
D. J. B. H.	HAWKINS, Very Rev. Canon Denis (ob.)	C. V.	VOLLERT, Rev. Cyril, SJ

The Editors record with regret the obits (noted above) of five valued contributors who died in mid-career before this volume could be completed. May they rest in peace.

Abbreviations

(1) THE BOOKS OF THE BIBLE

Old Testament (OT)

Gen	Deut	1 Kg	1 Par	Neh	Job	Cant	Jer	Dan	Abd	Hab	Mal
Ex	Jos	2 Kg	2 Par	Tob	Ps	Wis	Lam	Os	Jon	Soph	1 Mac
Lev	Jg	3 Kg	1 Esd	Jdt	Prov	Ecclus	Bar	Jl	Mic	Agg	2 Mac
Num	Ru	4 Kg	2 Esd	Est	Eccl	Is	Ez	Am	Nah	Zach	

New Testament (NT)

Mt	Lk	Ac	1 Cor	Gal	Col	1 Tim	Phm	Jas	2 Pet	2 Jn	Jude
Mk	Jn	Rom	2 Cor	Eph	1 Thess	2 Tim	Heb	1 Pet	1 Jn	3 Jn	Apoc
				Phil	2 Thess	Tit					

(2) PATRISTIC QUOTATIONS

Note : Works which do not appear in the following list are given in full the first time they are quoted, and an abbreviated title is given thereafter.

Ambrose	*De Sacramentis*	de. sac.
Clement of Alexandria	*Protrepticus*	Protrep.
	Paedagogus	Paed.
	Stromata	Strom.
Clement of Rome	*epistula prima*	I Clem.
ps–Clement	*epistula secunda*	II Clem.
Epiphanius	*Panarion haeresium*	Haer.
Eusebius	*Historia ecclesiastica*	HE
Hippolytus	*Refutatio haeresium*	Ref. haer.
	Traditio apostolica	Trad. apost.
Ignatius	*epistula ad Ephesios*	Eph.
	— — *Magnesios*	Magn.
	— — *Philadelphenos*	Phil.
	— — *Polycarpum*	Pol.
	— — *Romanos*	Rom.
	— — *Smyrnaeos*	Smyrn.
	— — *Trallenses*	Trall.
Irenaeus	*adversus haereses* (Harvey)	adv. haer. H
Justin	*apologia prima*	apol.
	apologia secunda	append.
	dialogus cum Tryphone	dial.
Origen	*contra Celsum*	c. Cels.
	de principiis	princ.
Tertullian	*adversus Marcionem*	adv. Marc.
	apologeticus	apol.
	de anima	de an.
	de baptismo	de bapt.

Common titles such as *epistula, homilia, sermo, tractatus* may be abbreviated as *ep., hom., serm., tr.*

(3) STANDARD WORKS OF REFERENCE

AAS	*Acta Apostolicae Sedis*
AA.SS	*Acta Sanctorum*
AB	*Analecta Bollandiana*
AER	*American Ecclesiastical Review*
AL	*Archiv für Liturgiewissenschaft*
ASS	*Acta Sanctae Sedis*
Bfr	*Blackfriars*
Bi	*Biblica*
BS	*Biblische Studien*
BZ	*Biblische Zeitschrift*
CAP	Charles, *Apocrypha and Pseudepigrapha*
CBQ	*Catholic Bible Quarterly*
CCL	*Corpus christianorum latinorum*
CCS	*Catholic Commentary on Holy Scripture*
CE	*Catholic Encyclopedia*
CIC	*Codex Iuris canonici*
CR	*Clergy Review*
CSEL	*Corpus Scriptorum Ecclesiasticorum Latinorum*
D	Denzinger-Bannwart, *Encheiridion Symbolorum*
DAC	*Dictionnaire d'Archéologie chrétienne*
DAFC	*Dictionnaire Apologétique de la Foi catholique*
DbR	*Dublin Review*
DBV(S)	*Dictionnaire de la Bible* (Vigouroux) *Supplement*
DCB	*Dictionary of Christian Biography*
DR	*Downside Review*
DSp	*Dictionnaire de Spiritualité* (1935–)
DTC	*Dictionnaire de Théologie catholique*
DV	*Douay Version*
EB	*Encyclopedia Biblica*
EHR	*English Historical Review*
ER	*Études religieuses*
ERE	*Encyclopedia of Religion and Ethics*
ET	*Expository Times*
ETL	*Ephemerides theologicae Lovanienses*
GCS	*Griechischen Christlichen Schriftsteller*
HDB	Hastings' *Dictionary of the Bible*
HJ	*Hibbert Journal*
HL	Hefele-Leclerq, *Histoire des Conciles*
HPR	*Homiletic and Pastoral Review*
HTR	*Harvard Theological Review*
HUCA	*Hebrew Union College Annual*

ICC	*International Critical Commentary*
IER	*Irish Ecclesiastical Record*
ITQ	*Irish Theological Quarterly*
JBL	*Journal of Biblical Literature*
JE	*Jewish Encyclopedia*
JEH	*Journal of Ecclesiastical History*
JRB	*Bulletin of John Rylands Library*
JTS	*Journal of Theological Studies*
Kn	Knox, *New Testament*
KTW	Kittel, *Theologisches Wörterbuch*
LTK	*Lexicon für Theologie und Kirche*
MGH	*Monumenta Germaniae Historica*
MN	*The Month*
Med St	*Medieval Studies* (Toronto)
NRT	*Nouvelle Revue théologique*
OCA	*Orientalia Christiana Analecta*
OCP	*Orientalia Christiana Periodica*
PG	*Patrologia Graeca*, Migne
PL	*Patrologia Latina*, Migne
PO	*Patrologia Orientalis*, Graffin-Nau
PW	Pauly Wissowa, *Real-encyclopädie*
RAC	*Reallexicon für Antike und Christentum*
RAM	*Revue d'Ascétique et de Mystique*
RB	*Revue Biblique*
RBn	*Revue Bénédictine*
RHE	*Revue d'Histoire ecclésiastique*
RSPT	*Revue des Sciences phil. et theol.*
RSR	*Recherches de Science religieuse*
RevSR	*Revue des Sciences religieuses*
RT	*Revue thomiste*
Std	*Studies*, Dublin
TQ	*Theologische Quartalschrift*
TS	*Theological Studies*
T&S	*Texts and Studies*
TU	*Texte und Untersuchungen*
WV	*Westminster Version*
ZKT	*Zeitschrift für katholische Theol.*
ZKG	*Zeitschrift für Kirchengeschichte*
ZNTW	*Zeitschrift für neutestamentliche Wissenschaft*

The *Summa Theologica* of St Thomas is referred to by Arabic numerals for part, question and article; the body of the article being referred to by c, and the answers to objections by @1, @2, @3, e.g. 3a:69:9c; 1–2æ:73:5@2. An asterisk in the Bibliography denotes that the author is not a Catholic.

List of Articles in Volume Two

C

CATECHISM, THEOLOGICAL AUTHORITY OF THE When the printing press had made the multiplication of books easy, it was not long before religious *compendia* of various kinds appeared, and the Council of Trent (Session 24, cap. VII) ordered that a catechism should be prepared as a guide for parish priests in expounding the doctrines of the faith to the people. Bishops were ordered to see that the work when completed was translated into the vernacular and put into use. Three Dominicans, Leonardo Marini (later archbishop of Lanciano), Francesco Foreiro (author of a commentary on Isaias) and Egidio Foscarari, bishop of Modena, took part in the compilation, along with the archbishop of Zara, Muzio Calini. Their labours were ended at the close of 1564 and then Pius V handed over the work to a special Congregation over which Cardinal Sirleto presided. It was printed by Manutius and came out in September 1566. St Charles Borromeo's Synod of Milan in 1565 ordered that all clerics over the age of 14 should have a copy of the Bible and also 'the catechism which is to be published at Rome, as soon as it shall be out' (decree 22). The Synod of Rouen in 1581 bade parish priests preach to their people on the efficacy of the sacraments 'according to the doctrine that is laid down in the Roman Catechism' (decree 4:1). At Bordeaux in 1583 the Synod (decree 18) went into further detail. The parish priest was to expound to his people from this Roman or Tridentine Catechism (of which he must have a copy in Latin and French) the more general doctrines about the articles of the creed, the commandments, the meaning of the Our Father and the sacraments.

The pastoral nature of the catechism will be apparent from the decrees cited. In their Introduction the authors of the *Catechism* say that they, 'having undertaken to instruct pastors in the knowledge of those things which belong more especially to their office and are accommodated to the capacity of the faithful, wished that those things only should be brought forward which may assist the pious zeal of pastors'. Thus the *Catechism* is in no sense a complete doctrinal statement nor a scientific expansion of the Profession of Faith. It has not the sanction of infallibility, as have the anathemas of a Council, and incidental errors may be found in the *Catechism* of Trent, as when it claims (on the authority of the pseudo-Denis and a False Decretal attributed to Pope Fabian) that chrism alone, without imposition of hands, is the matter of Confirmation. Other *Catechisms* such as those of Bellarmine or Canisius (1544), or in England those of Lawrence Vaux (1570) and of Henry Turberville (1648), have the authority of their compilers and approvers and

might in general be said to be safe in their doctrine. One would not on that account regard them as entirely free from error. Had the *Catechism* of Trent been so widely used as to have behind it the authority of practically every bishop in the Church, it might then be said to speak with the ordinary teaching authority of the Church, but in fact it was far less widely used than the work of Canisius, since it was not composed in the form of question-and-answer.

Hence, when theological objections are raised on the ground that the Church has committed herself in the *Catechism* of Trent to the idea that the Apostles' Creed (*see* APOSTLES' CREED) was made by the Apostles themselves or to a statement of the ends of marriage which makes the first of these to consist in 'the hope of mutual aid, that each helped by the other, may the more easily bear the ills of life', it is not necessary to admit that in fact the Church *has* committed herself. Pastoral ways of exposition are not perforce technical expressions of precise doctrine, and though in general they will be sound, and good for their time, they will not be irreformable.

At the Vatican Council of 1870 a scheme was put forward for a catechism which should be uniform for the whole of Christendom, but this plan did not gain final approval. Benedict XV set up a commission to produce such a work, but, when it was completed, it was issued under the authority of the chairman of the commission (Cardinal Gasparri) alone and not as a document of the Church. This *Catholic Catechism* (1930, English translation 1932) was adopted by the bishops of Mexico as the official catechism for their country but did not find much favour elsewhere. A reaction against theological catechisms led some German and Austrian theologians to propose that what they called the message of Christ (*see* GOSPEL KERYGMA) could be presented by the pastors of the Church in independence of theology proper. This thesis soon led to an opposition being set up between the theology of the message and 'school-theology' (or what was taught to those in training for the priesthood). Debate about this distinction naturally led to an exploration of the concept of Tradition (*see further* TRADITION).

Bibliography. An English translation of the *Catechismus Romanus* was published by Dr J. Donovan of Maynooth in 1829 and was often reprinted (*Catechism of the Council of Trent*, last reprint 1908). An American version was made by Frs McHugh and Callan (1923). J. A. Jungmann SJ, *Handing on the Faith* (English translation, 1959) contains much recent information, but no separate discussion of the theological authority of the catechism is known to the English Catechetical Centre.

J. H. C.

CATECHUMENATE The means of entry into the Catholic Church has from very early times been carefully organized. This organized process of making disciples is called the catechumenate. Some historians suppose that the Church learnt the advantages of having such a closely organized system from Marcion at Rome about 140 and that the system spread from there, being established as a three-year period according to the *Traditio apostolica* of Hippolytus early in the 3rd cent. (So Abbot Capelle, in 1933.) More recent discoveries at Qumran would suggest that the catechumenate may have been organized much earlier than the time of Marcion, seeing that something very similar was in use among the sectaries of Qumran. The *Manual of Discipline* (6:13) directs that anyone who seeks affiliation must be examined before being allowed to begin his training ; he must then enter into a covenant ' to return to the truth and to turn away from all wickedness', and only then is he to be instructed in the rules of the community. After a year of probation he is to be proposed for membership, and the community then takes a vote on his admission. Terms like ' enlightenment' and ' opening of the ears' were in use at Qumran, as among the early Christians, for this process. In view of this close parallel, it is unsafe to take the NT references to ' catechesis' and its practice in any sense other than technical.

Luke wrote his gospel for one Theophilus, to give him the backing or guarantee for the events about which he had heard in receiving his catechesis (Lk 1:3). Apollos (Ac 18:25) had been instructed (in Egypt, probably) in the way of the Lord and was able to preach ' the facts about Jesus', before Aquila and Priscilla took him in hand and completed his instruction, which had stopped short of Christian baptism.

It is now generally agreed that the Pauline use of the word ' catechize' is exclusively in the sense of ' giving someone instruction in the content of the Christian faith', the more general sense of ' learning by hearsay' not being used by him. This amounts to an admission that the word was a technical term with Paul (Rom 2:18 ; Gal 6:6 ; 1 Cor 14:19) ; what the term described was a process which was comparable (Rom 2:18) to a rabbi's training of his disciples. The activities of ' ministers of the Word' such as John Mark, who prepared people for baptism after they had been won to Christianity by the preaching of an apostle, seem to have been organized about the time that the word ' catechesis' acquired its technical meaning. Luke's usage of the word conforms to Paul's, except for the problematic instance of Ac 21:21-4. How soon the instruction of catechumens was given a fixed duration may still be a matter for debate, and would have varied from place to place, but a 1st-cent. origin for the practice itself must now be regarded as most probable. The use of the verb κατηχοῦμαι in an official letter of the Prefect of Egypt in the 2nd cent. (*Princeton Papyrus* II:20:3) occurs in a context where the meaning can only be, ' I have received detailed information' ; it

might be that the growth of Christian catechesis in Egypt (where the catechetical school of Alexandria was founded about 175) has helped to deprive the word of its vaguer meaning even for profane use.

Gradually a differentiation was introduced between the crowd of hangers-on or ' fellow-travellers' who came to Mass and were regularly sent out after the reading of the Scriptures and those who had given their names at the beginning of Lent as candidates for baptism, who would be prepared by a course of instruction during that season. The latter were called *competentes* in the West, or sometimes *electi*, and in the East φωτιζόμενοι ; the former remained *audientes* and might be in that category for several years. The Council of Elvira required two years from most people, but three from a man who had been a *flamen* of the pagan gods. The lists of forbidden occupations which are to be found in the Church Orders such as the *Apostolic Constitutions* (8:32) show that a man had to desist from any of these before he could be an *audiens* ; his perseverance in the matter would be observed by the Church authorities and taken into account when he gave his name for the course of instruction. It is easy to see how this systematization of the catechumenate brought it somewhat closer to the institution of public penance. The similarity is of some theological importance, for just as there can be controversy about the moment of absolution in the process of public penance, so there can be too over the catechumenate a theological debate about the moment from which an individual could be counted a member of the Church.

Cyril of Jerusalem in his *Procatechesis* (13 ; PG 33:353) calls the candidates ' sons and daughters of one Mother'. Ambrose in his panegyric of the catechumen Valentinianus (*De obitu Valentiniani* 52 ; PL 16:1374-5) says that the dead man ' had Thy Spirit, and how should he not have received Thy grace ?'[1] He also prays for this grace on the grounds that in life Valentinianus had not denied it. Ambrose is obviously aware that while catechumens are not fully inside the Church they somehow belong to it. Augustine carried the analysis a stage further. Against the later developments of Pelagianism he had to argue that the sanctification of the individual is a multiple notion ; the sanctifying grace of baptism is a free gift, but there are others before it and even the first act of faith is from God. ' Catechumens are, I suppose, in some way sanctified by the sign of Christ and the prayer at the imposition of hand, and, although what they are given to eat is not the Body of Christ, yet it is holy, holier indeed than our ordinary food, for it is sacramental. The sanctification of a catechumen, if he fail to be baptized, does not avail for his entry into the kingdom of heaven or for the remission of his sins'[2] (*De peccatorum*

---

[1] Qui habuit Spiritum Tuum, quomodo non accepit gratiam Tuam ?
Solve igitur servo Tuo munus gratiae Tuae quam ille nunquam negavit.

[2] Nam et catechumenos secundum quemdam modum suum per signum Christi et orationem manus inpositionis puto sanctificari, et quod accipiunt quamvis non sit corpus Christi sanctum est tamen et sanctius quam cibi quibus

remissione 2:26:42 ; CSEL 60:113). (The catechumens in certain baptismal rites were given salt at
their renunciation of the world, but Augustine may
be referring to the giving of blessed bread.)

Suarez championed the view (*Opera* XII:*disp.* 9:18)
that catechumens were members of the Church,
relying on the argument that what had been good
enough to make the patriarchs members of the
Church that began with Abel (*see* ABEL) was good
enough to make catechumens, who were in exactly
the same dispositions as the patriarchs, somehow
members of the present Church. His authorities
were the pseudo-Denis (*De ecclesiastica hierarchia* 3 ;
PG 3:460) and Augustine (*De baptismo* 4:21 ; CSEL
51:255). 'I do not hesitate to prefer a Catholic
catechumen who is on fire with divine charity to a
baptized heretic, but even within the Catholic
Church itself we prefer a good catechumen to a
baptized rogue, and in so doing we do no wrong to
the sacrament of baptism which the one has and the
other has not yet, nor do we consider the rite of
catechumens superior to the rite of baptism. Cornelius the centurion not yet baptized was better than
Simon who was baptized'.[1] The language of
Augustine's view is certainly striking. He distinguishes a Catholic catechumen from a Donatist,
and thinks that this Catholic one may have divine
charity. In his Tract 4 on Jn 1 (PL 35:1411) he
recurs to the same idea.

Modern Catholic teaching is summed up in the
phrase of Canon Law (canon 87) that by baptism
one is established as a person in the Church. A
person has rights as well as duties, and so this definition might leave room for the idea that a catechumen, though somehow within the Church (as
Augustine seems to say), was not a person therein
and therefore had not the rights of a baptized
Catholic. Church legislation (canon 1239:2) allows
that a catechumen who dies without baptism
through no fault of his own, can receive Christian
burial. The idea behind this seems to be that the
one link (that of faith) between the catechumen
and the Church has been forged ; the other (that
of baptism) has not, but at least there was the
intention there of going on to baptism if death had
not intervened. If membership of the Body of
Christ is a notion with rigid frontiers, then the
catechumen is outside ; but if it is a notion which
admits of analogical treatment, then he may be
somewhat more fortunate. The development of
biological knowledge (*see* BIOLOGY : IMPACT UPON
THEOLOGY) may help to a deeper understanding

on the part of the theologians of the future of how
the individual can be a member of the Body of
Christ.

In the past the Church has at various times had
to insist on the absolute necessity of baptism. The
Messalians, for instance, in the 5th cent. despised
baptism, as may be seen from the *Acts of Polyeuc-
tus* (cited by Vööbus in his *History of Asceticism in
the Syrian Orient*, 137). Later, Pope Zachary had
to write to St Boniface in Germany (PL 89:945)
about one Sampson, an Irishman, who was teaching
that by the imposition of the bishop's hand alone
and without the water of renewal and the sacramental invocation a man could become a Catholic
Christian. Zachary commented : 'If he said that,
the Holy Ghost has left him'.[1] It may be that some
idea of having confirmation before baptism, as
happened sometimes in Syria, had filtered through
to the Far West, or it may be that some text from
the re-baptism controversy had been misunderstood. The Syrian practice itself, the evidence for
which was gathered by Dom Connolly (in T &S
VIII, xlii–xlix), seems to have been followed by
Chrysostom, as his *Baptismal Catecheses*, discovered
by L. Wenger (1957), bear witness.

Bibliography. B. Capelle OSB, 'L'Introduction
du catéchumenat à Rome', RTAM V (1933) 129–54 ;
*F. L. Cross, *St Cyril of Jerusalem's Lectures on the
Christian Sacraments* (1951) ; A. Paulin, *Saint Cyrille,
catéchète* (1959) ; J. H. Crehan SJ, *Early Christian
Baptism and the Creed* (1948).   J. H. C.

CATENAE are chains of passages from the writings
of the Fathers, ranged around the text of a book of
Scripture by a scribe who had the works of many
of the Fathers at his disposal and who selected what
he thought useful for the interpretation of the text.
Sometimes the comments are set in paragraphs or
columns alternate to the text and sometimes they
surround the text, which is written in the centre
of the sheet in a larger hand. The late Cardinal
Faulhaber, who had worked on the catenae in his
earlier days, estimated that about one-half of the
writings of the Fathers exist in the form of catenae,
or in other words, that catenae contain as much
again as all the writings of the Fathers which exist
independently as complete works. Many catenae
are still unpublished, and as the Church is committed
to following the unanimous consent of the Fathers
in the interpretation of Scripture (D 786), their
importance for theology cannot be exaggerated.

Procopius of Gaza (*c.* 475–538) is generally taken
as the first great exemplar for the production of
catenae. His collections on Is ; Cant ; 1–4 Kg ;
1–2 Par and the Octateuch are extant. It must be
borne in mind that it was far easier for these
scholiasts to collect passages from the Fathers on

alimur, quoniam sacramentum est. Sanctificatio catechumeni si non fuerit baptizatus, non ei valet ad intrandum
regnum caelorum aut ad peccatorum remissionem.

[1] Nec ego dubito catechumenum catholicum divina
caritate flagrantem haeretico baptizato anteponere ; sed
etiam in ipsa intus Catholica bonum catechumenum malo
baptizato anteponimus. Nec ideo tamen sacramento baptismatis quo iste nondum ille iam imbutus est facimus
iniuriam ; aut catechumeni sacramentum sacramento baptismi praeferendum putamus, cum aliquem catechumenum
aliquo baptizato fideliorem melioremque cognoscimus.
Melior enim centurio Cornelius nondum baptizatus Simoni
baptizato.

[1] Scripsit reverenda fraternitas tua reperisse presbyterum
nomine Sanpson genere Scotum, errantem a via veritatis,
affirmantem sine misterica invocatione aut lavacro regenerationis posse fieri Catholicum Christianum per episcopalis
manus impositionem. Qui dicit hoc vacuus est Spiritu
sancto.

the OT than on the NT, since so many of the Fathers had written by preference on the OT, seeking its typical sense and its forward reference to the Christian religion. The age was that of the *Digest* of Justinian. Cyril of Alexandria had quoted a string of patristic texts at the Council of Ephesus, Leo the Great had included in his *Dogmatic Epistle* a collection of supporting passages from the Fathers (*paternae auctoritates*), and with learning in decline it was natural that men should seek to preserve what they felt to be the best of the past. The making of catenae went on in Greek and Syriac lands much longer and to a much greater extent than in the West ; here the work of Victor of Capua (d. 554) on the Heptateuch and on the gospels, of which fragments survive, is one of the very few examples. In Alexandria, where scholiasts had commented on classical texts for centuries, the making of catenae seems to have flourished, and it is no accident that there are exegetical works of the Alexandrian Fathers, Didymus, Ammonius and Cyril, which survive only because they were used in catenae.

The use of material from catenae is beset with difficulties, as the attribution of passages to authors can be trusted only when the scribe's accuracy in this can be checked by reference from time to time to the known works of the authors cited : Chrysostom and Origen are often invoked by inferior scribes who did not really know where their citations came from. Lesser authors, such as Asterius and Eusebius Emesenus, whose works seem to have been in confusion already in ancient times, often provide a refuge for the puzzled scribe. Much of what the scribes copied down is worthless, but there is valuable dogmatic material lying unused amongst the dross. If theology is to benefit by renewed recourse to the Fathers, the catenae will have to be made available once more. Editing of catenae was begun by the Jesuits Peltan, Poussines and Cordier in the 17th cent., by Patrick Young at Oxford (a *catena* on Job), by Cramer in the 19th cent. and by Sickenberger and Staab in this cent. Catholics have been more prominent in this work, and quite naturally, as they have more interest in the argument from tradition which the catenae exemplify.

Bibliography. R. Devréesse, in DBS *s.v.* Chaînes ; K. Staab, *Die Paulus-katenen* (1926) ; the same, *Paulus-kommentaren aus der griechische Kirche* (1932) ; the same ,' Die griechische Katenen zu den katholischen Briefen ', in Bi 5 (1924) 296–353 ; J. Sickenberger, *Titus of Bostra on Luke*, in TU XXI (1901) ; the same, *Niketas of Herakleia*, TU XXII (1902) ; the same, *Fragments of Cyril of Alexandria on Luke*, TU XXXIV (1909) ; J. Reuss, *Matthaeuskommentare aus der griechischen Kirche*, TU LXI (1957).

J. H. C.

CATHOLICITY of the Church. (*See also* CHURCH *and* UNION OF CHRISTENDOM.) In this article will be treated (I) the origin and early use of the term ; (II) its inclusion in the creeds ; (III) its place in modern theology ; and (IV) its Scripture foundation.

I The Origin and Early Use of the Term CATHOLIC as applied to the Church. It is, of course, one of the common Greek words for ' universal ', καθολικός from καθόλου, over the whole world. Akin to this term was the word οἰκουμενικός which meant ' over the whole civilized world '. The latter term came to be used for general councils, while the former very quickly came to be a favourite attribute of the Church. In its earliest use, as in St Ignatius of Antioch (*Smyrn.* 8:2) and the *Martyrdom* of St Polycarp (8), it has the meaning of ' universal ', as opposed to purely ' local ' communities. But very soon it began to be used as a term of commendation for the Church universal, in contrast with any purely local group out of harmony with that Church universal. Thus, from being purely ' universal ', it began more and more to carry with it the notion of ' true Church ', as opposed to heretical or schismatical groups, which never were throughout the world. It is thus used in the Muratori Fragment, St Cornelius (Eusebius HE 6:43.3), Pionius (*Acta*, passim), St Cyprian (frequently), and frequently from the 3rd cent. onwards. The term acquired enhanced doctrinal importance in the writings of St Optatus and St Augustine against the Donatists. St Augustine's view is well expressed in the often quoted phrase, which was to have so deep an influence on Newman, ' *Securus iudicat orbis terrarum* ' (*Contra Ep. Parmeniani*, 24; PL 43:101). It is used very commonly in the Latin Church everywhere from the 5th cent. onwards.

II Its Use in the Creeds. ' Catholic ' as an attribute of the Church was introduced into some of the Eastern creeds at a very early period. It is in the Dêr Balyzeh liturgy (which, according to some, repeats a simple 4th cent. creed), and in the Creed of the Council of Antioch (these creeds given in English in J. Stevenson, *A New Eusebius*, 131 and 356 ; also in J. D. N. Kelly, *Early Christian Creeds* 131 and 210), and in the *Apostolic Constitutions*. It was not until the late 4th cent. that it occurs in Western creeds, when it was first found in Nicetas of Remesiana, and from that time often in Spanish and Gallican creeds.

III Its Place in Modern Theology. During the Post-Reformation period, Catholicity was understood mainly from an apologetic standpoint, as one of the marks proving the truth of the Church. The Church was contrasted with every merely local or particular body, serving one nation or class. The aspect most underlined in this argument was that of geographical universality. The Church in principle extended to all nations, and in actual fact embraced a greater variety of races and peoples than any other religious body of people in this world.

At the present day, there is a more directly dogmatic interest in the word, especially as having an important relationship to the oecumenical question. In the earlier apologetic period, it tended to be seen as similar in meaning to the note or mark of unity, with the added circumstance of unity throughout the world. Today the real theological meaning of catholicity is seen to be complementary to that of unity. Catholicity suggests multiformity within unity. It is often feared by non-Catholic oecumenists that unity might mean absorption of the many by the one. This would be unity without catholicity. Catholicity safeguards the multiformity, without destroying the basic, essential unity.

The basic theological reason underlying catholicity, i.e. the universality of Christ's redemptive power, is well expressed by Newman in his *Lectures on Justification* : 'Christ came for this very purpose, to gather together in one all the elements of good dispersed throughout the world, to make them His own, to illuminate them with Himself, to reform and refashion them into Himself. He came to make a new and better beginning of all things than Adam had been, and to be a fountain-head from which all good henceforth might flow' (ed. 1892, 193). Everything human that is naturally good is capable of being purified from all taint of sin, and raised up to share in Christ's redemption. The doctrines of Incarnation and Redemption both imply this. Incarnation means that created flesh and blood is not in itself evil, but can even be assumed by God. Redemption means that everything other than sin itself can be renewed and restored.

From the *Incarnational* point of view, the Church is not limited to any one culture, or to any one nation or race. It is not limited to any one language or class. It is not confined to any one vocation or human interest or talent. The Church is at home under every lawful form of government. 'She has had trial of East and West, of monarchy and democracy, of peace and war, of imperial and of feudal tyranny, of times of darkness and times of philosophy, of barbarousness and luxury, of slaves and freemen, of cities and nations, of marts of commerce and seats of manufacture, of old countries and young, of metropolis and colonies' (Newman, *Discourses to Mixed Congregations*, ed. 1892, 247).

From the point of view of *Redemption*, the strongest basic principle of catholicity is the universality of sin. Universal sin requires a universal remedy. Every nation and culture stand in need of a redeemer in the same way. Moreover, since God wishes to save all, His Church must be intended for all.

Catholicity as a mark of the Church does not imply that the Church is actually found in every human nation, race and situation. All that is required is its universal aptitude, and God's desire that the Church's Gospel should be preached to all. No particularisms have any right within the Church, even though occasionally, through men's narrow-mindedness, they may exist.

The great importance of the notion of Catholicity as a basis of true oecumenism is obvious. The Eastern Christians with their special rituals have as much right within the Church as the Latins. What applies to actual Eastern rites applies in principle to other nations and cultures, such as the far Easterns and Africans. They also have a right to bring their special cultures within the ambit of the Church. This is the basis on which the Church might make concessions to any groups with special traditions, such as that of the Church of England, which would make it easier for them to enter the Church.

By the admission of all that is good in the human world, the Church is the richer for its catholicity. It cannot but rejoice, therefore, in accepting within its bounds cultures and values other than those of the West. By so doing, all members of the Church will be the richer, and such expansion will be to Christ's external glory.

IV Its Basis in Scripture. The word 'Catholic' is not applied to the Church in the Scriptures. But there is no doubt about the notion of universality in our theological sense having its roots there. In later OT literature and all through the NT, there is a movement away from the earlier Jewish exclusivism to universalism. Our Lord's own mission was, indeed, first to the Jews. The Jewish vocation was to receive the Gospel, and themselves to mediate it to the Gentiles. This vocation was for the most part refused, and, even during Our Lord's lifetime, he several times turned from the unbelieving Jews to believing Samaritans or Gentiles. 'Believe me, I have not found faith like this, even in Israel' (Mt 8:10). 'You yourselves will be cast out. Others will come from the east and the west, the north and the south, to take their ease in the kingdom of God' (Lk 13:28, 29). 'I tell you, then, that the kingdom of God will be taken away from you, and given to a people which yield revenues that belong to it' (Mt 21:43). It is with the same mind that Jesus on two well-known occasions uses the Samaritans as examples of virtues which he finds lacking among the Jews.

In the young Church after the Resurrection the same order is found. The Apostles preach first to the Jews ; and, only when the Jews have had their opportunity, do they preach to the Gentiles. But very soon it is made clear that now there is 'no more Jew or Gentile, no more slave and freeman, no more male and female ; you are all one person in Jesus Christ' (Gal 3:28). 'Here is no more Gentile and Jew, no more circumcised and uncircumcised ; no one is barbarian, or Scythian, no one is slave or freeman ; there is nothing but Christ in any of us' (Col 3:11).

The first non-Jewish place where the Gospel is preached is Samaria (Ac 8). A command to go to the Gentiles is implied in Peter's dream, followed by the conversion of Cornelius (Ac 10). Many Greeks were converted at Antioch (Ac 11:20 ff.). The Council of Jerusalem lays down a ruling which will make it easier for Gentiles to find their way into the Church (Ac 15:1-5).

A doctrinal basis for this catholicity of the Church's mission is, of course, the universality of sin and redemption. Nowhere is this more forcibly expressed than in the epistles of St Paul, especially the Epistle to the Romans. The thesis of this epistle is that everyone, Jew and Gentile, has sinned, and all alike need redemption through the blood of Christ. The same is implied in all those passages which proclaim that Christ died for everyone. It is a natural consequence that the apostles should be sent to baptize all, and preach the Gospel to all nations (Mt 28:19 ; Mk 16:15–16 ; Lk 24:47 ; Ac 1:8).

It is because God wishes the salvation of all mankind (1 Tim 2:4 ; Tit 2:11) that St Paul was especially called by Jesus Christ 'to be the instrument of bringing my name before the heathen and their rulers, and before the people of Israel too' (Ac 9:15). St Paul's whole life and preaching was to make 'known to the Gentiles the unfathomable riches of Christ, of publishing to the world the plan of this mystery, kept hidden from the beginning of time in the all-creating mind of God' (Eph 3:8–9). He was called to teach both Jew and Gentile that the promise and blessing God gave to Abraham were for all nations of the world, on condition only that they believed in Christ (Gal 3:7 ff.). 'Thus, in Christ Jesus, the blessing of Abraham was to be imparted to the Gentiles' (Gal 3:14), and Christ is 'our bond of peace ; he has made the two nations one, breaking down the wall that was a barrier between us, the enmity there was between us, in his own mortal nature' (Eph 2:14–15). For this reason, in all matters not essential to the faith, we must not 'insist on having our own way. Each of us ought to give way to his neighbour, where it serves a good purpose, by building up his faith' (Rom 15:2).

It is clear that the Fathers in insisting on the importance of catholicity as essential to the true Church were faithfully reflecting the Gospel as recorded in the Scriptures.

Bibliography. J. H. Newman, *St Athanasius*, ii:65 (Catholic : The Name and Claim) ; *Discourses to Mixed Congregations*, ed. 1902, 246 ff. ; *Development of Christian Doctrine* (1878) 279 ff. ; C. Journet, *L'Église du verbe incarné*, II (1951) 193–288 ; H. de Lubac, *Catholicism* (Eng. ed. 1950) 144 ff. ; K. Adam, *The Spirit of Catholicism*, ch. IX ; A. D. Sertillanges, *The Church* (1922) 66 ff. ; R. Hasseveldt, *The Church : A Divine Mystery*, tr. William Storey, 168 ff. ; G. Thils, *Les Notes de l'église dans l'apologétique catholique* (1937) ; Y. Congar, 'Catholicité', in *Catholicisme* II (1949) 722–5 ; cf. also apologetic text-books on the Church.

H. F. D.

CAUSALITY OF THE SACRAMENTS The Passion of Christ was a general and all-embracing cause of salvation to men (*see* ATONEMENT), but this cause needs to be applied to individuals in a more specific way. The power of the Passion is applied to the living by means of sacraments which somehow produce in men of each successive generation a conformity to that Passion. Thus argued St Thomas (*Summa* 3a:52:1:@2). The teaching of the Church, in elaboration of this position, is that (I) the sacraments are true causes of grace and not mere by-products of grace already received, nor (II) are they simply the occasions of God's acting to confer grace directly. The medieval analysis of the sacramental process into the sign, the grace and (III) a middle term (called *res et sacramentum*) led to a further determination of the exact purpose of the sacraments.

The post-Tridentine theologians engaged on a lengthy (IV) dispute about the manner in which the sacraments may be said to cause grace, without much attention to their ultimate purpose. In modern times there has been, with the liturgical revival, greater interest in the question (V) how Christ may be said to be present as principal author of the sacramental action.

I That the sacraments are true causes of grace, and not simply the badges of a Christian calling and the external acknowledgment of a justification that has been received already by faith, was defined by the Council of Trent (D 849). Mk 16:16 couples baptism with faith as a means of salvation, and the other sacramental texts of the NT (e.g. Jn 3:5 ; Ac 22:16 ; Tit 3:5, etc.) were traditionally interpreted as giving baptism a causal role in the work of salvation. When this was rejected by the extremists at the Reformation, who looked on sacraments as no more than 'badges of a Christian calling', the Anglican article XXV (following Luther) declared that they were more than that, being in fact 'certain sure witnesses and effectual signs of grace and God's goodwill to us, by the which He doth work invisibly in us and doth not only quicken but also strengthen our faith in Him'. This was not enough for Trent, whose decree is dated to 1547, whereas the Anglican article first appeared in 1538, being elaborated out of a more jejune statement of the Confession of Augsburg. Trent (D 851) insisted that sacraments confer grace 'by the work wrought' (*ex opere operato*) and thus tore apart the ambiguity which lurked in the Anglican phrase 'effectual signs'. After Trent (in 1553) the Anglican article had a clause added rejecting *ex opere operato* as contrary to Scripture, but this clause was dropped in 1563.

II The occasionalism which seems to have been accepted by some medieval thinkers as an explanation of the sacraments went with a view of grace that did not distinguish adequately between the divine indwelling, which is uncreated, and the beginning, growth or revival of sanctifying grace, which the various sacraments bring about, and which is not uncreated. If God does it all, then the sacrament cannot be more than an 'adornment of the soul' in preparation for, or in acknowledgment of, God's act. But if God has willed to use the co-operation of what would otherwise be beggarly elements, then the role of the sacraments needs to be very carefully surveyed.

The Occasionalist view is often an incredulity towards the idea that God *could* use water, oil and the rest as means of grace, and from the days of Naaman the Syrian (who thought Abana and Pharphar, the rivers of Damascus, much superior as healing agents to the glaucous Jordan) down to modern times it has been a standing objection to the doctrine of the sacraments. If God has chosen to use these means, it is not for men to tell Him what He ought to have done, and so the refutation of Occasionalism is really a matter of considering the institution of each sacrament (*see* BAPTISM, etc.). If Christ did this and said this, we have to accept it. If it be urged that

Occasionalism is the best way of avoiding a magical view of the sacraments, the proper answer seems to be that one should rather tackle the question of the *obex* or obstacle to grace which the indisposition of the recipient of a sacrament can provide and which has no parallel in magical theory. Those theologians who somewhat incautiously accept the suggestion that the Christian mysteries derived some of their conceptual background from pagan mysteries regard these pagan origins as so much *praeparatio evangelica*, even though they were no better than magic in their crude reality. The view of Justin (*apol.* 66:4) that diabolical influence introduced into pagan mysteries an imitation of the Christian sacraments may not be true of the pagan rituals themselves, but it is probably true of the ideology which went with those rituals and which must have gained greatly by elaboration in competition with, and in imitation of, what the Christians taught. Simon and Menander (both Samaritans like Justin) must be allowed to count for more in this process of borrowing than earlier theologians were willing to allow ; the recently discovered evidence of Gnostic writings is plain enough.

From the beginning (1 Cor 1:12) Christianity has repudiated the idea that the conferring of a sacrament sets up a special magical relationship of dependence upon its minister such as was believed to arise in the pagan mysteries between initiator and initiated. It is piquant to notice that St Paul's information about such beliefs spreading among the Corinthians was given to him by 'those of Chloe', probably those priests of Demeter who were in charge of such initiations themselves.

III The middle term, or *res et sacramentum*, which is the immediate result of the valid conferring of a sacrament, and which is itself the cause of grace in those who are adequately prepared to receive it, was established in theology in the 12th cent. (between 1140 and 1146), at the beginning of speculation about the sacraments (PL 176:140). In three sacraments this middle term was taken to be the character conferred by baptism, confirmation and holy orders. In sacramental marriage there is a quasi-character, for the relationship of the partners is a permanent likeness of that bridal relationship which exists between Christ and His Church. In the central sacrament of the Eucharist the middle term, on the way to the grace that is the goal of the sacrament, is obviously the real presence of Christ under the veils of bread and wine. Berengar's denial of this probably led to the coining of the new idea. In the sacrament of Penance the middle term was said by St Thomas (*Summa* 3a:84:1:@3) to be the interior repentance of the penitent, which along with the outward sign of the confessing of sins and the judicial absolution produced the remission of the sins confessed. This idea was rejected by others, Lugo for instance (*De Sacramentis, disputatio* 2:8), claiming that peace of conscience was the middle term. As this middle term is at one and the same time signified by the outward sign and itself signifies the grace to be received from the sacrament, it is obvious that some

difficulty will occur in the two sacraments of Penance and Extreme Unction, where disagreement about the nature of the sacramental grace is found. It is admitted by some moral theologians that both these sacraments can be validly received by those who are indisposed to receive their grace and that therefore the sacrament may 'revive' when the obstacle to grace has been removed. Thus it ought to follow (on their view, at least) that *something* is received by such indisposed men, even something more than the outward sign, for that by itself could not 'revive'. Hence they can admit (though many others would deny this conclusion) that even in these two sacraments of Penance and Extreme Unction there must be a middle term, though there might be disagreement about its nature (*see* SACRAMENTS).

It was the great innovation of St Thomas that he assigned to the sacraments a purpose that was positive and liturgical rather than the traditional negative purpose of being remedies for particular weaknesses of soul. Bede had popularised the medicinal view of the sacraments (PL 92:469) and St Thomas shared this view when he commented on the *Sentences* of Peter Lombard. But when he came to write the *Summa* he had found more light on the subject ; the medicinal idea is not entirely dropped (*Summa* 3a:62:2 and 5), but is overshadowed by the new notion of participation in the worship of the Mystical Body. Baptism is the beginning of this for the individual, Confirmation activates it and Priesthood makes the worship possible, while the Eucharist is the supreme act of worship. Christian Marriage is a permanent likeness of the reciprocal love that exists between Christ and the Church. Penance restores a man to the legitimate worship of the Church and Extreme Unction enables him to carry on such worship, when prevented from being bodily present at it, and maybe restores him to participation in it if God wills. To illustrate this positive purpose of the sacraments St Thomas appealed to the analogy of physical life and growth (*Summa* 3a:65:1 ; 72:1 ; 73:1). By linking the sacraments with the corporate life of the Church St Thomas took a step which was to prove an inspiration to his followers in this 20th cent., but which was not appreciated by the Nominalist philosophers of the later Middle Ages, who when they turned to theology were apt to regard the sacraments as no more than so many transactions between God and the individual soul.

It has become the fashion of late to regard the Church itself as being somehow a basic or original sacrament, a middle term between the outward rites and the grace received in all the seven sacraments. When St Thomas said that by the sacraments we are brought into conformity with the Passion of Christ, he may or may not have been aware of St Leo's saying that the Passion of Christ goes on to the end of time and is reproduced in the life of the Church, but he was on the same ground as Leo in what he said. The worship of God to which we are deputed by the sacraments centres round the representing of the Passion of Christ in the Mass. A collect from the *Leonine Sacramentary*, which St Thomas (*Summa*

3a:83:1c) cites in its present form, declares that ' as often as the commemorating of this Victim is renewed, the work of our Redemption is carried out '. The original word used (*exseritur* and not *exercetur*) meant rather that the work of Redemption was being applied or brought forth, but this nuance of meaning had been lost by the time of St Thomas.

Before St Thomas the idea was abroad that the sacraments make the soul conform to the likeness of Christ in His Passion, but it was thought of as a one-to-one correspondence between Christ and the individual ; the intervention of the Church did not then seem so important. An eloquent passage of a work attributed to Alexander of Hales sets this out : ' When a man is baptised, he is conformed to the likeness of Christ's death (Rom 6:5) ; by confirmation he is made like to Christ struggling against His enemies ; by the Eucharist he is made like Christ who goes about His sacrifice ; by Orders like to His priesthood ; by Penance he is conformed to Christ making satisfaction ; by Matrimony to Christ as He is spouse of the Church ; by Extreme Unction to Christ as He rose again, imbrued with the oil of the fullness of grace ' (*Quaestio de sacramentis in genere*, in *Franciscan Studies* XI [1951] 83). Here the idea of the sacraments having to do with the collective worship of the Church is not envisaged. Alexander also cites (without much enthusiasm) a scheme of parallels which makes each sacrament correspond to one of the seven (theological and cardinal) virtues ; this reappears in St Thomas, but he does not seem to use it to any effect.

In view of this close connection between sacraments and the Church it might be expected that the scholastic dispute about the nature of sacramental causality would have some light thrown upon it by the teaching which in recent times has been elaborated about the nature of the Mystical Body. Physical or moral causality was championed (after Trent) for the sacraments, while the Mystical Body has been said to be neither a physical nor yet merely a moral body but something in between, or else superior to both. One mystery of faith may be expected to throw light on others (D 1796), and it is not surprising that in recent times there has been a tendency to look for some species of sacramental causality that is neither physical nor moral.

IV The dispute about the nature of sacramental causality started with Vitoria (whom Cano followed) and Cajetan, and it raged in the 17th cent. A moral cause is understood to be one which by suggestion, petition or command moves a physical cause to the production of an effect. Such a moral cause can operate only in the activity of intelligent beings, whereas physical causes are efficient in any grade of reality. By rejecting (in *Summa* 3a:62:1c) the idea that the sacraments operate in the manner of a traveller's cheque or of any symbol that is used for an investiture, St Thomas was thought by some to have rejected moral causality in favour of physical, though he never uses this latter word. It is certain that in the Middle Ages there was abroad an idea of consecration by contact which would now be

repudiated by theologians. Christ was thought to have sanctified the waters of Jordan by touching them when He went to be baptised by John, and every baptismal font was a Jordan wherein new Christians were born to grace. Similarly, and more surprisingly, it was held that a consecrated particle of the Eucharist would consecrate the chalice of wine into which it was immersed, and this idea prevailed for several centuries, as Mgr Andrieu has shown (*Immixtio et consecratio*, 1922). This was physical causality *in excelsis*. The rhetoric of a preacher, who must at present remain unknown, was responsible for the wide extension of this same idea. St Thomas (*Summa* 3a:62:4@3) quotes the passage under the impression that it was a sermon by Augustine. It is found among the works of Maximus of Turin (PL 57:557 ; *serm.* 12 *De baptismo Christi*), though there is some doubt whether he wrote it. ' Wonder not that we claim that water, a corporeal substance, avails to purify the soul. It does avail ; it reaches into all the dark places of conscience. Itself subtle and refined, by the blessing of Christ it is made yet more subtle and by the dew of the Spirit it percolates through the hidden springs of life to the evil that is in the soul. The flow of blessing is more subtle than the movement of the waters '.[1] St Thomas had a somewhat garbled text of this passage before him and does not quote the final sentence which would have shown that the ' flow ' of grace was comparable only by analogy with that of such physical agents as water.

The introduction of the idea that the sacrament was an instrumental cause refined away some of the crudity of earlier conceptions, and this was due to William of Auxerre in the first days of the application of Aristotelian notions to theology. St Thomas picked up a distinction which is adumbrated in one place only in Aristotle and made out that the minister was the ' conjoined instrument ' and the sacrament the ' separated instrument ' of the divine action. Obviously they could not both be instruments in the same way, though this fact is often forgotten by participants in this dispute. Gradually, as the distinction of moments, between the middle term of the sacrament and its end term (or between *res et sacramentum* and *res sacramenti*), made its way in scholastic theology, there came the idea that the instrumental causality required for the production of these was unique and not to be paralleled exactly anywhere. St Thomas (*Summa* 3a:63:5:@1) speaks of the character (which is the middle term for three of the sacraments) as having ' a kind of instrumental force ' (*quaedam instrumentalis virtus*), and in his *Commentary on Romans* (lectio 3, cap. 4) he says that the death of Christ is salutary for us not only by meriting for us but also by a kind of efficient causality (*per modum cuiusdam efficientiae*). It is also to be noted

[1] Nec miremini quod aquam, hoc est substantiam corporalem ad purificandam animam dicimus pervenire. Pervenit plane ; penetrat conscientiae universa latibula. Quamvis enim ipsa subtilis et tenuis, benedictione tamen Christi facta subtilior, per occultas vitae causas ad scelera animae spiritus rore pertransit. Subtilior enim est benedictionum fluxus quam aquarum meatus.

that St Thomas did not include in his formal definition of a sacrament (*Summa* 3a:60:2c) the idea that it was a cause of grace.

Augustine in his argument with the Manichees (*Contra Faustum* 19:16 ; CSEL 25:513) threw out a phrase which has much to do with the medieval speculation, and that in its turn influenced post-Tridentine theologians who were debating quite as much what the mind of St Thomas was as the actual nature of sacramental causality. Augustine says : 'God is eternal, but the water and the visible activity which takes place when we baptize, and which begins and ends, is not eternal. Yet the power which operates through this abides for ever and the spiritual gift which is introduced (into the soul) by these means is eternal'.[1] Speculation was thus guided towards the consideration of baptism as the exemplary sacrament to the pattern of which the others must conform. In this lay an occasion of confusion, for whereas the character conferred by baptism is a (passive) power to receive other sacraments, there is a sense in which one may speak of the power of the sacrament of Order operating through the priest who absolves a penitent. Scotus (*Reportata* IV:1:4:8) took the position that the reception of a sacrament was the introduction of a disposition necessarily leading to grace, as a result of a divine compact by which God had bound Himself to see to it that the sacraments conferred what they signified. If this view were to be established, then there could be no talk of physical causation, for the good pleasure of God is not subject to physical necessity. Thomists and Scotists of the 17th cent. argued to and fro over this position.

In an attempt to clear up the controversy Billot introduced a new element of confusion, suggesting that the causality of the sacraments might be termed 'intentional'. The highly ambiguous word *intentio* was used in the Middle Ages as an equivalent for the Arabic word in Avicenna which denoted that physical force which among Oriental (and Jewish) peoples was thought to flow from person to person, e.g. by the imposition of hands. This ma'na, as it might now be called, was hardly to be compared with sacramental grace, yet the adoption of the word by Billot—in an honest attempt to find a more precise word than moral causality—led some to think that he was trying to bridge the gap between physical and moral causes.

Billot was impressed by a remark of St Thomas (*Summa* 3a:62:4:@1) that, 'just as in words that are heard there is a kind of spiritual force which arouses the human intellect, so there is a spiritual force in the sacraments, seeing that they are directed by God to a spiritual effect'. Speech is effected by sounds to which an arbitrary meaning is attached, as everyone since the days of Herodotus (2:2) has believed, and hence the force of the comparison is to suggest that the sacraments, though their matter and form are

[1] Deus aeternus est, nec tamen aqua et omnis illa actio corporalis quae agitur cum baptizamus et fit et transit aeterna est. . . . Virtus tamen quae per ista operatur iugiter manet, et donum spiritale quod per ista insinuatur aeternum est.

elevated by God to serve the purpose of communicating grace, do not produce that grace by physical causation. Billot's opponents insisted that in three of the sacraments at least the character conferred was a physical quality in the soul and not a mere juridical title to grace. If they are right, then there is a physical, albeit spiritual, reality which distinguishes the members of the Church from those who are not members. From this one might infer that the Church is a body physical and not a body mystical (*see* BODY, MYSTICAL). Others would resist the inference on the ground that there can be a real change (that might be called physical) in the spiritual being of the recipient of a sacrament without his being incorporated into a physical unity of believers. Grace certainly builds upon nature, and the sacramental grace upon a reality of some kind which is the middle term between itself and the outward sign. This is clearly where the mystery of the sacraments lies, but it is now being recognised that some light may be thrown upon it by subsuming it into the greater mystery of the Church.

V The presence of Christ in His Church, which is taken for granted by theologians, naturally raises the question of His presence in the sacraments of the Church. There is of course His real presence in the sacrament of the Eucharist, and as all other sacraments somehow look towards the Eucharist, a question naturally arises about the extension of the notion of presence to them. Scheeben made a distinction between the three character-giving sacraments (which he called hierarchical, as they built up the Mystical Body by drawing to the members the graces of the Head) and the other sacraments. In these three, he said, the middle term is a 'truly real internal sign, inhering in the soul of the recipient', while in Penance, Matrimony and Last Anointing it was only 'a moral relation, such as a state of freedom from sin, the marriage bond, or the resoluteness necessary for the last conflict'. This would provide (if somewhat untidily) a compromise solution of the earlier controversy about physical and moral causality, which does not necessarily mean that it is to be condemned, for God need not act in the tidy way that theologians think He would act. But since the time of Scheeben the theology of the Mystical Body has been much developed (*see* BODY, MYSTICAL) and there has been a more general acceptance of Matrimony as a permanent sacrament. Furthermore, although the Church as Bride of Christ may be said to become 'one flesh with Him', there is yet a physical distinction between Christ and His Mystical Body which cannot be obscured.

Dom Odo Casel, starting from a comparison with the pagan mysteries, argued that just as the participants in those had some idea of the gods and goddesses being present with them at their initiations, so the Christians had a purified idea of the presence of Christ as principal author of their baptism ; His dying and rising again were somehow present to them as they went down into the water and emerged. But how ? No satisfactory definition of this presence has been produced to clarify the original idea of

Casel. It cannot be that Christ was simply an example present in the minds of the catechumens, for that would reduce sacramental grace to the level of the Pelagian *doctrina et exemplum*. Nor can it be that the Passion of Christ is completely outside of time, for that would mean that the Incarnation also was adrift from its anchor in history. Recent attempts have been made to argue that the human soul of Christ was present *in visione beatifica* at every sacramental event where His Passion was to be applied, since a single act of charity inspired all His saving work ; but this mystical idea comes up against St Thomas's distinction between Christ as *viator* and *comprehensor* (*Summa* 3a:19:3:@1), and Casel himself thought that this way out would not provide him with a sufficiently full notion of presence. Appeal was made to a phrase in the papal encyclical of 1947 on Christian worship (AAS 39 [1947] 551), where it was said that the faithful ' should come into vital contact with the sacrifice of Christ '. St Thomas (*Summa* 3a:22:5:@2) had said that the priesthood of Christ was eternal because ' the power of that Victim once sacrificed remains for ever ', but this brings us back to efficient causality once more as an explanation of the way in which the Passion of Christ is ' present ' in the conferring of the sacraments, and therefore the problem may be said to await further clarification. Casel's ideas have had this advantage that they are centred round the Eucharist rather than baptism, and thus the argument is not complicated by questions relating to the sacramental character.

St Thomas (*Summa* 3a:79:1c) was prepared to say of the Eucharist that the effect which the Passion of Christ had in the world was produced by the sacrament in the soul of the individual.[1] Efficient causality is not the whole explanation of Christ's presence in the Eucharist, but it can be extended to the other sacraments in a way that the real Eucharistic presence cannot. Thus the debate has come back to the old question of the manner of this efficient causality, but now there is much more care to discern the various elements in the chain of causation. The sign produces the middle term (though how a sign can produce anything other than new knowledge is a mystery) and the middle term produces through the co-operation of Christ (and negatively of the individual recipient) the sacramental grace. Underlying much medieval and later speculation was the analogy of human birth ; the parents supplying the materials of the body and God infusing the soul, even as the Church supplies the sign and the middle term of a valid but as yet unfruitful sacrament which God will crown with His grace. A modern parallel might be added to this analogy to illustrate the function of the *obex* or indisposition of the recipient, which is a bar to the reception of sacramental grace. Augustine (*ep.* 98:10 ; CSEL 34:532) introduced the term *obex* into currency by saying that infants at baptism do not block proceedings by a disposition contrary to faith, even if they have as yet no faith of their own.

It is here that progress can be expected in theological speculation.

The idea that Christ is the proximate offerer of each Mass may point the way to a new line of speculation on sacramental causality. This idea was either not fully considered or else rejected by St Thomas and Scotus, but favoured by Suarez and the Salmanticenses, as also by popular piety of more recent times. It was taken up by Garrigou-Lagrange and seems to have the support of recent papal pronouncements (AAS 46 [1954] 669 and 48 [1956] 716) which speak of an act of Christ in each Mass. As the connection of each sacrament with the worship of the Church becomes clearer, it is to be hoped that the manner of operation of the sacraments will itself be clarified ; as it is, we are still not far advanced beyond the profound saying of Augustine (*contra litteras Petiliani*, 3:49:59 ; CSEL 52:212) : ' Christ has not rested from baptising, but what He once did by bodily service He now performs by the invisible operation of His majesty '.[2]

Bibliography. For the medieval period, apart from the *Summa* of St Thomas, there are useful collections of texts in W. Lampen OFM, *De Causalitate sacramentorum iuxta scholam franciscanam* (1931) ; H. Simonin OP, with G. Meersseman OP, *De Sacramentorum efficientia apud theologos Ordinis Praedicatorum* (1936) ; M. Gierens SJ, *De Causalitate sacramentorum textus scholastici* (1931) ; the same, ' Zur Lehre des heiligen Thomas über die Kausalität der Sakramente ', in *Scholastik* 9 (1934) 321–45 ; K. Lynch OFM, ' Quaestio de sacramentis, attributed to Alexander of Hales ', in *Franciscan Studies* XI (1951) 74–95 ; D. van den Eynde OFM, ' Stephen Langton and Hugh of St Cher on the Causality of the Sacraments ', in *Franciscan Studies* XI (1951) 141–56 ; N. M. Haring SAC, ' Berengar's Definitions of *Sacramentum* and their influence ', in *Med. St* 10 (1948) 109–46.

The post-Tridentine debate was summed up by Billot in his *De Ecclesiae Sacramentis* (many editions between 1902 and 1929). It can also be studied profitably in the *Cursus theologicus* of T. Compton Carleton SJ (1664), since Fr Carleton was teaching Englishmen at Liège who had to return to England and engage in controversy about Anglican sacraments, and he viewed the scholastic dispute of the times from a practical angle. The modern discussion of mysteries and presence began with Dom Odo Casel of Maria Laach, who propounded his views in many articles from 1922 onwards. Theological discussion of them was conducted by B. Poschmann, ' Mysteriengegenwart im Lichte des hl. Thomas ', in TQ 116 (1935) 53–116 ; T. Filthaut, *La Théologie des mystères* (1954) ; B. Neunheuser OSB, ' Mysteriengegenwart, ein Theologoumenon ', in *Archiv für Liturgiewissenschaft* III (1953) 104–22 ; J. Gaillard OSB, ' La Théologie des mystères ', in RT 57 (1957) 510–51 ; J. Nicolas OP, ' Réactualisation des mystères ', in RT 58 (1958) 20–54. The role of the Church in relation to the sacraments is to be found discussed in M. J. Scheeben, *The Mysteries of*

---

[1] Effectum quem passio Christi fecit in mundo, hoc acramentum facit in homine.

[2] Nec baptizare cessavit Christus, sed adhuc id agit, non ministerio corporis, sed invisibili opere maiestatis.

Christianity (written in 1865, translated into English 1947) ; O. Semmelroth SJ, *Die Kirche als Ursakrament* (1954) ; the same, *Vom Sinne der Sakramente* (1960) ; K. Rahner SJ, *Kirche und Sakramente* (1961) ; H. Dondaine OP, 'La Définition des sacrements', in RSPT 31 (1947) 214-28 ; P. Wegenaer OSB, *Heilsgegenwart* (1958) ; B. Fraigneau-Julian PSS, *L'Église et le caractère sacramentel* (1958) ; L. Audet, *Étude sur le caractère sacramentel* (1938) ; E. Schillebeck, *Christus, Sakrament der Gottbegegnung* (1960) ; while there are general summaries in B. Leeming SJ, *Principles of Sacramental Theology* (1961²) ; W. Van Roo SJ, *De Sacramentis in genere* (1960²).

J. H. C.

CELIBACY In this article clerical celibacy is treated historically, the teaching of the Church on the counsel of perfection which consists in the forgoing of marriage being treated under CHASTITY. The present article has five sections : (I) the developments of the early centuries, (II) the early legislation introducing celibacy in the West, (III) the effective restoration of the law in the 11th cent., (IV) the position in England and (V) later legislation.

I In the first three centuries the clergy were not bound by any written law of the Church to abstain from marriage and to observe the state of celibacy, but from the early 3rd cent., as can be seen from Tertullian (*De exhortatione castitatis*, 13), the ideal of clerical continence was widely honoured and observed in the Western Church. About the year 300 the Council of Elvira in Spain forbade the use of marriage to all clerks in sacred orders (can. 33), and in the course of this century the counsel, if not the strict obligation, of celibacy was reaffirmed by other councils at Rome and in Africa. The Council of Nicaea in 325 commanded the clergy to permit no females who were not close relatives in their houses, but, though it forbade clerics to marry after ordination, the council did not forbid those of the clergy who were already married to exercise their conjugal rights. In 386 Pope Siricius ordered bishops, priests and deacons not to co-habit with their wives under pain of suspension.

By the early 5th cent. the counsel had become a general law of the Church, and celibacy was generally of obligation in the West. Pope Leo the Great (440–61) extended the obligation to sub-deacons, and repeated the precept ordering the married clergy not to live with their wives.

In the Eastern Church the ideal of clerical continence was also widely respected in the first four centuries, and many of the clergy, perhaps a majority, were unmarried, but celibacy was never imposed as an obligation. The first legislation on the subject dates from the Council of Ancyra (can. 10) in 314, when deacons were forbidden to marry after ordination unless they had previously expressly reserved the right to do so. The Council of Neo-Caesarea (c. 314–25) ordered (can. 1) that any priest taking a wife was to be deposed from his order. At Nicaea a proposal to forbid the use of marriage to those bishops, priests and deacons who were already married was rejected, but the obligation imposed on deacons at Ancyra was now extended to subdeacons. The legislation of the Eastern Church in this matter was completed at the Council *in Trullo* in 692, which permitted marriage before ordination but commanded bishops on their consecration to separate from their wives, the wives being ordered to retire to convents far removed from their husbands' places of residence.

II The early legislation of the Western Church was frequently repeated in the councils of the 5th and 6th cents., but the barbarian invasions and the consequent collapse of the Roman Empire led inevitably to a rapid decline in public order and a general collapse of ecclesiastical discipline. Under the Frankish kings of the later 8th and the early 9th cents. the law of celibacy was revived and was more generally observed in France and Germany. This was largely due to the work of St Boniface and the Anglo-Saxon missionaries who, with royal support, reformed the hierarchy, revived the canon law and in a series of national church councils attempted a general reform of the clergy ; but the dissolution of the Carolingian empire in the later 9th cent., aggravated by the incursions of the Norsemen and the Hungarians, marked the beginning of a new dark age which was to have disastrous consequences for the Church and the clergy.

In the 10th cent. the Church lay entirely at the mercy of the lay power. Bishops, abbots and priests were most commonly the nominees of the feudal lords who had little regard for clerical morals or the requirements of the canon law. The obligation of celibacy was generally disregarded, and married bishops and priests were now the rule rather than the exception. But the law itself was not forgotten and was frequently recalled by the authors of the contemporary collections of canon law. Individual bishops attempted to impose the obligation in councils and synods at Mayence in 888, Trosly (909), Augsburg (952), Winchester (975) Poitiers (1000), Pavia (1023) and Limoges in 1031. But the extent of the evil, the number of offenders and the low cultural level of the clergy generally, made the application of the law and the imposition of any effective sanction impossible.

III The effective restoration of the law of celibacy first became possible after the reform of the papacy by the German emperor Henry III in 1046. From the time of Leo IX (1048–54) the popes embarked on a wide programme of reform which aimed at freeing the Church at all levels from lay control, making papal authority effective and restoring clerical morals by eradicating the twin evils of simony and clerical marriage. The 11th-cent. reformers equated clerical incontinence with heresy, and the guilty clergy were known as Nicholaitans. The origin of this term and its early application are somewhat obscure. There is a reference in Apoc 2:14-15 to a sect of this name whose chief offence was the sin of fornication, and Irenaeus (in *adv. haer.* I:xxiii, H) identified the founder of the sect with Nicholas, the proselyte of Antioch, who is mentioned in Ac 6:5.

Pope Leo IX was chiefly concerned with the problem of simony, but in the third of his reforming councils, held at Mayence in 1049, he issued the first papal decrees against clerical marriage. In 1059 Pope Nicholas II suspended all married priests from the service of the altar and forbade the faithful to assist at their masses. This ruling was repeated and enlarged by the Pope's successors, and above all by Pope Gregory VII (1073–85) in a series of synods held at Rome in 1074, 1075 and 1078.

The papal reform of clerical morals was supported by the contemporary monastic reform which began with the foundation of the monastery of Cluny in Burgundy in 911, and the monastic revival in Lorraine and in Germany in the 11th cent. In Italy, Peter Damiani, 1006–72, a hermit, a rigorous ascetic, a powerful polemicist and the founder of the order of Fontevallana, was the chief agent of the popes in the attempt to impose celibacy on the clergy of northern Italy. In Milan he was helped by the contemporary revolt of the proletariat, the Pataria, against the aristocratic and worldly clergy who dominated the city. Peter Damiani was a prolific writer, and more than thirty of his treatises were devoted to the theme of celibacy, in which he emphasised the canonical tradition and called on the popes to impose sanctions sufficient to secure the observance of the law. But the evil was too widespread, and the Gregorian reformers of the late 11th cent. appear to have made little headway in their attempt to break down the long tradition of clerical marriage. The real turning-point in the re-establishment of the law of celibacy came in the first part of the 12th cent., when the diocesan bishops were won over to the principles of the papal reform. The movement was once again assisted by the contemporary monastic revival, above all by the astonishing development of the new religious orders, the Cistercians and the orders of regular canons, the Augustinians and the Premonstratensians. The codification of the canon law by Gratian (c. 1140) provided the reforming bishops with a detailed programme of reform which placed a special emphasis on the law of celibacy.

The earlier papal legislation on the subject was repeated and enlarged in the 1st and 2nd Lateran Councils, the first oecumenical councils in the West in 1123 and 1139. The legislation of these two councils introduced a decisive phase in the attack on clerical marriage. Until this time the clerical state was only an impediment to matrimony and the clergy were still able to contract marriages which were valid, if unlawful. In 1123 Calixtus II ordered all such contracts to be broken, and Innocent II at the 2nd Lateran Council declared all clerical marriages to be null and void. Some doubt as to whether this legislation applied to the marriages of sub-deacons was resolved by a decretal of Celestine III (1191–8). Two canons of the 4th Lateran Council held in 1215 reminded the bishops of their duty to see that the law of celibacy

was observed by the clergy under their jurisdiction, and detailed the manner in which offenders were to be punished. There is clear evidence that this obligation was taken seriously by the bishops, particularly in England, in the course of the 13th cent.

IV The English Position. This gradual re-establishment of clerical celibacy can be followed in some detail in the Church in England. There can be no doubt that clerical marriage was widespread in this country before the Conquest. In the 10th cent. two archbishops, Oda of Canterbury (942–58) and Wulfstan of York (931–56), decreed that incontinent clergy should lose their goods and be denied burial in consecrated ground. Clerical marriage was prohibited in the codes of Aethelred (979–1016) and Cnut (1016–35). In the first part of the 11th cent. a number of reforming bishops, mostly of foreign origin, attempted to enforce the rule of celibacy by compelling the canons of their cathedral churches to live a community life, sharing a common refectory and sleeping in a common dormitory. None of these measures appears to have had any lasting effect. The first serious attempt to deal with the problem in England begins with the reform of the old English hierarchy by William the Conqueror, and with the appointment of Lanfranc, a former monk of Bec and abbot of Caen in Normandy, as archbishop of Canterbury in the year 1070. Among the English bishops contemporary with Lanfranc, Wulfstan of Worcester (1062–95), the one bishop of English birth who survived the drastic reform of the hierarchy, ordered the married clergy of his diocese to give up their wives or resign their churches.

In the third of his reforming councils held at Winchester in 1076 Lanfranc introduced legislation designed to make clerical marriages impossible in the future. All canons, the clergy of the cathedral chapters and of the collegiate churches, were ordered to put away their wives. No unmarried priest was to marry, and no bishop was to ordain any cleric to the diaconate or the priesthood without a previous promise of celibacy. But the 'upland' clergy, the parish priests, were not as yet commanded to separate from their wives. The reform was carried a stage further by St Anselm, Lanfranc's successor at Canterbury; in two councils held at London in 1102 and 1108 the obligation of celibacy was imposed on all the clergy, including sub-deacons, clerical marriage was explicitly forbidden and the sons of priests were forbidden to inherit their fathers' churches.

There is sufficient evidence to show that in the course of the 12th cent. the observance of celibacy made steady progress, at least among the higher clergy, in England. In the late 11th and early 12th cents. a number of English bishops were married men. Sampson, bishop of Worcester (1096–1112) was the father of Thomas II, archbishop of York (1109–14). Thomas II was succeeded at York by Thurstan (1114–41), a zealous reformer, a devoted bishop and a patron of the new religious orders, who was himself the son of Anskar, a canon of London, and the brother of Audoen, bishop of Evreux.

Richard de Belmeis, bishop of London (1108–27), made two of his sons canons of his cathedral. There is no case of a married bishop in England in the second half of the century. Hugh de Puiset, bishop of Durham (1153–95), had several sons, but they appear to have been born before their father's promotion.

It must be remembered that in the then state of society a married priest was not necessarily a man of evil life. The married clergy had for long ensured the succession of the priesthood, since they seem commonly to have been succeeded by their sons ; in this way they ensured the essential religious services and supplied the religious needs of the people. In the life of the hermit Wulfric of Hasel-bury in Somerset, written by John, abbot of Ford, about 1180–6, there are several references to Brictric, the priest of the parish. He was a married man and a good priest, who spent the greater part of the day and part of the night in prayer in his church. He had a son, Osbern, who served Wulfric at the altar and eventually succeeded his father in the church of Haselbury, dying about the year 1172. A neighbour-ing priest, Segar, had four sons, all of whom became monks at Ford abbey. St Aelred, who became a monk of Rievaulx in 1134, and abbot of the monas-tery from 1147 to 1167, was descended from a long line of married priests who served the church of Hexham, which passed from father to son for at least three generations. Aelred's grandfather, Eilaf I, became a monk and treasurer of Durham, and his son Eilaf II, after serving Hexham for many years, was received into the community at Durham before he died.

After the 4th Lateran Council the bishops in England made a determined and persevering effort to apply the Church's law, and by the middle of the 13th cent. clerical marriage in England was no more than an occasional scandal. There was no bishop with wife or children, and the obligation of celibacy appears to have been generally observed by the higher clergy. There remained the problem of clerical incontinence, a problem that was to continue to the end of the Middle Ages. Bishop Grosseteste of Lincoln (1235–53) warned the archdeacons of the diocese that many of the clergy were said to keep *focariae*, or hearth-mates, as these clerical concubines were called. That lapses were not infrequent is evident from the records of episcopal visitations contained in the bishops' registers, but the occasional nature of this evidence makes it impossible to esti-mate the proportion of the offenders at any given period. It is probably true that there was a greater falling away in the 15th cent. The records of a visitation in the diocese of Lincoln in the time of Bishop Alnwick (1426–49), which covered some 550 parishes and which was spread over a period of 6 years, showed 37 cases of priests accused of inconti-nence, the majority of them belonging to the unbeneficed clergy. This evidence, which is not untypical, would seem to indicate that the number of offenders in any one year was very small indeed.

V Later Legislation. The Council of Trent (1545–1563) in Session XXIV (c. 9) *De Matrimonio* repeated earlier legislation when it declared that major orders constitute a diriment impediment to marriage, but the council left unsettled the question whether the impediment results from the tacit or implicit vow of celibacy taken by the ordinand, or simply from the ecclesiastical law. The institution of the seminary system by the Council, which for the first time made provision for the adequate intellectual and spiritual formation of the secular clergy, has proved to be the most efficacious means of inculcating the discipline of celibacy.

During the Modernist crisis in the early years of the present cent., as Pius X noted in the encyclical *Pascendi*, some attempt was made to question the Church's right to impose the obligation of celibacy on the clergy. The question was again raised by small bodies of the clergy in Germany and Italy at a later date. In a consistorial allocution of 16 Decem-ber 1920 Benedict XV solemnly declared that the Holy See would never in any way mitigate ' the holy and salutary discipline of ecclesiastical celibacy ' (AAS 12 [1920] 585).

Bibliography. E. Jambart, ' Célibat des clercs, droit occidental ', in *Dictionnaire de droit canonique* III, 132–45 ; E. Herman SJ, ' Célibat des clercs, droit oriental ', *ibid.* III, 145–56 ; E. Vacandard, *Études de critique et d'histoire religieuse* (1913); A. Fliche, *La réforme grégorienne* (3 vols., 1924–37) ; *D. M. Stenton, *English Society in the Early Middle Ages* (1952²) ; *F. M. Stenton, *Anglo-Saxon England* (1951²) ; *C. N. L. Brooke, ' Gregorian Reform in Action ; Clerical Marriage in England (1050–1200) ', in *Cambridge Historical Journal* XII (1956) 1–21 ; * M. Gibbs and J. Lang, *Bishops and Reform, 1215–72* (1934) ; *A. Hamilton Thomson, *The English Clergy and their Organisation in the Later Middle Ages* (1947). The controversy at the Reformation was principally between Bishop Ponet, *Defense for the marriage of priestes* (1554) and Thomas Martin DCL., *A traictise on the pretensed marriage of priestes* (1554), to which Ponet replied with *An apologie fully answering by Saints and aunceant Doctors a blasphemous Book gathered by D. Stephen Gardiner . . ., D. Smyth of Oxford, Pighius and other papists, as by ther books appeareth, and of late set forth under the name of Thomas Martin.* This work was left unfinished by Ponet at his death and Matthew Parker seems to have completed it. Much of the argument is about patristic evidence imperfectly understood, and there is a plea that, if the reformed clergy have not entered valid marriages, they are wrongfully deprived by the Queen on the ground of their marriages.

G. C.

CERINTHUS This heretic, though possessed of a Minoan name with its *-inthos* termination, was said by tradition to have been an Egyptian (Hippo-lytus, *Ref. haer.* 7:33 ; GCS 26:220), and even an Egyptian Jew (Epiphanius, *haer.* 28:2–6 ; GCS 25:313–20). Irenaeus, citing Polycarp, makes him a contemporary of John the Apostle at Ephesus, by relating the story of John leaving the public baths there when he caught sight of Cerinthus, 'for fear lest the bath-building collapse while the enemy of truth was within' (*adv. haer.* III:iii:4 H). Irenaeus later (*adv. haer.* III:xi:7 H) makes Cerinthus a follower of the Nicolaites, whom he calls Gnostics. With the mounting evidence now available that Gnosticism was rife in the 1st cent. it is obvious that these traditions have to be taken more seriously than was customary fifty years ago. Erik Peterson now locates Cerinthus firmly in the apostolic age.

His system of theology is not quite clear. It certainly included the belief that the creator of the world was not God but the angel who delivered the Law to the Jews ; thus it was thought that the imperfection of the world could be explained. The Virgin Birth was denied ; Jesus was born to Joseph and Mary, while the Christ descended on him at the baptism and remained until the passion. This was a dividing of Jesus from Christ in the manner which John condemns in I Jn 4:3. In spite of this division Cerinthus apparently believed in the resurrection of Jesus (according to Epiphanius), though holding that Jesus (without the Christ) was simply a man superior to others in wisdom and justice. Origen's view (in his *Dialektos*) that Jesus yielded up His Spirit on the cross and received It back after His meeting with Magdalen on Easter morning (when He ascended to His Father to receive It back), would not be so very different from this Christology.

Cerinthus was a chiliast (Eusebius, HE 3:28), and the presbyter Gaius (*see* ALOGI) used this fact to attack the Apocalypse of John as if it was written by Cerinthus to bolster up his system. Papias is cited by Andrew of Caesarea (PG 106:217) as upholding the divine inspiration of the Apocalypse, and it seems clear that some defence of it would be called for at a very early stage, owing to such passages as Apoc 21:1 ; 22:2. Papias was himself compromised in the matter of chiliasm by his taking the allegory of the fruitful vine (Irenaeus, *adv. haer.* V:xxxiii:3 H) in a literal sense, and it is easy to see how the attack on the Apocalypse could have been renewed by the Alogi. A trace of the polemics of that time may be found in the nickname for the followers of Cerinthus, who were called Merinthians or fishing-lines. Acceptance of circumcision and of baptism for the dead, both ascribed to him, may have been part of his Jewish outlook. The chiliasm certainly was, for it is found in the *Apocalypse of Baruch* just before this time, and its attraction for a Jew such as Papias is similarly to be explained, though the circulation of an eschatological saying of the Lord about 'what eye hath not seen' (1 Cor 2:9) is now proved by the Gospel of Thomas (saying 17) to have occurred in non-Jewish quarters.

Consonant with his Jewish outlook Cerinthus accepted the gospel of Matthew but none of the others and nothing of Paul. Epiphanius, who records this fact (loc. cit.), gives an example of his exegesis when he tells that Cerinthus used Mt 10:25 (about the disciple being content to be as his Master)

to prove the necessity of circumcision for Christians. The law of Hadrian which forbade circumcision to all and that of Antoninus Pius which forbade it to those who were not of Jewish race must have led to a decline in the following of Cerinthus.

Bibliography. The material about Cerinthus from antiquity was collected by the article on him in DCB ; G. Bardy, 'Cérinthe,' in RB 30 (1921) 344–73 ; E. Peterson in *Enciclopedia cattolica* s. v. Cerinto ; *R. McL. Wilson, *The Gnostic Problem* (1958) ; for an earlier view, *R. Casey, 'The Study of Gnosticism', in JTS 36 (1935) 45–60.

J. H. C.

CERTAINTY After a general introduction (I), the article will discuss (II) the relevance of Certainty to theology, (III) Certainty in Ancient Philosophy, (IV) Certainty and Self-knowledge, (V) Certainty and Empiricism, (VI) Moral Certainty, and finally (VII) some modern views.

I General. St Thomas defines certainty as *firmitas adhaesionis virtutis cognoscitivae in suum cognoscibile* (in *III Sent*:26:2:4c). It will exist when someone is firmly, reasonably, and rightly persuaded that a given proposition is beyond doubt. Being relational it may be viewed from the standpoint of either of its *relata* : thus the person may say either, ' I am certain that *p* ', or ' *p* is certain '. Attempts have been made to distinguish these two aspects by special terminology, such as the use of the words ' certitude ' and ' certainty ' respectively, but really the two utterances quoted express the same fact. A proposition cannot be certain in itself, since many demonstrable propositions are not known to be such. Nor can a person's state of mind in itself constitute certainty, since his inability to doubt a proposition does not prove its indubitability, if we may ignore the derivative sense in which mistaken claims to certainty are themselves certainties. True, the Laws of Identity and Contradiction appear to be so evident that no one can doubt them, and some states of mind are self-guaranteeing since they involve no more than knowledge of one's own state of mind ; but even in these instances it is not alone the *a priori* character of the proposition nor the absolute conviction of the mind that constitutes the certainty : there is always an implied reference both to conviction on the part of a subject and to a justification for this conviction grounded in the subject-matter.

Many questions in the Theory of Knowledge concern certainty : are all propositions open to doubt ? if any are certain, which are they ? are they necessary propositions, whether analytic or synthetic ? or are they reports of immediate experience ? do they include any statements about the ' external world ', about the past, or the future, any propositions of science, or of history ?

II Relevance to Theology. Complete scepticism, were it possible, would deprive faith of all rational foundation and generally render all sciences, including that of theology, impossible. But, more particularly, the dogmatic theologian is committed to the certainty of what are called the *praeambula fidei* :

the existence and veracity of God and the fact of revelation. The believer must be firmly persuaded, if he is to overcome the temptations to relinquish his faith ; and he must know the *praeambula* to be beyond doubt in order to justify the completeness of his act of faith and his tolerance of difficulties which he cannot yet resolve. Kierkegaard, who maintains that becoming a Christian demands an infinitely passionate interest for which the certainty of proofs is neither necessary nor sufficient (*Concluding Unscientific Postscript*, 25, 33, 55), and Pascal in his wager (*Pensées*, 233) seem to be allowing the importance of the subject-matter to make up for the supposedly merely probable character of the argument, contrary to the rational procedure (cf. G. Colombo, DR 77 [1959] 18–37). Of course, the temporal order of conversion may not correspond to the logical order of argument, and it is undoubtedly true that the arguments can seem uncompelling to one without interest and goodwill : it has even been claimed that without the illumination of grace no one would be capable of seeing the signs of credibility *as* proofs with full assurance (P. Rousselot, RSR 1 [1910] 241–59 ; 4 [1913] 1–36 ; but, for the relations between reason and faith, *see* FAITH *and* APOLOGETICS).

The certainty of the *praeambula* was eventually defined at the First Vatican Council (e.g. D 1785, 1806). It has always been recognized that the fact of revelation, though certain, was not evident. There has been more variety of opinion about the existence of God, which has sometimes been supposed (notably by Descartes, *Principia Philosophiae* IV:ccvi) to have a higher certainty than the ' moral certainty ' attaching to the fact of revelation. We shall see that this last distinction is of doubtful value. Moreover, the general distrust of the Ontological Argument makes it highly doubtful whether God's existence is evident in the sense of *per se notum*, and the wide spread of atheism and agnosticism (*see* ATHEISM) suggests that all arguments so far advanced leave room for sincere, if not for prudent, doubt. This much is clear : the fact of revelation presupposes the existence of God and is therefore open to all the imprudent doubts to which that is liable and, in addition, to further imprudent doubts in its own right.

There will be no discussion here of (i) the extrinsic or derivative certainty which attaches to the content of faith, or (ii) the certainty which is necessary in moral matters if sin is to be avoided (or committed) : *see* PROBABILISM.

III Certainty in Ancient Philosophy. During much of his writing life Plato's answer to scepticism based on the conflicting reports of the senses and the varying views of men was to accept it as regarding the things of everyday life and their properties, but to reserve the realm of Ideas as one in which certainty was possible. Partly this corresponds to the superior certainty which some moderns would assign to analytic and definitional statements : but Plato thought of such propositions as having a special and higher realm for their subject-matter. Aristotle differed from Plato in at least two respects. He did

not think that the highest and most divine things were also the most evident for us : it was one thing to be prior in nature, another to be prior from the point of view of our understanding (*Metaph.* α 1, *de partibus animalium* 644 b 25). Secondly, he insisted that different standards of accuracy were appropriate to different subject-matters (*Eth. Nic.* 1094 a 12 ; 1098 b 1) : thus it was no blemish on a proposition of natural science or ethics that it could not be applied to every single case (i.e., in Aristotle's terminology, that it did not possess necessity), since it was only intended to be ' for the most part ' true. This led to later distinctions of types of certainty, such as that of metaphysical (or logical), physical and moral certainty.

IV Certainty and Self-knowledge. Scepticism, of its nature, will not admit defeat : it flourished as a school of its own and in the later Academy. St Augustine's answer was to appeal first to his own existence : *si fallor, sum* (*De civ. Dei* 11:26–7 ; CSEL 40:551). Much later Descartes used self-consciousness to solve the methodical doubt by which he proposed to test all his beliefs for their certainty : implicit in the single intuition which he expressed by the words *cogito ergo sum* there was certain knowledge of the existence and veracity of God, of the truth of whatever I clearly and distinctly perceive to be true, of a large number of necessary truths so perceived, and of the general reliability of the senses. It is a subject of controversy how far Descartes is committed to assigning a certainty independent of this intuition to truths such as the Law of Contradiction and the Principle of Sufficient Reason (as it came to be called), which are involved in bringing out what is implicit in the intuition, but in any case the importance of the Cartesian approach (as Leibniz saw) is that it succeeds in finding self-evidence not only among necessary truths but among truths of fact : my own existence is contingent but certain (Leibniz, *Nouveaux Essais*, iv). Descartes himself owed much to scholasticism and his views were developed by post-Kantian scholastics (e.g. S. Tongiorgi, *Institutiones Philosophiae*, Kleutgen, *Philosophie der Vorzeit*) into the thesis that three fundamental truths at least are required for a theory of knowledge : the self, the possibility of truth, and some form of the principle of contradiction.

There are well-known weaknesses in Descartes's position. The hypothesis that our senses deceive us all the time can perhaps be shown to be senseless without invoking God's veracity. His arguments for God's existence rest on doubtful principles concerning the causes of ideas. The proposition ' I exist ' may seem to lack content (A. J. Ayer, *Problem of Knowledge*, 50). It is some defence to say that he is concerned not with deductions from propositions but with the rich content of an intuition (*Discours*, ed. Gilson, 292 ff., 314) : at any rate he succeeded in pointing out that our reflective activity itself has complex presuppositions which often render incoherent suppositions that can at first sight be entertained.

V Certainty and Empiricism. Locke and Hume

thought that our knowledge was limited to the content of our ideas and the relations between them. In Hume's case this led to a theoretical scepticism : apart from analytic truths we can know only what appears to us to be the case. For Hume no causal proposition can be known for certain, not even the principle of causality. All that we take for most certain—the existence of external bodies and of our own minds (as opposed to our momentary thoughts)—is strictly indefensible. In our non-philosophic moments, of course, we cannot help believing in these things and employing causal reasoning. What we can and ought to avoid is reasoning which is neither experimental nor concerned with mathematics : it can only be sophistry and illusion (*Inquiry concerning human Understanding, ad fin.*).

Kant's answer was a defence of the concept of substance, the principle of causality, and the like : he showed them to be necessary presuppositions of any coherent experience, but he thought they could not be extended outside experience to justify reasoning, for example, about creation. Concerning God, Freedom and Immortality he had, in his famous phrase, abolished knowledge to make room for faith (*Kritik der reinen Vernunft* B xxx).

VI Moral Certainty. Elsewhere Kant said that God's existence was morally certain, a term defined as applying to *das, dessen Aufhebung alle Moralität aufheben würde* (' any factor whose removal would take away all morality ': *Werke*, XVI:442). The term has been used in a variety of significations, (*quantum sufficit ad practicum vitae usum :* ' what meets the practical needs of life '), Descartes, *Principia Philosophiae* IV:ccv ; what we know from the testimony of others, Euler, *Lettres* 119 ; *omne quod multis indiciis confirmatur, quae vix concurrere possunt nisi in vero :* ' anything which is confirmed by many indications which could not easily be convergent unless directed upon the truth ' (Leibniz, *Opuscules* 515), but among theologians has usually indicated a certainty *either* requiring a moral attitude (the rejection of imprudent doubt) *or* resting on knowledge of how men behave (as historical arguments must). If the *praeambula fidei* are morally certain, then the fact of revelation will be so in both of these senses, the existence of God in the former only.

It seems odd, however, to make the type of certainty involved depend upon the magnitude of the temptation to imprudent doubt ; nor is it clear that other reasoning in matters of fact differs in principle from historical reasoning. It is true that Hume (*Essay on Miracles*) and Bradley (*Presuppositions*) supposed that no historical testimony could outweigh a scientific truth : but it is obvious that science relies on testimony, just as the scrutiny of testimony must be scientifically controlled. In both history and science, as in everyday life, there are many propositions which could be denied without self-contradiction but which *we* cannot deny without absurdity. Often such absurdity (like that of a mistake in mathematics) may need to be elicited by reasoning, which (in the case of matters of fact) may depend on a variety of considerations, each one individually open to question but in the mass admitting of no other explanation.

R. Whately used the methods of Hume's *Essay* to cast doubt—in 1819—on the existence at any time of Napoleon (*Historic Doubts relative to Napoleon Buonaparte*). The example was chosen, no doubt, as something indubitable, in the way that the occurrence of two European wars in this century is indubitable for us. Any argument to show that there may not have been such wars will use principles, such as the liability of human witnesses to some types of error, which are less certain than the occurrence of the wars and which rest upon grounds (common experience, memory, etc.) which we must suspect if we are to suspect the occurrence of the wars. We cannot allege the *fact* of human fallibility if we question these facts ; and, if we allege the logical possibility of human error, we must admit the possibility of logical error about logical truths ; thus, if anything is certain, some facts of history may be certain.

Somewhat similar is Newman's account (*Grammar of Assent*, cap. VIII) of certainty in all concrete matters, scientific, ethical, and spiritual as well as historical : it rests on the cumulation of independent and convergent probabilities permitting a sort of inference which is called informal because any attempt to state it formally would omit some of the probabilities, would inevitably appeal to the *judicium prudentis viri* for the assessment of those it mentioned, and would invoke principles which would themselves be liable to question and defence in the same manner. Involved in such a certainty (and in attempts to give as full a defence of it as possible) would be not just one or two self-evident facts and logical principles but the whole or most of our thought and experience.

It follows, of course, that some certainties of this kind may be easier to arrive at than others : we come to see fairly soon that it would be absurd to suppose the Aeneid a medieval forgery, while it may take a man a lifetime to see that the world requires a creator or that the Church is divinely established : yet all three truths may be equally certain.

VII Some Modern Views. The phenomenalist claim that the only certain statements of fact are reports of sense-data is now for the most part abandoned, but some still think that these statements are the evidence for all others, so that the question of the nature or validity of the inference still remains (cf. Ayer, *Problem of Knowledge*, cap. 2). Followers of Wittgenstein naturally question whether incorrigible reports could be statements : as regards certainty, they are apt to point out the logical resemblance between some *a priori* and some empirical statements. There are empirical statements (e.g. about the best-established facts of history) which we could not suppose false without destroying the concepts involved in the expression of that supposition ; or (as N. Malcolm puts it, *Mind* LXI (1952) 189) reflection can make me aware of the fact that I shall not call anything proof or evidence of the falsity of such statements. Wittgenstein (*Philosophical Investigations*, 221) was also opposed to regarding knowledge of one's own states of mind as a suitable subject for certainty ; this was a part of his reaction away from the Cartesian bias that has bedevilled all subsequent philosophy (*see* DESCARTES AND HIS INFLUENCE). Gabriel Marcel, though making a Socratic approach to philosophical problems by being content with finding out the right questions to ask, has nevertheless guided the attention of many modern thinkers to an application to problems of certainty of the distinction Bergson made popular between an open and a closed system. Marcel would say that while the judgment of credibility is like the closing of a gap or the summation of a mathematical series, the act of faith is an opening of the mind towards the Infinite ; the certainty of each act will therefore be somewhat different in character (*see* APOLOGETICS).

Bibliography. Apart from works cited in the text one may mention : P. Wilpert, *Das Problem der Wahrheitssicherung bei Thomas von Aquin* (1931) ; H. F. Davis, ' Newman on Faith and Certainty,' in JTS 12 (1961) 248–59 ; A. Chollet, in DTC s.v. Certitude ; S. Harent, op. cit. s.vv. Croyance (cols 2364–65) and Foi (cols. 206–15) ; G. Marcel, *The Mystery of Being* (2 vols. 1950) ; P. Flanagan, *Newman, Faith and the Believer* (1945); J. H. Newman, *Grammar of Assent* (1870) ; the same, *University Sermons* (1843, revised 1871) esp. sermon XII.

B. McG.

CHALCEDON There are five sections of this article, (I) the doings of Eutyches, (II) the calling of the Council, (III) its transactions, (IV) its definition of the faith and (V) its other decisions.

Hoping to pacify the Antiochenes, who had refused to accept the decisions of the Council of Ephesus (431) and were exceedingly critical of his own doctrinal statements, St Cyril of Alexandria (d. 444) in 433 subscribed to a formulary of reunion, composed, it would seem, by Theodoret of Cyrrhus (*c.* 393–*c.* 458). In virtue of this agreement Cyril recognized as orthodox the Antiochene doctrine which was wont to speak of Christ's ' two natures ' and his ' one πρόσωπον ' and he left many under the impression that he had abandoned formulas such as μία φύσις and ἕνωσις φυσική that were characteristic of Alexandrine theology. His gesture, however, did not prove to be as conciliatory as he had genuinely hoped. First of all not a few of the Antiochenes persisted in their refusal to anathematise Nestorius. Secondly some of Cyril's more ardent followers took umbrage at what they regarded as a betrayal of Alexandrine orthodoxy. To the latter Cyril tried to explain his attitude in a manner that revealed his own embarrassment : though he upheld the fundamental orthodoxy of the Antiochene formulary of reunion, he committed himself to views which implied that formulas such as ' *the union is made out of two natures* ' and ' *one nature after the union* ' were in the last resort more accurate descriptions of the true doctrine. Divorced from

their context these formulas could be interpreted as proofs that Cyril had repudiated the agreement of 433. As subsequent events proved, fanatic attachment to them when wedded at the same time to strong anti-Nestorian susceptibilities, could give rise to a new heresy.

I The Case of Eutyches and the Robber Council of 449. The embers of anti-Nestorianism, which had been slumbering during Cyril's last years, burst into flames early in the episcopate of his successor, Dioscorus (d. 454). Rumours were being circulated that Ibas of Edessa (d. 457) and Theodoret were ' dividing ' Christ. Dioscorus rudely took Domnus of Antioch to task for favouring heresy and the latter complained of Dioscorus's interferences and calumnies to Flavian of Constantinople (d. 449). The East was all agog.

At Constantinople Dioscorus had a valuable ally in the archimandrite Eutyches (*c.* 378–454), who, though friendly to Cyril, had strenuously opposed the agreement of 433. In a short time Eutyches won over not only the majority of the monks but also the Grand Chamberlain, Chrysaphius, and other highly placed courtiers, to the anti-Nestorian cause. He even dared to denounce the new outbreak of Nestorianism in the East to Pope Leo I (d. 461), who congratulated him for his zeal in language that was very guarded. Events suddenly took a different turn, however, when Eusebius of Dorylaeum denounced Eutyches for heresy to the Home Synod of Constantinople in November 448. Eutyches was condemned and deposed for refusing to avow that Christ had two natures. He immediately appealed to Leo, who, about the same time, was informed officially of the case by Flavian in his capacity as president of the Home Synod. On examining the acts of the synod, the Pope endorsed the sentence that had been passed on Eutyches. The latter, however, through Chrysaphius, was able to influence the Emperor Theodosius II to summon the bishops to a synod at Ephesus in August 449 for the purpose of settling the question. Although the Emperor had expressed his intention of entrusting the presidency of the synod to Dioscorus, Leo decided to send his legates to the assembly. He gave them a copy of his famous *Tome*, namely, the letter dealing with the doctrinal issues then at stake which he had previously sent to Flavian, with instructions that it be read before the assembled bishops. It was unfortunate that Renatus, the ablest of Leo's legates, died on his way to Ephesus. The other legates, chiefly because they did not know Greek, were quickly outmatched by Dioscorus, who, far from ensuring that Leo's *Tome* be read in public, arranged instead for the reading of the acts of the Home Synod of 448 (which had been previously altered so as to put Eutyches in the most favourable light possible). The result of this manoeuvre was the reinstatement of Eutyches and the deposition of Flavian and Eusebius. At subsequent sessions Ibas and his defenders as well as Theodoret and Domnus were deposed and Cyril's *Twelve Anathemata* were given formal approval. These enactments were accompanied by scenes of violence against which the papal legates protested in vain. One of Leo's representatives, Hilarus, managed to escape to Rome, bringing with him Flavian's appeal to the Pope. About the same time Leo also received appeals from Eusebius and Theodoret. In his indignation Leo called the Ephesine assembly the Robber Council (*latrocinium*) but his efforts to persuade Theodosius to annul its decisions proved to be unavailing. The situation might easily have led to a rupture between the East and the West had not events changed their course as a result of the Emperor's unexpected death in July 450.

II The Calling of the Council of Chalcedon. Theodosius was succeeded by his sister, Pulcheria, who decided to marry Marcian, a valiant Illyrian general, and had him proclaimed Emperor in August 450. Chrysaphius was removed from office and the new rulers expressed their intention of convoking a general council as soon as possible to establish peace in Church and State. Leo, who had previously favoured the idea of holding a council in the West, began to plead that changed circumstances now made a council unnecessary. Marcian, however, was inexorable. In May 451 he issued an edict commanding the bishops of the Empire to meet at Nicaea in the following September. Leo was induced to withdraw his opposition and he consented to appoint legates to whom he gave explicit instructions concerning the *agenda* of the council : since most of the bishops of the East had subscribed to his *Tome*, he was of the opinion that the chief business of the council should consist in healing the wounds caused by the Robber Synod and in reconciling the lapsed ; with a view to disarming the opposition of the upholders of Alexandrine orthodoxy, he thought it advisable that the council should confirm formally the decrees against Nestorianism enacted at Ephesus under Cyril's presidency in 431.

In order to convenience Marcian, who wished to attend the council in person and yet was unable to absent himself from Constantinople on account of the danger of war, the seat was changed from Nicaea to Chalcedon, a town on the Bosphorus within easy reach of the capital.

III The Transactions of the Council. The council sat in session from 8 October to 1 November 451. It was attended by more than five hundred bishops and a commission consisting of eighteen state officials represented the Emperor. In the early sessions Flavian's orthodoxy was upheld ; Dioscorus was definitively deposed and other leaders of the Robber Synod were duly punished. The creeds of Nicaea and Constantinople were confirmed ; the letters of Cyril to Nestorius (*Obloquuntur*) and to John of Antioch (*Laetentur coeli*) and Leo's *Tome* were accepted as *de fide*. The bishops of Illyricum and Palestine had objected to certain passages of the latter, which, in their opinion, implied the Nestorian error of 'dividing' Christ. In the session in which the *Tome* was formally approved by the assembly, they publicly withdrew their objections, stating that they had received satisfactory assurances concerning Leo's orthodoxy from the papal legates.

The imperial commissioners were persuaded that peace could be established definitively only through the unanimous acceptance of an unambiguous doctrinal formulary. The bishops, however, were utterly unwilling to entertain the idea of composing a new confession of faith. After much patient negotiation the commissioners finally won over the assembly to their point of view. A select committee of the bishops produced a formulary which the majority of the council was willing to accept as *de fide*. The papal legates, however, opposed it and they threatened to withdraw from the council if it were not brought into line with Leo's *Tome*. The commissioners, anxious at all costs to avoid a rupture with the West, induced the bishops to accede to the legates' request. A revised formulary was framed and accepted as *de fide* by the whole assembly.

IV The Definitio Fidei. The Fathers of Chalcedon clearly intended this doctrinal formulary to be an explanation of the creed of Nicaea (as confirmed at Constantinople in 381) but they phrased it so as to bring out both what the Church affirmed and what it denied with regard to Christ's person and natures. The formulary positively upholds (1) the unity of Christ's person ; (2) that one and the same Christ is to be 'recognized' in two natures unconfusedly, unchangeably, indivisibly, inseparably, because the difference of the natures is by no means abolished on account of the union ; nay ! the property of each nature is preserved, both natures 'concurring' into one πρόσωπον and one ὑπόστασις. The negative aspects of the council's purpose are reflected in other statements. Thus the clauses which condemn those '*who deny the title of Theotokos to the Virgin*' and assert '*that He who was born of holy Mary was a mere man*', advocating '*a duality of Sons*' and dividing Christ into '*two πρόσωπα*' certainly envisage the errors of Nestorius. Again the exclusion of the view which confuses the divine and human natures so as to render the divine nature passible, and the rejection of the opinion that before the Incarnation there were two natures which became one nature at the Incarnation contemplate the errors of Eutyches.

The formulary is a synthesis of the Christological formulas of the Eastern and Western Fathers. Most of them occur in the above-mentioned letters of Cyril. The phrase '*not as though He were parted or divided into two πρόσωπα*' is found in one of the writings of Theodoret. The phrase '*in two natures*' (ἐν δύο φύσεσι) occurs in Leo's *Tome* and was inserted into the formulary at the request of the legates and of the commissioners ; it explicitly excludes the errors of Eutyches and Dioscorus.

In speaking of two φύσεις and one πρόσωπον or ὑπόστασις the Fathers of Chalcedon certainly distinguished the concept of φύσις from that of ὑπόστασις. Though they did not define how exactly the one concept differs from the other, the background of the council shows that φύσις necessarily means *nature* in contradistinction to πρόσωπον/ὑπόστασις which in the circumstances can only mean *person*. One result of the formulary was that the expression ὑπόστασις could no longer be used with impunity as a synonym for φύσις.

V Other Decisions taken at Chalcedon. Among the disciplinary measures adopted by the council was the famous canon 28 : the bishop of Constantinople (381) was invested with effectual patriarchal jurisdiction over Asia Minor and Thrace. The papal legates protested against this enactment and Leo, though subsequently asked by the council to do so, resolutely refused to disavow them. Theodoret and Ibas were fully reinstated in their sees.

Conclusion. The Council of Chalcedon failed to achieve all the great hopes that had been placed in it. Though it showed the utmost deference to St Cyril's authority and incorporated many of his formulas in its doctrinal formulary, it estranged his more ardent followers whose intransigence eventually led them into the heresy of Monophysitism. It is certain that the council did not intend to reject the formulas of Alexandrine orthodoxy but rather to exclude a false interpretation of them such as Eutyches had given. Many regrettable misunderstandings could have been avoided, however, had the council defined the precise meaning it attached to the expressions φύσις and πρόσωπον/ὑπόστασις.

Bibliography. *E. Schwartz, *Acta Conciliorum Oecumenicorum*, II, 1–6, 1932–8 ; P. Galtier in A. Grillmeir—H. Bacht, *Das Konzil von Chalkedon*, I, 1951, pp. 343–87 ; I. Ortiz de Urbina, ibid., pp. 389–418 ; *R. Sellers, *The Council of Chalcedon*, 1953.

A.K.

CHARISMS may be defined as those free supernatural gifts of God which are given to an individual not for his own benefit nor for the strengthening of the hierarchical functioning of the Church but for its edification and growth in holiness. The theological problems which they raise are many and have been but little treated. A beginning may here be made by considering (I) the NT idea of charisms, (II) their continuation in the Church after apostolic times, and (III) their diagnosis.

I In the NT the word is used 17 times, once in 1 Pet 4:10 and 16 times in St Paul. The close resemblance of this Petrine passage to Rom 12:6 suggests that there was something in the apostolic catechesis about these gifts. It is not easy to discriminate in these two texts between what might be called graces of status (which are attached to an office in the Church) and those given at random for the edification of the faithful as a whole. Peter, after mentioning hospitality as a duty (which would naturally fall to be performed at the Agape, *q.v.*), asks that if anyone speak he should behave as the spokesman of the oracles of God, while if he minister, he should depend on the strength which God administers to him. Here the thought seems to have passed naturally from Agape to Eucharist, and if so the two functions are those of the one who officiates and of the one who helps him. If, however, it is still the Agape which is the scene of these gifts, then they may be charisms such as the speaking with tongues or the like.

Six times Paul uses the word in a wide non-technical sense (Rom 1:11 5:15–16 ; 6:23 ; 11:29 and 2 Cor 1:11). The passages in 1 Tim 4:14 and 2 Tim 1:6 are more easily taken of the grace attached to the ecclesiastical status of Timothy. There remain the five instances of the word in Paul's treatise on charisms (1 Cor 12), two isolated references earlier in that epistle (1 Cor 1:7 and 7:7) and the catalogue in Rom 12:6. The treatise was written for the Corinthians because some of them had been in the past carried out of themselves by pagan orgiastic worship and now looked for something of the same kind from Christianity. Paul gives them a sure diagnostic by laying down that all Christian manifestations must square with the dogmas of the faith (1 Cor 12:3, cf. Rom 12:3). He then gives a classification which is not easy to understand but which is probably to be taken as reminiscent of an early Trinitarian formula, on the lines of which it is built (there are other such in 2 Cor 13:13 and Eph 4:4–6). Charisms, ministries and deeds of power are 'attributed' or appropriated to the Spirit, the Son and the Father respectively, and they are not completely distinct from each other. In the succeeding verses Paul enumerates nine different charisms in what seems to be a descending order of importance, as he places speaking with tongues and the interpretation of this phenomenon last of all. He was writing at a time when an inspired NT did not yet exist but was in process of formation (his own letter was to be one of its parts) and his 'word of wisdom' and 'word of Gnosis' may refer to the pre-eminent charism of the inspired writing of the Scriptures. Faith that will move mountains, a gift of healing and deeds of power are all public benefits, as the person who has such faith (for instance, St Teresa of Avila in her foundations) is not usually consoled by having it nor strengthened in the theological virtue of faith ; it is more a matter of confidence in God, which is required for the undertaking of spiritual works on behalf of others. Prophecy and discernment of spirits are both social gifts for the benefit of the Christian community, the activities of Barnabas and Agabus in Acts illustrating the one and Paul himself the other in his treatment of the sons of Scaeva and the pythonical girl of Phillippi.

After Paul has enlarged upon the doctrine of the Mystical Body, he returns (1 Cor 12:28–30) to his list of charisms and now seems to assign them to different offices in the Church. It is more likely that he wants to impress on the Corinthians that hierarchical graces of status come first (for apostles, preachers and teachers) and only then is there a place for charisms strictly so called, whether of healing, of discernment or of speaking with tongues. No one at least has claimed that there was ever in the Church a permanent office of glossolalist. The other two lists which Paul gives (Rom 12:6–8 and Eph 4:11) are more certainly hierarchical save for the mention of prophets each time. It is possible that in more normal times (for Corinth seems to have been a special case) Paul would have put together in the category of prophecy all these charismatic phenomena, since they were appropriated to the Spirit and were for the edification of the faithful. Peter, in his discourse at Pentecost (Ac 2:17–20), by his use of the passage from Joel certainly classes the Pentecostal speaking with tongues as prophecy and seems to expect a continuation, even though quite random, of such phenomena (see CCS 823 c). In 1 Cor 14 (see CCS 880 b–f) Paul argues that speaking with tongues is to be regarded as a lower sub-group of prophecy. The word 'prophecy' did not then connote a knowledge of the future ; it was used (e.g. in 1 Mac 4:14) to denote any spiritual insight.

Paul's statement in 1 Cor 7:7, that each one has his own charism from God (the context being his own practice of celibacy), need not be taken as contradicting his teaching about the exceptional nature of charisms. Everyone who is baptized receives sanctifying grace for himself, to keep in being his status as a cell in the Body of Christ, but there is also a further gift of God, which each cell has, to help to bind it to the others ; this may be a grace of status, when the individual has an office in the Church, or it may be just 'for edification', in many people not rising above a certain threshold and so not manifesting itself, but in some being quite exuberant and unable to be hidden. Thus the choice of a life according to one or several of the evangelical counsels would be in a wide sense charismatic, while the gift of healing would be more precisely so. On these lines Paul's language can be interpreted without any departure from consistency. If one bears in mind that the Spirit breatheth where He will, this idea of general possession of charisms at a subliminal level with an occasional and apparently random surging over the threshold may be found most adequate to fit in with the language of the NT.

II The non-continuation of charisms after apostolic times is often now held to be a fact, and reasons are quickly assigned for it, e.g. that the very existence of the Church came to be a sign to the nations which did not need the embellishment of more gaudy charisms. Gregory the Great is cited for this view (PL 76:721), but what he really says is not quite so sweeping. He claims, while discoursing on Job 41:13, that before the coming of Leviathan there will be a darkening of prophecy, a withdrawal of the gifts of healing, less power to sustain prolonged fasts, no miracles and a silence in place of the words of doctrine.[1] He can hardly have expected all this to have begun at the close of the apostolic age. Calvin used the idea of the fading of the charisms to evade the plain evidence of Jas 5:16 for the sacrament of Extreme Unction. He argued (Institutiones, IV:19:18) that the grace of healing vanished with all other miracles, as God had meant these to be no more than temporary while the gospel was first being preached. After that the ingratitude of men caused their withdrawal, and with them went, so he implied, the practice of anointing the sick. He somewhat over-

played his hand, for he went on to taunt the Catholics of the time : 'Why did they not set up another Pool of Siloe, if they thought that what was told in the NT was meant for later practice ?'[2] The existence of Lourdes today is a sufficient answer to that taunt. Yet the lessening of charisms after the apostolic age might be no more than the normal accompaniment of the fact that there was to be no inspired Scripture after that time, and that bishops were not to inherit all the prerogatives of the apostles.

In his praise of charity St Paul had implied (1 Cor 13) that prophecy would come to an end, but he does not say that this will be immediately after the death of the last apostle. None the less, some Christians of the 2nd cent. seem to have taken him in that sense, for when Clement of Alexandria cites the passage (Quis dives salvetur, 38 ; GCS 17:184) a phrase has been added to the text, saying that gifts of healing will be left upon the earth. This would imply a belief, on the part of some, that other charisms had already faded away. Origen (in Ioannem 2:204 ; GCS 6:92) compares the argument from Christ's miracles with that from prophecy as evidences for Christianity and speaks all the time as if for him prophecy means no more than what was in the OT. The saying in Mt 11:13 and Lk 16:16 implies that prophecy ended with John the Baptist, and in fact the Gospel of Thomas (saying 53) gives a total of 'twenty-four prophets (who) spoke in Israel, and all of them spoke concerning You'. Jewish tradition reckoned with no more than 23, and John the Baptist must have been added to the traditional number. On the other hand, when the Church is engaged in rejecting the Montanists, it is never made quite clear that prophecy has in fact stopped. In the anti-Montanist treatise cited by Eusebius (HE 5:17) the daughters of Philip, Ammia and Quadratus are clearly taken to have been orthodox prophets of the Christian period. The Montanists are challenged to show their succession-list of prophets since the death of Maximilla (she had said : 'After me there shall be no prophetess but the end of the world') ; the basis of this argument, that the prophetical charism must go on to the end of the world, is explicitly stated. One cannot say what authority the anonymous writer had, but his position was accepted as orthodox by Eusebius.

It is clear from 1 Jn 4:1 and 1 Thess 5:20–1 that prophecy was kept under strict control by the authorities of the Church, but in the second of these passages it is laid down that prophecy should not be 'annihilated'. Ignatius envisages the possibility (Eph 20:2) that God will give him a revelation ; this must be private in character (see REVELATION) and not an extension of the deposit of faith. Polycarp (according to the account of his martyrdom, 16:2) was accepted as a prophetical teacher, some of whose sayings had come true, but this gift is seen as distinct from his position as bishop. In the same way the prophetical activity of Silas and Barsabbas (Ac 15:22, 32) is regarded as distinct from their position in the

---

[1] Nam prophetia absconditur, curationum gratia aufertur, prolixioris abstinentiae virtus imminuitur, doctrinae verba conticescunt, miraculorum prodigia tolluntur.

[2] Cur non aliquam natatoriam Siloah destinant in quam certis temporum vicibus se immergant male habentes ?

Church as leaders. In the course of time it would be almost inevitable that charisms such as prophecy and the gift of healing would be felt to need a proper initiation or ordination such as was given to those who held positions in the hierarchy of the Church ; grace of status for these would seem to be in exactly the same case as charismatic healing. Thus in the *Testament of the Lord* (1:47) the idea of an ordination for charismatics has to be rejected : 'If anyone appear in the people to have a gift of healing or of knowledge or of tongues, a hand is not laid on him, for the work is manifest. But let them have honour.' The *Canons of Hippolytus* (53, 54) say that a man with the gift of healing is not to be ordained until it is clear that the gift is from God. The Ethiopic version of the *Traditio apostolica* (alone extant here of the versions) says : 'If someone says : "I have acquired the grace of healing and prophecy," they shall not lay hand upon him until his deed make evident that he is trustworthy.' The *Apostolic Constitutions* (8:26:2) has assimilated the charismatics to exorcists. 'The one who has a gift of healing has been made manifest by God through a revelation, and his gift is plain to all.' He is not to be ordained, any more than the exorcist, unless he is needed as a deacon or priest. In those times the exorcist was expected to look after the mentally unstable, who were kept in a separate pen during Mass, and who would otherwise be a trouble to the rest of the congregation. Such work would call for qualities that might be easily assimilated to those of the charismatic.

The treatise on charisms in the *Apostolic Constitutions* (8:1–2) clearly supposes that they will continue in the Church. The Apostles are represented as saying that charisms were first given to themselves, 'and then of necessity provided for those who found faith by our means, not for the help of those who wrought them but for the conviction of the unbelievers, that where they have not been persuaded by argument they may be abashed by the power of miracles'. Those who have such charisms are exhorted not to be puffed up, for, if there were no more unbelievers, then their gift would become superfluous. Prophecy and healing are the chief charisms envisaged in the work, and among the prophets are mentioned Our Lady, Elizabeth and Anne, and the daughters of Philip.

Among modern theologians there has been the widest diversity about the part charisms should play in the Church. A writer in the DTC (XI:2471, s.v. Paul) thought that they were destined to disappear or to play no part at all in the social life of the Church after the apostolic age. On the other hand, P. Lemonnyer claimed that they were not at all temporary phenomena. It was one of the preoccupations of Cardinal Newman to bring out the permanence of miracles in the Church. In his Anglican days he had lectured on the prophetical office of the Church, and as a Catholic he issued a revision of his *Essay on Miracles* in which he was at pains to defend against Gibbon and others the miracles related by Eusebius from the early centuries of the Church (*see* MIRACLES). The canonical requirement of certain miracles before the proclamation of a new saint (*see* CANONISATION) is an unspoken commentary on this matter of the continuity of miracles in the Church. Some confusion may have been due to the wider use of the term charism, as shown in Vatican I (D 1837) where it is used of papal infallibility, but the main fact, that the Church is meant by God to be marked with charismatic gifts as long as there are pagans to convert, should not be in doubt. Vatican II (*Constitutio de ecclesia*, II:12) laid it down that charisms, whether of an ordinary kind or not, should not be sought for ; if given, they should be received with gratitude. It would be presumption to expect them as a result of apostolic labours. The decision about their true nature and about the use to be made of them belongs to the Church authorities.

III The diagnosis of charisms is not easy. In the decree of canonization of Gemma Galgani (AAS 24 [1932] 517) the Church expressly stated that the declaration of her sanctity did not imply the supernatural character of her stigmata. The same problem arises over many cases where charisms seem to occur in conjunction with what on other grounds must be accepted as sanctity. Thus Ignatius of Antioch (*Phil.* 7:1) wrote : 'When I was amongst you, I cried out with a loud voice that was the voice of God : "Give heed to your bishop, and to his priests and deacons".' Here one can accept the doctrine without having to believe that Ignatius was speaking charismatically when he gave expression to it, though one may recognize the probability that he was. The account in Hermas (43:1–21 ; GCS 48:40) of the way to test a prophet shows how the early Church set about the problem, while the exaltation of prophets in the Didache (13:1–7), where the testing of a prophet is said to be the unpardonable sin, could well be a reaction against such treatment. The papyrus fragment (*Oxyrhynchus Papyri*, 5), which cites Hermas and then goes on to claim that prophets are somehow new instances of the Incarnation, is another sign that not everyone was ready to submit to the somewhat severe attitude of the Church towards charisms. Private revelations (*see* REVELATION) are often claimed by enthusiasts but do not find favour with the Church. Examples abound from the days of St Bridget of Sweden to those of Anne Catherine Emmerich.

The same problem of diagnosis had existed for OT prophecy, as Justin remarked (*dial.* 82:1), and Caiphas was often used as an instance of the charism of prophecy without the sanctity of life that should go with it. The gifts which according to Eph 4:8 Christ gave to men after His Ascension were more abundant and diverse than what had been dispensed in OT times, but they needed testing in much the same way. 'One must needs put to the test all the fruits of a prophet. Does a prophet, I wonder, dye his hair ? Does he paint his eyelids ? Is he fond of fine clothes ? Does a prophet gamble with dice at tables ? Does a prophet lend money at interest ?' These questions put by the anti-Montanist writer (Eusebius, *HE* 5:18) show the Church hard at work over her diagnosis after a century and a half of life.

Irenaeus (*adv. haer.* III:xi:12, H) speaks of some who in his time rejected all idea of charisms in the Church and would not accept Paul's treatise on them. They are like, he says, to those who will not communicate with the brethren because there are some who come there with feigned intent.

It might be possible to argue *a priori* that a lessening of charisms was to be expected in modern times, from some words of the encyclical of Leo XIII against Americanism. Fr Hecker, the publication of whose *Life* in a French version had occasioned the dispute, spent the three years immediately preceding his ordination almost without opening a book and yet was judged to know enough theology to be ordained. His reliance on the inner guidance of the Holy Spirit in this and other matters was defended on the ground that the outpouring of the Spirit was more abundant now than of old. Commenting on this the Pope said that no small temerity was needed to judge of the activity of the Spirit. Yet who could go back to the history of the apostles and the primitive Church and then claim that they were granted a smaller outpouring of the Spirit than the present time ? (*Tablet* LXI [1899] 350). External guidance was in God's ordinary Providence needed to supplement the inner motion of the Spirit, and this had been acknowledged by Fr Hecker, though not by his French admirers. Charisms are for the greater unity of the Church ; they help to hold it together, binding its new members to the old, as Ignatius (*Eph.* 9) saw when with his bold metaphor he spoke of the Holy Spirit as the rope which helped to haul up the stones for the building of the Church, the windlass being the cross of Christ.

Bibliography. B. Maréchaux, *Les Charismes du Saint-Esprit* (1921) ; A. Lemonnyer OP, ' Charismes ', in DBS ; H. Pope OP, ' Prophecy in NT times ', ITQ 7 (1913) 400–16 ; F. Prat SJ, *La Théologie de Saint Paul* I (Appendix D) ; X. Ducros, ' Charismes ', in D Sp. ; Cardinal Newman, *Essay on Miracles* (1873). J. H. C.

CHARITY, THEOLOGICAL VIRTUE OF
Questions concerning the scriptural, dogmatic and theological development of the Church's teaching on the virtue of charity find their proper setting in the wider question of Pneumatology—the section of theology concerned with the Holy Spirit (q.v.) as the distributor, within the Church and according to the measure of Christ's giving (Eph 4:7), of created grace and of the supernatural virtues and gifts. Pneumatology, in its turn, has to be seen in the light of the doctrine of the Mystical Body (*see* BODY, MYSTICAL), more precisely in terms of Christ's role as head of the Church and in terms of his capital grace (cf. S. Tromp, *Corpus Christi quod est Ecclesia. Pars altera, de Christo Capite Mystici Corporis*, 500 ff.). This approach to the virtue of charity would meet the recent criticism of Karl Rahner (*Theological Investigations*, I, 188) : ' There is hardly any mention of Christ in the tractate *de Virtutibus Theologicis* : the discussion moves merely in the

thin atmosphere of pure theological metaphysics '. Bearing in mind these wider horizons this article seeks to give a reading of the Church's understanding of the virtue of charity, particularly as this understanding is seen reflected in the teaching of the doctor of charity, St Augustine (*La Charité dans l'enseignement de Saint Augustin* : *Dossier rassemblé par l'abbé M. Huftier*, Monumenta Christiana Selecta, Vol. V, 1959), of St Bonaventure (*Questions Disputées* : *de Caritate, de Novissimis*, édition critique by P. Glorieux, 1950), and of St Thomas (*Quaestio disputata de Caritate*, edited by P. A. Odetto, Turin, 1949). Using the classical intellectual model of object-act-habit, the nature of the virtue of charity is established (I). Another intellectual model, that of the causes, is used to clarify questions concerning the existence of the virtue (II). A final section is devoted to the effects of the virtue (III).

I Nature of the Virtue of Charity. As a theological virtue charity has God for its object, that which terminates charity. As a virtue perfecting the will charity is concerned with the goodness of God. This infinite goodness can be considered as the source and end of natural existence and as such is the object of the natural love of the creature for its Creator. But this same infinite goodness can be considered as the object of God's beatitude. When considered as the object of God's beatitude the infinite goodness of God is the object of charity (St Thomas, *Quaestio disputata de Caritate* 7:c).

From this understanding of the object of the virtue of charity there follows the distinction between the natural love of God and that love of God that has its proximate source in the virtue of charity. The creature, by reason of its nature, has a capacity for the love of God as the source whence it came and to which, by means of its operations, it seeks to be united as to its last end wherein it finds happiness and rest. Indeed this natural love of the creature for its Creator is said to be innate in the rational creature, since by nature the will is determined to this love of God ; such love is spontaneous and is the source of all other loves (*Quaestio disputata de Caritate* 1:c). It cannot be said, however, that the creature by its nature has a capacity to love the infinite goodness of God as this is the object of God's beatitude. Being infinite the beatitude of God is something that transcends the capacity of all creatures. For such a capacity to exist in the creature there is required the elevation of the creature, in the Son of God, to the dignity of divine sonship, which alone makes the creature heir to the happiness of God. It is not according to nature but according to the grace of divine adoption that the capacity to love the divine goodness as the object of God's beatitude exists in the rational creature. Hence the love that springs from the virtue of charity is said to be a supernatural love of God and the virtue of charity is said to be infused.

Although the natural love of God and that love of God that has its origin in the virtue of charity are distinct, there is a real connection between them ; for both are participations of the beatitude of God and the latter supposes the former. Against the errors of Baius (q.v.) and others, the magisterium of the Church (D 1034 ; 1297 ; 1394–1408 ; 1523) has been careful to preserve the validity of the natural love of God as the locus in which the love of God that is grace can be realised. There is parity here with the situation that arises in regard to the knowledge of God. Unless the possibility for a natural knowledge of God is safeguarded (D 1785), it becomes impossible to ensure the insertion in man of that knowledge of God by His self-manifestation in revelation, which is pure grace.

In the object of charity, as in the object of any habit or power, two aspects, the formal and the material, can be distinguished. The formal is that aspect according to which the object is referred to the virtue ; whilst the material aspect is concerned with the manner in which the formal aspect is present in the object. The formal aspect of the object of charity is the goodness of God as the object of God's beatitude. There is but one formal aspect of the object of charity ; whereas, in regard to the material aspect, it is meaningful to speak of a plurality of objects of charity. For the formal aspect of the object of charity is found in God essentially and only by way of participation in all that is not God. Where the formal aspect of the object of charity is found essentially, there is the principal object of charity ; where it is found by participation we have the secondary object of charity. It is in terms of the material aspect of the object of charity that there is the dual enunciation of the precept of charity—to love God above all things, and to love our neighbour as ourselves. Love for the secondary object of charity is relative to love for the principal object, that is, that the beatitude of God may be in it by way of participation.

The formal aspect of the object of charity is found essentially in God and by way of participation in all that is not God. But it is important to notice the manner of this participation. The creature is called 'to enjoy a beatitude very similar to that with which the most holy and undivided Trinity is blessed' (Pius XII, *Mystici Corporis*, D 2290) not as an isolated individual but as forming part of a whole, as a member of the household of God, as a citizen of heaven. The secondary objects of the virtue of charity share in a common beatitude of which the author is the principal object of charity : 'God embraces and beatifies the citizens of heaven' (Leo XIII, *Divinum Illud*, ASS 29 [1896] 653).

When the object of the virtue of charity is seen as a common good, the love that has its source in the virtue of charity appears in its true light. It is a love that is not concerned primarily with the utility of the individual, not the self-love of concupiscence. Rather it is a love of benevolence in which the goodness of the object is loved for its own sake. Such a love of benevolence in one who is a part of a whole manifests itself by seeking to preserve and extend the common good of the heavenly city, and by striving to overcome all that is hostile to that common good. For the part to seek to possess for

its own utility the good of the whole is a travesty of true love for the common good. In this way the damned seek to possess the beatitude of heaven (*Quaestio disputata de Caritate* 2:c). So there is a sense in which the love of charity is a disinterested love, altruism (q.v.). But there is also a sense in which this same love of charity is interested, for by the nature of things the citizen realises his destiny within the common beatitude of the heavenly city. It is a false question if it be asked whether the love of charity can be qualified as *eros* or *agape*, without taking into consideration that those who have the virtue of charity are called to share in a common beatitude. Perhaps it was the great part that the vision of the heavenly city had in the mind of St Augustine that earned for him the title of doctor of charity.

The act of charity is the union of the soul with the infinite good as the object of God's beatitude. Because it is an act of the will this union is an affective one. In connection with affective union St Thomas (*Summa* 1–2ae:28:1:@2) distinguishes two other unions, one of which is the cause of affective union, the other its effect. As cause of the affective union between the soul and God, which is the act of charity, there is the union by way of resemblance that grace (q.v.) establishes between the soul and God. A similar situation is found in the natural order where love of one's neighbour supposes a union by likeness in nature. The presence of sanctifying grace in the soul produces that prior union by resemblance on which the further union, this time by operation, rests (*Quaestio disputata de Caritate* 2:@7). Theologians differ among themselves regarding the nature of the distinction, whether real or virtual, between sanctifying grace and the virtue of charity. All however agree in requiring the presence of sanctifying grace as the condition for the affective union of the soul with God that is realised in the act of charity.

The union that is the consequence of affective union is effective union. As St Thomas (*Quaestio disputata de Caritate* 2:@6) points out, effective union between the soul and God does not enter the definition, the *ratio*, of charity. It is true that, where effective union, the meeting of two people who love one another, is absent, affective union gives rise to the desire for effective union, and when it is present affective union finds rest in the fruition of effective union. But it is necessary to keep the distinction between affective and effective union in mind if the nature of the act of charity is to be understood.

The affective union between the soul and God can be described as the attraction that the supreme good exercises on the will and as the surrender of the soul to this attraction. Together attraction and surrender result in a kinship, harmony or connaturalisation, all of these terms being attempts to express in words the unique reality of the affective union that comes about in the act of love.

In the act of charity the object has a dual function. It terminates the act of charity in that this act is the affective union of the soul with God. Also it has a role to play as the specifying principle of the act of charity. This act is an immanent operation and so supposes as its principle a union of subject and object. The supreme good as the object of God's beatitude must be present in the will as determining or specifying the finality of the will. As the result of the soul's elevation by sanctifying grace there is the orientation of man to his supernatural end. However, before this finality or orientation can become operative, a further determination of the will is required. It is the function of the object to do this. For the object to exercise this function its goodness must be apprehended by the mind and presented to the will by the mind. This is what is meant when the act of charity is said to be an *elicited* love. And it is here that theological faith has its part in the act of charity. Left to its native powers the mind of man is incapable of grasping the beatitude of God and God as beatifying the citizens of heaven. Only in the light of faith can the mind accomplish the specification of the will that leads to the act of charity. In this specification of the will by the mind, both apprehension and judgment, the *liberum arbitrium* or judgment of value, are involved. This judgment of value is concerned with assessing, in terms of the will's finality, the attraction of the goodness of the object. And at this point the virtue of charity comes into play.

Because the act of charity is an act of elicited love involving appreciation or judgment of value, the question of the attitude of the person making this appreciation is of paramount importance. As Aristotle pointed out long ago and as is confirmed by experience, appreciations are largely determined by subjective dispositions. A sore throat explains why a pipe has lost its customary attraction for the smoker. In this connection the traditional definition of virtue as that by which a person has the right attitude (*bene se habet*) has its place.

The virtue of charity is that supernatural disposition of the will which results in a person having the right attitude to God as his last end. This disposition of the will is able to ensure that here in this life, where the attraction of the supreme good is not evident and where there is room for choice in the good in which final happiness is placed, the correct choice is made. Even in heaven, when the attraction of God's beatitude will be evident, the virtue of charity will still have its role to play, for surrender to that supreme goodness will be eminently free and personal, supposing in the subject the right attitude to God. In heaven the act of charity will still be an elicited love.

The necessity for the virtue of charity was called into question by Peter Lombard. His reason for doing so was that Scripture and Tradition so closely associate the Holy Spirit with man's ability to love God with the love of charity that the virtue of charity seems superfluous. But as St Thomas (*Quaestio disputata de Caritate* 1:c) points out, the special nature of the act of the will, its auto-determination, requires in the will both uncreated charity, the presence of the Holy Spirit, and created charity, the virtue of charity. The idea of the will being moved to

produce its act by an agent other than itself is alien to the nature of the voluntary act. If the Holy Spirit were the sole principal agent in man's act of charity, man's role would be reduced to that of being the instrument used by the Holy Spirit. It is indeed true that the Holy Spirit moves the soul to produce acts of charity, but He does so in a manner that is in harmony with the voluntary nature of the act of charity ; this supposes in a person the right attitude to God as his last end and the disposition of the will that lies behind such an attitude. St Thomas further points out that in the unilateral view of Peter Lombard where no place is left for the virtue of charity it is difficult to see how the meritorious character of the act of charity in this life can be preserved ; nor is it possible to explain certain psychological factors, e.g., the pleasure experienced by the soul when it produces an act of charity.

Outside this context of the role of the Holy Spirit in the act of charity, to deny the necessity for the elevation of the will by the supernatural virtue of charity (D 800 ; 821) would have the heretical consequence of making the object of charity fall within the capacity of man's nature. All the acts of the will go back to that basic act, of the will as nature, that is its finality. And similarly all the dispositions that the will is capable of receiving, other than those infused by God, in their turn go back to that fundamental disposition of the will wherein by nature it has the right attitude to its natural end.

In conclusion it should be borne in mind that the virtue of charity is not a medium that comes between the soul and God in their affective union. In the act of charity is realised the immediate affective union of the soul with God. Where the virtue of charity functions is in the specification, the determination of the will that leads to the act of charity. At the source of the act of charity as its proximate principle stands the virtue of charity : virtue not only makes its possessor good, it also makes his action good.

II Existence of the Virtue of Charity. This question is discussed in the light of the causes of the virtue, and in the first place of its efficient cause. The disposition of the will that means that a person has the right attitude to God as his supernatural end, the attitude proper to the member of the household of God and the citizen of heaven, is the effect of the immediate action of God. The efficient cause of the virtue of charity is God. The divine action brings the virtue of charity into existence in the will, not by developing the possibilities latent in the will but by producing there a resemblance to God's charity. St Thomas (*Quaestio disputata de Caritate* 1:@5) recalls that God is said to be charity not simply because He is the cause of charity, as He is the cause of the virtues of hope and patience, but more particularly because God is charity essentially. Of this uncreated charity the virtue of charity is a created participation. Hence its existence and preservation depends directly on God. It is an infused virtue differing from the virtues that man can acquire by developing the possibilities inherent in his nature.

Theologians commonly teach that the virtue of

charity is produced in the will when sanctifying grace is given by God to the soul (D 483). And as they discuss the question whether the sacred humanity of Christ, more particularly His human will, has a part in the production of grace in the soul, this same question can be moved when it is a matter of the efficient cause of charity. On this point there is a difference of opinion among theologians. In his recent study, *De Christo Capite Mystici Corporis* (1960) 286–311, Sebastian Tromp makes a strong case for the place of the human will of Christ, elevated by the virtue of charity and with reference to the anointing of His human nature by the grace of union, as the physical instrumental cause used by God in the production of grace and the virtues and gifts. This author sees the capital influence of Christ on His Church largely in terms of this role of His human will as the instrument used by God in the production of grace, and so of the virtue of charity, in the souls of those who are members of His Mystical Body (op. cit. 496–500).

The final cause of the virtue of charity is the glory of God and of Christ : ' Blessing and honour and glory and power, through endless ages, to him who sits on the throne, and to the Lamb ' (Apoc 5:13). From the teaching of the Council of Trent on justification (D 799) another factor in the final cause of charity is eternal life. The motive of God producing the virtue of charity in the will is that man should be able to enjoy a beatitude very similar to that with which the holy and undivided Trinity is blessed. In this beatification of the citizens of heaven the beatitude of the holy Trinity and that of Christ's humanity are manifested and glorified.

The formal cause of the virtue of charity, what St Bonaventure (*Quaestio disputata de Caritate* 1:c ; 14) calls the substance or essence of charity and which is not to be confused with the *ardor caritatis*, is that perfection or disposition that has to be present in the will if a person is to possess the virtue of charity. St Thomas (*Quaestio disputata de Caritate* 5:c) defines this perfection as that disposition of the will that gives a person the right attitude to his last end. It is important to notice that what, in the case of other virtues, is the final cause, is the formal cause of charity. Virtue is defined as that which enables man to live rightly, and to live rightly man must realise his destiny of sharing in the beatitude of God. But the formal cause of virtues other than charity is a disposition that gives the right attitude to some matter other than man's last end. Thus the virtue of justice is that disposition of the will that causes a man to seek to give to each his due. Even in the theological virtues of faith and hope the formal causes are dispositions that enable man to adopt attitudes of belief and trust in God when He reveals His truth and promises a share in His beatitude. Only in the virtue of charity is the disposition immediately concerned with the infinite good as the object of God's beatitude. This point is decisive in determining the role of charity among the virtues and in explaining why charity is said to be the queen and mother of the virtues. It is also important in the question of the perfection and growth of charity. The ultimate perfection of the virtue of charity, its actuality, is not that it should always be producing acts of charity but that this disposition giving the right attitude to the last end, this created resemblance to uncreated charity, should be present in the will (*Quaestio disputata de Caritate* 12:@9). Growth in the virtue of charity has to be seen in terms of this disposition coming to resemble more nearly the perfection of the source whence it originates.

There is no material cause of the virtue of charity in the sense of the matter out of which the virtue is made. Taken in a wide sense however, the category of material cause can be applied to charity and its use is helpful in clarifying the states or conditions in which the virtue can be found. The right disposition to the last end that is the essence of charity can be found in its subject, the will, in such a way that it does not prevent the will from receiving further dispositions that give rise to attitudes to the last end other than the attitude proper to charity. Such is the case with the virtue of charity as it modifies the will in this life, or charity in its pilgrim state. In heaven, where charity is in its terminal state, the disposition that is the virtue of charity so modifies the will as to make it incapable of receiving any other dispositions in regard to its last end. It follows therefore that in its pilgrim state charity is present in the will in such a way that it can also cease to be there. For when a disposition that gives rise to an attitude in regard to the last end, other than the disposition of charity, is present in the will, the virtue of charity ceases to be in the will. Not that the other disposition directly removes the virtue of charity, as in painting a wall one colour may replace another ; but when a person places his last end in something other than sharing in the beatitude of God the will is averted from God and by this very fact is incapable of receiving the influence of the divine action producing the virtue of charity. Any disposition of the will in regard to the last end that is opposed to the disposition of charity can be qualified as the state of mortal sin ; one mortal sin is sufficient to deprive the will of charity. From this it follows that once the virtue is present in the will it cannot in its essence or substance be diminished. That which would diminish the virtue, mortal sin, results in the total removal from the will of the virtue.

That charity in its pilgrim state can be increased is the common teaching of the Church. The problem here is to see the nature of this increase. The perfection of the other virtues is increased by charity and in some cases by the gifts of the Holy Spirit. But there is nothing in the genus of virtues and gifts that can perfect charity since, by reason of its formal object, it is the supreme principle in the order of operations. If it is meaningful to speak of the virtue of charity being increased, it must be within its own specific perfection that the increase takes place. Such increase is possible. The virtue of charity is a participation by resemblance of the uncreated charity of God. This resemblance admits of degrees according as it approaches nearer to its divine exemplar.

Only in the case of the virtue of charity in Christ's human will was this resemblance maximal from the beginning ; in all others it can be increased whilst in this life. And as God is the efficient cause of charity, so too He is the cause of its increase.

Growth in the virtue of charity supposes the co-operation of man. With the help of actual grace he can, by using the virtue to produce acts of charity both in terms of its principal and secondary objects, make his attitude to his last end more personal, more deeply rooted in himself. In turn this results in it being more difficult for his will to receive dispositions opposed to charity ; he is less easily influenced by external factors such as public opinion, or by prejudices arising from his individual situation. But this action of man does not go beyond preparing himself to receive the action of God increasing the virtue of charity ; he can never claim to be the physical cause of that increase. By way of merit too man plays a part in the increase of his charity. Actions whether elicited by charity or commanded by that virtue are meritorious. St Augustine (*ep.* 189 *ad Bonifacium*, 2 ; PL 33:854) says that charity merits both increase in this life and in the next life its crown.

Although there are the two states of the virtue of charity, there is but one numerical virtue. The difference between these states has to be measured not by the virtue of charity but by its subject the will. Because of the beatific vision (q.v.) the specification of the will is such that all its possibilities of receiving dispositions in regard to its last end will be actualised. This will mean that charity can never cease to be present in the will and so the possibility of mortal sin will be removed for ever. Further the *ardor caritatis* will be such that no action will escape its influence, and so all possibility of venial sin is removed. The crown of the virtue of charity, the special perfection that it will have in its terminal state, is this power to bring within the field of its formal object—the infinite good as the object of God's beatitude—all man's actions. By nature (*voluntas ut natura*) the will has, as its primary act, love for the supreme good. All subsequent acts of the will (*voluntas ut ratio*), whether elicited by itself or acts elicited by other virtues but under the command of the will, are participations of this essential or source-act of the will. So by the law of causality this primary act of the will must be present in all the subsequent acts of the will. But the crown of charity is something much more than this causal presence of the will in all human acts (*see* ACTS, HUMAN). It supposes that the formal perfection of charity, its resemblance to uncreated charity, will be communicated to all man's actions ; charity will be the unifying principle operative in them.

The exemplary cause is a category that can be applied to the virtue of charity in several ways. The virtue has both a created and an uncreated exemplar, and the latter can be considered either essentially or notionally. The created exemplar is the virtue of charity as it is found in the human will of Christ. St Thomas (3a:7:c), discussing the fullness of Christ's

grace, says that grace was bestowed on Him as upon a universal principle in the genus of such as have grace. Where, therefore, charity is found outside Christ it must be as a participation by resemblance of His created charity. The virtue of charity has this Christological dimension. It has too an ecclesial dimension, for as a member of the Church, as part of a whole, man's virtue of charity resembles more closely that of Christ.

The uncreated exemplar of the virtue of charity is the charity of God. In regard to the production, preservation and increase of the virtue, this exemplar is the essential charity of God. But there is a sense in which, when speaking of the exemplary cause of charity, reference should be made to the Blessed Trinity. The Holy Spirit is the exemplar of the charity of the Church, the temple of the Holy Spirit, as the filial charity of the Word is the exemplar of the charity of all who through Him, with Him and in Him love the Eternal Father. In this wonderful way, as St Thomas (2-2ae:23:6:c) says, charity attains God Himself that it may rest in Him.

III Effects of the Virtue of Charity. The principal effect of the virtue is that it makes possible and is the measure of union with God in the act of charity. As the First Epistle of St John teaches against the error of the Gnostics, union with God is not to be found in some esoteric knowledge but by loving God and man with the love of charity. ' God is love ; he who dwells in love dwells in God, and God in him' (1 Jn 4:16). This union is at once a love and a friendship, a friendship with God and with all who share in or who are capable of sharing in the beatitude of God. The same Epistle states the supposition of that union : ' Love springs from God ; no one can love without being born of God' (1 Jn 4:7).

Another effect of the virtue of charity is that it assimilates its possessor to Christ in His messianic function of making satisfaction for sin and of meriting grace. For it is charity that gives to man's voluntary actions their satisfactory and meritorious character. This assimilation to Christ that charity brings about is not univocal but analogous. Christ's satisfaction is universal ; whereas man's satisfaction (*see* PENANCE) is relative to the temporal punishment due to sin ; and man's merit (q.v.) is restricted to the increasing of his own grace (apart from what he does as a member of Christ).

In terms of the Church and so of the Holy Spirit a further effect of charity has to be noted. The virtue ensures the harmonious insertion of the member within the life of the Church, a theme dear to St Paul who speaks (Eph 4:6) of ' each limb . . . building itself up through charity ' and who describes (Eph 4:3) the attitude created by charity as ' eager to preserve the unity the Spirit gives you '. Leo XIII in his encyclical *Mirae caritatis* (ASS 34 [1901-2] 648) calls charity the form of the Communion of Saints (q.v.) and Pius XII (*Mystici Corporis*) refers to this ecclesial effect of charity when he says : ' For in that Body there can be no good and virtuous deed performed by individual members which does not, through the Communion of Saints, redound also to the welfare of all' (AAS 35 [1943] 236).

The effect of charity on the other virtues a person may possess is traditionally expressed by saying that charity is the form or quasi-form of these virtues. This does not mean that charity is the intrinsic form of other virtues ; were this so it would necessarily enter into their definition. Charity is said to be the form of the other virtues because it adds an extrinsic perfection to the acts that stem from those virtues : it makes them meritorious (*Quaestio disputata de Caritate* 3:@19). In the natural order the end is attained by acts. In the supernatural order acts have not this power of immediately attaining the end ; instead they have their efficacy in so far as by them the end is merited ; eternal life, at which these acts aim, is attained because God rewards man for these acts with the possession of his supernatural end. It is from the operative presence of charity in them that supernatural acts attain their end in this way.

Lastly there is the effect of the virtue of charity on the will itself. The will is capable of many loves : filial, spousal, parental, etc. The virtue of charity present in the will is the measure or norm of all these other loves. Hence St Augustine's definition : *rectissima affectio animi nostri* ' the most noble longing of our spirit '. The role of charity within the will is to order all the other affections of the will by uniting them to its own proper object, the supreme good as the object of God's beatitude. Charity is a virtue which, when our affections are perfectly ordered, unites us to God, for by it we love Him (St Augustine, *De moribus Ecclesiae* 1:11 ; PL 32:1319).[1]

Bibliography. Among recent works on charity by Catholic scholars the following deserve special mention : C. Wiéner, *L'Amour pour Dieu dans l'ancien Testament* (1959) ; C. Spicq, *Agape dans le nouveau Testament*, 3 vols (1958-9) ; V. Warnach, *Agape : Die Liebe als Grundmotiv der neutestamentlichen Theologie* (1951) ; G. Gilleman, *The Primacy of Charity in Moral Theology*, English translation (1959) ; L. B. Geiger, *Le Problème de l'amour chez Saint Thomas d'Aquin* (1952) ; G. Didier, *Désintéressement du chrétien* (1955) ; W. Heinen, *Fehlformen des Liebesstrebens in moral-psychologischer Deutung und moraltheologischer Wuerdigung* (1954). See also bibliography appended to the article on ALTRUISM.   E. H.

CHASTITY is the virtue which inclines a man (or woman) to control his (or her) sexual activity in accordance with the moral law. It therefore varies in its scope according as it is practised by the married, by those who have vowed virginity and by those who have not yet adopted either state of life. The renunciation of marriage by the clergy as part of their office is treated under CELIBACY. The Church is committed to a bi-metallism in her commonwealth, where the gold of virginal chastity and the silver of nuptial chastity have equal currency,

as Cyril of Jerusalem once expressed it (*catechesis* 4:25 ; PG 33:488). Where all use of sexual activity has been freely given up, the virtue is exercised more completely than by those who enjoy the free use of marriage, but it is the same virtue for both ; only its exercise is different. Here will be given (I) some account of the originality of the Christian ideal of chastity in the pagan world into which Christianity made entrance, (II) the heretical exaggerations of that ideal, leading to (III) the Manichean attempt to make virginity a duty for all, to the exclusion of the married state of virtue. In contrast with this will be given (IV) the teaching of the Church on the difference between chastity exercised as a counsel and the moral duty of chastity in married life. A final section (V) will deal with the post-Reformation attack on the idea of chastity as a counsel.

I The originality of Christian chastity can be seen at once from the vocabulary it created for itself. Words like *castimoniales* (for the people who vow chastity) are Christian Latin formations brought into the language because what they describe is new. By contrast, the word *parthenos* is found in inscriptions from the Jewish catacombs in Rome where it means ' one who has not been married before, but is now marrying for the first time ' (cf. Lk 2:36) ; it has an overtone of regret in the case of one Jewish girl who died before she could be married. The classical virgin goddesses (Athene, Artemis and others) and their virgin priestesses are brushed aside by Professor Marrou in his study of the subject as so many ' formal survivals, empty of all living content '. The elder Pliny (*Naturalis historia*, 5:15) writes of the Essenes : ' They are the most extraordinary people in the world, for they live without women and renounce all sexual desire '.[2] It is the Jewish writer Josephus, however, who points out that the Essenes did not condemn wedlock in principle (*Bellum Iudaicum* 2:120, 160) and that one sect of the Essenes did in fact marry. The female skeletons found in the graveyard at Qumran are facts ; the interpretation to be put upon them varies as one thinks that the dwellers at Qumran were or were not Essenes. Pliny may be repeating idle gossip, or Josephus may have been playing up to his Western readers when he says that the reason for the Essene disdain of marriage was a belief that women were never faithful to one man. It may be that some adumbration of the idea of the perfection of Christian chastity will be found to have existed among Jewish sectaries before the preaching of Christ, but on the whole it is safe to rely on the witness of Galen, who, in a fragment preserved in an Arabic version of his works, speaks with surprise and admiration of 'Christians who out of reverence abstain from all sexual relations, some of them for their whole lives '.

The teaching of Christ (Mt 19:12) was given in reply to the disciples' complaint that marriage would be unprofitable if there was to be no divorce. Christ's answer is at once a warning and a spiritualizing

---

[1] Virtus illa . . . quae ipsius animi nostri rectissima affectio est, si in alio est, favet ut coniungamur Deo, si in nobis est, ipsa coniungit.

[2] Gens sola et in toto orbe praeter ceteras mira, sine ulla femina, omni venere abdicata.

of their ideas ; abstinence from marriage should not be just a way of avoiding entanglement but rather the response to a special grace of God. Origen (in Mt 14:16 ; GCS 40:324) takes the grace of virginity to be a charism (see CHARISMS), but when he comments on Rom 1:12 (JTS 13 [1912] 213) he seems to draw back from this idea. Christ's words really mean : ' He who has the capacity, let him receive it ', and this certainly implies a grace from God. In Gal 5:23 Paul lists chastity among the fruits of the Spirit. 1 Cor 7:7 implies that both matrimony and virginity have graces from God but that these are different. Paul, who discoursed on this topic to Felix (Ac 24:25), must have been very much alive to the novelty of Christian chastity.

II Exaggerations about virginity must have begun very soon, as the warning in *I Clem.* 38:2 implies that there were some at Corinth who regarded those not vowed to virginity as second-class Christians. The ' virgin ' of 1 Cor 7:36-8 may be the daughter of the man who is being given advice by Paul, or his virginal bride or even the daughter of a deceased brother ; the case is uncertain (CCS 874 g). There are a few bogus Scriptural sayings from early times which indicate that chastity soon led to the most varied heresies. The coming of the promised Kingdom ' when the two shall be one and the outside as the inside, and the male with the female neither male nor female ' (*II Clem.* 12:2) shows one of these exaggerations, in this case probably an exaltation of virginity within the married state (*see* AGAPETAE). Another precept (*II Clem.* 14:3) ' Guard your flesh that you may partake of the Spirit ', may come from Encratite sources among the Gnostics ; here were produced some of the bogus Acts of Apostles (John, Andrew, Thomas) where many episodes are recounted of Apostles separating wives from their husbands in order to consecrate them to a chaste life. The husbands resent this and persecute the Apostles in consequence ; in fact the whole narrative is the Greek love-romance of the period in reverse. The extreme perversion in this direction seems to have been that of the Adamites as described by Epiphanius (*Haer.* 52 ; GCS 31:313).

Some of the Apostles had been married, but according to 2nd-cent. opinion as recorded by Clement of Alexandria (*Strom.* 3:6:53 ; GCS 52:220) they took their wives with them ' as sisters, to serve as fellow-deaconesses in dealing with women '. Clement knew of a tradition that the wife of St Peter had suffered martyrdom before him (*Strom.* 7:11:63 ; GCS 17:46), and it may be that he had other traditions about Peter. The text of 1 Cor 9:5, where Paul speaks of having the power to take about a sister with him, acquired in the East an addition : ' But this is neither fitting nor just ' ; it is cited thus by Aphrahat (*hom.* 6 ; P Syr 1:266) and by the Armenian version of 1 Cor.

Another saying, much used by the Gnostics, was : ' I am come to dissolve the works of the female '. Somewhat parallel to this was the maxim, ascribed to Nicholaus (Clement, *Strom.* 3:25 ; GCS 52:207) or to a tradition of Matthias, that, ' it is a duty to

give no thought to the flesh '. This highly ambiguous saying was used in various directions by early heretics. The collection of maxims known as the *Sentences of Sextus* is probably from the same period and contains the following (saying 273 ; T&S 5 [1959]) : ' You may see men cutting off and casting away their own members in order to keep the rest of their bodies strong. How much better to do so in order to be chaste '. This would suggest a literal interpretation of Mt 19:12, and we know from Justin (*apol.* 29) that some Christians took it so.

The closing paragraph of the Gospel of Thomas represents Our Lord saying about Mary Magdalen : ' I shall lead her so as to make her masculine, that she may become a living spirit like unto you (the Apostles). For every woman who makes herself a man shall enter into the kingdom of heaven '. In the middle of the 4th cent. the Council of Gangra (in the preamble to its decrees) shows that some Christians were trying to live up to this saying. It recounts how certain women had left their husbands under the plea of continence but had then lapsed into adultery ; others had thought to be made just by assuming male dress and cutting their hair short for religious motives. A misuse of Gal 3:28 may have helped in this aberration.

The Marcionites seem to have exacted a profession of virginity before they would baptise anyone. If a man who had separated from his wife in order to receive their baptism lapsed by returning to his wife, he could be baptised once again on renewing his undertaking. Macarius Magnes (*apocriticus* 3:47) records that one Dositheus of Cilicia summed up the Encratite doctrine of the wrongfulness of marriage in the words : ' By sexual intercourse the world had its beginning ; by continence it will receive its end '. St John in his vision (Apoc 14:4) had seen virgins given a certain preference, but he did not see them as the whole Church. Tertullian (*adv. Marc.* 1:29 ; CSEL 47:330) is explicit that this is exactly what Marcion did. ' No flesh is washed in his church unless it is a virgin's, a widow's, a bachelor's, or unless it has bought baptism by divorce '. [1]

III The Manichean attempt to make perfect chastity a duty for the *electi* instead of a counsel was given a theoretical basis in the idea that procreation was evil in that it led to the imprisonment of yet one more soul in a material body. It may have owed something to the practice of the Marcionites, for Manichean heretics seem to succeed to Marcionite in some parts of Asia towards the end of the 3rd cent. Porphyry (*De abstinentia*, 4:20) claimed on philosophical principles that sexual intercourse was a defilement since it involved a combining of opposite natures, but this was too abstruse an argument for popular appeal ; the Manichean idea of light-particles being imprisoned in the newly formed body was more easily understood by the multitude (see ALBIGENSES, BOGOMILS). Augustine (*De moribus Manichaeorum* 2:65 ; PL 32:1373) charges them with holding that procreation was a great sin but that intercourse itself

[1] Non tingitur apud illum caro nisi virgo, nisi vidua, nisi caelebs, nisi divortio baptisma mercata.

was not, and with practising intercourse during what they thought was the safe period.[1] As he had been a Manichee for nine years, he must have known the facts (*see also* D 235).

IV The Church made perfect chastity a counsel, as against these heretics, while still insisting that for the unmarried who had not yet chosen their state of life, as well as for the married, there were duties of chastity which differed in their exercise from the complete renunciation of virginity. The parable (Mt 13:23) of those who brought forth thirty-fold or sixty-fold was made use of here to illustrate how there were many mansions in heaven. The hundred-fold was reserved for the martyrs but virgins came next in merit. In the *Deprecatio Gelasi* (a prayer for all states in the Church, going back to the 5th cent.) 'those who practise virginity' are prayed for after the preachers of the gospel and before civil rulers. As early as Tertullian (*De carnis resurrectione* 61 ; CSEL 47:123) one can find the idea of the virgin as bride of Christ : 'How many virgins are there who are brides of Christ ?'[2] By the 4th cent. the custom of consecrating such virgins with the veil (*flammeum*) as if they were being married by the solemn pagan rite of *confarreatio* was well established (cf. Jerome, *ep*. 147 ; CSEL 56:322 and Ambrose, *De virginibus* 1:11 ; PL 16:206). Athanasius (who is probably the author of the treatise on virginity ascribed to him in antiquity) supplies some justification for this by saying (TU XIV:2:36) that whereas every husband who cleaves to his wife is one flesh with her, every man or woman who cleaves to Christ is one spirit with Him.

The *Leonine Sacramentary* has a *Velatio nuptialis* which immediately follows the prayers *ad virgines sacras* and which is the source of much of the modern nuptial mass. The long blessing of the married couple, now unfortunately truncated, is the first popular Christian statement of a philosophy of marriage : 'Thou didst fashion for Adam a helpmeet with Thy own hands that the bones formed from his bones should display a body like unto his but of marvellous diversity'. A reminder is given to the bride that she is called, 'not only to what is lawful between spouses, but also appointed to the charge of holy children according to the observance that is of God'.[3] She has to keep the precepts of eternal law. She marries chastely in Christ as one of the faithful and not as a pagan who has not the ideal of Christian chastity. This blessing survived whole in the *Gelasian Sacramentary* (and in its derivatives of Gellone, Fulda and Berlin) long enough to make it possible for later theologians to draw out from it the hierarchy of the ends of marriage which will be

discussed under PROCREATION. Augustine knew that there was a sanctity of the married as well as that of virginity for he asks the virgins : 'How do you know that your married sister is not already a St Crispina while you are not yet a St Thecla ?' (*De sancta virginitate* 44 ; CSEL 41:290). Preachers who commented on Mt 5:28 took pains to show, as did Chrysostom (*hom*. 17 on Mt ; PG 57:257), that no law forbade a husband to look with desire upon his wife but the law did bind him in all other ways.

Neo-Platonism among the Fathers may have led to some depreciation of marriage in favour of virginity, but the greatest danger came from the work of Pelagius. In his commentary on St Paul (T &S IX:2:376–9) he took Eph 5:18–26 as an argument for complete continence as the most perfect thing for married Christians. As this work masqueraded for so long under the name of St Jerome, it is easy to see how medieval theologians came to regard the use of marriage as sinful unless it were excused by an intention of procreating children. Jovinian went in the opposite direction and put marriage and virginity on the same level. Jerome in his reply (PL 23:218) was too narrowly rationalist and too little dependent on the tradition of the Church. He argued that if it is good not to touch a woman (1 Cor 7:1), then it is evil to touch her. If this evil is tolerated, that must be in view of the avoidance of a greater evil. He did not think that the contrary to what is 'good' may be a lesser good, even though its contradictory should be evil. Pope Siricius in his letter to the church of Milan (PL 13:1171) was more judicious, setting forth the traditional doctrine that marriage was good but virginity was better : 'We acknowledge marriages without any despite, for we attend them to conduct the veiling, but virgins consecrated to God, who are after all the offspring of marriage, we honour with greater respect'.[4] The evidence here given that there was a *velatio nuptialis* already practised in church (cf. also Ambrose, *ep*. 19 ; PL 16:984) suggests that the prayers which accompanied it may be of much greater antiquity than their presence in the *Leonine Sacramentary* would require.

St Thomas (*Summa* 2–2ae:184:3c) supplied a theoretical background to the traditional doctrine. Commandments remove the natural obstacles to the love of God, counsels those which impede its exercise while not being naturally contrary to it. Chastity (*Summa* 2–2ae:186:4c) removes the care of a family and the danger of the growth of sexual desire which, as Aristotle (*Eth. Nic.* 1119 b 7–12) taught, is fostered by indulgence. Continence would not have been praiseworthy in Paradise (*Summa* 1a:98:2:@3), for while sexual pleasure would then have been greater, the disturbance to reason caused by lust would have been absent (*see* CONCUPISCENCE).

St Thomas makes clear the distinction of counsels from precepts (*Summa* 1–2ae:108:4c) by saying that precepts have to be carried out as a *sine qua non* of reaching the goal of loving God above all things,

---

[1] Nonne vos estis qui filios gignere, eo quod animae ligentur in carne, gravius putatis esse peccatum quam ipsum concubitum ? Nonne vos estis qui nos solebatis monere ut quantum fieri posset observaremus tempus quo ad conceptum mulier post genitalium viscerum purgationem apta esset eoque tempore a concubitu temperaremus . . . ?

[2] Quot virgines Christo maritatae ?

[3] Meminerit se non tantum ad licentiam coniugalem sed ad observantiam Dei sanctorum pignorum custodiae delegatam.

[4] Nos sane nuptias non aspernantes accipimus, quibus velamine intersumus ; sed virgines quas nuptiae creant Deo devotas maiore honorificentia veneramur.

whereas counsels point out ways by which a man can more expeditiously reach that goal ; they are short-cuts, but not for everyone. Christianity is a law of freedom and therefore it is fitting that there should be such options for the Christian. The precepts are in fact negative in substance, whatever their form, for they indicate that lying, thieving, dishonouring one's parents and the rest are acts which will debar the doer of them from attaining his end in life. In the nature of things there cannot be a positive precept which has the same necessary linkage with the end of life, save the general law of seeking that end itself by loving God above all things. No one can say of a means to that end that it is the one thing necessary ; there are always other things that must not be neglected. Hence necessary rules have to be negative, while positive means to the end have to be judged according to their fitness, more or less, for attaining that end, regard being had to the capacity of the individual for corresponding with the grace of God.

The reason why the counsels are short-cuts to the goal lies in the fact of a triple concupiscence (of the eyes, of the flesh and through pride of life) in human nature since the Fall. If men had still the gift of integrity, there would be no special place for these counsels. Protestantism first rejected all counsels because of its doctrine of justification by faith alone, as this militated against all meritorious works. Later it was the habit of some to reject them through an untheological optimism, as if man was back in Paradise and therefore did not need them. Now there is a slow return towards accepting them, since they are practised by Protestants in France and Germany, as well as in England.

V The Reformation attack on the counsels was aimed chiefly at the celibacy of the clergy, but it involved a general repudiation of virginity as a counsel of perfection. The Council of Trent defined (D 980) that virginity was a better and happier state than marriage. This definition, to which an anathema was attached, is often overlooked since it comes at the end of a series of propositions about matrimony. Article XXXII of the Anglican Church, after speaking of celibacy of the clergy, said that it was lawful for all Christian men ' to marry at their own discretion, as they shall judge the same to serve better to godliness '. Appeal was made to Heb. 13:4 (' Marriage honourable in all ') which was read as an assertion, whereas from the parallel clause which follows it in the text it must be read as an exhortation (to the married) to keep marriage honourable in all things, at all times. Those who commented on the Article in the 19th cent. defended it in this manner : ' There grew up early in eastern lands from the same principle that recommends and makes a merit of every kind of abstinence and of self-denial for its own sake, and not as a means to an end, a notion that single life was purer and more acceptable to God ; and this maxim of a visionary philosophy soon found its way into the Church '. Anglican nuns were rejecting this Article in practice at the very time when its defence was written, and a contemporary response

of the Sacred Penitentiary declared that the vow of chastity of an Anglican nun did not lapse if she became a Catholic, but continued, unless dispensed in proper canonical form. Yet the lack of an adequate distinction between precepts and counsels bedevilled even the ethical discussions of Oxford philosophers about the right and the good as late as 1930.

Bibliography. *Chastity, a Symposium*, translated from the French by L. Sheppard (1955) ; R. Metz *La Consécration des vierges dans l'église romaine* (1954) ; R. Plus sj, ' Chasteté ', in D Sp.s.v. ; H. Doms, *Vom Sinn des Zölibats* (1954) ; *C. and K. George, *The Protestant Mind of the English Reformation* (1961) ; *J. G. MacBride, *The Thirty-nine Articles* (1853) ; J. Fuchs, *De castitate et de ordine sexuali* (1959). The encyclical of Pius XII *Sacra virginitas* (AAS 46 [1954] 161–91) and the condemnation by the same Pope of modern hedonism in an allocution (AAS 43 [1951] 851–3) were used for some reiteration of the traditional teaching of the Church by the Second Vatican Council.

J. H. C.

CHRISM. *See* SACRAMENTALS

CHRIST, MISSION OF, AND DIVINITY OF
That Jesus Christ, the man of Nazareth, is truly God is a mystery of faith which, even when communicated to us, we cannot comprehend ; that He was the Messias, or anointed messenger of God to the Jews, is something that is capable of proof from the facts of history now, as it was in the days when these proofs were originally presented to the Jews by the first Christian preaching (*see* GOSPEL KERYGMA). This article will therefore proceed on two levels ; first there will be presented the evidence for the Messianic character of Christ as prophet (I), priest (II) and (III) king. The arguments to support this evidence (IV) from the miracles of Christ, and (V) from the fulfilment of His prophecies will next be given, with a note (VI) on the title ' Son of Man '. Then (VII) the revelation of the divinity of Christ in the Synoptics, in Paul (VIII) and in John (IX) will be considered, with finally (X) some treatment of the acceptance of Christ as God in the prayer and practice of the early Church.

I Christ as Prophet. Moses foretold (Deut 18:15) that God would raise up from among the Jews, ' another prophet like unto me, and him you shall hear '. It is now clear from the Qumran findings that there was some expectation of the fulfilment of this prophecy at the time of Christ, and it is not surprising that the early preaching (Ac 3:22 and 7:37) made much of the passage. In Mt 21:10 (though not in the parallel passage of Mk and Lk) the crowds acclaim Jesus as *the* prophet, just before the cleansing of the Temple. In Jn 6:14, after the feeding of the five thousand, there is another acclamation of the same fact. In Jn 7:52 Nicodemus is urged by other members of the Sanhedrin to search the Scriptures and see that *the* prophet (this is the reading, generally accepted as original, of Pap. 66) will not come from Galilee. A case could be made out for saying that the pattern of Matthew's gospel is such that it presents Christ as the second and greater Moses. The words spoken at the Transfiguration, 'Hear ye Him', fit into this pattern as an echo of what was promised by Moses, 'Him you shall hear'.

The work of a prophet was understood by the Jews to comprise not only the issuing of warnings about the future but also the 'speaking for God' (according to the alternative derivation of the word προφήτης) which meant the announcing of God's message. This Christ began to do at Nazareth, where according to Lk 4:16-22 he took to Himself the words of Is 61:1 and claimed that He was anointed of God to preach release to captives and sight to the blind, and to give good tidings to the poor. Mk 1:14 sums up this activity as 'preaching the gospel of God'. Mt 4:13-17 relates the fact that the preaching was transferred from Nazareth to Capharnaum. The anointing here spoken of by Isaias as a preliminary to the preaching was more fully elaborated by Jewish tradition, as may be seen in Justin (dial. 8:4) where Trypho says that the Messias will not know of his mission nor have any power until Elias comes to anoint him. Justin (dial. 49 and 51:3) gives the Christian acceptance of this idea, using the words of Christ which refer to John the Baptist (Mt 11:14): 'If you will receive it, he is Elias that is to come'. The other passage in the gospels (Mt 17:10 and Mk 9:11) about John as Elias is given more full exegesis (dial. 49:1-7), on the basis that Elias will in his own person precede the Second Coming (see ELIAS), while John took his role at the First Coming. There are no real grounds for concluding, as Cullmann has done, that in the Synoptics John is himself taken to be the second Moses and the prophet that is to be heard ; the words of the Benedictus : 'And thou child shalt be called the prophet of the Highest' (Lk 1:76 DV), are not correctly rendered, since the article is not used in the Greek before the word 'prophet'. John is simply a prophet ; he is not the second Moses. The promise at his conception (Lk 1:17) that he would go forth in the spirit of Elias makes clear that the Synoptics could not have taken him for the second Moses. The contrast between Christ calling John Elias and John himself saying, 'I am not Elias' (Jn 1:21-5), has been familiar to theologians since the days when Jerome commented upon it ; given the Semitic way of putting out a qualified statement by alternate (and apparently opposed) assertion and denial, this contrast reduces itself to the declaration that John is fulfilling at the First Coming the role of Elias which that prophet will himself somehow fulfil at the Second.

The title of 'the Coming One' that is used for Christ (Jn 1:29 ; 3:31 ; 6:14 ; 11:27 ; Ac 19:4) seems to originate with John the Baptist. It fitted in with the text from the Psalms used by the crowd on Palm Sunday (Mt 21:9 ; 23:39 and parallels) and had been taught (Mt 11:3 and Ac 19:4) by John to his disciples. Stephen with his talk about the coming of the Just One (Ac 7:52) picked out an uncommon Greek word (ἔλευσις) which seems

to have a technical sense and to refer to 'the Coming One', whom thus Stephen identifies with the Suffering Servant. Why it gained such a wide circulation is hard to say, but it may have served as a shortened form of the fuller designation of Christ as the one whom Moses had taught them to expect.

II The priestly functions of the Messias are claimed for Christ in the Epistle to the Hebrews, which is an elaborate treatise on this theme. The claim made by Jesus that Ps 109:1 was to be regarded as referring to the Messias (Mt 22:41) naturally led to the application to Him of the verse in the same psalm which speaks of priesthood after the manner of Melchisedec. In Jn 10:36 and 17:19 the doctrine is proclaimed that the Father has sanctified Jesus, and that Jesus sanctifies Himself (or sets Himself apart for God's purpose), where the word used (ἁγιάζω) is the one employed in the OT (Ex 28:41) for the ordination of Aaron and his sons as priests. That this act of sanctifying should be claimed for the Father and for the Son will be relevant at a later stage (section VII), where the godhead of Christ is to be considered. Here it may suffice to note that the sanctification is not exclusively a hallowing unto death, though it certainly includes that.

Passages which indicate that Jesus freely took upon Himself the role of Suffering Servant (Ebed Yahweh, as in Is 53) are not confined to John's gospel, and the parallelism between Jn 10:17-18 and Lk 12:50 is significant. This 'baptism' which Jesus desires is again mentioned in Mk 10:38. The voluntary presentation to God of a victim is certainly a priestly work, even when the victim is oneself. In His reply to Caiaphas (Mt 26:64 and parallels) Jesus associates with the Son of Man the priestly prerogative of sitting at the right hand of the Father (as described in Ps 109:1). At the Last Supper also Jesus had (according to the Synoptic tradition and Paul) predicted His atoning death and associated it with the act of worship which He at that moment performed (Mt 26:28 and parallels, 1 Cor 11:24). The language of Jn 2:17-22 about 'the Temple of His Body' also implies the priestly character of Jesus's Messiaship. It fits in with what is said (Heb 9:11) about Jesus using a 'tabernacle not made by hands', and it is also of importance to notice that John's conclusion of the incident (Jn 2:22) shows that when the disciples came to understand the Scripture which Jesus had quoted (Ps 68:10), they must have realised that much of this psalm, including its use of the title 'servant' (παῖς), could be appropriated to Jesus. (When John uses γραφή in the singular with the article, he means a particular text of Scripture ; for the book of Scripture he uses the plural).

At Qumran there was a belief in two Messiases, the priestly Messias being (according to the Manual of Discipline 9:10 and Order of the Future Congregation 2:18) the superior of the kingly or lay Messias ben David. After the revolt of 132, when Bar-Kokeba had been taken by some to be the lay Messias, this idea of there being two Messiases was strengthened among the Jews. The OT prophecies of the suffering Messias were then referred to Bar-Kokeba (who was put to death by the Romans), while the other prophecies could be held to apply to the priestly Messias who was still to come ; thus in controversy with the Christians it was hoped that embarrassment would be avoided. Not all the Jews had accepted Bar-Kokeba as a Messias, and hence, although the *Testament of the Twelve Patriarchs* (in the 2nd cent.) has the theory of the two Messiases, Trypho apparently knows of only one. He is emphatic that the Messias will be ' a man from among men ' (Justin, *dial.* 48:1), but he has not heard of two. Justin claims that the doctrine of the two comings of Christ is foreshadowed in the Blessings of Jacob (Gen 49), and elsewhere (*dial.* 114:2) he says that Christ is the antitype to Jacob and Israel, thus establishing Him as Messias from Jacob and Messias from Israel.

III Christ as king is addressed with the title Lord (κύριος). In Mark there is but one instance (11:3) which is beyond cavil, for in most cases the word used means no more than ' Sir teacher ' (Mk 10:51), though 5:19 (' what the Lord hath done to you ') might possibly be counted as a genuine instance. The episode of the entry into Jerusalem is one where the royalty of Christ is brought out, and it is quite in context if He should say quite simply : ' The Lord hath need of it '. The attempt to explain away the word here by saying that it means the owner of the beast is faced by the fact that we do not know if the owner was a friend of Jesus or if he did need it (for it cannot be gratuitously supposed that Jesus would speak a lie), whereas it is quite in keeping with His claim to be Lord of the Sabbath that He should act here in apparently high-handed fashion. Mt 21:3 has the same title as Mark in the parallel place and it might be said that there is a Hebraic *inclusio* here, the episode starting with this command and ending with the refrain (Mt 21:9) : ' Blessed is He that cometh in the name of *Kyrios* '. In Matthew (22:41–6) this leads up to the dialogue with the Pharisees (a piece of Haggadah) about David and his Lord ; in this the words of Ps 109:1 are claimed by Jesus to apply to the Messias, and in this way they are claimed for Himself. This exegesis of their Master was followed by the preachers of the primitive Church (Ac 2:34 ; 3:21 ; 5:31 ; 7:55 ; Rom 8:34 ; 1 Cor 15:25 ; Col 3:1 ; Eph 1:20 ; Heb 1:3 ; 8:1 ; 10:12 ; 1 Pet 3:22 ; Mk 16:19 ; 1 Clem 36:5 ; Barnabas 12:10). It is probably the explanation of the curious note which Luke attaches to the beginning (Lk 9:51) of the section which he composed to lead up to the Passion : ' It happened in the fulfilling of the days of His taking-up (*analepsis*) '. Christ was according to this to be manifested as Lord by being taken up to the right hand of the Father through His Passion and Resurrection. This is the Johannine idea too, and it is at the end of John's gospel (20:28) that Thomas confesses Him with the title *Kyrios*, equating it with the name of God. In this act he is partially anticipated by Magdalen (Jn 20:13) who speaks of ' My *Kyrios* '. In John's epilogue (21:7 and 12) it is to be understood that the use of *Kyrios*

by the apostles now, after the confession of Thomas, has a higher significance than that of ' Master '. Jn 6:23 and 11:2 are footnotes by John in which the title of the *Kyrios* may be used because they are quite obviously afterthoughts added to the narrative and its use there is not anachronistic. Luke is more puzzling. He has some passages (1:43 ; 2:11 ; 7:13 ; 7:19 ; 10:1 ; 11:39 ; 12:42) where the later apostolic usage of calling Christ the *Kyrios* is allowed to slip into the reporting of scenes where it was as yet not an established practice.

The theory was put forward by Bousset in 1921 that *Kyrios* as a title for Christ was not native to Palestine but came in at Antioch in a Hellenistic *milieu*, which was already familiar with its use in emperor-worship, in a way that was absolutely foreign to the Jews of the homeland. The theory has been rejected by de Grandmaison and Cerfaux, and, were it not for the fact that Bultmann has swallowed it whole, it would not merit further attention. The use of the term *Kyrios* in the early part of Acts is crucial for Bousset. Peter's direct acceptance of Christ as *Kyrios* (Ac 2:36), Stephen's invocation (Ac 7:59) and the description of the Samaritan baptisms (Ac 8:16) have all to be rejected as later interpolations by a Hellenistic hand. Arbitrary treatment of texts in this way was possible in 1921 but it has rightly been ruled out by a later generation. Positive evidence of the invocation of Jesus as Lord in the Aramaic-speaking church of Palestine is available from the phrase quoted in 1 Cor 16:22, where Paul uses the words *Marana-tha*. This Aramaic phrase means : ' Come, our Lord '. If the words are divided in a different way (*Maran-atha*) it would mean : ' Our Lord comes ', but in view of the recurrence of the phrase (in Greek, this time) in Apoc 22:20 and in *Didache* 10:6, the invocatory form is the more probable. That Paul should have used an Aramaic phrase when writing to a Greek-speaking church shows that the phrase was of long standing when he wrote and that it had currency among Christians in the way that certain Latin tags now have among Catholics. This points back to a Palestinian origin, and it was special pleading by Bousset when he urged that it might have come from the bilingual church of Antioch. If from a bilingual church, why was not the Greek form current ? Other attempts to neutralise this evidence, such as the suggestion that it means ' Come, teacher ', are simply absurd, as Rawlinson pointed out. *Mari* in Aramaic was capable of polite use to one held to be somehow superior, but in a liturgical context it can only have had the meaning of an invitation to the Lord Christ to fulfil the word of Mt 18:20 or, beyond that, to hasten the Second Coming. Bultmann, selecting an *effugium* which Bousset had himself abandoned, claims that the phrase is an oath taken before God and that it does not refer to Christ at all. Apoc 22:20 then becomes very difficult to explain, and the assertion of Bultmann has no supporting evidence.

The dialogue (in Mt 22:42–5 and parallels) about the Messias as Son of David has the critics in suspense.

Some think that Jesus is teaching that sonship in the Davidic line is of no account, while others, with Cullmann, allow that Jesus's attitude to the title Son of David is consonant with His attitude to that of Messias generally. He does not rebuke those who call Him 'Son of David' (in Mt 9:27; 12:23; 15:22; 20:30; 21:9; 21:15). The pedigree-books which circulated in Palestine showing His descent from David (they are mentioned in the Talmud and probably supplied the material for Mt 1:1–17 and Lk 3:23–38) were no doubt multiplied by the 'brethren of the Lord' and led to some trouble in the time of Domitian (Eusebius, HE 3:19). Outside Palestine the title seems to have had little importance, though it is used in Paul's preaching to Jews (Ac 13:34–6; Rom 1:3; 2 Tim 2:8) and it has echoes in Apoc 3:7; 5:5; 22:16. In the fourth gospel it occurs only once (Jn 7:42) and then on the lips of those who raise an objection against a Messias coming from Galilee.

The distinction of two Messiases, the king from the line of David and the priest from the line of Aaron, may have been known in the time of Jesus, for it is in the Qumran documents (especially the Zadokite work). It was certainly appealed to after 135, when the acceptance of Bar-Kokeba as Messias by Akiba and his subsequent death in the failure of the revolt led to a difficult situation for Jewish exegesis. Rabbi Johanan ben Torta opposed the identification with Bar-Kokeba from the outset (TB *Pesachim* 112a, *Berakoth* 61b; *Iebamoth* 108 b).

IV The miracles of Christ are here treated only so far as is necessary to present their evidential value for His Messianic claims; for a general treatment of the subject, *see* MIRACLES. That the narration of Jesus's miracles is a substantial part of the gospels, and so substantial as to defeat all suggestions of wholesale interpolation, is quite plain. Matthew devotes two chapters (8 and 9) to giving a series of ten miracles which stand in relation to the three preceding chapters (where the Sermon on the Mount is given) as corroboration of the doctrine there expounded. The Jews had a tradition (*Pirke Aboth* 5:8, cf. TB *Yoma* 21) that ten miracles were worked by God in favour of the Temple (and ten more for Moses), and Matthew seems to set out a rival series of ten to show that a greater than Moses or the Temple was now upon earth. In Mark the space given to miracles is about two-fifths of the whole gospel (i.e. 156 verses out of 395), and the place of miracles in the preaching of Peter (which Mark follows) is given by Ac 10:38. Luke is naturally dependent on these two, and since his purpose is to offer evidence, or a guarantee, to Theophilus of the truth of Christ's claims about which he has been catechised, it must needs be that he was himself convinced that he was narrating facts. John introduces two great miracles (the man born blind and Lazarus) which are not recounted by the Synoptics. This has made them suspect to some critics, but it must be recalled that Lazarus was sought out by the Jews (Jn 12:10) that he might be put to death and that the Synoptics had therefore good reason for passing over his story

while he was still in danger. When John came to write, the whole story could be told, just as John was also free to give the name of the apostle who cut off Malchus's ear, while the others had been silent about it.

John is much preoccupied with the question of testimony and makes it clear that he considers all the miracles he recounts to be signs of the truth of Jesus's Messiaship. There is a crescendo of passages (Jn 3:2; 5:36; 14:11; 15:24) where the miracles are put forward as the ultimate proof if all else (such as the appeal of Jesus's personality) should fail. It may be that 'signs' is a term wider than the miraculous (which is only to say that there are other ways in which God can authenticate His messenger), but it is clear that for John all miracles are 'signs'. In view of the downright appeal in Jn 14:11: 'If you will not believe Me, believe the works', it is hard to see how some Catholics can regard miracles as an unnecessary adjunct to Christ's claims; to John, and to Jesus as John presents Him (e.g. in Jn 5:21), they are essential. This emphasis may be more pronounced than what one finds in the Synoptics, but the difference is largely accounted for by the lapse of time between their writing and John's, and it should also be remarked that in Luke especially there are not wanting indications (e.g. at Lk 19:37) of kinship with John. Luke in that passage describes the crowd of disciples, 'praising God with a great voice for all the deeds of power which they saw', very much as John says (Jn 12:17–18) that the crowd 'bore witness that He had called Lazarus from the tomb'. This is but one of many indications that Luke was in possession of some Johannine material which the two earlier Synoptic writers had not used.

Outside the gospels there are witnesses to the miracles of Jesus in early Christian writers such as Quadratus (cited in Eusebius, *HE* 4:3), who claimed that some of those healed by Jesus had lived on into his own time. Jewish sources (TB *Aboda Zara* 27 b and Midrash on Eccles 10:5) are aware that miracles had been done and there are various tales in the Talmud of punishment visited on Jews who called in a Christian to pray over their sick. Josephus, in his famous notice of Jesus (*Antiquities* 18:3:3), speaks of Him as a 'doer of startling works', and the sarcasm makes it obvious that he had heard of the miracle-stories. Josephus adds that the prophets had foretold Christ's resurrection and 'a myriad of marvels about Him', which shows that he saw the appropriateness of miracle-working by the Messias. So did Antipas (Mk 6:14; Lk 13:32 and 23:8).

The attempt to rob the miracles of Christ of their probative force by passing them off as so much 'faith-healing' comes up against the insuperable difficulty that no such attitude of expectancy in the subject of the miracle was possible in the water that was turned into wine, in the withered fig-tree, in the tempest that was stilled or in the dead Lazarus. It could have been present, but clearly was not, in the man born blind, who did not know (Jn 9:25 and 36) what the claims of Jesus were. That Jesus should refuse to do miracles at Nazareth because of the lack of faith there (Mk 6:5) shows that in the economy of salvation He made it a pre-condition (at least sometimes) that there should be some readiness to believe in Him before He worked a miracle ; that such faith was a pre-condition, and not a contributory cause in the working of the miracle, may be seen from the way in which He endeavours to elicit such dispositions in Martha (Jn 11:25–27) before the raising of Lazarus.

It is also urged that there was in the time of Christ an inextricable confusion between disease and diabolical possession and that the diagnosis of disease was rudimentary. In Lk 13:11–17 Christ says that the woman whose body had been curved for eighteen years had been bound by Satan. Some exegetes want to sidestep the difficulty by saying that here Christ is conforming Himself to the way of thinking of the time, but it seems more reasonable to understand the episode as one of paralysis caused by a mental state, and then to allow that this mental state was rightly diagnosed by Jesus as having been induced by the Devil. It should be noticed that in the catalogue of those healed given by Mt 4:24 the possessed are distinguished not only from those diseased but also from the hysterical. Ancient diagnosis of the outward symptoms of a disease was well developed, though the explanation of causal factors and the treatment were infantile in comparison with modern times. Celsus (who was born in 25 BC) distinguishes three kinds of dropsy, and knows that epilepsy differs from paralysis and phrenzy (of which again he distinguishes three kinds). That an angel could produce a disturbance in (and even a ligature of) any bodily power in man was the accepted doctrine of the Middle Ages (e.g. in St Thomas, *Summa* 1a:111:4:@2) and no advance in medical science has made it obsolete. The fact that stigmata have been induced by hypnotism in modern times is sufficient to show that where a human mind has such power, an angelic mind must have more.

The argument from the miracles of Jesus to His Messianic claim was presented to the disciples of John when they asked if He was the Coming One (Mt 11:3–5 ; Lk 7:20–2) ; Luke states and Matthew implies that the occasion was one on which many were cured of 'diseases, vexations and evil spirits'. The argument is taken up in the apostolic preaching and is shown to be part of the catechesis by Heb 2:3–4.

V The fulfilment of prophecies made by Christ will be considered here only in part. The prophecies of the Passion and Resurrection will be examined here, while those which concern the fall of Jerusalem will be considered in the article on PAROUSIA. It is the fashion of some critics such as Bultmann to dismiss all the prophecies of the Passion as so many historical compositions made up after the event. Cullmann has replied to this charge by arguing that the presentation of Christ as the Suffering Servant was not widespread in the early Church and that thus a motive for the forgery would be lacking. The matter is, however, not quite so simple. The

first note of acceptance by Christ of the role of Suffering Servant (Is 53) is given in the reply to John at the Baptism : 'It becometh us to fulfil all justice' (Mt 3:15). The δικαιοσύνη (justice) here meant is certainly not the Pauline, for Matthew never uses the term in that sense. It is best taken as 'all that belongs to the role of the Just One, who is described in Is 53:9 and 11'. (C. R. North has revived, with wide agreement, this old interpretation of Christ's words.) The use of 'the Just One' as a title for Christ (Ac 3:14 ; 7:52 ; 22:14) by Peter, Stephen and Ananias, and possibly in the episode of Pilate's wife (Mt 27:19–24), shows that there was an early acceptance of Christ in this role. The title survives in 1 Jn 2:1 and perhaps in Jas 5:6, while 1 Pet 3:18 knows of it, and indeed the use of Is 53 by Peter is quite extensive.

The taking away of the Bridegroom (Mt 9:15 and parallels) is a hint of the Passion that is plain enough, and if it be regarded as a later insertion, the whole episode of the argument about fasting would likewise have to go. The explicit prophecies of the Passion begin at Mt 16:21 and are prefaced by the note (in Mt and Mk, but not in Lk) that this was the beginning of Jesus's teaching about His Passion. It was spoken frankly (Mk 8:32) and was followed by the rebuke to Peter (a reason why Peter above all should have stressed the preaching of Is 53 later on). The second prediction (Mt 17:22 and parallels) is received with blank incomprehension (Mk 9:32), and the disciples fear to ask for an explanation, while in Mt 17:23 their reaction is said to be great grief. The two emotional states are not incompatible, but it speaks ill of the supposed forger if one supposes that he could leave untidy ends about like this. The third prediction (Mt 20:18 and parallels) is the most detailed, covering at least eight separate features. The mathematical odds against such a grouping of events being forecast by random methods are such (*see* PROPHECY, ARGUMENT FROM) that it is reasonable to conclude that here the alternatives are presented quite sharply : either the prophecy was made by favour of God, or it is a forgery made up after the event. Lk 18:31 adds that, 'all things will be accomplished that are written by the prophets for the Son of Man', and that they did not understand what it all meant even yet. It cannot be said that there is much resemblance between the language of this prophecy and that of Is 53 or of other notably prophetic parts of the OT.

The third prediction of the Passion is immediately followed (Mt 20:20–8 and Mk 10:35–45) by the promise to John and James that they will drink the chalice of the Lord (and Mark adds that they will receive the baptism with which He is to be baptised), while Luke (12:50) has recorded (in another context) a saying about the baptism which the Lord desires to receive. Close upon this comes the parable of the wicked husbandmen with its pointed saying about the killing of the Son (Mt 21:38 and parallels). This is stated by the Synoptics to have provoked the high priests to arrest Jesus, though they had to forbear through fear of the crowds. It is hard to see how a forger could have manufactured this sequence of narratives. Indeed, a case could be made out for saying that Matthew has arranged the second half of his gospel (from 16:1 onwards) so as to present the gradual rejection of Christ. If the prophecies were a later addition, the narrative would jump from the confession of Peter to the Passion with no real coherence. The prophecies must be at least as early as the original draft of Matthew's gospel. One can go further and say that the presence of the guards around the tomb (which is necessary to the whole of the resurrection-narratives in the Synoptics) supposes that there have been prophecies about the Passion and Resurrection (Mt 27:62-6). The apocryphal gospels of Peter and of the Hebrews make much of the episode, and the traditions on which they drew cannot have been manipulated by the supposed orthodox Christian forger. Further external corroboration of the prophecies of Christ can be found in the much-discussed inscription from Nazareth which gives an imperial rescript forbidding tombrobbery, and in the Talmud there are stories about what Rabbi Zadok began to do forty years before the destruction of the Temple, through fear that it would be destroyed. The forgery hypothesis makes so many difficulties as to be unacceptable.

VI A Note on the Title Son of Man. This title was used by Jesus to describe Himself, but was not used by the disciples themselves, save for Stephen (Ac 7:56) ; yet it must follow from Jn 12:34 that the crowd, which repeats the title after Him, understood what it meant, at least vaguely, for they ask : ' What is *this* Son of Man you are talking about ? ' and not : ' What do you mean by Son of Man ? ' The vision of John (Apoc 1:13 ; 14:14) clearly connects the Christian Son of Man with the account in Dan 7:13-27, and it is now generally accepted that Daniel is the source of Jesus's use of the title. That it should have a collective aspect in Dan 7:27 is not a difficulty, for the title to be appropriate to Christ must also indicate at least vaguely His mystical Body (*see* BODY, MYSTICAL). Its use by Jesus was not confined to descriptions of Himself as the suffering Servant, but it had an eschatological reference also, indicating that glory was to be the outcome of the suffering. Even judgment (Jn 5:27) was somehow the prerogative of the Son of Man. Perhaps the most illuminating use of the title is at Lk 17:22, where different ' days of the Son of Man ' are distinguished. These are taken as parallel to the ' days of Jahwe ' of the OT, in the sense of special visitations. Jesus, then, took up a title which had been neglected in orthodox Jewry, though the apocryphal *Enoch* was familiar with it and with its source in Daniel. It has not so far been found in use at Qumran.

That ' Son of Man ' should mean simply ' a man ' or ' the man *par excellence*, the archetypal Man ' has been urged by some, but apart from Ps 8:5 (cited in Heb 2:6) the title does not readily lend itself to this meaning in the NT. Paul may have won from it his idea of Christ as the second Adam (1 Cor 15:45 ; Rom 5:12), possibly owing to a need to enter into

polemic against Philonian ideas. Philo himself was quite indifferent to the OT prophets (whom he seldom cites in his voluminous works), and for him the origin in Daniel would have been of no significance. Christ's use of the title (Jn 1:51) to indicate the ' bridge-role ' of His Incarnation is in harmony with the Pauline developments. Later still, it is to be noted that Papias in his exegesis of the gospels drew upon the whole of the OT account of creation as a typological record of Christ and the Church (frag. 6).

The discussions on the title have been very extensive in recent times and are well summarised by A. J. Higgins in the *Studies in Memory of T. W. Manson* (1959) 119-35. Bultmann quite arbitrarily distinguishes between Son of Man sayings which concern the Parousia and those which concern the Passion and Resurrection ; these are spurious, those are genuine for him, while Glasson has argued exactly the opposite thesis, that the Passion-sayings are the genuine ones. That Jesus should have chosen such an obscure title for some of His principal utterances may be seen as part of the ' delayed-action ' effect of His teaching. He needed to instruct the disciples gradually, so that there should not be created a sudden *furore* and the inevitable clash with the authorities precipitated before the disciples had had a fair opportunity to assimilate His teaching.

VII The revelation of the divinity of Christ in the Synoptics is progressive. The voice from heaven at the Baptism must be a primitive datum in that narrative, for only thus can one explain the choice of the moment of baptism for the very earliest confession of faith, as performed by the Ethiopian (Ac 8:35-8). The variant in the so-called Western text of Lk 3:22 (' Today have I begotten Thee ') cannot be due, as Bultmann claimed, to Hellenistic mythology about the Virgin Birth, for in that case the angels ought to have chanted the words at Bethlehem, or Gabriel at Nazareth, and they would have no relevance here (see CCS 683 b and 750 f). Justin, who had that reading (*dial.* 88:8), gives the reason for it : ' The voice said His begetting commenced for mankind from that time from which the *gnosis* of it was destined to start '. This gives a clue to the probable origin of the variant, for the Gnostics cherished it and in the Gospel of the Ebionites it can be found alongside the genuine words : ' in whom I am well-pleased '.

The voice at the Transfiguration (Mt 17:5 and parallels) is sometimes discounted on the ground that this episode has been set further back in the life of Christ, and that it is really a post-Resurrection story which has been adapted to the Galilean ministry by the Synoptics. It is true that Lk 9:29 describes Jesus as having His countenance changed, in the same terms that are used for the Emmaus apparition by Mk 16:12, but the differences between the Transfiguration and the apparitions after the Resurrection are enormous. The most obvious difference is that after the Transfiguration is over the disciples find ' only Jesus ', in His usual form, whereas in the Resurrection stories this does not happen. Again, in the Resurrection-apparitions there is no attempt to describe the radiance which surrounds Jesus, whereas at the Transfiguration each of the Synoptics describes this in his own terms. Matthew's description of the angel at the Resurrection is in similar terms, but he never thinks of extending this to the risen Christ. Nor do figures from the OT appear with Christ after the Resurrection, as they do here. Finally, it cannot be said that John has ignored the Transfiguration, for he does claim (Jn 1:14) to have seen 'the glory of the Lord', using the same term which occurs in Lk 9:32 for what the three disciples saw at the Transfiguration. Only a pre-conceived theory that the Transfiguration could not have occurred can really make the modern questionings intelligible.

The Transfiguration bears some relation to the experience of Moses on Sinai (Ex 24:16-17) and the words spoken to the three disciples are as fundamental for them as the commandments were for Moses. Yet even here the disciples of Christ are more favoured by God than was Moses, for they can speak freely with Christ in His Transfiguration and are not overcome with fear until the lightsome cloud comes down and the voice of God is heard. As already noted, the injunction to hear Him shows that a greater than Moses is now being proclaimed to the disciples. The adjective used for the Son ('beloved' or 'chosen out') recalls Is 42:1 and the Servant of Jahwe, but it may be that the original phrasing of the voice is that given in 2 Pet 1:17 (according to *Vaticanus* and the Bodmer Papyrus) : 'My Son, My Beloved, is this one, in whom I am well-pleased', and in that case the two titles of Son and Servant are kept separate, the one transcending the other. The insistence of John's gospel that so much of what Jesus taught was not understood immediately by the disciples helps towards an understanding of the divine pedagogy which made the transition possible from Servant to Son in the disciples' progress to a full knowledge of what Jesus was.

The idea that 'beloved Son' is synonymous with 'only-begotten' was argued by C. H. Turner (in JTS 27 [1925] 113-29) on the evidence of patristic usage of the word *Agapetos*, and his case has been generally accepted as conclusive by later writers. The origin of the usage may be traced to the parable of the Wicked Husbandmen (Mk 12:6 ; Lk 20:13) where the word occurs. The parallel place in Matthew, as one might expect in a Hebraic gospel, lacks the word, the transference of meaning being possible only in Greek.

The foremost declaration by Jesus Himself of His Sonship is made in His prayer to the Father (Mt 11:25-7 ; Lk 10:21-2). It must be noticed that the early Church soon inverted the statements here made, reading : 'All things are given Me by My Father, and no one knoweth the Father save the Son. . . .' Thus Justin (*dial.* 100), Irenaeus (*adv. haer.* II:4:5 H ; IV:11:2 H) and Tatian, though Irenaeus is well aware of the alternative reading (*adv. haer.* IV:11:1 H). It may be that polemic with Marcion (who attacked the Father-Son relationship)

led to the re-phrasing, or it may be simply due to a tidiness of mind which saw in the knowledge of the Father by the Son a subordinate instance of what was given to the Son by the Father. Cerfaux and others think that the transposition was first made by Gnostics who wished thus to secure a lodgment in the gospel for their own *gnosis*, which could be represented as coming from the Father to the Son and then to themselves. It cannot be said that the use of Mt 11:27 in the Gospel of Thomas (saying 61 or 62) bears this out.

That Christ should in speaking of the Father-Son relationship claim an equality of nature with God (indicated in the text by the parallelism of its structure) is not surprising ; as W. C. Allen noticed in his *Commentary on Matthew* (*ad loc.*), 'this usage as a traditional saying of Christ is as strongly supported as anything in the gospels'. Only a selective treatment of the gospels, such as Bultmann's, would set it aside as a Hellenistic accretion—quite arbitrarily, since it has all the marks of a Jewish author upon it, with its reminiscence of Dan 2:23, 28, while the logion concludes with an echo of Jer 6:16. The relationship involves a sharing in the fullness of revelation and a pre-existence of the Son with God. 'The aorists are to be explained as referring to pre-temporal acts of God wrought in eternity,' as Allen so rightly claims. In controversy with the Christians, the Rabbis made use mainly of Matthew's gospel, and it is of particular significance that one finds in the Talmud (TB *Sanhedrin* 38a) this answer given to the question why God created Adam by himself rather than create several men together : 'That the Minim (Christians) might not say there are many ruling powers in heaven.'

Peter was honoured in the early Church with the epithet 'the possessor of knowledge' (ὁ ἐπιγνούς), and this usage seems to be justified by what is said of him in Mt 16:17, that the Father has imparted to him special knowledge of Jesus as Son of God. The Gnostics put up Thomas (Gospel of Thomas, saying 12) as the maker of a wiser confession than Peter or anyone else, thus showing the importance which in very early days was attached to Peter's confession. The Gnostic Thomas is made to say : 'My mouth will in no way bear to say what you are like,' whereas Peter is represented as proclaiming that Jesus is 'like a righteous angel'. That Peter should have coupled with his confession of Jesus's godhead an acceptance of Him as Messias is not surprising in view of the way the two titles are coupled by the heavenly voice. Mark has omitted the second and higher title (Mk 8:29), but the opening words of his gospel show that he knew this belief to be fundamental and the general practice of curtailing what redounds to Peter's praise is sufficient to explain the omission here. The report in Jn 6:69, where Peter confesses that Jesus is 'the Christ, the holy One of God' (thus the Bodmer papyrus), is more likely to be describing a different (and earlier) occasion than the confession at Caesarea Philippi. The title 'holy One of God' is used by the demons in the synagogue of Capharnaum (Mk 1:24 ; Lk 4:34) and, apart from a possible use in Ac 3:14, is not found again in the NT. What is almost a synonym occurs (in Ac 2:27 ; 13:35) from the Psalms, but these terms are not sufficient to indicate complete possession of godhead. Peter, then, is led on to a confession of the true godhead of Christ, but some modern Catholic theologians have questioned whether he himself fully understood the import of his confession at the time he made it. Might he not, as the OT prophets, have spoken a sentence the plenary sense of which he did not understand ? Suarez has a similar view of the incomplete faith of the disciples after the walking on the water (Mt 14:33 ; Mk 6:51), calling it *fides inchoata*.

The climax of the trial of Jesus before the Sanhedrin is His own admission of godhead (Mt 26:63–4 and parallels), where it should be noted that to call oneself Messias was not held to be blasphemy by the Jews ; thus Trypho in Justin (*dial.* 49) says that the Jews expected the Messias to be a man from among men (cf. *Psalms of Solomon*, 17:22–49). The Talmud was careful (TB *Sanhedrin* 66a) to say that if a son cursed his parents by the divine name he was to be punished, but if he used an attribute of God in his curse the sages would not hold him liable. Matthew and Mark report Caiaphas as putting the two questions together, about Messiaship and godhead, whether this was the way the charge had been formulated for him from the reports (given by Judas ?) of what Peter had said in Mt 16:16, or whether there was a deliberate intention to trap the Prisoner by a process of tacking two questions into one. Luke has the questions separate, the second (Lk 22:70) being an inference drawn by the assembly from Jesus's words about the coming of the Son of Man.

The command to baptise (Mt 28:19), where Son and Spirit are put on an equality with the Father, is often regarded as a later insertion into the gospel, but against this is to be weighed the fact that Justin (*apol.* 61:9) accepted it as apostolic, and his own baptism took place at Ephesus about 130. Whether the critic supposes that there was no command to baptise coming from Christ, or that the apostles changed the command that was given to them, he is involved in very serious difficulties in accounting for the evidence ; on the other hand the words (Mt 28:18) which introduce the command are no more than a recall to what was said in Mt 11:27, and the early awareness of the command (*see* BAPTISM II) makes a dating of the command as late as the end of the 1st cent. impossible.

VIII St Paul calls Jesus the Son of God in his sermons (Ac 9:20 ; 13:33) at Damascus and Pisidian Antioch. As this is the very beginning of his ministry, it is reasonable to suppose (in the light of Ac 22:10) that he had been taught this doctrine when he was catechised by Ananias. He appeals to Ps 2:7, as did the Voice at the Baptism of Christ. That he handed on this catechesis is shown by 1 Thess 1:9. In Rom 1:3–4 he affirms that the ' gospel of God ' is concerned with teaching about this Son of God, and here, as also in Gal 4:4–6, appears the antithetical

statement : sonship of David according to the flesh ; sonship of God in the unity of the Spirit. One cannot say that the stressing of such an antithesis is due to Paul himself, for it is the mainspring of the early Christian hymn which he cites at 1 Tim 3:16, the six lines of which are antithetically opposed in the order : ab ; ba ; ab.

At the same time Paul makes no secret of the fact that he received a revelation of God about the divine sonship of Jesus (Gal 1:16) : ' It was God's good pleasure to reveal His Son in my regard,' and this at the time of his conversion. The communication from God did not annul or make useless the human catechising, but in Semitic fashion Paul wishes it to be understood by his two disparate statements that both sources had contributed to his knowledge of the mystery. The combination of the two sources may be seen expounded in 1 Cor 2:4–13 ; the traditional *kerygma* is not a tradition of men but a Spirit-given tradition.

Isaac as a type of Christ was singled out by Paul (Gal 3:16 ; 4:28 ; Rom 8:32 and probably Ac 20:8 and Heb 11:17–19) for his miraculous birth and for the mystery of his being sacrificed by his father. Some have conjectured that Paul found in contemporary Jewish theology speculations current about the sacrifice of Isaac and adapted them to Christ, but it cannot be shown that these speculations were strictly contemporary, and in contrast there is the express declaration of Christ (Jn 8:56) that Abraham rejoiced to see His day. Now it is the constant idea of the Fathers that this joy of Abraham was owing to his having somehow glimpsed the typological value of his act in offering Isaac. Paul, too, may have had some point of contact with this Johannine tradition, or he may have had the same idea by personal revelation. In either case, his use of this OT type would strengthen his teaching about the Father-Son relationship *in divinis*. In the Synoptic parable of the Wicked Husbandmen (Mt 21:33 and parallels) there was a Lord who did not spare his only son, although the sacrifice was not intentional. In 1 Cor 9:7 there is a suggestion that Paul was aware of the parable, and it may be that Luke's emphasis (Lk 20:13) on the fact that the son was an only son is due to Paul's preoccupation with this aspect of Christology.

The capital passage in Phil 2:6–11 is often thought to be a citation from an early hymn, and authors have speculated how far Paul may be thought to have modified the wording. Christ was pre-existent ' in the form of God ', and because He did not think it a ' snatching-matter ' to be equal to God (as Adam made the apple a ' snatching-matter ') He poured Himself out, taking the form of a slave, and when He had come to be in the likeness of man and was seen by all to be a man, He humbled Himself, becoming obedient unto death. The underlying contrast here is with the disobedience of the first man, Adam. Yet there are strong assertions of the equality of Christ with the Father, and this in terms which are most probably pre-Pauline, since ἴσα and Μορφή are found nowhere else in Paul. Much discussion centres on the word Μορφή whose meaning lies between 'nature' and 'quality' and may be related to the word 'image'. Christ is called the image of God in Heb 1:3 without any derogation from His equality with God, and the Spirit was traditionally called the image of the Son ; it would not therefore be surprising to find the idea at work here also. Such equality along with difference is the idea which underlies the elaborate phrase of 1 Cor 8:6 and some of the Pauline doxologies (*see* DOXOLOGIES).

The progress of revelation in the time of the apostolic teaching can be seen in 1 Cor 15:24-8. Here Paul begins with the well-used passage from Ps 109 about Christ being at the right hand of the Father until all His enemies be subdued, but he goes on from there to new considerations. What is to happen when all things are set beneath His feet ? Then will the Son hand over the kingdom to the Father, and—most mysterious of all—He will then Himself be subject to the Father who subjected all things to Him, that God may be all in all. It is not the vision of a neo-Platonist who plans the world as a Coming-out-from-God and a Return-to-God, nor is it an absorption of the Son into the Father counterpart to His generation from the Father before time was. It must regard the Person of the Son and not His divine nature. Obedience is the characteristic of a son to a father among men ; the Fatherhood of God (from whom all fatherhood is named) would seem to require by analogy a harmony of succession in the personal relationship of the Son towards Him. It is not merely that the mediatorial role of the humanity of Christ has ceased with the gathering-together of the elect for eternal happiness, but that to all eternity the Son is truly Son to His Father, in the union of the Spirit. This does not imply subordination, and the Arians derived no comfort from this text (see Pelagius *ad loc.* in T&S IX:2:218-219). Chrysostom (PG 61:341) expounds it without a qualm : ' As is fitting for a Son and for God, thus does He obey, not in human fashion, but in a completely free manner and enjoying all power'. Likewise the Ambrosiaster (PL 17:265) : ' Then will Christ show Himself as God, but on account of the unique *auctoritas* of the Father He will be God of God and the exalted and ineffable *auctoritas* of the unique beginning will stand forth. That is the subjection of the Son to the Father ; that is God's being all in all. Yet the Son is not subject to the Father as a creature is subject to the Son. Then will the Son show that He is not the One from whom all things are but the One through whom are all things'.[1] Similar ideas can be found in Cyril of Jerusalem (PG 33:672 and 33:912), though Gregory of Nyssa (PG 44:1304-25) prefers to see this subjection as an act of the whole Christ, head and

[1] Tunc et Christus propter unicam auctoritatem Patris Deum quidem se ostendet sed de Deo, ut unius principii sublimis et ineffabilis auctoritas maneat. Hoc est subicere se Filium Patri, hoc est Deum esse omnia in omnibus. Non tamen sic subicitur Filius Patri sicut Filio creatura. Tunc Filius ostendet illis non se esse ex quo sunt omnia sed per quem sunt omnia.

members, than as a mystery within the relationship of the divine Persons.

The nearest parallel in the NT to the Prologue of John's gospel is the Pauline passage (Col 1:15-20) where Paul's Christology is developed to the full. Language is borrowed from what the OT had to say about the Wisdom of God (' first-born before all creatures ') in the hope that the audience would see how the new revelation was in continuity with the past ; Wisdom had been described as God's *paredros* or throne-companion, and now the Son was gone up from earth to sit at the right hand of the Father. Immediately from the naming of Christ as the crown of all creation, through whom all things were made, the thought goes to the mediatorial and redemptive work of Christ, as John's does. That Paul by calling the Father ' God ' and the Son ' Lord ' in such passages as 1 Cor 8:6 does not mean to diminish the status of the Son is plain from what he says here about the Pleroma inhabiting in Christ (*see* PLEROMA). In fact his choice of titles seems to reflect the OT variation between Elohim and Jahwe.

If Paul couples the divinity of Christ closely with His salvific mission, the use of such titles as ' our God and Saviour Jesus Christ ' (Tit 2:13) and ' our God and Lord Jesus Christ ' (2 Thess 1:12), which modern criticism (e.g. in Cullmann) is beginning to recognize as probably authentically Pauline, is at once made intelligible. That Paul should call Christ God outright, without any added title, as he seems to in Rom 9:5 (*see* CCS 857e), may have been somewhat disconcerting for his audiences, but he had a way of doing the same thing by implication, as it were to lessen the shock. Thus Rom 10:12-13 applies to Christ the words of Jl 2:32, which in their original context were meant for Jahwe. Again, the claim in 1 Cor 10:4 that ' the Rock was Christ ' would have been understood by one versed in the OT as a claim that one of the divine works was being attributed to Christ. In 2 Cor 12:8 he speaks of having prayed to the Lord (Christ), and for a Jew this would be understood as acknowledging Christ to be divine. A similar usage, borrowed from Paul, may explain why Lk 11:49 attributes to ' the Wisdom of God ' what the parallel passage in Mt 18:34 has Christ speaking directly. The ultimate justification for such practices was the action of Christ Himself in the Synoptics, where He claimed the right to forgive sins and the lordship of the Sabbath (rights which for a Jew belonged to Jahwe), and compared Himself to the Shekinah (Mt 18:20), which the Jews expected to be present when two or three of them gathered in the study of the Law (*see* SHEKINAH).

IX The gospel of John sets out to teach that Jesus is Son of God (Jn 20:31) and its teaching has become more systematic with the lapse of time since the Synoptics ; one cannot say that it has changed in the essentials. Jesus is rightly called Lord (Jn 13:13) and master, as Mt 23:8 had suggested, and the parallelism between Christ's relation (as man) to His Father and the apostles' relation to Himself (Jn 13:16 ; 15:20 ; cf. Mt 10:24) is clearly set forth. It is, however, not merely a parallel with the humanity of Christ, for at the end (Jn 20:21-2) it is restated to the accompaniment of what must be recognized as a creative act. Christ breathes upon the apostles that Spirit which had (Gen 2:7) first awakened into life the human creature. John implies that the apostolic mission of the Church is not that of a human society but is in some way divine, being the continuation of Christ to men. John is full of the notion that the disciples did not at once understand the full import of what Jesus said to them, and it can be inferred from this that, even without new revelations, the knowledge of what has happened to the apostles, one by one, in the course of time has cast a new light on the words of Jesus recalled from long ago. The appeal to the collective witness of the apostles (Jn 1:14 ; 21:4), made by one of themselves, is justified by a word of Christ (Jn 17:20) which may have seemed less relevant when the gospels first came to be written and when the believers could not be counted in their generations.

What have been called the *Ego eimi* sayings mark a similar growth in depth of meaning. At the stilling of the storm (Mk 6:48) Jesus says : ' It is I, fear not '. John follows the Synoptics in reporting this (Jn 6:20), but Jn 8:24 (in view of its likeness to Is 43:10) takes the believer very much further, to the throne of God itself. That the Jews misunderstand the intent of the saying and seem to think that Jesus has broken off in the middle of His sentence is part of the Johannine irony. A much bigger shock awaits the Jews (Jn 8:58) when they hear Jesus repeat this phrase to them. The account of its use in the garden of Gethsemani (Jn 18:5-7) is probably meant to convey that, however unwilling to believe, the Jews felt the force of language associated with the godhead. The use of predicates with this declaration (e.g. I am the Vine, the Door, etc. ; Jn 15:1 ; 10:7, and often) has parallels with the OT declarations of Wisdom and also with the supposed revelations of pagan deities. Thus the idiom would have suggested to both Jews and Greeks the presence of a self-revealing God. It cannot be said that John has invented these sayings. Most of them come from the Jerusalem ministry, which is not reported in the Synoptics, but in their gospels there are not lacking signs (e.g. Lk 24:39) of the same idiom's being used. The frequent ' I say unto you ' in Mt 5:22-44 has a suggestion of the same idea, and the original instance (the walking on the water) is in both Matthew and Mark.

Philo's Logos was an archetypal Man in whose image the human race was made ; John's Logos is the revelation of the Father. Those who receive the Logos on earth are born again of God (Jn 1:12), and it is the salvific purpose of the Incarnation which comes immediately into focus when John speaks of the Logos ; the Word declares the Father. (It is even probable that this is said at the outset of the Prologue Jn 1:4, if the reading there adopted by all the pre-Nicene Fathers can be taken to mean : ' What has come to be in Him is Life.') That the Church should ultimately come to teach that the Son proceeds from the Father by intellectual genera-

tion (*see* TRINITY) is due to this designation of Christ as the Logos or Word of God. It should be borne in mind that much of the criticism which was addressed to the gospel of John in the last hundred years has fallen to the ground through making false assumptions about the date of the gospel. It cannot now be maintained that the gospel is later than A.D. 100 by more than a year or two, yet it was the fashion of the critics to place it in the middle of the 2nd cent., Renan wanting 125, Loisy 160, Schmiedel 140, and so on. Thus it was possible to argue then that Justin, in whose writings there is a non-Philonian concept of the Logos (*dial.* 128), was a contemporary of the gospel and that the ensuing Christian Logos-doctrine was an amalgam of John and Justin, John being Philonian and Justin not. It is now clear that Justin has the Johannine doctrine and that it is not Philonian. For Philo the Logos is an intermediary being, not a divine Mediator who has taken flesh.

The sources of the Logos doctrine are to be sought in the OT, where the psalms have occasional glimpses of ' the Word of God ' (Ps 32:6 ; 106:20 ; 147:16-18) in its creative or healing activity. In Wis 9:1, 16:12 and 18:15 there are passages which come closer to what John has to say ; the warrior-Logos of the last passage bears a close relation to John's vision of the Logos as described in Apoc 19:13-15, while Philo, when he has the opportunity in a parallel passage (*De praemiis et poenis*, 95), has nothing to say about such a personified Logos. That John was not alone in preaching a Christian Logos may be seen from the fragment of the Jewish-Christian *Kerygma Petrou* (in Clement of Alexandria *Strom.* 2:15:68 ; GCS 52:149), where Christ is called Law and Logos. This work is dated to the early part of the 2nd cent. The texts from Qumran so far published show considerable similarity with some of the Johannine imagery ; there are phrases about ' doing the truth ', and truth and error are compared to light and darkness, but there is no suggestion of a personal Word. ' God will purge by His truth all the deeds of man . . . sprinkling upon him a spirit of truth,' says the *Manual of Discipline* (4:20), but here truth is a crucible, not a person, and the sprinkling is not the indwelling of a person. The Scrolls, then, make the Johannine Logos-doctrine appear much more appropriate to the contemporary background of Jesus's preaching, but they do not provide any anticipations of its central mystery.

The metaphysical relationship of the Son to the Father which John outlines is one of mutual indwelling (Jn 14:11), so that to see the Son is somehow to see the Father (Jn 14:9). It is not an identity of persons, for there is communication by the Father to the Son (Jn 3:35 ; 10:29), but yet there *is* an identity which is stated quite simply (Jn 10:30) as an identity of being. Even before the elaboration of technical terms by Christian theology, it would follow from what John says that the Son is another than, though not other than, the Father (as St Thomas says : *alius, sed non alienus*). Athanasius used this text more than fifty times in his writings against the

Arians (*see* CCS 799 j). The Son's obedience, as depicted in Jn 5:19 ; 14:9, is part of His salvific mission, and John does not attempt to describe (as Paul did in 1 Cor 15:28) how this obedience arises out of the very Person of the Son ; yet he hints at the same idea by saying (Jn 3:21) that one who does the truth comes to the light, for his works are done in God. If this is true of the Christian, how much more must it be true of Christ Himself ? His works are divine, and when He renders up the kingdom to the Father, then will it be most manifest that the source of His work is in the divine relationship of Father and Son.

X The prayer and practice of the early Church witness to the godhead of Christ chiefly by the use of doxologies (*see* DOXOLOGIES), wherein He is set on an equality with the Father. 'We call God Father and Son and Holy Spirit, proclaiming their power in unity and in rank their diversity,' wrote Athenagoras (*Legatio*, 10), and about the same time a hymn was in use which has come down to us on a 3rd-cent. papyrus (PO 18:507) : 'As we sing to Father, Son and Holy Spirit, may all the powers join with us to say : Amen. To the only giver of all good things be power and praise ; Amen.' The practice of singing *Gloria Patri et Filio et Spiritui sancto* after each psalm was noted as a novelty to himself by Cassian (PL 49:94) when he left the East and came to Gaul. How long it had been in use there one can only conjecture, but it is most probably to be ascribed to anti-Arian teaching (*see* ARIANISM).

The earliest practice at baptism (Ac 8:37 and 22:16) was to have the candidate declare his faith that Jesus was the Son of God. For a convert from Judaism that would have been enough, but in time the Father came to be named with the Son and finally the Holy Spirit, as has been argued at length by the present writer in *Early Christian Baptism and the Creed* (1950). It may be that the invocation of the Son of God at baptism led to the practice (which is widespread in the *Letters* of Ignatius) of referring to Jesus simply as 'God'. In *Rom.* 6:3 Ignatius speaks of 'the passion of my God', in *Eph.* 1:1 of 'the blood of God', and in bidding farewell to Polycarp (*Pol.* 8:3) he calls upon 'Jesus Christ, our God'. Elsewhere (*Eph.* 4:2) Ignatius tells the Christians to 'sing with one voice to the Father through Jesus Christ', affording an indication that prayer was beginning to be stereotyped into the formula that later became the norm.

The *Homily on the Pasch* by Melito has made it possible for the present generation to see very much more of preaching in the 2nd cent. than was possible before. Melito has a passage (84–5) which recalls the Good Friday *Improperia* of a much later time, attributing all the favours of God towards Israel to Jesus who has been by Israel denied. The conclusion to the homily (now available from the Bodmer papyri) addresses Christ as 'Alpha and Omega, undiscoverable beginning and incomprehensible end', but then, just as one might be thinking that Melito was a Monarchian who made no distinction at all between Father and Son, there comes the phrase : 'He bears the Father and He is borne by the Father', which puts an end to the premature speculations about Melito's unorthodoxy which were based on an imperfect text. In an obvious allusion to the Shekinah, to Ps 18:6–7 and to the prophecy of Malachy (1:11), Melito (45) exclaims : 'Not in one place nor within narrow bounds is the glory of the Lord established, but to the very ends of the earth has His grace been poured out, and there has God the all-mastering set up his tent, through Jesus Christ, to whom is glory unto the ages : Amen'.

The opening words of the so-called *II Clement* are : 'Brethren, we must think about Jesus Christ as about God, as about a judge of living and dead'. Meant probably for a Roman audience of the mid-2nd cent., this homily provides a sufficient commentary on the famous words of Pliny, that the Christians sang hymns to Christ, 'as to a god '. It would have been hard for a pagan like Pliny to understand the juxtaposition of divine attributes and mortal deeds which was found in the contemporary Christian worship of Jesus, unless he assimilated it to what he already knew of the demi-gods of paganism.

The *Dialektos* of Origen (discovered in 1942 and published in 1949) has thrown a great light on the 2nd-cent. belief in the godhead of Christ, for it shows Origen interrogating a bishop in some backward region of the East and helping him to overcome his naïve difficulties about the Trinity. 'How are the Father and the Son two, if God is one ?' asks Origen, and when the bishop can only stammer out something about their *dynamis* being the same, Origen helps him to see how the mystery is at least possible. In Eden God told Adam and Eve that they, though they were two, were to be one flesh. St Paul says that the just man who clings to Christ is made one spirit with Him. Cannot the bishop now raise his mind and see how the Father and the Son, though two, may yet be one, not in flesh, nor even in spirit, but in some higher way ? About the same time Hippolytus was causing trouble for Pope Zephyrinus by calling him a believer in two gods. Gradually the work of development of doctrine was proceeding and the simple articles of faith were being linked up by establishing the connections between each, very much as when a man goes to dwell in some new city ; after having found in its thoroughfares the main axes of his daily routine he will gradually come to find how to pass from one to the other and to fill up the gaps in his local knowledge until the whole city is like a map before him.

Bibliography. J. Lebreton SJ in DBS s.v. 'Jésus-Christ (1948) ; L. Cerfaux, *Christ in the Theology of St Paul* (1960) ; J. Jungmann SJ, *Die Stellung Christi im liturgischen Gebet* (1925) ; A. C. Cotter SJ, 'The Divinity of Christ in Apologetics', in TS 3 (1943) 369–384 ; E. Dambrowski, *La Transfiguration de Jésus* (1939) ; *V. Taylor, *The Person of Christ in NT Teaching* (1958) ; the same, *The Names of Jesus* (1953) ; *O. Cullmann, *The Christology of the NT* (1959) ; S. Losch, *Deitas Jesu und antike Apotheose* (1933) ; *W. Manson, 'The *Ego eimi* of the Messianic

Presence', in JTS 48 (1947) 129–36 ; *A. J. Higgins, ' The Son of Man ', in *Studies in Memory of T. W. Manson* 119–35 ; L. Cerfaux, Matthew 11:25–7, in ETL 30 (1954) 740–6 and 31 (1955) 331–42 ; the same (editor), *L'Attente du Messie* (1958).   J. H. C.

CHRISTMAS This article will present (I) the main facts about the introduction of the feast, (II) its theological import and (III) some account of the development of its significance in the patristic homilies for the feast.

I The earliest evidence for Christmas as a liturgical feast is in the Roman document known as the Filocalian calendar or the Chronographer of 354, where one reads the simple entry : ' On 25 December, Christ is born in Bethlehem of Judaea '.[1] Duchesne reasoned that this list of feasts kept at Rome was drawn up before 336 and his arguments have been generally accepted. Another fixed point in the history is the imperial decree of 389 (of Valentinian, Theodosius and Arcadius) which listed the public holidays for the law courts and mentioned both Christmas Day and Epiphany (*Codex Iustiniani* 3:12:6:3).[2] Just one year before the imperial decree John Chrysostom, preaching at Antioch (PG 49:358) speaks of the feast as being kept in the West ' from Thrace to Cadiz ' but new to the East, having been introduced within the last ten years. Antioch, therefore, was ready for the imperial decree when it came, but elsewhere in the East the Church does not seem at once to have made use of the public holiday for liturgical purposes. Thus in Egypt it is clear from Cassian (*Collationes* 10:2 ; CSEL 13:286) that the feast was not divided between 25 December and 6 January but was kept wholly on the latter day.[3] He was writing about 427, and by 1 January 433 the feast of Christmas had been taken up in Egypt, for Paul of Emesa preached two sermons, one on that day and one on 25 December 432, about the feast. At Constantinople Gregory Nazianzen in his sermon for 6 January 380 speaks of having celebrated the birth of Christ beforehand (*orat.* 39:14 ; PG 36:349) and of having been himself the *exarchos* of the feast. There is no real justification for taking this word to mean that he was the very first to celebrate that feast there ; rather does it point to his having presided at the liturgy of the feast as a bishop should. The evidence for Jerusalem is very complicated. The journal of Etheria is defective just at the vital place, but it is fairly safe to infer that she did not witness any keeping of Christmas there ; her account begins, after a gap in the text, with what happened on 6 January. The Armenian *Lectionary*, which gives the ritual borrowed from Jerusalem about 400, has for 25 December a feast of David and James (Conybeare, *Rituale Armenorum*, 527). The life of St Melania (63, the Greek text in AB 22 [1903] 44) shows that at the time of her death Christmas was being kept there, i.e. in 439. Later still, Cosmas

Indicopleustes (PG 88:197) shows that by 535 Jerusalem had gone back to the unitary feast of 6 January.

To go behind the date of 336 to search for the origins of the feast, at Rome or elsewhere, is extremely hazardous. The calendar on the statue-base at Rome which is generally said to be that of Hippolytus has the words γενεσις χριστου opposite the date of 2 April ; it is by no means clear whether this *genesis* is the conception or the birth of Christ, since the Greek word is ambivalent. A rough sketch of this portion of the calendar can be found in DAC VI:2423. In the *Commentary on Daniel* 4:23 (GCS 1:242) Hippolytus's text is somewhat uncertain. There are those who think they can be fairly sure what he wrote at that point and who make the text agree with the statue. Others, mindful that in his *Commentary on Apoc.* 20:1 (GCS 1:ii:238) he gives 25 December, the sixth day of the week, the seventh hour as the time of the birth of Christ (if one may trust the Old Slavonic version which alone is extant), would say that Hippolytus already knew of the Roman custom of keeping Christmas. Attempts have even been made to accept both dates, it being argued that the interval (2 Apr.—25 Dec.) would be according to ancient beliefs about the duration of a pregnancy. The *de Pascha computus* (a work of the year 243) has the birth of Christ on 28 March.[4] It works with a 16-year cycle for Easter and is apparently trying to correct the work of Hippolytus (CSEL 3:266). At the base of such datings seems to be the idea that the life of Christ had to be a complete number of years, with no fraction left over. He died at Passover, and therefore He must have been born then too, but it was important to decide in which year of the cycle His birth fell. From one Passover to another would be counted a complete year, evan though by the profane calendar of Rome the days of the month might not be the same.

Given the pagan practice at Rome of sacrificing to a person's *genius* on his birthday, and given also the widespread cult of astrology among the people (*see* ASTROLOGY), one would naturally expect the Church to be slow to sanction anything approaching a public celebration of the birthday of Christ. Indeed, one would look to popular enthusiasm as the probable origin of such a celebration, with ecclesiastical approval coming in somewhat later in the story. The archaeologists point out that when a grave-inscription is found to give the length of a man's life in years, months and days, it may be taken for granted that he was a pagan. Christians did not observe curiously the exact length of life God had granted their kindred. Clement of Alexandria (*Strom.* 1:21:145 ; GCS 52:90) echoes this sentiment when he blames some Christians as being over-busy about the exact date of Christ's birth, wavering between 20 May and 19 April. Origen (*hom.* 8:3 in Lev. ; GCS 29:396) agrees with Clement.

---

[1] VIII Kal.Ian. natus Christus in Betleem Iudeae.
[2] Dies etiam natalis atque epiphaniorum Christi.
[3] Non bifarie sed sub una diei huius festivitate.

[4] Ad diem nativitatis Eius perveniemus, qui dies sexta sedecennitate in tertio decimo versu invenitur V kal. April., feria IIII.

In the *Protoevangelium Iacobi* (8:3) Zachary, father of John the Baptist, is made to be the high priest, and thus the date of Elizabeth's conception is linked to that of the Day of Atonement. The narrative runs thus : ' The high priest took the vestment with the twelve bells and went into the Holy of Holies and prayed concerning (Mary). And lo, an angel of the Lord appeared, saying unto him : Zachary . . .' If, then, John the Baptist is conceived 23 September and born 24 June, the times that correspond for Christ will be 25 March, more or less, and 25 December. It was open to any careful reader of the Protoevangelium to make this deduction, but one cannot be sure when first it was made. (Chrysostom has it in PG 49:358, but did he originate it ?) The bogus correspondence of Cyril and Pope Julius (to be found PG 96:1436–44, also PG 1:861 and PL 8:966) supposes that Christmas is being kept at Jerusalem, owing to a tradition coming from James (i.e. from the *Protoevangelium* ?), but that it is difficult for the bishop to go three miles to Bethlehem and fifteen miles (to the Jordan, for some commemoration of Christ's baptism) on the same day. Will the Pope tell him what he is to do ? This forgery must come from a period when Jerusalem was keeping both the birthday of Christ and His baptism on the same day. It could be a justification for Juvenal (who was bishop there 422–58) changing the unitary celebration into two separate ones. If so, the forgery is quite early evidence for the tendency to follow the lead of the Roman liturgy in other churches.

The idea that Christ was baptized on His 30th birthday may come from the variant reading of Lk 3:22, where the words ' This day have I begotten Thee ' are attributed to the heavenly voice by some of the MSS, especially the non-African Old Latin (a b c ff² l r). One or two of these must transmit a very early Latin rendering of the passage, for they have the phrase *Iesu baptizante et orante*, where the active participle for the normal passive must come from a time when ' dipping ' rather than ' baptizing ' was the meaning of the word. Justin (*dial.* 88:8 and 103:6) has the words in his account of the baptism, and many patristic works copy them (e.g. Augustine, *De consensu evangelistarum* 2:31 ; CSEL 43:132). It was open to anyone who was puzzled about this variant to say that it was meant to convey to us that the baptism was on the same day as that of Christ's birth. Heretics, of course, took the words to mean that the godhead did not come to be in Christ till He was baptized. From this somewhat tortuous history it must be clear that the feast involves many questions of theology.

II The theology of Christmas is thought by some to be extremely simple. The pagans had a festival of the Sun (*Natalis invicti*) placed by the emperor Aurelian on 25 December (in the year 274) and the reaction of the Christians was to have this counter-feast of Christ, the rising Sun of Justice. It must be admitted that what is probably the earliest Roman representation of Christ shows Him (in the mosaic under St Peter's) as the charioteer of the Sun, a counterpart to Apollo, and this is much

earlier than the reign of Aurelian. Moreover, the scholiast of the medieval Syriac chronicle of Denis bar-Salibi says just that ; the Christian celebration of 6 January was moved to 25 December to meet the pagan challenge of *Sol invictus*. Yet the late Dr Baumstark could write quite categorically : ' In its primitive meaning Christmas was the feast of the Nicene dogma ' (*Comparative Liturgy*, 162). This hypothesis prejudges the historical question about the introduction of the feast in a manner that no liturgical scholar would now consider prudent. It might be that the early Church saw no more harm in thinking of Christ as the Sun of Justice, whose birthday could be kept at the winter solstice, than the present age does in speaking of Christ the worker to those whose minds are filled with the debris of Marxist terminology. It does not seem reasonable to date the mosaic of Christ the charioteer to the reign of Aurelian or after that, and there is still earlier the passage from Melito of Sardis (about the middle of the 2nd cent.) where Christ and His disciples are compared to the sun and the stars. ' The boundless Ocean, the measureless abyss, this is the baptistery of the sun, the watch-fire of the stars and the bathing-place of the moon . . . The stars are dipped in the baptistery of the sun, like goodly disciples ' (*De baptismate*, frag. 3). The fragmentary commentary that is found in the Egerton papyrus (written down in the early 3rd cent. and probably composed about the middle of the 2nd) speaks of Christ as ' the true sun that enlightens us ', and we are assured by a fragment of Papias (frag. 6) that the whole work of the six days of creation was to be understood in terms of Christ and the Church (cf. also Phil. 2:15).

The OT is as promising a source for the theology of Christmas as the stress of conflict either with pagan sun-worship or with Arianism. The canticle of Habacuc (Hab. 3:2–4), besides giving scripture-warrant for the ox and the ass at the crib, has a sun-girt theophany to tell of ; Ecclus 42:16 echoes this, while Mal 3:20 (LXX) has the Sun of Justice Himself, with healing in His wings. The Shekinah, usually represented as light or as a source of light, was in very early times brought into relation with the birth of Christ. In the *Protoevangelium Iacobi* the idea is used : ' A great light shone forth in the cave . . . and after some time the light waned and the infant appeared '. As the late Fr Burrows put it in a brilliant essay (*The Gospel of the Infancy* [1940] 101–10) : ' The Shekinah became a Christological concept '. With that to start them off, Christian Fathers had at hand a remedy against heretics and pagans when they needed it. Somewhere in the trackless regions of the 3rd cent. after the death of Origen, the rivalry of concepts, in which Christian sun-theology was found to be speaking almost the same language as the pagan sun-worshippers spoke, it must have occurred to some unknown to keep a sun-feast for Christ. Ephrem (whose liturgical background is somewhat more primitive than that of the Fathers of Nicaea) knows of only one birth-feast, and that is on 6 January, but he still links it with the winter solstice, for the twelve days that intervene (25 Dec.–6 Jan.) are to be taken, he says, as a sign of the twelve apostles of Christ (cited by Epiphanius, *haer.* 51:22 ; GCS 31:285).

There is a tract or sermon, discovered by Dom Wilmart among some Latin versions of Chrysostom (JTS 19 [1918] 305–27), which he thinks must date from the latter part of the 3rd cent., and in which the author is contrasting the *Natalis invicti* on 25 December with the Christian's belief : 'They call it (the day) the birthday of the undaunted one. But who is so undaunted as Christ who subdued death and triumphed over her ? And as for their calling it the birthday of the sun, He is the Sun of Justice, and of Him Malachy spoke : There will rise up for you that fear His name a Sun of Justice and healing is in His wings'.[1] The appeal to the OT here comes quite naturally as a reply to the pagan challenge and it does not seem unreasonable to think that the use of these OT texts would have been familiar before that challenge was made. Even at Qumran there could be an expectation that the victory of the Sons of Light would be accompanied by 'lightning flashing from one end of the world to the other. . . . Then in the era of God, His exalted grandeur will give light for evermore, shedding on all the Sons of Light peace and blessing'.

When once the calculation about Zachary and John the Baptist had been established, Augustine could point out (*serm.* 194 ; PL 38:1016) that John has his birthday when the days begin to shorten while Christ had His as they begin to lengthen, thus fulfilling John's word about decrease and increase (Jn 3:30). Gradually the existence side by side of Christmas and Epiphany came to be understood as a distribution of the honours due to Christ, His humanity being honoured at Christmas while the manifestation of the divinity was more properly honoured at Epiphany (*see* FEASTS). But the Monophysite heresy could have no such sharing of honours. The fragment of a letter attributed falsely to Hippolytus (GCS 1:ii:282) makes this clear : 'Those who say there are two natures are forced to adore the one and not the other ; they have to be baptized into the one that is divine and not into the human. When *we* are baptized, *we* confess one nature of divinity in flesh'. This argument seems to suppose that, as Epiphany was the day for baptisms admitted by all, the Chalcedonians (who kept both Christmas and Epiphany) would be receiving baptism on the day which according to them was sacred to the divinity of Christ alone, since on that day the divinity was manifested by the three miracles (of Cana, of the voice at the Baptism, and of the star of the Magi). It would seem that the stubborn attachment of Jerusalem to the one combined feast of 6 January even after an experiment with the keeping of 25 December, may have been due to

Monophysite beliefs or tendencies. Liturgy and theology were in close alliance in those days.

The opposite heresy, manifested by dropping the Epiphany and keeping only 25 December is chronicled by Filastrius (*haer.* 112 ; CSEL 38:111) who writes *c.*385 : 'There are some heretics who question the day of the Epiphany which is kept 6 January, saying that they should keep only the birthday of the Lord on 25 December. Others say that Epiphany is the day of the Baptism, others again that it is the day of the Transfiguration on the mountain'.[2] Those who wanted to keep Christmas alone may have been followers of Aetius (*see* AETIUS) who took a very low view of the position of Christ. Gregory of Nazianzus distinguished three nativities of the Logos (*orat.* 40 ; PG 36:361), the taking of flesh, the Baptism and the Resurrection. He does not suggest that the Church should keep the feast of the eternal generation of the Son by the Father, for that would be to place it in time and to go along with the Arians who said that time was when the Son was not.

The difference between the Paschal cycle of feasts and the Christmas-Epiphany group was expressed by Augustine (*ep* 55:2; CSEL 34:170), when he said that the former were sacramental, while Christmas was not sacramental but only commemorative. Perhaps in his time men were conscious that the dating of the Nativity was not, in spite of the calculations about Zachary and John the Baptist, based upon a firm historical tradition. On the other hand, Zeno of Verona (*tract* 8 ; PL 11:412) contrasted the eternal generation of Son from Father which no man could scrutinise with the temporal which was rightly the subject of a tradition.[3] Gregory of Nyssa (*epitaphios* 1 ; PG 46:789) thought that St Paul had established the order of feasts, first of all the Theophany of the Son, then Stephen, Peter, James, John, as apostles and prophets, while after these it was fitting to celebrate Basil as one of the shepherds and teachers, according to 1 Cor. 12:28. An attempt to make of the Epiphany at least a sacramental feast may be found in the *Stowe Missal*, where the *Canon dominicus papae Gelasi* has a phrase for introduction into the *Communicantes* on that day which speaks of 'celebrating the birthday of the chalice of Our Lord'. The miracle of Cana, commemorated in the Epiphany, would thus be a sign or foreshadowing of the Eucharist, just as the descent of Christ from the cross into the tomb and to Limbo was a sign of the Christian's going down into the waters of baptism. No such sacramentalization of the feast of Christmas can be observed. The best that can be done in this sense may be found in the *Leonine Sacramentary* (in Mohlberg's edition, n. 1241)

---

[2] Quidam dubitantes haeretici de die Epiphaniorum Domini, qui celebratur VIII Id. Ian., dicentes solum Natalem debere eos celebrare Domini VIII Kal. Ian. Quidam autem diem Epiphaniorum baptismi, alii Transformationis in monte quae facta est esse opinantur.

[3] Duas nativitates esse Domini nostri Iesu Christi . . . disce : unam quam tibi non licet quaerere, alteram quam legitime si possis permitteris edocere. Prima . . . in Patris et Filii tantum conscientia manet.

---

[1] Sed et Invicti natalem appellant. Quis utique tam Invictus nisi Dominus noster qui mortem subactam devicit ? Vel quod dicant solis esse natalem : Ipse est sol iustitiae de quo Malachias propheta dixit : orietur vobis timentibus nomen Ipsius sol iustitiae et sanitas in pennis Eius.

where the claim is made that whatever Christian piety may practise takes its start from this feast and is contained in its mystery ; but no specific elaboration is offered.

III The Christmas sermons of the Fathers were numerous and have in part been mentioned in discussing the origins of the feast. One may note the sermon by Jerome (now accessible in PL Supplement, 2:191–2) in which with his usual self-assurance he claims to have the whole world on his side in opposing the ritual practice of Jerusalem. Augustine's thirteen sermons (*serm.* 184–96 ; PL 38:995–1021) are a good instance of how not to repeat oneself when facing year after year a familiar occasion. Even the last of these has some novelty, with its study of the three women, a wife (Elizabeth), a widow (Anna) and a virgin, who salute the Incarnate Child. A sermon by Optatus has been rediscovered (edited by Dom A. Wilmart in Rev. SR 2 [1922] 271–302) which must have been preached on a unitary feast of Christmas-with-Epiphany in 362 or 363, when persecution of Christians had begun once more. He has the simple language of Tertullian for the Incarnation, describing Christ as *homo Deo mixtus* (man combined with God), a phrase which would not have found favour at Chalcedon. He is also the first to envisage the medieval picture of wicked dragon and beautiful princess, for he says that the devil who had entered into Herod was downcast and grieved at the birth of Christ, for the Church (Ecclesia) was then snatched from his jaws and united to God.[1]

Ambrose in his *De Virginibus* (3:3 ; PL 16:219–22) composed a sermon which he put into the mouth of Pope Liberius, reminding his sister that she had heard an address such as that, on the occasion of her first profession. Most critics agree that it really represents what Ambrose himself would have said on the feast. Gradually the custom began of collecting the sermons of the Fathers on this feast. If they were of uncertain authorship, then it was felt to be the simplest thing to put them down to Augustine, Basil or some other great preacher. The same plan was resorted to in the making of Catenae for the NT (*see* CATENAE). Much of the theology of the Incarnation was preserved and passed on in this way. One of these collections has recently yielded a previously unknown Greek sermon (by Proclus ?) of anti-Nestorian drift which takes the form of an interrogation of Nature, of the patriarchs and prophets, of Lazarus and the man born blind, of Peter and Thomas, on the mystery of the Incarnation. They are made to reply with words of Scripture and to stress that one must accept the fact and not seek to understand the *how*. This sermon was published in RBn 58 (1948) 221–63. The tendency was to treat of the whole mystery of the Incarnation at Christmas, for the Annunciation was not kept as a feast until somewhat later. There is a sermon by Abraham of Ephesus (probably *c.* 550) wherein the claim is made that this is the first

---

[1] Diabulus in Herode deiectus dolet ecclesiam suis faucibus ereptam et Deo coniunctam.

time the *Euangelismos* (as the Greeks called the Annunciation) was being thus honoured (PO 16: 443).

Leo the Great, coming after the debellation of Nestorius and Eutyches, is able in his ten sermons to call Christians repeatedly to rejoice in the true doctrine which lies between the two opposed heresies (*serm.* 21–30 ; PL 54:190–234). One development can be seen in his work : the idea that the birthday of the Head is that of the Body too (PL 54:213) and the Spirit who overshadowed Mary is the same Spirit who presides at baptism. From this, and from the ideas of Gregory of Nyssa cited above, it may be seen that the practice of starting the liturgical year with Christmas would appeal to many, as in fact it did (*see also* ADVENT). The *Gelasian Sacramentary*, whatever its history, is witness to this practice. Some of its Prefaces, in the Christmas liturgy (as those in the *Leonine Sacramentary* also) are like the perorations of patristic sermons. One of them (8, in Mohlberg's edition) was claimed by Baumstark as giving the key to his reconstruction of Christmas as the feast of Nicaea. It is indeed strongly Trinitarian in character, but as it occurs in a Mass (*in nocte*) where the post-communion speaks of a threefold celebration being fitted to the mystery of the Trinity, it is clear that this Trinitarian bias is linked with the saying of three Masses for Christmas, a custom which cannot be traced back before Gregory the Great (*hom. in evangelia* 8 ; PL 76:1103). Later theologians will say that the Incarnation was the work of the whole Trinity ; an appeal to the Trinity could therefore be made at any time.

Bibliography. H. Frank OSB, 'Frühgeschichte des römischen Weihnachtsfestse', in AL 2 (1952) 1–24 ; H. Engberding OSB, 'Der 25 Dezember als Tag der Geburt des Herrn', in AL 2 (1952) 25–43 ; *A. McArthur, The Evolution of the Christian Year (1953) ; H. Rahner SJ, 'Das christliche Mysterium vom Sonne', in Eranos Jahrbuch X (1943) 305–404 ; A. Baumstark, Comparative Liturgy (1958) ; A. Strittmatter OSB, 'Christmas and Epiphany', in Thought 17 (1942) 600–26 ; for earlier discussions, see C. C. Martindale SJ in CE s.v. Christmas ; B. Botte OSB, Les Origines du Noël et de l'Épiphanie (1932) J. H. C.

CHURCH In one sense all the articles of this Dictionary are concerned with the theology of the Catholic Church, and some of them are devoted to a consideration of separate items in the theology of that mystery. Moreover, there has been given under the heading BODY, MYSTICAL, a full-length treatment of the mystery of the Church. Here it will be necessary simply to co-ordinate the various articles, written and to be written, on the different aspects of the Church and to add a few details not covered elsewhere.

The 'little flock' or 'one fold' of Jesus, described by Paul as 'the household of the faith' (Gal 6:10) and even 'the Church of God' (Gal 1:13 ; 1 Cor 10:32), is already in the NT the new Sion (Heb 12:22) and the heavenly Jerusalem (Apoc 3:12 ; 21:2).

When through the revelation to Peter (Ac 10:13) and the discussion that followed it (Ac 15:14) the apostles have learned that the new ' people of God ' is to include Jew and Gentile without discrimination, the way is open to the adaptation of extensive tracts of the OT for the purpose of defining the nature and sketching the history of the true Israel. For Paul, who often uses the word ' mystery ' in the singular, this was the most vital truth of Christ's revelation (e.g. Eph 5:32 ; Col 1:26), which began with the apparently simple comparison of Himself to the Bridegroom (Mt 9:15 ; Mk 2:19 with Jn 3:29), by which He left the disciples to wonder at first whether He was claiming for Himself all that was said in the OT about the nuptial relationship of Jahweh and Israel. In II Clem. 14:2 after the citation of Gen 1:26 one has the plain assertion : ' The female is the Church '. The *Epistle to Diognetus* (11:5 ; 12:8) alludes to the same idea, while we are assured that Papias (frag. 6) interpreted the whole story of the days of creation in terms of Christ and the Church. It is here that the primitive theology of the Church must be sought.

The Church (*see* CATECHUMENATE) had very soon organised itself and what were later called the marks of apostolicity (*see* APOSTLES, APOSTOLIC SUCCESSION) and catholicity (q.v.) were being appealed to ; while the need for unity was brought out by the early heresies (*see e.g.* BASILIDES, ARIANISM). This mark of unity will be treated under the heading of SOLIDARITY which is the nearest our language comes to the *Sobornost* concept of the Eastern churches. For the Church as means of salvation see SALVATION and also ARK OF NOE IN LITURGY ; while the height of the teaching authority of the Church will be discussed in INFALLIBILITY and its special hierarchic structure in BISHOP ; CARDINALS ; POPE, PRIMACY OF THE ; PETER AT ROME ; HIERARCHY IN EARLY CHURCH. The holiness of the Church (q.v.) can be understood from the study of her means of reconciliation (*see* ABSOLUTION, CONFESSION) and of her liturgies which are framed in diverse fashion (*see* ADDAI AND MARI, LITURGY OF ; AFRICAN LITURGY ; BASIL, LITURGY etc.) for the celebration of the sacrifice of reconciliation on earth. The sacraments are each treated under their own titles, while the concept of the treasury of the Church will be examined in INDULGENCES, THEOLOGY OF. The uncovenanted manifestations of God's grace are considered under the heading CHARISMS.

The doctrinal mission of the Church is dealt with under the headings CREEDS, APOSTLES' CREED, TRADITION, DEVELOPMENT OF DOCTRINE, DOGMA, DOGMATIC FACT, RULE OF FAITH. The article immediately following this has the principal treatment of the problem of CHURCH AND STATE, but certain aspects of it are considered under the headings GALLICANISM, TOLERATION, CONCORDATS, ERASTIANISM. The councils of the Church are briefly considered under their individual titles for their theological importance, while the position of the laity in the Church comes up for attention under the heading FAITHFUL AS A SOURCE OF DOGMA. The idea of a twofold or three-

fold aspect of the Church is discussed under COMMUNION OF SAINTS, where the ordinary terms Church militant, suffering and triumphant are explained. A more recent attempt to apply this distinction to the problem of invalid ordinations needs however to be noticed here. It has been advocated by some Anglicans that relay-race, or pipe-line, metaphors to illustrate the idea of succession are not sound and that one should regard ordination or episcopal consecration not as an act by which the earthly Church authorises one of its members to perform certain functions but as the act of the universal episcopate, with Christ as the great High Priest, incorporating a new member into their number. It has even been claimed that according to Cant 1:4 one church was black, imperfect and empirical, the other comely and archetypal. But that is not how the two were distinguished in antiquity. There is a significant passage in Asterius (*hom.* 26 ; edited by M. Richard [1956], 208) : ' The tabernacle of Moses and the temple of Solomon are types and figures of the two churches of Christ, that in the world and that in heaven. Of the church in the world Moses's tabernacle is the figure, and of the heavenly one the Temple that was on the mountain ; two churches in number but one in the grace of faith. It was for the church on earth that Christ said : " Upon this rock I will build My Church," and of the heavenly Church the apostle says (Heb 12:22) : " You are come nigh to Mount Sion and the city of the living God. . . ." Just as the tent of Moses was changed from place to place and became a sojourner, while the temple of Solomon built on a mountain remained unshaken and untroubled, standing in one place for what time it was the temple of God, even so the Church of Christ on earth makes sojourners of the devout and is set up in " parishes ", while the Church that is above, made up of the first-born in heaven, hath no sojourners there but makes of the friends of God permanent dwellers '. This is the true view and it makes the hierarchic ' building upon the rock ' a function of the earthly Church, not of the heavenly ; in accord with the whole of ancient tradition it regards the present Church as ' sojourning ' or makeshift but none the less bound to the heavenly one, even as the sacrifice that was carried out on a temporary altar here was made acceptable on the heavenly altar (*see* ALTAR).

For the *communicatio idiomatum* that went on from about the 6th cent. between the Church and the Blessed Virgin one may cite the *Antiphonary of Bangor*, where a hymn (95) proclaims the Church to be ' a virgin most fruitful and mother undefiled, joyful yet full of fear in her submission to the Word of God '. The Armenian service for dedicating a church (Conybeare, *Rituale Armenorum*, 21) could be mistaken for a litany of the Blessed Virgin. The whole subject has been studied by H. Coathalem, *Le Parallélisme entre la Sainte Vierge et l'Église dans la tradition latine jusqu'à la fin du XIIe siècle* (1954).

For the theological significance of the rite of dedicating a church building, *see* CONSECRATION. Problems of membership of the Church, touched on under BIOLOGY, IMPACT ON THEOLOGY ; BAPTISM and BODY, MYSTICAL will be considered under SALVATION OF NON-CATHOLICS. In the articles on ANGLICANISM, PROTESTANT THEOLOGY and CONTINUITY, ANGLICAN various alternative ideas of the Church are considered.

Bibliography. The works cited under the various articles listed here should be consulted. There is a great need of a full-length treatise on the Church which would overcome the dislocation of the subject-matter by separation into two parts, one apologetic and the other dogmatic. The *Église du verbe incarné* of Mgr C. Journet (2 vols, I² [1955], II [1951]) is a praiseworthy modern attempt in this direction. See also L. Cerfaux, *The Church in the Theology of St Paul* (1959). J. H. C.

CHURCH AND STATE The problems created by the existence side by side of two powers, spiritual and temporal, have varied from age to age. This article will attempt to summarize the more important of them in seven phases, (I) before Constantine, (II) from Constantine to Justinian, (III) from Justinian to Charlemagne, (IV) in the Middle Ages, (V) during the Reformation, (VI) in the period of the absolute monarchies, and finally (VII) in modern times, with special attention being given to the English aspects of the problems.

I Before Constantine the main problem for Christians was to reconcile the teaching of Christ (Jn 19:11) on the heavenly origin of the authority of the State and the apostolic command to pray for rulers (1 Tim 2:2), with the awkward and even gruesome facts of imperial administration with its official promotion of emperor-worship as a bond of the empire. Clement closes his epistle (*I Clem.* 60-1) with a prayer for the emperor (Domitian) : ' May we have peace . . . as we are become obedient to Thy all-majestic and all-virtuous name, and to our governors and rulers upon this earth. Thou, Lord, hast given them the authority of the kingdom by Thy magnificent and unutterable strength, that we might recognize the glory and honour Thou hast given them and might be subject to them, while in no way going against Thy will. Grant them, Lord, health, peace, concord and steadfastness, that they may wield the rulership Thou hast given them without offence'. The prayer goes on to ask for the emperor and his *legati* wise counsel and that they may find mercy, but there is as yet no word of their possible conversion. The prayer follows Jewish models, and the fair treatment by Domitian of the grandsons of Jude (Eusebius, *HE* 3:20) may have counted for something in its composition ; it does more than re-echo the teaching of Rom 13:1-7.

The Jews had been exempt from the more extreme practices of the emperor-worship, and Tacitus, who governed the province of Asia about 114, could put into the mouth of Titus the sentiment that Christianity was a branch of Judaism ; when the root was destroyed, the branch would wither (*Histories* fragment 2). It may be that until the time of Hadrian, when the laws against the Jews were

tightened, Christians had been able to derive some protection from this confusion. The new situation arising when people realized that Christianity was not a Jewish sect would naturally provoke such inquiries as that of Pliny to Trajan (*ep.* 10:96) and that of Granianus to Hadrian. The reply of the latter to Fundanus (in Justin, *apol.* 68), now accepted as quite authentic, is of great importance : ' If our subjects of the provinces are able to support by evidence their *supplex libellus* against the Christians, so as to answer to it before a court of justice, let them take this course, but they must not fall to beseeching and mere clamour'. The existence of a specific law against the Christians has been much debated ; the spasmodic nature of the persecutions tells against it (*see* MARTYRDOM), but by the end of the 2nd cent. there are references to something like it. Athenagoras (*legatio*, 7) says : ' They (the philosophers) can speak and write as they will about the divinity, while a law is set against us'. The placing of Christian bodies on the same footing as philosophical schools (*see* APOSTOLIC SUCCESSION II) may have been tolerated after Hadrian, but was not countenanced by Marcus Aurelius.

In the collection of maxims for guidance in Christian living known as the *Sentences of Sextus* (edited by H. Chadwick, 1959) and coming from about the middle of the 2nd cent., there is remarkably little that bears on the attitude to be taken up in public. Saying 364 urges : ' When threats are uttered by a tyrant, then most of all be mindful whose child you are'. Saying 343 : ' Do not sharpen the anger of the multitude ', may be advice for those on trial, but one cannot be sure. The collection can be taken as showing that the average Christian was far more concerned with conquering his appetites and seeking wisdom than with facing persecution. Hippolytus, commenting on Dan 6: 11 (GCS 1:168), stresses the fact that Daniel did not give up his practice of praying thrice in the day when the king of Babylon forbade it, though he might have dissimulated. Heretics of the time were ready to teach that a Christian need not confess his faith before men.

In all this early material it is not easy to find what the Christians really thought the State was for. They might have answered with St Paul that it was for the restraint of evil-doers, but gradually, from the time of Tertullian (*apol.* 32), another idea begins to be put forward. ' We know that the end of the world and its calamities is being held back by the respite which the Roman empire gives us '.[1] The metaphor used implies that Christians are allowed a furlough from the eschatological crisis by the continued existence of the empire. This idea is taken up by Augustine (*de civ. Dei* 20:8 ; CSEL 40:446) and by Jerome, who linked it with 2 Thess 2:6 and the power which holds Anti-Christ in check (*see* ANTI-CHRIST). Armenia became a Christian nation before it was part of the Roman empire, but it would be true to say that the problems of Church

[1] Clausulam saeculi acerbitates horrendas comminantem Romani imperii commeatu scimus retardari.

and State in this period are those of the empire ; its need for a moral force of cohesion made Diocletian (who thought that paganism was the answer) a more calculating persecutor than any previous emperor, and it was by a realisation, however gained, that Christianity might provide this force, that Constantine turned seriously to the new creed.

II From Constantine to Justinian the Church is faced with the new problem of a friendly, even a patronising, State hastening to suppress those heretics who threaten imperial unity. When the emperor is himself a heretic, the Church goes into opposition and sometimes into the wilderness. The rescript drawn up by Constantine and Licinius at Milan in 313 (Eusebius, *HE* 10:5 and Lactanius, *de mortibus persecutorum* 48) declares that 'facility should be refused to no one whatever who gives up his mind either to the religious observance of the Christians or to that cult which he feels best suited to himself'. This was not an edict but an instruction for provincial governors, who were expected to promulgate it with local variations of detail. It marks the first acceptance of the idea that the State should not interfere in affairs of religion. But immediately a material problem forced Constantine to further action. Possession of buildings which the Church had used before the persecution had to be settled. In Africa there were rival claimants, Catholics and Donatists (for the circumstances, *see* DONATISM). 'All these things must be handed over to the corporation of the Christians forthwith, by thy intervention and without delay', said the rescript, but to whom should they be given in proconsular Africa ? There was a precedent, for the emperor Aurelian on the occasion of an earlier dispute had ordered the church buildings at Antioch to be given to 'those of the persuasion who were in receipt of letters of communion from the bishops of Italy and the city of Rome' (Eusebius *HE* 7:30). This Constantine followed, but immediately the Donatists appealed against the decision. Constantine then wrote to Pope Miltiades and to Mark (probably his archdeacon) saying that he had ordered Caecilian, bishop of Carthage, to come to Rome with ten supporters and with ten of the Donatist bishops and that he had summoned Reticius of Autun, Maternus of Cologne and Marinus of Arles to form a panel of judges with the Pope and Mark, to hear the case. The Pope quickly turned this meeting into a local council by associating with it the neighbouring bishops of Italy, thus early manifesting a desire to escape from imperial leading-strings. The Council of Arles, provoked by Donatist recalcitrance and attended by three British bishops, went a step further in its 7th canon : 'Concerning governors who are members of the Church when they come into office'. It is enacted that 'when once they begin to go against the discipline of the Church, then they should be excluded from communion. The like should be observed with those who wish to enter public life'. The Church could not help being suspicious of the great imperial machine of government, even when it had ceased to be lethal.

Much of Constantine's action in Church matters is subject to controversy, and it is gradually coming to be realized that there are two sources of bias in the reporting of the facts ; the lawyers of his Chancery remained pagan and did much in the drafting of his laws to tone down or conceal what was in favour of the Church (as A. Ehrhardt has shown), while Eusebius (who is our chief authority from the side of the Church) was concerned to conceal his own condemnation (for leaning towards Arianism) at a council prior to Nicaea (*see* ARIANISM). Thus the bishops of Syria had excommunicated Eusebius at a council of Antioch, referring him to a greater council that should meet at Ancyra. The emperor intervened to have the council meet at Nicaea, for greater convenience of access, and to invite bishops from the West to attend it. As he controlled the only rapid means of travel, the *cursus publicus*, it was natural for the Church to acquiesce in such imperial interference as this, but it would be false to ascribe the council to imperial initiative. At the council the emperor described himself in a famous phrase as 'bishop of those that are outside'. He cannot have meant that he was in charge of all Christian missions to lands outside the empire, for he took no special care of Armenia or Ethiopia, nor can he have been thinking of the pagans within the empire. 'Those that are outside' may refer to people or to things, but the point is hardly worth all the argument that has been spent on it, for the most likely sense is that the emperor was claiming to control what people did outside church, while the bishops dealt with them when they were inside. In 342, at the Council of Sardica (canon 5) it was stated that people were often finding sanctuary in churches and when they did so, it was right, the Council said, to petition the emperor for their pardon. It may be that Constantine's words gave rise to the custom ; legal acceptance of right of sanctuary came at the end of the 4th cent. 'Bishops have the primacy in places that are sacred', wrote Sozomenos (*HE* 2:34 ; GCS 50:100), and the principle was upheld through the ages (*see* CORONATION I).

Enforcement by the State of Church decisions about heresy might be considered to be a consequence of the principle which Constantine had laid down by his distinction between 'inside and outside'. At all events it soon became the fashion, and with it went the concern about the emperor's own faith which was inevitable once the principle was admitted ; no emperor was likely to apply sanctions in favour of a theological position which he did not accept for himself. Hence the appearance of the court-bishop in the person of Eusebius of Nicomedia (*see* ARIANISM), and the prohibition (in the Council of Sardica, can. 21) of journeys to the court by bishops '*propter desideria et ambitiones*' (from greed and ambition). 'Whatever I will, let that be taken as a canon,' is the tactless remark attributed by Athanasius to Constantius (PG 25:732). 'Accept this, or go into banishment.' This was to be the fate of many bishops and of some Popes in this period. Confining the powers of the Church within four walls was clearly an unsatisfactory solution, even when the emperor was a Catholic. If he came to church, he might be dealt with by a bishop such as Ambrose or Basil refusing to start Mass until he gave way on some disputed point, but once outside, the old trouble began again.

Gradually the Church began to formulate the rights of religion which extended beyond the walls of the place of worship. The Council of Sardica wrote to Constantius (CSEL 65:181) asking that he should decree that no magistrate or provincial judge might sit in judgment on matters of religion, sentencing the clergy to hardship and violence.[1] Osius in his last days wrote to the same emperor in 356 (PG 25:745) telling him that he stood under the judgment of God. In words that anticipate the famous *Duo sunt* of Gelasius he said : ' Keep yourself pure for that day. Do not meddle in ecclesiastical affairs and do not give orders to us about them but rather learn about them from us. God has put the kingdom in your hands, but to us He has entrusted the Church. One who derogates from your authority opposes himself to God who gave it, and likewise you should fear lest in drawing to yourself the business of the Church you have to render an account to God for a most grave offence '.

The imperial answer to these warnings, given by Constantius, can be read in the *de regibus apostaticis* of Lucifer of Calaris (CSEL 14:35) : ' If I had done evil ; if, as Lucifer says, I had become a heretic, God would have taken the kingdom from me before now '. Lucifer answers : ' I must tell you that Solomon lived on after his sin of idolatry, and I hope you realize that you are now such as he was after his sin '. God left Roboam alone for twenty years and Manasses for fifty-seven, but He judged them in the end ; He may now wait patiently, allowing His faithful ones to be proved by persecution, but He is still master. In this attitude of Lucifer may be seen the germ of the idea that the emperor, apart from the private account which he has to render to God for his life with wife and family, has as it were a public conscience, and in this too he must as a Christian seek the guidance of the Church. The office of the Lord Chancellor in England grows out of the same idea.

If the Church had to keep the emperor's conscience, private or public, she had also to judge of sin in her own members, and particularly among the ranks of the hierarchy. The problem of the exemption of the clergy arose very soon, as can be seen from a letter of Ambrose to the emperor Valentinian II in 386 (*ep.* 21 ; PL 16:1003). He recalls that the preceding emperor, Valentinian I, had ruled that ' in matters of belief or ecclesiastical discipline he should be judge who is not rendered unfit by his office nor governed by a different law '.[2] That is, as Ambrose claimed, bishops should be judged by bishops. With this went the system of appeals to the Pope which is evidenced by the Council of Sardica (can. 3). In that age the emergent nationalism of Copts in Egypt (in the Meletian schism) and of Berbers in North Africa (among the Donatists) was opposed both to the central government of the empire and to the universal Church ; a bishop, therefore, who became involved in these movements would be likely to meet with condemnation from both authorities, and the State would easily accede to the action of the Church against him, but when the aspect of things changed, and the Church found herself favouring one or other national group against an Arian emperor, it was important to have already established this independence of judicial powers.

The edict (27 Feb. 380) of Gratian, Valentinian and Theodosius which expressed the desire that all the peoples of the empire would adopt ' that faith which the apostle Peter preached to the Romans and which the pontiff Damasus now follows ', set up an established church for the first time. The edict was addressed to the inhabitants of Constantinople (*Codex Theodosianus* 16:1:2) and spoke of ' our initiative which We derive from the Judge in heaven '. Just one year later the city of Constantinople was the scene of a Council which in its notorious 3rd canon decreed a primacy of honour after Rome to the church of Constantinople ' owing to its being the new Rome '. If there had been *hybris* in what Theodosius did, *Ate* came close behind. The nucleus of Byzantinism, with a church subservient to the State, was already here. Pope Damasus was not officially represented at this Council, though from his letters (*ep.* 5 ; PL 13:365) it appears that he had briefed Ascholius of Thessalonica to act for him, and Ascholius did not sign the decrees of the Council, perhaps through disagreement with canon 3.

The fate of Priscillian (*see* PRISCILLIANS) is an example of the way in which Church and State now deal with ' mixed matters '. There was certainly an aspect of the case which called for the application of the criminal law. Mark of Memphis seems to have been a Manichee and something of a magician who, coming to Spain, made disciples of Agape and Helpidius ; these in turn instructed Priscillian, and he is described by Jerome (*ep.* 133:4 ; CSEL 56:248) as a magician turned bishop (*ex mago episcopum*). The law on *maleficium* was severe, and fear made judges quicker to act ; on the other hand, Priscillian was a bishop. The Council of Saragossa in 380 (can. 3) called down anathema on those who received the Eucharist into their hands but did not consume it ; one might suppose that some of the Priscillians were taking it away for magical uses. Although many of the details are obscure, the affair of Priscillian is an exact rehearsal for the Albigenses later on. Church and State combine against them ; there are churchmen who urge moderation (in this

---

[1] Decernat clementia tua ut omnes ubique iudices quibus provinciarum administrationes creditae sunt . . . a religiosa observantia se abstineant neque posthac praesumant atque usurpent et putent se causas cognoscere clericorum et innocentes homines . . . frangere atque vexare.

[2] In causa fidei vel ecclesiastici alicuius ordinis eum iudicare debere qui nec munere impar sit nec iure dissimilis.

case, St Martin of Tours, Ambrose and Pope Siricius) and ultimately judgment is given by the secular power. Thus early, the whole problem of the overlapping of interests has been posed, and posed within the framework of the Roman civil law. **III The ideal of Justinian** was set forth in his code of law, wherein the edict of 380 on orthodoxy (cited above) was given pride of place and the whole code was considered to be so absolute and complete that all commentaries on it were forbidden. It must be admitted that the device of taking the Church under the wing of the State produced a tough and enduring polity which lasted for nearly a thousand years ; in the Anglican experiment of the same kind it lasted, if not for so long. In spite of the monolithic quality of Justinian's *Code* he was constrained to add to it certain *Novellae*, of which the 6th (16 March 535) determines more fully his theory of the position of the Church. Addressing his obedient Patriarch, Epiphanius, he says : ' Nothing will be so great a concern to the emperors as the good life of bishops, since they are constantly to pray to God for the emperors. If this duty is everywhere faithfully discharged and meets with a generous return from God, and if on the other hand the imperial government worthily and efficiently embellishes the commonwealth that it has inherited, there will then be a blessed harmony from which all possible benefits will flow to the human race'. [1] In the very next year Pope Silverius, and after him Vigilius, Pelagius I, Martin, Honorius and Constantine I, were to feel the impact of this policy in their own persons. The teaching office of the Church is quietly ignored or else turned into a department of State. Bishops are confined to cathedral and sacristy for all the good they can do. The Western ideal had been formulated in the *Duo sunt* of Gelasius I and enough had been done, particularly among the Catholics of North Africa, to deepen the understanding of this principle that, when the time of conflict came, there were those who could withstand the imperial aggression. Gelasius had said : ' There are two powers by which at the highest level this world is governed, the sacred authority of the Popes and the kingly power. Of these so much the weightier is the duty of the priests in that they are destined at the divine scrutiny to render an account even for the kings of men themselves'. Emperors might think they must see to it that the Pope kept to his prayers, but the Popes knew from this letter that they would have to answer for the imperial conscience, at least in its public acts. [2]

St Augustine had spent 13 years writing his book

De civitate Dei for practical ends and was not concerned to present a single watertight conception of either Church or State. None the less, he was used as a quarry of ideas by the West for centuries and furnished many of the answers to Byzantine claims of dominance. ' We do not wish to have dealings with the powers that be,' he wrote in a moment of weariness at the burdens the State thrust upon the Church (care of orphans, curbing of civil administrators, hearing of civil disputes in ecclesiastical courts) and it may well be that he came to think that the State should on its part aid the Church by undertaking the suppression of heresy. A gradual change has been noted in Augustine's thought on this important topic (*see* TOLERATION). Against the Manichees he held (*ep.* 23:7 ; CSEL 34:71) that the State could not force the free will of man in matters of faith, but at the end, under the influence of the words *Compelle intrare* (from Lk 14:23), he accepted the coercion of the Donatists by the State. ' What worse death can the soul suffer than by its being allowed to go astray ? ' he asked (*ep.* 105:10 ; CSEL 34:602), and the sentence echoed down the ages.[3] He may have meant simply to bring an argument *ad hominem* against the Donatists who had begun the business of appealing to the State ; they had gone to an orthodox emperor (Constantine), but what would come of appeals to emperors who were anything but orthodox ? The interminable theological disputes of Byzantium are an answer to that question.

Justice was the giving to each his due, but Augustine knew that God must have His due also, and this left him in the dilemma of deciding either to omit justice from his definition of the State or else to deny that Rome had been a State at all. He chose a new definition of the State as a community of men bound by an agreement about the objects of their love. ' Set justice aside, and what are kingdoms but great banditries ? ' he asked, and the drift was that of Newman's sentence : ' There never was a kingdom, except Christ's, which was not conceived and born, nurtured and educated, in sin ' (*Sermons on Subjects of the Day*, 273). This pessimism coloured much of later theological thinking. It drove some to cling to the empire of Byzantium as to a State of holiness, while others were turned against civil authority as such. Not until the Thomist thinking about natural law and the natural end for men and States was it possible to envisage a Christian theory of the State which would leave the State real freedom in its own order. Augustine's view was foreshortened ; he saw (*De civ. Dei* 19:10 ; CSEL 40:388) the peace and happiness of the naturally good life as ' altogether misery ' in comparison with heaven and had not come to the vision of Aquinas (in his commentary on the last book of the *Ethics* of Aristotle) of an unending progress towards, or receding goal of, natural happiness that led a man on towards God, so that grace did not destroy nature, but perfected it.

Conflict between Rome and the Byzantine ideal came in the time of Gregory the Great. It has

[1] Nihil sic erit studiosum imperatoribus sicut sacerdotum honestas, cum utique et pro illis ipsis semper Deo supplicent. Nam si hoc quidem inculpabile sit undique et apud Deum fiducia plenum, imperium autem recte et competenter exornet traditam sibi rempublicam, erit consonantia quaedam bona, omne quicquid utile est humano conferens generi.

[2] Duo quippe sunt . . . quibus principaliter mundus hic regitur : auctoritas sacrata pontificum et regalis potestas. In quibus tanto gravius est pondus sacerdotum quanto etiam pro ipsis regibus hominum in divino reddituri sunt examine rationem.

[3] Quae est peior mors animae quam libertas errandi ?

recently been argued that Gregory took occasion from the mission of Augustine to England to open a campaign against the use by Constantinople of the title of 'universal patriarch', a title which had been used as early as 518 and which had not hitherto provoked any reaction in Gregory. The question belongs properly to a discussion of the Roman Primacy (q.v.) but it is also of importance for the development of ideas about Church and State. To be able to escape from the Caesaro-papism of Byzantium by strengthening the links of the Papacy with the new Western nations was ultimately of great value, as can be seen from the way in which Pope Sergius (in 692) was able to reject a demand that he should accept the decrees of the Byzantine council known as the Quinisext. The imperial emissary sent to bring the Pope to Constantinople under arrest had to seek refuge ignominiously under the Pope's bed when the Roman populace sought to impede his action.

Pope Constantine I in 710 made the journey to Constantinople, but even so he did not accept the Greek canon law, for on his return to Rome he had the decrees of the first six general councils inscribed in the portico of St Peter's where they were seen by Bede's abbot, Ceolfrid. This automatically excluded the decrees of the Quinisext, which the emperors were anxious to extend to the West. Ever since the middle of the 5th cent. there had been difficulty of communication between East and West, since the unity of the Mediterranean world was then broken by the pirate fleets of Vandal Carthage, while the *canalis Italiae* (the land-route through Jugoslavia) was rendered unsafe by barbarian inroads.

Gregory II in 729 could answer the emperor in firmer tones, as the power of Lombard and Frank was growing. 'It is not for the emperor to meddle in the affairs of the Church, to cast his vote in judgment on priests, to consecrate or handle the sacred elements of the mysteries, nor even to receive them without the interposition of a priest.' The line followed is exactly that of Gelasius, but now the accent is much firmer. The imperial reply was generally to appeal to the figure of Melchisedec and to say (e.g. in PG 90:113): 'I am both king and priest'. The way taken in the West to counter this idea was the careful separation of coronation-anointing (which was being adopted in the 8th cent.) from that of an ordination (*see* CORONATION). Still one finds that a council in the West (MGH *Concilia*, II:142) in 794 could use towards Charlemagne the acclamations: 'May he be king and priest; may he be the temperate ruler of all Christians'.[1] It should be noted, however, that this Council of Frankfurt was simply quoting the letter of Paulinus of Aquileia written on behalf of the bishops of Northern Italy, and the proximity of Aquileia to Ravenna may have accounted for the Byzantine style of the wording. The same council of Frankfurt declared that the controverted Quinisext meeting was 'neither a general council nor the seventh of that

series'. For other cross-currents affecting this problem of Church and State prior to Charlemagne, *see* FALSE DECRETALS.

IV The beginning of the Middle Ages can be dated from the crowning of Charlemagne as emperor by Pope Leo III in 800. The theories built up around that event are many, but there has come to be something of a consensus about the idea that it was meant to favour an East-West balance of power which would free the Papacy from the danger of Byzantine imperial control. The Roman populace had obviously been coached in what they were to shout in their acclamations, while Charlemagne himself said that he would not have gone into St Peter's on that Christmas Day if he had known what was going to happen there. The idea that the Pope escaped from one imperial danger only to be made subject to another cannot be maintained, since the story of the oath of purgation taken by Leo III in answer to the accusations that had been brought against him has been shown to depend on later forgeries for its colouring. This forgery was no doubt devised to further in the West the Byzantine idea (*see* Justinian's 6th *Novella*, cited above) that the Pope was to be judged by the emperor, while the emperor himself was accountable to God alone. There was a good deal of Byzantine ideology in the court of Charlemagne, as may be seen from the prologue to the *Libri Carolini*, but the Pope must have realized that the danger from the West (where he had Anglo-Saxon and Celtic kings to deal with, as well as Frankish) was less than that from the East. Alcuin, who supplied many of the leading ideas of Charlemagne, appears from his letters (especially *ep.* 177 and 202; MGH Epp. IV:292, 336) to have had a vision of a Christian empire in the West, but not of one where the emperor was in absolute control. In the Anglo-Saxon realms from which Alcuin came it was then the practice that the Archbishop signed the Acts of a Council first, then the King, then the bishops and finally the *duces* who had been present; something like this is implied by Alcuin's words: 'There are three most exalted persons in this present world; the apostolic Lord, the emperor with his secular power in the second Rome, the royal person of Charlemagne' [2] (*ep.* 174; MGH Epp. IV:288). It is true that by urging on Charlemagne the task of defending the faith (both against the barbarian invaders of Saxony and the heresy of Felix of Urgel) he was leaving dangerously little scope for the papal power, but it can hardly have been his intent to put the Pope in second place.

The problem of the proprietary church affected the medieval outlook on the relations of Church and State, at all levels. In 796 Charlemagne had written to Leo III: 'As I did with your predecessor, I desire also with Your Holiness to enter into a pact of sonship which shall be unbroken in faith and charity, so that the apostolic blessing will everywhere follow me while the Holy See of the Roman Church

[1] Sit rex et sacerdos; sit omnium Christianorum moderantissimus gubernator.

[2] Tres personae in mundo hucusque altissimae fuerunt; apostolica sublimitas, . . . imperialis dignitas et secundae Romae secularis potentia, . . . regalis dignitas. . . .

shall be defended by my zeal'. From this to the baron who kept a priest to say Mass of Requiem for his ancestors was not a great step. External deference might be paid to the ecclesiastic, but the paymaster might often show his displeasure at the sharpness of the gospel-message. It is in the light of this ever-present problem that one has to see the attempts made by men such as Gregory VII (in his *Dictatus Papae*) to break out of what was becoming a stranglehold and to assert the freedom of the Papacy. The Investiture contest, ended by a compromise in the Concordat of Worms (1122), had been due to the ideas that on the one hand a bishopric was in the royal gift like any other fief and on the other that only the central authority of the Church, the papacy, was strong enough to stand against the domination of a local church by the secular power. The details of the struggle do not concern the present article, but it should be pointed out that the concept of a marriage between ruler and subjects at accession (*see* CORONATION II) was also appealed to by the symbolism of the bishop's ring (*see* BISHOP XI) ; only gradually would these two relationships come to be defined more precisely and held apart.

Throughout the Middle Ages disputes between Church and State turn much more upon the persons (kings and bishops) than upon the theories concerned. In his study of the English bishops (1070–1532), in *Medieval Studies presented to Aubrey Gwynn* (1961), Fr David Knowles shows how freedom of election to bishoprics, guaranteed in Magna Carta, was whittled away in practice. The action of Urban V in reserving all appointments to himself (1363) was anticipated by the Statute of Provisors (1351), which forbade precisely that, and which remained a point of contention between Church and State until the Reformation. Immunity of clergy from civil sanctions had been a cause of dispute between Henry II and St Thomas of Canterbury, but the support given to the cause of immunity by Pope Alexander III at that time was withdrawn later on by Innocent III, who allowed the imposition of penalties by the civil courts, save for the death penalty itself.

The view that the existence of the State was due to the Fall of man was rejected by St Thomas Aquinas (*II Sent*. 44:1:3) with a distinction ; kingly power would not have been needed in Paradise to make good the defects of its inhabitants or to punish them for misdemeanours, but it would have been required for their guidance. The State was therefore natural to man. In commenting on the *Ethics* of Aristotle St Thomas found further reasons for calling it natural. Man had two goals of happiness, one supernatural and one natural, the latter being expressly termed *felicitas civica* or happiness in society. Here was a beginning of the idea that the State was independent and supreme in its own order. When St Thomas accepted the dynamic concept of a constantly receding goal of natural happiness (with the happiness of search supplying for the complete happiness of possession) he was indicating the point at which in the social order the Church could come

in to supplement the State, just as, for the individual, grace came in to supplement nature, but there was no attempt made to follow this up. If he had himself completed his *de regimine principum*, instead of having to leave it (after book II, 4) to his disciple Tolomeo of Lucca, perhaps some development would have taken place.

The use of the term 'Mystical Body of Christ' to designate the Church (*see* BODY, MYSTICAL) in the Middle Ages led to some extension of the idea to the State. Similarity of ceremonial (e.g. in the use of a marriage-ring) for king and bishop may have prompted this. The likeness of the inauguration oath to marriage-vows, the right of prince or bishop to use but not to alienate the property of realm or diocese, all these were pointers to the idea of a mystic marriage. Lucas de Penna (1320–90) stated these ideas extensively, though he was not their pioneer. Walter Burley in his commentary on Aristotle's *Politics* (*c.* 1338) could say that 'the manifold made up of king, nobles and wise men of the realm rules, rather than the king alone. . . . They rule in and with the king, and for the deep love of citizens towards the king there is great concord amongst them and the kingdom is strong, as may be seen in England today'. Sir John Fortescue (*de laudibus legum Angliae*, 12) claimed that the mystical body of the people was joined together and united into one by the Law. The Law, or citizen-charity ; that was the dilemma when the theorists looked round for what might for the State take the place held by grace in the Mystical Body of Christ. Not even Lyndwood was able to stress the difference between body politic of the realm and body mystical of the Church. For that we must wait for Cardinal Pole in his reply to Henry VIII. 'As far removed as is heaven from earth, so far does the body of the Church (which is the Body of Christ) differ from the body politic which is merely human' (*pro ecclesiasticae unitatis defensione*, 18). It is plain today that the Church is not simply a moral unity, but in some way surpasses that unity while falling short of physical. One might instance the fact that whereas the State exists for the good of the individuals who form it, the Church exists with another goal in view, its growth to the full stature of Christ, into which the salvation of the individual is subsumed.

V The Reformation was really the culmination of a process rather than a new beginning. The ideas of Marsiglio of Padua and the theories contained in the writings of the Norman (or York) Anonymous had been long maturing the events of the 16th cent. The principle *cuius regio, eius religio* was simply an assertion that the new nationalism counted for more than the right worship of God. The grouping by nations in the universities spread to the Councils of Constance and Basle (*see* BASLE *and* CONSTANCE), and in 1433 (HL 7:838) it was decreed at Basle that provincial (i.e. national) councils should control the archbishops and bishops of a country just as the great council itself claimed to control the Pope. William Sulbury wrote to Martin V in 1425 to say that if the Papacy did not take up the work of reform, the secular powers would, and in the end they did. The stream of conciliar theory flows straight from D'Ailly and Gerson to Marc'Antonio de Dominis and to Archbishop Laud. Cranmer's idea of consulting the universities about Henry's divorce was a mere transposition of what the University of Paris had done in 1394, when it consulted all its members on what the Pope and anti-Pope should do to end the schism.

Marsiglio of Padua wrote his *Defensor pacis* in 1324, yet it proved to be a blueprint for the Reformation. Thomas Cromwell promoted an English version (1535), and its modern editor, C. W. Previté-Orton, finds that, 'in his contributions to the debate of English divines in 1540 Cranmer is the most radical and Marsilian'. Hooker too is adjudged by him to have borrowed much from Marsiglio. The concept of State sovereignty comes in, though as yet lacking a term, with the phrase *legislator humanus superiore carens* (human lawgiver devoid of any overlord), and this legislator is identified by Marsiglio, though not by Cranmer, with the general assembly of the citizens, after the manner familiar to a free commune such as Padua was. God holds the sanction for the divine law, but He has entrusted none of this to the Church, and the priest or bishop in the sacrament of Penance is not a judge of sins ; confession is a useful practice but not necessary for salvation. General Councils can declare doctrines but not legislate independently of the State, and they should be convoked by the Emperor. Marsiglio was initially an imperial partisan, and in 1328 Lewis of Bavaria seemed to be acting according to the theories of Marsiglio, for he declared John XXII deposed and appointed an anti-pope by democratic decree of the assembly of the sovereign Roman people. Emperor and theorist soon fell out, and the *Defensor* remained in cold storage till the Reformation (D 496–500). A refutation of Marsiglio was produced by Pighius in his *Hierarchiae ecclesiasticae assertio* (1538). Marsiglio was an Aristotelian, and the Greek city-state offered an easy parallel to Padua, which after all claimed the Homeric hero Antenor as its founder. There was to be no appeal to mystical bodies in Church or State and no use of OT texts nor any allegorizing of the two swords (Lk 22:38). Interdependence of Church and State is viewed thus : 'Priesthood depends on principate for the justification of its civil acts and for guardianship from wrongdoing (so that it may not do wrong to others or suffer wrong in this world) ; principate depends on priesthood, for it receives doctrine from that source and the sacraments which prepare men in this world and remove what is contrary to salvation in the world to come' (*Defensor*, II:30). The Tudor picture, with the lay Vicars-general, the suppression of canon law, the clerical preoccupation with baptism, the Eucharist and the ministry of the word, is not so different from Marsiglio ; one feature has been added, the cult of OT parallels. Luther might revel in these and from his reading of Augustine produce a picture of the warfare between the mystical bodies of Christ and the devil, but the Anglican

reformers were nearer to Marsiglio. Cranmer at his trial declared : 'Every king in his own realm is supreme head of the Church'. 'Was this ever so in Christ's Church ?' he was asked. 'It was so.' 'Then what say you by Nero ? Was he head of Christ's Church ?' 'Nay, it is true ; Nero was head of the Church, that is in respect of the temporal bodies of men, of whom the Church consisteth' (*Works*, II:219). He did not add that he had accepted the claim of Henry VIII to have power over men's souls also.

Archbishop Parker had among the many MSS which he collected a more complete blueprint for the erection of State superiority over the Church. This was the so-called Norman, or York, Anonymous, a group of tracts written about 1100 to exalt the position of kings in the Church. Melchisedec was king and priest ; Christ fulfilled the type of Melchisedec, but it was kings who in the present dispensation stood for the divinity of Christ while bishops had to represent the work of Christ as priest, which belonged to His humanity. So ran the argument of this work. The amnesty at a coronation showed that a king could forgive sins, while his entry into the sanctuary with gifts of bread and wine on that occasion showed that he offered sacrifice with the priests (MGH *Libelli de lite*, III:663–78). The deposition of Saul for performing priestly sacrifice (1 Kg 13:13) was conveniently overlooked. So was the admonition which the bishops spoke to the king at his crowning (*see* CORONATION II). Lancelot Andrewes used the work in his glorification of James I against Bellarmine, and it must have been an encouragement to many Anglican theologians who read it in its Cambridge home. 'In marked contrast to Wyclif, whose doctrine of Election and Dominion strengthened the royal, but also the centrifugal, feudal powers at the expense of the ecclesiastical, the Anonymous in his devotion to the royal power had the astuteness to preserve and even to enhance the episcopate as a means of reinforcing that royal power. He strengthened the king in proving the indelible character of unction as it effected the bishop, insisting however that the unction imparted a royal or royal-priestly rather than a purely Apostolic sacerdotal power, and that as the king was the recipient of the same unction in a more representative way than any of his bishops, he was both more royal and more priestly than they' (G. H. Williams, in *The Norman Anonymous*, 199). Marsilius had made the community the origin of power in his State, and he had to be bowdlerised to suit Henry VIII, but the Anonymous is the true parent of the theory of the divine right of kings, though he is scarcely acknowledged as such by some of its historians.

The defence of Catholic principles was undertaken (for the English scene) by Cardinal Allen. He was willing to allow that the temporal and the spiritual powers were sometimes so distinct, 'that the one hath no dependence of the other nor subalternation to the other in respect of themselves (as it is in the Churches of God residing in heathen kingdoms and was in the Apostles' time under the pagan emperors), yet now where the laws of Christ are received and the bodies politic and mystical, the Church and civil State, the magistrate ecclesiastical and temporal, concur in their kinds together (though ever of distinct regiments, natures and ends) there is such a concurrence and subalternation betwixt both that the inferior of the two (which is the civil State) must needs (in matters pertaining anyway either directly or indirectly to the honour of God and benefit of the soul) be subject to the spiritual and take direction from the same' (*Defence of English Catholics*, II:11). Allen saw that the new missionary perspectives were presenting the Church with a new Church-State problem, but for him Europe was still Christendom. He did not envisage its passing away, but he had seen that it was not necessarily part of the established order of things.

The deposition of kings by the spiritual power had come about in the Middle Ages after their excommunication, and England had had the experience of King John and his troubles with the Pope. Even Henry VIII had, as Allen claimed, shown a desire, before his death, to be reconciled to the Church which had excommunicated him (ibid. II:124). That Pius V in 1570 should have excommunicated Elizabeth was not surprising ; the captive English bishops had been calling for it as best they could. The precedents were there and no particular theory of papal power had to be invoked. But, not long before that, Francis de Vitoria had openly challenged the view that the Pope was a temporal overlord of kings. He would not allow (*Relectio de Indis* 2:3) that the Pope could rightly make over the Indies to Spain by the use of that power. He used Mt 20:25 for his argument and pointed out that the pastoral office of the Pope was limited, because there were others who were not of his fold. Vitoria based the deposing power on the Pope's duty to avert spiritual harm from Christian nations even by intervening in their disputes and giving sentence for one side against the other, but his governing idea is that of the perpetual state of war with the Turks, which was the condition of Christendom at his time. Who, if not the Pope, was to see that the Christian nations did not weaken themselves by strife, regardless of the ' cold war ' condition under which they lived ? Vitoria limited this indirect power of the Pope, for he held that it did not apply in the Indies, where the Pope had no spiritual jurisdiction (according to 1 Cor 5:12). Ironically it was the victory of Lepanto, one year after the excommunication of Elizabeth, which removed for a long time the Turkish danger and with it the main reason for the active intervention of the spiritual power. Gregory XIII in 1579 granted to Frs Campion and Persons a mitigation of the Bull of excommunication, to the effect that *rebus sic stantibus* (in the present conditions) it did not bind Catholics to co-operation with its terms, though it still affected the Queen. It was owing to this change that the martyrs in England were asked by the government (often under torture) what they would do if the Bull was renewed. This was an invasion of

the rights of conscience and a ' wresting with suppositions ', as Campion called it at his trial, which was beyond the lawful authority of a civil power (*see* CONSCIENCE).

VI Absolutism was the product of the new theories of sovereignty and of the divine right of kings. It could be argued that the Papacy by excommunicating Elizabeth had forced the English monarchy into a position where it had to rely on divine right, and thus came to the inevitable collapse of 1649. A Royalist of the time put it that ' every one of the Regicides had a Pope in his belly to give him a dispensation from his oath of allegiance '. Bellarmine and John Knox were in agreement on the proposition that only the spiritual power could decide with authority whether in a particular case men are bound in conscience to obey their rulers. Luther, with his eschatological vision of temporal princes curbing the power of anti-Christ, had encouraged absolutism, for he did not set much store by the externals of worship and was quite content to see them administered by a department of the State. The Anglican cult of regality helped, though in a less degree, in the same direction. Only from Calvinism was there any support for the idea of two separate powers whereof the spiritual was the higher (Calvin, *Institutes* III:19:15). Buchanan stands here with Bellarmine against Barclay. During the Civil War some of the ideas of Fr Persons and his associates were revived by the Parliamentarians, and in 1687–8 James II tried to bring about (prematurely, as it proved) an alliance of Catholics and Radicals, an alliance which was in the end to carry through Catholic Emancipation and to disestablish, at least in part, the Anglican church. From the circumstances of their position English and Irish Catholics did not succumb to that acceptance of absolute monarchy which can be noticed in so many European Catholic writers of the 17th and 18th cents, especially when they come to treat of rebellion or tyrannicide (*see* REBELLION).

Of European monarchies France and Poland achieved some understanding of the separation of the Church from matters of State, France with the Edict of Nantes, which mitigated the urge to religious uniformity in the interests of national unity. Most of all, in the 17th cent., it was in America that the principles became clear to all by being worked out in practice. First of all in the Catholic colony of Maryland the oath for the Governor, devised by Lord Baltimore in 1636, required him to undertake ' not to trouble any person believing in Jesus Christ ' and to make no distinction in respect of religion in conferring offices. The Toleration Act of the same colony, passed 21 April 1649, was in the same spirit. Roger Williams, an Anglican banished from Massachusetts for heresy in 1635, went to Rhode Island, where he was later able to instil into the government of that State principles of toleration, but on the assumption that Churches were no more than moral unities like trading corporations. Penn in Pennsylvania followed the example of Maryland in 1682, adding to his fundamental law a clause : ' To the end that . . . atheism may not creep in under pretence of conscience, be it enacted that . . . every first day of the week people shall abstain from their usual and common toil . . . that they may dispose themselves to read the Scriptures at home . . . or frequent meetings of religious worship abroad. . . .' Penn's association with James II and the Declaration of Indulgence is significant in this connection. His influence can be judged from the fact that, when absolutism came to an end in France in 1789, the French were urged to imitate the Pennsylvanians in the matter of religious freedom.

The revocation of the Edict of Nantes by Louis XIV in 1687 was the ruin of English Catholicism for a century ; it sent over a stream of Huguenot refugees who did much to embitter Protestant feelings, while it stood in direct contradiction of the principles which James II had put into his Declaration of Indulgence. Some of its rigour may be put down to Gallican and Jansenist ideas, for even Bossuet was infected with these. The papal condemnation (D 1322 and 1324) by Pope Alexander VIII in 1690 of the idea that Gallican *instituta* are not amenable to papal guidance came too late to avert that tragedy. The weakness of the 18th-cent. Papacy in the face of the Bourbons and the Hapsburgs led to an exaggerated importance being given to the profession of Catholicism by the State as such. Overt support of the Church by the absolutist states had to be paid for in other ways. The appointment of bishops, the spread of national influence by Catholic missionaries in the Far East or the Far West, the diversion of ecclesiastical revenue to State purposes, all these were expected by the monarchs who protected the Church. To take but one random example : in 1741 a boy of 15, the Infante Luis, who was already a Cardinal deacon, was made civil administrator of the archdiocese of Seville, the spiritual care of it being entrusted to an archdeacon. In 1754 the young man decided not to make a career in the Church and renounced his charge. This provoked Benedict XIV into the remark about the Bourbons that they never take the trouble to learn ('I loro principi nulla studino e nulla imparino'). The same period (1741–53) was taken up with intense negotiation for a Concordat with Spain, the Holy See finally agreeing to surrender to the monarchy the right of presentation to all except 52 Spanish livings, the number surrendered being about 10,000.

Hontheim (otherwise Febronius), who advocated for the Church a system of two-tier democracy which was not desired by the absolutist governments for themselves, eventually recanted in 1778, but in a very limited sense. He was willing to give up the idea that the clergy were given power to govern by the faithful and the pope by the clergy, and these propositions were later declared to be heretical by Pius VI (D 1502–3), but when Hontheim said that 'in all that concerns the faith, the sacraments and ecclesiastical discipline the Church makes its decisions *suo iure*, without the co-operation of the civil authority', he was leaving out of account the many mixed matters in which the Church claimed independence (e.g. schools, appointments to bishoprics, etc.). Even the British government of Hanoverian times was willing to take the Catholic Church in Minorca under its wing, after the fashion of the times, when that island came under British rule. A plan to that effect was prepared as may be seen from the *Life of William Wake* (by Norman Sykes, 1957). This making of Catholicism the State religion was little more than a pretext for getting the 'mixed matters' such as marriage and education more securely under State control (*see* CONCORDATS).

VII In modern times there have been several changes of importance in the Catholic theories of Church and State. First of all, it is now no longer held that the Church should impose on offenders penalties other than spiritual. The new Canon Law of 1918 (canon 6) established the principle that ecclesiastical penalties, whether spiritual or temporal, which were not expressly mentioned in the new law, should be regarded as abrogated. As the Code in its penal sections made no mention of, for instance, the ancient penalties of loss of goods, testamentary disabilities, or even death, for apostasy from the faith, but confined itself to requiring that apostates be 'declared to have lost all reputation', it is clear that the Church was modifying her position in the modern age. Flogging had also been a punishment inflicted by the Church for certain offences, and this too was abrogated by the new Code. In some countries laws had been enacted by the State to protect clerics from such penalties, and these laws were a cause of friction with the Church which has now been removed. Controversies, between Church lawyers, about the right of the Church to inflict the death-penalty which had continued for a century or more, were thus robbed of all importance.

In the Lateran treaty of 1929 Pius XI claimed for the Holy See, 'a minimum of territory, just enough for the exercise of sovereignty, because a territorial sovereignty of this sort is universally recognised as an indispensable condition for all real sovereignty of jurisdiction' (Allocution of 11 Feb. 1929). He adduced the example of St Francis of Assisi, 'who had just enough body to retain his soul in union with it'. This act, set alongside the 76th proposition of the *Syllabus* of Piux IX (D 1776), is a sufficient indication of the care needed in interpreting that document. (This 76th proposition declared that it was erroneous to suppose that the abrogation of the civil rule (*civilis imperii*) of the Holy See would promote the liberty and happiness of the Church.) Some Catholics had in the 19th cent. taken the line that the temporal power of the Pope was a matter of divine law, so that he could not divest himself of it, even if he would.

Pius IX, in laying down certain principles for guidance in delimiting the spheres of faith and reason (D 1674), admitted that it was 'tolerable and perhaps true' to make a distinction between philosophy and the man who philosophises, in the sense that philosophy had a right to carry on its own business freely, with its own axioms and methods, and coming to its own conclusions. Yet this liberty had a limiting condition, for it should never be possible for a philosopher, or even for his philosophy, to go contrary to the teaching of divine revelation or to call it in question because it was mysterious. In other words, there is only one truth, not two, and philosophy does not cover the whole of it. These principles, laid down for the individual, can be carried over to the State, for the State is entitled, as a perfect society in its own order, to go about its business freely, with its own axioms and methods ; but it must recognize its limiting conditions. In face of a plurality of religions, a modern State cannot do more than proceed on principles of reason, while having care not to go against divine revelation. In the abstract it might seem that this last part of the State's duty is impossible of fulfilment. As Newman wrote to Gladstone in 1845 : ' The State has not a conscience. Is he (Gladstone) to impose his own conscience on the State ? . . . He must deal with facts. It has a thousand consciences, as being, in its legislative and executive capacities, the aggregate of a hundred minds—that is, it has no conscience'. Yet in practice the State depends for its well-being, if not for its very existence, on the sanctity of an oath (for loyalty, for law-courts and for much else) and this oath is indeed possible to all those who have reasoned themselves into accepting the existence of God, but in fact few men do so without some aid from revealed religion. Here, then, is a beginning of the State's deference to revelation. Furthermore, in countries of the Common Law (i.e. in most of the succession-states from the former British Empire), there is a latent Christianity in the legal system arising from the manner in which that system began. Often the requisite deference to divine revelation on the part of the State will be no more than a recognition of this latent element in the law.

Negative deference of the State towards revealed religion is sometimes a mark of a modern society. The heads of the State do not embark on some measure which they know will be condemned by the authorities of the Church. If, on the other hand, they go ahead with such a measure, there is still the possiblity of a papal condemnation, even in modern times. It has not often been remarked that Pius XI in 1933 issued such a condemnation of the legislation of the Spanish republican government against the freedom of religious Orders in Spain (AAS 25 [1933] 272). By saying that the law had no force against the rights of the Church, he equivalently showed that it could not be binding on Spanish Catholics. This fact may have had some bearing on the revolution of 1936. In 1937 (D 2278) Pius XI made further declarations to Mexican Catholics on the abuse of State authority. Thus, although in article 24 of the Lateran Treaty (AAS 21 [1929] 220) the Holy See declared that it would remain aloof from the temporal disputes between States and from Conferences called to settle them, the right of intervention on moral or religious grounds was expressly reserved. The aloofness was due to the events leading up to the Treaty of London

(of 1915) when the Italian government of the time bargained for the exclusion of Benedict XV from the future peace conference. In return for this aloofness, Italy in 1929 accepted that the Vatican City should have full rights of neutrality in any future war, and thus in 1939 the Pope was not deprived of his diplomatic contacts with the Allied powers as Benedict XV had been deprived of contact with Austria and Germany on Italy's entry into the war in 1915.

The American Declaration of Independence (1776) was signed by 34 Episcopalians, 13 Congregationalists (who were the Established Church in Massachusetts), 6 Presbyterians, 1 Baptist, 1 Quaker and 1 Catholic. This Catholic, Charles Carroll, said later: ' To obtain religious as well as civil liberty I entered zealously into the Revolution, and observing the Christian religion divided into many sects I founded the hope that no one would be so predominant as to become the religion of the State '. Distrust of the Anglican Establishment in Virginia led to the First Amendment (1789) that, ' Congress shall make no law respecting an establishment of religion, or prohibiting the free exercise thereof ; or abridging the freedom of speech or of the press . . . .' Preaching and the issue of church journals were envisaged under the freedoms mentioned, but the school question was not yet in sight, as compulsory education was still in the future. Thus the so-called separation of Church and State was in practice a reluctance to favour one religion rather than a contempt for all. Prayers at the meetings of Congress, national days of prayer or fasting, chaplains in the armed forces, sermons to Congress by different religious ministers in turn, all these religious acts on the part of the State are on record from the very beginning of the United States. Thus many religious activities were encouraged by a State which had no religion, but it must at the same time be admitted that the positive encouragement of Christianity in other directions was lacking, largely through fear of establishment. Leo XIII in his encyclical on the Christian constitution of States (D 1874) seems to envisage precisely this case when he admits that fear of a greater evil may cause a State to keep an equality between religious bodies among its citizens. It is to be remarked that, even in Italy, during the debates on the republican constitution of 1947, a Catholic deputy (Dossetti) could say that article I of the Lateran Treaty did not make Italy a confessional State but simply said that the Catholic religion was the religion of the majority of Italians.

The American standpoint on Church-State relations represents a return to the pre-Reformation English conception in so far as it has abandoned all idea of absolute State sovereignty. The Founding Fathers when they were approached by the Church about the appointing of a bishop to care for American Catholics, instead of rebuffing the approach as papal aggression, or claiming to appoint the bishop themselves, said that, ' Congress should not intervene in the ecclesiastical affairs of any religion '. This fits in very well with what the bishops used to declare to the crowned monarch in medieval England, as noted above. Through William Penn, John Locke and the Commonwealth men they were in touch with the genuine tradition of the Common Law, which the Reformation epoch of absolutism had obscured in England. Robert Aske and the men of the Pilgrimage of Grace would recognise as familiar what the Americans were doing. The Anglican Church (*see* ANGLICANISM) has lost a great part of the established position which it came to enjoy vis-à-vis the State after the Reformation. If the coronation were now to be shared by the three principal religious bodies in turn, parliamentary control of Anglican public worship abolished and the appointment of bishops left to that Church, instead of being in the hands of the Prime Minister, the English position would very soon approximate to the American.

The Common Law differs from Roman civil law in giving far less importance to the idea of *patria potestas*. Hence in Church-State relations there has been in countries of the Common Law far less of the paternalism of the State in respect of the religion of its citizens. Whereas a Spanish theologian might argue that it was for the State to guide all citizens with paternal authority in the religion of the Spanish State, as if they were all children, the English lawyer did not see the Church-State problems in that light at all, save during the Reformation period, when an access of Byzantinism had temporarily obscured the true spirit of the Common Law. With the great increase in numbers of the Catholic Church in Common-Law countries this absence of paternalism on the part of the State will make for the greater liberty of the Church, if at the same time it seems to some to deprive the Church of certain protections.

This debate, which still continues at the present time, about the exact relationship of Church and State, will probably be intensified as the organization of the world into larger and larger units goes on. Pope Nicholas I in 865 while writing on this subject to the emperor Michael used some wise words : 'The Holy See, I do admit, may change its opinion into a better formulation, when, having regard to the epoch, the conditions of the time and its needs, it decides in the manner of a good steward to make some regulation' (D 333).[1] Thus it might be contended that there is a basic position which the Church holds to in her requirements from the State, an ideal which some have called the 'thesis', in opposition to the 'hypothesis' or adaptation of that basic position to the changing circumstances of every age. The distinction of 'thesis' and 'hypothesis' was brought up by Taparelli d'Azeglio in the days of Pius IX, but some would claim that it is incorporated in the work of Leo XIII (D 1874). More will be said later about this distinction (*see* TOLERATION) ;

[1] Non negamus Apostolicae Sedis sententiam posse in melius commutari cum ipsa . . . pro consideratione aetatum vel temporum seu gravium necessitatum dispensatorie quiddam ordinare decreverit.

for the present it is enough to point out that if one were to take, for instance, the declaration of Boniface VIII (D 469) on the two swords as a statement of the 'thesis', one would still have to divest it of its temporary application to the dispute with Philip IV of France, having regard to the qualification of his own words made by the Pope at that time (cited in D 468, note 2). Others might deny that it is really possible to abstract from their concrete situation principles on this matter which can be expressed in terms that are any more than the vaguest generalities. Some attempt has here been made to outline some of these principles, but the difficulty of doing so will be obvious.

Bibliography. H. Rahner SJ (editor), *Kirche und Staat im frühen Christentum* (1961) ; E. Peterson, *Monotheismus als politisches Problem* (1935) ; S. Ehler and J. Morrall, *Church and State through the Centuries*, a collection of documents, (1954) ; *S. Greenslade, *Church and State from Constantine to Theodosius* (1954) ; *N. Q. King, *The Emperor Theodosius and the Establishment of Christianity* (1961) ; *Norman Baynes, 'The Political Ideals of St Augustine', in *Byzantine Studies* (1955) ; W. Ullmann, *The Growth of Papal Government in the Middle Ages* (1955), a German translation, with revisions (1960) ; *T. Parker, *Christianity and the State* (1955) ; *F. Gavin, *Seven Centuries of the problem of Church and State* (1938) ; *F. Ganshof, *The Imperial Coronation of Charlemagne* (1948) ; C. W. Previté Orton, 'Marsilius of Padua', in *Proceedings of the British Academy*, 21 (1935) 137–84 ; *E. Kantorowicz, *The King's Two Bodies* (1957) ; B. Tierney, *Foundations of Conciliar Theory* (1955) ; G. H. Williams, *The Norman Anonymous* (1951) ; *F. W. Maitland, *English Law and the Renaissance* (1901) ; A. P. d'Entreves, *The Medieval Contribution to Political Thought* (1939) ; J. Heckel, 'Marsilius von Padua und Martin Luther', in *Zeitschrift der Savigny-Stiftung*, kanonische Abteilung, LXXXVIII (1958) 268–336 ; *J. Bohatec, *Kalvins Lehre von Staat und Kirche* (1937) ; *Anson Phelps Stokes, *Church and State in the United States* (3 vols., 1950) ; D. Binchy, *Church and State in Fascist Italy* (1941) ; J. Courtney Murray SJ, *We hold these Truths* (1960) ; R. Hull SJ, *Medieval Theories of the Papacy* (1934) ; Cardinal Allen, *The Defence of English Catholics* (2 vols., 1914) : T. Kenny, *The Political Thought of Cardinal Newman* (1957). J. H. C.

CIRCUMCISION The main question that has to be discussed about circumcision is (I) that of the manner in which it can be considered to have remitted Original sin before the coming of Christ. After this one has to determine if possible (II) whether it also gave grace and (III) why it was abrogated in the Christian dispensation. Finally (IV) a word must be added about the dogmatic implications of the feast of Christ's circumcision.

I The remission of Original sin was associated with circumcision for all Jewish males from the time of Abraham (Gn 17:10–14), but the teaching of the Church is that circumcision was not in that time the exact equivalent of Christian baptism (D 845).

What is the exact difference ? Not merely that the rite itself is different but that circumcision did not operate as a sacrament (*see* CAUSALITY OF SACRAMENTS). From the time of Justin (*dial.* 23:4) there is a constant tradition which regards the circumcision of Abraham and of his descendants as 'a sign and not a justification'. Irenaeus (*adv. haer.* IV:xxvii:1–2, H) echoes Justin, amplifying his statement to the effect that the rite was a sign not only to the Jews themselves (by which they were set apart from neighbouring races) but for Christians also, in that it typified what was to come in baptism.

Augustine in his controversy with the Pelagians stressed the similarity between circumcision on the eighth day and the practice of infant baptism. This was rather a change of emphasis than a new departure in doctrine. All typological relations involve similarity and therefore also difference ; earlier Fathers had emphasized the difference between circumcision and baptism, while Augustine turned to the similarity. Some of his medieval disciples developed his ideas into the view that circumcision removed Original sin but did not confer grace. St Thomas (*Summa*, 3a:62:6:@3) had no difficulty in refuting this, even though something very like it appears in an *obiter dictum* of Innocent III (D 410). To put a distinction between the negative and positive effects of the sacrament of baptism and to allow to circumcision the negative effects while denying the positive was altogether too mechanical a view of sacramental grace.

II The conferring of grace through circumcision was more carefully investigated after the discovery of America (*see* AMERICA, THEOLOGICAL IMPORTANCE OF), when the undeniable existence of so many races who had no chance of contact with Israel in OT times forced theologians such as Suarez to consider much more carefully the way in which Original sin could have been remitted for them. Suarez (*opera*, 20:75–88) held that before Abraham there was in the law of nature (and therefore available to those across the Atlantic) a law and promise of God that Original sin would be remitted for children whose parents used 'any sign at all that was a protestation of their faith'. The promise to Abraham thus became a more exact determination by God of what had been there all the time. In this view it was necessary to regard the faith of the parents as the principal factor and the rite as accessory ; it also required some anthropological evidence that such a law of nature was to be traced in primitive peoples, whereby they showed that they were aware of some obligation to dedicate their children by some external rite to the worship of God or to sanctify them in some fashion. Suarez did not offer this evidence, though he may have been relying on reports of early missionaries such as Jose de Acosta. Suarez relied instead on the theological argument that there could not have been any intrinsic virtue in the rite of circumcision as practised by the Jews, for if there had been they would have devised some form of female circumcision, but they did not. (The use of such a female rite in Ethiopia was known

to St Ignatius and there is mention of it in his instructions for the first Jesuit mission to Ethiopia.) In this view circumcision became an occasion of grace rather than a cause, very much as baptism is for those non-conformists for whom baptism is a sign that the child has been received under the covenant in the faith of its parents. The likeness of much Reformed Christian theology to what Catholics were willing to allow for Jews in OT times may be seen from the text of St Gregory (cited by St Thomas, *Summa* 3a:70:4:2) which asserts that the children of the patriarchs were justified (*sola fide*) by faith alone.

For those who held that the sacraments of the Church were simply the occasions or conditions of grace rather than direct causes (and this view was held by Durandus and others, *see* CAUSALITY OF SACRAMENTS) there is no clear difference between these sacraments and a rite such as circumcision. After the insistence of Trent that there is to be accepted a clear difference between OT rites and Christian sacraments, it would seem that this equiparating of the two in the matter of the causation of grace is no longer possible. Suarez (*opera*, 20:162–175), who draws a distinction between the faith of Jewish parents and their intention of doing what God wants (saying that the first was not needed, but that the second was), was himself falling into the snare of equiparating OT and NT sacraments, a snare which he readily held out to the followers of Durandus.

III The abrogation of the law of circumcision, decided on (Ac 15:9) at the Council of Jerusalem, is generally held to be the result of a new revelation and not merely the elaboration of what was already present in the teaching Christ gave to the Apostles. The words to Peter in Ac 10:13, 'Do sacrifice and eat', are reminiscent of what Noah did on coming out of the Ark, just as the sheet full of animals recalls the circumstances of Noah. In 1 Pet 3:19 the saving of Noah is said to prefigure baptism, and 1 Clem 9:4 says roundly that Noah preached regeneration to the whole world. Thus the moment of revelation to Peter was fraught with great doctrinal consequences and the early Church learned that baptism looked back not simply to the circumcision of Abraham but to an earlier sacrament of nature in Noah, who in the Jewish mind stood for the pagan who kept the natural law.

For a time the rite of circumcision was for a Christian 'dead but not death-dealing' (*mortua sed non mortifera*) ; it was in the Pauline sense a dead work but did not at once involve its recipient in sin and was in fact carried out upon Timothy by Paul himself (Ac 16:3). Exactly when it became a sinful act might be disputed. The Church teaches (D 712) that it is so now, after the promulgation of the gospel (if done as a religious rite), but in a given situation it might be difficult to say when this promulgation became effective. In missionary lands the question has been sometimes raised whether circumcision that is practised by pagans as a rite of puberty should be tolerated ; indeed an Anglican bishop pleaded for its incorporation into a ritual of Christian observance.

For his diocese of Masasi Dr Lucas elaborated a whole ritual of introduction to manhood for Christian boys culminating in circumcision. Catholic theologians, intent on discriminating between baptism and circumcision, have not studied its place as a rite of puberty ; there is a problem of missionary adaptation involved in the prompt condemnation (e.g. among the Kikuyu) of male, and still more of female, circumcision, when these are widely regarded as a 'sacrament of nature' for boys and girls. If nature truly demands or encourages such a rite, then grace should somehow build upon nature. Confirmation cannot reasonably be delayed until the onset of puberty, while baptism has taken place in infancy. On the other hand, it might be argued that there is warrant in antiquity for taking confirmation as a spiritual circumcision. The use by Christians of Jos 5:2–12, with its account of the crossing of Jordan and the subsequent circumcision, enabled them to see in this second circumcision (which took place within the Promised Land) a type of confirmation. Justin abundantly illustrates this (*dial.* 12, 24, 113, 114), and it may be implied by some NT passages, especially Col 2:9–15. (Baptism is already likened to the crossing of the Jordan in the *Odes of Solomon.*) Confirmation was understood to be a perfecting of the new Christian, and after this, what more could be required ? There could thus be a case for using confirmation as the Christian equivalent for pagan rites of puberty.

IV The feast of Christ's circumcision, which has been abolished in the recent liturgical reforms, might seem to be out of keeping with the condemnation of the practice by the Church. It is true that the feast, which obviously depends on the fixing of the birth of Christ to 25 December, was not kept until the end of the 4th cent. If the prayers in the *Missale Gothicum* and *Bobbio Missal* can be taken as representative, there was little fear of the feast being an incitement to return to Jewish practices ; the Preface for the day declared that Christ took on Himself the yoke of circumcision in order to free us from the yoke of the devil.[1] Thus the motive for holding the feast on that day, a day on which pagan rites were still practised in the 4th cent., was aptly coupled with the act of Christ. In some liturgical sources (the *Gelasian Sacramentary* in particular) there are prayers for this day with the rubrical heading *Prohibendum ab idolis.* The day was designated by the *Gelasianum* as no more than *Octabas Domini*, and the circumcision of Christ was not mentioned in the prayers, whereas the *Canon dominicus papae Gelasi*, as given in the *Stowe Missal*, had a special clause to be inserted in the *Communicantes* on this day, with the words : *Diem sacratissimam celebrantes circumcisionis Domini.* Irish observance of the Feast of the Circumcision is further guaranteed for the 7th cent. by the gospel book of St Kilian which has the note : *Finit in circumcisione*, at Lk 2:40, while the *Lectionary* of Luxeuil confirms this. On the other hand, the *Capitulare evangeliorum* of Würzburg (which repre-

sents Roman usage of about 650, transmitted through an Anglo-Saxon medium) has for 1 January the portion Lk 2:22–32, with the heading : *In octabas Domini, ad sancta Maria martyra.* This may imply that the Roman Pantheon was the stational church for the day, or it may indicate some obscure development in the cult of Our Lady. The Ambrosian liturgy of this time, as evidenced by the *Capitulare epistularum* in MS Vat. Reg. 9, was occupied on this day with the danger from idolatry, for the epistle was taken from 1 Cor 8:4 and following, while the day was designated simply *In Kalendas Ianuarias.* Thus the theological moment of the feast would seem to be principally that of providing a counterweight to the idolatry of the day (it still had this in India recently), and this the more easily as the eighth day of Christmas was mentioned in the gospel (Lk 2:22). There would seem to be no desire to glorify the practice of circumcision. There has been no reason given for the recent abolition of the feast. **Bibliography.** Many theologians treat of circumcision in their treatises on the sacraments in general. St Thomas, *Summa* 3a:62 and 70 ; Suarez, *Disputationes de sacramentis* (in volume 20 of the *Opera*) ; *L. S. Thornton, Confirmation, its Place in the Baptismal Mystery* (1954) ; *W. V. Lucas, Christianity and native rites* (1949) ; J. H. Crehan SJ, *Early Christian Baptism* (1950), for the relation of proselyte baptism to circumcision ; *S. Perowne, Hadrian* (1960), for the Roman attempt to forbid circumcision, and the Jewish revolt.   J. H. C.

COLLECTS The theological importance of the Collect (i.e. the first prayer said by the priest at Mass) is that it is thought by many to demonstrate in the clearest fashion the true nature of liturgical prayer. The priest is said to perform in reciting it his function of mediator, 'gathering together and presenting to God the prayers of the people'. This is the theory of modern liturgists, who have generally abandoned the older view of Batiffol and Duchesne that the late Latin word *collecta* meant the rallying-point whence the pontifical procession set out for one of the main basilicas of Rome on certain feast-days. This older view regarded the Collect as the prayer said at the rallying-point before the procession moved off.

Abbot Capelle and others broke away from this view and appealed to texts such as the saying of Walafrid Strabo[2] that, 'we call them collects because we gather together, i.e. we conclude, their essential petitions with summary brevity' (PL 114 ; 945). In this view the early Christian use of *collecta* as an equivalent for the Greek *synaxis* has to be brushed aside as a passing fashion of no importance. Yet the evidence for this usage is too widespread to be thus dismissed as unimportant. For Augustine (*Breviculus*, 3:17 ; CSEL 53:82) '*collectam et dominicum*' is a description of what we should call Mass, while for Jerome (*ep.* 51:1 ; CSEL 54:397) the usage is the same ; even in Cassian (who does use the

---

[1] Iugum legis in sua carne suscepit ut iugum diaboli a nostra cervice discuteret.

[2] Collectas dicimus quia necessarias earum petitiones compendiosa brevitate colligimus, i.e. concludimus.

word to designate a special form of prayer) there is evidence (*Institutiones* 3:1 ; CSEL 17:44) of the more general sense of the word (and also in Ambrosiaster, on 1 Cor 16:1). It is still not clear how Latin-speaking Christians of the 5th cent. came to apply this word *collecta*, which they had used for their eucharistic meeting, to the first prayer that was recited when the meeting took place.

A piece of ritual is described by Cassian, who was holding up the Eastern monks as an example to the West (*Institutiones* 2:7 ; CSEL 17:23) : ' Before they kneel down they pray for a short time and remain standing in supplication ; after this they kneel for a very brief moment on the ground and then rise with great speed. Standing upright once more they hold out their arms and remain long in private prayer '.[1] He contrasts this with the lazy habits of the West, where prostrations were an opportunity for sleep. It is sometimes hastily assumed that Cassian is here describing the *Oremus* : *flectamus genua* proceeding, which still survives at Mass on Ember days, and that the *Collecta* which came after the genuflection was meant to sum up the silent prayers which had been made by individuals during the time of kneeling. It will be obvious from his words that the time of kneeling was no more than an instant and cannot have been a time of private prayer. On the other hand, Cassian does refer to a practice of ' gathering together prayers ' (*Conlationes* 18:11 ; CSEL 13:517), and mentions that after the singing of a psalm someone had to ' bind up the prayer ' (*orationem colligere*). What this meant may be seen in the Psalter Collects (recently edited by A. Wilmart OSB), where a short prayer that sums up the ideas expressed in the psalm is provided to follow each psalm. The variety of these Collects shows that the practice was widespread (it is envisaged in the *Regula Magistri*, but not in St Benedict's) and probably began as an improvisation. A similar practice was followed for other Scripture readings, and in the *Bobbio Missal* and *Missale Gothicum* the *Collectio post Prophetiam* is a short prayer which looks back to a reading from the OT. Survivals of this usage may be seen in the Collects which follow the Prophecies in the older form of the Easter Vigil, though in the course of time some of the Collects have been separated from the Prophecies they were meant to ' bind up '.

From this evidence it would seem that the function of the Collect is not for the priest to gather together and transmit to God the private prayers of the people, but rather for him to teach the people, while praying to God, what the lesson is that they should derive from the foregoing reading or ceremony. The legislation of the Council of Agde (canon 30), which was held in 506, envisages Collects of this kind. ' After the antiphonal singing of psalms let Collects

be recited by bishops and priests in due order '.[2] Somewhat later the Council of Macon in 627 fulminated against the followers of Columbanus for their multiplication of Collects (MGH, *Scriptores rerum Merovingicarum* IV:125) which it went so far as to call heretical. Perhaps the idea was that what had once been bound up and concluded ought not to be concluded again. There could not have been any objection to a repeated transmission by the priest of private prayers to God.

Bibliography. B. Capelle, *Collecta*, in RBn 42 (1930) 197–204 ; R. Hierzegger, *Collecta und Statio* in ZKT 60 (1936) 511–54.   J. H. C.

COMMUNICATIO IDIOMATUM In this phrase, which concerns correct modes of speech about the Incarnation, ' idiom ' (Gk *idioma*) is a property, understood loosely as any attribute which pertains to a nature, so that it can be predicated of the subject or person possessing the nature. Hence it embraces not only essential properties, but also all contingent attributes ; for example, ' idioms ' of human nature are the nature itself, its constituent principles, qualities, parts, accidents and actions. Thus we can say of a human person that he has a soul, a body, hands and feet, that he is learned, that he walks, thinks, speaks, dies, etc. *Communicatio* is the Latin rendering of the Greek *antidosis* (exchange). As used by classical authors, e.g. Lysias, Xenophon, Demosthenes, Isocrates, *antidosis* often signifies a law whereby a citizen, charged with a special tax or with a public service to be performed at private expense, could challenge any other citizen, whom he judged wealthier than himself, either to exchange his possessions or to take over the commission. The term was subsequently adapted by early Greek Fathers to the theological sense of an interchange and hence mutual predication of divine and human attributes pertaining to the incarnate Word (Petavius, *De Incarnatione*, 4:15).

Such communication of properties is possible only in the mystery of the Incarnation, because its ontological basis is exclusively the hypostatic union. According to Catholic dogma, Jesus Christ is a divine person subsisting in two natures, divine and human. It is clear that we can attribute to a person whatever really is his, for person is the ultimate subject of attribution ; since the God-man is a single person subsisting in two natures, we can ascribe to Him not only these two natures, but also all the properties of each nature, for they all belong to the same person and are His. However, as the two natures remain integral and distinct in their union, one cannot be predicated of the other, and properties cannot pass from one nature to the other. Indicating the incarnate Word, whether I call Him God, the Logos, the Second Person of the Trinity, Jesus, the Son of Man, or simply *this man*, I correctly say that He created the world, is eternal, all-powerful, infinite, begotten of the Father (according to His divine nature), and also that He was born in time,

---

[1] Antequam flectant genua paulisper orant, et stantes in supplicatione maiorem temporis partem expendunt. Post haec brevissimo puncto procidentes humi, summa velocitate consurgunt ac rursus erecti expansis manibus . . . suis precibus immorantur.

[2] Post antiphonas collectiones per ordinem ab episcopis et presbyteris dicantur.

that He was hungry, that He walked upon the waters, that He suffered and died (according to His human nature). But I utter nonsense if I say that His human nature is His divine nature or that eternity is origin in time or that adoration is thirst.

Since the communication of properties is no more than a consequence and, indeed, an expression of the dogma of the hypostatic union, the NT employs it abundantly throughout, e.g. ' The Word was made flesh' (Jn 1:14), ' The author of life you killed' (Ac 3:15), ' If they had known it, they would never have crucified the Lord of glory' (1 Cor 2:8) ; cf. Heb 1 and 2:9 ; Col 1:14-20. The Fathers quite naturally employ the same manner of speech, and also justify it theoretically (Petavius, loc. cit.).

To assure orthodoxy in *communicatio idiomatum*, theologians have painstakingly drawn up lists of rules governing predication about Christ (on the basis of patristic usage, Petavius op. cit., 4:16 ; theological elaboration, St Thomas, *Summa*, 3a:16). In summary form, these rules are applications of the general principle that only concrete, not abstract, expressions may be employed : ' God has died for our sins,' ' This man (Christ) is omnipotent' ; but not : ' The Godhead has died,' ' Christ's humanity is omnipotent'. The reason underlying this principle is that concrete terms designate properties as found in the subject possessing them, whereas abstract terms designate properties apart from any subject. Furthermore, negative propositions are to be avoided : ' God (the Word) has never slept' or ' Mary's Son was not omniscient'. Such assertions would mean that Jesus as man did not require rest or that as God He was not all-knowing.

The communication of idioms is not a mere affair of terminology which we are free to take up or discard as we please. It necessarily follows from the dogma of the hypostatic union ; unless we speak in this fashion we lapse into heresy. In fact, it served as a test of orthodoxy in the controversies with Nestorians, Eutychians and Adoptionists, and later clarified the issue in the polemic against Ubiquitists.

Bibliography. A. Michel, ' Idiomes (Communication des)' in DTC VII, 595-602 ; I. Backes, *Die Christologie des hl. Thomas v. Aquin und die griechischen Kirchenväter* (Paderborn 1931) ; A. Van Hove, ' De quibusdam communicationis idiomatum applicationibus' in *Divus Thomas* (Piac.) 40 (1937) 510-16.   C. V.

COMMUNION, HOLY The reception of the Eucharist. ' The Eucharist', says St Thomas, ' effects two things : the first is the consecration itself. . . . The other effect, wrought in the soul of the worthy recipient, is to unite man with Christ.'[1] The Scriptural term, *koinonia* (1 Cor 10:16, 17), is rendered *communicatio* (Vulgata), ' fellowship' (WV)

' participation' (Kn), ' communion' (DV). The Divine Saviour, sacramentally present by the consecration, shares fellowship with the communicant. This bond of love with Christ is also the bond between Christians : ' The unity of the Mystical Body, the Church', adds St Thomas,[2] ' this Sacrament both betokens and produces'.

Besides increasing sanctifying grace, Communion gives us spiritual life, doing whatever food does for the natural life—maintaining and increasing vitality, restoring health, affording pleasure.

Communion is *sacramental*, if actually received, as distinguished from *spiritual*, in desire only. Communicating entails being in the state of grace, as a result of confession (Can. 856). Communion knowingly received in mortal sin is designated unworthy, sacrilegious. The priest is the ordinary minister, the deacon the extraordinary one (Can. 845, 1, 2). In the Latin Rite Communion is distributed only in the form of bread (Can. 852), but Catholics may communicate in all rites (Can. 866, 1).

The common teaching of the Church on the need of Communion in the full economy of salvation, based on Jn 6:48-59, has passed into the precept of the Church (IV Lateran Council, 1215 ; D 437), obliging all Catholics over seven to communicate at least once a year, around Easter. The same doctrine underlies the precept to receive Viaticum when in danger of death (Can. 864, 1, 2). Except as Viaticum it is not permitted to communicate twice on the same day (Can. 857).

St Pius X was hailed at his canonization (29 May 1954 : AAS 46:311) for inaugurating a springtime of Eucharistic life : he overcame the prejudice of a wrong practice, and resolutely fostered frequent and even daily Communion of the faithful : Decree, ' Sacra Tridentina Synodus', 20 December 1905 : ASS 38:401-6 : D 1981. He also lowered the age for First Communion from about twelve to about six or seven : Decree, ' Quam Singulari' 8 August 1910 : AAS 2:577-83 : D 2137-44. Both directives passed into the Codex, Can. 863, Can. 854, 5.

Recent impetus in the spread of frequent Communion stems from the Constitution *Christus Dominus* and its Instruction (6 January 1953 : AAS 45:25-32 and 47-51), which modified the Eucharistic fast (now no longer broken by drinking water) and which sanctioned Mass in the evening on occasions. By *Motu proprio* (19 March, effective 25 March 1957) Pius XII : (*a*) permitted local Ordinaries to allow afternoon Mass daily, local need demanding, (*b*) set the Eucharistic fast for all as three hours from solid food and alcohol, one hour from non-alcoholic drinks (water not reckoned) before Mass or communion at any time of day or night ; (*c*) permitted the sick to celebrate or communicate after taking non-alcoholic liquids, or medicines solid or liquid, without any limitation of time.

The ancient Communion on Good Friday is restored by the new Holy Week Order (16 November 1955 ; AAS 47:838-48), which also restored the

---

[1] ' *Effectus huius duplex est, quorum primus consistit in ipsa consecratione sacramenti : . . . Alius vero effectus . . . quem in anima digne sumentis facit, est adunatio hominis ad Christum.*' *De Articulis Fidei et Ecclesiae Sacramentis*, 620 : *S. Thomae Aquinatis Opuscula Theol.* I, ed. R. A. Verardo (1954), 149.

[2] ' . . . *Unitas corporis mystici, idest Ecclesiae, quam hoc sacramentum et significat et causat*' (ibid.).

name *antiphona ad communionem* for the *Communio* verse and directed that according to ancient usage psalms may be sung with this antiphon as refrain while communion is being distributed.

For the theology of the practice of 'offering communion', *see* MASS, THEORIES OF.

Bibliography. P. Browe, *Die Häufige Kommunion im Mittelalter* (1938) ; J. A. Jungmann, *The Mass of the Roman Rite (Missarum Sollemnia)* II (1955), 'Communion of the Faithful : Frequency' 359–67.

G. E.

COMMUNION OF SAINTS This article will deal with (I) the Catholic Doctrine of the Communion of Saints ; (II) the historical question of the insertion of the dogmatic formula *Communio Sanctorum* in the Apostles' Creed ; and (III) the Patristic evidence for the belief in the doctrine in the early Church.

I Catholic Doctrine. By the Communion of Saints the Church understands the supernatural union which exists in and through Jesus Christ between all the members of the Church, in Heaven, in Purgatory and on earth, by which they all share in the same spiritual gifts. This union is not just of the moral and affective order ; it is a mysterious organic unity of ' those who have been sanctified in Jesus Christ' (1 Cor 1:2)—that is to say, of all who share in the fruits of Christ's redemption, either because they possess, or are called to the possession of the gift of eternal life in Heaven, and are members of the Mystical Body of Christ (*see* BODY, MYSTICAL). All who participate in the fruits of Christ's redemption share in one and the same divine life which extends far beyond the Church militant on earth to the Church triumphant in Heaven (Rom 12 : 4–6 ; 1 Cor 12:12–31 ; Eph 1:22–3 ; Col 1:18–22 ; 2:19 ; 3:15), because all who have been sanctified are branches of one and the same vine, Christ Himself (Jn 15:1–10). All 'who have been sanctified in Jesus Christ' share amongst themselves the benefits they have received from Christ, so far as their position within the Church militant on earth, the Church suffering in Purgatory, or the Church triumphant in Heaven permits (1 Cor 12:25–31 ; Eph 2:13–22 ; 4:3–6, 16). By the power of their intercession with God the saints in Heaven can procure all manner of graces and spiritual benefits both for the souls in Purgatory and for people, especially the faithful, living on earth ; the faithful on earth can unite themselves by their prayers and good works with the saints in Heaven in their worship of God, and merit remission of punishment for sin due to the souls of the just in Purgatory (*see* VENERATION OF SAINTS and INDULGENCES). The Communion of Saints is thus at once a communion or fellowship with holy persons in Christ, and a communion or sharing in the same holy things or spiritual riches, especially the Sacraments, which we owe directly to the merits of Christ's redemption.

When we say the Apostles' Creed we profess our faith in the existence of the Communion of Saints. But this universally accepted doctrine has never been formally defined in all its generality by the Church as a dogma of faith. Many of its particular and most important bearings have, however, been defined, and the definitions presuppose the mysterious unity of life existing between the members of the Church on earth, in Purgatory and in Heaven. Hence there can be no doubt that the doctrine itself has been at least implicitly defined by the Church. Without mentioning the formula *Communio Sanctorum* the Second Council of Lyons (1274), defined that the souls of those suffering in the cleansing fires of Purgatory can benefit from the intercession of the faithful on earth : ' The intercessory prayers of the (living) faithful, in the form of offerings of the Sacrifice of the Mass, prayers, alms and other works of piety which, according to the customary practices of the Church, are offered by the faithful for each other, can avail to relieve the punishments (endured by the Holy Souls) ' (D 464). The Council of Trent defined in the twenty-second Session that the Sacrifice of the Mass is offered not merely for the benefit of the faithful on earth, but also ' for those who have died in Christ, but are not yet fully cleansed from their sins ', and that the offering of the Mass for these intentions is in accordance with the Apostolic tradition (D 940, 950). In the twenty-fifth Session the Council issued the Decree on Purgatory stating once more that the souls in Purgatory can be helped by the intercessory prayers of the faithful and especially by the Sacrifice of the Mass (D 983). In the Decree on the invocation of the saints and veneration offered to relics and sacred images issued at the same Session, the Council defined that ' the saints reigning with Christ offer their prayers to God on behalf of men ', and that ' it is good and useful to invoke the saints in prayer and to have recourse to their prayers, aid and help on account of the benefits to be sought by them from God through His Son Jesus Christ' (D 984). It was also defined at the same Session that it is good to venerate the bodies of the martyrs and other saints living with God for such veneration brings many benefits to men from God (D 985). Those who deny that the Saints in Heaven are to be invoked, or who consider that the Saints do not pray for men, or that the invocation of the Saints is a form of idolatry, were condemned (D 984). It was stated that these practices of venerating the Saints accord with the customs (*usum*) of the Church, and that they had come down from the earliest days of the Christian religion, '*a primaevis christianae religionis temporibus receptum*' (D 984). Finally the Council defined that the power to grant indulgences was conferred by Christ Himself to the Church, and that she had used this divinely given power from the earliest times (*antiquissimis temporibus*) ; accordingly, the Council ordered that the use of this power was to be continued, as it had the full approval of the Church (D 989). It is to be noted that, though these Decrees bear upon the more general doctrine of the Communion of Saints, not one of them actually contains the formula *Communio sanctorum*.

The Catholic Doctrine of the Communion of Saints is based on the principle that in honouring and praying to the Saints in Heaven we are honour-ing and praying to God through Jesus Christ, for we honour and pray to the Saints as the members of Christ. Honour is due to 'the whole Christ', and thus we are honouring not just the isolated persons of the saints but Christ in and through His saints. We venerate the saints because God is in them ; since God is in them we can find help in them. They help us not through their own strength, but through the strength they have from God (Karl Adam, *Das Wesen des Katholizismus*, 151 ff.). Thus to some extent God sanctifies the faithful through the agency of the saints, and the saints worship God by assisting the Holy Souls and the Faithful on earth. In helping the Holy Souls by their prayers and good works, the faithful are in their turn sharing the spiritual wealth they have in Christ with those members of the Church who are in urgent need of their help ; this is a way in which the faithful on earth can worship Christ in those members of His Church He has fully redeemed but not as yet glori-fied. The faithful are also able to assist each other by the merits of their prayers and good works, and by thus living as one amongst themselves they are honouring Christ. They are living in closer union with Christ the more they serve Him in His members on earth. It is, then, union with Christ which establishes the Communion of all the Saints with each other, so that those alone are excluded from this Communion who are not united to Christ and are in no way members of the Church. For St Thomas even the angels, who were never redeemed by Christ and have no membership with Him through His Church, are none the less within the Communion of Saints because they are under the power of Christ and benefit from his *gratia capitis* (*Summa Theologica*, 3a:8:4c). The doctrine of the Communion of Saints is closely linked with the doctrine of divine Grace and of the Mystical Body, for in Christ all live with the one divine life of sanctifying Grace. The riches that each merits for himself and which each possesses, he merits and possesses not just for his own individual benefit, but for the benefit of all the members of the Church.

II The 'Communio Sanctorum' in the Apostles' Creed. The formula 'Communion of Saints' is not found in the great Nicene-Constantinopolitan Creed which is recited or sung every Sunday during Mass, nor is it to be found in the ancient text of the original Roman Baptismal Creed (conventionally referred to as R), the most ancient of all the early local Creeds, from which our Apostles' Creed originated. This early Roman Creed concluded with profession of belief *in Spiritum sanctum, sanctam ecclesiam, remissionem peccatorum, carnis resurrectionem* (J. D. Kelly, *Early Christian Creeds*, chapter 4). The reasons for the insertion of the *Communio Sanctorum* into the Apostles' Creed, that is to say into the present or Received Text (conventionally referred to as T), where it now stands as the second clause of the Ninth Article, 'I believe . . . the Holy Catholic Church, the Com-munion of Saints', are still unknown, though they

are the subject of widespread discussion and of many interesting conjectures (*see below*). Scholars are by no means agreed even about the meaning which the formula may have had in the minds of those who were responsible for its insertion into the Creed. The one thing of which we are certain, however, is that it was the last of all the additions to have been made to T. The earliest existing document known to us in which we have the Apostles' Creed in its present form, complete with the *Communio Sanctorum*, is a handbook of Christian doctrine called the *De Singulis Libris Canonicis Scarapsus* written by St Priminius, the founder and first abbot of the monastery at Reichenau, near Lake Constance, whose work was well known during Carolingian times. The *Scarapsus* was written some time between 710 and 724 (cf. Kelly, op. cit., 398 ff.). There are, however, many conjectures as to the sources from which St Priminius may have derived the formula. It is found much earlier than the 7th cent. in Christian literature. St Niceta, Bishop of Remesiana (Bela Planka in Yugoslavia), who died in 414, had used the expression 'Communion of Saints' in his *Explanatio Symboli*, one of the most important sources for our knowledge of the history of the Apostles' Creed :

> What is the Church but the assembly of all the Saints ? For, from the beginning of the world, patriarchs, prophets, apostles, martyrs and all the other saints who have been, are or will be, form but the one and only Church : sanctified in the unity of the same faith and of the same life, marked with the same Spirit, they have become one body of which Christ is the head. Believe then that it is in this one Church that you have 'the com-munion of saints' (PL 52:871).

The expression 'Communion of Saints' is found yet a little earlier in a small treatise entitled *De Sancto Spiritu*, 1, 2, attributed to Faustus of Riez which was written about 400. Faustus writes :

> After the Holy Spirit, this is what we read, up to the end of the Creed : we must believe the Holy Church, the communion of saints, the remission of sins, the resurrection of the body, life everlasting (CSEL 21:104).

It is interesting to note, however, that Rufinus omits the Communion of Saints from his famous *Commentarius* on the Apostles' Creed which was written about 404.

Whatever the reason for its insertion into the Apostles' Creed may have been (whether it was, as some think, to defend the practice of venerating the saints and martyrs, or, as others suggest, a reaction against the ultra-rigorist Donatist theories about Church membership, or for yet another of the reasons that have been put forward), it seems certain enough that the insertion originated with the Church in Gaul during the 6th, or perhaps as early as the middle of the 5th cent. (P. Bernard : *Communion des saints*, DTC III:451-2).

Historians have discussed the question as to what precisely was the doctrine in which the Church desired the faithful to express their belief, when she sanctioned the universal adoption of the formula *communio sanctorum* in the Apostles' Creed in association with the profession of faith in the Catholic Church.

Some historians think that the formula bore originally a purely sacramental meaning. Thus they consider that *sanctorum* is to be regarded as a neuter plural referring to holy things, and not as a masculine plural referring to holy persons. According to this view the Communion of Saints referred originally to the sharing by all the faithful in the same sacraments, and especially to their common life in the possession of the Holy Eucharist. This view is sometimes attributed to St Thomas because in his *Expositio in Symbolum Apostolorum* he says that the 'communion of saints' is a *communio bonorum*, that is to say, a sharing in the *Bonum Christi* which we receive through the sacraments, 'through which the power of Christ's Passion operates, and which bring us grace for the remission of sins' (Art. 10, Marietti edit., sec. 987–8). St Thomas is supposed to have derived this idea from some early medieval writers, notably Yvo of Chartres and Peter Abélard. In modern times this opinion has been advanced by Theodore Zahn (*Das Apostolische Symbolum*, 88).

Other historians consider that *sanctorum* is to be regarded as a masculine plural noun and that it undoubtedly refers to holy persons. This is certainly the meaning of *sanctorum* in the passages quoted above from St Niceta and Faustus of Riez, and it is the sense in which it is used by St Augustine (*Sermo* 52: 6 ; PL 38:357), and the commentators on the Creed in the 5th and 6th cents. The Church always taught the doctrine of the close union existing between all members of the Church, on earth, in Purgatory and in Heaven, and she could use no simpler formula for the faithful to express their belief than *Communio Sanctorum*. But the word 'saints', taken in the masculine to refer to holy people, can still be interpreted in two ways. It might be understood to refer exclusively to members of the Church on earth, and some think that the faithful came to be called 'saints' in opposition to the Donatist doctrine, that, as the Church on earth is nothing but a sorry mixture of good and bad people, we cannot regard the Church on earth nor the faithful as holy or sanctified. This is the view of the Anglican historian, H. B. Swete (*The Holy Catholic Church, the Communion of Saints, A Study of the Apostles' Creed*, 147–69). Another view suggests that during the 5th and 6th cents., when the formula was being inserted into the Apostles' Creed, the word 'saint' had lost its primitive Biblical meaning of one redeemed in Christ, and had come to be used exclusively of the blessed in Heaven. The formula *Communio Sanctorum* was inserted into the Creed as a consequence of this change of meaning, in order to preserve the traditional doctrine that there is a supernatural or mystical communion of life between the Saints in Heaven and the faithful of earth. This

view seems to fit the ways in which St Niceta and Faustus of Riez use the term 'Saint'. P. Bernard favours this opinion (op. cit.). Albert Michel considers that the formula was more probably understood by the Church in a rich sense which combines the main points of all the views mentioned above, for the Church believes in the Communion between the members of the Church in Heaven, in Purgatory and on earth, and the Communion by which the members of the Church share in the holy fruits of Christ's Passion, the Communion in these fruits being the condition of the Communion of Holy Persons (*La Communion des Saints*, 4–6). Michel's study of the Patristic evidence for the belief in the Communion of Saints makes his opinion the most satisfactory of all.

III The Patristic Evidence for the Belief of the Early Church. We cannot expect to find a comprehensive account of the doctrine of the Communion of Saints in any of the early Christian writers, but we do find, especially in the primitive doctrine of the unity of the Church, a clear understanding of the fundamental importance of the basic ideas and principles, from the systematic development of which the doctrine gradually took shape. For example, the whole burden of the Epistle of St Clement to the Corinthians is the unity of all the members of the Church in Christ : ' Therefore let the whole of our Body be maintained in Christ Jesus, and let each submit to his neighbour's rights in the measure determined by the special gift bestowed on him'. He likens the Church to an army of soldiers in which 'the great cannot exist without the small, nor can the small without the great. A certain organic unity binds all parts, and therein lies the advantage' (1 Clem 38 and 37, translation by J. A. Kleist). St Ignatius of Antioch repeatedly exhorted the faithful to mutual prayer, and wrote, sometimes in glowing terms, commending the offering he was about to make of his life as a martyr to the special care of the prayers of the communities to whom he addressed his letters (*Rom.* 4–9 ; *Phil.* 5 ; *Magn.* 14). In the *Epistle to the Magnesians* he states the basic theological principle of the Communion of Saints quite unmistakably : 'Just as the Lord, therefore, being one with the Father, did nothing without Him, either by Himself, or through the Apostles, so neither must you undertake anything without the bishop and presbyters ; nor must you attempt to convince yourselves that anything you do on your own account is acceptable. No ; at your meetings there must be one prayer, one supplication, one mind, one hope in love, in joy that is flawless, that is Jesus Christ, who stands supreme' (*Magn.* 7, translation by J. A. Kleist).

We find the first developments of the doctrine in the efforts of Clement of Alexandria to show how it is that a Christian martyr's death is offered in satisfaction for sin, in his clear awareness that the merits of Christ and the Apostles are applied to the Church, and his efforts to explain the mystical union between the Church triumphant in Heaven and the Church militant on earth which he conceives as modelled on the Church in heaven (*Strom.* 7:12:80 ; 7:12:7–8 ; 4:8:66). Origen developed these ideas and explained how Christ redeems the world with the aid or co-operation of those He has redeemed ; and he developed the theology of martyrdom showing the benefits a martyr's death brings to the whole Church. Tertullian and St Cyprian developed the themes of the unity of all Christians with the Church ; Tertullian stressed the idea that the Church is Christ Himself (*De paenitentia*, 10).

The doctrine appears in its fully developed form with the writings of St Basil, St Gregory of Nyssa, St Gregory Nazianzen and St John Chrysostom in the East, and St Hilary, St Ambrose and St Augustine in the West (P. Bernard ; op. cit., 439–43). St Augustine in particular presents the most comprehensive and detailed account of the doctrine in many of his Sermons (cf. especially *Serm.* 341:9 ; PL 39:1499–1500). In the *Enchiridion*, which is based largely on the Apostles' Creed, he writes : ' And we are to understand here (9th article of the Creed), the whole Church, not that part of it only which wanders as a stranger on the earth . . . but that part also which has always from its creation remained steadfast to God in heaven, and has never experienced the misery consequent upon a fall. This part is made up of the holy angels . . . and it renders assistance to the part which is still wandering among strangers : for these two parts shall be one in the fellowship of eternity, and now they are one in the bonds of love, the whole having been ordained for the worship of the one God ' (ch. 56). Later he writes about the holy souls in purgatory : ' Nor can it be denied, that the souls of the dead are benefited by the piety of their living friends, who offer the sacrifice of the Mediator, or give alms in the church on their behalf . . .' (ch. 110, translation by Marcus Dodds).

Finally, in his synthesis of the teaching of the Fathers, St Thomas conceived the Communion of Saints not merely as a communion in the merits of Christ (as some authors state), but also as a communion of all the persons within the Church based on their communion in the graces they have received from Christ's redemption through the sacraments. He conceived the union of people amongst themselves as one of the fruits of Christ's redemption, and as based on it : he does not omit it from his doctrine of the communion of saints. Thus he says in his *Expositio in Symbolum Apostolorum* : ' It is to be understood not only as the power of the passion of Christ communicated to us, but also the merit of Christ's life. And whatever good the saints do is communicated to those who live together in charity . . . and thus it is that those who live in charity share in all the goodness there is in the world ; but more especially he for whom the good was specially offered (by the intention of the person offering). For one person can make satisfaction for another . . ., so therefore the Communion of Saints involves two things : one, that the merit of Christ is applied to all, and the other that the good of one person is communicated to another person. . . .' (Art. 10,

Marietti edit., sec. 997–8. Cf. A. Michel : op. cit., chapter 5).

Bibliography. K. Adam, *Das Wesen des Katholizismus* (1940) ; *F. J. Badcock, ' Sanctorum communio as an Article of the Creed', in JTS 21 (1920) 106–22 ; P. Bernard and R. Bour, ' Communion des saints ', in DTC III, 429–80 ; B. Capelle OSB, ' Les Origines du symbole romain ', in *Recherches de théologie ancienne et médiévale* II (1930) 5–20 ; J. de Ghellinck SJ, *Recherches sur les origines du symbole des apôtres* (1949) ; *J. N. Kelly, *Early Christian Creeds* (1950) ; J. P. Kirsch, *Die Lehre von der Gemeinschaft der Heiligen im christlichen Altertum* (1900) ; A. Michel, *La Communion des saints* (1956) ; the same, ' Symboles, origines historiques ', in DTC XIV, 2925–39 ; G. Morin OSB, ' Sanctorum communionem ', in *Revue d'histoire et de littérature religieuse* (1904) ; J. Sollier, ' Communion of Saints ', in CE (1908) ; *H. B. Swete, *The Holy Catholic Church, the Communion of Saints* (1916) ; *T. Zahn, *Das apostolische Symbolum* (1893) ; D. E. Lamirande OMI, *La Communion des Saints* (1954). E. A. S.

COMMUNISM IN THE CHURCH This article will deal with the various attempts at Christian communism. Modern atheist communism will be discussed under MARXISM. The experiment of the early Church at Jerusalem (I) will be considered, and after that (II) the teaching of some of the Fathers on property-rights as due to Original sin. A note on Circumcelliones (III) will lead to a brief consideration (IV) of the medieval heresies about property, though the article on POVERTY will deal with them more fully. Finally a section will be devoted (V) to St Thomas More's *Utopia* and one (VI) to the Jesuit state in Paraguay which aimed at putting Utopia into practice.

I Communism in the apostolic Church (Ac 2:44; 4:32–5 ; 5:4) is not easy to understand. Those who had possessions in land or house-property made sales (but how often or how much they sold we are not told) and deposited the price with the apostles who then made distribution to the needy among the faithful. The words of Peter to Ananias (' When it was sold, was it not in thy power ? ') and the story of Barnabas (Ac 4:37) imply that there was no compulsion in the matter of the sale. It is obvious, too, that such a system would soon exhaust the charitable resources of the Jerusalem Christians, and in fact it is not long before other centres are being drawn in to the support of the ' saints at Jerusalem '. St Paul regards this as the discharge of a debt (Rom 15:26–7), other lands having received salvation from the Jews (without the burden of circumcision) and being thus beholden to the Jewish Christians as to ' founder's kin '. The voluntary nature of the contribution is clear from 1 Cor 16:2.

Parallels with the Qumran community have been noted by writers on the Dead Sea Scrolls, though the practice of Qumran and of the Essenes was so complicated as to make assertions of identity somewhat premature. The *Damascus Document* (18) calls for members of the community to pay two days' wages a month to a fund for social services and there is envisaged a ban on business dealings with those who were outside the sect. Property was not surrendered but was to be administered according to Mosaic law as interpreted by the priests. There were penalties for false declarations and fines could be imposed on members, who must therefore have been able to pay. To find similarities between Qumran and the early Christians may not be difficult, but both are far removed from the wholesale communism which the ancient literary sources (Pliny, Philo and Josephus) report of the Essenes. Some scholars think that the literary sources are at fault and should be interpreted in the light of Qumran practice, but not all are agreed about this. In any case one is left with the conclusion that both Qumran and the early Christians were aiming at social assistance and not at communism.

The *Didache* (4:8) and the *Epistle of Barnabas* (19:8) both reproduce as one of the prescriptions for the Way of Life the advice that those who share in what is incorruptible should be ready to share also their corruptible possessions with one another and should call nothing their own. As this Way of Life has foundations in the Qumran literature, it is easy to see that, whatever may be the case about Ac 2:44, some cross-fertilization between Jewish and Christian ideas has come about by the end of the 1st cent. Justin (*apol.* 14) treats the Christian readiness to render material aid as a carrying out of what he calls the suggestion ($\dot{v}\pi o\theta\eta\mu o\sigma$ $\dot{v}\nu\eta$) of Christ (Lk 6:30) ; the use of this rare word for ' counsel ' may mean that the Christians of the 2nd cent. were already elaborating the distinction between precept and counsel and had adopted an almost new term for the latter.

II Patristic teaching on property-rights was usually well balanced. It was the heretics who exaggerated, as is clear from Clement of Alexandria (*strom.* 3:2 ; GCS 52:198) and from the account of the Apostolici in Epiphanius (*haer.* 61 ; GCS 31:380). The abbot Dorotheus, writing in the 6th cent., can say roundly : ' Christ did not proclaim : " Be ye penniless as My Father in heaven is penniless " ' (PG 88:1784). Cyril of Jerusalem taught his catechumens (*catech.* 8 ; PG 33:633) that they must not think that riches were the work of the devil simply because in the temptation scene he had offered the whole world to Christ. Poverty was a counsel of perfection, to which the Spirit moved some (*catech.* 16 ; PG 33:945).

Ambrose has one passage (*serm.* 8:22 on Ps 118 ; CSEL 62:163) which has been taken up in modern times as a source of the idea that property came in with Original sin. ' God our Lord wished this earth to be the common possession of all men and to provide a living for all, but avarice made a division of property-rights '.[1] Chrysostom could declaim that *meum* and *tuum* were cold words and where they

are absent there is no fighting nor quarrelling. He goes on to say (*hom.* 12 on 1 Tim ; PG 62:564) that necessary things such as baths, market-places and porticos are public property and ought to have given men an example of the wrongfulness of avarice in smaller things. This sentiment would certainly classify Chrysostom as being in favour of common ownership of public utilities, but hardly more than that. It is ironical to notice that the examples he gives are precisely those chosen by Tacitus to illustrate the *delenimenta vitiorum* of Roman civilisation in Britain. Basil, too, has strong words about greed (*hom. in tempore famis* 8 ; PG 31:325). Animals have in common the fruits of the earth, and men might learn from them ; they should also be inspired by the example of the early Church. This appeal to the practice of the church at Jerusalem is quite constant in the Fathers but it is always to a voluntary system of renunciation (see the *Rule* of St Benedict, ch. 33-4).

One of the False Decretals (q.v.) which was ascribed to Clement of Rome (in Hinschius's edition, 65) did great damage throughout the Middle Ages. It found its way into the *Decretum* of Gratian and was taken as genuine by the Scholastics ; in particular it seems to have had a great influence on Scotus. It purports to be a decision about common life and was held to be binding on the clergy in some way. It says : ' Common life is necessary for all and most of all for those who desire faultlessly to wage war for God and to imitate the life of the apostles and their disciples. The use of the things of this world ought to be common to all men. But by reason of sin one man has said " This is mine ", while another man said " This other thing is mine ".' [2] The intention of the forger may have been to commend common life to those who wanted to follow the life of the counsels, but his words can be applied to the clergy generally. One can see in the sermons of Augustine how he used the narrative of Ac 2:44 and 4:32-5 to justify the practice of the clergy at Hippo who lived in common. In *serm.* 356 (PL 38:1574) Augustine can be seen using the passage (Ac 4:32) with much effect. From Augustine innumerable later bishops in the West would derive their understanding of the text. To them it would seem natural that Clement should have written what they found in the Decretal. Another forged Decretal (Hinschius, 143) in the same sense as the pseudo-Clement was ascribed to Urban I. In the course of the Middle Ages many attempts were made (*see* POVERTY) to enforce on the clergy the abdication of all possessions as being an apostolic duty inculcated by Clement. Writing against the Lollards on *The Repression of Overmuch Blaming of the Clergy* (edited by C. Babington [1860] II:316) Pecock said : ' Thilk ensaumpling was under counseil oonli, and to al the

---

[1] Dominus Deus noster terram hanc possessionem omnium hominum voluerit esse communem et fructus omnium ministrare, sed avaritia possessionum iura distribuit.

[2] Communis vita omnibus est necessaria, et maxime his qui Deo inreprehensibiliter militare cupiunt et vitam apostolorum eorumque discipulorum imitari volunt. Communis enim usus omnium quae sunt in hoc mundo omnibus hominibus esse debuit. Sed per iniquitatem alius hoc dixit esse suum et alius istud. . . .

lay peple as weel as to clerkis'. He also pointed out that there was no unanimity among the Fathers on the matter.

III The Circumcelliones have been taken up by a modern communist writer as providing a remote ancestor for modern communism, but in fact so little is known for certain about them that such a pedigree will not add lustre to the offspring. Augustine defines them as those *qui circum cellas vagantur* (who wander round granges) and tells how when the faithful reproach the Donatists with their association with these marauders, the Donatists reply with attacks on the monks (*enarratio in Ps 132* ; PL 36:1730). One of his letters (*ep.* 108 ; CSEL 34:632) shows that the bands contained runaway slaves, while the *Life* of Augustine by Possidius (PL 32:41) makes the curious statement that they professed continence. Further evidence from Optatus (*de schismate Donati* 3:4 ; CSEL 26:81) discloses that they were in the habit of calling themselves 'sons of the martyrs', 'soldiers of Christ' and 'saints'. They are given a Punic name *cutzupitae* in Augustine's *ep.* 53 (CSEL 34:154), and it may be that they were originally a Berber group of rigorist Christians who rejected what they deemed to be the laxity of the orthodox. This would bring them into alliance with the Donatists, for whom they seem to have acted as a guerilla army. A belief in the wrongfulness of private property would provide those who regarded themselves as saints with a suitable excuse for plundering outlying granges in what was then the prosperous North African hinterland. The Romans never properly pacified this area and militant revolution was endemic. The Circumcelliones are merely a temporary phase of this, drawn into alliance with the heresy of Donatism.

IV The medieval Scholastics were naturally exercised about the position of some of the Fathers that property had come in with the Fall of man. St Thomas (*Summa* 1–2æ:94:5:@3) deals with the adage of Isidore that common ownership of all things and common liberty are part of the law of nature, by arguing that private ownership and slavery were not brought in by the natural law but by the work of human reasoning for advantage in living ; this, he claimed, was an addition to the natural law, not a detraction from it. His argument is carried further in *Summa* 2–2æ:66:2 c, where the reasons are given for regarding private property as an advantage in living : people take more care of what is their own and put forth more energy to win it (from the soil) or to make it ; disputes about things held in common are more frequent than about what has an individual owner. This amounts to saying that private property depends on the *ius gentium*, a position which has been defended in modern times by some of his followers (e.g. Fr Vermeersch). At the same time St Thomas considers that what would now be called social justice may limit the use of private possessions. The modern development of these principles will be discussed under MARXISM.

With so much written in Scripture and patristic tradition in condemnation of riches, it is not surprising that there were medieval heresies which set communism in a favourable light. John XXII (D 494) condemned as heretical the idea that Christ and the apostles had no possessions either individually or in common, and in 1368 Urban V had to reject (D 577) the claim that the law of charity took away all rights of ownership. Wyclif was condemned for saying that the Pope and his clergy were heretics because they had possessions (D 616). There was a strain of idealism in all these exaggerations, but this was often marred by the fact that justification was sought from those same principles for confiscations of Church property by kings and their courtiers.

V The Utopia of St Thomas More has caused much perplexity among Catholics. It seems to advocate a form of communism, described in the book by the narrator, Raphael Hythloday, as an ideal. What many fail to notice, and what the late R. W. Chambers pointed out with great clarity, is that the ideal is that of unaided reason. More is bent on sketching a commonwealth which is governed by reason but not yet touched by the Christian revelation. It gives him an opening for his irony, when he can suggest, as he often does, that reasonable men do thus and thus in the light of a vague deism, but Christian Englishmen cannot go even as far as that. It is plain that More in his later life abominated the communistic experiments of the Anabaptists of Westphalia, for he wrote (in the *Defence of the First Argument Against Tindall, Works* 656) that one of their enormities was to say 'that no man should have any thing proper of his own but that all lands and all goods ought by God's law to be all men's in common, and that all women ought to be common to all men'. He was not here repenting at leisure of his youthful follies, for, as Chambers shows, there are similar inconsistencies between the views expressed in *Utopia* and More's contemporary practice (e.g. in the matter of bodily penance).

More did not shrink from making his ideal commonwealth a place of compulsion. Those to whom higher motives do not appeal will be committed to penal servitude and even to death, but there is the impulsion of a religious fervour among the Utopians, founded on no more than a belief in God and in an immortality where He will reward or punish. The state is not founded on terrorism but there is a tight rein kept upon discussion that would undermine the belief in God and immortality on which the working of the State depends. If More is, in part, protesting with his communism against the great landowners of his own time in England who were enclosing the old common fields, yet he is trying to establish what directives unaided human reason can discern for the State. This at once poses the question how he can have supposed that Christian revelation brought in the notion and the lawfulness of private property. The answer must have been, though More does not give it (and is not called upon to give it in the framework of his book), that in Christianity there is a new concept of human dignity and of the human person, and that this new concept debars a statesman from treating men as they are treated in *Utopia* ; some private property is required to set off and to maintain the dignity of the person. Utopians are sub-personal for they have not received that notion into their philosophy. Followers of the religious life among Christians may give up all rights to property, but then they also give up, for a higher end, much that belongs to human dignity. That More allowed his Utopians to have divorce and euthanasia, both affronts to the dignity of the human person, confirms this conclusion.

V The Paraguayan Utopia of the Jesuits (1607–1767) was gradually evolved under pressure of circumstances as well as from missionary zeal, being judged necessary to protect the Guarani Indians against Spanish slave-hunters and also against their own natural indolence. It was a state of semi-communism, for, though herds and plantations were the property of the Reduction (or settlement), tools and gardens belonged to the family and it was possible for a man by extra work, e.g. at wood-carving, to earn money from the Spaniards which he could spend on buying finery for his wife. Music and colourful processions gave these otherwise indolent people an interest in their work and they enjoyed under this regime peace and a quiet prosperity. The missionary narratives of the time compare it with the life of the early Christians at Jerusalem, and clearly some of the inspiration was drawn from that. As the settlements began before Campanella published (1620) his *Città del Sole*, it cannot be claimed that the idea of the settlements was due to him. The presence of a Scotsman (or Irishman) among the first missionaries, Fr Thomas Fields, may indicate that one amongst the missionaries had read *Utopia*, but there is no certainty of this. The chief pioneer in the moving of the settlements from where they were within reach of slave-raiders to the virgin lands where they would be safe was a Spaniard, Ruiz de Montoya.

Each settlement held some 2,000 people or more, with no more than two missionaries. The Indians had a Corregidor (or governor), two Alcaldes (or judges), a Banneret and other officials and the missionaries acted as a court of appeal, but the whole administration was rather like that of the prefects in some large public school with a headmaster remaining in the background. As a means of bringing primitive people to a state bordering on civilization, it was an admirable system ; its segregation was necessary to secure the mere survival of the Indians in the face of Spanish or Portuguese exploitation, and it may be that the experiment did not last long enough to change fundamentally the indolent character of the Guarani. It seems certain that, in spite of many calumnious tales about the Reductions, they served as a pattern for some of the idealistic experiments in America and elsewhere in the 19th cent. Even the *kibbutzim* of the Zionists may have drawn some inspiration from Paraguay, thus by a *recirculatio* linking up modern times with the early Christian Church at Jerusalem.

Bibliography. *A. J. Carlyle, ' Community of Goods ', in *Dictionary of Apostolic Church* (1910) ; E. Surtz SJ, *The Praise of Pleasure : Communism in More's Utopia* (1957) ; *R. B. Cunninghame Graham, *A Vanished Arcadia* (1901) ; *T. Büttner, *Circumcellionen und Adamiten* (1959) ; M. Fassbinder, *Der Jesuitenstaat in Paraguay* (1926) ; R. O'Sullivan, ' The Social Theories of St Thomas More ', in DbR 191 (1936) 46–62 ; *R. W. Chambers, *St Thomas More* (1935) ; *J. H. Baxter, ' The Martyrs of Madaura, in JTS 26 (1925) 21–37 ; *B. H. Warmington, *The North African Provinces* (1954).

J. H. C.

CONCELEBRATION is the carrying out of a sacramental rite by more than one minister, and while eucharistic concelebration is the more usual topic of theological discussion, there are cases of concelebration at the anointing of the sick and at an ordination which deserve some notice. A distinction is often made between sacramental and ceremonial concelebration, the difference being whether the presence of a second or third minister is regarded as essential to the rite or not, but this distinction cannot have been operative until theological thought had reached the concept of essential and non-essential parts of the rite. The first part of this article (I) will therefore trace the history of concelebration at the Eucharist until in the Middle Ages the distinction of essential and non-essential parts of the rite has become operative. Next will be discussed (II) the theological significance of sacramental concelebration with reference to the Eucharist, and finally a note will be added (III) about concelebration in other sacraments.

I The ancient rite of concelebration is first depicted in the *Didascalia Apostolorum* (2:58:3), where bishops are advised that a visiting prelate should be asked to celebrate the Eucharist : ' But if he be a careful man and decline that honour in favour of yourself, then let him say the words over the chalice'. This idea of sharing in the sacramental work was not taken up by the *Apostolic Constitutions* of the 4th cent., although in general they follow the *Didascalia*, for they direct that the visiting bishop should merely be asked to give the blessing to the people. What Eusebius records (*HE* 5:24) of Anicetus ' yielding the Eucharist to Polycarp ' when the latter visited Rome, seems more like a complete substitution of one bishop for another. Similarly in the *Statuta ecclesiae antiqua* (33) the direction that visiting bishops should be admitted both to preach and to consecrate the offerings envisages a substitution rather than a collaboration.

Some memory of the *Didascalia* may have lingered, even outside the region of Syria or Cilicia for which it was composed, since the next piece of evidence shows that there was some practice of concelebration at Rome in the 6th cent., when the *Liber pontificalis* was being put together. This work projects the practice back into the past, attributing its institution to Zephyrinus (198–217). He is credited (in very ungrammatical Latin) with having arranged that deacons should hold glass patens in front of each priest at a concelebration, as they stood round the bishop who was the chief celebrant, deferring to him in what was his prerogative.[1] When it came to the communion of the people the priests (who had communicated themselves from their own offering on the glass paten) were to take consecrated offerings (in the form of small crescents or circles of bread) from the bishop's altar to communicate the people. The famous ivory at the Fitzwilliam Museum in Cambridge shows something like this happening in the 9th cent., save that the priests who stand round have folded corporals in place of the glass patens to hold their obleys. The ivory was carved at a date when the liturgical year began with Advent (and not with Easter or 1 January). This practice would best be described as a synchronization of separate Masses, rather than a concelebration, for each of the priests deals with his own obley. The use of *corona* for the bread of the Eucharist (a use attested for the time of Gregory the Great) and of *sacerdos* for priest in the *Liber pontificalis* shows that the evidence it supplies cannot really belong to the 3rd cent., but the existence of gold-glasses (*see* ART AND EARLY CHURCH) about that time suggests that glass patens may not have been unknown in the 4th cent.

The Council of Neo-Caesarea (canon 14) in the 4th cent. forbade the country clergy to join with the bishop and the city clergy at their Eucharist.[2] The reason of this may have been the danger of over-crowding in small city churches. If the contemporary Council of Arles (canon 19) has the same situation in mind, its direction that visiting bishops are to be ' given a place that they may offer ' is at once comprehensible.[3] They should not be crowded out, but simple priests from the countryside might be.

The word *concelebrare* was in use in Christian Latin of the 4th cent. (in Hilary, Filastrius and elsewhere), but it does not refer to a special way of offering Mass. It keeps to the quite general meaning of keeping high feast with a large crowd assembled together. In the *Leonine Sacramentary* L 295=GR. 117) there is one prayer where the word is used,[4] and here the general sense is the only one possible.

The episode that is narrated in the life of St Columba (*vita Columbae* 1:44) seems to be a concelebration, though the passage has been variously interpreted. A Munster bishop named Cronan

came to Iona, but he concealed the fact that he was a bishop. On the Sunday Columba asked him to consecrate the Body of Christ in the usual way, but Cronan suggested that both should act together, as if they were both priests. Columba then went with Cronan to the altar, but looking close into his face Columba said : ' Christ bless thee, brother, break this Bread alone as a bishop does, for now we know that thou art a bishop '.[5] The underlying assumption seems to be that two priests concelebrated on a Sunday, yet Dom Gougaud argued that the story meant no more than that Columba joined Cronan at the Fraction, having previously left him to say Mass by himself. This view comes up against the fact that *proinde* means ' straightway ' and does not allow of the lapse of more than half the time of Mass before the action indicated by *accedens* is to take place. Warren translated the passage on the supposition that there was a concelebration, and Dom Gougaud, while criticising Warren's translation, did not offer an alternative version of his own.

At Rome before 800 there was on four feasts in the year (Easter, Whitsun, St Peter's Day and Christmas) a concelebration of Pope and cardinals that is described in *Ordo III* (in Andrieu's numbering). At this the cardinals each held a corporal on which the archdeacon laid three obleys. They stood in a half-circle round the Pope and spoke the whole Canon with him ' so that his voice might be the better heard '. They consecrated with him, but made no ritual gestures.[6]

More than fifty years later the *Ordo S. Amandi* has elaborated this practice, substituting bishop and priests for Pope and cardinals and increasing the number of feast-days to eight.

There are some who think that this individual manner of concelebration cannot be primitive, since they hold that the various versions of the *Traditio apostolica* of Hippolytus take us back to the earliest Roman practice and that these require the joint activity of many about the one altar while one chief celebrant speaks the words. There are so many imponderables here that no safe inference can be made about the primitive rites of concelebration. The Coptic and Ethiopic versions of Hippolytus direct that on the consecration of a new bishop he is to celebrate the liturgy at once. The deacons bring him the offerings and he lays his hands on them, accompanied in this gesture by ' all the priests ', and then he goes on to speak the words of the Canon

---

[1] Fecit constitutum de ecclesia et patenas vitreas ante sacerdotes in ecclesia et ministros supportantes, donec episcopus missas celebraret ante se sacerdotes adstantes ; sic missae celebrarentur, excepto quod ius episcopi interest tantum clerus substineret omnibus praesentes ; ex ea consecratione de manu episcopi iam coronam consecratam acciperet presbiter tradendam populo.

[2] Vicani presbyteri non possunt in dominico offerre praesente episcopo vel urbis presbyteris, neque panem dare precationis neque calicem.

[3] De episcopis pergrinis qui in Urbem solent venire, placuit eis locum dari ut offerent.

[4] Hostias Domine tuae plebis intende, et quas in honorem sanctorum tuorum devota concelebrat, proficere sibi sentiat ad medelam.

[5] Alia die dominica a sancto iussus Christi corpus ex more conficere, sanctum advocat ut simul quasi duo presbyteri dominicum panem frangerent. Sanctus proinde ad altarium accedens repente intuitus faciem eius sic eum compellat : Benedicat te Christus, frater ; hunc solus episcopali ritu frange panem ; nunc scimus quod sis episcopus.

[6] In diebus autem festis . . . habent colligendas presbyteri cardinales ; unusquisque tenens corporalem in manu sua, et venit archidiaconus et porregit unicuique eorum oblatas tres. Et accedente pontifice ad altare dextra laevaque circumdant altare et simul cum illo canonem dicunt, tenentes oblatas in manibus, non super altare, ut vox pontificis valentius audiatur, et simul consecrant corpus et sanguinem Domini, sed tantum pontifex facit super altare crucem dextra laevaque.

alone. It is strange that the bishops who have just taken part in consecrating him are not given any mention in the account of the Eucharist which the new bishop apparently celebrates with his own priests. The Latin version is not perfectly grammatical, but can be understood with the help of the Oriental versions. It seems to require, like them, that the new bishop speak the Canon by himself after his priests have joined with him in laying hands on the offerings.[1]

The term 'fellow-liturgist', which becomes current in the Eastern churches of the 6th cent. and later, is not in itself sufficient to establish sacramental concelebration as a fact. The liturgy of St Basil (in the new Coptic MS, which is dated 660–80) has in the Memento of the living a prayer for 'thy servant archbishop Benjamin, and his fellow-liturgist Colluthus, the holy bishop, and those who with them dispense the word of truth'. Here the common activity of those prayed for is the teaching of God's word and not the celebration of the Eucharist. The letters of John VIII to Photius (MGH *Epistulae Karolini aevi*, V:181–2) tell of an episode when the papal legates refused to join with Photius in his Eucharist,[2] but here the practice envisaged by the legates may well have been a joint Eucharist where each celebrant had his own obley and consecrated that, after the Roman practice ; if Photius wanted something different, they may have refused on the ground that this was not what they were used to. It would be hazardous to reconstruct the rite on negative evidence such as this.

Another episode which has been appealed to as evidence for concelebration comes from the Council of Constantinople in 680 (in Actio XIV). Here some discussion took place about Latin copies of the *Acta* of Chalcedon, and one speaker recalled how there had come to Constantinople some forty years ago Fortunius, archbishop of Carthage (who was probably as much of a Monothelite as the then patriarch, Paul). Fortunius was going to celebrate Mass in Sancta Sophia when there arose a question of precedence. Was he to sit in front of the metropolitans in residence, or behind them ? This was settled by reference to the Latin *Acta* of Chalcedon (when such questions must have been common) and the patriarch made him sit in his proper station according to what was found in the *Acta*.[3] The episode does not throw much light on the ritual used at the Mass, as the question in dispute was one of sitting, nor does it appear whether Fortunius was the principal celebrant or not, though the wording seems to imply that he was on this occasion. No doubt the prelates would sit during the chanting of epistles and psalms, but what they did when the

offerings were brought forward must remain a matter for conjecture. The language used by Fortunius was probably Greek, since Carthage had been under Byzantine rule after 533 until its fall to the Arabs in 692.

Apart, then, from the evidence of the *Didascalia*, there appears to be no ancient record of a *shared* celebration, where different but equal ministers carried out different parts of the one liturgy, whereas the main trend of what evidence is available is to show that different and equal ministers might join in celebrating a synchronized liturgy where each carried out all the spoken parts for himself, though only one stood at the altar and performed the ritual gestures.

II The theological meaning of sacramental concelebration is subject to much dispute. Where the early historical evidence is so read as to make it appear that there was a shared celebration, ambitious theories have been launched which would claim that the essential act of consecration in the Eucharist was an act of the whole body of priests—and even of the faithful there present—in which the individual minister had only a part. But when the early evidence is seen to incline towards the idea of individual consecrations synchronized, then these theories are deprived of support. Appeal is sometimes made to another sacrament, that of Orders, for support, since it might seem that 1 Tim 4:14 indicates a shared ordination of Timothy by all the priests. Modern research has established, however, that the word πρεσβυτέριον was used as an abstract noun, to denote the office conferred, and that to construe it here as a collective, for the body of priests taking part, would be against all probability.

In the medieval theologians there seems to be little trace of the idea of concelebration as a corporate act. The *False Decretals* (letter of the pseudo-Anacletus) lay it down that bishops should not say Mass alone but should take witnesses with them, ' that it may be proved that they offer sacrifice to the Lord perfectly in the places sacred to God '.[4] Durandus, in his *Rationale*, appeals to this idea of witnessing though with some uncertainty. ' It was the custom in the primitive church for others to consecrate the Body of Christ by word and action along with the bishop, perhaps for a testimony, as nowadays in an ordination Mass the newly ordained do with their ordainer '.[5] His use of *forte* shows that he was guessing. Pope Innocent III (PL 217:873) brought forward the pedagogical motive for concelebration, claiming that the Apostles had learnt the rite from Christ by joining with Him at the Last Supper, just as priests at their ordination went through the whole rite slowly with the ordaining bishop.[6] From the rubrics in some Pontificals (e.g. in Andrieu, *Pontifical*, III:349) it appears that this action of the newly

---

[1] Qui cumque factus fuerit episcopus, omnes os offerant pacis, salutantes eum quia dignus effectus est. Illi vero offerant diacones oblationem quique imponens manus in eam cum omni praesbyterio dicat gratias agens : Dominus vobiscum ; et omnes dicant : Et cum spiritu tuo.

[2] Quod dicitur . . . missos nostros tecum minime consacrare. . . .

[3] Exinde instructus idem Paulus fecit eum ordinabiliter sedere.

[4] . . . ut Domino perfecte in sacratis Deo sacrificare locis probentur.

[5] Consueverat primitiva ecclesia simul cum pontifice verbis et manibus corpus Christi conficere, forte ad testimonium, prout hodie in missa de ordinibus cum ordinatore faciunt ordinati.

[6] Ostendunt apostolos tunc a Domino ritum huius sacrificii didicisse.

ordained was not always held to be a real concelebration but only an imitation of what the bishop
was doing.[1] The drawback about this pedagogical
theory is that it cannot be primitive, for the *Gelasian
Sacramentary* (Mohlberg, 29) in its Mass for the
ordination of priests shows (in the *Hanc igitur*) that
the new priests are not reciting all the words of the
Mass with the bishop. Nor can it be claimed that
the apostles joined with Christ in consecrating at the
Last Supper. The *Pontifical of Apamea* (a work of
A.D. 1214 which was used in Syria for the Latin rite
by Crusading bishops) directs that a newly consecrated bishop is to concelebrate with his consecrators,
but this is not extended to priests at ordination. The
legends of the Grail made it seem to medieval
theologians that the Last Supper was known in all
its circumstances, and it may be from these that the
idea of the apostles concelebrating with Christ took
its rise.

St Thomas is on much firmer ground when he
justifies concelebration as the visible sign of the unity
of the Church (*Summa* 3a:82:2). The Eucharist is
the sacrament of unity and makes many one in
Christ. Just as the Apostles were united with Christ
(note that he does not say they concelebrated) at the
Last Supper, so the newly ordained are united with
their bishop at the Mass of ordination. Previously
(*Summa* 3a:67:6) he had rejected plurality of ministers
at baptism on the ground that this would involve a
change in the formula from 'I baptize' to 'We
baptize'. For St Thomas the ordination Mass has
but one consecration, not several, and he cites with
approval Innocent III who said that the intention of
each celebrant should be directed upon the same
instant of consecration. He does not consider
whether this manifestation of the unity of the Church
ought to be repeated more frequently than the
random necessity of ordination services may require ;
this topic has come to the fore in recent times.

In the modern liturgical movement opinions have
been put forward that would urge an extension of
concelebration to those occasions when the clergy
assemble in large numbers. Arguments were drawn
from the effects of the Mass and it was urged that
the celebration of a single Mass, at which one
hundred priests were present, participating devoutly
with the one celebrant, was of the same value in the
eyes of God as one hundred Masses celebrated by
those priests singly. This was rejected by Pope
Pius XII as an erroneous opinion (AAS 46:669
and 48:716) in 1954 and 1956, since it did not
pay attention to the nature of the act of offering the
Mass. 'In the offering of Mass there are as many
acts of Christ as there are priests celebrating Mass,
but the acts of Christ are not multiplied according to
the number of priests devoutly hearing the Mass of
priest or bishop celebrating'.[2] The reason given
was that it is only the celebrant who bears the person
of Christ at Mass ; priests or laity who may have

[1] Et dicunt totum submissa voce, sicut si celebrarent. . . .
[2] Quoad sacrificii eucharistici oblationem tot sunt actiones
Christi quot sunt sacerdotes celebrantes, minime vero quot
sunt sacerdotes missam episcopi aut sacri presbyteri cele-
brantis pie audientes.

active parts in the celebration cannot be equated
with the celebrant. The so-called priesthood of the
laity differs not merely in degree but in kind from
priesthood strictly understood. Since this condemnation little attempt has been made further to elaborate
the way in which Christ may be considered to act in
each Mass. It may be that when the theology of the
divine missions has been developed and the nature
of the *Epiklesis* in the Mass better understood, some
progress will be made here.

It is sometimes claimed by moral theologians that
the right to take a Mass stipend is the acid test for
theories of concelebration, but in the recent papal
condemnation the argument was drawn back from
considering the fruit of the Mass to the nature of the
act itself. The regulation of stipends is a matter for
the positive law of the Church. Benedict XIV in a
decree of 24 December 1743 for the Greek Melkites
laid it down that each priest taking part in a concelebration could take a stipend for the Mass, after
warning the donor that other priests would be
sharing in that Mass and receiving the consent of the
donor thereto. Benedict had forbidden these Melkites to have more than one Mass on each altar in
the day, and, to provide for overcrowding in
churches, he allowed them to concelebrate in such a
way that each participating priest should be vested
and should recite the whole of the liturgy, including
the words of consecration. Benedict was not innovating but rather insisting that the Melkites keep to
their older custom of one Mass on each altar, in the
face of a demand for more frequent Masses to suit
the devotion of priests and the piety of the faithful,
which at that time was being influenced by eucharistic devotions from the West (*see* ALTAR). Theologians who set out to argue how the infinite fruit
of the redemption can be applied in a limited way
by each Mass should make some attempt to draw
analogies from the work of modern mathematicians
who have been able to distinguish different orders of
infinity and to use a series of transfinite cardinal
numbers. It is clearly unsatisfactory to argue that
concelebration must reduce the fruit of the Mass for
each priest taking part as a celebrant in the consecration. Another line of theological speculation, suggested by Mgr Davis (*see* **Bibliography** below),
would be to deepen the distinction between the
Eucharist as a sacrifice and the other sacraments.

In 1963 the Vatican Council in its Constitution on
the Liturgy (para. 57) reorganized the discipline of
concelebration to allow of its more frequent use at
gatherings of clergy, while enacting that each priest
shall retain his right to celebrate Mass individually, a
right that was not expressly determined before. The
decree adds *obiter* that concelebration is a fitting
manifestation of the unity of the priesthood. A new
rite for it will eventually be drawn up. In this work
regard will have to be shown for the principles
outlined above and decisions taken on points of
uncertainty.

III Concelebration in other sacraments has been
studied by theologians chiefly for the light it may
throw on what happens at the Eucharist. Thus it

has been argued that, just as the co-consecrators of a new bishop act by a silent imposition of hands, so the silent imposition of hands over the offerings at the Eucharist (which the versions of Hippolytus's *Traditio apostolica* ascribe to the clergy who are in attendance on their bishop) may be held to be a consecration, even though no words are spoken by these priests. This argument was flatly rejected by Pius XII (AAS 48:717), who said that in a previous papal constitution (AAS 37:131) he had laid it down that the co-consecrators must do the actions and pronounce the essential words by which the power and grace of episcopate are transmitted, and that it is not sufficient that they unite their intention to that of the chief consecrator and declare that they accept what he has said and done. Although this papal constitution was naturally not retrospective, it cannot be considered to be contrary to existing traditions.

The consecration of the holy oils on Maundy Thursday was taken by Amalarius (1:12:26) to be an instance of concelebration. An *ordo* of Rouen, cited by Menard (PL 78:328), directs that the oil of the sick is to be blessed by bishop and priests together, and in the rubric of the *Gregorian Sacramentary* (in Wilson's edition, 49) the same direction is given, along with a prayer which was presumably spoken in unison by the company.[1] This practice caused difficulties for the medieval theologian (St Thomas, *Supplementum* 29:6@1). Why should a bishop be needed to bless the oil, when a priest can consecrate the Eucharist by himself? The answer given is not, as one might have expected, that the consecration of oil is a corporate act of the Church as a whole at which the bishop has to preside, although something of this idea may underlie the appeal to the text of Ps 132:1 about the oil that flows down Aaron's beard. Christ is the head, the bishop is apparently represented by the beard and the parish clergy by the hem of Aaron's garment.

The administration of the Last Anointing is given to the priests of the Church by the text of Jas 5:14, and Trent (D 910) affirmed this over again when it had been questioned by Cajetan. The use of the plural here ('priests') is defended by Salmeron on the ground that while one can anoint, the prayers of several will be more efficacious than the prayer of one. The modern rubrics for this sacrament do indeed speak of the parish priest 'calling together his clerics' before he sets out to anoint a sick man, but this can seldom happen in practice. Plurality of ministers has been kept more strictly in some of the Eastern Churches. For the corporate aspect of the sacrament of Penance, *see* CONFESSION. In this case, as in that of the Last Anointing, it is the element of supplication which is corporate, rather than the act of administering the sacrament. If this distinction can be used for the Eucharist also, it would show that intercessions at Mass could come from different ministers but that the essential act of consecrating should come from all the celebrants together if there is to be a true concelebration.

[1] Et benedicit tam domnus Papa quam omnes presbiteri.

Bibliography. J. M. Hanssens SJ, 'De concelebratione eucharistica', in *Periodica* 16 (1927) 143–154 and 181–210 ; 17 (1928) 93–127 ; 21 (1932) 193–219 ; K. Rahner SJ, 'Die viele Messen und das eine Opfer', in ZKT 71 (1949) 257–317 ; the same, 'Die Frage der Konzelebration', in *Münchener Theologische Zeitschrift* 6 (1955) 81–106, in reply to J. M. Granero, 'Novum Pascha', in *Estudios ecclesiasticos* 28 (1954) 211–37 ; various authors, 'Qu'est-ce que la Concélébration?', in *La Maison-Dieu* 35 (1953) 9–78 ; J. H. Crehan SJ, 'The Many Masses and the One Sacrifice', in CR 43 (1958) 415–21 ; H. F. Davis, 'The Pope and Private Masses', in CR 42 (1957) 2–14.   J. H. C.

CONCEPTION, IMMACULATE It is an article of faith in the Roman Catholic Church that the Virgin Mary was preserved from Original sin—that mysterious, sinful condition in which human nature is inherited by all Adam's descendants. Other human beings begin their existence already in a state of sin, even before they have performed a single personal act of their own, and can be delivered from it only by being united through faith and baptism to Christ, the Redeemer (*see* SALVATION). She, however, who was destined to be the Mother of God, did not begin her life in a sinful state, but in a state of holiness, thanks to a grace given in the first moment of her existence. Hence she is said to have been conceived immaculate.

The Immaculate Conception must not be envisaged as making Mary independent of the redemptive work of Christ. Such an understanding of it constituted the greatest obstacle to its acceptance during the 13th and following cents., as we shall see. On the contrary, the initial holiness of the Mother of Christ was the finest fruit of Christ's redemptive activity, which preserved her from an evil that she would otherwise have inherited.

It is often thought that the Immaculate Conception implies that Mary herself was virginally conceived. The doctrine does not refer to Mary's conceiving of Christ, but to her own conception by her parents ; and it does not imply anything extraordinary on their part, but rather on the part of Mary herself : namely, that by an exceptional, privileged grace she inherited human nature in a state pure and holy, untainted by sin.

This doctrine is not stated in Scripture. Neither is there evidence that it was held as a doctrine in the Apostolic Church. On the contrary, it is clear that it developed only gradually in the course of many centuries of reflection. This article will attempt to trace this development. The first stage was the emergence of the idea of Mary's holiness in the Patristic Church (I). The second was the maturing of this idea to its full strength, in the Byzantine world and, somewhat later, in the Latin (II). The final stage was that in which the general idea of Mary's immense holiness was specified as including preservation from Original sin. This development had already begun in a crude form in the ancient Eastern world with the legend of Anne and Joachim, and the feast of Mary's Conception (III). But Byzantine thought on Mary even at its greatest moment (the 8th cent.) never formulated a clear and firm notion of the Immaculate Conception (IV). This was a work which the Latin Church, provoked by a controversy over the feast in the 12th cent. (V), achieved through the scholastic discussions of the 13th and following cents. (VI). The crucial point was the reconciliation of the Immaculate Conception with the doctrine that all men have been redeemed by Christ. Duns Scotus showed how this could be, early in the 14th cent., after which the belief steadily gained a firmer hold in the Church until its official definition in 1854 (VII). The theological reasoning which underlay this historical development remains, however, difficult to formulate (VIII).

I The Church Fathers' ideas on Mary's holiness constitute the pre-history of the doctrine. In the beginning, they do not seem to have had any distinct doctrine about Mary. The Scriptural image of her was an enigmatic one that had to be deciphered gradually. In the earliest Christian centuries, it seemed possible to suppose that, on the score of personal holiness, she was not significantly different from anyone else. Thus, several of the early Church Fathers took it for granted that Mary had been guilty of faults like all other human beings, and in their homilies on the Gospels, they even used her as a type of sinful humanity in opposition to the holiness of Christ. Tertullian declared that Christ had denounced Mary's lack of faith when He asked, ' Who is My Mother . . . ? ' (Mt 12:48 ; cf. *adv. Marc.* 4:19 ; CSEL 47:482, 483. *De carne Christi* 8, PL 2:766-9). At the same time, Origen was teaching that Mary's faith had been shaken by the death of Christ (PG 13:1845), and on numerous other occasions he found her faith at fault. This exegesis was followed by later writers for several centuries, who also blamed her for questioning the angel Gabriel, for calling her twelve-year-old Son to account in the Temple, for an inopportune request at Cana and for attempting to interrupt Him in His preaching. Marius Victorinus proposed her as generically typifying womanly weakness (*In Ep. ad Gal.* 2 ; PL 8:1176-7) and St Hilary of Poitiers supposed that God would blame her on the Day of Judgment (*Tract. in ps.* 118 ; CSEL 22:384). St John Chrysostom is one of the severest of Mary's critics ; his Gospel homilies find fault with her on many occasions (texts in H. du Manoir's *Maria* I, 94f.).

When thus gathered together, these observations seem to compose a dark portrait of the Mother of Jesus. Remember, however, that they were dispersed among references to her which were, on the whole, laudatory. Moreover, they do not seem to represent a definite teaching of the Church ; rather, they reflect the absence of any firm and positive doctrine about Mary's state of soul. The brief glimpses of Mary that are given in Scripture are in many cases, when considered in isolation, susceptible of various interpretations. The early preachers, groping for the sense of the Gospel stories, and seeking to find in them a personification of the great

Christian vision of Christ's redemptive mission to sinful mankind, were understandably inclined to seize upon the Mother of Christ as representative of the race of sinners from which He was born, and by whom He was not received. Tertullian calls her expressly ' a figure of the Synagogue ' (*de carne Christi* 7 ; CSEL 70:212). The absence of any firm doctrine to the contrary, together with the rhetorical power of such a personification, readily explain its attractiveness. But, generally speaking, even those who thought they could discern some fault in Mary's conduct commonly looked upon her as being, in the final analysis, a saint despite her supposed defects. And in proportion as reflection upon the Scriptural text brought to light profounder reasons in favour of Mary's holiness, the inclination to put a bad construction on her actions receded and at last disappeared altogether.

There are signs of an approach towards recognition of Mary's special holiness in the middle of the 2nd cent., when Justin and Irenaeus (and after them, an endless stream of others) include her in their portraits of Christ as the Second Adam. She is represented both as the virgin soil out of which His body was formed, and as the Second Eve, whose faith and obedience initiate the movement of man's restoration, just as Eve's faithlessness (or misplaced credulity) and disobedience started man's fall. The image of the virgin soil is indeed pregnant with the potentiality of an Immaculist interpretation, but there are no grounds for suspecting that it was so understood at this early date. The representation of Mary as an example of faith and obedience is more significant, for it represents a first posing of Mary as a type of Christian holiness, even though it says as yet nothing whatsoever about the degree of perfection to be attributed to her.

The next significant development was the recognition of Mary as the type and model of the Christian virgin. As the practice of consecrated virginity developed in the Church, particularly during the 4th cent., the Blessed Virgin of the gospels was early perceived as the Scriptural type for the way of life inculcated in Mt 19:10-12 and 1 Cor 7. Origen sounded the note (on *Mt* 10:17 ; GCS 40:21-2), which was amplified by St Alexander of Alexandria, and St Athanasius (text in *Le Muséon* 42 (1929) 197-275). The latter presented Mary as a model of holiness, without however making her out to be faultless. His imitator (?), St Ambrose, in *De virginibus* (II:6-19 ; PL 16:208-11 ; edited by Faller, *Florilegium patristicum* (1933) 37-52), paints Mary in terms of pure praise that leave no room for faults. Finally, Augustine formulated for the first time (and still hesitantly) the idea that Mary had led a perfectly sinless life : ' All men have sinned . . . except for the holy virgin Mary, whom I do not wish to be brought into the question when sin is being discussed ; for whence do we know what greater grace of complete triumph over sin may have been given to her who merited to conceive and bear Him Who was certainly without any sin ? ' (*De natura et gratia* 36:42 ; CSEL 60:263-4).

This sober, cautious, but expectant reverence set the tone of many subsequent centuries in Western thought. Nevertheless, in relating the question of Mary's holiness to her being the Mother of Jesus, Augustine touched the key that would open the way to the next great development in the idea of this holiness : recognition that it was not only faultless, but immense.

Before leaving this period we must notice the early tradition about Mary's freedom from the pains of childbirth (see VIRGIN BIRTH). Some would regard this as a sign of belief in Mary's exemption from the effects of Original sin. In view of the contemporary vagueness so specific an interpretation is perhaps improbable. Nevertheless, this tradition does manifest an awareness of the privileged condition of the Mother of Christ, and the remarkable concordance of this early notion with the doctrine that was to be formulated centuries later is itself of the greatest significance.

II The maturing of the concept of Mary's holiness was accelerated by the Council of Ephesus (431). Convoked to pass judgment on the title *theotokos* (Mother of God), which had come into wide use during the preceding century, the Council ruled that it was theologically accurate when rightly understood, and that its usage was justified. The controversy drew attention to the title, and men began to reflect more consciously on Mary's being Mother of God as the reason for, and measure of, her holiness.

The rich development in the veneration of Mary during the next few centuries, especially in the Greek-speaking world, is attested by the multiplication of prayers addressed to her, hymns honouring her and sanctuaries dedicated to her. Legendary stories about her life and miracles proliferated and strongly influenced the popular image of Mary. Most important of all, feast days began to be observed in her honour. These celebrations, arising out of popular devotion, fostered that same piety, and made it more conscious and articulate regarding the beliefs that inspired it.

In the homilies composed for these feasts, there appears a new note of enthusiasm in the praise of Mary's dignity and sanctity. It had precedents, e.g. the hymns of St Ephraem (cf. Jouassard, in *Maria* I, 88, n. 9). But now a new energy is unleashed ; orators spoke as men driven by an impulse more profound, and captivated by a vision more noble, than was adequately declared by any of the particular assertions they made. They range over earth, sea and sky, and scrutinise the Old as well as the New Testament, seeking for comparisons by which to praise the holy Virgin. Nothing seems too extravagant for them, and they often finish by lamenting their inability to do justice to their object : ' Though her praises are heaped up without end, they do not attain the measure of the truth, or even draw remotely near to it ; for her beauty infinitely transcends all speech and thought' (Germanus of Constantinople ; PG 98:294).

This new tone, discernible in St Sophronius of Jerusalem (d. 638), reached its full vigour during the 8th cent. with St Andrew, Bishop of Crete (d. 740), St Germanus, Patriarch of Constantinople (d. c. 733), John, Bishop of Euboea (d. c. 750) and St John of Damascus (d. 749). The intentions of their exuberant rhetoric, which is more inclined to glorify Mary's holiness than to define it, cannot be reduced to a doctrinal summary, but must be illustrated by examples.

Very often Mary's holiness is touched upon in connection with her motherhood, her predestination or her virginity. The first case is represented in this line from Sophronius : ' By the splendour of your purity ($\kappa\alpha\theta\alpha\rho\acute{o}\tau\eta\varsigma$) you have surpassed men, angels and all creation ; for you have received the Creator of all things, you out of all creation have carried Him, have brought Him to birth and as Mother of God have brought Him into the world' (PG 87:3237). Elsewhere, and by others, Mary is called the virginal soil from which the body of the New Adam was formed, the dough from which the Bread of Life was made, the living book in which the Word of God was written by the Holy Spirit, God's new and most agreeable paradise, the Ark of the New Covenant, the Temple, the Sanctuary, the earthly palace of the heavenly King.

Mary is represented from the point of view of predestination as one designated by God for her sublime office, and made suitable for it by His agency. St Germanus has her parents present her in the Temple with the prayer : ' Receive this child whom you have chosen, predestined and sanctified . . . whom you have picked from among our unworthy number like a lily among thorns' (PG 98:299).

Her virginity is seen as typifying the state of her soul. ' She kept her soul virginal like her body' (John of Damascus, PG 94:1160). ' [God the Word] . . . entered the womb, resplendent with virginal holiness, of Mary the holy, radiant and godly-minded virgin, who was free from all stain ($\mu o\lambda\acute{u}\sigma\mu\alpha\tau o\varsigma$) in body, soul and spirit' (Sophronius, PG 87:3160–1).

Some texts speak more directly of her holiness. St Andrew of Crete says she is ' purer than gold or any other sensible substance' (PG 97:1097), she is ' the gate of heaven, elevated above the heavens, queen of the entire human race . . . higher than all things save God alone' (ibid. 1100). St Sophronius : ' Many saints preceded you, but none was filled with grace like you, none was exalted like you, none was purified in advance ($\pi\rho o\kappa\epsilon\kappa\acute{a}\theta\alpha\rho\tau\alpha\iota$) like you, none was flooded with light like you. . . . You surpass all that is most excellent among men, and all that God has given to all' (PG 87:3248).

In sum, the Byzantines of the 8th cent. saw Mary's holiness as flawless, immense, transcending all created holiness and second only to that of God. It lay even beyond the possibility of comparison or comprehension. Further advance in this line of thought was not possible.

In the Latin Church, where the decision of Ephesus had attracted less attention, the note of fervent acclaim so characteristic of the Byzantine homilies is not heard until much later. The history of Marian thought in the Dark Ages is not well known yet, but it seems clear that for many centuries after Augustine the declarations of Mary's holiness continue to be brief and moderate. In the 8th cent. the note strengthens, perhaps influenced by Byzantine thought, which then was in its full maturity. Paul Warnfridus, the Deacon from Lombardy (c. 720–c. 800), proclaimed that 'in the praise that she deserves, this most holy Virgin transcends the measure of human speech' (PL 95:1566). Two generations later a Frankish monk, St Paschasius Radbertus (c. 785–c. 860), is speaking in similar tones and at much greater length, to such a point that his veneration for Mary can be compared to that of the great Eastern writers. But not until the 12th cent. did Latin thought reach this level on a wide scale. Then, however, it made up for lost time, in homilies, hymns and finally a new literary genus, the *de laudibus beatae Mariae Virginis*, which flourished in the late 12th and 13th cents.

But the most significant work of the Latins consisted in the effort of scholastic theologians to formulate in precise and objective language the truth which inspired the enthusiasm of preachers and poets. Thus, St Anselm (c. 1033–1109) declared, in lines that were to become classic : ' It was fitting that she be clothed with a purity so splendid that none greater under God could be conceived' (*de conceptu virginali* 18 ; edited by Schmitt 2:159). In the next century John of La Rochelle OFM enunciated (c. 1238) the principle (to which however he did not commit himself) : ' Whatever good could be conferred on Mary was in fact conferred on her' (in Alexander of Hales, *Summa theologica* [1948] 4:112a). St Bonaventure (1221–74) revised his *confrère's* principle to say more cautiously : ' It is fitting to suppose that God gave to (Mary's) soul whatever it was fitting for her to receive' (in *III Sent.* 3:1:1:2 obj. 6 ; Quaracchi ed. 3:66a ; cf. 61a). The Dominicans were still more cautious. St Albert (c. 1200–80) : ' Holiness was received into (Mary) more than anyone else ; for she drew so near to Holiness itself that the (flesh) which was to be united to God was taken from her' (in *III Sent.* 3 ; Borgnet edition 28:51 b). This was reformulated by St Thomas (c. 1225–74) to read : ' Being the closest of all to Christ, the source of grace, Mary received a greater " fullness of grace " than anyone else' (*Summa* 3a:27:5c).

But those who affirmed Mary's holiness in a global way did not necessarily intend to declare her exempt from the law of Original sin. The latter point simply did not occur to the earlier theologians, and it would be quite illegitimate to seize on a general statement about Mary's perfect holiness and, by applying a mechanical logic to it, deduce that the author implicitly affirmed the Immaculate Conception. Many who spoke strongly on the former theme hesitated when the latter point was posed specifically. Hence we must make a special inquiry into the ideas on this precise point.

III The Legend of Anne and Joachim ; the Conception Feast. The earliest glimmering of the idea of Mary's Immaculate Conception is perhaps to be seen in an ancient Christian legend, which names Mary's parents as Joachim and Anne, devout Jews who were afflicted at having no children. In answer to their prayers Mary is born, after having been duly announced by an angel. The story was included in an apocryphal gospel of the 2nd cent., misnamed *The ' Proto-Evangel' of St James*.

This naïve account of marvels giving lustre to Mary's early life displays a remarkable sense of the holiness befitting her from whom Jesus would be born. It is manifested in a kind of mythical fashion by the separation of her person from all profane contact. At birth she is placed in a ' sanctuary' arranged by her mother in her room. From there she passes to the Temple, without ever having set foot on the earth. The Holy Spirit dwells in her, and even her food is brought by an angel, who thus safeguards her from any dietary ' impurity' (cf. Laurentin).

The original form of the story seems to have supposed (without, however, making an issue of the point) that Mary's conception was not only miraculous but virginal. This too is perhaps inspired by the intention of preserving her from any stain, and can thus be regarded as a primitive approximation of the Immaculate Conception (although one must not exaggerate its precision by attributing to the 2nd-cent. narrator a conscious linking of Original sin and carnal intercourse, such as was to occur in a later theology).

Out of this legend there originated, somewhere around the year 700, in the Eastern empire, a feast in honour of Mary's conception. It was *not* a feast of the 'Immaculate' Conception ; it merely celebrated her coming into the world. Presumably, it was modelled upon the earlier feast of the conception of John the Baptist (which likewise had been marked by an angelic announcement). While the legend of Anne and Joachim undoubtedly occasioned the feast, the main impulse which brought the latter into existence was the desire to honour the holy Virgin. The liturgy and homilies for this day, although they did not hesitate to borrow from the apocryphal narratives, gave chief attention to what was in reality the substance of the event, the coming into existence of the future Mother of God. And although the story of Anne and Joachim is presumably the creation of imagination, it should not be dismissed as senseless fantasy. It represents a tentative phase in the growth of Christian thought about Mary, expressing, in the imaginary form which alone was available to simple minds, an authentic, if still unrefined, sense of her holiness, which, it was felt, had to go back to the very beginning of her existence.

Further, the necessity of providing Scripture readings, homilies and chants for this feast obliged men to reflect seriously on its meaning. Naturally, they were led to speak of the holiness of the infant just conceived ; hence these writings witness to Byzantine thought about Mary's relation to Original sin. They continue, however, to be quite vague on the point, as minds were evidently not yet preoccupied with it. Often the liturgical compositions for the Nativity and Dormition of Mary are more significant on this point than those for the Conception feast.

IV The Byzantine ideas about Mary's relation to Original sin are difficult to assess because they were never expounded directly and precisely. There were many theologians, especially in the earlier period, to whom it did not even occur to raise the question. In the case of others, who strongly emphasised Mary's perfect holiness and sinlessness, it may be that her preservation from Original sin was taken for granted as so obviously included in the total picture of her sanctity that special mention of it seemed unnecessary. The doctrine of Original sin never received, in the Greek world, the intent consideration that it got from the Latins, where the Pelagian heresy drove the genius of St Augustine to fix attention upon it. (However, it would be erroneous to suppose, as many have, misled by Petau, that the Greeks were unaware of the doctrine of Original sin. Jugie has given ample evidence to the contrary in *L'Immaculée Conception . . .*, 25 ff.).

On the other hand, it may also be that the Greek Fathers avoided a precise declaration of Mary's freedom from Original sin because they were simply uncertain about this point. That her holiness contrasted with the general sinfulness of the human race, they were sure ; that it was incomparably great, to the point of being indescribable, many of them avowed ; but whether she had been like this from the very beginning, or whether she had had to be converted from an initial state of sin to the state of holiness by the action of divine grace, perhaps they would have hesitated to say.

Ordinarily, a Byzantine orator's views regarding the Immaculate Conception cannot be determined by one crucial text, but only by a convergence of indications. This makes brief surveys of a period difficult and misleading. One can better perceive the tone of Byzantine thought on Mary's sinlessness by examining in comparative detail the declarations of St Andrew of Crete (d. 740). He is perhaps the first for whom a solid case can be made that he exempted Mary from Original sin ; but he was surpassed by few, if any, of those who followed him. When all his relevant statements are compared, they seem to presuppose an immaculist doctrine, which, moreover, rises so near to the surface of his thought that it seems imminently on the point of breaking out into a clear declaration.

When speaking of Mary as the dough from which Christ, our bread, is formed, he says that this dough was unaffected by the leaven which fermented the whole mass (PG 97:812). He calls her ' the perfect reproduction (πανόμοιον . . . ἴνδαλμα) of the original beauty (of mankind)' (ibid. 1068), a matter (ὕλη) suitable for the incarnation of God, a divinely perfect clay used by the maker of all things, who is a perfect artisan, ' the only pure one' (μόνη ἄγνη, ibid. 1309), 'the only one who is

perfectly blameless' (μόνην πανάμωμον, ibid. 1308). He applies to her Cant. 4:7, which was to become classic in this matter in the West : ' Thou art beautiful, my beloved, and there is no stain in thee' (1097). Finally, there is an almost inescapable implication in his homilies on the Dormition. The fact that she underwent death, which is a punishment for sin, is there explained, not by any reference to sin, but by her conformity to the laws of nature, which Divine Providence had fixed, and to the lot of her Son (PG 97:1053 and 1081).

Of special interest are the terms in which Mary is called immaculate by Andrew and his contemporaries. Besides ἄχραντος (undefiled) which had already been used by St Epiphanius (315–403), they call her καθαρά (clean, pure), ἄγνη (pure, chaste), ἄσπιλος (unstained), ἀμόλυντος (unstained), ἀνέμπαφος (untouched), ἀχήρατος (integral) and ἄμωμος (blameless). They also used intensive compounds such as πανάμωμος (lit.'utterly blameless') and ὑπεράμωμος (lit. ' exceedingly blameless ') ; and this list is doubtless incomplete. Such appellations were based first of all on Mary's virginity ; but it is evident that they were understood to connote a spiritual integrity also. In a strict sense, they would have implied complete preservation from sin ; but how strictly they were intended is always difficult to measure.

What we have compiled from Andrew could be matched, more or less, in others, such as St Germanus of Constantinople (d. 733) or St John of Damascus (d. 749). One may hesitate about how firmly and strictly to take their assertions, but it cannot be denied that their thought inclined favourably in the direction of the Immaculate Conception, and that it had advanced so far by the 8th cent. that at most only another step was needed to reach it. From a different point of view, this doctrine harmonises so perfectly with their teaching that it appears to do no more than express the presupposition which underlay their declarations and gave them coherence and explanation.

From the 9th to the 15th cent. no substantial progress has been noted in the Byzantine portrait of the Mother of God (Jugie, *L'Immaculée Conception . . .*, 163). The East would have to pay a price for this failure to achieve a firmer expression of its belief. Beginning in the 16th cent., there occur Orthodox theologians who deny Mary's exemption from Original sin. By the 19th cent. the ancient Byzantine doctrine of Mary's perfect holiness had been forgotten, and Pius IX's definition of the Immaculate Conception was assailed in Russia and the East as an invention of Rome.

V Express formulation of the question, whether Mary had been exempted from Original sin, did not occur until the Latin Middle Ages, when the idea of Mary's perfect holiness encountered the doctrine of the universality of Original sin. Whereas the East had taken the lead in the appreciation of Mary's eminent holiness, the West had been more conscious of the ' law of sin ', due mainly to the influence of St Augustine. Confrontation of the ' Eastern ' and ' Western ' doctrines resulted in a conflict, out of which the hitherto latent doctrine of the Immaculate Conception finally issued forth into clear light.

At the beginning of the 5th cent., the doctrine that all men had become sinners through the sin of Adam, a doctrine which the Church had received from St Paul (especially Rom 5), had been obscured by the self-confident asceticism of Pelagius. St Augustine responded triumphantly in defence of the tradition. In his pioneering efforts at explanation, he tended unfortunately to make Original sin more or less equivalent to concupiscence—an identification that was sorely to pain early scholastic theology, which, moreover, failed to take note of the tentative and qualified tone of Augustine's assertions. In any event, Augustine impressed unforgettably upon the Latin Church the doctrine that sin is really inherited by *all* Adam's natural descendants. He made no exception for the Virgin Mary. True, he practically never relates the topic to her ; but, when challenged by Julian of Eclanum on the case of Mary, he seems to have maintained (reluctantly, it seems, in a laconic but involved sentence that is not very clear : *Opus imperfectum contra Julianum* 4:122 ; PL 45:1419) that Mary needed to be ' born again ' like all others.

Later writers of the Augustinian school likewise make no effort to exempt Mary from the universal law of Original sin. During the seven hundred years between Augustine and St Bernard, there seems to have been at most only a single voice that made an exception for Mary, and even this one case is quite uncertain. The actual text of *De partu Virginis*, by St Paschasius Radbertus (*c.* 785–*c.* 860 ; see above, II), declares : ' She did not contract Original sin, being sanctified in the womb of her mother ' (PL 120:1371). There is no evidence that this passage had any subsequent influence. If authentic (which is quite doubtful), it would be significant mainly as a sign of a natural tendency in Catholic thought about Mary to come to the idea of the Immaculate Conception.

Generally, however, the theologians of the Dark Ages seem to have assumed that Mary was, in respect to Original sin, no different from anyone else. Not that there was any positive tradition of her initial sinfulness ; it simply occurred to no one to make an exception for her from the law of sin which was, of itself, universal. Hence even St Anselm, who had so exalted Mary's purity, found it a problem to explain how Christ's humanity could be sinless, since His Mother had been born with Original sin (*Cur Deus homo* II:16 ; Schmitt edition II:116). It was this problem, in fact, that gave rise to the treatise on the Blessed Virgin in the early scholastic *summae* (which otherwise had almost nothing to say of her).

The answer given to this problem throughout the 12th cent. started from a datum of the patristic tradition, that a purification was wrought in Mary at the moment of the Incarnation (cf. e.g., St Leo I in PL 54:196). St Anselm explained Mary's purification by her faith in the coming Saviour (*Cur Deus homo*, loc. cit.). Later on, however, in developing his theory of Original sin, Anselm would propose a different answer, based on the virgin birth ; cf. *de*

conceptu virginali II:11, 12, 18, 19). Anselm's contemporaries, on the other hand, more commonly taught that the flesh which Mary transmitted to her Son was cleansed from sin either by the action of the Holy Spirit, or by the contact of Christ's own divinity, in the Incarnation. It was out of this unpromising beginning that the doctrine of the Immaculate Conception was to evolve.

The first step came when the *Summa sententiarum* (before 1141) made the point, which was accepted without challenge, that not only the flesh assumed by Christ, but Mary's entire person, were purified at that moment (PL 176:73). The same work added, however, the significant reservation that the '*fomes peccati*', or proneness to sin left in man by Original sin, was not taken away from Mary by this purification. About 1170 Peter of Poitiers retorted that all power to sin was purified out of Mary at the Incarnation. Moreover, he proceeds to take the portentous step of speaking about a previous purification, which had taken place before her birth, cleansing her of Original sin itself (*IV Sent.* 7 ; PL 211:1165).

The notion that Mary had been purified of Original sin before her birth had apparently become a commonplace of pious literature (cf. *Virgo Immac.* 5, p. 34). Its background was the belief, which goes back at least to St Ambrose (*in Lucam* 2:23 ; CSEL 32:53), that John the Baptist was sanctified by the Holy Spirit at the moment when, as an infant in the womb, he ' leaped ' at the sound of Mary's voice (Lk 1:44 ; cf. 1:15). A similar sanctification came to be postulated for Jeremias on the basis of Jer 1:5. Since it was granted that Mary surpassed these two saints in holiness, it was supposed that the privilege thus given to them would not have been denied to her.

The idea that Mary had undergone two purifications or sanctifications, one before her birth and the other at the Annunciation, provided the framework in which scholastic discussions of Mary's holiness were to be carried on until the time of Duns Scotus. And very soon after the framework had been set up, the question was raised whether Mary's first sanctification should not be pushed back still further, to the very beginning of her existence, so as to exclude Original sin from her altogether. This question did not arise spontaneously out of the scholastic discussions, but was forced into them by the appearance of the controversial feast of Mary's Conception. For the Eastern feast had somehow been transplanted to England during the 11th cent. (very likely through the intermediary of the Normans, who since 1016 were in contact with southern Italy, where the feast was celebrated by people of Greek descent). From England it spread to Normandy, and then throughout France, into Spain, Italy, Germany and Belgium before the end of the 12th cent. (Le Bachelet, col. 1033).

From the beginning this new feast provoked opposition. The Norman rulers of England suppressed it for a while in the course of a general reform of the English Church after the Conquest of

1066. But the classic attack on the feast came from St Bernard, in a letter (1139/1140) to the cathedral canons of Lyons, who had recently adopted the feast. Bernard protests that the latter 'is neither known to the liturgy of the Church, nor approved by reason, nor recommended by any ancient tradition' (*Letter 174*; PL 182:333). It was the legitimacy of this new feast, rather than the question of Mary's relation to Original sin, that was the focal point of attention, and would remain so for a long time. Nevertheless, the doctrinal issue inevitably emerged, already in Bernard's letter. He admits that it is reasonable to suppose that Mary was sanctified before birth, but not that her conception itself was holy : ' Are you going to say that in the marital embrace itself, holiness mingled with the conception, so that (Mary) was conceived and sanctified simultaneously ? Reason will not admit this ; for how can there be holiness without the Holy Spirit ? Or how can the Holy Spirit be associated with sin ? Or how can sin have been absent where *libido* was present ? ' (ibid. 335).

Opposition made it necessary for the promoters of the feast to formulate the reasons in its favour ; so it was that Mary's preservation from Original sin came to be declared explicitly and indubitably for the first time. The finest, and one of the earliest, of such assertions was composed by the English monk Eadmer, who had been secretary to St Anselm. Geenen conjectures that it was written about the same time as St Bernard's letter (1139–40 ; *see Virgo Immaculata* 5, p. 91). The burden of this charming *plaidoyer* is that God was well able to preserve Mary from the sin involved in conception if He willed to do so, and that He did in fact so will. The grounds for His willing it are that Mary had been made the ' repository ' (*reclinatorium*) of the divinity, the ' propitiatory ' for the whole world (i.e. the holy place where sins are forgiven) and the queen of the universe (including the angels, some of whom had been preserved from all sin).

These early discussions were written in function of vague and confused notions, which varied moreover from one author to another, about the nature of Original sin, and of conception itself. Most, but not all, supposed that in the conception of a child, only the body is formed at first, while the soul is infused forty or eighty days later. Nearly all agreed that Original sin was transmitted from parents to children through the body, the soul being infected by its union with the body. Some were so crude as to imagine Original sin as a quality inhering in the body itself. Following a suggestion of St Augustine (cf. e.g., *De peccatorum meritis* 2:11 ; CSEL 60:82), it was frequently supposed that the sinful condition of the offspring was brought about, at least in part, by sinful passion of the parents in their intercourse. Hence the question on which the discussion of Mary's conception often focussed, whether it was possible for sin to be kept out of the conception of a child, embraced at once, in a confused fashion, both the supposedly sinful act of the parents and the sinful state of the offspring. (An example of

this confusion can be seen in St Bernard's text, above.)

VI Scholastic Theology. The confusion and crudity began to dissipate when the argument about celebrating the feast, which had been carried on mainly by preachers and contemplatives, was taken over by the scholastic theologians and transmuted into the theological question about Mary's initial sanctification. As early as the beginning of the 13th cent. (between 1200 and 1206), the question of celebrating the feast was introduced into a scholastic commentary on the *Sentences* by Stephen Langton (text in *Beiträge zur Geschichte der Philosophie und Theologie des Mittelalters* 37:1:106). About 1230, Robert Grosseteste asked whether Mary may not have been sanctified ' in the very infusion of her rational soul' (text in Bonnefoy, *Le Vénérable . . .*, 15). He left the question open.

But it was the Paris Franciscans of the 1240s who first investigated Mary's sanctification in a profound and thorough manner (Alexander of Hales OFM, *Summa theologica*, Quarracchi edition, Pars 3, inq. 1, tr. 2, mem. 2–3 ; vol. 4:111–26). By exploiting St Anselm's theory of Original sin, which had been little noticed during the 12th cent., they freed the discussion from the misleading assumptions of the earlier authors. Anselm had insisted that there can be no sin in a foetus not yet animated by a rational soul, because sin is essentially a lack of due justice in the will. He thought, however, that Original sin can be transmitted by means of the parental *semen* ; the sin involves a corruption of human nature, which, engendering persons by its reproductive powers, causes them also to be corrupt (*De conceptu virginali* 2–4, 7, 8, 10, 23, 27).

Except for Grosseteste, all the scholastics until almost the end of the century rejected the thesis that Mary had been exempt from Original sin. (It must be remembered, however, that scholastic theology was not yet very widespread, being concentrated chiefly in Paris.) St Bernard's authority is cited ; but his reasoning—that conception is a process so sinful that it must have a sinful result—tended to be abandoned in the measure that the Anselmian theology prevailed. Many different arguments were given against Mary's preservation from Original sin ; the critical issue, however, was brought to the fore by St Thomas.

That Mary had been sanctified even before her birth ' can reasonably be argued ', he grants (*Summa* 3a:27:1c). This would have occurred presumably soon after the infusion of her soul (*cito post conceptionem et animae infusionem* : *Quodlibet* 6:5:1), although the exact moment is not known (*Summa* 3a:27:2:@3). But St Thomas will not admit that Mary was completely preserved from Original sin. In all five works in which he discusses the matter, from the beginning to the end of his career, he maintains that Mary contracted Original sin (*III Sent.* 3:1:2 ; *Quodlibet* 6:5:1 ; *Summa* 3a:27 ; *Compendium theologiae* 224 ; *Expositio super salutationem angelicam*). Even the *fomes* which results from sin remained in Mary until Christ, descending into her at the

Incarnation, eliminated it ; although God had never allowed it to lead her into the least sin (*Summa* 3a:27:3c).

The principal reason on which St Thomas bases his position is that, ' if she had been conceived without Original sin, she would not have needed to be redeemed by Christ. Thus He would not be the universal Redeemer of men' (*Compendium* 224). But that Christ is the 'Saviour of all men' is a doctrine of Scripture (1 Tim 4:10 ; cf. *Summa* 3a:27:2c). For St Thomas, the decisive consideration was the doctrine of faith that all men need to be redeemed by Christ from the sinful condition infecting the human race. It did not occur to him, or to anyone else yet (except perhaps Grosseteste), that redemption from sin could take the form of complete preservation from it.

The profoundest and most reliable interpreters of St Thomas, Cajetan (*c.* 1511) and John of St Thomas (soon after 1631), agree that his principles do not require that Mary contracted sin in actual fact, but only that there was in her, by reason of her descent from Adam, a kind of 'necessity' of contracting it, so far as this depended on her. Correspondingly, they maintain that Mary's sanctification was said to occur 'after animation' in the order of *nature*, but not necessarily in the order of time. For while, in the *Sentences*, St Thomas specified that it would not have accorded with the plan of Redemption for Mary to be sanctified 'in the very instant of the infusion of her soul' (art. 1, sol. 2), afterwards he avoided this specification, and confined himself to saying, 'not before animation, therefore after it', which makes good logic only in terms of the order of nature. Nevertheless it is clear that St Thomas himself did suppose that Mary had been subject to Original sin in actual fact, for he says that she 'contracted' it (*Summa* 3a:27:2:@2), was soiled (*inquinata*) by it (ibid.), incurred its stain (*macula* : ibid. c). The texts adduced by del Prado to prove that St Thomas taught the Immaculate Conception are in some cases inauthentic, in others irrelevant (they refer to Mary's sinlessness after having been purified).

VII Triumph of the Belief. Despite theological objections the Conception feast continued to gain in popularity, and towards the end of the 13th cent. theoretical defenders of Mary's sinless conception reappeared : Raymon Lull (even before 1280, but especially at Paris in 1298) and William of Ware (before 1300). Ecclesiastical patronage was given to the belief (1295-1300) by St Peter Paschasius, archbishop of Granada. But it was Duns Scotus, an Oxford Franciscan, who successfully answered the crucial objection, and turned the tide of theological opinion in favour of the Immaculate Conception.

Scotus maintains that preservation from Original sin would have made Mary not less but more dependent on Christ as her Redeemer, since it is through Him that it would have to have been brought about (*Opus Oxon.* 3:3:1, ' *ad rationes opinionis affirmativae*' ; Balic, *Elementa . . .*, 35). Furthermore, Scotus turns the objection into an argument favourable to the privilege, pointing out that complete preservation from sin would be the most perfect possible work of mediation, which is to be expected of Christ, the most perfect Mediator (ibid., 22).

Scotus did not claim to have demonstrated the *fact* of the Immaculate Conception, but only that it was a possibility. But it was definitely his personal opinion : 'Which of these . . . possibilities actually occurred, God knows ; but to me it seems right (*probabile*) to attribute to Mary that which is finer (*excellentius*), if it is not opposed to the authority of the Church or Scripture' (ibid., 31). In effect, however, Scotus himself had shown that the doctrine was *not* opposed to the teaching of the Church or of Scripture, because it did not offend against the universality of the Redemption.

This was enough to decide the case. Scotus's position would be controverted soon after his death (1308) and on into the 17th cent., but it gained ground ineluctably. The great mass of the faithful, without understanding all the theological implications involved, were drawn instinctively toward the doctrine that exempted Mary from all stain, once they knew it was allowable to hold it. For theologians the way was more difficult, for it was not easy to find a decisive reason for an opinion that seemed to be supported more by pious instincts than by any clear article of the Faith. Since, moreover, one party felt that the honour of the Mother of God was at stake, while the other feared for the purity of the Faith, it is understandable that their controversy became perhaps the most bitter that has ever gone on among Catholic theologians.

The chief fruit of this controversy was a greater precision in the understanding of the implications and conditions of Mary's privilege. A major question that is still unresolved, however, was raised about Mary's relation to the sin from which she was preserved. The earliest proponents of the Immaculate Conception, including Scotus in particular, reconciled this doctrine with the Redemption by declaring that Mary, 'for having been begotten from Adam in the usual way, would have contracted Original sin if she had not been prevented by the grace of the Mediator' (Scotus, *Op. Oxon.* 3:3:1, 'ad rationes opinionis affirmativae' ; Balic, *Elementa*, 35). This view, often reformulated in the terms, 'Mary ought to have contracted . . .', came to be designated awkwardly by the term *debt of sin* (*debitum peccati*), and was unfortunately identified by Cajetan, *De conceptu Virginis* (1515), with the notion of an 'infected flesh' in Mary. Since the 16th and 17th cents., the theory of a 'debt of sin' in Mary, despite the patronage of Duns Scotus, has ironically been rejected by nearly all Scotists, and adopted by nearly all Thomists (although the latter have separated it from any implication of an actual defect in Christ's Mother). The Church was cautious and gradual in taking a position regarding the belief, as can be seen by the earliest official pronouncements on the subject, issued by Sixtus IV (D 734), Trent (D 792), Pius V (D 1073) and Alexander VII (D 1100).

At the beginning of the 19th cent., veneration of Mary, conceived without sin, was still growing in ardour, and opposition to the belief had almost disappeared. This very fact was a convincing sign that the 'pious belief' was in fact integral to the Catholic Faith. So judged Pope Pius IX, who on 8 December 1854, solemnly defined that '. . . the doctrine which holds that the most Blessed Virgin Mary was preserved from all stain of Original sin in the first instant of her Conception, by a singular grace and privilege of Almighty God, in consideration of the merits of Jesus Christ, Saviour of the human race, has been revealed by God and must, therefore, be believed firmly and constantly by all the faithful' (D 1641).

VIII The theological justification of this doctrine is not easy to establish or even to formulate. Mary's preservation from Original sin is not explicitly stated in Scripture, but is contained only implicitly in the Scriptural image of Mary, viewed against the background of the great Christian doctrines on sin, grace, holiness, etc. Moreover, the derivation of the Immaculate Conception from these other truths cannot be demonstrated by any simple rational argument. Historically, it was not by conscious logical deduction that this doctrine was first attained. The crucial argument of Scotus which led to the acceptance of the belief was not a positive 'demonstration', but the solution of an objection. The positive force producing assent resided in the conviction, already settled in Christian thought long before Scotus, that Mary should be regarded as being as holy as the Faith allows (if this vague expression may be used to designate a conviction that was vague enough to defy precise formulation). The work of Scotus consisted in removing the barrier that restrained many from attributing flawless holiness to Mary : namely, the fear of infringing upon the doctrine of the Redemption.

The basic conviction itself seems to have been engendered mainly out of the demands of Christian piety. This, however, does not make it a kind of devout 'wishful thinking'. When the Gospel message has been incarnated in the lives of the faithful, its hidden implications begin to make themselves felt in the form of inclinations which may be experienced before the reason behind them is adverted to. Especially in the case of very delicate implications, or those which depend on a complex set of 'premisses,' Christian piety is likely to have quicker and surer perceptions than the reasoning of theologians.

These inclinations involve genuine knowledge, but of a type that is confused and obscure. Hence it becomes conscious only with difficulty, and grows in clarity and firmness slowly and hesitantly. That is why the Church's sense of Mary's holiness required time and the combined reflections of many thinkers, first to make itself felt, then to mature unto its full strength, and finally to manifest its precise meaning. This also explains why the objections encountered by the doctrine of the Immaculate Conception in the scholastic period constituted a normal phase in the process of clarification of a truth imperfectly grasped. They are likewise significant as proving that the doctrine did not conquer the Church on a wave of uncritical enthusiasm, but only after a searching scrutiny had given assurance of its inner coherence with the more basic Christian doctrines.

But the Immaculate Conception is held to be not merely compatible with the Faith, but an integral part of it ; hence there is need to make clear the hidden reasoning which underlay and authenticated the instinct of Christian piety which led to the belief. This reasoning, however, cannot be set forth adequately in a syllogistic construction. Attempts to fashion such a 'demonstration' of the Immaculate Conception based on Scripture have in the past produced many abusive interpretations of the sacred texts (especially Gen 3:15, Cant 4:7 and Lk 1:28, although there is indeed a valid sense in which each of these can be invoked).

Belief in the Immaculate Conception is not a conclusion from a single line of reasoning but arises from the convergence of several considerations. These depend in some cases on delicate undertones of the Biblical portrait of Mary, which in their turn depend on the most fundamental notions, values and outlooks of the Christian faith. Thus, the meaning one sees in the dialogue between Mary and Gabriel cannot be unaffected by the circumstance that one has a Catholic or Lutheran or Pelagian conception of grace, holiness and the relation of God's initiative to man's actuality. Likewise one's personal response to the values in question, including his piety, cannot fail to affect the rectitude and sensitivity of his perceptions in this delicate matter. As a consequence, all that can be done by way of argument for the truth of the Immaculate Conception is to point out, and in some measure clarify, the chief considerations on which the belief seems objectively to be based, and on which anyone wishing to make an appraisal will need to reflect lengthily for himself.

The indispensable background is the paradoxical Biblical doctrine on grace : that man's moral rectitude is, on the one hand, a free correspondence to the demands of God, and on the other hand, God's work in the human soul. Hence, there is a perspective in which it can be asked whether an individual has accomplished God's will for him ; and there is another in which it can be said that he is precisely as good and holy as God wills him to be.

Approaching the case of Mary in the first perspective, we must note that God required holiness of the people chosen to be His. The OT visualized this holiness as an external cleanliness and separation from whatever could 'defile', e.g. 'unclean' food, contact with gentiles, etc. But this external cleanliness and separation was only a symbol of interior freedom from all that defiles the soul, as is brought out most appositely in 2 Cor 6:14–7:1 (cf. Mt. 15:1–20 ; Mk. 7:1–23). The requirement of sinlessness on the part of those brought into close association with God would apply with special urgency in the case of Mary, called to the intimacy with God

Incarnate that a mother has with her child ; for this is not a mere physical proximity but a profoundly personal relationship.

But did Mary actually correspond to this high exigency ? The portrait of her given in Lk 1–2 is that of one who responded faultlessly to the divine word brought by Gabriel. In contrast, moreover, to the prophet who was stricken with the sense of his own sin by the vision of the Lord (Is 6), Mary is addressed with unprecedented reverence as one on whom God's favour has been lavished. To this is added the assurance that she ' has found favour with God ' (Lk 1:28, 30). To realise the import of this portrait and these solemn praises, one must keep in mind, first, that they occur in the context of that solemn moment when, through the Virgin's intermediary, God fulfils (and surpasses) His ancient promises to visit and dwell with His people ; second, that the Scriptural writers usually represent a truth in a concrete illustration rather than by declaring it abstractly.

All these indications favour the supposition that Mary's sanctity was flawless ; but they would remain perhaps indecisive without some sign that it was (in the second of the perspectives noted above) God's determined will to make her so. This sign Christian instinct has seen in Mary's virginity, itself a kind of physical holiness, and a symbol of a profounder holiness of spirit. For God, who preserved her virginity by a miracle, values the soul's integrity above that of the body.

The considerations here adduced have their proper force, not when assembled in the mode of an argument, but only when they express exigencies experienced by an integral Christian mind. The subjectivity inherent in such a mode of knowledge makes one hesitate about the certitude of an implication he seems to perceive. In fact, it is not for the individual believer, but for the teaching office in the Church, to certify that a given doctrine pertains to the sacred truth that has been entrusted to the Church's custody. The definition of Pius IX was needed therefore to give this belief a certitude it would not have had by its inherent evidence.

Bibliography. General surveys : *The Dogma of the Immaculate Conception*, edited by the present writer (1958), has articles by specialists on the major topics ; M. Jugie and F. Le Bachelet, in DTC (s.v.) provide a historical survey, now superseded in many details ; T. Harper SJ, *The Immaculate Conception* (1919). Collections of material : *Pareri dell'episcopato cattolico* (1851–4) 11 vols ; A. de Roskovany, *B. V. Maria immaculata* (1873–81) 9 vols ; C. Balic OFM, *Virgo Immaculata* (1955–8) 18 vols ; the same, *Bibliotheca Immaculatae Conceptionis* (from 1950, in progress) ; articles that appeared on the centenary of the definition in 1954 are listed in the bibliographies of ETL 30–32 (1954–6) and in two chronicles by R. Laurentin in *La Vie spirituelle, supplément* 8 (1955) 453–81 and *La Vie spirituelle* 101 (1959) 538–63 ; also in G. Besutti, *Bibliographia mariana* III (1952–7). On Scripture : G. Bonnetain in DBV(S) s.v. ' Immaculée Conception ' ; A. Peinador, ' Las

pruebas de la Escritura ', in *Estudios marianos* XV (1955) 53–77 ; C. Journet, *Esquisse du développement du dogme marial* (1954). On the Fathers : G. Jouassard, in *Maria*, I (edited by H. Du Manoir, 1949) ; W. Burghardt SJ, ' Mary in Western Patristic Thought ', in *Mariology*, I (edited by J. Carol, 1955) ; M. Jugie, *L'Immaculée Conception dans l'Écriture et dans la tradition orientale* (1952) ; I. Ortiz de Urbina and H. Rahner SJ, surveys of Eastern and Western texts in *Katholische Marienkunde* (edited by P. Sträter, 1952) ; L. Scheffczyk, *Das Mariengeheimnis in Frömmigkeit und Lehre der Karolingerzeit* (1959). For the legend of Joachim : E. Amann, *Le Protévangile de Jacques* (1910) ; E. de Stricker SJ, *La Forme la plus ancienne du protévangile de Jacques* (1961). For the origin of the feast : Mgr H. F. Davis, ' Origins of Devotion to the Immaculate Conception ', in DbR 118 (1954) 375–92 ; S. van Dijk, ' Origin of the Latin Feast ', in DbR 118 (1954) 251–67 and 428–42 ; M. Jugie, ' La Fête byzantine de la conception de Sainte Anne ', in *Alma socia Christi* V (1952) 29–40. Medieval works : Eadmer, *Tractatus de conceptione S. Mariae* (critical text by H. Thurston and T. Slater SJ, 1904) ; G. Hinger, translation of Eadmer's treatise (1954) ; A. Burridge, ' L'Immaculée Conception dans la théologie de l'Angleterre médiévale ', in RHE 32 (1936) 570–97 ; Mgr H. F. Davis, ' Theologia Immaculatae Conceptionis apud primos defensores in Anglia ', in *Acta Congressus Mariani* (1954) ; J. Bonnefoy OFM, *Duns Scot, docteur de l'Immaculée Conception* (1960—a work arising out of a bitter controversy in Rome about the role of Scotus in the development of this doctrine) ; C. Balic OFM, *Ioannis Duns Scoti theologiae marianae elementa* (1933) ; J. de Blic SJ, ' Saint Thomas et l'Immaculée Conception ', in *Revue apologétique* 57 (1943) 25–36 ; N. del Prado, *Divus Thomas et bulla : Ineffabilis Deus* (1919). Later developments : on the ' debt of sin ', M. Llamera OP, ' El problema del debito ', in *Estudios marianos* XV (1955) 169–223 ; J. Bonnefoy OFM, ' La negacion del *debitum peccati* en Maria ', in *Verdad y Vita* 12 (1954) 113–71 ; E. Carroll, ' Mary Immaculate in the *magisterium* since 1854 ', in *Carmelus* II (1955) 1–53 ; M. G. des Lauriers, ' L'Immaculée Conception, clé des privilèges de Marie ', in RT 55 (1955) 477–518 ; D. Frénaud, ' La Grace de l'Immaculée Conception ', in *Immaculée Conception*, VIIème *congrès*, Lyon (1955) 221–49 ; O. Casado Fuente, *La Immaculada Concepción en su problematica teológica* (1958) ; *G. Miegge, *The Virgin Mary* (from a Waldensian standpoint, translated 1955) ; *Sir Thomas Kendrick, *St James of Spain* (1960) has a valuable account of the forging of historical evidence that went on in Spain in the 17th cent. in connection with this theological controversy.

              E. O'C.

CONCORDAT This article will deal (I) with the general notion of a concordat, (II) its nature as a practical solution of a problem, (III) its matter, (IV) the underlying theological assumptions, (V) some examples from the past, and (VI) from the present age.

I In general, the term ' concordat ' signifies agreement, but it is normally reserved for agreements made between the Catholic Church and the governments of countries. The agreements concern matters in which both Church and State have a legitimate interest, and their purpose is to safeguard the rights and interests of either party. In actual fact, a concordat is a method adopted by the Church to secure freedom for Catholics to practise their religion and to obtain a civil guarantee for the exercise of certain fundamental rights (*see* CHURCH AND STATE).

Historically, concordats have been made by a national hierarchy with a government. In 1288 the bishops of Portugal concluded such a concordat with King Diniz. A similar agreement was made in 1273 between the bishops of Norway and King Magnus VI, and this was ratified by Gregory X at the 2nd Council of Lyons. The Portuguese hierarchy made a further concordat with King Manuel which was confirmed by Leo X in 1516. More recently, however, all concordats have been made by the Pope.

II Concordats as Practical rather than Theoretical. Concordats reflect the varying relations between the Church and secular Powers. They are impossible with a totalitarian State which looks upon the Church within its dominions as wholly subordinate ; they are unnecessary where there is complete separation of Church and State, as in the U.S.A. They presuppose some mutual recognition, and on the State's part an understanding—if not always an acceptance—of the Church's spiritual character and mission. They are an agreement between two ' perfect ' societies that acknowledge one another's status.

They are not an *ideal* solution. Ideally, the State should accept the special status of the Church, never transgress the limits that the Church lays down as necessary for her work, and protect and support the Church in it. But they are a practical method of dealing with particular difficulties. A concordat is usually a *treaty of peace* rather than an *alliance*. It is made, normally, to put things right after difficulties have occurred or rights been questioned.

III The matter of a concordat may be threefold. In the first place, there are clauses which directly concern the Church's spiritual activity : among them the appointment of bishops by the Holy See, freedom of communication between the bishops and the Holy Father, rights of religious orders and societies, freedom for religious teaching, the recognition of the Catholic religion as that of the State or of the majority of the people.

There are, secondly, clauses affecting temporal interests : the acceptance of the Church and religious orders as juridical personalities, rights of, and perhaps exemptions for, Church properties, State salaries to clergy as compensation for Church property previously confiscated. And finally, there are mixed questions, chief among them education and marriage. Education may be left in the hands of the Church, and civil recognition given to Catholic marriages.

IV Is a concordat a bilateral contract between two equal parties or should it be regarded, on the Church's side, as a concession ? Canonists and jurists have debated this with some energy. Many have argued that the parties are not equal because of the unique character and mission of the Church. The Holy Father, they contend, cannot agree to any limitation of his spiritual jurisdiction nor can one Pope bind his successor who receives the fullness of spiritual power. Consequently, the obligation to maintain the concordat is one of justice on the part of the State, in their opinion, but only of fidelity on that of the Holy Father. As regards the temporal clauses there is no difficulty ; they bind in justice. In practice, however, there is little difference between the two views. The Pope concludes a concordat, accepting certain obligations, and history will show how faithfully the Church has often observed concordats long after the civil Power has given her occasions for complaint and abrogation.

V Some Examples. Concordats were rarely made till the 18th cent. They have arisen out of the special problems of the lay or secular State. Till then there are only six instances : the two most notable being the Concordat of Worms in 1122, which settled the investiture quarrel, and that of 1516 between Leo X and the French king, Francis I, after the long controversy over the Pragmatic Sanction. There were fifteen in the 18th cent. : among them five with Sardinia, two with Spain, one each with Poland, Portugal and the Two Sicilies. There have been many more in the 19th and 20th cents. These have included the 1801 concordat between Napoleon and the Holy See which restored the Church in revolutionary France ; concordats with German States ; and from 1850 onwards eight concordats with States in Latin America which laid, in some cases, a favourable basis for relations between those countries and the Church.

VI In recent years concordats have become a normal procedure, by which the Holy See safeguards the position and rights of Catholics in different countries. A concordat does not of course imply approval of the government in question or of its political system. It is, in the strict sense, an agreement involving the recognition of mutual rights and interests and a presumed willingness, on the State's part, to give tangible expression to that recognition. The two best-known concordats in the last four decades have been that with Germany in 1934 and the concordat annexed to the Lateran Treaty of 1929.

Bibliography. Documentation can be found in I. Lo Grasso, *Ecclesia et Status, fontes selecti* (1952) ; particular concordats may be studied in works on the period, e.g. D. Binchy, *Church and State in Fascist Italy* (1941) ; E. E. Hales, *Napoleon and the Pope* (1961) ; the denunciation of the French concordat by Pius X in February 1906, a crucial instance for modern times, was undertaken in the letter *Vehementer nos*, published in the ASS 39 (1906) 1–16 an unofficial work which preceded the AAS.

J. M.

CONCUPISCENCE in its psychological context signifies the internal tendencies that precede and activate desires, or that accompany and modify acts of the will. In theological usage, concupiscence refers to the inordinate internal movements that are the result of the 'wounding of nature' brought about by Original sin. It includes all—and particularly the sensible—evil tendencies to which mortal man is subject. It will be dealt with here in its (I) pre-Christian significance ; (II) as the subject of theological speculation ; and (III) as the object of moral instruction.

I In Homer concupiscence (*epithumia*) has a neutral meaning—a desire or inner tendency toward some satisfaction. However, as the classic Greek ethic was dedicated to the achievement of moderation in human conduct, the Homeric man felt the need of subjecting his passionate feelings to control, although he attributed their origins to divine influence (*Iliad* 3:139). In agreement with Pythagoras, Democritus describes unchecked sense-desire as folly which interferes with man's peace of mind (*ataraxia*) and destroys his self-possession (*autarchia*). Platonic dualism, ontologically separating the body from the soul, divides the latter into three parts : rational, irascible and concupiscible. Concupiscence is the movement within the two lower parts of the soul that is outside the control of reason (*Republic* IV:435B–442A). For Aristotle concupiscence is an irrational function of the sense (animal) appetite to be distinguished from rational desire lodged in the will (*Nicomachean Ethics* 1102a). The Stoics considered concupiscence as an irrational appetite in the soul, proceeding from a mistaken judgment in favour of a false or apparent good. Together with fear, lust and sadness, concupiscence was one of the four affections which had to be rooted out through the practice of self-control for the achievement of peace of mind (Seneca, *ep.* 116:1). The later Stoics frequently identified concupiscence with lust. The Neoplatonists, pursuing a dualist concept of the soul imprisoned in the body, likewise insisted on ascesis as an annihilation of natural, corporeal tendencies, particularly of sexual desires (Porphyry, *Abstinentia* 4:20). While the Stoics considered legitimate sexual activity justifiable (but not necessary, e.g. Epictetus, *ep.* 3, 127) the Neoplatonists favoured absolute continence (Porphyry, ibid. 1:41). Most influential for patristic thought was the doctrine common to Hellenistic religious circles which postulated a threefold division in man's nature. Between the flesh (*sarx*) and the spirit (*pneuma*) intervened the *psyche* (volitional faculty) which, while satisfying man's necessary corporeal desires, had to free man's spirit from inordinate appetites or concupiscence.

In the OT, man is considered as a simple unity, hence his evil-doing was blamed upon an evil heart (*cor malignum*) rebelling against God's law. Later Jewish thought describes concupiscence as an internal movement whence arises disobedience to God's will. The Rabbinic literature speaks of the *jeser hara* (internal evil movements) which can be overcome only by God's help. Despite the account of the fall (Gen 3:7–11), no speculation on the connection between concupiscence and Original sin is to be found in the OT. Philo (*fl. c.* A.D. 40), in an amalgam of Greek dualism, the Stoic four affections, and Rabbinic thought, traces concupiscence to unreasonable desires which can be brought under control by ascesis aided by man's contemplation of God's Law.

II The theological consideration of concupiscence has its foundation in doctrines concerning Original sin and the temptational powers of the devil known through revelation. The first approaches to this aspect of concupiscence are to be found in the apocryphal literature. In the Qumran texts, besides an insistence on the influence of evil spirits, a connection is made between the body (*basar*) and sinfulness (*awel*). The older Jewish Apocrypha trace man's moral corruption to the union of the sons of God (Gen 6:1–6), and later the demons (*Book of Henoch*, 6–9), with the daughters of men,[1] while the later Apocrypha speak of an hereditary moral weakness that has its origin in (*a*) an evil heart which is accompanied by a physical weakness implanted in Eve by the devil (*Apocalypse of Moses*), (*b*) a carnally centred concupiscence (*Apocalypse of Baruch* II) and (*c*) an inclination to evil that pre-existed the fall (*IV Esdras*).[2]

In St Paul concupiscence is viewed in relation to man's salvation history (Rom 5:12–21). It is an inner movement, resulting from the effects of Adam's sin ; but it is not identical with Original sin. Paul contrasts *sarx* (flesh) and *pneuma* (spirit) (Rom 7:4–6), but does not mean simply a war between the flesh and the spirit (Gal 5:17). *Sarx* for Paul is the godless, unredeemed state of man in contrast to the man who is spiritual, that is, redeemed in Christ from the powers of Satan (Gal 5:19–25). Concupiscence is present even in those regenerated through sanctifying grace ; it is experienced as a lack, a potential source of sin connected with man's moral and religious relationships (Rom 6:6 ; 7:3). It has an intimate bearing on death (Rom 8:6). Finally, Paul stresses the 'Powers of evil' which utilize the tendency of the flesh toward sin (Gal 5:16–20 ; Eph 2:3), and puts the blame for sinfulness not so much on carnal infirmities as upon the rejection of God through the acceptance of the lawless realm of evil (anomia : Rom 5:19 ; 7:25). In Jas, concupiscence is the source of temptation (4:1–3), which destroys the love of God and leads to death (1:12–15) ; and in 1 Pet there is a reference to carnal desires which war against the soul. In 1 Jn the things of the world constitute the concupiscence of the flesh, of the eyes and the pride of life which, militating against the divine will, annihilate man's love of God (2:1–17).

A true attempt to analyse the nature of concupiscence is made by Irenaeus who retains the Platonic dualism in its popular Greek formulation of spirit (*pneuma*), soul (*psyche*) and body (*plasma*), with the opposition between the appeal of the divine Word (*Logos*) through revelation, and earthly attractions.

[1] Cf. J. Daniélou, 'Démons' in *D. Sp.* III (1955) 154–8.
[2] J.-B. Frey, 'L'État originel et la Chute de l'homme d'après les conceptions juives au temps de Jésus-Christ' in RSPT 5 (1911) 507–42.

He sees concupiscence as a sensual weakness ; but in contrast to docetist and gnostic doctrines, while insisting on its corporeal origins, he maintains that concupiscence is possible only because of prior pride and disobedience in the soul. Despite the realism of his description of the complicity between pride and gross desires that constitute 'sensual wisdom' he is an optimist who sees man as a child being gradually educated by God for union with the Word (*adv. haer.* V:xii:2–3H). For the Alexandrian Fathers generally (Clement, Origen), concupiscence, while natural to the body, but susceptible of satanic stimulation, is a blocking-off of the true gnosis or knowledge leading to contemplation of God. The Greek synthesis is supplied by Gregory of Nyssa who sees man's carnal condition as a deviation from his original status as the image of God. While the body is the source of man's sensible affections which are usually perverse, these tendencies can be combated by ascesis whose motivation is supplied by a striving for *apatheia* and thence, the reformation of God's image in man, leading to contemplative union with God in ecstatic love (cf. J. Daniélou, *Platonisme et théologie* (1944). St Athanasius, on the other hand, conceives of man as endowed from creation with a spark of divine grace (*charis*) which he lost in the Fall ; he has thus tumbled down into the baseness of created being (*physis*) which is good in itself, but corruptible. He is now weighed down with concupiscence in a multiplicity of worldly cares, bad habits and a false sense of liberty which keep him from ascending to God by ascesis and contemplation (*Contra Gentes* 3–4 ; *De Incarnatione* 3–6 ; PG 25:8–9 and 104–5). With Tertullian, Hilary of Poitiers, Ambrose and Jerome, the Western Fathers generally follow a dualistic anthropology, and locate the source of concupiscence in man's affections. While considering internal, bodily movements as natural, they speak of tendencies toward uncontrolled indulgence as the result of the weakness induced by Original sin. Man's freedom consists in his ability, with grace, to direct these natural movements (*anti-passiones*) away from the suggestions of the devil (temptation) and through self-denial to the exercise of virtues.

Pelagius denied Original sin as the source of concupiscence, and considered the root of sinfulness in bad habits inherited by the human race from imitation of Adam's disobedience. Augustine in reaction to the consequences of this over-optimistic view of human nature, insists upon Original sin as the root of a damaged, vicious quality in man's nature, that has so weakened his moral liberty that he is incapable without grace of keeping God's commandments as he should (*Contra Julianum* 1:16 ; PL 44:651 ; *De nuptiis et concupiscentia* 2:23 ; CSEL 42:275). Even after regeneration through baptism, man is still the subject of concupiscence in both body and soul. Combining Pauline doctrine with his own sinful experience, Augustine is pessimistic in his views of man's inordinate appetites. In particular he relates concupiscence to sensual and sexual desire (*Contra Julianum* 3, 52 ; PL 44:729 ; *De nuptiis et concupiscentia* 1, 28 ; CSEL 42:240) and

thus influences later patristic and early medieval thought (Faustus of Riez, Maximus the Confessor, Gregory the Great, Bernard of Clairvaux) to consider sexual concupiscence as the cause of Original sin.

Anselm of Canterbury (d. 1117) traces concupiscence to a simple punishment for Original sin (*De conceptu virginali* 22 ; PL 158:453), while Prepositinus of Cremona (d. 1210) insists on the natural character of concupiscence as the source of urges proper to the body. It is Thomas Aquinas who clarifies the Augustinian position, locating concupiscence in an inner movement of the body with its immediate effect on the soul. It reflects the lack of original grace which was caused by Adam's sin. Thomas sees the material element of sin in the appetites or concupiscences, and the formal element in the will. Without the gift of Original justice, the will is affected inordinately by the movements of man's lower nature. Hence he is prone to sin, which tendency the presence of grace in the soul after regeneration will correct if employed by man's free will (*De malo* 4:2 ; *Summa* 1–2ae:30–1 ; 73:6 ; 82:3).

Luther identified concupiscence with sinfulness : nature is irremediably corrupted by Original sin, whence an invincible concupiscence has removed true freedom of the will in favour of a slavery to the powers of evil (*De Servo Arbitrio*; *Werke* 3, 216). The Council of Trent, while admitting that Original sin had corrupted man's nature, denies the Lutheran thesis that concupiscence is irremediable. Concupiscence is not sinfulness in itself, though it is the outcome of Original sin and inclines toward actual sins. With grace, however, which man can freely accept or reject, concupiscence can be overcome. While human nature, even after regeneration, remains wounded, the continual exercise of virtue aided by grace can enable man to achieve progress in divine charity (Trent, Session 5 ; cf. D 792, 804, 828).

Baius saw in concupiscence a vicious, inborn habitude which is accompanied by ignorance in the mind, malice in the will, disobedience of the lower faculties and rebellion of the sexual instincts. Outside of faith and charity these tendencies are uncontrollable (*De peccato originali* 2, 3, 15–17). His teachings were condemned by Pope Pius V (1567), who made it clear that even the works which precede justification are not necessarily sinful (see BAIANISM). The contrast between either *vitiosa cupiditas* (sinful cupidity) or *laudabilis caritas* (meritorious charity) is false. Even unregenerated man is free, and can possibly achieve a truly moral life outside the realm of faith and salvation (D 1097).

For Jansenius, baptism remits the formal element of sin, but leaves the material element which is concupiscence, and comprises libido, cupidity, voluptuousness and delectation. These tendencies weigh heavily on the soul, causing it to concentrate on created things, which is sinful. The libido is St Paul's 'law of sin.' Creatures therefore cannot be loved even moderately without sin. All creature comforts must be extirpated. In faith and grace man must concentrate on the love of God alone (*Augustinus*, II:7–25 *De statu naturae lapsae*, 1641).

Modern Catholic theologians since Trent follow two divergent courses in explaining the effects of concupiscence. All agree on three elements that enter into consideration : *viz.* the inordinate movements of the appetites (sensible and rational), the necessity of grace, and the liberty of choice between good and evil. Some, with Pascal and the older French Oratorians, stress the evil effects of Original sin which manifest themselves in concupiscence as a rebellion of man's human desires. They see the rigoristic self-denial and a repudiation of all worldly satisfactions. Others, with St Francis de Sales, insist more on man's ability with grace to channel the urges of concupiscence towards good works which emanate from man's love of God in all things. Each school, however, recognizes the danger in pushing its contentions to an extreme. Each likewise insists on ascetical practices, prayer and self-denial as necessary to overcome the results of concupiscence. Some contemporary theologians see in concupiscence a natural phenomenon that existed in man even when endowed with integrity and Original grace, but which now, because of the damage brought about by Original sin, inclines man more towards evil than good. Concupiscence thus tends to be an interference with man's freedom that springs from a de-ordination in his appreciation of values. Others ask whether the essence of concupiscence does not consist in a fundamental opposition between wounded nature as such, and man's restored, supernatural destiny. Regeneration in grace removed the guilt of sin, but it has not fully repaired human nature's innate orientation toward the supernatural. This is the source of an existentialist anxiety—the *lacrymae rerum*—that can be overcome only by using grace to harness the urges of concupiscence consciously in striving for a life in Christ even in this world. Concupiscence will thus become an internal experience by means of which the Christian can unite himself to the passion and death of the Saviour.

III In moral theology, concupiscence is considered as one of the elements that modifies man's freedom in the performance of a human act. It is a movement of the (sensible) appetite or passion that precedes and gives rise to an act of the will in pursuit of a pleasurable good ; or one that is engendered and fostered by the will in the accomplishment of something evil. Antecedent concupiscence, in so far as it lessens or destroys deliberation, diminishes or eliminates freedom and hence sinfulness in an otherwise evil act. Thus sudden unpremeditated rage, or instantaneous, violent desire could relieve one of some or all responsibility for an evil act. Consequent concupiscence is voluntary and blameworthy if the object to which the will is turned is evil.

First movements of the concupiscible appetites (*motus primo-primi*) whose object is evil, but which precede advertance and deliberation, are not sinful.

Even when these incipient movements toward evil are first taken under consideration by the intellect and will as a desirable good (*motus secundo-primi*), they do not immediately constitute grave sin ; but they may give rise to venial sin, in as far as, upon being apprehended at least in part as evil, they are not rejected. It is only when the object of concupiscence is in itself grave and receives sufficient consideration on the part of the intellect and consent on the part of the will (*motus deliberati*) that serious or mortal sin is committed.

As a moral concept, concupiscence is an immediate source of temptation that must be provided against by prayer, self-denial and the practice of virtue.

Bibliography. A. Chollet, DTC III (1908) 803–14 ; C. Baumgartner, DSp II (1952) 1334–73 ; P. Wilpert, s.v. ' Begierde ' in RAC II (1954) 62–78 ; K. Rahner, ' The Theological Concept of *Concupiscentia* ' in *Theological Investigations* I (1961) ; J. Metz, LTK II (2nd ed., 1958) 108–12 ; H. Davis, *Moral and Pastoral Theology* I (8th ed., 1959) 20–7.   F. X. M.

CONFESSION The main theological questions about the sacrament of Penance have been treated under ABSOLUTION, while ATTRITION and CONTRITION deal with the scholastic disputes over its efficacy. Here some attempt will be made to show (I) how the act of the penitent in coming forward to confess his sins came to be made spontaneously. The necessity of confession for all post-baptismal mortal sins (II) will be explained, and (III) the theological background of the precept of yearly confession elucidated.

I Spontaneous confession was rarely the practice in the early Church. Confessionals were not provided in churches until after the Council of Trent, and it would be quite incongruous to think of the Apostles sitting down to hear confessions from six to nine on a Saturday evening. The discipline of the Church was at first quite the opposite ; the sinner had to be sought out by the bishop and did not come forward of his own accord. The portrayal of Christ as the Good Shepherd (at least eighty-eight times in the Roman catacombs) indicates that the rescue of the Lost Sheep was very much in the thoughts of the early Christians. The story of John the Evangelist and the Christian boy whom he reclaimed from a life of brigandage (told by Clement of Alexandria, *Quis dives salvetur*, 42 ; GCS 17:190) shows us the apostle ' giving the boy a solemn assurance that he has found pardon for him from the Saviour '. In the days when Christians were but a small enclave in each of the cities of the Roman empire, such personal care for one of their number who had fallen away was possible. It was also understood to be a duty.

From the beginning the instruction given in Mt 18:15–20 was taken to be concerned with the forgiveness of sins. The opening verse was read as saying : ' If thy brother sin, go, show him his fault between thee and him alone ' (WV). It is only with Codex Bezae that the words ' against thee ' are added ; Origen, Cyril of Alexandria, Basil and Jerome ignore them, while the parallel text in Lk 17:3 resisted emendation more successfully still ; a good majority of the Old Latin MSS omit the words (a b f ff² i l). Only in later centuries did this instruction for the bishop on how to forgive sins become transformed into general advice for all on how to show fraternal charity. The first step was the private interview. This was followed by a second interview to which the bishop went accompanied by one or two deacons. Origen is a sufficient witness to this second step (*hom. on. Josue* 7:6 ; GCS 30:333, and *hom. on Ps* 37 ; PG 12:1371). In the latter text he speaks of the resentment sometimes shown at the presence of these witnesses : 'Sometimes we do not suffer witnesses to be present while we are being rebuked, but make this a fault in our corrector and say : "You ought to say what you want to me in private." We cannot bear the wrath of the bishop who rebukes us'.[1] Reasons such as this may have led to the disuse of this second stage. The third stage was to tell the Church, or pronounce that the sinner was out of communion with the Church. Finally, he was written off as being no better than heathen or publican.

The important thing in this gradual treatment of the sinner is that it was left to the judgment of the bishop when to proceed from one stage to the next. If he thought that the sinner showed sufficient resolve to amend at the first private interview, he could end the matter then and there. If the sinner was obdurate, he had then to proceed to the next stage in his own time. The idea which some modern theologians have formed of the early Church, as dealing out an excommunication for all who sinned mortally and disregarding venial sins entirely, does not answer to the facts. The bishop might hear of a husband's adultery from the complaints of a wife (as Augustine shows, PL 38:511) and seek out the sinner privately ; if he owned up and promised reform, he would no doubt be assigned some period of penitential exercises and perhaps abstention from Holy Communion, but there might be cases where the bishop would make these exercises private also. There is even a statutory declaration of the Council of Elvira (can. 14) that certain offenders 'are to be reconciled after a year but without public penance',[2] and this is echoed by the Councils of Ancyra (can. 1–2) and Neo-Caesarea (can. 9). Origen in his commentary on Matthew (GCS 40:261–70) says : 'The one who is for the first time admonished and acts so as to deserve to be "gained" is set free by the admonition of the one who "gains" him and is no longer bound in the toils of those sins for which he was admonished, and thereupon he will also and rightly be judged by those who are in heaven to have been set free'. All the elements of the sacrament of penance are here ; the admonition is the bishop's act, it causes freedom from sins, it is valid in heaven, and it is the private

admonition 'between him and thee', before the Church has been told.

The only trace of a formula used for absolution in early times occurs in Aphrahat (*hom.* 14:44 ; P Syr 1:708) in a passage where bishops are being blamed for their respect of persons : 'If a man sin and offend God and yet conciliate the gaolers, they set him free, saying : "God is merciful and forgives your sins. Enter, come to the Eucharist". But if one has even in a small way done them injury, they say : "You are bound and accursed in heaven and earth. Woe to him who even speaks to you"'. These may not be the exact or full formulae, but they give some idea of them.

The move towards spontaneous confession seems to have come through a pondering of the medical aspect of confession. Origen (*hom. on Ps* 37; PG. 12:1386) urges self-accusation 'since some are almost choked by their peccant humours'. Aphrahat (*hom.* 7:4 ; P Syr 1:317) echoes this. Augustine has the same idea put more extensively (*Enarratio in Ps* 66 ; PL 36:809) : 'Your conscience had a gathering of poison ; the imposthume had swollen ; it pained you and would not let you rest. The doctor applies the poultice of his words and sometimes he uses the knife. Admit the healing hand, make your confession. Let all the poison escape and flow out in your confession. Now rejoice and be glad ; what remains will soon be healed'.[3] That words are always used and only sometimes resort is had to the amputating knife expresses in a suitable metaphor the distinction already pointed out between the private transaction between sinner and bishop and the resort to public penance. The medical analogy is responsible for many developments in the sacrament of Penance, notably for the wide use of the so-called Penitential Books (*see* PENANCE), but its chief value is for the part it played in persuading the faithful to confess spontaneously. It is now enshrined in canon 888 of the Code of Canon Law.

It was not easy for the habit of self-accusation to be formed. In the early centuries there is much evidence of accusation by other Christians, and in the *Didascalia Apostolorum* (a manual of advice for bishops, from Coele-Syria in the early 3rd cent.) there is an instruction on how this should be received: 'First of all, believe them not ; and secondly, do you, the bishops and deacons, be wary of them, and, when you hear them saying anything against one of the brethren, take knowledge of him against whom they bring the accusation, and make inquiry prudently and weigh his conduct ; and, if he is found blameworthy, do according to the teaching of Our Lord which is written in the gospel : Reprove him between thyself and him ...' (in Connolly's translation, 102). While the Church remained a small community in each town, it

---

[1] Interdum ne duos quidem cum arguimur adesse patimur testes, sed culpamus arguentem et dicimus : Oportuerat te soli mihi dicere quae velis. . . . Episcopi arguentis iracundiam ferre non possumus.

[2] Post annum sine poenitentia reconciliari debebunt.

[3] Conscientia tua saniem collegerat ; apostema tumuerat ; cruciabat te ; requiescere non sinebat. Adhibet medicus fomenta verborum et aliquando secat. Tu agnosce medici manum : confitere. Exeat in confessione et defluat omnis sanies ; iam exulta, iam laetare ; quod reliquum est facile sanabitur.

would be possible for the bishop to tell, by noticing when one or other of his flock abstained from receiving Holy Communion for some time, what sick members he had in his church. But, as numbers grew, this method would become unpractical, and more stress would be laid on self-accusation. (That freedom from sin was required for reception of the Eucharist in these times may be gathered from Origen (on Ps 37 ; PG 12:1386) : ' Are you not afraid to come to the Eucharist and receive the Body of Christ, as if . . . there was no unworthiness present in you. Do you think you will escape the judgment of God ?' Those formally excommunicated would be kept away by the deacons, but others had to be left to the reproaches of their own conscience as here.)

Gradually the element of inquisition declined in favour of spontaneous confession. It may still be observed in the Irish tract of the 7th cent. *De XII Abusivis Saeculi* (TU XXXIV:54) ascribed to Cyprian : ' It is fitting that a bishop should pay careful attention to the sins of all over whom he is placed as watchman, and when he has noticed them he should correct them by word and act, if possible, and if he cannot, according to the rule of the gospel, he should turn away the workers of iniquity'. Mt 18:15 is then quoted in its ancient form. Even today, the *Pontifical*, in its rules for the visitation of a parish, reminds a bishop that he should carry out these duties, though in practice he may often delegate them to missioners.

The two tendencies which develop, to regiment sinners in the discipline of public penance, and the recourse to private absolution from a ' soul-friend' as from one's own doctor, will be discussed under PENANCE.

II The necessity of confession for all post-baptismal mortal sins is the doctrine of the Church in the Council of Trent (D 899 and 917). In some ways this could be seen as a deduction from the duty of receiving the Eucharist as *viaticum* before death (*see* EUCHARIST), and the equally important duty of putting oneself in a state of fitness to receive, according to 1 Cor 11:28–9 and the traditional way of understanding this text as evidenced by the citation from Origen given above. The patristic homilies on the text (e.g. by Chrysostom *hom.* 28, PG 61:233) make it clear that the *dokimasia* required is that of self-accusation and not self-chastisement. One of the patristic documents appealed to at Trent was the letter of Leo the Great to Theodore of Fréjus (*ep.* 108 ; PL 54:1011–14). Leo sets Penance as parallel to baptism. For post-baptismal sins ' the pardon of God cannot be obtained without the intercession of the priests'. [1] He speaks of intercession, since absolution was given by a prayer of invocation, and not by a judicial sentence as it now is in the Western Church.

The necessity of confession, as St Thomas pointed out, is a hypothetical necessity, for if one have no mortal sins there has not been a shipwreck of the

[1] Indulgentia Dei nisi supplicationibus sacerdotum nequeat obtineri.

soul and thus the ' second plank after baptism' is not required for salvation. But in his theological reasoning about the necessity (*Summa* 3a:84:5:@2) St Thomas was not entirely convincing in the eyes of later theologians. Suarez (vol. XXII, *disp.* 17:2 and 35:1–2) elaborated the argument from the judicial aspect of confession ; the priest must take cognisance of mortal sins if he is to have power to ' retain' them, in the sense of Jn 20:23, as he sometimes has to do. This line of argument is sounder than that from the medical aspect of the sacrament, for one can urge that confession may be a good means to be rid of a disease of the soul without proving that it is the only one, if perfect contrition can offer another way out. As the Vulgate reading of Mt 18:15 obscured for all these theologians the application of that text to confession, no one thought of arguing from the absolute and unlimited nature of Christ's command : ' If thy brother sin, go, show him his fault'. The objection that, if the command is unlimited, it would refer to venial sins also, can be met by the consideration that venial sin and mortal sin differ in kind and not merely in degree (*see* SIN), and that Christ is speaking of sin in its proper sense and not of the analogate, which came to be called venial sin in later times. From this text, then, one might derive an argument for the necessity of seeking out all mortal sinners among the brethren, and hence, on their part, of submitting to such a quest.

There are occasions when the Church takes the will for the deed in this necessary duty of confession. Such a *votum sacramenti* (desire of the sacrament) has been known and accepted at least since the time of Denis of Alexandria. His letter to Fabian of Antioch (19–21 in Feltoe's edition) tells of an old man who had given way in the persecution by conforming to pagan worship. On his death-bed he sends for the priest who is himself ill and cannot come. The boy who summoned him is sent back to the old man bearing the Eucharist, and without any absolution the old man receives his viaticum. It is clear from the account that the old man wanted absolution ; he tells the boy : ' Get me a priest ; hasten and get me absolution'. A similar use of the *votum sacramenti* is manifest in the canonical rule that concerns a priest who might be unable to find another priest to hear his confession (can. 807) ; this rule is of considerable antiquity.

Suarez defended the adequacy of an *implicit* desire of absolution as being sufficient to dispose a sinner who had perfect contrition to receive the Eucharist. He uses the analogy of what would now be called hire-purchase (*disp.* 17:3) ; the sinner who is contrite, and who intends to confess but is prevented, does not receive a conditional forgiveness (which would remain suspended until he carry out his intention) but he enters now into the state of grace, though he still has to carry out what he has undertaken. If a sinner has contrition and the purpose of keeping all the commandments, and yet he does not advert to the existence of this particular commandment of the Church about confession, Suarez would say (against Melchior Cano and others) that his desire is sufficient. The matter is of theological importance, for, although in the days of Augustine (*De vera religione* 12 ; PL 34:142) one could demand that a heretic should have a formal desire of being reconciled to the Church before he could gain remission of his sins, it is possible now that a man who has been validly baptized in heresy could be quite ignorant of the existence of such a commandment while being fully ready to obey it if it were made known to him. St Thomas (*Summa* 3a:69:4:@2) argued from the case of the centurion Cornelius (Ac 10:47) that an implicit desire of baptism was sufficient and in his earlier teaching about Confession (IV *Sent* : 17:3:5:1) he had accepted the sufficiency of an explicit desire of the sacrament : ' Where confession is the object of the penitent's desire, he is freed from guilt, but when he afterwards makes his confession and receives absolution, his grace is increased '. [1] Suarez applies St Thomas's doctrine of implicit desire for baptism to the case of confession. If it is accepted, then the salvation of some of those outside the Church who have sinned mortally but have never gone against Christ's revelation as they have seen it may be made somewhat easier to envisage (*see* SALVATION OF NON-CATHOLICS).

III The precept of annual confession was imposed in the Middle Ages by the Fourth Lateran Council (D 437). It was a natural sequel to the precept of an annual reception of the Eucharist, imposed at a time when piety was growing cold. The earlier practice of annual confession is somewhat obscure and its history has been bedevilled by the tendentious and unreliable work of H. C. Lea (exposed by Fr Thurston) which was, and still is, taken far too seriously by Catholic writers on the Continent.

It is from England that some of the earliest evidence comes for the regular practice of confession. The *Dialogues* of Egbert of York (in Haddan and Stubbs *Concilia*, III:413) from the middle of the 8th cent. record that ' from the time of Pope Vitalian and Archbishop Theodore of Canterbury the custom, thanks be to God, has become established in the English Church, and was regarded as having the force of law, that not only clerics in monasteries but also laymen with their wives and children should betake them to their confessors and by tears and the mortification of carnal concupiscence along with the bestowal of alms should purify themselves during these twelve days, that they might the more spotlessly partake of the Lord's communion on Christmas Day '. This confession before Christmas must have been connected with the observance of Advent as a lesser Lent (*see* ADVENT IV). Lenten practice for the 9th cent. can be studied in the various MSS of an *Ordo* for private penance given in H. J. Schmitz *Die Bussbücher* (II:55–7) which depict German usage after the time of the Anglo-Saxon mission. ' Every priest ought to forewarn those who are accustomed to confess to him that at the head of the fast they

should begin to come up to renew their confession. He must point out to each a fitting penance or practice to be maintained until Maundy Thursday, bringing home to them at the moment that they must on no account make light of the duty of hastening to the reconciliation on that day.' A third example is that of Chrodegang of Metz (*c.* 754) who in the rule which he drew up for the canons of his cathedral enacted that ' twice in each year shall our clergy make an entire confession to their bishop, once at the beginning of Lent before Easter and the other time between the middle of August and the Kalends of November '. The words about ' Lent before Easter ' are not idle, as the Irish Church had three Lents a year and it may well be that the practice of a triple confession and communion each year was based on this triple Lent.

The Anglo-Saxon practice of regular confession to a fixed confessor was no doubt learned from Irish missionaries and came ultimately from Egyptian monastic practice in the Thebaid. The evidence of the *Penitentials* is complex and has been little studied, but it would be a fair summary if one said that, what England was doing in the 9th cent., Europe was doing in the 11th. The language itself bore witness to the practice, for the parish was termed a ' shrift-shire ' (*scrift scir*) or district within which the parish priest had the right to hear the confessions of his subjects. The coming of the Friars was to see this exclusive right limited in various ways. The growth of casuistry (q.v.) was at the same time limiting the authority of the ' shrift-book ' or *Penitential* which had hitherto guided the confessor. The gradual decline in the frequency of communion would of itself explain how a thrice-yearly practice of confession came to be no more than an annual duty. At the same time, confession of venial sins out of devotion and a desire for spiritual progress was becoming more and more common among monks and nuns, and eventually the practice spread to the laity also. Pius XII (AAS 35 [1943] 235) claimed that in this movement the Church was guided by the Holy Ghost.

Bibliography. P. Galtier SJ, *Aux Origines du sacrement de pénitence* (1951) ; J. H. Crehan SJ, ' Private Penance in the Early Church ', in MN 175 (1940) 190–9 ; H. J. Schmitz, *Die Bussbücher und die Bussdisciplin der Kirche* (2 vols : 1883, 1898 ; reprinted 1958 and still indispensable) ; H. Thurston SJ, ' Confession in the Dark Ages ', in MN 171 (1938) 13–22.   J. H. C.

CONFIRMATION The sacrament of confirmation was defined by the Council of Trent to be a true sacrament and not a mere idle ceremony, nor a rite whereby youths at puberty made profession of their faith ; its ordinary minister was a bishop, and it was not derogatory to the Holy Spirit to attribute some virtue to the chrism (D 871–3). This article will therefore deal (I) with the distinction of confirmation from baptism, (II) with opinions about its matter and form, (III) with its effects, and finally (IV) with theological problems concerning its minister. The

---

[1] Secundum quod in voto poenitentis praecessit (confessio) a culpa (eum) liberavit ; postmodum autem in actu confessionis et absolutionis gratia augetur.

canonical details about the circumstances required to allow of confirmation by a priest will not be discussed.

I The distinction of confirmation from baptism as a second sign of a specific grace instituted by Christ to be part of the process of Christian initiation has been the subject of much scholarly debate in recent times, particularly among Anglicans, some of whom wish to put the existence of such a sacrament beyond all doubt. For a Catholic the short answer to such a problem is to say that Trent, by putting an anathema on those who denied it was a true sacrament, was defining a dogma of faith, but retrospectively and as a matter of historical theology it is possible to see that the tradition of the Church warranted the action of Trent. The argument will be one of converging lines of proof, from NT evidence, from OT typology, from the early Fathers, Greek and Latin, and from the liturgies.

The most obvious place in the NT where a distinct rite is spoken of is Heb 6:1–4, where the Jewish Christians are reminded of their initiation into Christianity and how it included ' teaching about dippings and imposition of hands '. The ' dippings ' may cover a catechesis about the difference between John's baptism and that of Christ, such as was found necessary at Ephesus (Ac 19:1), or possibly a liturgical instruction about the meaning of the threefold immersion and its likeness to Christ's descent into death and His three days in the tomb. In Heb 9:10 the word ' dippings ' is used of Jewish lustrations, but it is by no means proved that proselyte baptism existed before the fall of Jerusalem, and this can hardly be intended here. The ' imposition of hands ' is clearly a part of the initiation which is common to all, and this at once excludes all ideas of ordination, or of a penitential imposition of hands, as what is meant here. The comment of the pseudo–Primasius (PL 68:720), though made late in the 9th cent., is apt enough : ' He means the imposition of hands by which the gift of the Holy Spirit is held to be perfectly received, and this is conferred by bishops after baptism as a confirmation of unity in the Church '. [1] The word *confirmation* was first used by the Council of Riez (439) to apply to this rite, having previously been used for the giving of the chalice at communion to those who had already partaken of the eucharistic bread. It is to be noted that the 9th-cent. commentator is trying to see what this rite ' confirms ', and selects unity as the answer. This commentary on the Pauline epistles, being a corrected form of that by Pelagius, had a wide vogue all through the Middle Ages.

The action of Peter and John in Samaria, where they lay hands on those whom Philip has previously baptized, can now better be appreciated if it is already established from Heb 6:1–2 that there were two rites of initiation and that laying on of hands was the second of these. Attempts have been made by some

Protestants to explain away the episode (along with that at Ephesus, Ac 19:1) as an exceptional performance for the purpose of associating the converts in these two places with the work of the apostolate. (Why Ephesus and Sichem should be singled out as homes of future apostles cannot be shown, nor what the evidence is for saying that the rite was one for making apostles, since there is none). Any attempt to argue by analogy from the commissioning of the Seven (Ac 6) or of Paul and Barnabas (Ac 13:1) can be met by the obvious fact that Heb 6:1–2 shows that laying on of hands was part of the initiation of Christians and that the suggested analogy is false. The connection of Apollos with the affair at Ephesus and the likelihood that he may have had a hand in the Greek of Hebrews (supposing that Paul dictated it in Aramaic) would serve to bind together these evidences still more.

It is disputable whether the apostolic laying on of hands was also an anointing. Some have thought (e.g. Umberg, in 1920) that Christ's laying hands on the sick was accompanied by a pouring of oil on their heads, and that the apostles imitated this practice. Mk 6:13 does not seem to have any direct connection with Mk 7:32 and 8:22, as one might expect if this view were correct, nor do Jewish precedents offer much help.

It has not escaped notice (by Bishop Chase of Ely) that the ' confirmation episodes ' of Acts correspond to Luke's schematism for the propagation of the gospel (Jerusalem, Judaea and Samaria, and the ends of the earth). The affair of the Samaritan converts and that of Cornelius in Caesarea answer well enough to ' Judaea and Samaria ', and Ephesus may be taken as typical of the gentile cities of the dispersion, while for Jerusalem itself, though no account of a confirmation there is given, it is certainly implied in Peter's words to the crowd at Pentecost : ' You shall receive the gift of the Holy Ghost ' (Ac 2:38), words which are paralleled by Ac 8:15 ; 10:47 and 19:2, while ' the gift ' is expressly spoken of at Ac 8:20 ; 10:45 and 11:17. Rather than supposing Luke to be giving random instances of the apostles dedicating converts to missionary activity (as Dr Lampe suggested), we may take it that he is following out a definite plan in his selection of these ' confirmation episodes ' for his narrative.

The gift that was bestowed upon Timothy (2 Tim 1:6) by the imposition of Paul's hands may be the gift of priesthood, and then the passage will be a parallel to 1 Tim 4:14, but this is denied by some, who argue that the context here, with its mention of Lois and Eunice, is one of common assurance in the Christian faith and not one of special prerogatives. The Spirit is spoken of as ' not a Spirit of cowardice, but of power, love and sobriety ', and this squares with the ordinary notion of the gifts which are brought into prominence by Confirmation.

The language of John (1 Jn 2:20 and 27) about the anointing which has been bestowed upon Christians has to be taken as metaphorical by those who, with Galtier (in DTC, VII:1356, 1369), claim that oil was not used for this sacrament in apostolic times, but it

---

[1] Impositionem manuum appellat per quam plenissime creditur accipi donum Spiritus sancti, quod post baptismum ad confirmationem unitatis in ecclesia a pontificibus fieri solet.

can hardly be denied that the passage gains in significance if it be assumed that oil *was* used.

The account of the baptism of Christ in the gospels is to some extent exemplary for the early Church, even though He receives the baptism of John and by His own word (Mt 3:15) is carrying out what was laid down in the OT for the Just Servant of Isaias 53. It is after the dipping in the Jordan that the Spirit descends, and Luke makes this more emphatic by recording that Jesus prayed between His baptism and the Descent (Lk 3:21). The fancies, which arose as early as the time of Justin (*dial.* 88) and which have influenced the apocryphal gospels, about a descent of the Spirit on the water at the time of the baptism, so that the water seemed to be on fire, may have led to the candle ceremony and its immersion into our fonts at the Easter vigil, but they are an obvious excrescence due to a desire to see that the Spirit was operative *at* baptism and not merely *after* it. Attempts have also been made to press the wording of Mk 1:10, where the descent of the Spirit is said to have taken place ' *immediately*, as He was coming out of the water ', but the use of this adverb is a stylistic trick of Mark's, which he uses eleven times in this chapter alone, and it cannot bear the weight of the theories built upon it.

The argument from OT typology for the existence of a second rite in the process of initiation is drawn chiefly from the parallel with Josue. Josue, whose name was written in Greek as Jesus, led the Israelites into the Promised Land across the Jordan (and this crossing is a type of baptism) and then circumcised them with stone knives. Justin (*dial.* 24:2 ; 113:3–7 ; 114:4) appeals to this event as a type of Christian initiation, and the question must be answered of what he found in the Christian rite to correspond to this circumcision. The stone knives he explains first as the words of Christ and then more precisely as ' the words of the apostles of the cornerstone ', words which circumcise our hearts from idolatry and all mischief. He certainly means some rite which was carried out by apostolic tradition, and as there was such a rite following upon baptism, it would be most natural to take this as the term of comparison. The exaltation (*hypsosis*) of Jesus spoken of in Jn 12:32 looks back to the passage about the brazen serpent (Jn 3:14) but in John's gospel so many depths of meaning lurk that one cannot exclude the idea that the exaltation of Josue (Jos 3:7), which occurred on Nisan 10, as did this one of Christ, and which was to show, ' that as I was with Moses, so also shall I be with thee ', is also being considered. John has elsewhere (1:45 ; 7:52, etc.) signs that he is not unfamiliar with the presentation of Christ as the New Moses. If this be accepted, then one could trace back the typology of Josue and the circumcision into apostolic times (cf. also *Odes of Solomon*, 39). Certainly, if a reason has to be assigned for the fixing of the initiation-ritual to the passover season, this is the most apt, the beginning of the Eucharist being then linked with the time when the manna ceased (Jos 5:12). The rite following upon baptism which effected a change in the heart by turning it

away from evil can therefore best be understood as being confirmation ; that this is even closer to the ideas of the NT may now be shown from a consideration of 2 Cor 1:21–2.

St Paul in this passage, which was assiduously read to the newly baptized in their Easter week catecheses, speaks of God as ' He who strengthens us with you unto Christ and anoints us, the very one who sealed us and gave us the earnest of the Spirit in our hearts '. There is some duplication of detail here, and even if one takes the sealing to be the rite of baptism, it is still possible to see that the anointing which confirms is something distinct. The ' earnest of the Spirit ' is often taken to be the same as a pledge, but in Roman law the *arrha* or *arrabon* was the money paid as a manifest proof that the contract had been entered upon (*Digest*, 18:1:35). In a baptismal context the contract is that which the candidate makes with God, professing his faith before he is baptised. If God pays the first instalment on this contract at baptism, then it is natural to look to another rite for the strengthening and anointing. It is not by accident that the Greek name for confirmation (*bebaiosis*) was taken from the verb used here for ' strengthening '. One need not press Paul's words by claiming that he knew of the use of oil at confirmation, but his language could easily have led to its adoption later on.

Justin's account of baptism (*apol.* 61) is commonly thought to show that he knew nothing of confirmation, but in fact, after he has digressed about pagan imitations, he comes back (*apol.* 65:1–2) to the rite and tells how ' the newly baptized is brought to the brethren and that they pray for themselves, for the newly baptized and for all men everywhere, and then exchange the kiss of peace '. Now this prayer for the newly baptized could very well be the prayer of laying on of hands. The ' president ', as Justin calls him (for he is very reticent, and with reason, about the ranks of the hierarchy), is with the brethren, and if he prayed over them before giving them the kiss of peace, this would be exactly what the earliest liturgical texts describe. In view of Justin's full acceptance of the Josue typology in his dialogue, it seems reasonable to conclude that he would have known of a confirmation-rite, however he might have named it.

Early heretics certainly have a rite of the imposition of hands, for Clement of Alexandria (*excerpta ex Theodoto* 22:5 ; GCS 17:114) cites part of the formula used by the Valentinians in the imposition of hands which accompanied baptism. Irenaeus (*adv. haer.* I:xiv:2 H) gives the whole of this formula as one in use among the Marcosians, some of whom anointed the candidate after baptism, while others (ibid. I:xiv:3 H) considered it superfluous to bring the candidate to the water but poured a mixture of oil and water over his head and then anointed him with oil and balsam. Professor Lampe has tried to evade the significance of these heretical imitations of the Christian rite by suggesting that they derived their usages, not from ' a good old Catholic tradition ', but from the pagan mysteries ; yet he does not offer any evidence for this. Against him is the fact that

Marcus and his followers certainly derived their liturgy from Catholic usage and this in itself sets up a presumption that they derived their initiation-rites also. Moreover, Irenaeus is at pains to show what it was that they derived from the mystery religions when he describes the practice of setting up a marriage-chamber and of making the neophyte go through a spiritual marriage there. This was a *mystagogia*, the rest was not.

Irenaeus himself gives an important comment on the sacrament of confirmation when he is speaking about the Corinthians : ' They were fit only for milk and not for strong meat. . . . The apostle was able to give them that food—for on whomsoever the apostles imposed hands, to them the Spirit was given and He is the food of life—but they could not yet receive the Spirit because the senses of their souls were still weak and unpractised in the exercise that leads to God' (*adv. haer.* IV: lxiii:1H). Professor Lampe argued that Irenaeus had here introduced a confusion of thought, an element which was really in contradiction with the ordinary view (which he himself elsewhere held) that the Spirit was given at baptism. The passage to which Professor Lampe appealed for this ' ordinary' view (*adv. haer.* III:xviii:1H) says that our bodies by the washing of baptism receive the unity which makes for incorruption, while our souls receive unity by means of the Spirit. This seems to distinguish two stages which are roughly parallel to those given in the previous passage, where the transition from milk-food to meat is spoken of. The clue to the mind of Irenaeus lies not in supposing that he was ignorant of the practice of confirmation in the church of his time, but in his anthropology, which could find room for senses of the soul and for a unity of soul higher than that of an immortalised body.

With Tertullian the place of confirmation is clear. After a reference to the episode of Paul at Ephesus he continues : ' A hand is imposed (on the baptized) which by its blessing calls and invites the Holy Spirit'.[1] The best that Professor Lampe can do with this evidence is to suggest that the Church in Africa had on its own taken up the precedent of Paul at Ephesus and made it into a local practice, or else that it was ' an old custom whereby the bishop, as the local head of the Christian community, laid his hand in blessing on the head of the new member'. But, if an old custom warranted confirmation in Tertullian's day, when did it begin ? The evidence of Tertullian points straight back to apostolic times. Cyprian, a little later in time and also a North African witness, is quite as explicit in his letters (*epist.* 73:9).

From the East the evidence is more complex. There are statements such as that of Theophilus of Antioch (*ad Autolycum* 1:1:2 ; PG 6:1041) : ' We are called Christians because we are " chrismed " with the oil of God ', where it is hard to make the claim that the writer is simply using a metaphor

[1] Manus imponitur per benedictionem advocans et invitans Spiritum sanctum. *de bapt.* 8

and not referring to a rite of the Church. Cyril of Jerusalem devoted the third of his post-baptismal catecheses to confirmation, which he puts on the same footing as baptism and the eucharist. He speaks of the candidate after his baptism and his anointing, being girt with the panoply of the Holy Spirit, and this phrase is echoed by Ephrem (on Joel 2:23), who explains that the gifts promised to the Jews in type were possessed by Christians in reality, in particular ' the oil wherewith those who have been baptised are anointed when they receive the armour of God '. Hippolytus too, when he comments on the typology of Susanna's bath (*in Dan.* 1:16 ; GCS 1:26), makes out that the oil she took with her typified ' the power of the Holy Spirit with which believers after their baptism are anointed as with scented oil '.

The complexity of the Eastern evidence is due to the fact that there are a certain number of cases where confirmation seems to have preceded baptism. These were collected by Dom R. H. Connolly in his edition of the *Liturgical Homilies of Narsai* xlii–xlix and the *Didascalia apostolorum* (xlix–li), but have not been dealt with by dogmatic theologians at all. The evidence is all Syrian and much of it is linked with Edessa. One clue is provided by Ephrem, who is cited by Connolly as saying : ' When the leper of old was cleansed, the priest used to sign him with oil and lead him to the waterspring. The type has passed and the truth is come '. One might claim on the strength of this that there was in Syria a conscious rearranging of the order of rites. If the typology of Josue (as given above) be true for Palestine (whence Justin came) and a connection be thereby established between Jewish circumcision and Christian confirmation, it would be an understandable confusion that in Syria the connection of the two rites as type and antitype was accepted, but the order of the two was taken to be that usual among Jews of the late 2nd and early 3rd cents., when proselyte baptism followed circumcision. As Connolly observed, the Nestorian church inserted an anointing after baptism in the 7th cent., while the *Apostolic Constitutions*, though based on the *Didascalia*, improve on this work by adding a direction that the bishop shall afterwards anoint the baptised, and this at the end of the 4th cent., probably at Antioch (cf. Chrysostom on Ac 10:47 ; PG 60: 187). The aberration did not therefore last for many centuries, nor did it spread, save possibly to Armenia.

II The earliest liturgical formula for confirmation is that found in the *Traditio apostolica* of Hippolytus, but there are serious doubts about the state in which this formula survives in most of the versions of that work. Nothing so easily suffers interpolation as a liturgical text, as a visit to any sacristy would prove, and there is in existence another formula in a MS dating from about 500, the composition of which, from its polemic intent, must have been about a century earlier. This is an Arian fragment which attacks the Catholics for saying that the Son is equal to the Father, while in their liturgy they subordinate the Son to the Father. Proof is then offered by the citation of a formula for the *benedictio* (or confirmation) : 'God the Father of Our Lord Jesus Christ, who has regenerated thee of water, shall Himself anoint thee with the Holy Spirit'.[1] The Ethiopic version of Hippolytus corresponds to this, saying : 'God, who hast made these worthy of the washing of new birth, and of the forgiveness of sin, make them worthy to be filled with Thy Holy Spirit'. It is curious and perhaps significant that the Sinaitic Syriac of Jn 3:5 puts 'spirit' before 'water' in its version of that famous baptismal text. If the usual formula was of the pattern just cited, one can see how in a region where confirmation was given before baptism there would be a natural tendency to put the Spirit before water in the text of the gospel. The Latin version of the *Traditio apostolica* couples water and spirit together as parts of the baptismal rite, while praying that the bishop's imposition of hands may be for grace that the baptized may serve God.[2]

The *Gelasian Sacramentary* has a prayer after baptism which is practically the same as the one cited above from the Arian fragment, save that now regeneration is said (under the influence of Tit 3:5) to be from water and the Holy Spirit, and the remission of sins is mentioned. This is headed by a rubric direction that the priest is to use this prayer while he does the post-baptismal anointing. In the original Gelasian, and in the *Sacramentary of Angoulême*, this prayer is followed by one for the bishop's use when he confirms. The bishop's prayer starts in exactly the same words as the priest's, but stops half-way and changes into a prayer for the seven gifts of the Spirit. As this second prayer is not found in the other Gelasian documents (Prague, Rheinau, St Gall, Paris, Berlin) nor in Milanese, Gallican or Irish sources, it must be regarded as a makeshift, provided when the theology of confirmation required some precise expression of how the Spirit was given, seeing that He had already come at baptism. The priest's prayer is assigned to the bishop in the *Sacramentary* of Bergamo and in the *Ordo* of Beroldus, both Ambrosian documents, and this seems to be its right attribution. Magistretti once suggested that it was taken over by priests when they began to usurp the anointing after baptism from the absent bishop.

Ambrose himself (*De Sac.* 3:2:8) discoursed of confirmation to the newly baptized on the Thursday in Easter week, when the lesson read was from 2 Cor 1:20-1 : 'There follows the spiritual seal, which you have heard mentioned in the lesson today. After the font, it remains for the perfecting to take place, when at the invocation of the bishop (*sacerdos*) the Spirit is bestowed, the Spirit of wisdom and understanding, of counsel and of strength, of knowledge and of piety, the Spirit of holy fear'. All the elements of the later theology of confirmation are here assembled.

[1] Deus et pater domini nostri Iesu Christi, qui te regeneravit ex aqua, Ipse te linet Spiritu sancto.
[2] Deus qui dignos fecisti eos remissionem mereri peccatorum per lavacrum regenerationis Spiritus sancti, inmitte in eos Tuam gratiam ut Tibi serviant secundum voluntatem Tuam. . . .

The matter of confirmation is variously assigned, some taking it to be the imposition of hands, some (e.g. St Thomas, *Summa* 3:72:2c) the anointing, some both of these combined. If one envisages the pouring of oil on the top of the head, opportunity is certainly given for the bishop to intervene by signing the candidate on the forehead as the oil runs down, and in a country where oil is abundant, this practice may at times have been followed (as seems to have been done in Milan, according to Ambrose *De myst.* 6:29). Some again wish to distinguish two meanings of the term 'matter' of the sacrament, so that what remains after the sacrament has been conferred is the matter (and this undoubtedly is the oil), but the action used for conferring the sacrament may also be called its matter, and then the matter is the imposition of hands. This final compromise is rejected by those who hold that an imposition of dry hands cannot by any means be reconciled with the use of oil. Others, noting precisely the places where the singular (hand) is used and where the plural (hands), think that a way out can be found by that means. At the present day some, e.g. M. Schmaus, adopt the view put forward by T. B. Scannell in the *Catholic Encyclopedia* in 1908, that the imposition of dry hands was the original matter in early days and that the Church added to this the anointing.

It may be possible to give some coherence to these changes in the matter of the sacrament if it be looked upon as primarily a blessing or *benedictio* of the baptized. (This is the technical term used for it in the Arian fragments of *c.* 400, and it is Tertullian's word (*De bapt.* 8) : 'imposition of hands, which by way of *blessing* calls down and appeals to the Holy Spirit'. This definition was given universal validity in the West by being taken up by Isidore (*Etymologies* 6:19:50). If the Church at first uses the Jewish way of blessing, by extension of hands over the one to be blessed, and then slowly elaborates her own rite of blessing the baptised, that is not to be wondered at. The Jewish blessing by imposition of hands is quite clearly shown in Gen 48:14 (where Jacob blessed Ephraim and Manasse) and in Lev 9:22 (where the whole people are blessed). These impositions of hands are certainly not ordinations. A similar rite was used for dedicating animals for sacrifice (Ex 29:19 and 2 Par 29:23) ; the rite was similar in all three instances, and its meaning had to be derived from the context. That the Church should eventually introduce into the rite a signing with the cross is only to be expected. The East, according to Basil, *De spiritu sancto* 66, regarded the rite as a blessing, for he there says that it is by an unwritten tradition that the baptismal water is blessed, the chrism also and *the one who is baptized*. Similarly, in the early baptismal ritual which is added to the Ethiopic version of the *Traditio apostolica* (in Duensing's edition, 119) the prayer for the rite of confirming is headed by the title : Prayer of the *blessing* for imposition of hands on the baptized.

The form of the sacrament will, on this view, have to be some kind of specification of the act of blessing, distinguishing it from other blessings of various types. The common view since the Middle Ages, that the form is found in the words, ' I sign thee with the sign of the cross and confirm thee with the chrism of salvation ', gives adequate room for this specification of the blessing. It cannot however be the primitive form in the Latin rite, if it be true that the Council of Riez (439) was the first to use the term *confirmatio* for this sacrament. (It may be that St Patrick was really the first to use the term when he wrote his letter of protest to the soldiers of Coroticus about the slaughtered converts, ' whom I begot unto God in the Christian band and confirmed in Christ '.[1] In his *Confessio* he uses the older term of *consummatio* twice (38 and 51)).

The prayer that is associated with the general imposition of hands on the candidates in the modern *Pontifical* is the most primitive of all the prayers in the rite. As noted above, it is found in the Arian fragment, in Ambrose, in the Ethiopic of Hippolytus's *Traditio apostolica* and in the supplementary *Ordo* there given. One might add that the *Testamentum Domini* (Maclean's edition, 127 and 219) has it in an enlarged form, while the *Canons of Hippolytus* have this : ' To those who have been given remission of their sins, grant now a first instalment of Thy kingdom, through Jesus Christ Our Lord '.[2] The *Missale Gallicanum Vetus* introduces it with the words *Infusio crismae* and the *Bobbio Missal* with the direction *Suffundis crisma in fronte eius dicens* (' You pour chrism on his brow as you say . . .'), but neither makes clear that the prayer is reserved to the bishop. Firmilian in his letter to Cyprian (*ep.* 75:18) speaks of baptism as being ' for the purgation of man ', while imposition of hands is ' for receiving the Holy Spirit ', a division which fits in very well with the wording of this prayer. Nowhere can one find support for the Latin version of Hippolytus (where the prayer asks that the baptised ' may always do Thy will ') save in the Egyptian rite of the 6th cent., which was published by Baumstark in *Oriens christianus* I (1901) 45, and which asks that they ' may serve Thee in purity all their days ', as well as asking for them to be filled with the Holy Spirit.

That the act of anointing should have a formula distinct from the prayer for laying on of hands is only to be expected. In the Ethiopic version of Hippolytus this formula is Trinitarian, while in the supplementary *Ordo* it is simply descriptive : ' Anointing of salvation and seal of the grace of the Holy Ghost '. The Latin of Hippolytus has the Trinitarian formula, while the Egyptian service-book just referred to has an elaborate anointing of the several senses with descriptive phrases, of which the last is the most significant : ' The perfection of the giving of Holy Spirit and the *lorica* of innocence.'

III The effects of confirmation, as distinct from those of baptism, are variously described in the

sources, but can best be summed up as a perfecting of baptism and the plenary reception of the Holy Ghost. This phrase occurs[3] in the recent teaching of the Church (AAS 27 [1935] 15), and, though one cannot rightly speak of the reception of the Spirit on a quantitative basis, it is correct to say that there are different functions attributed to Him in these receptions ; at baptism the Spirit Himself is the forgiveness of sin (as the Church teaches in the *Roman Missal*, post-communion for Whit Tuesday), while at confirmation He is the crowning of the baptized, their consecration to the cult and service of Christ and a first instalment of their heavenly life. All these functions are ascribed to the Spirit by the Fathers, as may be shown here summarily.

Irenaeus (*epideixis* 7) says that ' those who are bearers of the Spirit are led to the Word ', and the anointing is often spoken of as being the sign of that kingly priesthood to which 1 Pet 2:9 refers. Salvian (*De gubernatione Dei* 3:2:8 ; CSEL 8:44) claims that, as God in the OT called chosen men by a kingly anointing to the royal office, so all Christian men, after they have received the chrism of the Church, are called to the kingdom of heaven. In the epistle to Senarius (PL 59:403) this is amplified : ' The baptized person is anointed that he may realize that the mysteries of priesthood and the kingdom have been brought together in himself '. The typology of this sacrament is found by Hilary in the laying on of hands by Christ when the children were brought to Him. Commenting on Mt 19:3 (PL 9:1024) he says : ' The rich gift of the Holy Spirit was destined to be bestowed on the peoples by imposition of hands and by prayer. . . . The unconscious desire of the infants, who were to be checked (by the apostles), pressed forward blindly to realise the type of the future '.[4] Even the words of Christ, that these infants belong to the kingdom, were taken to indicate the effect of the sacrament, an anointing with the glory of the kingdom of heaven (PL 9:927). The same typology seems to be in Cyprian's mind when he speaks (*ep.* 73:9) of the baptized being *offered* to the bishop that he may perfect them through prayer and imposition of hands. As Leo XIII remarked, the laying on of hands is capable of various meanings and must be further specified before it is fully significant (D 1963), and it is eminently right that Christ, who laid hands on the sick to heal them and on His apostles to make them bishops (*see* BISHOP), should lay hands on infants to give them the first instalment of their life in the heavenly kingdom.

The first instalment of heavenly life is given at confirmation according to the *Catechesis* of Theodore of Mopsuestia (*Woodbrooke Studies* VI:68) : ' After you have received the grace of baptism and worn a white garment, the priest draws nigh to you and signs you on the forehead and says : '' So-and-so is

---

[1] *Quos in numero Deo genui et Christo confirmavi. Epist. ad Coroticum, 2.* The word *numerus* at this period denotes an army unit of battalion strength.

[2] *Da potius, quibus iam dedisti remissionem peccatorum, etiam arrhabona regni Tui, per Dominum nostrum Iesum Christum.*

[3] Complementum baptismatis, et in quo datur plenitudo Spiritus sancti.

[4] Munus et donum Spiritus sancti per impositionem manus et precationem erat gentibus largiendum. . . . In typicam consummationem prohibendorum infantium subrepit instinctus.

signed in the name of the Father and of the Son and of the Holy Spirit ". . . . The priest says this so that it may be an indication to you that it is in the name of the Father, Son and Holy Spirit that the Holy Spirit descended on you also (as upon Christ) and you were anointed and received grace ; and He will be and remain with you, as it is through Him that you now possess the first fruits. At present, indeed, you receive only in symbol the happiness of the future benefits, but at the time of the resurrection you will receive the full grace, from which you will become immortal and impassible. . . .'

Theodore seems to have taken 2 Cor 1:21, with its phrase about the ' earnest of the Spirit ' in a way that would imply that Confirmation was primarily of eschatological significance, giving us the hope of bodily immortality and integrity of soul which were lost in Adam. It is more usual in Western theology to look to the Eucharist for the promise of these gifts. Theodore may have been making his own deductions from the teaching of the Council of Laodicea (canon 48), which said that ' after baptism the newly baptized should be anointed with heavenly anointing and become sharers in the kingdom of Christ '. It would be open to any North Syrian to take the conciliar phrase about the kingdom in an eschatological sense, and this is what Theodore may have done, though he does not seem to have had many imitators here.

Victorinus of Pettau, commenting on Apoc 5:8 (CSEL 49:66) and explaining why the angels sang a *new* song, says : ' It is a novelty that the Holy Ghost should seal men, a novelty that they should receive a priesthood of petition and should look for the kingdom of great promise '.[1] From such a saying (and Victorinus in his backwater of the late 3rd cent. represents the teaching of a much earlier time, e.g. in the *Didascalia Apostolorum* (Connolly, 146)) one might derive the idea that confirmation bestows a status in the Church which the baptized as yet lack, and the later practice (when confirmation was separated from baptism) of not allowing the baptized to take part in the offertory at Mass during Easter week, until they had been confirmed on the Saturday *in deponendis albis*, could be explained as an application of the idea that only the confirmed could rightly take part in *active* worship. This deferring of confirmation from Easter eve till the Saturday following is taken for granted in the *Sacramentary of Prague* and in the letters of Alcuin (e.g. PL 101:261). This simple change broke the primitive sequence of the sacraments, for now (during Easter Week) the baptized received the Eucharist before they were confirmed. The wording of 1 Pet 2:9, where the kingly priesthood is said to be for the purpose of proclaiming the great deeds of Christ's salvation, is reminiscent of Ps 107:22 (106 in LXX), where such proclamation means announcing them to God in the liturgy. It may be that this is the source of the idea that confirmation gives a right to active worship,

or, as St Thomas put it, that the character imparted by confirmation is a participation in the priesthood of Christ (*Summa* 3a:63:6c and 3a:72:5c), along with the duty of actively professing the faith even under difficulty.

The linking of confirmation with the seven gifts of the Spirit is apparent in the prayer for confirmation in the *Gelasian Sacramentary* (and hence in Alcuin, PL 101:614), and it is often said that the specific mission of the Holy Spirit at confirmation is to confer those gifts. This cannot be quite true, for Trent (D 799, 904), although *obiter*, does envisage the giving of these gifts at baptism, or perhaps their implanting then, to be developed later. Origen (*hom* 3 on Isai ; GCS 33:253) finds a spiritual analogy in the seven women (of Is 4) who seize upon one man, and says quite simply : ' The seven women are the Spirit of God ' ; this may be the reason why that passage is read at the Easter vigil.

The metaphor of sealing can be applied to confirmation if it be understood (as it is by Clement of Alexandria in *Eclogae propheticae* 12:9 ; GCS 17:140) as the affixing of a seal upon a vessel that has just been filled with the Spirit of God (at baptism) and must be preserved from loss. A surprising use of this metaphor has recently come to light in the Valentinian *Gospel of Truth* (36:17) : ' Those whom the Father has anointed, they are complete. For it is the full jars that are wont to be anointed. But when the anointing of one jar shall be loosened, it is wont to leak '. K. Grobel, in his version of this document, notes that seal and anointing are taken as synonyms. In the *Odes of Solomon* there are some passages (4:8 ; 8:16 and 42:25) which speak of sealing as if it might be the affixing to a jar of such a seal, while in *Ode* 36:3-5 the newly baptized say : ' I was named the illuminated one . . ., and He anointed me from His perfection '. These ideas lingered in the East, and in a Syriac *Exposition of Baptism* by Moses bar Kepha (in the 9th cent.) it is said : ' He is sealed with *myron* upon the organs of sense that they may not be the entrances of sin '. In the West the separation of confirmation from baptism (a separation that has taken place by the time of the *Prague Sacramentary*, which has confirmation a week after baptism) would lead to the obscuring of the idea that the one sacrament perfected and made secure the other.

The rough distinction between infancy and adult age, which is made use of quite generally when pointing out the difference between the effect of baptism and that of confirmation, can claim patristic authority in the passage of Irenaeus cited above about milk and strong meat. Certainly, unless there is a difference of kind between the two sacraments in their effect, one could find no adequate reason for holding that they really were two sacraments. Suarez (*disp.* 34:1:2) made this clear, saying that without such a difference the two sacraments would be parallel to priesthood and episcopacy within the one sacrament of Orders. The change-over from the passivity of infancy (in the baptized) to the activity of lay priesthood, which is confirmation, seems great enough to establish such a difference of

---

[1] Novum est Spiritu sancto signari homines ; novum sacerdotium accipere obsecrationis et regnum expectare immensae repromissionis.

kind. If the difficulty be put that there is no notable decrease in the number of the confirmed who fall away, by comparison with those who were baptized but not confirmed, it may be answered that this is due to ignorance of, and failure to correspond with, the specific graces of confirmation. One may appeal to the medieval English synods, such as that of Worcester (1240), which decreed that parents should be excommunicated if they had not had their children confirmed one year after birth 'since the baptised have much warfare against the prince of darkness', while that of Exeter (1287) ordered parents to fast on bread and water every Friday if they had not had their children confirmed within three years from the day of birth. Such zeal would be out of place if confirmation were a mere adjunct of baptism.

IV The minister of confirmation was in early days a bishop, when the whole rite of initiation was conducted in the presence of the bishop and its final stage could be described by Ambrose as 'going up to the bishop'; hence too, the Welsh name for confirmation, *Bedydd Esgob* or bishop's baptism. Yet, as it was the practice of Mediterranean peoples from Homeric times to anoint their bodies after a bath, it must have been quite natural for the baptized to be given such an over-all anointing after their immersion, and this would be carried out by the priest or deacon (by a deaconess for women, as the *Didascalia* directs) before the baptized went up to the bishop. He may (in the East), or may not at first (in the West), have added an anointing of his own, or, as at Milan, he may have marked a sign of the cross on the brow still moist with its anointing. It is not easy to interpret the unguarded statements of patristic writers about post-baptismal anointings, and it is certainly unwise to attempt, as some have done, to wrest all of these statements to fit a pre-conceived pattern, so as to make *all* anointing after baptism the work of the bishop. The *Liber pontificalis* in its two recensions has strangely different things to say on this point. It first tells us that Sylvester I 'determined that chrism should be made by a bishop, and that it should be the prerogative of bishops to sign the baptized, on account of heretical influence'.[1] It would thus appear that in the early 6th cent. it was thought that, prior to Sylvester, priests could have confirmed. The later recension makes out that Sylvester : 'determined that a priest should anoint the baptized with chrism when he came from the water because of the chance of his passing away'.[2] This would imply that a post-baptismal anointing by a priest was then familiar (as the service-books show it was after 700) and that it was felt that this must be due to the Pope who was known to have regulated the administration of confirmation.

The Council of Orange (441) in its 2nd decree

laid down that no one with the right to baptize should ever travel without chrism. The reason given is that 'our rule is to use chrism once only (and that at baptism). If it be omitted then, the bishop is to be told at the time of confirmation. Nowhere in the Church is there more than one sacrament of confirmation. We say this not as prejudging any issue but as regarding repeated anointing with chrism as unnecessary'.[3] The rendering here given is based on the interpretation given by D. Van den Eynde in 1939 of a particularly troublesome decree. The Council of Riez in 439 had (canon 5) given priests the right to confirm within their parishes, and this Council in its first canon gave the same right to priests in the case of heretics (validly baptized) who might return to the true faith on their death-beds.

At a still earlier stage, the letter of Innocent I (*ep* 25:3 ; PL 20:554) had laid it down that a priest might anoint the baptized with chrism that had been blessed by a bishop, but he was not to sign them with the same oil on their brows, for that was the bishop's prerogative (D 98). It would be about this time that the prayer for anointing given in the Arian fragment was in use. If this prayer was gradually taken over by priests when they anointed, one can understand how a slightly different prayer might originate which could be used by the bishop for the solemn signing or *consignatio*, and also how the old anointing prayer should be found in such books as the Stowe Missal which were intended for the use of priests and not of bishops.

The anonymous author of the *Quaestiones Veteris et Novi Testamenti* (101:5 ; CSEL 50:196) claims that 'in Alexandria and throughout Egypt, if the bishop is not there, a priest performs the consignation'.[4] The same statement is found in the comment of Ambrosiaster on Eph 4:12, and although neither of these works can be assigned a locality, both can be claimed as evidence that in the West an existing prerogative of the bishop was being challenged, on precedents drawn from the East, about the end of the 4th cent. An isolated inscription (now lost) bears witness that a neophyte was confirmed by Pope Liberius, i.e. at some date between 352 and 366 (see the *Corpus* of Latin Inscriptions, XI:4975). Canons 38 and 77 of the Council of Elvira (which direct that a bishop should 'perfect' the candidate where others have baptised) may be taken to imply that priests were usurping this function, but in the absence of a contemporary commentary on the legislation, one cannot be sure.

The Prayer-Book of Serapion gives some idea of the part taken by an early 4th-cent. bishop in the rites of initiation. Serapion had provided himself with a prayer for the blessing of the chrism ' where-

---

[3] Inter nos placuit semel chrismari. De eo autem qui in baptismate, quacunque necessitate faciente, non chrismatus fuerit, in confirmatione sacerdos commonebitur. Nam inter quoslibet chrismatis ipsius non nisi una benedictio est : non ut praeiudicans quidquam, sed ut non necessaria habeatur repetita chrismatio.

[4] In Alexandria et per totam Aegyptum, si desit episcopus, consignat presbyter.

---

[1] Constituit crisma ab episcopo confici, et privilegium episcopis ut baptizatum consignent propter hereticam suasionem.

[2] Constituit ut baptizatum liniret presbyter chrisma de aqua levatum propter occasionem transitus mortis.

with the baptized are anointed' and with a prayer to be said over the baptized 'after their baptism and their coming-up'. This latter asks that they may receive the blessing of God and may be joined to the angelic choirs and that they may be preserved unto the end. The conjunction of these three requests makes it most probable that this prayer was used by Serapion while he performed the act of confirming, and, as he invokes God as the helper of all who come under His mighty hand, it would seem that Serapion imposed his hands in the act of blessing the candidates.

The blessing of chrism by a bishop is vouched for as early as the synod assembled by Cyprian in 255 at Carthage (*ep* 70:2) ; here it is laid down that 'those who are baptized must also be anointed, that by receiving the chrism, i.e. the anointing, they may be the anointed of God and may have within them the grace of Christ. Now it is the Eucharist at which the baptized are anointed with an oil that has been hallowed on the altar, and he who had no altar and no church could not sanctify the creature of oil ; wherefore there can be no spiritual anointing among the heretics, for it is clear that oil can in no way be sanctified nor Eucharist held among them'.[1] F. Dölger made exceeding heavy weather with this passage, not noticing that the Old Latin of Heb 1:9 (in *Codex Palatinus*, which has African sympathies, and in Cyprian's *Testimonia* 2:6) has the word *ungere* (to anoint) with two accusatives in the active voice, one of which is here retained with the passive. The passage makes it sure that the bishop blessed the oil, for Cyprian knows of no private Eucharist apart from the emergency of Mass in a prison-cell.

The building of separate *consignatoria*, or rooms where the bishop confirmed the newly baptized, seems to have begun in the 4th cent. There may have been such provision at Salona, Aquileia and at the Lateran. At Naples a *consumatorium albatorum* was built in 616. The absence of any distinctive feature such as a font makes it hard for archaeologists to identify these buildings.

Bibliography. *A. J. Mason, *The Relation of Confirmation to Baptism* (1893) ; *A. Wirgman, *The Doctrine of Confirmation* (1897) ; *F. H. Chase, *Confirmation in the Apostolic Age* (1909) ; F. Dölger, *Das Sakrament der Firmung* (1906) ; B. Welte, *Die postbaptismale Salbung* (1939) ; F. Gillmann, *Zur Lehre der Scholastik vom Firmung* (1920) ; *G. W. Lampe, *The Seal of the Spirit* (1951) ; *L. Thornton, *Confirmation, its Place in the Baptismal Mystery* (1954) ; J. H. Crehan sj, 'The Sealing at Confirmation', in TS 14 (1953) 273–9 ; the same, 'Ten Years' Work on Baptism and Confirmation', in TS 17 (1956) 494–515 ; D. Van den Eynde OFM, 'Le Concile d'Orange', in RTAM 11 (1939) 97–109 ; M.

O'Dwyer, *Confirmation, a Study in the Development of Sacramental Theology* (1915) ; N. Adler, *Taufe und Handauflegung im NT* (1951) ; A. Adam, *Das Sakrament der Firmung nach Thomas von Aquin* (1958) ; I. de la Potterie sj, 'L'Onction du chrétien', in Bi 40 (1959) 12–69 ; J. R. Gillis, *The Effects of Confirmation* (1940) ; J. Hanssens sj, *La Liturgie d'Hippolyte* (1959) ; J. Lecuyer CSSp., 'La Confirmation chez les Pères', in *Maison-Dieu* 54 (1958) 23–52 ; F. Dölger, 'Die Firmung in den Denkmälern', in *Römische Quartalschrift* 19 (1905) 26–41 ; the same, 'Öl der Eucharistie', in *Antike und Christentum* II (1930) 184–9 ; *H. M. Banting, 'Imposition of Hands in Confirmation', in JEH 7 (1956) 147–59 ; J. B. Umberg sj, *Die Schriftlehre vom Sakrament der Firmung* (1920) ; E. Doronzo OMI, *De Baptismo et Confirmatione* (1946).　　　J. H. C.

CONGRUISM The article has three parts : (I) the points of agreement between Congruism and 'pure' Molinism, (II) their differences, and (III) the position taken by Lessius between the Congruism of Bellarmine and Suarez and the Molinist position. The term 'Congruism' is used to denote those theological systems which explain the efficacy of grace by its 'congruity' or adaptation to the interior dispositions and the exterior circumstances of time and place of the recipient of the grace. The word is derived from St Augustine (*Ad Simplicianum*, l.1,q. 2,n.13. PL 40:119). He distinguishes between a call of divine grace which is 'congruous' and one which is not. The former is a special act of divine mercy which infallibly secures the consent of the human will. The latter implies that the recipient is indisposed to follow the call of grace. 'God does indeed call many, but has mercy on those whom He so calls as it is fitting for them to be called, that they do in fact follow. The call comes to others, but because it is one that does not move them and one that they cannot take in, they may be said to be called but not to be chosen. God has no frustration in His mercy ; the one to whom He shows mercy is called in such a way as God knows to be congruous for him, so that he does not reject the call'.[2]

In his later writings, when he is treating *ex professo* of the conciliation of grace and free will, St Augustine makes hardly any use of this distinction.

I The Agreements between Congruism and Molinism. Understood in a very wide sense the term Congruism has been applied to very various theological systems : (*a*) Molinism in general, (*b*) Augustinianism of different varieties, (*c*) mitigated Thomism, (*d*) Scotism. (Thus in LTK, VI [1961] s.v. Kongruismus.) In a more restricted sense it is often used of all forms of Molinism. In the proper sense of the term it refers to the special form of this system taught by St Robert Bellarmine, Suarez and

[1] Ungi quoque necesse est eum qui baptizatus est, ut accepto chrismate id est unctione esse unctus Dei et habere in se gratiam Christi possit. Porro autem eucharistia est unde baptizati unguntur oleum in altari sanctificatum. Sanctificare autem non potuit olei creaturam qui nec altare habuit nec ecclesiam. Unde nec unctio spiritalis apud haereticos potest esse, quando constet oleum sanctificari et eucharistiam fieri apud illos omnino non posse.

[2] Etiam multos vocat, eorum tamen miseretur, quos ita vocat, quomodo eis vocari aptum est, ut sequantur. . . . Ad alios autem vocatio quidem pervenit ; sed quia talis fuit qua moveri non possent, nec eam capere apti essent, vocati quidem dici potuerunt, sed non electi . . . Nullius Deus frustra miseretur ; cuius autem miseretur, sic eum vocat, quomodo scit ei congruere, ut vocantem non respuat.

numerous other theologians after them. It is with this special form of Congruism that we are concerned here. This system does not differ from the 'pure' Molinism of Molina, Lessius and others in its characteristic explanation of the infallibility of efficacious grace by reference to God's *Scientia media* (*see* MOLINISM, SCIENTIA MEDIA). The chief points of difference are in their divergent opinions on the question of predestination to glory and the predefinition of salutary acts (*see* PREDESTINATION). In consequence there is also a difference in the importance attached by the two forms of Molinism to antecedent congruity of grace ; but this difference is chiefly one of emphasis, at least in regard to the systems of Suarez and Molina. Before discussing in detail the differences between 'pure' Molinism and Congruism we shall indicate their fundamental points of agreement.

These are : (1) all graces bestowed by God, considered antecedently to the consent of the will, are *potentially efficacious*, even if in fact they do not secure the consent of the human will. They are, therefore, a true gift of God. This potential efficacy derives solely from their character of a supernatural motion. The resultant consent of the will, if it occurs, adds nothing to their efficacy. Thus Molina : 'Our free will and inclination bestow no force on the assistance given by grace, but rather does that assistance impart a power and inclination to the will, to produce consent'[1] (*Concordia*, 493 ed. Rabeneck, 1953). (2) Grace possesses *efficacity of connection*, through the determination of the will of the recipient. This is an act of the will already elevated by grace (i.e. *gratia excitans* or *operans*) and not a purely natural act. (3) Efficacious grace, considered antecedently, prior to the determination of the will, possesses *efficacity of infallibility* (*efficacia infallibilitatis*). This means that it not merely can, but in fact will, issue in the production of a salutary act. This infallible connection *in actu primo* between efficacious grace and a salutary act is threefold. (*a*) *Objectively* there exists a connection between certain graces and certain corresponding salutary acts. (*b*) God *sees* this connection by *scientia media* antecedently, by a priority of nature, to his actual bestowal of the grace and its acceptance by the human will. *Scientia media*, therefore, provides a medium by which God can infallibly secure the consent of the human will by the selection of a grace that will be accepted, in preference to another which will be refused. Such an efficacious grace is often called a 'congruous' grace. (*c*) In regard to the *divine will*, an efficacious grace already *in actu primo* implies a decisive intention of bestowing it, for the salutary act which it produces is God's gift. It also implies a special act of divine beneficence, inasmuch as God elects to bestow a 'congruous' rather than an 'incongruous' or merely sufficient grace.

Strict Molinists and Congruists are at one in claiming that this explanation satisfactorily harmonizes

with the teaching of revelation on grace and free will. It safeguards the existence of a truly sufficient grace which can, however, be rejected by man. It safeguards efficacious grace as a special gift of divine benevolence, and as an infallible means by which God can conduct the elect to salvation. It respects human liberty. It explains how the determination of the will to good, and the election of and predestination of the just, is primarily the work of God conferring grace.

The divine knowledge through *scientia media* of the antecedent connection between a particular grace and a definite salutary act presupposes an objective relationship between the two. Molinists of all schools, including Congruists, are at one in rejecting those systems which ground this objective relationship on the intrinsic efficacy of grace, and prescind from the circumstances in which it is offered. Thus the Thomistic system which explains efficacious grace by physical predetermination is said by them to be incompatible with free will and the existence of sufficient grace. The system of moral predeterminism is rejected on the grounds that it is either prejudicial to free will, or fails to explain efficacious grace. Against the condetermination theory of the Scotists the objection of incompatibility with free will is also urged. The Augustinian theologians and others who appeal to a 'victorious delectation' are criticised like the Thomists, for failing to safeguard human freedom and the existence of sufficient grace.

In place of a grace which is intrinsically efficacious Molinists and Congruists appeal to one which is congruous. The congruity provides the link between potential and actual efficacy, and is the object of *scientia media*. Here we must distinguish between antecedent and consequent congruity. Antecedent congruity signifies that the grace offered is adapted in a special way to the interior dispositions of the recipient, to his physical and moral condition, and also to the external circumstances of time and place in which he is situated at the moment when the grace is offered. All graces must possess this kind of congruity in some degree, otherwise they would not be true graces. Its significance is stressed not only by the Congruists Bellarmine and Suarez, but also, if less emphatically, by Molina (*Concordia*, Q.14,a, 13,d.53,m.4 ; ed. Rabeneck, 598f). He and his followers hold that strong antecedent congruity is more a mark of extraordinary grace, and that in any case the antecedent moral certainty which it provides is inadequate to explain the objective infallible connection between grace and its effect. Either it provides only conjectural certainty, or, if absolute certainty, then it is hard to see how this is compatible with human freedom. Suarez held that if antecedently congruous grace of this intense nature were necessary for an efficacious divine call, anything less than it would not even be sufficient grace (*de auxiliis, opusc.* 1,lib.III,c.XIV,n.8 (Paris 1858), t.11, p. 224). With Molina and most Molinists he sees the infallible connection, not in antecedent, but in consequent congruity, i.e. that which is logically, *in signo rationis*, consequent on the prevision of consent.

---

[1] Arbitrium et influxus noster nullam vim conferunt gratiae auxiliis, sed potius auxilia vim et propensionem arbitrio tribuunt ad consensum eliciendum.

In this way Suarez interprets the teaching of St Augustine on congruity. Augustine 'considered not only the congruity that the divine calling in itself has with a man's nature or character (and this is congruity at its first stage), but above all he dealt with that harmonization which consists in this, that the calling is given when it is going to work. This is congruity at its second stage and is congruity properly so-called, for it is most adapted to a man; he finds it better to be called, even though feebly, when he is likely to reply, than to be called strongly when he is not likely to follow'[1] (op. cit. p. 225). On this view, therefore, which is common to most Molinists, the difference between efficacious and merely sufficient grace is not intrinsic and antecedent, but ultimately derives from its extrinsic and consequent congruity. God's infallible foreknowledge of the efficacy of grace derives neither from the nature of the grace, antecedently to consent, nor from the antecedent condition and disposition of the will, but from his knowledge of conditionally future acts *in actu secundo*, or as already elicited by the will. This theory supposes that such acts have some kind of determinate entity which makes them the object of certain knowledge. For explanations offered by Molinists of this entity, *see* SCIENTIA MEDIA.

II The Points of Difference between Congruism and Molinism.

Molina's theory allowed him to say that for grace to be efficacious it is dependent on the human will: 'Grace, to be efficacious, depends on the will of the one to whom it is offered. That grace is called efficacious to which a man consents'[2] (cf. *Auctarium Bellarminianum*, ed. X. Le Bachelet [1913] 19). This doctrine was unacceptable to St Robert Bellarmine. He laid much more emphasis on intrinsic and antecedent congruity than did either Suarez or Molina. He attributed Molina's opinion to the influence of certain medieval scholastics (Henry of Ghent, Thomas of Strasburg, Biel). While rejecting physical predetermination as an explanation of the infallibility of efficacious grace, he was prepared to accept what he called moral determination of the will. By this he meant that God moved the soul, not by any physical determination of the will, but by interior graces of inspiration and persuasion which He saw were intrinsically congruous to the recipient, and by the provision of appropriate external circumstances for the divine call. In the light of *scientia media* God knows infallibly which of these graces would be effective, by inducing the free consent of the will. This divine knowledge is antecedent, even logically, to the prevision of actual consent. It is founded on the divine penetration of the nature and dispositions of the created will, of the graces which could be offered to it, and of the manifold circumstances in which they could be offered. Bellarmine considered that all these facts, as known to God, were adequate to overcome the difficulty that a contingent action of a free cause is of its nature antecedently undetermined and unpredictable. 'Since in no contingent cause taken by itself is there determination, Aristotle said rightly about future contingent beings that they had no determinate truth. He had regard to their contingent cause alone. But if one were to take along with the contingent or free cause all that can intervene or provide a hindrance and were to have regard to the inclinations and dispositions of the cause itself and of all the circumstances and obstacles —and this God alone can do—there would then be some kind of determination, and it would on that account be true to say: "This thing will come to pass at such and such a time"'[3] (*De gratia et libero arbitrio*, IV:15 [Rome 1840] p. 530; cf. *Auctarium Bellarminianum*, 101–10). Once God has moved the soul by prevenient graces of illumination and inspiration towards a particular good, He continues to move it to the acceptance of that good, provided the soul allows itself to be moved by non-resistance to the divine motion. In this way every good act is the work of God. The contribution of the will is negative rather than positive. 'Hence it comes about that the will is truly free and determines itself, although God set it in motion and put it to work, since the movement from God is under its own control, or in other words . . . our will makes use of the movement from God. If the will allow itself to be moved on the presentation of an object, it is God who sets it off and moves it to posit its act, while if it do not let itself be moved, then God does not set it off or move it. From this St Thomas concludes (*Summa* 1–2æ:10:4:@3) that when once God has given His impulse, it is impossible that the will should not be moved, but that this is not absolutely speaking impossible. The reason is that the will can render itself indisposed, by a negative determination, to receive the impulse from God'[4] (*De gratia et libero arbitrio*, IV:16). As has been said,

---

[1] Non enim consideravit tantum congruitatem, quam vocatio secundum se habet cum ingenio vel natura hominis, quae est congruitas quasi in actu primo, sed etiam ac praecipue proportionem illam consideravit, quae in hoc consistit, quod vocatio tunc datur, quando operatura est, quae proprie consistit in actu secundo, et maxime congrua dici potest, quia maxime congruit homini cui melius est vocari, quando responsurus est, etiamsi remisse vocetur, quam fortiter vocari, cum consensurus non est.

[2] Gratia ut sit efficax pendet ab arbitrio eius cui praestatur; illa enim dicitur efficax cui homo consentit.

[3] Et quoniam in ipsa contingente causa praecise considerata, nulla est determinatio, ideo vere dixit philosophus de futuris contingentibus, non esse determinatam veritatem; respexit enim ad ipsam solam causam contingentem. Tamen si quis coniungat cum causa contingente, vel libera, omnia quae possunt occurrere et impedire, et videat propensiones et aptitudines tum ipsius causae, tum omnium obiectorum et circumstantiarum, quod solus Deus facere potest, existet inde aliqua determinatio, et ratione illius verum erit dicere: hoc erit tali tempore.

[4] Atque hic fit, ut voluntas sit vere libera, et se ipsa determinet, tametsi Deus illam moveat, et applicet ad opus, quoniam ipsa Dei motio in eius potestate est, sive . . . Dei motione voluntas nostra utitur. Nam si se moveri sinat ab obiecto proposito, Deus eam applicat; et movet ad actum eliciendum; si non sinat, Deus eam non applicat, neque movet. Et ideo S. Thomas (in 1–2æ:10:4:@3) concludit, posita Dei motione impossibile esse ut voluntas non moveatur; absolute autem non esse impossibile. Quia videlicet potest voluntas non se disponere per negativam determinationem ad motionem Dei recipiendam.

the fundamental difference between Congruists and strict Molinists is that the former almost exclusively hold also the doctrine of predestination to glory antecedent to the prevision of merits. Thus Suarez, Bellarmine, Arriaga, Tanner, Ruiz, Silvester Maurus, Mayr, Billot. Molina (equivalently) and the majority of his followers, explicitly, including Lessius, Vasquez, Becanus, Petavius, Franzelin, expound the theory of predestination to glory consequent on the prevision of merits (*see* PREDESTINATION). According to the doctrine of antecedent predestination God has, in his eternal love and mercy, decreed that a certain number of rational creatures shall possess eternal glory each in a determined degree. This divine election is logically prior to the prevision of their final state of merit or demerit. Those not thus chosen are permitted to lapse into final impenitence, and their punishment is a manifestation of divine justice. The elect are to merit glory in their respective degrees through supernatural acts which God prepares for them by efficacious graces. These acts therefore are said to be *formally predefined*. According to this theory, therefore, the order of divine predestination is (*a*) glory, (*b*) merits, (*c*) efficacious graces. In the order of execution in time the order is reversed, (*a*) efficacious graces, (*b*) formally predefined merits, (*c*) glory. The control of grace is dependent on *scientia media*.

Those who hold predestination to glory consequent on the prevision of supernatural merits maintain that the divine will to decree glory or not does not become absolute prior (logically) to the prevision of the final state of merit or demerit at the hour of death, and that the degree of glory is commensurate with the supernatural merits thus foreseen. Consequently they do not admit the reversal of the orders of predestination and execution. In both the order is : (*a*) graces, (*b*) merits, (*c*) glory. They hold that as God has not selected the present order of supernatural providence precisely in order to secure the salvation of certain creatures, with the consequent negative reprobation of the rest, it follows that the merits of the just are not formally predefined, but only virtually. In other words, the divine will has for its immediate object the manifestation of the divine goodness by the bestowal of certain particular graces. *Scientia media* reveals which of these would be accepted and become efficacious in any particular order. In choosing this particular order rather than another possible one, God does in fact predefine the merits of the just, but only *virtually*, by the selection of graces which will in fact by the consent of the will be efficacious.

III The Intervention of Lessius. In the year 1610 Leonard Lessius sj, a Belgian theologian who was an enthusiastic follower of Molina, published a work entitled *De gratia efficaci, de praedestinatione, etc.* In this book he went, verbally at least, even further than Molina in asserting the opinion of predestination consequent on the prevision of merits. After the book was denounced in Rome St Robert Bellarmine was charged with its examination. While not accepting all the criticisms of the censor he

reported unfavourably of it to the General of the Society, Aquaviva, and sent a copy of his observations to Lessius. In a communication to the General, entitled *De gratia congrua*, Lessius defended his opinions, maintaining that efficacious grace, considered antecedently to consent, is not, or need not be, intrinsically different from grace which is inefficacious or non-congruous. He concluded that ' the denomination by which grace is said to be congruous and efficacious depends on the determination of the will '. This grace, he urges, is a special benefit of God, inasmuch as He bestows it with full knowledge and in view of a future consent. He denied that God chooses congruous graces for the elect, and non-congruous ones for those not elected to glory in the manner taught by the partisans of the theory of antecedent predestination. The real point at issue between Lessius and his critics, who included Suarez as well as Bellarmine, was not so much the system of election to glory through prevision of merits by itself, as the way in which Lessius proposed it. His critics considered that his teaching seemed to imply that not merely election to glory was posterior to foreseen merits, but predestination also, considered as the preparation of the means of obtaining salvation.

The outcome was that in 1613 the General, Aquaviva, in a letter to the Society of Jesus, laid down that the doctrine held by numerous Jesuit theologians, and defended before the Popes in the Congregations *de Auxiliis*, should be observed. In particular it was enjoined that for the future the theologians of the Order should teach that there is a distinction in *actu primo* between sufficient and efficacious grace, in the sense that God, in the light of *scientia media*, and with the efficacious purpose of effecting good in us, deliberately selects those means and bestows them in the manner, and at the time, in which He foresees that they will infallibly produce their effect, *and that he would make use of other means if He foresaw that these would be inefficacious* ; ' *aliis usurus si haec inefficacia praevidisset* '. Morally, therefore, and regarded as an act of beneficence, more is always contained, *in actu primo*, in efficacious than in sufficient grace. In this way it is God who is the cause of our good act ; He does not merely give us the power to perform it.

This decree gave rise to discussion. It appeared at first sight that formal predefinitions of good acts were imposed by the phrase *aliis usurus si haec inefficacia praevidisset*, even though nothing in the document had imposed the doctrine of antecedent predestination. This ambiguous phrase was therefore omitted when the decree was confirmed in the next General Congregation of the Society in 1616. On this occasion it was explained that Aquaviva had not intended to impose the opinion that God predetermines or predefines any good work of ours independently of the co-operation of our free will, nor that there is any real entity or physical mode in *actu primo* in efficacious grace which is not found in sufficient grace. This interpretation did not exclude pure Molinism. After another confirmation in 1651, the decree received a further interpretation in 1657 in which it was stated that it was sufficient if the decree were observed in its principal intent, which was to assert that efficacious grace is distinguished from sufficient grace *in actu primo* by its character of a special benefit. Since the 19th cent. this decree has been regarded as antiquated, so that Jesuit theologians are at liberty to defend either Congruism or Molinism.

Bibliography. L. Molina, *Liberi arbitrii . . . concordia* (edited J. Rabeneck, 1953) ; St Robert Bellarmine, *De gratia et libero arbitrio* (many editions); the same, *Auctarium Bellarminianum* (edited by X. Le Bachelet, 1913) ; F. Suarez, *De gratia* (vol. VIII of collected works, 1856) ; *opusculum* I : *De concursu* ; *opusculum* II : *De scientia Dei futurorum contingentium* ; *opusculum* III : *De auxilio Dei efficaci* (these three are in vol. XI of collected works, 1858) ; L. Lessius, *De praedestinatione* (in his *opuscula*, 1626) ; J. B. Franzelin, *De Deo uno* (1876) ; H. Lange, *De gratia* (1929) ; C. Mazzella, *De gratia* (1880) ; B. Beraza, *De gratia* (1916) ; G. Schneeman, *Controversiarum De gratia initia et progressus* (1881) ; H. Quilliet, in DTC III, s.v. *congruisme*.   F. C.

CONSCIENCE The presence in our language of two separate terms, conscience and consciousness, which are lacking in Romance languages, and of the terms right and law (a distinction which is lacking in German), shows that the problems of conscience have received great attention in English thought. Man rises above the level of animal agents in his possession of free will. This does not make him a completely random agent (*see* FREE WILL) ; he is aware even in his most arbitrary moods of a distinction between what he wants (immediately) and what he *really* wants. Catholic theology has analysed this distinction and studied its background, thereby coming to consider man as receiving in his nature, and according to the capacity of that nature, the impress of God's eternal law, which presents itself to him not as a compulsion but as a motive drawing forward his will to its acceptance. This law in man is called the natural law, inasmuch as it speaks for his nature in the sense of what he was meant to be, and offers him the possibility of becoming a complete, integrated personality. The practical judgment of his understanding which presents or applies the law to him is called conscience.

Conscience indicates approval or disapproval of acts to be done in the future and also of those done in the past. It may not always be certain in its decisions, and then, if a man has to act one way or another in the given situation, he will have to act on a probable conscience (*see* PROBABILISM). His conscience may be certain but erroneous, owing to his own ignorance or prejudice, and in that case he is bound, say Catholic moralists, to follow his conscience, unless it is possible for him to overcome his error. If he cannot, he is said to be in a condition of invincible ignorance. For the disturbance in the working of conscience caused by the fall of man, *see* ORIGINAL SIN. Rousseau might hold that to

follow nature was to be benevolent and humane, and Sade that it was to be cruel and bestial, but the Church has kept to a middle way.

This article will consider the teaching of the Church about conscience : (I) in the New Testament, (II) in the Fathers, (III) in Scholasticism. Developments caused by the Reformation (IV) will be examined and the work of the principal English thinkers who have been concerned about it will come under review, William Penn and Bishop Butler (V), and Cardinal Newman (VI) whose influence has lasted until the present day.

I Conscience in the New Testament is a term that has come into Christian use from Greek popular speech. It is practically unknown in the OT (Eccl 10:20 is the only place where the LXX uses the Greek word *syneidesis*). Menander (*Monostichoi*, 654) has a line which declares that ' to every mortal his conscience is a god ', and the Corinthians seem to have used the word in their complaints to St Paul, for in replying to them (1 Cor 4:4) he seems to be saying : ' It is all very well to talk to me about your consciences ; I have a conscience, too, and it is clear. But that is not the point. Baptism into Christ is of far more importance than what you call conscience '. The Greek idea of conscience, exemplified by the *daimonion* of Socrates, was that of a pain or regret for evil done and not a forward-looking directive about what was to be done. In 1 Cor 8:7-12 and 10:25-9 Paul gives his teaching on the Christian duty of respecting the consciences of those who are weak and who will easily become victims of what theologians are wont to call ' the scandal of the little ones '. In Rom 13:5 he couples the idea of conscience with the very Jewish notion of the wrath of God, as if the internal pain of conscience gnawing at a man for his sins, was the counterpart to the punishment of the wicked which God administers in world-history. Thus Paul found a place for the idea in early Christian theology.

In 1 Tim 4:2 and Tit 1:15 Paul shows that the scar upon the conscience caused by unrepented sin weakens not only that agent but also upsets the mind or the power of choice in matters of future conduct. In Heb (9:9 ; 9:14 ; 10:2 ; 10:22 ; 13:18) the theme is developed that one cannot worship God with a burdened conscience. Here, finally, the expression ' a good conscience ' comes into use, though it is to be understood in the sense of an absence of reproach rather than of positive reassurance. The speeches of Paul (Ac 23:1 and 24:16) offer a justification for this idea that to him ' good conscience ' meant the absence therein of reproach or pain. With 1 Pet 3:16, 21 and 2:19 the meaning is more difficult to establish. Mr C. A. Pierce, in his otherwise excellent monograph on *Conscience in the NT* (1955), does not quite succeed with his analysis of these Petrine passages. The baptismal passage (1 Pet 3:21) defines the candidate's part in baptism as ' the pledge unto God through the resurrection of Christ, where one's conscience is good '. The words συνειδήσεως ἀγαθῆς are almost used as a genitive absolute. Cyril of Alexandria

(PG 74:792) paraphrases the passage as 'the good pledge proceeding from a right conscience'. The goodness of conscience was therefore felt here in patristic times to be something more than an absence of reproach or pain for evil done, since it was 'right' and had to do with the profession of faith in the mysteries of Christ. It would be possible to say that Peter understood his words to imply that candidates must have nothing on their consciences at baptism, but it is much more likely that he meant their goodness of conscience to be a sincerity of belief coming from the inner man. Peter's use (in 1 Pet 2:19) 'if for conscience of God a man sustain sorrows', though ambiguous, is more commonly taken to mean that a man who has his conscience directed towards God may suffer tribulation in this life. Here again, some association of conscience and faith seems to be required.

II Conscience in the Fathers soon became a term denoting the approval for right-doing (or being in the right way) which a man experienced, as well as the pain of remorse or a shrinking from sin. Justin (*apol.* 29:3) speaks of the Christian who asked the Prefect of Egypt to allow him to be castrated as a rebuttal of the calumnies circulated against the Christians. When the Prefect refused, Justin says, the man 'remained as he was, content with the approval of his conscience and that of his fellow-believers'. Later in the Apology (*apol.* 44:1) he draws a picture of Adam with God saying to him : 'Lo, there are set before thee good and evil, choose the good'. This he links with the Platonic axiom (*Republic* 617e) : 'Responsibility belongs to the one who chooses ; God is without blame'.

Clement of Alexandria has passages (*Strom.* 4:6:37 ; GCS 52:265, and *Strom.* 7:4:27 ; GCS 17:20, where Euripides is cited) in which the old pagan idea of conscience as a remorse is uppermost, but at the same time he is well aware that Christianity has given it a more positive content. He cites 1 Tim 1:18 on faith and good conscience and says that heretics 'have defiled with their disbelief the conscience that comes from God' (*Strom.* 2:6:29 ; GCS 52:129). In his picture of the Christian athlete (*Quis dives salvetur* 3:6 ; GCS 17:162) this hero is to finish his course in the stadium as the last trump sounds and to come to receive the crown of victory from Christ 'with a good conscience'. Now at the games there had to be positive performance as well as the avoidance of fouls or disqualifications. In *Strom.* 7:12:79 (GCS 17:56) he sketches a distinction that was to become traditional among later Christian thinkers : fear can produce an abstention from evil, but when conscience is 'informed by charity' (as the Scholastics would put it), a man will then go forward to do good. Clement's phrase is that charity comes to abide in the will. The true Gnostic goes forward through his good conscience and hastens to join Christ in eternal thanksgiving. Origen (on Jn 8:46 ; GCS 10:368) goes so far as to claim that the Christian should be able to apply the words of Christ to himself and to go about 'with the freedom of speech that a clear conscience gives,

saying even to the devils : " Who shall convict me of sin ? " '

Jerome (on Ez 1:7 ; PL 25:22) provided, through a mistake of his copyists, the word *synderesis* which was to become the stock term of the medieval Scholastics. He said that the Platonists (Christians, presumably) explained the vision of the four living creatures as an allegory of man : the shapes of cow, lion and man refer to the powers of lust, anger and reason in man. 'The fourth power, which the Greeks call conscience, and which like a spark was not extinguished when Cain was thrust out of Paradise, they establish as that which makes us aware of sin when we are overcome by lust or anger'.[1] Jerome used the word συνείδησις but the copyists mistook it, with lasting consequences. Conscience as an innate habit or innate power was taken for granted by the Scholastics because they had read of it in Jerome, or in works deriving from him.

Augustine was responsible for another elaboration of the Western understanding of conscience by his remark (*De Genesi ad litteram* 12:34 : CSEL 28:430) that the joy of a good conscience is a Paradise on earth.[2] In his theory of the divine illumination of the human intellect he wavered at times between a supernatural enlightening by grace and a natural *concursus* of God with the human reason, and he bequeathed his confusion to posterity.

III The Scholastic treatment of conscience, under the impact of the *Ethics* of Aristotle (*see* ARISTOTLE, PLACE OF), was to analyse and to catalogue its working parts. With the two words *synderesis* and *conscientia* to play with, it was easy for St Thomas to say (II *Sent.* 24:2:@3) that *synderesis* was an habitual knowledge of the principles of moral action, while conscience was the application of the natural law which those principles contained to some particular action. It was taken for granted (e.g. in the *Summa* of Albertus Magnus, 2:16:99) that this application of principles was of two forms, either a prompting to do good or an aversion from evil. In this assumption the Scholastics were simply drawing upon the legacy of the Fathers, for Greek philosophy had known but the one motion, away from evil. The practical syllogism, which Aristotle had expounded (*Eth. Nic.* 1144a 31 and elsewhere), found a ready welcome from the intellectualising exponents of Scholasticism (cf. St Thomas *Summa*, 1a:79:12–13). There was, however, the voluntarist school who said with Bonaventure (II *Sent* 39:2:1c) that just as the intellect had light from God which served it as a medium for judgment (*iudicatorium naturale*), so the will or affections had a natural bias towards good in the objects of choice and this could be called *synderesis*. This 'drift' of the will could be checked by blindness of mind, as among heretics, or by onset

---

[1] Plerique iuxta Platonem rationale animae et irascitivum et concupiscitivum . . . ad hominem et leonem ac vitulum referunt. Quartamque ponunt . . . quam Graeci vocant συντήρησιν quae scintilla conscientiae in Cain quoque pectore postquam eiectus est de Paradiso non extinguitur, et qua victi voluptatibus vel furore . . . nos peccare sentimus.

[2] Laetitia quaedam conscientiae bonae Paradisus est in ipso homine.

of passion, and could be finally blocked in the damned. Thus for St Albert and St Thomas the dictate of conscience was the conclusion of a practical syllogism where *synderesis* supplied the major premiss and experimental knowledge the minor, whereas for Bonaventure conscience was a habit rather than an act of judgment, a habit, moreover, that was in part natural (for the principles of morality were common to all) but in part acquired, and here the influence of the ' drift ' in the will could be of great assistance in forming or extending the habit.

The problem of the erroneous conscience and the obligation to follow it now began to come under examination. Alexander of Hales (*Summa*, 2–2æ:3 : 3:3) listed five kinds of action, good acts which could not ever be undertaken for a bad end (such as to love God above all things), and bad acts (such as fornication) which could never be undertaken for a good end. The conscience that erred about these ought not to be followed, he thought, but, if the acts were such that, though good, they might be undertaken for a bad end (such as almsgiving for show), or bad but undertaken for a good end (such as visiting brothels to reclaim the inmates), then an erroneous conscience which considered such acts and came to a wrong decision about them was binding until it was further enlightened. Finally a fifth class of acts was indifferent between good and evil. The traditional *Glossa* on Rom 14:23 took that text to mean that every act against one's conscience was sinful. This Alexander would have denied when the act was love of God on the part of one who thought such love to be wrong, or fornication on the part of one who thought it to be right. St Thomas (*Summa*, 1–2æ:19:5c) said that this was an unreasonable position. He appealed to Aristotle (*Eth Nic.* 1146a 28–30) who had propounded the enigma that the passionate fool may be virtuous, for he thinks he is doing good while he sins from passion. Aristotle suggested (ibid. 1146b 31) that one might make a distinction between having knowledge of the right and using that knowledge, but St Thomas did not at once take up this suggestion. Instead, he appealed (*Summa*, 1–2æ:19:6:@1) to a principle he found in the pseudo-Denis that goodness in acts comes from the rightness of every circumstance in the act (*integra causa*) and evil from any single defect. Thus he accepted that the passionate fool would do wrong if he went against his conscience, when it told him to give way to passion, but would not do right for he was seeking an apparent but not a real good. The obvious objection to this position—that it leaves the agent with the prospect of doing evil either way—is faced by St Thomas in *Quaestiones de veritate* 17:4:@8. His answer is that the agent is faced, not with an absolute dilemma, but with a hypothetical one, the hypothesis being that he does not get rid of his erroneous conscience, which he can do (or could have done, had not his ignorance grown upon him by habit). In his *Commentary on the Ethics* (*ad loc.*) St Thomas does consider the distinction between having and using knowledge and pictures the passionate fool as subject to two practical

syllogisms at the same time, saying to himself : ' All pleasures are good and this is one of them,' but also : ' Reason should fix the time and place for pleasure in a man's life, and this is neither '. The passionate man *has* both in his mind but *uses* only one (cf. also *Quaestiones de malo* 6:1:@18). Thus the ethical debate is turned aside into a discussion of psychology. The Franciscan psychology (in Alexander and Bonaventure) with its emphasis on the ' drift ' of the will would give a quite different account of this dilemma (cf. Alexander, on III *Sent.* 3:12).

The old distinction between the conscience that turns a man away from evil and that which moves him to good appears again in St Thomas when he comments (*Quaestiones de veritate*, 17:4 c) that we are not bound to follow the counsels of perfection, and to omit to do so is not a sin.[1] Although he held (*Summa*, 1–2æ:18:9c) that every individual human act done with knowledge and deliberation was either good or evil, and that there were no indifferent human acts, this refusal to follow the counsels looks very much like one ; it is not a sin, and yet can one say that it is good ? It is quite fair to postulate that in many particular cases there will be laziness or negligence which will make the refusal sinful, at least venially (*see* SIN) ; one may still wonder if all cases are covered by such a supposition. Scotus and the Franciscan school were willing to say that all refusal to follow a counsel was a venial sin, but they did not carry everyone with them in this. Suarez (*De legibus*, 1:14:10 ; *De religione*, 1:9) allowed that, if a man said to himself that Christ was wrong when He counselled him to leave all things, that might be a sin of contempt, but if he simply did not want to follow, that could not be sinful, since no law made it so. He urged the text of 1 Cor 7:28 (for which *see* CHASTITY), but the controversy has gone on in spite of that, for the notion of an imperfection (which cannot be called, even in an analogical sense, a sin) has been fashioned to meet the case, though not all theologians accept it as a way out. For an account of the recent controversies one may refer to P. R. Brouillard, 'Pour l'Histoire de l'imperfection morale' (in NRT 58 [1931] 217–38). What all seem to accept is that a man's conscience does not bind him to follow a counsel in the same way that it binds him to avoid evil.

That a conscience should be aware of a claim upon it, yet not aware of any moral compulsion to accept that claim, is established by the case of the non-follower of the counsels. The recurrence of this attitude of mind when a man appeals to the maxim that an uncertain law cannot be regarded as binding and so sets up for himself a ' probable opinion ' will be discussed under PROBABILISM (*see also* CASUISTRY), but the inter-connection of the cases deserves to be noticed here. It may be suggested that the unwillingness of the Reformers to see the distinction between counsels and moral laws was also responsible for their rejection of casuistry.

When St Thomas (*quodlibet* 3:27) put himself the

[1] Ad consilia dicimur non ligari, quia qui consilium praeterit non peccat.

difficulty that a heretic's conscience could tell him to preach against the Catholic faith and thus bring him into a line of action which would be in fact against the law of God and yet right for him to follow, he did not answer the problem put, giving a parallel case instead. A priest, he said, may be in mortal sin ; if he has an obligation to say Mass and does so in a state of sin, he adds to his sin, while if he omits to say Mass, he sins by neglecting his obligation. The dilemma is unreal, said St Thomas, for he can receive the sacrament of penance and then say Mass. We are to conclude that the heretic could do likewise. In other words, St Thomas did not envisage the possibility of heretics who were in absolutely good faith ; if their consciences told them to preach heresy, that must come of ignorance which was ultimately their own fault. What may be called long-term heresy was perhaps not familiar in his time, and so he has really little guidance to offer on its problems. It is only in the period of the Reformation that principles about the rights of consciences come to be worked out.

The good which conscience prompted a man to do was for St Thomas bound up, however remotely, with faith. His view (expressed in *Summa*, 1–2æ:89:6c and *Quaestiones de veritate*, 24:12:@2 ; 28:3:@4) was that a pagan, when he first came to the use of reason, was obliged in conscience to submit himself to God and thus to do what in him lay to strive towards a supernatural end, even though he would not know that this end was supernatural. ' If he does not direct himself to his appointed end, in so far as he is at that age capable of discernment, he sins mortally by not doing what is in his power '.[1] The theology of this view was partly feudal (a man must be subject to his liege before he can receive commands from him) and partly due to a desire to clear up the position of the infidel in the matter of salvation (*see* SALVATION), but it was also derived from a conviction about the harmony that existed between man's natural and supernatural ends (*see* APOLOGETICS IX). After the discovery of the Americas (*see* AMERICA, THEOLOGICAL SIGNIFICANCE OF) and still more of the Chinese civilisation, the theologians of the late 16th cent., such as Suarez and Vasquez, abandoned this position. Suarez (*De bonitate et malitia actuum* 6:1:12) simply affirms that it is the common opinion that a pagan who is ignorant of the truth can sometimes do good actions ; his turning to God is to be understood to be no more than virtual. Vasquez (on *Summa* 1–2æ : disputatio 149) agrees with this. Not all the virtues of pagans are vices, said the Church (D 1025) in her condemnation of Baius. The stage was being set for the great debate on the assistance of divine grace (*see* GRACE).

IV The Reformation, with its principle of *cuius regio, eius religio* (change your religion with your flag), made liberty of conscience a vital issue in a way that the Middle Ages had not known. In England St Thomas More at his trial in 1535 spoke

for the rights of conscience : ' Ye must understand that in things touching conscience every true and good subject is more bound to have respect to his said conscience and to his soul than to any other thing in all the world beside ; namely when his conscience is in such sort as mine is, that is to say, where the person giveth no occasion of slander, of tumult, and sedition against his Prince, as it is with me ; for I assure you that I have not hitherto to this hour disclosed and opened my conscience and mind to any person living in all the world '. The limitations of the right of conscience included in More's statement are those which he had legislated for in his natural-law kingdom of Utopia. There, if a man had opinions against the very foundations of the Utopian state, concerning immortality, for instance, which provides an other-worldly sanction for law, he had to keep silent about them in public, though he might discuss them privately with the learned.

Elizabeth, in spite of the often-quoted words about reluctance to make windows into men's souls, followed the example of Edward VI in setting up a High Commission (19 July 1559) to punish for spiritual offences even, ' such as to the Commissioners or six of them should seem to be suspect persons ', at the same time empowering them to use torture, which was a thing contrary to the ideas of English law and to Magna Carta (ch. 29). (One may recall the indignation of St Thomas More when his enemies said that he had used torture on those awaiting trial under his care as Lord Chancellor. The first royal licences for its use appear in the time of Thomas Cromwell.) The Elizabethan Commission was an imitation of the inquisition set up in 1551 by Edward VI, ' to pluck up with all speed and celerity the noxious seed of heresy . . . without the noise and form of a judicial proceeding '. By contrast the proceedings of the reign of Mary were all, in spite of their severity, according to the ordinary process of law ; it can be shown that torture was sometimes used in her reign, but not for matters of religion (cf. D. Jardine, *The Use of Torture* [1837]). If this was the practice of the Reformation, it is easy to judge what a change of principles had come about. *The Execution of Justice in England* (1582) was Burleigh's *apologia* for the change, but still in 1592 one may read (in Verstegan's *Letters*, 52) : ' The frequent use of torture being disliked by all the people, Topcliffe has authority to torture priests in his own house '. Allen's *Defence of English Catholics* replied to Burleigh, while Richard Hooker, who set out to meet Allen's arguments, could not make up his mind what to say, as his modern investigators have shown, and left his work unfinished because of that.

The Puritans did not stand for the rights of conscience in the same way as Catholics when they opposed the established Church. For them to admit that individuals could be of different minds about texts of Scripture would be equivalent to an admission that Scripture was itself obscure, and this they could not allow. They were still back in the position of St Thomas in holding that those who

---

[1] Si non ordinet seipsum ad debitum finem, secundum quod in illa aetate est capax discretionis, peccabit mortaliter non faciens quod in se est.

had doubts of conscience about accepting their whole position should be able to set aside their doubts easily. The practice of the Puritan settlements in New England (e.g. in Massachusetts Congregationalism was the established Church) was in keeping with this outlook. It was in the Catholic colony of Maryland that real freedom of conscience was first put into practice (*see* CHURCH AND STATE). In some instances desire for freedom of conscience can be traced to an indifference to the truth of Christianity, as when Michael Servetus opposed Calvin, or when Lord Herbert of Cherbury brought out his *De veritate* (1624) with its plea for confining religious belief to what was common to all religions. Yet one cannot accept the view that toleration of the erroneous conscience was at first a political expedient taken up by those indifferent to religion and afterwards blessed and upheld by Christian principles as an absolute value (*see* TOLERATION). The writings of George Cassander (1511–66) and Robert Persons (1546–1610) on the Catholic side prove the opposite. It was a book by Cassander which Fr Petre SJ in 1687 gave to the Anglican bishop of Chester to win him over to accepting the Declaration of Indulgence of James II.

V Penn and Butler. William Penn the Quaker was perhaps the pioneer from the Protestant side in promoting liberty of conscience, and this added to his unpopularity in his own day. In his tract *The Great Case of Liberty of Conscience* (1670), he defined this liberty as ' not only a mere liberty of mind in believing or disbelieving this or that principle or doctrine but the exercise of ourselves in a visible way of worship, upon our believing it to be indispensably required at our hands that if we neglect it for fear or favour of any mortal man we sin and incur divine wrath '. He made a limiting condition to this absolute freedom : ' yet so as not to contrive or abet any contrivance destructive of the government and laws of the land tending to matters of an external nature ', though one can see that the one word ' external ' here could give rise to many perplexities. Penn as the son of an Admiral was from youth a friend of James II and had much influence on his Declaration of Indulgence (1688). This Declaration was enormously popular with Dissenters, as one may see from Luttrell's *Diary* for that year, and after the accession of William III there had perforce to be some admission of the rights of conscience, even though Catholics were excluded from its scope.

Bishop Joseph Butler was born in 1692 of nonconformist parents and became the great theoretician of conscience in Anglican theology. His *Sermons*, his *Dissertation on Virtue* and the part devoted to conscience in the *Analogy of Religion* were of immense importance, not only to Newman as a young man but to the whole development of English ethics. ' His chief merit,' as Professor Broad has said, ' is as a moral psychologist ; he states with great clearness the principles according to which decent people do feel and act and judge, though they could not state these for themselves.' His polemic against Hobbes,

who had tried to reduce morality to self-interest, leads him to make of conscience a supreme arbiter which guides a man to give the right proportions to benevolence and ' cool self-love ' in his life (*see* ALTRUISM IV). By his saying (in Sermon III) that any plain honest man who asked himself if a contemplated course of action was good or bad would know at once the right answer, Butler gave hostages to the Intuitionist school of morals, while by his insistence on the ' manifest authority ' of conscience, he led on to Kant's categorical imperative (*see* KANT). Butler was no believer in the ' greatest happiness of the greatest number ' slogan of the Utilitarians, for he wrote (*Dissertation on Virtue* 16) : ' Though it is our duty to endeavour to contribute to the ease, convenience and even cheerfulness and diversion of our fellow-creatures, yet from our short views it is greatly uncertain whether this endeavour will in particular instances produce an overbalance of happiness on the whole '. God can be a Utilitarian, but man should not.

VI From Newman to the Present Time. Newman may be termed the *doctor conscientiae*, as others were termed ' subtle doctor ' or ' irrefragable ' in the Middle Ages. In his sermon on Dispositions for faith (*Sermons on Various Occasions*, V) he spoke of conscience thus : ' Whether a man be born in pagan darkness or in some corruption of revealed religion . . . he has within his breast a certain commanding dictate, not a mere sentiment, nor a mere opinion or impression, or view of things, but a law, an authoritative voice, bidding him do certain things and avoid others. I do not say that its particular injunctions are always clear, or that they are always consistent with each other ; but . . . it commands, it praises, it blames, it promises, it threatens, it implies a future, and it witnesses of the unseen. It is more than a man's own self. The man himself has not power over it, or only with extreme difficulty ; he did not make it, he cannot destroy it. He may silence it in particular cases or directions ; he may distort its enunciations ; but he cannot, or it is quite the exception if he can, he cannot emancipate himself from it '. Newman adds to this that ' in spite of all that this voice does for them, it does not do enough. . . . It inspires in them the idea of authoritative guidance, of a divine law ; and the desire of possessing it in its fullness, not in mere fragmentary portions or indirect suggestions '.

Newman thus supplied the best answer to Kant. Where Kant had tried to account for the phenomena of moral activity without allowing room for any intuitions by man of his own acts (of himself judging or choosing), Newman took his reader into the sanctuary of conscience and asked : ' Do you see what I see ? ' If there are intuitions, they cannot in the nature of things be the subject of argument and proof ; one can do no more than draw attention to them, and this Newman did. Much of the modern theorizing about the finality (or end-seeking) which may be observed in human intellectual and voluntary activity was anticipated by Newman's writings. In his short essay on conscience, written in reply to

Gladstone after 1870 and included in *Difficulties of Anglicans* (II, 246–61), he compares the authority of conscience and that of the Pope. ' All sciences, except the science of Religion, have their certainty in themselves . . . but the sense of right and wrong, which is the first element in religion, is so delicate, so fitful, so easily puzzled, obscured, perverted, so subtle in its argumentative methods, so impressible by education, so biassed by pride and passion, so unsteady in its course, that in the struggle for existence amid the various exercises and triumphs of the human intellect, this sense is at once the highest of teachers, yet the least luminous ; and the Church, the Pope, the Hierarchy are in the divine purpose the supply of an urgent demand. Natural Religion, certain as are its grounds and its doctrines as addressed to the thoughtful, serious minds, needs, in order that it may speak to mankind with effect and subdue the world, to be sustained and completed by Revelation. . . . The Pope, who comes of Revelation, has no jurisdiction over Nature' (*see also* REVELATION).

While extolling conscience, Newman was careful to point out that the ' liberty of conscience ' which Popes had condemned (D 1613, 1690) was a term to be taken in a Pickwickian sense ; it was to be set between inverted commas and meant the right of self-will. ' When men advocate the rights of conscience, they in no sense mean the rights of the Creator, nor the duty to Him in thought and deed of the creature ; but the right of thinking, speaking, writing and acting, according to their judgment or their humour, without any thought of God at all. They do not even pretend to go by any moral rule, but they demand . . . for each to be his own master in all things, and to profess what he pleases, asking no one's leave, and accounting priest or preacher, speaker or writer, unutterably impertinent, who dares to say a word against his going to perdition if he likes it, in his own way.' Newman, who firmly believed in the argument from conscience to the existence of God, would have resisted all attempts to treat conscience as something self-explanatory ; for him it was essentially a proof that man's nature was not a closed system but rather one which was ' open at the top ', awaiting the completion of divine grace.

Modern errors about conscience often go back to Kant. For him the erroneous conscience was a mere chimaera ; the man who suffered from it had simply failed to search his heart. But the application of the Kantian maxim (that one should act from a principle that one may at the same time will, should become a universal law : *Metaphysics of Morals*, 421), coupled with the undoubted fact of erroneous consciences, led many honest men to think that all human consciences were equally sacred ; their owners might cultivate invulnerability and everyone else should hold aloof from the untouchable. In reality freedom of conscience means a freedom to become a person, to become one in whom there is a harmonizing of the elements of human nature. The concept of person was brought into ethical thought by Christian thinkers ; it is

a by-product of revelation. Kant's other maxim : so to act as to treat other human beings always at the same time as an end and never merely as a means (*Metaphysics of Morals*, 428), is itself a result of Christian thinking in his predecessors. Hence the paradox, that those who want to stand up for human rights, even to the point of allowing licence, must appeal to Christian principles to do so, and these principles from another point of view forbid that licence (*see* FREEDOM OF THOUGHT). There is the further paradox that it is in the countries of the Common Law (England, the United States, etc.) that personal rights have been more strongly developed than in those countries which are wedded to the Roman civil law with its exaggerated notions of the paternalism of the State, yet it is these latter which have been traditionally Catholic until the recent past. As noted above, both More and Penn found that some external check on liberty of conscience was necessary, but the rights of a conscientious objector are more likely to be upheld under the Common Law than elsewhere.

In recent times Catholic teaching has stressed the rights of consciences against the claims of totalitarian states. When the Fascist régime in Italy issued a manifesto (in the article *Fascismo* of the *Enciclopedia Italiana*) claiming that the State was a super-person, possessed of ends of its own that were higher than those of an individual, and proceeded to act accordingly, Pius XI (AAS 23 [1931] 291), in his letter of protest, condemned ' outrages against the wholesome and precious freedoms of religion and of consciences '. Some Catholics may have appealed to St Thomas (*Summa*, 2–2æ:64:2c), who said : ' The individual person is compared to the whole community as a part to the whole', but he limited this principle a little later (2–2æ:64:6c) by saying : ' Abstracting from circumstances, it is never lawful to kill a man, for in every man however sinful we should love the nature which God has created '.[1] His views may have been in part conditioned by feudalism (*see* FEUDALISM AND THEOLOGY), but when he tried to abstract from such conditions and view man as he would have been in Paradise (*Summa*, 1a:96:4c) he restricts very considerably the authority of the State over the individual person. A more detailed condemnation of totalitarian claims was given by Pius XI in a letter to the Archbishop of Milan (AAS 23 [1931] 147–9), where the distinction was made that, though Catholic societies do not engage in politics as such, they claim the right to instruct men's consciences about such action ; this assertion was made more forcibly (D 2278:4) in the Encyclical to Mexico in 1937 (*see* REBELLION, THEOLOGY OF).

In 1943, having in view what had been happening in the newly erected kingdom of Croatia, Pius XII included in his Encyclical *Mystici Corporis* a passage about freedom of conscience which merits attention : ' If we desire prayers to be made . . . that all those

[1] Secundum se considerando, hominem nullum occidere licet, quia in quolibet etiam peccatore debemus amare naturam quam Deus fecit.

in error should return speedily to the one fold of Christ, we none the less proclaim that this must take place of their own free motion, for no one should believe if not freely. Therefore if any who are not believing Catholics are compelled by force to enter the church-buildings, to approach the altar and receive sacraments they certainly do not become true members of the Church, for that faith without which it is impossible to please God must be the freeest service of intellect and will' (AAS 35 [1943] 243). This reiteration of Catholic teaching, the problems of Catholics in various resistance groups during the war of 1939–45 and the position of Catholics under Communist rule, all combine to make the need of a *Summa* on conscience a paramount need of modern times. What has been attempted here cannot claim to be that but it may hope to point the way.

Bibliography. P. Rousselot SJ, *Quaestiones de conscientia* (1937) ; *C. Pierce, *Conscience in the NT* (1955) ; Alexander of Hales, *Summa theologica* III (edition of 1924) ; the same, *Glossa in IV libros Sententiarum*, vols 2 and 3 (1953 and 1955) ; G. Cassander, *De officio pii viri . . .* (1561) ; T. Hanley SJ, *Their Rights and Liberties* (about Maryland, 1959) ; J. H. Crehan SJ, 'Libertas Anglica et veritas Catholica', in *Thomistica Morum Principia* (1960) ; the same, 'Catholic Toleration in Maryland', in MN 185 (1948) 205–15 ; E. D'Arcy, *Conscience and its Right to Freedom* (1961) ; V. Buranelli, *The King and the Quaker* (on Penn and James II, 1962) ; J. Lecler SJ, *Toleration and the Reformation* (2 vols, 1960) ; O. Lottin OSB, *Morale fondamentale* (1954) ; various German authors, *Die Vollmacht des Gewissens* (1956), a discussion on conscience and the duty of a soldier ; L. Vereecke, *Conscience morale et loi humaine selon Vasquez* (1958). J. H. C.

CONSECRATION The term is used for the sanctifying of both men and things. A man can be said to be consecrated to God, and Augustine gives evidence of this when he says (*De civ. Dei* 10:6 ; CSEL 40:455) : 'Man himself, when he is consecrated on God's account and dedicated to God, is a sacrifice'.[1] Primarily, however, the word refers to the sanctification of the elements of bread and wine at the Eucharist. In Latin usage the earliest extant instance of this seems to be in a letter of the Arian bishops at the council of Sardica (c. 340) which is now preserved among the works of Hilary (*frag.* 4:9 ; CSEL 65:55) ; the phrase used is *consecratum Domini corpus*, the consecrated Body of the Lord, and it undoubtedly refers to the Eucharist. This article will consider (I) the development of the words of consecration in the Mass, with some attention to the theological importance of the changes introduced (for the Orthodox theory of consecrating by invocation of the Holy Spirit, *see* EPIKLESIS), and then a minor section (II) will be given on the consecration of churches and its theological meaning. The consecration of altars has been treated under the word

[1] Ipse homo Dei nomine consecratus, et Deo devotus, sacrificium est.

ALTAR and that of bishops under BISHOP. For the theology of Christ's presence in the Eucharist *see* TRANSUBSTANTIATION.

I The words of consecration at Mass are drawn from the gospel narrative of the Last Supper and are present in all liturgies save for some Nestorian forms (*see* ADDAI AND MARI). The words are arranged so that the priest speaks the formula in the person of Christ, saying : 'This is My Body' (and not : 'This is the Body of Christ'). The fact that no one has ever tried to make such a change away from the actual words of Christ has a negative theological importance as showing that the action of the Eucharist has always been looked upon as being somehow the action of Christ. In the Latin liturgies the account in Mt 26:26 has been the primary source, with additions from 1 Cor 11:23. If the Old Latin versions of these passages are compared with the words of the Canon of the Mass as this is found in the earliest form (in the *Stowe Missal*), the approximation of the two texts, as Professor Ratcliff has recently shown, is much closer than if one starts with the present Roman Canon (which differs slightly from *Stowe*) and the Vulgate text of Matthew. It is now commonly accepted by liturgists that the Mass was celebrated in Greek at Rome until about the time of Pope Damasus (366–84), and as this Pope was instrumental in producing the Vulgate, it would seem that the wording of the consecration, with its Old Latin affinities, must therefore have been by origin an African or a Spanish product (*see* AFRICAN LITURGY). The oldest form of the Roman Canon is to be found in the Irish group of texts, *Stowe Missal*, *Bobbio Missal* and *Missale Francorum* (*see* E. Bishop, *Liturgica historica* 92–3), and in Ireland there was certainly some knowledge of the Old Latin gospels, even though the Vulgate generally prevailed over them. Visigothic Spain had great influence on Ireland in the matter of the transmission of texts, though it should be noticed that the Canon in the *Stowe Missal* is headed : Mass-canon of Pope Gelasius (*Canon dominicus Papae Gelasi*).

The first addition to the gospel narrative is a note of time : 'the day before He suffered', which is not so precise in Eastern liturgies where the phrase is : 'the night on which He was betrayed' (1 Cor 11:23). Western authors are generally agreed on this linking of the Supper with the Passion, following Cyprian (*ep* 63 ; CSEL 3:708) and Irenaeus.

The next phrase that is added without Scripture warrant is the mention of Christ's 'holy and venerable hands'. This must be of great antiquity, for attention to the hands of Christ is a mark of very early piety. The *Epistle of Barnabas* (12:2–4) sees in the extension of Christ's hands on the Cross a fulfilment of Is 65:2, while in Irenaeus (*epideixis* 46) the appeal is to Ex 17:9 and the raising of the hands of Moses. The same idea is reproduced by Justin (*dial.* 91 ; 112 ; 131) and Victorinus of Pettau (*De fabrica mundi* 5 ; CSEL 49:5). Cyril of Jerusalem (*Catech. mystagog.* 2:5 ; PG 33:1081) speaks of Christ being nailed in His undefiled hands and feet (ἀχράντων) and from this it would seem to be the usual practice to add an adjective of respect if the hands of Christ were mentioned. Later on, in lands under Keltic influence, the anointing of a priest's hands at ordination becomes customary. The first evidence is in Gildas (*De excidio Britanniae* 21 ; MGH *Auctores*, 13:82) from about the year 545, then in the *Missale Francorum* (*c.* 700), in the *Lanalet Pontifical* (*c.* 900), the *Benedictional of Archbishop Robert* and other works from these islands. It may well be that the designation of the hands of Christ as holy and venerable in the Mass-canon was a reason for the adoption of this anointing at the ordination of one who was to use those words at Mass.

The next phrase *elevatis oculis suis ad caelum et ad Te Deum patrem suum omnipotentem* (raising His eyes to heaven and to Thee, His almighty Father) has been added to the gospel account of the Supper from the story of the multiplication of the loaves (Mt 14:19), where the Old Latin reads *aspiciens in caelum*. It has been conjectured by Professor B. Gärtner that the multiplication narrative was originally put together for liturgical purposes to be recited in place of the Jewish Haggadah that was customary at the Paschal meal. Even without this hypothesis one can see that the two narratives have obvious parallels and borrowing for one from the other would be easy. This addition to the gospel account has already been made by the time of Ambrose (*de sacramentis* 4:21) and the *Apostolic Constitutions* (8:12) in the later 4th cent., whence it passes to the Alexandrian anaphoras of St Cyril and St Gregory Nazianzen and to others. The liturgy of St Basil (*see* BASIL, LITURGY OF) has in place of this apparently untheological description the highly charged word ἀναδείξας which means, 'having consecrated it to His Father' or 'having set it apart'. The Latin canon is not quite so technical in its language, but there seems to have been intended by its wording a side-reference to the sacerdotal prayer of Jesus (Jn 17:1) as well as to the multiplication of the loaves, for the words of that text are *sublevatis oculis in caelum dixit : Pater*. The purpose of the addition would then be to suggest that what Christ as man did with the bread and wine at the Supper was part of His worship of His Father. (One of the Old Latin MSS of Jn 17:1 reads *adlevatis oculis*, which comes still nearer to the Canon.)

The mention of 'giving thanks' (*gratias egit*) alongside *benedixit* has been brought into the Canon before the consecration of the bread from the parallel narrative of what Christ did before speaking words over the cup (Mt 26:27) or perhaps from Lk 22:19. Ambrose (loc. cit) already has the addition, but as he is paraphrasing the liturgical text, or perhaps citing it freely, one cannot always depend on the turn of phrase found in his homily being a faithful quotation. It must, however, be observed that the word for Eucharist in some of the Latin versions of early conciliar decrees is *gratia*, and hence the placing of the words *gratias egit* in the forefront of the liturgical narrative probably had a theological significance ; this was Christ's thank-offering to the Father.

The introductory words to the formula for the chalice, *simili modo posteaquam coenatum est*, have come from the Old Latin of 1 Cor 11:25, but the designation of the chalice as 'this glorious chalice' (*hunc praeclarum*) is a borrowing from Ps 22:5, which was regarded as a prophecy of the Eucharist by Cyprian (*ep* 63:11 ; CSEL 3:710). The insistence that it was *this* chalice which Christ took is theologically quite remarkable, for it does emphasise the identity of the Eucharist with the Last Supper, however that identity may be explained.

The words *mysterium fidei* added to the formula for the chalice are not likely to have been an interjection spoken by the deacon as he assisted the priest at Mass. It is true that they are found 1 Tim 3:9, where deacons are said to 'have the mystery of faith', but the comment by Pelagius (T&S 9:2:486) at this point is simply that the mystery of faith is the fact that the passion of Christ is the redemption of the human race. He makes no allusion to the Eucharist, although there is some evidence that before his time the addition had been made to the Mass-formula at this place. The *Apostolic Constitutions* (8:12:36) have the words : 'This is the mystery of the New Testament ; take and eat. This is My Body', but the mystery-phrase is not there repeated with the chalice. Perhaps the phrase as there used might give warrant for the construing of the chalice formula as 'mystery of faith of the new and eternal Testament'. The *Sacramentarium Rossianum* (of the 10th cent.) omits the whole of this phrase from its Canon, a fact which suggests that the copyist (who could scarcely have made the omission by accident, or left it uncorrected) considered that those six Latin words were to be taken together. The dependence of one genitive upon another is not unwonted in Latin. The Matthaean formula : 'This is My Blood of the covenant' was elaborated in the Pauline catechesis, becoming : 'This chalice : a new covenant in My Blood'. The further qualification of the covenant as eternal comes from Heb 13:20. To combine all these scriptural elements into one formula for the Mass is a task that leaves room for some variety of choice. That the shedding of blood should be 'for you' (Lk 22:20) or 'for many' (Mt 26:28) leads naturally to a formula stating both together, but between the references to the covenant there has to be a choice.

The command to renew the sacrifice of Christ (from 1 Cor 11:26) was repeated at the Eucharist from the time of Justin (*apol.* 66) and Irenaeus (*adv. haer.* IV:29:5 H). The Old Latin of Paul's text runs : *Hoc facite, quotienscunque biberitis, in meam commemorationem*. The change of this formula to *Haec quotienscunque feceritis, in mei memoriam faciatis* of the *Stowe* and *Bobbio* Missals is not without theological significance. When communion under one kind was the rule, the command to drink was not operative, for the laity at least, and hence the change to *feceritis* would then be acceptable. Conversely, one might argue that, as the Latin canon in this form goes back to the time of Gelasius I, no dogmatic necessity was then felt for insisting on communion under both kinds. An alternative explanation of the change might be that in the liturgies derived from the *Apostolic Tradition* of Hippolytus one finds the words (e.g. in the Ethiopic version) : 'Take and drink of it, and when ye do this make a memorial of Me'. The Latin version from Verona has made of this : *Quando hoc facitis, meam commemorationem facitis*, and has no mention of drinking. It is clear that in the Ethiopic version 'do this' refers to drinking, but when communion from the chalice was less commonly practised and the command to drink was omitted, the words 'do this' would acquire a more general reference to the whole act.

In the *Testament of the Lord* there is another liturgy derived from Hippolytus, which has the strange sentence (inserted after the words over the bread) : 'When ye shall do this, ye make My resurrection'. This would be suitable for a Sunday Eucharist, and there is some likelihood that those who used this *Testament* had their liturgy on that day only in early times, adding Saturdays and fast-days later. Yet behind the abrupt wording of the sentence there may be theologically important ideas, for the Resurrection of Christ was represented typologically by the wave-offering (Lev 23:10–16) of the new corn, first-fruits of the harvest. As the Syriac word used in the *Testament* here for 'make' and 'do' can also be translated 'offer', the probability is that the 4th- or 5th-cent. user of the book thought he was offering the Risen Lord as 'the first-fruits of them that sleep'. In some other liturgies (e.g. the Alexandrian *anaphora* of Mark and that of Gregory Nazianzen) there is introduced a mention of the Resurrection at this point : 'As often as ye eat . . ., ye proclaim My Death and confess My Resurrection'.

The power of the words of Christ to effect the consecration is simply declared by Ambrose (*De sacr.* 4:23 ; CSEL 73:56) : 'Before the consecration, it is bread ; but when the words of Christ are there, it is the Body of Christ'.[1] One of the first signs of special solemnity attaching to the moment of consecration is found in the short treatise in Irish that was inserted at the end of the *Stowe Missal* not long after 800. 'He offers it (the chalice) to God, and the people kneel, and here no voice cometh, lest it disturb the priest, for this is the right of it that his mind separate not from God while he chants this lesson. Hence its *nomen* is *periculosa oratio*.' The lesson is defined as beginning with the words *Accepit Jesus panem*. The chanting of the words of consecration is common in Eastern liturgies and there are some other signs that this was once the Western practice too.

The *Penitential* of Gildas (mid-6th cent.) has a ruling that if any priest through mistake change the sacred words where there is a sign to denote danger, he must do a penance of three vigils. This is copied by the *Penitential* of Cummean (13:21) : 'If he stumble over the Mass-prayer that is called *periculosa*, for the first time he is given fifty stripes, the second

time a hundred, the third time he keeps a vigil'.[2] Similar directions are found in the pseudo-Roman *Penitential* and in that of Bobbio which belong to the tradition of Columbanus and come from the 7th–8th cents. From these it is plain that Edmund Bishop was very wide of the mark when he claimed (in his appendix to R. H. Connolly : *The Liturgical Homilies of Narsai*, 129) that concern about the moment of consecration was 'not so much as thought of' in the West as late as the 9th or 10th cents.

Innocent III sent the Decretal *Cum Marthae* to the archbishop of Lyons to reassure him that, although the words *mysterium fidei* were not found in Scripture, they really belonged to the consecration of the chalice and did not imply a denial of the real Presence. This Decretal was much used in the later Middle Ages and contributed to dogmatic development about the importance of the words of consecration. William Woodeforde (1397) appealed to the fact that the complete formula for the chalice could not be found in Scripture against the heresy of Wyclif : 'It shows how wrong that opinion is which claims that nothing is to be believed unless it can be clearly deduced from Scripture'. The Western world was content to accept the formula of consecration as a datum of Tradition. Florus of Lyons (PL 119:52) in Carolingian times had expressed this view for them : 'In these words, without which no country, no people and no tongue, in fine, no part of the Catholic Church can confect or consecrate the sacraments of the Body and Blood of Christ, the Lord Himself laid down a tradition for the apostles and they for the whole Church generally'.[3] For medieval arguments about the moment of consecration, see the article by V. Kennedy cited below.

II The dedication of a church is so complicated a rite that it is not always easy to determine what exactly is being consecrated and how. The instructions of Pope Gelasius to a Bishop Valentinus (in 495–6) for a dedication are puzzling (there are several letters of the same type from this Pope) : 'If the place where the new building is belongs to your diocese, you may, as the petition asks, dedicate it by the saying of Mass, taking care to receive first as free gifts what had been offered there and letting it be known that no rights remain to the owners save that of a procession, which is certainly the right of Christian persons'[4] (Loewenfeld, *Epp. Romanorum Pontificum ineditae*, 15). The main thought here would seem to be not so much to set the church

---

[1] Antequam consecretur, panis est ; ubi autem verba Christi accesserint, corpus est Christi.

[2] Si titubaverit sacerdos super orationem dominicam quae dicitur periculosa, si una vice, L plagas ; secunda, C ; tertia, superponat.

[3] In his verbis sine quibus nulla lingua, nulla regio, nulla civitas, i.e. nulla pars ecclesiae catholicae conficere potest, i.e. consecrare sacramenta Corporis et Sanguinis Domini, ipse Dominus tradidit apostolis . . . et apostoli generaliter omni ecclesiae.

[4] Si ad tuam diocesim pertinet locus in quo facta constructio est, divinis eam sicut petitur dedicabis ministeriis, ita ut quae illic oblata sunt primitus donatione suscipias, denuntiaturus non illic quidquam dominis reservari nisi gratiam processionis quae kristianis conpetit sine dubitatione personis.

apart for God as to transfer it completely out of private ownership.

The letter of Pope Vigilius to Profuturus of Braga in 538 (PL 69:18 and 84:832) is in reply to a question whether on the restoration of a ruined church which had had no relics deposited in it there has to be a renewal of consecration : ' We judge that it would do no harm if at least blessed water was scattered over it ; for the consecration of a church where there are no relics consists, as we know, in the solemnisation of Mass and in that alone '.[1] For the nature of this ' blessed water ' see ASPERGES.

The same kind of sprinkling seems to be postulated by the reply of Gregory the Great to Mellitus of London (ep. 11:56 ; MGH *Epp.* II:331) directing that where pagan temples are taken over, the idols are to be destroyed, the place sprinkled with blessed water, altars built and relics introduced. Consecration by the placing of relics in a church grew apace during the Dark Ages, and where relics were not available, *brandea* or small squares of cloth which had touched the body of a martyr were used instead. The parallel between sanctifying a man (an archbishop) by giving him a *pallium* which had touched the tomb of the Apostle and the hallowing of an altar by *brandea* is fairly close. The same explanation may with some diffidence be invoked for the rite of enclosing particles of the consecrated Eucharist in an altar. Directions to do this are found in the Council of Chelsea in 816 (Hadan and Stubbs, *Concilia* 3:580), in the *Sacramentary* of Drogo of Metz (*c.* 825–35), in *Ordo Romanus* XLII and in the *Roman-German Pontifical.* If a man could go about with the Blessed Sacrament reserved in a vessel hung from his neck, that same Sacrament could be placed in an altar. (The custom of carrying about the Eucharist in a *chrismale* or *gerulum* can be abundantly illustrated from the Penitentials and seems to go back to the 4th cent. Cf. Hilary *frag. hist.* 9 ; CSEL 65:55). To place three particles of the Eucharist in a sealed recess of the altar may seem quite an outlandish rite, but it marks the beginning of the desire of the faithful to have the Eucharist reserved for worship.

The Zacheus-motif in the consecration rite is well marked in the English sources (*Lanalet*, Egbert and the *Benedictional* of Archbishop Robert), which have an anthem sung about him at the start of the whole service. ' This day salvation is come to this house ', and : ' I must abide in thy house today ', are two lines from the text which figure in the anthem. It may be that the burial of the Eucharist in the altar was understood to be a literal carrying out of this promise. In *Lanalet* too, the gospel for Matins at the vigil that is to precede the dedication is taken from this passage. A more primitive use can be seen in the old Armenian lectionary (Conybeare, 526) where Jn 10:22–42 is appointed for the annual dedication feast of 23 September.

The inscription of the alphabet on the floor of the church by the bishop with the foot of his crozier is a Keltic rite, as Fr Thurston clearly proved and as Mgr Andrieu in his edition of the *Ordines Romani* has come to accept. That the alphabet should be done twice, in Greek and in Latin, is an exuberance of the same type as what takes place according to the *Gelasian Sacramentary* (312) at the *traditio symboli*, where the Creed has to be recited first in Greek and then in Latin. The symbolism of the action denotes that the Church is founded upon Christ who is the beginning and end of the alphabet, Alpha and Omega. In the Armenian ritual for a dedication (Conybeare, 9) there is a prayer which suggests the same thought : ' Now therefore, Lord, through Thy Son Jesus Christ, there hath been built . . . a temple of Thy holy name, which Thou didst ordain should be made and be builded, by the apostolic preaching of the true faith in the holy Trinity, to found the same'. Defence of the West against the surviving elements of Arianism would be effected by this indication that the church was founded on true faith in the divinity of Christ.

The anointing of the walls in twelve places and the setting up of candles or crosses there may be a conscious imitation of OT practices, for Gen 28:16–18 (and 31:13) is appealed to in the prayers that accompany the rite. One may remark, however, that in *Lanalet* the bishop is directed to use the formula taken from ordination-anointings : *Sanctificetur hoc templum per istam unctionem et nostram benedictionem* ; this suggests that consecrating the church was looked upon as a species of ordination. Other ideas of consecration present in the ritual include the statement of the *Gelasian Sacramentary* (706) in the Dedication-Mass that though God is present everywhere, yet He wills that places be set apart by consecration so that the house of prayer may itself excite the minds of petitioners to invoke His name.[2] This is perhaps the clearest early definition of the purpose of church architecture and must have had a profound influence.

The antiquity of the practice of consecrating churches is attested for Jerusalem by the Armenian lectionary and by Etheria (*Itinera Hierosolymitana* 48 ; CSEL 39:100), where the OT parallels (2 Par 7:8) are emphasized. This takes us back to the 4th cent., and indeed from Eusebius (*De laudibus Constantini* 9 ; GCS 7:221) it is clear that Constantine's great buildings were dedicated on completion. The so-called Dedication council (see ARIANISM) met at Antioch in 341 on the occasion of the dedication of a church there. The Book of Kells illustrates the temple of Solomon by a reproduction of one of the small rectangular churches typical of Irish monasteries, thus indicating that the OT parallel was still understood to apply. Bede (*HE* 3:23) telling how Cedd consecrated the monastery church of Lastingham (*c.* 664) strikes a new note by record-

---

[1] Nihil iudicamus officere si per eam minime aqua exorcidiata iactetur, quia consecrationem cuiuslibet ecclesiae in qua sanctuaria non ponuntur celebritatem tantum scimus esse missarum.

[2] Cum ubique sis totus et universa tua maiestate contineas, sacrari tamen loca tuis mysteriis apta voluisti, ut ipsa orationum domus supplicum mentes ad invocationem tui nominis incitaret. . . .

ing that he fasted for the whole of Lent to prepare for the work, ' purifying the place by prayer and fasting from its former filth of crime'. This was, says Bede, the accepted practice of Northumbria and must be of Keltic origin, though it has not left its mark in the service-books, save for the rubric, which is still in the *Pontifical*, directing that the consecrating prelate and those who ask him to perform the consecration should fast the previous day and that the people of the place should be invited to do so.

Bibliography. F. Hamm, *Die liturgische Einsetzungsberichte* (1928) ; B. Capelle OSB, 'L'Évolution du *Qui pridie*', in *Recherches de théologie ancienne et médiévale* 22 (1955) 5–16 ; H. Schürmann, *Die Einsetzungsberichte* (1955) ; E. Bishop, Appendix VI to *Liturgical Homilies of Narsai*, edited by R. H. Connolly (1909) ; *H. Chadwick, ' On Luke 22:17–20 ', in HTR 50 (1957) 249–58 ; *E. C. Ratcliff, ' The Institution Narrative of the Roman *canon missae* ', in *Studia patristica* II (1957) 64–82 ; S. Benz OSB, ' Zur Geschichte der römischen Kirchenweihe ', in *Enkainia* (1956) ; H. Thurston SJ, ' The Alphabet and the Consecration of Churches ', in MN 115 (1910) 621–31 ; the same, ' The Blessed Sacrament and the Consecration of Altars ', in MN 112 (1908) 351–62 ; M. Andrieu, *Ordines Romani* IV (1956) ; V. Kennedy CSB, ' The Moment of Consecration ' in *Medieval Studies* 6 (1944) 121–50.   J. H. C.

CONSTANCE, COUNCIL OF This council, which was convoked by the anti-pope Baldassarre Cossa (who used the title of John XXIII), met at Constance on 5 November 1414. It was the time of the Western Schism and in the early stages of the Council the whole discussion was about the way to end the Schism. Three alternatives were considered, to subdue the recalcitrant by force, to decide between the claimants by judicial process, or finally to get John himself, Benedict XIII (Pedro de Luna) and Gregory XII to abdicate and then to hold a conclave and elect a new Pope. It was this last alternative that was chosen. One glimpse of the proceedings from the English standpoint is gained from the notice that Richental's chronicle gives of Robert Hallum, bishop of Salisbury, who died at Constance. ' He was the bishop who dared to say openly to Pope John that he was not worthy to be Pope for the wicked crimes he had committed, and then he recounted them to his face ; for he stood in fear of no man.' As John felt he was being abandoned by the council he took to flight, but was brought back and then undertook to accept deposition on 29 May 1415. Gregory XII sent envoys to the council who first of all read out Gregory's Bull for convoking the council (to legitimate proceedings) and, when this had been accepted by the council, they read out the formal act of abdication of their master. Pedro de Luna was dealt with by sending a mission to him to arrange his abdication and, after a long delay, when it was clear that Pedro would not abdicate, he was deposed by the council (26 July 1417). Those

taking part in the council numbered, at John's abdication, 2 patriarchs, 27 or more cardinals, 49 archbishops and 250 bishops, while at an earlier stage there were already 282 doctors of theology taking part as well.

There are three main theological issues with which the council was concerned : (I) the form of polity proper to the Church, (II) the errors of Wyclif and Hus, and (III) the incidental condemnation of tyrannicide.

I The form of polity proper to the Church was asserted by Pierre D'Ailly, one of the principal theorists of the council, to be mixed, but fundamentally democratic. All office derives from the community ; the cardinals (who represent the aristocratic element) should be elected from the nations, and the Pope when elected by them should pledge himself by an oath to act ministerially for the community. The decree *Sacrosancta* of 6 April 1415 incorporated these ideas : ' This holy synod . . . being lawfully assembled in the Holy Spirit . . ., representing the Catholic Church militant, has power directly from Christ, and all persons, even a Pope, are bound to obey it in matters relating to faith and the ending of the Schism and general reformation. . . .' As noted above, the abdication of Gregory XII, three months later, was offered when the council had accepted convocation by himself, and in his convocation he did not accept its earlier proceedings, but only those that were to follow. Canonically, therefore, the decree *Sacrosancta* was no better than a *senatusconsultum* ; it failed to achieve the status of law. Among the men of the time who accepted the supremacy of the council over the Pope was Aeneas Sylvius Piccolomini (the later Pius II) who took up this position while writing his *De concilio Basiliensi*, though he lived to repent of this youthful enthusiasm (D 717). In the course of his work he admits that the Pope (Eugenius IV) at the time of writing did not accept conciliar supremacy : ' Eugenius declares that so far is he from being obliged to obey a council that he acts then most meritoriously when he treats conciliar decrees with despite' (edition of 1525, 16. The book was reprinted in England in 1690 for controversial purposes). The Gallicanism (*q.v.*) of the 17th and 18th cents. was a direct descendant of this conciliar movement and its claims were finally ruled out at the First Vatican Council (*see* POPE, PRIMACY OF).

Secondary to the question of conciliar supremacy was the representation of the nations in a council. In its 40th session (11 November 1417) Martin V was elected Pope by the Cardinals and by a group of 30 deputies, drawn 6 apiece from the 5 nations (Italy, France, Germany, England, Spain) into which the personnel of the council had been organized. It was expressly said that this arrangement should not continue but was simply to serve the turn at a crisis when the Papacy was vacant after the removal of three contestants. The French, not unmindful of Agincourt, led an attack on the right of the English to count as a nation in the council. The English reply, given in Filastre's diary of the council, is a very curious document. 'There are 8 kingdoms (in the English nation), England, Scotland, Wales, the kingdom of the sea, and the four great and notable kingdoms in Ireland, namely Connaught, Galway, Munster and Meath, as the registers of the Roman curia list them in the catalogue of Christian kings. There is also the notable principality of John, prince of the Orkneys and other islands, about 60 in number, as large as or larger than the realm of France.' Going over to the offensive against France, the English delegates claimed that there should be only four nations in the Church, divided by the points of the compass. The Northern nation would then be England, with Norway, Sweden and Denmark, while France and Spain would be the Western; Germany, Hungary, Bohemia and Poland would be the Eastern, and Italy ' with the Greeks who belong to our obedience, such as the Cypriots and the Cretans in Candia ', the Southern. When the decrees for reformation of the Church were read (21 March 1418) the Cardinal of Ostia (vice-chancellor of the Church) said : ' By command of the nations I reply that they accept the decrees just read. Every nation sanctions the concordat Our Lord the Pope has made with it '. It may prove in the future that the attempt of Constance to incorporate a ' United Nations ' structure into the architecture of the Church was not so much wrong-headed as premature, and the modern episcopal committees of each nation seem to have possibilities for good that were first envisaged at Constance.

II The condemnation of Wyclif by Thomas Arundel, archbishop of Canterbury in 1396, was followed by the treatise of William Wideford, or Woodeforde, OFM, *Contra errores Wiclephi in Trialogo* (1396). Eighteen heads of error were enumerated by the Council of London and certain divines were asked to write a reasoned refutation of them. Woodeforde had been an associate of Wyclif's at Oxford and, when Wyclif was preparing his exposition of the *Sentences* as a young man, he would write out his arguments on a text and leave the writing with Woodeforde, who would then hand it back to him the next day with counter-arguments set against each of his. It was therefore quite natural that Woodeforde's treatise should be the most complete refutation of Wyclif's later errors. The work was printed in 1525 along with Aeneas Sylvius on the Council of Basle and had great influence. The English condemnation was used as the basis of that issued at Rome by John XXIII in 1412, though now Hus was joined to Wyclif as the protagonist of heresy. Meanwhile a group of Oxford theologians had produced a list of 267 errors found in the writings of Wyclif. Always in the forefront of these lists there appeared the heresy of the persistence of the bread in the Eucharist after consecration (*see* CONSUBSTANTIATION). When Sir John Oldcastle was condemned (25 September 1413) by the archbishop of Canterbury, this and the question of confession to a priest made up the sum of his errors. At Constance the Wycliffian material was given to a commission of theologians who drafted the 45 articles (D 581-625)

which were promulgated in the 8th session (4 May 1415). Theological notes were not attached to these articles at the time but these may be determined (D 661) from what is said in the (unofficial) memoranda of the theologians who worked on the draft (printed e.g. in Labbe, *Concilia* XVI:848-938). Martin V by his Bull *Inter cunctas* (22 February 1418) adopted the conciliar condemnation and called on the bishops to regard as heretics those who held the 45 Wycliffian propositions or the 30 ascribed to Hus (D 627-56), though later in his Bull he admits that some of the propositions were ' scandalous, rash, seditious, offensive to pious ears ', and therefore not strictly heretical. The idea of the Pope seems to have been to close the legal gap and to anticipate the possibility that some stubborn Lollard would appeal from the council to a future Pope.

When the final session of the council was drawing to a close (22 April 1418), the Pope was lobbied by a group of Poles who wished for a papal condemnation of John Falkenberg OP, a German who had satirized the Poles for calling in the Turk to help them in warfare against the Teutonic Knights, and who was thought to be encouraging the assassination of the Polish king. Martin replied to them that he intended to abide by all that the council had decided, as a council, in matters of faith and that he ratified all such decrees.[1] They asked to have this in writing and it was immediately written down by a papal notary. The incident does not seem to have been planned by the Pope, and his *obiter dictum*, while valuable as indicating his attitude, has not the solemnity of a formal declaration by decretal letter and will not bear the weight that is sometimes put upon it by historians.

One defect of this piecemeal condemnation of Wyclif was that the final article of the London condemnation of 1396 was lost in transmission somehow, though what it said was most important in the light of what followed at the Reformation. ' Whatever the Pope and his cardinals are able to deduce clearly from Holy Scripture, that and that alone is to be believed or acted upon at their behest, and whatever they claim over and above is to be condemned as heretical.' This championing of *scriptura sola* was a portent the council failed to understand.

The commonly accepted view is that no direct influence of Wyclif on Hus can be proved, since Wyclif died at the end of 1384 and the Bohemian courtiers who came with Queen Anne on her marriage to Richard II (January 1382) cannot in the space of those three years have made contact with him. On the other hand there is the almost contemporary treatise *Quonam pacto doctrina Wiclephi in Bohemiam venerit* (anonymous, printed in 1525 with Aeneas Sylvius, *De concilio Basiliensi*) which tells of a Bohemian student ' *ex domo quam putridi piscis vocant* ' (from the house of Faulfis, i.e. Jerome of Prague) who

[1] Quod omnia ac singula determinata, conclusa ac decreta in materiis fidei per praesens concilium conciliariter tenere ac inviolabiliter observare volebat, . . . ipsaque sic conciliariter facta approbat ac ratificat.

went to Oxford and read there the book of Wyclif, *De realibus universalibus*, returning to Bohemia to join in the anti-German revolution of the University of Prague which led to the founding of Leipzig (1409). One may presume that long before 1400 the theology of Wyclif was being studied in Bohemia. In 1398 Hus wrote a marginal comment on a treatise of Wyclif : ' Wyclif, Wyclif, you will make many a head shake with doubt ', thus punning in the Czech language on the name.

III The condemnation of tyrannicide at Constance was a half-measure which had little theological importance. The Duke of Burgundy had murdered the Duke of Orleans, brother of the French king. A Paris theologian, one Jean Petit, wrote a justification of the murder. Nine propositions, said to be found in this work, were submitted to the council by Gerson on behalf of the French king, and these were condemned in a general way on 6 July 1415, the day of the execution of Hus. None the less, on 30 April 1416 the bishop of Arras put in an appeal on behalf of the Duke of Burgundy. On 4 May he was allowed to tell the council that the nine propositions were not formally contained in the work of Petit. The matter was still being argued on 16 November 1417 and again on 8 January 1418, being really political. The first proposition said : ' It is lawful for any subject, without any manner of commission or command, both by natural, moral and divine law to kill or procure the death of any tyrant, who . . . is working against the bodily health of his king '.[1] The case envisaged was parallel to what Burgundy had done ; it will be seen at a glance that what the council condemned (D 690) on 6 July 1415 was not this case at all. Moreover, the condemnation on 6 July 1415 was agreed to by the deputies of four nations (the Spanish envoys had not yet come), by the president of the council (the cardinal of Ostia) and by the king of the Romans. This approbation might be challenged as not having been given *conciliariter* in the sense intended by Martin V later on. In its condemnation the council laid more stress on the breaking of an oath of loyalty and the absence of any commission than on the actual killing, and it did not make any distinction between a usurper and a good king gone wrong (*see* FEUDALISM AND THEOLOGY).

Bibliography. The *Acta concilii Constanciensis* (4 vols, 1896–1928) were edited by H. Finke, who died before completing his work. The older edition *Magnum Constantiense concilium* (6 vols., 1692–1700) by H. von der Hardt is still useful. *Miss L. Loomis, The Council of Constance* (1961), has provided English versions of the most important of the documents. B. Tierney, *Foundations of Conciliar Theory* (1955) ; *E. F. Jacob, Essays in the Conciliar Epoch* (1943) ; *J. Dahmus, The Prosecution of John Wyclif* (1952) ; W. Ullmann, *The Origins of the Great*

---

[1] Licitum est unicuique subdito absque quocunque mandato vel praecepto, secundum leges naturalem, moralem et divinam, occidere vel occidi facere quemlibet tyrannum qui . . . machinatur contra salutem corporalem regis sui.

Schism (1948) ; *R. Betts, ' English and Czech Influences on the Husite Movement ', in *Transactions of the Royal Historical Society* 21 (1939) 71–102 ; J. P. McGowan, *Pierre d' Ailly and the Council of Constance* (1936) ; J. E. Morrall, *Gerson and the Great Schism* (1960) ; unpublished Manchester dissertations by pupils of Professor Jacob include ' Robert Hallum, Bishop of Salisbury ', by F. Hodgkiss and ' Richard Ullerston, Canon of Salisbury ', by A. H. Wood. The volume of the Fliche-Martin *Histoire de l'Église* that deals with Constance (XIV, 1 and 2) is by E. Delaruelle, E. Labande and P. Ourliac (1963 and 1965). A critical edition of J. Hus, *De ecclesia*, appeared in 1956 and a life of *John Wyclif* by K. McFarlane (1952) with a sketch of the Lollard movement up to 1413 ; the canonical aspect of the Council is treated by Mgr L. Cristiani in *Dictionnaire de Droit canonique*, s.v. Constance, vol. IV:390–424. A recent controversy is summed up by J. Gill SJ, ' The Fifth Session of the Council of Constance ', in *Heythrop Journal* 5 (1964) 131–43. J. H. C.

CONSTANTINOPLE, COUNCIL OF The first ecumenical council of Constantinople (381) presents some difficulties to the theologian, since its ecumenicity was not recognised in the West until 518 at the earliest, and the creed which is ascribed to it (under the title of Nicene-Constantinople Creed) has been widely called into question. For the second ecumenical council at Constantinople in 553, *see* THREE CHAPTERS. For the third, in 680, *see* MONOTHELITES, and for the fourth, and its aftermath (869–79), *see* PHOTIUS. Here will be treated (I) its proceedings, (II) its ecumenicity and (III) its creed.

I Its Proceedings. The council of 381 left *Acta* which were extant at the time of Chalcedon (451), for when the Fathers of that council called for the adoption of the creed of Nicaea (' that of the 318 bishops ') and that of Constantinople (' that of the 150 bishops '), they saluted the first with the cry : ' In this we were baptized ; in this we ourselves baptize ', while the creed of Constantinople is said to have been read out from a book (ἀπὸ βιβλίου ἀνέγνω: *Acta conciliorum oecumenicorum* II:i:2:79). Six canons of this council were known to the Greek collection of John Scholasticus (*c.* 565) and a seventh was added in later collections such as that of Photius. The Old Latin versions of the canons contain only the first four of these, one dealing with the faith of Nicaea, one with the need for bishops (and especially metropolitans) to avoid meddling in affairs outside their own territory, one with the rank of Constantinople as second see after Rome, and one with the deposition of Maximus the Cynic from the episcopate. Canon I is vouched for by the fact that at Chalcedon (*Acta conciliorum* II:1:2:127) it was said that the 150 Fathers drew up their creed ' for the taking away of the heresies which were then sprouting forth and for the confirming of the faith ', and this is exactly what canon I does, visiting with anathema the disciples of Photinus, those of Apollinaris and the Pneumatomachoi. (In Turner's Greek canons, for which *see*

Bibliography, the eighteenth says that it is right to call Pneumatomachoi any who will not accept the consubstantial Trinity as set forth in the Tome of Antioch.)

The limiting of spheres of interest, which is settled by canon II, was natural after the primitive period when letters of communion went to and fro, and bishops were instituted to vacant sees, without much regard to boundaries at all. This canon II enumerates the regions of the Eastern empire (the larger units of Diocletian's reform, which were called *dioikeseis*); they were Egypt, Oriens (i.e. Syria, etc.), Asia, Pontus and Thrace. The canon does not touch the West. Of lands outside the Roman empire (i.e. Scythia, Abyssinia, Armenia, Persia) it says that they should continue their traditional practice. Nothing is said about the overriding possibility (laid down at Sardica) of an appeal to Rome. As Maximus had been instituted bishop of Constantinople by Peter of Alexandria and was to be deposed by canon IV, it is clear that this general canon had to be enacted first, to show the iniquity of what Maximus had procured for himself. In the days of Arian predominance, it had been very important to secure the support of some leading figure, however remote his territory might be, if one wished to gain acceptance in a vacant see. The deposition of Maximus was not recognized by Ambrose, who held a council later in the same year, at which Maximus was upheld. After some negotiation Pope Damasus granted him recognition (so, at all events, declared Pope Boniface I *ep* 15, *Ad episcopos Illyriae*; PL 20:783).

II Its Ecumenicity. The rank of Constantinople was a matter of concern to Rome, and in the declaration of Damasus on the primacy of Rome (D163) the words : ' The Roman church is set before others not by any conciliar decree but by the word of the Lord in the gospel . . .',[1] may be read as a direct answer to canon III of Constantinople. (There is no doubt that C. H. Turner and E. Schwartz are right in seeing in this decree the work of Damasus himself.)

Leo the Great (*ep* 106 *Ad Anatolium*; PL 54:1005) said that canon III had never been submitted to the Holy See : ' Your argument is in no way helped by what certain bishops put into writing, as you say, some sixty years ago ; nor was this writing brought by your predecessors to the knowledge of the Apostolic See. It is this argument, void from the start and unreliable, that you now seek to support, though tardily and to no purpose '.[2] Leo wrote in 452, and Anatolius had spoken of what was enacted at Constantinople sixty or seventy years before. Gregory the Great (*ep* 7:31 ; MGH *ep* 1:479) went a little further and claimed that no *acta* of this council were

[1] Romana ecclesia nullis synodicis constitutis ceteris ecclesiis praelata est, sed evangelica voce Domini. . . .

[2] Persuasioni enim tuae in nullo penitus suffragatur quorundam episcoporum ante sexaginta—ut iactas—annos facta conscriptio, nunquamque a praedecessoribus tuis ad Apostolicae sedis transmissa notitiam, cui ab initio sui caducae dudumque collapsae sera nunc et inutilia subicere fulcimenta voluisti.

available in Rome, though he accepted what the council had done against Macedonius (leader of the Pneumatomachoi). Elsewhere (*ep* 1:24 ; MGH *ep* 1:36) he accepts this council as one of the Great Four which may be compared with the four gospels. To reconcile Gregory's two statements it is necessary to suppose that he had knowledge of the creed of Constantinople along with the first canon, but that (officially at least) he did not find in his archives a copy of the *Acta* of that council. Nectarius, whose name stood in the first place on the list of signatories of the *Acta* (since he had been chosen to replace— after the brief interlude of Gregory Nazianzen—the deposed Maximus as patriarch of Constantinople) was known at Rome from the letter of Boniface I cited above, which Gregory the Great must have found in his archives. Here it was said that the election of Nectarius ' had not received our official approval ' (*in notione nostra non esset*, the word *notio* having a legal sense, as in *sine notione populi Romani, sine iudicio senatus*). While the work of the council against the Macedonians would be appreciated, its disciplinary proceedings would be subject to some suspicion. Pope Hormisdas in 518 (PL 63:429) and Vigilius in 540 (PL 69:25) took a similar line with this council.

No Western bishops were present at Constantinople for the council, save for the Spanish bishop Agrius whose name occupies the penultimate place on the lists (Latin and Syriac) and who may have been a court bishop in attendance on the emperor, who was himself Spanish. From the letters of Damasus (*ep* 5 ; PL 63:365) it appears that he had briefed Ascholius of Thessalonica to represent him at the council, but this bishop did not sign the *Acta* at all ; it may be that he withdrew when the proceedings against the Macedonians were complete, not wishing to be compromised by what was to follow. These doctrinal proceedings were clearly of much greater import than the record they have left would suggest. Gregory of Nazianzen in his autobiographical poem (PG 37:1143) gives a picture of 'West' lined up against 'East' in the matter, but for him the West must have meant the Greek islands, Thrace and the Asian coastlands. A careful analysis of the bishop-list for this council by N. Q. King has shown that the absentees (and there were 36 of them) who did not sign the *Acta* were chiefly from the regions just mentioned. It is the creed of Constantinople which best illustrates the nature of the dogmatic proceedings.

III The creed of Constantinople follows for most of its length that found in the *Ancoratus* of Epiphanius (118 ; GCS 25:147). Unless this creed has been introduced subsequently by a scribe into the text of Epiphanius, it must be accepted as having been in use in Cyprus for baptisms at the time when the *Ancoratus* was written (374). Some elements of the creed of Epiphanius can be traced in the *Catecheses* of Cyril of Jerusalem, but the differences are quite large, and, as Canon J. N. Kelly has shown, the hypothesis of Hort and Harnack, that Cyril proclaimed his own creed at the Council as a witness to his orthodoxy and that this creed was then made official, can scarcely be maintained. Epiphanius was not himself present at Constantinople, and one cannot, therefore, simply transfer the hypothesis to him. In his introductory remarks Epiphanius, whose accuracy as a historian is not great, says that ' this creed was handed down from the holy apostles and from all the holy bishops of that time in the Church, the holy city, who were more than 310 in number '. No one can be sure what exactly he means ; the ' holy city ' seems to be an expression he frequently uses for the Church as a whole and cannot refer to Jerusalem, but he does not tell us what time he is referring to. He may be thinking of Nicaea, but one cannot be sure of that. Canon Kelly has concluded that the true text of Epiphanius had a version of the Nicene Creed at this point and that the solitary MS has been altered to carry the Constantinople creed instead, but there are objections to this conclusion. What we read in Epiphanius is not quite the creed of Constantinople ; it has two clauses which come from the original Nicene Creed (born of the Father before all ages, *that is from the substance of the Father* . . . through whom all things were made, *the things in heaven and the things on earth*). Now if a scribe was bringing the text of Epiphanius, as he thought, up to date, there is no reason why he should leave in or insert these clauses which had been dropped from the creed of Constantinople, presumably as the need for them was no longer felt.

It may then be tentatively suggested that the Fathers at Constantinople took as a model for their own creed this Epiphanius creed (there were four Cypriot bishops at the council), removed the anathemas which came at its end, substituting for them what is now canon I of the council and touching up the wording of the creed in the two places already noted. The framework of the Constantinople creed is certainly that of Nicaea (for which *see* ARIANISM IV), but where the Nicene Creed laconically expresses belief in the Holy Ghost there has been an expansion into clauses : ' the Lord and lifegiver, the One who proceeds from the Father and the One who is to be adored along with Father and Son and glorified along with them, the One who spoke through the prophets '. Whether, as here suggested, these clauses originate in Cyprus and are adopted at the council, or are due to the council itself, matters little. The heresy of Macedonius had denied all except the last of these clauses, and that was needed against the Marcionites and Manichees (*see* CCS 35f). The Fathers at Chalcedon (*Acta conciliorum* II:i:2:128) thought that their predecessors at Constantinople had been ' making clear from Scripture (in their creed) what they believed about the Holy Spirit against those who were trying to set aside His lordship '. This emphasis on Scripture may delicately suggest that consideration was given to the idea of using the term *homoousion* once more, to declare the Holy Spirit consubstantial with Father and Son, but that it was rejected as likely to lead to a recrudescence of Arianism (cf. Socrates HE 5:8 ; PG 67:577).

Such a term was in use for the Holy Spirit in an Egyptian creed known to Macarius (who died in 390 at the age of 90), and it is found again in the creed of the *Antiphonary* of Bangor in Ireland.

The imperial view of what was done may be found in the βασιλικὸς τύπος of Justinian from the end of 543 (PG 110:784), where it is said that : ' Theodosius, when Macedonius was denying the godhead of the Holy Spirit, and Apollinaris his disciple was blaspheming against the theology of the Incarnation, called together the 150 Fathers and himself shared in their gathering, and when the aforesaid heretics had been condemned, he procured that the true faith was proclaimed '. The Apollinarists are included in the anathema of canon 1, and it has been thought that the elaboration of the words of Nicaea about the Son being made flesh (with the addition of *from the Holy Spirit and the Virgin Mary*) was due to Apollinarist dangers. At Chalcedon (*Acta conciliorum* II:i:1:91) Diogenes of Cyzicus claimed that this was so. Some Egyptian bishops tried to shout him down, not for his facts but for the very idea that additions should be made : ' No one accepts additions (to the creed) ; no one accepts diminishing thereof '. To which some Eastern bishops retorted : ' That is what Eutyches said '. It is unlikely that Constantinople saw anything like the complicated process of drafting that went on at Chalcedon where a deputation of 23 bishops withdrew to the church of St Euphemia to produce the ὅρος or doctrinal statement required. To select a formula in current use and then debate on minor changes in it seems much more in keeping with what is known of the obscure proceedings of Constantinople. What it did has lasted, and the later use of its creed is discussed under CREEDS, but how it did it remains very much in the dark, and yet it is of great importance to the theologian, for this was the second ecumenical council ; what Nicaea did was either to be followed now and so become a precedent, or discarded as a temporary expedient and perhaps never be tried again.

Bibliography. The study of Constantinople in HL II:1–48 is now somewhat superannuated and should be used with care ; *E. Schwartz, *Acta conciliorum oecumenicorum* II:i and ii (1927) on Chalcedon gives many references to what happened at Constantinople ; the same, ' Über die Bischofslisten der Synoden von Chalkedon, Nikaia und Constantinopel ', in *Abhandlungen der Münchener Akademie* XIII (1937) has been superseded by *N. Q. King, ' The 150 Fathers of Constantinople ', in TU LXIII:635–41 ; J. Lebon, ' Les Anciens Symboles à Chalcédoine ', in RHE 32 (1936) 809–76 ; *J. N. Kelly, *Early Christian Creeds* (1960 2) ; *C. H. Turner, ' Greek Canons of the Council of Constantinople ', in JTS 15 (1914) 161–78 (this was an edition of some 21 canons from two Patmos MSS ; they are identical with penitential regulations found in Basil's third letter to Amphilochius, except for canons 18 and 21. The canons are followed by a full list of bishops present at the council) ; the same, *Monumenta Iuris antiquissima* (1939), vol. II, part iii, has the Latin *Acta*.   J. H. C.

CONSUBSTANTIATION is the name for a theory of the Eucharist which supposes that, after the consecration, the substance of the bread and wine remains (whether it be 'impanated' or personally united to Christ or not), whereas in the orthodox explanation (*see* TRANSUBSTANTIATION) the elements are simply converted into the Body of Christ.

The analogy with the Incarnation, used by some of the Fathers who had to combat the Monophysite view that the humanity of Christ was taken away by the advent of the Logos, will be considered first (I) ; then (II) the position taken by some of the Reformers such as Ridley, who appealed to this analogy, and finally (III) the revival of the theory by some of the Tractarians.

I The analogy of the Incarnation with the Eucharist may have been first appealed to by Eutyches himself, for he apparently cited a passage from the *Catecheses* of Athanasius (PG 26:1325 and 86:2401) which spoke of the advent of the Logos upon the bread and wine at the Eucharist. If the faithful believed that this advent did away with the substance of bread, let them do likewise for the Incarnation ; this seems to have been the argument. It must at once be noted that there would be no argument at all if the belief in a substantial change, however it might be further described, had not been already in possession. Naturally, the orthodox Fathers had some trouble in refuting the argument from this analogy. One attempt at a reply must be considered in detail.

Pope Gelasius in his treatise on *The Two Natures in Christ* (*c.* 492) had to deal with the parallel. The capital text is in paragraph 14, but he works up to this by degrees. He says (§ 4) that it is absurd to claim that human nature is so transformed into godhead that 'its proper character ceases to exist' (*ut proprietas eius esse desierit*). In § 7 he argues that the union of the two natures must imply that one of them is destroyed or else both are mixed (*aut unius abolitio est aut utriusque confusio*). That his language is not that of technical philosophy but of common human usage appears from § 10 where he argues : 'If substance goes, then each thing ceases to be what it is' (*sublata substantia, pariter res quaelibet illa tollitur*). Then in § 14 he deals with the parallel at length. He admits that something of the bread and wine remains, and his words (*esse non desinit substantia vel natura panis et vini*) really mean no more than this, as he is speaking non-technically. He goes on to say : 'Just as, by the action of the Holy Spirit, they (the bread and wine) change into the divine substance while there remains what is proper to their nature ; so the principal mystery (of the Incarnation), the mighty power of which is shown forth by the Eucharist by reason of what is agreed properly to remain there, shows us that Christ remains one (i.e. not mixed with the godhead) because true and entire'.[1] The technical, or nearly technical language of Trent, about the permanence of the species in the

Eucharist while the substance changes, had not been developed in the time of Gelasius. He does not refuse the parallel of Incarnation and Eucharist but he lacks a precise formulation of what it is that remains. Even the text, as it has come down to us, wavers at this point and what has been reproduced is only the most probable wording of the phrase *permanente tamen.* . . . The fact of substantial change is allowed (*transeant in divinam*), but *something* must remain to justify the symbolism of eating, and that something may be compared to the human nature that remained in Christ and was not absorbed into the godhead. A more common parallel for the union of godhead and manhood in Christ was, even at this early time, the written word of God, where divine inspiration and human literary style were combined into a single work. It is right to learn from the comparison of one dogma with another (D 1796), but there are limits to be put to the area within which comparisons can operate ; the Monophysites had gone outside this area.

With Theodoret this is still more clear. In his *Eranistes*, or dialogue between an orthodox Christian and a Monophysite, he gives the argument from analogy with the Eucharist (PG 83:168), in the words of Eranistes the challenger. The reply, after a warning that the matter falls under the *disciplina arcani* and that therefore it cannot be gone into fully, is that, after the consecration or sanctification of the elements, they do not utterly lose hold of their own nature, 'for they abide by their former substance and shape and quality, and can be seen and touched as they could before', but none the less, 'adoration is paid to them as being that which they are believed to be'. As J. Garnier observed long ago in his essay (PG 84:427-33) on Theodoret's faith in the Eucharist, a full statement of Theodoret's view must have been given in his *Liber mysticus* (or catechesis on the sacraments), which is now lost. Here he has to aim at refuting an adversary. But why does he not give a straight denial to the parity that the adversary has adduced between Incarnation and Eucharist ? Because something does remain of the elements after they are consecrated, he thinks he can accept the parity and use it to refute the Monophysite view of the Incarnation ; to refuse the parity would seem to remove all basis for discussion. Origen (*Commentary* on Mt 15 ; GCS 40:58) had provided one term for what remained when he called it 'the material element' ($\tau\grave{o}$ $\dot{v}\lambda\iota\kappa\acute{o}v$), but Theodoret is clearly anxious here to keep to the popular level and does not enter into technicalities. His phrase about 'abiding by their former substance' (which does not say simply that it stays) shows that he would have accepted some form of substantial change, had he been treating the question theologically.

The pseudo-Chrysostom, in the *Epistula ad Caesarium monachum* (PG 52:755-60), appealed to the same comparison of Incarnation and Eucharist, but whether he was writing from the orthodox or from

---

[1] Sicut in hanc, scilicet in divinam, transeant sancto Spiritu perficiente substantiam, permanente tamen suae proprietate naturae, sic illud ipsum mysterium principale, cuius nobis efficientiam virtutemque veraciter repraesentant, ex quibus constat proprie permanentibus, unum Christum, quia integrum verumque, permanere demonstrat.

the Nestorian point of view must remain uncertain. A Latin version of the letter was brought to England (like some secret weapon) by Peter Martyr Vermigli and given to Cranmer ; it was cited by Ridley in his disputes about the Eucharist but was not published until 1685, when the original Latin from which Vermigli had copied was found in the convent of S. Marco at Florence. A few Greek fragments were then available but not the Greek which should represent the text of the vital passage. Enough Greek, however, is left to show that it could never have been written by Chrysostom. ' Before the bread is hallowed, we call it bread, but when by means of the priest divine grace hallows it, it is no longer to be called bread but is found worthy of the title of Body of the Lord, even while the nature of bread remains in it ; and we speak of one body of the Son and not two.' The final words may be an attempt to qualify what is said about the nature of bread remaining, whereby ' nature ' would be reduced to meaning ' natural properties ', but without the Greek original it is really impossible to guess what the writer was at ; it must be confessed that the Latin version, when it can be compared to the Greek, does not show great fidelity.

II The Reformation controversy was prepared by two currents of ideas coming down from the Middle Ages. There was the fear of too carnal a view of the Eucharist (see CAPHARNAITES), and this was exploited by the Reformers, who backed it up with passages from Augustine where he was emphasising the meaning of the Eucharist as symbolic of the union of the faithful in the Church. With these texts the Reformers could offer a view that suggested a material element (bread and wine) and a spiritual element (unity with Christ) and thus escape all appearance of carnality. This tendency was exposed for the first time by Guitmund of Aversa (c. 1090) in a tract, *De corporis et sanguinis Christi veritate*, where he attributes it to some of the followers of Berengarius. ' They say that the Body and Blood of the Lord are there contained in a hidden manner and are subject to impanation so that they may be consumed ' [1] (PL 149:1430). This is the first occasion when the word impanation is found. Later in the same work (PL 149:1482) Guitmund rejects the view as being devoid of theological reasons and contrary to the teaching of Christ, of the prophets and apostles.[2] In English the word ' impanation ' seems first to have been used by Edmund Geste in his *Treatise against the Privy Masse* (1548).

The other tendency that was at work among the Reformers, though less openly, was a philosophical one. Ockham (*De corpore Christi*, 5) had claimed that in the Eucharistic consecration there were two operations, the coming-to-be of the Body of Christ and the cessation of the substance of bread ; these two were *unum per accidens*, i.e. not absolutely

[1] Berengarii alii dicunt ibi corpus et sanguinem Domini revera sed latenter contineri, et ut sumi possint quodammodo ut ita dixerim impanari.

[2] Impanari vel invinari Christum nulla expetit ratio, nec prophetae praedixerunt nec Christus ostendit nec apostoli praedicaverunt.

inseparable. In his *Reportata* (4:6) he went further and said that consubstantiation involved fewer difficulties and was an easier theory to hold, but that the teaching of the Church was against it. The story that Tunstall of Durham, in the days of Edward VI, had admitted to Bernard Gilpin his conviction that Innocent III had been misguided in committing the Church to transubstantiation, probably means that he was an Ockhamist in this matter. St Thomas (*Summa* 3a:75:2 and 3a:75:7:@1) had considered the transformation to be instantaneous (cf. also IV *Sent*. 11:1:1), but for Ockham this was a case for distinguishing between what God naturally does and what He can do by His absolute power. When the theory of consubstantiation had thus received the philosophical blessing of Ockham, the question of evidence from Scripture and Tradition that this was what in fact God had chosen became more acute. Wyclif (D 581) had been condemned for holding consubstantiation and the error was refuted by St John Fisher in his writings againts Oecolampadius (1527).

Cranmer accepted the theory and, when Vermigli (Peter Martyr) arrived in England (20 December 1547) with his patristic evidence for it, the two men were in harmony. Bucer (himself a Lutheran) at Strasbourg had advised Vermigli, ' when he spake of the Eucharist to use more dark and ambiguous forms of speech that might be taken in a larger acceptation, urging to him that this was the course he himself took, and that a certain good man [said by Strype to be most probably Cranmer] had persuaded him that by this means the great controversy concerning the real presence in the sacrament might be at an end ' (Strype, *Cranmer*, 586). In February 1548 Vermigli was incorporated D.D. at Oxford (from Padua), and at the end of March 1548 he became Regius Professor of Divinity. In this capacity he was used by Cranmer to publish the new Zwinglian views of the Eucharist which had been adopted by the King's Council after the great debate of bishops and peers at the close of 1548. In this debate Ridley maintained (fol. 26b of the MS) that : ' Of the common breade before, it is made a divine influence. The natural substaunce of breade remaynes as it was before'. It was Ridley, too, who provided the longest catena of patristic passages in support of consubstantiation. When Cranmer and the Council went over to a Zwinglian view, Vermigli was much embarrassed but followed them more the less (*see Clergy Review* 43 [1958] 607 and 44 [1959] 424). Geste (op. cit. 86) seems to have been a forerunner of the change. He put to himself the difficulty : ' If Christ's Body be in the breade, then it is enbreaded and His Blood enwyned, whych was alway taken for a great heresy '. His answer is : ' Notwythstandinge Christ's Body be presented in the bred, it is not placely, as ther placed, spaced and measured, but ghostly . . ., howbeit it is not enbreaded, no more than the deytie is recompted enfleshed for that it is substancially in us. . . . The impanation of Christ's Body . . . is not in simple any presence indeferently of the said Body in the bred, no more than the Incarnation or enfleshing of Christ's godhead is indeferently any presence thereof in man's fleshe and nature '. Though Cranmer had changed from consubstantiation to a theory of dynamic presence at the moment of reception, he kept going back to Ridley's book in his hesitations, and thus confused the historians. When Vermigli had debated publicly at Oxford (1 June 1549) on the question, Bucer wrote to him (*Scripta anglicana* 549) : ' Most of those who read the Acts will be entirely of opinion that you assert that Christ is altogether absent from the Supper and that the only presence is that of His power and Spirit '. The remedy for this suggested by Bucer was to alter the *Acta* of the disputation.

Richard Cheyney, archdeacon of Hereford under Edward VI and bishop of Gloucester under Elizabeth, consistently held a belief in consubstantiation. Edmund Campion (who had been ordained deacon by him) in his public letter to him alludes to this when he says : ' Of all the leading heretics you have the mildest form of madness '. It appears from a letter of Geste to Cecil (printed by Darwell Stone, II:210) that in 1566 while the present XXXIX Articles were being drafted, Cheyney objected strongly to the clause added in article XXVIII, saying that : ' The body of Christ is given, taken and eaten in the Supper after an heavenly and spiritual manner only '. Geste thought that, as he had penned this clause himself, he might persuade Cecil to have the word *only* left out, for then Cheyney could continue in his belief unmolested. In May 1571 Geste returned to the charge, but without avail, and Cheyney never subscribed to the Articles at all, though he lived on for some time after their promulgation. Geste does indeed say in his second letter : ' My lord of Gloucester is pronounced excommunicate by my lord of Canterbury, and shall be cited to answer before him and other bishops to certain errors ', but Cecil must have decided that ecclesiastical trials for heresy were not to be encouraged at that juncture. Geste was himself troubled about admitting article XXIX that the wicked are in no wise partakers of Christ, but he got no satisfaction from Cecil and eventually subscribed to it, though he had complained that it was against Scripture. The rejection of consubstantiation by the Articles is neatly shown by a question and answer of the contemporary *Catechism* of Dean Nowell : ' Why dost thou not grant that the body and blood of Christ are included in the bread and cup, or that the bread and wine are changed into the substance of His body and blood ? Because that were to bring in doubt the truth of Christ's body, to do dishonour to Christ Himself and to fill them with abhorring that receive the sacrament, if we should imagine His body either to be enclosed in so narrow a room, or to be in many places at once, or His flesh to be chewed in our mouth. . . .' This tacking together of Lutheran and Catholic doctrines, for the rejection of both, and heaping up of Capharnaite and philosophical objections to Catholic doctrine shows the position finally accepted by the Anglican reformation.

III In modern times one has to note the reaffirma-

tion of belief in consubstantiation by the Evangelical Church in Germany (1957) in these terms : ' The crucified and risen Lord allows Himself in His body and blood to be received by us with bread and wine '. In England there was one stage in the Oxford Movement when consubstantiation was advocated by Dr Pusey and others, though they did not state their view with quite the same clarity as the Germans just cited. Archbishop F. Temple in his visitation charge of 1898 on the Eucharist discussed the case of Mr Bennett (1867-72) which was decided by the Privy Council. Mr Bennett had taught that Anglicans should adore Christ present in the sacrament under the veils of bread and wine. Temple commented : ' The Privy Council refused to condemn this doctrine. Though it be not explicitly taught in our formularies, there is nothing in those formularies which explicitly forbids a man to hold or to teach it. It is difficult, if not impossible, really to distinguish between this doctrine and the Lutheran doctrine commonly called Consubstantiation, and it is important that it should be clearly understood that it is not unlawful to hold it and to teach it within the Church of England ' (cf. Darwell Stone, II:583). Cheyney of Gloucester would no doubt have been grateful for such a pronouncement.

The growth of eucharistic devotions in the Anglican Church must have led many who could not accept the Catholic doctrine to acquiesce in some form of consubstantiation. Language about 'the sacramental veils ' is itself Catholic (the expression is English and comes from Aelred of Rievaulx, PL 195:227, *tegumentum sacramentorum*), and those who wanted to have Benediction with the reserved sacrament had of necessity either to accept Catholic doctrine on the Eucharist or to go in for this Lutheran doctrine ; it is well known that Luther made no bones about adoration of the Eucharist, even when he was teaching consubstantiation with emphasis.

Behind Pusey was the memory of Newman's Letter (1838) to the Lady Margaret Professor at Oxford on the Eucharist (printed in *Via Media* II: 189-249). Here Newman lamented that ' the thin and empty ears of Zurich and Geneva think it scorn unless they devour and make a clean end of the pleasant and fair pastures of Catholic doctrine which are our heritage '. He cited Hooker with approval for the view that Anglicans should accept a Real Presence, though not a local one, and should refrain from defining it further. ' The Bread and Cup ', he said with Hooker, ' are His Body and Blood because they are causes instrumental, upon the receipt whereof the participation of His Body and Blood ensueth ' (op. cit. 232). And again : ' This bread hath in it more than the substance which our eyes behold '. Newman was distressed to find the Professor ' unable even in thought to distinguish this from Consubstantiation . . ., and, in spite of Hooker and Cosin, denying that individuals holding it are safe and consistent members of the Church of England ' (op. cit. 235). Later, in his *Apologia*, Newman said of Transubstantiation : ' I did not believe the doctrine until I was a Catholic '. Pusey, too, in some of his

moods, came to accept it, thinking (mistakenly, as Darwell Stone points out, II:541, n. 1) that he had found a difference between the post-Tridentine theology of transubstantiation and the medieval. For further details of this, *see* TRANSUBSTANTIATION.
Bibliography. The tract of Gelasius, *De duabus naturis* is not in Migne ; it may be found in A. Thiel, *Epistulae Romanorum pontificum* (1868) ; St John Fisher, *De veritate corporis et sanguinis Domini* (1527) has a refutation of the Lutheran position ; A. Gasquet and E. Bishop published in *Edward VI and the Book of Common Prayer* (1891) the account of the House of Lords debate of 1548, but with some inaccuracies ; their account should be supplemented by *J. Tomlinson, *The Great Parliamentary Debate of 1548* (1915) ; E. Bueschor, *The Eucharistic Teaching of William of Ockham* (1950) ; P. Shaughnessy, *The Eucharistic Doctrine of Guitmund of Aversa* (1939) ; H. Weisweiler SJ, 'Die Impanationslehre des Johannes Quidort', in *Scholastik* 6 (1931) 161–95 ; *Darwell Stone, *The Doctrine of the Holy Eucharist* (2 vols 1909) ; A. Michaud, 'S. Gélase et le monophysisme eucharistique', in *Revue internationale de théologie* 7 (1899) 303–9 was answered by J. Lebreton SJ, in ER 117 (1901) 489–99 ; *H. Dugdale, *Life and Character of Edmund Geste* (1840) is the only biography of this divine who was the architect of much Anglican eucharistic belief ; there is no life of Cheyney and no notice of him in the *Dictionary of National Biography* ; *L. Waterman, *The Primitive Tradition of the Eucharist* (1919) sought to revive belief in consubstantiation among the Episcopalians of America ; J. Koch, 'Neue Aktenstücke zu dem Ockhamprozess', in *Revue de théologie ancienne et médiévale* 7 (1935) 353–80 and 8 (1936) 81–93 ; 168–97, has further evidence of Ockham's views ; the homily of Aelfric which was published by Abp Parker in 1566 as a proof of the antiquity of his own eucharistic views (*A Testimonie of Antiquitie*) has been shown to be quite Catholic in sense by T. Bridgett–H. Thurston, *History of the Holy Eucharist in Great Britain* (1908). Parker was right in suspecting that the homily was 'overmuch cumbered with monkery' ; it does in fact speak of 'how bread may be turned to Christ's Body, wine is turned through one blessing to Christ's Blood'. *Turnekynde* is the word used by Geste for transubstantiation ; it may have a much longer history than one might think. **J. H. C.**

CONTEMPLATION The word contemplation translates the Latin *contemplatio*, and this is the patristic translation of the Greek *theoria*, which means 'considering'. Plato held that to behold beauty itself is the highest human experience, and that the 'theoretic life', the life of 'gazing at' or considering truth, especially the highest truth, which is one with beauty and goodness, is higher than a life devoted to riches or worldly honour. After brief historical sections (I to III) the article will discuss modern theories (IV), with some criticism (V) and a conclusion (VI).
I Early Greek Tradition. Clement of Alexandria baptized the word *theoria* which, with the conviction that the 'contemplative' life was higher than the 'practical', became characteristic of the Greek Christian spiritual tradition. The 'practical' or 'active' life means asceticism and the acquisition of virtuous habits, while the 'theoretic' life becomes practically identical with communion with God in prayer. This distinction became classical, being found for instance in Augustine Baker's *Sancta Sophia* where the active life becomes 'mortification' and 'prayer' takes the place of 'contemplative life'.
II Western Tradition. This has three origins : St Augustine, a convert from Neo-Platonism ; John Cassian, who brought to the West the tradition of the Desert Fathers ; and Pseudo-Dionysius the Areopagite, translated into Latin on various occasions in the Dark and Middle Ages and representing the quintessence of one line of Eastern theory. St Benedict says little about contemplation but accepts Cassian's teaching, for which contemplation is the *raison d'être* of monastic life. From St Gregory the Great onwards, Cassian and St Augustine dominated the Western scene until the influence of Pseudo-Dionysius began to make itself strongly felt in the 12th cent.
III Middle Ages. By St Gregory the tranquil life of the cloister is contrasted favourably with the life of ecclesiastical administration—tending to a shift in the meaning of our terms, since formerly the two 'lives' were really two constituents of the single life of a man seeking God. On the later view, the contemplative life is that of those who choose the direct worship of God (indirectly serviceable to their fellow men) in preference to the direct service of man (indirectly promoting God's glory). St Thomas Aquinas (*Summa*, 2–2æ:188:6c) preferred to both these the 'mixed' life in which direct preoccupation with God 'overflows' into a service of others which is inspired and directed by this preoccupation.

It was agreed that the heart of contemplative life was prayer, liturgical and private. Prayer was direct communion with God in act. Gradually there emerges a distinction between contemplative and other kinds of prayer (e.g. 'vocal prayer' and meditation). St Thomas (*Summa* 2–2æ:180:3@1) teaches that contemplation is a simple gazing at the truth (*simplex intuitus veritatis*). Thus the act of contemplation, in Christian prayer, will be a 'gazing at' the supreme Truth, God. This act of simple intellectual apprehension differs from reasoning about God and the things of God. But St Thomas teaches that the immediate vision of God is not granted to us in this life. The act of contemplation therefore presupposes faith in God as revealed in Christ, and is a 'union with God as unknown', by which we 'know concerning God what he is not' (*Contra Gentiles*, 3:49). It is motivated by supernatural love, and the knowledge of God which it gives is other and higher than what can be attained by study and reflection. Contemplative prayer, then, will be a kind of prayer in which such contemplation preponderates over the use of the imagination and meditation.

IV Modern Period. There are three important names : St Ignatius of Loyola, St Teresa of Avila, St John of the Cross. If the early Middle Ages were the 'Benedictine centuries', the period from the Council of Trent to 1900 and beyond may well be regarded as the Jesuit age. The Society founded by St Ignatius became the great teacher of systematic meditation and of the doctrine that prayer is subordinate to ascetic practice. A common Jesuit view was that contemplative prayer was legitimate but hardly consonant with the apostolic vocation of the Society.[1] Contemplation tended to be identified with its more advanced stages ; one expected to find it accompanied by extraordinary phenomena and to regard it as somewhat dangerous. A more traditional attitude was maintained by a line of distinguished Jesuits from Lallemant to Grou.

St Teresa was a great 'mystic', not a trained philosopher or theologian. She wrote largely from experience, and her terminology is adapted to her own prayer. She rarely describes as 'contemplative' any prayer 'lower' than one in which there is experienced 'passivity'—e.g. her 'prayer of quiet', in which the person praying finds that without effort on his part his mind and will are quietly and consciously centred in God apprehended by faith.

Her younger disciple, St John of the Cross, was also a great contemplative and his experience informs his teaching. But two other elements have moulded it. One was the observed fact that friars and nuns living a fervent life and meditating assiduously tended to run into a crisis when meditation became virtually impossible. The other was his theological competence. He distinguished two 'dark nights' of the soul : the (active and) passive dark night of the senses (cf. the crisis referred to above), and the (active and) passive dark night of the spirit. These passive nights, it should be observed, are not only crises in prayer ; they are crises in a man's whole spiritual development. St John of the Cross holds that prayer is a function of the spiritual life, that life and prayer develop together and affect each other ; thus 'contemplation' takes its place as a feature of a normally developed spiritual life.

Our concern here is with the passive night of the senses. It is both a loss of appetite even for the practice of devotion, and an inability to meditate, not due to any real loss of fervour or temporary indisposition. St John explains that God is impelling the soul to a pure adhesion to him by faith and charity. No imagination or thoughts about God can be more than a substitute for that direct union with him for which the soul, moved by him, is yearning. The right sort of prayer for such a person is one of unreflecting loving attention to God as apprehended by faith : 'contemplation'. As this is a prayer which those who have successfully passed the crisis can normally practise at will, some later

authors give to it the name 'acquired' or 'active' contemplation, thus distinguishing it from St Teresa's prayer of quiet and other 'higher' kinds of contemplative prayer. But in theological (not psychological) terminology this so-called active contemplation is passive or 'infused', being possible only by God's impulsion and utterly dependent on grace. Grace in its essence is imperceptible to ordinary reflection. A person in the 'prayer of quiet' is not necessarily praying better than one who, lacking such experience, tries to 'attend lovingly' to God.

V Criticism. There are fervent people, earnestly seeking God's will, who not only cannot meditate during prayer-time but appear to fail even to attend lovingly to God. They will say that in prayer they get absorbed by involuntary distractions ; their attention wanders involuntarily and they 'come to ', finding that they have been occupied with mundane thoughts. Such involuntary absorbing distractions are distinct both from voluntary distractions, where both attention and intention are astray, and from merely superficial irrelevant ideas and images which do not seriously impede conscious attention to God and should in practice be entirely disregarded.

A director will advise the victim of involuntary distractions to persevere at all costs, but without strain or anxiety, with his prayer ; accepting distractions as a salutary humiliation. But theoretically, and perhaps practically, there may be more to say. The persons in question are not 'tepid souls' ; they really will to serve God with unlimited obedience and love. They may begin their period of prayer by trying to make an act of faith in God's presence in their souls and to offer their prayer in love and surrender to God. When they become conscious of distractions they try to redirect their attention to God—this may happen over and over again. They do not 'throw up the sponge' and deliberately provoke or surrender to distractions. Thus the intention with which they began to pray, an intention to 'attend lovingly to God', remains intact and is probably frequently renewed ; they would not retract it for anything but duty or charity. This intention is not affected by involuntary distractions but persists unperceived even while distractions are at their height. There is good reason for saying that this intention is the essence of prayer, and that therefore their prayer has been uninterrupted.

But is such distracted prayer contemplative ? It might be objected : whatever their intention may have been, there has been little or no attention to God.

The answer involves a distinction, familiar at least since St Francis de Sales, between our surface consciousness and the deeper life of the human spirit. It is comparable with the modern psychological distinction between consciousness and the subconscious ; but whereas for the moderns the subconscious is infra-rational, the spiritual writers are thinking of something superior to the level of argumentative thinking. Our surface consciousness is occupied with sense data, imagination, emotion, reasoning thought, particular acts of will. But

---

[1] St Ignatius himself means by 'contemplation' something entirely different from the traditional meaning of the word ; he means by it an intense and warmly felt realization of a scene from, or mystery of, the gospel.

'below' (or 'above') this level there is the will's more abiding, more general orientation. Thus, the organization and execution of a journey may involve many particular decisions, and attention to a host of 'absorbing details'. But the whole sequence of thought, decisions and actions is governed by the object which 'inspires' them all. The deeper will is actuated throughout by this object, which gives unity to the pervading intention of the whole journey and each of its constituents. And since the human will does not work blindly but is informed by the intelligence, it would seem that below the surface the cognitive powers have had the object of the journey continually before them.

Similarly in a period which begins with a real intention to devote the period to praying, and during which this intention is not voluntarily retracted but renewed from time to time, the basic will, or the 'apex' or 'fine point' of the soul, has been set on God throughout. This can only be because the intelligence, by faith, is occupied with God. Thus in this involuntarily distracted prayer there is a real loving attention to God above (or below) the level of surface consciousness, and not essentially affected by the distractions. Such prayer would be genuinely contemplative—and, of course, a work of grace.

VI Some Final Reflections. If contemplation is the voluntary active adhesion of the deepest self to God revealed in Jesus Christ as He is preached by the Church, it is a constituent part, indeed the essence, of all Christian prayer, whatever its superficial aspect. The vast difference between the prayer of a saint and that of a beginner is one of purity, depth and duration, not of essence. Moreover, there will be an element of contemplative prayer in all devoted service of God, since all such service is inspired by an intention to love and seek God, His will and His glory. Contemplative prayer is not the privilege of a specialised élite. It is the heart of Christian life, actuating the theological virtues at their deepest level.

Bibliography. The article 'Contemplation' (*Dictionnaire de spiritualité*, 1932 ff.) is invaluable for the history and various modern presentations of the theory ; *The Cloud of Unknowing* is published along with (*a*) *The Letter of Privy Counsel*, (*b*) a quaint rendering of Pseudo-Dionysius's *Mystical Theology*, (*c*) Baker's commentary on *The Cloud* (1943) ; de Caussade, *On Prayer* (1948) ; Bremond, *Histoire littéraire du sentiment religieux en France, VIII* (1928), Ch. ii on Piny ; Anon., *Contemplative Prayer*, in CR 3 (1932) 196–211, 278–91, 366–82 ; H. J. Chapman, 'Contemplative Prayer', in *Spiritual Letters* (1946), Appendix I.   B. C. B.

CONTINUITY, ANGLICAN The Anglican claim to continuity with the Catholic Church is generally based on the statement of the Preface to the *Ordinal* of Edward VI : 'It is evident to all men diligently reading Holy Scripture and ancient authors that from the Apostles' time there hath been these orders of ministers in Christ's Church—bishops, priests and deacons. . . . And therefore to the

intent these orders should be continued and reverently used and esteemed in this Church of England, it is requisite that no man (not being at this present bishop, priest, nor deacon) shall execute any of them except he be called, tried, examined. . . .' This article, while not giving a lengthy treatment of the question of Anglican orders (for which *see* ORDINATION), will give (I) a brief survey of the chief innovations of the Reformation settlement which break that continuity, and (II) some account of the apparent instances of continuity being maintained (*see* ANGLICANISM for an historical outline).

I The innovations of the Elizabethan settlement are those to be examined, since the Henrician and Edwardian changes had been extinguished by the reconciliation of the realm to the Holy See through Cardinal Pole in November 1554, when Parliament was absolved from heresy and schism. The chief innovation was the subordination of Church to State after a new pattern. 'When Queen Elizabeth began her reign, those that were nearest about her and more prevailed in counsel, inclining to have a change of religion, that thereby also other changes of dignities, offices and livings might ensue, and desiring to reduce all to the Queen's disposition, but yet finding great difficulty and resistance in many of the Calvinists to give the accustomed title of headship, in respect of John Calvin's reprobation thereof ; they devised a new form and feature of words, whereby covertly to give the substance without the name ; that is to say, the whole spiritual power and jurisdiction of Supreme Head under the name of Visitrix or Supreme Governesse, as in the oath of the same statute is set down, where every man . . . is bound to swear that he believeth in his conscience that the said Queen is supreme governess in all causes ecclesiastical in this sense, and that there is no other spiritual power or ecclesiastical jurisdiction over souls in England but this of the Queen or such as cometh from her' (R. Persons, *Answer to Cooke*, [1606] 58). Thomas Lever is generally credited with the suggestion to the Queen of the new title, but what is seldom noticed is that *both* titles had been used for Henry VIII, both that of Head and that of Governor. That Persons was not writing a merely partisan brief may be seen from the way in which Sir W. Holdsworth in his *History of English Law* (1:590) sums up : 'In order to create the illusion that the new Anglican Church was indeed the same as the medieval church, it was necessary to prove the historical continuity of these two very different institutions'. Referring to the work of F. W. Maitland and his refutation of the historical claim, he says : 'It was not until a historian arose who, besides being the greatest historian of this century, was both a consummate lawyer and a dissenter from the Anglican as well as from other Churches, that the historical worthlessness of Henry's theory was finally demonstrated' (op. cit. 591).

Thus the novelty of the new settlement was to give the Queen the whole power of jurisdiction which had been held by the Pope and the bishops before. It was sometimes urged by apologists for the new settlement that the Queen was not empowered to minister God's Word and the sacraments and thus had not the ' power of Order ', but it does not appear that this had been claimed by Henry VIII (Wilkins, *Concilia* III:762). Persons did suggest that the Queen might lawfully appoint a woman as her Vicaress-general to administer the Church (*Answer to Cooke*, 48) but he was here drawing attention to the dislike of female rule expressed by Chemnitz, and by others such as John Knox and the Calvinists Gilby and Goodman.

That doctrinal novelty was taken for granted by Anglicans appears from Jewel's reference to his own work when he writes about it to Peter Martyr (February 1562) : ' I have recently published an *Apology* for the change of religion and separation from the Roman church '.[1] The main change was an acceptance of the fallibility of the Church. Not everyone put this clearly to himself, but the one bishop, Cheyney of Gloucester, who ' was in judgment for the unerring of general councils ', was himself excommunicated in 1571 and seems to have been suffered to die in peace some years later. ' When the Council of Carthage was objected to him, how it erred about the baptism of heretics, he said that the Holy Ghost was promised not to one province but to the whole Church ' (Strype, *Annals*, I:i:422). T. Rogers in a semi-official commentary on the XXXIX Articles in 1586 said, on Article XIX : ' The visible Church may and from time to time hath erred both in doctrine and conversation '. The infallibility of the Church and its exercise by Pope or Council had not then been defined, though it was clearly accepted by the bishops at Trent in the care they took before committing the Church by their definitions (*see further*, INFALLIBILITY). Cranmer confused the issue in a fashion that was characteristic : ' While it is true the Church doth never wholly err, yet this Holy Church is so unknown to the world that no man can discern it ' (*Works*, 377).

Ultimately, of course, the idea that the Church is the congregation of the saints, wherever they are, in which the gospel is rightly taught and the sacraments are rightly administered, must lead to an impasse. A Scandinavian theologian, Einar Molland, has recognized this : ' In cases where the Church has to choose between the right gospel and the rightly interpreted and rightly administered sacraments on the one hand, and on the other the formal continuity of ordination, she must choose the Gospel and the Sacraments ' (in *Union of Christendom*, 18). The invisibility of the Church makes continuity a myth. For the humanist theologian such as Cranmer or Parker, the idea that one could not work back to the primitive Church adequately by one's own historical means was repugnant ; they felt that they could safely discard the existing notions of Tradition which had just been reinforced by Trent. Cranmer's appeal to ' ancient authors ' in the Preface to the *Ordinal* seems to have been based on the pseudo-Denis and his *De ecclesiastica hierarchia*, but the

[1] Edidimus nuper Apologiam de mutata religione et discessione ab ecclesia Romana.

worthlessness of this as a source was not yet understood. Strype (*Memorials of Cranmer*, I:437) shows Cranmer confident that his new rite of Orders was according to the doctrine of the Church fifteen hundred years ago ; this would take him back to the supposed time of Denis, A.D. 50. Pilkington (*Works*, 585) defended the borrowing from Denis.

The use of the word *continue* in the Preface to the *Ordinal* was probably a calculated ambiguity. It could mean ' to carry on with what has hitherto been the practice ' (and this Cranmer certainly did not intend), or it could mean ' to take up once more from the point where it was dropped ', and this seems to represent his real intent, though many of his readers must have taken the first sense of the word. Such calculated ambiguity was urged upon Peter Martyr by Bucer who said that ' a certain good man ' had taught him to do this, and Strype notes (*Memorials of Cranmer* I:586) that this was probably ' our Archbishop '. The Catholic reaction to such reversion to what was thought to be primitive is expressed in an anonymous document preserved by Strype (*Annals* I:ii:453) : ' If any in that (ancient) time disagreed from his forefathers, he is according to Irenaeus's rule to be judged suspected. As in Canterbury Cranmer disagreed from all his predecessors, in Exeter Myles Coverdale. And those men who suddenly now will leap from this point unto the Apostles' time, saying that they agree with them, they are much like as he that would challenge kindred of Constantyne the Great and would from his father skip up straight to Constantyne, saying : " I am Nicholas, and my father is William, and so I came of Constantyne "'. Continuity in this sense was not the plain man's continuity at all. Jewel said of his colleagues that ' they had restored all things, as much as possibly they could, to the ancient purity of apostolical times and to the similitude of the primitive church ' (cited by Strype, *Annals* I:ii:68). Given the state of historical knowledge in 1560, this was a hazardous boast and at the same time made it clear that continuity was not really the aim.

To mark the break in continuity the Convocation when it met in February 1559, being still Catholic, put together five articles which were to be submitted to Parliament (Strype, *Annals* I:i:81). The fifth said : ' The authority of handling and defining concerning the things belonging to faith, the sacraments and discipline ecclesiastical hath hitherto ever belonged and ought to belong only to the pastors of the Church whom the Holy Ghost for this purpose hath set in the Church, and not to laymen '. When the Lord Keeper Bacon communicated the articles to the House of Lords, he suppressed this one. Soon after (I Eliz. 1:cap. 35) Parliament enacted that : ' No manner of order, Act or determination for any matter of religion . . . made by the authority of this present Parliament shall be accepted, deemed, interpreted or adjudged at any time hereafter to be any error, heresy, schism or schismatical opinion ; any other decree to the contrary notwithstanding '. This enactment of their own infallibility, to the exclusion of the traditional authority of the Church, does not seem to have struck the members as ludicrous.

Innovation in church services was soon recognized by English Catholics after the accession of Elizabeth. A petition of the English nobility to the Council of Trent was presented in June 1562 and the reply of a committee of the Council given in August of the same year. Cardinal Hosius, Peter Soto and twelve other learned divines formed the committee. They decided that : 'It is by no means lawful for you, without great sin and the displeasure of God, to be present at these prayers and preachings of the heretics. It would be far better to suffer even the most severe hardships rather than by any sign whatever to consent to these wicked and disgraceful rites. The purpose of the iniquitous law is to bring death to souls, to confirm the schism, to shake and weaken the solidity of the Catholic Church and the see of Rome (which was set up by Christ as supreme head of His Church on earth), and anyone who obeys this iniquitous law, does what in him lies to approve it by tacit consent, he forwards it and becomes a sharer in the same schism '.[1] The document was published by C. G. Bayne as Appendix 46 in his *Anglo-Roman Relations 1558–65* (1913).

The late Fr J. H. Pollen SJ disposed of the story (which he traced to Elizabeth herself) that the Popes had offered to approve the *Book of Common Prayer* if it were to be accepted by the Queen as coming to her from papal authority (in MN 100 [1902] 274–80). The tale goes back to some French intrigue of 1560 which the Queen revived from time to time for her own purposes. It is obvious that such a story could easily create confusion in the minds of those who had heard something of the Tridentine decision just cited but who did not know its exact wording.

II The signs of apparent continuity depend in the main on the consecration of Parker as archbishop of Canterbury. There was a flaw about this according to the civil law, as Bonner showed when he challenged the legality of proceedings against himself taken in October 1563 by Horne, whom Parker had consecrated to be bishop of Winchester. Bonner's grounds were that the *Ordinal* of Edward VI had no Parliamentary approval and that the consecration of Horne had not been according to the statute, 25 Henry VIII cap. 20 (which called for four bishops as consecrators). Eventually, in 1566, a law had to be made to give legal sanction retrospectively to what had already been done. The preamble to this (8 Eliz. I cap. 1) recites how 'overmuch boldness of speech and talk amongst many of the

[1] Minime vobis sine magno scelere divinaque indignatione licere huiusmodi haereticorum precibus illorumque concionibus interesse. Ac longe multumque praestare quaevis vel atrocissima incommoda perpeti, quam profligatissimis sceleratissimisque ritibus quovis signo consentire ; cum enim impia lex in animarum exitium lata ac schisma confirmare et ecclesiae catholicae integritatem Romanaeque sedis (quae a Christo summus ecclesiae suae vertex in terris est praefinita) nephario convellere et labefactare conatur, quicunque iniquae legi paret, illam quoad eius fieri potest tacita consensione approbat, in eamque conspirat, atque eiusdem schismatis particeps est.

common sort of people being unlearned hath lately grown upon the making and consecrating of archbishops and bishops within this realm '. It was no doubt in this *milieu* that the 'Nag's Head' story originated, though it does not appear in print until later. No credence is to be attached to it. Cecil was aware of the legal difficulties, as he made clear by annotating a document drawn up before the consecration ; he notes : 'There is no archbishop, nor iiii bishopps now to be had, wherefore *quaerendum* etc.', and also, about the *Ordinal* : 'This booke is not established by parlement'. Eventually Barlow, Scory, Coverdale and Hodgkin carried out the consecration, Barlow acting as chief consecrator. Scory and Coverdale had been consecrated according to the Edwardine *Ordinal* on the same day (30 August 1551). Hodgkin was a Henrician bishop, but only a suffragan. There is no record of the consecration of Barlow, who was elected bishop in 1536 and should have been consecrated at that time. The lack of record has been the subject of bitter polemics ; it is a difficult question, turning on the degree of carefulness one has the right to expect in keepers of records of those times, and here judgments can vary widely. It certainly would have been strange conduct to make Barlow the principal in the rite if there was any doubt about his position. Whatever the position of Barlow, it is clear that lack of continuity was felt, because the royal commission to the four bishops contained a dispensing clause : 'Supplying by our supreme royal authority if in what you do at this our behest . . . aught be lacking for the carrying out of this commission either by statute law of this our realm or from what the ecclesiastical laws require in this part. . . .' This is enough to indicate that the royal *fiat* was intended to make up for lack of continuity.

The hierarchy of bishops, priests and deacons was in apparent continuity with the past, but, as a Russian theologian pertinently asked of the Anglicans in conversations of 1956 : 'What was the point of securing the recognition of the consecration of Archbishop Parker if the sacrament of Orders did not exist ? The Orthodox cannot recognise the other five sacraments as being on a lower plane, only described as sacramental rites' (*Anglo-Russian Theological Conference* [1958], 113). Yet this is exactly the position that the first Anglicans took up. Episcopacy might have been taken away without touching the essence of their Church : 'If it had pleased Her Majesty to have used no bishops at all, we could not have complained justly of any defect in our Church', wrote Whitgift (Strype, *Life of Whitgift*, III:222). Jewel (*Works*, III:335) agreed : 'If there were no bishops left alive, yet would not therefore the whole Church of England flee to Lovaine '. Pilkington too, while allowing that good bishops were a blessing of God, said : 'Because God and His truth hangs not on man nor place, we rather hang on the undeceivable truth of God's word in all doubts than on any bishops, place or man' (*Works*, 598). It was only under pressure from the Puritans, and notably after Bancroft's sermon at St

Paul's (9 February 1589), that Anglicans began to urge the divine right of bishops.

Ironically enough, it was a distinction in Stapleton (*Relectio principiorum fidei . . . : Controversia I:5*) between the essence (or *definitio intrinseca*) and the *plena essentia seu descriptio* of the Church that was seized upon by Bramhall to explain how Anglicans regarded episcopacy. For Stapleton the strict essence included the idea of hierarchy, but Bramhall let this be a point of perfection, or of the *plene esse* of the Church. This distinction has become popular again in recent controversies, for, if Methodists and others are to be urged to accept episcopacy with a view to their reconciliation with the Anglican Church, it is much more likely that they will accept it as belonging to the perfection of the Church than if they are told that it is a condition *sine qua non*. After a High Church offensive in *The Apostolic Ministry* (1946 and 1957) by Bishop Kirk and others, there was an effective evangelical reply by Norman Sykes in *Old Priest and New Presbyter* (1956), where the gradual change of front of the early Anglicans was established.

Continuity in canon law was not secured. Cranmer was busy with a *Reformatio legum* but did not finish his work. In 1571 (cf. Sir J. Neale, 'Parliament and the Articles', in EHR 67 [1952] 510–21) the project was taken up again, and 'the Archbishop laboured to get the Queen's allowance to it [the *Book of Canons*] but had it not'. In 1604 James I did give his royal approval, but Parliament did not sanction the work. Hence, as Lord Hardwicke said in 1737 : 'The Canons of 1604, not having been confirmed by Parliament, do not *proprio vigore* bind the laity'. One of the motives for pressing on with new Canons in Elizabeth's time was the matter of clerical marriage. Sandys wrote to Parker (Strype, *Annals* I:ii:118) : 'No law was made about the marriage of priests, but it was left as it were *in medio* ; the Queen would wink at it but not establish it by law, which is nothing else but to bastard our children'. It is at present understood by English civil lawyers that medieval canon law might still be in force for the Anglican clergy in matters where it is not in conflict with any statute of the realm. In 1621 Archbishop Abbot, who shot a keeper with his cross-bow while out hunting, was held to have incurred the canonical irregularity of bloodshedding and sought a royal pardon. A more recent case was that of Bishop Winnington-Ingram of London, who claimed jurisdiction over the crypt chapel of the House of Commons (with a view to forbidding a non-conformist holding a baptism there). The Law Officers of the Crown disagreed about the case and the Government resigned (in 1923) before a decision was reached. Here the claim to jurisdiction rested on the fact that the chapel retained its status as a consecrated building, and for this the medieval understanding of consecration and its loss was used. Such matters as right of sanctuary and the seal of confession are ill-defined in law because of the obscurity about this survival of canon law.

Bibliography. L. Hicks SJ, 'The Ecclesiastical Supremacy of Queen Elizabeth', in MN 183 (1947) 170–7 ; the same, 'Elizabethan Royal Supremacy', in MN 184 (1947) 216–28 ; the same, 'The Consecration of Archbishop Parker', in MN 182 (1946) 131–43 ; *N. Sykes, *Old Priest and New Presbyter* (1956) ; *H. F. Woodhouse, *The Doctrine of the Church in Anglican Theology 1547–1603* (1954) ; *M. Maclure, *The Paul's Cross Sermons* (1961) ; C. Hoare, *Continuity* (1938) ; *G. H. Williams, *The Radical Reformation* (1962) ; E. Messenger, *The Reformation, the Mass and the Priesthood* (2 vols, 1936–8) ; P. Hughes, *The Reformation in England* (3 vols, 1950–5).   J. H. C.

CONTRITION This is considered as the main part of repentance after grave sin. So we shall explain (I) the Catholic notion of repentance, chiefly according to Trent ; (II) the definition of contrition and its necessity for all remission of sin ; (III) the qualities required in all contrition ; (IV) the distinction of contrition into perfect and imperfect ; (V) the notion of perfect contrition, that it justifies, and how it justifies ; (VI) perfect contrition and the sacrament of Penance.

I Catholic Notion of Repentance. Trent (D 798, 801, 807, 894, 897) explains the Catholic idea of repentance. It is an act universally necessary for sinners. It can be described as a free movement of the will, hating and detesting the sinful act, turning from it to God's mercy with the hope of forgiveness based on faith, and with a firm purpose of leading a good life.

The occasion of this teaching was the Protestant idea of repentance as an initial torturing of conscience that is changed into consolation on the perception of God's promise that leads to faith (*Confessio Augustana*, art. 13). Calvin stressed in addition the fact of a new life according to God's will. This notion, the Protestants said, is evangelical, as opposed to the Catholic teaching, which is also evil and hypocritical. For it suggests that man can free himself while (in the Protestant supposition) he knows that he cannot.

The Catholic notion is derived from the OT and NT through the tradition of the Fathers and Scholastics. Thus Ps 50 ; Dan 3:39–40 ; Bar 2:11 ff. show the required elements, which can be multiplied by any reading of the prophets. It is this, then, that is understood in the NT passages like Mt 3:3–8 ; Lk 17:2–3 ; Ac 2:37–8 ; Mt 21:29–30 ; Ac 8:22–3 ; 26:18–20. Nor, of course, is it Catholic teaching that man frees himself, but that he disposes himself with the help of God, co-operates with God.

II The Definition of Contrition given by Trent (D 897) reads : '. . . contrition is a sorrow of the soul and a detestation of the sin committed, with a purposing not to sin for the future'. This definition sees mortal sin as an act by which God has been offended, and as a present resultant state of privation of grace entailing eternal loss. Following this mental apprehension there is sorrow, sadness (at least spiritual, though it may also be sensible) at the fact and state of sin perceived as evil. So there is a hate or detestation of the sin in the will, a wish that it had not been committed, a desire that it and its effects be abolished. Such a hatred carries with it a firm purpose in the will to avoid such evil, i.e. not to sin again (though the possibility could be speculatively foreseen).

These three constituent elements are accepted by all, though there is a dispute whether all are formal constituents, or only follow upon a formal constituent of sorrow (Billuart) or of detestation (Suarez). The majority of theologians accept them all as formal constituents because Trent and Scripture show them simply as constituting contrition. (Thus we find detestation of sin in Ez 18:31 ; Ps 50:6 ; Is 38:15 ; sorrow in Jl 2:13 ; Is 38:15 ; Ac 2:37, and firm proposal in Ez 18:21-4, 31). These ideas are also traditional (cf. St Gregory, PL 76:1256 ; St Augustine, PL 36:409) though, as usual, without the later precision and systematization. It is commonly held that the firm proposal can be virtual if the penitent does not explicitly advert to the future. This can only be true if his sorrow is truly universal, and so implicitly detests all sin, even for the future.

The need for contrition for all forgiveness of mortal sin is defined Catholic teaching. Trent (D 798-9) described man's movement to God, including contrition as a required disposition or preparation for justification. Then in Session XIV (D 894-7) it described the part of the penitent in the sacrament, and, against the Protestants, defined his acts of Contrition, Confession and Satisfaction to be necessary for the remission of sin (D 914). The scriptural basis for the definition can be found in e.g. Ps 50, the Prophets, the words of John the Baptist, Lk 13:1-5 ; Mt 11:20-2 ; Ac 2:8, 26.

Since the elements of contrition constitute the very process of conversion, they are the necessary means of forgiveness, in addition to being commanded by God. Cano, Soto (d. 1560) and others of their school held that contrition must always be formal contrition. Scotus (d. 1308) and others defend virtual contrition (i.e. contained in some other act) as always sufficient. The main view now is that, since contrition is part of the process of conversion, it is *per se* required and should be always formal and explicit. It can only be supplied either by what contains it (e.g. charity, as elsewhere indicated) or *per accidens*, e.g. when a man unintentionally forgets the explicit detestation.

III The qualities required in all contrition are that it be supernatural, universal, supreme or *appretiative summa*. It must be supernatural because it is a salutary act, an act leading to salvation. So it is defined that it must proceed from a principle of grace (*see* GRACE). It is controverted whether it must also be supernatural in its motive. The common view is that it must ; but, despite the condemned proposition (D 1207), some probability cannot be denied to the other view. In this a naturally known motive (e.g. that sin offends God) could give rise to contrition supernatural in its principle, grace, much as the convert's judgment of the need for believing, or his pious will to believe,

are held to be supernatural, although they follow only a rational process and motive.

It must be supreme. This does not refer to the intensity of the sorrow or detestation, or to its duration ; it refers to the appreciation or valuation that lies behind it, so that the will is presented with an efficacious motive and detests sin effectively. This valuation will differ in perfect and in imperfect contrition. In perfect contrition, proceeding from charity, the valuation will be absolutely supreme, regarding sin as the greatest evil and God as the greatest good. In imperfect contrition, proceeding from e.g. the foulness of sin or the fear of hell, the valuation is that sin is a greater evil than any other evil (e.g. death), fear of which might lead a man to sin. In that sense the detestation of sin is greater than any other. Some few theologians held that supreme intensity was needed for supreme detestation (Hickey, Pallavicini) ; others (Baius, Estius) said that perfect contrition which was already supreme and could justify a sinner in the sacrament, needed supreme intensity to justify outside the sacrament.

This quality is needed so that the conversion may be efficacious. For if any good is seen in sin, or if any evil is feared more than sin, then the will of man has not a fully efficacious motive ; its aversion-conversion will be defective. Supreme intensity of affection is not required, for that concerns the natural and spontaneous reaction of the will to good and evil. So, while it is desirable and an ideal, it is not free and cannot be commanded. Nor is it needed, if the intellect presents an efficacious motive to the will.

Finally, contrition must be universal, that is to say it must detest all actual mortal sins. For sin is to be detested as an offence against God. This is a universal notion, applicable to all mortal sin, so that a man would not be sorry for one if he were not sorry for all. Furthermore sin is remitted by the infusion of grace, and so one mortal sin cannot be remitted without all being remitted. Hence contrition must be universal. Virtual universality will *per accidens* suffice ; though for sacramental confession and to make firm proposals about duties arising from repented sin (e.g. restitution), a consideration of the sins themselves is obviously needed.

IV Contrition divided into perfect and imperfect. Hitherto we have considered contrition as a general term for the central act of repentance, referring only to its division into perfect and imperfect when speaking of its qualities. Here we treat that distinction up to Trent, leaving the rest for the article on ATTRITION or imperfect contrition.

The words *atteri* and *attritio* ('to be attrite' and 'attrition') are first found in Simon of Tournai and Alain de Lille in the 12th cent., but the idea is traditional. The Fathers describe the process of conversion as having many stages or elements. The sinner disposes himself under the influence of God, so that he turns from sin and to God until he is sincerely repentant. In this many acts and motives can be discerned—fear, hatred, desire, faith, love, hope, etc. . . . For the graver sins the Church's intervention (*Actio Poenitentiae*) is required, and means that the Church collaborates with the sinner, leads him through the process of canonical penance and finally completes it with her reconciliation and absolution. The Fathers emphasize that in all conversion it is God who justifies and gives grace. The precise question as to what sorrow is sufficient is not asked, but the aim is sincere and complete conversion through the *Actio Poenitentiae*, and that will mean contrition. Hence love of God is always sought, and will normally be achieved even before the end of the Church's penance and the giving of absolution.

In the 11th cent. theologians like Yves de Chartres began to divide the interior acts of the penitent from the exterior act of the Church, which was thought of as the external sign of the internal act. Abelard (d. 1142) then separated them further so that interior repentance led to charity and justification, while the Church's act was conceived only as remissive of temporal penalty. Consequently, he said, only charity is sufficient for contrition ; fear is insufficient. At the end of the 12th cent. the word 'attrition' was used by Alain de Lille (d. 1202) in the sense of incipient or imperfect contrition. The imperfection was described by him and by others in various ways —because it lacked the proposal to confess and to sin no more, because it lacked intensity, because it was forced and not entirely free. It was accepted that only perfect contrition would justify ; but eventually this problem was posed : 'What if a sinner, only attrite, received the sacrament thinking he was contrite ?' (cf. St Bonaventure [d. 1274], IV *Sent* : 17, ii:2:3). No fully satisfactory explanation was given, but they conceded that he would be justified, becoming contrite. Somehow *ex attrito fit contritus*, the attrite becomes contrite.

St Thomas (d. 1274) was able to synthesize the data of preceding theologians (*see also* ABSOLUTION). He distinguished attrition as a partial conversion (detesting sin as an offence against God greater than any evil) from contrition, in which the whole process of conversion to God through the Church is found. (cf. IV *Sent*:17:2:1:*solutio* 1, '. . . sorrow of the will with the proposal to confess and make satisfaction'). The universal necessity of a link with the Church's absolution is to be noted. This contrition is perfect and justifying when it is joined with charity and so with grace. Hence, normally, charity is one of the dispositions of a sinner receiving the sacrament (IV *Sent*:17:3:2:*solutio* 1:@2 ; IV *Sent*:21:2:2). But it can happen that man receives absolution not so fully disposed (we would say 'only attrite'). The sacrament, with dispositive causality, completes the process of repentance giving the sinner grace and justification (IV *Sent*:22:a:1:*solutio* 3). Doronzo (II, 297) notes that St Thomas makes no mention of good faith being needed for this sufficiency of attrition (against Galtier, n. 400).

It will be seen that this viewpoint is ontological rather than psychological ; it considers efficacy rather than the varying motives. But charity is the distinguishing mark of sufficient from insufficient contrition, at least in this sense that a man cannot be justified unless his sorrow includes an act of charity or unless the sorrow he brings to the sacrament is compatible with the charity which the sacrament will produce (cf. IV *Sent*:20:1:1, *solutio* 1:@1 ; *Summa*, 1–2æ:113:5:@1 ; 3a:85:5:c and @1 ; cited by P. Anciaux, *Le Sacrement de la pénitence* [1957] 76). Others hold that for St Thomas there is a distinction of motive (Doronzo, II, 9 ; Dondaine, 8).

Scotus developed the question further, distinguishing clearly two ways of justification. The first is by contrition that merits *de congruo* by its charity (i.e. not as if by strict merit and justice, but as a suitable disposition that God would accept and complete). The second way is by the sacramental absolution given to one whose dispositions are without that merit, without charity. Yet the sinner must be attrite, repentant and opposing no obstacle to God's grace. By this Scotus focussed attention on charity as a distinguishing motive. Unfortunately he also obscured the essential uniformity of the penitential process as St Thomas had explained it, a uniformity in which the interior repentance and the activity of the Church always go together. His line of thought was widely followed, though at times exaggerated into laxism by some Nominalist writers (cf. Dondaine, 24–6). It was already common by the time of Trent, defended by theologians like Soto and Cano, though with some doubts.

The sense of Trent itself (cf. Dondaine, Perinelle) was to be widely disputed later (cf. ATTRITION) but this much seems clear. While not canonizing either view the Council used both. It firmly set all repentance into the context of the sacrament, as St Thomas had done, and then spoke in terms of charity and fear to explain the two sorrows that are sufficient, perfect contrition and attrition (D 898). Hence such a way of distinguishing the two contritions became general. The later history concerns mainly the sufficiency of attrition, and will be treated under ATTRITION. For the rest of this article we shall deal only with perfect contrition.

V Perfect Contrition reconciles to God. The common notion of perfect contrition is that it proceeds from charity, love of God in himself. This does not, of course, exclude loving the goodness of God by which we profit (e.g. his wisdom, mercy, etc.). Some Scotists, however (cf. Brancatus *De Poenitentia*, Disp. 8, 2, 20 ; Minges, *Compendium Theologiae*, III, 512), go further and think that contrition from motives other than the goodness of God can be called perfect contrition, as long as they are motives regarding God in himself (e.g. justice, religion). This is commonly rejected because of the way Trent and Scripture speak of perfect and justifying contrition. Only charity seems intended.

The fact that perfect contrition justifies is theologically certain from Trent (D 898). Trent teaches that contrition can sometimes be perfected by charity and so reconcile to God even before the sacrament is received, though not without including the desire of the sacrament. For this desire is a condition *sine qua non* of charity, once Christ institutes the sacrament as a necessary means. Compare also D 880, 893, and the condemnation of Baius's assertion that there could be an act of charity without remission of sin (D 1031-3, 1070).

The OT justifies this teaching not only because adult remission of sin would there have to be *ex opere operantis* (and so, obviously from his most perfect act, charity) but also because of texts like Deut 4:29 ; Prov 8:17. In the NT the connection of our love with being loved by God, or indwelt by God, is equally stated and demands grace (cf. Jn 14:21-3 ; 1 Jn 4:7-13). Tradition confirms this by the idea of Baptism of desire and by explicit statements (e.g. St Chrysostom, PG 50:607 ; St Augustine, PL 38:211 ; St Gregory, PL 76:1241).

How perfect contrition justifies is variously explained by the theologians. Trent answered the Protestant accusation that Catholics taught a man to be justified by his own efforts. The council stated clearly that ' nothing of what precedes justification, whether faith or works, merits the grace of justification itself' (D 801). A few theologians (Dominic and Peter Soto, Vasquez, etc.) would think of charity as a partial, formal cause of justification ; but this seems true only of the grace infused by God. Man's activity is only dispositive, and charity, or perfect contrition, acts as an efficient, meritorious and material cause. For this disposition is the most perfect that man can achieve with the aid of God's grace. While, therefore, it cannot merit *de condigno*, or in strict justice (D 801), it is a disposition that makes it congruous or fitting that God should justify man. So it is said by many to merit justice *de congruo*, and infallibly at that. This is not because of its intrinsic perfection but because of God's promise that he will love those who love him (cf. Galtier, n. 90). It must be noted that there is a necessary relation in such charity to the sacramental absolution. This is expressed by saying that perfect contrition justifies but only if it includes *votum sacramenti*, the desire of the sacrament, explicit or at least implicit. The further point about the priorities and mutual causality of grace and charity is intricate and controverted (cf. St Thomas, IV *Sent*:17:1:4: *solutio* 2, and modern comments on this text).

VI Perfect Contrition and the Sacrament of Penance. A few words will suffice in addition to the points already touched. From what has been said it is clear that some contrition is needed in the sacrament of Penance. The notion given above of perfect contrition should show its obvious sufficiency when it is present as one of the dispositions of a sinner receiving the sacrament. In fact the only question raised was why the sacrament was needed, and how it entered in. The solution found was that Christ had made the intervention of the power of the keys necessary, so that the desire of the sacrament was to be included in perfect contrition (cf. ABSOLUTION and **II** and **IV** above). The point that perfect contrition, though desirable and to be sought, is not universally necessary as a disposition for receiving the sacrament is treated under ATTRITION.

Bibliography. E. Doronzo, *De Poenitentia* II

(1951) ; P. Galtier, *De Poenitentia* II (1950) ; P. Anciaux, *La Théologie de la pénitence au XIIe siècle* (1949); the same, *Le Sacrement de la pénitence* (1957) ; A. Perinelle, *L'Attrition d'après le Concile de Trent et d'après Saint Thomas d'Aquin* (1927) ; H. Dondaine, *L'Attrition suffisante* (1943); J. de Blic, ' Sur l'Attrition suffisante ', *Mélanges de science religieuse* 2 (1945) 329-66 ; M. Flick, *L'attimo della Giustificazione secondo S. Tommaso* (1949) ; C. R. Meyer, *The Thomistic Concept of Justifying Contrition* (1949) ; P. de Letter, ' Two Concepts of Attrition and Contrition ', TS 11 (1950) 3-33.   J. McD.

CONVERSION A man can turn his mind and his will ; conversion can therefore be analysed as either religious or moral. When a conversion towards God follows upon an aversion the process is principally one of change of will, but when it follows upon a state of ignorance or indifference it can be described as more genuinely intellectual or religious. The end-state to which religious conversion moves is discussed under the word FAITH, while the lines of thought that a convert follows are treated under APOLOGETICS. The reverse process is treated under APOSTASY, and it is there made evident that the dynamics of theology are of much greater difficulty than the statics ; movements of the spirit are harder to analyse than the abiding realities. The whole process, repentance, faith and baptism, which is to be studied under the Tridentine term JUSTIFICATION, is understood by the Church in a way that differs from the Lutheran fiduciary faith, and Trent was mainly concerned with refuting this view, not with the analysis of conversion-movements in the individual or the group. Strict Lutherans, such as Flacius Illyricus, favoured *monergismus* (sole-working) which attributed all the movement to God, while Melancthon came nearer to the Catholic idea of joint-working (D 797), which he called *synergismus*. Here religious conversion (or the movement towards a Christian faith in God) will be studied (I) in Scripture and (II) in Tradition, and then more briefly moral conversion (III) from sin to grace, and (IV) from the way of the precepts to that of the counsels (sometimes styled a second conversion) will be examined, with a final note on (V) the psychology of conversion.

I Religious conversion is described in the NT by the term ἐπιστροφή which in 1 Thess 1:9 and 1 Pet 2:25 has acquired the meaning of a religious and not merely moral conversion. The change is not just from sin to doing good but to faith in the living God. In much the same way the word ' conscience ' (*q.v.*) changed, acquiring a connotation of true belief alongside right action. There was a gradual realisation that the change from idolatry to Christian faith was not quite the same as the change from sin to good works (Ac 14:15-16). Even in the OT (e.g. Is 30:15, LXX) there is the idea that conversion involves a deepening of knowledge. In 2 Tim 2:25 Paul speaks of God, ' granting men repentance unto the knowledge of the truth ', thus emphasizing the two phases of conversion. This phrase is echoed by the Jerusalem critics of Peter in Ac 11:18, who speak of 'repentance unto life'. In 2 Cor 7:10 Paul proclaims : 'Sadness according to God worketh repentance unto salvation, and this abides'. On his way to the Council at Jerusalem (Ac 15:3) he speaks everywhere of the 'conversion of the Gentiles', and the fact that he had already, at Lystra, told them that God had borne with their idolatry in the past shows that he did not regard conversion (which must from this point onwards be accepted as a technical Christian term) as being simply a change from evil to good.

II Christian tradition accepted some loans from the philosophy of the time. Plato had used the idea of 'turning-round' when developing his myth of the cave-dwellers who had to judge of the outside world by shadows and could not turn round to see the realities (*Rep.* 518c–519b). This περιαγωγή is almost equivalent to the Christian idea of religious conversion. What holds the soul back, according to Plato, is the leaden weight of the appetites, but what it is seeking is greater knowledge. Clement of Alexandria (*Paed.* 1:6 ; GCS 12:108) claims that the Christian catechesis 'turns the soul round unto faith' (and the word used is Plato's), while elsewhere (*Strom.* 6:3:34 ; GCS 52:448) he speaks of God doing miracles to promote the conversion of the unbelieving soul. He counts (*Strom.* 6:3:28 ; GCS 52:444) threats, promises, commands and miracles as God's weapons for producing conversion and cannot therefore have regarded it as simply an affair of morals. The personal narrative of Justin (*dial.* 8:1) tells us how a Christian Ancient broke in on his philosophic meditations, showing him that Christianity is the whole of which his Platonic philosophy had been a part (Justin, *append.* 13:2–3), and 'a fire is suddenly kindled in my soul, and desire takes possession of me for the prophets and those men who are the friends of Christ'.

In an age that was singularly lacking in introspection the conversion of Paul did not excite much analytical treatment. Hippolytus considers it typologically. Commenting on Gen 49:27 (GCS 1:71), he says that Paul was typified by Benjamin : 'In the beginning he persecuted the Church and at evening he gave us our spiritual food'. Origen was frankly allegorical in his analysis of conversion. Somehow, for the word is never used by Philo, he found that the mystical meaning of the name Jephone was 'conversion'. 'Caleb therefore is the son of conversion. Instruction is first from Moses and then from Jesus' (*hom. on Jos* 18:2 ; GCS 30:407). After conversion came the study of the Scriptures. But the name Phenenna also signified conversion, while Anna (the other wife of Helcana) signified grace. Origen therefore gave an elaborate analysis (*hom. in* 1 *Kg* 1:5 ; GCS 6:8) of the interplay of grace and human effort in the work of conversion : 'First a man should marry the one that is more elevated and nobly-born, i.e. grace, for she is the first to be joined to us by faith, as Paul says (Eph 2:8). But a man should also be married to Phenenna, i.e. to conversion, for after the coming of grace the improvement

that faith brings causes a conversion in one's moral life. This is the order of marriages, but the order of begetting children is different. Phenenna is the first to bear children to us, since it is from conversion that we produce our first offspring and beget by our acts and labours the first shoots of the just life. The first work of justice is to be converted from sin, for unless we are first converted and turn aside from evil, we cannot achieve paternity by Anna and beget the offspring of grace. . . . Phenenna has children, but they do not stand before God, since the offspring of conversion are not such as can stand before God and cleave to Him, yet they are not completely void and estranged from the things of God. . . . Each of us then is first converted from sin, and then after his conversion begets the works of justice. Afterwards Anna is through rivalry and the emulation of the good aroused in our regard and puts up prayers to God that she may bear children too who will stand before God. . . . Unless the work of conversion goes before, we shall not merit the grace of the Spirit nor be able to produce from it the gift of the Spirit'. This *tour de force* was available to the West in the version of Rufinus, and it must have had its influence on those who came to think of the passage of the soul from sin to grace as if it were bound to traverse a zero-point where neither sin nor grace was found (*see also* GRACE, PELAGIUS).

St Thomas has in various places discussed the conversion of Paul. In the commentary on the Sentences (II *Sent.* 28:1:4:@3) he regards the sudden light from heaven as an occasion which induced Paul to dispose himself for the infusion of grace. In *De veritate* (28:3:@4) he says that it cannot easily happen that a man with Original sin upon him should avoid yielding to actual sin (which, however, seems to envisage the case where this freedom from actual sin was possible) and he adds (ibid. @19) that Paul consented to his grace at the very instant of its infusion. In the *Summa* he has come to the view (1–2æ:113:10c) that there was not only the miraculous external intervention of God but an internal one as well. Here he lays down a distinction between *conversio imperfecta et perfecta*, as if he regarded the case of Paul as non-typical. Nowhere does he seem to consider the words spoken by Christ to Paul ('I am Jesus whom thou dost persecute', Ac 9:5) as a shortened form of apologetic argument suggesting the identity of the Suffering Servant and His members in the new Israel and thus supplying a brief argument from prophecy. In the controversies about grace that followed Trent, the theology of conversion was occasionally illuminated by the lightnings of the theological storm, but its centre was elsewhere.

III Moral conversion is practically the only type understood in the OT. Repentance (μετάνοια) brings a man from an evil life and from idolatry to the service of God (e.g. Os 6:1–4 and 14:2–4). At times (Is 63:17) God is Himself blamed for their falling-away, but this is due to the Jewish failure to discriminate between primary and secondary causality in God, whereby He was blamed for what He could have prevented but did not. Yet the whole message of a work like Jona is to enhance the value of human efforts towards repentance. The preaching of John the Baptist was aimed at the same mark, and what John said (Mt 3:2) was taken up by Christ (Mt 4:17), was given by Him to the Apostles as the burden of their preaching (Mt 10:7) and then proclaimed by them to Jerusalem (Ac 2:38 ; 3:19). The approach of the kingdom is given as a motive for repentance, but the initial emphasis is on ' Repent ' rather than on ' Believe '.

Hermas with his Jewish outlook takes it for granted in his parables about conversion (66:1–69:8 ; GCS 48:64–9) that this is always the overcoming of an evil life and he does not envisage the case of a conversion from philosophic doubt to religious faith, even though one such (that of Justin) was taking place at the time of his writing. He holds (66:4 ; GCS 48:64) that the process of conversion is a long one, requiring much penance. For the conversion of Augustine, which is just such a ' lingering slow, sweet skill ' on God's part, *see* AUGUSTINE I.

The conversion of St Patrick, as described for us in his *Confessio*, stresses the moral aspect of the process. He was the son of a deacon and had presumably been baptized, but he ' did not know the true God ' at the age of sixteen. ' We did not keep His commandments and did not obey our priests who used to remind us of our salvation. . . . The Lord opened the sense of my unbelief, that I might at last remember my sins and be converted to Him ' (*Confessio*, 1–2). ' I lived in death and unbelief until I was chastised and humiliated by hunger and nakedness day after day ' (ibid. 27). ' He that is mighty came and in His mercy lifted me up and placed me on the top of the wall ' (ibid. 12). There is no Pelagian nonsense about all this, but it may be significant that one of the Patrician canons (can. 29) requires that ' if one of the brethren wishes to receive the grace of God, he shall not be baptized until he has kept the forty days' fast '.

The importance of the moral aspect of conversion is shown in the story of Marius Victorinus, told by Augustine (*Confessiones* 8:2 ; CSEL 33:173). He had the intellectual conviction that Christianity was true, but could not bring himself to decide that it was worth while for himself (*see* APOLOGETICS XIII for the analysis of these two judgments). He kept saying to his friend Simplicianus : ' You know that I am already a Christian'. Simplicianus would reply : ' I shall not count you a Christian until I see you within the walls of the Church.' At this Victorinus would say : ' It is the walls then that make the Christian ', for he feared to alienate his pagan friends.

IV Conversion to a life of perfection was canvassed as a possibility by Clement of Alexandria (*Strom.* 7:10:57 ; GCS 17:42) when he wrote of ' a first change in the direction of salvation from paganism to faith, and a second from faith to Gnosis, and this is made perfect in charity '. *Conversio* in this sense is first met with in some conciliar decrees

of the 6th cent. (Arles in 524, can. 1 and Orleans in 538 and 549, cans. 6 and 9 respectively). The first of these runs : ' No layman should receive the dignity of the priesthood unless he has first undergone a period of *conversio* and is thirty years old '.[1] The period of *conversio*, later fixed at one year, seems to be linked with the introduction of celibacy for priests. The *Rule* of St Benedict (58 and 73 ; CSEL 75:133 and 164) speaks of the *conversio morum* that a monk undertakes, though the word used in many MSS and favoured by modern editors is *conversatio*, which seems to have meant almost the same thing. The whole monastic observance was summed up in the term *conversatio* which began by a *conversio*. The idea of a second vocation long after a person has embraced the life of the counsels is a further extension of this concept, but presents no theological dilemmas.

V The psychology of conversion has been studied since the Reformation, for the Lutheran idea of inner assurance was one of its key-concepts. The resolution of religious doubts or the abandonment of a vicious life, achieved by a subjective assurance of salvation through the blood of Christ, was the essence of an evangelical conversion. Long before the conversion of Whitefield (1735) or of the two Wesleys (1738) the sudden inrush of a transforming assurance was being proclaimed by Anabaptists who used all the extravagances of patristic times about the nuptial mystery of Christ and the Church to explain what had happened to themselves at the moment of adult baptism.

The Council of Trent, reacting against this position of the Lutherans (D 802, 822), determined that ' no one is able to know with the certainty of faith which admits of no falsity that he has gained the grace of God '. It did not, however, intend thereby to put an end to the debate that was then current among Catholics about the Scotist theory which claimed that one could have this knowledge *fide particulari acquisita* ; Lainez did in fact defend this theory in the Council and was not censured for it. The condemnation fell on the idea that such certainty could be given *fide catholica infusa*, i.e. one could not make an act of faith about it, adding to one's personal creed a clause saying : ' I am saved '. It is clear from this condemnation, however, that Catholics tended to look askance on the introspective search for certainty of salvation and on the narratives of conversion that displayed it.

Modern times have brought a new interest in the psychology of conversion, attempts being made now to generalise the phenomena, as if conversion to (e.g.) Buddhism and Catholicism must exhibit the same essential pattern. This, of course, means looking at conversion from a purely human point of view, as if the grace of God played no part in it. The subconscious, individual or collective, has been put forward as an explanation of what happens in a religious or moral conversion. The evidence for the

---

[1] Presbyterii honorem nullus laicus ante praemissam conversionem vel ante XXX annos aetatis accipiat.

operation of a collective subconscious in man is, however, such as to require its being situated in the animal side of man's nature ; the lower the position of an animal in the scale of being, the greater the pull of this collective force. For the individual subconscious there is this to be said, that it can gather up impressions and fleeting half-judgments without our being fully aware of their being gathered in, but the process is never *completely* unconscious. On the other hand, it has been recognized since the famous analysis by Augustine (in his *Confessiones* and also in *De spiritu et littera* 53–60 ; CSEL 60:209–20) that God can guide what happens in the subconscious. 'No one has in his own power what comes into his mind', says Augustine, and he draws a picture of the entrance-lobby of the mind, where suitors for attention gather to accost the owner when he comes that way, jostling one another in a mob (*Conf.* 10:8 ; CSEL 33:200). He wants one particular idea and the mob comes up, crowding round and saying : 'Perhaps I am that one'. In this analysis Augustine leaves room for the action of God, who can bring forward from the depths of consciousness the one thought that will dissolve a human perplexity. The modern psychologists have notably failed to make use of all this Christian analysis, being too busy with their own cherished ideas about the factor that brings up directive ideas from the depths. Some decided for the crisis of adolescence, as if all conversions took place then ; others for a sublimation of sexual desires, or for the idea that the convert's chosen dependence on the Church was a substitute for a childish dependence on his mother ; others, again, have said that the convert hypnotizes himself. Now, while it is true that Christian mystics (e.g. Gregory of Nyssa, PG 44:729) have described certain states of soul as experiences of vertigo and helplessness, it has to be admitted that such language is metaphorical ; what is being described was *like* that, but obviously not due to the physical causes that produce vertigo. Every similarity in nature is accompanied by a degree of difference, and it is the differences that the psychologist allows to escape him. What a psychologist calls 'transference' is a multiple phenomenon ; it would be more proper to introduce distinctions than to rest content with a single and question-begging term. A distinction similar to that between upcast and downcast analogy (*see* ANALOGY OF BEING I) would be pertinent here. Ignatius Loyola may have borrowed from *Amadis de Gaul* the idea of keeping a vigil of arms before the statue of Our Lady, but he was not simply transferring his love for a lady of the court to another object ; he was integrating his life and becoming a human person, perhaps for the first time.

The psychologist would have a happier time studying the cases of pseudo-conversion that sometimes occur. As St John wrote : 'They went out from amongst us, but they were not of us' (1 Jn 2:19). God does not withdraw the gift of faith unless there is sin against faith itself, but there can be cases of would-be converts who are accepted on the strength of their preliminary judgments (that the claims of the Church are credible and that it is worth while to accept them) but who have not believed on the divine authority of God revealing (*see* APOSTASY). The rice-Christian can have his counterpart on the intellectual level. Gibbon, swept off his feet by reading Bossuet and Robert Persons at the age of 16, was received into the Church by Fr B. Baker SJ at the old Sardinia Street chapel in 1753 ; when he informed his father, he was sent to stay with a Calvinist minister in Lausanne who had instructions to bring about his perversion gently. He may have made a real act of faith, for he clung to some Catholic practices for a long time in Lausanne, but it might be said that it was only his intellect that was convinced.

Bibliography. H. Pinard de la Boullaye SJ in D Sp s.v. conversion ; *A. D. Nock, *Conversion* (1933) ; the same, in RAC s.v. Bekehrung ; S. De Sanctis, *Religious Conversion* (1927) ; *F. W. Bullock, *Evangelical Conversion in Great Britain from 1696 to 1845* (1959) ; Mgr R. A. Knox, *Enthusiasm* (1950) ; *W. James, *The Varieties of Religious Experience* (1902); Edward Hutton, 'The Conversion of Edward Gibbon', in *Nineteenth Century* III (1932) 362–75 ; narratives of individual conversions are too numerous to mention, and range from Newman's *Apologia* to the pamphlet with the title *How I came home* (by Lady Herbert of Lea) ; H. Bouillard SJ, *Conversion et Grâce chez Saint Thomas* (1945); the same, 'La Grâce actuelle chez Saint Thomas', in RSR 33 (1946) 92–114 ; G. Bardy, *La Conversion au christianisme durant les premiers siècles* (1949) ; M. Leahy (editor), *Conversions to the Catholic Church* (1933) ; J. M. Oesterreicher, *Walls are crumbling* (1953, on conversions from Judaism) ; M. Piette, *John Wesley and the Evolution of Protestantism* (1937) ; P. Aubin SJ, *Le Problème de la conversion* (1963), a study of the use of Greek terms for conversion in the early Church ; J. McCann OSB, *The Rule of St Benedict* (1952) ; the same, English translation of *Commentary on the Rule of St Benedict* by P. Delattre.   J. H. C.

CORONATION The chief theological interest of the rite of coronation is its bearing upon theories of Church and State, to the article on which this survey will be subsidiary. The article comprises three parts, (I) the introduction of the king into the sanctuary, (II) the compact between Church and State and (III) the attempt to make coronation a sacrament.

I The rights of the emperor in the Christian sanctuary, if they had been a prolongation of the observance of pagan times, would have been much greater than in fact they were. The union of emperor-worship with various forms of paganism made the emperor the temple-sharer or throne-companion of the gods or goddesses invoked, but in Christianity no such equality prevailed. At the death of Constantine, his body was buried at Constantinople in the church of the Apostles which he had had built, 'to secure that emperors and bishops should not be kept away from the relics of the Apostles', as Socrates recorded (PG 67:180). Sozomenos comments (HE 2:34 ; GCS 50:100) on the same event that bishops were to be buried alongside the emperors, 'episcopacy being, I suppose, of equal honour with royalty ; or rather having the primacy in places that are sacred'. This idea that the bishop is sovereign in the sanctuary and that the emperor is there on sufferance was exemplified by the action of Ambrose in refusing to start Mass in the presence of the emperor if the latter persisted in his denial of the rights of the Church (PL 16:1120), but it had perhaps never been formulated before this.

An imperial edict of 425 (*Codex Theodosianus* XV:4:1) forbade the adoration of the imperial image when it might be found in a church, as this act should be reserved for the majesty of God. Hereafter the practice grew of having the emperor depicted in churches as adoring Christ, being crowned by Christ, building or guaranteeing the church, but never alone in majesty. Familiarity with the picture of the emperor kneeling to receive the crown from the hands of Christ may have led to the use of the adjective 'God-crowned' ($\theta\epsilon\acute{o}\sigma\tau\epsilon\pi\tau\sigma$) which became a habitual description of the emperor after the time of Justinian. The earliest surviving picture of such an action is said to be a miniature in a Paris MS (*graecus* 510), where, however, it is the angel Gabriel who performs the coronation of Basil I (867), but many earlier mosaics and fabrics depicting this must have perished.

Byzantine royal customs were translated to the West after 800, Charlemagne being greeted in that year (*see* ACCLAMATIONS) with the words : 'God-crowned, great and peace-loving' (*a Deo coronatus, magnus et pacificus*). The words Alcuin wrote to Charlemagne in June 799 (MGH *Epistulae* IV:288) show that to an Englishman at least the primacy of the spiritual power was not impaired by this change. Alcuin says : 'There are three persons who up to now are the most exalted in the world : the first is the apostolic dignity ; the second is the imperial majesty and secular power of the second Rome ; the third is the royal state in which the providence of our Lord Jesus Christ has placed you to rule the Christian people '.[1] The English practice that would be familiar to Alcuin had been determined at the Synod of Chelsea in 787 whose 11th Canon directs that the kings shall 'obey their bishops from the heart and with great humility, because to the bishops are given the keys of heaven'.

II The Compact between Church and State.
The rubric in Anglo-Saxon coronation *Ordines* which runs *Regis status designatur* introduces an admonition spoken to the king by the bishops when they are in the act of enthroning him, and this admonition is very much in keeping with what the Synod of Chelsea prescribed. The bishops say : 'In as much as you look forward and see the clergy nearer the altar, in so much may you be mindful to give them

greater honour in the places that belong to them '.[2] This declaration reiterates what Sozomenos had said about the primacy of the bishops in sacred places. Misguided attempts to make of the declaration an appeal to the king to reward the bishops if they stick to their duties at the altar would mean that the king (as Wycliffe held) should regard as null a bishop who was in mortal sin. It would also require an impossible sense (in that age) for the word *propinquiorem*. This admonition is found in the *Ratold* coronation Order of the mid-10th cent., which was probably the parent of the 'Edgar Order' used in England from 973.

Immediately after the admonition (in the *Leofric Missal*, in 'Ratold' and 'Egbert') the king is told that it is right for him to secure the peace of the Church and of all Christian people. This is a reminder of what happened at the beginning of the ceremony (in 'Ratold'), when the bishops asked the king to uphold for each of them and for their churches canonical privilege and due law and justice, the king undertaking this even before he is elected by the acclamations of the people. The theory at work here is aptly expressed by the Irishman Sedulius (PL 103:329) in his book on Christian rulers : 'In a good ruler there should be the praiseworthy intention . . . that the heads of churches should lawfully hold their places and the royal clemency should give aid to them for this purpose so that they may be able to carry out their office to the full in accord with the law of God and the sacred canons, nor should secular authority hinder them in this but rather encourage them to keep the faith of God and to fulfil their practice of justice '.[3] The circle of Sedulius at Liège may have been responsible for the first appearance of such a royal promise at the crowning of Louis the Stammerer (8 December 877), the ritual of which is preserved (MGH, *Capitula* II, 364).

This is not the place to launch hypotheses, but it should be pointed out that there are a number of signs, apart from this text of Sedulius, which suggest that the whole rite of coronation, and especially the pact, came to the Continent from Irish sources, themselves indebted to Visigothic Spain. The pre-Christian custom of Irish rulers going through a 'marriage' with their people on accession must have counted for something in the process, as well as the Irish love of OT precedents, as witnessed by the (still unpublished) *Liber ex lege Moysi*. Hincmar of Reims, who knew his Irish authors, crowned Charles the Bald as king of Lotharingia in 869 in a rite in which *seven* bishops took part, each saying one of the blessings. All this is suspiciously Keltic. If one can trust the medieval *Book of Lismore*, St Patrick himself

---

[1] Tres personae in mundo altissimae hucusque fuerunt, id est apostolica sublimitas . . ., alia est imperialis dignitas et secundae Romae saecularis potentia ; . . . tertia est regalis dignitas in qua vos domini nostri Iesu Christi dispensatio rectorem populi Christiani disposuit.

[2] Quanto clerum sacris altaribus propinquiorem prospicis, tanto ei potiorem in locis congruis honorem impendere memineris.

[3] In bono rectore debet laudabilis intentio esse . . ., quatenus praepositi ecclesiarum Dei suum locum legitime teneant, eisque ad hoc adminiculum regia clementia tribuat, ut officium suum secundum mandata Dei et sacrorum canonum instituta pleniter agere valeant, nec eis saeculares potestates impedimento fiant sed potius ad fidem Dei servandam et cultum iustitiae perficiendum faveant.

blessed Angus as king of Munster at Cashel. The episode there recounted tells of the point of the saint's crozier going through the king's foot. When Patrick saw the blood flowing at the end of the ceremony he asked the king why he had not spoken, to which the reply was : ' I thought it was a rite of the faith '. The incident seems to be depicted on the Cross of Kells, which is much earlier than the written source.

III The claim that coronation was a sacrament arose out of the fact that it included an anointing and an investiture, just as the consecration of a bishop did. What is more, in the Anglo-Saxon rites (in the *Leofric Missal*, in ' Egbert ' and Lanalet) the coronation took place after the Gospel at Mass, and not before Mass as everywhere else. To the unlettered spectator this would make the two rites scarcely distinguishable. It is not surprising to find that St Peter Damian, when enumerating various sacraments, included coronation as one of them (PL 144:899). The regal theorists such as the *Anonymous of York* (or, as some think, of Normandy) were quick to take advantage of this idea. ' King and priest have in common the anointing with holy oil, the Spirit of holiness and the power of the blessing, though the sacrament of the king and that of the priest differ in part ' (MGH, *Libelli de lite*, III:665). ' The king by the sacrament of blessing is made the Lord's anointed ' (ibid. 672).[1]

A canonical opinion, drawn up by Grosseteste in reply to Henry III who had asked how the sacrament of anointing increased the royal dignity, makes clear the position of the medieval Church. The anointing confers no priestly status ; it brings an increase in the seven gifts of the Holy Ghost to enable the king to act with heroic virtue. Pope John XXII, in a letter to Edward I, expressly denied that the coronation anointing impressed a character on the soul, as confirmation does (Mollat, 5149). None the less, regalist propaganda went on with the assertion that the king was the image of the divinity of Christ just as the bishop was the image of the humanity of Christ, both of them thus being linked to Melchisedech who was king and priest. Grosseteste's plain words rebut this : ' The holy anointing adds this to the king's majesty that from the sevenfold gift of the Spirit he should be endowed beyond others of his kind with godlike and heroic virtues in all his regal acts '. This would make the rite a sacramental which depended on the collective prayer of the Church (*see* SACRAMENTALS) but refuse it all claim to be a direct channel of grace by itself.

Lyndwood, in deciding the case how far the king can give the title to a benefice without the action of the bishop, has to meet the objection of some lawyers that the king is an ecclesiastical person or a *persona mixta* and can therefore act on his own in the matter.

His answer is that while the king can deal with the temporalities, no one, not even an ecclesiastic, and still less the king, who is a secular person, can institute to the spiritualities without the bishop (*Provinciale* III, titulus 2:Ut clericalis . . .). The suspension of all teaching of canon law by Henry VIII at the Reformation opened the door once more to the theories of the regalists and with the Royal Supremacy came in the idea of the Lord's Anointed who was king by divine right. English kings had been Lords of Ireland because they held it of the Pope ; but now they had to put the claim that they held Ireland ' of God '.

Bibliography. The coronation *Ordines* are best approached through C. A. Bouman, *Sacring and Crowning: the Development of the Latin Ritual for Anointing and Coronation before the 11th century* (1957); the text of the Ratold *Ordo* was critically edited by *P. L. Ward in EHR 57 (1942) 345–61 ; its importance was made clear by *J. Armitage Robinson in JTS 19 (1917) 56–72 ; the work of *P. E. Schramm in *History of the English Coronation* (1937) has been criticised by Bouman and Ward as arbitrary and his work on Charlemagne has been subjected to a complete refutation by J. Déer, ' Die Vorrechte des Kaisers in Rom ', in *Schweizer Beiträge zur allgemeinen Geschichte* 15 (1957) 563–80 ; Sir Francis Oppenheimer, *The Legend of the Sainte Ampoule* (1953) shows how wide is the theological interest of the subject of coronation ; the Keltic background was studied long ago by John, Marquis of Bute, in *Scottish Coronations* (1902), and since then Irish scholars seem to have avoided the subject ; P. L. Ward published his criticisms of Schramm in ' Coronations in Medieval England ', *Speculum* 14 (1939) 160–78 ; *W. Ensslin, ' Zur Frage nach den ersten Kaiserkrönung ', in *Byzantinische Zeitschrift* 43 (1950) 369–72 and A. Grabar, *L'Empereur dans l'art byzantin* (1936) throw light on the imperial practice.   J. H. C.

COSMOGONY The origin of the universe has been a source of speculation from early times to the present day. Creation myths figure prominently in the mythologies of many primitive societies ; in more advanced cultures theologians, philosophers and scientists have occupied themselves with the question from many different points of view. In this article we shall be concerned mainly with the scientific evidence bearing on the origin and age of the universe in so far as this is relevant to theology. (For a study of the Genesis account and the theological development from it, *see* CREATION.) The discussion here will be divided into four parts : (I) a brief statement of the theological data ; (II) the historical development of views on the origin and age of the world ; (III) modern views on cosmogony ; (IV) some special problems concerning the nature of time.

I The Theological Data. The 4th Council of the Lateran (1215) laid it down that : ' God by His almighty power from the beginning of time established together both kinds of creature, spiritual and

---

[1] Habet itaque rex et sacerdos communem olei sancti unctionem et sanctificationis Spiritum et benedictionis virtutem. . . . Aliud erat in parte sacramentum regis, aliud sacerdotis.

Rex per benedictionis sacramentum efficitur Christus Domini.

corporeal ; that is to say, angels and creatures of this world ' (D 428).[1] This was repeated by the 1st Vatican Council in 1870 (D 1783). The primary purpose of these decrees was to define that all things have been created by God and that this creation was a free act. The words ' from the beginning of time ' are, however, generally regarded by theologians as formally defining, in addition, that the universe had a definite beginning and that its age is finite.

[*Editorial note.* St Thomas (*Summa*, 1a:46:2c) held that the non-eternity of the world was a truth of faith and not a conclusion demonstrable by reason. On the other hand he held (*Summa*, 1a:46:1c) that the reasons given by Aristotle for its eternity were not proofs either but only persuasive suggestions. The Lateran Council was concerned to check Catharist ideas that either matter or the devil were outside the creative activity of God. The wording of its decree seems to have been influenced by a passage in the *De mirabilibus sacrae Scripturae* (PL 35:2151). This work was very popular among early medieval theologians. It purported to be by Augustine but was in fact by an Irish Scripture scholar of 655. Its opening passage about creation (' God, existing alone outside time, precedes all creatures ') may have been thought to recall the paradoxes about time which are found in the 11th book of Augustine's *Confessiones*, but it was known to St Thomas (*Summa*, 3a:45:3:@2) that the work was not by Augustine.]

For the idea, prevalent among Christians of all persuasions in the 19th cent. but rejected by Leo XIII (D 1947), that the inspired account of creation in Gn 1–2 was meant by God to teach men truths of science, *see* CREATION Ib, *and also* INERRANCY. The French, who suffered most from it, have called this idea *concordisme*, but it was also manifest in England in works such as Cardinal Wiseman's *Lectures on Science and Religion* (1836).

II The Historical Background. Until the early 19th cent. the views of most Christians on cosmogony were based on the Book of Genesis. It was assumed that the world was created literally in six days, some time between 4000 and 6000 B.C., and no scientific evidence was available which would cast any serious doubt on this estimate. The first definite evidence that a much longer time-scale was required came from the geological investigations of James Hutton (*Theory of the Earth*, 1795), ably supported by his disciple John Playfair. These showed that the present geological structure of the earth's crust could not have been produced in the relatively short time allowed by the traditional view and that the earth must, in fact, have existed at least for many hundreds of thousands of years. Despite some initial theological opposition this view steadily gained ground. It was strongly reinforced by the publication of Charles Lyell's *Principles of Geology* (1830–2) and had become accepted by most Christians, both Catholic and Protestant, by about 1850.

[1] Deus . . . sua omnipotenti virtute simul ab initio temporis utramque condidit creaturam, spiritualem et corporalem, angelicam videlicet et mundanam. . . .

The geological evidence, at that time, suggested that the earth was very old but gave no indication of its actual age. During the second half of the 19th cent. this problem was investigated by Lord Kelvin, who calculated the length of time which the earth must have taken to cool down from a molten state to its present condition and found this to be between 25 and 100 million years. A somewhat similar calculation for the age of the sun, based on the rate at which it is losing energy, seemed to show that its age also must fall between these limits. At the end of the century Joly calculated the age of the earth by an independent method based on the rate at which salt accumulates in the ocean and found an age of about 80 million years. It is now known that all these methods were based upon false premisses and that the good agreement between them was merely coincidental. The actual age of the earth and sun is to be measured in thousands of millions rather than in tens of millions of years.

At the same time that Hutton was pursuing his geological researches the French astronomer Laplace was attempting to explain the origin of the solar system by means of his Nebular Hypothesis, which postulated that the solar system was formed by the contraction and condensation, in successive stages, of a vast cloud of primeval gas. This theory later encountered a number of serious difficulties and for a time was generally abandoned. More recent work has, however, tended to rehabilitate it in a modified form.

The 19th cent. saw also the formulation of a new physical principle which seemed to throw light on the origin of the universe. This was the second law of thermodynamics, which states that in any isolated system—i.e. one for which there is no exchange of energy between the system and the rest of the universe—the free energy tends constantly to diminish and the entropy to increase. The precise significance of these terms need not detain us ; the net result will be that the energy of the system becomes progressively more disordered (in a somewhat technical sense) and is therefore less capable of producing new ordered structures. If now we generalize this law and apply it to the universe as a whole, it would seem to follow that the earlier stages of the universe must have been in lower states of entropy than the present and that if we go back far enough in time we shall reach a stage in which the entropy was the lowest possible. Beyond this the second law would forbid us to go. It appears therefore to represent an absolute beginning. Writers on apologetics have sometimes used this as an argument for the existence of God, even giving it the special title of ' the entropological argument '. It cannot, however, be regarded as in any way conclusive, since : (*a*) although the law applies to isolated systems within the universe, it is not certain that it can be applied to the universe as a whole ; (*b*) it is not, in any case, one of the fundamental laws of nature, arising out of the properties of matter as such ; it results from the particular way in which energy is partitioned, at the present time, between matter and radiation. There is no absolute reason, so far as can be seen, why it should not be reversed during some other phase of the history of the universe. The most that can be said is that the law suggests the possibility that the world was created, a finite time ago, in a state of minimum entropy.

III Modern Scientific Cosmogony. Two events in particular have made possible the modern advances in scientific cosmogony. The first was the discovery of radioactivity at the beginning of this century, and the steadily increasing knowledge of nuclear reactions which has resulted. The study of radioactive changes in uranium and thorium have made it possible to date the various geological strata with considerable accuracy and to assign a total age to the earth of between five and seven thousand million years. Evidence based upon other types of nuclear reaction shows that the age of the sun must be about the same or a little more. More tentatively, it has been estimated that the oldest stars which have yet been identified are about twenty-five thousand million years old.

The second great advance came with the building of the 100-inch telescope at Mt Wilson in California shortly after the First World War. This was more powerful than any previously existing, and it made possible a much more detailed study of the heavenly bodies. In particular, it showed that the stars are not scattered uniformly throughout space but are aggregated into well-defined systems known as galaxies, each containing something between a thousand million and a million million stars. The galaxy to which our solar system belongs has a maximum diameter of about 100,000 light years and its distance from the nearest neighbouring galaxy is over a million light years. (A light year is about six million million miles.) It was subsequently found that light reaching the earth from the more distant galaxies is appreciably redder than that from the nearer ones and that the amount of reddening is proportional to the distance away of the galaxy. It is now almost universally agreed that this phenomenon is a Doppler effect—i.e. it is due to the fact that the galaxies are receding from the earth and that the velocity of recession is proportional to their distance from the earth. If this is true—and no other generally acceptable explanation of the reddening has been proposed—it follows that the whole universe is in a state of expansion. As time goes on, the existing galaxies will become progressively farther separated from each other until, eventually, only a few will be visible at all from this earth even with the most powerful telescope. Conversely, it would seem to follow that as we work backwards in time towards the remote past, we shall find the galaxies approaching more and more closely to each other until eventually a condition is reached in which they were packed together in the smallest possible volume.

This consequence of the recession theory was pointed out by Hubble in 1929. He calculated, on the basis of data available at that time, that if the rate of expansion has always been uniform, the epoch of maximum density must have been about two thousand million years ago. It is now known that this age is too small, since it was based on an erroneous estimate of the distances of the other galaxies. More recent estimates, based upon observations with the 200-inch telescope at Mt Palomar, put the epoch of maximum density between ten and fifteen thousand million years ago. The hypothesis of uniform expansion is the simplest, but it is not the only possible one ; by making suitable assumptions concerning the variation of rate of expansion with time, it would be possible to lengthen or shorten the time which has elapsed since the epoch of maximum density within fairly wide limits.

One of the first cosmologists to propound a specific theory of the universe on the supposition that it was once in the state of maximum possible density was Canon Lemaître of Louvain, in 1931. He postulated that at one time all the matter of the universe existed in the form of a single gigantic atomic nucleus. This nucleus, being highly unstable, exploded into small fragments which expanded as a cloud of gas, out of which the galaxies, stars, etc. gradually condensed. A later modification of the theory, by Gamow, supposed that the initial state was a dense cloud of neutrons rather than a single atom.

Not all cosmologists would admit that the universe has expanded from a state of maximum density or from any other 'singular' state. An influential school led by Hoyle, Bondi and Gold holds that the structure and density of the universe have always been much the same as they are now. It is true that the existing galaxies are receding steadily from each other, but to compensate for this, new matter is being continuously 'created' (i.e. is coming into existence *de novo*) throughout the universe. The rate of production of new matter is just sufficient to balance the thinning out due to expansion. On the average, as one galaxy disappears from view another is being formed out of new matter. The large-scale structure of the universe therefore always remains more or less constant. The universe has been, or could have been, in existence for an infinite time.

At the present time (1964) there is no decisive scientific evidence in favour of either the evolutionary or the steady-state theory, but it may be possible to decide between them in the fairly near future. It is therefore of interest to ask whether, in the event of an evolutionary theory's becoming established, this would necessarily imply an absolute beginning to the universe. In the past, some scientists have held that it did, notably Sir Edmund Whittaker in his book *Space and Spirit* (1946). Whittaker believed that astronomy had proved that the universe has evolved from a state of maximum density and minimum entropy, and that this could not have been produced from any conceivable previous state ; hence it must have been created directly by God. Few cosmologists today would agree that this conclusion necessarily follows. There are at least two alternative possibilities which cannot be ruled out : (a) that, previous to the present phase of expansion, the universe had been contracting throughout an infinite time until it reached the state of maximum density from which it is now expanding ; (b) that the universe is an oscillating system which alternately expands to a maximum volume, contracts to a minimum, expands again to a maximum, and so on *ad infinitum*. At the present moment, on this theory, we would be in a fairly early stage of one of the phases of expansion. It is very doubtful whether, even in principle, either of these types could ever be disproved by scientific observation, provided, of course, that a sufficiently long period of oscillation was postulated. Conversely, if the evidence were ever to favour the steady-state theory, it would still not be possible to prove that the age of the universe is actually infinite. There would still be two ways in which its age could be finite. Firstly, the state might not be absolutely steady ; there might be a very gradual evolution from a singular state in the remote past. If this beginning were sufficiently far back in time, the discrepancy from a perfectly steady state might be so small that it could never be detected by any conceivable scientific test. Secondly, God might have created the universe at any arbitrary time in the past, in such a way that it would look as if it had been previously existing. At the first moment of creation there might, for instance, have been stars at various stages in their evolution ; there might have been light rays travelling away from each star, looking as if they had been previously emitted from these stars at some previous epoch when, in fact, neither the stars nor the light existed. This, of course, would remove the question from all possibility of empirical verification and would seem to be a rather desperate expedient for safeguarding the finiteness of the universe. If pushed to extremes, it could be used to maintain that the whole world was created a few thousand years ago and that all the fossils, flint implements, cave-paintings, etc. which are dated to an earlier period were created by God *in situ* as if there had been animals and men so many years ago.

It seems clear then, that science can neither prove nor disprove an absolute beginning for the universe. The most it could hope to do would be to establish the existence of a singular state at some epoch in the past—probably a state of maximum density and minimum entropy—which could be regarded as an appropriate moment for creation, even though it could have been preceded by an earlier phase of existence. We cannot, however, exclude the possibility of an absolute beginning which was associated with no singularity or with one so far back in time as to be undiscoverable by any possible scientific observation or reasoning.

IV The Problem of Time. We have so far assumed that the question : ' What is the age of the universe ? ' has an unambiguous answer, even if in fact we can never discover it for certain. This assumption is not, however, as simple as it might seem. It presupposes that there is a single universal time-scale which is the only valid one. For Aristotle

and the medievals there was no difficulty on this point. They believed that all processes in the universe were ultimately controlled by and geared to the rotation of the outermost sphere of the heavens, which was therefore the absolute measure of time. This rotation, being subject to no conceivable hazards or external influences, was necessarily and absolutely constant throughout the whole range of past, present and future. It was therefore the clock by which all other processes were measured. The age of the universe was simply the number of rotations of this clock. We know now that this view was based upon false premises.

An ideal clock would consist of some cyclic process which had been insulated from all disturbing influences and which could continue indefinitely at a rate which could be regarded as absolutely uniform. There is, in fact, no such process, so far as is known, which has continued uniformly and uninterruptedly from the beginning of the world. To obtain an estimate of the age of the universe it is necessary to ask the hypothetical question : How many cycles of a (*de facto* non-existent) ideal clock would have occurred, from the first moment of creation until now, if such a clock had operated continuously throughout this period ? The question is made more complicated by the fact that, on the evolutionary theory, no usable clock could have existed or functioned under the conditions in which the universe began.

There are several different types of clock available at the present time. The most accurate, and the one which most nearly approaches the ideal, is the atomic or molecular clock which measures time by means of atomic vibrations. The earth's rotation on its own axis provides another standard. If the earth were a perfectly rigid uniform sphere this also would be an exceedingly accurate clock ; in practice, however, it fluctuates appreciably owing to tidal and other effects, some of which are not yet fully understood. The period of the earth's orbit round the sun—the year—provides yet another independent unit of time which, when suitable corrections have been made to allow for the disturbing effects of other planets, is very satisfactory. The question arises whether all these, and other possible time-scales, agree with each other. Do the units of time determined by these different processes always bear a constant ratio to each other ? Within the limits of present-day observation they do, but it is not certain that they have always done so. In 1933 E. A. Milne put forward a theory that there are two different time-scales in the universe ; one (measured by the uniform rotation of a rigid body) according to which the age of the universe is infinite ; the other (measured by atomic vibrations) according to which it is finite. Each of these is valid in its own right. The universe is therefore both finite and infinite, depending upon which particular scale is being used. The theoretical basis of Milne's conclusion is now generally rejected ; nevertheless there is some evidence, based upon the possible variation of some of the so-called ' cosmological constants ' with time, which suggests that the conclusion itself might possibly be true.

One other possibility may be mentioned. If the universe is an oscillating system which periodically returns to a state of maximum density, it is conceivable that during the period when it is in this state there would be no physical processes occurring which could provide a basis for time measurement, even in principle. In this case there would be no temporal continuity between the previous phase of contraction and the subsequent phase of expansion. All the old temporal processes would have been wiped out before the new ones could begin. The new phase would then be, in real but qualified sense, an *initium temporis*—a new beginning to time and history.

In conclusion, then, it can be said that modern cosmology suggests the possibility that the world may have been created in a state of maximum density and minimum entropy some time between, say, ten and fifty thousand million years ago. This is a tentative conclusion which might have to be radically revised if the steady-state theory should become more strongly supported by the available evidence. In any case, it must now be recognized that the relation between time-scales and physical processes is a more complex one than was formerly realized. It is possible that the question whether the age of the universe is finite or infinite is not capable of an absolutely unambiguous answer.

Bibliography. For historical background : C. C. Gillispie, *Genesis and Geology* (1951) ; F. C. Haber, *The Age of the World : Moses to Darwin* (1959). For modern scientific theories : G. C. McVittie, *Fact and Theory in Cosmology* (1961) ; G. J. Whitrow, *The Structure and Evolution of the Universe* (1959).

J. L. R.

COUNCILS, GENERAL, HOW MANY ?

This article will deal with the list, giving some observations on it (I) ; terminology (II) ; the problem of drafting a list (III) ; its solution (IV).

I The List of Ecumenical Councils.

A ANCIENT CHURCH

1	Nicaea	I	325
2	Constantinople	I	381
3	Ephesus		431
4	Chalcedon		451
5	Constantinople	II	553
6	Constantinople	III	680–1
7	Nicaea	II	787
8	Constantinople	IV	869–70

B MEDIEVAL CHURCH

9	Lateran	I	1123
10	Lateran	II	1139
11	Lateran	III	1179
12	Lateran	IV	1215
13	Lyons	I	1245
14	Lyons	II	1274
15	Vienne		1311–12
16	Constance		1414–18
17	Basle–Ferrara–Florence		1431–42
18	Lateran	V	1512–17

C MODERN CHURCH

19	Trent		1545–63
20	Vatican	I	1869–70
21	Vatican	II	1962–5

Observations : (i) Twenty ecumenical councils in about 2,000 years : on an average one per century. In fact, however, things have not run quite so smoothly. The first council came only after the Church was some 300 years old ; and the gap between Trent and the Vatican is another 300 years. These big intervals are counterbalanced by two councils in the 5th cent., six in the 150-odd years beginning with 1123 and two a generation apart in the 16th cent. (ii) The council of the Apostles at Jerusalem (Ac 15:6–30) is not listed, not because it was not ecumenical (on the contrary, it was supremely so, being the prototype and pattern of the whole series) but because it belonged to that unique and never-to-be-repeated phase of the Church's career when it was being spread and governed by the Apostles in person (cf. C. Journet, *The Church of the Word Incarnate*, I [1955] 127–53 ; E. Haible, ' Die Vergegenwärtigung des Apostelkollegiums' in ZKT 83 [1961] 80–7). (iii) The first eight councils form a block apart : all were 'materially' convoked by the Roman or Byzantine emperors ; all were held in the Eastern half of the Empire—Nicaea, Constantinople, Ephesus and Chalcedon ; all were composed almost exclusively of Easterners. The remaining twelve councils were distributed through the Italian-, French- and German-speaking sectors of Europe (none in Spain, England or Scandinavia). That six that have met in Rome eloquently witnesses to the prestige of the papacy. In every sense, the Roman Pontiffs were the sole architects of Lateran I–IV and Lyons I and II. The immense and beneficent influence of Trent—that ' outwardly modest act of self-examination and self-renewal '—is assuredly attributable to the fact that the popes threw the full weight of their authority behind the execution of its decrees. (iv) The first and the twentieth ecumenical councils can be bracketed together as being pre-eminently assemblies of bishops ; not that their members were exclusively episcopal : at Nicaea I, the Emperor Constantine played a prominent role ; at the Vatican, though no secular rulers were invited, there were the Generals of Religious Orders with a handful of others who were not bishops. In between these two councils the circle of participants widened more and more—in favour of abbots, of delegates from chapters and universities, of princes and lay-magnates and, finally, of proxies for the absentee bishops. The climax was reached at Basle, which looked very much like a general Christian forum or parliament (*see* BASLE, COUNCIL OF). Bishops were outnumbered by ten (even by twenty-five) to one. By Trent the circle had contracted once more and bishops enjoyed their rightful, absolute preponderance.

II Terminology. In the ecclesiastical sense, a council is an assembly of bishops deliberating and deciding on matters concerning the Church. Councils are of various sorts : diocesan, provincial, plenary, national, general and ecumenical. The diocesan council or synod is not a council in the strict sense, because it is not a gathering of bishops but of local clergy under their bishop who alone legislates, consulting them or not as he thinks best. Suffragan bishops foregathering under the presidency of their metropolitan form a provincial council. When bishops of many ecclesiastical provinces come together under a papal legate or perhaps a primate or patriarch, one has a plenary or national or regional council. In the terminology of some writers (e.g. I. Salaverri, *De ecclesia Christi*, n. 581, in *Sacrae Theologiae Summa* [1958], vol. I, 690–1), *general*, as applied to councils, is contrasted against *ecumenical*. Thus they will qualify as *general* a ' spoilt' ecumenical council, i.e. a large and representative gathering from which the papal ratification was withheld, e.g. Pisa, 1409. However, it seems preferable to follow our practice in this article of understanding *general* as synonymous with *ecumenical*. The ecumenical councils of the Middle Ages describe themselves simply as *general*. Trent designates itself by both terms (e.g. Session IV, D 783: ' *Sacrosancta oecumenica et generalis Tridentina Synodus, in Spiritu Sancto legitime congregata . . .*'). An ecumenical council is a gathering of bishops from all quarters of the Church, under the pope, to deliberate and decide on matters concerning the Church. It wields supreme authority over the universal Church. What the metropolitan is to the provincial council, and the primate to the regional council, the pope is to the ecumenical council, as visible Head of the visible Church.

III Problem of drafting a List. For the free-lance historian to draw up a list of general or ecumenical councils is a formidable and tortuous task. Ransacking the accumulated records of 2,000 years, he would muster scores of likely-looking councils; he would then have to pick his way painfully through the congested claims of each—a quite endless process if nothing more than purely human considerations are invoked. To grasp this, one need only pause a little over the list at the head of this article. Do any councils figure there that all Christians would salute as ecumenical? Perhaps the first six. But then agreement would halt. The Greeks, for example, would intercalate the 692 synod of Constantinople in between the sixth and seventh councils. They rate it either as ecumenical in its own right or at least as a prolongation of the fifth and sixth ecumenical councils. They dub it ' Quini-Sext' (*penthekté*), and tendentiously they held it ' in Trullo '—in that same domed hall of the imperial palace which housed the fifth and sixth; thus they emphasized its equality with its august forerunners. With most of the West, Catholic and Protestant, the Greeks accept Nicaea II, which, however, was rejected by that stalwart guardian of orthodoxy, the Emperor Charlemagne (768–814). Repudiating the eighth ecumenical council, which healed the Photian Schism, the Greeks put in its stead another synod of Constantinople (879–80). Of course they turn their backs on the remaining twelve councils, not excepting even Lyons

II and Florence which for a while bridged the gap between East and West. The Lutherans would particularly want Trent struck off the rolls, but might be prepared to substitute Wittenberg (1536): cf. A. Ebneter, ' Luther und das Konzil ', in ZKT 80 (1962) 1–48. In general, Protestants would object to all the councils under B and C except the anti-papal sessions of Constance and Basle, which they would cherish. The Gallicans challenge the ecumenicity of Lateran V because it proclaimed the pope above a general council, while the Ultramontanists are embarrassed by Basle and Constance because their more turbulent sessions vociferated the contrary proposition—the superiority of council over pope. One is bewildered by apparent anomalies: Lateran IV was deliberately summoned as an ecumenical council and it enjoys this status (indeed it is one of the most resplendent in history); on the other hand, Seleucia-Rimini (359), Ephesus (449—the notorious *latrocinium Ephesinum*) and Pisa (1409) were all likewise planned as such; yet this title has not been accorded to them. Constantinople I (381) complicates things still more: this was intended to be no more than a regional council of Oriental bishops; yet, in fact, it is ecumenical. Gregory the Great (540–604), while declaring it such, because it formulated its famous Creed with its article on the godhead of the Holy Ghost, refused to endorse the canons it promulgated—the first instance of a pope's recognizing the ecumenical status of a council together with parts of its transactions, but withholding recognition from other portions.

Can membership be cited as a criterion of ecumenicity? Hardly—whether one considers either (*a*) provenance or (*b*) numerical strength. As to (*a*), in the ancient councils, most countries of Western Christendom did not have even a single, national representative; to the medieval councils, barring Lyons II and Florence, most sectors of the Orient did not send a solitary, native bishop. As to (*b*), some acknowledged ecumenical councils are numerically quite dwarfed by non-ecumenical councils. At a Lateran council of 1116, an eye-witness counted 427 bishops and abbots from many countries—yet no one treats this as ecumenical. By contrast, at the epoch-making sessions V and VI of Trent, only 59 bishops were present (cf. Jedin, *Geschichte des Konzils von Trient*, [1957] II, 258).

Does the secret of winning ecumenical recognition lie in the fact that a council has resolved some burning issue of its age? Thus, Lateran I settled the clash over investiture; Lateran II, the schism caused by Anacletus II; Lateran III dealt with Barbarossa; Constance terminated the Great Schism of the West. But, by the same token, the synod of Sutri (1046) under the aegis of the Emperor Henry III (1039–56), should be acclaimed as ecumenical: it achieved a task of high importance and necessity, disentangling the knotty situation arising from three claimants to the papal tiara. Yet it is graded by all as a merely local council.

IV Solution. The attempt to establish which are the authentic ecumenical councils by weighing up merely natural and historical 'pros' and 'cons' plunges one into a maelstrom of difficulties, queries and anomalies from which there is no issue. Here we are confronted with a problem in many respects parallel with that concerning the *canon of Scripture* (q.v.). Rival catalogues of sacred books are proposed by Jews, Protestants and Catholics. Within the Church herself, some books ('deutero-canonical') achieved recognition only after centuries of debate. The infallible Church alone enjoys the competence to settle all doubts and to state authoritatively (this she did, for example, at Trent—D 783 f.—and the Vatican—D 1787) what books are divinely inerrant and have the Holy Ghost as chief author.

So it is with general councils. In importance to the Church they rank little lower than Sacred Scripture—indeed St Gregory the Great avowed that he revered the first four councils just as he did the four Gospels,[1] and St Leo regarded the decrees of Chalcedon as 'furnished by the Holy Ghost'.[2] According to the institution appointed by Christ in His divine wisdom, the foregathering of the successors of the Apostles around the successors of St Peter in a general council is the most illustrious means to set forth in a clearer light the beneficent truth of Christianity, and to introduce more effectively into one's living its holy law. (These words are a translation of the pastoral letter issued from Fulda, 6 September 1869, by the German bishops. It was the eve of the Vatican Council. Text: *Collectio Lacensis* vii, col. 1192.) It belongs, then, to the Church's gift of infallibility that she should be able to discern which councils, and which portions of them, are ecumenical. She, the Mystical Body of Christ, has as her Soul the Spirit of Truth to guide her in general, and, in particular, to attune her to His action in history, so that she can pick unerringly where and when His efficacious and infallible assistance has lighted. Though her authority is essentially not only monarchic but also collegiate (*see* G. Dejaifve, in NRT [1952] 477 f. [1959] 927, *also* W. de Vries in *Scholastik* 37 [1962] 341–70), her insight into the ecumenicity of councils is nevertheless most palpably expressed through the Roman Pontiffs. Towards general councils they have exercised a threefold role. It is here that we find our handiest touchstone of ecumenicity.

(i) The pope must *convoke* the ecumenical council. In fact, the Roman or Byzantine emperors were the 'material' or literal conveners of the first eight councils; and on 30 October 1413, the German Emperor Sigismund announced the council of Constance to the whole Christian world. Nevertheless, the pope remains always at least the formal convener: by some juridical act (such as sending his legates) acknowledging and legalizing the material convocation. (The distinction between material and formal convocation is a theological interpretation of extant historical evidence dictated by the doctrine of

papal primacy: just as the bishop is convener of his synod, and the metropolitan of his provincial council, so the pope must in some sense have convened the general councils of the Church. Of course, allowance must be made for the merely gradual attainment of explicit, theoretic awareness by the Church of the full range of papal authority.) St Celestine at Ephesus was a convener in the most elevated and active sense of briefing the council and setting it its task.

(ii) The pope must *celebrate* (i.e. direct, preside over) the council—either personally or vicariously, through his legates. This right follows indefeasibly from his position as visible Head of the Church; it is as obvious as the right of the bishop to preside over the diocesan synod, or the metropolitan over the provincial council. In some, particularly the early, councils, the Emperor or his vicegerent enjoyed a presidency, sometimes of privilege and pure form, sometimes of protection, to ensure, by physical force, the maintenance of order and the freedom of speech; but always from the outside. The pope, however, was the controller of the council's internal doctrinal affairs; he was the president vested with divine authority to feed the flock of Christ. His precedence is strikingly attested in this fact that either he himself or his legates, even when they were simple priests, even in the Eastern Councils (A) were the first to sign the decrees (Hefele, in HL I:92 and 48–51, declares that Ephesus is the solitary exception to this rule; and there Cyril signed before the three papal legates, because —so it is argued—he was a sort of 'super-legate', being Celestine's plenipotentiary for the whole Nestorian imbroglio).

(iii) The pope must *confirm* the council. This definitive and formal ratification of conciliar decrees is the chief of the three papal prerogatives vis-à-vis an ecumenical council. Without this solemn pontifical confirmation no edict in the Church can be supreme, universal, irreformable. Without the vote of the Head, the will of the whole episcopal college cannot be recorded. Since the papal signature alone can ensure the ecumenicity of a decree, it is anything but a matter of empty protocol—as history abundantly proves. On the one hand, the councils were most eager to secure the papal approbation. (As at Chalcedon, so at Constantinople III, the conciliar Fathers would not rest content with the signature of the pope's legates; they wanted to have this expressly endorsed by the pope personally, whom they hailed as bishop of the first See of the ecumenical Church (πρωτόθρονος τῆς οἰκουμενικῆς ἐκκλησίας), as giver of strength and health to the members of the Church, as august and holy head (ὦ σεβασμία καὶ ἱερὰ κεφαλή)—Mansi, *Concilia* XI:683–8); on the other hand, the popes were decidedly fastidious as to what they did ratify. Thus, apparently, Damasus, and then, certainly, Leo the Great and Gregory the Great accepted the Creed and nothing else from Constantinople I (cf. Hefele, HL I:62–3); Leo repudiated the notorious 28th canon of Chalcedon; Gregory X amended the

---

[1] '. . . sicut sancti Evangelii quatuor libros, sic quatuor concilia suscipere et venerari me fateor', *ep* XXV; PL 77:478.
[2] '. . . instruente Spiritu sancto, irreprehensibiliter definita sunt . . .', *ep* CLVI; PL 54:1128.

decrees of Lyons II ; John XXII had no scruple about revising the reform legislation of Vienne before finally enforcing it ; Martin V and Eugenius IV gave only qualified approval to the transactions of Constance and Basle respectively. So decisive is this papal ratification that, when given, it invests with ecumenicity the decrees of provincial councils (this has happened at least twice in history : when a St Zosimus ratified the anti-Pelagian enactments of the 16th council of Carthage (D 101-8) ; and again, when Boniface II did the same for the second council of Orange (D 174-200)) ; or when withheld, it strips of ecumenicity the transactions even of veritable general councils.

The answer to our question : how many general councils ? is that there are twenty-one to date, those listed at the head of this article. We are serenely confident that these, and these alone, are ecumenical councils, because they are the only ones honoured with recognition by the infallible Church. We discover this recognition concretely, by noting which are the councils that the Roman Pontiff has not only (in some sense) convoked and celebrated, but also and especially confirmed as ecumenical. In practice, the only matter over which Catholic theologians can quarrel is the two-fold historical question : (i) is there enough evidence to prove that the pope did in fact ratify this would-be general council, and, if so, (ii) did he ratify the whole, or only some portion, of it ? [1]

The convoking of Vatican II has naturally stimulated discussion among theologians on the subject of this article. H. Küng in TQ 141 (1961) 50-77 has argued for a participation of the laity in ecumenical councils on the ground that such councils are to represent the Church as a whole, and while the bishops do this in an eminent sense they do not do so completely. The dictum of Constantine at Nicaea I that he was ' bishop of those that are without ' (see CHURCH AND STATE) comes up for consideration here. J. Ratzinger has replied to Küng (in Catholica 15 [1961] 292-304) to the effect that councils are to represent the Church in its one particular aspect of proclaiming the gospel and protecting it, and that this does not call for lay participation. What should be taken into account is that the laity were present as spectators in very early councils such as the one made known to us by the Dialektos of Origen ; they could at least applaud or show resentment at what was said.

Bibliography. Conciliar collections were produced by J. Hardouin Conciliorum collectio regia maxima (1715), by J. D. Mansi, Amplissima conciliorum collectio (reprint, 1899-1927) and (for the 3rd, 4th and 5th councils) by E. Schwartz, Acta conciliorum oecumenicorum (1914-40). General works include H. Jedin, Ecumenical Councils in the Catholic Church (1960) ; F. Dvornik, The Ecumenical Councils (1961) ; the same, The Photian Schism (1948) ;

B. Tierney, Foundations of Conciliar Theory (1955) ; O. Rousseau (editor), Le Concile et les conciles (1960) ; *S. H. Scott, The Eastern churches and the Papacy (1932) ; J. Forget, in DTC III:9636-76 (s.v. conciles) ; L. Jaeger, The Ecumenical Council, the Church and Christendom (1961) ; T. H. Thielen, What is an Ecumenical Council ? (1960) ; W. de Vries, ' Konzil in ostkirchlicher Sicht ', in Stimmen der Zeit 170 (1962) 401-17 ; the Histoire des conciles, a French amplification of Hefele's German work by H. Leclercq and others has reached eleven volumes and still has to cover Western councils since Trent.

J. P. K.

CREATION The act of creation may be defined as the production of a thing to the extent of its entire being, and it involves essentially two elements : an act on the part of the Creator which goes beyond any activity of which we have experience (since all the activity which we know extends only to a process of change and not to the total production of a thing), and a relation of total dependence of the created thing on its creating cause (since all that is real in it is produced by that creating cause). The scope of this article goes no further than an investigation of these two elements and their immediate implications as they are found in Catholic theology. The first part of the article will be concerned with the positive teaching of Scripture and the pronouncements of the Church, and the second part with some philosophical considerations based on the findings of the first part. In the first part we shall follow the method of simple textual analysis. In section (I) we shall study what is revealed in the OT about creation, treating of (a) the Genesis account of creation, (b) some of the Prophets, and (c) the Wisdom literature and the Books of Machabees. In section (II) we shall treat of the NT, and pass thence to treat in section (III) of the Church's teaching, considering (a) some of the early Church documents, (b) the teaching of the 4th Lateran Council and of the 1st Vatican Council, and (c) pronouncements that have been issued since that Council. The first part will conclude with a short summary of the teaching of the Church about creation (IV). The second part deals with (V) God the Efficient Cause of All Things, (VI) Created Things, and (VII) God, the Final Cause of Creation.

I The Old Testament. (a) Genesis account of creation. Before examining the two accounts of creation in Genesis it will be worth while to recall a basic principle of theological research : that we must not look for categories of thought belonging to one age and culture in a previous age or different cultural background. For example, we are not to look for the precision of the Vatican Council in early Church documents, nor for the type of history that is written in Europe today in the historical writings of the early Jews. Needless to say this in no way vitiates the value of the early pronouncements of the Magisterium nor the value of early history ; it only calls for a proper use of the rules for interpreting historical documents (see THEOLOGY).

---

[1] Apropos of Constance and Basle, there is some mild discrepancy of view between, say, Hefele and Jedin on the one hand, and Bellarmine de conciliis, in his Controversiae vol. II, and Forget on the other.

It is of great importance to remember this when studying the Book of Genesis.

On 30 June 1909, the Biblical Commission issued a series of 'replies' concerning the historicity of the Book of Genesis. Their general purport was that we must hold to the 'literal-historical' interpretation of Genesis. This means that we must recognize in the Book a hard core of historical fact as opposed to mere religious fiction, particularly on points which 'touch the foundations of the Christian religion', and thus we must hold the historical truth of the creation of all things by God at the beginning of time (cf. CCS, 48 e–l). This, however, does not imply that allegorical elements are not present in the account. We must, as ever, distinguish the substance of the account from its literary embellishment.

It is now generally recognized that the author of Genesis worked from pre-existing sources, and we find the elements of two sources in the section which concerns us: there are really two accounts of creation. The first, 1:1–2:4a, has the characteristics of the so-called Priestly Code, the second, 2:4b–25, those of the Yahwehistic Code.[1]

'In the beginning God created heaven and earth.' This is the fundamental statement of Genesis 1. The Hebrew phrase, berē'šît, 'in the beginning', seems to indicate an absolute beginning to the exclusion of any pre-existing matter on which God might work. It is from this that we argue to creation in the strict sense rather than from the word for 'created', bārā', which, though used in the Bible exclusively of divine actions, is not only used of creation but also of other kinds of divine making. 'Heaven and earth' do not denote merely land and sky, but are rather a Hebraism denoting universality, 'all things', the kosmos of the Greeks for which Hebrew has no equivalent. So it might be better to translate: 'In the beginning God made all things.' Hence without seeking any philosophically refined notion of creation, we find in these opening words of Genesis a simple statement that God is the only cause of the visible world.

Certain writers, such as Loisy, Holzinger and Gunkel, have suggested that the statement should be construed, 'in the beginning, when God made the world, the earth was void and empty', suggesting that God worked on some independently existing matter. This interpretation demands a reading of the Hebrew text so complex as to be altogether unlikely in such a document as Genesis.

There follows the later (in point of origin) of the two accounts of creation. The author of Genesis gives preference to this more detailed and developed narration of the beginnings of the world. It is divided up into a series of seven days, in the first six of which God creates and on the last takes His rest. The work of creation proceeds through the division of light from darkness, of the upper from the lower firmament, of the dry land from the waters, through

the creation of the first organic matter of the vegetative order, of the luminaries of heaven, through the production of animal life to the climax of the creation of man in God's own image and likeness. There is an ascending order from the most primitive creatures to the climax in God's most perfect creation, man. Then comes (2:4b) the second and earlier account of creation, beginning this time with man and then describing the world God made for him to live in. The impression one has of this second account is that its originator is not so much interested in creation as such, but rather in the beginnings of human history. This may well be the reason for its being placed second, as providing a better starting-point for the subsequent narrative.

One of the first questions which arises on comparing these two accounts is: which gives the correct order of creation? Clearly it is not the first, since this gives the creation of light (3), before the creation of the causes of light, the luminaries of heaven (14). In the second we have the creation of man before that of other living things. This seems to be ruled out by the findings of geology and kindred sciences. It would seem better, then, not to look for a strictly *historical* order in the narrative, but rather for a *literary* order chosen for the purpose of the writer. This, it must be insisted, in no way destroys the historical value of the Genesis accounts. The facts are historically true; the order of their narration belongs to the literary presentation of the subject.

The 'days of creation' referred to in the first account have given rise to much speculation. Many opinions about their exact meaning have been put forward from the earliest times. Among the Fathers we find very different schools of thought. The Alexandrian Fathers favour an allegorical interpretation: Clement says that the creation of all things was simultaneous and that the six days are merely employed to point out the gradation which is to be found in created things. Origen carries this interpretation to an astonishing degree of allegorical complexity. The schools of Edessa and Antioch, on the contrary, reject almost any idea of allegory in their interpretations. God created all things in the course of six days, and St John Chrysostom, for example, suggests that the inerrancy of the Bible is at stake if we depart from the exact literal understanding of the narrative. The Cappadocian Fathers suggest the creation of all matter in one instantaneous act followed by the ordering of all things from this primitive matter through the six days. Among the Western Fathers, St Ambrose follows this last view, while St Augustine says that the literal understanding is impossible and that the succession as described in the account must be understood allegorically. The discussion continues to the present day, and must remain an open one. It would seem, however, that we can exclude the two extreme views: that which says the whole account is pure myth, because the Church has declared such an opinion to be untenable in the light of her teaching and doctrine; and that which demands a strictly literal reading, because of

[1] For a detailed analysis of these sections we must send the reader to CCS, 'Genesis', or, for a fuller treatment, to P. F. Ceuppens OP: *Quaestiones Selectae ex Historia Primaeva*, chs. 1 and 2.)

the multitude of difficulties it involves, such as the anomaly already mentioned of the creation of light before the causes of light. Nor does it seem possible to understand the 'days' as periods of 24 hours for scientific reasons. It has been suggested that these days may correspond to the geological ages of the world. This, however, is impossible again because the order would not correspond with the findings of geology, and also because the Hebrew word translated as 'day', *yôm*, is never used of long periods. Perhaps a fruitful suggestion about the significance of the days of creation is that the author of Genesis, although he is writing history, is not writing a scientific account of the order and manner of the beginning of the world. The history he has to narrate is that everything came into being as a result of God's creative word. A scientific account of the manner of this coming-to-be was no concern of his. He has also a religious purpose in mind. He is writing with an eye on the preservation of the purity of Jewish religion by recalling the transcendence of Yahweh and the excellence of the Law of Yahweh. One of the most cherished Jewish practices was the correct observance of the Sabbath. Thus in choosing a framework for his narrative the writer of the first account chooses the Jewish week and represents even God as resting on the seventh day at the end of His work.

From a number of vexed questions confronting the exegete certain clear conclusions present themselves to the reader of Genesis. (i) The sacred writer intends to show the utter dependence of the world on God, and that God, its total cause, created it without any pre-existing matter. (ii) We see clearly the absolute independence of God from created things and His transcendence over matter: He speaks, and the effect is produced. There is none of the strife between a demiurge and some intractable material elements found in most other early cosmogonies. (iii) We see very clearly also the excellence of all that God has made and in particular of His masterpiece, man. The author of the first account is careful to remark on the goodness, even in God's eyes, of each item in creation. The first two of these conclusions (which we have already referred to at the beginning of this article) are constantly recurring themes of scripture, especially of the OT. There are many other questions arising from Genesis which cannot be discussed here but which are of importance, in particular those which arise from the theory of evolution (*see* EVOLUTION).

(b) *Some prophets*. Witness to the Jewish belief in God as creator of the universe abounds in the writings of the prophets. In Jeremias and in Deutero-Isaias especially we find eloquent declarations of the doctrine. Jeremias is concerned particularly with the election of Israel and with God as her saviour. It is in this framework that his references to creation come: the God who has chosen Israel and boasts that He will save her is the all-powerful God who has created and who still governs this world. It is especially as the Lord of the elements and seasons that His authority is invoked: ' Thus saith the Lord, who giveth the sun for the light of the day, the order of the moon and of the stars for the light of the night: who stirreth up the sea, and the waves thereof roar. The Lord of hosts is his name. If these ordinances shall fail before me (i.e. if God's governance of the world should fail, just to imagine the impossible), saith the Lord: then also the seed of Israel shall fail, so as not to be a nation before me for ever' (Jer 31:35–6 DV). 'Shall a man be hid in secret places and I not see him, saith the Lord? Do not I fill heaven and earth, saith the Lord?' (Jer 23:24 DV). 'Are there any among the graven things of the Gentiles that can send rain? Or can the heavens give showers? Are not thou the Lord our God, whom we have looked for? For thou hast made all these things' (Jer 14:22 DV).

The latter part of the Book of Isaias is nowadays generally recognized to be the work of a second writer and is usually referred to as Deutero-Isaias. It is in this part of the book that we find numerous references to God as creator of the world. We may give a few examples. Isaias is a bringer of comfort to a people in a state of despair at the end of a long exile, who can see no relief for their sufferings. It is the all-powerful Yahweh, creator of heaven and earth, who is going to bring them deliverance and lead them back to Jerusalem. The majesty and serenity of the message is impressive: ' . . . He shall gather together the lambs with his arm. . . . Who hath measured the waters in the hollow of his hand and weighed the heavens with his palm? Who hath poised with three fingers the bulk of the earth and weighed the mountains in scales and the hills in a balance?' (Is 40:11–12 DV), and in the same chapter (40:26): 'Lift up your eyes on high, and see who hath created these things. . . .' The language is figurative, but the message could hardly be clearer. God has shown His almighty power in creating the world; He is well able to lead His chosen people home. Two further examples speak for themselves: 'For thus saith the Lord that created the heavens, God himself that formed the earth and made it, the very maker thereof, who did not create it in vain, who formed it to be inhabited: I am the Lord; and there is no other' (45:18 DV). 'Hearken to me, O Jacob, and thou, Israel, whom I call: I am he, I am the First, and I am the Last. My hand also hath founded the earth, and my right hand hath measured the heavens: I call them, and they shall stand together' (48:12–13 DV). In such formulae the prophets teach the chosen people, ever striving to keep pure and unadulterated the faith of the Jewish people in the one God, creator of heaven and earth. In such language also God speaks to His wayward people who are so easily infected by the polytheistic tribes around them.

(c) *Wisdom literature and Machabees*. We take now the Wisdom literature and Machabees as together representing the most advanced expressions of belief in creation. The Book of Psalms constantly declares the transcendence of God over all creation: ' O Lord, our Lord, how admirable is thy name in the whole earth! . . . For I will behold thy heavens, the work of thy fingers : the moon and the stars which thou hast founded' (Ps 8:2, 4 *passim* DV). 'The heavens show forth the glory of God : and the firmament declareth the work of his hands' (Ps 18:2 DV). Here we have a statement that creation mirrors the glory of God, that He is the exemplar and final cause of created things. In Ps 103 we have a hymn of creation of unsurpassed beauty, showing God presiding over and in the work of His hands. It rises to a climax of praise and wonderment : 'How great are thy works, O Lord ! Thou hast made all things in wisdom : the earth is filled with thy riches' (Ps 103:24 DV). Ps 138 shows us the omnipresence of God to all His creation, and in particular to man in his actions and his inmost thoughts, and man's utter dependence on God. The creation of man is made explicit : ' Of my soul thou hast full knowledge, and this mortal frame had no mysteries for thee, who didst contrive it in secret, devise its pattern, there in the dark recesses of the earth' (15 Kn). In Prov 8:24 the Wisdom of God is personified and described as present with God ' before He made anything from the beginning' (8:22), and as taking an active part in the designing and creation of the world : ' When He prepared the heavens I was present. . . . I was with Him forming all things' (8:27–30 DV). The writer presents the traditional teaching of the Jews, now in a more polished literary form, yet still with the characteristic anthropomorphism of the OT. We hear reaffirmed the wise manner in which God designed the world. The dependence of the world and the transcendence of God are again shown in Wis 11:23 ff. DV : ' For the whole world before thee is as the least grain of the balance, and as a drop of the morning dew that falleth down upon the earth'.

Finally, in the era immediately preceding Christ, we have one of the clearest and most striking professions of Jewish belief in God, the creator of all things out of nothing, a belief on the basis of which a pious Jew is ready to face martyrdom : thus the mother of the Machabees exhorts her son : ' I beseech thee, my son, look upon the heaven and earth and all that is in them : and consider that God made them out of nothing, and mankind also : so thou shalt not fear this tormentor . . .' (2 Mac 7:28–9 DV). This statement is, of course, not covered by the guarantee of inerrancy since it is an explicit quotation ; but there can be no doubt that it embodies the belief of the faithful Jews of the Machabean period and is firmly approved by the sacred writer.

Before summarizing our findings thus far we must briefly consider the classical objection to creation *ex nihilo* from the OT. In Wis 11:18 DV the author appears to affirm that God formed the world, not out of nothing, but out of some pre-existing, formless matter : ' For thy almighty hand, which made the world of matter without form, was not unable to send upon them a multitude of bears. . . .' The objection is of little force since the author in no way denies that God is responsible for the unformed matter also. In perfect accord with the distinction

we have already noticed in Genesis between the work of creation and that of ordering, the author may here be presumed to be speaking of the wonderful manner in which God has produced a world in which we see harmony and order. That God is responsible for the world in the totality of its being is not here in question. The author is merely explaining that God punishes evil-doers in a manner which He sees to be in accordance with their crimes, using the very things by which men have sinned to punish them. Thus again is clearly demonstrated the complete mastery which God exercises over the world.

In brief, then, the OT teaches that God created all things out of nothing, that He is the total cause of all things, that all creation is dependent on Him in its entire being, and that God transcends all that He has made. There is evidence also that God is held to be wise in His creation and ordering of the world, and that He is quite free and independent of other beings in His designs.

II The New Testament. Though it might at first seem strange, the NT does not often speak explicitly of creation as such. No doubt this is due to the fact that in a religious atmosphere as developed as that of NT Judaism, creation is one of those basic truths taken for granted in all religious thought and not needing to be alluded to explicitly. In the preaching of Our Lord it is always there as a background to the themes of Providence, God's Paternity and His Father's relations to the world. Such themes in the NT are corollaries of, and presuppose, the root notion of creation and total dependence. However, there are a certain number of passages in which we read of creation explicitly. The most celebrated is, of course, in the prologue of St John's Gospel : ' . . . and the Word was God. . . . It was through him that all things came into being, and without him has come nothing that has come to be' (Jn 1:1–3 Kn). The same thought is echoed by St Paul in Col 1:14–18. St Paul is not here primarily concerned with creation, but with the divinity of Christ, as indeed is St John in his prologue. He argues that Christ must indeed be God since all things have come to be through Him, whether heavenly or earthly, visible or invisible ; in Him they all subsist. St Paul therefore implies that it is only God who has created all things. Further confirmation comes from Heb 1 where the sacred writer declares that it is through His divine Son that God has now spoken to us, ' a Son, whom he has appointed to inherit all things, just as it was through him that he created this world of time', and again, ' all creation depends, for its support, on his enabling word' (2–3 Kn). The upshot is clearly that creation is a divine prerogative. In Ac 17:24–5 we find another clear statement about creation. St Paul is addressing the members of the Areopagus on the subject of the existence of a unique and supreme God. He identifies Him as ' the God who made the world and all that is in it, that God who is the Lord of heaven and earth . . . he, who gives to all of us life and breath and all we have '. Earlier in his speech at Lystra St Paul had again identified God as He 'who made sky and earth and sea and all that is in them' (14:14 Kn).

God's governance of the world, and in particular of human destiny, is a frequent topic especially of St Paul. One example will be sufficient. God calls freely whom He wills to salvation : 'He has chosen us out in Christ before the foundation of the world . . .' (Eph 1:4 Kn). This introduces us again to the notion of creation in time. St John, too, gives us the words of our Lord in His last discourse where He prays the Father to exalt Him 'in that glory which I had with Thee before the world began' (Jn 17:5 Kn), and again : '. . . in that love which thou didst bestow upon me before the foundation of the world' (25 Kn). We conclude that the world has not always existed but that God brought it into existence.

The world created by God witnesses to His divine perfections : '. . . from the foundations of the world men have caught sight of his invisible nature, his eternal power and his divineness, as they are known through his creatures' (Rom 1:20 Kn).

Another theme which receives further development in the NT is that of the finality inherent in the world, expressed, of course, not in philosophical terms, but in the more concrete manner of Scripture. 'For of him and by him and in him, are all things . . .' (Rom 11:36 DV). 'In him' translates the Greek εἰς αὐτὸν which might be better translated 'unto him', since the Greek accusative suggests direction towards. The world's purpose or end, then, is to be found in God. The perfect world-order is expressed by St Paul in 1 Cor 3:23 (Kn) : 'Everything is for you, . . . and you for Christ, and Christ for God'. In Apoc 22:13 (Kn) God gives solemn expression to this in the words : 'I am Alpha, I am Omega, I am before all, I am at the end of all, the beginning of all things and their end'.

We may summarize, then, what we have found about creation in the NT : God is the creator of all things, visible and invisible, and it is a proof of Christ's divinity that He has created all things with His Father. God preserves and governs all His creation and has a special paternal care for men. He has created the world wisely and with perfect freedom. God's perfections are mirrored in creation and it is through the things that He has created that we are able to know Him. The world and all it contains find their final purpose and meaning in Him who is their creator and last end.

III The Church's Teaching. (a) *Early Church documents.* The earliest of the official Christian professions of faith is the so-called Apostles' Creed. Its very first statement concerns belief in God the creator. There are variant forms but these do not affect the primary statement : 'I believe in God, the Father almighty, Creator of heaven and earth'. In the Greek texts the word which is translated 'omnipotens' in the Latin version, and 'almighty' in English, is παντοκράτωρ which has a rather fuller significance : 'He who holds all things in His hands'. This strikingly conveys the notion we have

already discovered in the OT of the total dependence of all things in their existence and activity upon God. There follows at once the explicit statement of belief in creation as such : 'creator of heaven and earth'. Formulae of this nature date back at least to the second half of the 2nd cent. It cannot be doubted that they contain in substance the professions of faith used in Apostolic times. Other early creeds and professions of faith contain similar statements (D 13, 15, 19). The Creed of Nicaea professes belief in the one God who made 'all things, visible and invisible' (D 54).

(b) *The later Councils.* (i) The Fourth Lateran Council (1215) was concerned with the errors of the Albigenses (*q.v.*) who, like the Manichees, held that not all things are derived from God, but that there are two principles of creation : one Good, responsible for all spiritual beings, the other Evil, responsible for the evil, material elements in lower things. The Council came out with a clear statement of the Church's belief : 'We firmly believe and straightforwardly confess that the true God is only one . . . Father, Son and Holy Spirit . . . the one principle of all things, the creator of all things, visible and invisible, spiritual and bodily, Who by His almighty power, from the beginning of time, created out of nothing both types of creature, spiritual and corporeal, that is to say angelic and mundane ; and then human, as constituted commonly from spirit and from body' (D 428). The Church thus rigorously excludes dualism from her doctrine of creation, and insists that the Three Persons of the Trinity act as one principle in creating.

(ii) The Vatican Council (1869–70) stated once more the teaching of the Church in opposition to modern errors, of which rationalism, agnosticism and pantheism were amongst the most serious (*see* VATICAN COUNCIL). In chapter 1 of the 3rd Session the Council set forth in the clearest manner the Church's doctrine. First the distinction of God from the world was set forth : God is 'in fact and by His nature to be declared distinct from the world . . . unspeakably transcending all things which exist outside Him, or can be conceived to exist' (D 1782). In this general way all forms of pantheism are excluded. Then follows the clear and highly evolved positive doctrine of creation, the fullest and most scientific yet seen : 'This one, true God, in His goodness and almighty power, by His utterly free design and from the beginning of time, created out of nothing both types of creature, spiritual and corporeal, that is to say angelic and mundane, and then human as constituted commonly from spirit and from body ; this (He did) not to increase nor to acquire His own happiness, but in order to manifest His perfection through the good which He imparts to creatures' (D 1783). Using to a large extent the words of the Lateran Council, the Vatican brings in the purpose of creation, bearing in mind the false ideas of the followers of Hermes (*see* APOLOGETICS XVII) and Günther (*see* GUNTHERIANISM), and also God's freedom in creating against the same schools of thought. At the end of the Session various

Canons were propounded to deal with individual errors : first a general one against all who deny the existence of God, the creator of all things. Next are impugned all who are ' not ashamed to affirm that nothing beyond matter exists '. Against pantheism in general : ' If anyone shall say that the substance or essence of God and of all things are one and the same, let him be anathema '. The Council goes on to condemn three special types of pantheism : (*a*) ' substantial ' pantheism (the Alexandrian Neo-Platonists and perhaps also Spinoza), according to which the world is constituted simply by some form of emanation from the divine substance ; (*b*) ' essential ' pantheism (especially the views of Schelling and kindred spirits) : the antinomies of subject and object, finite and infinite, etc. are resolved into the ultimate essence of all things, itself indifferent, but producing all these contrasts in its evolution ; (*c*) pantheism of ' universal being ' (Hegelian absolute) : God is simply universal being which through an ' idea ' and a dialectical self-determination becomes all things successively. The next Canon condemns pantheism in all its forms in so far as they deny explicitly the fact that God has produced every form of being ' in its entire substance out of nothing '. Finally we have two Canons directed against the theories of Günther and Hermes concerning the freedom and purpose of God in creating. Thus those are condemned who say that God created the world as necessarily as He loves Himself, and not with a will free from all necessity, or who deny that the world was founded for the glory of God (D 1801–5). This concludes the Council's work on the subject of creation. Here at last we have a full statement of the teaching of Revelation on creation : full in the sense that it deals in one place with all the principal statements comprised within the doctrine of the Church. Moreover, it is presented in a language at once precise and unambiguous, yet unaffected by any one school of thought within the Church.

(iii) Since the 1st Vatican Council there have been two pronouncements of importance. The first we have already alluded to in our discussion of Genesis : the replies of the Biblical Commission of 1909 (*see* CCS, Sutcliffe : ' The Replies of the Biblical Commission ', 47a–54m).

The second document of importance is the now famous encyclical letter of Pius XII, *Humani Generis* of 1950, dealing with errors and dangerous tendencies in modern thought. The Pope first recalls the mistaken conclusions, sometimes drawn from modern evolutionary theories, leading to ' monistic or pantheistic speculations which represent the whole universe as left at the mercy of a continual process of evolution ' (AAS 42:562 ; CTS ed. par 5). Later, when dealing with ' some specific theological errors ', he deprecates the doubts entertained by some theologians : ' We are told that the world had no beginning ; that its creation was a necessary event, owing its origin to an act of liberality which the divine Love could not refuse ' (ibid. 570 ; CTS ed. par. 25). One notices immediately that the nature

of the errors is not as new as the theories which are supposed to be their foundation and justification. The root of so many theological errors is the same : the unbridled desire for human autonomy to the detriment of man's essential dependence on God.

IV A summary of what we have discovered about creation from a study of Scripture and Church documents will conclude this first part under seven headings : (1) God and only God (the Trinity acting as one principle) has created all things out of nothing. There is no evil principle involved nor any pre-existing material. (2) As a result, all creation is radically dependent on God in its entire being. (3) God created the world in time in the sense that the existence of the world cannot be traced indefinitely into the past. We need say no more on this point here ; it has to be examined in the latter part of the article. (4) God was entirely free in creating the world : free from any external coercion, free as regards the laws of His own nature to create or not to create, to create this or any other world. (5) He has created wisely and not at random ; and all that He has created is good. The Church has never declared this to be the most perfect of all possible worlds. Indeed Catholic theology has almost always held that God could have created a better world, though His choice of this particular world is a choice which is infinitely wise. (6) His purpose in creating was His own Glory, through the participation by His creatures of His own perfections. (7) God is also the examplary cause of the world, in the sense that the beings existing in the world mirror the perfections of the Divine Nature, which in its turn can be known through and in them.

P.F.H.

V God, the Efficient Cause of All Things :

What can reason make of the doctrine of creation revealed to us by God ? We use the word ' creation ' in two senses : (i) to refer to the act by which God produces the very being of all things in the spiritual and material universes without drawing them either from His own Being, or fashioning them from some pre-existent materials ; and (ii) to refer to the things produced by God's creative act. We begin, then, by treating of ' creation ' in the first of these two senses, which theologians usually call its ' active ' sense.

We are incapable of understanding the inner nature of God's creative act, or even of thinking directly of the act itself, for, being one identical reality with the divine Being, this act is as mysterious to us as God Himself. But just as we can think about the divine Being by means of ideas derived not from God Himself, but from the things of this world, so, too, we can think about God's act of creating by means of ideas we derive from the activities of finite agents, and especially human persons (*see* ANALOGY). Now the activity of a finite agent is always other than its being or substance, and since our minds think in terms of finite things, we always think of activity as other than being. Hence we differentiate in our thinking between God's activity and His Being ; since our idea of God's activity is different from that of His Being, we think of His activity as if it were other than His Being. It is, however, essential to avoid the common anthropomorphic error of treating being and activity as distinct in God, and to avoid transferring this distinction from our minds into God we have to be guided by the demands that the nature of Perfect Being make on our judgments, and not by the wholly inadequate concepts we form of Perfect Being. We must begin thinking about God's creative act on the firm foundation of a judgment denying that the distinctions we cannot help making in the course of our thinking are to be found as such in God (*see* ATTRIBUTES OF GOD). We must rise above the limitations of imaginary pictures of a god fashioned to suit our human ways of thinking, to affirm that, despite the logical distinctions we have in our minds, in God Himself being and activity are one and the same reality. The contrast between the affirmations of the judgment and our conceptual representations of those affirmations corresponds to the contrast between the things we know and our ways of conceiving those things. The truth of the judgments we make about things, and in which we express what we know of them, is to be distinguished from, and treated as independent of the ways in which we happen to represent conceptually what we affirm about those things in our judgments, for judgments are statements about things, not about how we conceive them. (We have a similar difficulty in attaining a knowledge about things perceived sensibly : to the naked eye railway lines seem to converge and meet on the horizon, but we realize that we must follow our judgment, not our sense impressions, and affirm that they run parallel up to and on the horizon.) When we are speaking of God and of His creative act, our attention must be focussed on the truth or falsity of the affirmations we have to make about Perfect Being, and not on the way in which we make an abstract conception of the truths we affirm. Thus my statement that God is merciful is always true, no matter how imperfect my concepts of mercy and of divine mercy happen to be. Similarly the truth of the statement that God's creative act is identical with His Being, is in no way impaired by the fact that in making the statement we cannot but conceive God's creative act as though it were different from His Being, because what we affirm of God is not our human way of conceiving Him, but solely the truth of what is stated.

To understand the differences between the way in which we conceive of God's creative act and the way in which we have to judge of it, we must see first of all how we conceive the activity of finite beings, for our conception of God's act of creating is derived from our ways of conceiving a finite agent's act of making something. The production of something new by a finite agent always involves processes of change, for a finite agent can only produce something new out of some pre-existent materials which he transforms in various ways until they become what the agent wants to make them. These changes are brought about successively by processes which go on in time, so that not only is the desired effect produced gradually, but the activity of the agent has to be both maintained for the length of time required to realize the effect, and constantly changed in order to produce what is required at each stage of the total process of its making. For example, when an artist produces a statue he puts forth numerous activities of mind and body which are not merely distinct from each other, but also from the being or substance of the artist himself. His activities are successive, following one upon the other in a temporal sequence. The statue is eventually produced as initially conceived, thanks to numerous transformations wrought by the skill of the artist in the materials which he selected for his work. Furthermore, the artist himself is by no means unaffected or unchanged by his own activities : he learns and acquires much in the way of skill from the experience of his work. An artist must be constantly producing new works, either to acquire the skill he lacks or to maintain that which he has already acquired. Thus for a human agent to be producing new works is also to be acquiring much for himself and so to be constantly changing. The mere process of producing new works redounds to the benefit of the artist, no matter how intent he may be on losing himself in perfecting his work.

The essential difference between the human act of making and the divine act of creating is that a man makes one thing from something else, whereas God does not make *from* anything : God's act is not the production of something new from something old, but the production of the very existence, the entire being of all things by an act which is unique because devoid of all change. When we speak about creation we are accustomed to say that God created all things 'out of nothing'. The preposition 'out of' or 'from' used in this kind of expression, in which we say that A comes from B, can be understood to denote either causality or sequence. If we understand it in a causal sense, the expression might be taken to mean that an effect B comes from an agent A as its efficient cause, or out of A as the matter from which it was formed. When we say, however, that God created all things 'out of nothing' we are not using the 'out of' in any causal sense, for non-being cannot be a cause ; nor are we using it to denote sequence or order, for there is no order or relationship of any kind between sheer nonentity and being. St Thomas points out (*Summa Theologica*, 1a:45:1@3) that in saying that God creates things 'from nothing' we can understand the negation asserted by the word 'nothing' to bear either on the verb 'create' or on the preposition 'from', so that the phrase can be understood to mean either that things are not created at all, or that they are created, but not from anything. Taken in the first sense, we would be saying that a being is not created at all, and this is true of God alone for He alone is uncreated being. In speaking of God's creative act the expression must, then, be understood in the second sense to mean that things are made, but not from anything at all, i.e. neither from pre-existent materials nor from God's own being.

Creation is the act by which God produces all things, visible and invisible, in being, without the aid of anything whatsoever. A created thing owes its entire being to God, for it is, and it is what it is, as a result of God's creative act. Unlike the human act of making something, God's creative act involves no change of any kind either for God Himself or for the things created by Him (for they are not produced from anything else), and therefore it is an act which is outside time. We cannot conceive what such a production is in itself for it transcends our experience completely. Notwithstanding the incalculable multiplicity of the things He brings into existence, and the unceasing creation of human souls which goes on in time, God's creative act itself is one, timeless, act. Nay more, it is not just *an* act, i.e. a passing act, one which began, endures and will come to an end, for it is not an act distinct from, or accidental to, the Being of God : it is identical with His eternal Being, so that it is itself eternal and utterly simple, being devoid of any succession and multiplicity whatever. Though God is free to create or not create, His creative act is none the less identical with, and not something adventitious to, His Being. His act of creating does not involve any kind of change in God Himself, so it is not incompatible with the divine immutability. God is not different in any way for having created things from what He would have been if He had never created anything. It is necessary to realise that with God there is no succession of any kind. Before the universe was created there was no such thing as succession, time or even duration. Succession and time were created by God with the universe. We cannot picture to ourselves a changeless and timeless agent, but we must hold firmly to the affirmation that God did not come to decide to create after previously not having decided to create. There was no period of the divine existence during which God was first able to create, followed by another during which He deliberated doing what He had not done before, and another during which He is doing what He had decided, followed finally by a period during which He looks back on having completed what He had resolved to do. It is meaningless to think of a time of some kind which existed before anything changing was created, even if our imagination disposes us to picture a duration existing on its own without anything as its source ; and it is meaningless to think of God as if He were enveloped in some sort of time of His own, even if we do imagine Him as if He were a being in time. God did not exist *before* the world came to be, and He will not exist *after* it has ceased to be : He does not even exist *while* the world continues to be. God is outside all succession : succession came to be with the things that God made and it envelops them, but not Him. God's eternity is not endless time : it is the fullness of Being which is so unalterably itself that we can only say of God that He is, never that He was or will be. God's act of creating is only an aspect of that fullness of immanent perfection which

is Living Being, so that it is eternal and changeless like Himself. God is unchangeable even in the free acts of His will. It is pointless to argue, as one would with reference to a finite being, that because the effects of His creative act are things which begin to be, the divine creative act itself must have begun to be, for we must determine the nature of God's act of creating not by the kind of things He produces as the acts of human agents are determined, but by the Being He is, seeing that His activity is really one with His Being.

Creation is the divine act of producing the entire being of everything that is. It is, in its most striking and obvious sense, the initial instantaneous production of things in their primeval existence. But since finite beings depend on God not merely for coming to be, but also for their continuing to be, as well as for the performance of all their activities, God's creative act must not be confined to the first origin of things : it includes the conservation of things in being and activity throughout time and the divine providential direction of all things to their final destiny (*Summa Theologica*, 1a:104:1:@4). What we call God's act of conserving things in being is not really different from His creative act : it is His creative act itself looked at from the point of view of the temporal endurance of its effect (*Contra Gentes*, 3:65). Thus in the richest sense of the term, ' creation ' is the production of the entire being of things. God's timeless creative act has effects enduring throughout time for He brings into being things which of their nature have a successive, because changing, manner of existence. His timeless creative act produces time itself. When we speak of God conserving things in existence throughout time we are not referring to an act of God which is really different from the act of creating them in the first instance, nor to an act of God which itself endures in time (like that of a finite agent producing finite effects), but to the enduring effect of God's timeless act of creation. The initial existence of created things, their subsequent history in time and their final destiny are all simultaneously present to God in His creative act ; God does not have to wait after creating things until they reach their final ends (as an artist has to wait until he finishes his work), nor does He have to anticipate their reaching their end, nor does He have to look back on the first beginning of things when they have reached their end. The whole temporal being of created things is just present to God in a non-temporal manner, i.e. in the eternity of His creative Act and Being.

We cannot understand how the succession of events that are unfolded in time and that make up the history of the world are all eternally present to the Being of God. Examples are of little value here, but we can profitably think of God as remotely like the perfect artist having a perfect and changeless image in his mind of the statue he is carving, and which exists unchanged in his mind all the time he is carving it. The artist's idea shapes the statue without being in any way improved during the process of its formation, so that it is not itself shaped by the spectacle of the statue coming to be. The example is useful in that it helps to show what we mean in speaking of the immutable presence of created things to God, but it limps because, even though it is not being made in time, the mental picture the artist has endures in time in the artist's mind. With God, however, all things are just present to Him without even enduring in time, for they are present in His eternal Being, which is without even continuing to be.

Not only does creating involve no change in God, but it does not even involve a change in created things. Since He produces the very being of all that He creates, since He does not form them from anything at all, God's creative act produces its effect instantaneously. A finite agent produces its effects as the result of the numerous changes it brings about in the materials on which it works to realize its effects. Change always presupposes something pre-existing which lacks the particular determination the agent works to impart (thus the sculptor works to impart a special shape to the marble). Change presupposes some privation in an existent thing. Creation, on the other hand, presupposes not merely some privation, but utter privation of all finite being and existence, so that before things were created there was not anything from which to produce them, and hence there was not anything from which God could initiate a process of change. A thing can change from being A to become B, and we can speak of a transit of a thing from A to B. But there is no transit from nothingness to being. The transit from non-being to being that we imagine to take place as God creates things is not really a transit at all; to speak of such a transit as being real is devoid of meaning. Creating is therefore a pure positing of things in being, without there having been anything before. It is, then, an act which produces its effect instantaneously and which, so far from beginning in a process of change, initiates things and all change processes.

To create is an act proper to God and to God alone, for only Infinite Being can produce the entire being of all things which exist without the help of anything whatsoever, and still be able to produce countless other universes, apart from those He does create, without the need of anything whatsoever from which to produce them. Hence a created being proceeds directly and immediately from God, and equally it depends directly and immediately on God for its being. Theologians are generally agreed that the hypothesis of God using an instrument in creating is to be discounted as incompatible with the very idea of creation. An instrumental cause is only in place (a) where something is produced as the result of a process of change wrought in the materials from which the effect is to be produced, and (b) where the causal power of the agent is limited in some way so that he is not able to produce by himself alone the effect he has in mind. But in creating the world God had nothing to work on, nothing to transform. Hence there would have been no role for an instrument to perform in God's work of creating things.

God created all things Himself and created them exactly as He wished them to be, for He had no obstacles to overcome and nothing to condition His creative activity. God is the sovereign master of the entire work He produced and so far from being subjected to the limitations of the things, He created them entirely subject to His power and providential control.

VI Created Things. We now treat of 'creation' in what theologians call its 'passive' sense, i.e. the things produced by God as the effects of His creative act. Created things owe their entire being to God, and exist in a state of complete dependence on Him. For St Thomas the createdness of things is this relationship of dependence on God (*Summa Theologica*, 1a:45:2:@2 and 45:3). Creation is not essentially the actual commencement of finite existence, or the actual producing of things from nothing; for though in fact things did commence to exist and there was a first moment of time, so that (theoretically at least) it should be possible to trace the origin of the world back to its first moments, God could have created the world everlastingly so that it would never have actually commenced to exist. The created world might have existed always, so that it would always have been and be in the state of being created (*see* COSMOGONY).

God's act of creating is not a transitive action, i.e. nothing actually passes from God to the things created as happens when an artist makes a statue; although they are maintained in their status as creatures by God, created things do not receive anything passing from God to themselves. Their createdness consists in their being established in existence by the immanent act of the divine will and set in a relationship of dependence on God. Since creation, unlike change, does not involve any movement, the createdness of finite things cannot consist in anything but this real relationship of dependence. The relationship is in some way distinct from the substance of created things. Many theologians conceive it as really distinct from the being of created things, as something other than their being and so as an accident. Since, however, the relationship is demanded as a condition of the existence of a finite thing (and does not presuppose its existence), it is not one of the predicamental accidents envisaged by Aristotle. Some theologians adopt the simpler view of Scotus and say that the relationship of createdness is only logically distinct from the being of created things: it is the thing itself considered as dependent on God.

The relationship between God and creatures is not symmetrical, because though it is one of real dependence in the creature, it is only a logical relationship in God, for God has not made Himself dependent on, nor beholden in any way to, the creatures He has produced.

Created things bear witness to the omnipotence of God, 'to his eternal power and divinity', for God has designed the universe that it should manifest to all minds both the wisdom and the might of its creator. God created what He willed, and made everything as He willed it to be, endowing each and every thing with just those qualities He willed them to have. God could not possibly fail to realize what He intended in creating things, for His creative power is infinite like His Being. But how are we to think of God's omnipotence ? What is God able to create ? For those who regard the will as a power which is complete in itself, divine omnipotence must mean that God could create absolutely anything He might happen to choose, and thus in this view it would be His will that is *solely* responsible for making things not only to be, but to be what they are. That is creatable which is chosen by God and solely because it is chosen by Him. Some things have been so created by God, for example the truths of logic and mathematics, and the irreversibility of history, as to be necessary. Created necessities are not rooted in anything but the free choice of God's will so that they are not inherent necessities. God could have made a world in which these would either not be, or not be necessary as they are now. The vast majority of theologians reject this conception of divine omnipotence: they argue that will in God is, and can only be, what will is as such, a power rooted in mind, and since mind is a power rooted in being, so too is will. God must will His own Being, and He wills created things as reflections of His own Being. As God knows His own Being, whatever He wills to create must be known by His mind and thus willed in order that it might manifest the perfections of His own Being. Hence God could create whatever is an intrinsically possible reflection of Himself, i.e. anything which is not inherently contradictory or absurd. The ultimate ground of the possibility and of the necessities inherent in created things is thus the divine Being itself. Divine omnipotence, therefore, means that God can create anything that is a possible likeness to His own Being ; ultimately an absurdity is absurd because it is out of keeping with the necessities of being as they are in God Himself. We often say that God could not create a square circle, or that He could not reverse the course of history because such things are impossibilities. To be incapable of the impossible is no real limitation to God's omnipotence, because it is not a real incapacity or powerlessness in God. St Thomas reminds us that ' it is better to say that what involves contradiction cannot be done, rather than that God cannot do it ' (*Summa Theologica*, 1a:25 ; 3–4).

Because all the beings that God creates are reflections of His own Being, and because a finite being can be at its very best only a faint manifestation of the perfection of God, God creates an enormous multiplicity of things to have a creation capable of showing forth His glory and omnipotence the more vividly : ' Because His goodness could not be adequately represented by one creature alone, He produces many and diverse creatures, that what was wanting to one in the representation of the divine goodness might be supplied by another. For goodness, which in God is simple and unvaried, in creatures is manifold and divided ; and hence the

whole universe together participates in the divine goodness more perfectly, and represents it better than any single creature whatever' (*Summa Theologica*, 1a:47:1). Similarly St Thomas shows that God established the inequalities there are between things to manifest His wisdom, and he rejects Origen's theory that inequality is not the work of God manifesting His goodness, but the result and punishment of sin. The wisdom of God is manifested by the splendour of the whole universe which comprises beings of numerous kinds, whereas the standardization of all created things to one pattern would scarcely be an evident manifestation of the supreme wisdom and infinite splendour of God (cf. *Summa Theologica*, 1a:47:2).

VI God, the Final Cause of Creation. God knows and loves Himself necessarily. The proper object of the divine intellect is the divine Being, and since in God intellect and Being are one reality, God's knowledge is His Being. God's intellect requires nothing other than the divine Being itself for its eternal act of knowing. Again, since the Being of God is infinitely good, God necessarily loves Himself with a love that is Himself and unchangeable like Himself. God does not need anything other than Himself in order to realize a love that would be perfect. God's love of Himself is not a divine form of egoism, as is sometimes imagined. Egoism is disordered love of self, or love of self that is excessive because based on an exaggerated esteem of self. But since God is infinite goodness He could not love Himself excessively : infinite good calls for infinite love. It would be a disorder if God did not love Himself with a love that is infinite and perfect. So far from being egoism, God's love of Himself is His sanctity ; we say that God's sanctity is perfect because He could not possibly not love Himself with infinitely perfect love.

God was under no necessity to create anything, for He is infinitely perfect in Himself and has need of nothing other than Himself. He was free to create or not to create. But granted that He did decide to create, that He has eternally decided to do so, He must have a reason or purpose for doing so, for creating could only be a free act of His will provided God intended some known end, and it could only be an act of supreme wisdom provided He decided to create beings which could achieve that end. This end or purpose could not, however, have been anything other than God Himself, for seeing that His love is of Himself, all His activity must inevitably be inspired by love of Himself. God could only seek something other than Himself from love of Himself, or as an expression of the love He has for His own Being. In other words God did not create things in order to attain something other than Himself, for He had no reason to seek anything other than Himself. Hence the only possible purpose God could have had in creating (*finis Dei operantis*) was the love of His own infinite goodness and the manifestation of His Glory. God did not create things because He needed them, nor because they can give Him anything that would enrich Him, nor because He needs to express Himself outwardly in finite things. God created things for His own glory, i.e. to communicate to finite beings something of the perfection and glory which is His, that they too may rejoice in the supreme act of loving and glorifying God as He loves and glories in His own infinite Being. As St Thomas says, God does not love creatures for any good He finds in them, for His love for creatures cannot be an effect produced in God by creatures themselves : God's love for Himself is creative of the goodness there is in created things, so that His love of creatures is as a reflection of His love for Himself : ' *Amor Dei est infundens et creans bonitatem in rebus* ' (*Summa Theologica*, 1a:20:2). Thus God wills good to creatures not for their own sakes, but for love of Himself. This is no derogation to creatures, for the noblest love God could have for creatures is that of loving them in His love for His own infinitely perfect Being. Divine love of self is not sterile, but the most fruitful source of good. Thus the ultimate purpose for which God created all things is not for their own sakes, but for Himself. It is only indirectly that God wills good to creatures, i.e. inasmuch as He Himself is the greatest good to all things. God's creative act is thus unique by reason of its ultimate purpose which is not to attain anything He has not, but solely to bestow on creatures something of His own life and happiness which is achieved in their glorifying Him.

Creation in God is absolutely free and therein lies perhaps the supreme mystery of divine Love. God does not create out of any necessity, nor from any inward striving for some end other than Himself, but from the completely free act of His will. This idea of creation is the exclusive possession of Christianity. God was, furthermore, free to create just what He willed, and as many beings or as many universes as He willed, granted that He willed to create at all. There are no limits to His creative power, and He is under no obligation to create one kind of universe rather than another. Leibniz's conception of God having to create the best possible world has never had the support of Catholic theologians ; St Thomas points out that one can only talk of the best possible world provided one knows first of all just how it attains the end for which it was created. St Thomas thinks of the created world as being ' excellent ' (*Summa Theologica*, 1a:47:2:@1). God would not have been in any sense the poorer nor the less holy if He had never created anything at all, for by creating things He has brought benefit not to Himself but solely to His creatures. Creating was an act of pure and supreme liberality on God's part.

It is sometimes objected that God created things in order that they might render Him honour and glory, so that He must evidently stand in need of what He demands that all men and creatures should render Him, the acclamation of unceasing worship. Framed in this way the objection presupposes that creatures can give God something He does not possess, and that He will be without, if they do not give it to Him. God's glory, however, is not increased by the creature's acts of rendering Him worship, nor is it diminished by their failure to worship Him. God demands that creatures should worship Him not for His own needs, but for theirs. If they are to be what God made them to be, men should be doing freely, by their own choice, what all created things are doing by their very nature, i.e. paying tribute to God by the splendour of the existence which is theirs as a gift from on high. God commands men to worship Him because this is conducive to their well-being as creatures, not that they might add to His glory by so doing, but that they might enjoy God's glory as He enjoys His own. God's creation is the manifestation of His glory and it necessarily manifests His glory because it has been made by Him for this purpose. The material world manifests the glory of God to men ; it is as expressive of the majesty of God as it could be, notwithstanding the blindness of many who cannot perceive what is of itself perfectly perceptible. Thus God does not have to win honour and worship from men because He stands in need of their recognition, as a man might seek recognition from his companions for his deeds, and suffer some loss if he fails to secure it. God ' seeks ' His own honour and glory only in the sense that He communicates something of His perfection and glory to what He creates, and commands men to render Him the worship which is His due, that they too may become by their own acts of mind and will what all created things are by their very nature, outward manifestations of the glory and majesty of God.

Bibliography. P. F. Ceuppens OP, *Quaestiones Selectae ex Historia Primaeva* (1953) ; L. Pirot, *La Sainte Bible*, vol. 1 (1946) ; R. de Vaux OP, *La Bible de Jérusalem—La Genèse* (1953) ; E. Mangenot, ' Hexaméron ', in DTC, col. 2326–54 ; F. de Hummelauer SJ, *Commentarius in Genesim* (1895) ; J. Chaine SJ, *Le Livre de la Genèse* (1951) ; *T. B. Chetwood, God and Creation* (1928) ; *S. R. Driver, *The Book of Genesis* (1948) ; E. F. Sutcliffe SJ, ' Genesis ', in CCS, 136a–161e ; A. Vacant, *Études théologiques sur les Constitutions du Concile du Vatican*, tome 1 (1895) ; H. Pinard SJ. ' Création ', in DTC, col. 2034–201 ; St Thomas Aquinas, *Summa Theologica*, 1a:44–9 ; *Contra Gentes*, 2:1–45 ; *De Potentia*, 3–5 ; St Bonaventure, *In IV Sent.*, liber 2, dist. I ff ; Suarez, *Disputationes Metaphysicae*, Disp. 20, (vol. 25, in the edition of 1866) ; Lessius, *De Perfectionibus Moribusque Divinis* (1619) ; C. Mazzella SJ, *De Deo Creante* (1908) ; D. Palmieri SJ, *De Creatione* (1910) ; L. Janssens OSB, *De Deo Creatore* (1905) ; M. Daffara OP, *De Deo Creatore* (1947) ; M. Schmaus, *Katholische Dogmatik*, vol. 2 (1949) ; J. Stufler SJ, *Why God Created the World* (trans. from German by E. F. Sutcliffe, SJ, 1937) ; A. D. Sertillanges OP, *L'Idée de création* (1945) ; D. J. B. Hawkins, *The Essentials of Theism* (1949) ; R. Jolivet, *Essai sur les rapports entre la pensée grecque et la pensée chrétienne* (1955) ; E. Gilson, *The Christian Philosophy of St Thomas Aquinas*, (trans. from French by L. K. Shook, 1957, part 2, ch. 1) ; G. Lambert SJ, ' La Création dans la Bible ', in NRT 75 (1953) 258–81 ; R. Guelley, ' La Portée religieuse du dogme de la création ', in NRT

75 (1953) 803–14 ; M. Flick SJ, 'La Struttura del trattato "de Deo Creante et Elevante"', in *Gregorianum* 36 (1955) 284–90 ; Z. Alszeghy SJ, and M. Flick SJ, 'Gloria Dei', in *Gregorianum* 36 (1955) 361–90 ; B. Vawter CM, *A Path through Genesis* (1957) ; A. Gelin, *Problèmes de l'ancien Testament* (1952) ; P. Denis OP, *Les Origines du monde* (1951) ; M. Flick SJ and Z. Alszeghy SJ, *Il Creatore* (1962 ²).   E. A. S.

CREEDS As the several creeds used by the Church have been treated at different points in this work (*see* APOSTLES' CREED ; ARIANISM, for the creed of Nicaea ; CONSTANTINOPLE, for the history of the Nicene creed as transformed by the first council of Constantinople), the subject of the present article is the use made of creeds by the Church, or their function in her life. The use of creeds at baptism (I), at Mass (II) and for solemnizing various changes of status in the Church (III) will be examined, and a note added (IV) on the theological importance of minor creeds such as the so-called Athanasian and the *Te Deum*.

I Baptismal creeds are a primary datum of the Tradition of the Church. At the culmination of the catechesis (*see* CATECHUMENATE) the candidate is entrusted with the formula of a creed which he learns by heart and is able to pronounce before receiving baptism (*see* BAPTISM, IV (*d*) and XV). From the time of the revised text of Ac 8:37 (before 150 at the latest) there was Scripture warrant for requiring an elementary Christ-creed before baptism (*see* Crehan, *Early Christian Baptism*, 7–11), while it seems very probable that St Paul (Eph 5 : 26) is alluding to the same practice by his mention of 'the word' as an accompaniment of purification (Crehan, op. cit. 18). The rendering : 'water to which His word gave life' (KV) imports into the text far more than is there present.

Tertullian for the Latin world gave the idea legal precision when he wrote (*de fuga* 12) : 'The sun marked the day of the incurring of the debt for our Redemption. Our setting free was enacted in Hell and the formal contract was in heaven'.[1] The darkening of the sun at the Crucifixion was the sign of the contract. Christ went down to Hell and set us free (and therefore in imitation of this we go down into the water), but the contract is valid in heaven, where the Trinity has witnessed it. In the West the idea of a *pactum fidei* is universally accepted from the 3rd cent. onwards. Clarus of Mascula in 256 (CSEL 3:459) speaks of 'baptizing the faith of those who believe' ; Niceta of Remesiana in his instruction on the Creed (ed. by A. E. Burn, 51) calls on the candidates to 'keep the pact which you have made with the Lord'; Ildephonsus of Toledo (PL 96:158) has the idea that the pact has two parts, a renunciation of the devil and a pact of faith with God.

In the East one can find some echo of the same ideas in Clement of Alexandria (*eclogae propheticae* 13 ; GCS 17:140) and Origen (*exhortatio ad*

[1] Sol cessit diem emptionis nostrae. Apud inferos remancipatio nostra est et stipulatio nostra in caelis.

martyrium 17 ; GCS 2:16) where the word συνθῆκαι is used for what takes place at baptism. This word recurs in the newly-discovered *Dialektos* (4:28) where Origen begs of Bishop Heracleides and the others present at their meeting : 'Let us abide by the contracts'. Didymus of Alexandria towards the end of the 4th cent. in his *De Trinitate* (PG 39:716) is careful to make clear that, while we pay out our faith at baptism, this is not the purchase price of redemption which is a free gift to all of us. In Basil (*hom* 13:3 ; PG 31:432) baptismal regeneration is simply described as 'the gift', a phrase echoed in Gregory of Nazianzen (*oratio* 40:18 ; PG 36:381) and Chrysostom (hom. 10 in Mt ; PG 57:185). One may see in this difference of emphasis between East and West a result of their differing outlooks, mystical and practical, or even legal. This does not mean that the East neglected to insist on a credal profession at baptism ; the evidence of the Fathers at Chalcedon is quite to the contrary. They cry out (*Acta conciliorum*, II:i:2:79) : 'This (the Nicene creed) is the faith in which we were baptized ; this is the faith in which we baptize'.

II The creed at Mass is first found in the *Stowe Missal* (of late 8th cent.) where it is sung between gospel and offertory, exactly as now in the Roman rite. This Irish service-book is no doubt dependent on a Spanish forerunner, as frequently happens with liturgical traditions, but the only Spanish trace that has been discovered is slightly different in character. The Visigothic king Reccared, on his conversion from Arianism in 589, proclaimed the creed of Nicaea and Constantinople at Mass, and it was decided to make the practice customary, but the place chosen for it was before the *Pater noster*, a place which is still kept in the Mozarabic rite (PL 85:556). There can be little doubt that the Irish custom was followed by the Anglo-Saxons, from whom it passed to the Franks in the days of Alcuin and Charlemagne, when it was desired to meet the challenge of the Adoptionists.

The attempts of Walafrid Strabo to trace its history (PL 114:947) are misleading and come from a time when the historical study of the liturgy was hardly begun. Pope Benedict VIII accepted the custom for Rome in 1014 (PL 142:1060) at the request of the Emperor.

As with so many liturgical usages which have come via Spain and Ireland to general adoption in the West, there must be supposed an Eastern origin for the practice of professing one's faith at Mass. The *Testamentum Domini* (Syriac, from the late 4th cent.) gives an account of the instructional service (lessons, gospel and sermon, with dismissal of catechumens) corresponding to the first part of the Mass (I:28) and then directs : 'After that let the bishop teach the mysteries to the people. But if he is not present, let the presbyter speak so that the faithful may know to whom they are approaching and who is their God and Father'. There follows a form of creed, here called *Mystagogia*, all concerned with the mysteries of Christ, though it contains several references to the Father. In the Cooper-

Maclean edition (1902) this creed fills four pages of print. At the end a rubric directs that the Eucharist is to follow this creed, but that the recitation of the creed is not to take place every time, being reserved for ' Pascha on Saturday, the first day of the week and the days of the Epiphany and Pentecost '. The purpose of the recitation is said to be (ibid.) ' that the people may know of whom in the holy things they are partaking and what memorial they are making through the Eucharist'. Thus the creed at Mass was meant to look forward to the Eucharist rather than backwards to the gospel which had just been read. It was also meant more as an instruction for the faithful than as a proclamation and in some liturgies is called μάθημα. In the Coptic and Greek liturgy of St Gregory (Renaudot, *Liturgia orientalis* I:36 ; I:123) and in the Ethiopic anaphora (ibid. 520), just before the giving of Holy Communion, there is a form of creed recited by the participants where they profess their faith that this is the true Body of Christ, born of the pure virgin, suffered under Pontius Pilate, never confused with, nor disjoined from, His divinity, and given for the remission of sins and for life eternal. One might consider this creed as simply an expansion of the primitive usage whereby the priest at Communion gave the Body of Christ into the hands of the recipient with the words *Corpus Christi* and received the answer : *Amen*.

The 2nd Canon of the 3rd Council of Toledo in 589, at which Reccared made his profession of faith, directed that : ' Out of reverence for the holy faith and for the strengthening of the weak minds of men . . . the Eastern creed of the Council of Constantinople, i.e. of the 150 bishops, should be recited. Before the Lord's Prayer is pronounced this creed should be chanted by the people to give a plain testimony of the true faith and to secure that the people come to partake of the Body and Blood of Christ with hearts that have been purified in faith '.[1] This instruction was amplified by Isidore of Seville and passed into Spanish tradition. It is a valuable indication of how theological Tradition operated ; in an age when the oath was generally held in honour, the recitation of this creed before Communion by some heretic who had entered the assembly of the faithful would be regarded as a great crime. Not merely at baptism but throughout life the articles of this creed would be present in the minds of believers. Eusebius (*HE* 6:43) narrates that Novatian made his adherents swear at the moment of Communion that they would not go back to Pope Cornelius. From this it would seem that the solemnity of the moment was understood and valued in the Church from very early times.

The Der-Balyzeh papyrus when first discovered (1908) was thought to give very early evidence for the use of the creed at Mass, but time has brought a correction to this view. The papyrus is now dated to the late 6th cent., and its latest editor, C. H. Roberts, has rearranged it so that the leaf which carries an elementary creed, headed by the rubric : ' He confesses (this) creed ', is now seen not to be part of the Mass at all. It may be a form of service for Communion to the sick, or possibly a baptismal *Ordo*. The leaf itself has lost some fifteen lines of writing which went before the creed, but this would hardly be sufficient for the whole service of exorcism and renunciation prior to a baptism.

III The Creed was used in other Solemnities.

When Communion was taken to the sick, it was the Irish practice to call for a recitation of the creed, if the *Book of Dimma* (c. 650) may be trusted. Here the priest has to say : ' Taught by the authority of God and prompted by divine schooling, let us make bold to say : "I believe in God the Father almighty. I believe also in Christ His Son. I believe also in the Holy Ghost. I believe in life after death. I believe that I shall rise again " '.[2] This is very similar to the Der-Balyzeh creed, both having as sole addition to the Trinitarian form a declaration of belief in the resurrection of the body. The *Book of Mulling* (which is prior to 697) has a set of prayers for Communion to the sick and directs that a creed be chanted, but the wording of the creed is not given, save for the first four words which, however, are the same as in *Dimma*. The *Bobbio Missal* in its explanation of the Creed (n. 591) has a few words in praise of faith which show that it would be quite natural for Irish bishops such as Mulling and Dimma to make a profession of faith just before death.[3] ' Faith promises heaven and its kingdom after the death of the body, and therefore whoso shall persevere in confessing such faith as this need not fear from the wrath that is to come.' The ceremonial profession of faith for a bishop on his death-bed (*caerimoniale episcoporum* 2:38) is probably developed from this rite.

At the entry upon office of a pope there was a credal statement to be accepted. The custom can be traced back to before the time of Gelasius (492–6), but how much earlier than his time the custom is can be (and is) debated at great length. Gelasius wrote to Laurence of Lychnida, a bishop in Macedonia (*epist. Romanorum pontificum* ; CSEL 35:225) as follows : ' It is customary in the Roman Church for its bishop when newly entered on office to set forth the profession of his faith as an example to the holy churches in the following form'.[4] The word *praerogare* appeals to the Roman constitutional theory of the *centuria praerogativa*, a group in the Assembly

---

[1] Pro reverentia sanctissimae fidei et propter corroborandas hominum invalidas mentes, . . . secundum formam orientalium ecclesiarum, concilii Constantinopolitani, hoc est centum quinquaginta episcoporum, symbolum fidei recitetur ; ut, priusquam dominica dicatur oratio, voce clara a populo decantetur ; quo et fides vera manifestum testimonium habeat et ad Christi corpus et sanguinem praelibandum pectora populorum fide purificata accedant.

[2] Divino magisterio edocti et divina institutione formati, audemus dicere : Credo in Deum Patrem omnipotentem ; credo et in Iesum Christum filium eius ; credo et in Spiritum sanctum ; credo vitam post mortem ; credo me resurgere.

[3] Fides post sepulcrum generis caelum atque regna caelorum promittit ; ideoque qui in tali confessione permanserit a superveniente ira timere non potest.

[4] Mos est Romanae ecclesiae sacerdoti noviter constituto formam hanc fidei suae ad sanctas ecclesias praerogare.

which set an example by its vote for the groups that were to vote after it. In the *Liber diurnus* (edited by T. Sickel in 1889) from the papal chancery, are three formulae for a profession of faith (73, 84 and 85), and the detailed discussion of them would be far too complicated to be attempted here. It must suffice to note that these formulae have received additions from time to time ; that is entirely in accordance with Roman legal practice, for the praetor's edict was compiled in exactly the same way, *iure tralaticio*. Some of the additions are Chalcedonian and anti-Nestorian, but to subtract these and then to claim that the residue is a Roman creed of the 4th cent. is much more hazardous a proceeding. The theological importance of the custom is that it makes clear that there was no inhibition in Rome about adding to a formulation of the faith, even in a time when some bishops (at Chalcedon) were claiming that the creed should be treated like the Scripture and kept free from all additions. For the question of the *Filioque* addition, *see* HOLY GHOST.

IV The Athanasian creed, which begins with the words *Quicunque vult*, is now admitted to be a Latin composition and not a Greek, while Ambrose and Vincent of Lerins are favoured candidates for its authorship. What is certain is that it was in use by 542, when it is cited by Caesarius of Arles at the head of a collection of homilies which he compiled for the use of his parish priests. Caesarius says : ' Since it is necessary that not only the clergy but also the laity should have knowledge of the Catholic faith, we have for that reason in this Book of Homilies written down the Catholic faith as the holy Fathers have defined it, which we should ourselves frequently read and explain to others'. There follows in the MS published by Dom Morin the creed with the heading *Fides catholica sancti Athanasii episcopi*. Caesarius was a monk of Lérins and may have learnt this creed in his monastery. From one of its sentences about the Incarnation (*nam sicut anima rationalis et caro unus est homo, ita deus et homo unus est Christus* : just as rational soul and body make up one man, so divinity and humanity make one Christ) it might be inferred that the creed was meant for expository purposes rather than as a form of prayer. The canon of the Council of Autun (*c.* 670) orders that : ' If any priest, deacon, sub-deacon or cleric, shall not have repeated without mistake the symbol which under inspiration of the Holy Ghost the apostles handed down to us and the Faith of St Athanasius the prelate, let him be condemned by his bishop'. This points to the use of this creed as the basis of doctrinal instruction by the clergy who should be ready at any time to expound what they know by heart. The view of C. H. Turner that the *Quicunque* is really a hymn and not a creed at all depends on its use at Prime in the divine office. Though this use accounts for many MSS of the creed, yet they are not so early as the one which tells us of its employment by Caesarius, while an *epistula canonica* of the early 6th cent. (PL 56:890) enacts that clerics who fail in their ' by heart ' examination on this creed must abstain from wine for forty days.

From England there is the testimony of Denebert, bishop of Worcester in 798, who uses this creed as a profession of his faith to the archbishop of Canterbury, Ethelheard (Haddan and Stubbs, *Councils* III: 525). His words ' as I learnt I will expound ', imply that he had it by heart.

The habit of collecting creeds and writing them successively in one MS can be illustrated from several surviving MSS of the 8th and 9th cents. One such, from Reichenau, was studied by K. Künstle in 1900 (*Forschungen zur christlichen Literatur* 1:4). The nucleus of the collection is Spanish, but it has passed through Irish hands, for the Irish canons and an Irish *Penitential* have been added by them. The idea seems to have been much the same as that which guided the canonists (*see* CANONICAL COLLECTIONS), and the creeds ascribed to Jerome, Ambrose, Augustine, Gregory Thaumaturgus, Damasus and Isidore were eagerly copied so that later (and perhaps less fortunate) generations might have a full picture of the faith as held in the age of the Fathers. The destruction wrought by the Vikings or the Moors may have had a part in spurring on this work of collection.

The *Te Deum* was from the first meant to be sung. It is a chanted creed and not a recited one. Cyprian of Toulon (*c.* 530) in his ungrammatical Latin refers to it as ' the hymn which the whole Church has accepted and sings daily '; in it we use the words *Tu es rex gloriae, Christe*. (MGH *epist. Carolingii aevi* I:436).[1] It is mentioned in the Rule of St Benedict (XI ; CSEL 75:58), and its manner of composition, with the ending of each verse arranged to fit the *cursus* of accented but no longer quantitative Latin speech, shows that it can hardly go back to Ambrose and Augustine, even though some of the MSS (such as the Latin psalter given by Charlemagne to Pope Hadrian I in 772) ascribe it to these two. Nicetas of Remesiana is now very much the most favoured candidate for its authorship, but from his remote see in Old Serbia to Monte Cassino or to the Irish monastery of Bangor (in whose *Antiphonary* of *c.* 680 the *Te Deum* is found with the heading *Hymnus in die Dominica*) the passage of this canticle must have been somewhat uncertain.

The Jerusalem church in the 5th cent. had a collection of 14 Odes or canticles drawn from Scripture, for Hesychius produced a commentary on them. Similarly in Alexandria 14 canticles were held in honour, for the second scribe of Codex Alexandrinus copied them out about the same time. Of the 14 there were usually two, the *Prayer of Manasses* and the *Gloria in excelsis* which were not strictly scriptural. What seems to have happened when this custom of singing canticles reached Ireland by way of North Africa and Spain is that other non-scriptural canticles were added and among them the *Te Deum*, the *Quicunque vult* and even the Nicene creed. The *Antiphonary of Bangor* has the two canticles of Moses, the *Benedictus*, the *Song of the Three Children* and the *Te Deum*, all very much on a footing, while the Irish *Liber hymnorum* includes

[1] In hymno quem omnes ecclesia toto orbe receptum canit cottidie dicemus ; Tu es rex gloriae, Christe.

Te Deum and *Quicunque vult*, but by a curious accident the preface (in Old Irish) to this latter has been lost and in its place stands a paragraph which was clearly meant as an introduction to the Nicene creed. The implication is therefore that this collection had once included both Nicene and Athanasian creeds *as canticles*. Until the history of the early chants has been explored more fully, it will be impossible to establish what exactly was the reason why the *Quicunque vult* became a canticle after having been a clerical profession of faith. Structurally it resembles the *Te Deum* in that it has a Trinitarian part followed by a Christological part, and both creeds in their execution have attended to the accentual *cursus* for line-endings, but the clue to its transformation into a canticle is probably to be sought in its musical history.

In the Trinitarian piety which grew up in the West as a reaction against the lingering Arianism of the 5th and 6th cents. there is a kerygmatic or proclamatory quality which made men want to sing of the great mystery, hailing the dawn as a gift from the Father of lights, from the Son who enlightens our darkness and from the Spirit of light and fire. One can find a first trace of it in the anonymous commentary on the Nicene creed published by C. H. Turner (*Monumenta iuris antiquissima*, II:i:330) which says : 'He who does not believe this and does not to his life's end keep this profession and proclaim it to the faithful in the liturgy and manifest it to pagans, at the bidding of the Father, at the bidding of the Son and by the urging of the Holy Spirit, he shall be sent to Hell and expiate his sin there for ever'.[1] The note added to the *Te Deum* in a MS of the 13th cent. (British Museum, Harleian 2253) calls for it to be sung at the Consecration during Mass. Such joy in the Trinity has since the Reformation become a rare mark of popular devotion, though the Anglo-Saxon practice of singing *Te Deum* at a coronation (it can be traced back as far as the crowning of King Edgar by St Dunstan in 973) has not yet been lost.

Bibliography. *C. H. Turner, *The History and Use of Creeds and Anathemas in the Early Centuries of the Church* (1910²) ; J. H. Crehan sj, *Early Christian Baptism and the Creed* (1950); G. Morin osb, 'L'Origine du symbole de Saint Athanase', in RBn 44 (1932) 201–19 ; B. Capelle osb, 'Alcuin et l'histoire du symbole de la messe', in *Recherches de théologie ancienne* 6 (1934) 249–60 ; *A. E. Burn, 'The Authorship of the *Quicunque vult*', in JTS 27 (1926) 19–28 ; *M. Frost, 'The Irish Text of the *Te Deum*', in *Church Quarterly Review* 102 (1926) 136–41 ; S. Salaville, 'Les Textes grecs du *Te Deum*', in *Échos d'Orient* 13 (1910) 208–13 ; H. Schneider, 'Die biblische Oden im christlichen Altertum', in Bi 30 (1949) 28–65 ; J. Jungmann sj, *Missarum sollemnia* (1957). **J. H. C.**

---

[1] Haec qui non crediderit, et istam confessionem usque ad finem vitae non semper tenens et fidelibus dixerit in confessione et gentilibus demonstrarit, iubente Patre, iubente Filio, Spiritu sancto urguente, in Gehennam missus perpetuas luet poenas.

CREMATION This article is divided into two parts, (I) history and (II) the Church's attitude towards, and legislation against, cremation.

I History. Cremation is a funeral rite in which the dead body is reduced to ashes by burning. Archaeological research and historical records make it clear that the practice of cremation has existed for many centuries among both civilized and uncivilized races. Certain nations employed this means of disposing of the dead so completely as to exclude inhumation. Other nations, like the Greeks in Homeric times, seem to have resorted to both methods. Cremation was certainly practised by the primitive Chanaanites but the Semitic tribes, who later occupied their territory, used inhumation. The Jews established their cemeteries outside their city walls and buried all the dead including the bodies of their enemies slain in battle.

Cremation appeared among the Romans only during the time of the Republic and, although it was to become the common mode of disposal during the Empire, burial (inhumation) did not wholly cease to exist. With the Christianization of the Empire cremation disappeared. From the earliest times the Church has been opposed to cremation. It endeavoured to give the dead the same care and homage which was accorded to the body of Christ, and the early Christians readily undertook grave risks and paid large sums of money in order to recover the bodies or ashes of the martyrs and give them burial (H. Leclercq, in DAC s.v. Incinération). So intense was the desire of the Church that the dead should be completely inhumated that in 1299 Boniface VIII issued a decree of excommunication against those who removed the bones from the flesh of the famous dead, a practice employed to facilitate transportation. No more was heard of cremation in the Church until the end of the 18th cent.

Whether the reason for its reintroduction into Christian countries was due to anticlericalism, freethinking, Masonry, or a desire to throw off the restraint of the Church, is difficult to ascertain. By a parliamentary decree cremation was allowed in Italy in 1874. Similar legislation appeared in France (1887), Denmark (1892), Great Britain (1902), and at later dates in other European countries and in America.

II The attitude of the Church towards cremation is not founded on any purely aesthetic objection. Nor does cremation offend against divine law. Why, then, has the Church made several enactments against this practice ? Certainly not because it would seem to militate against the dogma of the resurrection of the body. The resurrection of the cremated body is as intrinsically possible as that of the body allowed to corrupt by inhumation. Athenagoras in his treatise *De Resurrectione Mortuorum* emphasized, as early as the 2nd cent., the fact that God who brought men's bodies into being, could easily bring them together again, however great the extent to which the component parts had been dispersed (PG 6: 979). Assuredly certain Church legislation has been directed against those who held cremation to be a public profession of their irreligion and materialism (cf. the decree of the Holy Office, 19 May 1886.) When, however, such an idea is far from the mind of those who employ cremation and the rite is used, for example, because it is deemed more hygienic, the Church has other reasons to advance for Her opposition. Not only is inhumation in consecrated ground part of the Christian tradition, following the manner in which the body of Christ was buried, but it is more consonant with Scripture (e.g. Eccl 38:16) and the respect due to the Christian. For the Christian body has been the dwelling-place of the Holy Spirit, (1 Cor 3:16), it has been sanctified by the reception of the Sacraments and especially by the reception of Holy Eucharist. Conjugal love, filial piety and friendship are more deeply wounded by the harsh destruction of the body by cremation and it is a significant indication of this, perhaps, that the bodies of those killed in war are still buried in the earth (cf. E. Valton in DTC s.v. Crémation). Moreover, many of the rites and prayers of the Church, which are both ancient and beautiful, would lose their import when applied to a body that was to be cremated. It was for these reasons that the Instruction of the Holy Office, 19 June 1926, referred to cremation as 'this barbarous practice'. The mind of the Church is expressed quite simply in canon 1203, § 1, which states that the bodies of the faithful departed are to be buried and that their cremation is condemned. The symbolism of the funeral chant *In Paradisum* is ill-suited to the committal of a body to the fire.

Finally the arguments that inhumation is both unhygienic and a great devourer of useful land have many times been shown, in recent years, to be not necessarily true. From a medico-legal point of view, cremation may impede the course of justice. It may render the detection of certain crimes impossible by forestalling exhumation and the subsequent examination of the dead person.

The private relaxation in 1964 of canonical severity towards cremation was not a change of doctrine or of traditional attitude, but a recognition that, in a matter which is not determined by divine law, considerations of necessity or hardship may be allowed their force. It is also a sign that the use of cremation as a gesture of anti-clericalism in Italy and France is on the decline.

Bibliography. *Sir Henry Thompson, *Modern Cremation* (1891) ; *P. H. Jones, *Cremation in Great Britain* (1945) ; H. Noldin and A. Schmitt, *De Praeceptis* (1957[31]) ; E. Valton, in DTC, s.v. Crèmation ; H. Leclercq, in DAC s.v. Incinération ; G. de Ninno, in *Enciclopedia Cattolica*, s.v. Cremazione.
G. S. D.

D

DANTE Dante is considered here only in relation to theology, and this under three heads. (I) Dante's knowledge and use of the Bible and other theological sources. (II) The tension in his thought between faith and reason. This tension remained, in a sense, with him to the end, but as it is most apparent in the prose works of his middle age, the *Convivio* and the *Monarchia*, a separate paragraph (III) will deal briefly with the *Divine Comedy* as the poet's final theological synthesis.

I Dante's Knowledge of the Bible and Other Sources. The earlier works, the *Vita Nuova* and the verse written before Dante's exile from Florence in 1302, represent an original development of the courtly love tradition. Two features of this development may be noted : the strikingly Christian handling of courtly love themes in the *V.N.* ; and Dante's attempt, in much of the other pre-exilic work, to express philosophical and moral teaching in the vernacular. The chief source of this teaching was certainly the *Nicomachean Ethics*, read in translation with St Thomas's commentary. At this time Dante must have become acquainted with other philosophical sources, Aristotelian and Neo-Platonist (cf. *Convivio* 2:12) including, probably, some *opuscula* of Albert the Great. His debt to Boethius is important. But there is no evidence of Dante's giving serious attention to theology proper during early manhood, or indeed until well on in middle age—until his studies in preparation for the *Monarchia* (c. 1308-10) the third book of which is certainly theological. It is well in general not to exaggerate his theological learning, nor to antedate such as he eventually acquired. The firmest elements in his culture were literary and philosophico-scientific. He turned to theology and to the Bible (which he came to know thoroughly in the Vulgate) broadly for two reasons : polemical—to uphold the Emperor's *de jure* independence of papal authority in temporal matters ; and personal and artistic—to resolve his own religious difficulties (*see* II) and to articulate rationally the Christian themes which found expression in the *Comedy*. Thus in *Mon* 3:4 Dante appeals to Augustine against the papalist writers' abuse, as he thought it, of the 'mystical' sense of Scripture, and ibid. 2: 4 he adopts St Thomas's definition of miracle ; and 'il buono frate Tommaso' (read especially in the *Contra Gentiles*) was probably the theologian most consulted by Dante while composing the *Comedy*. Other authors mentioned with reverence in this work, and no doubt read on various points of doctrine, are Bernard, Richard of St Victor, the pseudo-Areopagite, Bonaventure, Gregory the Great, Augustine and Jerome. The influence of the Bible on the *Comedy* was of course enormous. Dante's

reverence for Scripture was that of a devout Catholic, but it has its particular tone and stresses. The Bible is all inspired by God and, along with Church authority, is the sufficient guide for Christian living (*Mon.* 3:4 ; *Par.* 5:73-8 ; 29:91-3). It propounds mysteries accommodated to our imagination (*Par.* 4:43-5), which, if accepted on faith, may be partly understood in this life (*Mon.* 2:7 ; *Par.* 24:142-7) and are the object of vision in the next (*Par.* 2:43-5 ; 6: 19-21). It is shamefully neglected by the Roman curia (*Par.* 9:133-8) and often garbled by preachers (*Par.* 29:88-126). According to *Mon.* 3:3 both OT and NT existed *ante ecclesiam*. The parts of Scripture most used and loved by Dante are the Gospels, the Pauline and Catholic Epistles, and the Sapiential books ascribed to Solomon.

II The 'tension' mentioned above appears chiefly with regard to four points : (*a*) God's knowledge of matter ; (*b*) the authority of ecclesiastical traditions ; (*c*) the purpose of man's life *in this world* ; (*d*) the salvation of the virtuous unbaptized. Of these (*a*) has the least importance ; Dante's difficulty about God's knowledge (*Con.* 4:1) was an effect of his first contacts with philosophy, and he seems to have overcome it, along with other metaphysical difficulties, in later years. Point (*b*) involved two questions : (i) Does the Emperor receive authority directly from God or through the Church ? (ii) Can the Church *de jure* own property and exercise temporal jurisdiction ? In *Mon.* 3:11 both questions are answered in the Church's disfavour. The *Comedy* is less explicit ; but of course it continues, and intensifies, Dante's campaign for a detachment of the Church from temporal involvements and for a return to evangelical poverty (*Inferno* 19:91-6 ; *Purgatorio* 32:94 ss. ; *Par.* 9:127-32 ; 21:127-42 ; 27:22-57, etc.). As to (*c*) it is in *Mon.* 3:16 that Dante distinguishes most sharply between the *duo ultima*, the end of man as mortal and his end as immortal ; but the distinction went deeper than political issues, involving as it did a certain dualism—due in part to Averroistic influences—which Dante later largely overcame (cf. *Purg.* 25:61-75) but which, in *Con.* and *Mon.*, inclined him to exaggerate the *autonomy* of the will in the acquisition of virtue and the *sufficiency* for man, precisely as mortal, of a temporal happiness. And this attitude underlies the difficulty noted as (*d*) a difficulty later resolved, in principle, in *Par.* 20:118-32.

III In the 'Comedy' the tensions in Dante's thought are largely resolved in a cosmic vision of man's ascent to, or final revulsion from, the 'Primal Love'. The basic contrast here is no longer between faith and reason, or Church and Empire, but between good and evil ; and the handling of the Christian themes of damnation, purification and beatitude, though magnificently original in mode and temper, is substantially orthodox. A small exception to this may be a residual Pelagianism in the representation of the pagans in Limbo : Grace was always the weakest point in Dante's theology. But human life is now placed firmly in the context of man's eternal destiny, and the fundamental themes of the Trinity and creation, of the Incarnation, Redemption and the life of glory are treated with a precision unparalleled in secular literature.

Bibliography. There is no satisfactory theological commentary on the *Comedy*, but the Penguin Classics, ed. D. L. Sayers, continued by B. Reynolds, 1949–62, contain much of value. On particular aspects of Dante's thought : *Convivio*, ed. G. Busnelli-A. Vandelli (1934), for its learned if tendentiously 'Thomist' notes ; *Monarchia*, ed. G. Vinay (1950) ; E. Gilson, *Dante et la philosophie* (1939) ; B. Nardi, *Nel mondo di Dante* (1944) and *Dal 'Convivio' alla 'Commedia'* (1960) ; *C. S. Singleton, *Dante Studies* : I *Problems of Structure* (1954), II *Journey to Beatrice* (1958) ; K. Foster, *God's Tree* (1957), chs. 1, 3, 4 ; 'Dante's Vision of God', *Italian Studies* 14 (1959) 21–39. The greatest official tribute to Dante is Benedict XV's encyclical *In praeclara* (AAS 13 [1921] 209–17).   K. F.

DEACON The theological problems concerning the diaconate can be reduced to four, which will be discussed here : (I) the sacramental character of ordination to the diaconate, (II) the remission of sins and eucharistic consecration by deacons, (III) the ordination of deacons by a simple priest, and (IV) the admission of women to the diaconate.

I That the diaconate is a sacrament is generally taught today by theologians, though not all are fully aware of its history. For a sacrament some kind of institution by Christ is required (*see* SACRAMENTS), and, while it was formerly assumed that the Seven of Ac 6:1–6 were the first deacons, that is not to be lightly taken for granted, since the text nowhere calls them by that name. Irenaeus (*adv. haer.* III:xii:13 H) indeed says that Stephen was the first deacon (*electus est ab apostolis primus diaconus*) and uses similar words about Nicolaus (*adv. haer.* I:23 H), and the Council of Neo-Caesaraea in 314 (canon 14 ; Turner, *Monumenta iuris antiqui* II:ii:140) laid it down that there should never be more than seven deacons in a city, whatever its size. (Rome kept to this number in 251 ; cf. Eusebius HE 6:43). On the other hand, if it be supposed that Christ gave the apostles a commission to make deacons when the time was ripe, it can hardly be maintained that Ac 6:1 shows them carrying out this commission, since the reasons for that episode are purely circumstantial, as the text shows. Further, when deacons are met with (in Phil 1:1) for the first time under their proper name, they are the helpers of bishops and they maintain this role in the letters of Ignatius. The help they render to bishops is certainly not that of ministering to the widows of the community (*Smyrn.* 10:1 ; Phil. 11). In one place (Phil. 10:1) Ignatius regards the deacon as a legate or

messenger appointed by an individual church. Chrysostom (*hom.* 14:3 in Ac ; PG 60:116) took the view that it would be anachronistic to call the Seven deacons. I *Clem* 42:5 appeals, not to anything that Christ did, but to an adapted version of Is 60:17, when giving a justification of the office of deacon. Ignatius does indeed say that the deacon serves the bishop as Christ in His humanity served His Father (*Trall.* 3:1), but in this general way Christ may be said to have assumed the role of each of the minor Orders as well (and later piety did say this very often), whereas no one would claim that these minor Orders are sacraments.

The ordination of deacons is described in the so-called *Traditio apostolica* of Hippolytus, where a form of prayer is given which does not help much towards the idea that the rite was a sacrament. It asks for 'spirit, grace and diligence' for the candidate, but looks forward to his 'obtaining the exalted priesthood, having served the degrees of ordination'. The preamble declares that the deacon 'is not ordained to acquire the great Spirit of which the presbyters partake', while it emphasizes that his function is simply the service of the bishop. This phrase, 'not for the priesthood but for a service', echoes through the medieval theologians with a wonderful harmony ; it is found in Hugh of St Victor (PL 176:427), and in Peter Lombard (PL 192:903), whence it passed to St Thomas (IV *Sent.* 24:2:1).

It cannot be said that the remarks on deacons in I Tim 3:8–13 show the office to be so closely associated with the priesthood as to be somehow part of the same sacrament. Deacons require a *dokimasia* (or scrutiny) before entering on their office, and this office is a *bathmos* (or stepping-stone). The account of this word in the *Lexicon of Patristic Greek* does indeed show that by the 4th and 5th cents. (in Basil and other Greek legislators) the word has taken to itself a technical sense and refers to sacred Orders as distinct from those minor Orders that are not sacred, but this usage is rather a reflection of popular belief than the source thereof. The fewness of deacons by comparison with the multiplication of other grades had by then given them a scarcity-value in the Church which enhanced their status.

The *Constitutio* of Pius XII in 1947 (D 2301) laid down matter and form for the ordination of a deacon and treated this as a sacramental ordination, but it expressly stated that no retroactive force attached to the decree ; it cannot therefore be taken as a definition of what has always been the case, and the opinion of Durandus and Cajetan, that the diaconate was not part of the sacrament of Order, remains uncondemned. It is further to be noted that, while the *Constitutio* established the formula of ordination in these words : 'Send upon him, we beseech Thee, Lord, the Holy Spirit, that he may be strengthened by the gift of Thy sevenfold grace in the task of faithfully carrying out Thy ministry',[1] the original wording of this prayer as found in the *Leonine*

[1] Emitte in eum, quaesumus, Domine, Spiritum sanctum, quo in opus ministerii tui fideliter exequendi septiformis gratiae tuae munere roboretur.

Sacramentary (Mohlberg, 951) has a not unimportant difference. It does not speak of *Thy* ministry, and the adjective ' sevenfold ' is taken with gift, not with grace. Thus the *Leonine* does not provide any warrant for regarding the diaconate as ' Christ's ministry ', in the sense of something started by Him.

The Council of Trent was very circumspect in what it said about Orders, and in its canons on the subject deacons are not mentioned, though it is declared (D 966) that a hierarchy of bishops, priests and helpers (*ministri*) is of divine origin. The *capitulum* (D 960) which leads up to this canon aims at destroying the Reformers' idea that the Church was a rabble of equals and had no structure, while elsewhere in the decree (D 958) there is the somewhat restrained assertion that deacons are mentioned in the NT. All this amounts to in terms of institution by Christ is that He must have indicated to the Apostles (either directly or through the operation of the Spirit) that there should be some kind of gradation between themselves and their subordinates and that this should be passed on to the Church as a permanent thing. Trent also directed an anathema (D 964) against those who said that a priest (*sacerdos*) could ever be a layman again, but did not suggest that the same was true of deacons.

The 2nd Vatican Council (*Constitutio de ecclesia* 3:29) said that deacons are strengthened with a sacramental grace (*gratia sacramentali roborati*). This phrase of studied ambiguity was chosen in order not to decide, one way or another, whether the diaconate was a sacrament.

II The sacrament of penance concerned the deacon in early times, in this way. He was the helper of the bishop, and the bishop had to seek out the sinner, either going alone to him (*see* CONFESSION) or taking with him one or two as witnesses. He took deacons for this task, as the *Apostolic Canons* (16 in the Ethiopic, and 22 in the other versions) expressly say when they ask for the ordination of deacons, ' that by the testimony of two or three every word shall be established ' (cf. Mt 18:16). The *Didascalia* (ii:44 ; Connolly, 109) supposes the same work to be theirs, when it directs that the deacon is to be ' the hearing of the bishop ' and that bishop and deacon are to shepherd the people as one body, like Father and Son (*see also* the account of Polycarp, *vita* 27). This is repeated later (ibid. iii:13 ; Connolly 148) where bishop and deacon are told to be ' of one counsel and of one purpose, and one soul dwelling in two bodies '. Hence one can understand Cyprian saying (*ep.* 18:1 ; CSEL 3:524) that if a priest cannot be found and a sinner is dying, the deacon can receive his confession and impose hands on him with a view to his penance, so that he may go to the Lord in the peace of the Church.[1] Where the reconciling of a sinner was a combined and public operation in which the deacon took part, it would not seem unusual to delegate even the essential part of it to him in an emergency (*see also* Regino of Prüm, PL 132:247). One can make

this fact the basis of an argument to claim that therefore the deacon must have been recognized as having received the sacrament of Order, but if bishop and deacon were really regarded as ' one soul in two bodies ', this would not follow. A boy was used as the means of reconciling the lapsed Serapion, according to Denis of Alexandria (*Letters*, ed. Feltoe, 20), and no one would say that the boy was in Orders.

Deacons carried the Eucharist to those absent from the *synaxis* in early times (Justin, *apol.* 65). They helped in the breaking of the bread (according to Hippolytus) and in the distribution of the Eucharist at Mass. ' Whenever the deacon approaches the presbyter, he shall hold out his robe, and the presbyter himself shall take the bread and deliver to the people with his hand.' (Thus the Ethiopic version of the *Traditio apostolica*, 35). These tasks are subordinate, and when the deacons take on themselves the main work of *offering*, this is roundly condemned as an abuse by the Council of Arles in its canon 16 (Turner, *Monumenta iuris antiqui*, I:ii:392). ' About those deacons who, as we have learnt, are offering the Eucharist in many places, it is resolved that this must cease.' [2] As Turner argues, the word *offerre* is used later (in canon 19) in the sense of celebrating the Eucharist, and therefore it must have the same sense here. Similar abuses have been found from time to time. There are records of papal dispensations for irregularity incurred by deacons who administered other sacraments ; thus in 1335 Benedict XII pardoned an English deacon who had performed the Last Anointing for a woman who was unconscious, while in 1327 John XXII pardoned one who had heard the confession of a priest and absolved him at the urging of the priest who had told him he could do it. The documents are published by G. Mollat in *Mélanges Andrieu* (1956) 361–3. From such abuses to the real power of deacons there can be no argument.

III The ordination of deacons by a simple priest took place quite often in medieval times. Dispensations were issued by three popes to Cistercian abbots to ordain their subjects thus (*see* J. M. Canivez in *Dictionnaire de droit canonique*, III:783, s.v. Citeaux). If it could be shown that no priest ever ordained another priest, then one would have an argument for excluding the diaconate from the sacrament of Order, but in view of the facts available (*see* ABBOT, ORDINATION BY) it is quite clear that sometimes (though more seldom) priests did ordain priests. The *Apostolic Canons* (can. 1) and the *Traditio apostolica* of Hippolytus (24) both insist that it is the bishop alone who ordains deacons ; this may be due to a desire to show that he is the bishop's man when once ordained but, whatever the motive, the fact remains that a bishop was expected to act. In the time of Augustine a more spiritual idea of clerical ordination (as distinct from priesthood itself) comes to the fore. He wishes to show (*De bono coniugali* 24:32 ; CSEL 41:226) that a wife cannot divorce a husband even when she finds that she cannot conceive a child by him, and he puts this parallel: ' If there is a clerical

---

[1] Si presbyter repertus non fuerit et urgere exitus coeperit, apud diaconum quoque exomologesin facere delicti sui possint, ut manu eis in poenitentiam imposita, veniant ad Dominum cum pace.

[2] De diaconibus quos cognovimus multis locis offerre, placuit minime fieri debere.

ordination for the purpose of gathering together the Christian people (of a village), the hallowing of their ordination remains in those men, even though the gathering of the people does not ensue, and likewise, if one of them is deposed for any fault, he is not deprived of the hallowing of the Lord that he has once received, though it remain to judge him'.[1] Augustine is not thinking simply of priests here, for deacons would be required to marshal the people in church for a new parish and to watch over those admitted to communion. He clearly required the act of a bishop for the conferring of the *sacramentum Domini*.

IV The first woman deacon on record is Phoebe, 'deacon of the church that is at Cenchreae' (Rom 16:1), while the remarks of 1 Tim 3:11 about what is required of women may refer to women-deacons, as they are embedded in a paragraph about what is required of deacons. Chrysostom (*hom.* 11 on 1 Tim; PG 62:553) interprets the passage in this way, though Moffat and Knox translate as if the sentence dealt with the deacon's wife. Deacons were often married men, and there is legislation in the Council of Ancyra (314) about this; if a deacon wishes to marry, he should say this publicly before the bishop imposes hands on him, and his omission to do so is to be taken as a profession of chastity. This canon (can. 10) was known in the West (Turner, *Monumenta iuris antiqui*, II:ii:80) and may have been the origin of the idea that ordination carries with it a vow of chastity even though nothing is said about this in the service. It cannot be shown that the wife of a deacon was always regarded as a deaconess, but this may often have been so. The Council of Nicaea (can. 19) regards the deaconess as not receiving imposition of hands, being in line here with what Hippolytus said about widows: 'They shall not lay hand upon her, because she does not offer the sacrifice' (*Trad. apost.* 26). Yet Chalcedon (can. 15, *Acta conciliorum* I:ii:161) decided that, 'if she receive the laying on of hands and remain in her ministry for a time but then wanton with the grace of God by giving herself to marriage, let such a one be anathema, along with her partner'. The service-books (e.g. *Constitutiones apostolicae*, 8:28) describe her duties as helping at the baptism of women and supervising the entry of women to the liturgy by their own door (cf. also Epiphanius, *haer.* 79:3; GCS 37:477). The addition of a few words in some late Greek MSS. of the NT, at Tit 1:9, shows that bishops were expected to exclude such women from the sanctuary; 'Let not women enter the sanctuary to engage in the divine liturgy'.

The position of deaconess remained roughly parallel to that of deacon until the rise of communities of nuns in the 6th and 7th cents. Theologians are therefore left with a choice: either they say that the principle invoked by Durandus (IV *Sent.* 24:1:9),

that where a task needs a special grace, there ordination to it is a sacrament, applies to both men and women in the diaconate, or that it applies to neither. The *Testamentum Domini* (2:20) directs that a deaconess shall take the Eucharist to a pregnant woman who is unable to come to church, and in 1:23 it places the deaconesses within the veil at the Eucharist, so that the prohibition of the Council of Laodicea (can. 44) against this practice and the enlarged text of Tit 1:9 cannot have had effect everywhere. One cannot say, then, that deacons had a task to perform within the sanctuary but deaconesses had not; it would seem that they stand or fall together. Theologians have therefore to make up their minds if they think the evidence warrants them in looking on the diaconate as part of the sacrament of Order, and, if it does, then women have some part in Order along with men. Future developments in the diaconate are to be expected, but the theology of the matter needs to be clarified first. The desire of many to have a permanent (and married) diaconate, which should not be a stepping-stone to the priesthood, would be helped by the idea that the diaconate was not part of the sacrament of *sacerdotium* or priesthood, but, as this article may have shown, the tradition about this is in need of considerable clarification.

Bibliography. A. Kerkvoorde OSB, *Où en est le problème du diaconat?* (1961); J. Colson, *La Fonction diaconale aux origines de l'église* (1960); P. Gächter SJ, *Die Sieben*, in ZKT 74 (1952) 129–66; W. Croce SJ, *Die niederen Weihen*, in ZKT 70 (1948) 257–314; B. Fischer, *Die niedere Klerus bei Gregor dem Grossen*, in ZKT 62 (1938) 37–76; T. Klauser, Diakon, in RAC III; J. Lecuyer, in D Sp s.v. Diaconat; the same, *Sacerdoce selon Théodore de Mopsueste*, in RSR 37 (1949) 481–516.

J. H. C.

DEAD, PRAYER FOR THE The Catholic doctrine that those who die 'in the Lord' can be helped by the prayers of the living did not break suddenly on a world that had no inkling of it, in the way that the doctrine of the Trinity could be said to have arrived. This article will therefore deal (I) with the OT anticipations of the doctrine, (II) with the pagan contrasts and parallels, (III) with its gradual formulation in the early Church and finally (IV) with its establishment as a permanent feature of the liturgy.

I The Jewish people were brought gradually by divine Providence to a belief in human survival of death (cf. E. F. Sutcliffe, *The Old Testament and the Future Life*, 1946) and it is therefore quite natural that it is the latest of their inspired Scriptures which has an express witness to the idea that the living can help the dead (2 Mac 12:39–45). The soldiers of Judas fallen in battle had been found to have pagan amulets hidden under their clothing. To expiate this sin the sum of 2,000 drachmas was collected and sent to Jerusalem to pay for a sin-offering. The writer then points out that the purpose of this act was to benefit the dead themselves, lest some might think that it was rather the purging of the sin from the surviving

---

[1] Si fiat ordinatio cleri ad plebem congregandam, etiamsi plebis congregatio non subsequatur, manet tamen in illis ordinatis sacramentum ordinationis et, si aliqua culpa quisquam ab officio removeatur, sacramento Domini semel imposito non carebit, quamvis ad iudicium permanente.

army that was contemplated. 'He made a propitiatory offering for the fallen that they might be loosed from their sin' (see CCS 579e). The Latin version of this passage has turned this particularized statement into a general axiom : 'It is a holy and wholesome thought to pray for the dead that they may be loosed from their sins'.

The Jews had been forbidden (Lev 19:28 ; 21:5 ; Deut 14:1) to practise such rites as the shaving of the head to baldness, clipping the beard and making incisions in the flesh on behalf of the dead. The texts do not say precisely that these things were done to help the dead but simply that they were done on the occasion of a death. Pagan infiltrations were no doubt to blame ; the extravagance of Egyptian mourning rites was proverbial in classical literature. Jewish mourning lasted for seven days (Ecclus 22:12) or possibly for thirty (Deut 34:8) and the signs of mourning were regulated (Ez 7:18 ; Is 22:12).

II Paganism of the time of Christ had some idea of a purgation that the soul would undergo after death by the action of air, water or fire, for it is embodied in Vergil's vision of the underworld (*Aeneid* 6:740) ; there does not, however, seem to be any idea that the living can help in this process. In fact, it is commonly supposed that after purgation the soul re-enters the land of the living as someone else : such is the sense of the epitaph of Laberius, priest of Cybele : 'What I was I am now no longer, but what I am not now I shall be once more ; birth and dying, life and death, 'tis all one' (*Corpus inscriptionum latinarum* VI:13528).[1] The scholia of Servius on the Vergilian passage mentioned make it clear that in the mystery religions the initiate was taken through a triple purgation ritual (by leaping through fire or fumigation by sulphur, by washing, and by being hung aloft or fanned with great fans) so that he might be deemed insured against real purgation in after-life. Perhaps 'those who get themselves baptized for the dead' (1 Cor 15:29) at Corinth were treating Christian baptism as if it were a pagan rite and had the idea that it could be transferred to those who had died before the gospel had reached their country, but it cannot be said that there is any trace of such transference of merits in paganism itself. In the works of Macrobius (commentary on the *Somnium Scipionis* I:13:16) it is laid down that the departed sinner cannot improve his lot : 'Those who leave this life defiled with sin are like men who fall from a precipice ; they have no chance of rising up again'.[2]

Some features of pagan belief may have passed over into what may be called the folklore of Christianity. The figure of Hermes $\psi\upsilon\chi\omicron\pi\omicron\mu\pi\acute{o}s$ is replaced by that of St Michael as early as the end of the 4th cent., when the *History of Joseph the Carpenter* (an Egyptian product) makes him the escort of the

dead. The pagan and Manichean concept of 'customs-house officers', who hold up the soul on its way and examine its baggage of good deeds and bad, is also used by Origen (*hom* 23 on Lk ; GCS 49:144) who pictures them sitting at the boundary of the world and searching whether travellers have with them 'anything of theirs'. Cyril of Alexandria (*hom* 14 ; PG 77:1073), if the work is really his, adopts the same idea, and it was a widely practised superstition to place in the hand of the dead person a note addressed to these 'searchers'. This idea of angelic escorts of the dead was not repudiated by the Church and is used in the *In paradisum* of the funeral liturgy ; the Christian theology of guardian angels would give it justification. But there were other practices which the Church refused to follow. The funeral banquet at the graveside was thought by pagans to bring solace to the dead if some portion of food and drink was left for them. Augustine had several times to combat this rite (*De moribus ecclesiae* 34:75 ; PL 32:1342 ; *Civ. Dei* 6:6 ; CSEL 40:282 ; *Ep.* 29 ; CSEL 34:114). Two sermons attributed to him but probably by Caesarius of Arles (*serm.* 190 and 191 ; PL 39:2101) are aimed at checking this *refrigerium* and it is made a reproach against the Christians by Faustus the Manichee that they still practise it (Augustine *Contra Faustum* 20:21 ; CSEL 25:561). The pagan feast of the *cara cognatio* on 22 February was supplanted by that of the *Cathedra Petri*, though the calendar of Polemius Silvius (of 448) records both together. The liturgy for this feast as set forth in the Mozarabic missal (PL 85:722) and kindred works (such as the Milan palimpsest edited by Alban Dold, *Schabcodex M* 12 *sup.* [1952]) shows a distinct intention to attack the pagan customs of the day. 'Their greatest devotion was to venerate the spirit of Romulus, stained with his brother's blood.'[3] In place of this a Christian prayer for the dead was interposed, though the feast itself did not warrant it : 'Grant rest to the spirits of the faithful departed, that this commemoration of them which their dear ones observe may give comfort to them and to ourselves advancement in virtue'.[4] The Council of Tours in 567 (canon 22) forbade the offering of food to the dead on this day, and, though the provenance of the Milan palimpsest is not certain, it may well come from such a milieu as this. In the long struggle against paganism the bishops seem animated by the saying that where God has His church the devil has also his chapel.

III The early Christian idea that, once removed from the body, the soul of the just enters into eternal rest is formulated in Apoc 14:13 (the Vulgate has altered the meaning of the passage by faulty punctuation, see CCS 969j). What the Christians said positively, an educated pagan of the time could say conjecturally, as may be seen in Tacitus *Agricola* (46) : 'If the spirits of the great do not die with the body,

---

[1] Quod fueram non sum sed rursum ero quod modo non sum :
　　　ortus et occasus vitaque morsque itid' est.
[2] Animas vero ex hac vita cum delictorum sordibus recedentes aequandas his qui in abruptum ex alto praecipitique delapsi sint, unde nunquam facultas fit resurgendi.

[3] Quibus maxima esset religio Romuleos manes colere fratris cruore perfusos.
[4] Requiem fidelium spiritibus tribue defunctorum, ut facta per caros suos commemoratione illis refrigerium conferat his profectum.

may you have rest in peace'. This ἀνάπαυσις of the Christians was not the perpetual drunkenness which Plato had derided (*Republic* 363c), though some of its appurtenances may be found in such popular works as the *Acts of Perpetua and Felicitas* (1:3 ; T &S, 1:2:66). It is all the more striking that in the prayer for a departed soul in Serapion's *Sacramentary*, a prayer which asks for the deceased to be taken to the place of repose, the language is borrowed from Scripture (Ps 22:2 LXX ; Mt 8:11) rather than from these popular fancies. The style of this prayer differs from that of the rest of Serapion's collection and it may thus be much earlier than the other prayers, which come from *c.* 350.

Jewish and Gnostic ideas about the seven spheres were adapted in Clement of Alexandria (*Strom.* 5:6:36 ; GCS 52:351 ; 6:16:140 ; GCS 52:503 ; *Excerpta ex Theodoto* 63 ; GCS 17:128), who says that the dead had their repose in the seventh sphere until they were called to the vision of God which they would enjoy in the eighth sphere. The apocryphal *Fourth Esdras* (7:79, dating from the end of the 1st cent.) appears to be the source of this idea, and its characterization of the progress through the seven spheres was used by some of the Fathers ; Ambrose (*De bono mortis* 11:48 ; CSEL 32:744) in his description of the fourth sphere is simply quoting what this *Esdras* book says (7:79). Numenius of Apamea, the precursor of the Neo-Platonists, whose work was known to Origen, has a similar notion of the ascent of the just souls to beatitude through the spheres, sinners being delayed for punishment on the way. Christians of the early centuries were willing to treat these ideas as so much *praeparatio evangelica*, since the doctrine they were dealing with was not so far removed from the scope of natural reason as the major doctrines of Trinity and Incarnation. In his work *Contra Vigilantium* 6 (PL 23:344) Jerome repudiated in no uncertain language this apocryphal Esdras book which Vigilantius had cited to prove that ' after death no one should dare to pray for others '.[1] The book survived, though most of its MSS have this offending section omitted. It was used by Gildas as scripture, and must have been familiar in 6th-cent. Britain.

The heretic Aerius denounced prayer for the dead as unprofitable, and in refuting him Epiphanius (*Haer.* 75:7 ; GCS 37:338–40) appealed to the Tradition of the Church as justification for the practice. Chrysostom (*hom* 3 on Phil ; PG 62:204) makes an explicit claim that the practice was ordered by the Apostles ; the faithful departed should be remembered at Mass, though dead catechumens, who were not worthy of this honour, might be helped by almsgiving. He used Ps 6:6 (' Who shall confess to Thee in Sheol ? ') to argue that, as the dead could not help themselves, those on earth must help them. An eloquent testimony of the practice among the faithful is given by the Christian chapel at Dura-Europos, where one of the plasterers has left his name, and an appeal to put the Lord in mind of him, just by the doorway. He must have done this

[1] Quod post mortem nullus pro aliis audeat deprecari.

while the plaster was still wet, during the construction of the chapel, and he added the year, A.D. 232 (*Excavations at Dura, 5th Season* [1934] 239). Soon after this there is the letter of Cyprian (*ep.* 60:5 ; CSEL 1:695) to a colleague, asking that he join in a pact that whosoever survives the other should undertake the work of intercession for his soul.

In the Church Orders there are some attempts to set down an explicit ordinance for the commemoration of the dead. The *Didascalia* (6:22:2) has a brief allusion to this, but in the Ethiopic and Coptic versions of the *Statutes of the Apostles* (Horner's edition, 215 and 355) there are extensive rules : ' Concerning the memorial of those who have fallen asleep : the third day shall be observed with psalms and prayers, because of the Resurrection of the Lord. . . . They shall observe the completion of a month in likeness of the old ordinance, even as the people mourned for Moses thirty days. . . .' This regulation does not belong to that part of the document which can be traced back to Hippolytus, but it may well belong to the 3rd cent. and be valid at least for Egypt. Priests and deacons are reminded in the same passage that : ' If you should be invited on their days, eat in comely fashion and the fear of God, as having power to intercede for those who have departed from this world'. This caution about funeral feasts would have been worded much more severely in Western lands where the practice (as noted above) was not tolerated by the Church.

If an attempt be made to trace the practice of prayer for the dead back to the Apostles, an important landmark is the episode in the *Acts of Paul and Thecla* (from about 160) where the queen Tryphaena is represented as learning in a dream from her dead daughter : ' Thou shalt take in my stead Thecla the stranger, that is desolate, that she may pray for me and I be translated into the place of the righteous '. That this work of fiction is not innovating here may be judged from the fact that Abercius, at about the same time, was directing that the inscription on his tomb should invite the passer-by to pray for him ; he died at the age of 72 late in the 2nd cent. and must have known what was Christian practice for some fifty years previously. The variant reading in Rom 12:13, where μνείαις has come into the text for χρείαις and thus made it into a command to ' take part in the commemoration of the faithful ', must have arisen before the middle of the 2nd cent. It is strongly supported by the Latin version and Latin patristic quotations, and it found its way into some of the Greek uncials (DFG). The change must be due to the influence of current practice on scribes who had no clue to the meaning of the original text, which spoke of the needs of the faithful at Jerusalem. A transformation due to a similar cause took place in the text of Jude 23.

IV The liturgy for the dead has two refrains : *Requiem aeternam* and *lux perpetua* which are pseudoscriptural, both coming from the so-called *Fifth Esdras* (T &S 3:2:5). Edmund Bishop (in *Liturgica historica*, 189) claimed that the use of these refrains was ' Franco-Gallic' and first found in Alcuin's supplement to the *Gregorian Sacramentary* (from about 786), but Cumont has shown that a single Christian cemetery in North Africa (at Ain-Zara near Tripoli) had the formula used on graves twenty-six times, all of them dating from the 5th or 6th cents. The *Stowe Missal* which has a Mass-formula *pro mortuis pluribus*, asks that the dead may obtain pardon of their sins and ' the everlasting joy of light ' (*gaudia perpetua lucis*). It speaks of the offerings, ' which we bring to Thy altar for the commemoration of Thy faithful ', and the phrase (*pro sanctorum tuorum N. commemoratione*) is a clear echo of the Latin version of Rom 12:13, for the word *sanctorum* is used in the old sense of ' the faithful generally ', and not in its later sense of ' the saints in heaven '. Finally, the same *Missal* in its Canon has the following Memento of the Dead : ' Be mindful . . . of all those who are at rest, who have gone before us in the peace of the Lord, from Adam until the present day, whose names have been called by God and are known to Him. For them and for all those who rest in Christ we beg of Thy mercy a place of rest, of light and of peace '.[1] There is every likelihood that this, the oldest form of the Canon of the Mass, goes back to Pope Gelasius himself. In his *Deprecatio* (PL 101:560) there is a petition ' for the repose of the faithful departed ' (*pro refrigerio fidelium animarum*). The use of the word *pausantes* is also a sign of antiquity. De Rossi has an inscription from A.D. 353 that uses it (*Inscriptiones christianae* I:72:n. 117) ; it seems to be a Christian formation from the Greek 'ανάπαυσις and was used in Ireland in place of *defuncti* for many centuries.

The *Sacramentary* of Serapion has the prayers for the dead after the consecration and in this it is in agreement with the liturgy in the *Apostolic Constitutions* (8:12:43 and 8:13:6). The liturgy of St Basil (in the Coptic version from the 7th cent.) has, following upon the epiklesis and intercessions for the living, a remarkable prayer for the dead : ' Since, Lord, *it is the precept of Thy only-begotten Son that we take part in remembering Thy holy ones*, deign to be mindful of our fathers who have been pleasing to Thee from the beginning, patriarchs, prophets . . . and in like manner be mindful of all who have gone before us to their rest, both priests and layfolk of all degrees, and grant them rest in the bosom of Abraham, Isaac and Jacob in a grassy place by the waters of repose, whence pain, grief and sorrowing have been removed. (Here recite the names.) Grant them rest with Thee.'

In liturgies of Spanish and Irish inspiration, on the other hand, the memory of the dead seems to have come at the offertory. In the *post-nomina* prayers of the *Missale Gothicum* and of the Mone-masses from Reichenau (*c.* 650) there are frequent mentions of the dead. The *Missale Gallicanum vetus* (from Luxeuil, *c.* 700) has the present-day prayer for the dead almost verbatim incorporated in its *post-nomina*

prayer for the first Advent mass. A ruling of the Penitential of Cummian imposes a penance on the deacon who neglects to bring up the offering at the uncovering (of the altar), ' while the names of the departed are being recited '. The transfer of these prayers to their present place after the consecration may be connected with the moving of the kiss of peace, for the *post-nomina* prayer was followed by one *ad pacem* in these missals. Edmund Bishop, on the strength of the recurring words *cari nostri* in these prayers, claimed them all for Gallican, since ' strong affection and deep sense of family relationship characterize the French people '. But among Celtic peoples they have no monopoly of that, and it seems clear (*see* II *above*) that the words are due rather to the Christian desire to supplant the pagan festival of *cara cognatio*, and this either in Rome, Spain, or North Africa.

The practice of keeping the list of dead upon the altar during Mass is first evidenced in a preface of the *Bobbio Missal* which speaks of ' those faithful departed whose names we have written for remembrance . . . or whose names are seen to be written on the altar ' (n. 440). From this usage develops the *Liber vitae* of Durham (now Cotton MS Domitian A vii) with its list of Saxon kings and other names to the number of 3,000, coming down to about A.D. 850. The Necrology of Remiremont, from about the same time, shows, as Fr Thurston argued, that the Mass for the Dead was often copied into such a list of names, thus providing the origin for the present practice of having a separate missal for such occasions. In the *Hanc igitur* of the Mass in this Necrology there is a change of wording to introduce a reference to the names in the list ; from such practices to the medieval use of chantries was no long step.

The *Leonine Sacramentary* (nn. 1138-60) has a collection of prayers with the heading *super defunctos*. These may be from the early Roman Masses for the dead, though Spanish origins are not to be excluded. The theological importance of these prayers is great, for they envisage exactly the belief of present-day Catholics that prayer for the dead helps to remit the temporal punishment due to sins of the deceased which have been forgiven. Some of the prayers are for one who intended to take on himself public penance but died before he could do so. ' Free him from all his sins, that he may not lose that reward of penance which his heart desired but which was denied to him by human mortality.'[2] In another of these prayers it is laid down that to God alone it belongs to afford relief to the soul after death.[3] When at Florence and at Trent the Church came to define the value of prayer for the dead (D 693, 950, 983), it is easy to see that the age-old tradition of the liturgy was her principal resource. The varieties of racial and national temperament may have left their

---

[1] Memento . . . omnium pausantium qui nos in dominica pace praecesserunt ab Adam usque in hodiernum diem, quorum nomina Deus nominavit et novit. Ipsis et omnibus in Christo quiescentibus locum refrigerii lucis et pacis ut indulgeas deprecamur.

[2] Ab omnibus absolve peccatis, ut paenitentiae fructum quem voluntas eius optavit praeventus mortalitate non perdat.

[3] Deus cui soli competit medicinam praestare post mortem.

mark on that liturgy, but the central belief that prayers and especially Masses for the dead do by God's mercy bring them relief can be seen to be constant from Cyprian in the 3rd cent. (who threatened to deny such aid to one Victor, *ep* 1:2 ; CSEL 1:466) down to the English yeoman of 1500 who willed ' to my daughter Elizabeth, if she will say daily for my soul the third part of the Jesu Psalter, she shall have for her labour twenty shillings '.

The origin of All Souls Day is commonly traced to Cluny and to the year 998, but Fr Thurston showed that already in 800 the monasteries of St Gall and Reichenau had entered into a compact that every year on 14 November each would hold a solemn commemoration of the dead of both houses, and that each priest would celebrate three Masses on that day. The innovation at Cluny seems thus to be simply the transfer of such a commemoration to the day following All Saints. When the pagan associations of the *cara cognatio* were lost from men's minds, the Church saw no danger in allowing the rise of a Christian commemoration of all the faithful departed. At the Council of Trent suggestions were made that the Offertory verse in the Mass for the dead was superstitious and should be reformed, but no action was taken. The image of the lion's mouth is scriptural (Ps 90:3), and Sedulius had written of Christ (*carmina* 2:89 CSEL 10:168) : ' The fury of the envious dragon and the mouth of the wicked lion have been trampled by the only-begotten Son of God '.[1]

Apart from the OT warrant for the practice, prayer for the dead derives its justification from the Tradition—and largely a liturgical Tradition—of the Church. If that Tradition picked up the language of paganism it transformed the concepts behind that language. The Roman emperors (e.g. in the *Code* of Theodosius 5:13:4) granted an *indulgentia*, a remission of taxation for so many years, on notable occasions ; the Church took the word, but applied it to the relief of the departed souls, as in the ancient and familiar collect : ' Grant them the pardon which they have always desired ; *indulgentiam quam semper optaverunt* '.

Bibliography. H. Thurston SJ, *The Memory of Our Dead* (1915) ; E. Bishop, *Liturgica historica* (1918) 96–103 ; the same, *Book of Cerne* (1902) 266–75 ; T. Klauser, *Die Cathedra im Totenkult* (1927) ; F. Cumont, *Lux perpetua* (1949) ; the same, *Le Symbolisme funéraire des Romains* (1942) ; H. Frank ' Der älteste erhaltene römische *Ordo Defunctorum* ', in *Archiv für Liturgiewissenschaft* VII (1962) 360–415 ; A. C. Rush, *Death and Burial in Christian Antiquity* (1941) ; A. Stuiber, *Refrigerium interim* (1952) ; J. Fischer, *Studien zum Todesgedanken in der alten Kirche* (1954).   J. H. C.

DEISM is a term used to denote a philosophico-religious movement of European thought in the 16th, 17th and 18th cents. Although the movement was

[1] Zelum draconis invidi : et os leonis pessimi : calcavit unicus Dei.

not homogeneous, it can be said to be characterized in general by the denial of some or all elements of the supernatural, the assertion of the self-sufficiency of human reason, and the exaltation of a humanism entirely or partially closed to divine intervention. The history of the movement can be roughly divided into two periods. The first, that of Socinian deism, began shortly after the middle of the 16th cent. and ended with the English Restoration in 1660 ; the second period, which may be termed the period of classical deism, extended from 1660 to the end of the 18th cent.

The first-known use of the word ' deism ' occurs in the dedicatory letter prefixed to the second part of Pierre Viret's *Instruction chrestienne* (1564) where deism is opposed to atheism and appears to be identical with Socinianism and anti-Trinitarianism. It is this unitarian meaning that the word deism generally retained until 1660. This Socinian movement was begun by Italian academicians of the 16th cent. ; after being expelled from their native Italy, they spread the movement through Switzerland and from there to France and all of Europe.

The partial rejection of the supernatural and of revealed religion that had characterized Socinian deism continued to grow until it produced the classical deism that flourished after 1660. This classical deism was nothing less than a complete and unequivocal denial of the supernatural in all its forms and aspects ; the idea of God was retained, but His role was more and more reduced to the Being who began the universe and then had nothing more to do with its governance and conduct. With regard to Christianity the classical deists either rejected it in its entirety or regarded it as the perfect natural religion.

Classical deism received its first full expression in England. Already in 1624 Lord Herbert of Cherbury in his work *De religione laici* had given voice to the doctrine, but the movement did not reach its full force until after 1660 when the word deism began to be a commonly used word in England. Charles Blount, whose writings were largely repetitious of the ideas of Lord Herbert, acted as the catalyst for the movement, while John Locke, though disclaiming deism personally, furthered deistic attitudes in his work *The Reasonableness of Christianity* (1695). The clearest expression of classical deism is to be found in John Toland's *Christianity not Mysterious* (1696) wherein the position is maintained that any supposed Christian dogma which cannot be justified by natural reason is not a part of true Christianity. Anthony Collins in his work *A Discourse of the Grounds and Reasons of the Christian Religion* (1724) attacked the credibility of Christianity, while his *Discourse on Freethinking* (1713) emphasized the deistic demand for freedom of investigation. Thomas Woolston expressed the deistic attitude toward miracles in his work *Discourses on the Miracles of Our Saviour* (1727-9). Matthew Tindal in his *Christianity as Old as Creation* argued against the necessity of any revelation, reducing Christianity to a natural religion.

From England classical deism spread to France where, however, it was chiefly referred to as ' theism '.

The chief proponents of French deism were Voltaire, d'Holbach and the Encyclopedists. French deism reached its culmination in the worship of the goddess of reason in Notre Dame during the French Revolution. From France classical deism spread into Germany and was there propagated by a number of writers among whom Samuel Reimarus and Gotthold Lessing were especially influential. In the 19th cent. deism ceased to exist as a distinct movement ; its followers either embraced atheism or were absorbed into the German pantheism begun by Hegel. At the present time the only traces of deism are found in Masonry.

Bibliography. The best general introduction to deism and its background is contained in two books by Paul Hazard : *The European Mind* (1953) and *European Thought in the Eighteenth Century* (1954). The history of Socinian deism has never been fully investigated, but a useful beginning may be found in ' The Genesis of Modern Deism ' in Harold R Hutcheson's edition of Lord Herbert of Cherbury's *De religione laici* (1944), to be supplemented by Clement Welsh's ' A Note on the Meaning of " Deism " ', *Anglican Theological Quarterly* 38 (1956) 160–5. A detailed history of English deism is included in Leslie Stephen's *History of English Thought in the Eighteenth Century*[3], 2 vols. (1902) ; no single work adequately covers the history of French and of German deism. An interesting plea for the reassumption of the word ' deism ' into current language is to be found in B. Romeyer's ' Déisme ' in *Catholicisme* III 546–7.   R. F. S.

DEMIURGE: from the Greek δημιουργός— originally, one who works for the people, skilled workman, handicraftsman (Liddell and Scott, s.v.) ; hence, ' maker, producer, creator '. In some Greek cities the title of a magistrate (PW, s.v.). Since Plato, and probably earlier, the word had been used in reference to the maker of the *cosmos*, a divine artificer. The concept will be examined under the following headings: (I) Greek (and Roman) philosophical usages, (II) Jewish, (III) gnostic and near-gnostic speculations, and (IV) Christian anti-gnostic arguments.

I The Demiurge in Ancient Philosophy. In his enigmatic and difficult dialogue, the *Timaeus*, Plato introduced into philosophy[1] a Demiurge as the image of a creator-god. He does not appear to have been the first to use the word in this sense. Plato's meaning is obscure and controversial ; at any rate, the Demiurge is conceived on the model of a human craftsman, who works in materials not of his own making, and is limited by the nature of the material at his disposal. Into the pre-existent chaos he introduces order (κόσμος), working on a pattern which is eternal and perfect. The general force of Plato's image is to stress the part of intellect (νοῦς) in world-making, against the stress laid by Ionian cosmology on the part of nature (φύσις).

This stress on the governing role of intelligence in the *cosmos* was inherited by much of later Greek

[1] cf. F. M. Cornford, *Plato's Cosmology* (1937).

philosophy, but the concept of the Demiurge became less prominent, though his name still appears on occasion (e.g. Cicero, *De natura deorum* II:58 'artifex', 142 'opifex'). The most important development of the concept took place in the later schools of Platonism. Here the archetypal ideas which served as the pattern for the Demiurge's work in Plato's *Timaeus* are decisively placed within the divine mind which is also creative. Plotinus in effect identifies this Νοῦς, the divine intelligence, with the Demiurge (*Enneads* V:1:8 ; 9:3). This is the source of the world-making soul (ψυχή), and this latter hypostasis is also spoken of as producing (ποιητής—*Enneads* II:3:18).

II The Demiurge in Jewish Thought. The Jewish idea of creation differs in important ways from the Platonic theory of the Demiurge's work ; nevertheless, Greek-speaking Jews could draw on the language of Plato and later Greek thought to express their understanding of the OT creation-story. Although the LXX does not use the word in reference to the Creator, Philo's exposition of the creation-story is cast in terms distinctive of the Platonic tradition. In his account (cf. *De opificio mundi*, 4:16) God is the source both of the intelligible world of the archetypal pattern, and of its copy. When he wished to create (δημιουργῆσαι) the visible world, he first created the intelligible world to serve as its pattern. An idea common in late Jewish speculation, that of God using intermediaries in the work of creation, appears here in one of its many forms.

III The Demiurge in Gnostic Mythology. Some of these speculations about an intermediary between the supreme divinity and the created world, especially on the heterodox fringes of Hellenistic Judaism, encouraged a belief in a ' second god '. These intermediate hypostases were often conceived as the agents of divine creative activity. The idiom of such speculations is sometimes very close to the language of gnostic or neargnostic sects. Among the multifarious sects described by Irenaeus in *adv. haer.* it is the Valentinian system[2] which has the most clearly conceived cosmogony in which the Demiurge occupies a key place. He is both lord and maker of the lower realms of reality, here called ' material ' or ' earthy ' (ὑλικόν, χοϊκόν) and ' animal ' (ψυχικόν) respectively, distinguished from the third and highest realm, the ' spiritual ' (πνευματικόν). The Demiurge himself is an offspring of the world of spirit, from which he takes his origin as the consequence of a primal, pre-mundane fall and disintegration in that world. In the teaching of the Valentinian schools he is identified with the Creator-God of the OT, and is therefore also the God of the Mosaic Law. The contrast between the Creator and Lawgiver of the OT and the God of the NT is fundamental to the less mythological and less cosmologically orientated teaching of Marcion. The Valentinian *Letter to Flora* (ed. G. Quispel, *SC*) in Epiphanius (*Panarion* 33:3–8 ; GCS 25:451) contrasts the Old Law as ' just ' with the ' perfection ' of the New. Although representing a more favourable attitude to the OT than Marcion,

[2] cf. G. Quispel, ' The Original Doctrine of Valentine ', in *VC* I (1947) 43–73.

its author also insists on its having its source in an inferior power. This he identifies with the Demiurge, who differs in nature both from God and from the Devil (ibid., 33:7).

Cosmological ideas similar to those embodied in the Valentinian myth are to be found in some of the treatises of the Hermetic corpus ; they appear to have been among the commonplaces of later Hellenistic philosophy. The gulf between a supreme Noûs and a second, lower Demiurge, and the two worlds to which they belong, is sharply stressed in the most ' gnostic ' of these treatises, the *Poimandres*.

IV Christianity and the Demiurge. In Christian literature the term is sparingly used in reference to the Creator. It occurs once in the NT (Heb 11:10), and a number of times in the writings of the Apostolic Fathers and the Apologists of the 2nd cent. It may be that after this time Christian writers preferred to avoid it, as being too reminiscent of the meaning the term had borne in gnostic contexts. Much of later 2nd- and 3rd-cent. Christian thought was avowedly anti-gnostic in purpose. The need to meet gnostic speculations about a Demiurge had two chief consequences in the development of Christian theology: (i) the insistence on the unity of the Scriptures and their single, divine authorship. Against gnostic and Marcionite attempts to drive a wedge between OT and NT, and their respective Gods, Christian writers stressed the unity of the Old and New Testaments and the identity of Jahve and the Father of Jesus Christ. They also explored the relation of the Old Law to the New. Writers like Justin and Irenaeus laid great stress on the continuity of divine revelation in the scriptures, on its development and its gradual unfolding in history.[1] The OT was held to anticipate, foreshadow and prepare the NT, and this was seen as the fulfilment of the OT ; (ii) reacting against the dualistic aspects of gnostic cosmology, Christian writers rejected the separation of a visible, ' psychical ' and ' material ' world from the world of ' spirit ', and the subjection of the former to a power inferior to God. They insisted on God's dominion extending over all realms of creation, and on their all having one origin in God's creative action. St Augustine's polemic against Manichaean teaching may be regarded as the last phase of this controversy. *See also* CREATION, GNOSTICS.

Bibliography. Apart from general works on gnosticism (cf. bibliography to GNOSTICS), the best treatment is in *RAC*, 3:694-711 (with bibliography) ; also the shorter article in *LThK* s.v. ; A. J. Festugière, *La Révélation d'Hermès Trismégiste*, 2 : *Le Dieu cosmique* (1949) ; A. H. Armstrong and R. A. Markus, *Christian Faith and Greek Philosophy* (1960) chs. 1 and 3.   R. A. M.

DESCARTES, INFLUENCE OF : Descartes (1596–1650) was the founder of ' the method of rightly conducting the reason, and seeking truth in the sciences ', concerning which he published his celebrated *Discours de la Méthode* in 1637. Though

[1] cf. R. A. Markus, ' Pleroma and Fulfilment: the Significance of History in St Irenaeus's Opposition to Gnosticism', *VC* VIII (1954) 193-224.

it is an integral part of his system of philosophy, the Cartesian method of ' conducting the reason ' can be considered on its own. In the words of Fontenelle, Descartes ' a amené cette nouvelle manière de raisonner beaucoup plus estimable que sa philosophie même '. The influence that Descartes has had on theology has been due, in fact, to his method of investigating truth rather than to his philosophical system itself. Indeed, the widespread adoption of his method brought about revolutionary changes in our Western philosophy and culture, and attacked the very roots of theology in that the method involved (I) a rejection of the Catholic idea of divine faith, and (II) a total rejection of the traditional idea of scholastic theology and philosophy.

I The Wrong Idea of Faith. Descartes was unquestionably a sincere Catholic, and an unquestioning believer in the teaching of the Church. He never had any intention of introducing revolutionary changes into theology itself, though he hoped that his philosophy would be acceptable to the Church as apologetics on two points in particular, in proving the existence of God (*see* GOD, EXISTENCE OF), and in meeting difficulties raised against the Real Presence of Christ in the Eucharist (*see* EUCHARIST). His life-work consisted in his effort to reconstruct philosophy on lines that would establish it as a purely human science entirely independent of any authority extrinsic to reason itself, and especially that of faith and theology. His method was devised to make reason what it had never been in the Middle Ages, entirely self-sufficient, and to inspire philosophers with confidence in their abilities to discover the truth about any question of philosophy or science. In doing this he introduced (1) a new theory about the relations holding between faith and reason, or theology and philosophy, and (2) a new conception of reason.

(1) Descartes drove a wedge between faith and reason which separated them so completely as to divorce them from each other entirely, and deprive them of any right to be re-united. He made reasoning an activity which is self-contained and bounded by its own laws, having nothing to do with the non-rational truths of revelation. He put the truths of faith outside the reach of his methodic doubt as too exalted to be examined by ' the impotency of reason ' (*Discours*, part 1). He declared the truths of faith to be above reason, but in explaining the meaning of ' above ' he went to the extreme of putting them outside the mental order altogether, making them intrinsically unthinkable by the mind. No doubt Descartes was not aware of the logical consequences of his views about the transcendence of the truths of faith, but his mistaken ideas of the true nature of this transcendence prepared the way for the later rationalist agnostic conception of faith, according to which the act of religious belief is irrational and in no proper sense of the word an act of knowing. In Descartes' view faith shows us the way to Heaven, and the act of faith is an act of the will by which we submit to God's teaching concerning the conduct of our lives.

(2) Descartes established reasoning on the sole foundation of purely natural certitudes, and devised his method to fit the mind for the investigation and discovery of all the truths of philosophy and science, on the condition that it follows the method of reasoning that is natural to it. This method consisted in the exclusive use of 'the clear and distinct ideas' of the mind, of 'simple and easy' steps of reasoning in a chain of deductions with links which are clearly and distinctly (or intuitively) perceived with perfect geometrical clarity, and of the memory supporting the work of reason by retaining an intuitive recollection of all the reasonings which have led up to any proved proposition under consideration (*Discours*, part 2 ; *Regulae ad Directionem Ingenii, passim*). In reason thus methodically conducted we have the key to universal knowledge. In the Cartesian idea, philosophy is concerned solely with the life of man on earth and his future well-being in this world. As Gouhier says, re-echoing the lamentation of Pascal, 'Descartes secularized God by making him accessible to, and necessary for, reason rightly conducted, and prepared the way for the "God without mysteries" of the 18th-cent. rationalists'.

II The War on Scholasticism. The philosophy of the Scholastics was declared by Descartes to be vain and futile. It was vain for it had solved no problems, and it was futile for, having no conception of the method of rightly conducting the reason, it was incapable of producing certitude about anything. Descartes declared war on the Scholastics for their failure even to appreciate the need of the proper, natural method of reasoning, and he derided the Aristotelian Logic as useless for the investigation of the unknown (*Discours*, part 2, and *Regulae, passim*). He attacked the solidarity which the Schoolmen had set up between faith and their Aristotelian philosophy, on the score that it had created untold confusion by transforming human errors into divine truths (especially errors in physics and astronomy), and led the Church to treat salutary reforms as dangerous heresies. He had in mind the condemnation of Galileo, whose heliocentric theory he had expounded in his early treatise on *Le Monde*. He denied also the necessity of any intellectual preamble to faith, on the score that the only preparation required is of the will.

Descartes' *Méthode* was instrumental in bringing what we call 'Modern Philosophy' into life, and in a modified form it shaped philosophy in England through the work of John Locke. The widespread diffusion of this famous Method resulted in the virtual collapse of scholastic theology for two hundred years, and raised the problem of the relations between faith and reason in a form in which it is presented by many philosophers to this day.

Bibliography. *Oeuvres de Descartes* (published by Adam and Tannery, 13 volumes, 1897–1913) ; *Discours de la Méthode* (text and commentary), edited by E. Gilson (1925). English translation in the *Everyman's Library* ; E. Gilson : *Études sur le rôle de la pensée médiévale dans la formation du système cartésien* (1930) ; H. Gouhier, *La Pensée religieuse de Descartes* (1924), and *Essais sur Descartes* (1937). E. A. S.

DESCENT INTO HELL The first part of the fifth article of the Apostles' Creed is perhaps the most neglected part of theology in modern times. By contrast, in the early Church it was one of the most prominent. The Creed confines itself to saying that Christ went down to Hell, and this will be treated in the first section (I) of this article. What He did there (II) will next be considered in the light of the Tradition of the Church, and (III) certain theological consequences of this teaching will be noted.

I The fact of the Descent is taken for granted by St Peter in his very first sermon (Ac 2:27), where Ps 15:10 is applied to Christ, as showing that His soul went to Hell but did not abide there. In 1 Pet 3:19 and 4:6 the Descent is somehow connected with the saving acts of Christ. Some have held that this Petrine doctrine was derived from Jewish apocrypha, for in *Enoch* 69:26 there is a tale about the dead rejoicing because the name of the Son of Man was made known to them. But there are too many other NT references to the Descent for it to be explained away thus as an importation into Christian thought due to the whim of an individual. In Jn 5:25, 28 Christ says that all those who are dead are shortly to hear His voice. This saying cannot be set aside simply as a forecasting of what is to happen to Lazarus ; the perspective runs on from the events of Bethany to what happens at the Descent, and from there to the final judgment of the world. As E. G. Selwyn forcibly argued : ' The hour now is, because the life-giving powers of the Son of God are already evident, but it is still coming, because He has not yet conquered death and Hades ' (*The First Epistle of Peter*, 348).

In Eph 4:8–9 it may be true that Paul does not identify the captives who were led away to heaven, but Irenaeus (*epideixis*, 83) is quite clear that by captivity, ' he means the destruction of the rule of the apostate angels '. The passage is the more impressive as Paul seems to take it for granted that his audience will follow the allusion. Similarly in Phil 2:10, Rom 10:7 and 2 Tim 1:10 he can afford to be allusive about the same matter, as if it already formed part of the general catechesis.

Justin (*dial.* 72) and Irenaeus (in five places : *adv. haer.* 3:22:1 ; 4:3:61 ; 4:50:1 ; 4:55:3 ; 5:31:1 H) quote a passage which they claim was formerly found in the text of Jeremias (once Irenaeus attributes it to Isaias) and which had been cut out by Jewish controversialists: it ran as follows: ' The Lord remembered His dead people of Israel who lay in their graves, and went down to preach to them His own salvation '. It is strange that no trace of this text is found in the LXX of Jeremias, if what Justin alleges is true, but it must now be admitted (in the light of the Qumran scrolls) that some tampering with controversial texts was practised by the Jews, for the Isaias scroll at 53:11 has a reading which favours the Christian argument (and which is found in the LXX), but this reading has disappeared from all later Hebrew manuscripts. Moreover, the Greek fragments of the OT found at Qumran present a type of text which is often in agreement with Justin.

II The nature of Christ's activity in the Descent is described by Melito of Sardis (*hom. Passionis*, 102) as dissolving death, triumphing over the devil, trampling on Hades, binding the strong one and bringing man to safe harbour in heaven. Earlier in the same homily (68) he says that this was one of the works of Christ in which He resembled Moses, for as Moses bound Pharaoh in the toils of grief, so Christ bound the devil. The parallel of Moses and Christ is part of the primitive Christian preaching, and it may be that this triumphal note in the account of the Descent goes back a very long way. In the *Odes of Solomon* (17:8 and 31:1–2) this triumph is celebrated, and one may infer that those who used these popular chants at the close of the 1st cent. were quite familiar with the doctrine of the Descent. The language of Is 45:1–3 about Cyrus as the agent of Jahwe in the restoration of Israel was very quickly applied to Christ's Descent. 'To open doors and to unbar the gates I myself will go before thee and make thy ways plain ; I will break down the gates of brass and cut asunder the bars of iron ; and I will give thee the treasures of darkness, the hoards of secret places.' Kissane notes in his comment on this passage that the language is reminiscent of the Exodus ; for Moses, God rendered useless the weapons of the Egyptians and allowed their treasure to be despoiled, and a similar favour will be shown to Cyrus on behalf of Israel. In the *Epistle of Barnabas* (11:4) this passage is used as a prophecy of baptism. The practice (for which *see* BAPTISM, III c) of regarding baptism as parallel to Christ's Descent provides the link required by Barnabas between the prophecy of Isaias and what he regards as its fulfilment.

The salvation of those in Limbo is described in the *Odes of Solomon* (42:21–22): 'Those who had died ran towards Me and cried: " Son of God, have pity on us ... and bring us out from the bonds of darkness, and open to us the door by which we shall come out to Thee. . . . Thou art our Redeemer ". And I heard their voice, and My name I sealed upon their heads'. This would imply that the preaching to the dead (1 Pet 3:19) was not just a proclamation of His triumph but an offer of a last-minute salvation. Hermas (93:5 ; GCS 48:90) says that the apostles went down to evangelize and baptize the dead. Clement of Alexandria cites this text with the comment that the apostles were imitators of their Master in this action (*strom.* 6:6:45 ; GCS 52:954). Ignatius (*Magn.* 9:3) also accepts the salvation of the prophets, though he seems to connect it with Mt 27:52, rather than with an act of preaching. Apocryphal works of the 2nd cent. (e.g. *Epistle of the Apostles*, 27 ; *Gospel of Peter*, 10:42) make much of this preaching and quite overlook the difficulties in the text of 1 Pet 3:19, where 'the spirits in prison that once were disobedient' could more easily be taken of the fallen angels, as Dean Selwyn argued in his essay on the passage. Marcion (according to Irenaeus, *adv. haer.* 1:25:2 H) so disliked the story that he changed it, making out that Cain and the men of Sodom and Egypt listened to the preaching, while the patriarchs and prophets looked upon it as a

temptation and disbelieved it. His anti-Semitism must have made him unwilling to accept the retrospective salvation of so many Jews.

The liturgy of Hippolytus (*Trad. apost.* 4:8) in its Latin version speaks of four works of Christ in His Descent: that He broke asunder the bondage of the devil, He trampled on Hades, He enlightened the just and set up a trophy.[1] This enumeration is fairly close to that of Melito quoted above, and it may betoken a liturgical tradition of some importance. The trophy which Christ set up is further described in the pseudo-Hippolytus homily on the Pasch (1:55): 'He took up His firm stand on the confines of the world, going forward Himself in triumphal procession over His enemy, as a trophy of His victory'. All the efforts of the 2nd-cent. Christians in Rome to set up a trophy for Peter's victory over death take on a new significance if it can be seen that the trophy for Christ Himself was already an accepted matter of belief among them. On the *tropaeum* in Hades, cf. also Alexander of Alexandria, PG 18:599. The doxology of the *Didascalia Apostolorum* (Connolly, 258–9) shows liturgical practice of the early 3rd cent. running over into the formation of a creed with a clause about the Descent: 'Jesus Christ, who was crucified in the days of Pontius Pilate and slept, that He might announce to Abraham and to Isaac and to Jacob and to all His saints the end of the world and the resurrection that is to be for the dead, and rose from the dead that He might show and give to us, that we might know Him, a pledge of the resurrection. . . .'

The first formal and dated creed to have a clause about the Descent is that of Sirmium (359), which has the following: '. . . who went down into the nether regions and set to rights their affairs, to whom at His approach the warders of Hades showed fear and trembling'. The author of this creed was, according to Socrates (HE 2:30 ; PG 67:280), Mark of Arethusa from Coele-Syria (the country of the *Didascalia*). The creed of Aquileia (in Rufinus, PL 21:356) has the three words *descendit ad inferna* and Rufinus gives it as his opinion that these words do not occur in creeds of East or West. About the East he was clearly wrong, but in the West there are not many imitators of Aquileia until the 6th cent., when the ' Athanasian creed ', Martin of Braga and the *Antiphonary* of Bangor give evidence of the acceptance of this clause. The *Bobbio Missal* (246) has the clause in its baptismal creed, and it may be that the line of transmission, from Syria, through Spain to Ireland, is for this clause the same as has been noted for various liturgical forms and practices of the Dark Ages (*see* ADVENT, AZYMES, CREEDS).

Augustine, though at first he had accepted the usual view of 1 Pet 3:19 (e.g. in *De haeresibus*, 79 ; PL 42:45), took up an entirely new line of interpretation in his letter to Evodius (*ep.* 164 ; CSEL 44:522–31). The preaching to the disobedient spirits in the days of Noah, he thought, might be understood as taking place at the time of Noah, Christ in His divine nature engaging in a theophany

---

[1] Ut vincula diaboli dirumpat, infernum calcet, iustos inluminet et terminum figat.

such as was canvassed by some of the Fathers for other OT occasions. The 'spirits' were to be thought of as imprisoned in their bodies and fettered by sin. Thus one might evade the difficulty of Lk 16:26, where Lazarus is said to have been happy in the bosom of Abraham, even before Christ had gone down to Hades. No one would now make much of a difficulty like this, but the view of Augustine was followed by many theologians in the West, as may be seen from St Thomas (*Summa*, 3a:52:2:@3). Suarez (*Opera* XIX:736) and Bellarmine (*Disputatio de Christo* IV:13) returned to the earlier tradition.

St Thomas, as a result of his following Augustine, is forced to make the doctrine of the Descent and its manner depend on texts such as Zach 9:11 ; Col 2:15 and Os 13:14, where the spiritual sense has to be invoked to a considerable extent. It is curious that he did not make the direct inference from Mt 12:29 that Christ was the one who entered the castle of the Strong Man and bound him. His way of avoiding the difficulty arising from the promise to the Good Thief (Lk 23:43), which seems to cut down the time available for the Descent, is neat and not without merit (*Summa*, 3a:52:4:@3) ; it envisages a descent of the Thief in company with Christ.

III Theological consequences of the doctrine of the Descent were of many kinds. In a liturgical text published by A. Dold (*Das Sakramentar im Schabcodex M* 12, 1952) which is either Spanish or Breton work of the 7th cent., there is a *post-Sanctus* for Easter in which the claim is made that the entry of Christ into the nether world caused a cessation for the moment of the pains of Hell.[1] 'The pains of the damned were stilled for a while through the surprise and their tortures had no sting. The very place of pain trembled before its Judge, for at the presence of Thy light the dire nature of the dark was quelled and feared that its judgment was even then come.' The same passage is found though imperfectly in *Missale Gothicum* (281) and in the Mozarabic Missal, PL 85:501. This dramatization of the Descent is simply a prolongation of what is said in the creed of Sirmium (cited above) ; the warders of Hades were no doubt connected in the popular mind with Mt 16:18, especially in the East where the words for 'gates' and 'warders' can be easily interchanged, both in Aramaic and Syriac. The influence of Job 38:17 as a prophecy of the Descent helped also in the same direction ; the clause about the Descent in the creed of the synod of Constantinople in 360 shows a verbal reminiscence of this passage. The 4th-cent. *Apocalypse of Paul* (44) may be the ultimate source of the idea of a day's remission for Hell.

A much more extensive dramatization of the Descent can be traced to an Englishwoman, Lady Katherine of Sutton, Abbess of Barking 1358–76, who in her desire to stir up popular devotion devised a most interesting para-liturgy (*The Barking Ordinale*, I:107 ; II:378). After the third responsory of

---

[1] Attonita paululum miserorum steterunt supplicia nec habuerunt tormenta cruciatum. Et iudicem suum ipsa etiam poena contremuit quia natura terribilium tenebrarum praesentia tui fulgoris hebetata iam tum timuit iudicari.

Matins for Easter, she, with all her nuns and with some priests and clerks, went to the chapel of St Mary Magdalen, bearing palms and unlighted candles. Here they were shut in, to represent ' the holy patriarchs who had gone down before the coming of Christ '. Then a priest with two deacons and cross-bearer came to the door and intoned the anthem *Tollite portas* (Ps 23(24):7). He knocked thrice on the door while the anthem was repeated, and then he led out those who were within, all going in procession to the Easter sepulchre, where the drama of the Three Maries and the *Quem quaeritis* was then carried out. It may also be that the vigil kept by individual Christians in St Patrick's Purgatory at Lough Derg was considered to be an imitation of the Descent of Christ ; it is remarkable that in the early testimonies to the place emphasis is laid on the fact that the island was infested with evil spirits. Those who kept vigil may have been regarded as doing battle with these under the protection of the *lorica* of Christ. (Cf. also the dialogue of Christ and Adam in the Book of Cerne, 196–8.)

In the 4th cent. use was made of the doctrine of the Descent against Apollinaris. When he taught that the divine Word took the place of the human mind of Christ (*see* APOLLINARIS), he was asked how Christ could have been recognized by the patriarchs, if His Descent concerned His human soul alone, and that soul was without the higher functions of mind and was confined to those proper to animal and vegetative life. This *ad hominem* argument is used in a treatise ascribed to Athanasius (PG 26:1125). From what has already been shown of earlier statements of the doctrine it will be quite clear that the Church did not devise this doctrine out of pagan myths simply in order to deal with Apollinaris ; fanciful reconstruction of the history of dogma on these lines was once a German fashion, but is now discredited. In fact the history of this doctrine provides a very valuable instance of the fact that the popular elaboration (in apocryphal gospels, such as that of Nicodemus) of the Descent comes *after* the doctrine has been officially taught in the NT, and not before such official teaching. In the light of this fact, the growth of *Transitus* literature after the official acceptance of the Assumption in the liturgy (*see* ASSUMPTION) is easier to understand aright.

The extent of Christ's saving activity in the Descent was disputed by the Fathers. Cyril of Alexandria (*hom. Pasch.* 7 ; PG 77:552) says that everyone was rescued. Origen (*contra Cels.* 2:43 ; GCS 1:164) on the other hand speaks of Christ ' converting those who would or those whom He knew were more fit ', thus leaving the question open. In another work (*hom. in* 1 *Kg* 28 ; GCS 6:293) Origen says that before the Descent of Christ, ' none could go to where the tree of life grew, for none could pass the fiery sword of the angel. But now, if we get rid of the cargo of our sins, we shall go through the fire and not go to the place where the patriarchs were detained '. Thus the perspective changes from the immediate effect of Christ's Descent to its long-term value to all Christians.

When Gregory the Great (*ep.* 7:15 ; MGH *Epp.* I:459) wrote to correct the views of George the priest, he may have been confronting one who had confused these immediate and long-term effects. Gregory says: ' When Christ went down to the lower regions, He set free from their prison-house only those whom while they were living in the body He had kept safe by His grace in faith and good works '.[1] The Old Latin reading of Ecclus 24:45 (not found in the LXX, where it should come between 24:32 and 24:33) no doubt helped Gregory in his ruling. It said: ' I will go through all the lower parts of the earth, and look upon all those that sleep, and I will enlighten all those that hope in the Lord '. (For the value of this Old Latin version, *see* CCS 396e–g).

Abelard, in the light of his view of the death of Christ as redemptive by its appeal to the love of mankind (*see* ABELARD), was not inclined to favour a strong theology of the Descent. He seems to have held that it was potential and not actual, and this opinion was condemned (D 385) at the Council of Sens (1140). When the 4th Lateran Council of 1215, in its profession of faith, inserted the words *descendit in anima* (D 429), it is commonly thought to have been reaffirming what had been enacted at Sens against Abelard. Pico della Mirandula revived the idea of Abelard, saying that Christ was not truly present in Hell but only made His will effective there. One can readily admit that the location of the Descent presents difficulty, but that does not make the fact itself unacceptable. Mathematicians work with square roots, even though these numbers are incommensurable with the series of natural numbers ; in much the same way the theologian can work with the concept of the Descent without having to decide its location.

A modern Calvinist finds in the doctrine of the Descent a substitute for Purgatory. Br P. Emery (of Taizé) writes (in *L'Unité des croyants*, 72) that the Descent is an act outside the plane of history ; its effects extend, as do those of the Passion and Resurrection, to all generations before and after the coming of Christ. Hence anyone who has not been in a position to believe in Christ during his earthly life will somehow be given, after death, the opportunity of deciding for or against Christ. In this way the rigours of strict Calvinism with its negative reprobation may be avoided, but St Thomas would not go all the way with Br Emery in universalizing the efficacy of the Descent. Asking whether Christ emptied Purgatory at His Descent (*Summa*, 3a: 52:8:@2) St Thomas says that He did not, for the Descent was not in itself a work of satisfaction ; it took on that character from the Passion. Now the Passion of Christ is a generic work of satisfaction and has to be made efficacious for each individual by some factor which properly belongs to that individual.[2] It is therefore not necessary to suppose that

the Descent freed all who were in Purgatory but only those who while alive had shown faith in Christ in some way. The difference here is one of fundamental significance and turns upon differing theologies of justification, whether internal or extrinsic to the soul. (*See* PURGATORY *and* JUSTIFICATION.)

In theologizing about death, Fr K. Rahner puts forward a new theory of Christ's Descent. This was, he says, ' not a soteriological act on behalf of the saved who had lived before Christ ' but was to establish ' an open, real-ontological relationship to the world in its oneness '. He thinks this theory is in accord with the NT and appeals to Ac 2:24 and 31. But those two passages merely state that Christ was not able to be vanquished by death and did not see corruption. The theory will have to be supported by much more careful treatment of the sources of doctrine if it is to merit consideration. The insistence in these sources upon the activity of Christ in His Descent must be given some place in any theological development which is going to remain true to the tradition of the Church.

Humanist speculation about Christian borrowing from the legend of Herakles in this doctrine, as canvassed by Professor Toynbee (*Study of History*, V:474), does not merit serious consideration. The verbal parallels with Seneca are remote ; Cerberus and the Styx are absent from the Christian account, where Christ is supremely free and not, like Herakles, under command (cf. Seneca, *Hercules furens*, 596).

Bibliography. U. Holzmeister sj, *Commentarius in epistolas Petri* (1937) ; J. Chaine, in DBS s.v. Descente ; ★E. G. Selwyn, *The First Epistle of St Peter* (1946) ; ★B. Reicke, *The Disobedient Spirits and Christian Baptism* (1946) ; A. Grillmeier, ' Der Gottessohn im Totenreich ', in ZKT 71 (1949) 1–53 and 184–203 ; ★F. Loofs, in ERE s.v. ' Descent to Hades ' ; ★J. Jeremias, ' Zwischen Karfreitag und Ostern ', in ZNTW 42 (1949) 194–201 ; ★K. Young, *The Drama of the Medieval Church* (2 vols., 1933) ; ★J. N. Kelly, *Early Christian Creeds* (1950) ; E. Peterson, ' Die Taufe im Acherusischen See ', in *Vigiliae christianae* 9 (1955) 1–20 ; F. Cabrol, ' La Descente du Christ d'après les liturgies gallicanes ', in *Rassegna Gregoriana* 8 (1909) 233–42 ; ★J. A. MacCulloch, *The Harrowing of Hell* (1930) ; K. Rahner, *The Theology of Death* (1961) ; ★E. K. Rand, ' Sermo de confusione diaboli ', in *Modern Philology* 2 (1904) 261–78, a critical text of an important patristic work.   J. H. C.

DETERMINISM. *See* FREE-WILL.

DEVIL After dealing with the OT doctrine (I) of the tempting spirit and with that of the NT on Satan (II), this article will examine briefly (III) the theological aberration of the patristic age which took Gen 6:1–4 to be an account of diabolic procreation. The traditional Catholic idea of discernment of spirits as a necessary part of the Christian life (IV) will then be considered, (V) some notice will be

---

[1] Descendens ad inferos Dominus illos solummodo ab inferni claustris eripuit quos viventes in carne per suam gratiam in fide et bona operatione salvavit.

[2] Passio Christi . . . erat satisfactoria in genere, cuius virtutem oportebat applicari ad unumquemque per aliquid specialiter ad ipsum pertinens.

taken of diabolic phenomena as they bear on theology, and finally (VI) a note will be added on the nature of the devil's sin.

I The serpent of Gen 3:1 is identified as the devil by Wis 2:24 which ascribes to the devil the entry of death into the world, a fact which is elsewhere (Ecclus 25:24) imputed to a woman. The general attributes of angels are frequently described (*see* ANGELS) in the OT, and the angelic nature of the devil is implied by Zach 3:1, where he is introduced as the adversary of the angel of God in the prophet's vision of Jesus the high priest. This passage was used by the Fathers typologically (cf. the newly recovered commentary of Didymus on Zacharias, edited by L. Doutreleau from the papyrus in 1962), and it may have given them the idea that the fall of the devil was somehow due to his being shown the Incarnation in prospect. In Job 1 and 2 the devil is depicted as an angel of evil propensity who has God's permission to tempt Job by all manner of physical hardships. The story (for which *see* CCS 320e) represents this angel as coming before God in the midst of the other angels, but his function is that of being man's adversary ; the name Satan was originally a common noun that meant 'adversary'. From these chapters it might not appear certain that Satan was here being depicted as an evil angel, but this is simply due to the unsystematic nature of Hebrew thought. What God permits in the way of evil and what He orders are not fully distinguished by the Hebrew mind, but later (Job 4:18) it is made quite clear that God 'lays wickedness to the charge of His angels'. Eliphaz is shown as repeating this idea (Job 15:15) in the words : 'Lo, in His holy ones He putteth not trust'. In 1 Par 21:1-8 the devil is said to have prompted David to hold a census, which is then found displeasing by God. It is true that the parallel account of this census (2 Kg 24:1) represents it as instigated by God, but this is but another case of Hebrew failure to distinguish what God allowed to Satan from what He positively ordered. Ex 30:12 makes it quite clear that a census was an infringement of the divine prerogative, in atonement for which the temple tax was instituted.

The Book of Tobias introduces the activities of a devil named Asmodeus who has killed the seven husbands of Sara (Tob 3:8). The angel Raphael puts this devil to flight (Tob 8:3) and leaves him bound in the upper parts of Egypt. The Vulgate has an expanded text at Tob 6:17 and 8:7-9, in which it is taught that the devil has power over those who enter upon marriage relations for impure motives (*see* CCS 302h). The means by which Tobias puts the devil to flight are, according to the LXX text (Tob 6:8 and 8:3), the burning of parts of the fish in the marriage chamber. The text does add that Tobias was safe because he married 'not for harlotry but for truth', yet there is no expansion of this into what Jerome put in his version. (Jerome did not accept the book as canonical, and so he added to it freely.) In CCS 305h it is suggested that the use of the fumigants may be regarded as a sacramental of the OT, but this is far-fetched. The detail is simply

a part of the story and could be paralleled from the literature of paganism. There is no sign that the Church ever encouraged its use, though an extensive blessing of the nuptial chamber was practised in, e.g., the Sarum ritual.

II The gospels, even though they do not in general care much for the exact chronology of events, seem to show a gradually mounting intensity in the conflict of Christ with the devil. The temptation (Mt 4:1-11 ; Lk 4:1-13 and Mk 1:12-13) is the beginning of this struggle and it takes the form of an inducement to launch a bogus-Messianic campaign in one way or another. When this fails, there is the attack through the 'brethren of the Lord', who claim that Jesus is beside Himself, and this is linked by Mark (though not by Matthew and Luke) with the accusation of His being in league with the devil. The attack through the possessed man in the synagogue of Capharnaum (Mk 1:23-8 ; Lk 4:33-7), whether it happened before or after the last-mentioned episode, is clearly a development from the failure of the direct temptation of Christ. If He cannot be brought to start a Messianic campaign before His proper time, then it may be possible to launch one by having Him proclaimed by the possessed and then getting Him to acquiesce in this. Obviously it was not in Our Lord's own interest to have the campaign started too soon, before He had time to complete the training of the apostles on whom so much would depend.

The muzzling of the devil in the possessed man is followed up with a counter-attack on the evil spirits, when the disciples are themselves sent out with power to cast out devils (Mt 10:8 ; Mk 3:15), thus multiplying the occasions of exorcism. In reply to this onslaught, devils of greater power are brought into action, and an episode ensues where the disciples are powerless to cast out the devil from the 'lunatic boy' (Mt 17:14-21 ; Mk 9:14-29 ; Lk 9:38-43). They are taught that for this kind of devil greater effort is needed. Soon after this defeat of the devils, one of the disciples is himself taken over by Satan (Lk 22:3 ; Jn 13:27) ; Judas must have taken part in the earlier exorcisms, but now falls a victim himself, after a temporary control of Peter had been obtained (Mt 16:23) and then lost. Judas betrays Christ, and the Passion then follows inevitably. A final assault (Jn 14:30) is made by the ruler of the devils on Christ Himself, as had been foreshadowed in Lk 4:13, but this proves unavailing, and the judgment of the devil is then begun (Jn 16:11). The Resurrection of Christ was a triumph over the devils (Col 1:13 ; 2:15), Christ making them a laughing-stock. For this triumph, *see* DESCENT INTO HELL.

In the early days of the Church, incidents are recorded of encounters with the devil on the part of Peter (Ac 5:3 ; 8:23) and of Paul (Ac 13:8 ; 16:16). Paul sometimes alludes (2 Cor 12:7 ; 1 Thess 2:18) to other devilish impediments put in his way (*see also* ANTICHRIST), and tells of some who have deserted Christianity for Satan (1 Tim 5:15). A recrudescence of the power of Satan is anticipated for the last age of the world (*see* ANTICHRIST). The handing over of a sinner to Satan is practised by Paul (1 Cor 5:5 ; 1 Tim 1:20) and seems to have been the making him liable to an infliction of physical disability, on a par with the temporary blinding of Elymas (Ac 13:11) ; this disability was looked on as the work of Satan who was given permission by God through the apostle to inflict it. Something of the kind is envisaged in the story of the woman bent double (Lk 13:16) whom Satan had bound for eighteen years. These NT narratives are dismissed by many modern critics as so much mythology, and some Catholic commentators have said that, in the last-mentioned example, Christ is speaking on the level of contemporary Jewish understanding and is not describing the woman's condition as He Himself understood it. This condescension would not be unparalleled in the NT, but it seems quite the most natural interpretation to take the statement literally ; one can easily see that psycho-somatic maladies may sometimes have an entirely spiritual cause, even though in other cases their causation may be due jointly to bodily and to mental disturbance. If stigmata at the present day are found to have been induced by human suggestion in an apt subject (as did happen in 1933 ; cf. A. Lechler, *Das Rätsel von Konnersreuth*), and are on other occasions to be put down to divine intervention, it does not seem absurd to hold that some maladies can be due either to natural causes or to diabolic disturbance.

The Qumran documents show that Satanic afflictions were expected as a punishment for wrong-doing ; ' the reward of all who walk in evil ways is a multitude of afflictions at the hands of the angels of destruction ', says the *Manual of Discipline* (4:1), while the *Zadokite Work* (12:2) asks that a man who is dominated by evil spirits to such an extent that he utters words of apostasy should be put to death in accordance with Lev 20:27. (If he was possessed but did not speak such words, he might be left alone, while being kept under observation.) The sons of Sceva (Ac 19:13) provide evidence for the practice of exorcism among contemporary Jews, though the designation of Sceva himself as a ' high priest ' may mean no more (as Burkitt has shown in *Beginnings of Christianity*, IV:241) than that he was one who knew by family tradition how to pronounce the Tetra-grammaton and used this knowledge in such exorcisms.

The *apotaxis* or renunciation of Satan that was demanded of catechumens in early times is witnessed by Hermas (36:9 ; GCS 48:33) in a passage that amplifies very considerably the Jewish doctrine of the Two Ways and provides the first evidence for a Christian doctrine of discernment of spirits. Use of the word in II *Clem* 6:4 and in the *Acts of Thomas* (along with the parodies in Apollonius of Tyana) warrants the conclusion that this renunciation must have been in use at baptism from the second quarter of the 2nd cent. at the latest ; it may have been in use earlier, for the language of Lk 14:33 may have an overtone of technicality. The practice of exorcis-ing the catechumens several times in the course of their instruction is mentioned in the Ethiopic version

of Hippolytus *Trad. apost.*, and more elaborately in the *Testamentum Domini* (2:7). Tertullian already has the phrase *pompa diaboli* (De idololatria 10 ; CSEL 20:40), and it seems originally to have con-noted the processions of the pagan gods, attendance at which was so difficult to avoid in many towns. The idea that diabolic influence was the driving force of pagan worship soon spread among the Christians. It is in Justin (*apol.* 23:3, and often), and it led to the more ready acceptance, by some of the Fathers, of a Jewish myth that must now be discussed.

III The story in Gen 6:1–4 of the ' sons of God ' and the ' daughters of men ' was taken by many Jews to refer to a descent of angels upon the earth in search of female partners. *Enoch* 6:1–5 has a circumstantial account of the myth ; the fallen angels numbered two hundred, their progeny were giants, who brought in war and the use of swords among men. The inconvenience of this legend for Christian use was that it did not provide an explanation of the fall of Satan, since it was clearly placed at a time after Adam had been expelled from Paradise ; in fact *Jubilees* (7:21) says that the Flood was due to this sin of the angels with the daughters of men. Origen (*contra Cels.* 5:55 ; GCS 3:58) rejected the tale and adopted the interpretation that the ' sons of God ' meant the descendants of Seth, while the ' daughters of men ' were the children of Cain. An early Syriac commentary on *Genesis* (published by A. Levene, 1951) which follows Ephrem and Theodore of Mopsuestia, agrees with Origen. Yet there were a number of Fathers who accepted the story. Justin was the first, and he seems to have been beguiled by the readiness with which it could be made to explain how pagan myths were really due to diabolic prompting. All their stories of the amours of Zeus could then be explained as alternative versions of the Jewish tale. The wild improbability of the legend, involving as it does the idea that angelic beings could assume bodies, was felt by some of its users, for the *Testament of the Twelve Patriarchs* (Ruben 5:6) seeks to obviate this : ' The watchers, i.e. the devils, appeared to the women when they were with their husbands, and the women lusting in their minds after their forms gave birth to giants, for the watchers appeared to them as reaching even to the heavens '.

Chrysostom (PG 53:187) pleaded for a demy-thologizing of the tradition (ἀνατρέψαι τὰς μυθολογίας), pointing out that men are called ' sons of God ' in Ps 8:16, in Ex 4:22 and Is 1:2 and that the sin of the devils is earlier, according to Wis 2:24, than the days of the Flood. Cyril of Alexandria (*Glaphyra* 2:2 ; PG 69:52) notes that there are different readings of Gen 6:2 ; Aquila translated it as ' the sons of the gods ', Symmachus as ' the sons of the powerful ones ', while some MSS. (and among them, as we now know, the *Codex Alexan-drinus*, in the corrector's hand) actually had the ἄγγελοι and not sons (υἱοί). Augustine (De civ. Dei 15:23 ; CSEL 40:109) rejected the tale as it implied an impossibility for angelic natures. He said that 2 Pet 2:4 was not to be taken to refer to this tale but to the apostasy of Satan and his followers from

God in the beginning. The text of 2 Peter does not specify the sin of the angels, and the parallel passage (Jude 6) says only that they ' kept not their principality but forsook their own habitation'. As the Canticle of Moses (Deut 32:8) speaks of God ' establishing limits for the nations according to the number of the angels of God ', there had grown up a Jewish idea that each angel was assigned to a particular tribe or people, St Michael being for the Jews (Dan 12:1), and that some of them abandoned their charge when they sinned. It is this view that found most favour with the Fathers (cf. Origen, *hom.* 9 in Ezech. GCS 33:409). The motive of this desertion of their charge is said by Origen to be pride, and, as he regarded *Enoch* as an apocryphal work (commentary on Jn 6:42 ; GCS 10:151), it is safe to say that he had no inclination to accept the legend of angelic fornication. It cannot be claimed (as some recent Catholic scholars have maintained) that the rejection of this legend by the Fathers begins only in the late 4th cent. Even among those of the Apologists who accept the tale (such as Athenagoras, *legatio* 24) one can find the other story accepted: ' Some angels fell a-lusting after maidens . . ., and he, the chief of them, became heedless and wicked in the administration of his charge'. What is true is that, towards the end of the 4th cent. one finds Filastrius stigmatizing as heretical the assertion that angels had commerce with women (*haer.* 108 ; CSEL 38:69) ; until then the Church does not seem to have impeded the free discussion of the story. For a recrudescence of these ideas, cf. D. 1261.

IV The discernment of spirits was practised by Jews before the coming of Christ, for they were familiar with ' the good inclination ' and 'the evil inclination ' which came to a man. Hermas, as noted above, has the basic idea of discernment along with much else that is Jewish in origin. Irenaeus (*epideixis* 12) says that Adam ' had his discretion still undeveloped, wherefore he was easily misled by the Deceiver'. The classical period of Christian teaching on this discernment was that of the Desert Fathers. Those coming to the wilderness in search of sanctity soon found that they needed a ' soul-friend ' who would save them from the pitfalls of that difficult life. It is reported of Macarius that ' he was held worthy of the divine gift of being able to treat with contempt the devils ' (Palladius, *The Book of Paradise*, in the version of Wallis Budge, 160) and such a man would be sought out by those who were tempted. Did not the last petition of the *Pater noster* ask for freedom from the evil one ? And was not the danger of a solitary life more acute than that of an active life in cities ?

It was in the desert that account had to be taken of diabolic temptation *sub specie boni* (under the appearance of good), a temptation reserved for those who had advanced some way towards sanctity and who had overcome direct temptation to evil. The turning-points in the conflict between Christ and the devil, as narrated in the gospels, were carefully studied and to this was added the fruit of experience. ' It is a customary deception of Satan, says one of

these Fathers, that he produceth avarice under the guise of love of family ' (Palladius, op. cit., 140). Water was regarded as an element hostile to man and therefore as the abode of devils. Before they drank, the desert hermits blessed the water in their cups (Palladius, op. cit. 134), and this exorcism has survived as a rubrical practice in the Mass. The exorcism of baptismal water and of the oil of anointing was elaborated in the liturgies of the time. Sometimes the advocacy of false doctrine was ascribed to the devil. There was a widow in the desert, says Palladius (op. cit., 980) who went to pray, and Satan put to her this question: ' Why do you pray like a man and say: " Glory be to the Father and to the Son and to the Holy Ghost " ? You should say: " Glory be to thee, Mary, mother of Christ ". The widow replied: " There is dust in thine eyes, Satan. Why should I forsake the Lord and worship a handmaiden ? " '

It was the task of those ordained to the office of exorcist to guard the possessed, who were admitted to the liturgy but were kept penned up in a separate part of the church. Epileptics and mental defectives generally would be included in this group, the diagnosis between cases being left to the exorcists. ' Let the church have a house of the catechumens, which shall also be the house of the exorcists, . . . not separated, but so that those who are in it may hear the lessons and psalms ' (*Testamentum Domini*, 1:19). In 251 at Rome there were, according to the letter of Pope Cornelius (in Eusebius HE 6:43), forty-two ' exorcists and readers '. It was Origen who had made difficult the treatment of epilepsy as a disease. In commenting on the lunatic boy (in Mt 13:6 ; GCS 40:193) he said that doctors might put down the disturbance to the action of the moon on the moist elements in the man's head, but one should not give way to such astrological fancies and insult a creature of God such as the moon, for the unclean spirit is at work on these sufferers. Thus the desire to discredit astrology and superstition led to a disregard of ordinary medical diagnosis ; Athanasius (PG 27:1388) seems to follow Origen, though we are told that Posidonius, the son of Philostorgius, went back to the medical theory (Philostorgius, HE 8:10 ; GCS 21:111). The Council of Elvira in the early 4th cent. (canons 29 and 37) ordered that *energumeni* were not to be allowed to light lamps in the church, nor ' to minister with their hands ' there. These seem reasonable precautions and may signify that in Spain at least there was no fear that such people were possessed. It was also agreed by this council that they could be given communion when dying and, if they were catechumens, could be baptized before death. A similar ruling may be found among the Apostolic Canons. In the Ethiopic version of the *Statutes of the Apostles* (Horner, 187), in what may be a garbled interpretation of Hippolytus's treatise on charismata, the doctrine of St Paul is reproduced (1 Cor 14:22): ' Signs are not for the faithful but for the unbelieving, for Jews and Gentiles. Casting out demons is no gain for us, but is done by the working of Our Lord

Christ. To those that believe, this grace shall be given '.

It was generally understood on the basis of Jn 12:31 ; 16:11 (cf. CCS 805c) that the Christian shared somehow in Christ's triumph over the devil (*see* ATONEMENT). Ambrose (*De Tobia* 33 ; CSEL 32:536) has this in terms of money-lending. Eve borrowed the money, and the human race had to pay with usury, until Christ came. He did not owe anything to the devil, but paid our debt. He could say : ' The prince of this world cometh and findeth nothing of his own in Me '.[1] The leading of the monster by a hook (Job 40:25) was applied to this triumph often (e.g. PG 26:880), but some of the metaphors used proved dangerous tools in the hands of amateur theologians ; too much care was shown in elaborating them and not enough in diagnosing true from false possession.

V Diabolic phenomena are by the modern *Rituale* described (*titulus* XI) as of three categories: knowledge of things distant or secret ; speaking fluently in an unknown tongue ; and the display of superhuman strength. It is pointed out that the exorcist should not be eager to believe that he has a case of possession before him and that the concurrence of all three signs is a stronger indication than the display of one of them alone. These rules contrast with what Chrysostom described when he was dealing with the case of his friend Stagirus (PG 47:426). Here the signs are twisting of the hands, rolling of the eyes, foam at the mouth, a changed voice, trembling of the whole body, catalepsy enduring for a time, and wild dreams. Even the signs now given need cautious interpretation. It is possible for the unconscious memory to retain snatches of an unknown language that has been heard when the body was in a trance or under an anaesthetic ; extra-sensory perception seems to be a natural but abnormal phenomenon which might account for some knowledge of things distant ; and drugs can give a man more than normal strength. It is unlikely that natural causes of all three phenomena should occur at one and the same time, but the diagnosis would normally be extended to include some inquiry into the past history of the subject, whether, for instance, he had renounced his will freely at some time past into the hands of an unknown power ; this might be by a formal act, as is recorded of the notorious Aleister Crowley, or by the practice of automatic writing, which would induce such a habit. A practising exorcist, with twenty years' experience in Paris (Fr J. de Tonquédec), has put it on record that 90 per cent of his cases were pseudo-possession, where medical aid was needed by the subject.

The worship of the devil has been practised from time to time among those who have fallen away from Christianity (*see* MANICHEES for the rejection of dualism by the Church, as in D 428), and perhaps never more so than in the latter part of the 19th cent. among the Decadents of France. Much mystification

[1] Dominus aeris solutor alieni nihil ipse debebat qui poterat dicere: Ecce venit huius mundi princeps et in Me suum non invenit nihil.

still surrounds their doings, and the forgeries of Leo Taxil and Diana Vaughan (which in their time led astray many ecclesiastics) are quite unreliable. Some of those who were deceived continue, however, to repeat a remark taken from a letter written by J.-K. Huysmans to the Abbess of Solesmes in 1900: ' Il y a un fait très certain—nous en avons eu ici des preuves—c'est que l'abominable Taxil a plus menti lorsqu'il a déclaré que le culte luciférien maçonnique n'existait pas, qu'il n'avait menti en racontant les invraisemblables bourdes dont il a berné les catholiques '. One may venture to judge that the ' preuves ' which satisfied Huysmans in that hour of crisis (it was the moment when the expulsion of the religious Orders was being decreed in France) would not satisfy the historian of today.

Witchcraft had been reckoned a grave sin from the time of Ex 22:18 and was generally taken to involve dealing with the devil. Some Catholic countries, such as Ireland, remained remarkably free from scares about witchcraft and prosecutions for it, even during the two centuries (1450-1650) when the scare was at its height. The Rhineland, the Low Countries and Lorraine were, however, marred by it, while at the same time it must be noticed that some lands which went over to the Reformation found that one of their first concerns thereafter was to bring in legislation against witches and to base this on the OT. Denmark, Scotland and Transylvania are examples of this. In Germany it was the *Cautio criminalis* (1631) of Fr Friedrich Spee von Langenfeld SJ that brought about a reaction towards moderation. Two theological causes may be assigned for the witch-scare, one being the Protestant over-emphasis on OT legislation just mentioned ; the other is the passing away of the danger to the Church from the survival of paganism. While that lasted, it was urgent for the Church to impress on men that witchcraft was not all-powerful and that the greater part of it was trumpery anyhow, but, when in the later Middle Ages paganism had ceased to be a pressing danger, the canonical injunctions found in Burchard of Worms (PL 140:576 and 837) or Regino of Prüm (PL 132:284), which had dissuaded men from attaching belief to the powers of witches, tended to be forgotten. (*See also* ASTROLOGY *and* MAGIC.)

VI The devil and the Incarnation of Christ are brought together by the theological opinion that the devil's sin was one of envy, when he was given foreknowledge that it was human nature that was to be united with the divine nature of the Second Person ; he wanted this divine favour for his own angelic nature instead. This opinion was elaborated by Suarez (*Opera* II:881), but he did not originate it. Papini (*Il diavolo*, 58) traces it back to Catharinus, who in 1552 published a tractate, *De gloria bonorum angelorum et lapsu malorum*. As Papini recognized, there was ample patristic testimony to the idea that the devil sinned by envy of man, even though the Fathers do not elaborate the details of that sin in the way that Catharinus did. But what has not been noticed is that it was Augustine who sent theologians away on another trail by his psychological analysis expressed in the three words, *causa invidendi superbia*: the cause of envy is pride. In this passage (*De Genesi ad litteram* 11:14 ; CSEL 28:346) he admits that some describe the sin as envy, and then adds his reason for not following them. As Augustine was far more introspective than most theologians of his or of many succeeding ages, it is natural that his explanation of the order of precedence among the passions should have been accepted. St Thomas (*Summa*, 1a:63:1:@4) carried it even further by an argument designed to show that pride could arise not only through ignorance but also through lack of due consideration, thus avoiding the equation of virtue and knowledge. With the coming of the modern age and its tendency to introspection, the Augustinian theory has been abandoned by many.

The patristic tradition that made envy the reason of the sin begins with Justin. Irenaeus (*adv. haer.* 5:26:3 H) cites an unknown work of Justin with approval for the idea that before the coming of Christ the devil had not blasphemed, but when he heard from Christ's teaching that eternal fire had been prepared for him and for all those who stood fast in their apostasy from God, then he broke out into blasphemies. This apostasy is described by Irenaeus as envy of mankind: 'The devil . . ., being envious of mankind, became a castaway from the divine law ; envy is indeed entirely foreign to the divine nature' (*adv. haer.* 5:24:4 H).[1] Cyprian (*De zelo et livore* 4 ; CSEL 3:421) and Gregory of Nyssa (*Oratio catechetica* 6 ; PG 44:456) both keep to envy as the cause of the sin, while Epiphanius (*haer.* 39:9 ; GCS 31:78) reports the suggestion that before the advent of Christ the devil had not blasphemed, but that when Christ 'rejected his conversion', he broke out into blasphemy.

St Thomas (*Summa*, 1a:63:2c) follows Augustine and Anselm in making the sin of the devil pride and envy. He reasons that for a spiritual creature there cannot be affection towards all sins, but only towards those that are spiritual, although the devils tempt men to all kinds of sin and thus incur the guilt of all those kinds. He finds great difficulty (op. cit., 3c) in accounting for the possibility in an angelic spirit of a sinful desire to be like unto God, and yet from Is 14:14 he inferred that such was the desire of the devil in sinning. The whole theology of analogy (*see* ANALOGY OF BEING, VI) cries out that assimilation to God is a good thing, and so the devil must have desired this out of due order.

St Thomas does not subscribe to the idea of a mystical body of the devil, an idea that has been urged by some modern French writers such as Bernanos. He says (*Summa*, 1a:114:3c) that the devil is the cause of all sins only indirectly and as their remote origin. One cannot make sinful action the exact counterpart of action under the influence of the grace of Christ. Men have sinful appetites and give way to them, even without the prompting of the devil, since they have free will. He uses great ingenuity in working out an angelic psychology

[1] Diabolus . . ., invidens homini, apostata a divina factus est lege; invidia enim aliena est a Deo.

to account for the instant character of the sin of many devils (*Quaestiones de malo* 16:4, and *Summa*, 1a:63:5c and 8c), but he is too near the time of the Albigenses to have any inclination towards making a parallel between good works done 'in Christ' and sins done with diabolic aid.

Suarez was more inclined to rest his theory on passages of Scripture (Ez 28:2 and Is 14:14) taken in a spiritual sense, than on the evidence of the Fathers, which he admits to be uncertain. Most of all he trusts to Jn 8:44, where he takes the words about being a murderer from the beginning to refer, not to the slaying of Abel, but to the primordial act of envy towards mankind which was the grudging of the hypostatic union. Naturally, this opinion proceeded on the assumption that the Scotists were right about the motive for the Incarnation (*see* INCARNATION), and therefore the criticism addressed to the theory by some modern theologians—that it supposes in the devil a desire of destroying his own existence—is quite misplaced. Only on a strictly Thomist view that the two natures in the one Person of Christ have an unique existence would this be a difficulty to the theory ; on the Scotist view there would be none.

From the much wider knowledge of the Fathers available to us than was at the disposal of Suarez it is possible to see that his theory fits better their accounts of the devil's envy than he himself realized. The patristic idea that repentance was open to the devil until the Incarnation had become a fact (or until man had been created) would also appear to be most consonant with this theory. Basil (if it be he) says (*hom.* on Is 14:19 ; PG 30:609): 'Perhaps there remained some chance of repentance even for the devil, before the creation of man. Even though the malady was of long standing, perhaps his pride could have been healed, had he taken himself in hand by means of penance, and then he would have been restored to his pristine condition. But after the creation of the world and the planting of Paradise, with man dwelling in it, and God's command, and the devil's jealousy, and the slaying of the one whom God had honoured, then all chance of repentance was barred to him '.

The very frequency with which, in retreats based on the *Spiritual Exercises* of St Ignatius, appeal has been made to the Suarezian theory, has made it a common opinion among theologians, though St Ignatius himself (whose text was fully worked out before 1552) does not appeal to it directly. One may cite a passage from the *Notebooks* of G. M. Hopkins SJ as an example of a very skilful use of the theory: 'Being required to adore God and enter into a covenant of justice with Him, (the devil) did so indeed, but, as a chorister who learns by use in the church itself the strength and beauty of his voice, he became aware in his very note of adoration of the riches of his nature ; then when from that first note he should have gone on with the sacrificial service, prolonging the first note instead, and ravished by his own sweetness and dazzled, the prophet says, by his beauty, he was involved in spiritual sloth and spiritual luxury and vain-glory ; to heighten this he summoned a train of spirits to be his choir, and, contemptuously breaking with the service of the eucharistic sacrifice, which was to have a victim of earthly nature and of flesh, to raise a hymn in honour of their own nature, spiritual purely and ascending, he must have persuaded them, to the divine ; and with this sin of pride aspiring to godhead their crime was consummated ' (*Devotional Writings*, 179–80).

Bibliography. F. Suarez SJ, *De angelis* (printed in vol. II of his *Opera*, 1856) ; G. Papini, *Il diavolo* (1954) ; various, *Satan* (a symposium of the *Études carmélitaines*, translated with some omissions and reinforcements, 1951) ; St Anselm, *De casu diaboli* (in PL 158) ; Palladius, *The Book of Paradise* (translated by E. A. Wallis Budge, 1904) ; J. Laver, *The First Decadent: J.-K. Huysmans* (1951) ; G. M. Hopkins SJ, *Sermons and Devotional Writings* (1959) ; J. de Tonquédec SJ, *Les Maladies nerveuses et les manifestations diaboliques* (1938) ; D. J. Saunders SJ, ' The Devil and the Divinity of Christ ', in TS 9 (1948) 536–53 ; L. M. Estibalez SJ, *Discernimiento de Espiritus* (1960).   J. H. C.

DEVOTIO MODERNA The New Devotion which spread over western Europe from Holland at the close of the 14th cent. was important theologically less for the new propositions which it put forth than for the spirit which it sought to infuse into the lives of theologians themselves. After a brief outline of the principal features of the movement (I), there will be an assessment (II) of its theological importance in its own day and (III) an indication of some of its theological consequences.

I The Devotio moderna begins with the ' conversion ' of Gerard Groote (1340–84) in 1374 ; after this he had ten years of apostolate, though he was never more than a deacon, and in his preaching of a devout life lived in common with much reading of the Scripture and meditation of the Passion of Christ, he is able to influence Gerard of Zutphen (1367–98) and through him Thomas à Kempis (1380–1471). Florence Radewijns (c.1350–1400), a priest of Deventer, was his associate and the founder of the Windesheim community in 1387. Groote's turning away from the cult of solitude, urged on him by Ruysbroeck, seems to have set the new movement going in an anti-mystical direction. It had little to do with Scholasticism, the Canon Law, the liturgy or the hierarchy of the Church, but concentrated on deepening the spiritual life of the individual, chiefly with the help of Augustinian materials. The gathering together of a community was thought of as the making of a *civitas Dei*, as if one could take literally what Augustine had written; the *Soliloquia* attributed to Augustine were in common use, and the letters of Groote are full of citations from Augustine. On the other hand, in a sermon *De nativitate Christi* he attacks St Thomas, though without naming him.

Those who lived in common were to practise poverty, though not at first under vow ; they often kept a dormitory or hostel for students and sometimes taught in schools themselves ; they compiled devout anthologies from their reading (and these, under the name of *rapiaria*, form the principal literary memorial of the movement) ; they copied out the Scriptures, and later they engaged in printing. Though not humanists at the outset, they soon welcomed the current of Italian humanism when it reached them, and Erasmus owed as much to them as he ever did to Valla.

Some of the aims of the movement are not so far removed from what Protestant reformers would later demand ; the opposition to monks and friars who lived under vow, the preaching against clerical extravagance, the reading of the Scriptures in Dutch and the practice of confessing their sins to each other (which the brethren followed according to Jas 5:16) are all signs of what is to come in the 16th cent., but there are also wide differences. The career of John Standonck shows this clearly ; he acquired the spirit of the movement at Gouda and then reformed the Collège Montaigu at Paris which was to shelter in quick succession St Ignatius and Calvin. The activity of Windesheim in reforming and calling back to their true estate so many convents and monasteries in Flanders, the Rhineland and Burgundy, before the days of Luther, is also a proof of this difference. The household of St Thomas More owed something to the movement, and Margaret Clement (daughter of the Margaret Giggs whom More had adopted) became in 1609 the first Superior of St Monica's, Louvain, which was an offshoot of the famous Windesheim foundation there known as St Ursula's. Radewijns was called ' the pope of the Lollards of Deventer ' and there are some resemblances between these and the brethren (*see* LOLLARDS). Wessel Gansfort (1419–89), whose interests may be judged from the titles of some of his lost works (*Libellus pro Nominalibus, De triduo Christi in sepulcro, Liber de futuro saeculo*), was a pioneer in spreading ideas about the priesthood of all men (which he exalted above the sacramental priesthood) but he is wrongly credited by some with a preference for *Scriptura sola* (cf. H. Oberman, *The Harvest of Medieval Theology*, 408–12) and claimed as a father of the Reformation. The very first words of his treatise on the Eucharist declare that during Mass one should neither read nor pray but simply keep in mind the Passion of Christ. Gansfort was not original in saying this, for in the *Lives of the Brethren*, one of them, John Ketel, in the rules he drew up for himself, makes exactly this prescription. Luther, when he came to know the works of Gansfort (about 1520), said that if he had known them earlier he would have been open to a charge of plagiarism. This rhetorical outburst won for Gansfort a place on the Index of Prohibited Books, but it need not be taken as literally true.

II The chief theological ideas of the *Devotio* may be counted as five, though it is not claimed that the Brethren subscribed to a creed which emphasized these ideas. The first is that of Christocentric devotion, manifested in the work which above all others gave the movement its lasting influence, the *Imitation of Christ*. (The controversies about its authorship do not enter into this judgment, but one must recall that by many in the 16th cent. it was held to be the work of Gerson.) Devotion of this kind tended to turn theological investigation away from Trinitarian subjects and in particular from the work of the Holy Spirit. It also, as has been noted above in the case of Gansfort, led to a neglect of the liturgy in favour of methods of meditating on the Passion during Mass. The second idea that is prominent is the giving of the primacy to will over intellect. The moral philosophy of the Ancients was the only thing that the Brethren wanted to take over ; the *Ethics* of Aristotle was the one work of pagan antiquity which Groote cherished. The activism of the movement was a consequence of the acceptance of this primacy, and one notices in the *Spiritual Exercises* of St Ignatius the remark that, ' in acts of the will, when we speak vocally or mentally with God . . ., there is required greater reverence than when we use the intellect '. This greater attention to the will led to the later 16th-cent. controversies about the relation of the will to grace (*De auxiliis gratiae*), and Molina could fairly say that he was asking questions that were new and that had not been posed by Augustine or Aquinas.

On the negative side there was in the movement a lack of interest in the mystery of the Church which went with its greater concern for the individual. Dean Colet (who may have been touched by the movement) wrote on the Mystical Body, but after his day the stress of controversy with the Reformers about the visible nature of the Church precluded devout speculation on the mystery of the Church, even had there been the inclination towards it. There was also, as noted above, the anti-mystical trend. Ruysbroeck may have spoken ' heavenly secrets ' to Groote when they met, but the chronicle goes on to say that Groote did not understand him. The influence of this tendency on the theology of the times was to encourage the cult of tidiness of ideas, as if a Dutch interior was being arranged by the artist in theology.

Stress on the individual undoubtedly led to developments in the theology of conscience (*see* CONSCIENCE). Debates at Trent about personal assurance of salvation (D 802) were not ended by the condemnation there of Lutheran excess in the matter, and not all theologians were content to accept the compromise which Cardinal Pole had learnt from Gentian Hervé (it was known to St Ignatius too) and which was to ' pray as if all depended on God and to work as if all depended on ourselves '.

III The theological consequences of the *Devotio* are harder to assess. The activism led very soon to an attack on the doctrine of Indulgences by Gansfort, who made himself notorious for this in Paris and in Rome long before Luther (*see* INDULGENCES). There is an apparent paradox in the fact that men like Gerson and Gabriel Biel should be so indebted to the *Devotio* (Biel was for many years head of the Brethren at Butzbach). Polemic against *genera* and *species* (as found in the *Imitation*) seems to have been aimed more at the Scotists than the Nominalists ;

the latter, with their veneration for the *potentia Dei absoluta*, were, in spite of all their distinctions, welcomed by Gerson, who wanted to exalt an acquired contemplation in which the will of man is freely united with that of God, while rejecting the mysticism of Eckhart and Ruysbroeck wherein man and God are conjoined in an essential union of being.

When Suarez (*Opera* XVI:1019) came to defend the doctrine of the *Exercitia spiritualia* of St Ignatius, he had to address himself to the passage cited above about the greater reverence which should belong to the acts of the will. St Thomas had held that prayer was rather the work of the intellect than of the will, but Suarez counters this by making a distinction on the lines of Newman's famous one of notional and real assents : ' If the work of the mind on divine matters is merely speculative, it does not excite the affections nor does it deal with God as with a person, but only as an object of speculation, and in such a task reverence is not so necessary and not ordinarily produced to such an extent '. The undoubtedly infused contemplation manifested in the life of Ignatius (cf. J. de Guibert, *La Spiritualité de la compagnie de Jésus*, 33–50) did not debar him from indicating a parallel if lower way to others, while at the same time his great devotion to the Church (cf. H. Rahner, ' Esprit et Église ', in *Christus* 5 [1958] 163–84) kept him from the extravagances of Eckhart.

The eucharistic theology of the movement is hard to seek and the *Expositio canonis missae* of Biel can hardly be taken as representative of the whole movement. The Brethren were to communicate about twenty-five times a year, according to one set of rules for their observance, and at other times of the year the kissing of the pax-brede when it was brought round the congregation at Mass was held to constitute an act of spiritual communion. The originality of the teaching of St Ignatius on frequent communion is plain here. Biel made it clear that he did not regard the sacrifice of the Mass as renewing the physical sufferings of Christ *in poenam* but only as a representation of them to win God's pity ; modern strictures on the eucharistic theology of the later Middle Ages seem therefore ill-directed. The inculcation of meditation on the Passion at Mass was precisely to stress the representational character of the sacrifice.

That Erasmus and Ignatius could both be in some ways indebted to the *Devotio*, though opposed to one another, shows how lacking in precise tenets the movement was. If one were to take the axiom *Facienti quod in se est Deus non denegat gratiam* (God does not refuse grace to one who does his best), one might find that the general optimism of outlook that goes with such an axiom was foreign to the movement as a whole, yet the axiom was certainly held by Biel and by all the early Jesuits, though it was not welcome to Erasmus, any more than it was to Luther. The Christian humanist could look upon Vergil as one who ' had done his best ', but a sense of impending doom and of the frailty of human nature is more characteristic of the movement as a whole. St Thomas More asked Erasmus to do something against

Luther, and in his reply (*Ep.* VII:8, of 1527) Erasmus said: 'If I treat the matter (of grace and free-will) according to the mind of the monks and theologians, who allow too much scope to human merits . . ., I shall certainly speak against my conscience'.

The *Theologia Germanica* of Bp. Berthold of Chiemsee (1528 and 1531) was written against Luther and had a considerable influence, but the view it put forward of human free-will was not very different from his. Berthold says (*c.*37) that we can will what is good but, since the Fall, we cannot by our will alone bring this velleity to execution. God supplies His grace to preserve our freedom.[1] This would be to write off all the virtues of the pagans as so many vicious acts, as Biel and others had already seen. By appearing in both Latin and German Berthold's work spread widely the somewhat melancholy outlook on human destiny which has been noted as characteristic of one wing of the movement.

The links between Holland and Britain in those times were strong, and both countries had their Lollards. Yet the *Devotio* does not seem to have exercised an immediate influence in England. Walter Hilton's writings show more favour to the mystics than would have been welcomed in Holland, and Margery Kempe does not seem to have been interested in the Brethren, for all her voyaging in 'Dewtcheland'. She heard Dutch sermons but did not understand them. W. Atkinson translated the *Imitation* into English (1502), at least the first three Books, while the translation of Book IV was done by Lady Margaret. Another translation was made by Richard Whytford (1530), who also translated *The Golden Epystel of S. Barnard* (a favourite of the movement, and not really by St Bernard but by William of St Thierry). His other works of devotion (*Fruyte of Redempcyon*, *Preparacion unto Houselynge*) are in the same spirit. Protestantism later took over the *Imitation* (with omissions) pleading that the 'Auctor, howsoever living in a Popish time, was yet in hart no Papist'. Cranmer worked through Erasmus on the Psalms, making his own annotations as he went, while on the scaffold Thomas Cromwell recited the prayer Erasmus had composed 'for a time of serious illness'.

The *Devotio moderna* could never by itself have led into the devout humanism of the 17th cent. and the Baroque age (see BAROQUE IV *and* V), if there had not been added to it the elements supplied by St Ignatius, love of the Church, freedom from a gloomy view of human nature and a greater readiness to give scope to the mystics, all of which can be found in the *Spiritual Exercises*. St Francis Borgia, who produced the first book of meditations on the gospels of the *Temporale* and *Sanctorale* of the Missal (1563-6) was doing something that would never have entered into the minds of the Brethren. St Francis of Sales, with his remarkable balance, was a great antidote to the gloom of the *Devotio*, and he set his personal stamp on devout humanism in France.

---

[1] Velle possumus bonum . . ., sed pro nostra voluntate exequi nequimus. Praesumendum est: Deus pie porrigat homini gratiam qua suum liberum arbitrium bene conservet.

Bibliography. W. Mulder SJ, *Gerardi magni epistulae* (1933) ; A. Hyma, *The Christian Renaissance* (1924) ; the same, *The Brethren of the Common Life* (1930) ; P. Debongnie, 'Dévotion moderne', in D Sp (1957) ; the same, 'Les Thèmes de l'Imitation', in RHE 36 (1940) 289-344 ; *H. A. Oberman, *The Harvest of Medieval Theology* (1963) ; *Helen C. White, *The Tudor Books of Private Devotion* (1951) ; the same, *The Metaphysical Poets* (1956) ; A. Renaudet, *Préréforme et Humanisme à Paris 1494-1517* (1916) ; *W. Miller and J. Scudder, *Wessel Gansfort: Life and Writings* (2 vols., 1917) ; A. Codina SJ, *Los Origenes de los ejercicios espirituales* (1926) ; *E. F. Jacob, 'Groote and the Beginnings of the New Devotion', in JEH 3 (1952) 40-57 ; J. Huijben and P. Debongnie, *L'Auteur ou les Auteurs de l'Imitation* (1957) ; D. Knowles, *The Religious Orders in England* III (1959) ; M. Muller, *St Francis de Sales* (1936).

J. H. C.

DIVORCE In its proper sense, divorce is the dissolution of a true marriage bond and includes separation from bed and board, with the right to remarry. It was recognized as a legitimate practice by almost all ancient peoples ; and it is given legal sanction, though limited with safeguards particularly in favour of the woman, in the 17th-cent. Code of Hamurrabi (art. 137-42). It will be dealt with here in its Christian context as found (I) among the Hebrews, (II) in the early Church, (III) among Oriental Christians, and (IV) modern Catholic thought.

I Among the Hebrews, divorce was a legitimate practice and is taken for granted in the OT. The law in Deut 24:1-4 prohibits a woman divorced by her husband from returning to live with him if she has had relations with another. The passage mentions as grounds 'something shameful' (*'erwah dābār*) in a wife and gave later rabbis, as well as Christian exegetes, opportunity to dispute its meaning. It also speaks of a 'bill of divorce' (*sēfer K'erītūt*: document of cutting off) which a woman had to show as proof of freedom to marry another (cited also in Is 50:1 ; Jer 3:8) and was probably worded according to Osee: 'She is not my wife ; I am not her husband' (2:4). A high priest could not marry a divorcee (Lev 21:7, 14 ; Ez 44:22) ; and a woman could not divorce her husband, but she could leave him (Jg 19:2-10). But divorce is called an evil in Mal (2:14 ff.) and Sir (42:9), yet the last urges a man to divorce an unfaithful wife (25: 25).

In both Greece and Rome divorce was legitimate for both husband and wife, by mutual consent as well as by repudiation, and laws were gradually introduced to protect the rights of a woman dismissed for reasons other than adultery.

II In the NT, Jesus condemned divorce in decisive terms (Mk 10:2-12 ; Lk 16:18) and this absolute prohibition is reflected in St Paul (1 Cor 7:10 f, 39). However in Mt. 5:32 Christ forbids divorce 'except for somethin gshameful' (*mè 'epí porneìa*) usually interpreted as fornication, and in 19:9 'apart from the matter of something shameful' (*parektos logou porneías*). Most Greek and some Latin fathers interpreted this passage to mean that Christ made an exception and allowed divorce for adultery on the part of the wife—an interpretation accepted in practice by most Orthodox and Protestant churches. Some exegetes, starting with Lowther Clarke in 1929 (*see* Bibliography), prefer to take *porneia* in the technical and rabbinical sense of marriage within the forbidden degrees of Lev 18:11-15. The exceptive clause can then be taken to mean that the breaking of such 'incestuous' marriages is not against the general prohibition of divorce, and its insertion into the Matthaean text might be variously explained. Ac 15:21, 29 probably records a prohibition of such marriages by the Council at Jerusalem, but there is no sign that the conciliar decree was retroactive. 1 Cor 5:1-5 is not much help, as the union there was one that even pagans would repudiate.

In the early Church, Hermas (*Mandate* 4:1, 5 f.; GCS 48:26) and Tertullian (*adv. Marcion* 4:34 ; CSEL 47:534-5) accept the Matthean pericope as a command that a husband repudiate an adulterous wife. Justin (*append.* 2:2) allows a Christian wife to repudiate a pagan spouse. Basil (*Ep.* 188:9 ; 217:77 ; PG 32:677, 804) takes for tolerable the custom that a husband can divorce an adulterous wife, but not *vice versa*. Asterius of Amasea praises the husband who repudiates an adulteress (*homil.* 5 in Mt 19:9 ; PG 40:237) as does Theodoret of Cyr (*Graecarum affectionum curatio* 9 ; PG 83:1053), while Clement of Alexandria (*Strom.* 2:23:145 ; GCS 52:143) and Origen (*Commentarius in Mt* 19:9 ; GCS 40:341) admit that some bishops permitted a second marriage after divorce to prevent greater evils, even though it was against the Scriptures. Epiphanius (*adv. haer.* 59:4,9 ; GCS 31:369), though he repudiates divorce, seems to tolerate remarriage in certain extreme situations.

In the West, Ambrosiaster (on 1 Cor 7:10 ; PL 17:218) permits a second marriage to a man divorced from an adulterous wife, but not to the woman, even if separated from an adulterer, apostate or profligate ; but Ambrose, recognizing the difference between divine and secular law (*in Lc* 8:5 ; CSEL 32:394), says: ' You repudiate your wife *quasi iure*, and think it *licit* because human law does not prohibit it ; but divine law forbids it '. The same attitude is taken by Chromatius of Aquileia (*Tract. in Mt* 10 ; PL 20:351). Even so absolute a moralist as St Jerome attempted to attenuate the guilt of Fabiola who had remarried after separating from a profligate first husband (*epist.* 77:3 ; CSEL 55:38) ; but while admitting that the abuse of divorce was widespread among Christians, he testifies to the indissolubility of the marriage bond: ' *Volumus, nolumus, sustinenda est* ' (in Mt 3 ; PL 26:281), signifying that no matter what her faults, a wife is to be retained. She may be put away for adultery, but remarriage is not permitted, not even for a wife whose husband is imprisoned (*vita Malchi* 6 ; PL 23:56).

It was only gradually, however, that the Church broke with the civil law, both Roman and barbarian. Even the Christian emperors could not change ingrained custom although they did attempt to limit divorce. Constantine recognized the legitimacy of divorce for a free spouse whose husband was reduced to slavery, or a homicide, magician or ghoul ; and for the husband whose wife was an adulteress, procuress or who practised evil medical arts (*Cod. Theod.* 3, tit. 16). Although Justinian forbade, Justin II had to recognize the legitimacy of divorce by mutual consent, contenting himself with tightening the limiting legislation. In the codification of the barbarian laws, the Burgundians, Visigoths, Bavarians, etc. retained the basic right to divorce for incompatibility, vice, or simple antipathy, while injecting safeguards for the injured party.

It is with Augustine that the theological foundation for the indissolubility of marriage is clearly elucidated. At first he was inclined to permit marriage after the divorce of an adulteress (*De sermone Domini* 1:45 ; PL 34:1252 ; cf. *Retract* 1:18:9 ; CSEL 36:92) considering it an excusable fault (*De adulterinis coniugiis* 1:25 ; PL 40: 469 ; *De fide et op.* 19 ; PL 40:221). In consideration of Eph 5:25-33, however, he finally insists upon the sacramental character of marriage which, he maintains, renders it indissoluble (*De Gen. ad litteram* 9:7 ; CSEL 28:275).

In the early synodical law, no permission to remarry after divorce is discernible. The Council of Elvira (A.D. 304) forbids a Christian woman remarried after divorce to be given communion before the death of her original partner, except on her deathbed (can. 9) ; and Arles refuses the right to remarry, to a man after divorce (can. 10), while Carthage XI commands penitential discipline for the man or woman who remarries after divorce (can. 8). Pope Innocent I, following the *Apostolic Canons* (48), allows absolution only after the death of a divorced partner (*Ep.* 2:15), and Leo I (*Ep. ad Nicetam Aq.*) prescribes that if a woman has taken a second husband after the disappearance of her husband in captivity, she must return to her first husband if he reappears and desires her. Gregory I insisted that although the civil law permitted a married person to divorce an unwilling spouse in order to enter a monastery, this was in conflict with the law of God (*Epist* lib. 6, 48 ; lib. 11, 45 and 50).

In the synodal legislation from the 5th to the 9th cent., two currents are discernible: one attempts to compromise with civil legislation such as the Synods of Verberie (A.D. 756) and Compiègne (A.D. 757) ; the other affirming the indissolubility of marriage. In general likewise the Penitentials support the prohibition of divorce, and those that seem to tolerate it are challenged as inauthentic, e.g. by the Synod of Paris in A.D. 829. The decision attributed to Pope Gregory II making divorce licit for post-marital impotence (MGH, *Epist* III:276:3) was interpreted by medieval canonists to refer to a *ratum non consummatum* marriage, since in other rescripts Gregory insisted on indissolubility (MGH,

Epist III:453), as did his successors Zachary, Stephen II and John VIII. This is the stand of the Carolingian theologians such as Hincmar of Rheims and the Pseudo-Isidore, and of the 11th-cent. Gregorian Reform. One of the last opponents of indissolubility is found in the canonical treatise *Exceptiones Petri* of 1110–20 (I:37) but with the Scholastics the doctrine repudiating divorce for *ratum et consummatum* marriage is certain. Both the Council of Trent (Sess. xxiv, can. 5 and 7), the Code of Canon Law (1016 ; 1961), and recent popes have confirmed this position.

III The Byzantine Church, generally speaking, followed the Justinian legislation legitimizing divorce for high treason, criminal attacks on the life of a spouse, frivolous wifely conduct, intentional abortion, prolonged disappearance, incurable lunacy, entrance into a monastery, impotence (Novel 22 and 117), but abolishing divorce by mutual consent. Justin II repealed the latter injunction, and the Council in Trullo of 692 restored it (can. 87) while accepting most of the Justinian legislation. This is also the case with the *Nomocanon in xiv titles* which since the 10th cent. has been recognized as the authoritative law of the Church. In the thirteenth century Bishop Demetrius Chomatianus of Bulgaria denied that the law of indissolubility proclaimed by Christ was meant for the Christian Church ; and at the close of the Council of Florence, when questioned by Pope Eugene IV regarding the practice of divorce in the Byzantine Church, the Emperor suggested that, with a doctrinal union finally achieved, it would be best to leave that problem to the future. Current practice in the Orthodox Churches varies, but an attempt has been made to limit divorce to cases of proven adultery by Macarius Bolgakov, Patriarch of Moscow (1879–82) ; and N. Milasch, in his *Ecclesiastical Law of the Oriental Churches* (1905), says that death alone—physical, moral or religious—can sever marriage.

In the Protestant Churches divorce is recognized as legitimate in keeping with the civil law, though some, such as the Anglican and Episcopalian, limit the right to remarriage to cases involving adultery.

IV Modern Catholic Theology. Earliest evidence for a Christian marriage ceremony is supplied by St Ignatius of Antioch: ' Let bride and groom effect their union with the consent of the bishop, so that their marriage will be godly ' (*ad Polyc.* 5:2), thus indicating the Church's acceptance of the Roman concept that *nuptias consensus non concubitus facit—* consent not cohabitation makes a marriage. However, as the primary end of marriage was considered to be the procreation and education of children, and grave difficulty could be raised about sincerity of consent, the performance of the conjugal act came to be considered proof absolute of the consummation of the marriage, and this was based on a literal interpretation of the scriptural texts that speak of husband and wife as ' two in one flesh ' which St Paul designated as a ' mystery in Christ and in the Church '. It is on this basis that, with St Augustine, indissolubility is claimed for a marriage *ratum* (with consent, legitimately given) and *consummatum* (perfected with the conjugal act).

In modern Catholic thought a sacramental marriage, *ratum et consummatum* between two Catholics, or two baptized persons, is considered indissoluble, although there are a few theologians who believe that the Pope's power to ' bind and loose ' gives him the right to dissolve even such a marriage. The Church likewise considers marriage between two non-baptized persons as indissoluble by the law of nature, to which, however, the Pope can make an exception ' in favour of the faith ' of the Catholic, usually a convert with whom the pagan partner will not live peaceably. This is known as the Pauline Privilege, several varieties of which have entered into Catholic practice more recently. As there is doubt among theologians regarding the sacramental character of a marriage entered into between a baptized person and a non-baptized person, such marriages likewise seem to come under the Pope's dispensing power.

While the Church does authorize separation from bed and board where cohabitation becomes impossible between a couple bound in a sacramental marriage, and will tolerate the obtaining of a civil divorce because of the civil effects involved, it denies the right of remarriage to either party, no matter what may have been the cause of the separation. Annulments obtained in ecclesiastical tribunals signify that, from the beginning, there was no true marriage, for lack of consent or some other impediment. Despite difficulties with worldly potentates down through the ages, from Lothaire and Constantine VI, through Henry IV and Philip Augustus, to Henry VIII and Napoleon I, the Church's doctrine and practice have been homogeneous: a sacramental marriage, entered upon with free and full consent and properly consummated, is indissoluble. The history of the Church is cluttered with annulments (declarations that no true marriage ever existed) and various privileges ' in favour of the faith ' (affecting non-sacramental marriages), but divorce in its strict sense has been repudiated as contrary to the law of Christ. However, in the solution of problems involving divorced persons desiring to make peace with Christ in the Church, the all-but-plenipotentiary power of the supreme pontiff is receiving greater attention, and legitimate ways are being sought to mitigate impossible marital situations with an eye to the spiritual well-being of the parties. The Church's teaching on divorce will likewise be a principal factor in the discussions dealing with ecumenism and the eventual reunification of the Christian churches.

Bibliography. A. Villien, DTC s.v. divorce 4, 1455–78 ; A. Lehmkuhl, in *Cath. Encyc.* 5, 54–64 ; G. H. Joyce, *Christian Marriage* (1933) ; L. Hartmann, ' Divorce ', in *Encyc. Dict. of the Bible* (1963) 580–5 ; G. Delling, ' Ehescheidung ', in *Realencyc. für Antike und Christentum* 4, 707–19 ; J. Douglas, *Church Quarterly Review* 123 (1936) 105–11 ; P. Gasparri, *Tractatus canonicus de matrimonio* (4th ed., 1932) ; *Codex Iuris Canonici*, canons 1016, 1961 ; J. M. T.

Barton, Napoleon's 'Divorce', in CR 43 (1958) 321–32 ; H. Thurston and G. H. Joyce sj, 'Did Pope Gregory II sanction bigamy ?', in Mn 157 (1931) 320–31 and 540–3 ; J. Dupont, *Mariage et Divorce dans l'Evangile* (1959) ; *W. Lowther Clarke and F. Gavin, *New Testament Problems* (1929) 59–64.

F. X. M.

DOCTRINE, DEVELOPMENT OF The subject will be treated in the following sections : (I) the state of the question, (II) the inseparability of change from the Church's earthly existence, (III) historical and psychological causes of new formulations of doctrine, (IV) the driving force behind this progress, namely the wish, not to change, but to retain and safeguard, (V) the fact of genuine progress in dogma, (VI) the gradual realization among Church leaders and theologians of the idea of development of doctrine, (VII) late scholastic theology concerning development of doctrine, (VIII) modern approaches to this question : (i) Newman ; (ii) Newman's notes of a genuine development ; (iii) present-day theories concerning development ; (iv) modern heterodox views on the subject, (IX) conclusion.

I The State of the Question. The existence of development in Christian doctrine has not always been recognized among Christians. Change of any kind seemed to be the antithesis of a final revelation. At all times the Church has protested against heresies that they were innovations on the pure Gospel, and she has always maintained that pure Gospel without alteration or adulteration. During the Reformation and post-Reformation periods, each side of the controversy tended to accuse the other of innovation. The Reformers declared that they were returning to the primitive gospel and purifying the Church of medieval corruptions ; while Catholics declared that the contrary was true : that Catholics had not changed, and that the Catholic doctrines of the 16th cent. were identical with those of the earliest centuries. As will be explained later, Catholics have for a long period come more and more to recognize the inevitableness of some development, and most of the discussion has been with regard to its manner and limits. The last century provoked some new complications, with the introduction into scientific thought of the notion of evolution. Newman's Sermon on Development (1843) and his *Essay* (1845) had preceded by some years Darwin's *Origin of Species* (1859) ; but the proximity of the dates led some people to suspect some connection. Such suspicions were expressed in the 19th cent. and especially in the early 20th cent. during the Modernist crisis. On the other hand, the persuasiveness of Newman's arguments, together with the immense advance of existential thinking and the growing influence of Newman, have ensured for the notion of doctrinal development permanent citizen-rights in Catholic theology.

II The Inseparability of Change from the Church on Earth. Newman wrote in his *Essay on the Development of Christian Doctrine* (ed. 1897 ; 40) : ' In a higher world it is otherwise, but here below to

live is to change, and to be perfect is to have changed often '. Those that are in the midst of the process of living are not immediately aware of the changes of which the purpose is to save and preserve. The Church from the beginning has been a great living community. It has at all times been keenly conscious of its life. It has known itself as the community loved and created by the Father, redeemed by the Son and indwelt by the Holy Spirit. From the beginning the members of this community have recognized that the Gospel by which they live, and which they proclaim to the world, is Jesus Christ, yesterday, today and for ever. They have wished to know nothing but Jesus Christ, and Him crucified. They have been conscious that they are of the family that had lived with the Word of God, whom they had seen with their eyes, and touched with their hands, whose eye-witnesses they had been as they passed on the words of life (cf. 1 Jn 1:1 ff.).

With Christianity a large body of truth has been ' poured about in all quarters of the world ' (Newman, *Discourses to Mixed Congregations*, ed. 1892 ; 174). The Apostles had preached this word as they passed from city to city fulfilling their mission to preach the Gospel of Christ to all the world. They had understood it as their duty to protect, preserve and declare the Word of Christ, to add nothing, to subtract nothing and to alter nothing. But how this would be done in each successive age, when languages and thought-forms began to change, no one had stopped to think. The Apostles could speak Aramaic to the Jews, and Greek to the Gentiles, and they could speak in concepts current in these civilizations. Yet even St Paul had felt the need to adapt himself to the Greeks at Athens. In doing this he did not feel that he was being unfaithful to the revelation which had come to him from Christ.

It probably never occurred to the Apostles to consider how far this process of adaptation, begun by St Paul, would develop. It would hardly have occurred to them to consider how far new modes of expression would become necessary in order to convey the old truths of the Gospel. Still less would it occur to them that the continual need to explain and to refute misunderstandings would lead, at least among the ordinary people, to a clearer grasp and understanding of many aspects of the original deposit. The need for continual articulation would lead Christians to recognize that they already held a great deal more by implication than the first words of revelation might suggest. The process of explanation and adaptation thus beginning would be rightly called ' development ', in its root meaning of ' unwrapping ', ' unfolding ', ' bringing to light ' aspects of the Gospel which had not been adequately and for all time expressed in the earliest form of words.

The saving truth of Christianity is conveyed, not in a textbook or catechism, but first in a series of spoken sermons and addresses, and later in the literature of the Bible. It was at an early stage, but still one step removed from the earliest preaching, that the most basic truths came to be formulated and expressed in a creed. The early creeds were the simplest forms of what later came to be called developments (see CREEDS).

III The historical and psychological causes that provoked new formulations. One of the factors has already been mentioned, i.e. the desire to give Christian converts a short summary of the principal truths of the faith in the form of a creed. Even to do this involved judgments of relative importance, and also certain simplifications and clarifications which 'unfolded', as it were, for the simple faithful the central and vital doctrines of the Gospel.

A second factor was the need to protect the original message against heretical and erroneous interpretations. This was the chief factor at work during the early centuries when Sabellians, Modalists, Arians, Pelagians and others gave forth their corruptions of the Gospel as the true teachings of Christ. To answer them, many doctrines which had been stated only obscurely or with insufficient explicitness had to be openly and clearly defined. This is what happened at the four great councils of the 4th and 5th cents. The first critical test-case of development, as we now see, was the struggle over ὁμοούσιος and ὑπόστασις. The conciliar decisions came to be the key to Scripture and Tradition, not seen as additions or alterations to the earliest revealed expression of the Word of God, but as true and clear interpretations of their real meaning. They used different words from those used by the Apostles, since they wrote at a different time, and in a different environment, and with a different immediate purpose. But, though the words were different, these 'new' definitions were such that the Church has always believed that the Apostles would be the first to approve of them, and say: 'Yes, that is our meaning.' Not that these new definitions would be in any way complete or final. They were formulated for a definite limited purpose, and that purpose did not include any attempt, as if such were possible, to make a complete and final statement of the whole doctrine. They would, however, be final in the sense that they would always remain true as far as they went. But no one has ever expressed, nor ever will express, in human words, all that is included in the doctrine of the Incarnation or in that of the Trinity. The conciliar definitions and creeds might be called minimal statements of what every Christian should believe.

When these creeds were formulated, it was never thought that any particular development was involved. The Council Fathers would have been horrified at the thought that they were introducing new doctrines. They would have declared that they were simply saying what the Scriptures had said in clear, succinct language. If they had been blamed, as they sometimes were, for going beyond the Scriptures, they would have protested that they had been forced into it by the obstinacy of heretics.

After the age of the great heresies a third factor began to be dominant. This was the rise of scholastic theology. Formal theology and controversy did not invariably lead to stalemate. Points that remain controverted have no chance, of course, of being defined. But, in many cases, particularly in sacramental theology, agreement was reached. In such cases as the definition and number of the seven sacraments, this was almost exclusively due to theological discussion. In other cases, as in that of transubstantiation, the eventual definition had been provoked both by a desire to preserve the truth against error and by the development of theology.

A final factor, operating at all periods of history, was the process of long, maturing contemplation of the figures, events or words of revelation. In the case of Marian devotion, for instance, Newman spoke of 'the inquirer into heavenly truths' dwelling 'in the cell and the oratory, pouring forth his heart in prayer, collecting his thoughts in meditation, dwelling on the idea of Jesus, or of Mary, or of grace, or of eternity, and pondering the words of holy men who have gone before him, until before his mental sight arises the hidden wisdom of the perfect' (Newman, *Discourses to Mixed Congregations*, ed. 1892 ; 343). This has in more recent times been classified under the term 'consent of faith', or 'consent of the faithful', or 'sense of faith'. Whereas, in the other types of development, it is the theologian who goes before the ordinary faithful, in this it is more often the ordinary devout Christian who has preceded the theologizing of the men of learning. The theologians tend rather to put a brake on the advance of the doctrine. This is how doctrines held commonly by the faithful over many centuries, as, e.g. the Assumption, may be among the last to be proclaimed by definition as part of the original revelation.

IV The driving force behind this progress has been the urge to safeguard. It cannot be too strongly emphasized that, throughout the process of development, the driving force has been the urge to preserve, to keep pure and uncontaminated, the original deposit. Early councils showed this by prefixing to their definitions some such expression as *Credimus*, with the meaning : 'This is our Catholic Faith.' The implication has always been that they were referring, not to a new faith, but to the faith which had always been. Hence the meaning was never, 'Henceforth we shall believe this' but 'This is the faith of the Church, part of our Christian faith from the beginning'. The Council of Trent declared that it was expounding the true and ancient doctrine concerning faith and the sacraments. Elsewhere it declared that the doctrine it was defining was that which the Catholic Church had been taught by Jesus Christ Himself and His Apostles, which she had learnt from the Holy Spirit, and had kept intact, to preserve it until the end of the world. Pius IX, speaking of the Immaculate Conception, said it was revealed by God, and so to be believed firmly by the faithful. Even where Pius XII allows a certain growth, he says it is only a growth into an understanding of what was already revealed.

From this it is clear that the Church's 'developments' have always had it as their purpose to enable Christians of a later time to understand clearly what was revealed at the beginning. It is not a new revelation but only a new emphasis or clarification. In every age the Church's first wish is to remain true to herself, and true to the revealed body of truth entrusted to her keeping, which is to be her faith and life. To do this she must spell out this revelation to every age, and in answer to every attack or misunderstanding. The expression of a truth which is suitable in one age may not be best adapted for people of another. The need for new modes of expression in answer to new needs will lead to a deeper subjective understanding of the ancient truth. Such clearer or deeper expressions of a truth are not new truths, nor are they new knowledge, except in the sense that they enable us to understand and state more clearly what was already implicitly understood and imperfectly expressed. The new expressions do not make the older ones untrue. They are merely more articulate for a different age. One is reminded of a man trying to make his meaning clear by multiplying the explanations. From beginning to end he knows more than he is at any one moment able to express. The result of his efforts is both to enable others to understand his view, and progressively to clarify his own knowledge for himself.

V The Fact of Genuine Progress in Dogma. It has sometimes been stated that there is no development in doctrine in the Christian Church, that apparent developments have been no more than convenient new formulations of what had all along been explicitly held. The Anglican Bishop Bull, in opposition to Petau, and later some 19th-cent. Anglicans in opposition to Newman, contended that the 4th-cent. conciliar definitions constituted no progress on the doctrines of the ante-Nicene Church. At the most, it was contended, they put the earlier explicit doctrines into a new technical language. It was argued by J. B. Mozley (*The Theory of Development*, 1878) that Newman had exaggerated the unorthodoxy and unclearness of much of ante-Nicene theology in order to create for himself a case for development in the early centuries and so prepare his reader to accept the later additions of Rome. Many Catholics have adopted the same position, contending that so-called Roman 'additions' were neither additions nor developments, but that they had been explicitly held in the Church from the beginning. This seems to have been the position of Bossuet, and even today it is defended by some Catholics. Those who hold this view must maintain that even extreme cases of apparent development, like papal infallibility and the two modern Marian definitions, are no more than new statements of what was held explicitly in the oral tradition from the beginning.

As will be explained more fully later in this article, Newman went to the other extreme, and believed that there is some degree of development involved in every doctrine definition and in every new credal formulation. This is the view here defended.

So, for instance, the 4th-cent. credal statements concerning Christ's true Godhead were developments. Such included the statement that He is true

God, consubstantial with the Father, equal to the Father, God of God and Light of Light and eternal creator of the world. These are all interpretations of the words of Scripture, in harmony with the ancient living Tradition. They are expressions in human words chosen from the language of the early centuries to convey certain aspects or necessary implications of the original revealed message.

Similarly there were developments regarding the Word's human nature, that it was distinct from, and unconfounded with, the divine nature, and that it was identical with our own human nature in all except sin. It was also a development when it was declared that He had no human person, but that the eternal Person of the Son of God existed and acted as Person in the human body assumed from the Virgin. It was likewise declared that He had a human soul and will. Nevertheless there was only one Person, with two natures hypostatically united.

There were developments in the early centuries regarding justification, grace and original sin. The greater part of the Church's explicit doctrine in opposition to Pelagianism was a comparatively late development. Though based on Scripture, in the light of Tradition, the developed teaching on grace and original sin is not found expressed clearly during the first three centuries.

A good example of the fact of development is perhaps specifically the doctrine of Original sin. This doctrine, accepted by most Christian denominations, is not easily found on the face of Scripture or early Christian writings. Traditionally it is connected with the fall of our first parents ; yet there is not a great deal from which the doctrine could be deduced in the Genesis account of the first human beings. Death and suffering do indeed appear as the punishment of sin, but it is not clearly stated that the whole race is involved in this sin. Wis (1:13 ; 2:24) states that death came into the world through the envy of the devil. Ecclus (25:33) blames women for the origin of sin and the consequent universal mortality.

Apart from a few passages laying the blame for death on our first parents, there are several passages which insinuate that, after Adam has set the example, man's heart has turned aside to every manner of sin. However, some men, like Noe, appear as just men, without the suggestion that they too had been at one time contaminated. The notion of inherited guilt comes into the Book of Thanksgiving Songs and the *Mishna*.

In addition there are a host of passages emphasizing the universality of sin, without giving any explanation. Yet some of these passages, e.g. those from Job, including sometimes the angels, appear to prove too much, since they seem to assert the unworthiness of every creature merely through being a creature. On the other hand the Lord's Prayer tells everyone to pray for forgiveness of sin. The redemption is spoken of as universal, and baptism is laid down as a necessary condition for salvation. On the basis of such texts we see a gradual development of the doctrine of Original sin. The 2nd-cent. Fathers see death and corruption, in which everyone is involved, as the result of sin. St Irenaeus and many Greek Fathers understand that we all lost something in Adam, e.g. the image of God, the Word of God, the full likeness to God, the Spirit. From the 3rd cent. baptism comes to be especially associated with the washing away of a state of sin.

The final development of the doctrine is more or less reached with St Augustine and the Councils which, under his influence, condemned Pelagianism. There is still further development of theology, but little further progress in defined doctrine.

Another clear example of a development, this time of a doctrine much less explicit in its Scripture origins, is that of the doctrine of the state of the disembodied soul after death until the resurrection of the body.

To these random examples of doctrinal development we must clearly add the papal and Marian doctrines defined during the 19th and 20th cents.

VI The gradual realization of the idea of development in doctrine. Some realization of the principle is already apparent in St Irenaeus's defence of Christianity against the Gnostics. Where the Gnostics claimed that their new teachings were faithful interpretations of the Gospel, St Irenaeus appealed, not solely to the letter of the Scriptures, but to the traditional understanding of its meaning, as found in the ancient sees of Christendom. He thereby unconsciously admitted that a 2nd-cent. explanation could be the best and most faithful statement of the original doctrine underlying the Scripture text. If he had not implicitly accepted the principle of development, his only refutation of heresy would have been the letter of Scripture.

A more explicit recognition of the principle of development is found in the sermons of St Gregory of Nazianzus (*Or.* 31:26 ; PG 36:161), where he asserts that, whereas the OT proclaimed the Father clearly and the Son obscurely, the NT proclaimed the Son clearly and the Spirit obscurely. ' Now the Spirit dwells among us, and gives us a clearer demonstration of Himself.' St Gregory, however, fails to distinguish between development by new revelation (OT to NT) and development by explanation.

A still clearer advance in the understanding of development is found in the *Commonitorium* of St Vincent of Lerins. Paradoxically it occurs in the same tract in which he elaborates his celebrated dictum that the test of Christian truth is its unchangeableness : ' In the Catholic Church itself great care must be exercised that our faith should be that which has been held always, everywhere and by all ' [1] (*Commonitorium* 2:3, in Moxon's edition, 10). He himself asked the question : ' Perhaps someone will say : Is there then no growth of religion in the Church of Christ ? ' He answered : ' Yes, but so that it be a true growth of faith, and not a change. For it is characteristic of change that it is a transfor-

[1] In ipsa item catholica ecclesia magnopere curandum est ut id teneamus, quod ubique, quod semper, quod ab omnibus creditum est.

mation from one thing to another. Let then the understanding, knowledge, and wisdom whether of individuals or of all, whether of one man or of the whole Church, increase and advance much and forcefully according to the various ages and centuries, but provided it keeps to its own order, preserving the same doctrine, the same meaning, and the same understanding ' (*Commonitorium*, 23:28, in Moxon's edition, 88).

Systematic theology was led to the question of doctrinal development through the controversy that arose over additions to the creeds. In their opposition to the West over the Western introduction of the *Filioque* clause into the Nicene Creed, the Greeks would quote the Council of Ephesus (canon 7) with its prohibition of ἕτεραν πίστιν, and that of Chalcedon, which had stated : ' It is unlawful for anyone to present, write, compose, devise, or teach other Creed ' than the one they had sanctioned (cf. T. Herbert Bindley, *The Oecumenical Documents of the Faith* [1950] 255). St Paulinus of Aquileia defended the addition of the *Filioque* on the ground of the need in new circumstances to make more precise the Church's teaching concerning the Holy Spirit, and he quoted the precedent of the Council of Constantinople (cf. Mansi, *Concilia*, XIII:836 and J. N. D. Kelly, *Early Christian Creeds*, 301).

It was this controversy with the Greeks that brought the matter to the notice of St Thomas. The latter defended the promulgation of new creeds from the need to instruct people about the truths of the faith in answer to any errors that arise and endanger the soundness of the Christian people's faith. The only new aspect of the later creed is that, under the pressure of heretics, the implicit content of the old creed is explained more fully (*Summa*, 1a:36:2:@2). St Thomas similarly defends Our Lady's motherhood of God on the grounds that, ' though it is not found expressly stated in Scripture that the Blessed Virgin is the Mother of God, it is found expressly that Jesus Christ is true God . . . and that the Blessed Virgin is the mother of Jesus Christ. . . . And so it follows of necessity, from the words of Scripture, that Mary is the Mother of God ' (*Summa*, 3a:35:4:@1).

VII Late scholastic theology concerning the development of doctrine. The late scholastic theories on the subject were an elaboration of the explanation of St Thomas. The question was discussed as a reply to the question, ' Are theological conclusions definable ? ' By theological conclusions the theologians understood either conclusions from two revealed premisses or conclusions from one revealed and one metaphysically certain premiss. As long as there is no definition by the Church, a believing Catholic can be certain by reason of a natural inference from revelation that such conclusions are true. Could such conclusions be defined by the Church, and so be accepted on faith as part of the original revelation ?

Fr Marin-Sola (*La Evolución Homogénea del Dogma Católico*, 1952) divides the theories of the Scholastics into four groups. The first group, containing John of St Thomas and most Thomists, answered the question affirmatively. They held that, until it is defined by the Church, such a conclusion, whether from two revealed premisses or from one revealed and one premiss of reason, could only be known with the certainty of human reason. Before being defined, it could not be categorically declared to be revealed. It could not then be accepted with the divine faith on which we accept Christ's revelation. However, the Church, with her infallible guidance from the Holy Spirit, could define such a conclusion. Once the Church has done this, we would have the Holy Spirit's assurance that the conclusion was truly implicitly contained in the revealed premiss or premisses. What was a theological development until defined would now be accepted as a doctrinal development, since the conclusion now defined by the Church would (a) not go beyond the original revelation ; yet (b) bring new understanding or certainty in this particular aspect of revelation, such as had not existed before.

The second theory, that of Molina, is diametrically opposed to this. According to Molina, no theological conclusion from revealed premisses can ever be defined, because the element of reasoning which is introduced adds something new to the original revelation. Such a conclusion could never be defined, and if defined it could not be accepted on faith. Molina's position was virtually the complete denial of all doctrinal development.

A third opinion was that of Vasquez and Vega. These theologians went still further to the other extreme. Not only could any theological conclusion be defined, as the Thomists had asserted, but it could and should be accepted as of faith by anyone who saw the force of the argument, even before the Church had defined it. Their argument was in effect : ' Either a theological conclusion is doctrinally identical with its revealed premiss or not. If it is, then it is of faith ; and the Church's definition merely asserts the truth of what we have already discovered by reason on the basis of revelation. If it is not, then no definition of the Church can make it identical.'

Suarez thought the truth should be found somewhere between the first and third views. He thought that there were two kinds of theological conclusions. The first kind were mere explanations of terms, and introduced nothing really new. Such purely explicative conclusions he regarded as already revealed in a confused way when their premisses were revealed. Hence, for such conclusions, he agreed with Vasquez and Vega that they should be accepted by everyone who accepted the premisses, whether or not the Church defined them. At least this would apply to anyone who realized what they were, namely no more than explanations. But, with regard to those conclusions which by virtue of human reasoning really advanced our knowledge, Suarez claimed that we should accept these on faith if the Church defined them ; but we could not accept them on faith if the Church had not defined them. In those cases where the Church defined them, Suarez claimed that there was here equivalently a new revelation. He agreed

that revelation had ceased with the death of the last Apostle. Nevertheless, he thought that, since, by virtue of her infallibility, the Church could define such a conclusion, the resultant dogma must be not revelation but its equivalent.

Clearly the Suarezian position raised a new problem. Was Suarez right in his contention that the use of reason to gain a deeper understanding of the original revelation led to what was equivalently a new revelation when it was defined by the Church ? In other words, does the definition of the Church in some way give us new knowledge ?

Professor Owen Chadwick (*From Bossuet to Newman*, 1957) thinks that the course of scholastic post-Reformation theology in its attitude to this question indicated two mutually exclusive tendencies. There were those who believed that the power of reasoning could attain to new and deeper understanding of revelation merely by the application of theology. This could be done either by the individual or by the Church ; and the Church had no greater power of reasoning than had the individual. Such was the opinion of Vasquez. For such a view, the definition of a dogma by the Church did no more than help to a new understanding those individuals who had not succeeded in reaching it by their own reason. Logically then, any new definition would have been of faith even before its definition, to anyone who had been able to deduce it. Such a view elevates the function of theology, and minimizes that of ecclesiastical definition.

The second scholastic tendency, as Professor Chadwick sees it, is the tendency to displace theology as a developing factor in favour of the Church's infallible power to define. As will be seen from the above analysis, the Thomists generally agreed that, where real reasoning was involved, a theological conclusion could never be accepted as of faith until the Church had defined it. The Thomist argument had always been that a theological conclusion is deduced by the power of reason, and therefore its certainty cannot be greater than a rational, or metaphysical, or natural certainty. Psychologically, we may accept this with absolute certitude, in fact we must do so if we see the force of the argument. But we do not accept it on faith. Though subjectively there can be no degrees of certitude, there can be different degrees of objective claim to our assent. Faith claims our assent with the authority of God. The conclusions of reason claim our assent with the authority of reason. Since God cannot be deceived, and reason is sometimes deceived, we are bound to say that, once we recognize the voice of God, we must admit His claim on our assent as greater. This is what is meant when scholastics say that the certainty of faith is greater than the certainty of reason. The Thomists declared that the Church has power to add the certainty of faith to those conclusions the theologians had already discovered by reason. In general the Thomists did not agree that the Church's definition gave any new knowledge over and above what had been discovered from revelation by the use of reason. It merely gave certainty that our rational deduction had not led us into an erroneous understanding of revelation. It will be remembered that Suarez had said that, wherever a genuine process of reasoning, as opposed to mere explanation of terms, is involved, the resulting definition of the Church is equivalently a new revelation. Since public revelation ceased with the death of the last Apostle, Suarez could not openly say that such a definition is a new revelation. His terminology, ' equivalently a new revelation ', was too bold for theologians after him. Marin-Sola (op. cit.), the author of the fullest modern scholastic monograph on the subject, objected strongly to Suarez's innovation. But Marin-Sola did not deny the power of the Church to define in such cases. On the contrary, he was convinced that Suarez mistook the function of reason in his suggestion that a process of genuine reasoning would lead to something new, not already in the premises. At the other extreme, Marin-Sola disagreed with Vasquez for reasons already mentioned. He admitted with Vasquez that the theologian who deduces by evident reasoning that a certain truth is truly contained in the revealed datum would have full certainty that such a truth is revealed. But his certainty has come to him through a process of reasoning, and is not made possible by an act of faith. Reason, after all, is fallible, where the definition of the Church is infallible. The certainty of faith, which enables us to accept the Church's definition by the same faith as we accepted its premises is made possible by the fact that the Holy Ghost intervenes divinely to prevent the Church from misunderstanding the Deposit. To prevent a misunderstanding of the Deposit is not the same as making an addition to that same Deposit. Professor Chadwick (op. cit.) is not convinced by Marin-Sola's reasoning. He thinks that Suarez was right, and that the claim that the Church's definition can enable us to accept a truth with the certainty of faith, on the assumption that a proof from reasoning that the truth is revealed would not give the same certainty, is virtually dethroning reasoning and substituting for it the Church's authority.

VIII Modern Approaches to this Question. (i) *Newman.* The first radically new and non-scholastic approach to this question was introduced into Catholic theology by John Henry Newman. He had been led to the notion of doctrinal development while still in the Church of England, in his defence of Christian doctrine or dogma, in opposition to the doctrinal liberal, Hampden, in the mid-1830s. Hampden had adopted the extreme liberal view that denied all authentic Christian doctrine, except such as could be expressed in the actual words of Scripture. In other words, he denied any revelational authority to the creeds. Hampden based his theory on a philosophy of language paradoxically similar to the one held by Newman. Both Newman and Hampden recognized the limitations of language, especially when used to convey supernatural truth. Hampden was, however, not completely consistent, since he allowed that the words of Scripture did enshrine truth about God and His Son,

Jesus Christ. But he did not believe that we could to such an extent grasp the truth of Scripture as to be able to explain with certainty the meaning of any Scripture statement in language other than the exact words of Scripture. At least, if we did use such language, we could never, even on the word of the Church, be certain that our language was anything more than human opinion. Creeds then could not be imposed.

Now, although Newman was also convinced that human language was incapable of adequately expressing human thought, and still more incapable of fully expressing supernatural truth, he was nevertheless convinced that there could be no Christianity without dogma and creeds. ' I do not allow,' he wrote, ' that there *is* no creed at all contained in Scripture, though I grant it is not on the surface. But if there *be* no divine message, gospel, or creed producible from Scripture, this would not lead me one inch toward deciding that there was none at all *anywhere*. No ; it would make me look *out* of Scripture for it, that is all. If there is a Revelation, there must be a doctrine ; both our reason and our hearts tell us so ' (*Discussions and Arguments*, 132).

However, Newman did believe that much, if not all, Christian doctrine could be gathered from the letter of the Scriptures, even if not expressly found there *ipsissimis verbis*.

Newman's controversy with Hampden clarified his own concepts. He agreed with Hampden that Christian doctrine was an interpretation of the implications of the letter of the sacred text. Such an interpretation was, of course, a human one. But it could be authoritatively adopted by the Church as a sound one ; and, when so adopted, it must be recognized by all as dogma. It is important to realize that the idea of doctrinal development first arose in Newman's mind as part of the answer to radical doctrinal liberalism. The fact that he later found it a useful instrument to remove certain difficulties Newman felt in Roman Catholicism did not alter the fact that it was in the first place his answer to latitudinarianism.

Newman further agreed with Hampden that there are few developments which are purely an explanation or translation of terms. Even Hampden would presumably admit that the original text of Scripture could be translated into another language and still remain the Word of God. But, as soon as one left the field of exact translation and entered that of doctrinal interpretation, one had accepted the legitimacy and inevitability of development.

Newman's early tentative efforts to outline a theory in defence of dogmas and creeds, against Hampden, are reflected in some lectures published in 1838 on *Holy Scripture in its Relation to the Catholic Creed.* Five years later, he wrote a sermon on *The Theory of Developments in Religious Doctrine*, published in his *Oxford University Sermons* (1843). This remains to this day an indispensable work for the full understanding of Newman's theory. It was by another work on development, *An Essay on the Development of Christian Doctrine* (1845), that he prepared the way for his own conversion to the Catholic Church.

Newman's theory of development is affected by four factors : (*a*) we have no direct contact with our sources ; (*b*) the object of revelation is basically one, i.e. Jesus Christ ; (*c*) human language can express a simple, unified object only in complex language, with multiple words and phrases ; (*d*) there are especial difficulties inherent in the attempt to express supernatural truth in earthly human language.

With regard to the first factor, it is this that makes the essential difference between the development of theology and that of the natural sciences. The imperfections of human language make it difficult for us to express even purely natural truths. But we can continually correct our earlier attempts at formulation by referring back to the sources. For the source of natural science is continually present for our observation. Natural science is a kind of dialogue with nature. Nature is always there, and we can practically always consult it. In the realm of Christian doctrine, on the other hand, we have no direct contact with the objective source ; for the source of our doctrine is none other than Jesus Christ, the Son of God made man. His Godhead remains hidden from human eyes. We can of course see traces of God in His creation. But knowledge through such traces is natural theology, not what we call Christian doctrine. The latter is that message from God embodied in Jesus Christ. Its recognition is based on the faith that in Christ God has spoken. A return to the sources here then can only be a return to the accounts that have come down to us of Christ, His life and death and His words.

The second factor is the unity of the ultimate object of revelation. Since the object is one, the ultimate idea given to us is one. It was not in the first place a series of propositions. 'Particular propositions, then, which are used to express portions of the great idea vouchsafed to us, can never really be confused with the idea itself, which all such propositions taken together can but reach, and cannot exceed' (*Oxford University Sermons*, ed. 1892 ; 331). Again, Newman says of creeds and dogmas, that they 'live in the one idea which they are designed to express, and which alone is substantive' (op. cit., loc. cit.). Again, 'the Catholic dogmas are, after all, but symbols of a Divine fact, which, far from being compassed by those very propositions, would not be exhausted, nor fathomed, by a thousand' (op. cit., 332). Newman regarded it as the fault of the heretics to confuse the revealed fact with certain fixed statements. 'And here we see the ordinary mistake of doctrinal innovators, viz. to go away with this or that proposition of the Creed, instead of embracing that one idea which all of them together are meant to convey ; it being a definition of heresy, that it fastens on some one statement as if the whole truth, to the denial of all others, and as the basis of a new faith' (op. cit., 337). According to this view of heresy, heresy would share with a certain narrow conservative Catholic theology the conviction that the original revelation was a list of propositions. It

would differ from that theology merely in the number of propositions it accepted.

The Newman theory of development depends upon Newman's understanding of the object of Revelation. The latter is a Person, one Person, and not a series of formulae or propositions. Formulae are no more than means by which we have contact with the Object of Faith, with the true Idea of that Object, that they are from differing aspects trying to express. 'As God is one, so the impression which He gives us of Himself is one ; it is not a thing of parts ; it is not a system ; nor is it anything imperfect, and needing a counterpart. It is the vision of an object. When we pray, we pray not to an assemblage of notions, or to a creed, but to One Individual Being ; and when we speak of Him we speak of a Person, not of a Law or a Manifestation. This being the case, all our attempts to delineate our impression of Him go to bring out one idea, not two or three or four ; not a philosophy but an individual idea in its separate aspects' (*Oxford University Sermons*, ed. 1892 ; 330). Elsewhere Newman speaks of the danger of forgetting the 'One Thing Needful' in one's over-anxiety about correct faith, ceremonial observances, or acts of charity and piety. It is the one Person of Christ who is the Object of our worship, and the recognition of this is the true purpose of orthodoxy (*Lectures on Justification*, ed. 1892 ; 314).

The third factor is the nature of language. We become conscious of the Divine Object in the way in which we are made conscious of objects of the senses. Descriptions multiply in an attempt to describe what we see. But we still see and describe the one object. It does not become more than one object for all our multiplication of descriptions of different aspects. Newman was convinced likewise that, ideally, the articles of the creed and dogmas should generate in our minds not a multitude of ideas or visions, but one. 'Religious men, according to their measure, have an idea or vision of the Blessed Trinity in Unity, of the Son Incarnate and of His Presence, not as a number of qualities, attributes and actions, not as the subject of a number of propositions, but as one, and individual, and independent of words, as an impression conveyed through the senses' (*Oxford University Sermons*, ed. 1892 ; 331).

One of the most obvious causes of development of doctrine is, of course, development of theology. Theology uses language and inference to increase the theologian's personal understanding of the faith. Where some new expression of the faith made by theologians seems to pinpoint some important aspect of the original revelation, usually in answer to heresy, the Church may authentically endorse it. It is in this way that a truth reached by theological reasoning can sometimes lead to a new expression of doctrine, or, as we often say, a new dogma. Thus the term 'consubstantial' as a means of expressing the mode of identity within the Godhead of Father and Son was at first a theological interpretation of the Gospel revelation, which arose in the attempt to rebut Arianism. Arianism was seen to be so dangerous that the Church decreed the use of this term in her official Creed.

Other stimuli to doctrinal development may be ' the habitual and devout perusal of Scripture, which gradually acts upon the mind ; again, the gradual influence of intercourse with those who in themselves are in possession of the sacred ideas ; again, a continual round of devotion ; or, again, sometimes, in minds both fitly disposed and apprehensive, the almost instantaneous operation of a keen faith' (*Oxford University Sermons*, ed. 1892 ; 333). The latter was considerably developed by Newman in later life, and has come to be known as the *consensus fidelium* or the *sensus fidei*.

It will be seen from what has been said that development in Newman's theory is not the drawing of a conclusion from premises, after the manner of formal logic. It is better described as the drawing out of some new aspect, or the bringing to view of some new facet, of the one original divine fact revealed to us from the first. If we call that original fact ' Jesus Christ ' or ' The Word made Flesh ' or by any other name, the whole official teaching is but a development or bringing out of some aspect of it. It cannot be a purely metaphysical analysis of the notion, based on human philosophy and reasoning. It must be a development of that basic object of faith, in so far as it is described to us in the words of Scripture, and as understood in the light of Tradition.

If it is asked : ' How do we get at this original fact ? ' Newman's answer is that it is conveyed to us through a multitude of propositions, which conspire together to form a simple, unified impression or idea within us. If we are asked in turn to describe or express this idea, we can only do so by a similar way in reverse, i.e. through many propositions. This is the way Scripture gave it to us in the first place. But we do not repeat the identical words of Scripture, in parrot-fashion. For what we describe in our own words is not the original propositions of Scripture but the one truth underlying them.

The manner of arriving at this original fact is similar, as said before, to the way we arrive at knowledge of a person. The fact that we use a thousand propositions to describe that one person, or that others use as many to describe him to us, does not alter the ultimate impression of unity which results.

If Newman's theory is right, it would seem that all Christian doctrines that have ever been queried, and afterwards authentically accepted, are developments.

To apply all this in the concrete to Christian revelation, we would say that, when Christ spoke to us His divine saving Word, His good tidings of salvation, He used a great number of human expressions, each possessing a certain divinely guaranteed analogy to divine truth, in order to convey to our minds, with the help of God's grace, a new understanding of what we need to know about God. The inner heart of the knowledge He imparted to His Apostles was not commensurate with the actual words He used. It was not just a list of propositions, each representing a different truth. Rather it was a series of propositions pointing to something beyond themselves, i.e. to that unified body of truth we call Christianity.

If today we wish to correct our modern expressions by a return to the sources, we cannot do as the scientist does : go back directly to the original objective truth. We can only hope to return to the knowledge possessed by the Apostles. But this is not identical with saying that we merely go back to the words of the Apostles. With the help of all their words we hope to return to the underlying knowledge expressed in those words—to the ' impression ', as Newman said in his Sermon on Developments in Doctrine, underlying all the expressions. To reach this ' impression ', we must study their words carefully—as far as possible all their words—and we must study them in the light of early tradition. Only thus have we a hope of getting underneath the letter to the central truth never fully expressed, which the Apostles themselves were expressing to the best of their opportunity and ability.

One can see from this one great difference between the Newmanic approach and the scholastic. The scholastics asked the question : ' Could a theological conclusion be defined ? ' Such a way of putting the question betrays that they set out from the supposition that the original deposit was a series of propositions, any one of which could serve as a premiss in a syllogism. For Newman, as will now be clear, the starting-point of the development was not any proposition or series of propositions but the knowledge underlying all the propositions, which they intended to convey, but which at the time would only be partially reflectively perceived. If one takes as an example the doctrine of the infallibility of the Pope, the scholastic would ask the question : ' Can this be deduced by strict syllogistic reasoning from one or more revealed propositions ? Can it be deduced from the promise of Our Lord to Peter ? Or can it be deduced from a complex syllogism using several Scripture passages ? Or can it be argued from the promise of the Spirit of Truth to guide the Church ? ' Newman would ask a different question. He might ask, for instance : ' Does this doctrine emerge from a full understanding of Our Lord's choice of St Peter, together with a deep appreciation of His command to Peter and the Apostles, the nature of the Church He founded, the work He wished it to do, and the manner in which He intended to stay with that Church through His Spirit. In short, does the conviction of the Pope's infallibility, as defined in the First Vatican Council, come from a fuller and more explicit ability to put into words a most important aspect of the Church, as revealed by Christ and believed in Christian tradition ? ' Similarly, with regard to the doctrine of the Immaculate Conception, Newman would not look for some Scripture text from which it can be deduced. He would rather ask : ' Does this doctrine emerge from a full understanding of Mary, the predestined Mother of God, as we know her in the sources of revelation ? Does it follow from a true and full understanding of the

Incarnation, as actually decreed by God for the saving of our fallen race ?'

For Newman, then, the questions proposed by the scholastics were unreal. They were based on a propositional, and therefore abstract, understanding of the original revelation. Not that this makes them false. But it tends to make them inadequate. Newman's position can be better appreciated if one considers the unity of the ultimate Christian revelation, in contrast with the multiplicity of the words conveying it. Christianity is one Gospel, not many. Yet it can only be conveyed by many words. No number of words ever succeeds in adequately and finally expressing it. Every sentence strives to make its contribution to articulating the truth underlying the whole. Paradoxically, its basic unity demands a great catholicity of expression, without which even its unity will fail to be grasped. For this unity is nothing less than Christ. The whole of the Scriptures ultimately have but one subject-matter. Christ is the inner Gospel which all its texts are striving in one way or other, in one aspect or other, to express. By studying the gospels, Christians learn the Gospel ; and that Gospel is one, it is the Word made flesh. When Christians study the epistles of St Paul, it is still Christ they are seeking. The same is true of all the books of the New Testament. One of the paradoxes of human speech is that the greater the inner unity of the idea we are trying to express, the greater the variety of words that are needed to convey it truly. At least this must be true of the simple concept underlying all reality—that of God. In this understanding of Christian doctrine, all the Marian doctrines are seen by Catholics as aspects or suppositions of the central revealed truth, Christ.

In the post-apostolic history of the Christian Church, as each succeeding generation, by learning, and meditating upon the tradition handed down to them, reaches its own image of Christ impressed on its mind and heart, new spontaneous and living ways of expressing it arise. These new modes of expression are affected by the prevailing language and mental climate in which each generation lives. By adapting their expressions to their listeners, they enrich for each age its understanding of Christ. These adaptations and expressional enrichments may be called developments. They are new and living expressions of what is ancient and eternal. They have no desire to alter the Christ whom they express, but merely to ensure in others a lively knowledge of Him.

In his 15th *Oxford University Sermon*, written in 1843, Newman distinguished between the many outward expressions and the single inward impression. The perfect Christian has not as many faiths as there are articles. All the articles of his creed express the same faith. He does not believe a series of truths, but One Truth. 'Religious men, according to their measure, have an idea or vision of the Blessed Trinity in Unity, of the Son Incarnate and of His Presence, not as a number of qualities, attributes and actions, not as the subject of a number of propositions, but as one, and individual, and independent of words, as an impression conveyed

through the senses' (*Oxford University Sermons*, 331).

Newman, with his normal unconcern for technical language, at some times *compared* the underlying Christian message to a philosophy, and at other times *contrasted* it with philosophy. It is like a philosophy in so far as, underlying all its different expressions, there is a basic unity. It is unlike a philosophy in so far as it is not something abstract, but deals with facts and persons—ultimately with the Person of Jesus Christ. In the first sense, Newman wrote about the deposit of faith : 'What is meant by the *depositum* ? Is it a list of articles that can be numbered ? No, it is a large philosophy ; all parts of which are connected together, and in a certain sense correlative together, so that he who knows one part may be said to know all, as *ex pede Herculem*' (from an essay of 1868 published in JTS 9 [1958] 332). In the second sense, Newman wrote : 'Revelation sets before it (the mind) certain supernatural facts and actions, beings and principles : these make a certain impression or image upon it.' The two senses are harmonized in so far as the given element comes to us not by any intuition but by means of concrete events and propositions, and yet by means of these a single unified image or idea of immense depth and richness is gradually impressed upon the minds of Christians. This is mostly verified of Christians taken together as the whole community of the Church. Individual Christians only attain to the realization of the ultimate unity by degrees and imperfectly.

Newman compared the underlying unity to the unity of the world of nature. He described it as our inward idea of divine truth, or the inward belief, or the great sight, or the true inward impression. Just as a disciple who understands a philosophy perfectly will be able to answer questions of many different kinds by the application of the principles of the philosophy, so is a Christian who understands his faith able to answer many questions referring to its application in new fields, without necessarily departing from the original doctrine and principles. But the analogy of a philosophy must be corrected, since a philosophy is abstract, whereas Christianity deals with a real concrete truth. The God whom we have learnt to know through Christian revelation is not an abstraction. This we realize when we pray to him. 'When we pray, we pray not to an assemblage of notions, or to a creed, but to One Individual Being ; and when we speak of Him we speak of a Person, not a Law or Manifestation. This being the case, all our attempts to delineate our impression of Him go to bring out one idea, not two or three or four ; not a philosophy, but an individual idea in its separate aspects' (*Oxford University Sermons*, ed. 1892 ; 330).

The development of truth, or of 'ideas' (in Newman's terms) comes about inevitably with every attempt to answer objections, or to explain, or even to express the thoughts that come to one in meditation. No one maintains that, in the field of doctrine, such development comes about through the inspiration of the Holy Spirit. So, likewise, no one maintains that all apparent development is faithful. In the case of developments of doctrine which are accepted by the Church in conciliar or papal definitions, the Holy Ghost merely intervenes negatively to prevent the defining of an unfaithful development. But the process of attempting to develop is natural and inevitable. ' As the mind is cultivated and expanded, it cannot refrain from the attempt to analyse the vision which influences the heart, and the Object in which that vision centres ; nor does it stop until it has, in some sort, succeeded in expressing in words what has all along been a principle both of its affections and of its obedience' (*Arians of the Fourth Century*, ed. 1890 ; 144). It is an attempt to explain and analyse one's vision of Mary, the Mother of God, that was a great factor in the development of Marian doctrine.

It is not so easy to test this form of spontaneous informal development, in order to discover whether it is faithful to the original or a corruption. If all rational inference proceeded by syllogisms, one would only have to test it by the rules of formal logic. Quite different tests must be used to certify informal reasoning. What is to be tested is not a visible reasoning process but a complicated historical process of thought, which cannot easily and clearly be captured. It is almost impossible to put one's finger on the starting-point of the process. If an individual reasons his way to a new conviction informally, it is seldom that he can tell you how and where the process began or how it proceeded. Newman always claimed to be unable to capture and put on paper the process of reasoning which led him to the Catholic Church. In the case of doctrinal development within the Church, it is made still more difficult by the fact that this informal reasoning process is a co-operation of many minds over many centuries, living in all the vicissitudes of real life.

(ii) *Newman's notes of a genuine development*. Since the human mind, for all its spirituality, functions through a living organ, which cannot be entirely exempted from the laws of life here below, Newman thought there might be some analogy between psychological and biological development. One must be careful not to press the analogy too closely, but analogy can frequently be a useful pointer, if only to suggest terms and categories in which our minds can operate.

It was undoubtedly on the analogy of biology that Newman hit upon his seven notes or tests of genuine development. In this field he was a pioneer. Previously, since the time of Aristotle, no one had proposed any test of reasoning except logic. But logic is helpless unless in the presence of clearly defined starting-points, which it can use as premisses. Also logic is helpless except when dealing with propositions. If the original truth revealed to us could not be reduced to so many propositions, then formal logic is useless to test any statement that claims to be a true explanation of development of it. These tests devised by Newman from the analogy of biology are a series of converging signposts pointing n the direction of some truth.

Newman does not pretend that these tests were actually used by the Church before the latter marked with its stamp of approval some development. These are merely tests which, so Newman suggests, could be used. In real life, it is what Newman called our illative sense that makes the decision that we have grounds enough to accept a certain position as true. Strictly speaking, we make our decision by using our illative sense. In the case of supernatural truth, the Holy Spirit in the Church guarantees the conclusion arrived at by the normal informal reasoning of the Christian theologians and the body of the faithful. We do not accept the doctrine of Original sin on the basis of Newman's seven tests. But rather our conviction that St Augustine was right in his contention that this doctrine was part of the deposit comes from the fact that the councils of the Church accepted it, and that these councils have the protection of the Holy Spirit.

So the seven tests have rather an apologetic value, showing to the theologian and the inquirer that the institution which is being tested has remained true to itself over the centuries. They could also be used as a true test for any doctrine not yet defined by the Church but defended by her theologians. They could thus be a test of the faithfulness of a new view, say, of the sacraments or of the Church, which might be put forward by one or more of our 20th-cent. theologians.

Putting the matter in a concrete way, we could thus describe it. We might take as the original Gospel, say, the Word was made Flesh for man's Redemption. This would, of course, have to be understood in the concrete way in which it was revealed to us. Taking this then as our starting-point, we might ask the question : ' Does the doctrine of Original sin, or of the state of happiness of the disembodied soul, or the doctrine of the Trinity, appear as a faithful interpretation of some aspect of that original Gospel ?' Or we might ask the same question in regard to some of the re-thinking which is going on in our present-day theological world. How does the theology of a Congar or a Cullmann appear as a faithful development of that original Gospel ?

Newman's reply is to apply his seven notes : (i) identity of type ; (ii) continuity of principles ; (iii) power of assimilation ; (iv) logical sequence ; (v) anticipation of its future ; (vi) conservative action upon its past ; (vii) chronic vigour.

If we were to apply these tests to a specific doctrine or theory we might ask questions of this nature. First, regarding *identity of type*. Newman does not mean that we must compare the doctrine in mind with Scripture and see if it is identical. If that were so it would not be a development. Newman's tests are concrete and historical, like the world in which we live. How, we might ask ourselves, would the secular world react to this newly expressed doctrine ? Would it tend to reject it in the same way as it formerly rejected primitive Christian doctrines ? Would this new doctrine impress serious minds in the same way today as it impressed such minds in the first centuries ? Would it tend to arouse in them a similar hatred of sin and fear of guilt ? Would it lead people to admire the same form of life that early Christians admired ? Does it appear to worldly men as foolish, just as early Christianity appeared foolish ? Is it part and parcel of a religion that is still liable to divide families, as Our Lord said Christianity would divide families ?

Or, on the contrary, would people of the world say to this new presentation : ' Now at last you speak a language worldly people can understand. Now at last the age-long obstacles that have kept worldly men from Christ have been removed. Now we can all qualify as Christians.'

Or, to take the second note : here we must ask the new theology whether it is based on the same principles as early Christian doctrine. For example, is it still based on the principle of faith as, ' the absolute acceptance of the divine Word with an internal assent, in opposition to the informations, if such, of sight and reason ' ? In modern language, we might ask : ' Is it based on the analogy of faith ? ' Does it still follow the traditional principle that, since faith has to do with truth, reason can be used in its development ? Is it true to the incarnational or sacramental principle ? Is it based on Our Lord's manifest intention in His Incarnation of making us share what He is in Himself, i.e. the principle of grace ?

Take the third note. Does it recognize all truth as from one source, and so admit the essential goodness of matter and its capability of being baptized ?

As regards the fourth note, is it a doctrine which can be shown to be logically consequent upon others already accepted ? Or, as regards the fifth note, is it so new that nothing in the past has appeared which might be regarded as an anticipation of it ? With regard to the sixth note, does it tend to strengthen and preserve Christianity ? Finally, is it a sign of the Church's life ?

The criticism has often been made that these ' tests ' are vague and unscientific—that they were put forward by Newman half-heartedly. That they are extremely difficult to apply in a clear, scholastic, fully articulate way, Newman would be the first to agree. But this is because ideas in real life are as difficult to capture as any other living thing in this world of ours. All growth is difficult to capture, the Church's growth included.

Professor Owen Chadwick (*From Bossuet to Newman*, 1957) thinks that by implication Newman's theory supposes continual new revelation. Newman himself did not think so. He was convinced that a Christian of the 4th cent., for example, could speak more clearly and more surely about the Holy Ghost than one of the 2nd, and yet there had been no new revelation. It had come about through a deeper and clearer understanding of the revelation that had already been handed down in the 1st cent.

Something should here be said of what is perhaps the only serious challenge to Newman's seven notes. This dates back to January 1847, to an article by J. B. Mozley in *The Christian Remembrancer* (pub-

lished in book form under the title *The Theory of Development*, 1878). Mozley's claim was that Newman's tests might be valid to distinguish between sheer corruption and faithfulness, but gave no guidance to help us to detect exaggerations. Now it was precisely the Anglican complaint about Rome that it had admitted exaggerations into its doctrinal teachings. Mozley distinguished between the doctrines defined in the early centuries, which were no more than new formulations of the original doctrines of the Scriptures, and many of the doctrines defined by the Church of Rome in more modern times, which were the kind of addition to the original that might be termed exaggerations.

Surely Newman's answer to this would be that an admitted exaggeration is either in some essential matter or in something purely secondary. Exaggerations in secondary matters, such as theological opinions or popular devotions, do not involve the Church as such, since these are not officially taught by the Church in Christ's name. They are no more than inevitable human imperfections in an institution which is partly human, and so continually in need of self-reform. On the other hand, an exaggeration in an essential matter, in some doctrine officially preached by the Church in the name of Christ, would be excluded in fact, we believe, by the preserving action of the Holy Spirit. It would also be *seen* to be excluded, because exaggeration of such a kind would clash with several of the notes. The type would no longer be preserved, the past would no longer be conserved in its original form, and the new development would not follow with logical sequence.

(iii) *Present-day trends in the theology of doctrinal development.* The great modern monograph on the scholastic theology of doctrinal development has already been mentioned, that of F. Marin-Sola. His effort might be regarded as a 20th-cent. attempt to present a Thomist synthesis of the main scholastic theories. Marin-Sola's basic contention was that anything deduced from the original revelation by a process of pure syllogistic reasoning must be virtually revealed, and so was capable of being defined.

Other characteristic 20th-cent. analyses and critiques of doctrinal development seem to proceed consciously or subconsciously on Newman's lines. This is notably so in the case of Karl Rahner's essay on the subject published in his *Theological Investigations*, vol. 1 (1961). He contends that, in spiritual development, as in all development of living things, the laws of development can never be adequately discovered until the process or stage of the process has been completed. He admits that certain *a priori* tests can be applied in the Church, and ultimately by the Church, but that they are in the end no more than appeals to the Church herself. In the order of nature, prescinding from the Holy Spirit's guidance, the danger of error from the human factor is always there. But the Church relies on the ever-present Spirit to safeguard her against that factor.

As regards the manner of development, Rahner's explanation is in many respects conceived on Newman's lines. He points out that revelation did not originally come in the form of a number of propositions. In his language, it was the great saving event or happening. It is indeed communicated to us by means of propositions, but, together with the words, there is committed to the hearer the Apostles' experience. The listener rightly grasps more than the minimum content of the words ; he grasps in fact concomitantly all that further content of the sphere of unreflexive awareness not yet propositionally objectified. He hears it further as something known to the speaker. Most of the progress in biblical theology concerns subjects such as the biblical concept of man or of God. All this theology is only partly articulate in the actual words of Scripture. Further, when what a man reads is fitted into the rest of his experience he is able to understand new aspects of it. So the biblical theologian does not hope to find something which is not in Scripture, but he does hope to see more deeply and clearly the meaning of that Scripture. He is further enabled to express it more fully.

The same is true of the Church's doctrine. There is at first a development of theology. But, if this leads to a growth in understanding of the revealed Word of God, what was at first a development in theology may be accepted by the faith, on the Church's guarantee, and become a development of doctrine. The final result, as Rahner points out, is both more and less than the original. It is more in so far as the original is reflectively formulated and elucidated. It is less in so far as it can never express more than what is ' reflexively and remotely a part ' of the original.

This doctrine of Rahner appears to be essentially identical in principle with that of Newman, yet expressed in a manner that helps it to be harmonized with the scholastic theories.

Other modern theologians who have adopted similar theories of development are Taymans SJ, Liégé OP and Dublanchy (*see* Bibliography). Taymans argued that, in all our knowledge of reality, our understanding of a thing is only partially made explicit. Things we are conscious of in a non-explicit way we possess, but inadequately. As we contemplate them our possession gets deeper and clearer. Every statement we make affirms virtually more than it states. For every statement has a background, without which it would not be the statement it actually is. Taymans also stated, like Newman, that the ultimate object of our faith-knowledge is one, i.e. Christ present by faith.

Liégé argued that theology frequently was helped in its development by the *sensus fidei*. The faithful often have a grasp of some aspect of the faith that theologians have not yet succeeded in expressing and satisfactorily proving until after a period of time. When the faithful appear to be arguing from theological reasoning, the chief factor contributing towards the acceptance of the doctrine as homogeneous with the original deposit is the fact that it has been accepted by the faith of the Christian people. A similar view seems to underlie much of the

writings of Y. Congar, especially at the time of the Second Vatican Council.

There is a nearness to real life in these new theologies of development, which makes them better exponents of the real living historical growth of doctrine than the earlier scholastic theories. Fr Dillenschneider, notably, is convinced that it is on Newman's lines alone that one can explain the development of Marian doctrines in the Church.

(iv) *Modern heterodox views on development.* Heterodox views on development of doctrine have usually been based on an idea of progress not compatible with a divine revelation. For, on the supposition that there has been a divine revelation, the only progress we can make in its regard is towards a fuller understanding of that revelation on our part. The idea of progressing towards new truths or towards fundamentally different understandings of the original deposit is unacceptable, as it would involve substituting a new, humanly acquired truth for a divinely revealed truth. In the fields of science and philosophy it is man's ambition to progress to new truth or to the correcting of earlier error. In the field of revelation we can certainly try to exclude our own misunderstandings of that revelation, but we cannot hope either to correct it or to add to it.

In classical liberal Protestantism many views have been put forward involving the reinterpreting of Christian truth according to an essentially new philosophy. Such systems imply that we reach a view of Christianity essentially superior to that handed down by the Apostles, or even to that taught by Jesus Christ. Such views seem to be involved in the theologies of Lessing, Kant, Fichte, Hegel and several consequent types of Hegelianism. Something similar is found in the reinterpretation of Christianity characteristic of Schleiermacher. The same is true of most systems of liberal Protestantism, from Sabatier and Harnack right up to Bultmann at the present day. Similar views were defended in the Catholic Church by Günther in the 19th cent., and by many of the Modernists in the early years of the 20th cent. (*see* GUENTHERIANISM).

Such views are not, strictly speaking, entitled to the term ' development ', since development means ' unfolding ', and one cannot unfold more than was originally given. So that any view which alters or exaggerates or increases or ' corrects ' the original is not a development but a corruption, from the point of view of the original deposit. In the First Vatican Council false views of dogmatic progress were condemned, when the opinion was anathematized that, ' with the progress of knowledge a different meaning from that understood by the Church in former times or now can be given to dogmas proposed by the Church ' (D 1818). The same Council asserts positively the need for maintaining the same meaning as in former times, but it quotes Vincent of Lerins in support of its admission that there can be general growth in our understanding and power of expressing the original dogma (D 1800).

IX In conclusion it should be said that (*a*) it is impossible satisfactorily to account for the apparently changed appearance of Christian doctrine and practice except on some theory of doctrinal development ; and (b) that the only line of thought in this matter that can account for the actual growth of the Church's doctrine in its historical concreteness is that inaugurated by Newman.

The whole question of development of doctrine has come to possess an overwhelming oecumenical importance in this later 20th cent. All the main groups of Christians have ' developed '. Not all the ' developments ', it seems, can be genuine ; otherwise we should not still be divided. Since the Reformation Christian communions have both grown apart from one another and, to some extent at a later period, grown towards each other once more. It is admitted by all orthodox Christians that one of Newman's notes, i.e. identity of type, should be a characteristic of genuine developments, and that it can, with God's help, be recovered, where it has been lost or obscured, by a new study of scriptural and patristic sources. It would appear that all of Newman's notes could be used as a test of sound Christian theology. Sound theology will, in turn, help towards the restoration of unity in doctrine.

Not the least important among the developments of theology which we hope will contribute to Christian unity will be a development of the theology of development itself. The present trend away from an exclusively scholastic approach will certainly make an understanding of Catholic doctrinal developments easier to our separated brethren. But there is also a sense in which this may be true in reverse. Believing non-Catholics have been using their minds during the period of separation, as before, in trying to penetrate more deeply into the full meaning and implications of Christian doctrine. We should not assume that all these ' developments ' are corruptions. It may come to be seen that genuine explicitations of Christian, and therefore Catholic, theology have arisen among the separated brethren. There is no a priori impossibility of their being eventually accepted as Catholic expressions of the faith. This would not mean that the Holy Spirit has ' inspired ' Protestant theological developments, any more than we claim that the Holy Spirit inspires Catholic theological developments. In no case would any development, whether it took place in the Church or among the separated brethren, be regarded as guaranteed by the guiding Spirit until it has been defined by Council or Pope. But, in the realm of theology, we can all help one another.

Bibliography. J. H. Newman, *Oxford University Sermons* (1843, revised ed. 1892) ; the same, *Essay on the Development of Doctrine* (1845, revised ed. 1897) ; the same, ' On consulting the Faithful in Matters of Doctrine ' (an article in *The Rambler*, 1859, reprinted with introduction by J. Coulson, 1961) ; J. Walgrave, *Newman the Theologian* (1960) ; J. Guitton, *La Philosophie de Newman, essai sur l'idée de développement* (1933) ; H. F. Davis, ' The Catholicism of Newman ', in *Newman Centenary Essays* (1945) ; W. Ong SJ, ' Newman's Theory on Development ', in TS 7 (1946) 2–45 ; P. J. Donnelly SJ, ' Theological

Opinion on the Development of Dogma ', in TS 8 (1947) 659–99 ; T. Lynch, ' The Newman-Perrone Paper on Development ', in *Gregorianum* 16 (1935) 405–47 ; A. Stephenson SJ, ' Development and Immutability of Christian Doctrine ', in TS 19 (1958) 481–532 ; H. F. Davis, ' Is Newman's Theory of Development Catholic ? ', in *Blackfriars* 39 (1958) 310–21 ; F. Taymans d'Épernon SJ, ' Le Progrès du dogme ', in NRT 71 (1949) 687–700 ; H. de Lubac SJ, ' Le Problème du developpement du dogme ', in RSR 35 (1948) 130–60 ; L. de Grandmaison SJ, *Le Dogme chrétien* (1928) ; F. Marin-Sola OP, *L'Évolution homogène du dogme catholique* (2nd ed. from Spanish, 1924) ; M. Blondel, ' Histoire et Dogme ', in *La Quinzaine* 56 (1904) 145–67 ; 349–73 ; 433–58 ; *O. Chadwick, *From Bossuet to Newman : the Idea of Doctrinal Development* (1957) ; C. S. Dessain, ' An Unpublished Paper by Cardinal Newman on the Development of Doctrine ', in JTS 9 (1958) 324–35 ; H. Rondet SJ, *Do Dogmas change ?* (1961) ; K. Rahner SJ, *Theological Investigations* I (1961) 39–77 ; C. Journet, *Esquisse du développement du dogme marial* (1954) ; L. Barmann SJ, ' Newman and the Theory of Development ', in AER 143 (1960) 121–9 ; C. Dillenschneider, *Le Sens de la foi et le progrès dogmatique du mystère marial* (1954) ; P. Liégé OP, in *Catholicisme* III:957–62, s.v. Dogme ; Y. Congar OP, in *Catholicisme* IV:1059–67, s.v. Fait dogmatique ; G. Biemer, ' Newman an das Vaticanum II ', in *Wort und Wahrheit* 16 (1961) 409–19 ; E. Dublanchy in DTC IV:1606–50, s.v. Dogme.

H. F. D.

DOGMA This article is not intended to be a full-scale discussion of all that is implied in the word, but rather as a definition of the way in which the word is used in Catholic teaching. The article therefore is in three parts : (I) a note on the etymology of the word, (II) definition of dogma and (III) certain precisions and implications.

I Etymology. The word is derived originally from the Greek verb δοκέω meaning ' form an opinion '. The word has two substantival derivatives with a strong divergence of meaning : δόξα which has the general meaning of ' opinion ', ' mere opinion ', and δόγμα with the stronger sense of a teaching which has a certain authoritative basis. In classical Greek it refers either to something decreed by law, or in philosophical use, a fundamental tenet or axiom. In Biblical use the LXX uses the word of royal decrees (e.g. Est 3:9 ; Dan 2:13). In the NT it has the sense of ' edict ' or ' decree ', e.g. the edict of Caesar Augustus (Lk 2:1), or the authoritative decisions of the Council of Jerusalem (Ac 16:4). In ecclesiastical use up to the 4th cent. it refers indifferently to fundamental teachings of faith and morality. But from the 4th to the 5th cents. the sense hardens and it is reserved for truths which are the object of faith, as distinct from laws and obligations with a foundation in revelation. This use has remained constant in the Church since then. Cyril of Jerusalem (*catechesis* 4 ; PG 33:453) speaks of ' the ten dogmas ', and these are almost the articles of the Creed.

II Definition. A dogma is a truth revealed by God and proposed as such by the teaching Church for the belief of all Christians. Its denial constitutes heresy.

The definition clearly contains two elements: (*a*) the truth is one which is part of the deposit of revelation (*see* REVELATION). A dogma is therefore a statement of what is to be believed by Christians simply on the authority of God who reveals. (*b*) The official proposal by the teaching Church that this truth constitutes an element of this revelation, and therefore must be accepted on faith.

Dogmas are therefore distinguished: (*a*) from matters of ecclesiastical discipline and morality on the one hand, and from statements about belief which are not guaranteed or asserted as belonging to divinely revealed truth, e.g. dogmatic facts (*see* next article). Dogmas are distinguished: (*b*) from less definite statements of belief, e.g. the teaching of individual bishops, or of the Pope when not intending to invoke infallibility, the teaching of theologians, etc. They are also to be distinguished in this respect from *Creeds* (*see* CREEDS), which are the official confessions of faith, in brief and compendious form, which are part of the Church's official cult or worship. A dogma then is a statement of divinely revealed truth, issued by the solemn *magisterium* (the Pope or General Council in solemn definitions) or by the ordinary *magisterium* (the Pope's ordinary teaching of matters already defined, or the universal teaching of the Catholic episcopate). So a further element in the notion of dogma appears: it is a matter in which the Church invokes, as a guarantee of truth, her infallible teaching authority. Dogmatic statements therefore rely for their certainty on the special 'assistance' of the Holy Spirit (*see* INFALLIBILITY), and consequently are irreformable.

III Further precisions. Divine revelation is contained in Scripture and Tradition. Revelation as a body of truth was complete with the death of the last Apostle. Dogmatic development has however continued and will continue in the Church (*see* DOCTRINE, DEVELOPMENT OF). It constitutes an always clearer and fuller understanding of what is contained in this divine revelation. Dogmas do not change in the sense that what was once believed ceases to be believed and something new is substituted. The object of belief changes in so far as its formulation becomes more precise and more adapted to the understanding of each age. What is expressed is the same truth, of absolute, and not merely relative value. But the expression may have been made more precise in order to exclude erroneous or false statements of belief. Dogmatic definition occurs in the Church most often in this context of heresy or error, in order to make even clearer the Church's understanding of the truths which God has revealed.

It is not to be thought therefore that any dogmatic statement is exhaustive of revealed truth on the topic concerned, and false notions of theology can easily occur when this is not appreciated. A dogmatic definition is often concerned with one side of the coin (e.g. many of the decrees of the Council of Trent), and may leave much to be said in other respects.

Do dogmatic statements jeopardize the purity of primitive revelation and its inspired language? The justification of such dogmatic formulae from a theological point of view comes from a double guarantee: (i) the fact that divine mysteries can be expressed in human terms is implicit in the notion of revelation itself; (ii) for the faithfulness of such statements to this revelation the Church relies on the divine guidance (*see* INFALLIBILITY) expressed by Our Lord in Jn 14:26: 'He who is to befriend you, the Holy Spirit, whom the Father will send on my account, will in his turn make everything plain, and recall to your minds everything I have said to you' (Kn). From the purely rational point of view, the possibility of expressing mysteries in human terms is often explained in terms of analogy (*see* ANALOGY).

In her dogmatic formulations the Church makes use of certain abstract terms, and often ones which are used in fairly definite philosophical or theological systems. Does this imply any acceptance by the Church of all their philosophical implications? Clear examples of such terms are: *person, nature, matter and form, trans-substantiation*. The Church has always made it clear that in employing for the sake of exactness certain philosophical terms, she does not intend to endorse the systematic implications of these terms, but uses them in the ordinary and common understanding of them. Thus for example, the definition of the Council of Vienne in 1311, that the rational or intellectual soul is *per se* and of its nature the *form* of the human body (cf. D 481), does not involve the Church in an endorsement of all the implications of hylomorphism, as Pius IX made clear in a letter to the Rector of the Catholic University of Lille (ASS X [1877] 257–9). Similarly, the notion of *trans-substantiation* which in Catholic teaching replaced the notion of *conversio*, or rather, made it more exact, does not imply the Church's dogmatic commitment to the Thomist or any other philosophical account of substance and change. As early as the 2nd cent. one can see the Apologists combining terms from Platonic, Stoic and Aristotelian systems for Christian usage.

However, the common and ordinary sense of words changes and dogmas do not change. How do we explain this? Not all would agree, but it seems that philosophical expressions used in dogmatic definition do not lose all speculative content, and though they endorse no one school, they employ words in the sense that all Catholic philosophical and theological schools would agree on, that is to say, they are to be understood in the sense they hold at the time of the definition in educated circles as expressing some philosophical truth which is thought by the Church to be beyond dispute. The Church has a high regard indeed for the value of such terms (cf. Pius XII, *Humani Generis*, D 2311–12), in the sense in which they are used by the Church, and as capable of expressing absolute and unchanging truth (cf. ibid.). Hence, in an indirect way the Church also rejects philosophical systems which are so relativistic that they are unable to provide a vehicle for the unchanging truth contained in revelation (cf. *Humani Generis*, D 2323, and see MODERNISM). In consequence of this the Church regards dogmatic definitions as irreformable, in the sense that their meaning cannot be altered, though they remain always open to further precision.

Finally, it is often thought that dogmas are purely a matter of intellectual import and demand only a purely intellectual assent. And thus it is often said that the Catholic approach to revelation is purely intellectualist, and her insistence on the minutiae of understanding exaggerated. Two considerations are here useful. First, since the Church regards revelation as God's living dialogue with man in an approach of love, the attitude which is impatient of such careful search for the exact meaning overlooks the intrinsic value of God's word to man and its loving acceptance. Secondly, the content is by no means purely intellectual, but is an account precisely of God's gift of Himself to man in the Church, and His loving advances to and designs for man's happiness in a communion of love, now based on faith, but to be perfected in the union of the blessed vision of God in heaven.

Bibliography. R. Aubert, *Le Problème de l'acte de foi*[3] (1958) ; S. Cartechini SJ, *De Valore Notarum Theologicarum* (1951) ; L. de Grandmaison SJ, *Le Dogme chrétien* (1928) ; H. Dieckmann SJ, *De Ecclesia* (1925) ; E. Dublanchy, art. ' Le Dogme ', DTC IV, 1574–1650 ; A. Gardeil OP, *Le Donné révélé et la Théologie* (1910) ; A. M. Henry OP (editor), *Initiation théologique* (1957), Chapter 1 in Vol. 1 ; H. Pinard, art. ' Dogme ', DAFC I, 1121–84 ; T. Zapelena SJ, *De Ecclesia Christi*[2], Part 2 (1954) ; R. Garrigou-Lagrange OP, *Le Sens commun, la philosophie et les formules dogmatiques* (1922) ; D. Deneffe SJ, ' Dogma, Wort und Begriff ', in *Scholastik* 6 (1931) 381–400 and 505–38.

P. F. H.

DOGMATIC FACTS This article is concerned with certain matters which come within the range of dogmatic definition by the Church, although not themselves dogmas of faith, in the sense of the statements of the Church's understanding of divine revelation (*see* DOGMA). Section I explains the various senses in which the term is used. Section II discusses the historical background to the narrow sense. Section III discusses the Church's vindication of her right and competence in this field. In section IV a note will be added concerning Anglican Orders and whether the Bull of Leo XIII, *Apostolicae Curae*, provides an example of definition of a dogmatic fact. In the last section (V) we shall examine briefly the kind of assent which is required to such definitions on the part of members of the Church.

I Meaning of Dogmatic Facts. It is part of Catholic belief that the Church, when defining matters of belief, is an infallible teacher in proposing what has been divinely revealed by God (*see* INFALLIBILITY OF THE CHURCH). This office of the teaching Church is for the practical purpose of expounding

and defending what God has revealed, for the guidance of her members. This divine assistance is clearly concerned primarily and directly with divine revelation, the contents of which are therefore said to be the ' primary object ' of infallibility. There are other matters, however, closely connected with this body of dogmatic teaching which can be described as ' functions ' of dogma and contingent facts. On these, for the effectiveness of infallibility, the Church needs to be able to have certain judgment. A simple example is the validity of the election of a particular Pope. The dogma of papal infallibility would be of little use in the Church's teaching if there could be a genuine and insoluble doubt about the validity of a papal election. One would know that ' the Pope ' was infallible, but this would be of no use if we could never be certain who really was the validly elected holder of that office. We shall see other examples. Dogmatic facts are said, therefore, to come under the ' secondary object ' of infallibility. The link between the facts and revelation is here contingent rather than logical, as in the case of truths said to be ' virtually revealed '. Authors usually distinguish :

(*a*) Dogmatic facts in the broad sense : e.g. valid election of a Pope, legitimacy of the acts of a General Council, etc. The certain knowledge of such facts is clearly not revealed, but certainty is required for the practical exercise of infallible teaching. Without this one could never be certain of what was or was not an infallible definition.

(*b*) Dogmatic facts in the narrow sense. The discussions about dogmatic facts received considerable impetus in the 17th cent. after the condemnation by Innocent X of five propositions from the book *Augustinus* of Cornelius Janssens. We shall see more of this in section II. Largely as a result of this controversy the question of dogmatic facts has been seen to be of great importance with regard to the understanding of the genuine and clear meaning of a text or a proposition of some kind.

In this specialized sense, therefore, the Church claims the competence not only to define revealed doctrine but to judge other expressions of belief as orthodox or erroneous, not merely on the face value of the text, but of the text *as expressing the author's own meaning*. Such a decision clearly does not come within the province of revelation itself, but is a contingent fact. However, it is also clear that, unless the Church could decide with certainty on the meaning of the author, revealed truth could not be successfully defended against purely personal judgments, leading to heterodoxy.

We shall also examine another possible candidate for inclusion among decisions of this kind in the question of the force and meaning of the Bull, *Apostolicae Curae*, by which Leo XIII put an end to the discussion of the validity of Anglican Orders.

II The Condemnation of ' Augustinus '. Cornelius Janssens (1585–1638) was a reader in theology at the University of Louvain and later Bishop of Ypres. After a lifetime of study of the works of St Augustine he produced a book which he called

Augustinus, on the real understanding of Augustine's teaching on grace. The book was published in 1640, after its author's death. It was condemned in a general way by Urban VIII in 1642 because of the Calvinistic flavour of its teaching. This condemnation, promulgated in 1643, was hotly debated and declared by the followers of Janssens to be spurious. As a result of the controversy thus aroused, the matter was again referred to Rome, to Innocent X.

After two years of deliberation judgment was given in the constitution, *Cum occasione* (31 May 1653), and in particular, five propositions extracted from the work were condemned as heretical (cf. D 1092-6). These were concerned with the nature of grace and the extent of Christ's sacrificial meriting.

A ready-formed opposition party was found in Antoine Arnauld and his friends, in particular the convent at Port-Royal under its abbess, Mère Angélique Arnauld. The controversy that developed was of a most complex nature and for a full account the reader should see the article of J. Careyre, 'Jansénisme' (DTC VIII, 318-529). The general line of argument followed by the Jansenist party was that the *Augustinus* could be understood in several ways, a Lutheran and Calvinist sense, a Pelagian sense, but also in the genuine orthodox sense intended by its author. Hence there was a show of submission to the condemnation, in so far as the Protestant sense was condemned, but a resistance in that Arnauld declared that this was not in fact the genuine meaning of Janssens. The 'five propositions' were not a faithful interpretation of the *Augustinus*. Arnauld's letter 'à un duc et pair de France' (10 July 1655) elaborated this argument and rallied considerable support for the Jansenist party.

This position called out a clarification of Innocent's condemnation from his successor, Alexander VII, in the form of a constitution, *Ad sacram beati Petri sedem* (16 October 1656) in which he insisted that the five propositions were condemned 'in the sense intended by Cornelius (Janssens) himself'—'*in sensu ab eodem Cornelio intento*' (cf. D 1098). Alexander's intention was explicitly to cut through the cavilling of the Jansenists. This clear condemnation however was not accepted by the Jansenists, and it was reinforced in 1665 by a formula for submission for the Jansenists repeating the condemnation '*in sensu ab auctore intento*' (cf. D 1099).

Arnauld refused to allow that the Pope could be certain on this point of 'fact', namely that the five propositions were a sure and certain declaration of the author's intention and meaning in the *Augustinus*. Each person must decide this matter for himself. This question of fact, he said, is outside the Pope's competence because not part of revelation. Jansenist resistance continued and in 1694 Innocent XII confirmed the condemnation and the formulary which must be accepted in its obvious meaning (cf. D 1099, note 3). The Jansenists had declared that a reverent but external silence was all that need be accorded to the condemnation. This final subterfuge was removed by Clement XI in the constitution, *Vineam Domini Sabaoth* of 16 July 1705. All sons of

the Church must hear the Church, 'not only by keeping silence . . . but by obeying interiorly' (*non tacendo solum . . . sed et interius obsequendo . . .*, D 1350). The faithful are called on to reject and condemn as heretical the meaning of Janssens's book, condemned in the five propositions, whose words exhibit this sense (*. . . sed damnatum in quinque praefatis propositionibus Iansenii libri sensum, quem illarum verba prae se ferunt . . .* ; cf. D 1350).

In this complicated and protracted controversy, it emerged quite clearly that the Church claimed competence not only to define doctrine, and condemn heresy, but also to judge whether the meaning of certain texts does *in fact* manifest such a heretical sense. In other words, the Church's infallible teaching authority goes beyond the production of formulae which are divinely guaranteed to be a faithful exposition of revealed truth. She can go further and see how far other expressions measure up to the genuine sense of revealed truth, on the grounds that she is able to judge the mind of an author as objectively expressed in certain words. In cases therefore of this kind, the object of the condemnation is not the mind of the author *tout court*, nor a disembodied verbal expression, but of the mind of an author as conveyed in the words he uses.

III Arguments which show this competence. Authors usually distinguish two types of argument to prove the assertion that such dogmatic facts form a part, if secondary, of the object of the Church's divinely constituted teaching authority. The first argument is theoretical and provides a clear example of the deduction of a theological conclusion (*see* THEOLOGY, NATURE OF).

The purpose of this infallible teaching authority is to act as a sure guide to the faithful in professing the true faith and avoiding contrary errors. Against whatever philosophical background one's thoughts may be developing, the communication of ideas is in our present human condition, tied to linguistic expression. Moreover, the whole concept of divine revelation implies a native ability in the human mind to reach objective truth of absolute validity, not merely relative in its truth-value to changing human needs and cultural backgrounds (cf. *Humani Generis*, D 2306, 2320, 2323). This in its turn implies *some* objective and permanent validity in the language in which such truth is expressed, an objective value which, given an understanding of the context of the human author, can be discerned as *the meaning* of that author as expressed in the terms he uses. Consequently, if the Church were incapable of reaching a firm decision, after careful examination, about the meaning of expressions used by writers or speakers, then the whole function of preserving the deposit of revelation from erroneous and misleading expressions would be stultified and nullified from every practical point of view. The purpose of an infallible teaching authority however is precisely this, to be able to present the truth adequately for the faithful and to preserve their faith from error in its objective content. Practical infallibility therefore implies and entails this competence of the Church to decide not on the inner mind of an author (who may deliberately mislead his hearers about what he really thinks) but on the obvious and objective sense which he expresses in his writing or speech, when this is concerned with revealed truth.

The second argument used to show the competence of the Church in declaring with certainty dogmatic facts is that the Church has in fact always at least implicitly claimed this competence ; implicitly in certain cases, more or less explicitly in the Jansenist controversy which we have already discussed. Other examples usually mentioned by the authors to show the Church's *implicit* claim are : (i) the vindication of certain terms she uses (e.g. θεοτόκος—D 113, trans-substantiation—D 877) ; (ii) the condemnation of terms or expressions which are plainly heretical (e.g. condemnation of Nestorian teaching at Ephesus—D 125 ; the judgment on Theodoret at the second Council of Constantinople—D 228 ; the condemnation of Abelard by Innocent II—D 387, and numerous other examples).

Clearly, the question now arises : how certain is it that dogmatic facts come within the Church's competence for dogmatic decision ? From the actual way in which it is presented here, it is a *theological conclusion*. That is to say, it has been *deduced* from principles which are themselves of defined faith, viz., infallibility of the Church's teaching authority. Thus it could be qualified as 'theologically certain' (*see* NOTES, THEOLOGICAL). However, it may be *implied* in the very nature of this infallible *magisterium*, and does in fact seem to be. In this case it could be given a higher theological qualification, such as 'proximate to faith'. If the Church makes any further elucidations of the doctrine of infallibility as defined by the first Vatican Council, this point may well receive further clarification.

IV The Question of Anglican Orders. A strong case can be made out for the consideration of Leo XIII's Bull, *Apostolicae Curae of* 1896 (ASS 19 [1896–7] 198–201), in which he gave a definitive answer to the question of the validity of Anglican orders (*see* ORDINATION) as an example of the definition or decision of a dogmatic fact. The purely dogmatic questions involved were the general ones about intention and form in the theology of the sacraments. The dogmatic fact decided would be principally the decision that *this form* (i.e. as contained in the Edwardine *Ordinal* of 1550 and its subsequent revisions) does not measure up to the requirements for a valid sacramental rite. For example, Fr Sydney Smith SJ (DAFC III [1162–228] : s.v. *Ordinations Anglicaines*) certainly thought that this constituted a case of a decision of dogmatic fact.

The case from its nature is quite clearly a candidate for consideration of this kind. It could in no way be said that divine revelation has anything to say about the validity of orders conferred with this form. But the requirements for a valid sacramental form are part of the Church's dogmatic teaching. And so, in some way at least, the case of Anglican Orders is a decision which involves this *function* of fact and dogmatic truth.

There can be little doubt that Leo XIII himself intended to decide the question definitively. In a letter to Cardinal Richard of Paris in November 1896, Leo wrote : 'It was our purpose to deliver final judgment and to settle completely that most important question of Anglican ordinations. . . . All Catholics should receive our decision with the utmost respect, as being perpetually fixed, ratified and irrevocable'. The definitive nature of the Bull is therefore clear. But one would not want to say that every time the Pope makes a firm decision on a contingent matter involving dogmatic truth we have a case of the definition of dogmatic fact. It could be argued that the case of Anglican Orders, unlike that of the *Augustinus*, is not of sufficiently *universal* importance to come under the category of dogmatic fact. To the present writer it seems that the vital question to ask in this context is : Is this the sort of decision in which the Church's mission as an infallible teacher could not be properly and effectively fulfilled without competence to decide infallibly ? Or is it rather a decision of essentially 'local' significance and import and therefore not involving the belief of all Catholics ? Without further clarification by the Church these questions cannot be decided definitively and remain a free theological debate. Admittedly the decision has reference only to the ordinations performed according to the Anglican *Ordinal*, not even to all non-Catholic ordinations, and this would argue against its being an instance of dogmatic fact. However, on the other side, though there is a clear limitation to the number of cases to which the decision applies, nevertheless it is a decision which seems to involve a decision about what does and what does not constitute a valid sacramental rite, at least with regard to the decision about defect of form. This seems to give it an import of universal significance, extending far beyond the declaration of certain ordinations as actually invalid. In this respect it bears very close resemblance to the decisions about the meaning of *Augustinus*. However, the precise point whether this is an example of infallible decision of dogmatic fact remains open to debate.

V The Assent demanded to Statements of Dogmatic Fact (*see* FAITH). The conclusion of our study of dogmatic facts is the affirmation that such definitions of the Church as fit this category form part of the secondary object of infallible teaching. Hence they are absolutely certain and must be accepted on faith by those who belong to the Church. This assent must be as firm and unconditional as the assent to an article of faith.

The type of assent required for dogmatic facts is usually characterized as 'ecclesiastical faith'. It is not classed as 'divine faith', since the object does not materially count as part of divine revelation. But reductively, or implicitly, the motive of ecclesiastical faith is also 'God revealing', since the assent is made not simply because of the Church's testimony, though this is its immediate motive, but because it is reducible to belief in the divinely revealed truth that the Church has a divine commission to teach infallibly what is revealed or what is so closely connected with revelation as to be necessary for the proper functioning of this teaching mission.

Bibliography. L. Billot SJ, *De Ecclesia Christi*[2] (1903) ; J. Carreyre, art. 'Jansénisme', DTC VIII, 474–522 ; Y. Congar OP, 'Fait dogmatique et foi ecclésiastique', in *Catholicisme* IV, 1059–67 ; H. Dieckmann SJ, *De Ecclesia*, Vol. II (1925) ; E. Dublanchy, s.v. 'Église', DTC IV, 2188–97 ; I. Salaverri SJ, *De Ecclesia Christi*[4] (1958) ; G. Wilmers SJ, *De Christi Ecclesia* (1897) ; T. Zapelena SJ, *De Ecclesia Christi*[2] (1954) ; A. Gits, *La Foi ecclésiastique aux faits dogmatiques dans la théologie moderne* (1940).

P. F. H.

DONATISM After a historical description of the schism (I), its theological import will be considered in its bearing on ecclesiology (II), on the doctrine of the sacraments (III), and on the Church's attitude to civil support in its affairs (IV).

I History of the Schism. Our leading authority for the origins and early history of the Donatists is St Optatus, Bishop of Milevis in Numidia, whose work in seven books (PL 7) is a reply to a treatise by the only Donatist controversialist of any weight, Parmenian, third Donatist Bishop of Carthage. Parmenian's own writings do not survive except as quoted by Optatus and Augustine. Optatus also quotes extensively from the civil and ecclesiastical documents concerned with the Donatists. The authenticity of these documents has been defended by Norman Baynes (JTS, 26 [1924] 37–44 and 404–6). They will be referred to here as occasion demands. They are conveniently printed by the Benedictine editors of St Augustine's works in an appendix to the volume of his anti-Donatist writings (PL 43:773–fin).

The schism was a direct consequence of Diocletian's persecution. Persecution always produced a tension in the Church between those who favoured leniency towards the lapsed seeking reconciliation and those who would treat them with a more rigorous severity. Sometimes it was the 'laxists' who withstood what they regarded as the excessively severe discipline of the bishops, as at Carthage under Cyprian during the Decian persecution (c. A.D. 250) or at Rome during Diocletian's ; sometimes it was the 'rigorists' who went into schism, like the Novatianists at Rome about A.D. 250, or the Donatists in Africa in A.D. 312.

The issue in this latter case was that of the *traditores*, clergy who had surrendered the sacred books to the civil authorities during the persecution. In A.D. 311 Mensurius, Bishop of Carthage, died, and was succeeded by his deacon Caecilian. Both were moderate men, who had expressed their disapproval of the zealots for openly courting martyrdom during the persecution, and had earned in return their hostility. Caecilian in particular had offended a wealthy and fanatical woman called Lucilla. She financed an opposition party led by the Numidian Bishop Secundus of Tigisis, and in A.D. 312 this man assembled in Carthage a council of seventy bishops, who cited Caecilian to appear before them. He refused, and was condemned in his absence as a *traditor*. His consecration was declared invalid because it had been performed by a bishop also pronounced a *traditor*, Felix of Aptunga. In his place Majorinus, a client of Lucilla's, was consecrated Bishop of Carthage.

Meanwhile Constantine had not only ended the persecution by his edict of Milan, but also instructed his representatives in Africa to distribute a very considerable imperial largesse to the Christians ; and it was Caecilian and his party in Carthage who benefited from this. So in A.D. 313 his opponents laid before the Emperor their claim to be recognized as the lawful representatives of the Christian Church in Africa, and asked for the case to be decided by the bishops of Gaul, on the ground that the Church of that province had not been troubled by the pest of *traditores*. Constantine, however, ordered the parties to appear before Miltiades, Bishop of Rome, and his synod, while instructing three bishops from Gaul to attend as assessors. The leading spokesman for the plaintiffs was Donatus of Casae Nigrae who had succeeded both Majorinus as Caecilian's rival Bishop of Carthage and Secundus of Tigisis as leader of the party, and from whom the schism derives its name. The Donatists later maintained that Donatus the Great, Bishop of Carthage, their eponymous hero, was a distinct person from Donatus of Casae Nigrae. Both Optatus and Augustine denied the distinction, which was probably only made for obscure tactical reasons.

The Roman synod acquitted Caecilian of all charges and declared him to be the lawful Bishop of Carthage. Donatus next took his case to the general Council of the West which met at Arles in A.D. 314. Here the Roman synod's judgment was upheld ; and while the Donatists were accorded a decree that bishops who had been *traditores* should be deposed, it was affirmed that the consecrations and baptisms they performed were valid ; finally Donatus himself was found guilty of the schismatical act of rebaptizing.

The issues were now thus clearly defined ; to the Donatists the Catholics were the polluted communion of the *traditores*, to the Catholics the Donatists were the infamous sect of the rebaptizers. In A.D. 316 these latter appealed to the Emperor from the ecclesiastical decisions, which, however, he simply ratified. In addition he ordered the proconsular authorities in Africa to inquire into the case of Felix of Aptunga, Caecilian's consecrator, and the effect of the inquiry, of which the *Acta* are preserved by Optatus (PL 43:780–6), was to clear him of the charge of being a *traditor*, so that even on Donatist premisses Caecilian's consecration should be regarded as valid.

At the same time facts very damaging to the Donatist cause seem to have been revealed by lesser members of the party with grievances. In particular an account of a small synod or meeting of twelve bishops at Cirta in A.D. 305, under Secundus of

Tigisis, showed that both he and his colleagues, who all took part later on in the proceedings against Caecilian, had all been *traditores* themselves. The later Donatists always maintained that the Council of Cirta was fabricated evidence ; and indeed the details alleged are so grotesque, and make these rigorists, from the very outset of their schism, into such barefaced hypocrites, that it would seem prudent to give them the benefit of the doubt (PL 43:793–800).

There is no doubt, however, that they were men of a determined and ruthlessly unscrupulous energy. Under the able leadership of Donatus they ignored the imperial displeasure with impunity. In many towns they took possession of basilicas built by Constantine for the Catholics, and soon made themselves the dominant Christian body in the provinces of Africa, Numidia and Mauretania.

In A.D. 345 the Emperor Constantius sent to Africa two commissioners, Macarius and Paulus, with imperial alms for the Churches. A violent reception awaited them from the Donatist strong-arm men, the Circumcellions, bands of religious terrorists who were to be the bane of Africa for the next seventy years or so. Augustine's letters are full of their outrages, which included throwing a mixture of lime and vinegar (a kind of *Urvitriol*) in people's faces, and also religious suicide by jumping over cliffs, for which they were accorded the honours of martyrdom. They drew their strength from the Punic, or more probably Berber-speaking, inhabitants of the remoter districts in Numidia, and the social, economic and cultural pressures behind the movement have been rightly investigated by modern historians. But it is a misleading oversimplification of all the issues simply to identify the Catholics with an alien, urban, Latin culture, and the Donatists with an indigenous, popular, rural resistance to the Roman domination. The Donatists were as Latin as the Catholics in their worship, only rather more conservatively so ; their leaders were men of normal Latin education ; they drew support from wealthy landowners whose religious convictions were imposed on their tenants. On the other hand the Catholics were not unrepresented among the poorer classes and in the remoter country towns and villages.

Macarius forcibly repressed the Circumcellions, and in A.D. 348 Donatus was exiled with many of his colleagues. He died in exile *c*. A.D. 355. From then on, the Donatists looked back to the 'tempora Macariana' as their heroic age of persecution ; the fact of being persecuted automatically vindicated, in their opinion, their claim to righteousness.

The exiles were allowed to return in A.D. 361 by Julian the Apostate, and under Donatus's successor, Parmenian, who lived until *c*. A.D. 390, the Donatists attained their zenith. They also began to suffer the first serious strains of internal dissension. They were greatly embarrassed by their most gifted writer, Tychonius, a careful student of the Scriptures, who saw and publicly pointed out the inconsistencies of the Donatist position. Parmenian wrote him an open letter of remonstrance and refutation, and many

years later Augustine, who had great respect for Tychonius as an exegete, wrote a reply to this letter in three books (*Contra Epistolam Parmeniani*, PL 43:33–108).

But more damaging than Tychonius's indiscretions were the sub-schisms which soon broke out within the sect. The first permanent splinter group were the Rogatists, who, however, soon dwindled to an insignificant handful in West Mauretania. But when Parmenian died, there was a more serious schism in the Donatist see of Carthage itself. A faction hostile to his successor, Primian, consecrated a rival bishop, Maximian. The pattern of the original schism against Caecilian was very exactly repeated, to the glee of Catholic controversialists. For not only did the main Donatist body invoke secular aid against the Maximianists, though it was one of their chief points against the Catholics that they manifested their unrighteousness by doing precisely this against the Donatists ; they also, in order to repair the damage of this second schism, in effect recognized the sacraments of the Maximianists as valid, and received them back into communion without any rebaptism, thus again logically depriving their own continued separation from the Catholics of its *raison d'être*.

From A.D. 390 the sect began to decline, not without violent death-throes in the depradations of the brigand Bishop Optatus of Thamugadi, a prelate of quite legendary villainy who threw in his lot with the rebel Gildo. Augustine succinctly calls him 'the man who made all Africa groan for ten years' (*decennalis totius Africae gemitus* [*Contra Parm.* II:4 ; PL 43:51]). Frend, in *The Donatist Church*, tries heroically but with little evidence to paint him as a genial, though admittedly ruthless Robin Hood. No government could possibly wink at Optatus, and it is not surprising that the State's pressure on the sect became steadily more relentless. So too did the controversial skill and truly miraculous patience of Augustine, with his unwearied exposure of the real issues at stake, and his repeated challenge to public discussion of them.

The climax came with the great Conference at Carthage in A.D. 411, convoked by the Emperor Honorius at the request of the Catholic bishops, and presided over by the Imperial Commissioner, Marcellinus. The result was a foregone conclusion, not simply as the cynic might assume because both Emperor and official were Catholics, but because the Donatist case was so totally lacking in substance. A glance at the *Acta* of the Conference (PL 43:815 ff.) will show that Marcellinus treated the Donatists and their obstructive filibusters with the most magnanimous and courteous forbearance.

After the Conference, it was simply a long and never wholly successful mopping-up operation. Donatist church property was confiscated, bishops who refused to return to Catholic unity were subject to fine and exile. Those, however, who sought reconciliation, with or without their congregations, were received on the most generous terms, and allowed to retain their rank and jurisdiction.

II Donatism and the Nature of the Church. The

Donatist axiom was that the sins of heresy, schism and apostasy—and the *traditor's* sin was apostasy—not only cut the sinner off from the Church's communion, but also deprived him of any ecclesial status whatever, so that he could not validly administer any sacraments, particularly baptism and ordination. Hence the Catholic party in Africa, deriving from their invalidly consecrated 'father' Caecilian, a *traditor* ordained by a *traditor*, was wholly unchurched ; and as sin and its consequences are highly infectious, the overseas Churches which communicated with the African Catholics fell under the same condemnation by consenting to their sins, and were unchurched too. The Donatists therefore alone were the Church of Christ.

The implication, stressed by the Catholics and accepted by the Donatists, was that the Church was the society only of the just, without qualification the communion of saints. The practical human impossibility of living up to this implication was the great weakness of the Donatist position, to which they seem to have been singularly blind, and which the Catholics of course exploited *ad nauseam*.

The contrary Catholic position is stated clearly in the *mandatum* given by the Catholic bishops to the seven spokesmen who were to put their case in the Conference at Carthage. The leading spokesman was Augustine, and we can also see his hand in the *mandatum* itself. The Catholic representatives are above all to insist on the distinction between the *causa ecclesiae* and the *causa quorundam hominum*. The Church's case is to be pleaded on its own merits, for it in no way depends on the rights and wrongs of the case of Caecilian, Felix, Donatus, Secundus or any other individual.

The true Church is to be identified from the portrait of her given in the gospels, in the parables of the wheat and the cockle, sheep and goats, the catch of good fishes and bad, the grain and the chaff on the threshing-floor. It had been foretold by the Saviour that the Church would contain evil men mixed with good. 'The whole harvest on the threshing-floor, the whole flock, the whole catch of fish, is not to be cast away on their account ; rather should the bad be borne within the unity of the faith for the sake of the good' (*Coll. Carth. Acta* 4 ; PL 43:824).[1]

This doctrine is developed in detail by Augustine in his *De Baptismo contra Donatistas*. This is a sustained exegesis of Cyprian's *Epistola ad Jubaianum*, and the *Acta* of his Council at Carthage, *c.* A.D. 250, which had decreed that heretics coming to the Church were to be rebaptized. Cyprian was of course the basic authority for the Donatists. But besides refuting Cyprian's arguments for rebaptism, Augustine cites his authority and example in favour of ecclesiastical unity. Cyprian explicitly refused to impose his opinion about baptism on bishops who differed from him, and never took his undoubtedly embittered disagreement with Pope Stephen of Rome to the point of open rupture. Moreover, he remained in communion with bishops whose corruption and avarice he lamented. Thus his example illustrates the truth that absolutely anything is better than schism : 'Nothing is worse than the sacrilege of schism, for there is no possible justification for rending the unity of the Church' (*contra Ep. Parm.* II:25, PL 43:69).[2]

For schism is *the* sin against charity, which with its effect of unity is of the essence of the Church. Where we nowadays tend to see oneness of faith as the hallmark of Catholic unity, Augustine looked deeper and saw charity as the primary unifying principle. On the one hand he says: 'I think no one can be so lacking in sense as to consider that he who has not charity can belong to the unity of the Church' (*contra Cresconium* 1:34 ; PL 43:464).[3] On the other hand charity is the pearl beyond price which the Church holds out to those who come to her : 'When members of your party come to us, they are made partakers for the first time of the Church herself and in her of peace, charity and unity coming from her very own invisible fountain, the Holy Spirit' (ibid. II:19 ; PL 43:477).[4]

This doctrine of the Church, less *simpliste* than the Donatist, does more justice to the mystery of the Church. Sinners who lack charity, even if Catholic by faith and profession, do not belong, one might say, to the vital or inner unity of the Church, which is constructed precisely of the links of charity. Yet in another sense they do belong to the Church and have to be tolerated within its net by and for the sake of that unity and that charity. It is only at the last judgment that the exact *discretio* will take place ; only in its eschatological perfection that the Church will consist not only inwardly but also manifestly of the saints bound together by charity, and that the wicked will be manifestly excluded from all connection or membership.

A correlative of the Church's unity is its catholicity (*see* CATHOLIC CHURCH). The unity of the universal Church, found in all nations, is the visible manifestation of the universal dominion, the totality of Christ. It is the *totus Christus*. Donatism, by confining the Church of Christ to one corner of Africa, is a *reductio ad absurdum* of the prophecies and promises of Scripture. The Catholics of Africa made their case incontrovertible by simply being in communion with the other Churches of the *Catholica* throughout the world. 'The whole world can judge, and judge without a qualm, that they are not good, wherever they are, who break themselves off from the rest of the world' (*contra Ep. Parm.* III:24 ; PL 43:101).[5]

Securus judicat orbis terrarum ; the phrase that had such a stunning effect on Newman when he read it in Wiseman's article in the *Dublin Review* (1839).

[1] Non ergo propter eos tota messis, tota area, grex totus, piscatio tota damnata est . . . cum potius malos propter bonos pia unitate tolerare debeamus.

[2] Non est quidquam gravius sacrilegio schismatis ; quia praecidendae unitatis nulla est justa necessitas.

[3] Non existimo quemquam ita desipere ut credat ad Ecclesiae pertinere unitatem eum qui non habet caritatem.

[4] Cum ergo veniunt ad nos vestri, . . . accipiunt primitus ipsam Ecclesiam, et in ea pacem, caritatem, unitatem, per fontem ejus proprium atque invisibilem Spiritum Sanctum.

[5] Securus judicat orbis terrarum bonos non esse qui se dividunt ab orbe terrarum in quacunque parte terrarum.

It affected him, he says, like the voice saying : ' Turn again, Dick Whittington ', or the even more famous voice singing ' *Tolle lege* '. But in fact the comparison of Anglicans to Donatists is not a very just one since the cases are so dissimilar, as Newman himself saw and pointed out. That is probably why he had to wait six years after hearing his ' *Tolle lege* ' before rational conviction on patristic evidence carried him into the Catholic Church.

What one might call the juridical structure of the *Catholica* played little part in Augustine's arguments. A local Council (Cyprian's) must yield to the decision of a universal Council (probably Arles is meant) which settled the issue of baptism against Cyprian once and for all. So he appeals to the Donatists : ' Come to the universal Church which is at peace seeing that Cyprian did not desert it even when it was in peril ' (*De Bapt.* II:20 ; PL 43:140).[1] He certainly attached a particular importance to communion with the Roman see ; thus he says that Carthage as a metropolitan city has a bishop ' of no small prestige, since he is manifestly linked in communion with other lands but especially with the Roman church where the authority of the apostolic throne has ever prevailed ' (*Ep.* 43:7 ; PL 33:163).[2] But he scarcely seems to develop this into an argument.

III Donatism and the Sacraments.

When the question of heretical baptism first arose in St Cyprian's day, the holders of the Roman opinion that such baptism is valid did not support their contention with arguments ; they merely appealed rather stiffly to tradition. Cyprian and his colleagues, who had a number of arguments to back their case, countered that *consuetudo* could not override *ratio*. It remained for Augustine to work out fully the *rationale* of the Roman and Catholic practice. Here we can list only the chief points of sacramental doctrine that emerge.

(*a*) The first point of importance is that order is a sacrament just like baptism. Augustine does not prove this ; he assumes it as a premiss in argument, a premiss that was common to the Donatists as well. In so doing he is perhaps one of the earliest unequivocal witnesses to the sacramentality, in the strictest sense, of order. In an *ad hominem* argument, he adopts his rivals' language, and calls order *jus dandi baptismum*. They admit that someone who leaves the Church does not lose his baptism, but say that he loses his right to give it. But they do not say why this is so. ' For each is a sacrament ; each is given a man by a kind of consecration, the first when he is baptized, the other when he is ordained ; and thus neither may be lawfully repeated in the Catholic Church ' (*contra Ep. Parm.* II:28 ; PL 43:70).[3]

(*b*) The validity of the sacrament does not depend on the holiness of the minister, because in conferring it he is not giving something of his own, but acting as the proxy of Christ. There is only one baptism and that is Christ's, and it is from Christ that the sacramental sanctification comes to the recipient, not from the minister. Because it is Christ's baptism, it is also the Catholic Church's, whoever confers it, and whether inside or outside the Church's communion. But it can be received fruitfully only inside the Church's communion (by an adult). Thus a distinction is made between the sacrament (which includes in its scope the character) and the moral dispositions appropriate to it. ' The sacrament of baptism is one thing, and another the change of heart ; but a man's salvation is made up of both ' (*De Bapt.* IV:32 ; PL 43:176).[4] Each of these two co-efficients of salvation can, extraordinarily, be an efficient of it without the other. Baptism alone saves infants, without any *conversio cordis* ; this *conversio* alone will save an adult without the sacrament, as in the case of the good thief. [In *Retractationes* 2:18 ; PL 32:638 Augustine withdrew this example of the good thief, saying that he did not know whether the man had been baptized. He then preferred to consider the death as some form of martyrdom.] It will bring the grace of baptism before baptism, as it did to Cornelius. But it would not have saved him had he, on receiving the Holy Ghost, then despised the sacrament as something vain and superfluous. Similarly the sacrament will not save if *conversio cordis* is positively withheld—and this is presumed to be the case with someone deliberately seeking baptism in a sect outside the Church.

(*c*) Granted this distinction, and granted the efficacy of *conversio cordis* for salvation—what we nowadays call baptism of desire—it is difficult to say, as Augustine is frank enough to admit, precisely what the good is of the actual application of the sacramental rite—*sanctificatio sacramenti corporaliter adhibita*—(*De Bapt.* IV:30 ; PL 43:174). But that it certainly is of the utmost good cannot be doubted. It is a real co-efficient of salvation, not a mere ritual formality. Hence contempt of it or indifference is a real bar to salvation. Finally, this distinction is the basis of, but not the same as, the later theological distinction between *sacramentum tantum* and *res sacramenti* or *res tantum*, between the sacramental sign and the sacramental reality.

IV The Church's Attitude to Civil Support.

St Augustine's attitude to the coercion of heretics, schismatics and pagans by the civil power was from the beginning wholly pragmatic. It is a great mistake to try to work out any *a priori* principles from his practice ; he never had any. At first he differed from his fellow bishops in disapproving of it, because he thought it would do harm. Later he changed his mind because he thought experience showed that it did good. It must be borne in mind that civil involvement in the ecclesiastical dispute was from the very beginning just one of the facts of the situation.

[1] Venite ad Catholicam concordantem quam Cyprianus non deseruit fluctuantem.

[2] Non mediocris auctoritatis, cum se videret et Romanae Ecclesiae, in qua semper apostolicae cathedrae viguit principatus, et ceteris terris . . . esse conjunctum.

[3] Utrumque enim sacramentum est ; et quadam consecratione utrumque homini datur, illud cum baptizatur, istud cum ordinatur ; ideoque in Catholica utrumque non licet iterari.

[4] Aliud esse sacramentum baptismi, aliud conversionem cordis ; sed salutem hominis ex utroque compleri.

And the activities of the Circumcellions made it hard for the civil authorities with any propriety to play the Gallio and stand aloof.

The *locus classicus* for his views on the subject is his letter to the Rogatist Bishop Vincent, who had been an undergraduate with him at Carthage (*Ep.* 93 ; PL 33:321 ff.). He brushes aside all generalizations about the use of force ; its rightness or wrongness depends on the intentions of the user. Likewise, whether or not the suffering of violence is virtuous depends on what it is suffered for. ' You see that it is no longer a question of the fact that compulsion is used on some, but rather of the nature of that towards which they are compelled, whether it be good or bad. It is not a question of making a man good against his will, but of getting him, through fear of what he dislikes, willingly to accept what previously he did not.' (Ibid. 93:16 ; PL 33:329).[1] Granted that driving the horse to water will not make it drink—but you may well find that it decides to drink after all.

He makes the vital point that penal laws alone are useless, and indeed unjust. What is required is a combination of legal penalties and pastoral instruction. ' If fear was aroused in them and no instruction given, it would seem like a wicked tyranny [and this is a point persecutors have too often overlooked]. But when to a wholesome fear there is added instruction in the way of salvation, and, while the light of truth dispels the gloom of error, the bonds of vicious habit are broken by a strong fear, we have reason to rejoice in the salvation of many, as I have pointed out ' (ibid. 93:3 ; PL 33:322–3).[2]

Finally, the penalties he had in mind were fines and exile, never death. He vehemently opposed capital punishment for any crime against the Church—even if it happened to be murder (*Ep.* 133 to Marcellinus ; PL 33:509: *ep.* 134 to Apringius ; ibid. 510.)

Bibliography. Three modern works in English (none of them by a Catholic author) are W. H. C. Frend's *The Donatist Church* (1952), a book of immense historical learning, often displaying an odd combination of perceptiveness and perverseness in its judgments, especially on Augustine's anti-Donatist activities ; G. G. Willis's *St Augustine and the Donatist Controversy* (1950), a balanced study of the theological issues, and G. Bonner, *St Augustine of Hippo* (1963), an excellent theological introduction. See also P. Monceaux, *Histoire litteraire de l'Afrique chrétienne* (7 vols., 1923) ; P. de Labriolle, *Latin Christianity* (Eng. tr. 1924) ; H. I. Marrou, *Saint Augustin et la fin de la culture antique* (1938) ; H. Pope, *St Augustine and His Times* (1937). Other works of Augustine not quoted in this article are *Contra Litteras*

[1] Vides itaque jam non esse considerandum quod quisque cogitur, sed quale sit illud quo cogitur, utrum bonum an malum ; non quo quisque bonus possit esse invitus, sed timendo quod non vult pati . . ., volens teneat jam quod nolebat.

[2] Si enim terrerentur et non docerentur, improba quasi dominatio videretur. Cum vero terrori utili doctrina salutaris adjungitur, ut non solum tenebras erroris lux veritatis expellat, verum etiam malae consuetudinis vincula vis timoris abrumpat, de multorum sicut dixi salute laetamur.

Petiliani, lib. III (PL 43:245) ; *De Unitate Ecclesiae* (ibid. 391) ; *De Unico Baptismo contra Petilianum* (ibid. 595) ; *Breviculus Collationis cum Donatistis* (ibid. 613) ; *De Gestis cum Emerito* (ibid. 697) ; *Contra Gaudentium*, lib. II (ibid. 707).　　M. E. H.

DOORKEEPERS. See ORDERS

DOXOLOGY, a form of prayer in which one wishes glory to the Trinity, or to one or more of the Three Persons, was usual at the opening or conclusion of an early Christian's prayer. The habit was taken over from the Jewish *berakoth*. The familiar Jewish phrase : ' Blessed be the God of our Fathers ', gave place very soon among the Christians to : ' Blessed be the God and Father of our Lord ', as in 2 Cor 1:3 ; Eph 1:3 ; 1 Pet 1:3. In fact, the only Christians to speak of ' the God of our fathers ' in the whole NT are Peter (twice, in Ac 3:13 ; 5:30), Stephen (Ac 7:32) and Ananias (Ac 22:14). As soon as the Church's horizon widened beyond the people of Israel, such a change would have been imperative. Remnants of early Christian hymns, which are thought to be recognizable at Rom 9:5 ; 1 Cor 8:6 ; 1 Tim 3:16 ; 6:15–16 ; 2 Tim 2:12 ; Phil 2:6–11, though they do not all culminate in a doxology as they are quoted in the NT, yet probably had one in their original composition. The *Mishna* (*Berakoth*, 9) tells how at the conclusion of the Benedictions said in the Temple the words ' for ever ' used to be said. ' But when the Sadducees perverted their ways and asserted that there was only one world, it was ordained that the response should be " for ever and for ever ".' This is clearly the source of the ending to the Christian doxologies.

Bishop Westcott, who began the scientific study of doxologies (in an appendix to his *Epistle to the Hebrews*, 1889) enumerated sixteen of them in the NT. Three of these (2 Tim 4:18 ; 2 Pet 3:18 and Apoc 1:6) are certainly addressed to Christ alone. Three others (Heb 13:21 ; 1 Pet 4:11 and Rom 9:5) may be so. Two ascribe glory to God through Christ (Rom 16:27 and Jude 25). Four (Gal 1:5 ; Phil 4:20 ; Rom 11:36 and 2 Tim 4:18) are almost identical, word for word, while Eph 3:21 is unique for its mention of the Church. Some think that the ' unity of the Holy Spirit ' which finds mention in later Trinitarian doxologies originates from here and means the unity which the Spirit brings about, i.e. the Church. It should not be thought that, when a doxology occurs in a NT epistle, this must mark the end of one document and the start of another. Only a very mechanical criticism makes such a mistake. Doxologies can occur whenever the mind of the writer is caught up to a realization of the goal of all human existence, and this is not seldom in inspired writers, or even in preachers such as Melito (*Homily on Passion*, 10 ; 45 ; 65).

The first Trinitarian doxologies are reported by Justin (*apol.* 65:3 and 67:2) in his description of the Eucharist as he knew it (*c.* A.D. 130–50), and one of these is quoted by Clement (Quis dives salvetur 42 ; GCS 17:191). Julius Africanus, the friend and contemporary of Origen, speaks of a ' rule for sentences of this kind ', when he cites a Trinitarian doxology (he is appealed to by Basil, in *De Spiritu sancto* 73 ; PG 32:204), and Denis of Alexandria, writing to the Pope about A.D. 260, also appeals to ' the model and rule for doxologies at the Eucharist which we have received from the elders who went before us ' (*Letters* of Denis, edited by Feltoe, 198). It is significant that such a rule was established and in possession before the great Trinitarian controversies had begun to shake the Church. When they did, doxologies were often tampered with in MSS, and it becomes quite unsafe to draw conclusions from doxologies that have come down to us in the various derivative documents based upon the lost original of Hippolytus's *Traditio apostolica*. The way in which liturgical prayers could be used in dogmatic controversies is made clear by the Arian fragments published by Mercati (*Studi e Testi* VII [1902] 47–56). The doxology with which Hippolytus ends his *Contra Noetum* (PG 10:829) : ' Glory and might to the Son, with Father and Holy Spirit, in the holy Church . . .' is most nearly reproduced by the Ethiopic version of the *Traditio*, while the *Apostolic Constitutions* in characteristically Arian fashion suppress the ascription of might to the Son and alter the wording to remove the impression of equality between the Persons which the original formula may be presumed to have preserved.

The Jews had the Book of Psalms divided into five sections by doxologies (which are found at the end of Pss 41, 72, 89 and 106 [Hebrew numbering], while Ps 150 is itself an extended doxology), and this would make it quite natural for the Christians to close each psalm with the Trinitarian doxology *Gloria Patri et Filio et Spiritui sancto*. Cassian (PL 49:94) noted this usage when he came into the West for the first time from the East. The Christian titles of the psalms were first compiled in the 3rd cent., the oldest series being the Columban, and though one of these sets is due to Eusebius of Caesarea (being found in *Codex Alexandrinus*) it is possible that they originated in the West about the same time as the doxology came into use with the psalms. The variations in the Eastern form of the *Gloria Patri* (' *through* the Son *in* the Holy Spirit ' or ' *with* the Son and *with* the Spirit ') are abundantly discussed by Basil in his treatise *De Spiritu sancto* 59 (PG 32:176). When attempts were made to introduce a mention of the Holy Spirit into a traditional doxology which ascribed praise to the Father through the Son and which went back (e.g. via 1 Clem 61 and 64) to the NT, it is obvious that the resulting Trinitarian form would lend itself to Arian abuse, and this is what in fact happened.

Doxology as a term of art is first found in the Gnostic writers, who are referred to by Justin (*dial.* 7:3) and Irenaeus (*adv. haer.* I:8:8, H), and Hippolytus (*ref. haer.* 6:48:3 ; GCS 26:180). Examples of these doxologies can be found in the magical papyri, and the Church's need for controlling the use of doxologies must have been acute by the middle of the 2nd cent. The appearance about that time of the addition to Mt 6:13 (' For Thine is the kingdom, the

power and the glory ') shows what could happen ; a doxology which is found separate in the *Didache* made its way into Coptic, Old Latin and Syriac versions of the NT and even (by retroversion ?) into some of the later Greek MSS of the NT such as the Freer *codex*. The pseudo-Cyprianic prayer (CSEL 3:3:146) : ' Father in Son and Son in Father, through whom and with whom is Thine the power and the glory in holy Church . . .[1] may be an expanded form of this prayer.

The *Gloria in excelsis* is sometimes called the Greater doxology, as distinct from the Lesser (the *Gloria Patri*), and there are many problems about the original intent of the prayer ; was it to glorify the Son alone, or was it Trinitarian from the start ? These problems are still unresolved. Similar problems occur with the *Te decet laus*, a Trinitarian form of which is found in *Apostolic Constitutions* (7:48:3), and with the *Te Deum* itself.

Bibliography. A. Stuiber, in RAC IV: 210–25, s.v. Doxologie ; J. Jungmann SJ, ' *In unitate Spiritus sancti* ', in ZKT 72 (1950) 481–6 ; B. Capelle OSB, ' Le Texte du Gloria ', in RHE 44 (1949) 439–57 ; R. Connolly OSB (with J. Armitage Robinson), ' The Doxology in the Prayer of St Polycarp ', in JTS 24 (1923) 141–6 ; J. Lebreton SJ, *Histoire du Dogme de la Trinité* (1928) vol. II:189–248.   J. H. C.

DUNS SCOTUS AND HIS INFLUENCE

This article will give the elementary facts (I) about the life of John Duns, the state of opinion (II) about his authentic works and (III) a brief estimate of his importance in theology.

I The life of John Duns, son of Ninian, has become better known in the last twenty years. He was born at Littledean, Maxton-on-Tweed, in 1265 or 1266. There is documentary proof that he was ordained priest in the friary of St Andrew at Northampton by Oliver Sutton, Bishop of Lincoln, on 17 March 1291. Some have concluded that he must have joined the Franciscans in 1280, but an eleven-year course of study before ordination seems too long. His family belonged to the landed gentry of Scotland and had given property to the Franciscans earlier in the century, and one of his uncles had joined them.

His earlier teaching was at Cambridge and at Oxford (though perhaps not in that sequence). He had taught for some time in Paris, when in the summer of 1303 he was forced to leave, having refused to side with the French king against the Pope. He returned to Oxford for the year 1303–4 and then went back to Paris to become doctor of theology, the event being the occasion for his defence of the *Quaestiones quodlibetales*. His last year of life (1307–8) was spent at Cologne, where he died. His tomb in the Franciscan church there had the inscription:

> *Scotia me genuit* ; *Anglia suscepit*:
> *Gallia edocuit* ; *Germania tenet.*

II His major works are his commentaries on the *Sentences* of Peter Lombard, given in Oxford and

[1] Pater in Filio, Filius in Patre ; per quem et cum quo est Tibi in sancta ecclesia virtus, honor. . . .

in Paris. The *Opus Oxoniense* is now being edited from numerous MSS. by a Franciscan group led by C. Balic, and is styled by them *Ordinatio* ; since 1950 six volumes have appeared. The difficulties in the way of a critical edition are great, and this for the reason that Scotus was so popular an author immediately in his own day and was copied and recopied by his contemporaries. The preference given in the new edition to an Assisi MS. (137) may be sound, but the fact that it has a maximum number (75) of passages marked with the note: *Non in libro Duns*, and also a maximum (116) of additions marked: *Extra de manu Scoti*, does not inspire confidence. One can see that it may be the most carefully edited of the early codices, but this fact would not exclude the possibility that other MSS. were nearer to the original of Scotus and not in need of so much editing. The editors speak of one MS. being in the possession of Sir Sydney Cockerell in 1899 and add that they could not trace it. When they wrote in 1950, Sir Sydney was still alive, and not the man to be vague about what he had done with his treasures.

The *Reportata Parisiensia* are probably pupils' lecture-notes from the course Scotus gave on the *Sentences* at Paris, and what revision these notes were subjected to by Scotus himself must be a matter of minute investigation which is still to be made. There are also *Reportata Cantabrigiensia* still extant in the Todi MS., and these seem to be earlier than those of Paris or Oxford.

The *De primo principio* is an authentic *opusculum*, covering the same ground as some of the opening questions of the *Ordinatio* ; but the *De rerum principio* is not by Scotus. There is still a diversity of opinion about the *Theoremata* ; Fr Balic (1950) accepts this work as authentic, while Fr Longpré (1952) rejects it as anti-Scotist, containing propositions put by his adversaries. Balic urged that there was a reference in the *De primo principio* to a work which was described as *in sequenti, scilicet in theorematibus*, but unless it could be proved that this reference was set down by Scotus himself, little would be gained by it towards the proof that the *Theoremata* are authentic. it was the habit of scribes to add references, helpful or unhelpful, to what they were copying.

The commentaries on the *Metaphysics* of Aristotle, on the *De interpretatione*, *Sophistici elenchi*, *Categoriae* are all authentic, while that on the *De anima* is still open to question. Balic, who accepts it, admits that it was 'compiled and published' by a disciple, Antonius Andreas, from the work of Scotus. The *Quodlibet* (mentioned above) and some forty-six *Collationes* are genuine works of Scotus.

One of the earliest printed editions of the works of Scotus was by Thomas Penketh, an English Augustinian at Padua (1477 and 1481), but the best early edition was by Maurice O'Fihely (Venice, 1506, 1514, 1521 and Paris, 1513). He may be the source of the belief that Scotus was an Irishman. In earlier times the adjective did indicate Hibernian origins, as it did for the illustrious Eriugena, and it may be that some memory was preserved of the ordination on St Patrick's Day. This mistake was fortunate, since it led a group of Irish Franciscans in the 17th cent. to devote their energies to the continuation of the Scotist tradition. Hugh MacCaughwell (Cavellus), Anthony Hickey (Hiquaeus) and Luke Wadding all took part in this work and their monumental *opera omnia* of 1639 still remains the standard edition that is only slowly being replaced by that of the Franciscan Scotus Commission. The 14th and 15th cents. were so very much more under the influence of Scotus than of Aquinas that the MSS. and early printed editions of his works were multiplied beyond all measure, and Oxford was not the only place where the Reformers ' put Duns in Bocardo '.

III The influence of the thought of Scotus upon theology was in the direction of speculation upon the data of revelation. Thus his subtlety can be praised or blamed, but its origin should be sought in the doctrine of the Trinity. Nature and person are non-identical in God, and yet person is not added to nature as thing to thing. Here is the source of the formal distinction (*formalis a parte rei*), which is not a mere distinction in thought nor so wide as that between thing and thing. If it is found in God, surely it will have left some trace in God's world.

Scotus was an introvert and though he did not follow Augustine and such medieval disciples as Henry of Ghent in claiming that the human mind needs a freely given illumination from God to carry out its work of rational thought, he was willing to agree with Augustine against Aquinas that the human mind has direct awareness of its own states. He even ventured to support this from Aristotle, who (in *Metaphysics* D, 1010 b 3–10) had said that we know our waking state immediately, as we do the principles of reasoning. Scotus says (*Ordinatio* 1:3:4) that there is a conviction laid up in the mind that a faculty is not liable to error when dealing with its proper object unless it be indisposed.[1] He was fond of this idea of a *propositio quiescens in intellectu* and used it to work out an elementary theory of induction (*see* CERTAINTY). Scotus was also led by his bias towards introspection to take up a theory of being which put the emphasis on how the human mind thinks of being rather than on how being exists (*see* ANALOGY OF BEING, VII).

In Christology Scotus followed the Franciscan tradition of Bonaventure and others in seeing the Incarnation as the crown of all creation and not simply due to Adam's sin. Where St Thomas (*Summa*, 3a:19:1) stressed the instrumental character of the human nature of Christ (in this he was following John Damascene), Scotus held out for a separate actual existence of the human nature in the hypostatic union (*esse actualis existentiae*) on the ground that otherwise the reality of the death on the cross would be imperilled (*Ordinatio* III:6:1). In the opinion of many, this was a prolongation of the views set out by St Thomas in the *Quaestio disputata de unione Verbi Divini*, a work of the latest years of his life, when Scotus was a boy of seven. These debates naturally led to great speculation about the status of the human

[1] Ista veritas quiescit in intellectu quod potentia non errat circa obiectum proportionatum nisi indisposita.

nature during the three days between Calvary and the Resurrection, and ultimately to the dispute between Dominicans and Franciscans about the blood of Christ shed on Calvary (D 718), a dispute that was left undecided by Pius II in 1464.

The voluntarism of Scotus is often opposed to the intellectualism of St Thomas. Certainly Scotus was fascinated by the problem of freedom and necessity in God. Holding that freedom of will was a simple perfection which must therefore be found in God, he was not content to say that this freedom was exercised in the unnecessary act of creation, but carried the problem further back into the nature of God. Instancing a human example of freedom co-existing with necessity in the suicidal man, who while falling off a cliff nevertheless wills (or acquiesces, or is complacent, in) his falling, Scotus argued (*Quodlibet* 16) that God could be thought of as similarly ratifying by a free complacency His necessary love of Himself. Once this distinction had been secured in the being of God, it was open to Scotus to present human free-will as not an imperfection nor merely an accident due to the dullness of the human intellect, which cannot understand completely what is good for it. If freedom is thus not a vanishing quantity which has to diminish as one moves up the scale of being, it is clear that God may be supremely free, and the door is open to the theories of the Occamists about the *potentia absoluta* of God as distinct from His *potentia ordinata*. Scotus himself held (*Ordinatio* III:37:1) that the natural law is immutable, even for God, but he had perhaps given an opening to the Occamists here.

The ideas of Scotus about the individual existents of this world have been much illuminated by their being taken up by the poet G. M. Hopkins. 'There lives the dearest freshness deep down things', is a more acceptable presentation of the idea than the rugged *haecceitas* or this-ness.

'Each mortal thing does one thing and the same :
  Deals out that being indoors each one dwells ;
  Selves—goes itself ; myself it speaks and spells,
  Crying, What I do is me : for that I came.'
(*Poems*, 34)

Hopkins coined the word 'inscape' to mean the outward expression of this inner self-nature of each individual thing and made it an integral part of his poetical theory ; nothing like this has happened in recent times to make the theory of individuation opposed to Scotus appear attractive. Whether the physicists in their scrutiny of the inner constituents of matter find the Scotist theory as attractive as the poets do is another question, one which the scientists themselves have to answer when they have time for it. Not that it is for them to settle a metaphysical debate, but they can supply pointers towards the truth or untruth of the rival theories.

The infinity of God is established by Scotus philosophically by means of Anselm's ontological argument, used as a follow-up to the *a posteriori* proofs of God's existence from contingent being (*Ordinatio* I:2:2:25–32 and *De primo principio* 4). In thus giving Anselm's argument an indirect claim to

validity, Scotus anticipated the work of Leibniz. When Scotus goes on to distinguish between omnipotence as the object of faith and God's infinite power which can be proved by reason, he has made the work of his critics difficult (*Ordinatio* I:42:1) ; he was envisaging the problem of God's co-operation with creatures (*Quodlibet* 7:4) and considered that if one said that God can do all, the causality of creatures is endangered. This problem, he thought, could be solved only in the light of revelation.

That Scotus 'fired France for Mary without spot', as Hopkins has it in his poem, is the accepted conclusion of the historians of dogma, though in recent years there has been a sharp controversy about it between Fr Balic and Fr Roschini OSM. In 1938 an article by Roschini in the *Osservatore Romano* claimed M. Lazzari OSM (who died in 1348) as the first defender of the Immaculate Conception, Scotus being dismissed as not having advanced beyond the assertion of the possibility of the privilege. These claims were repeated several times, especially in *Duns Scoto e l'Immacolata* (1955). In reply to this last, Balic in *Antonianum* 30 (1955) 349–488 fully vindicated the claims of Scotus. It now appears that the treaties of Lazzari is completely lost and conjectures about its contents seem to be of doubtful value (*see also* CONCEPTION, IMMACULATE).

There are several other Scotist positions in theology which have been adopted in recent times by those who show no awareness that in fact they are following Scotus. Thus one may find a whole group of theologians, engaged in the debate about the natural desire of the vision of God, classified as neo-Scotists in spite of themselves by a chronicler of the debate (Fr P. Bastable, *Desire of God* [1948] ; and *see* SUPERNATURAL).

Bibliography. The works of Scotus in Wadding's edition (1639) fill twelve volumes ; the new edition of the *Ordinatio* has so far published five, covering *Sent.* 1:1–25. A new start has been made with vol. XVI, covering *I Sent.* 1–7. There is an edition of the *De primo principio* by E. Roche in *Franciscan Institute Publications*, philosophy series V (1949) ; a section of the *Ordinatio* : *On the Necessity of Revealed Knowledge*, has been edited by A. Wolter OFM in *Franciscan Studies* XI:(3–4 (1951) ; he has also edited a selection of *Philosophical Writings* (1960) ; O. Schafer, *Bibliographia de vita et operibus Scoti* (1955) covers 19th and 20th cents. ; M. Grajewski, *The Formal Distinction of Duns Scotus* (1944) ; E. Gilson, *Jean Duns Scot* (1952) ; T. Barth *De fundamento univocationis* (1939) ; *C. R. Harris, *Duns Scotus* (2 vols. 1927) is marred by the acceptance of the *De rerum principio* as authentic, but in spite of this the book has had a photographic reprint (1960) ; J. Finkenzeller, *Offenbarung und Theologie nach Skotus* (1961) ; A. Wolter, 'The Theologism of Scotus', in *Franciscan Studies* VII (1947) 257–73 and 367–98 ; F. Pelster SJ, 'Eine Munchener Handschrift', in *Franziskaner Studien* 17 (1930) 253–77 ; E. Longpré OFM, in *Catholicisme* s.v. Duns Scot (1952).   J. H. C. and G. R.

DYNAMISM *See* BOSCOVITCH

E

EASTER : THE FEAST OF The English name for the central celebration of the Christian year is uncommunicative and in no way indicates its nature. The Romance languages make the point more clearly : *Pâques, Pasqua.* Easter is the celebration of the Lord's Passover, of His total redeeming work, which runs from the events of the Last Supper to the Resurrection on the Sunday morning. This truth, long overlaid by a theological orientation that had its origins in the later Middle Ages and by the rupture of the liturgical scheme, has now been re-established in the Christian life of the people by the restoration of the Holy Week liturgy in 1955 and by the theological writing and reflection of the last twenty years. (This applies to the Western Church ; the East has always kept a stronger grasp of the primitive notions of Easter, and the Resurrection has always been the climax of its liturgical celebration.) Here the matter will be considered in four sections : (I) the NT evidence, (II) the early tradition of the feast, (III) the 4th-cent. development, and (IV) the loss and restoration of the pattern.

I The NT Evidence. It would be an anachronism even to ask the question : Was there a feast of Easter in NT times ? Yet all the elements of the later feast are to be found there. The synoptists all set the Lord's redeeming work firmly in a Passover context (Mt 26:17 ff. ; Mk 14:1 ff.; Lk 22:1 ff.) and St John even more clearly indicates that Christ's redeeming acts are His Passover (Jn 13:1 ff.). The emphasis on the first day of the week for the Resurrection (Lk 24:1 ; Jn 20:1) without doubt led to the celebration of the Lord's day well within NT times (1 Cor 16:2 ; Apoc 1:10), when the events of the last three days of Holy Week were recalled. That there may have been a tendency even in NT times to emphasize the annual celebration of the Passover may be inferred with some hesitation from 1 Cor 5:7–8, where St Paul speaks of 'keeping the feast' (ἑορτάζωμεν) of Christ the *Pascha* who has been sacrificed' (cf. the note by C. Spicq on this passage in *La Sainte Bible de Jérusalem*).

What is of greater importance is that the NT writers never separated the Passion from the Resurrection, and they saw the cross always in the light of the Resurrection. We are redeemed by both : Jesus Christ was delivered up for our sins and rose again for our justification (Rom 4:25, and cf. 2 Cor 5:15). It is in the same context that St Paul speaks of baptism (Rom 6:4), and this no doubt is the origin of the custom of associating baptism with Easter. Early typology of baptism as a crossing of the Jordan would also help to this fixation, in the light of the date given by Jos 4:19 for that event. It is thus

that the NT presents the mystery of Christ and provides all the elements of the paschal feast that began to emerge in the 2nd cent.

II The Early Tradition of the Feast. That there was a paschal feast in the 2nd cent. is indisputable, and the evidence is so well known that it would serve no good purpose to retail it here. What however is important is the nature of that celebration. First it must be said that the Quartodeciman dispute, which broke out between the East and the West in the second half of this century, had nothing to do with the content of the feast. It was simply a dispute whether the feast was to be kept on 14 Nisan whatever day it fell, or on the Sunday after it, as the whole Church except Asia Minor kept it. The *Pascha staurōsimon* (celebration of the Passion) kept in the East and the *Pascha anastasimon* (celebration of the Resurrection) kept in the West, are the invention of a 17th-cent. scholar. Everywhere it was a unitary celebration which recalled both the Passion and the Resurrection. This is clear from the homily of Melito of Sardis (*see* **Bibliography**). Writing about the middle of the century, he speaks of the mystery of the Pasch (τοῦ πάσχα μυστήριον) and in a rhythmical passage develops the theme of the Passover from Exodus to the Resurrection ; the Lamb was slain, though Lord of life : He was dead in the tomb, but ' deathless through His rising from the dead' (lines 10–19, and cf. lines 697–702). As we see from Tertullian, the feast was an all-night vigil (*ad uxorem* 2:4 ; PL 1:1407), which was preceded by two days of absolute fast, the days ' when the Bridegroom was taken away' (*ubi ablatus est Sponsus* ; *de ieiunio* ; PL 2:1006), thus revealing the depth of meaning which the feast had for the Church at this time. The Friday and Saturday were days of mourning when the Church felt itself bereaved of its bridegroom, to whom, as we may suppose, the Church was considered to be re-united with the celebration of the feast. From him too, as well as from other sources, we learn that baptism had already become associated with the feast, which concluded with the celebration of the Eucharist (*de baptismo* 19 ; PL 1:1331, cf. also Justin *apol.* 65).

All the elements of the paschal liturgy that are found scattered up and down Tertullian's works are combined in the liturgy of Hippolytus, in his *Traditio apostolica* (written *c.* 215, though surviving only in later versions), though he does not in fact say that this Christian initiation took place at paschaltide (chs. 21–3 : the headings in Dix's edition have been inserted by the editor). Nor in this place does he provide the elements of a theology of the feast. For this we must go to his consecration prayer (ch. 4), the most ancient we possess, where the *anamnesis* of the Lord's death and Resurrection is made. (Reference may be made to other texts of Hippolytus collected by O. Casel in *La Fête de Pâques dans l'Église des Pères*, 50–3, and to *Une Homélie inspirée du traité sur la Pâque d'Hippolyte*, edited by P. Nautin, 49–51 and especially the peroration, 62–3).

It should be noticed that in all this there is no question of a Good Friday. The Friday before Easter was marked, like any other Friday, by a synaxis of the word and by a fast that lasted until Sunday morning (on which fast cf. the letter of Denis of Alexandria, in Feltoe's edition, 94–102). This synaxis remained the only celebration in Rome until the veneration of the cross was added to it in the 7th cent. Though it is true that the lessons of Friday gradually reflected the Lord's passion (the present readings may go back to the 4th cent., if not earlier), there was never any suggestion in the Roman tradition that this was the celebration of the Pasch. In all this early period what we have to do with is a unitary feast of the Lord's passage from death to life, and this was celebrated in a single feast without any great attention to the historical details of the gospel. The point of view remains that of St Paul and St John, and the fact that it was the only feast of the year (with its prolongation in the 'fifty days', the *Pentecost é*) gave it a prominence that it was to lose in the 4th cent.

Yet the paschal feast celebrated the events of Christ's redeeming work, and it remained for the Alexandrines, principally Origen, to spiritualize its meaning, though by so doing they made it applicable to people's lives (Origen, *Contra Celsum* 8:22 ; GCS 3:239, and cf. Eusebius, PG 24:696, who was manifestly influenced by him). Athanasius in his *Festal Letters* is more concerned with practical matters, with a special emphasis on fasting, though in the first of them we note that he cites 1 Cor 5:7–8 and has the whole Passover context in mind (PG 26:1362).

III The Fourth Century. With this century a change begins to take place. The old theology of the feast is retained, but it is now in competition with a new train of thought. Greater attention was given to the historical aspect of the gospels. The positive and factual school of Antioch begins to make its voice heard (e.g. in the *Apostolic Constitutions*, viii:33:3, from *c*. 380), and with the uncovering of the holy places in Jerusalem there comes a greater concern for time and place. Yet this was not the only factor at work. There seems to have been a change of mood all over the Church—witness the gradual emergence of the feast of the Ascension (*see* ASCENSION) and of Pentecost as a separate commemoration of the descent of the Holy Spirit. In Rome the feast of Christmas (q.v.) is first heard of, significantly, in a calendar of martyrs. It was at first an entirely historical feast. The whole of this development is summed up in the *Peregrinatio Egeriae* (or *Etheriae*), by the nun from southern Gaul or northern Spain, who went to the Holy Land towards the end of the 4th cent, or early in the 5th.

In her vivid descriptions of what happened in Jerusalem we observe the concern of that church to build its liturgy as exactly as possible according to the times and places when and where the events it recalls actually took place. It is here that we find the tendency to break up the celebration into separate parts and to spread the feast over several days, in fact from Palm Sunday to Easter Day itself. It was this church that influenced the whole of the West, and to it we must attribute celebrations like that of Palm Sunday (which came to Rome from Carolingian Gaul) and the historical emphasis Holy Week has had ever since.

Yet if the feast was in competition with other influences, the original theology was still taught, as we can see from St Augustine (e.g. *serm.* 231:3 ; PL 38:1105 : ' the Resurrection of Christ is our renewal ' ; Easter is the mother of all vigils (*mater vigiliarum*), *serm.* 219 ; PL 38:1088 ; there is an echo of the *Exultet* in *serm.* 258 ; PL 38:1194–5). St Leo also, while giving full weight to the importance of the historical elements, is a faithful (and magnificent) commentator on the meaning of the feast. He constantly calls the whole celebration the paschal mystery (*sacramentum paschale*) and speaks of the *sacramentum dominicae passionis et resurrectionis* (*serm. de passione* 13 ; PL 54:358). The same teaching will be found in one of his contemporaries, Maximus of Turin (e.g. *hom.* 58, *de paschali sollemnitate* IV ; PL 57:363) : ' the risen Lord affords resurrection to all men '.[1] Lastly, and more important than all else, there was the *Exultet*, which was sung every Easter to the people and which gave them, as it still gives us, the whole teaching of the Passover and of the redemptive death and Resurrection of the Saviour.

IV The Loss and Recovery of the Pattern. But if the doctrine about Easter remained sound, it is possible to trace quite early the tendency to break up the unity of the *Pascha*. Already before the end of the 4th cent., the Thursday before Easter had established itself as a special day. St Jerome, writing in 399, speaks of Thursday as the day for the reconciliation of the public penitents, while using the ancient term for the Easter festival (*ante diem Paschae*, ep. 77:4 ; CSEL 55:40) and Pope Innocent a few years later bears witness to the same fact (*ep.* 25:7 ; PL 20:559). For St Augustine it is the day when the anniversary of the Lord's Supper is celebrated (*coena dominica anniversarie celebratur*: ep. 54:9 ; PL 33:204). By the 6th cent. the Holy Oils were being consecrated on Maundy Thursday, and although Rome kept its primitive synaxis of the word on the Friday, in the 7th cent. the veneration of the cross was added to it. Then began another phase. The times at which these rites were celebrated began to change, and from the time of St Gregory the Great onwards there was a tendency to celebrate them at an earlier hour. By the 13th cent., the Easter vigil was celebrated in the morning and the old unitary feast of the *Pascha Domini* was broken up. It was in this atmosphere that the

[1] Resurgens Dominus resurrectionem praestitit universis.

triduum Passionis (Thursday, Friday and Saturday) came into being, to be distinguished from the *triduum Resurrectionis* (Sunday, Monday and Tuesday), a division of which our liturgy still bears the marks. Other factors (e.g. economic) than the purely liturgical played their part in this change, the effects of which were increased by the spiritual atmosphere of the later Middle Ages, when the emphasis was on the 'dolorous Passion', and the Resurrection appeared as no more than an epilogue to the events of salvation. The ancient *Pascha Domini* had largely disappeared, and all attention was concentrated on Maundy Thursday and Good Friday. The ancient vigil, now celebrated in the early morning of the Saturday, no longer played any part in the piety of the faithful.

Yet the teaching of the texts remained, and with the growth of the liturgical movement they were being more and more exploited for the benefit of the people in homilies and books. From 1944 onwards the inherent incongruity of celebrating a night office in the morning was felt to be intolerable, and in 1951 came the restoration of the vigil. This was followed in 1955 with the restoration of the whole liturgy of Holy Week, and the Church was once more in a position to celebrate and live the *Pascha Domini*. It is significant that little change was made in the texts of the rites which, now restored to their original context, were able to make their proper impact. With the extension of the use of vernaculars in the liturgy, permitted by the liturgical *Constitutio* of the Second Vatican Council, the meaning of the paschal celebration will once more be completely intelligible to the people.

Bibliography. L. Bouyer, *Le Mystère pascal* (2nd ed., 1962, English translation, 1952) ; O. Casel, OSB, *La Fête de Pâques dans l'Église des Pères* (French version of *Art und Sinn der ältesten christlichen Osterfeier*, 1938) ; B. Fischer, 'Von einen Pascha-Triduum zum Doppel-Triduum', in *Paschatis sollemnia* (Jungmann Festschrift, 1959) ; H. Oster, *Le Mystère pascal dans la Pastorale* (1964) ; M. Righetti, *Storia liturgica*, vol. II (1955) ; H. A. Schmidt, SJ, *Hebdomada sancta* (2 vols., 1957): *A. Allan McArthur, *The Evolution of the Christian Year* (1953, esp. part III, 77–139) ; for rubrical commentary on the restored rite, C. Braga and A. Bugnini, *Ordo hebdomadae sanctae instauratus* (1956) ; A. G. Martimort, *L'Église en prière* (1961 : esp. 693–720 on *le Cycle pascal*). For the early texts, B. Lohse, *Die Passa-homilie des Bischofs Meliton von Sardis* (1958) ; A. Chavasse, *Le Sacramentaire gélasien* (1958) ; *G. Dix, *The Apostolic Tradition of Hippolytus* (1937) ; B. Botte, OSB, *La Tradition apostolique d'Hippolyte* (1963) ; H. Petré. *Étherie : Journal de voyage* (1948) ; *J. G. Davies and R. George, *Holy Week* (1963). For an analysis of the texts, J. D. Crichton, 'The Resurrection', in *The Furrow*, XI (1960) 207–16. For the theory of an NT link with the liturgy, *F. L. Cross, *I Peter, a Paschal Liturgy* (1954), exploited by E. Boismard, OP, in RB (1956) 181–90.   J. D. C.

EBIONITES This early Jewish Christian sect has recently come into prominence again among theologians on account of its affinities with the Qumran group. But while speculation about them is rife, it seems best to set down here (I) the more trustworthy evidence about them, and then (II) some of the possible theological deductions from these facts. That they had a founder called Ebion was denied by Gibbon and most historians have followed him ; Belloc took up Gibbon's challenge, on the strength of a passage from Tertullian (*De praescriptione haereticorum* 10:33 ; PL 2:46) and asserted the existence of Ebion, but he did not win much support.

I The evidence about the Ebionites comes first from Irenaeus (*adv. haer.* I:22 and IV:52:1, H) whose notes about the early heretics have to be taken very seriously now, since they have been confirmed very considerably from the new-found Gnostic writings of Nag-Hammadi. Irenaeus says that they accepted (as in the first article of the Apostles' Creed) the doctrine of creation, but agreed with Cerinthus and Carpocrates in denying the divinity of Christ. They accepted only one gospel, that of Matthew, rejected all the Pauline epistles and expounded the prophets in a strange fashion. They practised circumcision and followed a more Jewish way of life which included adoration of (or possibly towards) Jerusalem. Hippolytus (*ref. haer.* 7:34 ; GCS 26:221) follows this account in the main.

Eusebius (HE 3:27 and 6:38) distinguishes two varieties of Ebionites ; some deny the Virgin Birth of Christ, while others accept it and keep the Christian Sunday along with the Jewish Sabbath. Clearly, this indicates a gradual falling-back of Jewish Christians into their former faith, rather than a slow emancipation of a Christian group from Jewish teachings. Eusebius locates them in the time of Cerinthus, at the end of the 1st cent., but differs from Irenaeus by calling their gospel the *Gospel according to the Hebrews*. Epiphanius (*haer.* 30:13 ; GCS 25:349) reconciles these two testimonies by claiming that the gospel according to the Hebrews was that of Matthew. When he goes on to cite the passage about the baptism of Christ (a crucial episode for the Ebionites, for it was then that, in their view, the Spirit made Christ more than man), he gives a version that does not agree with what Jerome (in Is 11:2 ; PL 24:144) says he found in the Hebrew gospel which he had inspected at Aleppo. Jerome's version runs : ' When the Lord was come up out of the water, the whole fount of the Holy Spirit came down and rested upon him, and said to him : " My son, in all the prophets was I waiting for thee that thou shouldst come. . . . Thou art my first-begotten son, who reignest for ever ".' According to Epiphanius the passage ran : ' John saw the Holy Ghost in the likeness of a dove that came down and entered into him [Christ] ; and a voice from heaven said : " Thou art my beloved son ; in thee I am well-pleased " ; and again " This day have I begotten thee ". And immediately a great light shone about the place.' Jerome blusters about the copy of the Hebrew gospel that was preserved in the library at Caesaraea but does not claim to have seen it ; it may be that the one he saw at Aleppo was a still more embroidered version of the same episode. The insertion into the text of the words from Ps 2:7 and the mention of the great light are found in the Old Latin version of Mt 3:15 and Lk 3:22, and from these they have been taken by Hilary and Augustine, but they are also known in Methodius (*Symposium* 8:8 ; GCS 27:91).

Symmachus, the translator of the OT into Greek, was an Ebionite according to Eusebius and Jerome, and Palladius (*Hist. Lausiaca* 64) tells a circumstantial tale of the lady Juliana who sheltered Origen in Cappadocia (238–41) and who passed on to him the commentaries of Symmachus on Matthew, along with a MS. which was written in *stichoi* and which may have been Symmachus's translation of the poetical books of the OT. Epiphanius (*De mensuris et ponderibus* 16 ; PG 43:264) tries to make out that Symmachus was a Samaritan who went over to the Jews but this can hardly be right.

The book of Elkesai was, on the evidence of Origen (in Eusebius, HE 6:38), regarded as having come down from heaven ; it was brought to Rome by one Alcibiades about A.D. 220 and contained instruction about baptizing people a second time ' with their clothes on ' for the remission of their sins. Epiphanius claimed that those who used the book were Ebionites (*haer.* 30:17 ; GCS 25:356) though he also attributes it to the sect he called the Ossenes (*haer.* 19 ; GCS 25:222). The book taught that it was a matter of indifference whether one professed one's faith when put to the question. Worship was to be towards Jerusalem, but the sacrifices of the Temple were explicitly rejected. The internal date of the work was the third year of Trajan (101), though earlier scholars were reluctant to accept this as probable.

The use of the title *Ebionim* at Qumran (in the *Habacuc Commentary* 12:1 and in the Commentary on Ps 37:11) where it seems to designate the central core of the community who practise poverty as a virtue, at once makes it plausible that the somewhat early dating for the Jewish-Christian Ebionites in the documents may be right after all. ' God will sentence him (the wicked priest) to destruction even as he plotted to destroy the Poor ', says the *Habacuc Commentary*, and the similarity of this title for the community to that used by Gal 2:10 for the ' founder's kin ' at Jerusalem has given rise to much speculation.

II Speculation about the Ebionites ranges from a complete identification of the Qumran community with Jewish-Christian Ebionites (by J. Teicher in *Journal of Jewish Studies* 2 [1951] 65–99 and 3 [1952] 111–18) to a guarded acceptance of similarity between Qumran and the Christian Ebionites by Professor M. Black. The latter makes out a good case for accepting the evidence of Epiphanius (*haer.* 19:5 ; GCS 25:223) that there was a Jewish sect of Nasaraeans quite distinct from the Christian Nazoreans or Ebionites. These Nasaraeans have some affinities with the Samaritans and may also have influenced the development of the Mandaeans. These last, who are so beloved of German exegetes, have been shown by Lady Drower, who knows the writings of the sect most thoroughly, to have been anti-Christian rather than forerunners or offshoots of Christianity.

It is sometimes urged that the Ebionites were indebted to the Essenes, and this is a favourite argument of those who want to see in the Qumran community an Essene body. Certain currents of opinion may have been common to various Jewish groups such as the Essenes, the people at Qumran and the Ebionites, without involving these in complete solidarity. An opposition to the Temple sacrifices, the desire to make use of frequent washings, a belief in the two spirits that beset a man, drawing him to good or evil ; all these are common Jewish traits among the sects which stand to one side of orthodox Jewry in the 1st cent.

Ebionite views are of importance as showing what doctrines the Church had to defend against them in these early times. Epiphanius says, for instance, that the Ebionites advocated divorce (*haer.* 30:18 ; GCS 25:357) ; this may account for the emphasis on the impossibility of divorce in the work of Hermas (29:6 ; GCS 48:26), a work which is Jewish-Christian but orthodox. The Christology of the Ebionites may be responsible for the emphasis on the Virgin Birth which can be noticed in the credal passage of Ignatius (*Eph.* 18–19) ; to insist on that truth would be the easiest way of meeting the suggestion that it was only at the baptism that the godhead descended on Christ. The curious form in which the Talmud (*Shabbat* 116 b) cites the saying of Christ (Mt 5:17) about the Law, may be due to Ebionite adaptation. ' I came not to take away from the Law nor to add to it ', is not exactly what Christ said, but it would serve to persuade a Jewish Christian that he had still to keep the whole of the Law.

It is difficult to use the pseudo-Clementine *Homilies* and *Recognitiones* for the reconstruction of Ebionite beliefs, for these works in their present form come from the 3rd cent., and in order to work back to their earlier form, in the formative period of the Ebionites, it is necessary to make personal judgments about individual passages where the element of subjectivity is large. Epiphanius does indeed say that the Ebionites used a book called *The Ascents of James*, which attacked the Temple sacrifices (surely uncalled for after the destruction of the Temple in A.D. 70) and indicated Paul as no true Hebrew but a proselyte from Hellenism (*haer.* 30:16 ; GCS 25:354). There is also much use made of the person of James in the Clementines, but both they and the Ebionites may have used the *Ascents* independently. Lightfoot conjectured that the grand finale of the *Ascents* was an account of the martyrdom of James and, if this were true, the work could very well have been written before A.D. 70, as the account seems to be that of a contemporary and was available to Josephus when he began to write.

To throw a blanket over the problem of the Ebionites and Qumran by saying that both were Gnostic is easily accomplished but calls for a justification that is difficult to find (*see* GNOSTICISM). One may appeal to Cerinthus as a link (*see* CERINTHUS), for he is alleged by Irenaeus to have been, in part at least, in accord with the Ebionites. Others see in Elkesai the Gnostic impact upon the Ebionites, whether that be supposed to come in the traditional year (101) or later. The Elkesaite formula for baptizing ' in the name of the great and supreme God and in the name of his son the great king', suggests that it was devised early in the 2nd cent. at the latest, for it would have been found expedient later on to have three names in the formula.

When Irenaeus said the Ebionites interpreted the prophets *curiosius*, he probably meant that they departed from the traditional interpretation of the Church. The word *curiose* is used three times elsewhere in his book and in those passages it means ' outside one's own sphere ', ' more than normal ' ; the Greek original can only be guessed. Preoccupation with the prophecy of Moses (in Deut 18:18) that God would ' raise up out of the midst of the brethren a prophet like unto me ' was common to the Ebionites, to the orthodox Christians (as may be seen from the pattern of Matthew's gospel and from the sermons of Peter and Stephen in Ac 3:22 ; 7:37) and to the sectaries of Qumran, one of whom copied out this passage along with another of similar import. In the *Clementine Homilies* (3:53) there is what purports to be a saying of Christ : ' I am He of whom Moses prophesied, saying : " God will raise up.... " ' Stress on the words ' like unto me ' would have made it possible for the Ebionites to affirm that Christ was no more than man, but, as the text was in the Kerygma from the beginning, it cannot be made to serve as proof of the dependence of the Ebionites on Qumran.

One may fairly put down to the existence of the Ebionites that strong line taken by the orthodox in the 2nd cent. which involved the claim that Christians were a third race, neither Jewish nor Hellenistic ; something of the kind was needed to avoid the confusion created by Ebionite clinging to as much of Jewish practice as could be preserved. The *Epistle to Diognetus* (1) undertakes to answer the question why Christians are a third race, and the *Apology* of Aristides (2:1) accepts the fact. The insistence on typological interpretation of the OT which is so marked in Melito (*hom. Passionis*, in the new passage between lines 191 and 193) seems to be due to the same desire to meet the challenge of the Judaizers. Melito says : ' What is said and done (in the Exodus) is nothing, apart from parable and typology. . . . What is said is parable, what is done is a fore-type, and just as the present happening is made known by the fore-type, so the discourse has light shed on it by the parable '. He then applies this rule : ' The People were a fore-type of the Church and the Law was the writing of a parable '. Only the existence of a strong Ebionite challenge could make these views of Melito understandable. The more that is discovered about the sure teaching of the Ebionites, the more easy it will be to understand the early theological development of the Church.

Bibliography. The article Ebionism in DCB is still of great value ; J. Fitzmyer SJ, ' The Qumran Scrolls, the Ebionites and their Literature ', in TS 16 (1955) 335–72 (reprinted as ch. XIII in *The Scrolls and the NT*, 1958) ; *M. Black, *The Scrolls and Christian Origins* (1961) ; J. Daniélou SJ, *Théologie du Judéo-christianisme* (1958) ; Lady E. S. Drower, *The Secret Adam* (1960) ; *H. J. Schoeps, *Urgemeinde, Judenchristentum, Gnosis* (1955) ; *H. Kosmala, *Hebraer, Essener, Christen* (1959).   J. H. C.

ECK, INFLUENCE OF Johann Eck (1486–1543) is the only Catholic opponent of the Reformation whose works are cited by Calvin in his *Institutes*. His *Encheiridion locorum communium adversus Lutherum* (1525) saw some ninety editions. He was the chief theologian consulted in the drawing-up of the catalogue of Luther's errors in the Bull of Leo X (D741–81) in 1520 and had previously been in public disputation with Luther at Leipzig. These few facts show the importance of the man for the theology of the 16th cent., yet there has been but little attention paid to his work in recent times. Here a brief list (I) of his works will be given and (II) some attempt made to show the importance of his leading ideas.

I Eck's work was at first outside the realm of dogmatic theology and would have marked him out as a progressive, had he died young. He wrote in defence of the morality of taking interest up to five per cent, which he claimed did not amount to usury, and he worked upon what might be called the new logic of the times. As an obvious man of ability he was called upon to meet the challenge of Luther and faced him at Leipzig in 1519, where he forced his adversary into four principal positions which were to mark the whole of the Reformation : that Scripture was the sole rule of faith ; that the Church was solely a spiritual reality (a soul without a body) ; that the universal priesthood of the baptized was above any hierarchical priesthood ; and that the Pope was anti-Christ. It is interesting that neither justification nor the sacrifice of the Mass came to the fore at this time. His first controversial work was *De primatu Petri* (1520). In 1522 he wrote *De paenitentia et confessione* ; in 1523 a defence of Henry VIII's book on the seven sacraments and a work *De satisfactione*. In 1526 his *De sacrificio missae* was printed, with a dedication to Sigismund, King of Poland. At the Augsburg meeting of 1530 he put forward some 404 articles of religion as a challenge (which the Reformers did not take up) and was instrumental in having the *Confessio Augustana* rejected as unorthodox. From 1530 to 1539 he issued five volumes of sermons in German, on the gospels of Sundays and feasts, on sacraments and commandments, which were meant to provide the clergy with a Book of Homilies to combat the errors of the time. In 1539 he produced a German translation of the Bible (not entirely his own work), and at Worms (1540) and Ratisbon (1541) he again defended the true faith. He visited England in 1525, where he was the guest of both More and Fisher. On his return to Germany he dedicated to More a revised edition of his *Encheiridion* (1 February 1526).

II His influence as a theologian can be measured by the reflection of his personality that may be observed in the letters of Erasmus. In 1518 Erasmus writes to John Lang (*Letters*, III:410) : ' I wonder what came into Eck's head that he should fight with our Eleutherius ? ' (This was Erasmus's name for Luther, and the same letter calls the Roman monarchy the plague of Christendom.) In 1520 he writes to Luther that the dispute with Eck has gone far enough[1] (*Letters*, VIII:xlvii) ; this may have been an attempt to urge caution on Luther. In 1530 John Henckel has met Eck at Augsburg (*Letters*, IX:58) and reports that he has a list of some hundred heretical propositions and that these include some taken from the writings of Erasmus, while at the same time Eck writes to Erasmus (*Letters*, IX:53) urging him to take up arms against the heretics ; it is true that four of the propositions on his list may be from the works of Erasmus, but Eck did not know this until it was pointed out to him. If they are his, then it must be said that they are scandalous. Erasmus is upset by this (*Letters*, IX:279) and grows sarcastic about Eck, but is still afraid. Eck, for all his abruptness, may have kept Erasmus from final apostasy. Erasmus suspected (*Letters*, IX:370) that Eck had been in Paris to move Aleander against himself, but no such visit seems to have taken place. In all this Eck appears as the consistent champion of orthodoxy.

The Leipzig dispute with Luther shows Eck's clearsightedness as a theologian in the way he forced Luther back on his heretical pre-suppositions. After some sparring about the Roman primacy (in which Luther is saying, very much as Cullmann today, that Jerusalem and not Rome had the primacy) Luther has to say that Scripture is above all human evidence, and for him Scripture (1 Cor 15:25) made Christ alone the head of the Church, to which Eck replies that this is the true Bohemian touch, to want to understand Scripture better than Pope and Councils, than doctors and flourishing universities, in spite of the fact that the Holy Spirit has not deserted the Church.[2] Luther did not like being thus compared to Huss and Wyclif, but the charge was just. In a letter of 14 February 1521 (*Briefwechsel*, 254) Luther wrote to a friend : ' We are all Hussites without knowing it, and that goes for St Paul and St Augustine '. This shows that he did not want to try to refute the charge directly.

Eck also forced Luther to admit that he did not regard general councils as infallible (session of 7 July, *Leipziger Disputation*, 129). It may be a consequence of this admission that on 18 December 1519 Luther wrote to Spalatin : ' I have just discovered the principle of the priesthood of the faithful '. In the dispute itself he had said that the primitive churches were governed by a general agreement between the priests (*communi presbyterorum consilio*), and from this it was but a step to putting the whole body of the faithful in place of the hierarchy of the Church.

The Leipzig disputation went on to deal with Purgatory, and here the subject of Scripture and Tradition came to the fore. Luther said that he admitted the text in 2 Mac about Purgatory, but since the book was not canonical, it was no good for anyone outside the Church (*Disputation*, 145). He went on to claim that the Church cannot give a book more authority than the book has in itself and that a council cannot make into Scripture what is not Scripture by its own nature (ibid. 147 and 152). To all this Eck replied that a council had the gift of the Spirit to understand the Scriptures (ibid. 159) and that though the Church cannot make gospels, still it is the Church that secures our unwavering faith for the four gospels, to the exclusion of such works as the gospel of Nicodemus, of Bartholomew or of Thomas. Luther was thus shown to be with his *scriptura sola* in the line of descent from Wyclif and John Wessel and the ground was already prepared for the decree of Trent on the subject.

Eck's encounter with Melanchthon at Worms in 1540 provided Trent with a similar preparation for the definitions about concupiscence and Original Sin. Eck forced him to admit that, in the baptized, concupiscence was to be regarded (according to Luther) not only as a penalty but as something deserving eternal death unless it should be pardoned (*Colloquium Wormatiense*, fol. C ii) ; while Eck himself took up the Tridentine position that it was a remainder of sin and that it was ever inciting to sin (ibid. fol. I iiii).[3] At one point Eck remarked that he had not read Occam for twenty-six years (i.e. since 1514), and indeed his bent was towards patristic and scriptural sources rather than scholastic.

Eck's treatise on the Mass (1526) was in part a defence of what Henry VIII had written against Luther, and, coming as it does just after Eck's visit to England, it may be that More and Fisher had put him in the way of doing this. He insists (*De sacrificio*, 64 and 212) that the Mass is not a memorial of the Last Supper but of the Passion and death of Christ ; there are two kinds of representative image, one which the Church has worked out for Good Friday (when in her liturgy she tries to bring before the minds of the faithful the Passion of Christ in one way), and another kind of representation (the Mass) which is also an offering, and by this the effects of the Passion are applied to the faithful. He meets Luther's charge that Christ did not offer at the Supper by showing that what He then did was in some sort a fulfilment of the wave-offering (Lev 23:11). Trent (D 938) without appealing expressly to this parallel taught that there was an offering by Christ at the Supper (though some nine of the bishops voted against this assertion).

Liturgical history was then in its infancy, and Eck is naïve in his attempt to derive the word *missa* from Hebrew and in his regard for the pseudo-Denis. None the less, he gathers a good array of patristic passages, starting with Ignatius (*Smyrn.* 8), in defence

---

[1] Satis cum Eccio litigatum est.

[2] Hoc est verum Bohemicum, plus velle intelligere sacram Scripturam quam summi Pontifices, concilia, doctores et universitates in magno vigore existentes, cum tamen Spiritus sanctus ecclesiam suam non deseruerit.

[3] Ex peccato relicta ad peccatum semper inclinat.

of Tradition. His book ends with the note that he would have added a fourth part to show that each of the prayers of the Mass had authority in Tradition, but that Thomas Walden has already done this.

Brave words are now being used about the way in which Trent misunderstood the Reformers and deflected the course of theological development. It is for the users of them to substantiate what they say by demolishing the work of Eck, who does in fact seem to have put Trent on the right track after all.

Bibliography. Eck's dispute with Luther in 1519 is published from the authentic MSS. by O. Seitz, *Der authentische Text der Leipziger Disputation* (1903) and W. Gussmann published *Johann Ecks 404 Artikel zum Reichstag von Augsburg* (1930). For Worms (1540) one has to go to the original *Colloquium Wormaciense* (1542). Many of the works of Eck have been reprinted in the *Corpus Catholicorum*, vols. I, II, VI, XIII and XIV (1919–29). Thus J. Metzler SJ edited Eck's *De ratione studiorum suorum* of 1538 in vol. II of this *Corpus* (1921), and in vol. XVI (1930) printed three sermons which were preached at his funeral. This vol. XVI gave also a full bibliography of Eck. There is a good monograph by E. Iserloh, *Die Eucharistie in der Darstellung des Johannes Eck* (1950), but apart from this, there have not been notable works on Eck's theology.   J. H. C.

EDESSA, LITURGY OF

When the pilgrim Etheria visited Edessa (c.380–420) she reported that the church (cathedral) there was huge, beautiful and had a new design which made it truly a house of God.[1] (*Itinerarium* 19:2 ; CSEL 39:61). There were many *martyria* there, too, one of them being that of St Thomas. The church was visited by the Emperor Valens in 372 (Socrates, HE 4:18 ; PG 67:504) and the body of St Thomas, which had been brought back from India along the caravan route which passed through Edessa, was moved to a shrine in the church by Bishop Cyrus in 394. This was the heyday of Edessa. Ephrem was not long dead (*see* EPHREM, INFLUENCE OF) and the school of which he was the glory continued there until it withdrew to Nisibis in 489, now thoroughly Nestorian. Rabbula was bishop in this period (412–35) and spent himself in securing orthodoxy in his diocese. He had a great reverence for Jerusalem and perhaps he may be looked upon as the source of elements of the Jerusalem liturgy in Edessa.

The principal witness of the liturgy of Edessa is the lectionary (edited by F. C. Burkitt from the British Museum Add. MSS. 14528 of the early 6th cent.) which gives the outline of the liturgical year and an abundance of Scripture readings for each feast. Some fifteen extracts from various books of OT and NT are usually prescribed, amounting sometimes to as many as 440 verses. This points to a separate Scripture service, distinct from the Eucharist. Indeed, for Good Friday there was a three-hours' service of Scripture readings lasting from midday until 3 p.m. Christmas and Epiphany are separate

[1] Ecclesia ingens et valde pulcra et nova dispositione, ut vere digna est esse domus Dei.

feasts, and thereafter the lectionary goes straight to the ' Sunday of entry into the fast of the Forty '. The Great Week and the Week of Rest (Holy Week and Easter Week) have readings for each day ; the Ascension is separate from ' Sunday of the completion of Pentecost ', and then are given ' lessons when a man is tonsured to be a *Bar Kyama* ' (i.e. a son of the Covenant, or religious), for an ordination, for the consecration of an altar or church, for the commemoration of martyrs, of bishops and finally for the anniversary (7 May) of the vision of the cross by Cyril of Jerusalem in 351. The letter of Cyril about this vision is prescribed to be read on this day, but the heading given is : ' The day that the Holy Cross was seen in the heavens by blessed Constantine, the believing king '. As Cyril's letter was in fact directed to the Emperor Constantius, an Arian and a persecutor of the orthodox, a conflation has been carried out by Edessene piety and the vision projected back to the days of the father of Constantius.

There are no feasts of Our Lady, no Rogations and probably no Palm Sunday (for in spite of a lacuna, the title of the Sunday at the beginning of Holy Week is not the usual ' Sunday of the Hosannas '. Now it is known from the homilies of Severus of Antioch (PO 29:247) that in his time (c.512–18) Palm Sunday and the feast of 2 February were just being introduced at Constantinople ; they were copied from Jerusalem, but even there they were not ' something ancient '. Hence it must be concluded that Burkitt's lectionary goes back to a time near enough to Rabbula as to be representative of his outlook. The *Chronicle* of Edessa (compiled c.507) attributes to Peter, Bishop of Edessa in 498, the introduction of the feast of Palm Sunday.

It was the accession of Justin I as Emperor in 518 that began the imperial proscription of the Monophysites as heretics. This meant that the Melkites or orthodox (nicknamed King's-men) tended to use Greek for their liturgy and to be in harmony with developments at Constantinople (e.g. in the popularity of the Chrysostom liturgy) while the heretic Monophysites became rebels using the Syriac liturgy and keeping to the *anaphora* of St James. In 541 the rebels chose Jacobus Baradeus or Burdeana as their bishop, being from that time known as Jacobites. He died in 578. He has an *anaphora* to his name (in Renaudot, II:333) which in its *post-Sanctus* bears witness to his Monophysite faith. He is not to be confused with Jacobus of Sarug, Bishop of Batnae (d. 521) near Edessa, whose orthodoxy is now hardly open to question and who was author of many hymns and metrical homilies that came to be used in the liturgy in place of some of the long tracts of Scripture prescribed by Burkitt's lectionary. He, too, is credited with an *anaphora* (*Anaphorae Syriacae* II:i [1951]) which has a remarkable Christological passage (redolent of Chrysostom) in its *post-Sanctus* : ' Thou didst send to us Thy beloved only Son, as saviour and liberator, who shone forth from Thee in the virgin, as a ray of light that shines forth from the sun in an eye that is clear. He took the form of a slave from a holy womb though He is the very form of

Thy majesty. He became man as He himself wished, that He might make us gods since that was His good pleasure. He was born of a carnal womb that He might regenerate us from a spiritual womb. He became our brother that He might make us sons to Thee.'

Although the Edessenes told Etheria that their king Abgar had been promised by Our Lord that their city would never be captured by invaders from the East, the Persians in 609 did in fact capture it and were not driven out until 628. From then until the final overrunning of the whole of Osrhoene by Islam in 639 there was a brief restoration of orthodox Melkite worship. Under Islam there flourished yet another Jacobus, known as Jacobus of Edessa, a Monophysite, who was bishop there in the later 7th cent., went into exile where he engaged in much literary activity (e.g. editing the hymns of Severus of Antioch) and returned to his see for one year (707–8) before his death. There is a MS. of these hymns (British Museum, Add. MS. 17134) in his hand, written in 675, which contains his corrections of an earlier Syriac version of them by Paul of Edessa ; these hymns are available in PO 6 and 7 (edited by E. W. Brooks) and they represent perhaps the major collection of hymns from so early a time. The only parallel to them of equal date would be the *Bangor Antiphonary*.

Narsai taught at Edessa from 437 to 457, when he migrated to Nisibis. His liturgical homilies seem to have been written after this migration. Dom Connolly, who edited them (T & S 8:i:1909), found that the liturgy of Narsai had as its framework that of Addai and Mari (q.v.) but that within this framework the elements from Preface through Sanctus, Institution and Intercession to Invocation were variable. The large number of Syriac *anaphoras*, each of them covering just these five elements, bears out Connolly's conclusion, and the phenomenon of this East Syrian liturgy is thus the very opposite of what happened in the Latin West, where an invariable Canon was surrounded and decked out by a great variety of collects, post-communions, and so forth. Narsai, even at Nisibis, is probably drawing upon his knowledge of the practice of Edessa, for he appeals to traditions handed down by Theodore of Mopsuestia and makes no effort to distinguish between what others did and what he himself wanted done. After telling of the Institution, he says : ' Then the herald of the Church commands the people : " With your minds be ye praying. Pray in mind and in thought at this hour, for great peace is being accomplished with the accomplishing of the Mysteries " ' (op. cit. 18). Narsai also supposes that while communion is being distributed (op. cit. 29) there will be a chant : ' Come ye mortals, receive and be pardoned your debts. This is the Body and the Blood of our Lord in truth. . . .' The likeness of this to the *Sancti, venite* of the *Bangor Antiphonary* is obvious.

The importance of Edessa in liturgical development lies chiefly in the fact that heresy and rebellion against Byzantium went hand in hand after 518.

Links were established perforce between Syriac and Coptic rebels, while those heretics who had withdrawn Eastwards knew Edessa as their main point of contact with the Christian world. The formative period for the Syriac liturgy was the 6th cent., though little survives that was actually written down at that time. The fragmentary *anaphora* edited by Connolly (*Oriens christianus* 14 [1925] 99–128) from a British Museum MS. of that time is therefore of much interest. It was imperfectly edited by Bickell in 1873, and Brightman made a Latin version of what Bickell published. A long approach to the Institution narrative is one of its chief peculiarities. ' He left in our hands a pledge of His holy Body that He might be close at hand to us by means of His Body and might continually mingle with us by His majesty. For prior to the time of His crucifixion and the hour when He was prepared to be glorified, He took bread and wine, which His own will had produced, He hallowed them with spiritual blessing and left us this tremendous mystery and gave us a good example that we might ever do as He had done and live by His mystery.' This excursus on the meaning of the Eucharist is not matched in the surviving MSS. of later Syriac *anaphoras* such as those of Jacobus of Edessa or Jacobus of Sarug. It does, however, recall the language of Chrysostom and Cyril of Alexandria about ἀνάκρασις or the mingling of God with men (*see* EUCHARIST), and its mention of the glorification of Christ may recall Jn 13:31, which the Diatessaron connects with the Eucharist.

The Novella 137 of Justinian (from 565, renewing Novella 123 of 546, *Corpus iuris* III:699) ordered that the prayer of the Oblation must be recited in a voice that the people can hear. The motive may have been to encourage what is today called active participation, but in view of the example just given of the elaboration of doctrinal statements in the *anaphora* it is much more probable that the detection of heresy was in view. Those who refuse to speak up are answerable to God, says Justinian, but we will not leave them unpunished. The homilies of Narsai make it clear that the practice of whispering certain prayers was well established in his day, and what Justinian ordered was therefore a breach of more primitive usage. ' The priest fills the place of a mouth for all mouths, and as a mediator his voice interprets *in secret*. He calls upon the Hidden One to send him hidden power, that he may give power in the bread and wine to give life' (Narsai, *Homily* XXI ; Connolly, 56).

It has recently been argued by Professor Ratcliff that in *Homily* XXI (on baptism) and *Homily* XXXII (on priesthood) Narsai is using two different *anaphoras* whose elements do not correspond to the one he has commented on in *Homily* XVII (on the Eucharist). From the citation just given it can be seen that some preliminary form of *epiklesis* is supposed in *Homily* XXI, for the point reached by the narrative is that of the *Secreta* just before the Preface and *Sanctus*. It may not be altogether satisfactory to follow Narsai's order of narration as if it gave the exact order of liturgical pieces, but in this homily he undoubtedly speaks of two *epikleses* at different points, the one just mentioned and one that comes before the Fraction and *Pater noster*. When Professor Ratcliff claims that the *anaphora* of *Homily* XXXII ends with a *Sanctus* which is regarded as 'in some way contributing to, or effecting the consecration of the Bread and the Wine', he has failed to notice that at the conclusion of the *epiklesis* and the *Pater* there was, according to *Homily* XXI (which had a proper *Sanctus* in its right place), a response by the people : 'Holy is the Father ; holy is His begotten ; holy is the Spirit that is from Him ; to them is due holiness and praise from all mouths'. This second *Sanctus*, as it may be called, answers fairly well to what is found in *Homily* XXXII : 'Holy, Holy, Holy Power, hidden from all and revealed to all' (Connolly, 67). What Professor Ratcliff has discovered is much rather the beginnings of the *Sancta sanctis* which became a regular feature of Eastern liturgies later on as a prelude to communion. There is no evidence that the *Sanctus* was ever looked upon as consecratory.

A calendar of the feasts kept at Edessa in 411 is preserved in a MS. of the British Museum (Add. MS. 12150) written in that year. There are many martyrs of the West listed, spread out over the year from 26 December to 24 November. After that the Eastern martyrs are given, first a small group of protomartyrs, and then the rest in hierarchical order : bishops, priests, deacons and clerics. No attempt is made to assign days to these. There are no feasts of Our Lady and none of OT figures. The MS. is printed in PO 10:7–26.

A Syriac poem on the cathedral of Edessa, written in the 6th cent., offers opportunities for speculation about the original shape of that building. Etheria, as noted above, said that it was *nova dispositione* which may mean that it was novel to her, in contrast with what she knew in Spain or Aquitaine. It had been rebuilt after a flood in 524 and the poet is describing the restored church, but there is reason to suppose that it kept to its original pattern. One certainty that emerges from his poem is that it had a *bema* or episcopal throne in the centre of the nave. This was supported on eleven columns, to symbolize the apostles in the Cenacle at Pentecost. The church was surrounded by streams (Edessa being well watered), and thus the usual Syriac symbolism, which looked on the floor-space of the church as the world, the bishop's chair as Jerusalem and the raised sanctuary as heaven, was more aptly expressed. How far the Jerusalem liturgy of St James was influential at Edessa is a most difficult matter, depending largely on determining the original pattern of that liturgy, and as at present the Georgian and Armenian versions of it are regarded as the most trustworthy (*see* JERUSALEM LITURGY), one can hardly be sure what is Palestinian material in it, and what is not.

Bibliography. *F. C. Burkitt, 'The Early Syriac Lectionary', in *Proceedings of the British Academy* X (1923) 301–38 ; the same, 'The Old Lectionary of Jerusalem', in JTS 24 (1923) 417–23 ; A. Raes,

Introductio in liturgiam orientalem (1947) ; R. H. Connolly OSB, *The Liturgical Homilies of Narsai*, T & S 8:i (1909) ; A. Baumstark, *Comparative Liturgy* (1958) ; *E. C. Ratcliff, 'The Anaphoras of Narsai', in *Biblical and Patristic Studies in Memory of R. Casey* (1963) ; P. Peeters, 'Jacques de Saroug, Monophysite ?' in AB 66 (1948) 134–98 ; A. Grabar, 'La Cathédrale d'Édesse', in *Cahiers archéologiques* II (1947) 41–68 ; A. Raes, H. Codrington and others, *Anaphorae Syriacae* (in course of publication from 1939 ; vol. I includes Timothy of Alexandria, Severus of Antioch, Gregory Nazianzen, Chrysostom, the Twelve Apostles, Dioscoros and Cyril. Vol. II:i gives Jacobus of Sarug (1951) ; ii (1953) James of Jerusalem. When completed, this work will replace the 18th-cent. collection of *Liturgiae Orientales* of Renaudot ; *W. Wright, *The Chronicle of Joshua the Stylite* (1882) ; lives of Jacob of Sarug, Jacob of Edessa in DCB s.v. ; *M. Black, *Rituale Melchitarum* (1938). J. H. C.

EGYPTIAN LITURGY Egypt being the land of the papyrus, the fragments of liturgical texts written on that material and preserved in Egypt tell us far more about the early state of the liturgy in that country than we know about Latin or Byzantine liturgies of early date. These fragments have never been collected into one book and the study of them has to be conducted piecemeal, with some difficulty. The Egyptian church produced (I) a liturgy of St Mark (which in Coptic texts is attributed to Cyril of Alexandria), and (II) the prayer-book (or *Euchologion*) of Serapion of Thmuis has survived (in an 11th-cent. MS. at Mount Athos) ; there are fragments of other *anaphoras* (III) which cannot as yet be given an author's name, and a Coptic *anaphora* of Gregory of Nazianzen (IV) seems to be so-called simply because of its use of a prayer for the kiss of peace against which in two MSS. the name of Gregory has been written. These seem to be local Egyptian productions, and the arrival in Egypt of the liturgies of St James, St Basil and St Chrysostom led to a large contamination of sources, so that it was practically impossible for liturgists in the past (who had only medieval MSS. to work on) to know what was the genuine and primitive form of the Egyptian liturgies. These four sources will now be briefly discussed.

I The liturgy of St Mark is found on a Strasburg papyrus (published by M. Andrieu in 1928). Though this was only a single sheet giving the beginning of the *anaphora* down to the end of the intercessions, it did enable a comparison to be made with the much later texts printed by Swainson from the Rossano codex and from a Vatican MS. of 1207. It was at once obvious that these had been expanded by the addition of adjectives and parentheses borrowed from imported liturgies. Where the papyrus spoke of God having created seas and rivers, the later versions added 'springs and marshes' (not a very Egyptian trait to add), and were not content with the simple term 'Thy Catholic Church' but must change it to 'Catholic and apostolic Church that is from one end of the earth to the other'. What survives of this liturgy on papyrus is the Preface (to use a Western term) with its mention of the 'clean oblation' of Mal 1:11, and the intercessions which followed it. These end with a doxology in the papyrus, though all trace of this has disappeared in the later MSS., which must therefore have been purged as well as amplified. It may be that, as doxologies grew in theological importance (*see* DOXOLOGY), it was thought better to limit the frequency of their use and to eliminate them from the *anaphora*, save for the final doxology.

The intercessions are introduced by the papyrus with an important dogmatic phrase (which is lost in the later forms of this liturgy): the citation of Mal 1:11 ended with the word 'sacrifice', and the papyrus continues: 'In view of which sacrifice and oblation we beg and beseech Thee ...', thus showing how the intercessory power of the Mass was understood in the 4th cent. (for that is the date of the papyrus). The Greek words ἐφ᾽ ᾗ θυσίᾳ imply that the sacrifice is the cause or condition of granting the petition.

After the intercessions came the *Sanctus*, and then a parchment (John Rylands pap. 465, of the 6th cent.) takes up the same *anaphora* of Mark, starting just after the *Sanctus* and expanding the last words of that acclamation: 'Truly full is heaven and earth of Thy holy glory. ...' This is the normal Egyptian development, whereas in the West it was customary to expand with a *Vere sanctus.* ... Immediately there follows a prayer that this sacrifice may be filled with blessing from God through the Holy Spirit. This minor *epiklesis* preceding the narrative of the Institution was no doubt the warrant for the later Greek MSS., inserting, in the words spoken over the chalice, the phrase: 'He filled it with Holy Spirit'. The phrase is not found in this parchment, but the development from the preliminary *epiklesis* must be due to a quite natural theological reflection.

The *anamnesis* speaks not only of the Death, Resurrection and Ascension of Christ, but also of the session at the right of the Father and the Second Coming in glory. This is followed by the words: 'Thy own gifts of Thy own making we have offered to Thee', and then comes a simple *epiklesis* which lacks the long proclamation of the attributes of the Paraclete found in the later MSS. and which has but a single *Amen* by way of response from the faithful. By contrast, all the benefits of the Eucharist that are here prayed for, in the parchment, appear practically unchanged in the later MSS., and this must be taken to mean that theological development on the benefits of the Eucharist, as one would expect, had taken place very early in the history of the Church.

The parchment has a prayer for the resurrection of the dead, added by a different hand after the *epiklesis*. This prayer, which is not the exact equivalent of the intercession for the dead found in the later MSS. at a point before the consecration, asks for the dead to be gathered with the saints where pain, grief and wailing are no more, that they may enjoy what eye hath not seen nor ear heard. Apart from the

In paradisum at a funeral and one of the prayers for the dying, this theme is not very familiar in Western liturgy (*see* DEAD, PRAYERS FOR). These early sources do not supply us with the name of Mark, as they are incomplete, but the later MSS. leave us in no doubt, for one of the intercessions mentions 'Mark our holy Father, who showed us the way of salvation'.

II The prayer-book of Serapion was discovered not long before 1900 and was hailed by its editor, Bishop Wordsworth, as a complete answer to the contention of Leo XIII (in his condemnation of Anglican Orders) that 'either the Order of priesthood or its grace and power' has to be mentioned in the prayer of ordination (*see* ORDERS). Serapion's book had a prayer of ordination which did not seem to refer to either of these, but in fact it asks that the new priest 'may become a steward of Thy people and an ambassador of Thy divine oracles, and may be able to reconcile Thy people to Thee'. The significant thing here is that Serapion in his *anaphora* inserts between the two consecrations a short prayer in which the priest prays: 'Through this sacrifice be reconciled to all of us and be merciful, God of truth'. Thus the reference of his ministry of reconciliation is rather to the Eucharist than to Penance, and the requirement of Leo XIII is satisfied by Serapion's prayer.

Another feature of Serapion's *anaphora* which is of theological importance is the Logos-*epiklesis*, which comes after the consecration: 'God of truth, let Thy holy Word come upon this bread, that the bread may become the body of the Word. ...' Serapion may have adapted to his own purposes the simple Spirit-*epiklesis* already noted as existing in the liturgy of St Mark at this same point, but the survival of so remarkable a feature in a MS. so much later than its author is hard to explain. It cannot be a later insertion in the liturgy, since it corresponds to what Athanasius (PG 26:1325) wrote about the Mass: 'Whenever the great prayers and the holy supplications have been sent up, the Word comes on the bread and the cup and they become His Body and Blood'. Earlier still, the language of Origen (on Mt 26:26 ; GCS 38:196) and of some of the Gnostic prayers, suggests that this idea of a coming of the Word at the Eucharist was current long before an *epiklesis*, as such, existed.

Another early prayer used by Serapion is the one (found in *Didache* 9:4) asking that, 'as this bread had been scattered on the top of the mountains, and being gathered together came to be one, so also gather Thy holy Church out of every nation and country and city and village and make one living Catholic Church'. The same prayer is found with slight variations in the papyrus of Der Balyzeh (see below) and in some of the Ethiopic *anaphoras*. It is a vivid realization of what Paul said in 1 Cor 10:17. Serapion does not show great originality in his devising of prayers, but is not tied to one source. Part of the Preface leading up to the *Sanctus* is borrowed from the liturgy of St Mark, while his post-communion prayer asks that we may set aside the threat of sin 'by the Gnosis that is towards Thee', words that recall the prayer before communion in the liturgy of St Mark. Some terms, such as 'God of truth' and 'only-begotten' are, however, used frequently and seem to be his own favourites.

III Other liturgies have been recovered from papyrus, chief of them being the so-called Der Balyzeh liturgy (from its place of discovery). This was first published by Dom de Puniet at the eucharistic congress in London (1908), and not surprisingly, since he never saw the original three leaves of papyrus which are at Oxford, he inverted their order and sent off the liturgists of the world on an imaginary voyage in search of the affinities of such a monstrosity. Although the mistake was suspected by Schermann in 1912, no attempt to correct it was made until 1949, when a new edition of the papyrus was issued by C. H. Roberts, with a liturgical commentary by Abbot Capelle. Dom de Puniet made exaggerated claims for the document, and there were some who regarded it as the earliest of all liturgies, but these alarms have now receded and it has taken its place as a late 6th-cent. document giving the liturgy that was then followed in one village of the Egyptian hinterland, a liturgy with some affinities with St Mark but eclectic in character. The chief novelty of the papyrus is the *epiklesis* of the Spirit coming between *Sanctus* and consecration ; it reads like an expansion of the minor *epiklesis* noted at this point in the liturgy of St Mark (see above, I). A second *epiklesis* after the consecration, where the papyrus has a gap of fifteen lines, seems unlikely, though a petition for the fruits of communion cannot be excluded.

A Coptic papyrus, published in 1940 (*Coptica Lovaniensia*, 27), gives a liturgical fragment running from just after the *Sanctus* to the end of the words of consecration, and here again there is an *epiklesis* of the Spirit. More curiously still, the *epiklesis* is preceded by an *anamnesis* : 'We make memorial of His death, offering Thee these Thy created gifts, this bread and this cup, and we beg and beseech Thee to send upon them Thy holy Spirit. ...' Could it be that the whole complex was later on transferred to a position after the consecration ? A homily ascribed to Gregory Nazianzen and preserved in the 7th-cent. Amherst papyri (published by W. Crum in *Theological Texts from Coptic Papyri* [1913] 47) speaks in such general terms about the descent upon the bread that it is not attributed to one divine Person to the exclusion of another : 'The holy eagles, the clergy, do say unto God with the mere words of their mouth : "Be favourable ; come down upon the bread and the cup, and He heareth them and doth come"'. If this was a common way of looking at the *epiklesis*, one cannot expect from the Copts precision either in its placing or in its attribution.

The Arabic version of a Coptic liturgy which Baumstark edited (*Oriens christianus* I [1901] 1–45) was written down in the 10th cent., but its editor considered that it came from a Greek original not later than the 6th cent. Here again an *epiklesis* of sorts is found before the consecration : 'Perfect this sacrifice with the blessing that is from Thee, with

the descent of the Holy Spirit upon it. Bless with blessing and cleanse with cleansing these gifts that are set before Thee, this bread and this cup. Amen'. The post-consecration *epiklesis* asks that the Spirit be sent, 'upon us and upon these gifts' to effect the change for the remission of our sins and for eternal life to the participants. At the reception of communion, rules of precedence are set down ; the clergy are to approach first, then the newly baptized, the charismatics, the old men, middle-aged and young, and finally the women in the same three age-groups. A prayer which follows the Fraction and introduces the *Pater* is notable for its use of Heb 13:10 in an eucharistic sense, thus making more than questionable the idea of St Thomas that the altar there referred to was the cross of Christ.

A Berlin papyrus (13918) was edited by H. Lietzmann (dated about A.D. 540) along with Heidelberg pap. 2 and seemed to give the closing prayers of a liturgy akin to that of St Mark. Most remarkably, the prayer for the fruits of communion reproduced some ten words of Ignatius *Eph.* 20:2, and the editor argued that it was far more likely that Ignatius was citing a liturgical prayer of his own time than that the papyrus was citing him. Indeed, it is very rare to find in liturgies any citation from a patristic writer, however old.

The Coptic ostraca (flakes of limestone) that were edited by W. E. Crum (1902) have been very much neglected by liturgists. One of them (Crum, 4, with a counterpart at Leningrad) gives a Preface and *Sanctus* of great interest, especially since the nature of the material indicates that the text was meant for popular use. It thanks the Father, 'that Thou didst make us pass into being by Thine only-begotten Son, who of His own will came on to the earth to redeem the race of mankind'. The *Sanctus* itself concludes : 'Lord God almighty, who wast and art and art to come'. This use of Apoc 4:8 in the *Sanctus* is unparalleled. Another ostracon (519 in Crum, op. cit.) gives a set of communion anthems (in Greek) very similar to the collection that appears in the *Stowe Missal*, an indication that the liturgical trade-route from Egypt to Ireland carried such materials as these.

One interesting ostracon (Crum, 41) is an undertaking given by one who was probably a deacon to Bishop Abraham (probably about 600) : 'I or my father will sleep in the church and . . . its lamp from morning until evening, and perform its offices and prepare incense'. This must be the first mention in history of a sanctuary-lamp that was kept burning all day. The penalty for neglect of this undertaking is stated to be excommunication. Again, what is probably the first known usage of ideas which produced the *Dominus vobiscum* : *et cum spiritu tuo* of the Latin liturgy may be found in a 3rd-cent. Berlin papyrus (9794 ; reprinted in PO 18:429), where a prayer which is headed : 'Prayer of Peter and the other apostles' has intercalated into it the words : 'My spirit is with the divine Spirit'. Coming so early in liturgical history, this prayer falls within the time when a threefold division of body, soul and spirit was still generally accepted, and it is clearly this division which is presupposed by the salutation and its reply.

The great *Euchologion* of the White Monastery, though by no means fully preserved, is now available in PO 28, edited by Dom E. Lanne. It is of the 9th–10th cents., and does not indicate very violent change from the papyri of earlier times. The problem of Syriac influence on Egyptian liturgical forms has still to be investigated, whether it be that of Monophysite exiles after Chalcedon or of the permanent contact through the Syrian monastery in Wadi Natrun (the *patres heremi Sciti* who are commemorated in the *Stowe Missal*). From the archaeologists' reports, it does not appear likely that Egypt was familiar with the Syrian arrangement of the church with a *bema* or raised platform for the bishop's throne in the centre of the nave. The place of the pulpit in the Wadi Natrun churches was in the northeast corner of the nave, and the notion that the church should be like a ship is evidenced by the remark of Ibn Sebba that every church should have a barrel-vaulted roof in order to imitate Noah's ark.

Wadi Natrun yielded a MS. of the *anaphora* of Basil and of that of Gregory in Greek which could be dated by its discoverer, H. G. Evelyn White, to the time of the patriarch Benjamin II (1327–39). This showed that although Coptic versions of these liturgies had been made by the 6th cent. at the latest, there was still need for a Greek service-book eight centuries later. Even down to the present day many parts of the liturgy which are spoken out loud remain in Greek ; the biddings of the deacon, the responses before the Preface, the *Sanctus*, the *anamnesis*, the formulae at the consignation and at the blessing with the sacred species are all Greek. Thus, in spite of the strong nationalism of the Monophysite Church, the vernacular did not prevail over the Greek as it did in Syria. The survival may be due to a desire to stress the continuity of their Church with that of Athanasius and of Cyril, but this can hardly be the full reason.

IV The anaphora of Gregory Nazianzen seems to have been so-called because it contained a prayer for the kiss of peace which was ascribed to that saint ; two of the MSS. used by the editor of the Coptic version have Gregory's name alongside the prayer. The *anaphora* is remarkable theologically for its *epiklesis* : ' Change these presents through Thy own voice, Thou who art present to us, complete for us this holy mystery ; plant in us the thought of Thy holy service ; send upon us the grace of Thy Holy Spirit that He may sanctify these gifts and change them. . . .' The appeal is obviously to Christ's liturgy at the Last Supper when He used the consecratory words and made His offering. That He could send the Spirit would be an idea repugnant to medieval Greeks, but it does seem that this liturgy preserves a wording that would do justice to the dogmatic statements of Chrysostom (*see* EPIKLESIS) about what happens in the Mass. There is even some variation at the operative verb in the Coptic, where some MSS. read : ' That Thou mayst change ',

while others agree with the Greek in reading : ' That He may change '. The variation of a single letter in the Coptic makes the difference.

After the words of consecration the people respond with the three acclamations (in Greek) : ' We believe ; we confess ; we give glory '. In the post-*Sanctus* there is the theologically significant statement : ' Thou needest not my service but I am in need of Thy lordship '. The intercessions have been moved from their usual position here to a place between the *epiklesis* and the Fraction and are notably longer than in the liturgy of St Mark, or in its Coptic counterpart, which goes under the name of St Cyril. An *anaphora* of St Matthew which is found in the *Euchologion* of the White Monastery seems to be a local product, and it may be expected that the sands of Egypt have yet other treasures to give up to the liturgical scholar and that the value of Egyptian material as a laboratory for dating liturgical developments will be more appreciated with the passage of time.

Bibliography. For St Mark, the Strasburg papyrus was published by M. Andrieu in RevSR 8 (1928) 489–515, while the Rylands parchment is in *Greek and Latin Papyri of the John Rylands Library* III (1938) number 465. The later MSS. are most easily consulted in G. Swainson's *Greek Liturgies* (1884). The text of Serapion may be found in Funk, *Patres apostolici* II (190) or in JTS 1 (1900) 88–113 ; 247–77, while Bishop Wordsworth's translation and commentary *Bishop Serapion's Prayer-book* had a 2nd edition in 1910. The Der Balyzeh papyrus was edited by C. H. Roberts and Abbot Capelle, *An Early Euchologion* (1949). The Coptic *anaphora* of Gregory has been edited by E. Hammerschmidt, *Die koptische Gregoriosanaphora* (1957). Modern Coptic usage is described by O. H. Burmester in *Eastern Churches Quarterly* (1949) 1–39, while the same author dealt with *The Greek Kirugmata in the Coptic Liturgy* in OCP 2 (1936) 363–94. Mgr L. Lefort's *Coptica Lovaniensia* are in *Le Muséon* LIII (1940) 22–4. Some early liturgical papyri are collected in PO 4 and others again in PO 18. The churches of Wadi Natrun were described by H. G. Evelyn White, *Monasteries of Wadi Natrun* II (1933), while vol. I of the same work (1936) gave some new Coptic texts. H. Lietzmann printed the Berlin papyrus in *Festschrift für A. Jülicher* (1927). T. Schermann, *Ägyptische Abendmahlsliturgien* (1912) is now somewhat out of date, but still has some useful judgments. W. E. Crum, *Coptic Ostraca* (1902) has some liturgical notes by Brightman, and there are other Coptic documents edited by Crum in *Der Papyruscodex der Phillippsbibliothek* (1915) and in his *Catalogue of Coptic MSS. of the British Museum* (1912).   J. H. C.

ELIAS, THEOLOGY OF It is not proposed in this article to discuss all the exegetical questions concerned with the OT account of Elias, but to estimate his position in Christian theology. The main questions are (I) his translation to Paradise and his second coming, (II) his typological relation to John the Baptist, (III) his being taken as a prototype of those who follow the contemplative, and especially the solitary, life, and (IV) the cult of Elias as a saint who has not yet died.

I The translation of Elias to Paradise is narrated in 4 Kg 2:1–15 (for which *see* CCS 273 g), the date tentatively assigned to it being 851 B.C. The very last words of the last of the prophets (Mal 4:5) tell of his coming again before the great and dreadful day of the Lord, to reconcile son with father and neighbour with neighbour. As the revelation of future rewards and punishments was not far advanced by the time of Malachy, his language was confused and was not made clearer until the matter was set in its true light by Christ (Mt 17:10–13), who explained that Elias is indeed to come and restore all things (at the Parousia) but that for the nonce his anti-type, John the Baptist, was at work. Ecclus 48:9, in the praise of famous men, includes the taking-up of Elias and repeats (48:10) part of the promise of Malachy, while a much briefer catalogue in 1 Mac 2:58 says that he was taken up on account of his zeal for the law.

The shadow of Elias falls across the gospels, and although it is made clear (see below) that he stands to John the Baptist as type to anti-type, there are many signs that Elias was often in the thoughts of contemporary Jewry. Antipas thinks that Christ Himself may be Elias (Lk 9:8), and this opinion is cited by the disciples as being held by some (Mt 16:14). John is clearly filled with the thought of the parallel when he asks for fire to be brought down on the Samaritan village (Lk 9:54) and there are quite a number of witnesses to the text which adds the words : ' just as Elias did ', though the addition may be due to Marcionite anti-Jewish feeling. It is Luke who makes most of the parallel with Christ, for the words he cites (4:25–6) from the Nazareth episode, may be considered to have dictated his choice of the Naim miracle as one that must be put in his narrative, a miracle which brings out the likeness between what Christ does and the act of Elias in 3 Kg 17:17–24. Luke also (9:57–62) gathers three instances of discouragement offered to would-be disciples, which afford a good parallel to those which Elias (4 Kg 2:2–6) administered to Eliseus.

In the Synoptic accounts of the Transfiguration (Mt 17:1–13 and parallels) it is Luke who omits the explanation given to the disciples about Elias. The omission is natural when Luke has committed himself to suggesting a parallel between Elias and Christ ; it would only confuse if he now brought in other parallels. In both Mt and Mk Christ is reported as saying that Elias is going to come and restore all things, and this coming cannot be identified with the life of John the Baptist. It is clear from the words of Christ that there are two comings to be considered, the one of the anti-type of Elias, John the Baptist, and another at some later time, for the purpose of *apokatastasis* or restoration. John Chrysostom (*hom.* 57 on Mt ; PG 57:559) found no difficulty in separating the two advents of Elias, pointing out that the prophecy in Mal 4:5 calls Elias ' the Thesbite ', and that John the Baptist was not a Thesbite. It is

possible that Paul (Rom 11:5) in his talk about the final conversion of ' the remnant ' is thinking of Elias as the instrument thereof, since he grounds his hope on God's promise to Elias (11:2).

Irenaeus (*adv. haer.* V:v:1, H) gives it as the teaching of disciples of the Apostles that Enoch and Elias were taken to Paradise and abide there until the consummation. As a reason for this he suggests that their ' taking-up ' is a pledge of what will happen to those who walk in the Spirit. In view of the gospel texts just examined, one cannot dismiss this patristic evidence (as Spadafora does, writing on Elias in the *Enciclopedia cattolica*) as so much Jewish *midrash*. It is true that Victorinus (on Apoc 11:3 ; CSEL 49:98) appeals to the tradition of ' our elders ' (*veteres nostri*) for the view that the other person with Elias in Paradise is Jeremias (since Moses and Eliseus, whom others had proposed as candidates, were both certainly dead, whereas of Jeremias it was said [Jer 1:5] that he was to be a prophet among the Gentiles, and this did not happen when he was on earth). Victorinus may here be using some argument from Papias, who was himself probably Jewish, but the testimony of Augustine (*De civ. Dei* XX:29 ; CSEL 40:503) is not likely to have been due to Jewish folklore. He says : ' It is the constant belief and attestation of the faithful that in the last age the great Prophet Elias will bring the Jews to believe in our Christ '.[1]

The Jewish *Apocalypse of Elias* was known to Origen (on Mt 27:9 ; GCS 38:250), who said that 1 Cor 2:9 was a quotation from it ; Epiphanius (*haer.* XLII:12:3 ; GCS 31:180) thought that Eph 5:14 was also taken from the work, and neither of these Fathers thought it impossible that Paul should have known the book. One may reasonably suppose, then, that the imagery and background of Apoc 11:3–12 owes something to this Jewish apocryphal work, but the actual message, that Elias will preach against Antichrist and be done to death by him, reads more like a development of the words of Christ Himself. Information about the personal appearance of Antichrist was obviously welcome from whatever quarter it came (and in the late Hebrew version of this *Apocalypse of Elias* there is such a description), but the central fact, that Elias would come and be slain by Antichrist, would not be accepted by Christians simply on Jewish authority.

The *Carmen adversus Marcionem* (which cannot be later than the 3rd cent.) has a couplet about Elias (III:149–50): ' Noble is Elias who has not yet experienced the debt of death, for that he has again to come into this world '.[2] St Ambrose in the basilica which he built (386–9), and which now bears his name, had a reproduction of the translation of Elias in his fiery chariot (PL Supp. 1:588) with the legend : ' Elias mounts his horse-drawn fiery chariot, being carried to the heavenly court by favour of those

---

[1] Heliam magnum prophetam ultimo tempore Iudaeos in Christum verum, i.e. in Christum nostrum, esse credituros celeberrimum est in sermonibus cordibusque fidelium.

[2] Nobilis Elias qui nondum debita mortis
  Gustavit, quoniam rursum venturus in orbem est.

above '.[1] Another sign of the popularity of Elias is that Noetus is said to have proclaimed that he himself was Moses and his brother Elias (Filastrius, *haer.* 53 ; CSEL 38:28). This may have been an attempt to guarantee a supposedly new revelation by a second Transfiguration, but it is more likely that it was an appeal to popular belief in the return of Elias and (for Moses) to Deut 18:15. It is true that Hippolytus (*Contra Noetum* 1 ; PG 10:804) says that Noetus put forward his brother as Aaron, but there is much slapdash quality about Hippolytus's work, and he must be judged less reliable here.

There are five Christian sarcophagi showing the translation of Elias and a panel on the door of Sta Sabina in Rome. The mosaic of Christ as charioteer in the tombs under St Peter's owes most of its inspiration to the contrast with the pagan worship of Apollo, but there may have been some idea in the mind of the artist that there was a parallel between Elias and Christ ; a working-out of this parallel can be found in Aphrahat (P *Syr* I:965) at a date not too far removed from that of the Roman artist.

St Patrick in his *Confessio* (20) tells of his being beset by Satan at night and of his calling on Elias. He seems to have awakened himself by the cry and then to have found the sun shining upon him. The editors of the *Confessio* suggest that Patrick may have seen a mosaic or carving of the translation of Elias and noticed its likeness to pagan representations of Helios the sun-god. Irish devotion to Elias was most marked. An Irish litany (edited by C. Plummer [1925] 32) entreats God, ' by all the holy martyrs . . . from the beginning of the world to Elias and Enoch who will suffer the last martyrdom on the brink of doom. . . .' The Irish *De mirabilibus Scripturae* (found among the works of Augustine, PL 35:2180-3) enlarges on his fate. The Advent-fast in Ireland (*see* ADVENT) was known as the Lent of Elias. The remarkable Preface (or *Contestatio*) of Elias in the Mone masses has probably undergone Irish influence. These masses were written out in a *libellus* for some Burgundian monastery about 630-40, and at the end of one of them (in Mohlberg's edition of the *Missale Gallicanum*, 88) there is added this Preface. It goes through the whole life of Elias, ending with his translation. It may be true that apocryphal works such as the *Gospel of Nicodemus* and the *History of Joseph the Carpenter* were popular in Ireland and that these dilate upon the fate of Elias, but the essential fact of his coming at the end of time was sufficiently clear from the canonical gospels to make their acceptance of these embroideries seem harmless. Suarez goes so far as to say that the fact is *de fide*, or almost so (*disp*. 55:2:2 on St Thomas *Summa*, 3a.).

II Elias as prototype of John the Baptist was proclaimed by Christ Himself after the Transfiguration (Mt 17:12 ; Mk 9:13). The description of John's manner of life (Mt 3:4 ; Mk 1:6) is probably meant to indicate the parallel with Elias, for it is not the custom of evangelists to dwell upon trivial details for their descriptive value only, as might be the case

with a modern novelist. The Jezabel in the life of John, namely Herodias, also finds place in the narrative. Elias had escaped from his fate (3 Kg 19) by flight to Horeb, but John was imprisoned and beheaded ; none the less, Aphrahat (P *Syr* I:288) elaborates the parallel.

Justin (*dial.* 49:1) argues with Trypho that the anointing of the Messias by Elias which the Jews expected, had been carried out by John, and that it was quite simple to understand how the spirit of Elias had been given to John, for Josue had received the spirit of Moses (Num 27:18-20). Origen (on Mt 17:10 ; GCS 40:172) took occasion from the language of the gospels about John being ' with the spirit and power of Elias ' to argue that there was no transmigration of souls, for the soul of Elias had not entered into the body of John, but only his spirit or power. John's own forthright denial (Jn 1:21) that he was Elias never caused difficulty to the Fathers but merely provided them with a good pedagogical opening for expounding what is meant by typology. Augustine says quite categorically (*tract* 4 on Jn ; PL 35:1408) : ' What John was for the first coming of Christ, that Elias will be for the second '. Origen (loc. cit.) was careful to point out that the story of John's birth, so elaborately told by Lk 1:5-63, was meant to assure us that he was no reincarnation of Elias.

Typology found other features in which Elias and John were alike ; both went to the Jordan, Elias to cross it for his translation and John to baptize in it. Ambrose (*De Elia et ieiunio* 83 ; CSEL 32:463) has an elaborate comparison of the candidate for baptism with the sacrificial victim in the contest at Mount Carmel between Elias and the priests of Baal : ' You are that man upon the altar, washed with water and your sins burnt away that your life may be renewed. Fear not the fire that enlightens you '. There is also in Augustine (loc. cit.) the suggestion that the end of John the Baptist prefigures in its turn what will happen to Elias when he comes again. Not all theologians have been ready to admit a second level of typology (not now between OT and NT but between NT and the life of the Church) but this would seem to be a notable example of it.

III That Elias should be taken as a prototype of religious life is quite natural. One does not need the somewhat rabbinical arguments of Gregory of Nyssa (*hom.* 7 on Cant ; PG 44:924) to prove this, for Athanasius, seeking justification for his flight from persecution, found it in the flight of Elias to Horeb, which was the mountain of contemplation (*Apologia* 10 ; PG 25:657). He was praised by Ambrose (*De virginibus* I:3:2 ; PL 16:192) for having led a life of virginity ; this is not stated in the OT accounts, but might be inferred from his long period in solitude (thus Aphrahat, P. *Syr* I:833) or from his dependence (3 Kg 7:9) on the widow of Sarepta. Ammonas, the successor of Antony, held up Elias as an example to monks (PO 10:586). His experience on Horeb (3 Kg 19:11-12), where he was told to put himself in the presence of God and that then the Lord would pass by, was very soon seized upon by Origen (on Jn 4:24 ;

---

[1] Helias ascendit equos currusque volantes
Raptus in aetheriam meritis coelestibus aulam.

GCS 10:248) as a description of mystical experience, while his opening of the heavens after they had been shut up was taken by Origen (*De oratione* 13 ; GCS 3:330) as the bringing of the water of spiritual refreshment to the soul, in the manner later so fondly described by St Teresa.

Later mystical writers were much given to using the example of Elias. Maximus the confessor (in his *Capita theologica* 174 ; PG 90:1160) says that the seeker after God will not only go to Horeb, i.e. practise the virtues of the spiritual life, but also into the cave on Horeb, by becoming a true contemplative. Gregory Palamas went so far as to see in the bodily posture assumed by Elias (3 Kg 18:42), when he prayed for rain, a better means of uniting the mind to God. Certainly, from the 8th cent. onwards (when Peter the Athonite lived there) the example of Elias has been honoured at Mount Athos. The circumstances of his handing his cloak to Eliseus were often recalled, especially in Eastern monasticism, when the link of personal discipleship came to be established between one hermit or contemplative and his successor.

This is not the place to set forth the way in which the Carmelites came to regard Elias as their father-in-God, but one may note in passing that a fierce controversy raged between them and the Bollandists at the end of the 17th cent. on the subject of a historical continuity of contemplatives on Mount Carmel from the time of Elias until the arrival there of Albert of Jerusalem (*c*.1209). In 1696 Innocent XII imposed silence on both sides in the dispute and again by a Brief of 20 November 1698 which added the threat of excommunication. The ban was removed in 1715, just after the death of Papebroch, the Bollandist chiefly involved. The modern Carmelites are content to see a spiritual affinity between Elias and their Order and do not uphold a strict historical succession, as may be seen from the two volumes dedicated to the subject of Elias in the *Études carmélitaines* (1956). It is worth noting that English medieval writers, John Baconthorp, Thomas Netter of Walden and Thomas Bradley (one-time Bishop of Dromore and later an anchorite), were foremost in developing the likeness between Elias and the Order of Mount Carmel.

IV The present status of Elias is obviously the determining factor in the question of the cult that may be paid to him. The Irish Litany, as cited above, cheerfully invokes him as a future martyr, thus implying that he must be confirmed in grace and not liable to fall away when he comes for his final trial. Methodius (*De resurrectione* 1:22 ; GCS 27:246) says that he came to the Transfiguration with bodily presence but changed to a more glorious state ; this would not imply a resurrection-body. The Church has generally styled the feast of Elias that is allowed to be kept in certain places on 20 July (or thereabouts) the *raptus Eliae*, and the Preface of the mass allowed to the Carmelites in 1919 says simply : ' Carried off in a whirlwind of fire, he is to come as precursor of Christ's second coming '.[1]

[1] Qui raptus in turbine ignis praecursor est venturus secundi Adventus.

The power of his intercession even in his lifetime is shown by Jas 5:17, where the statement that Elias *was* a man like unto ourselves implies that now he is something better. The Church prays in the *Ordo commendationis animae* that the dying person may be set free, ' as Thou hast set free Enoch and Elias from our common burden of death '. This prayer is of great antiquity. It can be traced in MSS. as far back as the 8th cent., but the personages mentioned (Daniel, Susanna, the three children, Job) are all figured on the Podgoritsa cup (perhaps of the 3rd cent.) alongside Christ and Lazarus. St Thomas (*Summa*, 1a:102:2:@ 3) replying to the objection that there is no point in God's keeping a Paradise if there was no one in it, said that Enoch and Elias were there. Suarez (*disp*. 55:1:12) said that the word Paradise, when used by the Fathers, means many things. Dom Alban Stolz tried to explain the whole patristic idea of the religious life as an attempt to reach a local Paradise which was believed to exist (and to be the abode of Elias) across a desert somewhere in the Eastern world, but this explanation will not do for Egyptian monasticism ; its monks, thinking as they did that Jerusalem was the centre of the earth, cannot have hoped to find the Eastern edge of the world by pushing out into their own deserts.

Most theologians would agree with St Thomas (*Summa*, 3a:49:5:@2) that Elias cannot have anticipated the benefits of Christ's resurrection. All the patriarchs had to wait for this (see DESCENT INTO HELL) before being released from Limbo, and if Elias has to come again and die upon earth, he cannot have enjoyed greater privileges than the patriarchs. In short, his fate is a check to theologians who want to present too tidy a picture of the universe, and it leaves them with many awkward questions to answer. Perhaps God intended this.

Bibliography. Two volumes of *Études carmélitaines* (1956) deal with Elias from many aspects. Some of the contributions are weak, the chapter on the iconography, for instance, not having recourse to the Princeton index, and the Irish tradition being neglected elsewhere, but other contributors are quite thorough. For Jewish tradition, *M. R. James, *The Lost Apocrypha of the Old Testament* (1920) ; *E. R. Goodenough, *Jewish Symbols of the Greco-Roman Period* (vols. IX and XI, 1964). For Elias and Islam, L. Massignon, in the *Études carmélitaines* (vol. II, 1956). A monograph, *De reditu Eliae* (1938) by A. de Guglielmo, offers some help.   J. H. C.

EMANATIONISM : a theory about the origin of things ; involves assertion of their procession (*emanatio, emissio, ἀπόρροια, προβολή*) from a divine essence, sometimes also a denial of their creation from nothing. The theory will be considered under the following headings : (I) Gnostic emanation theories, (II) Christian trinitarian theology, (III) Cosmology. **(I) Gnosticism :** the doctrine of ' emissions ' from a godhead, according to Irenaeus (*adv. haer.* II:16:4, H) is characteristic of the teaching of a number of gnostic sects. Irenaeus defines this *emissio* (προβολή) as ' the manifestation of that which is emitted outside that which emits' (ibid.). The images of light emanating from a source which remains undiminished by the emission of rays, or of a word uttered, or an offspring conceived and brought forth are frequently encountered in expressions of emanation theories. In gnostic systems each emission is generally thought of as a degenerate issue of its immediate source (cf. *adv. haer.* II:22:3, H). In emanation theories of this kind the world thus appears as a stepwise process of descent from the supreme divinity, its source. The scale of being is also a scale of value, the lowest emanations in the order of beings having the least worth. In gnostic teaching the theory appears in two variant forms. (i) In the monistic version all things have a single source, from which they originate, gradually decreasing in value. Evil, in this version of the theory, is the final degradation in the descending scale of being, the effacement of value or the extinction of the primordial light. (ii) In dualistic versions of the theory the world originates in two opposed principles, one often described in terms of light and opposed to a primal darkness, the two being contrasted as good and evil. On definitions of 'emanationism' which insist on a single source, such theories would not qualify for this title; their family-likeness to (i), however, seems to make it preferable to include them here as a variant form.

(II) Trinitarian theology: the terminology and concepts of emanation found some utilization in early trinitarian thinking. The Word, as Second Person of the Trinity, was occasionally described as an 'emanation', or 'emission' of the Father, in language sometimes reminiscent of gnostic theogonies. Tertullian (*adv. Prax.* 8) discussed the use of the term 'emission' (προβολή) in reference to the procession of the Word from God, and decided that, although the term had been 'usurped' by Valentinian gnostics for their heretical teaching, it had a place in orthodox trinitarian theology. The important qualification on which he insists is that the term must here be understood as meaning procession, without implying separation of what emanates from its source. Notwithstanding this possibility of an orthodox trinitarian usage of the concept, and its vindication by Tertullian, the word had become suspect in Christian circles on account of its close association with gnostic speculation. From the time of St Athanasius it ceased to be used in this context, though some echoes of emanation-language occur later.

(III) Cosmology: in contrast with its fate in trinitarian thinking, the concepts, language and imagery of emanationism continued to play a large part in Christian thought in cosmology. The idea of a world having a divine origin and proceeding from this by a stepwise descent is one of the commonplaces found in many philosophical systems. It is especially characteristic of neo-Platonism. Thus Plotinus, though rejecting gnosticism, and particularly scornful of its tendency to multiply intermediaries between the soul and God (cf. *Enneads* V:1:3) nevertheless uses emanation language to describe the relation of the One, and of Nous, to other things, as well as the image of 'light from light' (*Enneads* VI:8:18).

The world in his view is a graded system of entities on a scale of being and value culminating in the One and proceeding from the one source. This notion could be assimilated by Christian thought, and is often found in the work of Christian thinkers influenced by Platonism. The most notable example of this adoption of the neo-Platonic universe is in the thought of the psuedo-Dionysius. The stepwise descent (πρόοδος) of beings from their source and their return to it (ἐπιστροφή) is central to his conception of the world-process. The metaphor of light issuing from its undiminished source is again a favourite image (*De divinis nominibus* IV:1). This kind of thinking had much influence in Christian circles, and not only in those primarily Platonic in outlook. St Thomas Aquinas adopted the scheme of *exitus* (*processus*)-*reditus* (πρόοδος—ἐπιστροφή) from the pseudo-Dionysius for the framework of his *Summa theologiae*, and the language and ideas of pseudo-Dionysian neo-Platonism had a very deep influence on his thought. Significantly, he casts his definition of creation in terms of *emanatio* (*Summa*, 1a:45:1c). The distinction between Christian emanation theories and heterodox emanationism hinges on the distinction between a procession of creatures from God (a) by will and intellect, not by natural ecessity (cf. *Summa*, 1a:19:1c) and (b) a procession from God who makes them out of nothing, not from his own essence. (*See also* CREATION; GNOSTICISM; GUENTHERIANISM; HEGELIANISM; *and* LIGHT, METAPHYSICS OF).

Bibliography. RAC 4:1219–28; LThK 3:841–2; A. O. Lovejoy: *The Great Chain of Being* (1936); A. H. Armstrong: *The Architecture of the Intelligible Universe in Plotinus* (1940). 				R. A. M.

EPHESUS, COUNCIL OF Everyone knows that the Council which met at Ephesus on 22 June 431 defined that the Blessed Virgin was Mother of God (Θεοτόκος), but when that has been said, the boundary that lies between fact and mystery has been reached for most people. The *Acta* of the Council have to be reconstructed out of the immense dossier which was published in a critical edition by Eduard Schwartz (*Acta conciliorum oecumenicorum* I) between 1920 and 1930. Though he was a conscientious editor, Schwartz was not free from certain fixed ideas about how the ancient Church must have conformed to the pattern of a Reichskirche such as he had known in Germany. His edition of the Council proceedings was contemporary with the publication of some Nestorian source-material which led to an attempted rehabilitation of Nestorius, an attempt which was countered by Pius XI, who issued his Encyclical for the fifteenth centenary of Ephesus in 1931 (AAS 23:493–517, esp. 503). This article will treat of the occasion (I) of the Council, its course (II), and the peace-making (III) which had to follow it. (For the Nestorian theology, *see* NESTORIUS.)

I The occasion of the Council was the preaching of Nestorius in favour of using the title 'Christ-bearer' for Mary in place of the more traditional 'God-bearer'. Nestorius had been elected to the headship of the church of Constantinople on 10 April (or perhaps 1 April) 428. He was a leading light of the church of Antioch, a stranger in the capital, who caused some upsets soon after his arrival. He pressed hard on the remaining adherents of older heresies (Arians and the like) and he found fault with those of the clergy who said Mass in private (*Acta*, I:i:7:172), though the clergy replied that every one of us does this when it is suitable or necessary. By contrast he showed some leniency with the refugee Pelagians who had settled in Constantinople (at a time when some of their followers had been banished to the Scilly Isles).

So far was Nestorius from thinking his stand heretical that he sent copies of his sermons to Rome, where they were received with some misgiving. Not immediately, however, for it was some time before the sermons could be translated into Latin for Pope Celestine to read, as (*Acta*, I:ii:7) he wrote to Nestorius later on. What may have counted for more in Rome at the time (in 430) was the act of Leo the Great, then a young man and archdeacon of Rome, who called into consultation Cassian, Abbot of a monastery at Marseilles and, from his origins in the country now called Rumania, a man able to deal with both Latin and Greek. His work *De Incarnatione Domini contra Nestorium* was prepared at Leo's request and betrays a very poor grasp of what was involved in the new theology of Nestorius, being altogether too crude, but it was taken as a valid appreciation of the problem by the Roman curia. Coming on top of this, the letters of Cyril of Alexandria to Rome could not fail to win acceptance. Cyril had the traditional bias of Egyptians against Constantinople.

In August 430 Pope Celestine held a Council in Rome at which it was decided to tell Nestorius that, unless within ten days of the receipt of the papal letter he should condemn his preachings and in a written profession of faith accept ' this faith of ours about the birth of Our Lord Jesus Christ ', he would be deposed (*Acta*, I:ii:6). Gennadius (*De viris illustribus*, 54) says that Celestine sent to the churches of East and West a *volumen* with the record of this synod, but it has not survived anywhere. All that is known about the proceedings of the synod are a few chance remarks, one of which describes the Pope as quoting against Nestorius a hymn [1] composed by Ambrose : ' Come, Redeemer of the Gentiles, manifest Thy virgin birth. Let each succeeding age take note ; for such a birth befits our God ' (PL 53:289). The inference from this hymn would be that the *lex orandi* had long ago sanctioned the idea expressed by *Theotokos*.

The execution of his decree Celestine left to Cyril of Alexandria. Obviously, there had to be someone charged with this who would be competent in the Greek language and the theology of Antioch, and also one who was of equal rank with Nestorius. It would not require any intrigue on the part of Cyril to secure the nomination. A *pro memoria* by Cyril for his agent, Poseidonios, sent to Rome, has survived (*Acta*, I:vii:171) and this confines itself to doctrinal

[1] Veni, Redemptor gentium; Ostende partum virginis. Miretur omne saeculum; Talis decet partus Deum.

issues ; Nestorius is attacked for saying that the union of the two natures in Christ was a συνάφεια, like, but closer than, that of God with the prophets of the OT, and with refusing to call it ἕνωσις, or an hypostatic union. Cyril took his time over the task given to him. He called a synod of his own in Egypt and drew up his famous twelve *anathemata* against Nestorius. Finally, on 30 November 430 Cyril's envoys delivered the papal letter to Nestorius, who had already safeguarded his retreat by persuading the Emperor to summon an Oecumenical Council (19 November 430) for Pentecost (7 June) of the following year.

II The proceedings of the Council did not begin punctually. After waiting for a fortnight Cyril gave notice that business would start the next day, 22 June. John of Antioch and the whole of his party of Syrian and Cilician bishops were still on the way to Ephesus, and the papal legates had not yet arrived. Recriminations about this action came later on from both sides, Cyril saying that many of the waiting bishops in Ephesus were poor and anxious to go home, and that anyhow he had had a message from John saying : ' Get on with the work ' (*Acta*, I:iii:6) ; while on the other side there is the protest of some 68 bishops, drawn up on 21 June, saying that they wanted the start to be postponed until John arrived. In the event, about 150 bishops met on the Monday morning. The Imperial Commissioner, Candidianus, seems to have tried to stop them from getting down to business, but the document from his imperial master which is preserved in the *Acta* (I:i:120) and which gave him his instructions, empowered him indeed to remove from Ephesus all monks and worldlings who might have gathered there on occasion of the Council in the hope of influencing its decisions, but told him quite definitely to keep himself outside the debates of the Council ; the Emperor wished the Fathers to deliberate in peace about doctrine, while all personal accusations should be sent back to Constantinople for treatment in the courts there. Having thus checkmated the Commissioner, Cyril proceeded to work.

Cyril put to the Council his own letter to Nestorius (the one beginning with the word καταφλυάρουσι) and had the members vote on its conformity with the faith of Nicaea. Then a letter of Nestorius was read and declared to be against the faith. Next the papal letter was read, and after it a second letter of Cyril (τοῦ Σωτῆρος), to which a list of twelve *anathemata* was attached (D 113–24). No vote was taken on this letter and hence the *anathemata* never gained approval as a dogmatic text of the faith. By an easy misunderstanding of what had been done on this day, later theologians, down to modern times, took the *anathemata* as the main result of the Council and theorized on that basis. The two Egyptian bishops, Theopemptos and Daniel, who had delivered the papal letter to Nestorius the preceding December, were now called upon to report how it had been received. A long list of patristic extracts was then put in, and a counter-list of passages from Nestorius (*Acta*, I:ii:45). A letter from Capreolus of Carthage was read, declaring that the Emperor had sent a most pressing invitation to Augustine, who had just died, and that it had been impossible to hold an African synod owing to the Vandal inroads. Nestorius was then thrice summoned to attend without avail and sentence of deposition and excommunication was pronounced on him in the name of Christ. About 200 bishops signed the *Acta*. It had been a hard day's work.

Next day the Imperial Commissioner heard the public criers going about the streets of Ephesus shouting the deposition of Nestorius, and had them silenced. There could be no better sign than this that what the Council had done on its momentous day was entirely independent of the imperial power. It was that day's work which lasted and which contained the infallible decisions of the Council. When the papal legates arrived, two sessions were held (10 and 11 July) at which the legates (Bishops Arcadius and Proiectus, with the priest Philip) took cognizance of what had been done. The most important statement here made was that of Firmus (from Caesarea in Cappadocia), who recounted how Pope Celestine had written to Cyril, to Juvenal of Jerusalem, to Rufus of Thessalonica, to John of Antioch and to the church of Constantinople about Nestorius, how the ten days' grace allowed by the Pope had long ago elapsed ; how even the time of Pentecost fixed by the Emperor had gone by ; and how the Council had therefore proceeded to execute what the Pope had ordered (*Acta*, I:iii:58). Celestine's own letter to the Council did not mention Nestorius, but was a homily urging them to stand by the traditional faith and saying at the end that the legates would 'be present at your proceedings and bring to execution what we have long ago decided' (*Acta*, I:iii:57).

Meanwhile the Antioch party had arrived on 26 June and proceeded to form, with the help of the Imperial Commissioner, a rival Council. It decreed the deposition of Cyril and of Memnon, Bishop of Ephesus, and a denial of communion to all the other bishops who had signed with Cyril (*Acta*, I:v:122). Forty-three bishops signed this decree, most of them being those who had come late with John of Antioch ; the sixty-eight who were in Ephesus at the start, and who wanted Cyril to wait longer, do not seem to have gone over to John in any strength. The chief gravamen alleged against Cyril in this decree is that of his 'heretical chapters, which are in agreement with the wicked tenets of Apollinaris, of Arius and Eunomius'. Now it must be admitted that in the collection of patristic texts which Cyril had produced (and on which his *anathemata* were based) there were some that went under the names of Athanasius and of Popes Julius and Felix which were forgeries, perhaps from the workshop of the Apollinarians (*see* APOL-LINARIS). In urging that the union of natures in Christ was a 'natural oneing' (or ἕνωσις φυσική) Cyril was attacking the συνάφεια of Nestorius, which suggested something like conjugal union as the image of the Incarnation. In so doing he left a flank undefended against the followers of Apollinaris, who might use his words about 'unity in the Person of

the Word' to argue that therefore (as their master said) Christ had no human soul. It would take a long time for this imbroglio to be cleared up.

It was at the session of 11 July that Philip, one of the papal legates, used of the Pope those words which were to be taken by Vatican I as the true expression of the papal primacy (D 112 and 1824 ; *Acta*, I:iii:60). This declaration, coming just before the legates signed the Acts of 22 June, was of greater theological importance than much of what the Council did. The other feature of importance was the appeal to patristic *florilegia*. Cyril may have picked up some unsound passages in his collection, but he has far more weighty genuine ones than Nestorius, who (in his *Bazaar of Heracleides*) keeps ringing the changes on three texts, one from Ambrose (*De fide* 1:94 ; PL 16:550), one from Athanasius (*ep. ad Epictetum* 7 ; PG 26:1061) and one from Gregory Nazianzen (*ep.* 101 ; PG 37:180) ; and these are single sentences taken from the collection presented to the Council by Cyril. Newman (in his Catholic edition of the *Via Media* I:312) wrote : ' At Ephesus the Council did not refer to a single passage of Scripture before condemning Nestorius, but principally to the Creed of Nicaea and to ten or twelve passages from the Fathers '. It was in fact his being cited at a Council as a witness to the faith that made a writer worthy to be called a Father (*see* FATHERS OF THE CHURCH), and the custom began here.

The meetings of the Council on 16 and 17 July were for the purpose of replying to the countersynod of John. Cyril and Memnon presented a statement of their grievance at having been declared deposed by John of Antioch for unknown reasons (*Acta*, I:iii:15). The council then at the motion of Juvenal of Jerusalem sent two deputations to the house of John, calling on him to come and make his charges in the full assembly. Each time they found the house guarded by men with drawn swords. They saw some clerics too, but these replied abusively : ' We are clerics, not postmen '. John refused to move. The situation had become like that of Sardica, with two rival Councils in the same place. Next day a final deputation was sent. This time the Archdeacon of Antioch met them and offered them a paper which they would not accept. He then gave them John's message : ' Do not you send to us, and we are not going to send to you, for we are awaiting an imperial decree '. The Council then excommunicated John (*Acta*, I:iii:23). On 22 July the Council had its final session, dealing with Charisius, a priest from Lydia, and others who had been Quartodeciman heretics and whose reconciliation had been carried out by friends of Nestorius. An exposition of the faith submitted to them by these Nestorians (*Acta*, I:vii:97–9) was produced and reprobated, the Council declaring that no additions to, or omissions in, the creed of Nicaea were to be tolerated (D 125 ; *Acta*, I:vii:105). It was this decree which was to cause so much trouble at Florence for the *Filioque*.

III The peace-making after the division of the Council took two years and much imperial interference, into the details of which there is no need to enter here. In their letter to the Pope (*Acta*, I:iii:8), written soon after 17 July, the bishops gave an account of what had happened and accused John of Antioch of 'playing for a draw', in that he hoped to have the deposition of Nestorius withdrawn in exchange for a withdrawal of his own excommunication of Cyril and Memnon. This did not happen, owing to imperial intervention. All three were put under arrest, but Cyril escaped (bribing his way out) and was home in Alexandria by 31 October, while Nestorius agreed to go into exile and retire from Constantinople for ever. Thus Cyril was left victor in the sense that he remained in possession of the field. The Emperor called on both parties to take part in a seven-a-side discussion at Chalcedon (since Ephesus was too far away for rapid communication, the weather was stormy and the road was infested with brigands [*Acta*, I:iii:43], as we are told in a letter of 13 August 431).

Discussion proved unavailing, but gradually the liberality of the presents made by Cyril to the courtiers of the Emperor began to have effect. A list of these presents—so many ostriches, so many pounds' weight of gold, carpets and ivory chairs—is extant ; it speaks of the wealth of the Patriarch of Alexandria and of the low standards of the court, both parties using the same method of gaining a hearing. The list seems to be due to a desire to show what hardships Cyril suffered, since he had to use such bribes in self-defence. He seems to have thought it no more immoral than a modern businessman would find the buying of time for advertising on television. The plot constructed by Schwartz, according to which Cyril was all the time using the Council to lower the status of the see of Constantinople, does not answer to the facts. It has been shown by many scholars that Cyril's commentaries on St John were written long before he heard of Nestorius, and yet they have exactly the same Christology which he set forth against Nestorius. Schwartz also made great play with a supposed forgery by Cyril. The fact is that one of his letters (*Acta*, I:i:110–12) to his supporters in Constantinople ends with a resounding appeal to fight the good fight, while the Latin version of the same (*Acta*, V:53) ends quite peacefully. Schwartz claimed that both versions were sent together and that only one of these (the peaceful one) was to be shown to the Emperor. It seems however that the Latin version has combined two letters, for the paragraph where the texts diverge begins with the words : 'I must make my purpose clear and so I write to you again'. One has not to exculpate Cyril completely, since there is no guarantee of impeccability for those who take part in infallible decisions, but the case against Cyril has been very much exaggerated.

The use of peacemakers, such as the centenarian Acacius of Aleppo (Beroea) and Paul of Emesa, succeeded where open discussion had failed. In A.D. 433, on 23 April, Cyril read to his congregation at Alexandria (*Acta*, I:vii:173) John of Antioch's letter to himself and his reply, re-establishing communion between the East and Egypt. He quoted Mt 13:38

and said that Nestorius, that cockle of impiety, had been plucked up out of the Church. The letter o John had a passage of some twelve lines which gave a full statement of the faith of the East about the *Theotokos* and this Cyril repeated in his reply, accepting it fully (*Acta*, I:iv:17). Nestorius was in exile, where he lived on until 451, and Celestine was dead, Sixtus III having been elected in his place on 31 July 432 (*Acta*, I:vii:143). The mosaics which he procured for Sta Maria Maggiore at Rome are still there as a reminder that the real gain for the Church from the Council was a development in Mariology. The Eastern formula (it is reproduced in Rouet de Journel, 2060) said in careful terms that there was one Son, one Lord, not two, and that there came about a union (ἕνωσις) of the two natures, so that Mary could rightly be called Mother of God. Nestorius's word 'connection' (συνάφεια) was not mentioned ; neither were the twelve *anathemata* of Cyril, but the Antiochenes were content that their formula made some of these look very awkward. Cyril did not seem to mind. The next Council (*see* CHALCEDON) would supply a balance to the doctrine defined at Ephesus, just as the second Vatican Council is doing for what was defined at Vatican I. While everyone was preoccupied with the Council in 431, a minor event was noticed by Prosper's *Chronicle* (MGH *Chronica* I:473) that would in time bulk as large as the Council in history : Palladius was sent as their first bishop 'to the Irish believing in Christ'.

Bibliography. The *Acta* of Ephesus were edited by E. Schwartz in 6 vols. (1922–30), vol. I having eight parts, of which the last contained a chronological table of events. The *Bazaar of Heracleides* was edited by L. Hodgson (1925) with G. R. Driver's translation of the Syriac. This translation was heavily criticized by R. H. Connolly OSB (in JTS 37 [1926] 191–200) who had himself translated large extracts of the work for J. Bethune-Baker, *Nestorius and His Teaching* (1908). E. Amann in DTC s.v. Nestorius (1931) was able to use the new edition of the Acta, and the same author, 'L'Affaire Nestorius, vue de Rome', in RevSR 23 (1949) 5–37, 207–44 ; 24 (1950) 28–52, 235–65 was unfinished at his death. G. Jouassard has a useful summary in *Maria* I ; 122–37, edited by H. Du Manoir (1949) ; *H. Chadwick, 'Eucharist and Christology in the Nestorian Controversy', in JTS 2 (1951) 145–64 ; *E. Schwartz, *Gesammelte Schriften* (1960) IV:126–34 ; the same, 'Cyril und der Monch Viktor', in Vienna Academy *Sitzungsberichte* CCVIII (1929) part 4 ; *E. Honigmann, 'Juvenal of Jerusalem', in *Dumbarton Oaks Papers* 5 (1950) 209–79. This last is an important study of one who was much more prone than was Cyril to use the Council to promote the growth in prestige of his own see.

J. H. C.

EPHREM SYRUS, ST Here are considered (I) his life, (II) his writings, (III) his theological method and (IV) his influence.

I Life. Born of a Christian family at or near Nisibis in Mesopotamia about 306, Ephrem grew up under the saintly Bishop James of Nisibis, who was present at Nicaea in 325 (though he cannot have taken Ephrem with him, as the Syriac *Life* relates). Most of Ephrem's references to historical persons and events occur in the *Carmina Nisibena*, where he expresses his veneration for James and his successors Babu (338), Vologeses (346) and Abraham (361), under all of whom he would have taught in the catechetical school of Nisibis. The same hymns reflect the long agony of Nisibis as a Roman frontier city, withstanding siege after siege from 337 until in 363 it was finally lost to the Persians. Ephrem then moved to Edessa, the cradle of Syriac-speaking Christianity, where he continued his activity under Bishop Barses. Tradition makes Ephrem a deacon (cf. Sozomen, H. E. III:16 and Ephrem's probable meaning in *Contra Haereses* 56:10) and a 'monk': but though he must certainly have lived in evangelical chastity, we cannot conclude from his expressions of admiration for the contemporary ascetics (whom in any case it is anachronistic to call 'monks') that he actually left his busy life as a teacher and controversialist to join them. The solution to this problem, however, depends on difficult decisions regarding the authenticity of certain works. Ephrem's diaconal activity will have been divided between teaching (mainly giving exegetical and *midrashic* commentaries on Scripture) in the Christian schools, and the liturgical function of instructing the people by means of the metrical homily (*memra*) and doctrinal hymn (*madrasha*). In these media his teaching was especially controversial, directed against (1) the Jews, with regrettable bitterness, (2) the native Syrian gnostic and encratite heresies of Bardesanes (q.v.) and Mani (*see* MANICHAEISM) together with that of Marcion (q.v.); and (3) Arianism, which began to afflict the province of Edessa about the time that Ephrem came there, and threw all into confusion. Unlike the heretics in class (2), the Arians do not seem to have formed an effective counter-church, and unity seems to have been largely restored, thanks above all to Ephrem. According to the *Edessene Chronicle*, he died on 9 June 373. Venerated as a saint and 'Harp of the Holy Spirit' by all Churches, he was declared a Doctor of the Universal Church by Benedict XV in 1920.

II Writings. Unlike Bardesanes, Ephrem knew no Greek, shows no debt to Greek philosophy, and expresses contempt for Greek thought (*Hymni de Fide* 2:24, etc.). Of the extensive literature in Greek under the name of Ephrem, on which his fame in the Greco-Latin Church is based, little can have even a possible relation to Ephrem himself. His authentic works are all in Syriac or preserved in Armenian versions. Scholarly study of Ephrem's theology is in its infancy because, with few exceptions, only since 1953 have reliable texts been published. Almost all the authentic works are now available, and on this firm basis it may be possible to establish the authenticity of some doubtful works which seem to stand close to Ephrem. As few of his writings can be assigned to a definite period in his life, they are here divided according to their form. Bibliographical details are

omitted, as they can be found in studies quoted in the Bibliography.

(1) Prose works. (*a*) Exegetical: authentic and complete are the commentaries on Genesis and Exodus, on the Diatessaron (two-thirds are extant in Syriac, the whole in Armenian) and on the Pauline corpus. Other commentaries on the OT, and fragments of one on Acts, are preserved in Armenian catenae, while of the extracts ascribed to Ephrem in a 9th-cent. Syriac catena, only partly published, some, especially on the Prophets, may well be genuine. As an exegete Ephrem has affinities with two traditions, that of Jewish *Midrash Haggadah* and that of the Antiochene school. Like Aphraates, he both repeats stories common to Jewish tradition and tells others of similar type; but he also soberly distinguishes the literal sense from the spiritual (cf. *In Gen.* 42–3), and in his typology often coincides with the common patristic tradition stemming from the same Judaeo-Christian origin. (*b*) Controversial; *Prose Refutations of Mani, Marcion and Bardaisan.* These are the only works of Ephrem which contain reasoned controversial argument, as opposed to the mockery or passionate exhortation of his doctrinal poems. (*c*) Sermons: the only important and certainly authentic prose sermon is the *Sermo de Domino Nostro*, of some Christological significance. (*d*) Ascetical works: the *Epistola ad montanos* may be authentic.

(2) Metrical homilies (*memre*): the six *Sermones de Fide* are certainly from the Nisibene period and reflect the dangers to the Christians both in the Persian War and also, apparently, from effective propaganda by the culturally far stronger Jews. By far the largest part of the works doubtfully ascribed to Ephrem are *memre*; those with the best claim are the first *Sermo de reprehensione*, the *Sermones Rogationis* (for rain) and a few sermons on the ascetic life, the *Testamentum Ephraemi* (at least its core) and the *Sermones in Hebdomadam Sanctam.* Dom E. Beck judges the latter to show a development of doctrine beyond what is found in the certainly authentic works, but they have a number of marked features peculiar to Ephrem.

(3) Doctrinal hymns (*madrashe*): Ephrem is said to have adopted this form from Bardesanes. The stanzas are in various metrical forms, usually with a refrain, with which the hearers would have responded as Ephrem sang the stanzas to his harp. Authentic are the *Carmina Nisibena*, of which 1–34 have many references to persons and events, both before and after Ephrem's move to Edessa. Other hymns in the series are dramatic disputes between Sheol and Satan about Christ's descent to Sheol; here Ephrem uses a Mesopotamian literary form which goes back to Accadian and Sumerian literature. Also datable are the *Hymni contra Iulianum* and one hymn which Dom Beck calls *De Ecclesia*, reflecting Julian's visit to the East in A.D. 361–3. Of the two major doctrinal series, the *Hymni contra Haereses*, against Marcion, Bardesanes and Mani, are probably from the Nisibene period, while the *Hymni de Fide adversus Scrutatores* reflect the Arian conflict of Ephrem's last ten years. Also authentic are the series on various mysteries of Christ's life, *De Nativitate*, *De Azymis*, *De Crucifixione*

and *De Resurrectione*, the eschatological series *De Paradiso*, the ascetical series *De Ieiunio* and three very beautiful sets of mixed content, the first two in Syriac under the conventional titles of *Hymni de Virginitate* and *De Ecclesia*, and the third a collection of fifty-one hymns preserved in Armenian, which include more examples of the poetic dispute, this time between virginity and married chastity. The doubtful hymns are very numerous, especially those ascribed to Ephrem in liturgical books. Some of the hymns *De Epiphania* which follow those *De Nativitate* are probably genuine, others not ; for the rest, the closest to him seem to be the hagiographical hymns *De Confessoribus et Martyribus*, *De Abraham Qidunaya* and *De Iuliano Saba* ; the question of Ephrem's being a 'monk' is linked to that of the authenticity of the latter two sets. The hymns *De Maria Virgine* come at least from the school of Ephrem, but Dom Beck judges that their doctrine is developed beyond that of the certainly authentic works (which in itself is the most developed Mariology of the 4th cent.).

III Theological Method. Ephrem is heir to a Judaeo-Christian tradition which developed largely in isolation from the Greek-speaking world. Despite tension with the Jews, Ephrem, like his older contemporary Aphraates, uses an OT Peshitta text and continues an exegetical tradition which frequently echoes the Targums and the Midrashim. In NT exegesis, Ephrem uses *testimonia* less intensively and more implicitly than Aphraates, but has the same love of typological parallelism between the two Testaments. For both writers, the displaying of parallels seems almost a sufficient end in itself in theological exposition. The main themes thus illustrated are the Person of Christ, the Cross and the Church of the Gentiles which has replaced 'the former nation'. While much of Ephrem's typology is common to earlier Greek Fathers, no individual influence on him can be traced, not even that of the *Didascalia*, which Aphraates, despite his greater isolation, almost certainly knew. (Similarities to the *Odes of Solomon* hardly impose the conclusion that Ephrem knew them.) Besides *testimonia* and typology, Ephrem (again like Aphraates) makes great use of symbolic titles of Christ, both in litany-like hymns and as the basis of developed figures. While some (e.g. King, Shepherd, Bridegroom) are common to all tradition, some others (e.g. Farmer, Physician, Medicine of Life) are divine titles, going back to ancient Mesopotamian religion, whence many of them passed also into Manichaeism, Mandaeism and Islam. Finally, Ephrem delights in poetic symbols drawn from life and nature, which he lets proliferate luxuriantly. Creation is God's harp on which He plays ; so, again, are the two Testaments. The history of salvation is a great Road, stretching ' from the Tree to the Cross, from the Wood to the Wood, from Eden to Sion, and from Sion to Holy Church, and from the Church to the Kingdom ' (*Hymni de Fide*, 26:4). The olive tree, source of light, nourishment and healing, serves Ephrem for hymn after hymn about the sacraments. The ' hovering ' or ' brooding ' of the Holy Spirit is symbolized in baptismal anointing, priestly

ordination and in the Eucharist. Doctrinal interpretation of Ephrem is made difficult by his delight in shifting and often many-levelled imagery, which he presents but does not explain. That this is deliberate is clear from his constant attacks on the ' inquirers ', as he calls the Arians ; it almost seems as if for him the evil of Arianism is prior to its error, consisting in the sacrilegious attempt to fathom the mystery of the Godhead by speculative theology at all. Ephrem's answer to this is an affirmation of symbolism as the only way we can glimpse the meaning of divine things. The Father is the tree, the Son is the fruit ; when we have considered this figure beside others, we shall conclude that Ephrem is orthodox in his theology of the Trinity and Incarnation, but the fact remains that with his indifference in the use of the words for ' person ' and ' nature ' he has made it possible for Orthodox, Nestorians and Monophysites all to claim him as their Father. (For summaries of Ephrem's doctrine so far available, *see* Bibliography.)

IV Influence. For all Syrian traditions Ephrem is the supreme Doctor, to whom all regarded themselves as faithful, just as the Copts to St Cyril ; Ephrem's ambiguities were perpetuated but were interpreted in conflicting ways. Whether or not he was for any time an ascetic, tradition soon made him the father of all Syrian monks, under whose name pullulated an ever-growing literature in both Syriac and Greek. Thus much of Ephrem's influence reduces to the magic of his name. His literary influence is better verified. Though the development of the fatally facile *memra* metre was to reduce the fresh Aramaic of the 4th cent. to the tedious mediocrity of later Syriac, and though Ephrem's subtlety and intensity were too personal to be copied, he had a true spiritual descendant in (the probably bilingual) Romanos Melodos, so that Ephrem is the grandfather of the Byzantine *Kontakion* and all that developed from it. Now that we have reliable editions, Ephrem is revealed anew as the greatest poet of the patristic age and, perhaps, the only *theologian-poet* to rank beside Dante. It may be that in the contemporary rebirth of symbolic theology Ephrem is going to speak more clearly and influentially than ever before.

Bibliography. For full bibliography see Dom E. Beck, art. *Ephrem* in DSp 4:788–800 and I. Ortiz de Urbina, *Patrologia Syriaca* (1958), especially the 2nd edition (1965).

Editions. The very unsatisfactory Syriac volumes in J. S. Assemani's edition (6 vols. Rome, 1732–43) are now almost entirely superseded. On this see F. C. Burkitt, *St Ephraim's Quotations from the Gospel*, T & S 2:2 (1905). J. Overbeck, *S. Ephraem Syri . . . Opera selecta* (1865) ; T.-J. Lamy, *S. Ephraem Syri Hymni et Sermones* (4 vols. 1882–1902), largely superseded ; *St Ephraim's Prose Refutations*, ed. C. W. Mitchell, A. A. Bevan and F. C. Burkitt (2 vols. 1912 and 1921) ; *Commentarius in Evangelium Concordans*, Syriac text, ed. Dom L. Leloir, Chester Beatty Monographs 8 (1963). In the CSCO (Louvain) are now published : Commentaries *In Gen. and Ex.*, ed. R. M. Tonneau, vols. 152–3 (1955) ; *In Evangelium Concordans* (Armenian), ed. L. Leloir, vols. 137 and

145 (1954–5) ; edited by Dom E. Beck are : *Sermones de Fide*, 212–13 (1961) ; *Hymni de Fide*, 154–5 (1955); *Hymni contra Haereses*, 169–70 (1957); *Hymni de Paradiso et Contra Iulianum*, 174–5 (1957) ; *Hymni de Nativitate et Epiphania*, 186–7 (1959) ; *Hymni de Ecclesia*, 198–9 (1960) ; *Hymni de Virginitate*, 223–4 (1962) ; *Carmina Nisibena*, 218–19 (1961) and 240–1 (1963) ; *Hymni de Ieiunio*, 246–7 (1964) ; *Hymni de Azymis, de Crucifixione, de Resurrectione,* 248–9 (1964). *Works* in Armenian (4 vols. 1836); *In Epistolas S. Pauli,* Latin version (1893) ; *In Ac. Apost.*, Latin and English, in F. Jackson and Kirsopp Lake, *The Beginnings of Christianity* I, 3:373–453 ; *Hymni B. Ephrem LI*, ed. L. Mariès and C. Mercier, PO 30:1 (1961). On the Greek and other versions, see D. Hemmerdinger-Iliadou and J. Kirchmeyer in DSp 4:800–22.

Theological studies, select list : L. Leloir, *Doctrines et Méthodes de Saint Ephrem d'après son Commentaire de l'Évangile Concordant*, CSCO 220 (Subsidia 18), (1961); the same, *Le Témoignage de Saint Ephrem sur le Diatessaron*, CSCO 227 (Subs. 19), (1962). E. Beck, *Die Theologie des hl. Ephräm in seinen Hymnen über den Glauben*, Studia Anselmiana 21 (1949) ; the same, *Ephräms Hymnen über das Paradies*, ibid. 26 (1951) ; *Ephräms Reden über den Glauben*, ibid. 37 (1953) ; *Ein Beitrag zur Terminologie des ältesten syrischen Mönchtums*, ibid. 38 (1956) 254–67 ; 'Das Bild vom Spiegel bei Ephräm', in OCP 19 (1953) 5–24 ; 'Die Eucharistie bei Ephräm', in *Oriens Christianus* 38 (1954) 41–67 ; 'Die Mariologie der echten Schriften Ephräms', in OC 40 (1956) 2–39 ; 'Le Baptême chez Ephrem', in *L'Orient Syrien* 1 (1956) 111–26 ; *Symbolum-Mysterium bei Aphrahat und Ephräm*, OC 42 (1958) 19–40 ; *Asketentum und Mönchtum bei Ephräm*, OCA 153 (1958) 341–60 ; 'Ephrem', in DSp 4:788–800 (1960). J. Teixidor, 'Le Thème de la descente aux enfers chez Saint Ephrem', in *L'Orient Syrien* 6 (1961) 25–40 ; the same, 'Muerte, Cielo y Seol en San Efrén', OCP 27 (1961) 82–114; 'La Verdad de la Resurrección en la Poesía de San Efrén', in *Anales del Seminario de Valencia* I (1961) 99–124. I. Ortiz de Urbina, 'Le Paradis eschatologique d'après Saint Ephrem', in OCP 21 (1955) 467–72. A. Vööbus, *Literary, Critical and Historical Studies in Ephrem the Syrian* (1958). R. Murray, 'The Rock and the House on the Rock' (extract from an unpublished work, *The Church in Aphraates and Ephrem*), in OCP 30 (1964) 315–362.					R. P. M.

EPIKLESIS *Epiklesis* is a Greek word meaning, roughly, 'invocation', and it has come to be used for a certain much-disputed part of the Eucharist, particularly in the Eastern churches. Its original meaning (I) must first be discussed, and then (II) the theological development of 'invocation' in the patristic age. Finally, the disagreement (III) between East and West since the Council of Florence will be noticed.
I The meaning of the word was debated at some length (1917–24) by two English liturgists, Mr J. Tyrer and Dom Hugh Connolly OSB (*see* Bibliography). The editors of the *Lexicon of Patristic Greek* have taken notice of this in their organization of the uses of the word. In Irenaeus (*adv. haer.* I:vii:2, H) the word seems to be used for the whole Eucharistic prayer of the impostor Marcus, and is there called a *logos* of the *epiklesis*. Dom Connolly wanted to take this and many other texts as meaning no more than a naming of divine names without any prayer of petition, but the sense of the passage is against him and the *Lexicon* has recognized this. There are, indeed, many texts of early Christian and Gnostic writings where 'naming of a name' or even 'incantation' would be the correct rendering, and baptismal passages where the word seems to refer to the candidate's profession of faith in the Trinity, whom he names ; yet in eucharistic contexts the simple sense of naming a name does not fit. Origen (in his comment, in JTS 9:502, on 1 Cor 7:5) does say that the Eucharist differs from the shewbread of the Jews, for, 'over it there has been invoked the name of God and of Christ and of the Holy Spirit'. Dom Connolly supposed that this invocation was carried out by the recital of the final doxology of the primitive Canon of the Mass, since no petition-invocation directed to the Trinity was known. He admitted that there was one such (in the Syriac *anaphora* of Theodore) but regarded it as a liturgical curiosity of no significance. This *anaphora* reads : 'May there come upon us and upon this oblation the grace of the Holy Spirit ; and may He dwell and rest upon this bread and upon this cup, and may He bless and sanctify and seal them in the name of the Father and of the Son and of the Holy Spirit' (Renaudot, *Liturgia orientalis* II:621). It may be dismissed as a Nestorian product of the 5th cent., but it is not quite without importance.

From Basil (*De spiritu sancto* 27:66 ; PG 33:188) it is clear that the term *epiklesis* was still in use in his day for what we should call the Canon of the Mass. He argues that 'the words of the *epiklesis* for the consecration of the bread of the Eucharist and the chalice of thanksgiving' have not been left us by the gospels in writing but have come down by tradition (*see* BASIL, LITURGY OF, II). Vaguer phrases, such as that of the *Didascalia* (6:22) directing that the bread of the Eucharist is to be sanctified by an *invocatio*, or that of Firmilian (in Cyprian *ep.* 75:10 ; CSEL 1:818) who speaks of a heretic woman who pretended to hold a Eucharist, hallowing the bread *invocatione non contemptibili*, should be judged in the light of what Basil says so clearly. It is strange that these examples, put forward by Tyrer, are the only ones that Connolly did not discuss.

Irenaeus (*adv. haer.* IV:xxxi:4 H) in a highly ambiguous passage says that, 'bread from the earth receiving the invocation of God, is no longer common bread but Eucharist'. The Latin version is clear, but the Greek original cited by John Damascene has *ekklesis* for *epiklesis*, to hold us in suspense. Connolly said of this passage that *epiklesis* is not used as a current term for the eucharistic prayer as a whole, and still less does it carry a reference to a special petition for consecration within that prayer. He did not offer a rendering of his own and it is hard to see what he could have suggested. Cyril of Jerusalem (*mystica catechesis* 1:7 and 3:3 ; PG 33:1072 and 1092) re-echoes this phrase of Irenaeus, but by his time theological development had begun and this must now be considered.

II The theological development in Cyril (ibid.) has come about by a comparison of the consecration of baptismal water with what happens in the Eucharist, and also by a contrast with the pagan invocation of demons in their sacrifices. In *catechesis mystica* 2:3 (PG 33:1080) he says of the oil of catechumens that the breath of the saints and the invocation of the name of God like a vehement flame burns and sets to flight the demons, and in the same manner, ' this exorcized oil receives such virtue by the invocation of God and by prayer as to burn away and cleanse all trace of sin '. There were in existence, by the time of Cyril, prayers of invocation to be said over the oil (the Coptic version of the *Didache* has one, at 10:7), and it must therefore be concluded that some prayer within the Mass could now be looked upon as a prayer for effecting change. There is even the mention of a descent of the Spirit (κάθοδος) as the result of *epiklesis* in the fragment of Peter of Alexandria (dated to 373) which is cited by Theodoret (HE 4:22 ; GCS 44:251). This is the time when, in the West, Ambrose was teaching that the words of Christ from the Last Supper are operative of the consecration in the Mass (*see* CONSECRATION). In John Chrysostom the two ideas can be seen side by side. On the one hand the institution words of Christ are operative (*serm.* 1 *De proditione Iudae* ; PG 49:380) while on the other (*hom.* 45 on Jn ; PG 59:253) it is the coming of the Spirit that makes the bread become heavenly bread. One may say that Chrysostom did not reflect upon the inconsistency, but it is not easy to prove such a negative. There is a similar inconsistency in Augustine (*De Trinitate* 3:4:10 ; PL 42:874) ; the bread is hallowed by the invisible operation of the Spirit and yet it is consecrated *prece mystica* ' by a heavenly or revealed prayer ', which in the context must mean the words of institution. It seems unlikely that two such great theologians among the Fathers would both be willing to remain in a fog of uncertainty about this important belief.

The recovery of the *Catecheses* of Chrysostom (edited by A. Wenger, 1957) makes it possible to discern what he was really thinking about the connection between the Trinity and the sacraments. In *Catechesis* 2:25 he speaks of an ἐπιφοίτησις or visitation of the Spirit to the baptizand as he goes down into the font, but in the next paragraph he says that the indivisible Trinity accomplishes all and that it is not the hand of the priest but the hand of Christ that touches the head of the candidate. In *Catechesis* 4:17 he looks forwards to the catechumens at Holy Communion ' having Christ dwelling in their souls, and His Father too, and the coming of the Holy Spirit '. He was therefore well aware that the works of the Trinity outside the divine sphere are done in common, though certain attributions could be made to one Person or another (*see* TRINITY). What is needed to complete the thought of Chrysostom is a doctrine of the missions of the divine Persons. If one said that in the Eucharist there is a mission of the Son

by the Father (i.e. a coming-to-be-present in a new manner of the Son for the purpose of our sanctification), and that there is also a mission of the Spirit by both Father and Son (since He proceeds from both), whether for the transformation of the elements or for the uniting of the faithful into one body, there would be a complete reconciliation of the apparently diverse statements Chrysostom made.

The *Dialogus de recta fide* of Adamantinus (in the Latin of Rufinus, written *c.*300) gives the substance of what has just been said, even if not in technical terms (2:20 ; GCS 4:109) : ' Christ hallows the material of His body by the bestowal of the Spirit '.[1] Perhaps Paschasius Radbertus (PL 120:1310) is consciously echoing this when he says : ' By the power of the Holy Spirit through the word of Christ His flesh and blood are brought into being in an unseen way '.[2]

Theodore of Mopsuestia in his *Catecheses* (edited by A. Mingana, *Woodbrooke Studies*, VI:104) says that the priest prays ' that the Holy Spirit may descend, and that grace may come therefrom upon the bread and the wine . . . so that they may be seen to be truly the body and blood of Our Lord '. But he continues : ' When the priest, therefore, declares them to be the body and blood of Christ, he clearly reveals that they have so become by the descent of the Holy Spirit '. This last sentence must refer to the use by the priest of the words of institution, since no known *epiklesis* has such a declaration in it. Theodore adds that, ' the priest prays that the grace of the Holy Spirit may come also on all those present . . . that they may be knit as if into one body. . . .' Ideally, then, one might expect Theodore's liturgy to have an *epiklesis* for consecration before the words of institution and another afterwards for the union of the Church. There are liturgies, especially those of Egypt, which have the prior *epiklesis*. The liturgy of St Mark has : ' Fill, O God, also this sacrifice with the Blessing that is from Thee, through the descent of Thy Holy Spirit, that He may make the bread the body and the cup the blood of the new covenant '. The papyrus of Der Balyzeh is equally explicit : ' Vouchsafe to send Thy Holy Spirit upon these creatures and make the bread the body of Our Lord . . .'; while Serapion of Thmuis says : ' Fill also this sacrifice with Thy power and Thy participation (μεταλήψεως)'. All these prayers come before the recital of the words of institution. Other examples are the liturgy of St Cyril (Renaudot, I:46) and that edited by L. Lefort in *Muséon* LIII (1940) 22–74.

The affinity between Egyptian and Syriac liturgies has been shown by H. Engberding (*see* Bibliography) who has compared the *epiklesis* in the Syriac and Ethiopic *Testamentum Domini* with the *anaphora* of Timothy and a Coptic service-book recently published (in PO 28:284), and has made clear that an original prayer for the hallowing of the

---

[1] Christus . . . materiam corporis Spiritus sancti largitione sanctificat.

[2] Virtute Spiritus sancti per verbum Christi caro Ipsius et sanguis efficiatur invisibili operatione.

communicants was transformed into a consecratory prayer. The Ethiopic runs : ' Lord, Father of Our Lord Jesus Christ, this Thy gift—it is not food and drink—which we offer to Thy holiness, grant that it may be to us not for judgment nor condemnation . . .', while the Syriac has changed this to : ' Lord, Holy Spirit, produce this food and drink of Thy holiness ; grant that it may be to us not in judgment nor condemnation. . . .' The Syriac *anaphora* of Timothy agrees entirely with the Coptic book and is half-way between the two versions of the Testament : ' Lord God, grant that this food and drink of Thy holiness may be for us not unto judgment . . .,' and in the Coptic service-book the prayer is placed as a post-communion. The MSS. of the Syriac *Testament* are not earlier than 800, and it must be accepted that someone has inserted into it a consecratory *epiklesis* where none was before. After this prayer both versions of the Testament have tacked on the *epiklesis* which comes from Hippolytus and which prays : ' Grant that all those who partake and receive of Thy holy things may be made one with Thee . . .'; and at this point some of the Ethiopic MSS. have an interpolated consecratory *epiklesis*.

In the West a halt must have been called to such changes of invocation in the Mass prayers by a canon (25) of the Council of Hippo in 393 which directed that at the altar all prayers must be addressed to the Father. Though this was a local ruling, it must have had wide influence (*see* AFRICAN LITURGY) in Spain and elsewhere. In the East no such rulings were made. Some of the liturgies cited above for having an *epiklesis* before the institution narrative (notably those of Mark and Cyril) have another *epiklesis* following the consecration ; this may be directed to the Father, asking Him to send the Spirit, or to the Spirit Himself. Where such duality of invocation prevails, there can have been no worry about a moment of consecration determined by the recital of the words of institution. But in the West, as shown in CONSECRATION, q.v., there came about, from the time of Ambrose to that of Gildas (380–550), a consolidation of the idea that this moment was decisive. It is in this period that the doctrine of Transubstantiation develops (q.v.), and that more especially in the West.

III The difference between East and West arose chiefly from the gradual neglect in the East of the procession of the Spirit from the Son. If there is no such procession, then neither can the Son be said to send the Spirit upon the gifts when His priest recites the words of institution in the person of Christ. The possibility of reconciling the two positions held by Chrysostom thereby vanishes. The second *epiklesis* is then made to emphasize that the Spirit proceeds from the Father, and sole consecratory power is ascribed to it.

Nicholas Cabasilas in his *Commentary on the Liturgy* 29 ; PG 150:428, claims that the words of Christ, ' do not take effect simply in themselves or under any circumstances, but there are many essential conditions, and without these they do not achieve their end '. To the Latin argument that Chrysostom had called them creative words, valid once for all, he replies that the words : ' Increase and multiply ', are equally creative but expect human co-operation and prayer before they are at any given time effective. What he cannot see is that the act of Christ in sending the Spirit may be repeated in each Mass, as modern Catholic theology teaches (AAS 48 [1956] 716). Nicholas tries to carry the argument over to the Latin ground by claiming (ibid. 30) that in the Roman liturgy there is an *epiklesis* after the consecration. He asks if the prayer *Supplices* aims at a *local* translation of the offerings or that they be enhanced in status ; if the first, that is not what is wanted at a liturgy (Of what benefit is it to us to pray that the holy mysteries may be taken away from us ?), and if the second, then it would be blasphemous to ask for transformation when it had already taken place at the institution narrative. It will not do if one answers this dilemma with Remy of Auxerre (PL 101:1262) by saying that the words of institution cause Christ's body to be present on the altar and that one must then ask (in the *Supplices*) for it to be united to His body in heaven. Nor does the answer of Bessarion satisfy, that there can be fond repetitions, after the manner of the Psalmist who asked : ' Wash me yet more ', when he had already been cleansed. Mgr Duchesne (in *Christian Worship* 5:182) simply admitted that Cabasilas was right. ' This symbolical transference [of the *Supplices*] is in a contrary sense to that implied in the Greek formulary ; it involves not the descent of the Holy Spirit upon the oblation, but the elevation by God's angel of the oblation to heaven. But in both cases alike it is after it has been brought near to, and has participated in, the Divine Virtue that it is called the Body and Blood of Christ '.

The true answer to Cabasilas seems to be that our *Supplices* prayer in its original form (as found in the *Stowe Missal*) is simply a prayer for the communicants ;[1] there is no adduction, real or symbolical, asked for. ' We humbly ask Thee, almighty God, that Thou wouldst enact by the hand of Thy holy angel on Thy heavenly altar in sight of Thy divine majesty that as many as partake of the holy Body and Blood of Thy Son from this altar of holiness may be filled with all blessing. . . .' The phrase *iube perferri* means : ' Bid it to be enacted ', the infinitive being impersonal, as in legal phrases such as *perlatum est ut. . . .* The ratification of the sacrifice in heaven may be regarded as necessary for fruitful communion but is not needed for valid consecration.

Mark of Ephesus (PG 160:1089) has a more philosophic defence of the Greek view of *epiklesis* ; he says that the words of Christ, spoken at the Supper, were effective of consecration for all time potentially but not actually ; the priest's invocation is needed to bring about the ἐπιφοίτησις of the Spirit at Mass, and the Spirit actualizes what Christ made

---

[1] Supplices Te rogamus et petimus, omnipotens Deus, iube perferri per manus sancti angeli Tui in sublimi altari Tuo in conspectu divinae maiestatis Tuae ut quotquot ex hoc altari sanctificationis sacrosanctum Filii Tui corpus et sanguinem sumpserimus omni benedictione et gratia repleamur.

possible. This position quietly assumes that there can be no mission of the Spirit by Christ Himself and would call in question whether the priest speaks the institution words *in persona Christi*. If he does, and if Christ *can* send the Spirit, then there is strictly no need of an *epiklesis* for consecration, whatever may be required for the achievement of the *res sacramenti*, i.e. the union of the faithful who partake of the sacrament. Western theologians have no reason to depart from the position of Fulgentius (*Ad Monimum* 2:9 ; PL 65:187) : 'When the advent of the Holy Spirit is asked for, that He may hallow the offering of the whole Church, nothing else, I think, is being requested than that the union of love should be for ever preserved unbroken by the grace of the Spirit in the body of Christ which is His Church'.

In dogmatic teaching the Church has come by degrees to clarify the question of the *epiklesis*. First of all, Benedict XII (D 544) rejected a gross error of the Armenians about it. At Florence on 26 June 1439 the Pope agreed that a definition about the *epiklesis* need not be included in the decree of Union. Instead, on 5 July Bessarion read out a prepared statement that 'the dominical words are they that change and transubstantiate bread and wine. . . .' The Greeks had already signed the decree and were waiting for the Latin bishops to sign. This proceeding was appealed to in the decree of union of the Ruthenians (1720) as something which 'the universal Church in the Council of Florence proclaimed' (*Collectio Lacensis* II:30). The decree of Trent about the Eucharist and its 'form' (D 886) was not brought up here, as it deals rather with the errors of the Reformers. The Maronite synod of the Lebanon (1736) affirmed the sufficiency of the words of institution, but added that the *epiklesis* was not altogether superfluous and could not be omitted without sin (ibid. II:196).

In 1822 Pope Pius VII in a letter to the Melkites (ibid. II:550) ordered that no one, not even bishops and patriarchs, should in future dare to defend the opinion that the *epiklesis* was necessary for consecration. Canonically speaking, the language of this prohibition is not so severe as it could be, and that may have been due to the lack of a formal definition of the Church about the *epiklesis*. When Pius X in 1910 forbade certain opinions which had been put forward in a periodical, *Roma e l'Oriente*, advocating reunion, among them was this : that for the Greeks the consecration did not take effect until the *epiklesis* had been said (D 2147 a). The reason given for rejecting this was that the Church has no power to alter the substance of the sacraments. This would imply that the Church was already fully committed on the point (and that 'substance' here means matter and form), but as stated above one cannot produce a strict definition of the matter. The reply of the Congregation of Propaganda (31 March 1729) to the Melkite patriarch of Antioch (ibid. II:439) that his priests should continue to use the *epiklesis* at Mass, 'seeing that these prayers were examined and explained in a Catholic sense at the Council of Florence

and not rejected by the Holy See', seems very far from what really happened.[1]

If one may venture to suggest a line of possible future development, this might come from the examination of the relation of the Eucharist to the Resurrection. There should be an invocation to God to accept the sacrifice in heaven as He did the death on Calvary by the Resurrection. The prayer *Supplices*, as shown above, is really asking for that 'enactment on the heavenly altar' which will make fruitful the communion of those gathered round the altar on earth. There are *epikleses* with a similar drift in old Gallican liturgies (e.g. the *post-pridie* of Easter in the Milan *schabcodex* M 12 a, edited by A. Dold) and also the *post-secreta* which is twice found in the *Missale Gallicanum vetus*, 8 and 46, and which asks 'that our offering may be a spiritual sacrifice *accepted* in the odour of sweetness'.

Bibliography. R. H. Connolly and J. W. Tyrer, 'The Meaning of *epiklesis*', in JTS 25 (1924) 139–50 and 337–64 ; S. Salaville in DTC s.v. Epiclese ; M. Jugie, *De forma eucharistiae* (1943) ; H. Engberding, 'Untersuchungen zu den jungst veroffentlichen Bruckstucken saidischen Liturgie', in *Oriens christianus* XLIII (1959) 59–75 ; E. Lanne, *Le Grand Euchologe du Monastère blanc*, in PO 28 (1958) ; *W. H. Frere, *The Anaphora* (1938) ; *E. Atchley, *The Epiclesis in the Liturgy* (1935) ; E. Stommel, *Studien zur Epiklese der Taufwasserweihe* (1950) ; J. Jungmann, *Missarum sollemnia* (1958) ; E. Renaudot, *Liturgia orientalis* (2 vols. 1716) ; J. Laager, in RAC s.v. Epiklese ; J. De Jong, 'Le Rite de la commission', in ALW 4 (1956) 245–78 and 5 (1957) 39–79 ; J. M. Hussey, *Nicholas Cabasilas on the Divine Liturgy* (1960) ; Bessarion's rejection of the Byzantine case was published in the *Beiträge zur Geschichte der Philosophie* edited by C. Baumker, Supplementband III:2 (1935) 1376–411.   J. H. C.

ERASTIANISM Thomas Luber (1524–83), who latinized his name as Erastus, was a Swiss physician who spent most of his life at Heidelberg, but who somehow managed to give his name to a heresy that is peculiarly English. The popular notion of Erastianism, that religion is the creature of the State, emerged in the 17th cent. during the Civil War, when Independents wanted parliamentary control of the Church of England (as against the Presbyterians), while on the royalist side many looked upon the King as sole head of the Church (as against the Catholics and the beginnings of a High Church party, who denied this). It can be asked (I) if Erastus was himself an Erastian, and (II) if not, how the heresy came to be fathered on him.

I Erastus himself was against the exercise of judicial powers by the Church, and his book *Explicatio utrum excommunicatio mandato nitatur divino* (published after his death, 1589, and translated, 1659) is an elaborate attempt to argue that Scripture has no knowledge of ecclesiastical tribunals. He claims that the Sanhedrin

[1] Per essere le suddette Preci state esaminate e spiegate in senso cattolico nel concilio generale di Fiorenza, e non riprovate dalla S. Sede.

was a civil magistracy, that the unclean were always admitted to Jewish sacrifices and that the power of the keys (Mt 18:15–18) was concerned with private injuries only. This text (for the correct interpretation of which see CONFESSION, I) meant, according to him, that if private correction was of no avail, the injured party must go to the Sanhedrin ; the binding and loosing entrusted to the apostles was simply a command to preach the gospel. With exegesis like this one could reach any goal that was desired. Erastus also held that the Church had not exercised the right to excommunicate for the first century and a half of her existence, but in this he was confuted by the appearance (in 1633) of Clement's letter to Corinth (I Clem 59:1) which says : ' If any disobey the words spoken by Christ through us, let them know that they will involve themselves in transgression and in no small danger '. Pope Victor was not an innovator in the practice of excommunication.

Erastus made one exception to his theory when the magistrate was not a Christian. ' In whatever nation the magistrate is Christian, pious and orthodox, there is no need of other persons who should set a governing us and call us to account or punish us for our misdeeds. But . . . under a profane government (as in the dominions of Turks and papists) they should make choice of pious, sober persons who (agreeable to St Paul's command) might arbitrate between contesting members, might take up quarrels, . . . might chide and admonish debauched flagitious men, and such of the ministry as walk disorderly ' (Propositions 74 and 75 of his book). In all this he was thinking of the harm done at Geneva by the Calvinist theocracy quite as much as of papal excommunications. He wrote his book in 1568 (i.e. before Pius V excommunicated Elizabeth), though it was not published until later.

The position of Erastus is far removed from a complete subservience of Church to State such as one may find in the words of Tyndale (Obedience of a Christian Man [1528] 178) : ' The king is in the world without law and may at his lust do right or wrong, and shall give accounts to God only '. The statute of 8 Eliz. I : ' All such jurisdictions, privileges, superiorities and pre-eminences, spiritual and ecclesiastical, as by any spiritual or ecclesiastical power or authority hath heretofore been or may lawfully be used over the ecclesiastical state of this realm, and the order, reformation and correction of the same, is fully and absolutely by the authority of the same parliament united and annexed to the imperial Crown of this realm ', was already far beyond what Erastus held, but it merely drew the logical conclusion from the Byzantine position of Henry VIII (see CHURCH AND STATE).

II The broader Erastianism of Hobbes or Selden, while perhaps borrowing some arguments from Erastus, is more in line with Cranmer, Tyndale and the regalist tracts of the Middle Ages than with Erastus himself. Grotius is sometimes cited as Erastian for his saying that ' imperial rule extends not only to profane matters but even to sacred ', yet here the whole work of ' ordering and reforming '

would be included (as in the Elizabethan statute just cited) whereas all that Erastus himself wanted was for the imperial power to take charge of ' correction '. It may be due to the principles of Erastus that the Anglican Canon Law drafted in 1603 never gained legal force, but when once the civil power had learnt to identify crime and sin, at least in practice, the way was open for the religious sentiment of the majority or of those in power to punish by civil means what was displeasing to itself on grounds of religion. The system reaches its nadir when Hobbes maintains that the State can support any religion it please out of motives of State policy.

Erastus thought that, once he had handed over matters of conduct to the care of the civil power, the purely religious matters of creed and sacraments would constitute a separate province for the Church. True, he would not allow the Church to condemn anyone who changed his creed nor to deny the sacraments to anyone who wanted them, but this realm of the liturgical is soon overthrown if there is no lex credendi and no lex supplicandi. Writing in 1900 the Anglican political theorist J. N. Figgis (who was the pioneer in distinguishing between Erastus himself and the later Erastianism) could regard it as self-evident that ' all coercive jurisdiction must be wielded either directly or indirectly by the State '. He may have regretted the intolerances of the later Erastianism, but, after the experience of totalitarian tyrannies of recent times, it must now be equally self-evident that his proposition cannot stand. Hitler's claim not to be persecuting but simply to be confining the Church to the sacristy was so hollow as to make reasonable men aware that a division of the powers or a pluralism is essential for harmony and that the Church must be recognized as a society that is fully equipped, as a society, to run its own affairs. Even the Medical Association can ' strike off ' a doctor, and could not exist without that power, yet that power would have to be denied to it by a loyal follower of Erastus.

Bibliography. There is no article on Erastianism in DTC nor in the Lexicon für Theologie und Kirche, thus showing that it is an English heresy. *J. N. Figgis, ' Erastus and Erastianism ', in JTS 2 (1901) 66–101 ; J. Lecler, Toleration and the Reformation (2 vols. 1960) ; *P. Geisendorf, Théodore de Bèze (1949); *J. N. Figgis, The Divine Right of Kings (1922).

J. H. C.

ERIUGENA John Scottus, or John Eriugena, was born in Ireland in the first quarter of the 9th cent. He received his early schooling in an Irish monastery, where he learned elementary Greek, which he later improved through the opportunities afforded by continental libraries : this at least is the most likely hypothesis. Certainly there remained many gaps in his knowledge of Greek. Nevertheless for his period, his learning, in this respect as in others, was truly remarkable.

He became one of the chief figures in the Palace School of Laon, and the friend of Charles the Bald. There is no evidence that he ever became a monk, and it is unlikely that he ever became a cleric. The first specific mention of him dates from 850–1, when he was invited by Hincmar, Archbishop of Rheims, to contribute to the controversy on Predestination, which he did with his *De Praedestinatione*. This was his only part in the debate, for his views embarrassed the Archbishop. Eriugena was later condemned for his views on the Eucharist by the Councils of Rome (1050), Vercelli (1051) and Paris (1051), but this was due to the fact that a work of Ratramnus was falsely attributed to him by Berengarius and others. True, a passage in Hincmar's writings (PL 125:296) seems to imply that he held doubtful views on the Real Presence, in the context of the controversy between Paschasius Radbert and Ratramnus, but, if he ever wrote a work on the Eucharist, it has been lost. In 860–2, at the request of Charles the Bald, Eriugena translated into Latin the works of Pseudo-Denis, already very badly translated by Hilduin. He later revised his first version from a better text (865–75). About 862–4 he also translated the *Ambigua* of Maximus Confessor, the *De hominis opificio* (*De Imagine*) of Gregory of Nyssa (as yet unpublished), and probably also the *Ancoratus* (*De Fide*) of Epiphanius. Then came his great work, *De Divisione Naturae*, or *Periphyseon*, as later recensions are entitled. There follow the *Expositiones super hierarchiam caelestem* of Pseudo-Denis (865–70), a *Homily* on the prologue to St John's gospel, and a *Commentary* (at least on certain chapters) on the same gospel. He may have written also a *Tractatus de Visione Dei*, no longer extant. Besides poems, some in Greek, he also wrote, before 860, *Adnotationes* on the *De Nuptiis Philologiae et Mercurii* of Martianus Capella, and a *Commentary* on at least part (iii, met. 9) of Boethius's *De Consolatione Philosophiae*.

Charles the Bald remained his patron to the end. After the King's death in 877 there is no further mention of Eriugena. Presumably he died about this time. Later accounts of his spending his last years in Britain, even dying a martyr there, as also stories of his earlier travels in the East, do not appear to have any solid foundation. He is one of the almost unknown figures of the Middle Ages, remembered for his learning, his translation of Pseudo-Denis and for the recondite thought and expression of his *De Divisione Naturae*. The heretic Amaury of Bene (d.1205) was said to have drawn the inspiration for his doctrines from this book (phrasing his pantheistic ideas in the language of Eriugena), and accordingly, Pope Honorius III in 1225 ordered all copies of the book to be burned. In 1681 Thomas Gale had it printed at Oxford, with the translation of the *Ambigua* as an appendix, and it was placed on the Index in 1684, where it still appears.

To understand Eriugena's doctrine it is essential to realize that he is in the Greek tradition of *apophatic* or negative theology, which emphasized the unknowability of God, who infinitely transcends all concepts. This tendency was strongly marked in Pseudo-Denis, Gregory of Nyssa and Maximus Confessor. Eriugena also uses *kataphatic* or affirmative theology, though he describes as ' metaphorical ' such affirmative terms as the scholastics later call ' analogical '. He prefers compounds of *super*, such as *super-essence*, which combine both theologies. The combination of negative and affirmative theology is his ideal method, though his preference is for negative theology as closer to the truth.

The Augustinian image of God in the powers of the soul is a theme which recurs frequently in the *De Divisione Naturae*, but formally this work is an exposition of ' Nature ', by which is understood all reality. The first Nature, ' which creates and is not created ', is God, One and Three, infinitely above all creatures which He freely creates, the efficient cause of all. The second Nature ' which is created and creates ', the first stage of God's ' descent ' or ' progression ', and which is a ' theophany ' or manifestation of God, refers to the primordial causes, the Ideas, which are identical with the Word in His eternal generation by the Father, though in logical moments He precedes them. Here Eriugena is speaking of exemplary or formal, extrinsic causality in the neo-Platonic sense. Thirdly, Nature ' which is created and does not create ', the second stage of the divine ' descent ' and of the divine ' theophany ', refers to contingent, individual realities. Man is the microcosm of spiritual and material reality. Because of the Fall, foreseen by God and consummated in the moment of Creation, *corruptible* nature was created, and man lost his spiritual body which had no sex, his knowledge and his incorruptibility. Fourthly, Nature ' which neither creates nor is created ', considers God as Final Cause, and describes the dynamic process of the ' return ' to God or the ' ascent '. The cosmic effects of Original Sin were reversed by the Redemption, which Eriugena describes magnificently. Corruptible nature is to ' return ' to its causes, in its destruction. The ' return ' to God, made possible by the Redemption, is also due to a natural tendency. Man, as the result of God's grace is to be ' deified ', while retaining his individuality, when God will be ' all in all '.

The language of Eriugena in the *De Divisione Naturae* is obscure and paradoxical at times. His neo-Platonic theory led him into error on some points, for example in his eschatology, where he interprets Scripture rather too freely. But it should be remembered that, though he had to forge a new technical language, none the less he succeeded in creating the first medieval theological synthesis. Many of his phrases, if not sympathetically set in their context, especially the context of his age where no real distinction was made between philosophy and theology, can lead, as they have led, to improbable assertions concerning his rationalism, pantheism, agnosticism —even his idealism and modernism. As a thinker he stands supreme among all theologians of his time both in West and East.

Bibliography. *Manuscripts, editions, literature* : J. F. Kenney, *Sources for the Early History of Ireland, i* : *Ecclesiastical* (1929) section on *Eriugena*; I. P. Sheldon-Williams, ' A Bibliography of the Works of Johannes Scottus Eriugena ', in JEH 10 (1959) 198–224.

Editions : H. J. Floss, *Opera*, printed in Migne,

PL 122, incomplete, unsatisfactory text, and containing non-genuine works ; C. E. Lutz, *Annotationes in Marcianum* (1939) ; H. Silvestre, 'Le Commentaire inédit de Jean Scot Érigène au mètre IX du livre 3 du "De Consolatione Philosophiae" de Boèce', in RHE 47 (1952) 44–122 ; L. Traube, *Poems*, in MGH, *Poetae latini aevi Carol.*, iii (1896) 518–56 ; J. A. Willis, *Annotationes in Joannem* (extra fragment), in *Classica et Mediaevalia*, 14 (1953) 233–6; I. P. Sheldon-Williams, *Periphyseon*, an edition of Book I being prepared for the series, *Scriptores latini Hiberniae*, published by the Dublin Institute of Advanced Studies.

Life, doctrine, influence : A. Brilliantov, *The Influence of Eastern Theology on Western Theology in the Works of John Scottus Eriugena* (in Russian) (1898) ; A. Schneider, *Die Erkenntnislehre des Johannes Eriugena im Rahmen ihrer metaphysischen und anthropologischen Voraussetzungen* (2 vols., 1921–3) ; H. Bett, *Johannes Scottus Eriugena. A Study in Mediaeval Philosophy* (1925) ; C. Albanese, *Il pensiero di Giovanni Scoto Eriugena* (1929) ; Dom M. Cappuyns, o.s.b., *Jean Scot Érigène. Sa vie, son œuvre, sa pensée* (1933) ; D. Nerney, s.j., 'Johannes Scottus Eriugena', in *Studies*, 24 (1935) 415–32 ; A. Little, s.j., 'Some Picturesque Philosophers : vii. The Episode of Eriugena', in *Studies*, 38 (1949) 209–17 ; A. Forest, 'La Synthèse de Jean Scot Érigène', in Fliche-Martin : *Histoire de l'Église*, XIII (1951) 9–30 ; M. Dal Pra, *Scoto Eriugena*, 2nd ed. (1951) ; J. M. Alonso, 'Teofanía y visión beata en Escoto Erigena', in *Revista Española de Teología*, 10 (1950) 361–89 ; 11 (1951) 255–81 ; F. Copleston, s.j., *A History of Philosophy*, II (1950) 112–135 ; L. Bieler, 'The Island of Scholars', in *Revue du Moyen Âge Latin*, 8 (1952) 213–34 ; J. Gross, 'Urund Erbsünde in der "Physiologie" des Joannes Scotus Eriugena', in *Zeitschrift für Kirchengeschichte*, 66 (1954–5) 254–71 ; P. Mazarella, *Il pensiero di Giovanni Scoto Eriugena* (1957) ; L. Scheffczyk, 'Die Grundzüge der Trinitätslehre des Johannes Scotus Eriugena', in M. Schmaus, *Theologie in Geschichte und Gegenwart* (1957) 497–518 ; Hans Urs Von Balthasar, *Kosmische Liturgie, Das Weltbild Maximus des Bekenners*, 2nd ed. (1961) ; L. Bieler, *Ireland, Harbinger of the Middle Ages* (translated from German) (1963).   P. O'C.

EROS The article is divided into six sections : (I) the idea of Eros in Platonism, (II) in the Christian Fathers, (III) a survey of the problem as it reached the Middle Ages, (IV) what the medieval thinkers took from the tradition, (V) the 12th cent. and (VI) the solution of the 13th cent.

I In pagan Platonism. Eros to the ordinary unphilosophical Greek meant simply sexual love, and could carry every shade and overtone of meaning appropriate to the different forms of that love, from the highest and most unselfish love between husband and wife (e.g. Alcestis and Admetus) to the lowest animal passion. Like all the great forces working in human nature, Eros to the Greeks was a god, a power higher and stronger than man, which at times mysteriously came upon him and possessed him. It was

Plato and his followers who gave this primitive conception philosophical significance and importance. For Plato, Eros is the passionate desire for the divine beauty which we once knew in the intellectual world, awakened in us by the images of that beauty which we encounter in the world of sense, and providing the first impulse and continuing driving force for our return to the vision of the divine, which is our true end. It is not a graspingly selfish or self-regarding desire, but a fruitful and creative one, productive of good not only in ourselves but in others. Eros, fulfilled, results in generation (*Symposium*). The philosophic lover makes his beloved better and more godlike, and in so doing becomes more godlike himself (*Phaedrus*). But Plato never speaks of an Eros of gods for men, though divine goodness is for him essentially ungrudging, productive and creative (*Timaeus*). Aristotle has little to say about Eros, but it provides him with the best analogy for the impulse which keeps the heavenly spheres rotating in a sort of ceaseless aspiration to the indifferent perfection of the Unmoved Movers. Plotinus on the whole follows Plato fairly closely in his doctrine of Eros, but makes two important additions : one that the One or Good himself is Eros of himself, and the other that he gives to all beings, in his necessary creation of them, the Eros which leads them back to union with him. But Plotinus denies to the Good any love or care for his own creation (because he is concerned to deny that the Good can in any way be passive to or affected by what comes from him). A later neo-Platonist, however, Proclus, in the 5th cent. taught a doctrine of the Eros of gods for men which makes it strikingly like Christian *agape*. The later neo-Platonists abandoned the doctrine of Plotinus and Porphyry that man's true self 'did not come down', was naturally divine in the sense of being incapable of fall or sin : they therefore felt more need for a doctrine of loving divine care and help to enable man to attain his true end, and developed one, perhaps to some extent under Christian influence, partly from the old idea of Eros as a cosmic unifying power, and partly from the account of the philosophic lover in the *Phaedrus*.

II The Christian Fathers. Those of them who were Greek-speaking, from Origen onwards, found Eros as understood by the Platonists an appropriate term to use in speaking of both the love of God for men revealed in Christ and the love of men for God. Origen went so far (in explanation of Ignatius of Antioch, *Rom* 7:2 ὁ ἐμὸς Ἔρως ἐσταύρωται : 'my Eros is crucified') as to consider Eros an appropriate name for Christ Himself, and he was followed in this by many later writers. The pseudo-Denys, who was influenced by Proclus and who knew the Platonic doctrine of Eros in its latest form which brings it close to *agape*, uses Eros particularly freely of God and His love for men ; and he is followed in this by St Maximus Confessor, who in his comments on the pseudo-Denys often elsewhere tacitly corrects his excessively Proclan tendencies. Nowhere in the Greek-speaking Christian tradition does there seem to be any sense of an intrinsic opposition between the Eros of the philosophers and the *agape* of the Christian revelation. The Greek Fathers would probably have generally agreed that *agape* was preferred to Eros in the NT as a name for Christian love because of the associations of the latter in ordinary unphilosophical Greek speech with all too human sexual passions, rather than because philosophic Eros and Christian *agape* were two different and opposed kinds of love.

The Latin-speaking West seems equally to have felt no need to make a fundamental distinction between the two. The three Latin words in current use for 'love' in the early Christian centuries, *amor*, *dilectio* and *caritas*, show no distinction of meaning corresponding to that made by modern writers between Eros and *agape*. The greatest and most influential of Latin Christian theologians of love, Augustine, certainly seems to have felt no need to distinguish them. It would be irrelevant here, and indeed impossible, to summarize adequately his profound and subtle doctrine of love. It undoubtedly springs primarily from his continual meditation on the NT and his own spiritual experience. But it shows clear influence of the Platonic doctrine of Eros in his conception of love as 'weight', the inclination which determines our course and carries us to our goal, and his insistence that right love must be ordered love, that is, love which directs itself to the true and genuinely desirable Good, which is God. It is in speaking of man's love for God that Augustine goes deepest and is most illuminating. But, of course, he never forgets that God's love for man is primary, and that we love Him wholly by His grace. 'In order that we might receive that love whereby we should love, we were ourselves loved, while as yet we had it not. . . . For we would not have wherewithal to love Him, unless we received it from Him by His first loving us' (*De gratia Christi*, XXVI:27 ; PL 44:374).

A quite different kind of influence of the late Platonic doctrine of Eros appears in Boethius, in his *De consolatione philosophiae*, II:metrum 8 ; PL 63:719. Here Amor appears as the power which holds the whole universe, and should hold human society, in unity and harmony, as Eros does in Proclus. This vision of the universe as held together in an ordered and harmonious unity, which human societies should imitate, by God's creative and sustaining love, is one which had great power throughout the Middle Ages and beyond.   A. H. A.

III In the medieval period. In this context Eros may be defined as the natural inclination of the human psyche as a whole to satisfaction or fulfilment. (Note in particular the terms 'natural' and 'as a whole' ; the inclination in question implies as such no intrinsic supernatural factor ; and our definition of it abstracts from the difference between man as animal and as rational, presupposing that man, at least in relation to the range of objects he can find desirable, is a psycho-physical unity.) From the theological point of view the question at once arises :

What is the relation of Eros, in this sense, to that total love for God which was Christ's first and greatest commandment ? Is God included, in any sense, among the *objects* of man's natural desire ? And, supposing that he is, how does the *motive* of this natural God-desire compare with the motive of Christian God-love or charity ? Is its dominant motive merely the satisfaction of subjective desire or is it God as good in Himself ? Does it tend to God ultimately only for man's sake, or can it be said to bear *principally* on God, so that by nature man would love God *more than himself* ? Note that this question involves the whole problem of the relation of nature to grace (*see* GRACE). God gives grace, all Christians agree, to perfect us in charity, in loving God above all things. But from this point of view natural love would seem to be radically perverse if it can only tend to God as good *for us*, i.e. in view of our natural love of ourselves ; and would thus have to be destroyed to make room for charity, and so grace would destroy, not perfect, nature (cf. St Thomas, *Summa*, 1a:60:5c, *and see also* ALTRUISM, CHARITY).

But the logical connection of these ideas only began to become clear in the 12th cent., and indeed was not worked out thoroughly by anyone before St Thomas. The chief reasons for this were, first, the lack of a sufficiently clear distinction between nature and grace ; and secondly a metaphysically undeveloped concept of creation. So long as their concept of nature remained indistinct, Western Christians were ill-equipped to deal *critically* with the idea of an inborn desire for God in things which they inherited both from their chief master in theology, St Augustine, and from neo-Platonist philosophy. So long as their belief in creation was not conceived in terms of an adequate philosophy of being, they could only grope towards a solution of the apparent contradiction between the command of charity, that God must be loved above all things, and the egocentrism of desire—an egocentrism that seemed borne out both by ordinary experience and by the abstract consideration that whatever one loves, one loves as somehow good *for oneself*.

The medieval developments of doctrine on this matter were virtually limited to the 12th and 13th cents. Our account, then, will concentrate on this period and divide in three sections : the tradition that the Middle Ages inherited (IV) ; the 12th cent. (V) and the 13th cent. (VI).

IV The chief influences on Western thought about love down to the 12th cent. were those of St Augustine and of Denys the Areopagite. Concerning Augustine, three points should be noted : (*a*) his stress on man's desire for God implicit in the craving for happiness (as in the saying : Thou hast made us for Thyself . . .) ; (*b*) his stress on the *actual* division of men's loving into *cupiditas* (*amor sui*, self-love) and *caritas* (*amor Dei*, love of God) ; (*c*) his analysis of the motivation of all loving in terms of end and means, corresponding to enjoyment (*fruitio*) and use (*usus*). Now one effect of (*b*) on the tradition deriving from Augustine was rather to obscure the notion of *nature* implicit in (*a*) ; the insistence that self-love was the normal *de facto* condition of fallen man tended to preclude the abstract consideration of human nature as such ; it tended, moreover, to stress the healing aspect of grace (*gratia sanans*), and so man's moral need of it, at the expense of its divinizing aspect (*gratia elevans*) as raising man to a higher order of being, inaccessible to his nature as such, quite apart from the factor of sin. Again, touching point (*c*), Augustine's very ethical and concrete way of expressing the requirements of *caritas*—God is owed a total love that would bear on Him alone as the absolute Good, as the object of *fruitio*—rather left in the shade the metaphysical questions involved, especially whether in any sense man's *natural* desire for happiness could be called theocentric.

That it could be so-called was certainly implied in the teaching of the 5th- to 6th-cent. neo-Platonist Christian Denys, whose writings, introduced to the West chiefly by John Scotus Eriugena (*see* ERIUGENA) in the 9th cent., greatly stimulated later medieval thought about love, St Thomas's in particular. Denys's special contribution may be summarized thus : (*a*) the whole universe is moved by a yearning for God, the necessary effect of its originally proceeding from God ; (*b*) God-love and self-love are virtually identical, the latter being each thing's share in love's unifying and cohesive force ; (*c*) the reunion with God, the term of love for the intellectual creature, is an ecstasy (*excessus*) consisting in a kind of transformation into God (*deificatio*).

V The 12th cent. added to these influences (and note that in Augustine they had involved an exceedingly thorough adaptation of love-themes found in the Bible) a new interest in classical authors, especially Cicero and Ovid. Naturally, the influence of these two worked in different directions and in rather different milieus, Cicero's chiefly in cathedral schools and cloisters, Ovid's in the world. The effect of Cicero's *De amicitia* is clear in Abelard, in the Cistercian Aelred of Rievaulx and even in St Bernard. The chief idea taken from Cicero was that true love is disinterested ; it finds its reward in itself.[1] Abelard in particular seized on this idea and drew it out to dangerous theological consequences ; charity required that God be loved solely for His intrinsic perfection, without any thought of heavenly reward or, even, of His prior love for us. This was a logician's, rather than a theologian's, position ; but its very extremism uncovered problems that theology would have to meet sooner or later. The difficulties arising from the contrast between egocentric desire and that objective 'absolute' element which seemed to give love whatever *value* it had were theoretical as well as practical. Moreover, they could be felt whether the object of one's attachment were God or a fellow-creature. Both intentions, the one 'mystical', the other 'human', came to brilliant expression in this century of, on the one hand, St Bernard, William of St Thierry and Richard of St Victor, and on the other of the Troubadours, with their cult of *fin amors*. The latter, on its theoretical side—as

[1] *Omnis fructus eius in ipso amore est* (*De amicitia* 9).

presented in the *De amore* of Andreas Capellanus (*c.*1180)—might be very summarily described (at the risk of exaggeration) as an attempt to harmonize the sexual instinct with the Ciceronian idea of friendship : to bring the element of desire in sex under the full influence of the 'objective' value-element in love, but with no loss to desire, indeed to its intensification. But this ideal was in conflict with Christian morality on two counts. For (*a*) as an ethic based on the ennobling power of love, it did not in principle exclude fornication ; and (*b*) conceiving sexual love as ideally an utterly free interchange, it tended to disparage marriage, where interchange is legalized and obligatory, as a morally inferior state (cf. Capellanus, *De Amore*, edited by Trojel, 143–55). But the interest of Courtly Love in the present context lies chiefly in its being a cult of sexual desire that was morally ambivalent. Potentially immoral, it could be reconciled with morality either through sublimation without reference to marriage (as later by Dante) or, indirectly, through a doctrinal development which would allow more intrinsic moral value to the sexual factor in marriage than traditional theology had done. But such a development was still, in the Middle Ages, a thing of the future. The harmonizing of natural desire with religion was sought almost exclusively, so far as doctrinal formulations went, by way of mysticism (desire being seen as consummated in charity) or of metaphysical theology (desire being seen as implicitly theocentric).

The former way was, of course, that of the greatest master of the early Cistercian *schola caritatis*, St Bernard (1090–1153). His thought on love reflects that of Augustine, but adds three stresses that are distinctive : (*a*) on the connection between love and gratitude ; (*b*) on man's capacity, under grace, to love God spontaneously and disinterestedly ; (*c*) on ecstasy as the ultimate term of charity. Behind (*a*) is Bernard's intense concentration on the outflowing goodness of God, apparent in his constant use of the Scriptural passage which Gilson has singled out as his text of predilection, 1 Jn 4:7–10 (cf. *La Théologie mystique de Saint-Bernard*, 35–8). 'God is charity' and 'God has *first* loved us', and *all* our loving should be a response to His. Note that for Bernard this duty of gratitude-love lies on all men, not on Christians only. The Christian, knowing that He who created also redeemed us, has a redoubled motive for fulfilling that duty ; moreover, he alone, in fact, is able to fulfil it ; but the love-capacity of man as originally constituted, in his unfallen state, was *totally* owed to God, in return—and so in gratitude—for a gift that itself was total ; and that same debt still lies on every man, though he can only repay it now through Christ (*De diligendo Deo*, ii–vi). The original gift is man's soul and body, the soul bearing the Giver's image, especially in free will. This is the basic human *dignitas* ; and it flowers into *scientia* when through self-awareness the soul recognizes its Exemplar ; and then into *virtus*, as this recognition leads to spontaneous and effective attachment. Such was the original pattern of man's way to God ; and it is still the Christian way, the only difference being that now God has shown man yet more of His love to counteract the pull of self-love due to the Fall. But this self-love is not all bad ; it is only out of control. The way to control it is to go to school—Christ's school of charity. Here natural love is trained, passed through stages which represent an increasing subordination of self-love to God-love, until the original ' image ' is fully restored and the soul, dynamically, in its loving, refers itself entirely to God, loving itself only *propter Deum*, but God *propter Seipsum* (ibid., viii–xiv). By love it is utterly absorbed into its Lover (*sic affici, deificari est*), though without losing its own substance or, let us note, the love due to this precisely because God Himself loves it. Thus the soul discovers, under grace, its *infinite* capacity for loving ; and also incidentally the full meaning of that *disinterestedness* of true love which pagan wisdom had glimpsed but could not explain ; for only with reference to God can one truly say : ' True love is content with itself ; it has a reward, but its reward is the object of its love ' [1] (ibid., vii).

Only two comments on this radiant synthesis are necessary here ; first, that Bernard has restated the old idea of a natural desire for God entirely in terms of the Biblical doctrine of man as God's image ; second, that his solution of the problem posed by the apparent egocentricity of human desire depended on his finding the image of God *primarily in the will* (*see* FREE WILL), not in the intellect, in the capacity for loving, not for knowing. This made for a solution having tremendous moral appeal, but open to philosophical objections which Bernard did not consider. Nor did his friend, the great William of St Thierry (*c*.1080–1148), really consider them for all his more intellectualist approach. Broadly, William's thought about love is similar to St Bernard's, and this is not the place to examine the admittedly interesting differences. It is enough to observe that (*a*) William is more speculative and metaphysical than Bernard, and more influenced by Denys's vision of a cosmic Eros with its source and its term in God ; (*b*) he finds the divine image in the intellect rather than in the will ; (*c*) and perfection in a union with the Holy Spirit such that the soul loves God with God's own self-love (*Teipsum in nobis amans*) ; yet he is (*d*) in essential agreement with Bernard (and the Augustinian tradition) in seeing nature as *de facto* self-loving unless ' healed ' by grace, and in interpreting the passage from self-love to God-love in terms of a restoration of the image of God in the soul. To these two doctrinal syntheses that of Richard of St Victor adds nothing very pertinent to our subject except his idea that love was essentially inter-personal, and so of its nature must transcend the limits of selfhood, be ' ecstatic ' or, as he likes to say, ' violent '. This theme he elaborates impressively, but without solving the questions it raises ; his temper was too unphilosophical for that.

[1] *Verus amor seipso contentus est ; habet praemium, sed id quod amatur.*

VI The 13th Cent. Let us recall the fundamental question we began with : Are natural Eros and charity mutually opposed ? The main Catholic tradition down to 1200 had answered, in effect, with a distinction : essentially, no ; *de facto*, yes. And the main effort of the 12th cent. had been to show how this *de facto* opposition could be overcome in practice. But this left the more speculative—and yet also, potentially, very practical—question unanswered : What does it mean to say that any creature's natural desire is essentially theocentric ? That this question came to the fore after 1200 was the natural result of the decisive new factor in Western culture : Aristotelianism. Men trained in this system could not but think in terms of nature—of specifically structured forms of being, each tending to its own proper actuality or perfection, the good for *it*. On such a view, what is natural love but a given nature's tendency to its intrinsic good ? And how can God be intrinsic to a created nature ? And even granted that the intrinsic good of a given creature came from some contact with God, would it not, precisely as this particular creature, still have to love that intrinsic goodness, its own perfection, principally, and God only as a *means* to it ? This objection seemed so strong to Duns Scotus that he swung to an anti-Aristotelian extreme, declaring, rather as Abelard had done, that even were God not man's good, He could still be loved by man. This St Thomas categorically denied (*Summa*, 2–2ae:26: 13@3, and cf. 1a:60:5@2). But he did so, not merely as an Aristotelian, but also and principally as a believer in creation. If all natures, he held, are created out of nothing, then whatever perfection, however 'intrinsic', a given nature may desire, is nothing but some kind of likeness to the Creator ; so that in tending to its *proper* goodness each creature is tending, in fact, to make itself as much like God as its nature allows (*Contra Gentiles*, 3:24) ; hence, consciously or unconsciously, it is loving God primarily ; God is the fundamental motive for its tending to anything at all. By *nature* then, every creature loves God more than itself ; hence sin is basically anti-natural, and charity is *nature's* restoration (*Summa*, 1a:60:5c ; 1–2ae:109:3c). St Thomas has preserved the insights of preceding centuries, re-set in the light of a more exact philosophy of being.

Bibliography. P. Rousselot SJ, *Pour l'histoire du problème de l'amour au moyen âge* (1908) ; E. Gilson, *L'Esprit de la philosophie médiévale* (1944, esp. ch. 14) ; R. Garrigou-Lagrange OP, *L'Amour de Dieu et la croix de Jésus* (1929, vol. I, ch. 2) ; K. Foster OP, *Courtly Love and Christianity* (Aquinas Paper 39, 1963) ; C. S. Lewis, *The Allegory of Love* (1936) ; M. D'Arcy SJ, *The Mind and Heart of Love* (1953) ; the same, *The Meeting of Love and Knowledge* (1958) ; A. H. Armstrong, ' Platonic Love and Christian Agape ', in DR 255 (1961) 105–21 ; the same, ' Platonic Love ', in DR 268 (1964) 199–208.

K.F.

ESCHATOLOGY. *See* PAROUSIA

ETHICS, CHRISTIAN The moral impact of Christianity on the world has been glanced at in the articles on CONSCIENCE and CONVERSION. As a supernatural system (*see* BEATIFIC VISION) Christian moral teaching soon developed a moral theology of its own (*see* CASUISTRY, PROBABILISM), but from its contact with philosophy there grew up a conviction that grace perfects nature, rather than that it dissolves it. This conviction will be treated here (I), and then its rejection (II) in the Lutheran worldview and among the Barthians of today, while (III) there will be added a note on how far the light of revelation may be considered to come to the aid of nature. Particular issues in ethics (e.g. DIVORCE) are not considered here but under their own headings.

I That grace should perfect nature seemed right to the Fathers of the Church. They noticed on the one hand an open or unlimited character about the philosophic notion of the good or the life of virtue and on the other they found (Phil 3:13) that St Paul looked on the moral life as a reaching out beyond what was naturally attainable. Gregory of Nyssa (*De vita Moysis* I:3) laboured this point. 'The one goal of virtue is that there is no goal fixed (τῆς ἀρετῆς εἶς ὅρος ἐστὶ τὸ ἀόριστον). Hilary of Poitiers (*De Trinitate* II:10 ; PL 10:59) had a sentence which became one of the favourite quotations of St Thomas Aquinas : 'He who goes out dutifully to look for a goal at infinity, though he will never arrive there, none the less he will always be gaining as he goes on'.[1] St Thomas used this in his *Expositio super librum Boethii de Trinitate* (2:1:@7) to argue that assimilation to God is indefinitely possible for the creature and that the human mind ought ever to be moving towards greater knowledge of God according to its capacity. This gave him an ethical system which was 'open at the top' and therefore admitted of being completed by the work of grace.

That contemplation was preferable to action the Christian thinkers took over from Greek philosophy. St Thomas (*II Sent.* 19:1:1:@2) refers expressly to the *Ethics* of Aristotle (*Eth. Nic.* 1177a 20) for this, and then goes on to say that as the happiness of active life continues until death, it is clear that contemplative happiness must extend beyond that point, but not in the body, and therefore in the soul. It was thus that an ethic of happiness was built up which allowed for an easy transformation-scene at the end of the argument, when the data of revelation could be brought in to show that the reality of this happiness far exceeded the outline which the ethical philosopher had vaguely discerned. The fact that revelation was seen to define more accurately the goal of human moral striving made it easy for St Thomas and other medieval thinkers to regard grace as perfecting nature.

The chance remark of Aristotle (*Eth. Nic.* 1099b 13) that, if there are to be any gifts of the gods to men, it would be reasonable to expect that happiness

[1] Qui pie infinita persequitur, etsi non contingat aliquando, tamen semper proficiet prodeundo.

would be god-given ; but that this is perhaps more fitting for some other inquiry than the present one, delighted St Thomas. When he came to comment on the *Ethics* (in 1269), he took this very seriously (*lect.* 14 on Bk I), though a modern Aristotelian scholar would consider that the mention of ' another inquiry' was simply a refusal on the part of Aristotle to go into a matter about which he was not greatly concerned. When in 1270 St Thomas was writing the *De unitate intellectus*, he was shown a strange work in Arabic, called *Theology of Aristotle* (in reality a compilation by a Christian neo-Platonist of the 8th cent.), and this seemed to be the ' other inquiry' that was meant by Aristotle. This conviction, that in his more secret doctrine Aristotle had found right (i.e. Christian) answers to the questions he left unanswered in the *Ethics*, did but confirm St Thomas in the view he had learnt from Albert the Great (whose lectures on the *Ethics* he had listened to, *c.*1250–2) that supernatural happiness and the god-given means thereto supplemented, but did not clash with, natural striving for virtue and a natural contemplation of God *in visione qua videtur aliquatenus in via* : ' with that kind of insight that is somehow accessible to us in this life '.

The acceptance of teleology in ethics by St Thomas led to a difficulty which became acute in the Thomistic revival of the 16th cent., and which has been renewed in modern times. If there is a natural desire for contemplating the divine nature, and no natural desire can go unfulfilled without supposing a defect in God's original creation, then it becomes urgent to show that this argumentation does not in fact establish the necessity of the beatific vision (*see* BEATIFIC VISION) which the unanimous teaching of the Church has held to be gratuitous. Three ways were found of avoiding this awkward (and indeed heretical) conclusion. Cajetan said that the desire was not natural at all but infused by God supernaturally, and he was willing to throw overboard the teleological ethics based on Aristotle. Francesco Silvestri (Francis, or Sylvester, of Ferrara) held that the desire was not for the vision of God-in-Trinity, but for more knowledge about God's nature in an abstract way. Suarez held that there was not a desire but simply a velleity for the vision, and that God was not bound to further this by the very fact of His having implanted it, but might do so if He chose. The debate between these three views still goes on.

The Roman lawyers had bequeathed to posterity a confusion about natural law ; Ulpian having held that it was what nature taught to all animals, while Gaius and Justinian regarded it as what was common to all societies of men. This confusion lasted into the Middle Ages, until St Thomas (platonizing here very considerably) expounded that natural law was a mundane analogue of the eternal law of God and a ' participation' thereof ; he did not shrink from Plato's word μέθεξις. All men might be thought to have impressed on their minds the primary precepts of this natural law, even though secondary precepts and the application of the primary to a given situation might not be easy to work out. With this went the view that *synderesis* (*see* CONSCIENCE) was sure and unerring in its pronouncements on the major proposition of moral syllogisms, and that error, when it did occur, came in the minor ; murder was on all hands known to be wrong, but when was killing murder ? In this appeal to moral reasoning and the application by conscience of basic laws to situations, the traditional Christian ethic is not far removed from the position advocated in modern times by a great Aristotelian scholar, Sir W. D. Ross. The Intuitionism that Ross is credited with is quite a misnomer, for he held that moral rules are *media axiomata*, arising from the application to particular circumstances of certain basic rules that are common to all ; if this application is at times made instantaneously, that may be the result of a conscience disciplined by moral habits, rather than a spontaneous activity.

II The Lutheran attack on natural law grew out of the study of Holy Scripture. Theft, murder and adultery were clearly matters for the primary precepts of the natural law, yet there were OT passages which seemed to show that it was right for the Israelites to despoil the Egyptians, for Abraham to sacrifice Isaac and for Osee to be united with a harlot. St Thomas (*Summa*, 1–2ae:100:8:@3) took the line that the application of general precepts to particular matter was sometimes liable to be changed by God (and by Him alone in matters which were of divine origin such as marriage), and sometimes by human jurisdiction (in matters that the natural law had left vague and undetermined). This solution did not satisfy all medieval thinkers, and there were soon those who made here an application of the distinction between what God habitually wills for man and what He could of His arbitrary power decide man should do. This distinction was enshrined in the words *potestas ordinata* and *potestas absoluta*, and owed something to contemporary theories of government. The Nominalists did not to a man accept this solution, though some of them did. Biel insisted that God's will is never divorced from His wisdom, though this wisdom may be hidden from men.

The easy hypothesis that Luther took from Biel a scriptural view of morality and opposed this to the vain teaching of Aristotle current in the theological schools of the time does not really fit the facts. Biel has some forthright declarations on the adequacy of reason. ' If God, who is divine rationality, did not exist (which is of course impossible), or if the divine reasoning was faulty, anyone who went against right reason, whether that was found in angels or in men, would be sinning '[1] (*II Sent.* 35:1:1). Nor did Biel oppose OT and NT laws as completely diverse ; he allowed that there was a

difference of degree, but both came into the same category of law. Christ may have abrogated the ceremonial law of the OT, said a disciple of Biel and teacher of Luther (Bartholomew of Usingen), but He did not abrogate the commandments, and, what is more, He gave His Spirit to the Church to guide it in establishing new laws in place of the old (*Libellus contra Lutheranos*, J 4).

For Luther it was the strong texts of Gal 4:5, 31 and Rom 5:20 that started him off on new ethical theories, and the Barthians of today recognize this. They formulate from Luther's teaching what some of them call a *koinonia*-ethic. By our solidarity in Christ a climate of trust is established, and the individual, by his membership of the Christian *koinonia*, is related to what God is doing in the world. He must aim so to live that God will recognize that he is on the track of what God Himself is doing. Hence there is never any one universalizable way of dealing with a given situation ; man must strive to become aware of God's claim upon him. Thus a ' situation-ethic ' is given its charter and full scope allowed to the inner light. Anything like universally valid principles of rational ethics becomes anathema. The position thus taken up is a comfort to those who fear that if they were to try to meet the humanist on the ground of reason the issue might remain in doubt.

The late Michael Foster, in an essay ' Ethics and Mystery' (*Mystery and Philosophy* [1957] 71–84), after setting out the biblical case for such a Lutheran ethic as has been described above, adds with frankness : ' Some parts of the Bible are difficult to reconcile with what I have said ', and he cites Rom 1:19 ; 2:14, pointing out also that, ' in the Wisdom literature of the OT, Wisdom deals with man as man and not as Israelite ' (op. cit., 74). While he admits that modern Jewish ethical thought follows the Wisdom tradition, he goes on to claim that the real conflict envisaged by the OT is between man's whole nature and God, not between one part of human nature and another. Quite apart from St Paul in the first two chapters of Romans, there is the whole Jewish theory of the two inclinations in man (the good impulse and the evil) to oppose to such a claim, and the new material from Qumran makes this still more obvious than it was in 1957. Barth himself in his commentary on *Romans* tries to slide away from the difficulty which its early chapters create for him by saying (quite without evidence) that St Paul meant to regard the gentiles as imperfect Israelites, with some inkling of the Law and therefore with some claim to the same privileges. Much work has been done in recent times on the Jewish idea of the Noachic covenant and its application to all gentiles, but there is no sign that Paul, or anyone else, thought of it as a watered-down version of the Israelites' own covenant. To abstain from idolatry, fornication and murder and to keep the Golden Rule (as in the D-text of Ac 15:20) was commonly regarded by Jews as the duty of gentiles, but no one suggested that this gave gentiles

---

[1] Si per impossibile Deus non esset, qui est ratio divina, aut ratio illa divina esset errans, adhuc si quis ageret contra rectam rationem angelicam vel humanam aut aliam aliquam si qua esset, peccaret.

any special status in the eyes of God ; they were, as Paul said, inexcusable if they ignored these commands.

III The light of revelation aids nature to discover the remoter workings of the natural law. This is a position which has become traditional among Catholic theologians. At the First Vatican Council it was defined (D 1786) that revelation is needed so that all men in their present condition may easily, with certainty and without admixture of error come to know those truths about God which are in themselves open to the scrutiny of reason. In a similar way it is held that ethical truths (which arise from an adequate idea of human nature and of God) are made accessible to all with the same clarity and certainty by the help of revelation. This has not been defined in so many words, but the distinction, which all theologians accept, between primary and secondary precepts of the natural law, does in fact require a position of this kind. The darkening of the intellect by Original sin is not selective, so that knowledge about God might be difficult and obscure while ethical truth might be plain ; rather is there a parity of cases.

The historical study of the impact of revelation on the various problems of morality has not been very much developed, and much remains to be done. Here it may be suggested that the idea of person (which is a Christian notion, due to revelation) has had a profound effect on all ethical thinking. The slow emancipation of the world from the idea of slavery, from notions of the rightfulness of torture used for the ends of justice, from the inequality of the sexes in marriage could be claimed as results of this process. Neither Greek philosophy nor Roman law really helped, and indeed the Roman civil law countenanced the continuation of all three abuses. Where so much depends on persuading large numbers of men (all of them marked by Original sin) that a course is right, it must be obvious that a Christian ethic has to work as a leaven rather than as a panacea, and that its effectiveness will not be judged by short-term views. (Attempts to reduce ethics to logic or questions about language are not considered here, as many would hold them to have failed and their discussion belongs rather to CONSCIENCE and GOD, EXISTENCE OF.)

Bibliography. D. von Hildebrand, *Christian Ethics* (1953) ; the same, *True Morality* (1955) ; *P. Lehmann, *Ethics in a Christian Context* (1963) ; *M. B. Foster, *Mystery and Philosophy* (1957) ; J. H. Crehan sj, ' Ethics, History of : II, Medieval ', in *Encyclopaedia Britannica* ; the same, ' Quid senserit S. Thomas de naturali beatitudine', in *Acta congressus Thomistici* (1950) ; J. Dunbabin, ' The Two Commentaries of Albertus Magnus on the *Nicomachean Ethics* ', in *Recherches de théologie ancienne et médiévale* 30 (1963) 232–50 ; *H. A. Oberman, *The Harvest of Medieval Theology* (1963) ; P. Bastable, *Desire for God* (1947) ; *H. V. Jaffa, *Thomism and Aristotelianism : a Study in the Commentary of St Thomas on the Ethics of Aristotle* (1952) ; J. Leclercq, *La Philosophie morale de Saint-Thomas* (1955) ; O. Lottin, *Morale fondamentale* (1954).

J. H. C.

ETHIOPIC LITURGY Ethiopia was converted to Christianity by Frumentius and Aedesius about A.D. 340, their mission starting from Alexandria. It is natural to suppose that the new converts would follow the liturgy of Alexandria and at first they must have had it in Greek. No MSS. survive from this early period, and indeed none are known to be earlier than the 15th cent., but by analogy with what happened to the Scriptures in Ethiopia one may obtain some guidance for the history of the liturgy. The Ethiopic Bible was gradually formed, most of the books being translated separately and from Greek, though the whole version was not completed until the 7th cent. One curious fact is that the Ethiopian version of the Psalms has at 37:21 an addition of some eight words which is found again only in the Greco-Latin Psalter of Verona ; this link with Verona is of importance when one comes to estimate the value of the Ethiopic liturgy, for in Verona and in Ethiopia were preserved the two most complete versions of the *Traditio apostolica* of Hippolytus. How the link is to be supplied between the liturgy of the two places is a matter for conjecture, but the most probable answer is that the Monophysite churches of Syria after 450 supply the connection. It is known that Ethiopia was then visited (c.480) by a group of Monophysite missionaries who are known in Ethiopic records as ' the nine saints '. At the same period the Latin version of Hippolytus may have been made for the Arian Goths of North Italy who would themselves be opponents of Chalcedon too. Other Greek works were translated direct into Geez, the ancient Ethiopic language, at this period ; there is a book of extracts from Cyril of Alexandria, known as the *Qerlos*, a version of the *Lausiac History*, the *Physiologus*, the *Book of Enoch* and other works, and one can hardly suppose that no liturgy at all was put into Geez from Greek amidst all this activity.

The *Senodos*, a collection of so-called Apostolic canons in eight books, is regarded as part of Scripture and contains various liturgical texts. Thus the *anaphora* of the twelve Apostles now in use is taken from the Mass for the consecration of a bishop that is found in the part of the *Senodos* which corresponds to the *Traditio apostolica* ; while the *anaphora* of Our Lord is drawn from the Ethiopic version of the *Testamentum Domini*, which is itself a derivative work based on the *Traditio apostolica*, but with many Syrian additions. The *Testament* was turned into Syriac from Greek by James of Edessa in the 7th cent., but the editors of the *Testament*, Cooper and Maclean, consider that the Ethiopic version was made direct from the Greek. In using these Ethiopic texts, however, one has to remember the verdict of the late Archdeacon Charles about the Ethiopic OT : ' It is unquestionable that our version was made in the main from the Greek—in the main, for there are certain phenomena in the MSS. which cannot be explained from this hypothesis alone '.¶ The fact that the MSS. are so late means that they have been copied and re-copied by those to whom Arabic was more familiar than Greek and who were probably in possession of Arabic versions of the works they were copying.

Besides these two ancient *anaphoras*, some seventeen others are known to have been used in Ethiopia : those of Our Lady, of Sts Basil, Athanasius, Gregory, Cyril, Epiphanius, Dioscorus, of Jacob of Sarug etc. The preliminary part of the Mass, or *pro-anaphora*, is invariable, but the *anaphora* used varies with the feast or season. An English version of the *pro-anaphora* was printed, along with the Ethiopic text, as an appendix to Swainson's *Greek Liturgies* (1884). From this one may see how elaborate are the opening prayers of purification (of the vestments, vessels and of the clergy themselves) which bespeak a firm belief in the Real Presence. The four readings, each with its ritual introduction, are taken from St Paul, from the Catholic epistles, from Acts and from the gospel. The entire neglect of the OT is remarkable and must be due to fear that Jewish practices might be too freely adopted from it if it were read publicly. It is to be recalled that one of the documents in the *Senodos* is a version of ' a discourse of St Gregory of Armenia against the Jews ', and other signs of anti-Jewish trends (such as the canonization by Ethiopia of Pilate) can be noticed. One of the preliminaries to the reading of the gospel is the recital of the (first part of the) *Hail, Mary*.

In the *anaphoras* the words of institution over the bread are usually : ' This bread is My body ', though the *anaphoras* of John the evangelist, of Chrysostom and of Gregory Nazianzen have the correct words. Over the cup the words are sometimes (e.g. in the *anaphora* of Our Lady) not given in direct form but merely as a narrative. The importance of the moment of consecration is emphasized in the *anaphora* of the Apostles by allowing the people to interrupt, just at the beginning of the institution narrative, with the words : ' We believe it '.

The *epiklesis* is sometimes directed towards asking graces for the communicants, as in the *anaphora* of John the evangelist : ' May this bread be the communion of Thy living Body . . . that to everyone who believeth . . . it may be for hope and for salvation. . . .' The *anaphora* of Gregory the Armenian has a similar *epiklesis*. In some of the later *anaphoras* (Jacob of Sarug and Dioscoros) there is a curious *logos-epiklesis* : ' May the Lamb come, may we see Him '. To a Monophysite, there must always be a danger of diminishing the distinction of the Persons in the Trinity, since he believes that after the Incarnation the divine nature somehow absorbed the human nature of Christ. Sometimes there are two *epikleses*, and one may conjecture that here the Spirit *epiklesis* has been inserted at a later stage to conform to other Monophysite churches where that prayer was regarded as consecratory (*see* EPIKLESIS).

Doctrinal passages of significance can be found here and there. The *anaphora* of Jacob of Sarug, after citing the words of Jn 6:58, goes on to speak of Our Lady : ' Thou didst say unto her : " Whoso maketh memorial of thee and calleth on thy name shall live in life eternal "'. This instance of advanced Mariology is much earlier than what could be found in the West in the same vein. There is in the *anaphora* of John the evangelist an intercession ' for all Thy apostles who ploughed the land of the nations with the ploughshare of Thy Cross and sowed the treasures of Thy word to the ends of the earth '. This image must be derived from the language of the prayer of ordination of bishops (as given in the Ethiopic version of the *Traditio apostolica*), which, as Connolly showed (T & S 8:4:24) uses an early patristic image that does not find favour with the later Fathers at all.

For centuries the head of the Ethiopic church was consecrated to the episcopate by the Copts of Egypt and thus no consecration-service in Geez was needed ; but in 1940 a *Pontifical* in Geez for the use of the Uniat church was printed in Rome as a provisional measure. In 1945 the Missal, edited by van Lantschoot and containing seven anaphoras, was issued. The music of the Ethiopic liturgy seems to be unmatched elsewhere, as are its spectacular features of dancing and rhythmic hand-clapping, but the elaborate ritual of dividing the altar-bread at the Fraction into a pattern of fragments can be paralleled in the Mozarabic (and to some extent in the Keltic) liturgy.

Bibliography. Three works by J. M. Harden, the Anglican Archbishop of Tuam : *The Ethiopic Anaphoras* (1928) ; *Ethiopic Christian Literature* (1926) ; *The Ethiopic Didascalia* (1920) ; Takla Mariam, *La Messe éthiopienne* (1937) ; E. Wellesz, ' Studien zür äthiopischen Kirchenmusik ', in *Oriens christianus* 9 (1920) 4–106 ; E. Cerulli, ' La festa del battesimo e l'Eucaristia in Etiopia ', in AB 68 (1950) 436–52 ; A. A. King, *The Liturgy of the Eastern Churches* (vol. I, 1946) ; the work of *S. Mercer, *The Ethiopic Liturgy* (1915) is almost worthless, as Harden proved.

J. H. C.

EUCHARIST Many aspects of the theology of the Eucharist are dealt with under other titles and these will be enumerated here before the general plan of this article is given. Thus the contribution made by distinctive liturgies is assessed under separate headings (ADDAI AND MARI, AFRICAN, AMBROSIAN, ANTIOCH, BASIL, BYZANTINE, EDESSA, EGYPT, ETHIOPIAN, GLAGOLITHIC, JERUSALEM, MOZARABIC), and on the chief sacramentaries of the Roman rite there are special articles also. The adoration of the Eucharist is treated under BENEDICTION, THEOLOGY OF and RESERVATION. Certain points of controversy on the Eucharist enter into the articles CONTINUITY, ANGLICAN and CONSUBSTANTIATION, while the manner of Christ's presence in the Eucharist will be treated under TRANSUBSTANTIATION. Parts of the Mass are dealt with under CANON, COMMUNION, CONSECRATION, EPIKLESIS, OFFERTORY ; and the theology of the sacrifice of the Mass will be treated under MASS. Here then it remains to discuss (I) the institution of the Eucharist, (II) early Christian faith in the Real Presence, (III) the heresies which led to denials of this Presence (though under RATRAMNUS, INFLUENCE OF, further details will be given) and (IV) the effects of the Eucharist as a sacrament.

I The institution of the Eucharist is narrated in the Synoptic gospels and in St Paul. It is customary now to treat these accounts as being basically two, one common to Matthew and Mark and the other to Luke and Paul. In 1 Cor 11:23–31 Paul gives the account which he had received at his conversion ; he writes it down about the year 55, during his stay at Ephesus, but he must have received it some twenty years before that. He agrees almost word for word with Lk 22:19–20 in the peculiarities in which Lk differs from Mt 26:26–8 and Mk 14:22–4. These peculiarities are mostly additions : the words : ' This is My Body' have the addition, ' that is for you' (τὸ ὑπὲρ ὑμῶν) ; the cup is said to have been given ' after they had dined ' : there is a command to ' do this for a commemoration of Me ' ; the words over the cup are : ' This cup, the new covenant in My Blood', whereas the other account gives : ' This is My Blood of the covenant which is being shed for many (i.e. for all) unto the remission of sins '. Much discussion of these differences and of their theological import has gone on since the publication in 1949 of *Die Abendmahlsworte Jesu* by J. Jeremias (English version in 1955). Actually this was the second edition (much enlarged) of a book which came out in 1935 and did not at the time attract much attention. The complete change in outlook of modern theology about eucharistic origins can be seen by comparing the space given to refuting theories of pagan origins (five columns) and expounding the NT text (three columns) in the article Eucharistia (*Enciclopedia cattolica*, 1950) and that given in the *Lexicon für Theologie und Kirche* (1961) where four columns are devoted to the text and none to the pagan parallels. The aim now is to find the OT setting for the Christian Eucharist, and the pagan practice, noticed by Paul in 1 Cor 10:20–2, is not viewed as having any influence on what was done in Palestine before the parting of the Apostles.

Attempts to assign priority to either of the two NT accounts of the institution are often made on the strength of what could not conceivably have been omitted had it stood in the prior version ; but this inconceivability turns out in many cases to be what the modern writer deems inconceivable. One may urge that the mention of remission of sin in Mt is more likely to be primitive, since it brings out the nature of this covenant as being the one foretold by Jer 31:31–4 ; the omission of this phrase in Mk would then be a simplification for Gentile readers or hearers. On the other hand it has been urged by J. Jeremias that one cannot have in Aramaic the words ' my blood of the covenant ' and that therefore the Mt-Mk account which has them cannot be primitive. Jeremias was answered by an Anglican Syriac scholar, J. Emerton, who pointed out (*see* Bibliography) that in the Sinaitic Syriac the phrase is present and that one may fairly project that idiom back into the Aramaic of the time of Christ. In the last edition of

his book (1960) Jeremias withdrew to the extent of admitting the phrase as possible but still harsh. Emerton thereupon followed up his former argument by showing that Christ would not want to say ' the blood of my covenant' since that would damage the reference to the covenant of Jahweh (Jer 31:32) and that there is adequate evidence in Syriac for the use of a possessive suffix with a noun followed by a genitive that does not act as further definition of that suffix. Since Christ in His manhood offered sacrifice, it is more fitting that He should call the covenant God's rather than His own. In Zach 9:11 (' Thou, by the blood of Thy testament hast sent forth the prisoners out of the pit ') the covenant is called Christ's prophetically, as it is linked to the harrowing of Hell (*see* DESCENT INTO HELL), but, while Zach 9:9 is used by the Synoptics in their account of Palm Sunday, this verse is not cited verbally.

The fitting of the Eucharist into the framework of the Paschal meal can be variously attempted (CCS 720 ab ; 739 de), but it is at least generally agreed now that it was the Pasch that was being celebrated and not some other festive meal. Jeremias has enumerated some ten signs that show the meal to have been a Pasch ; the reclining on couches, the use of red wine (implied by the choice of this for the Blood), the singing of the Hallel at the end, the partaking of a preliminary dish (Mt 26:23) before the breaking of bread, the natural way in which the words of Our Lord prolong the Haggadah of Passover spoken by the head of the family, and the idea (Jn 13:29) that Judas might have gone to give alms as was customary at Passover ; all this is hardly explicable unless the meal was a Pasch.

The theory taken by Dix (*Shape of the Liturgy* [1945] 50) from Oesterley, that the meal was a Chaburah, or weekly social meeting of the apostolic group, was put out of all reckoning by Dugmore (JTS 47 [1946] 107), while Jeremias has made equally untenable the idea of Box and others that there was a Passover-Kiddush held on the eve of the festival. The explicit preparation for the Pasch described in the Synoptics would be unintelligible on these hypotheses, and in fact they were originally put forward to satisfy what was thought to be the Johannine chronology (Jn 18:28) which seemed to put the eating of the Pasch on the Friday. It has been shown from Josephus (*Antiquitates* XIV:21 ; XVIII:29 and *Bellum* II:10) that the term Pasch could be applied to the whole festive week, having become interchangeable with the term Feast of Azymes, and that in fact there was a great festive meal on Nisan 15 according to Num 28:17 and 2 Par 30:22. Even if this explanation were rejected, it would still be possible to suppose that there were conflicting views on the date of the Pasch, the Sadducees (in charge of the Temple) having one official date, while the Pharisees (who were feared and deferred to by the Sadducees, TB Sukkah 48 b, Yoma 19 b) kept the feast a day earlier. The lunar calendar was fixed by watching for the new moon on a hill near Jerusalem (TB *Rosh-ha-Shanah* 24a) and this primitive system, however shocking to the modern scientific mind, would easily lend itself to controversy and abuse. It is not necessary to indulge in large hypotheses about a conflict between users of the lunar calendar and those who had adopted (as at Qumran) a solar calendar. The Christian evidence of a discrepancy in the dates (*Didascalia apostolorum*, in Connolly's edition 181) and Epiphanius (*haer.* 51:26 ; GCS 31:296), along with Victorinus of Pettau (*De fabrica mundi* 3 ; CSEL 49:4), who put the arrest on the Wednesday, provides an argument for saying that in fact there were two days for observing the Pasch in the year of the crucifixion, but it does not amount to proof and can hardly bear the weight of theory that has been imposed on it by some recent writers who have followed Mlle Jaubert. It is certain that the Montanists followed a solar calendar (Sozomen, HE 7:18 ; GCS 50:329), and the patristic passages just cited might be due to infiltrations from them.

The words 'Parasceve of the Jews' which are used three times (in Jn 19:14, 31 and 32) mean no more than 'Friday' or 'Jewish Friday', since the word *harūbtā* in Aramaic and Syriac meant 'evening' and hence also 'Sabbath-eve', i.e. Friday. Versions which render the term as 'preparation of the Pasch' are wrong and there can be no argument drawn from them to suggest that John and the Synoptics are at odds over the chronology. In Mt 27:62 the word Parasceve occurs, but this time, as C. C. Torrey has argued, it has its original meaning of evening or sunset-time, and the rendering should be : 'On the morrow, i.e. after sunset . . .', thus showing that Matthew was reckoning the days, after the Jewish manner, from sunset to sunset. It is to be noted that the African MSS. of the Old Latin regularly render the word *Parasceve* by the words *cena pura*. This was the Jewish term in North Africa (so Augustine *tract.* CXX:5 on Jn 19:41 ; PL 35:1954) and it implied that Friday was a day without meat at supper (hence *pura*).

The Pasch in its primary meaning of a memorial of the Exodus was associated in the Jewish mind with redemption. The *Pirke* of Rabbi Eliezer (29:14 d) says : 'By the atoning force of this blood they were redeemed in Egypt and they will be redeemed in the days of the Messias'. The Targum on Ex 12:42 (according to the Vatican codex, which may well reproduce the ideas of the 1st cent. A.D.) sees in the Pasch the commemoration of four nights, the night of creation, that of the appearance of Jahweh to Abraham (Gen 17:1–8) and the making of the first covenant, the night of the Exodus and finally the night when the Messias will appear. In Melito's *Homily on the Pasch* (lines 525–60) it is precisely these events which are brought up in sequence, as a reproach to Israel. The early Christian interest in the sacrifice of Isaac by Abraham (Gen 22:1–16) is shown by the selection of this portion to be read at a Three Hours service on Good Friday according to the early *Syriac Lectionary*. Numerous representations of Abraham and Isaac in early Christian art confirm this inference.

The nature of the covenant spoken of by Christ must have been understood by the Apostles, who witnessed it, in the light of what Abraham had done and Moses (Ex 24:4–8) too, for Moses had set up twelve pillars round the altar at the making of his covenant. There was also the prophecy in Is 55:3 ; this was appealed to by Paul (Ac 13:34) in the early days of his preaching, long before he came to write to the Corinthians. In the gospel accounts it is always *the* new covenant and not simply *a* new covenant ; it was the final Messianic covenant, and from this fact Paul had warrant for saying that it was to be kept in being 'till the Lord come'.

The meaning of commemoration (*anamnesis*) has been much debated, some holding that it means that God is to be put in mind of Christ's sacrifice by its renewal in the Christian liturgy. This is to stretch the meaning of the word too far. It is not used again in the NT, save for Heb 10:3, where the word has taken on the technical sense of Christian usage (for which see section II) and can hardly mean that God is put in mind of Israel's sins once a year, for the very purpose of Jewish sacrifices was that God should not be mindful of sins.

The absence of the command to reiterate in Mt and Mk has been assigned to various purposes. It has been suggested that Mt and Mk follow a liturgical text ; P. Benoît sums up this argument in the words : 'On ne récite pas une rubrique, on l'exécute'. Lietzmann would have it that Paul has made up the command in order to transform a simple fellowship-meal into a commemorative sacrifice. Against this it has been urged that the language of the command is not Pauline and that anyhow Paul is appealing to tradition for what he lays down. The strictly Jewish viewpoint of Mt (and also Mk) might be invoked for the omission ; it would not need to be said to a Jewish Christian that in what took place at the Last Supper (which was deliberately planned as the Christian Pasch) there was a command to reiterate, whereas with Gentiles the need would be obvious.

The silence of John about the Institution is traditionally explained by the fact of his including the long Haggadah about the promise of the Eucharist in his gospel (6:22–72). What is less often remarked is that, in his long account of the Last Supper, the place at which the Institution narrative should be inserted is, according to Tatian, after the words (13:32) : 'Straightway shall He glorify Him'. This would imply that Judas did not receive Communion, and, while the Fathers are divided about this, there is support for Tatian's view. The Haggadah itself is in reality a descant upon the theme of Ps 77:24, and the argument from lesser to greater is developed in terms of Moses and Christ, the bread from heaven, the giving and then the eating. It is not possible to separate the last section (6:51–9) from the rest of the discourse and to claim it as a later addition, for the word φαγεῖν is part of the text in the form in which it is given (6:31) and it must be commented upon in its turn. The thematic unity of the discourse, quite apart from its metrical structure (which has been examined by P. Gächter ZKT 49 [1935] 419–41), is a check to any theory of the composition of the whole by John out of isolated sayings of Our Lord. (On its theological import, *see also* CAPHARNAITES.) Outside the ruins of the synagogue at Capharnaum can be seen a circular mosaic pavement with a peacock depicted in its centre, a monument of Byzantine piety towards the teaching of John's gospel on the bread of eternal life, for the peacock was the accepted symbol of eternity.

One may thus gather from the institution-narratives that the Eucharist was Christ's Pasch, the new and final covenant, and that this belief can be traced back to within a very few years of the event itself.

II The earliest Christian faith in the Eucharist left its mark on other parts of the gospels. The phrase used in Mt 15:36 and Mk 8:6 at the feeding of the four thousand, to describe what Christ did there, is the same as that used by Paul in 1 Cor 11:24 for the Eucharist ; ' Giving thanks He broke ', εὐχαριστήσας ἔκλασεν is not quite normal Greek, as Jeremias has explained, and a liturgical overtone is suggested by this language. The inclusion of this, and of the other miracle of the bread (in Mt 14:15, Mk 6:35, Lk 9:12 and Jn 6:1), in the gospels must have been meant to show that, as Christ had done these miracles, so He could bring about a miraculous change in the bread of the Eucharist, thus making good His word that this was indeed His body. The objection urged by some that the minds of the apostles were unprepared for what He did at the Supper finds here its answer.

' The consumption of blood was a sinister, animistic horror for the born Jew ' writes Jeremias (op. cit. 145), but the apostles had been prepared for this, too, by the Capharnaum discourse (Jn 6:52–5) and would have understood from Jesus's comparison of Himself with the Paschal Lamb that His blood had to be applied, not to the door-posts and lintel (Ex 12:7), but to their own lips. This at least is what the early Church thought, as may be seen in the early Paschal homilies (edited by Nautin [1953] 77 and 83), and the same idea (that it is the blood applied to oneself that protects from the destroying angel) seems to have been used by Origen in his treatise on the Pasch (cited by Nautin, ibid.). The ῥαντισμός of the Blood of Christ (Heb 12:24 and 1 Pet 1:2), or sprinkling, was very soon taken (1 Pet 1:19) as being applied in the Eucharist ; Melito in his *Homily on the Pasch* (lines 401–2) is quite explicit : ' He sealed our souls with His own Spirit and the limbs of our body with His own blood '.

What Paul says (1 Cor 10:16–20) about ' table-fellowship ' with demons is sometimes brought up as an objection to the belief in the Real Presence at the beginning of the Church. The objection overlooks Paul's habit of using comparisons (such as that of Adam with Christ) which are not simply comparisons of equality. Theodoret, when he comes to this passage (PG 82:304), has no difficulty with the idea of communion with Christ, but has to explain how communion with demons is at all possible. Origen in his *Dialektos* (3) has a long development on the analogous nature of unity ; one human being can become one flesh with another, or one spirit with

Christ (1 Cor 6:17), and conceivably there is a higher unity, in which Father and Son are one God.

In *Acts* there is the difficulty of deciding what was understood by ' the breaking of bread ' (Ac 2:42, 46 ; 20:7, 11 ; 27:35). By the time of 1 Cor 10:16 it certainly means the Eucharist, but is there an earlier stage when the expression was used for the Agape, and did the Eucharist always follow the Agape ? No certainty can be reached about these questions on the evidence at present available (*see* AGAPE), but one cannot safely exclude the possibility that at the outset the Apostles celebrated the Eucharist only once in the year and that at the Pasch ; the demand of the faithful for a Sunday Eucharist (making the Sunday a little Easter) would be quite sufficient to explain their holding it more frequently. It is certainly difficult to take the ' breaking of bread ' in Ac 27:35 as eucharistic, whatever may be thought of the other passages. The reading at 2:46 is not quite certain.

From the time of Justin the Christians took the prophecy of Mal 1:11 to refer to the Eucharist (*dial.* 116:4–117:1). The dating of the *Didache* and its evidence are too uncertain to be of use here. The *Homily on the Pasch* of Melito (lines 255–60), after it has contrasted the slaughter of the lamb with the sacrifice of Christ, continues : ' Not in one place nor in a small compass is the glory of God established, but unto all the ends of the earth has His grace been outpoured, and here has the almighty God set up His tent ', through Jesus Christ, to whom be glory for ever '. Melito here combines the ideas of Malachy and of Jn 13:32, and he echoes the word of institution ἐκκέχυται. Some might say that he already shows the *disciplina arcani* (rule of silence about sacred mysteries) to be in operation, for recently this rule has been put forward by Jeremias to explain why the institution narrative is omitted from the fourth gospel, but it does not seem safe to presume that such a rule existed before the end of the 2nd cent., when the calumny about the Christians devouring the raw flesh of a child became common. The Apologists deal with this calumny (Justin, *apol.* 26 ; Minucius Felix, *Octavius* 28 ; Tertullian, *apol.* 7:1 ; Eusebius HE 5:1:14). Pliny (*ep. ad Traianum* 96:7) knew of it, for he stresses that Christian food was harmless. The use of the primitive title for Christ of ὁ παῖς σου (Thy child or servant) and the simple realism of early Christian faith could easily be twisted, by one who had lapsed, into a new form of the myth of Thyestes. On the other hand, it is hard to see how such a calumny could have arisen if there had not been this realistic faith.

The priesthood of Christ according to the type of Melchisedec (and therefore concerned with offering of bread and wine, Gen 14:17) was set forth in Heb 7:1–8:5 and was taken up by 1 *Clem* 34:5–36:2 and 40. In this last passage Clement speaks of the correct time, place and ministers for the liturgy in language which seems to refer to the Jewish temple ritual but which, being certainly written after the destruction of the temple, must be taken typologically to indicate how the Church was developing her liturgy. It has been denied by W. van Unnik (*Vigiliae christianae* 5

[1951] 204–48) that Clement knows of the *Sanctus*, but the reasons alleged are not convincing.

Ignatius of Antioch (*Eph.* 13:1 ; *Phil.* 4:1 ; *Smyrn.* 7:1) has a realist faith in the Eucharist as the Body and Blood of Christ and urges frequentation of the Eucharist as bringing victory over the devil. It is Justin (*apol.* 66:4) who sees in the Mithraic mysteries a parody of the Eucharist, and in the Mithraeum beneath Sta Prisca on the Aventine it is the picture of the Mithraic banquet which has been most defaced by the Christians who took over the building. Yet Justin does not play into the hands of the anthropological school ; he points out (*apol.* 66:4) that it is bread and water that are set out in the Mithraic mysteries and (*dial.* 70) that it is by twisting the OT prophecy of Is 33:16 that the devotees of Mithra have come to their cave-mystery. He does not say, as he could have done, that the initiate did not feed mystically upon Mithras but upon the bull he had slain, and perhaps he did not know of this.

With Justin the word ' eucharist ' has become a technical term, but it still has the overtones of 'prayer of thanksgiving' that made up its former meaning. In the account which he writes for the Emperor (*apol.* 66) he describes what took place at the Eucharist and continues : ' We do not take these as common bread and common drink, but, just as Jesus Christ our Saviour was made, and was, flesh and blood for our salvation, through a Word of God, even so we are taught that this food, over which eucharist has been made by means of a word—that comes from Him—of prayer, and from which our flesh and blood are by metabolism nourished, is flesh and blood of that Jesus who was made flesh '. Irenaeus (*adv. haer.* IV:xxxi:4 H) writes in manifest dependence on Justin ; hence his phrase about the Eucharist (ἐκ δύο πραγμάτων συνεστηκυῖα) ' compacted or put together of two elements, one heavenly and one from earth ', is no more than the echo of what Justin said about the word of prayer from God being used over bread and wine. The Lutheran use of the passage for evidence of consubstantiation is unwarranted ; the fragments of Irenaeus forged by Pfaff in the same interest should be mentioned here, though they were shown up long ago, as they still deceive the unwary theologian and are quoted as authentic by H. de Lubac.

By the end of the 2nd cent. the attitude of reverential awe before the Eucharist with which we are familiar is becoming common, and there are signs in Tertullian (*De corona* 3 ; PL 2:79) and Origen (*hom.* 13:3 in Ex ; GCS 29:279) that great care was taken lest fragments should be lost (*see further*, RESERVATION). One valuable indication of popular faith is found in the gold-glasses of early Christian times ; they sometimes depict Christ with an outstretched wand and the figure of Lazarus emerging from his tomb, while in other pictures (sometimes pictures on the same glass) Christ is seen with the wand raised towards seven baskets of loaves or seven water-pots. Clearly it was believed that in some way the power that restored Lazarus to life was being exercised upon the bread and wine of the Eucharist. These gold-glasses cannot be dated exactly, but they cannot be later than the 4th cent. (*see* ART AND THE CHURCH, VI) and lead on to such large-scale designs as the carvings on the doors of Sta Sabina in Rome.

The earliest liturgical prayer is said to be the work of Hippolytus (*see* CANON OF MASS) in his *Traditio apostolica*, but in the absence of the original Greek of that work it is not really safe to draw precise conclusions from one or other of the versions made of that work in later times by men who were not always free from their own prejudices. An important feature of this liturgy is its Jewish pattern, dividing it into three movements : thanksgiving, narrative of fact and petition. This pattern can be found on the prayer of the Levites (2 Esd 9:5–37), which was itself the occasion of a covenant, and again the liturgical document from Qumran (published in RB 68 [1961] 195–250) shows the same sequence : election of Israel and of Jerusalem, infidelity of Israel and punishment, prayer for pardon. The inference would be that the eucharistic prayer from Jewish Christian times was marked by the sequence : preface of thanksgiving, narrative of what Christ did at the Supper, petition for grace based upon the significance of Christ's act (*unde et memores . . .*).

A misunderstanding about early belief has been cleared up recently by K. Woollcombe in his discussion of the term ἀντίτυπος (*La Vie spirituelle*, supplement, February 1951) and cf. also the *Lexicon of Patristic Greek*. He is able to show that it was only after the 4th cent. that ἀντίτυπον meant the unconsecrated bread and wine (e.g. Anastasius of Sinai, PG 89:297) ; before that, it had been quite normal to use the term to describe what we would call ' the sacramental Body of Christ '. It never had the sense of ' mere symbol ' in those days. When it was turned into Latin (as in the *Traditio apostolica* of Hippolytus, TU 75:132) it caused difficulty : ' Let the offering be brought by the deacons to the bishop and let him eucharistize the bread as a sacrament (in Greek ἀντίτυπον) of the Body of Christ and the cup of wine mixed for an antitype (or in Greek, likeness) of the Blood which is shed for all who believe in Him '.[1] The use of *figura* by Tertullian (*adv. Marc.* 4:40 ; CSEL 47:559) need cause no difficulty when it is put alongside a passage such as the one from Hippolytus. Until the term *sacramentum* was well established, there was bound to be this uneasiness of language. Tertullian adds : *Figura autem non fuisset, nisi veritatis esset corpus* (It would not be a sacramental sign, unless it was truly His body).

III The heresies which tried to overthrow faith in the Eucharist arise from a one-sided interpretation of things that Augustine said about the Eucharist as a sacrament or sacred sign. It is sometimes the fashion to oppose Augustine and Ambrose as if they represent realist-symbolist and crude realist trends in their teaching. This is to neglect the fact that Augustine

---

[1] Offeratur oblatio a diaconibus episcopo et gratias agat panem quidem in exemplum—quod dicit Graecus antitypum—corporis Christi ; calicem vino mixtum propter antitypum—quod dicit Graecus similitudinem—sanguinis, quod effusum est pro omnibus qui crediderunt in Eum.

was made a Catholic by Ambrose whom he calls (*ep.* 147:52 ; CSEL 44:331) *plantator et rigator meus* (the one who planted and watered me). There are passages in Augustine which repeat the realism of Ambrose, especially those which give his catechesis. 'The bread which you see on the altar, when it has been sanctified by the word of God, is the body of Christ. What is in the chalice is the blood of Christ. . . . If you take it well, you are what you receive.' Here (*serm.* 227 ; PL 38:1099) Augustine cannot resist the pun : *Si bene accepistis* : 'If you take my meaning', or, 'If you receive worthily'.

The heretics, Ratramnus in the 9th cent. and Berengarius in the 11th, went astray largely through not having a fully developed terminology about the sacraments. They lacked the term *res et sacramentum* and so fell victims to a false dichotomy between the sign or *sacramentum* and its *res* or grace ; a middle term would have saved them. The theory of typology worked out by the Fathers for OT in relation to NT required that the OT type should have reality in and for itself, besides its forward reference to the NT anti-type. This is the warrant for making a middle term (*res et sacramentum*) in the theory of the sacraments, but it took a long time to discover this fact. Darwell Stone in his *Doctrine of the Holy Eucharist* (I:233) wrote that he had 'read the book of Ratramnus many times in the hope of being able to form some clear idea on this subject (Ratramnus's meaning), and can only confess his failure to reach a conclusion which seems to him to satisfy all the elements in his teaching, and to solve the problem whether he regarded the inner spiritual gift which the elements are made to be and convey as simply a mysterious power of effecting a spiritual union with Christ, or as Christ Himself present in those elements and to the communicant in spiritual fashion'. Those who have struggled with the phrases of Ratramnus will echo this verdict, yet his book, when printed in 1530, became the *vade mecum* of Ridley and of other reformers, to whom he was known as Bertram (*see also* CAPHARNAITES).

Another difficulty which beset those who debated on the Eucharist in the Dark Ages was the lack of a sufficiently wide acquaintance with the writings of Augustine. A group of his most forthright and simple catecheses on the Eucharist survives in a single MS. and was published by Dom G. Morin in 1917. It seems unlikely that this *Codex Guelferbytanus* was accessible to many in the time of Ratramnus or of Berengarius. One of these sermons (*serm.* 7 *in Die Paschae*) is as realist as anything that Ambrose wrote : 'What you see is bread and wine. Sanctification comes to it, and that bread will be the body of Christ and that wine will be the blood of Christ. The name of Christ, the grace of Christ effects this, and so you will see what you did see and yet its power then will not be as its power now ; for previously if it was eaten it filled the belly, now when it is eaten it builds up the mind'. Karl Adam, who had produced a monograph on Augustine's eucharistic theology in 1908, found it necessary to re-cast his work after the discovery of these sermons, which he did in a long article of the *Theologische Quartalschrift* (112 [1931] 490–536).

The work of Berengarius *De sacra coena adversus Lanfrancum* was first printed in 1834 by Neander and again in 1941 more accurately by W. Beekenkamp. It did not influence the Reformation controversy to the same extent as ' Bertram ' did, though the reply of Lanfranc (PL 150:407–42) has always been accessible, and in Cardinal Pole's last letter to Cranmer (as yet unpublished, in Lambeth Palace Library) he reproaches him with renewing over the Eucharist the heresy of the deacon of Angers, i.e. Berengarius. The arguments of Berengarius were mainly patristic, turning on the reading of certain passages of Augustine. He did put forward one argument from reason, that if Christ allows the faithful to see as bread what is no longer bread, He is deceiving them, and this Christ could not do. The answer to this is in the verse of the *Adoro Te* : *Visus, tactus, gustus in Te fallitur, sed auditu solo tuto creditur.* In Crashaw's version :

> Down, down, proud sense. Discourses die,
> And all adore faith's mystery.

Much play has been made with the profession of faith that Berengar accepted in the Roman synod of 1078. This is longer than the one he subscribed to (D 355) in the Roman synod of 1079 and contained the words : ' The Body and Blood of Christ, not only in symbol but in truth, are handled by the priest, broken and crushed by the teeth of the faithful '.[1] This might seem to show a very carnal view of the Eucharist, but at the time Lanfranc, in his refutation (PL 150:422), cites Augustine for the words : ' When we eat, we do not divide Him into parts ', and continues : ' Far be it from us to think of eating Christ in that manner. . . . We eat the flesh of Christ in such sort as to leave Him intact and living at the right hand of the Father '. It appears from Berengar's own work (in Beekenkamp's edition, 14) that he had used 2 Cor 5:16 to scout the idea of Christ's being present in the Eucharist in bodily wise. Hence the rather crude wording of the Synod. The liturgical argument of Berengar (op. cit. 161) based on the *Iube haec perferri* is a misunderstanding of that prayer (*see* EPIKLESIS).

The teaching of Trent (D 874) shows that in many of its ideas about the Eucharist the Reformation simply carried on from where Berengar had left off. Thus Trent insists that there is no contradiction in holding that Christ is, according to the natural mode of his existence, at the right hand of God in heaven and yet sacramentally present in the Eucharist, even though this sacramental mode of existence ' can scarce be put into words by us '. Minds enlightened by faith can envisage it, and anyhow, that is what the Fathers taught from the beginning. After dealing with the institution of the sacrament (D 875) Trent points out the failure of Cranmer's parallel between baptism and the Eucharist, saying (D 876) that, whereas all the other sacraments give grace by being used, in this sacrament grace—and the Author of

---

[1] Corpus et sanguinem Iesu Christi . . . non solum sacramento sed in veritate manibus sacerdotum tractari, frangi, et fidelium dentibus atteri. . . .

grace—are present before it is used by being administered to the faithful. Christ did not say : ' This will be My Body when you eat it ', but, ' This is My Body '. It is to be noted that three of the *anathemas* (D 883, 885 and 886) relate to this one section of the Council's positive teaching. For further discussion of Trent, *see* TRANSUBSTANTIATION.

IV The effect of the Eucharist is described in countless post-communion prayers of the liturgy. At first these speak of purgation, as they are composed in a theological climate that looks on the sacraments as so many remedies for the wounds of the soul (*see* CAUSALITY OF THE SACRAMENTS). Thus the *Leonine Sacramentary* (198) gives a prayer that is reproduced by many other liturgical books : ' By these heavenly mysteries may our vices be purged away and ourselves made more fit for receiving Thy gifts '.[1] At the same time, though less prominently, there is a suggestion here and there of that unity which St Thomas (*Summa*, 3a:79:1c, and also in the Mass for the feast of Corpus Christi) said was one of the principal effects of the sacrament. The *Leonine Sacramentary* expressed this (1116) with majestic simplicity : ' Grant, almighty God, that we may be counted as members of Him whose Body and Blood we have received in communion '.[2] It is this grace of union that makes the Eucharist truly the crown of all the sacraments, for, as M. de la Taille showed (*Mysterium Fidei, elucidatio* XLVII), following out an idea of Toletus, all the other sacraments involve a desire of the Eucharist ; they give some grace of unity, but this sacrament beyond the rest.

The importance of this *votum eucharistiae* in baptism is manifest, for the status of the baptized Christian who is yet outside the communion of the Catholic Church has to be pondered by the theology of ecumenism, and this factor must bulk largely in any such ponderation. Either the individual has consciously accepted that desire (which baptism of its very nature involves), or he has not. If not, there may or may not be culpable ignorance on his part. Thus it becomes somewhat easier to estimate the degrees of proximity to full union with the Church that may be proper to this or that category of non-Catholic Christians.

The pledge of heavenly immortality given by the Eucharist was singled out from the beginning as one of its principal effects. Ignatius (*Eph.* 20:2) calls it ' the medicine of immortality, an antidote stopping death and bringing life in Christ for ever '. The theme is developed by Irenaeus (*adv. haer.* IV:xxxi:4 H), and led, in the *Traditio apostolica* of Hippolytus, to the conceit that reception of this sacrament before breaking one's fast would be a safeguard against poisoning (TU 75:143). The words used at the distribution were then (ibid. 134) *Panis caelestis in Christo Iesu*.

St Thomas names peace as the second effect of the Eucharist, and this idea is borne out by the use of

Is 65:13–25 as a foreshadowing of the Eucharist. This passage was read on the Wednesday in Holy Week according to the *Syriac Lectionary* (dated *c*.475). Irenaeus (*adv. haer.* V:xxxiii:4 H) cites the concluding part of this passage to complete his picture of the millenium, which he holds out as a fulfilment of Christ's promise about drinking the new wine (Mt 26:29). The peace-giving reconciliation with God which every Jew was reminded of by his Passover was brought nearer to the Christian by his communion. In the liturgy of Serapion the priest had to ask for this expressly as he paused between the two consecrations, while in the ordination prayer for priests, Serapion prayed that the priest ' may be able . . . to reconcile Thy people to Thee, the uncreated God '.

Above all, the Eucharist was the sacrament of peace for the hour of death. The Council of Nicaea (can. 13) legislated that ' this last and most necessary provision for his journey ' (ἐφόδιον) should not be refused to the dying. It was claimed in the canon that this practice was ' the ancient canon law ', but it must be admitted that some local councils (such as that of Elvira in Spain *c*.307) had laid it down that certain grave sins, such as idolatry and adultery, should be punished by refusal of *viaticum*. The rigorism of the Novatians was not without its share in this attitude of the orthodox. Innocent I (D 95) has the word *viaticum* and it is used in the Latin versions of Nicaea. As the practice of public penance spread, it became the rule that a penitent, even though his period of penance was not complete, might be given his *viaticum* when in danger of death : thus the Council of Agde in 506 (can. 15). Keltic missionaries who carried the Eucharist with them on journeys (*see* RESERVATION) were presumably anxious to satisfy the need of the faithful for *viaticum*.

The necessity of the Eucharist for Christians is quite obvious, once these effects are clearly understood. ' Moses taught us of the lamb of the Pasch, which was slain ; he commanded us to smear the blood on the lintel of the door and the door-posts. And the smearing declared, therefore, the faith which now we have, which dwells in us, which He gave us in the pure and perfect Lamb. And for this cause, if we have our foreheads thus sealed with the hand, we shall be safe from those who wish to kill us.' Thus the *Traditio apostolica* of Hippolytus (in Horner's version of the Ethiopic, 185 ; and TU 75:144 and 149 for the Latin) is an early witness to this Christian practice of taking to themselves the protection of the Eucharist. Evidence of the practice can be found also in Cyril (*Catechesis* 23 ; PG 33:1124) and in the anonymous Paschal homilies (Nautin, I:159 ; II:79) of the 4th cent. One of these homilies (Nautin, II:91) develops the spirituality of the Eucharist as ἀνάκρασις or a mingling of bodies : ' Indictable for impiety against the Lord are those who do not prepare their bodies in readiness for mingling with His, which He gave us in order that, mingling with Him, we might be mingled with the Holy Spirit '. Cyril of Alexandria (on Jn 11 ; PG 74:528) has the same idea. Gregory of Nyssa (*Orat. catechetica* 37 ; PG 45:93) says that this ἀνάκρασις saves the body

---

[1] Sacris caelestibus, Domine, vitia nostra purgentur, ut muneribus Tuis possimus semper aptari.

[2] Quaesumus, omnipotens Deus, ut inter Eius membra numeremur cuius corpori communicamus et sanguini.

of man, just as faith and baptism save his soul. Chrysostom (*hom.* 15:4 on I Tim ; PG 62:586) uses it too, and the term 'interpenetration' (ἀνάκρασις) can be traced back to Denis of Alexandria (Feltoe, 240) in its Christological, if not yet in its eucharistic, usage.

The Council of Antioch in 341 (can. 2) ordered that those who come to church to hear the word of God but through some ἀταξία (or wantonness) of their own do not partake of communion, should be shut out until they repent. This would seem to envisage that all present after the expulsion of catechumens and penitents, communicated. While this Council had great influence on the formation of canon law, it was not mandatory. The *Penitential* of Theodore of Tarsus (12:1 ; Haddan and Stubbs III:186) declares that Greeks communicate every Sunday and are excommunicated if they omit three successive Sundays, while Romans are not so precise and have no excommunication for omissions. Gradually restrictions on the frequency of communion crept in ; classes of men (e.g. traders) were considered to be excluded almost by the terms of their occupation, while for the married, abstinence from sexual intercourse for some days was held to be a prerequisite. There can be no doubt that this latter ruling was due to an influx of Jewish ideas (1 Kg 21:5) into Christian thinking. Faustus of Riez (*serm.* 1 ; CSEL 21:226) asks that this abstinence should last for 'many days', but the *Penitential* of Egbert (Haddan and Stubbs III:423) requires no more than three.

The decline in frequency of communion belongs more to the history and sociology of the Church than to theology. Edmund Bishop tried to make out (T & S 8:i:92–7) that a feeling of awe in the presence of the Eucharist, which was inculcated by Chrysostom and others in the latter part of the 4th cent., was a departure from former traditions. Yet the compunction that Chrysostom requires (κατάνυξις) is by his own definition to be gained by the calling to mind of the benefits of God (*De compunctione* 2:7 ; PG 47:422), and for the conjunction in this attitude of both love and fear he gives warrant from St Paul and the Psalms.

The renewal of the practice of frequent communion, urged by Trent (D 944), was attacked by the Jansenists, who alleged various theological grounds for their attitude. In 1679 a decree of the Conciliar Congregation (D 1147) in effect left the practice to the judgment of parish priests and confessors, but in 1690 Alexander VIII ruled out one of the main Jansenist theological arguments (D 1313). In 1905 St Pius X (D 1981–90) stamped out the last embers of Jansenism.

The Encyclical of Pius XII *Mediator Dei* (AAS 39 [1947] 532) admits that it was the greater frequency of communion from the close of the 19th cent. which helped to produce the liturgical movement (*sacramenta latius crebriusque participata*). After discussing the sacrificial aspect of the Eucharist (for which *see* MASS), the Encyclical renewed the plea of Trent (ibid. 564) for frequent communion. It also defended

(ibid. 569) the cult of the Eucharist (*see* BENEDICTION). Some words that follow about the mysteries of Christ in the liturgical year were held to have condemned the *Mysterientheologie* of Casel (ibid. 580), but later it was suggested that only the excesses of that theory were in view. Christ, said the Pope, planned that men's minds should make contact with His mysteries and in a manner live by them. Now these mysteries are ever-present and operative, not in the dark and muddled way in which certain modern writers have prated, but in the manner that Catholic doctrine tells us. . . . They are examples of Christian perfection and sources of divine grace. . . .'[1] The declaration of the Holy Office (25 November 1948, published in *Ephemerides liturgicae* [1949]) did little to clarify the matter, as it simply told people to look at the plain words of the Encyclical.

The liturgical constitution of the Second Vatican Council (AAS 56 [1964] 113) goes back to Cyril of Alexandria (on Jn 11 ; PG 74:557) to express the final effect of the Eucharist, 'that they may be day by day through Christ their mediator brought to perfect union with God and among themselves, that God may be all in all'.

Bibliography. P. Neuenzeit, *Das Herrenmahl* (1960) ; J. Betz, *Die Eucharistie in der Zeit der griechischen Väter* I (1955) ; J. Bonsirven, 'Hoc est corpus meum', in Bi 29 (1948) 205–19 ; A. Jaubert, *La Date de la Cène* (1957) ; *J. Jeremias, *The Eucharistic Words of Jesus* (1955, new German edition 1960) ; *J. A. Emerton, 'The Aramaic of Mk 14:24', in JTS 6 (1955) 238–40 ; the same, 'Evidence of the Syriac Versions', in JTS 13 (1962) 111–17 ; I. van Woerden, 'The Iconography of the Sacrifice of Abraham', in *Vigiliae christianae* 15 (1961) 214–55 ; P. Benoît, *Exégèse et Théologie* I (1961) ; M. Baillet, 'Un Recueil liturgique de Qumran', in RB 68 (1961) 195–250 ; R. Le Déaut, 'De nocte Paschatis', in *Verbum Domini* 41 (1963) 189–95 ; *P. Heawood, 'The Time of the Last Supper', in *The Jewish Quarterly Review* 42 (1951) 37–44 ; *C. C. Torrey, 'The Fourth Gospel and the Pasch' (ibid. 237–50) ; *J. I. Packer (editor), *Eucharistic Sacrifice* (1962) ; *D. Stone, *History of the Doctrine of the Holy Eucharist* (2 vols., 1909) ; M. de la Taille SJ, *Mysterium fidei* (1931–2) ; H. Schürmann, *Der Paschamahlbericht Lk 22:7–38* (3 vols. 1953–7) ; *F. C. Burkitt, 'The Early Syriac Lectionary System', in *Proceedings of the British Academy* X (1921) 301–8 ; J. Coppens, in DBS (1934) s.v. Eucharistie.   J. H. C.

EUGENICS. *See* PROCREATION

EUTYCHES If ever a heresy began by accident, it was that of the Monophysites who were condemned at Chalcedon (q.v.) in 451. Eutyches was the archimandrite of a monastery at Constantinople, where he had ruled for some thirty years when he went astray. He was then a man of over seventy, and he blundered into heresy, as Pope Leo said,

---

[1] Quae profecto mysteria non incerto ac subobscuro eo modo quo recentiores quidam scriptores effutiunt, sed quo modo catholica doctrina nos docet, praesentia continenter adsunt atque operantur.

rather through want of learning than by subtlety of thought. He hated the Nestorians so much that he leaned over too far in the opposite direction. Here the growth of his heresy (I) will be treated briefly and (II) its treatment by the Church outlined. **I The growth of the heresy of Eutyches** was due to his fondness for the views of Cyril of Alexandria. There was a difference (for which *see* EPHESUS, COUNCIL OF) between what Cyril secured at the Council in 431 and his own more extreme views, which were codified in the famous *Anathemata*. Eutyches neglected to observe this difference, to his own destruction. The situation might be compared to what could have happened had W. G. Ward been able after the Vatican Council of 1870 to impose his own extreme views of papal authority on all the English seminaries and then, with the help of Mr Gladstone, succeed in calling a council of French and Spanish bishops to have his opponents condemned for heresy. Cyril had used a formula which with slight variations declared belief in ' one nature of the Word of God enfleshed' ($\mu\acute{\iota}\alpha$ $\Phi\acute{\upsilon}\sigma\iota\varsigma$ $\tau o\hat{\upsilon}$ $\theta\epsilon o\hat{\upsilon}$ $\lambda\acute{o}\gamma o\upsilon$ $\sigma\epsilon\sigma\alpha\rho\kappa\omega\mu\acute{E}\nu\eta$). Cyril thought the formula was traditional and that it came from Athanasius. In reality it was from the heretic Apollinaris, who had foisted it upon Athanasius (PG 28:28). Cyril sometimes used the word $\acute{\upsilon}\pi\acute{o}\sigma\tau\alpha\iota\varsigma$ for $\Phi\acute{\upsilon}\sigma\iota\varsigma$, and this fact may give a clue to what he made of the formula, but it was what others made of it that mattered in the long run.

Eutyches had a friend at court, Chrysaphius the eunuch and *spatharius*, whose godfather he had been. Whether knowingly or not, he became involved in the plans of the eunuch for the removal from the court of Pulcheria, sister of the Emperor Theodosius II and pillar of orthodoxy. She was the heir presumptive to the imperial crown and the plan was to have her ordained deaconess to prevent a possible marriage with some unwelcome courtier. (In the event, when Theodosius died, she married Marcian, who did in fact become emperor.) The other obstacle in the way of the eunuch to supreme power was the Patriarch of Constantinople, Flavian. Chrysaphius invoked against him the help of Dioscorus, Patriarch of Alexandria. The Emperor himself cared only for hunting and for his hobby of copying ancient manuscripts. This is the context into which must be inserted the heresy of Eutyches. He had been presented by Cyril with a copy of the *Acta* of Ephesus ; he had been active against Nestorius and his followers, and when (after the death of Cyril in 444, and of John of Antioch in 442) there had been renewed polemic against Theodoret of Cyrrhus (who was looked upon in Egypt as still three parts Nestorian), Eutyches joined in and even wrote to Pope Leo, from whom he had an encouraging reply sent on 1 June 448 (*ep.* 24 ; PL 54:736).

II The Treatment of the Heresy. It was Eusebius of Dorylaeum who began the downfall of Eutyches. In the synod of Constantinople (8 November 448) he presented a *libellus* accusing Eutyches of heresy. Eusebius had as a layman put up placards against Nestorius in 428 and seems to have been of the same energetic character now that he had become a bishop. After three canonical citations, Eutyches put in an appearance to answer the charge on 22 November. The crucial question put to him by Flavian was : ' Do you accept two natures after the assumption of manhood, and do you say that Christ is consubstantial with us according to the flesh, or not ?' (ACO II:ii:16). Eutyches replied that he had not come to discuss theology but to present his faith, and he offered a paper which he had prepared ; but, when asked to read it, he said : ' I cannot. That is impossible.' When the question was again put, he answered : ' I have never until today admitted that the body of Our Lord and God is consubstantial with us, though I do admit that the holy Virgin is consubstantial with us.' At this a bishop (Basil of Seleucia) broke in : ' If His mother is consubstantial, He is Himself too, for He is called son of man.' Asked again if he agreed that Christ was ' of two natures after taking manhood' ($\dot{\epsilon}\kappa$ $\delta\acute{\upsilon}o$ $\Phi\acute{\upsilon}\sigma\epsilon\omega\nu$ $\mu\epsilon\tau\grave{\alpha}$ $\tau\grave{\eta}\nu$ $\dot{\epsilon}\nu\alpha$ $\theta\rho\acute{\omega}\pi\eta\sigma\iota\nu$) he said : ' I accept that Our Lord was of two natures before the union ; but after the union I confess one nature.' This sentence became the slogan of the Monophysites for centuries in all lands, even though it seems to have been spoken in the heat of the moment. ' I never saw this clearly in the Scriptures nor in the Fathers, and if I pronounce your anathema,' he added, ' woe is me.' When pressed further, he said : ' Go and read Athanasius, and you will find that he does not say anything of the sort.' The synod deposed him from the priesthood and his monastic charge and excommunicated him, while he was uttering an appeal to Rome, Alexandria, Jerusalem and Thessalonica.

The position of Eutyches was, as he had said at his first summons, that he accepted the faith of Nicaea and of Ephesus, but that if perchance there was anything erroneous or misleading in the wording of these councils, he did not attach blame to them. Neither did he accept such error, preferring rather to search the Scriptures, for they were more reliable than the decrees of the Fathers. And in the Scriptures he found nothing about two natures. In his letter to Pope Leo he says that he is aware that ' our forebears, Julius and Felix, Athanasius and Gregory, the holy bishops, all reprobated the talk about two natures'. The listing of Julius, Felix, Gregory Thaumaturgus and Athanasius shows that Eutyches was relying on the catena of passages which Cyril had used at Ephesus, in which were certain *spuria* from these four Fathers, all of them in fact being forgeries from the workshop of Apollinaris (*see* EPHESUS, COUNCIL OF). The naming of Gregory might also recall a passage of the sermon of Gregory of Nyssa against Apollinaris (PG 45:1221) where he uses 2 Cor 5:4 to argue that in Christ the mortal part is swallowed up in the divinity ; but Gregory is here turning a poet's eye on the doctrine of the *communicatio idiomatum* (q.v.).

Chrysaphius must have rejoiced at the means given him of ruining the patriarch Flavian. The *Acta* of his synod were re-examined with the help of an imperial commissioner (13 April 449) in order to establish the fact that Eutyches had appealed to Rome. (The evidence of some of the bishops was that at the end of the hearing, amid a hubbub, Eutyches had said that if the Patriarch of Rome and of Alexandria told him to say the objectionable words, he would do so. But other bishops declared that they heard nothing of all this.) Flavian was now in a difficult position. Worse was to come. On 8 August 449, before Pope Leo could properly deal with the case, the Emperor had called together a synod at Ephesus which was to be known to posterity by the name Leo gave it of *latrocinium* or brigandage. Leo on 20 June wrote to Flavian that the Emperor for the peace of the Church was calling a synod, 'although it is quite clear that the matter in hand in no way calls for a synod to deal with it'.[1] Leo, however, sent legates, arming them with his famous *tomus ad Flavianum* in which he set forth the true doctrine of the two natures.

With his legates for Ephesus Leo sent a batch of letters, one to Pulcheria, one to the archimandrite of the monastery where she had taken refuge, one to Julian, Bishop of Cos, and one to Faustus and Martin, heads of other monasteries in Constantinople. Some of these Latin letters exist in a double recension, and a Greek version of one of the recensions is also extant. What Leo seems to have done was to entrust two separate carriers with his letters (which were not in exactly the same wording) or else to send out copies to other recipients, and the Greek version would be made from the copy which succeeded in reaching the addressee, or which he thought most useful for circulating among his friends. To Julian, Leo writes (*ep.* 35; PL 54:807) that Eutyches with his talk of Christ being in two natures before the union must be thinking that the human soul of Christ was pre-existing in heaven before the Nativity, but that this was simply to revive a view that had been condemned in Origen.[2] He urged Flavian to have patience with the heretic and to try to reclaim him. Leo seems to have felt that he was dealing with an obstinate old man [3] (*ep.* 38; PL 54:813) and that while the doctrine of the Church was clear, it might not be amiss to let the Emperor's meeting of bishops deal gently with Eutyches.

The reality proved to be quite different. Dioscorus presided at the 'brigandage'; Leo's *tomus* was not read to the 150 bishops, but instead, the *Acta* of Flavian's synod were read, to the accompaniment of groans and anathemas. It was said of Eusebius of Dorylaeum : 'Let him be cut in two ; let him be divided, even as he divided the natures.' Some of the proceedings of the council of 431 were read (including the *anathemata* of Cyril) ; Eutyches was declared to be restored and Flavian deposed ; Flavian appealed to the Pope, and the papal legate said but one word to sum up his reaction to the whole affair. It was the Latin word *contra-dicitur*, meaning in effect that he regarded it as quite invalid. Two days later Flavian died from his injuries, after he had been beaten by the soldiers and monks who overran the council and forced the bishops to sign a blank paper on which a space had been left for the addition (later on) of the sentence of the council. A group of fifteen bishops held out in the sacristy until evening, when they were coerced like the rest.

On 22 August there was another meeting (reported only in the Syriac *Acta*), at which Theodoret, Ibas, Irenaeus of Tyre and other bishops were deposed *in absentia* on a variety of charges. Irenaeus had had two wives (against 1 Tim 3:2), Sophronius had practised divination, and Ibas (of Edessa) had corrupted the writings of Cyril and had kept the books of Nestorius (which should have been destroyed). He had also said to his clergy : 'I do not grudge that Christ has become God, for just as He did, so have I become, since He is of my own nature.' This may have been a way of impressing on them the truth that Christ is con-substantial with us and that grace makes us partakers of the divine nature, but it was certainly provoca-tive. Even so was the remark of Ibas, in a sermon, that the Jews need not boast about their having crucified Christ, for they crucified but a man ; or the other remark (in a sermon on the Resurrection) : 'If God should have died, who would restore Him to life ?' (Syriac *Acta*, 45).

The papal legates did not attend this meeting. They had already departed to report to Leo the violence that had disfigured the first session, though their notary, Dulcitius, had been left behind on a sick-bed in Ephesus. Domnus of Antioch had also taken to his bed, and when visited by delegates declared his readiness to comply with all that should be decided in the session, but that did not save him from deposition. He was held (cf. the Syriac *Acta* edited by Flemming, 145) to have sinned by offering the advice that Cyril's *anathemata* should not be insisted on as a test of orthodoxy, as they would never be accepted in the East and as they had not been included in the statements of union agreed between Cyril and John of Antioch in 433 (*see* EPHESUS, COUNCIL OF).

Dioscorus, as a result of these depositions, now had in his hands (though subject to what Chrysaphius might think) the filling of the sees of Constantinople and Antioch, and his abetter, Juvenal of Jerusalem, was rewarded with the title of patriarch and with the subjection to himself of all the bishops in the three provinces of Phoenicia I and II and of Arabia. In the winter of 449 it might have seemed that the

---

[1] Imperator pro ecclesiae pace sollicitus synodum voluit congregari, quamvis evidenter appareat rem de qua agitur nequaquam synodali indigere tractatu.

[2] Arbitror enim talia loquentem hoc habere persuasum quod anima quam salvator assumpsit prius in caelis sit commorata quam de Maria virgine nasceretur . . ., sed hoc catholicae mentes auresque non tolerant.

[3] In senectute carnis suae mente sunt parvuli.

papacy was in a position of some peril. An accident in the hunting-field led to the death of the Emperor Theodosius (28 July 450), whereupon the title went to Pulcheria ; the eunuch Chrysaphius disappeared overnight and the new sovereign married Marcian, who was proclaimed emperor (25 August). Pope Leo, who had written in vain to Theodosius (*ep.* 43 ; PL 54:821) that a general council ' at which all the bishops of the whole world should assemble' must be allowed to meet, was now able to set in motion the arrangements for this council ; it met at Chalcedon in 451 (*see* CHALCEDON, COUNCIL OF). Eutyches was almost forgotten meanwhile. It was Dioscorus who was called to account at Chalcedon. Eutyches was of course condemned again, and after this verdict the new Emperor sent him into exile ; he passed through Palestine and may have died there on his way to the place appointed, but no one knows for certain. Thus the wheel had come full circle ; Eusebius of Dorylaeum, on beginning his attack on Eutyches said that he had been threatened to make him desist : ' He (Eutyches) keeps depicting for me the oasis to which I shall be sent as an exile' ; now it was the turn of Eutyches.

Some of the theological consequences of Eutyches need to be underlined. He had relied on Scripture alone against Tradition (see above). He had perpetuated the confusion between Cyril's *anathemata* (which were not made official teaching) and Cyril's letter to Nestorius (which had been canonized at Ephesus), and this confusion has been cleared up only in the present century. Leo, in his moment of danger, had appointed Pulcheria papal legate (*ep.* 45:3 ; PL 54:835) to deal with the Emperor about a general council, and at Chalcedon she was hailed as a second Helena. Her consort, Marcian, was the first emperor to be crowned by the Patriarch, in a ceremony of immense future import (*see* CORONATION). The later Monophysites (q.v.) did not espouse all the views of Eutyches. Severus of Antioch (in his *Letters*, PO 12:176) admitted two οὐσίαι after the union but held that these were not Φύσεις. It may be seen from Vigilius of Thapsus (*Contra Eutycheten* ; PL 62:103) that others allowed the two natures to remain in Christ until the Resurrection, or even until the Ascension. Theodoret of Cyrrhus (perhaps the ablest theologian of the time) in his appeal to Leo, after the ' brigandage' had deposed him, is quite eloquent in his tribute to the Roman primacy. In the course of his letter (*ep.* 52, among the letters of Leo) he says that his diocese (of which he had been bishop for twenty-six years and which contained 800 parishes) does not hold a single heretic and that he has himself received back 1,000 Marcionites in the course of his episcopate. That this heresy should have survived for three centuries is but one of the surprises of the East. **Bibliography.** The older sources, Leo's letters in the Ballerini edition and the *Acta* of Chalcedon in Mansi, vol. VI, have been in part superseded by the publication of *Acta conciliorum oecumenicorum*, series II, vols. 1–6 (1932–8) by E. Schwartz, but the

tendencies of this edition need to be checked with the help of the review of each volume, as it appeared, by P. Peeters in AB 1932–9. *E. Schwartz, ' Der Prozess des Eutyches', in *Sitzungsberichte der Bayerischen Akademie* (phil.-hist. Klasse) 1929, Heft 5, collected and discussed the evidence for the trial of Eutyches at Constantinople. Some chapters in the collective work, *Das Konzil von Chalkedon* (edited by A. Grillmeier and H. Bacht, SJ, 1951) deal with Eutyches. The Syriac *Acts* of the Latrocinium were published in an English version by S. G. Perry, *The Second Synod of Ephesus* (1881), and more elaborately by J. Flemming in a German version in the *Abhandlungen der Göttingen Akademie* (phil.-hist. Klasse, 1917). P. Galtier, SJ, ' Saint-Cyrille et Apollinaire', in *Gregorianum* 37 (1956) 584–609 examines the forgeries which misled Cyril. The part of Juvenal of Jerusalem in these events can be studied in *E. Honigmann, ' Juvenal of Jerusalem', in *Dumbarton Oaks Papers* V (1950) 209–79, and the general background in *T. Jalland, *The Life and Times of Leo the Great* (1941).   J. H. C.

EVE In Gen 3:20, the first woman is given the name Hawwah, from which comes the English Eve. The text connects it with the verb ' to be', *hayah*. It is not a proper name, but descriptive of her role as the one from whom all men derive their existence.

In Gen 1:27, it is said that God made ' man ', and made him male and female. No reference should be seen here to an original androgynous creation (and still less, of course, to the fact that such unity of sex might be the basis of man's likeness to God). The word ' adam ' is not used here as a proper name but in the generic sense of ' man ' ; the substance of the author's thought bears on the fact of the creation of mankind, and its creation in two sexes.

The account of the creation of woman is given directly in 2:18–24. The introduction prepares us for the author's main point : she is higher than the animals and is suited, as they are not, to be a companion for man. In the prevailing contempt for womankind, this was a doctrine which needed to be made clear. It is made even more explicitly in verses 21–4 : woman is of the same nature as man, and the relationship between them is so close as to find its natural fulfilment in matrimony.

Clearly, Eve's creation from Adam's rib is in the nature of a metaphor. The precise nature of the metaphor is not certain. But in seeking an answer, we should bear in mind first the fact mentioned above—that this account is different from the previous one of 1:27. There, the author was concerned primarily with the creation of the human race (as distinct from the animals, etc., also mentioned in that account) ; here he is concerned with the creation of woman specifically, woman as distinct from man. Presumably, therefore, his account of her creation is meant to answer the question, Why two sexes ? why woman in addition to man ? Secondly, we should remember that these chapters of Genesis are not due to verbal dictation by God, but are the inspired result of reflection on the existing state of humanity. This means that the author frequently presents an argument from effect as if it were an argument from causality ; he describes causes in terms of observed effects. We see this in the account of Adam's creation in this same passage : Adam is said to be created from dust, because it was observed that this was the 'raw material' to which he returned at death.

Applying this to the account of Eve's creation, we can see that the author will be less interested in describing the biological process of her origin than in stating the position of woman in relation to man. Now, as the author himself makes clear, the most striking thing about the relationship between man and woman is that they are intended to be 'two in one flesh' : the woman is intended to be 'bone of man's bone, flesh of his flesh'. And this truth is graphically represented by describing her origin as being from Adam's very flesh and bone.

At the same time, this indicates a certain secondary role in comparison to man. She is not taken directly from the earth, as he was, but from him. No doubt this is the sense of the reply of the Biblical Commission of 30 June 1909. In this reply, the Commission does not insist on the 'rib', but it holds that the woman was formed *ex primo homine*. This would seem to be supported by 1 Cor 11:9 (to which the Commission may be referring), in which St Paul argues from woman's origin *ex homine* to show that she has a secondary position in the Church.

The description of the creation of Eve, then, is intended to show the relationship between man and woman, particularly as that relationship is fulfilled in marriage : that woman is equal to man in nature, but subordinate to him in the family (*see also* EVOLUTION).

Bibliography. H. J. T. Johnson, 'The Bible, the Church and the Formation of Eve', in DR 69 (1951) 16–30 ; E. F. Sutcliffe sj, article on Genesis in CCS ; B. Vawter, *A Path through Genesis* (1957) ; for the relation of the creation of Eve to the origin of the Mystical Body of Christ, *see* S. Tromp sj, *Corpus Christi quod est Ecclesia* (English translation 1960).

L. J.

EVIL The problem of evil involves the ultimate intelligibility of the cosmic order. One general solution, *dualism*, denies in effect that intelligibility, by setting up good and evil as positive, opposing forces locked in an inveterate and perpetually indecisive struggle. Another, *monism*, makes evil, still conceived at least vaguely as something positive, an intrinsic part of the universe, a necessary part of the pattern of things in which, according to an optimist or pessimist viewpoint, good or evil ultimately triumphs.

In the fully theistic solution, found in historical Christianity alone, evil is neither a positive force or reality opposed to good nor an intrinsic part of any necessary cosmic plan, but it has the reality of a privation, and so it has a place in the designs of God, who permits it no less wisely than freely in His ordering of the universe to His own Good, which is necessarily the good of the universe itself.

Thus we shall examine briefly (I) the dualist and (II) the monist misconception, with a view to the fuller understanding (III) of the Christian solution and (IV) its synthetic presentation, clearly suggested by St Augustine, and fully elaborated in the writings of St Thomas Aquinas.

I Dualist Misconception. Exception made for the Jews, the statement of Plutarch (*De Iside et Osiride*, 45) that practically all ancient peoples and their philosophers admitted the existence of a good and an evil principle governing the world seems accurate enough. In the 6th cent. B.C. appears the Persian dualism of *Zoroaster*, for whom the world is a mixture of good and evil, thought and matter, truth and falsity, light and darkness, reflecting the inveterate opposition of twin spirits, one good and the other evil. Already we have the assumption that matter is to be equated with darkness and evil and hence that the body is not only inferior to spirit but irrevocably opposed to it as evil is opposed to good. This we see in *gnosticism* (*see* GNOSTICS), whose fundamental preoccupation is that of man with himself as a spirit imprisoned in a body or as light imprisoned in darkness : hence for it the material world is the work of a principle inferior to God and evil in itself. Gnostic dualism is very apparent in *Manichaeanism* (*see* MANICHEES), whose founder Manes died in the 3rd cent. For him the world is explained by the imprisonment of a part of light in darkness, light being good and darkness evil. Anterior to the world they were separate substances, and will eventually return to their primitive separateness.

The Greeks did not avoid a certain dualism. Matter for them is something eternal, uncreated and chaotic ; and it is the task of reason (*logos*) to impose on it form, harmony and order. Thus Heraclitus seems to see good and evil as opposing tensions or part of that conflict which is the father of all things, but into which reason seeks to introduce unity. Plato sees in matter the source of evil which is identified with disorder : thus the evil in the world is accounted for by the resistance offered by matter to information by reason or the idea. In an obscure passage in the *Republic* (379 c) Plato says that since there are more evil things in the world than good things, and since God can cause only good, there must be some other cause of what is evil ; this other cause irreducible to good is apparently matter. For Aristotle (*Ethica Nicomachea* 1106 b 29 ; 1177 b 30), God as the end of everything imparts movement, finality and order, but matter is the source of evil wherever it escapes the influence of this finality or is not penetrated by form or reason. Matter being eternal and uncreated, it follows that we have a certain dualism. Not only physical but also moral evil is thus accounted for, because reason is the form of human operations and passions. Thus we have the celebrated doctrine that virtue consists in a certain equality with the measure of reason, while vice consists in a want of harmony with this rule either by excess or by defect. Aristotle here glimpsed that evil consists in privation, but, not rising to the concept of the creation of the world *ex nihilo* he was not able to exploit the implications of this in harmonizing the existence of evil with the Goodness of the First Mover.

The Platonic idea of matter as the source of evil reappears in a somewhat different form with the Neo-Platonists. For Plotinus in his *Enneades*, evil is at the bottom of the scale of beings emanating from the One. It is being deprived as it were of particular determination and hence deprived of good, but it is still a positive reality and individual things are evil in so far as they have mixed with them this lowest possible degree of being.

Dualism persists in much modern thought and is reflected in much of modern literature and art, where the reality of evil is vividly realized and where at the same time there is no clear recognition of any intelligible order or purpose in the world. Thus good and evil appear in their ancient guises of positive forces locked in a perpetual and insoluble conflict.

II Monist Misconception. Most forms of ancient dualism are struggling towards a monism. This is evident above all in the Greeks with their passion for reducing everything to order. They strove, as is exemplified by Plato, to reduce matter itself to order, and, not succeeding, reluctantly conceded that it was the irreducible principle of evil. Even the dualism of Zoroaster derived from the monism of Mazdeanism for whom Ahura Mazda is the only supreme being. In ancient China Confucianism dating from the 6th cent. B.C. is fundamentally monist, for in spite of the opposition between Yin, the female principle, and Yang, the male principle, which is reflected in the opposition between heavenly substances which are good and earthly ones which are evil, Tao, the One, from which both Yin and Yang are derived, is neither substance nor person, but the expression of total order regulating alternating fortunes of good and evil (cf. A. Sertillanges, *Le Problème du mal* I: 61-9). Hence evil enters into the intrinsic constitution of the world pattern.

Evil has not only an essential but a dominating place in the pessimism of Schopenhauer for whom *the will to live*, running through everything but consciously perceived in man is the source of all misery ; while for Nietzsche the distinction between good and evil disappears inasmuch as oppression, cruelty, deception, not less than heroic self-sacrifice, must be cultivated in the evolution of the superman according to the drive of the *will for power*.

Certain forms of Christian theism are monistic, as that of Luther, Calvin and Melanchthon, the latter of whom says in his *Commentary on the Epistle to the Romans* that God is not less the author of the adultery of David and the treason of Judas than of the conversion of St Paul. The *optimism* of Leibnitz is not free from a similar blemish according to his famous concept of *metaphysical evil*. For him, God has made the best possible world, but there is a certain necessary (metaphysical) evil in creatures inasmuch as every creature is a limited being. Thus physical and moral evil necessarily result as intrinsic parts of the universe (cf. his *Theodicy*, Eng. trans. [1951] 136).

III Christian Solution. Not a philosophy but a religion, Christianity offers the solution to the problem of evil in the Old Testament doctrine of the creation by God of all things together with the doctrine of the Incarnation of the Divine Word, Whose assumption of a bodily nature disposes of the dualism opposing body to spirit as evil to good.

However, the reality of evil looms large in the Providence of God, not that He wills it for itself, but that He permits it freely, in order to take occasion to work good, this good being ultimately the final consummation of the Mystery of Christ in whom God will manifest His Justice and Mercy. Thus in Christ, in and for whom all things were created in heaven and on earth (Col 1:16), the Kingdom of God will triumph, when everything will be made subject to Him (1 Cor 15:24) that 'God may be all in all' (1 Cor 15:28). Death, the result of sin, will be overcome, for 'as in Adam all die, in Christ shall all be made alive' (1 Cor 15:22) ; and the power of sin itself will thus be brought to nought (1 Thess 2:8), those who will have done evil things being banished from the Kingdom for ever (Jn 5:29 ; Mt 25:32).

In this way the perplexity of the devout Jew at the prosperity of the wicked (Ps 91:8) and his confidence that the Justice of God will somehow be vindicated (Ps 7:15-16) receive a resounding answer and confirmation in the redemptive Incarnation, which includes the Resurrection and Second Coming of Christ ; for if sin has 'reigned unto death' it is that 'grace might reign by justice unto eternal life through Jesus Christ Our Lord' (Rom 5:21).

IV Synthesis. An impressive systematic presentation of this Christian solution has been worked out by Christian thinkers who have built it into a fruitful synthesis. Evil is a privation permitted to intrude into the work of God only for the sake of some greater good. In the light of Revelation this greater good is seen as the redemptive Incarnation. It is a synthesis which leaves the mystery intact, conscious that its final solution will be seen only by the Light of Glory.

The doctrine of creation *ex nihilo* provided Tertullian (*adversus Hermogenem* 3 ; PL 2:200) with a refutation of the idea that matter is eternal and hence opened the way to seeing that matter is not the source of evil which, as St Basil first saw clearly, was nothing but a privation (PG 29:340). St Augustine first came squarely to grips with the metaphysics of evil. He saw evil not as the work of God but as a defect, whose possibility is due to the fact that the world has been created from nothing (*De civ. Dei* 14:11; CSEL 40:27). Hence the cause of an evil will is nothing positive but rather something that deflects from its proper operation, and to seek such a cause in some positive efficient cause is like trying to see darkness or to hear silence (*De civ. Dei* 12:7 ; CSEL 40:577). Evil is indeed a reality though not having a positive nature in itself ; for it is found in the nature that it corrupts (*Contra Iulianum* 3:206 ; PL 45:1334). That evil exists is no argument against the Goodness and Omnipotence of God, but an omnipotent God would permit evil in His works only because His Goodness and Omnipotence are such that He exploits evil to produce good (*Enchiridion* 2 ; PL 40:230). Thus, when man abused the gift of freedom and sinned, he reduced himself to captivity, and from this captivity he was delivered and restored by the Word Incarnate (*De civ. Dei* 14:11 ; CSEL 40:28).

With St Thomas the lines of the synthesis are complete, and we shall endeavour to present them briefly as found in the works of the Angelic Doctor.

(*a*) *The Notion of Evil.* Evil being the opposite of good is conceived as its absence, just as darkness is the absence of light. However, since good means what is desirable, and since nothing is naturally desired except what has positive reality and being, it follows that evil as such is not being but the lack of being (*Summa*, 1a:48:1c) ; not indeed that any absence of perfection is evil, but only the absence of a perfection that should be found in the thing we call evil. It is not an evil in a man that he cannot run like a deer, but it is if he cannot see. Thus evil is not merely the absence of good but the absence of a requisite good, a positive privation (*Summa*, 1a:48:3c).

Evil being a privation cannot have an efficient cause which is of its nature adjusted to produce it as the generative action of a man is precisely adjusted to generate another man, for good bears no proportion to evil. Still good can efficiently cause evil in two ways : first in the process of producing good, as when a sculptor making a statue not only impresses a new form on the marble but destroys its old one. Thus evil often results by way of effecting good. Secondly it sometimes is the result of the defective action of some agent or of the unsuitability of the material in which it operates. Thus children are sometimes generated blind or deformed. In every case it is clear that evil results from good only accidentally (*Summa*, 1a:49:1c).

(*b*) *Division of Evil.* Evil can be a natural defect, a privation of form or of integrity or some deficiency in a natural operation, as being maimed, blind or lame, which is usually called nowadays *physical* evil but which St Thomas calls *malum naturalis defectus* ; or it can be the privation in a human action of its due ordination to God, which is *sin* or *moral evil*, called by St Thomas *malum culpae* (*Summa*, 1a:19:9c). In relation to the rational will the first kind of evil sometimes constitutes a punishment, and so on this level evil is divided into *malum poenae* and *malum culpae* (*Summa*, 1a:48:5c).

(*c*) *Evil and the Will of God.* It is clear that God can in no sense will moral evil or sin, for sin of its essence is contrary to the divine good, and therefore there is no possible higher good in relation to which He could will it, even accidentally. He can and does will the evil in a natural defect, but only accidentally. He wills the corruption of certain things and that certain natural causes operate defectively in willing the harmony and variety of the entire universe. Because secondary causes are created from nothing they are capable of deviating from their natural purpose, and so it is becoming that God should so govern the universe that their native defectibility becomes apparent : but in a way that makes for the order of the

universe as a whole, inasmuch as every created thing in its being and operation falls under the direction of Divine Providence (*Summa*, 1a:49:2c).

Further, because it pertains to the order of the universe to manifest God's Justice, God can will physical evil as a *malum poenae* (loc. cit.).

Finally, though moral evil is completely irreducible to good even as a means to obtaining it, God can permit it and takes occasion thereby to manifest His Justice and Goodness. If there were no sins in the world, many examples of heroic virtue would be lost (*Summa*, 1a:48:2:@3). Hence though sin can never be willed by God, He has not got to will always to prevent it, and can indeed permit it, and this permitting of it is good (*Summa*, 1a:19:9:@3).

(*d*) *Place of Evil in the Universe.* As such it is not part of the universe, because it is a privation (*I Sent.* 47:1:2:@1), but the above considerations show it has a place therein, not in the monistic sense of being an intrinsic part of the intelligibility of things, but because God can will that privation which is in a natural defect for the good He wishes to achieve, and He can permit sin in the pursuit of the due manifestation of His Goodness.

Thus the place of evil in the world remains mysterious (*see also* DEVIL), but its existence is understandable, for creatures are made from nothing : this disposes of the necessity of postulating uncreated matter or any other principle opposed to God to explain the existence of evil (*Summa*, 1a:49:3c). For problems arising out of the presence of pain and physical evil in the universe, *see* PROVIDENCE.

Given the revelation of the Incarnation, it is not difficult to see how these reflections of the Angelic Doctor are illuminated by, and themselves cast light upon, this central mystery of the Christian Faith.

Bibliography. E. Masson, in DTC 9:1679–703 s.v. Mal ; C. Fabro, *Enciclopedia Cattolica*, 7, 1902–6 s.v. Male ; C. Journet, *The Meaning of Evil* (1963) ; J. Maritain, *St Thomas and the Problem of Evil* (1942) ; F. Petit, *The Problem of Evil* (1959) ; A. Sertillanges OP, *Le Problème du mal* (2 vols., 1948, 1958) ; E. F. Sutcliffe SJ, *Providence and Suffering in the OT and NT* (1953) ; M. D'ARCY SJ, *The Pain of this World and the Providence of God* (1925). St Thomas treats of evil not only in the *Summa Theologiae* (professedly in 1a:48–9) to which we have almost exclusively referred, but also in most of his major works, as *II Sent.* dist. 34:3 ; *Contra Gentiles*, c. 7ss ; *Quaestiones Disputatae de Malo* ; *Compendium Theologiae*, c. 115, etc.   A. R.

EVOLUTION The theological climate in which evolution can be discussed is now quite different from what it was only a few decades ago. The encouragement shown to scientists by Pope Pius XII and the readiness of theologians to hear what the scientists have to say make for a better understanding. A Catholic scientist no longer needs to reassure the theologian that while dealing with secondary causes he does, of course, accept the divine *concursus* that holds all things in being, while the theologian has put the anxieties of concordism firmly behind him.

This present article will deal (I) with the necessary definitions, (II) with the history of evolution as a theory, (III) with the evolution of man, (IV) more especially with Adam and Eve, and finally (V) with the future of evolution.

I Definitions. The analyses and syntheses of nature which are involved in the study of evolution are regarded by the biologist as continuous processes of investigation into an ever-widening field of knowledge which is ever changing and posing new problems. There is no place here for a concept of final or absolute truth ; even as all in nature is to the biologist relative or perfectible, so are the truths deduced from the study of nature. As H. Levy (1938) stated : ' Truth is the summation of man's experience at any given moment ; it is a lantern that illumines his next few steps ; past truth becomes incomplete as a greater truth replaces it ; it is an instrument for the creation and working out of a human purpose, becoming sharper and more effective as that purpose itself becomes clearer, and as man's reading of natural processes becomes more and more accurate.' This is a working view of truth which the evolutionist will endorse and, inasmuch as it is teleological, it is not exclusive and is not confined to any empirical or mechanistic system of thought. Evolutionary theory is vital and important to an understanding of the nature of man and of his place in the universe. This article attempts to support this statement by explaining very concisely biological opinion about evolution especially at those points of contact with theology or theological opinion.

It is obvious that the word ' evolution ' has different meanings in different contexts even in biology. We may, however, give three working definitions. Firstly, organic evolution may mean that all living organisms are ultimately described by way of sequence of change from one or a few primordial ancestors, to give rise to the multiplicity of flora and fauna we know from palaeontology and see around us today. Secondly, organic evolution may mean that all things which are common to an archetype, or a basic plan of construction, such as the large phyla, are each descended from a common ancestor by changes occurring throughout biological time. Thirdly, as in the definition by K. Mather (1943), ' Evolution is the occurrence of persistent changes in the hereditary constitution of a population of organisms '. Most other definitions would be included in the above or extensions of one or more of them. None of these definitions mentions origins ; they begin with something living in the first place and this is all that is normally necessary in organic evolution. For cosmic evolution, *see* COSMOGONY. In a cosmic theory of evolution, however, life itself would have to be accounted for and there is an increasing number of biologists who nowadays accept spontaneous generation as a reasonable speculation. Evolution which includes spontaneous generation completes the picture as given by the cosmologist and the biologist, and asserts the continuity of all things from the very beginning of the universe up to the present time. Such a picture satisfies the basic conception of unity which is axiomatic to the scientist. Hence evolution is a theory of secondary causes and it could not be otherwise. But from evolutionary theory evolutionism, or a system of philosophy, may be developed.

In the definitions given above the word ' species ' is not mentioned. In the Darwinian and Neo-Darwinian periods most definitions of evolution would have at least mentioned this word. Previous to about 1930, while Mendel's theory was being vigorously developed to become the theory of the gene, while in fact modern genetics was being developed, there was perhaps a certain conflict between genetics and evolutionary theory. But, by about 1930, with a better understanding of the role played by mutations in evolution which enabled biologists to arrive at a better understanding of the part played by natural selection in nature, much of the conflict had disappeared. At the same time the primary study of the biologist, that of classification and taxonomy, had advanced, and inevitably the data of the taxonomist had to be interpreted in genetical and ecological terms. Almost immediately difficulties arose over the word ' species ', and while we may allow that there is a natural entity which we call ' species ', the concept of species even today defies precise definition. The result of these developments has been to shift evolutionary thinking from the biological species as such to a study of populations of organisms. In other words the species has been short-circuited and difficulties over its definition do not arise so frequently. Likewise the study of the gene or ' pure genetics ' has been extended to population genetics. The almost universal application of these newer concepts to evolutionary theory has thus resulted in a fundamental change of emphasis which has consolidated the theory along the lines of causal explanation and given it much greater credibility. Evolution is now thought to occur through population changes rather than through individual changes in individual species. The importance of the individual, while still necessary for evolution to occur initially, is thus greatly lessened. An essential feature of the newer approach is that evolution is looked upon as an ordinary process occurring in nature ; evolution is dynamic, not static. This conclusion of modern biology is important when we consider the evolution of man.

II History. Inasmuch as man within historical (and perhaps prehistorical) times has always had an appreciation of change, it has been held that an *idea* of evolution more or less not consciously understood, preceded any realization of the existence of an evolutionary process in nature (Fothergill, 1952, 1961). Man's natural curiosity, coupled with a developing philosophy of change from early times, has led to attempts to give concrete expression to what we can call evolutionary ideas for very many years. There has been an evolution of the idea of evolution, which reaches back at least 2,000 years.

In this short review it is possible to show that evolution did not begin with Charles Darwin, but that the modern theory is the heir of past ages, that it is a more exact and firmly based scientific picture of the living world, having its roots in earlier times. When we say that early writers had ideas of evolution, we do not mean evolution as we know it ; we merely mean that they had glimmerings of facts about evolutionary ideas. Fuller treatments of the history of evolution are given by H. Fairfield Osborn (1924) and P. G. Fothergill (1952). For descriptive purposes we shall divide the subject into an *Earlier Period* and a *Modern Period*.

(*a*) **The Earlier Period.** Man began to observe nature from the earliest times. We see this from the prehistoric cave drawings of animals and man, and many of these drawings have a distinct agricultural or hunting flavour. In later historical times a practical appreciation of nature and of art developed to produce men who speculated more about nature. Ancient philosophers, whether Chinese, Egyptian or Grecian, had quite definite ideas about the origin of things. The ancient Chinese conceived of five primary elements—water, wood, fire, soil, and gold, which existed at the beginning and out of which life arose. This is an example of living things arising out of something different. To Confucius the word *Yi* meant some kind of change in the natural world, a change from simple to complex. In his *Yi-Chang* he attempted to show that things originated from a simple source through gradual unfolding and branching. This is an old idea with a very modern ring about it.

The ancient Egyptians too considered *Khephera* as the Creator of all and *Nu* as the abyss of water from which *Khephera* raised all things to life. Man was imagined as becoming actual from the mind of the Creator through seven distinct stages before he became fully human. This resembles a process of evolution by stages. The ancient Greeks too had their primary elements. Empedocles has been called the 'father of the evolution-idea'. He taught that life arose gradually through an unconnected series of imperfect forms which were at first ill-adapted to live and reproduce and which appeared in the order : plants, animals and man. Aristotle superimposed his hylomorphic theory on these naturistic views of the earlier Greeks, and of him H. Fairfield Osborn said that he taught of an evolution from 'polyp to man'. Indeed, Aristotle's system of animals from which a detailed classification can be compiled, and his ideas of nature producing, or ordering, things in a sequence of perfection, in the order : lifeless, plant, animal and man suggest that Aristotle had evolutionary ideas. But this is a matter of opinion, for his philosophical system may not allow of the change of one *forma* into another. Other early writers such as Anaximander and Democritus also held views containing a germ of the evolutionary idea ; we may even say that the *Genesis* account of creation puts forth the beliefs of the Jewish people, and shows again a nothingless

void into which the Creator puts the Universe and Earth and subsequently follow on living things in a definite order, which is also an order in the scale of perfection, ending finally in man.

Aristotle's influence extended up to and into the Renaissance period. Eventually a new type of biologist, who investigated biology for its own sake, not necessarily as a part of philosophical speculation, came into being. Naturalists like Ray, Tournefort, Linnaeus and Buffon, all classified organisms and invented systems of classification. At first these classifications were simple and arbitrary, such as the division of plants into trees, shrubs and herbs, but they ended by becoming highly organized and complex systems such as the sexual and binomial system of Linnaeus, who began his work convinced that species were immutable but ended by thinking they were mutable. These classifiers worked hard on the investigation of resemblances and differences between plants and animals. They came to recognize that change in species could occur and they seemed to be attempting to find an overall explanation of why living things could be grouped together into what seemed natural units such as classes, genera, etc. A modern appreciation of evolution was not possible to them because it is evident that their knowledge of nature was not detailed enough to allow them to find an explanation. But their work followed on from the naturistic views of earlier writers, and we must remember that evolutionary theory is in a true sense a rationalization of classification.

The explanation which the Classifiers wanted was found for them, however, by their contemporaries, the Natural Philosophers. These thinkers came to recognize clearly and distinctly that change in the living world was a fundamental feature. Hence they were ultimately able to formulate an idea of evolution. But in order to do this it was apparently necessary to create a dichotomy. They separated what is called mechanism from vitalism. This advance in thought probably gave *direction* to the course of science. Cartesianism produced a shift in the mode of thought and the concomitant dichotomy found expression in Kant's principle that teleological explanations were not necessary in biology. In the *Critique of Judgment* Kant[1] was thus able for the first time to give a positive and unequivocal statement of the possibility of *genetic* evolution, and thus he gave the Classifiers the basis they needed for further exploration. It is essential to realize that one of the first definite statements about genetic evolution came from a philosopher, not from a biologist.

The Greeks dealt with nature as a whole, but Aristotle was largely concerned with 'being' as such. By the time we get to Kant we find that in Natural History at least the idea of 'becoming' had replaced that of 'being' (about 1790). As the work of the Classifiers increased and was crystallized

[1] See H. Bernard's trans. [1914] pt. 2, Append. Section 80, 337-8.

by Kant's statement, the way was then opened for the formulation of evolution and the emergence of a truly generalized evolutionary theory. This period in the history of evolution is well known. At first, genetic evolution was appreciated by relatively few people but it developed steadily and consistently through the works of men like Erasmus Darwin, Lamarck, Geoffrey St Hilaire, Alfred Russell Wallace, Charles Darwin, Mivart, T. H. Huxley and others. The focus of this period is of course on the writings of Charles Darwin and Alfred Russell Wallace. Darwin, in his famous *Origin of Species by Means of Natural Selection* (1859) for the first time brought together the lines of evidence for evolution and at the same time gave a causal explanation about the mode of evolution.

During this time also other sciences such as geology and palaeontology had made great strides and subsidiary biological sciences such as cytology had arisen, so that by the end of the 19th cent. the theory of evolution was recognized as a major biological theory with ramifications spreading far and wide into politics, literature, philosophy and theology. We are well aware of the vast polemical literature of the Darwinian era. There were those who doubted the philosophical bases of evolution and, as evolutionism began to develop, there were those who considered the theory theologically dangerous, if not inadmissible, because it was popularly thought to be necessarily materialistic and atheistic. While the theory, as a theory, is theologically neutral, the literature during the Darwinian period undoubtedly gave it an antireligious bias, and so the theologian was forced to examine it. The story of this period is so well known that we need say no more about it.

(*b*) **The Modern Period.** With the beginning of the 20th cent., evolution entered a new phase. Mendel's work on genetics was re-discovered, mutation theory developed, cytology expanded and research in all branches of biology related to evolution went on at an ever-increasing rate. The new discoveries of fossil men gave substance to the inclusion of man in the evolutionary scheme. The synthesis of these researches opened the way for the genetical and experimental investigation of evolutionary problems along new lines both in the laboratory and in the field. Genecological studies, that is, the study of the composition and behaviour of the species complex and of populations in ecological, taxonomic and genetical terms have been very fruitful of practical results and have led to greater understanding of the mode of evolution as it occurs among populations of organisms. At the same time the explanation of genetical theory ushered in the modern mathematical study of evolution, due to the pioneer work of Sir R. A. Fisher, S. Wright, J. B. S. Haldane and others. This work was a great step forward in the historical development of evolutionary theory by showing the relation between empirical and mathematical interpretations of biological events on the one hand and on the other a process in the

organic world which is historical by definition and philosophical by implication. The result of all these studies and researches has been the discovery of the four major causal factors in the evolutionary process, namely *mutations, recombination, selection* and *isolation*. There may be other factors at work not yet known, but the importance and operation of these four is well known.

Mutations represent the basic changes without which there could be only limited evolution. By mutation is meant any heritable change, however small, in the hereditary make-up of organisms. This does not mean to say that all mutations lead to evolution. Providing these mutations are reproducible they are present for evolution to work on. *Recombination* is the genetic phase of evolution, as it were. It is the sorting-out phase of the mutations which become thereby definitely incorporated into the genetic constitution of the organisms concerned and are enabled to play their part in evolution. *Natural selection*, to which great prominence is often given, and rightly so, is the sifting-out stage of the organisms through which favourable changes in organisms, which have become incorporated genetically, are related to the wider worlds of the internal and external environments of the organisms. Natural selection supplies the supreme test of survival to the evolutionary changes which have occurred. Thus it directs the course of evolution and for this reason it often seems to be *the* most important factor in evolution. Natural selection is not a conscious selection; of course, it is only analogically selective— but the net result is the same. It is, in effect, the resultant of all the causes which cumulatively determine whether an organism, or a group of organisms, shall live in a certain area and reproduce their kind and continue to do so. *Isolation* is the fixing and stabilizing factor of evolution. In a word, by isolating the organism or group of organisms either or both spatially or reproductively, it ensures that the organism naturally selected will continue to survive without biological and environmental difficulties.

The acceptance of these factors as the factors of evolutionary change led to the present position that it is primarily the population which evolves as a whole and not just individuals. This conclusion does not preclude the evolution of individuals on occasion or in special circumstances, but this group-activity is regarded as the normal way in which evolution works and by it evolutionary theory harmonizes better with the biological facts encountered in the field. In any case, as far as individuals are concerned, if they were evolving separately, they would very soon form a population. We should point out that it is no longer necessary to postulate evolution as occurring through the slow accumulation of small variations over a vast period of time. This was an early Darwinian idea, and of course some evolution may occur in this way. Mutations may lie hidden in a population showing little or no outward manifestation until favourable circumstances and opportunities arise, when they may quickly come to the surface and bring about a relatively rapid evolution. Modern causal evolutionary theory has moved a long way from the original Darwinian view of natural selection, but it includes this view, and it is true to say that without the discovery of a selective effect which influences the death-rate and survival value of organisms, which is what selection means, little or no advance in evolutionary theory could have been made. Modern evolutionary theory is basically due to this discovery coupled with the realization that mutations may be large or small. Hence it is no longer correct to say that there is no satisfactory causal explanation of the way in which evolution occurs. Modern genetic evolutionary theory is true in so far as the data on which it is based are true, and these are well known and well tried and rest on a solid basis of fact, observation and experiment.

(c) **Evidence.** What is called the formal or classical evidence for the occurrence of organic evolution is well known and forms the subject-matter of many standard textbooks on evolution. But there are one or two points which should be mentioned because, even today, a good deal of Catholic non-biological literature tends to give the impression that the evolutionary process is only vaguely understood, or that the evidence for it is not very conclusive. In the previous section we have outlined the genetical and ecological approach to the subject. It has thus become quite untrue to say that evolution has not been proved, at least to the entire satisfaction of the biologist. The presence of an evolutionary process in nature has been shown beyond doubt ; some species have even been synthesized from their probable evolutionary constituents. This is not a matter of opinion and Mather's definition of evolution which we gave earlier is completely true. It describes what we may call micro-evolution, or the evolution of the smaller units in nature such as varieties, species, genera and perhaps families in current classifications. Evidence for the occurrence of what we may call macro-evolution, or evolution of the larger groups such as classes and phyla is, in the nature of the case, less positive and direct. These groups of organisms at the present time are no longer genetically connected ; it is so long since they evolved from each other or from common ancestors that there is now no reproductive compatibility between them. This state is, of course, itself a result of evolution. Direct evidence of blood relationship cannot therefore be obtained ; through evolution their original genic composition has now wholly and completely diverged. The evidence for their evolution thus becomes less direct and circumstantial.

In evolutionary theory an exceedingly large number of facts have been discovered relating to comparative anatomy and morphology, classification, geographical distribution, embryology, serology, palaeontology, etc. These facts form the classical lines of evidence for evolution ; in each of them the facts remain restricted to the narrow field proper to them, but they become marvellously related, and give a much wider and more complete explanation, if evolution which individually they only suggest is postulated. We may mention the special case of palaeontology. If we accept the basic postulate that true similarity of structure is an indication of true relationship between organisms, which is one of the basic axioms of the whole of biology, then palaeontology, in certain cases where the records are fairly complete, may be said to be in a certain sense direct evidence for evolution. When dealing with these lines of evidence, let us not fall into the fallacy of division. The organism is a unity with itself and with its environment. The biologist merely divides the subject and the organism into various compartments as a working convenience in dealing with highly complex things. These classical lines of evidence for evolution when taken together cumulatively present only one conclusion with overwhelming force. They all point to a reality shown by direct evidence to be present in nature, that is, they point to evolution. Furthermore, the biologist has always worked on the basic axiom that nature presents a unity in diversity. Nature is not a conglomeration of events chaotically unrelated to each other. The result would be pure chaos. Naturally the higher up we go in the natural categories of orders, phyla, etc., the less compelling is the immediate evidence for evolution, and so what are called the 'gaps' occur. Physiologically, genetically, ecologically, cytologically, structurally, the gaps are what we would expect if evolution had occurred. Their very existence is itself evidence of evolution. The absolute number of units of classification diminishes very rapidly from the species up to the phylum ; there are upwards of a million species but only a few dozen phyla. This fact in itself makes it much more difficult to obtain comprehensive evidence such as we obtain directly at the species and generic levels. In any case there are strong biological arguments such as those given by G. G. Simpson (1960) and others which minimize the importance of the gaps. There is no biological reason why these different phyla should not have evolved from common prototypes. Indeed there is a very strong a priori probability that they have done so.

The theory of organic evolution is thus a very comprehensive one embracing the whole of the organic world, and by further extensions the whole of the cosmos. It unites organisms into one grand intelligible scheme. It gives a highly reasonable and intellectually satisfying explanation of a myriad of facts in biology which would otherwise compel the conclusion that nature is chaotic and meaningless. It points to order in nature ; it is the unifying factor in biological nature and as such is finalistic, pointing the way to the end in view.

III Evolution of Man. For a very good reason indeed Pope Pius XII in *Humani Generis* was careful to distinguish between the general biological theory of evolution and the evolution of man in particular. Providing the theory of evolution is not accounted for by the operation of chance alone, and provided the errors of a materialistic, atheistic or pantheistic form of evolutionism are recognized, one may be rightly satisfied that there need be nothing in biological (or even cosmic) evolution contrary to faith.

Evolutionists would have wished the Pope to go further by indicating the manifold advantages to theology of a general acceptance of evolution on the right lines. But it is important to remember that this was the first time a Pope had explicitly mentioned evolution in a public statement. It seems that the very least that may be said is that the Church officially does not see anything in the theory of organic evolution which is necessarily contrary to faith.

The case is rather different, of course, when we come to the evolution of man. Clearly evolutionary views of man will affect one's views about his nature, and biological ideas of his origin affect the teachings of religion on these matters. Thus evolution and theology meet. By this we mean that in the nature of the case alone what the biologist has to say about the origin of man is cognate to his origin as disclosed by faith. By the evolution of man is generally meant the evolution of his body. It does not really affect this issue if some evolutionist writes as though this were the whole man. Such a view leads to errors in evolutionism which may be contrary to faith, but this does not invalidate the general question of man's evolution. The human soul is not subject to the laws of evolution, and it is accepted by all Catholics and others that human souls are immediately created by God. This is indeed an article of faith, and it applies to the souls of newly-born infants (who are none-the-less corporeally the products of a completely natural biological process) as well as to the souls of our first parents. The human soul is thus truly unique, but the body is not necessarily so. The one undeniable point about which all persons will agree is that man has not always been present on this earth. As far as we know geologically, he was not in existence more than a million years ago. In order thoroughly to appreciate the biological position about the evolution of man it is necessary to understand what biologists themselves understand by evolution (see I above). In this section we wish merely to indicate some outstanding recent views about man's lineage and then to pass on to the more theological questions of Catholic sources and to the speculative but difficult question of Adam and Eve. Some of these topics will be dealt with from different points of view under the headings ADAM, POLYGENISM and ORIGINAL SIN, but all such views should be complementary with little overlapping.

(a) **The Lineage of Man.** Two important points should be borne in mind. Firstly, it is scarcely doubted by human evolutionists and anthropologists that man has evolved from some type or types of lower creature. This is not a controversial topic. Secondly, it is not known from what animal or animals he has evolved, the line of his evolution is not clear even today. There is much diversity of opinion about human evolution, but this evolution concerns the 'how' and not the 'fact' of his evolution. In the time of Charles Darwin and soon after it was commonly held that man and apes were closely related, but the present-day view has radically changed. No one now holds that man is descended from any existing type of ape. No one now believes (if indeed anyone ever did believe) that a missing link will ever be found, but a relatively large number of missing links have been found and it is on these that the ideas of man's origin are founded.

In the time of Charles Darwin only two fossil men were known. But his book *The Descent of Man* (1871) stimulated research, with the result that at the present time a representative sample of the remains of man and man-like creatures has been unearthed. There are hundreds, if not thousands, of hominid bones which have been found. The more important of these are listed below ; for fuller accounts the reader should consult textbooks, some of which are given in the Bibliography.

The fossil bones of hominids consist of various parts of the skeleton such as the skull, teeth, thigh-bones, pelvis and so on, which in the course of time have for some reason been preserved. The condition of these bones varies a great deal ; some of them are well preserved, others are not ; some are more or less whole, others are broken. Dealing with bones is a highly specialized study, but the results of this study may be accurate and are often surprisingly so. It is amazing what amount of information that even a small piece of bone, or a tooth, can reveal to the expert. There is often controversy about the various human fossils but this is about details of comparison rather than about principles. As Sir Solly Zuckerman (1954) maintained, human bones should never be confused with ape bones. In zoological terms man is a member of the family *Hominidae* and he is closest in zoological characters to the family *Pongidae*, which contains the gorilla, chimpanzee and orangutan. The characteristics possessed by these animals and man, both structural and functional, indicate that man belongs to the same stock as that of the apes, not by direct descent, but probably by descent from a common ancestor more or less far removed. Since the original divergence occurred, these animals have independently acquired each their own distinctive specialized characters which emphasize the collateral relationship and delimit the various types each to their group. These 'characters of independent acquisition', as Le Gros Clark (1955) calls them, are peculiar to members of one family or of one type. They indicate true relationship between the organisms possessing them. It is these characters which enable anatomists to determine the status of fossil men and to show the extent of their divergence from the collateral ancestor.

The fossils so far discovered show unmistakably that the hominids and pre-hominids fall into several more or less distinct types or levels called the Australopithecines, the Pithecanthropi, the Neanderthaloids and the *Homo sapiens* types. Both man and ape trace back to a highly generalized ape type which was spread over Europe, Asia and Africa in the Miocene period some thirty million years ago. These creatures may have been the common ancestors of both ape and man. If so we would expect to find some forms which are intermediate. In fact such have been found in the Australopithecines, or

Southern Ape-men, which are among the most interesting of recent fossil finds. The first one was discovered by R. Dart at Taungs, and was called the Taungs skull. Since then a relatively large number of similar forms have been found which have been the subject of much discussion, because they truly show an admixture of human and ape characters. Their brain was small, similar to that of the largest apes. While brain-size does not give an absolute measure of intelligence, generally speaking the larger the brain the greater the intelligence. On the other hand brain complexity is of more importance than size. While according to size the Australopithecines were ape-like, endocranial casts show that their brains were probably much more complex, perhaps as complex as those of some of the later hominids with much larger brains. It is also claimed that the Australopithecines used tools of a primitive kind. *Zinjanthropus* is a newer discovery from Africa which is similar to *Australopithecus*. The brain was much larger than that of *Australopithecus* and the creature apparently used primitive tools. While very ancient, its age is uncertain, varying from 600,000 to $1\frac{3}{4}$ million years.

Australopithecus lived about a million years ago. The important feature about these types is that structurally they were true intermediates between undoubted apes and undoubted men. If indeed they could manufacture and use hand-made tools, then they represent the most ape-like men so far discovered presenting unmistakable evidence of man's evolution.

The remaining hominid fossils fall into two fairly clear groups both as regards their characteristics and their age. There is some overlapping, of course. The *Palaeoanthropidae* are the oldest and they occur in the Lower and Middle Palaeolithic levels. The *Neanthropidae* occur in the Upper Palaeolithic levels and include contemporary man. The Palaeo-anthropidae may also be grouped into an earlier more primitive type and a later more advanced type. We may briefly mention the more important ones. *Pithecanthropus erectus* was first discovered in Java in 1894 by Dubois and later in the 1930s other forms were dug up. *Sinanthropus*, or Pekin man, was first found in 1927 in the Choukoutien Caves near Pekin. Subsequently a number of other bones were found in the same place. These types are practically identical with *Pithecanthropus*. They are included in the same genus. In structure they were man-like but with ape-like features giving them a rather brutish appearance. The brain was considerably larger than that of any ape but much smaller than that of modern man. Quartz implements and remains of fire hearths were also found in the fossil sites at Choukoutien. These creatures are often classed as true human beings. Another very interesting find was made in the Ternifine deposits in Algeria by Arambourg and Hoffstetter in 1954. This consisted of several jaws and a parietal skull bone of a pithecanthropoid type called *Atlanthropus*. There is also another pithe-canthropoid type from Europe consisting of the well-preserved lower jaw called Heidelberg man, or *Pithecanthropus heidelbergensis* found at Mauer in Germany in 1908. All of these fossils are very old, occurring in the Lower Pleistocene some 400,000 or 500,000 years ago. There are a number of others of similar type. The interesting thing about the Pithecanthropoids is that even half a million years ago they were widespread in China, Java, North Africa and Europe. They were primitive men much less advanced than *Homo sapiens*.

The later Neanthropidae include the well-known Neanderthal man. *Homo Neanderthalensis* now includes a large number of specimens with forms from the Neanderthal Valley, Palestine, Krapina, Spy, La Quina, Saccopastore, Ngangdong, Broken Hill, Steinheim, etc., etc. All of these forms are much more advanced both culturally and structurally than the Pithecanthropoids. In fact they present a mixture of Pithecanthropoid and *Homo sapiens* characters, with some characters distinctive to their own kind. They had beetle brows, rather prognathous jaws and brains as large as those of modern man, but they made advanced tools, used fire and buried their dead. The Neanderthaloids fall into two groups, one nearer the Pithecanthropians and the other nearer to *Homo sapiens*. In age they extend from the Middle to the Upper Pleistocene Period starting from about 200,000 years ago and, for a time, they were contemporary with the earliest types of modern man. Eventually they died out, leaving no trace of any descendants.

The Neanthropidae form *Homo sapiens*, or modern man ; they fall into two groups based on age. First, Swanscombe man, discovered in Kent in 1935, consists of well-preserved skull bones little different from those of contemporary man but with a smaller brain. Its age is about 250,000 years, which may mean that *Homo sapiens* was in existence before Neanderthal man. Fontéchevade man (discovered in 1947) is younger, about 150,000 years old. It consists of skull bones similar to the bones of Western man, with a brain only slightly smaller. The later Neanthropidae are recognizable in the Late Pleistocene Period less than 100,000 years ago and they comprise several forms of *Homo sapiens* as we know him today. The types include Grimaldi man, Cro-Magnon man, Chancelade man, Brünn man, Choukoutien man and Olduvai man. The descendants of some of the later types of these men may be identified today but, as a whole, they seem to have been largely submerged before the modern races of *Homo sapiens* arose.

It should also be remembered that anthropologists recognize the various palaeolithic culture industries which started in the middle of the Lower Pleistocene from the end of the first Glacial Period. Various implements, some of them beautiful and highly elaborate, which are the product of human skills, have been found forming industries such as the Abbevillian, Archeulian, Mousterian, Magdalenian, etc. These represent different and increasingly more complex human culture levels. The presence of implements such as these is unmistakable proof of the existence of man at that time and in some cases such implements have been found in association with, or near to, the various fossil men.

Humphrey J. Johnson (1956) pointed out that while a few decades ago modern man stood alone in the animal world, today this is by no means the case, and this is the important point about these fossil hominids. All the scientific evidence shows that since about half a million years ago (and much longer if we include the Australopiths) several species or types of men have come into existence and have died out completely, leaving no trace of descendants. These types undoubtedly show all gradations of structure between modern apes and modern man, but because of their brain-size and their industries we must acknowledge them as human beings. There is thus a high degree of probability that man has in fact evolved from some lower type. The degree of probability is high enough to establish the conclusion with practical certainty. Thus the biologist is entitled to assert categorically that man does not stand alone in the biological sense, that is, that he is truly a part of nature showing unmistakable signs of his natural origin. Physical man fits perfectly into the evolutionary scheme, so that the unity of nature is maintained. The scientist is thus justified in asserting that any modern account of the origin of man must take cognizance of the scientific conclusions. The scientific and the religious accounts of man's origin should be complementary.

(b) **Sources.** Since the early Darwinian days when evolution became a topic of general discussion, there have always been biologists who were good Christians and good evolutionists. Nevertheless there has been a very large amount of Catholic and non-Catholic literature devoted to destructive criticism of evolutionary theory. Unfortunately much of this was ill informed. It is amazing, therefore, that the Popes mentioned evolution only in recent times. In *Humani Generis* (AAS 62 [1950] 561–77) Pius XII left open the question of evolution. He asserted that the theory was not proved beyond doubt, but he did not attempt to assess biological opinion. However, he was at pains to show that certain aspects of evolutionism were in error. Clearly here he was condemning atheistic, materialistic and pantheistic evolutionary philosophies without denying that there can be a Christian form of evolutionism. Even this negative recognition is important. We may now say that the age of evolutionary polemic is over.

In this document it was the evolution of man which the Pope was particularly concerned about. Pius XII pointed out that Scripture has something to say about this matter and he re-affirmed the traditional Catholic teaching that human souls are specially created. He stressed also the traditional view of the unity of the human race by insisting that the doctrine of Original Sin, so far as we know *at present*, demands a single original progenitor for all men and women. The Pope wrote : ' This teaching of the Church leaves the doctrine of Evolution an open question, as long as it confines its speculations to the development, from other living matter already in existence, of the human body. (That souls are immediately created by God is a view which the Catholic Faith imposes on us.) In the present state of scientific and theological opinion, this question may be legitimately canvassed by research, and by discussion between those who are expert on both sides.' Such a statement amounts to a guarded recognition of the claims of evolutionists. It would seem to invite further research and discussion. While the Pope thus explicitly acknowledged the possibility of the evolution of man's body from some lower animal, he did not imply that, in the mind of the Church, the matter is certain, or even probable, but it is a statement of fact that to hold such a view is not contrary to Scripture as so far interpreted by the Church. By implication the Pope also acknowledges that our first progenitors may have arisen as a natural result of the process of reproduction (involving no direct supernatural intervention, except for the creation of the human soul) much in the same way as a baby is produced. The divine *Concursus* is always present, of course. Such an acknowledgment invites biological speculations as to the *modus operandi* (*see below*).

In *Humani Generis* Pius XII also pointed out that Scripture contains references to the origin of man which all acknowledge. As this topic now involves the theory of evolution, the relation of evolution to the Scriptures and to the writings of the Early Fathers on Scripture becomes important to theologians and biologists alike. In a sense, the question whether or not the Bible stands in opposition to modern evolutionary ideas may be settled immediately in the words of the Rev. Dr Meagher (cf. E. C. Messenger, *Theology and Evolution*, 18) who wrote : ' Is the Bible favourable to evolution ? My answer to that is in the negative. Is it opposed to evolution ? Again I answer negatively. Are the Fathers favourably disposed to evolution ? No, I do not think so, because they never thought of it.' Dr Meagher is undoubtedly correct : evolution as we know it is not mentioned in the Bible, or by the Fathers. But these sources do express views about the nature of man and his origin which form a part of the historical development of thought and ideas just as much as do the views of the early philosophers. If we look for germs of evolutionary ideas in one, we should also look for them in the others. It is cognate, therefore, to inquire whether the Bible and the Fathers in their treatment of origins show any glimmerings of evolutionary ideas and to see particularly if they oppose such ideas.

Studies of this kind are highly specialized and call for special skills which few biologists possess. Fortunately we may make use of three works which have given masterly summaries of the position. We refer here to E. C. Messenger's *Evolution and Theology* (1931), and *Theology and Evolution* (1949) and Canon H. de Dorlodot's *Darwinism and Catholic Thought* (1925). The present account is largely a short synopsis of some of the important views on evolution as expressed by these writers and their contributors.

Dr Messenger first dealt with spontaneous generation, a topic which ultimately concerns evolutionists too. While there is no positive evidence about its occurrence, it is widely believed in today. Many of the ancient philosophers thought that living things came from primary elements, often in a fixed order. It seems that, previous to Charles Darwin, Pasteur and Tyndall, it was the common opinion that spontaneous generation occurred. As regards the Fathers and early theologians, Messenger contends that their opinions were in agreement with popular opinion. They thought that living things arose from non-living due to secondary causes, to the power put into inorganic matter by the Creator. The Scholastics broke away from these views, however. Not all theologians would agree with Messenger on these points.

When we come to evolution Messenger points out that he has selected for comment those who belong to the literal school of interpretation of Genesis ; we give these below. St Ephrem (*see* EPHREM) taught that plants and animals were produced by the active power of the elements. St Basil thought that the earth produced the plants and animals. St Gregory of Nyssa (like the Alexandrian School) considered that all things were created potentially at once by the Creator, their subsequent appearance being brought about by the development of the potencies first created according to a fixed and necessary order of succession. St John Chrysostom taught that, according to Scripture, plants and animals were first produced by the operation of earth and waters as secondary causes at God's command. The teachings of St Augustine recall those of St Gregory of Nyssa, but there are differences. St Augustine considered that there was an actual creation of inorganic things but only a potential creation of living things. And so we may progress through the works of Bede, St John Damascene and St Bonaventure up to, but excluding, St Thomas Aquinas. St Thomas took a different view ; he taught that the terrestrial bodies took an active part in the production of plants and inferior animals, but that the higher animals were produced directly by God. These views are fundamentally similar to the naturistic views of ancient philosophers in whom we discerned glimmerings of evolutionary ideas. We may say that views of this kind are no less materialistic than those of modern evolutionary theory, nor do they seem to oppose an idea of evolution. Canon Dorlodot summed up these views as follows : ' Some authors explicitly profess the theory of absolute natural evolution of living things in the sense of St Gregory of Nyssa and St Augustine. Others repeat more or less in their entirety the assertions of St Basil ; lastly there are some who remain silent on the matter and limit themselves to expounding the order of appearance of the different creatures and the meaning of the six days of the Hexameron. But we have not been able to find a single Christian writer previous to the Scholastic Period who opposed the theory, or who endeavours to regard the *rationes seminales* of St Augustine simply as material or passive powers, as later writers endeavoured to do.' Since the time of St Thomas some of the later writers

agreed with the Early Fathers, others have followed St Thomas and, in modern times, others again have expressed truly evolutionary views.

In his second book Messenger published some reviews of his first book along with his own replies. The net result of the book is to make it clear that there is no fixed opinion either about evolution in general or about the ' evolutionary ' interpretations of Genesis given by the Fathers. These works thus sum up modern theological opinion, leaving open the question of evolution. There is no responsible suggestion that evolution is contrary to Faith.

IV Evolution of Adam and Eve. In discussions of the origin of Adam and Eve biology and theology come into close contact. In the present state of our knowledge all we can do is to speculate. We may now assume that the possibility of the evolution of physical man is accepted, but that there is room for further discussion, especially about the biological account of his origin as contrasted with the account in Genesis and Church documents. The following account is largely taken from the writer's own book, *Evolution and Christians*. We would ask the reader to bear in mind that it is written in an attempt to find biological explanations. Previous biological explanations of the origins of Adam and Eve have not been satisfactory. Most of them have been written to find suitable interpretations of Genesis, rather than to follow known biological processes. The present writer attempts to give possible ways in which Adam and Eve could conceivably have arisen, starting from the natural biological processes—those of reproduction and genetics. That these explanations are put forward by the writer does not necessarily mean that he prefers them. If we accept Adam and Eve as individuals who actually existed and from whom all men are descended, and if we accept the evolution of man, it is incumbent upon us to give explanations of that evolution which do not contradict either Genesis or known biological processes.

In 1909 the Biblical Commission in a decree approved by the Pope (D2121–8) answered eight questions about the historical character of the early chapters of Genesis. It decided in favour of the literal sense generally, contrasting, however, the *notitia popularis*, or the common understanding of the writer's day, with scientific history, and also showing that it was not every word and phrase in the account which had to be taken literally and that there were passages where the Fathers had held diverse opinions. It singled out four truths as of special moment : the creation of the world by God, the special creation of man, the formation of woman from man and the unity of the human race, along with certain other facts concerning Original Sin. The list of these goes back to Origen (fragment on Phm ; PG 14:1306) ; these the narrative taught as true.

In an address to the papal Academy of Science (AAS 33 [1941] 506) Pius XII spoke of the essential superiority of man over the beasts by reason of his possessing a spiritual soul. He spoke also of Eve as being formed from Adam, flesh of his flesh, to be his helpmeet. He added that so far science had not brought light that was clear and certain to the problem of man's origin but that it was for the future to see whether science, guided by revelation, would reach a definitive result in the matter.

In 1948 (D2302) a letter of the Biblical Commission to the Archbishop of Paris gave an authentic interpretation of the former decrees of 1909, allowing that it was difficult to estimate the exact literary genus of these early chapters, that the language was simple and figurative, on the level of a primitive people, but not devoid of historical content. Then in 1950 the encyclical *Humani Generis* (D2327–8) allowed that sober investigation into the origin of man's body was acceptable, though theories of polygenism demanded much more careful scrutiny : ' The faithful cannot follow that opinion which is put forward by its sponsors as claiming either that after Adam's time there were men on earth, properly so-called, who were not the lineal descendants of Adam, or alternatively that Adam was the name of a collectivity of ancestors. It is in no wise plain how such an opinion can be reconciled with the doctrine of original sin as this is presented to us in the sources of revelation and expounded by the Church '.[1]

In the light of these documents it is possible to hold that while Adam could not have been generated by an animal in the full and proper sense (the theological requirement), the reproductive process has not altered fundamentally since Adam's time, and that in his case, according to normal evolutionary ideas, the sex cells could have been produced only by prehominids, i.e. from animals near to man. If this were so, those cells (male sperm and female egg) could have been the instrumental causes of the production of Adam, inasmuch as they furnished *in potentia* the biological requirements for a man. In the ordinary course of reproduction the body resulting from the fusion of those sex cells would have lacked a human soul and the resultant creature would have been an animal. But those cells could also by divine action receive a human soul when the requirements for the formation of a human body had been biologically fulfilled. The biology of this theory will be discussed below.

These documents, while not being technically infallible pronouncements, must none-the-less be taken with due reverence. They indicate that the present human race is descended from Adam, who must be regarded as a single individual if difficulties with the doctrine of Original Sin are to be avoided. To find room for polygenism some have stressed the language of the encyclical (' It is in no wise plain '— as if some day it might be) and others have urged that the children of Adam are said to be *his in terris*, i.e. the present human race, not those of other planets. Some thinkers, both Catholic and non-Catholic, favour polygenism and consider that Adam was in fact a group or population of individuals (*see further* POLYGENISM). Such a population would

[1] Cum nequaquam appareat quomodo huiusmodi sententia componi queat cum iis quae fontes revelatae veritatis et acta magisterii ecclesiae proponunt de peccato originali. . . .

undoubtedly have been a coherent natural entity, behaving in a practical sense as a single organism. In an evolutionary sense a population shows an ecological and genetic unity due to its common environment and to its common genetic inheritance, which is not possessed by any other population. This biological unity could be possessed by both homogeneous and heterogeneous populations. Evolutionarily and genetically such unity would be achieved whether the population were descended from a single, or from a number of similar, individuals. At least the biological unity of the human race could still be preserved if polygenism were accepted. It may be, however, that the unity referred to by Pius XII is essentially of a spiritual nature bound up with Original Sin. Again, as we have already stressed, modern evolutionary research has shown that it is normally, or usually, populations which evolve, a conclusion which is supported by strong genetical evidence. It is in fact so much easier to understand and to visualize evolution in terms of population changes rather than as taking place through single individuals (or pairs of individuals). Thus a common opinion among evolutionists probably favours polygenism without in any way insisting on it.

We may mention some representative views of human evolutionists. No one really questions the uniqueness of man as contrasted with animals ; his intellectuality and his power of reflection alone assure this. P. Teilhard de Chardin SJ described the evolutionary change from animal to human as crossing the threshold of reflection which is the beginning of the process of hominization, or as an instantaneous and individual ' leap from instinct to thought '. He wrote : ' A mutation therefore as fundamental as that of thought, a mutation which gives its specific impetus to the whole human group, could not in my opinion have appeared half-way up the stalk. It dominates the whole edifice. Its place must therefore be *beneath* every recognizable verticil in the unattainable depths of the peduncle and thus beneath those creatures which (however pre-hominid in cranial structure) are already clearly situated *above* the point of origin and blossoming of the race.'

Teilhard seems to imply that crossing the threshold of reflection is so great a step that it could have occurred only *once* and that at the very beginning of the human stem before any branches were formed. There is no half-way house between reflection and non-reflection. In the biological sense alone a change of this kind is enormous. All evolutionary knowledge indicates that major break-throughs of this kind are not repeated. The chances of the conditions appearing again in order to bring about such changes are so astronomically small as to render it practically impossible. This fact in itself also rules out the probability of parallel evolution.

Teilhard's statement also implies that human beings were fully human from the very first moment of their conception and appearance ; forms such as the Pithecanthropoids and perhaps even the Australopithecines could be completely human. Thus the only true link between man and the lower animals would be a structural one. Nevertheless the fossil men always appear in a crowd, as it were, giving no indication, even a distant one, of the mutation, or mutations, which caused hominization. Teilhard therefore maintained that the problem of strict monogenism eludes science by its very nature. *The missing link in fact does not exist.* Though biologically probable, this conclusion does not of course deny monogenism ; it merely emphasizes the difficulty inherent in human evolutionary studies of finding the point at which man became man. Vallois (1957) considered that all the known hominids show an undoubted monophyletic origin and Arambourg (1948) thought that speculations on polygenism were outmoded. Le Gros Clark (1955) considered that polyphyletic origin was possible for the different races of man but he did not think it very probable. Consensus of opinion therefore is probably towards at least a monophyletic origin for man, that is, an origin from one group which may mean from one or from many individuals.

The theological difficulty involved in a polygenic or multiple origin theory is chiefly bound up with the doctrine of Original Sin. Pius XII pointed that there are inherent difficulties in reconciling this theory with Original Sin. Original Sin is the *result* of an actual sin. It is not an *act* committed by human beings on conception. It is a spiritual deprivation suffered by the race. The doctrine is an extremely difficult one, and rests on NT more than on OT teaching. But Christian tradition has always understood certain passages of St Paul and the practice from apostolic times of infant baptism as implying it (*see* ORIGINAL SIN).

Another possibility exists. Pre-Adamites may have existed, creatures perhaps like *Pithecanthropus* ; and Adam may have descended from a pair of these. This would require that all the Pre-Adamites ceased to exist after Adam's time and left no descendants. Some of the human fossil record at least indicates that ancient men and pre-hominids were widely scattered, and so the Pre-Adamites could also have been widely scattered. It is extremely difficult to see how they could all have perished by natural means in a short space of time leaving no descendants whatsoever. There seems to be little evidence to support the Pre-Adamite theory on this basis.

On the other hand, if we accept Adam as the first human being of all, and allow that genetics favours evolution within a population, there is still no serious genetical or evolutionary reason why all men should not have descended from a single pair. In many respects this is what biologists would expect. A further biological explanation of the origin of Adam and Eve may then be given. Perhaps part of the difficulty in visualizing this lies in our psychological conditioning and in our imagination. We tend to conceive of Adam as a man just like ourselves—we think of him in terms of Adonis rather than in terms of a *Pithecanthropus*. There is no real reason why Adam should have been exactly the same as ourselves in physique, since undoubtedly evolution has taken place within the human family and even within

Homo sapiens. If we can rid our minds of preconceived ideas then perhaps we can speculate objectively on the possible and tenable biological mode of origin of Adam.

Biologically the only way in which Adam could be produced is by means of sexual reproduction. This implies the prior existence of male and female gametes, or sex cells, which fuse. We know of no way other than this which occurs in human beings, or in higher animals. We are aware that both gametes, and even undifferentiated somatic cells, as tissue-culture experiments show, contain the potentialities of the individual. Human parthenogenetic development of the egg is theoretically possible but probably unknown in nature. (The Virgin Birth is of course miraculous.) If such reproduction happened naturally, the resultant individual would be female, not male. A male could only arise parthenogenetically from a male gamete and, because of the nature of the embryonic process which takes place in the uterus, male parthenogenesis in human beings is practically impossible. In any case the male gamete has to be deposited within the female first.

We may try to express the situation in modern terms. The fossil record indicates that scattered about part of the Afro-Asian Continental mass there were small populations of various kinds of man-like creatures. Perhaps in one of these populations mutations began to arise which gradually pushed the physical appearance of the creatures concerned away from the animal type towards the human type and which at the same time set in motion the development of the brain. If these mutations were recessive and small, according to modern population genetics, they could be present as heterozygotes for a long time before showing any major effects, but they would gradually accumulate and become dominant, ousting the original and more animal-like types. Thus a small population of man-like creatures would arise concentrated in one local and relatively small geographical area or even ecological niche. For similar mutations and a similar process of emergence under identical conditions to arise in other populations would be statistically extremely unlikely, if not impossible.

But once the specifically human characteristics had become dominant, the evolution of the population could have progressed rapidly until creatures very near to man physically had arisen. At this stage perhaps the last mutations necessary for the production of a physical man would have been brought together in the sex cells. If these gametes were acting as instrumental causes, then, through the divine action at the moment of conception the zygote could have received a human soul. Adam, his soul apart, would have arisen through a normal evolutionary channel. Such a picture does not necessarily introduce a gap into the evolutionary picture ; the laws of unity have not been upset. We can say that from amoeba to physical man, as it were, the process of evolution was complete and continuous. God could have willed the process to stop there, but instead something new was created, something which was not a part of the biological process occurred. Something was gratuitously *added* to the evolutionary process in that God created a human spiritual soul which had no biological connections with any organism previous to that which it now informed, in much the same way that every specially created human soul informs every product of a human biological conception, or fusion of gametes, without introducing a gap into the biological process of reproduction.

Adam would then have been born among a population of individuals much like himself physically but who lacked the essential human attributes of reflection and spirituality essential to human nature. Even speech could only have come gradually when there were people to talk to, nor is the reflective quality in man immediately evident. Some theologians would be disconcerted by such a method of origin because they see difficulties in the upbringing of a child by animal-like creatures. Though it would be difficult for us to imagine a 20th-cent. baby in the midst of apes, is it so difficult to imagine a baby in the midst of a *Pithecanthropus* population or a *Pithecanthropus* baby in the midst of Australopithecines? Some people claim that *Pithecanthropus* was a pre-hominid rather than a hominid; it would seem to be no more intrinsically unlikely to imagine a baby among such creatures than among Early Stone Age men. In such a population a primitive human baby, who had yet to discover speech and reflection, could be nurtured and grow up long before he had the mental ability to realize his specifically human faculties which made him different from his companions. Eventually, of course, his spiritual soul would exert its influence, giving him feelings and insights enabling him to 'walk with God' as he developed, until he really realized that he was 'alone' and needed a companion like himself (Gen 2:18).

Perhaps the biological origin of Adam occurred in some way such as this; but a greater difficulty arises in trying to explain the biological origin of Eve. Again we shall attempt a reasonable biological explanation based on genetic and reproductive facts as known. Part of the difficulty in explaining the origin of Eve lies in the fact that many early writers and commentators accepted literally that Eve was actually formed from a rib of Adam. But this is not now generally held; many authors have seen that the sense here is metaphorical. Cajetan, for instance, in the 16th cent., held such a view. The miraculous origin of Eve from a rib of Adam is not a *de fide* doctrine. The Biblical Commission was careful in its phraseology over this matter: *formatio primae mulieris ex primo homine* which may mean merely that there was a very intimate connection between Adam and Eve. Thus the field is left open for discussion as to the nature of the connection.

Many suggestions have been made, some on rather fanciful and biologically unsound lines. For instance, it has been suggested that Eve arose from one of Adam's chromosomes. But one chromosome does not contain the potentialities of a human being in any sense. Again it has been suggested that Eve devel-

oped from one cell of Adam. We have already mentioned the difficulties arising in human parthenogenesis; in all such explanations the further difficulty how Adam could nurture an embryo arises. For male cells to develop into a female would in any case also require an *ex nihilo* creation of an X chromosome. Biologically speaking, so long as a man remains male he is quite unable to produce, directly and unaided, another human being, male or female. Dr Messenger gave a parthenogenetic explanation of Eve's origin, but he did not really believe in his own explanation. M. Paquier (cf. *Theology and Evolution* [1949] 144) considered that an early division of the embryo of Adam could have produced Eve in much the same way as identical twins. Generally, however, identical twins are produced simultaneously in the very first stages of division of the fertilized egg. One twin does not have preference over the other, although, of course, they are born successively. If this occurred, it would be just as true to say that Adam was produced from Eve. Again, identical twins by their very nature are always of the same sex. If they were not, a further difficulty would arise in explaining the difference. It is clear that such explanations raise more biological problems than they solve.

There is, however, another approach to Genesis, if we take a metaphorical explanation of Eve's origin. We may note that the writer, or writers, of Genesis were not actually present at the Creation and all we would expect of them is that they expressed the Divine truths concerned in the light and language of their own knowledge and experience which, admittedly, was not advanced in a biological sense. In Gen 3:20 we read: 'And Adam called the name of his wife Eve; because she was the mother of all the living.' In the original language Eve's name was *Hawwah*, which is connected with the Hebrew verb *hayah* meaning 'to be'. *Hawwah* is not a proper name, but rather describes Eve as the mother of the human race in the same way that Adam really means 'man' and is likewise connected to the word *adamah* meaning 'earth'. In Gen 1:27 we read: 'And God created man to his own image: to the image of God he created him. Male and female he created them.' There would seem to be no suggestion here that man was created first and woman later. But Gen 2:21 gives a fuller account as follows: 'Then the Lord God cast a deep sleep upon Adam: and when he was fast asleep, he took one of his ribs and filled up flesh for it. And the Lord God built the rib which he took from Adam into a woman: and brought her to Adam. And Adam said: this is now bone of my bones and flesh of my flesh: she shall be called woman because she was taken out of man.'

We may note that Adam's companion must be very near to him, suited to him and not a *mere* animal. At the time these passages were written, women in general were held in contempt, fit only to be toilers for men, but verses 23 and 24 clearly reverse this view of the very low status of woman by showing how close Eve was to Adam—she was part of him, she had the same nature as he had. Thus the essential truth here would seem to be that man and woman are equal in dignity and made for each other. Adam and Eve are very closely connected to each other and the Biblical narrative expresses this by the metaphor of the creation of Eve from Adam's *body* (*see also* Eve).

And now, bearing this in mind, we may give an explanation of the formation of Eve which is biologically sound. In seeking to explain natural phenomena St Thomas Aquinas (*Summa* 1a:105:7:@2) cautions us against an appeal to the miraculous unless such is really required. It may be possible that Eve was formed in the most natural way of all, that is, by the ordinary method of sexual reproduction. First, we must acknowledge that, if we accept Adam and Eve as the first progenitors of all human beings, ' marriages' must have been between very close relations for the first few generations of human beings. What we call incest must in the nature of things have been inevitable and natural, however unnatural we may consider it in later times. If then, as we have supposed, Adam was the product of pre-hominid parents whose gametes acted as instrumental causes, and if he grew up among these pre-hominids very near to him in the physical sense, then he need not at first have been physically repulsed by the more advanced near-human females among them and thus he could have had a child by one of them. Later, perhaps even before such a child was born, a *psychic isolation mechanism* may have then arisen which raised a psychological barrier between Adam and the creatures amongst whom he lived, preventing him from associating with any other of these pre-hominids. The child he had produced would then have been the product of a fully-formed human male gamete and a near-human female egg which perhaps again carried the final mutations for the production of a human being. As a single gamete itself contains all the potentialities of the offspring, the child would have been human in the true and full sense of the term, generated directly from Adam in the most natural and intimate way, and perhaps could have received a human soul in the way we all do. Such a child may have been Eve. We may also note that such a close union of Adam with Eve would, in the biological sense, enhance the specifically human qualities of their descendants particularly in the first few generations.

Again Eve could have arisen in another natural way which involved reproduction. We have already mentioned that Adam could have arisen from the fusion of two near-human gametes carrying the final mutations necessary for the production of physical man which were in their own turn produced by advanced near-human pre-hominids. Such gametes carrying final mutations would be potentially human. They would have arisen in each sex as the result of a single meiotic division in which the chromosomes segregated in the normal way. (In the normal way, if a mother carries, shall we say, factors Aa, when meiosis is completed four nuclei are produced, two with A and two with a.) Hence, in the hypothetical case we are considering, four gametes would be produced by each parent, each carrying the necessary reciprocal final mutations for physical human nature. The female gametes would each carry an X sex chromosome while two of the male gametes would carry an X sex chromosome each, and two would carry a Y chromosome each. It is possible that a double fertilization occurred between these potential human gametes to produce one zygote carrying XY chromosomes and one zygote carrying XX chromosomes. As fertilization is a random process there is no reason why the XY, or male, combination should not have been produced first in time. The final result would be the birth of fraternal twins, one boy and one girl. These children could have been Adam and Eve. In this natural explanation, however, Eve is not perhaps as close physically to Adam as she would be in the former explanation, but inasmuch as Adam and Eve would here be carrying X and Y chromosomes of common descent they may have been close enough to enable Adam to say that Eve is ' bone of my bones flesh of my flesh'. The process envisaged here is completely different to M. Paquier's idea of the formation of identical twins mentioned earlier. In conclusion we would like to state that however fanciful on the surface these explanations may seem, fundamentally they are not biologically unsound and in the hypothesis that Adam and Eve did arise in a natural manner, they do not unduly stretch our imagination ; at the same time they emphasize the uniqueness of Adam and Eve and their closeness which Genesis would seem to require.

V Evolution in the Future. Some Views of Teilhard de Chardin. Some writers have attempted to systematize evolution and extract from it the utmost meaning ; we need only mention Henri Bergson, Sir J. S. Huxley and Pierre Teilhard de Chardin SJ in modern times. In some ways the most advanced of all these views are those of Teilhard who certainly attempted to give a lofty meaning to evolution on Christian lines. His views, which are now becoming generally disseminated, have aroused a great deal of controversy chiefly among theologians and philosophers. It is appropriate therefore, that we should finish this article by outlining some of the chief speculative views of this writer which have a bearing on theology or philosophy but without in any way attempting to give a critique.

Teilhard attempted to give a view of man as a phenomenon who has a place in the world because he is *the* product of the processes occurring in that world. This phenomenological approach, looked at from the point of view of one who considers that evolution is the basic natural process in the cosmos, forces one to seek an explanation of the nature of man in evolutionary terms. This explanation, far from being materialistic, ultimately converges on the essence of man's spirituality and gives greater cogency and urgency to the Christian phenomenon of man as a creature made for union with God under the stimulus of love. Teilhard looks at man first from the outside but seeks to find meaning for him in respect to his 'within'. This is done against a conscious background of Faith and of an understanding of the purpose of man's existence. Theologically man is made for God and biologically this is shown by his evolution towards an omega and towards the Omega. Thus biologically Teilhard's views become complementary to philosophical and theological explanations about the nature and purpose of man. A few days before he died in 1955 Teilhard wrote a synopsis of his ideas (printed as an appendix to *The Future of Man*, 1964) which represents his mature evolutionary thought based upon the Christocentric doctrine of 1 Cor 15:26–8.

Teilhard reverses older concepts of evolution whereby human evolution (anthropogenesis) was regarded as a by-product of biological evolution (biogenesis) which itself was a by-product of energetic evolution (cosmogenesis). He gives full play and importance to the consequences of the advent of reflection into the living world and of socialization in man (psychogenesis). Greater changes have taken place during human evolution since man learnt his powers, than in all the millenia before he evolved, and, clearly, the last hundred years or so have shown the immense power and significance of human thought and action at a vastly accelerated pace. Mankind is on the move, great forces are acting on him, of which some people are aware. Psychogenesis is not an epiphenomenon imposed by chance on the natural world ; human evolution is not a sub-effect but a super-effect of organic and cosmic evolution. It is the culmination of evolution in its penultimate phase proceeding inevitably to a final consummation. Whereas the chief characteristics of cosmogenesis and biogenesis are emergence and divergence, in human evolution convergence, a new factor, has developed, brought about by the sheer force of thinking matter which of necessity has now become spiritual, substantially and effectually. Evolution therefore is now emergent, divergent and convergent in its human totalization. Thus it is vitalized and intensified to the nth degree.

The law of unity on which science is based finds its complete expression in man at this stage of history. As Teilhard wrote : ' Unquestionably and in spite (or, rather at the price) of fearful tensions, the human world is decidedly caught today and for ever, in an irresistibly tightening vortex of unification. Economically, technically, mentally, we are forced (by the very force of each new idea and of each new invention—or under the impact of each new conflict) to become more and more one : one materially— and one spiritually.' Teilhard considers that this unitary process is the natural end-result of (*a*) cerebration (shown in the animal world by a constant and deterministic increase and development of nervous tissue until the human brain resulted, leading to an equally constant increase in complexity-consciousness) and, (*b*) socialization (foreshadowed in the animal world and instinctively developed among some groups of animals but reaching its real expression only within the human family). The totality of thought in the world handed on from

generation to generation by education, experience and communication has produced what may be called a new envelope surrounding living things, the *noosphere*, encircling the biosphere. The noosphere is at once the reason for, and gives impetus to, the increasing organization in the complex process of human evolution. Inasmuch as Teilhard sees the physical world dissipating itself by the release of energy and its fixation through entropy, he also sees the counteracting and counterbalancing force of re-converging thought in the noosphere setting the direction, and the pace, of man's future evolution. Man can only expand outwardly over the earth (and perhaps to some nearer celestial bodies) which limits his physical development, but his evolutionary convergence occurs by a turning-in on himself both personally and collectively in socialization, leading him personally to a centre and also collectively to a centre of centres. Teilhard wrote : ' To become ultra-reflexive (that is, " ultra-human ") by reaching some stage of mono-culturation—or else to resign and to die on the way—this, aside from any temperamental or philosophical considerations, must on purely scientific grounds be regarded as the biological fate of man.'

Within the noosphere this evolution is thus striving towards higher consciousness through complexity, and Teilhard considers it will ultimately die out unless its intensification shows unmistakably that man is really moving *somewhere* and *for ever*. Thus, by extending evolution on the one hand to include the cosmos, so that a single process appears evident in which gradually enlarging self-consciousness is throughout the guiding and decisive factor and, on the other hand, prolonging evolution within mankind, which thus becomes totally personal, collective and super-organized until consciousness is totally reflexive upon itself (super-centrated), Teilhard seeks to transcend death for *Homo sapiens*. This is accomplished by considering that there exists a supreme pole of attraction, the centre of convergence, the centre of centres, which is perceived as drawing man irresistibly to itself. This centre is the Omega point. As planetization (expansion of the noosphere on a planetary scale) continues, as the ' within ' and consciousness develop, spirituality is increased and can find its home only in a supreme point from which all things emerge. But man is still free ; he can choose to be or not to be. Long before Teilhard had synthesized his ideas, drawn from phenomena, of the existence of an Omega point, he had had ' mystical ' intuitions of the Incarnation not only as the Redemptive Measure, but also as engendering and fulfilling the physical and ' spiritual ' necessities of evolution (1916). Man is freely but yet of necessity drawn to Omega by natural cosmic processes, and he is drawn to Christ, from whom all things flow, by faith, grace and love. It was inevitable therefore that Teilhard should identify Omega with Christ and find the hope for the future and the fulfilment of man in the Divine God-Man who is ' All in All '. Even in 1916 (in *La Vie cosmique*) Teilhard could write : ' Since the birth of Jesus, since His growth, death and resurrection, the whole world continues to develop, because Christ has not yet completely formed Himself. He has not yet gathered to Himself the last folds of that robe of flesh and of love which is made up for Him by the faithful. The mystical Christ has not yet reached full stature. In the extension of this development is found the secret spring of all created activity. . . . Christ is the term even of the natural evolution of creatures.'

Thus Teilhard sought to counteract materialist evolutionary views and to show that speculative evolution leads to God. Science and faith converge on God, the Reality. He has attempted and, in some large measure, succeeded in giving us a great synthesis of biological and general scientific knowledge affecting us at vital points. It is not surprising, therefore, that Teilhard has many critics, but he himself was the first to acknowledge that his views needed correcting, clarifying and extending, and he left it to others to do this. For his purely scientific views there need be little contact with theology, but it is with his speculative ideas, drawn from his scientific conclusions, such as we have given above, that Teilhard has something to say to theologians. The power of Teilhard's appeal to the intellect would seem to force theologians to state the possible errors and inadequacies in his system in the synthetic and forward-looking spirit which Teilhard has shown is possible in evolutionary biology, and this task would have great value in bringing theologian, philosopher and scientist closer together to the ultimate benefit of humanity and to a deeper understanding of our ultimate purpose.

Bibliography. C. Arambourg, *La Genèse de l'humanité* (1948) ; H. de Dorlodot, *Darwinism and Catholic Thought* (1925) ; P. G. Fothergill, *Historical Aspects of Organic Evolution* (1952) ; the same, *Evolution and Christians* (1961) ; H. J. Johnson, *The Bible and the Early History of Mankind* (1947²) ; the same, 'The Origin of Man', in CR 41 (1956) 395–405, 477–84, 534–42 ; *H. Levy, *A Philosophy for Modern Man* (1938) ; K. Mather, 'Polygenic Inheritance and Natural Selection', in *Biological Review* 18 (1943) 36–44 ; E. C. Messenger, *Evolution and Theology* (1931) ; the same, *Theology and Evolution* (1949) ; *H. F. Osborn, *From the Greeks to Darwin* (1924) ; J. Piveteau, *Traité de paléontologie*, VII : Primates, Paléontologie humaine (1957) ; *G. G. Simpson, *The Meaning of Evolution* (1960) ; *Sir W. Le Gros Clark, *The Fossil Evidence for Human Evolution* (1955) ; J. Motherway sj, 'Theological Opinion on the Evolution of Man', in TS 5 (1944) 189–221 ; C. Vollert sj, 'Human Evolution and Theological Implications', in *Proceedings of the Catholic Theological Society of America*, VI (1951) 122–45 ; *D. Lack, *Evolutionary Theory and Christian Belief* (1957) ; P. Teilhard de Chardin sj, *The Phenomenon of Man* (1959) ; the same, 'The Antiquity and World-expansion of Human Culture', in *Man's Role in Changing the World*, edited by W. L. Thomas (1956) ; the same, *On the Biological Meaning of Human Socialisation* (address of 15 May 1952) ; the same, *The Future of Man* (1964) ; *S.

Tax (editor), *Evolution after Darwin* (2 vols., 1960) ; H. Vallois, *Fossil Man* (Eng. trans. 1957) ; Sir S. Zuckermann, 'Correlation of Change in Evolution of Higher Primates', in *Evolution as a Process* (1954, edited by J. S. Huxley, A. E. Hardy and E. Ford).

P. G. F.

EXTREME UNCTION This title is used, rather than last anointing, merely for convenience of reference, as most adult readers will still know the sacrament under that name. The Council of Trent called it *sacramentum exeuntium* (the sacrament for those leaving this life) and described it as the consummation of a Christian life (D 910 and 907), though it is truly a sacrament for the sick as well as for the dying : as Vatican Council II has emphasized (AAS 56 [1964] 119) by saying that it is not reserved for the hour of death.

Christ promised (in Mk 16:19) that His apostles would impose hands on the sick for their recovery. This power could have been casual and miraculous, or else sacramental and ordinary, and the preliminary mission of the disciples described in Mk 6:12–13 seems to have produced cures that could be called miraculous, while Trent (D 908) was content to regard the episode as a foreshadowing of the sacrament. This article will consider (I) the evidence for the existence of the sacrament drawn from Jas 5:14–15, (II) the patristic evidence, chiefly from the early liturgies, for a twofold blessing of oil for anointing the sick, (III) the instances of anointing which can be found in early lives, (IV) the gradual emphasis on the administration of this sacrament to the dying, (V) problems of its minister, and finally (VI), the scholastic controversy about its effects.

(I) The use of Jas 5:14–15 to justify the practice of anointing the sick is obviously dependent on the acceptance of that epistle as canonical Scripture (*see* CANON OF SCRIPTURE). In the East there was a general acceptance of it, but in the West it is absent from the Muratori fragment and from the (North African) Latin canon published by Mommsen, and in some quarters it may have fallen under suspicion for its Jewish character. Origen (*hom.* 2:4 on Lev ; GCS 29:296) is the first to cite the text and he sees in it a justification for the forgiving of sins by penance. When one takes into account Origen's exegetical habits and his dislike of the literal sense, and when one sees the controversial value of such an application of the text in those days of rigorism, it becomes quite unsafe to conclude from his handling of the text that he knew nothing of its connection with the practice of anointing the sick.

Appeals to the text in sermons where Christians are being urged to abandon their superstitious resort to magic in time of illness is common from the 4th cent. onwards. The first known passage is in the works of Isaac of Antioch (edited by Bickell, I:187) who belongs to the later part of the 4th cent. He is followed by John Mandakuni, Patriarch of Armenia (405–87) in his *Letter* 26 (edited by M. Schmid in 1871) : 'It is only through medicine, by burning and cutting, that you can allay your pain. And still more do you despise the graces of God, for the Apostle says : Is any man sick among you . . .' (op. cit. 222). The patriarch borrows freely from Ephrem and it is possible that this mode of argument was developed by Ephrem himself. It is found also in Cyril of Alexandria (*De adoratione* 6 ; PG 68:472) and will be met with later in Caesarius of Arles.

Pope Innocent I in his letter to Decentius of Gubbio (*ep.* 25:6 ; PL 20:560, of 19 March 416) quotes the text in the Old Latin version and says that it should be understood to refer to the faithful who fall sick and who may be anointed with sacred oil of chrism which has been blessed by a bishop. This letter soon passed into the canonical collections and established a norm for Latin Christianity. Decentius had asked whether bishops could anoint, since the text spoke of priests, and Innocent replies that not only *sacerdotes* but all Christians could *use* this oil. He may have meant no more than ' have the benefit of it ', but his words are not clear. The 8th-cent. epitome of canons in the Lucca MS. condensed Innocent's letter into the sentence : ' It is lawful for a priest to visit the sick man and anoint him with chrism '.[1] This shows that the anointing was not considered necessary to salvation but seems to take for granted that the minister would be a priest.

Caesarius of Arles was tireless in preaching about the need for this anointing, to exclude the resort to pagan magic. In his *serm.* 13 (*Corpus christianorum* 103:66) he speaks of the sick man going to the priest and asking for the oil that he might anoint himself, thus fulfilling the advice of Scripture. In *Serm.* 19 (ibid. 90) he seems to envisage the anointing being done in church by the priest, where the sick man might have priests and deacons praying over him and thus not only regain his health but also have remission of his sins. In *serm.* 50 (ibid. 225) he cries out : ' Anoint yourselves with blessed oil, take the Eucharist of Christ. Doing this, you will regain not only health of body but also health of soul '.[2] Here the first command might seem to imply that the patient anointed himself, but as the taking of the Eucharist required the ministry of a priest, so also in all probability did the anointing. In *serm.* 52 (ibid. 232) the language is less ambiguous : ' Instead of being anointed with blessed oil by priests, as the Scripture says, they do the opposite '.[3] The *Ordo ad visitandum et perungendum infirmum* in the Mozarabic ritual (Férotin, *Liber ordinum*, col. 72) bids the priest pray that, as he touches the sick man with oil at the command of the Apostle, the mercy of God may be shown to the sufferer. This ritual was in use *c.* A.D. 650–700, and is a sufficient commentary on what Caesarius had urged in the previous century. One must note, however, that the Spanish prayer introduces the idea that the sick man is near death : ' His sickness bends him towards his end and his declining

strength is trailing off towards extinction ',[1] says the prayer. One hopes the patient was unconscious while it was being said.

An Irish commentary on the epistle of James (PL Supplement, 3:81), which was compiled in the 8th cent. but was later taken for the work of Hilary of Arles, discusses the text at length. The sickness, it decides, is the sickness of sin. When one is burdened by thoughts, he should intercede for himself, but when he has done a sinful deed, he should ask that prayer be made in the language of the Churches. On the word *ungentes* the comment is that this has been the custom of the Church up to the present. By oil the pardon of mercy is symbolized.[2] The prayer of faith that is to save the sick man is glossed as the consent of the whole church, in obedience to Jn 16:23. Bede in commenting on Mk 6:13 (PL 92:188) may have had this Irish commentary before him to lend substance to his assertion that it was by apostolic tradition that the Church anointed the sick. Bede couples with the sick those who are possessed, and this was inevitable at a time when all medicine was psychosomatic and when sin was commonly allowed to be a cause of disease.

The Monophysite churches which separated from unity at Chalcedon took with them the same tradition of interpreting Jas 5:14–15. Severus of Antioch (*hom.* 79 ; PO 20:230) is quite emphatic in this sense and in the canons of James of Edessa (canon 14 in the edition of C. Kayser [1886] 17) it is laid down that the priest who visits the sick must take with him the ' oil of prayer and of grace ' and that it will not do to go with an empty chalice (to perform a *missa sicca* at the bedside). The distinction here made between the oil of prayer and what is called oil of unction bears upon the liturgical evidence for blessings of oil, which must now be considered.

II A twofold blessing of oil is provided for by Serapion in his prayer-book (5 and 17) ; one is for oil and water brought to church by the faithful, which they then take away to use (and to drink) in their own homes, while the other is for an oil that will be concerned in the forgiving of sins. This latter is headed : ' Prayer in regard to oil of the sick or for bread or for water ', and in its text asks that ' the oil may become to those who are being anointed with it, or are partaking of these Thy creatures, for a throwing-off of every sickness. . . .' Bede's life of St Cuthbert gives evidence that bread and water were taken to a sick man when he was anointed (PL 94:771) and the St Gall sacramentary (MS. 350, published by G. Manz in 1939) has prayers for blessing such bread and water for an anointing. The link between Egypt, St Gall and Wearmouth is not so far to seek when one considers the dependence of Keltic monasticism on Egyptian.

John Chrysostom (*hom.* 32:6 on Mt ; PG 57:385) illustrates the superiority of Church to home by the fact that the oil which the priest uses for anointing

---

[1] Presbytero liceat visitare infirmum et ungere chrisma.

[2] Oleo vos benedicto perungite, eucharistiam Christi accipite. Haec si facitis, non solum corporis sed etiam animae sanitatem recipietis.

[3] Cum, sicut scriptum est, oleo benedicto a presbyteris deberent perungere. . . e contrario faciunt.

[1] Quem languor curvat ad exitum et virium defectio iam pertrahit ad occasum. . . .

[2] Hoc usque hodie in consuetudine ecclesiae venit ; per oleum misericordiae indulgentia designatur.

the sick there is better than what the faithful take home to use for themselves. One may suppose that, just as the Church developed the use of holy water alongside the water of baptism, even so there grew up a usage of blessing oil for home use alongside the blessing of the ' oil of prayer ' which the priest used for the sick. Criteria for distinguishing between the two could be found in the mention of forgiveness of sins in the prayer for blessing the priest's oil, or in an appeal to the text from Jas 5:14 in the same. A clear instance of a blessing for the inferior oil would be that in the Mozarabic liturgy (Férotin, *Liber ordinum*, 69) for oil that is blessed on the feast of Cosmas and Damian.

The blessing in Hippolytus (in Horner's version of the Ethiopic, 141) is more difficult to assess. The oil is offered by the faithful and is blessed during Mass with this formula : ' Having sanctified oil, Thou shalt grant to all who are anointed or receive it that with which Thou didst anoint priests and prophets ; and in like manner strengthen those and all who taste, and sanctify them who receive it '. In the Latin version the prayer asks for health (twice) and does not mention sanctification at all. It is more likely that oil for home usage is in view, but it is not easy to say whether the Latin should have here priority over the Ethiopic version. What is more important is that in the fragmentary ritual which follows the *Traditio apostolica* in the Ethiopic (Horner, 168 and 176) are two versions of a prayer headed : ' Prayer of unction of oil which the chief priest consecrates for those who receive the washing and *for sick believers* '. The prayer itself is in substance that which is found later in the *Gelasianum* (Mohlberg, 382) for the blessing of oil of the sick, a prayer which survives today for use on Maundy Thursday. It runs : ' Stretch out Thy invisible hand upon the fruit of this olive with which Thou didst anoint the priests and the prophets ; and Thou hast given power to it with Thine own hand that it may be to those who are anointed with it for healing and benefit in all disease and every sickness and for extermination of every Satanic adversary, and make it the unction of Thy grace for remission of sin to those to whom has been given Thy Holy Spirit. . . .' It must be noticed that it is only the second of these two prayers which has the reference to forgiveness of sins, the first prayer being somewhat ambiguous on the point. The same prayer has turned up recently in an Egyptian *euchologion* (that is published in PO 28:393), the MS. of which was written in the 10th cent., and here the oil is described as ' oil of healing and of pardon by the grace of God '. The Hippolytean form of the prayer goes back to the 4th cent. and the Latin form (in the *Gelasianum*) is probably not much later, as it calls the oil *chrisma*, which would not be possible after *c.* A.D. 450.

The comparison of oil of the sick with the oil for the anointing of priests and prophets (in the OT), which this Hippolytean prayer makes, has been studied in detail by J. Hanssens (in OCA 155:416–20), who finds a first instance of it in the *Didascalia* (Connolly, 146). One might add that Aphrahat

(*demonstratio* 23 ; P Syr II:10) has it too, for he speaks of the fruit of the olive, ' in which is the sign of the hallowing of life by which Christians are made perfect, and priests and kings and prophets ; it lightens darkness, it anoints the sick and with its hidden hallowing it brings back the penitent sinner '. Syria and Egypt thus provide early ritual evidence for the blessing of an oil of the sick which was also a means of grace. How the prayer came to be used in the West is not very clear, but it may well have come by the liturgical trade-routes that operate from Egypt and Syria to Spain, Ireland and Anglo-Saxon England. [The Coptic prayer for blessing μύρον, added to *Didache* 10:7, is not meant for oil of the sick.]

Another ritual form, suggesting that the sick man is being prepared for a final combat with the devil, is found widely scattered in the West. It is in the St Gall sacramentary (MS. 350), in the *Missal* of Robert of Jumièges, in the *Leofric Missal*, the *Lanalet* and *Fulda Pontificals* and even in the Ambrosian rite. ' I anoint thee with blessed oil that as a soldier anointed with oil thou mayst be ready for combat to overcome the hosts of the air '.[1]

This phrase seems to be a pair of ruined hexameters and may therefore come from an Irish source, for versified blessings are usually Keltic. In the Greek churches (according to Symeon of Thessalonica, PG 156:206) it was customary to bless the oil of the sick on the Wednesday in Holy Week, a day which was looked upon by them and by the ancient Jerusalem church as the anniversary of the anointing of Christ at Bethany, an anointing done for His burial (Mt 26:12 ; Mk 14:8). This association can be shown to reach back into patristic times (for the Jerusalem church read Mt 26:2–16 on that day), and it might be held responsible for the linking of the sacrament of the sick with the approach of death. Eusebius (if he be in fact the writer), in a work that is extant only in a Latin version (*De resurrectione* 2: PG 24:1111), says while commenting on the passage from Mt 26 : ' Oil is poured on those who are on the point of death '.[2] His comment on Isai 25:6–7 (PG 24:268) is in harmony with this and is certainly genuine, but it is less clear. Ephrem (*Carmina Nisibena* 73) : ' Seal with the cross your dying friends that they may escape the second death ', is sometimes cited for the same idea, but does not mention oil. The fact that Christ spoke just before His death of the approach of Satan who had no rights over Him (Jn 14:30) would naturally foster the desire among Christians to have spiritual protection for their last hours. It may be that in some of the commentaries on this passage the clue to the origin of this theological speculation will be found.

III Instances of anointing in early lives are hard to assess. Rufinus in his version of the *Historia monachorum* (PL 21:445) tells of the monks of Nitria that they never met save for Mass ; when one of

---

[1] Ut more militis uncti praeparatus ad luctam aerias possis superare catervas.

[2] Immittitur enim gentibus qui moriuntur unguentum.

them was noticed to be absent, the others would go to his cell one by one, bringing some present that might gratify the sick man. This does not envisage anointing, but the very next sentence says that there was another exception to their rule of silence, namely the need for instruction, ' when like athletes poised for a contest they are anointed with the comforting preparation of discourse '.[1] This striking metaphor, which was not in the Greek that Rufinus had to translate, may have been suggested to him by the thought that they were after all anointed when sick, but that his text did not mention it.

Many famous men put off their baptism until death approached; the Emperor Constantine was not the only example. In such cases there could be no question of anointing. Elsewhere one finds mention of the laying on of hands on the sick; Augustine is said never to have refused to go and pray over the sick, laying his hands on them [2] (*Vita* 27 ; PL 32:56). One cannot be sure that he used oil for this, but it is not excluded. Ambrose (*De poenitentia* 1:8: 36 ; CSEL 73:136) turns on the Novatians with an argument from parity of cases. Why do they practise laying on of hands for the sick, while refusing it to penitent sinners ?

It is evident from the lives of saints that lay people and even women used to anoint the sick with oil. This is related of St Geneviève (AA.SS Jan. 1:142) but the writer (who may have been a contemporary of the saint) is careful to point out that she always had oil blessed by a bishop, being reduced to working a miracle when this was not available. It was the thesis of Puller's book that lay people gradually lost their right to anoint between 716 and 850, by which time the priests had established a monopoly. He took no account of the two oils, one for home usage (which was obviously used by lay people) and the other (oil of pardon) for priests only. The story told by Theodoret (*Historia religiosa* 8 ; PG 82:1376) about one Aphrahat (hardly the Persian sage, as the date of the event is 373–8) who cured the Emperor's horse by anointing it with oil when it was suffering from a painful illness, is a difficulty for those who want to maintain that all use of oil for the sick is the sacrament. Theodoret says that the oil was blessed just prior to its being used, and this makes the episode quite distinct from anything like a sacrament.

The incident told in the life of St Martin (Paulinus, *Vita Martini* 2:530 ; CSEL 16:54) is more to the point. At Trier Martin was asked to cure a girl. He prostrates himself in prayer until assured of God's help ; he asks for oil, blesses it, and then anoints the girl limb by limb and she recovers.[3] The wide fame of St Martin must have led to frequent imitation of his act, even had there been no previous habit of using oil for the sick. In many other lives there are

incidents of anointing. St Nepotianus visited Arthemius (MGH, *Scriptores rerum Merovingiarum* I:53) and anointed him, restoring him to health. The words used (*oleo sancto perunctus*) suggest that this was a sacramental use. The life of St Eugene of Ardstraw (AA.SS Aug. 4:627) relates that at the end of his days (at the close of the 6th cent.) he was anointed with blessed oil and his passing was fortified with the Eucharist.[1]

IV The gradual emphasis on the last agony is not easy to trace, and it must be remembered that in the Dark Ages most illnesses were looked upon as likely to be fatal. One text (from *c.* A.D. 450) is found in the *Liber de promissionibus et praedictionibus* (2:29 ; PL 51:803) which is variously ascribed to Quodvultdeus or to Prosper. The Latin is ungrammatical as it stands, but it seems to say that just as the widow of Sarepta (3 Kg 17:7) was helped by a miracle of corn and oil while waiting for the rain from heaven, even so the soul is rewarded which, while the body is failing, loves the chastisement of the Lord and keeps to its nuptial pledge, which is fortified with the sacrament of corn and anointing of oil and which then awaits that rain from heaven which is the grace of God.[2] In the various *visitationes infirmi* one can perhaps detect a change of emphasis as the centuries advance. In the *Stowe Missal* the prayers all ask for a cure, though one of them is open : ' Deign to renew Thy handiwork, either by new strength or by taking him to Thyself ' (*aut in reparando aut in recipiendo*). The prayer is found again in the *Book of Dimma*, but in the 9th-cent. additions of a visitation *ordo* to the *Book of Mulling* it has disappeared and the peace of the sufferer is asked for before his restoration to health.

The *Lanalet Pontifical* (*c.*925–50, but with much earlier material) has a very extensive *visitatio infirmi*, with separate anointings of the senses. Here one can see a wavering between asking for restoration of health and for protection against the assaults of the devil. Familiarity with stories such as that told by Augustine (*De civ. Dei* 22:8 ; CSEL 40:604) of the girl who thwarted the devil by the use of blessed oil would no doubt lead to a ready acceptance of this strengthening for combat as the chief effect of the sacrament. Some of the *ordines* edited by de Clercq from the 9th and 10th cents. have vague phrases (*ut salvus sis in perpetuum, ut salveris aeternaliter*) asking for eternal salvation as the result of anointing, and this change of emphasis in the *lex orandi* is probably more to blame for a similar change in the *lex credendi* than *vice versa*.

A whole philosophy of disease, which was lost to medicine by the Cartesian bifurcation of nature and is only slowly returning in the concept of psychosomatic illness, must be supposed by one who would

---

[1] Velut athletas in agone positos sermonis consolatione perungere.

[2] et si forte ab aegrotantibus ob hoc peteretur ut pro eis inpraesenti Deum rogaret eisque manus imponeret, sine mora pergebat.

[3] Oblato accedit benedictio sancta liquori :
Exim mutati congaudens unguine suci :
Singula contingit medicato chrismate membra.

---

[1] Gravi corripitur infirmitate . . . qua ingruente . . . venerabile corpus sacro oleo ungitur et exitus eius viatico non deficiente communitur.

[2] Sic repletur anima quae, corpore abscedente, Dominum castigantem diligens, unius tori fidem pudico amore custodi sacramento farris et olei unctione munita, secura expectans gratam pluviam cum ei dixerit Dominus : Euge serve bone. . . .

seek to explain the gradual change of viewpoint in the use of this sacrament from physical to spiritual efficacy. Puller's sweeping denial that there had been any thought of forgiveness of sins for the sick man before 850 is contradicted by the ritual prayers and by the very term ' oil of pardon '. Statements such as this of Ambrose (on Lk 14:2 ; CSEL 32:371), that the dropsical man by his bodily disease suffered a heaviness of soul and loss of spiritual ardour, may be matched in many patristic writings. They would all fortify the early medieval theologian in his belief that the spiritual effects of this sacrament were paramount and that the physical cure might or might not follow them, as God willed. The change in the Vulgate reading of Jas 5:15 (*alleviabit* for *allevabit* ; the Old Latin had *suscitabit*) went with this change in viewpoint and seems to have passed unnoticed.

The term *extrema unctio* is said to have been used by Sonnatius, Archbishop of Rheims *c.* 625–31, but the document (PL 80:444) is of very doubtful authenticity. When the medieval Orders such as the Cistercians and Dominicans arrange that their subjects receive anointing *after* viaticum, the purpose of the sacrament as a preparation for the final contest has been assured. William of Auvergne dilates on the subject (*De sacramentis,* 5) and, though Robert of Courçon (*c.* 1200) can still hesitate whether the anointing should come at the beginning of an illness or when the illness has become critical, the majority opinion is clearly that it should be kept for the crisis. The researches of Fr Weisweiler (*see* Bibliography) into the MSS. of the early Scholastics establish this ; he cites a Spanish tract *De VII Sacramentis* which says outright that as baptism was the entry into life, so this is the sacrament for departure.

V The minister of the sacrament was held by the Scholastics to be a priest, on account of the words in Jas 5:14, but some of them had read the life of St Geneviève (see above), and Peter Cantor commented on the story that this custom was now out of fashion ; he does not seem to have suspected that it was a quite different kind of anointing. He does, however, think that deacons might administer the anointing in emergencies (cited by Weisweiler, 539), on the ground that they do not have to bless the oil but merely use it, and that they can administer the Eucharist, even though they cannot say Mass. St Thomas (in *IV Sent.* 23:1:1) was positive that what St Geneviève did was not the conferring of a sacrament, and other similar tales of the Desert Fathers were likewise discounted. He did not think that deacons should confer this sacrament, for the pseudo-Denis said that their function was purgative and in this sacrament there was an illumination of grace. It is unfortunate that St Thomas did not reach the place for treating this sacrament in his *Summa,* for he had by then discarded the theory of the sacraments as remedies for seven wounds of the soul to which he subscribed in the days when he was commenting on the *Sentences* (*see* CAUSALITY OF SACRAMENTS).

The Eastern churches kept to a plurality of ministers in literal obedience to the text of Jas 5:14, but were wont to confer the sacrament in church, and

not in the home of the sick man, even as late as the 14th cent. They found a mystical reason for the use of seven ministers, in that Eliseus (4 Kg 4:35) lay seven times on the body of the child that he was restoring to life : thus Symeon of Thessalonica (PG 155:517).

St Thomas puts forward a singular opinion (in *IV Sent.* 23:2:2) when he claims that the personal merit of the minister contributes much to the efficacy of this sacrament. He is arguing that it should not be given to those who are mad, since they cannot co-operate by their devotion, and then he adds his opinion : ' The devotion of the recipient and the personal merit of those who confer it and of the whole Church are of much avail in securing the effect of this sacrament since it is given in the form of a petition '. This reason would debar the unconscious from being anointed, and here the practice of the Church has moved away from St Thomas.

The definition of Trent (D 929) laid it down that the proper minister of the sacrament is a priest. Trent was mainly concerned to reject the Reformers' idea that the ' presbyters ' of James's text were the elders of a church and not priests. At the same time the anathema was issued in such general terms that it seems to preclude the opinion of those medieval theologians who would allow deacons to administer the sacrament. There is no parallel with confirmation, for there the council spoke about the *ordinary* minister. If the diaconate is really part of the sacrament of Orders (*see* DEACON), it might be argued that deacons were not excluded by Trent any more than bishops, but, if the diaconate is not a sacrament, they could not be included as ' priests ' in any sense at all. It was proposed at the Vatican Council II, but in vain, that deacons be allowed to give this sacrament. Since Trent, some have put forward the idea that a priest might anoint himself, if he was alone and could not get help. As a public person in the Church he might be held fit to pray in his public capacity for himself as a private individual. The case of a priest's giving communion to himself when he has not time to say Mass before commencing a necessary journey does sometimes arise and offers a parallel which some might urge.

The objection of Waldensians and Wycliffites (D 424 and 669) to the sacrament seems to have been on the grounds that it was expensive in that it involved the calling together of seven priests who would all have to receive a stipend. The evidence of the *Ordines* would however suggest that the conferring of the sacrament by a single minister was already coming into practice before these complaints were made. The individualism of the later Middle Ages (*see* DEVOTIO MODERNA) may have weakened the sense of corporate action which had been more highly esteemed at an earlier age (*see also* CONCELEBRATION).

VI The controversy about the effects of the sacrament began from the obvious fact that not all those who were anointed recovered. St Thomas (*Contra Gentiles* 4:73) made bodily health a conditional effect, depending on whether it was expedient for the soul's welfare, and Trent (D 909) adopted his idea. What the sacrament did for those whom it did not cure was variously explained. St Thomas (loc. cit.) said that *pronitas ad malum* and *difficultas ad bonum* were consequences of sin which were diminished by the sacrament, if not removed, so that the subject was ready for his passage to eternal glory. The idea that preparation for eternal glory was the main effect is found in Master Simon (cited by Weisweiler from his MSS., op. cit. 345) and may have been due to an inference by him or by some earlier theologian, who reflected that if the sacrament was conferred in the crisis of an illness and did not always cure, but did always strengthen against the final assault of the devil, it must prepare the soul for its next state.

Some took the line that the prayers healed the body while the anointing affected the soul. Hugh of St Victor (PL 176:579) did not accept this, but did think that the spiritual effect came first and then the physical. Scotus (*IV Sent.* 20:1) seems to have been the first to psychologize about the state of the sick man and to show that he could not easily produce acts of true repentance while he was so ill. This psychologizing has been carried further by some modern theologians who would say that where the sacrament does not produce a physical cure it will always produce a calmness and resignation which are in effect the conforming of this dying Christian to the death of Christ. It would seem necessary for such an opinion to be upheld or rejected by a clinical investigation. Does this in fact happen ?

A curious medieval theory is found in the tract *De VII Sacramentis* already mentioned (Weisweiler, op. cit. 546). In logical accord with the idea that the sacrament is a preparation for eternal glory, this Spanish writer demands that a married man must always have his wife's consent to his being anointed, for thereafter he may not have sexual relations with her, ' for when once he has been anointed, he is dead to the world '.[1] The partisans of this extreme view do not seem to have been numerous, and one may find other theologians of the period (such as Robert Courçon, cited by Weisweiler, 545) urging that the sacrament should be given at the beginning of an illness rather than when it reaches its climax. It is artificial to oppose medievals and moderns as if the one group was all bent on waiting for the hour of death, while only in modern times did a saner theological view appear. It is true that some theologians of the recent past, chiefly Kern and Schmaus in

[1] Ex quo semel unctus est, mundo mortificatus est.

Germany, have championed the view that the primary effect of the sacrament is to prepare for glory, and they have even spun a fine poetic web about the idea, but pastorally they have not had a sweeping success. One of the most important contributions to the discussion has been that of F. Cavallera SJ, who examined the *Acta* of Trent (still unpublished on this point) and found that the original decree had directed the sacrament to be reserved for those who were on the point of death (*illis duntaxat qui tam periculose decumbunt ut in exitu vitae constituti videantur*). The discussion within the Council led to a change, ' only ' being made to give place to ' especially ' (*praesertim* for *duntaxat*). The area of theological debate was thus left unrestricted. The Second Vatican Council (AAS 56 [1964] 119) ordered that alongside the existing separate rites of *viaticum* and anointing there should be provided a continuous rite in which confession preceded anointing and *viaticum* came last of all ; this provision did not favour the idea of anointing being given for any and every illness (where *viaticum* would not be in place). The Council did state that ' anointing of the sick ' was an alternative and better name for the sacrament than ' extreme unction ', but did not contradict Trent on the point.

Bibliography. P. Palmer SJ, ' The Purpose of Anointing the Sick ', in TS 19 (1958) 309–44 ; H. Weisweiler SJ, ' Das Sakrament der letzten Ölung im Werken der Frühscholastik ' in *Scholastik* 7 (1932) 336–53 ; 524–60 ; T. Spacil SJ, *Doctrina Orientis de sacra infirmorum unctione*, in OCA 74 (1931) ; C de Clercq, ' Ordines unctionis infirmi IX et X saeculi ', in *Ephemerides liturgicae* 44 (1930) 100–22 ; A. Chavasse, ' L'Onction des infirmes dans l'église latine ', in RevSR 20 (1940) 64–122 ; 290–364, afterwards published in book-form ; J. Didier, *Le Chrétien devant la maladie* (1961) ; *F. Puller, *The Anointing of the Sick* (1904) ; J. Kern, *De sacramento extremae unctionis* (1907) ; *H. Porter, ' Origins of the Medieval Rite of Anointing the Sick ', in JTS 7 (1956) 211–25, and ' Rites for the Dying in the Early Middle Ages ', in JTS 10 (1959) 43–62 ; 299–307 (but these articles neglect the Eastern, Spanish and Irish evidence) ; Z. Alszeghy SJ, ' L'effetto corporale dell'Estrema Unzione ', in *Gregorianum* 38 (1956) 385–405 ; F. Cavallera SJ, ' Le Décret du Concile de Trente sur l'Extrême-Onction ', in *Bulletin de Littérature ecclésiastique* XXXIX (1938) 3–29 ; P. Browe SJ, ' Die letzte Ölung in der abendländischen Kirche des Mittelalters ', in ZKT 55 (1931) 515–61.

J. H. C.

F

FAITH We begin by considering the use of the word in Scripture, Tradition, and Catholic theology (I), then further analyse its meaning (II), and examine how in Our Lord's time men came to believe (III), what the Church tells us of the nature of faith (IV), how it develops in one who in childhood learned to believe (V), and how the adult convert reaches faith (VI). After seeing how, in spite of the darkness attaching to faith (VII), it is an unhesitating assent (VIII), we study the ultimate basis on which our faith rests (IX). Next we discuss the loss of faith (X), its necessity and religious value (XI), and its connection with the authority and unity of the Church (XII).

I Meaning of the Word. God has revealed Himself to us in and through His son, Jesus Christ. The revelation given us by Christ, his prophets and his apostles, is a call from God to man, a message meant not merely to increase our knowledge but also to draw us into union with Him in Christ. Faith is the corresponding movement of man towards God, the acceptance of God's invitation. In this encounter between God and man, it is God who takes the initiative by calling us to Himself, externally through His revelation, internally by His grace, which transforms us and empowers us freely to accept His invitation. Faith is both a gift of God and an act of man. In its strict sense it means accepting God's message as true. In its fullest development it means also acting in accordance with that message. In the Bible the word has many meanings. Taking the main Biblical meanings together, we may say that faith is the surrender of oneself to the new order offered by God, the submission of one's mind by belief in the truths revealed, a firm conviction of the sincerity of God's promises and of His power to fulfil them, the adoption of a new way of life. In short, it is the response which Christ wanted His hearers to make when He delivered His saving message. It is obvious that this reaction is complex, but what is also clear is that the first thing Christ demanded of His hearers was that they should take what He said as true and take it on His word. All further flowering of faith depends on this fundamental belief, and the Church, without denying the need of the other elements for justification, has reserved the word 'faith' for this mental acceptance of what God has revealed, while to the other acts which form part of the complete response to Christ's call it gives the names of hope, charity, obedience, etc. In the Bible, faith sometimes includes all these virtues, sometimes it is distinguished from them (as in 1 Cor 13:13 ; 1 Thess 1:3, 5:8 ; Heb 11 ; etc.) and used in its strict sense of believing what God says ; but always it includes this belief in the truth of God's promises

(cf. Abraham's faith, Gen 15:6), or in the claims of his messengers or in the doctrines revealed through them. In Catholic theology the word is used in these same senses. In its technical sense, with which this article mainly deals, faith is the accepting of God's revelation as true. In its fuller sense (as when we speak of living faith, justifying faith, the life of faith, etc.) it covers or connotes all the virtues which form part of the true Christian's attitude to God.

The meaning which the Church today gives to faith is the one it has had since the beginning of the Church. When the early Christians professed their faith at Baptism, the faith they affirmed was their belief in the Christian truths—the Trinity, the Divinity of Our Lord, the Resurrection, our salvation through Christ and so on. In the works of the Fathers the faith that justifies (though not by itself) is dogmatic faith, the acceptance of revealed truths, as is shown also by their use of 'the Faith' to describe the truths which Christians believe. (Cf. St Ambrose : *De Fide ad Gratianum*, PL 16:527 ff.; St Athanasius : *Expositio Fidei*, PG 25:199 ff.; etc.). It is true that by faith the Fathers often meant living faith, that of a person who has also the virtues of hope and charity. This is true especially of St Augustine, for whom the Christian is one who not only believes what God says (*credere Deo*) but also reaches out to God by joining love to faith (*credere in Deum*) : (cf. PL 35:1631, 36:988, 38:865). But even St Augustine is not constant in this use. In *De Fide et Operibus*, where he states that faith without works is dead, he uses the word not just of believing God but of believing 'in Him' : 'Go into eternal fire, which was prepared for the devil and his angels ; He (Christ) rebukes them, not because they did not believe in Him (*in eum*), but because they did not do good works' (PL 40:214). In the Fathers, faith is clearly distinguished from hope and charity, and it always means belief or dogmatic faith, though, if it is living faith, it means much more. Catholics of all periods distinguish between the dead faith of those who are in sin and the living faith which alone will save us ; but the Councils of Trent (D 838) and first Vatican (D 1791) insist that even the faith of the sinner is real Christian faith, a gift of God and a step towards salvation.

II Analysis of the Meaning. The divine revelation throws open to us a new life in union with God, a life beyond our natural rights and aspirations. Supernatural life involves a supernatural way of acting, and so for faith, by which we enter this new life, we need some new power which will step up our natural faculties. In those who are not yet justified this help takes the form of an actual grace, a short-term aid, enabling the mind to submit to God's word. But in those already justified, the divine aid takes the form of a virtue or permanent disposition which prepares the mind for the acceptance of God's revelation. This virtue of faith has been defined by the Vatican Council as ' a supernatural virtue by which, aided and attracted by divine grace, we hold as true what God has revealed, not because we see its intrinsic truth by our reason, but because of the authority of God, Who can neither deceive nor be deceived ' (D 1789). The act of faith which this virtue empowers us to make is directed towards the truth made known by God and received firmly and undoubtingly by the believer. Faith is not the outward profession of something we do not really consider true. Having faith in a doctrine is different from wishing it were true, or pretending or hoping it is true, or acting as if it were true. Faith is a firm conviction that what we believe is in fact true independently of us. Yet, in spite of the firmness of this conviction, when we make the assent of faith we do not see, but only believe, the truth revealed by God ; and for this reason faith is not a purely intellectual act. It is an act in which we give our assent only because, urged by God's grace, we freely agree to do so. We believe with our mind, not, however, because intellectually compelled (as happens with obvious truths) but because we choose to believe what we know to be God's word. Faith is therefore a deliberate act, not a reaction which we cannot prevent (cf. D 797, 1242). It is not a feeling or emotion which comes over us. In a convert the awareness that at last he has found the truth may cause a thrill, and at various times our faith may have an emotional effect on us ; but these feelings of joy and gratitude and satisfaction are not faith ; they need not accompany any single act of faith, they may be absent from a whole lifetime of real faith, and their presence is no guarantee of the truth of the doctrines which cause them. The Catholic's reason for believing the doctrines he professes is not that they appeal to him, though they may do so, but that he believes that they are the word of God.

The act of faith is, therefore, a deliberate opening of our minds to God. Yet, though deliberate, it does not depend on us alone. It depends on three things —first, the reasons which convince us that God wants us to accept these doctrines ; secondly, our decision to believe them because He affirms them ; and, thirdly, God's help without which we could not make this decision. Without God's grace we cannot will or reason ourselves into faith. It is something aroused in us by God, but not without our consent. Faith is not a disinterested admission of certain truths ; it is a personal response to God's call, an acceptance of Him as the source of all truth to whom we willingly open our minds. It is He who shows us why we should open them and prompts us to do so ; but the opening has to be done, with His co-operation, by us and of our own free will. Once we have opened our minds, the divine truth flows in, accompanied by a light which shows us that things are as we believe. This divine light, which comes from the virtue, is not measured by the grade of the believer's natural intelligence. And the certainty it brings of the truth of the divine doctrine is out of all proportion to the reasons that prepared the way for faith or the arguments by which we might seek to justify our faith to those who do not believe. In the state of faith we have no vision of the intrinsic reasons for the mysteries we believe. But the assurance that they are true will continue so long as we keep our minds open to the light by submitting to the testimony of God.

Faith, therefore, depends on God. He is its object, known to us through His revelation ; it is He who enables us to recognize the revelation as His and to accept it on His word. But it depends also on ourselves. We cannot believe unless we consent. This does not mean that we are free to choose the object of our faith. God has revealed Himself, and it is our duty to accept His message ; but we cannot accept it as His unless we are convinced that it is indeed from Him. How do we reach this conviction ? To answer this question we shall consider (1) how in the time of Our Lord men came to believe, (2) what guidance the Church gives us in this question, (3) how children today come to believe and grow up in the faith, and (4) how today adult converts pass from unbelief to faith.

III How in Our Lord's Time Men came to believe. It is especially in St John's Gospel that we find an answer to this question. In the Synoptics faith most frequently means confidence in Christ's power to work miracles. This confidence would normally presuppose belief in Christ's word, but the Synoptic writers tell us little of how people came to believe in Him, though passages like Mt 11:20–30 contain the main elements of St John's teaching on faith. St John never uses the noun ' faith ' (πίστις), but he frequently uses the corresponding verb ' to believe ' (πιστεύειν), and his Gospel is almost a commentary on the origin of faith. In it the works done by Our Lord are held up as proof of the credibility of His claims. Of those who heard His teaching, some believed, while others did not. The two disciples, going on the recommendation of John the Baptist and conversing with Jesus, believed before they had seen any miracles : ' We have found the Messias ' (Jn 1:41). Once Our Lord had begun to work miracles, ' many believed in his name, seeing his signs which he did ' (2:23). Some believed in Him on the testimony of the Samaritan woman, and many more because of His own word (4:39–41). When the leaders of the Jews refused to believe, Christ appealed to His miracles : ' The works which I do give testimony of me, that the Father hath sent me ' (5:36), and to the prophecies : ' For, if you did believe Moses, you would perhaps believe me also : for he wrote of me. But, if you do not believe his writings, how will you believe my words ? ' (5: 46–7). Even when they had recognized Him as a miracle-worker, the Pharisees failed to see the connection between these wonders and His claims. ' What do we, for this man doth many miracles? If we let him alone so, all will believe in him ' (11: 47–8). Some of the leaders did reach a kind of conviction, but were unwilling to take the final step because of the sacrifice involved. 'Many of the chief men believed in him ; but because of the Pharisees they did not confess him, that they might not be cast out of the synagogue. For they loved the glory of men more than the glory of God' (12:42–3).

The proof of Christ's claims was therefore patent for all to see, in His person, His teaching, His miracles (see APOLOGETICS). Some were easily convinced by His character or teaching ; others required the proof from His miracles ; but some remained unmoved even by these, for neither His teaching nor His works could by themselves cause faith. Believers had to be called by God. 'There are some of you that believe not. . . . Therefore did I say to you that no man can come to me, unless it be given him by my Father' (6:65–6 ; cf. 6:44). They had to be of His sheep. 'I speak to you and you believe not : the works that I do in the name of my Father, they give testimony of me. But you do not believe, because you are not of my sheep. My sheep hear my voice. And I know them and they follow me' (10: 25–7). Those who had made themselves sensitive to truth responded to its call. 'Every one that is of the truth heareth my voice' (18:37). Those who had listened to conscience recognized the voice of God in this new message. 'My doctrine is not mine, but his that sent me. If any man will do the will of him, he shall know of the doctrine, whether it be of God, or whether I speak of myself' (7:16–17).

Only those, therefore, who had the light to see were able to read and understand the evidence. Nevertheless, this light was offered to all, for Christ is 'the true light that enlighteneth every man that cometh into this world' (1:9). Those who were unable to believe had themselves rejected the light and had been made blind on account of their sins, as Isaias had foretold, 'that they should not see with their eyes nor understand with their heart and be converted' (12:40). Not every sin would cause this blindness, for Christ had come to call sinners to repentance. Mental blindness was the punishment of those who sought their own glory, of those whose self-reliance had shut their minds to the possibility that God should speak through 'this man'.

In the Acts of the Apostles we find the same process and the same judgment. The Apostles appealed to the credibility of their teaching, referring to the miracles worked by Christ or themselves and to the consonance of their doctrine with the prophecies of the Old Testament. Some listeners were convinced by the preaching itself. (Ac 8:37, 11:21, 13:43, 16:34, 18:8). Others required a prolonged study, 'daily searching the Scriptures whether these things were so' (17:11, 28:23). Others again were moved by the miracles (4:4, 5:14, 13:12). But the conviction was not brought about by the proof alone, and many who had examined it did not believe. 'What shall we do to these men ? For indeed a miracle hath been done by them, known to all the inhabitants of Jerusalem. It is manifest : and we cannot deny it' (4:16). Those who did believe were those whose heart the Lord had opened (16:14) and who were ordained to life everlasting (13:48). Those who failed to recognize the truth were those who had resisted the Holy Ghost (7:51) and become blind (28:27).

From the New Testament we see therefore that (1) the object of faith is Christ, the Son of God, and the truths He taught directly or through His apostles. (2) Christ and His Apostles offered proof that they spoke the word of God, a proof sufficient to convince many, but not enough to secure belief in all ; (3) some of those who heard needed little proof, some a great deal, and some demanded more than Our Lord would give ; (4) only those who were drawn by God became fully convinced and made the submission that is faith ; (5) the ability to recognize the truth of Our Lord's claims had no connection with natural intelligence ; there were learned and unlearned among both believers and unbelievers.

IV What the Church tells us about Faith. Before Our Lord left the earth He founded His Church, the assembly of all the faithful who believe in His name. To the leaders of His Church, the Apostles chosen by Him, and to their successors, He committed the task of preserving His message and preaching it throughout the world (Mk 16:15). At first the message was passed on by word of mouth, in sermons and conversations ; later, part of it was, under divine inspiration, committed to writing. The revealed truth has therefore its visible witness both in the written Word of the Bible and in the living Church, the believing Church and the teaching Church. Even when God intervened directly in the conversion of St Paul and of Cornelius, He at once sent them to the Church for further instruction (Ac 9:6–7, 10:5–6). It is therefore not only in the Bible but also in the living tradition of the Church that the divine revelation comes down to us. The gospels were not meant to supplant the Church, but to teach her and help her, with the guidance of the Holy Spirit, to preserve the message. It is through her that most people become familiar with the Bible and learn to love it. The Church presents the divine revelation not as her own message but as given her by Christ. She is therefore not the source but the custodian of the true doctrine, appointed by Christ to maintain the unity of faith without which there would be no real community of believers. Her faith is guaranteed by Christ, and by keeping our faith in line with hers we cling to the truth made known by Christ. The Church has not given us a treatise on faith, but in the course of history she has had to correct many errors on the object and nature of faith, and the pronouncements she has made are signposts to guide theologians in their speculations. The most important of these declarations were made in three Councils : Orange II, which dealt with the need of grace for faith ; Trent, which considered the connection between faith and justification ; and first Vatican, which defined the relation between faith and reason. From these and other decisions we learn, among other things, that :
(1) Faith is not any kind of vague feeling but a

supernatural intellectual virtue and act by which, on God's authority, we believe as true whatever He has revealed (D 1789, 2145).

(2) The truths revealed by God are contained in Scripture and Tradition (D 783, 1787, 1792) ; they are not the product of our own thought nor the fruit of our religious experience (D 1812, 2145).

(3) The principal truths to be believed are beyond human understanding and cannot be discovered nor proved by reason ; nevertheless, they do not contradict the findings of reason (D 1635, 1649, 1795-9, 1816-18).

(4) The acceptance of these doctrines on faith is not a blind arbitrary impulse but a reasonable act, for it can be shown that they are supported by the supreme authority of God (D 1637, 1790, 1791, 1812).

(5) That the doctrines to be believed have been revealed by God may be proved by signs external to us and capable of being grasped by any kind of intelligence. Internal experience and private inspiration are therefore not the only means by which people may be brought to faith (D 1790, 1812).

(6) The evidence in favour of revelation does not force the mind to believe ; so faith is a free, deliberate act by which we direct ourselves to God (D 798, 1791, 1814).

(7) God's grace is needed not only to make faith easier but to make it possible. Hence faith is a gift of God (D 178-9, 200-200a, 813, 1791, 1814).

(8) It is possible for us to resist this grace, so that faith is a free act and a step to salvation (D 797, 814, 1791).

Within the limits set by these and other pronouncements of the Church there is a wide field for speculation, and during this century probably no subject has been more discussed by Catholic theologians than that of faith. The problem which has exercised them most is that of the parts to be allotted to grace and to reason in the coming-to-be of faith. In the 18th and 19th cents. the main attack on Catholic belief came from Rationalists, who regarded faith as an insult to reason. Catholic writers replied that faith is fully justified by reason, because Catholics believe only those things which reason can show to have been revealed by God ; and to accept the testimony of God, the most authoritative of witnesses, is eminently reasonable. In their anxiety to show the reasonableness of faith these writers paid less attention to the part played by grace, though no Catholic writer ever ignored it. With the present century the attack on Catholic faith has swung to the other flank. Catholics were accused by the Modernists of crediting the human reason with powers it did not possess. The classic rational arguments for the credibility of the Christian doctrines were alleged to be invalid, and a new method of proof based on the appeal of these doctrines to the feelings was proposed as the only valid method. Catholics rejected this theory, but, as a result of the controversies which ensued, many Catholics began to feel that in the preceding period too much emphasis had been placed on the part of reason in the preparation for faith and too little on that of grace.

All Catholics agree that it is God who makes us believe. Whether we began to believe as children or only later, our faith is a gift of God (Jn 6:44, 6:65-6 ; Eph 2:8). It is something we cannot receive from our parents nor give to ourselves by study or desire, something we cannot communicate to others by argument or persuasion. A divine gift when we first receive it, it remains at every moment something which cannot be attributed to us alone. Nevertheless, God gives us faith in a manner that is in keeping with our independence as rational creatures. Our faith is a free act in which we pay homage to God by accepting his testimony. It is clear, therefore, that we cannot make an act of divine faith, that is, an assent of which the motive is God's authority, unless we are convinced that God has in fact given His word for the doctrines believed. If we have this guarantee, our faith, though it is a gift of God, does not run counter to our reason, for nothing could be more reasonable than to believe God. If on the other hand we have no such guarantee, we cannot believe the doctrine on God's authority. How sure a guarantee is required to make faith reasonable ? Must it be quite certain that God has revealed the doctrine, or is it enough that it be credible that He has done so ? On this the theologians are not agreed. Before examining their answers, we shall consider the kind of guarantee the ordinary Catholic has for his faith.

The approach to faith of an adult convert is an easier subject for psychological study than the development of faith in a child, and for this reason there is a tendency to regard the adult's road to faith as the ideal, and to look on the faith of a child as in some way defective. Yet Our Lord said : ' Whosoever shall not receive the kingdom of God as a little child shall not enter into it ' (Mk 10:15 ; cf. also Mt 11:25). And the great majority of Catholics have grown up as believers, without experiencing any break in their faith when they ceased to be children. Instead, therefore, of beginning with the faith of the relatively few who are converted in adult life and who have to overcome unusual obstacles on their way to faith, we shall take as normal the faith of those who have believed since childhood.

V Development of Faith in Childhood. Faith comes ' by hearing '. For children the ' hearing ' comes through the word of their parents, teachers and catechism. The divine message is a seed sown in the soul of each child who hears it, and, if the soul is properly disposed, the seed takes root. The soul of every baptized child is already made receptive by the virtue of faith which was received at Baptism. If the child is not baptized, his soul can be made receptive by actual graces. Thus the child is already prepared by grace for the coming of the divine message and, unless some extrinsic element, such as an irreligious education, intervene to prevent the seed from taking root, he will gladly receive the good news sent by God. Once he has made his first conscious acceptance of divine truth as God's word, the light of faith illumines his soul. From that moment until death, the child, and later the man, has no need to cast his glance continually over the reasons for faith in order to maintain his belief. Provided he has not dimmed or extinguished the light by a sinful life, the believer is convinced that his faith is true ; and he is so, not because of any study of apologetics, though this will confirm his faith, but because of the conviction that comes from the virtue infused by God. For one who believes, faith is its own justification because of the certainty it brings, so that no constant referring to the arguments for belief is necessary. Nevertheless, to those who do not believe, a faith which appeals to something other than rational arguments seems irrational, and it is useless to try to convey to them the certitude the normal believer enjoys. For their benefit, therefore, we have to show that the faith of a Catholic, and even of a child, is not unjustified and that rationally it is as defensible as his other mental acts.

We have already seen that the child is both naturally and supernaturally disposed to believe. All he needs is that the object of faith be put before him. At first, perhaps, he accepts the divinity of Christ and the truth of the revealed doctrines on human faith rather than divine, on the word of his mother rather than on that of God. Very soon, however, he becomes aware that these doctrines are not just his mother's but God's, and he learns to believe on God's authority : ' because Thou hast said it and Thy word is true '. Even if we consider only the human foundation of his faith, without taking into account the influence of grace on his mind, his faith is as reasonable as his assents on non-religious subjects. He knows that ' God has said it ' in the same way as he knows that Britain is an island—on human testimony. It is a natural law of his mind to be convinced by those whom God has given him as guides ; if he refused to do so, he would be abnormal. Knowing on their word that God has said these things, he believes because God has revealed them. His act of faith is a prudent and reasonable act. It is true that, both on religious and non-religious subjects, his informants may mislead him, for their testimony is not infallible. If when he grows up he finds that he has been believing on God's word some statements which are not really revealed, he drops his belief in them ; it never was an act of divine faith. But the fact that his parents or teachers sometimes misinformed him does not lead him to withdraw his assent to everything they ever taught him. He continues his true acts of faith and need never reach a stage at which he has either to give up faith or believe against reason. As he grows up, he finds the testimony of his teachers to the truths they taught him reinforced by more and more evidence. As his false beliefs are gradually swept away, his true beliefs are confirmed. Thus, without any break in his faith, his knowledge of the evidences in support of Christian belief becomes transformed from that of a child to that of a man. When his parents misinformed him, their authority went no further than themselves ; when, on the other hand, they were transmitting truths which are really revealed, their authority was not their own but that of the Church or the Bible, which they were reporting. Thus from the beginning a child who is correctly taught his faith has a view of the evidence for revelation, and this evidence (but not the child's view of it) is in itself sufficient to satisfy even an adult mind ; for the child it is reduced to a smaller compass to suit his capacity. Just as the map in his schoolroom represents all the geographical investigation that has gone to its composition, so the word of his teachers or catechism represents all the study of apologetics on which it is based ; indeed, represents the Church herself, the great sign given to mankind. As the child develops, his range of vision expands, his power of penetration increases, he sees the evidence in greater width and depth, and his early conviction is sustained without any interruption in his assent. There is no question of his having to suspend his belief and start anew by searching for motives of credibility suited to an adult (D 869). The transformation is gradual and the proof may be unfolded to suit the development of each mind, because the evidence for Christianity is susceptible of ever greater penetration and will stand up to examination by even the most acute intellect.

The believer has therefore a rational defence of his faith, a defence which will of course vary with his abilities and status. But this rational defence does not in fact lay bare his whole reason for believing. Even in non-religious questions people often have good reasons without being able to produce them, and this is much more true in matters of faith, where the mind of the believer is helped by grace. One of the effects of the infused virtue of faith is that it casts a new light on the reasons why we should believe, illuminating the revealed truth and its credibility, and making us feel the attraction of faith. Far from having to act against reason, the believer finds in faith the only course that will fully satisfy his reason, so that he has difficulty in understanding why unbelievers should be so blind. Provided he co-operates with grace by trying to lead a good life and keeping his religious knowledge in step with his mental development, no Catholic has to face the choice of abandoning his faith or doing violence to his reason by continuing to believe. This is true of those also who are not Catholics but who with real faith believe some of the revealed truths. Though the grace of God may lead them out of the Church of which as children they were members, and bring them into the Catholic Church, they will not thereby leave behind them the faith, that is, the true supernatural beliefs, of their past. Converts who with divine faith have hitherto believed some of the revealed truth do not give up this true faith on entering the Catholic Church. As Newman said : ' They come, not so much to lose what they have, as to gain what they have not ; and in order that, by means of what they have, more may be given to them ' (*Grammar of Assent*, 249).

VI The Convert's Approach to Faith. Though the faith of the adult convert is the same as that of any believer, his approach to faith is more difficult, especially if he has been brought up in a society hostile to the Church or even to God. There are, of course, some people who, even though grown up, and whether intellectual or not, come into the Church like children, drawn by divine grace and with almost no need for preparatory proof. The stronger the pull of grace, the more easily are people convinced, and in privileged souls like St Paul a special divine illumination makes other motives of credibility superfluous. But normally God draws souls to faith not by His grace alone but also through the ordinary use of their intellect and will, and so conversion normally presupposes a process of rational conviction, which will vary with the type of mind.

We have already seen that it was to the Church that Christ entrusted his message. If the Church herself has all the signs of being a divine creation, and if she affirms that the Christian message is of divine origin, we have a guarantee that this is so. Thus the problem of recognizing whether the doctrines are from God is in practice reduced to that of deciding whether the Church, which affirms them to be from Him, is herself accredited by God. And to do this it is not necessary for the inquirer to undertake a prolonged study of Scripture and history, a study beyond most people. The evidence for the genuineness of the Church's claim lies open in the Church as she exists today. ' She bears her unearthly character on her brow ' (Newman, *Difficulties of Anglicans*, I:v). If her present existence cannot be accounted for except by God's protection, her witness to Christ is true and His message which she preaches is from God (cf. D 1793–4).

The judgment that the doctrines taught by the Church are from God logically presupposes other judgments, such as that there is a God and that the supernatural is possible. St Thomas did not consider a natural knowledge of these truths to be necessary as a preliminary to faith. For those who cannot discover them by reason, faith is itself sufficient to cover all that its object presupposes (cf. *Summa*, 2–2ae:1:5: @3). But even a person who is capable of a natural knowledge of these truths may become sure of them all in one single conviction, without passing step by step through them. If the Church is what she claims to be, God exists and has given a revelation to man, and this revelation is that proclaimed by the Church. In one act of recognizing the Church as inexplicable in purely human terms, the inquirer may for the first time become fully convinced of all these truths ; in one final move all the pieces may fall into place to form the only pattern that makes sense.

To those who already have faith the arguments for belief are satisfying. Why do unbelievers fail to see their cogency ? Is it because they have not received light from above, or can it be explained without reference to the supernatural ? We know from Scripture that only those called by God can make the act of faith, but here the question concerns the judgment that comes before faith, the conviction that the doctrines are from God. The Church teaches that the motive of faith is the authority of God, not proof arrived at by human reason. But it teaches also that faith is a reasonable assent, not a blind plunge made without rational justification. For belief to be a reasonable act it must be backed by indications that

the statements to be believed have been made by God and so are worthy of credence. These signs do exist for the Christian doctrine, and theoretically they should be recognizable by all. Yet, when confronted with them, some people are convinced while others are not. Newman has analysed some of the reasons for this diversity and shown the effect of antecedent considerations, favourable or unfavourable, in our assents not only in religious questions but in all that touch us personally. While in theory an unbiased inquirer would make the correct judgment from the evidence, none of us is in fact unbiased in matters of this kind. Our interpretation of the evidence depends largely on the principles from which we start. And in questions of a religious nature our intellectual principles are to a great extent the product of our moral life. And so, unless the inquirer has a suitable mental and moral preparation—a recognition of his own insufficiency and a readiness to accept any help that God may give—it is unlikely that the signs of a revelation will have any meaning for him. And theologians of all schools agree that it is practically impossible for anyone to have the right outlook and the necessary goodwill without the help of grace. It would seem, therefore, that, while theoretically possible without the aid of grace, the recognition of a revelation as divine is in fact always the result of grace. This grace may consist in the providential direction of our lives along lines on which it becomes easy for us to see the meaning of the signs ; but it may also consist in light removing the obscurity of the evidence and in strength of will to follow the search wherever it may lead.

But is this enough ? Even with the help of these graces, can one who does not yet believe ever really grasp the fact that the Christian doctrine is from God ? Can a convert, before he has made his first act of faith, be really sure that the Catholic Church is the Church of God ? There is one school of theologians—that of Rousselot—which thinks this is not possible. Rousselot used the example of the inductive reasoning by which a scientist, from a multitude of little indications, suddenly perceives the scientific truth which explains them all. They are all signs pointing to this truth ; in advance it seems probable that they are such ; but it is only when we are sure of the truth itself that we can be certain that they are in fact signs of that truth. In a similar way, the signs of the divine origin of a revelation cannot with certitude be recognized as such until we have recognized the revelation as divine. And to admit a revelation as divine is to have faith. In other words, it is only when we have faith that we can be certain of the grounds of faith. Thus, for Rousselot, faith is not merely the acceptance of truths which we know to be revealed ; it is also the recognition that they have in fact been revealed by God. There are many writers, such as de Broglie, Karl Adam, Aubert and others, who, without accepting this extension of faith to cover also the judgment of credibility, agree with Rousselot that before faith the human reason cannot reach full conviction that God has given a revelation. It can perceive the fact of revelation as credible (and this, they say, is enough to make faith reasonable) but not as certain. When these writers speak of the fact of revelation as credible, they do not mean (as they and all theologians mean when they speak of the object of faith as credible) that it is the object of a reliable testimony. What they mean is that the fact of revelation is highly probable or, at least, cannot be proved with ineluctable evidence. This same terminology is found in many theologians of the 16th and 17th cents.

Rousselot's theory was the subject of much controversy when it first appeared (*see* APOLOGETICS). It has not been publicly censured by the Church, but can scarcely be reconciled with some of the official pronouncements (e.g. Vatican Council I, D 1790 ; Oath against Modernism, D 2145), which refer to the signs of revelation as certain and suited to any kind of mind. And the following passage in *Humani Generis* would seem decisive : ' Although God has provided so many wonderful signs by which even our natural reason can prove with certitude the divine origin of the Christian religion, nevertheless the human mind may often have difficulty in forming a firm judgment about the credibility of the Catholic faith. For a person may be so influenced by prejudice or passion or animosity that he may remain unmoved not only by the evidence of external proofs but even by the heavenly inspirations which God conveys to our minds ' (AAS 42 [1950] 562).

We may take it, then, that, though in practice we need grace in order to recognize the revealed doctrine as revealed, we can (and the normal convert does) reach this conviction before the act of faith. Nevertheless (and perhaps this is all that writers like Aubert and de Broglie mean to bring out), the proof that God has given a revelation or that the Catholic Church is the Church of that revelation is not a mathematical proof which precludes all possibility of denying the conclusion. No one has analysed this kind of proof better than Newman. It is the kind that can convince one who is not unwilling to be convinced, but which other people can, without appearing foolish, fail to see. In a proof of this kind the conclusion is not forced on us ; we have to draw it for ourselves, and we can do so only if properly prepared. It gives rise to, or, rather, permits, a certitude which is usually called moral certitude but sometimes probable or free certitude. This is the only kind of proof we can have on most historical and philosophical questions. Faced with a proof of this nature, our normal reaction is to say : ' I am perfectly justified in taking this conclusion as proven. Theoretically, of course, some other unthought-of explanation might be possible, but in fact no other is seriously conceivable '. If the matter at stake is not of great importance, we jump to the right conclusion at once and pay no attention to alternative but far-fetched explanations. If, however, our whole future is involved, as in religious assent, we cannot accept the conclusion without some hesitation and even fear. And so, before the act of faith, the mind will seldom, if ever, be completely at rest. There will be a conviction that, ' this *must* be the truth,

since there is no other plausible explanation of the facts ', but only faith will bring the assurance that ' this *is* the truth '. Inquirers often reach a point at which they see no reasons against the Church, yet feel that the truth of the Church should be more compelling. They have a fear that perhaps they have overlooked some part of the evidence. No amount of reading or discussion will bridge the space between this state of mind and the outlook of one who already believes. Only the will, drawn by the grace of God, can shake off this fear. Faith always involves a decision. Once the step has been taken, there comes, as an effect of the virtue of faith, an assurance which often surprises the convert and makes him wonder at his previous hesitation. St Thomas tells us that ' faith has its certitude from the light infused by God ' (*In Joan*. IV, lect. 5, n. 2). It is not merely a certitude of the doctrine believed on God's word. Faith throws its light back on to the rational and historical arguments which prepared the way for it. The believer sees them now in all their force and with a penetration which his natural powers could never give. There is this much truth in Rousselot's theory —that our certitude, even of the grounds of faith, is immeasurably firmer after faith than before.

From all this it is clear what an important part the will has to play in the approach to faith, not only after the judgment of credibility has been made but throughout the search. Only determination and fortitude will carry a person through to the end ; and we have just seen that the judgment of credibility itself is normally made at the behest of the will. However, the crowning act of the will comes once we have made the judgment that the message is indeed from God. It might seem that at this stage faith would follow as a matter of course ; but it is not so, for faith is not just the conclusion of a piece of reasoning. Our reason can show us that God is speaking to us and that it is our duty to listen, but the decision to do so is an act of the will made from the desire to please God. The devils are too intelligent not to conclude that the Christian doctrines must be true, but their assent is a grudging admission of truth and is not made out of respect or love for God. Religious faith is made out of veneration for God. Persuaded that God is calling him, the believer has welcomed the call and answered : ' Speak, Lord, for thy servant heareth ' (1 Kg 3:10). The decision to accept God's message is one we cannot make unless He draws us, but even in spite of His grace we can refuse.

VII The Veil of Faith. Of the part played by evidence and grace in the approach to faith, St Thomas says : ' The believer has sufficient inducement to believe, for he is induced by the authority of the divine teaching confirmed by miracles, and what is more important, by the inward attraction of God Who invites him. So he does not believe imprudently ' (*Summa*, 2a–2ae:2:9). But he adds : ' Nevertheless, he has not the evidence required for clear knowledge, and so the merit of his act is not taken away ' (ibid). The believer knows that what he hears is true, but he knows this not because he sees its truth but because it is God Who is speaking. Faith is not vision. St Paul describes us as walking with faith instead of a clear view, as seeing in a dark manner instead of face to face, and speaks of faith as ' of things that appear not ' (Heb 11:1 ; cf. 2 Cor 5:7 ; 1 Cor 13:12). The chief object of our faith is God Himself and the divine mysteries, and the 1st Vatican Council told us that, though our reason, enlightened by faith and helped by grace, can penetrate these to some extent, it can never really grasp them as it would an object proportioned to it (D 1796).

Though we have no proof of the mysteries we believe, we know we are not being misled, because it is God Who tells us of them. Some theologians would go further in describing the obscurity of faith. Faith, they say, is a step in the dark, not merely because we have to commit ourselves to God and let Him guide us, but also because even the fact that it is God who is leading us is to some extent hidden from us. If it were perfectly clear that God had given His guarantee for the revelation, there would be no merit in accepting it as true ; it would be an inescapable conclusion from evident premisses. Other theologians do not agree. It is true, they say, that the proof of the divine origin of the Christian message is not compelling ; it can be rejected by those who are unwilling to believe. The nature of the proof adds, therefore, to the obscurity, freedom and merit of faith. But, even if the proof were overwhelming, this would not destroy the essential freedom and merit of religious faith. We might indeed be compelled to admit the revealed truth on purely scientific grounds with the kind of faith that even the devils might have. But this would not be religious faith and would still leave us free to give or refuse the loving adherence to Divine Truth that religious faith entails.

VIII The Firmness of Faith. St Thomas frequently remarks (e.g. *Contra Gentiles* 3:40) that in faith the intellect is of necessity unsatisfied, not because it doubts whether or not it should believe, nor because it is uncertain of the truth of what it believes, but because of its nature the intellect strives to see truth instead of merely believing it. Whereas its normal function is to assent only when the evidence compels it, in faith it has no intrinsic proof of the mysteries it accepts as true. Faith is a voluntary submission induced not by evidence but by the desire to please God. Yet, though not moved by evidence of the things believed, our mind accepts their truth firmly and unhesitatingly. This firmness, on which the Creeds insist (e.g. Athanasian, D 40 ; St Leo IX, D 343 ; Lateran, D 428 ; Trent, D 994 ; Anti-Modernist D 2145), is essential to faith, which supposes a complete and unqualified submission of mind to God's authority, a readiness to accept as true the whole of God's revelation, even those parts which we do not yet know. The firmness of faith is therefore due to the motive of our assent, but in other ways it is due to the virtue of faith and to the will, which, moved by grace, makes the mind assent. In its objective foundation faith is the firmest and most

immovable of all our assents, for no natural judgment and no other testimony is as reliable as the word of God. Even subjectively, faith is in one sense the most decided of all our affirmations, for in it we exclude not only present doubt but even the present admission of the possibility of valid doubt in the future. And the believer, if he finds that something he had thought naturally certain is in fact against the faith, will reject his apparent natural certitude and cling to faith. Nevertheless, in spite of this firmness, faith is less capable of giving peace to the intellect than many of our natural assents. While in these the intellect is satiated because we have proof and a clear view of what we hold, in faith the mind longs to penetrate the veil and see for itself. Since the intellect cannot see the inner truth of the object believed, the firmness of faith does not necessarily prevent difficulties arising, some of which may seem plausible. But difficulties are not doubts. Faith is not incompatible with difficulties, even those we cannot fully solve, but it is incompatible with doubt. That is why, though the Church encourages her members to study the evidences for Christianity and to become more familiar with the doctrines they profess, she cannot permit them to harbour the intention of giving up the faith should it prove to be badly grounded ; for the mere admission that it might be badly grounded would show a lack of faith. One who believes with divine faith not only has the truth but knows he has it, and the possibility that he may eventually be proved wrong is not really conceivable to him.

Ordinary Catholics, whether learned or not, seldom have difficulties against the faith. Some of the saints have had to pass through long periods of darkness, when all that remained clear was their duty to believe ; but those on a lower spiritual plane are generally spared these trials. People who are not practising their religion may gradually grow weak in their faith, but the Catholic who is trying to lead a good life needs no effort to accept the doctrines of his religion. He may frequently find himself unable to answer objections against his creed, but such inability, whilst it may distress him, does not shake his faith. He knows he has the truth even though he cannot always defend it. This refusal to be moved by arguments against his faith is not due to insensitiveness nor to stubbornness. It is an effect of the virtue of faith and of the gifts of the Holy Ghost, especially of understanding and wisdom, which bring to good and even uninstructed souls an infused grasp of divine truth.

IX The Basis of Faith. To those who do not believe, the certitude and firmness with which we hold our beliefs seems exaggerated, because, they say, the basis of our faith is, at best, no stronger than that of other assents. We believe the doctrines of our faith because God has revealed them. But, if it is through human testimony or a study of the evidences that we know He has revealed them, the certitude of our faith can be no greater than that of human testimony or human reasoning. All Catholic theologians answer this difficulty by affirming that the certitude of our faith is not based on the natural knowledge we have of the grounds of faith. The knowledge which, before or independently of faith, we have of the motives of credibility gives us only a natural certitude of the fact of revelation, a certitude comparable to that obtained by other similar processes of reasoning. And it serves to show that it is reasonable for us to believe. But in faith our certitude is of a higher, more immovable kind, based on something else. In explaining how it comes about, theologians divide into groups. For Rousselot it is true that the firmness of our faith depends on our conviction that God has revealed, but this conviction cannot be reached by natural reasoning. It is only when seen through the eyes of faith that the signs of revelation are convincing. All other theologians maintain that without faith we can reach a natural conviction that God has revealed. But Thomists like Gardeil and Garrigou-Lagrange think that this natural conviction is not enough, because faith based on this would be a merely natural act. To be supernatural, faith must have a supernatural motive, i.e. God's authority known to us in a supernatural way. And, they say, the only supernatural way in which we can know it here on earth is by faith. Hence our faith must, in one single act, embrace not only the object revealed but also God Himself as revealing and guaranteeing this object. Another group of theologians prefers a theory elaborated in modern times by Pesch and Billot. According to these writers, for faith the only necessary knowledge of God's guarantee of the revealed doctrine is the natural knowledge obtained through the evidences. But this knowledge is not the cause nor motive nor measure of our faith. It is indeed by natural reasoning that we know that God has given His word, but how we know this does not come up for consideration in our act of faith. The sole motive of our faith is God's authority considered in itself, and, since this is the most reliable motive we could have, it is to this alone that the solid foundation of our faith must be attributed.

Nowadays few theologians would accept Billot's theory, and the modern trend is rather towards some modification of the Thomist theory. Most modern writers are convinced that the certitude normally possessed by the believer cannot be explained unless the believer has some supernatural experience of the motive of faith. We believe the revealed truths because of God's authority, the sole motive of faith. But we are certain that the doctrines are from God because in some supernatural way we are made conscious of His intervention. All agree that this is the result of faith and that it does not depend on our previous natural knowledge of the motives of credibility. But how faith has this effect on us they explain in various ways. Some think that God's action consists in attracting our whole being to Himself—our will drawn by the Good and our mind by the Truth Who reveals Himself—and that in the act of faith this attraction is obscurely felt by us. Others consider that it is in and through the signs of revelation, and especially through the life of the Church, that we become supernaturally aware of the action of God revealing Himself to us. Others combine these explanations.

These modern suggestions would seem to explain better the extraordinary assurance we have of the truth of our religion. The individual Catholic has no illumination nor intuition of each particular doctrine of his faith ; he believes each of them because it has been revealed by God, and it is through the Church that he knows with certainty which doctrines have been revealed. But, if he has no knowledge, except the obscure knowledge of faith, of each part of the revelation, he knows with the clarity of daylight that, in accepting God and the revealed system as a whole, he has not been deceived. The Catholic does not have to *believe* he is in touch with divine truth ; it seems obvious to him ; he sees it with a realization he did not have before he began to believe. Rousselot was wrong in saying that before faith we cannot be sure of the grounds of faith ; we can, and for this reason our faith is not irrational nor fideistic. But he was not wrong in saying that in the light of faith the old arguments take on a new brightness. When we believe, everything connected with the revelation contributes to make us see the hand of God in it. The external evidence, the whole tenor of the message, the feeling of security given by the Church, the sense of union with our fellow believers—in all this and much more we perceive the hand of God beckoning to us. All that is good in us is attracted and responds. St Thomas says that under the light of faith believers ' see ' that they should believe (*Summa*, 2–2ae:1:4:@3 ; 2–2ae:1:5:@1). And with this assurance given by God that the message is from Him and for them they accept unhesitatingly whatever it contains. It is this overwhelming conviction that God is guaranteeing our faith that keeps Catholics firm in their faith even when confronted with obscurities they cannot dispel. ' Will you also go away ? . . . Lord, to whom shall we go ? Thou hast the words of eternal life. And we have believed and have known. . . .' (Jn 6:68–70).

To sum up this and some of the preceding sections, we may distinguish four stages connected with faith. (1) Prior to faith we have the reasons which satisfy us that God has revealed the divine truth which He wants us to accept. This first element is a necessary preparation for faith, but it does not produce faith, though it shows us that belief is reasonable and will not conflict w h our normal intellectual life. At this stage, however, these arguments will not have greater certainty than we may acquire on ordinary historical questions. Our grasp of the evidence will be strong or weak according to our natural capacities and opportunities, but the strength of this grasp has no relation to the strength of our faith ; all that is required is that we be convinced, in whatever way, that God has testified to what we are to believe. (2) Under the influence of the divine attraction by which God draws us to Himself, we decide to obey His call and to accept the revelation on His word. (3) As soon as we give this consent, God gives the virtue of faith. Under its light we see now in a supernatural way, with a much firmer certitude, that the revelation really is from Him and for us ; we see in a new way the reliability of God's word and our obligation to believe. (4) Simultaneously with the reception of the virtue and under its power we make our act of faith, accepting all God's message as true because it is from Him.

The sole motive of our act of faith is God's authority. We believe that there are three Persons in God, solely because God, who has said so, cannot deceive nor be deceived. But our assurance that we are not mistaken in holding that God has spoken to us is caused by the virtue of faith, which enables us to see, in a manner that transcends all natural knowledge, that the revelation is a message from God to us. The act of faith is therefore directed to God alone as He reveals Himself ; but the virtue of faith illumines not only the divine revelation but also the signs in which God manifests Himself.

X The Loss of Faith. It is in the light of this influence of grace, in keeping us firm in our faith, that we must view the question of the loss of faith. The virtue of faith, given to us when first we receive sanctifying grace, remains in our souls unless we deliberately deny some article of faith. A soul which has committed a grave sin against some precept other than faith will retain the virtue of faith. Without faith there can be no charity nor supernatural life, but faith may remain without charity. Like all supernatural virtues, faith gives to the soul the power to act in a supernatural way, but it does not compel the soul to do the acts to which the virtue is directed. Many people who for a long time do not make an act of faith may therefore still retain the virtue, because they have never directly denied the faith.

The 1st Vatican Council defined that a Catholic can never have a well-founded cause for abandoning or doubting the faith (see APOSTASY). A Catholic may, indeed, deny some revealed truth without being aware that the Church holds it as revealed. It may also happen that when the Church in some country becomes heretical, many simple Catholics find themselves in an heretical sect without realizing that they are separated from the Church. Denials or defections of this kind need not be culpable, since there is no conscious denial of what the Church declares to be of faith. But, provided he is not suffering from some mental disability, a person who believes that the Catholic Church is the true Church and accepts all she teaches, and who remains faithfi to his duties, will not at any time arrive at the point at which his conscience tells him he must reject what he knows to be Catholic doctrine. And so anyone who knowingly does so has been guilty of grave sin. It may be that at the moment of defection there is no consciousness of guilt and no formal sin, because denial may seem to be called for on conscientious grounds. But, presupposing that he is morally responsible, the believer would not have reached this crisis had he not at some stage rejected God's help by committing grave sin. Sins against virtues other than faith, especially sins of pride and licentiousness, may lead to a loss of divine guidance, with a blinding of the intellect and a weakening of the will, so that the duty to believe becomes obscured.

XI Faith, the Foundation of our Spiritual Life. The loss of faith cuts all our contacts with the supernatural life. God has destined us for union with Himself in a way that is above our nature. Unless we seek Him in a supernatural way we cannot reach Him. And we cannot seek or love Him in a supernatural way unless we know Him in a supernatural way through faith. Without faith, therefore, we cannot reach our destiny. Faith is the foundation of all justification (D 801). In spite of the problem of the salvation of those who have not heard of revelation (see SALVATION OF NON-CATHOLICS), the great majority of the theologians of this century affirm that this act of faith, required for salvation by a responsible adult who is unbaptized or has sinned, is an act of faith in the strict sense, an acceptance on God's authority of the fundamental truth that God exists and will reward those who seek him (Heb 11:6). Today, however, theologians are seeking a solution to this problem in the fact that God gives His internal invitation to all men through His grace, and that the acceptance of this grace by the choice of good rather than evil is implicitly an acceptance of God and an embryonic act of faith.

St Thomas regards faith not merely as a means to salvation but also as a prologue to the eternal happiness for which we are destined. (*De Veritate* 14:2 ; *Summa*, 2–2ae:4:1 ; etc.). Whether on earth or in Heaven, eternal life consists in the loving knowledge of God and His Son. 'This is eternal life, that they may know thee, the only true God, and Jesus Christ, whom thou hast sent' (Jn 17:3). Thus living faith is the beginning of eternal life. 'He that believeth in me hath eternal life' (Jn 6:47, 3:36, 5:24 ; I Jn 5:13). Through faith we become united to God ; He is its chief object (*credere Deum*) and motive (*credere Deo*), and its purpose or aim is union with Him (*credere in Deum*). Though an intellectual act, faith is also a moral act, depending as it does on the will ; and, being a moral act which directs us straight to God, it is above all a religious act. In all three respects—intellectual, moral and religious—faith is the basis of our spiritual life.

As an intellectual enlightenment, faith gives us a share in the knowledge proper to God, making us disciples of the Divine Master (*Summa*, 2–2ae:2:3), from whom we learn of the things we hope to see clearly in Heaven. Thus, in faith we already possess 'the substance of the things to be hoped for' (Heb 11:1). Through it we base ourselves on the rock of divine truth, so that in faith we have 'a proof of the things we cannot see' (ibid.). The divine knowledge obtained through faith becomes our guide, with reference to which we can judge all else at its true value, combat temptation and avoid religious error. Thus, even considered as an intellectual act, faith is the support of all the other virtues ; the growth of our spiritual life depends on the depth of our faith.

But this intellectual act is also a moral act. It is the will that moves us to assent, and so faith, unlike knowledge based on evidence, is a virtue in the moral order. As St Thomas remarks, after St Augustine, ' whereas a person can unwillingly perform all the acts connected with the exterior worship of God, only one who is willing can believe ' (*In Rom.* 10, lect. 2). Because of this moral character also, faith is the foundation of the spiritual life. Being itself a surrender to God of the best we have, our spiritual faculties, it is a preparation for the service of God through the other virtues. Faith is a movement towards God, and in the normal act of living faith it is joined to love of Him. Even in dead faith there is an element of love, a love of divine truth or of God as truth (*Summa,* 2–2ae:5:2:@2) ; often there is something more, not indeed the perfect love which unites us fully to God, but at least a longing to love. The sinner who believes has chosen God, even though he remains untrue to his choice. Dead faith, however, is a movement towards God which stops short of its target, a foundation on which nothing can be built (*Summa,* 2–2ae:4:7:@4). The spiritual edifice cannot rise until the foundation, faith, has been perfected by hope and charity, and faith has become a living or loving faith. Without charity, faith avails us nothing, but in this life charity without faith is impossible. The two react on each other ; when faith is alive, the stronger our faith, the greater our love of God ; and, as we grow in love of God, our faith becomes more and more an act of love.

Faith, especially living faith, is a religious link between the soul and God. Through it man is raised above his own natural level and drawn into union with God. On the one hand God offers to man His infinite love and shares with him the secrets of His divine life. On the other, man responds by giving to God in humility and obedience the sacrifice of his most precious faculties, his mind and heart. Therein lies the merit of faith and the submission which makes it not a mere act of knowledge but an act of religion.

If faith is a union with God, it is in a special way a union with God-made-man, our Saviour Jesus Christ. Our supernatural life is the life of those redeemed by Christ, and so faith, the foundation of the supernatural life, must have a special relationship to Christ and to our redemption through Him. From the Scriptures we learn that it is through faith we are to be saved, because it is through it that our souls come under the influence of Christ and share in the fruits of His Passion and Death. Our faith is essentially Christian, not only because we believe in Christ and receive through His merits the grace to believe, but also and especially because it is through Him and in Him that we receive the testimony of God, which is summed up in Christ. ' Faith cometh by hearing and hearing by the word of Christ ' (Rom 10:17). This word which Christ gave personally to his contemporaries is given to us today by His Mystical Body, the Church, whose mission is to preach Christ.

It is therefore through faith that we put on the mind of Christ. But the union with Him which results is deeper and more mysterious than a union of minds, for it is through faith that we undergo His saving influence and become incorporated in Him. ' The power of the passion of Christ is linked to us by faith ' (*Summa,* 3:62:6 ; 3:49:1:@5 ; etc.). By faith alone we are not fully united to Christ (D 800). Faith by itself is merely a preliminary to this more perfect union ; nevertheless, without faith this union is impossible ; and to believe Christ's teaching is the first step towards possessing Him as our Redeemer. When faith is united with charity, the believer becomes a living member of Christ and recipient of the fruits of His Redemption (cf. St Thomas : *In Heb.* 3, lect. 3). Thus, through faith and love there begins in us a new life in Christ, a life which shows itself externally in the works of faith (Jas 2:18 ; Tit 1:16). But in addition to faith Our Lord demanded also an external profession and consecration in Baptism. ' He that believeth and is baptized shall be saved ' (Mk 16:16). Thus the faith which grafts us into our Saviour is a faith crowned by love, and so by good works, and externally professed in Baptism, which the Fathers and Trent call ' the sacrament of faith ' (D 799). (On all this section, cf. Domínguez : ' La Fe, fundamento del Cuerpo Místico en la doctrina del Angélico ', in *Ciencia Tomista,* 76 [1949] 550–86).

XII Faith and the Authority and Unity of the Church. This, then, is what Catholics mean by faith—a union with God through submission of our minds to divine truth. Outside of the Catholic Church there are many who have this kind of faith, a readiness to accept whatever God has revealed. But the characteristic part of the Catholic's faith is his belief that God has not left it to each individual to decide what has or has not been revealed. The Catholic believes that, as part of the revelation, God has given us in the Church an infallible guide on these matters ; and so, when the Church has vouched for the divine origin of some doctrine, he accepts it as divine truth and feels no need to question this decision. The Catholic's faith is therefore linked with the faith and authority of the Church. Because of this, there is in the belief of Catholics, and in the Church herself, a unity not found elsewhere. In spite of different grades of knowledge, the object of faith is one for all. Each Catholic believes implicitly, and is prepared to believe explicitly, the same as every other Catholic. The picture is the same for all. Some see its details more clearly, but all see the picture as a whole and accept all it contains, even the details they cannot make out. What the Church teaches and the faithful believe is the same now as in the early centuries—the truths revealed by God. But, as time goes on, the Church perceives more and more clearly the content of these truths (*see* DEVELOPMENT OF DOCTRINE). At all times she encourages her scholars to seek out the meaning of the divine message. If some of them go wrong, she intervenes to correct them, and by these infallible pronouncements the original revelation is kept free from corruption. As the Church's own understanding of the faith develops and will go on developing until the end of time, so also a similar development should take place in each believer (D 1800).

What we believe as children is the same as what we believe as adults—whatever God has revealed. But in the course of our life our knowledge or perception of that truth should become more perfect, in order that what we already believe implicitly may become more and more an explicit object of our faith.

Faith is a unifying element in the mind of each believer, giving him a point of reference, a principle by which he can judge all situations. Our faith not only tells us of the hidden mysteries of God ; it gives us also the answer to many problems that might perhaps be solved by reason, but which for most of us would without faith remain unsolved—problems concerning the purpose of life, the reason for suffering, the meaning of death. Through our faith we have a sure guide in all the questions that really matter. And, since all believers have this same guide, there arises a fellowship and unity of outlook among all the members of the Church. But the unity brought about by faith is deeper still. Not only do all receive through faith the same illumination from God ; through it all become members of the one body in Christ. Thus, through faith, the whole structure of the Church, the Mystical Body of Christ, is held together.

Bibliography. St Thomas, *Summa*, 2–2ae:1–12 ; *De Veritate* 14 ; R. Garrigou-Lagrange OP, *De Virtutibus theologicis* (1948) ; H. Lennerz SJ, *De Virtutibus theologicis* (1933) ; Cardinal Newman, *Grammar of Assent* (1870) ; *University Sermons* ; *Discourses to Mixed Congregations* ix, x and xi ; R. Aubert, *Le Problème de l'acte de foi* (1950–2) ; the same, ' Questioni attuali intorno all 'Atto di Fede', in *Problemi di Teologia dommatico* (1957) ; G. B. Smith, ' Faith and Revealed Truth ', in *Teaching of the Catholic Church* (1947) ; A. Gardeil OP, *La Crédibilité et l'Apologétique* (1928) ; J. Bainvel SJ, *La Foi et l'acte de foi* (1921–3) ; S. Harent SJ, ' Foi ', in DTC 6:55–514 ; M. D'Arcy SJ, *The Nature of Belief* (1934) ; F. Sheed, *Theology and Sanity* (1950) 297–302 ; H. F. Davis, ' The Act of Faith ', in ITQ 19 (1952) 102–15 ; C. Davis, ' Faith and Dissident Christians ', in CR 44 (1959) 201–19 ; G. de Broglie SJ, ' La Vraie Notion thomiste des *Praeambula fidei* ', in *Gregorianum* 34 (1953) 341–89 ; with *Précisions complémentaires*, ibid. 36 (1955) 291–2 ; E. Joly, *What is Faith ?* (1958) ; P. Rousselot SJ, ' Les Yeux de la foi ', in RSR 1 (1910) 241–59 ; 444–75 ; M. Nédoncelle, ' L'Influence de Newman sur Rousselot, in RevSR 27 (1953) 321–32 ; J. de Wolf, *La Justification de la foi chez Saint Thomas* (1946) ; H. F. Davis, ' Newman and the Certainty of Faith ', in JTS 12 (1961). J. Alfaro SJ, ' Cristo glorioso, revelador del Padre ', in *Gregorianum* 39 (1958) 222–70 ; the same, ' *Fides* in terminologia biblica ', in *Gregorianum* 42 (1961) 463–505 ; the same, ' Supernaturalitas fidei iuxta Thomam ', in *Gregorianum* 44 (1963) 501–42 and 731–87 ; Y. Congar OP, *La Foi et la Théologie* (1962) ; J. Pieper, *Über den Glauben* (1962) ; G. de Broglie SJ, *Les Signes de crédibilité de la révélation* (1964) ; various, *XIX Semana Española de Teologia* (1962) ; F. Durrwell, *In the Redeeming Christ* (1964) esp. ch. 6. There is an extensive bibliography of works on faith in *Teologia* (1950) 442–51 ; 625–42.

P. F.

FAITHFUL, THE, AS A SOURCE OF DOCTRINE As the Second Vatican Council has greatly elaborated the teaching of the Church on the position of the laity in the conservation and development of doctrine, the decree of this Council will be investigated first (I), and then the antecedents of the doctrine, in Newman particularly, (II) will be considered. A short section (III) will indicate the theological problem which still awaits solution.

I The Second Vatican Council in its decree on the Church (II:12) draws out the function of the laity as witnesses to the doctrine of Christ from the prophetical office of the Church. Prophecy is here taken rather in the sense of ' speaking for someone or something ' than of ' speaking beforehand and with prevision '. Such prophecy is a παράκλησις or a counselling and comforting, and the Church has never been without it. The decree (ibid.) shows that witness is borne to the truth by worship and by spreading abroad a life of faith and charity. It says that the totality of the faithful cannot fall away in faith. The reason for this is given (1 Jn 2:20, 27) as the anointing which all the faithful have from the Spirit ; this may be due to their baptism and confirmation (*see* CONFIRMATION). Parts of the Church may fall away in schism or heresy, but there cannot be a failure of the totality. Universal consent about a matter of faith or morals, from the most erudite bishop to the least educated of the laity, is a manifestation of this indefectibility. The faith once delivered to the saints (Jude 3) is thus preserved, as the Spirit of truth stirs up the faithful to an understanding of what they believe, to a right judgment about its deeper meaning and to practical wisdom in applying it in their lives.

The task of bringing salvation to men does not rest on the clergy alone (IV:30), but they are to take cognizance of and legitimize the operations and gifts of the faithful so that all may be united for a common task.[1] The word *recognoscere* that is used has extensive legal connotations, which warrant the translation given. The Council admits (IV:33) that there are places and circumstances where the laity alone afford an effective presence of the Church in her work of salvation ; one does not need to enlarge on these, nor does the decree. It may suffice to point out that lack of priests and the need for a permanent diaconate is not being considered here, for the text goes on to say that, besides the general apostolate which is common to all the faithful, there are special modes of co-operation with the clergy which may be needed in special circumstances, after the manner indicated in Phil 4:3 or Rom 16:3 ; the general apostolate depends rather on the measure of grace given by Christ (Eph 4:7). Thus it is envisaged that under certain aspects the prophetic office of the Church is to be exercised in special circumstances by

[1] Ita pascere fideles eorumque ministrationes et charismata ita recognoscere ut cuncti . . . unanimiter cooperentur.

the laity alone, however much they may depend on the teaching Church for their formation.

The warrant for this singling out of the laity as a source of doctrine is found by the Council (IV:35) in Ac 2:17–18 and Apoc 19:10. Christ as the great Prophet has endowed the laity with an understanding of the faith and with His grace (*sensu fidei et gratia verbi*), so that the power of the gospel may be made manifest in family and social life of every day. The context is somewhat different from what the theologians of the past had considered, for they thought rather of the laity as expressing in their devotions some aspect of the faith which might then be captured and fixed by scientific theologians and so become a new doctrine of the faith. This mention of family and social life as the *locus* of lay witness leads in another direction. The application of Jl 2:28–32 (in the Hebrew Enumeration, 3:1–5) to the Christian situation is not easy to follow, for St Peter did not elaborate this part of his text. Justin (*dial.* 87) is ready to see in the text a forecast of what was to happen after Christ had ascended to heaven and delivered gifts to men. 'It is possible,' he writes, ' to see amongst us both women and men who have charismata from the Spirit of God.' Justin may have written this before the outbreak of Montanism, but thereafter more caution would be needed in allowing scope to extraordinary charismata, and this caution is in fact shown by the Council in what it lays down (II:12) about their use (*see also* CHARISMATA). They are helpful to the Church and to be received with thanksgiving, but the decision about their validity rests with the hierarchy, who have also to decide about the use that is to be made of them.

Starting at the primary stage of family life, the Council twice points out that Catholic parents are to be preachers and witnesses of true doctrine to each other and to their children (II:11 and IV:35). Then the whole family is entrusted with the task of proclaiming the hope of eternal life and of convicting the world of sin (a work assigned in Jn 16:8 to the Holy Ghost), and these tasks may clearly be taken to call for charismata of the ordinary, if not of the extraordinary, kind. After the family comes the witness in society (IV:36), where all research into the secrets of nature is said to be capable of helping to the glory of God, while technology and cultural advancement may be perfected by grace in the way that all nature is meant to be (*see* ETHICS, CHRISTIAN). A distinction is laid down between what Catholics do as members of a state and what they do as members of the Church, but there should be a harmony of the two, and the idea that religious faith has to be shut out of public life is declared to be pernicious. Some words of Pius XII on the right and lawful sense in which a state is secular are cited in support (AAS 50 [1958] 220), words spoken to a group of Italians from the Marche, a region where Communism is strong, as Fascism was before it. The Church has to avoid taking over temporal concerns, even as she guards against losing her own rightful sphere to the secular.

This outward-looking witness of the laity to the faith that is in them does not exclude all consideration of the internal life of the Church. In what may prove to be the most important passage of the conciliar decree it is laid down that they have the right and sometimes the duty, according to their knowledge, ability and position, of giving their opinion about what concerns the good of the Church (IV:37).[1] No doubt this opinion is simply consultative, and not a suffrage, when put alongside the teaching office of the Church, and there may be some dispute about what constitutes *praestantia*, but the principle is now established that the laity are not simply passive recipients of doctrine, but rather to be compared to those communication-satellites which boost a message while passing it on.

When St Thomas dealt with prophecy (*Summa,* 2–2ae:174:6c and @3) he decided that there was no further need of prophecy after the time of the apostles, save for guidance in conduct ; faith had been sufficiently made clear to them. He viewed world-history in three periods, which started with Abraham, Moses and Christ ; each of these began in full clarity and thereafter some declension was to be found.[2] This was a neo-Platonic notion, according to which the first instance is always the best in any series of manifestations of, or emanations from, the divinity. Strictly, this would not allow for any development of doctrine (q.v.). His concession that private prophecy might be for the good of the Church in matters of conduct sets up too sharp a dichotomy in the present age when most of our heresies are moral. St Thomas would by his distinction leave room for the charismatic individual, whether it be Catherine of Siena, Ozanam or Edith Stein, to suggest new lines of conduct for the Church, but what the Council has accepted seems to go beyond this, for ' the good of the Church ' certainly includes faith as well as morals.

II The debate begun by Newman was in reality about the prophetical office of the Church, though it was precipitated by a remark in *The Rambler* of May 1859 that, ' even in the preparation of a dogmatic definition the faithful are consulted, as lately in the instance of the Immaculate Conception'. This remark was the basis of an *a fortiori* argument, designed to show that it would not be strange for the bishops to consult the laity in a practical matter about Catholic schools. When challenged, Newman defended his remark by a long survey of what happened to the Church in the days of the Arian heresy. His crucial instance was a passage from Hilary (*In Auxentium,* 6 ; PL 10:613), which he rendered thus : ' Up to this date the only cause why Christ's people is not murdered by the priests of Anti-Christ, with this deceit of impiety, is that they take the words, which the heretics use, to denote the faith which they themselves hold. The ears of the people are holier than the hearts of their bishops.'[3] The final sentence

---

[1] Pro scientia, competentia et praestantia quibus pollent, facultatem, immo aliquando et officium, habent suam sententiam de iis quae bonum ecclesiae respiciunt declarandi.

[2] In singulis statibus prima revelatio excellentior fuit.

[3] Sanctiores aures plebis quam corda sunt sacerdotum.

Newman left in its Latin form, perhaps not wishing to administer a shock to Wiseman and Ullathorne.

Newman had been interested in observing how traditional doctrines were preserved by the *sensus fidelium* (or common belief of the laity) ever since his stay in Rome in 1847, when he had talked to Perrone and Passaglia about the preparations for the definition of the Immaculate Conception. The laity were consulted by Pius IX over this, and it was this that impressed Newman. Perrone followed Gregory of Valentia in holding that the practice of the faithful in some devotion, or their taking offence at some new opinion, might be relied on as a sign of a continuing tradition. Had he been aware of the liturgical practice of early times, when the audience would interrupt the reader if he gave an unfamiliar twist to a Scripture passage, he might have been more emphatic in his statements. The appeal to popular devotion as a sign of tradition is practised by the Second Vatican Council in its decree on the Church (VIII:66), which begins a section on the intercession of the Blessed Virgin by citing the popular use of the prayer *Sub tuum praesidium* ('We fly to thy patronage . . .'), which is now known to have existed long before the dogmatic teaching of the Council of Ephesus in 431. It is found on a Rylands Papyrus (470), which was dated by a Jewish papyrologist (who had certainly no theological axe to grind) to the 3rd cent. at the latest; some Catholics wanted to put it at a later date, but only for considerations extrinsic to the normally accepted canons of dating.

In his Catholic preface to the third edition of his *Via Media* (1877) Newman issued what one might consider his *Retractationes* of his former Anglican thinking about the prophetic office. He showed that he now had no illusions about the limits of the *sensus fidelium*. 'Novelty is often error to those who are unprepared for it, from the refraction with which it enters into their conceptions. Hence popular ideas on religion are practically a match for the clearest dicta, deductions and provisos of the Schools, and will have their way in cases when the particular truth which is the subject of them is not of vital or primary importance. Thus in a religion which embraces large and separate classes of adherents, there always is of necessity to a certain extent an exoteric and an esoteric doctrine' (op. cit., lii).

In order to set right what may have been amiss in his Anglican work, Newman in this preface worked out more fully, but perhaps not completely, the distinction of the three functions of the Church, which he called regal, sacerdotal and prophetical; they answer roughly to the Schoolmen's idea of *potestas iurisdictionis*, *potestas ordinis* and *potestas docendi*. Newman clearly says that the Pope exercises the prophetical office (op. cit., xlviii), though elsewhere he supposes that theologians are its mouthpiece. He goes on to argue that the Church has inevitably to run the risk of superstition arising through a conflict between departments in her work: 'Considering . . . how intimately the sacramental system is connected with Christianity, and how feeble and confused is at present the ethical

intelligence of the world at large, it is a distant day at which the Church will find it easy, in her oversight of her populations, to make her Sacerdotal office keep step with her Prophetical' (op. cit., lxix). His Anglican sermon (*Sermons on Subjects of the Day*, [1843] V) on the three offices of Christ applies all three to the faithful, who therefore share in Christ's priesthood, in His prophetical office and His regal office, but the trilogy of thought, action and suffering (which this sermon indicates as expressing their share) does not really show how the participation takes effect.

Newman's *Rambler* article was delated to Rome as being unsound in its theology, by Bishop Brown of Newport, but the Latin wording of the sentences picked out as dangerous was incorrect; he was made to say that during the Arian heresy there had been ecumenical councils which had erred and that the whole body of bishops had remained silent, when in reality he meant that there had been several general councils (*see* ARIANISM) between the two ecumenical ones of Nicaea and Constantinople (e.g. Rimini) and that the common run of bishops was silent, without thus committing the whole *magisterium*. Newman, having ascertained with some difficulty the charges against his view, presented his defence in the appendix to the third edition of his *Arians of the Fourth Century* (1871).

After these misunderstandings are discounted, there still remains a point in which theologians like Franzelin disagreed with Newman. One may see it in the way that Franzelin cites the text of Hilary about the ears of the faithful (*see above*) as a difficulty against his own view, while Scheeben used it, in this following Newman, as an argument in favour of his. St John Fisher, when answering the earliest Reformation heresies, said that the faithful *in their practice* had preserved the doctrine of the sufficiency of communion under one kind, while theologians such as Luther opposed it. During the interval (1520–62) between the appearance of the heresy and the authoritative pronouncement against it at Trent one might say that here was a parallel to the Arian period, and that, as then the faithful went on clinging to their practice of equating Son and Father in their prayers in spite of some quite notable voices that would have dissuaded them, even so at the first onset of the Reformation.

Augustine appealed to the consent of the faithful in his dispute with Julian of Eclanum (*Contra Iulianum* 1:7:31; PL 44:662). Julian had dismissed this appeal with some contempt as the grumblings of the populace; Augustine replies that it is much more than that: 'All over the world mothers go with their little ones not only to Christ the anointed one, but to Christ Jesus the Saviour. This assembly of the saints to which I have brought you is not just a popular gathering, nor simply the children of the Church; they are also Fathers of the Church.'[1]

[1] Matres cotidie toto orbe terrarum non ad Christum tantum, id est ad unctum, sed ad Christum Iesum, id est ad Salvatorem cum parvulis currunt. Sed ecce, quo te introduxi, conventus sanctorum istorum non est multitudo popularis, non solum filii sed et patres ecclesiae sunt.

Thus the popular belief which underlay the practice of infant baptism could be trusted as a refutation of Pelagianism.

III The problem which remains is that of determining what share the faithful have in constituting the mind of the Church. Newman in 1868 drew up a paper in reply to a question about the mind of the Church, but it was not published until 1958. In this he speaks of the Pope sitting in St Peter's chair, or having a Council of Fathers and Doctors collected round him and of the deposit of faith being presented to *their* minds. This would suggest that the ordinary charismatic assistance (which is displayed in the prophetic function of the Church) is confined to them, but it would allow that they should take cognizance (in the manner envisaged in the decree of Vatican II) of what the faithful do and say which may enshrine some element of the original faith. The conservation of this element might then be itself attributed to the charismatic influence of the Holy Spirit. Why for instance, does the Western Church so entirely and without question associate the sign of the cross with the invocation of the Trinity? Is this an apostolic practice, and does it imply some point of dogma not yet determined?

There is always the possibility that new evidence may make more explicit the part played by the laity in past doctrinal assemblies. The *Dialektos* of Origen (recovered in 1949) gives a verbatim report of one such, giving us a record more than a century older than anything previously available. Here the laity are credited with διαμαρτυρία, or solemn attestation of what is enacted about the faith.

Bibliography. J. H. Newman, *On Consulting the Faithful in Matters of Doctrine* (reprint with introduction by J. Coulson, 1961); the same, 'An Unpublished Paper on Development', in JTS 9 (1958) 324–35; V. Blehl SJ, 'Newman's Delation', in DbR 486 (1960) 296–304; Y. Congar OP, *Lay People in the Church* (1957).   J. H. C.

FALL OF ANGELS. *See* DEVIL

FALL OF MAN. *See* ADAM, ORIGINAL SIN

FALSE DECRETALS, THE The forger Isidorus Mercator, who made the collection of conciliar decrees and papal decretal-letters in the 9th cent. (at Le Mans or Reims, between 847 and 852) which is now known as 'the False Decretals', chose to call himself by names that would recall two genuine collectors of canons, Isidore of Seville and Marius Mercator (*see* CANONICAL COLLECTIONS). His work was in three parts; the first was a collection of forged letters of popes from Anacletus down to Melchiades (311–14); the second was a series of conciliar decrees from genuine Councils (Nicaea to Seville II); the third a mixed gathering of later papal letters (from 314 to 731), many of them forged but with a genuine section comprising letters of popes from Siricius to Hormisdas (c.384–523). What matters for theology is the tendencies which the forger was trying to develop and the use made of his material by later theologians.

I The tendencies of the forger were to defend bishops and clergy in both their persons and their property, to limit the authority of metropolitans, and above all to protect the interests of the Frankish Church. 'Whenever the pseudo-Isidore called in the Papal See, it was always in the immediate interest of the bishops and never in the future interests of the Pope,' said Davenport in his monograph on the forger. The Decretals were viewed in a false light by Reformation controversy, because in the initial disputes about the primacy of the Pope between Luther and Eck, the latter had appealed to a forged Decretal of Anicetus. Lorenzo Valla (*De falso credita*, 1440) had delivered a powerful attack on the Donation of Constantine, a piece which the forger of the Decretals had incorporated into his collection from the bogus *Acts* of Sylvester. That Eck should take some of his evidence from so contaminated a source was made a matter for shrill denunciation by his opponents, and they returned to the attack contending that the entire papal case rested on this forged evidence. This was not true, and one can go through a work such as the *Disputationes Tridentinae* of Lainez and notice how, though from time to time he quotes a False Decretal, he always has other evidence from the Fathers alongside and is nowhere led by the false evidence alone.

One of the main tendencies of the forger was to attack the status of *chorepiscopi* or *episcopi vagantes*, who had episcopal consecration but no diocese, and this reflects the clash of Keltic Church with Frankish in the 9th cent. Augustine's meeting at the Synod of the Oak with the seven Keltic bishops must have had many a counterpart in the 7th and 8th cents., and if we knew more about the once-flourishing Breton Church (whose history has been neglected by almost all scholars save Duchesne and Henry Bradshaw), it might be possible to see more clearly what the forger was at. His preference for the position of a patriarch or primate of Gaul above that of metropolitans might then appear to be anti-Breton.

The forger contrived to set out extensive rules for the trial of a bishop and for his right of appeal to the Pope. This right was based on the perfectly genuine Council of Sardica (canon 7) but the forger elaborated it. He also laid it down that seventy-two witnesses were needed for the condemnation of a bishop, thus transforming the old custom (a relic of the idea of collegiality) that a bishop had to be tried by seventy-two of his peers, in memory of the Seventy-two Disciples.

A remarkable omission of the forger is that he had nothing to say about the relation of bishop to king at coronation rites (*see* CORONATION). The 9th cent. saw works like that of Sedulius Scotus, *De rectoribus christianis*, and Hincmar, *De regis persona* and the contemporary liturgies have the *admonitio* addressed by the bishops to the monarch whom they are crowning, yet the forger does not seem to have been interested in the theory of Church and State but only in practical measures for the protection of bishops; he was a lawyer rather than a philosopher.

II The theological use of the forged material

was, for reasons already given, not significant for the development of the papacy. As Davenport says: ' Without the False Decretals, Nicholas I was sure to have effected the same mode of government (as he did) and the principles of Nicholas I were the principles of Gregory VII and of Innocent III '. What may be admitted is that the principle of collegiality was to some extent obscured by the misapplication on the part of the forger of a text from Leo the Great (*ep.* 14 ; PL 54:671). Writing to the Bishop of Thessalonica, who was acting for him as papal legate in Illyricum, Leo said : ' We have entrusted our functions to your dear self in such sort that you are called to share in the burden, not to enjoy the plenitude of power '.[1] The forger turned this into a general rule for all bishops in relation to the Pope and ascribed it to a Decretal of Vigilius in the 6th cent. Leo's arrangement for Illyricum was quite well understood in his own day, for we have news (in *ep.* 42 ; PL 54:816) of an impostor, one Petronianus, going about through Gaul saying that he was Leo's representative (*diaconus*). Clearly the functions that Leo transmitted to his legate were papal ones, not the ordinary powers of bishops.

A side-effect of the forgeries was that the theology of confirmation in the Middle Ages was much influenced by the supposed Decretal of Pope Melchiades which said that, just as we are born again in baptism, so after baptism we are confirmed in view of the warfare of life.[2] Hence it was thought that the only gift of the Spirit to be developed by the sacrament of confirmation (*see* GIFTS, THE SEVEN) was that of fortitude. Recent theological work on the sacrament (*see* CONFIRMATION) has restored the true perspective.

The temporal power of the Pope was by medieval theories based largely on the Donation of Constantine. In the struggle with the Holy Roman Empire canonists often appealed to it and it is not surprising that in reply Otto III in a document of 1001 (MGH *Diplomata* II:ii:820) called it a forgery. It was only in 1433 that the charge was taken up more seriously by Nicholas of Cusa (*De concordantia catholica*, III:2) for the benefit of the Council of Basle. In 1435 Leonardo Therunda addressed a *Memoriale* to Pope Eugenius IV on the need for reform. Whence came royalty to priests ? It was from Charlemagne who gave and from Pope Zachary who accepted, and to give credit to the transaction they ascribed it to Constantine and Pope Sylvester.[3] When one considers that as late as 1890 there were not wanting those who defended the Temporal Power as belonging to the Pope by divine right (e.g. C. Collingridge, *The Theandric Kingdom* [1894]), it is clear that the forgery had a great influence on theories of Church and State, even if it left the dogmatic position of the

papacy very much where it was before. In 1436 with fine impartiality Therunda sent a similar *Memoriale* to the Council of Basle, elaborating the charge of forgery. Francis de Vitoria in the 16th cent. had no scruple in rejecting the thesis that the Pope was lord of the world (*dominus orbis*). It is commonly thought that the False Decretals were introduced into England by Lanfranc after the Norman Conquest. It may be that the practice English canonists had of breaking up decretal letters and grouping the component parts according to subject-matter (and not in chronological order of origin), when they made their collections of canons, led to a diminution of the influence of the forgeries. When anomalous sayings compiled by the forger were set alongside genuine papal *dicta* in the same subject-matter, it would at once be seen that there was a clash.

Bishop Reginald Pecock in his *Repressor of Overmuch Blaming of the Clergy* (*c.*1456), writing against the Lollards, took up a story they had produced that on the day when Constantine made his Donation an angel was heard to proclaim : ' This day is venom shed upon the Church '. Pecock's reply was to question the fact of the Donation by showing from Eusebius that Constantine was not baptized by Pope Sylvester and that the story of the angel could not be traced further back than the works of Gerald of Wales. Thus in medieval England it was in the interests of orthodoxy that the Decretals were challenged, while the Lollards wanted them to be true in order to use them more effectively in their attack upon the Church.

Bibliography. The only edition of the False Decretals is by *P. Hinschius, *Decretales pseudo-Isidorianae* (1863). The best monograph on them is by *E. H. Davenport, *The False Decretals* (1916), which is a much improved version of the Lothian Prize essay for 1914, A. J. Carlyle having helped in the improvement. The *Memorialia* of Therunda were printed as an appendix to F. Gaeta, *Lorenzo Valla : Filologia e Storia* (1955). A. Stickler, *Historia fontium Iuris canonici* I (1950) and W. Ullmann, *Medieval Papacy* (1949) supply some background material, while C. Duggan, *Twelfth-century Decretal Collections* (1963) shows how much research still remains to be done on the growth of canon law. J. H. C.

FASTING The canonical changes in the discipline of fasting are not proper to a work of dogmatic theology and are not considered here. The main theological issue which arises out of the practice of fasting is the motive (I) or theory inspiring that practice. There is also some theological bearing of the practice (II) on the doctrine of Tradition.

I The motive for refraining from food and drink during a whole day and night, or until sunset, or until the third hour p.m., may not have been clearly discerned by Christians at first. Fasting of this kind was a Jewish practice, and the occasions where it is mentioned in the very early days of Christianity (Ac 27:9, certainly Jewish, as the variants of the text bear witness, Ac 13:2 ; 14:23) show that Paul was following Jewish usage without much

---

[1] Vices enim nostras ita tuae credidimus caritati ut in partem sis vocatus sollicitudinis non in plenitudinem potestatis.

[2] In baptismo regeneramur ad vitam, post baptismum confirmamur ad pugnam.

[3] Cum in datoribus et receptoribus auctoritatis satis esse non crederent, Sylverstrum sanctum qui accepisset et Constantinum Augustum qui dedisset regni sibi quaesiti auctores sibi fecerunt.

reflection. It may be that his fast at the time of his conversion (Ac 9:9) was due to shock, but it is just as likely to have been the result of Jewish religious conviction. Cornelius before his conversion (Ac 10:30) is said by *Codex Bezae* and some supporting MSS. to have been 'fasting and praying the evening prayer' when he had his vision telling him to summon Peter. The Jewish custom was to fast on Mondays and Thursdays except for occasions when these week-days coincided with certain feasts ; a list of these feasts was handed down in the *Megillath Ta'anith* which was compiled before A.D. 70 (TB *Ta'anith* 10a).

A motive for Jewish fasting is assigned by Tacitus (*hist.* 5:4) ; it was to remind them of the hunger in the desert after the Exodus.[1] The first motive for Christian fasting was somewhat similar, to recall the days when the bridegroom was taken away (Mk 2:20 ; Mt 9:15 ; Lk 5:35). The days in question were obviously the days of the annual celebration of the death of Christ, but there was great variety in the manner of counting these days, as the Quartodeciman dispute showed in the 2nd cent. The letter of Dionysius of Alexandria (in Feltoe's edition, 94) deals with this matter as still a problem in the 3rd cent. Tertullian, in his (Montanist) treatise on fasting (*De ieiunio* 2 ; CSEL 20:275) puts forward as the orthodox Catholic position (which he is attacking) that the only prescribed days of fasting were those 'when the bridegroom was taken away', and that Jewish fasts were abolished for a Christian. The *Didache* (8:1) has this anti-Jewish polemic : 'The hypocrites fast on Monday and Thursday ; but do you fast on Wednesday and Friday.' While one cannot be sure when and for whom this author is speaking, it seems that the observance of a Good Friday fast must have led to a similar fast on the Friday of each week, and that the desire to be as good as, but different from, the Jews led to the addition of the Wednesdays. These weekly fasts may not have been so severe as the annual one, for Tertullian (loc. cit.) calls them half-fasts, indicating that they lasted only until the time of evening prayer (when the next day began for liturgical purposes) ; if one prolonged the fast until the next morning this would be a *superpositio* (ὑπέρθεσις). For the *statio, see also* ABSTINENCE II.

The idea in Is 58:4 that fasting is no good without works of mercy was accepted by Christians (though it does not seem to have been much noticed by contemporary Jewry) and soon led to the practice of giving away the food that had been saved by fasting. This is ordered in *Apost. constit.* V:20:18. The regulations in Hippolytus (*trad. apost.*, statute 39) for the meal of the widows suggest that individuals used to call together the widows and the aged for a meal at which they might enjoy what had been saved by voluntary fasting. The same source shows that it was difficult for a bishop to fast, since there would be many who brought to church bread for distribution as *eulogia* (or *pain bénit*), and, when they did so, it would be hard for the bishop to refrain from

[1] *Longam olim famem crebris ieiuniis fatentur.*

tasting it out of politeness, thereby breaking his fast.

The ascetic purpose of fasting was understood by Greek, Roman and Jewish philosophers alike. Seneca (*ep.* 8 :5) laid down the principle that the body should be treated harshly lest it rebel against the soul. Philo (*De vita contemplativa*, 35) reported of his heroes that some of them fasted for three and some for six whole days. Tertullian (*De ieiunio*, 1 ; CSEL 20:274) accepted the idea as a truth of physiology. Digestive and sexual organs are juxtaposed in the body because of their interaction.[2] Jerome (*Contra Iovinianum*, 2:7; PL 23:297) quoted the comic poet for the same idea.[3] It is indicative of the truth of the maxim to find Boswell in the midst of his life of pleasure appealing to it as a reason for combining all three (Boswell's *London Journal*, 137). Luther disagreed (*Werke* XL:115), saying he was most of all tempted when he was abstemious.

Self-denial went further in antiquity, for there was a general belief that a complete fast kept away evil spirits. Plutarch (*De defectu oraculorum* 417c) expresses the idea. Porphyry (*De abstinentia* 4:20 and in the fragment cited by Eusebius, *Praeparatio evangelica* 4:23 ; GCS 43:214) accepted that devils find entrance into human bodies through what is eaten, most of all when animal blood is consumed. On the fringe of Christianity the author of the *Clementine Homilies* (9:10 ; PG 2:248) gave currency to the notion, alleging that evil spirits found entry in that way in order that they might make use of the organs of the human body. It is in this connection that the text of Mt 17:21 and Mk 9:29 must be considered. By the absence of the verse from the Matthaean passage in *Vaticanus, Sinaiticus*, the oldest Syriac and some of the Old Latin MSS., a *prima facie* case is established for its having been inserted after Mt 17:20 in the other MSS. by borrowing from Mk 9:29. In the Marcan passage prayer alone is given as the means of driving out devils by some of the MSS., *Vaticanus* and *Sinaiticus* being the chief witnesses of this reading, along with the Georgian version, a citation in Clement of Alexandria (GCS 17:141) and one Old Latin MS., but the vast majority have the word 'fasting' added. In view of the manifest intrusion of this word in 1 Cor 7:5 (where married folk are urged to return to their prayers from time to time) it is most likely that ascetic trends in the 2nd-cent. Church led to the insertion of the word in Mk 9:29 also. Tertullian seems to have been familiar with the insertion ; he speaks of Christ having taught that fasting was to be used against stronger demons [4] (*De ieiunio*, 8 ; CSEL 20:284). Origen (*hom.* 24 on Josue ; GCS 30:448) couples prayer and fasting as weapons against the devil in a manner that might imply he knew the text in the longer form, though he does not cite it. The instruction to the exorcist that he should fast before starting his work (*Rituale*, titulus XI:1) and get others to do so does not mention

[2] *Specta corpus, et una regio est.*
[3] *Sine Cerere et Libero friget Venus.*
[4] *Docuit etiam adversus diriora daemonia ieiuniis proeliandum.*

the victim as having to fast. The Vulgate text of Mt 17:21 is cited. This may be taken to mean that the Church did not accept the pagan view that it was by means of the food eaten that the devil found entry.

Ecstatic fasting is a later development in the Church. Augustine (*De consensu evangelistarum* 2:27 ; CSEL 43:167) speaks of a fast that is of a higher order, where the mind is held aloft in spiritual delight and is aloof from bodily food. Clement of Alexandria (*Eclogae* 14 ; GCS 17:140) foreshadows this view. Jerome, too, speaks of having the world under one's feet when fasting (*Contra Iovinianum* 2:11 ; PL 23:301). Tertullian (*De ieiunio* 6 ; CSEL 20:281) argued from the experience of Elias at Horeb that fasting made of God one's familiar companion,[1] and from the story of Daniel's fast (Dan 10:2), which was followed by a vision, that Christians might expect the same result from theirs. A Lenten preface in the *Bobbio Missal* (141) brings in the fast of Moses, 'who abstained from bodily food that he might be more capable of receiving sweetness from God while he lived by the divine word'.[2] The *Missale Gothicum* (179) in a similar preface generalizes the idea : 'While the body is stinted, the soul has her fill ; our outward man is in pain while our inner man is set free.'[3] This preface is also in the *Gelasianum* (673) and the *Gallicanum vetus* (266). The Lenten preface of the Roman Missal provides a suitable summary of the purposes of fasting : restraint of vice, elevation of mind, reward by the strengthening of virtue. In the *Summa* of St Thomas (2–2ae:147:7c) the earliest of the motives mentioned in this article is not forgotten, though the others have come to assume larger proportions. He can say that those who afflict their flesh are assimilated to the Passion of Christ. The faithful have not forgotten this in their ordinary practice.

II The importance for Tradition of the practice of fasting is not often noticed, yet Tertullian, who wanted more fasting than the orthodox, had some trouble to justify himself. He claimed that traditional practices which had no warrant in Scripture required further substantiation by charismatic deed or utterance (*De ieiunio*, 10 ; CSEL 20:287).[4] Tertullian would have cited (and did) one of the new prophets when he wanted to justify his own traditions. He mocks (loc. cit.) at the orthodox for going 'according to the law of Peter' (*ex forma Petri*). With heavy sarcasm he attacks the foundation of this Petrine law (*De ieiunio*, 15 ; CSEL 20:294) by asking if Peter had had given to him the keys of the meat-market. Even so, says Tertullian, that does not prove that the kingdom of God is inside. This mockery must be viewed in the light of what we

[1] Deum praestat homini contubernalem.
[2] A carnalibus cibis ut Tuae suavitatis capacior esset abstinuit, de verbo Tuo vivens.
[3] Restrictis corporibus animae saginantur ; et in quo exterior homo noster adfligitur, dilatatur interior.
[4] Eorum quae ex traditione observantur tanto magis dignam rationem adferre debemus quanto carent Scripturae auctoritate, donec aliquo caelesti charismate aut confirmentur aut corrigantur.

now know of 2nd-cent. polemic against the Petrine position from the *Gospel of Thomas*; there (section 12) a carefully-contrived story (parallel to Mt 16:18) gives the primacy to Thomas. Tertullian's adversaries may be thought to have based their justification of limited fasting on the authority of apostolic tradition coming from Peter.

One could argue that Scripture (in this case Mk 9:29) had laid down the law for fasting, but the words there used by Christ do not amount to more than a promise that there would be fasting in the Church. It was for the apostles to determine when, and how, and how much. It was for them, even, to say what the comparison of bridegroom and bride really meant ; and, if we are to believe the hint in Papias (fragment 6), the Johannine school did this with a will. They worked out the comparison in terms of the Genesis story of Adam and Eve. At a later time Jerome (*ep.* 71:5 ; CSEL 55:6) can say that Church traditions, when they do not run counter to the faith, are so to be followed as they have been handed down, and that differences between one place and another in the matter of fasting do not mean that it is to be given up as something void for uncertainty.

Bibliography. R. Arbesmann, *Das Fasten bei den Griechen und Römern* (1929) ; J. Schuemmer, *Die altchristliche Fastenpraxis* (1933) ; *and see also* Asceticism. J. H. C.

FATHERHOOD OF GOD There is no feast in the liturgy of God the Father. The inner life of the Trinity is not generally presented to the faithful for their meditation. Its theological treatment belongs to the article Trinity, and here the theme is that fatherhood in which God stands to all men, and not the mystery of His eternal generation of the Son.

I The distinction between general and personal paternity is outlined by the language of Christ in the gospels. 'Your heavenly Father' (Mt 5:16, 45, 48 ; 6:1, 4, 8, 14, 15, 26, 32 and often) and 'My heavenly Father' (Mt 7:21 ; 10:32 ; 12:50 ; 15:13 and often) are kept distinct. The discourse of Mt 18:10–20 opens and closes with a reference to 'My heavenly Father', while at 18:14 there is, according to some MSS., a mention of 'your heavenly Father', but here the witnesses to the text are evenly divided, א DW and fam 1 with syrcur and the Latin wanting 'your', while Bθ fam 13 with syrsin and the Coptic have 'My'. What does not occur is 'Our Father', save in the opening words of the Lord's Prayer, where the wording is obviously arranged to suit the need of those who were to use the prayer. Jn 20:17 has the distinction quite explicitly : 'My Father and your Father', while Jn 8:41 shows that a general paternity of men could be attributed to God by contemporary Jewish thought. This is borne out by what Philo says (*De specialibus legibus*, II:247) about God being no father of iron heart and by what the Talmud (TB *Sotah* 12a) relates of a 1st-cent. Rabbi : 'He fixed his heart on his Father in heaven'.

St Paul (Eph 3:15) has what looks like a statement

of the relationship between the two paternities, where God's personal paternity is said to be the prototype of all paternity in heaven and on earth. The text was taken in this way as early as the time of Athanasius (PG 26:60), who says that the Father and Son are related in the proper and only true sense (κυρίως καὶ μόνον ἀληθῶς), while all others are denominated fathers in a secondary way. Two difficulties have been raised about this way of taking the text, that it is too early in the development of philosophical thought for Paul to have used the language of analogy (but *see* ANALOGY OF BEING, II) and that it is hard to see what paternity in heaven would mean. Clement was perfectly familiar with the ideas about analogy current in Middle Platonism, and he it is who uses technical language for the idea (*see below*). Paul speaks more concretely, and there is no reason to think that such a setting forth of analogy should have been impossible to him. Ac 3:25 shows that talk about 'every family on earth' was current in early Christian discourse ; the linking of heaven with this is not surprising in this epistle (1:10, 21 ; 2:6). Some of the Fathers took Paul to be speaking about physical and spiritual paternity (so Theodoret, PG 82:529, and Athanasius, *Orat. in Arianos* 1:23 ; PG 26:60), and, in view of 1 Cor 4:15, this is not impossible. Clement (*strom.* 6:7:59 ; GCS 52:461) seems to have taken the same way with the text, for he says : 'Just as all fatherhood runs back logically to God the creator, so too the teaching of our faith recurs to Christ the Lord.'

By the time of the Scholastic theologians there is established the axiom that all works of the Trinity *ad extra* (i.e. those concerned with created being) are common to all three Persons (*see* TRINITY) and St Thomas can say quite without comment : 'We say the *Our Father* to the whole Trinity' (*Summa*, 1a:33:3:1). Suarez (*Opera*, I:722) echoes this. To many this may come as a revelation quite parallel to M. Jourdain's discovery of prose. Augustine was quite confused about this ; he asked the catechumens (*serm.* 57:2 *in Mt* 6 ; PL 38:387) : 'Whom does He want us to call our Father, if not His own Father ?' and yet he continues : 'We have fathers and mothers on earth to bring us forth to labour and death ; we have found other parents, God our Father and the Church, our mother, from whom we are born to life eternal.' Here the spiritual fatherhood must primarily be that of Christ, who in the previous sermon (PL 38:379) is spoken of as giving rise to their conception in the womb of the Church, yet this is one of the divine works *ad extra* which on principle belong to the Trinity. The personal and the general fatherhood of God are not distinctly viewed by Augustine.

St Thomas (*Summa*, 1a:33:c) sees the whole range of fatherhood, from inanimate creatures such as the rain (which, as Job 38:28 implies, comes under the general fatherhood of God) up through man's physical existence (Deut 32:16) to his spiritual elevation (Rom 8:15–16). But this general relation of God to His creation is only a faint reflection of that primary fact that Father stands to Son as Begetter to

Begotten, and in his attempt to describe this latter relation (*Summa*, 1a:27:2:@3) St Thomas can speak of the Son accepting His whole being from the Father (following in this Jn 5:26) without at the same time suggesting that this acceptance implies any diminution of reality or status. Calvin would not acquiesce in this explanation, but said (*Admonitio ad Polonos*, in his *Opera*, IX:647) that such a passage of being from Person to Person[1] must imply that there were three essences in God. Thomas Whitaker (in his answer to Campion, 34) claimed that to say that the Son accepted His being from the Father was to deny the divinity of the Son.

II The distinct knowledge of the Father in His own Person is hinted at in the phrase used by Ignatius of Antioch (*Rom.* 7:2) about the living water within himself that said 'Hither, to the Father'. The practice of the Church, established as early as the first public prayers known to us, was to address the Father through Christ, who in His humanity was the high priest of us all. It must however be admitted that the doxologies with which prayers were generally concluded (*see* DOXOLOGIES) were always strongly Trinitarian.

The language of St Thomas (himself a contemplative of no mean degree) is studiously vague. He speaks (*I Sent.* 15:4:1) of the Holy Ghost coming to be present—though unperceived—in the human mind by the gift of charity, of the Son likewise by the gift of Wisdom and of the two producing a manifestation of the Father, who is the goal of our elevation.[2] The use of the neuter (*ultimum*) here does not encourage one to think in personal terms of the Father. A little later (*I Sent.* 16:1:2) he says that the invisible mission of the Holy Ghost produces an overflow of grace in the human mind and thus causes an experimental knowledge of this divine Person on the part of the one who receives the mission. Knowledge of the Father cannot be by way of His mission, for there is no such mission, but in *Summa*, 1a:43:4:@1 and @2, St Thomas speaks of the Father liberally communicating Himself to His creatures for their happiness, even while he denies that there is a mission of the Father.

St Augustine had entered into a polemic (*De Trin.* II:18:33) against those who said that while Son and Spirit might have been seen by the Fathers and Prophets, the Father Himself never was. St Thomas knew this polemic and also the attack on those (neo-Platonist ?) philosophers (*De Trin.* IV:15:20) who thought that they could by their own efforts win access to the light of God's incommutable truth and thus outdistance the Christians who did not claim as much.[3] Augustine in reply had taken

[1] Si essentiatus est Christus, non est ille Jehova.
[2] Sicut Spiritus sanctus invisibiliter procedit in mentem per donum amoris, ita Filius per donum sapientiae, in quo est manifestatio ipsius Patris, qui est ultimum ad quod recurrimus.
[3] Purgationem sibi isti virtute propria pollicentur, quia nonnulli eorum potuerunt aciem mentis ultra omnem creaturam transmittere ac lucem incommutabilis veritatis quantulacunque ex parte contingere, quod Christianos multos ex fide interim sola viventes nondum potuisse derident.

I Tim 6:16 to apply to the being of God and not to the Father in Person ; he accepted some experimental knowledge of the Son, and St Thomas (*Summa*, 1a:43:5:@2) followed him in this ; about knowledge of the Father, though he supposes it to be given, he is less communicative.

Rather disappointingly St Thomas in his comment on Eph 2:18 (if one can trust the *Reportatio* of his lectures thereon, lect. 5 on Eph 2) took the ' access to the Father' ($\pi\rho\sigma\alpha\gamma\omega\gamma\dot{\eta}$) which is there proclaimed, to be access to the Trinity as a whole, or to the being of God. Chrysostom (*hom.* 6 in Eph ; PG 62:44) had noted that $\pi\rho\sigma\alpha\gamma\omega\gamma\dot{\eta}$ (access) was not the same as $\pi\rho\dot{\sigma}\sigma\delta\sigma$ (an open road), referring to Jn 14:6 for his statement. The examples from the records of the mystics given by Poulain (*Graces of Mystical Prayer*, ch. XVIII) show that often these mystics were content to say that they had been made aware of the divine nature, but that sometimes they could distinguish (as e.g. St Ignatius Loyola did) between visions of the divine nature and of the Father alone, without the other Persons. The Church has in general kept to the rule of *Tribus honor unus* (a single veneration for the three Persons) in her devotions, and Benedict XIV argued that if there was to be a devotion to the Father as Begetter, there should be added one to the eternal Generation of the Son and another to the Procession of the Holy Ghost. Our sonship by adoption does not carry us into the heart of the Trinity in this life (*see* ADOPTION) in the way that this is possible to Christ Himself. The analogy of fatherhood is what may be called a downcast analogy (from God to ourselves), as Severianus of Gabala insisted (cf. a fragment of his, on Eph 2:18, in Cramer's *Catena*, VI:159). It is perhaps significant that (Mt 12:50) in praising those who do the will of His Father Christ did not make use of this one relationship of fatherhood along with the others, brother, sister, mother.

In the conciliar discussions of Vatican II about non-Christian religions, the question arose about the theological propriety of saying to them that there is ' one God and Father of us all' (Eph 4:6). The context at that place shows that only the baptized are meant, as Chrysostom (ad loc.) said. On the basis of Rom 8:20–2 Mersch and others had written of ' the grace of adoption penetrating to the depths of the universe, conferring a new manner of existence upon the whole world, that vast body wherein all humanity lives' (*The Whole Christ*, 144). This manner of speaking is hardly justified by the text itself, for as Chrysostom (ad loc.) points out, the elevation of creation is to come at and after the resurrection of the body. No doubt the last days are upon us, but in so far as we have not yet had experience of the resurrection of the body, it seems idle to speculate on the share in that resurrection which may have been imparted to creation. Lessius thought that flowers were somehow to share in the Redemption, and any gardener will be ready to see in the emergence of a new cultivated flower a triumph over the original wildness of nature ; yet between strict adoptive sonship (*see* ADOPTION) for

the baptized and this vague diffusion of grace over the whole of creation there seems to be no middle stage clearly discernible. Grace is certainly given outside the Church (D 1379) but it is given in view of baptism, whether of water or of desire (*see* SALVATION OF NON-CATHOLICS).

Bibliography. E. Guérry, *God the Father* (1947) is a devotional book, but has a page of theological comment as an appendix ; M. Catherinet, ' La Sainte Trinité et notre filiation adoptive ', in *La vie spirituelle*, 39 (1934) 113–28 ; S. Dockx OP, *Fils de Dieu par grâce* (1948) ; A. Poulain SJ, *The Graces of Mystical Prayer* (5th English edition from 10th French, 1950) ; E. Mersch SJ, *The Whole Christ* (1938) ; P. Galtier SJ, ' La Religion du Fils ', in RAM 19 (1938) 337–75.   J. H. C.

FATHERS OF THE CHURCH It is not the purpose of this article to give information on the lives and works of individual Fathers, but to consider what it is that the Church understands by the term ' Father of the Church', which is applied to some of her earliest writers. The four marks essential to this notion are by common consent of theologians laid down to be these : the author must belong to antiquity ; his doctrine must be Catholic ; it must have received approval, and he must have been marked by holiness of life. The first note causes no difficulty, it being agreed that the age of the Fathers ends in the West with Isidore of Seville (d.636) and in the Greek East with John Damascene (d.c.749). No such clear limit is assigned to the Syriac Fathers. The note of sanctity is equally clear ; thus the writer Firmicus Maternus in the 4th cent. is held by some to have written a treatise expounding astrological views subsequently to his (doctrinally sound) Christian work *de errore profanarum religionum*. If this were proved against him, he could not be considered as a Father of the Church.

The notes of sound doctrine and ecclesiastical approval may be examined together. When Cyril of Alexandria (*see* EPHESUS) presented the Council of Ephesus with a list of passages taken from Christian writers of the 4th cent., in order to show that Nestorius was not in line with traditional teaching, he was in fact appealing to certain Fathers of the Church. His authors were put forward as being sound in doctrine and, if the Council accepted the list, then posterity could know that these men were authors approved by the Church. There was at first no hand-list of approved authors, but the practice at both Ephesus and Chalcedon was to refer to those who attended the first Ecumenical Council at Nicaea as ' Fathers'. Athanasius in particular was much favoured as a quotable author, and Cyril was in fact misled into using as Athanasian certain texts that had been foisted on him by the followers of Apollinaris, or even by Apollinaris himself. Their anxiety to pass off partisan views as those of Athanasius means that the cult of the Fathers went back to the later decades of the 4th cent., and indeed this is borne out by the fact that Basil (*ep.* 140 ; PG 32:588) could write about ' what we have been taught by the holy

Fathers'. Gregory Nazianzen is the first to suggest (*orat.* 33:15 ; PG 36:233) anything like an equality between the Scriptures and the writings of the Fathers. The council of Ephesus, as Newman pointed out (*Via Media* I:312, note added to the 1877 edition), had to proceed on the evidence of creed and Fathers alone, without Scripture.

The *Decretum Gelasianum* (D 164–5), to be dated *c.*492, after listing the books of Holy Scripture added : ' The Roman Church does not forbid these writings also being received, namely the holy Councils of Nicaea, Ephesus, Chalcedon . . ., also the works of the blessed Cyprian, of Gregory Nazianzen, Basil, Athanasius, John Chrysostom, Cyril of Alexandria, Hilary, Ambrose, Augustine, Jerome, Prosper . . ., and also the works and treatises of all the orthodox Fathers who have in no point turned aside from communion with the holy Roman Church.' This list includes one (Jerome) who was a simple priest and one (Prosper) who was a layman. Thus, though the teaching authority exercised by the bishops of the Church often over-lapped with the works of the Fathers, yet they did not quite coincide. Ephrem had been the test case for the admission of a non-bishop to the list of Fathers, as he was *the* Father of the Syriac Church. He is not mentioned in the decree, as there would be few in the West who could then read his works.

To trace farther back into the past the idea of fatherhood, one may cite a passage from Clement of Alexandria (*strom.* 1:1 ; GCS 52:1) where he says that those who give us our elementary instruction we call Fathers (πατέρας τοὺς κατηχησαντάς φαμεν), and also the letter to Origen (in Eusebius, HE 6:14) from Alexander, later Bishop of Jerusalem : ' We regard as fathers those blessed men who went on the way before us, Pantaenus . . . and Clement.' This language would not sound unfamiliar to a Jew of those times who was aware of what rabbinical suc-cession meant to his faith. It was something different from a priestly succession in a liturgical office, and, though in the Christian Church succession from the apostles (*see* APOSTOLIC SUCCESSION) was the most highly prized, yet the master-disciple relationship was not unknown. The thesis of Gerhardsson in *Memory and Manuscript* on the place of this relation-ship in the first decades of the Church, while the gospels are being composed, has found some attackers and also stout defenders. It may be that in the future it will be possible to see more plainly the origins of the notion of fatherhood, when the present debate is concluded.

No single Father was held to be free from all error. The rule is set out by Vincent of Lérins (*commoni-torium* 28:39 ; in Moxon's edition, 115) : ' This is the way in which the Fathers are to be trusted. Whatever all or several of them with one accord, openly, often and persistently affirm as traditional, as it were giving the agreed opinion of the teachers in a school, that is to be taken as certainly approved doctrine. But when one of them, however much a bishop, or a martyr or confessor, goes outside or against the common agreement, that may be set aside as his own private and peculiar vagary of opinion . . . .'[1] For the part played by the Fathers in interpreting the Scriptures, *see* BIBLE, USE OF IN THEOLOGY.

The status of ' Father ', achieved by the possession of the four notes listed, marks off a writer from the common run of writers who may testify to the thought and interests of a past age. Not all the writers in Jerome's *De scriptoribus illustribus*, or in its continuation by Gennadius, are to be called Father. In Modernist days there had to be some emphasis on this difference (D 2086, 2146). To give the evidence for a doctrine, it was not proper for the theologian to lump together all the writings from a particular period, treatises of the Fathers with apocryphal Acts, heretical works and comments in pagan authors. The reason for the difference is that some assistance of the Holy Spirit was vouchsafed to the Fathers, even though they cannot be said to be inspired as the Scripture-writers were inspired. The Holy Spirit, animating the Church, saw to it that the doctrines to be handed on were not left without witness and that the Scripture was not left without a gloss. He did not override the whims and vagaries of individual Fathers, but left sufficient milestones on the wayside, and it was the duty of posterity to see that they were not moved (Prov 22:28). This text was frequently appealed to, e.g. by Eutherius of Tyana in his *Antilogia*, 15 (in the edition of Tetz, 29).

Bibliography. The best discussion is still that of O. Bardenhewer, *Geschichte der altkirchlichen Literatur* I (1913) ; B. Altaner, *Patrology* (1960) has some three pages (3–5) on the topic ; the *Commonitorium* of Vincent of Lérins, edited by R. S. Moxon (1915), and the *Acta conciliorum*, edited by E. Schwartz (series I on Ephesus, and II on Chalcedon, 1912–38), contain most of the vital texts.   J. H. C.

FEASTS It is perfectly natural that the Church should have an annual commemoration of the Passion (for which *see* EUCHARIST), but the origin of the cycle of feasts (the seasonal feasts rather than saints' days) is a matter of great obscurity, and efforts to open new lines of inquiry into this obscurity are only just being made. The special branch of theology which will some day be called heortology (from the Greek for feast) is rapidly growing and may be productive of great benefits to theology in general before very long. Here one may hope to do no more than disentangle two or three strands in that inquiry : (I) the dating of events in the life of Christ and the keeping of their anniversaries, (II) the finding of parallels to the Jewish calendar, (III) the making of a cycle (annual or triennial) of liturgical readings, (IV) the importance of Epiphany as the foremost

[1] Quibus tamen (patribus) hac lege credendum est ut quidquid vel omnes vel plures uno eodemque sensu manifeste, frequenter, perseveranter, velut quodam consentiente sibi magistrorum concilio, accipiendo, tenendo, tradendo firmaverint, id pro indubitato certo ratoque habeatur. Quidquid vero, quamvis ille sanctus, et doctus, quamvis episcopus, quamvis confessor et martyr, praeter omnes aut etiam contra omnes senserit, id inter proprias et occultas et privatas opiniunculas . . . secretum sit.

feast of the year alongside Easter and Pentecost, and finally (V) a theological conclusion.

I The public life of Christ was held by some to have lasted for no more than a year, from the Baptism to the Passion. Irenaeus (*adv. haer.* I:i:5 H) has recorded this of some of the Valentinians, and one view of the chronology of the Synoptic gospels would make it possible to work out a scheme that would fit in all the events therein narrated within the compass of one year. From this to the keeping of certain days as the anniversaries of particular events such as the Transfiguration or the beheading of John the Baptist would be but a step. Palm Sunday, the Ascension and the Descent of the Spirit fit into a pattern like this, but the trouble starts when one has to explain why there was no annual commemoration of so many other striking events, the Temptation, the walking on the water, the promise to Peter, the healing of the centurion or the raising of the daughter of Jairus. Those who support a chronology of the public life of Christ which requires two years or three for its deployment naturally look with little favour on this line of inquiry, but it is hard to deny that it may have had some influence on early practice.

The late Fr Sutcliffe, in his book *The Two-year Ministry* (1938), had no difficulty in showing that many of the orthodox accepted the idea that the public life lasted for no more than one year. His list (op. cit. 17–25) includes Clement of Alexandria (*strom.* I:21:145 ; GCS 52:90), who uses the text of Is 61:2 about the acceptable year, Tertullian (*adv. Iudaeos* 8 ; PL 2:615), Filastrius (*De haeresibus* 106 ; CSEL 38:65), and Prosper of Aquitaine, whose chronicle (MGH, *Auctores antiquissimi* IX:409) calls this belief the *usitatior traditio*. Irenaeus (*adv. haer.* II:xxxii:6 H) is at some pains to refute the application to Christ of the 'acceptable year' of prophecy, and one must suppose from the wealth of evidence that, in spite of the three Paschs of St John's gospel, it would have been quite easy for early Christians to set up a one-to-one relation between the events of the gospel and the holy days of their ecclesiastical year. Positive evidence that they did so is not so easy to find.

The most obvious case of the Ascension did not move the early Christians to celebrate its anniversary forty days after Easter (*see* ASCENSION) until the late 4th cent. ; previously they kept it on Pentecost as a part of that mystery. The story of the feast of the Transfiguration is still more complex, and its discussion (see below) depends on Jewish material and Jewish precedents. The feast of St Peter's Chair is in no way a commemoration of Mt 16:13–18, but is due to an effort to supplant the pagan feast of *cara cognatio* at Rome (*see* DEAD, PRAYER FOR THE).

II Jewish parallels are quite certain for Easter and Pentecost, but if there had been wholesale matching with the Jewish feasts, one would have the right to expect that the feast of Tabernacles had some Christian rival or copy, quite apart from Hanukkah and Purim. Origen (*c.Cels.* 2:2 ; GCS 2:128) has the general principle that the Jewish law about foods, sabbaths and new moons was a shadow of the truth,

and in *De oratione* (27:16 ; GCS 3:374) he again appeals to this fact, but this time he mentions yearly feasts, citing the law of Deut 16:16 which ordered the presence of every male Jew before the Lord in the place He should appoint three times in the year, for Azymes, Weeks and Tabernacles. On the other hand, his catalogue of Christian feasts (in his *c.Cels.* 8:22 ; GCS 3:239) lists Sundays, Fridays, Easter and Pentecost. The only Christian feast that ranked with Easter and Pentecost in antiquity was Epiphany. It therefore becomes crucial for this line of inquiry to show that Epiphany has been taken up as a Christian 'sublimation' or antitype of Tabernacles.

The four features of Tabernacles that are most distinctive are its practice of constructing booths of selected boughs, its procession of a water-libation from the pool of Siloe to the Temple, its all-night celebration with the illumination of Jerusalem (according to Is 60:1–3), and its connection with the vintage. The feast was held for a week in Tishri (roughly September), soon after the original Jewish new year (the custom of starting the year with Nisan in the spring began in the Babylonian captivity). A 2nd-cent. papyrus (*Corpus papyrorum Judaicarum* 452a) tells of one Amaranthus who gave 100 drachmas for the *pannuchis* (or all-night celebration) of this feast in a small Egyptian community, and a letter of Bar Kokeba during the revolt of 132 orders the collection of the right kind of boughs for the feast ; there can be no doubt of its solemnity for the Jews of the early Christian times.

Now in the year 335 Constantine held the dedication feast of his new basilica in Jerusalem for seven days in September (11 to 17), a feast at which Eusebius was present (*Vita Constantini* 4:44 ; GCS 7:136). Sozomenos writing after 439 tells us (HE 2:26 ; PG 67:1008) that the feast became an annual event, and he adds the important fact that baptisms were carried out during it. Etheria in her pilgrimage to Jerusalem noted (CSEL 39:101) that 'on these days of the Dedication the adornment of all the churches is the same as at Easter and at Epiphany, and on each day there is a procession to the several holy places as at Easter and Epiphany'. Her description of what happened on Epiphany (ibid., 75) is incomplete owing to a break in the text, but it does report that two processions took place, one during the night from Bethlehem to the Anastasis church at Jerusalem, arriving there, 'at the hour when one man begins to be able to recognize another', and the procession from Golgotha to the Anastasis after Mass there about the sixth hour. Other Jacobite or Nestorian churches had dedication feasts in November or December, as Professor M. Black has shown, and these may have been conscious attempts to copy the Jewish Hanukkah or *encaenia* (which is known, from Jn 10:22 and elsewhere, to have fallen in December) rather than postponements of an original September festival on Jerusalem lines. What is certain is that Constantine was not ousting an earlier Christian attempt to copy Tabernacles when he began his dedication feast in September 335. The borrowing of Jewish Sukkoth selections from OT for reading on the September

ember days (the *ieiunium mensis septimi* of the Leonine Sacramentary) is a later Western phenomenon, due probably to the absence of all knowledge of the Jerusalem liturgy there.

There is a curious English imitation of Tabernacles, due to the letter of Gregory the Great to Mellitus (cited in Bede, HE 1:30 ; Plummer, 65) which suggested that the new converts in England might be encouraged to build huts of branches near the church on certain festivals such as the dedication day and the feasts of martyrs, and to hold banquets there.[1] The 'wakes' or 'feasts' of many English churches are no doubt survivals of this Gregorian initiative, but it is not likely that Gregory had any other guide in what he said than his own reading of the OT. It may well be that his instruction fitted admirably the tendency of Keltic Christianity to imitate the OT, but one cannot think that he was aware in giving it of what Constantine had done at Jerusalem in 335.

III The making of a cycle of annual (or triennial) readings for the liturgy is by some held to be proved by the section-markings in the MSS. of some of the gospels. Archbishop Carrington must be credited with the discovery that the Vatican codex (B) had in Mark a quite different system of dividing the text to what was found in the other main MSS. of that gospel. He counted sixty-two sections ; fourteen comprised the Passion gospel and the other forty-eight were, he thought, arranged in a one-to-one correspondence with the Sundays of the year (a lunar year). In his first book *The Primitive Christian Calendar* (1952) on this topic he did not clearly distinguish between real time and liturgical time, implying sometimes that Christ had done all that is told in Mk 1–13 within the space of one year (as discussed in [I] above) and sometimes that the narrative of these events was to be read in instalments which lasted for a year. The theory postulated that the text-division had been made at a very early date (when the church where it was carried out had but one gospel to use), and this made it appear that some theology of the Christian year going back to apostolic times might be recovered. Fr Daniélou accepted Carrington's theory, even in its first form, but in his second book (*According to Mark*, 1960) the Archbishop gave up the attempt to link the text-divisions with real time and was content to keep to liturgical time. Fr Daniélou (*Theology of Jewish Christianity*, 345–6) thinks that the liturgical distribution of passages was made for a Jewish-Christian calendar starting with Tishri (September) and that, when this arrangement had to be transposed for the Julian calendar of the Gentile churches (starting in January), the Baptism of Christ, which was the first episode recorded in Mark, came to be fixed in the early days of January as the feast of the Epiphany. This would mean that the Little Apocalypse of Mk 13 would fall in December (the Passion gospel having been used as a separate series at Easter) and thus prepare the way for the liturgy of Advent (*see*

ADVENT). It may be that all this is true, but it throws back the formation of the liturgical year to so early a date that it is quite impossible to check the theory against known facts. The crucial point is the likeness of Tabernacles to Epiphany and the role of the latter in the beginnings of the Christian year. If the followers of Basilides in the 2nd cent. kept a feast of the Baptism of Christ on 6 January, as Clement says (*strom.* 1:21:145 ; GCS 52:90) they did, and if in this they had copied the Jewish Christians, as Fr Daniélou asserts, then why did the Christians in Jerusalem still keep mid-September as their time of baptism from 335 onwards ? One may say that they had these two baptismal seasons or days, but evidence for this is lacking.

IV The original idea of an Epiphany feast is a matter of some controversy. It has been proposed to see in it a feast of the Incarnation, on the ground that the most primitive feasts were not historical commemorations but 'feasts of an idea', and that the idea here displayed was the Nicene dogma, of God revealing Himself in one who was the image of His own substance. The principle itself of this priority is very much open to question. If the Church was really using Jewish feast-times and putting her own content into them, as she certainly did with Passover and Weeks, then the correspondence of OT events with NT events is more likely to have supplied that content. Solomon's dedication was certainly part of the inspiration behind what Constantine did at Jerusalem in September 335, and this was an event rather than an idea.

What has not been remarked is that when the Latin West received Epiphany from the East, it was thought of as *several* manifestations, for the word was in Latin a neuter plural (manifestations), as may be seen from Ammianus Marcellinus (a pagan author who reports [21:2:5] the existence of this Christian feast in Gaul in 361), from Cassian (*Collationes*, 10:2; CSEL 13:286), who describes it as being in Egypt both the baptism feast and the nativity, and from Filastrius of Brescia (*haer.* 112 ; CSEL 38:111), who says that the four major feasts are the Birth, the manifestations, the Passion and the Ascension, adding that some take the manifestation to be the baptism while others think of the Transfiguration. Ambrose, in a hymn which has been denied to him in the interest of the theory that idea feasts came first but which is vindicated for his authorship by A. S. Walpole (*Early Latin Hymns*, 62–9), sang of Christ the enlightener (*Inluminans Altissimus*) who made three manifestations, at Jordan, to the Magi and at Cana.

In the 2nd cent. Justin (*dial.* 88:8), while dealing with the Baptism of Christ, says that the Father declared His Son to be that day begotten because ' His birth for men was to be counted from the time when the knowledge of Him was to go forth'. Justin (along with *Codex Bezae*, the old Latin, Clement and Origen) read in his gospel (Lk 3:23) an exact citation of Ps 2:7 by the voice from heaven at the Baptism ; it was only logical to interpret its words : ' This day have I begotten Thee ', as an

---

[1] Die dedicationis vel natalitii sanctorum martyrum . . . tabernacula sibi circa easdem ecclesias . . . de ramis arborum faciant et religiosis conviviis sollemnitatem celebrent.

indication that the Baptism should be kept as a beginning of Christianity. The same idea is found in the *Epistle to Diognetus* (11:4–5), in a passage which Kirsopp Lake wanted to regard as a homily for the Epiphany. A. McArthur has recently revived this view, but, as the last two chapters of that *Epistle* are by no means proved to be detachable from the rest, it is not at all clear that they can be a homily for Epiphany, and still less that Epiphany was then looked on as a feast of an idea, namely of the manifestation of Christ by His Incarnation. McArthur is certainly right in wanting to have Epiphany kept as a baptism feast by the Church long before the 4th cent., and he is right to reject the hasty theories of Dom B. Botte (who thought that there was no notion of connecting Epiphany with Baptism in early times). The statement of Justin and the passage in the *Epistle* are sufficient to show that when the 2nd-cent. Church wanted to keep a feast of the manifestation, that feast would be concerned with the Baptism. That some 2nd-cent. heretics did keep a feast of the Baptism on 5 January is also established, and it would therefore seem likely that they were in this copying the practice of the orthodox rather than the reverse.

Why Cana should have been joined to the Baptism at Epiphany is not so clear. Jn 2:11 does call the event a manifestation of the glory of Christ, and Jn 17:6 would suggest that the whole public life of Christ was a manifestation. Ephrem in one of his Epiphany hymns speaks of the Bridegroom this day entering the Jordan ; once the idea of Epiphany as the nuptials of Christ and the Church had been produced, then the viewing of Cana as an incident to be recalled on this day would be natural. Besides the hymn of Ambrose cited above, Paulinus of Nola (*carmina* 27:45 ; CSEL 30:264), Peter Chrysologus (*serm.* 157 ; PL 52:613) and Maximus of Turin have Cana as a part of their Epiphany feast.

The star of the Magi was a heavenly manifestation at the Birth of Christ, and when the Church began to insist on the fact of the Birth, as against Gnostic views about the divinity coming upon Christ at the Baptism, it would be easy for some to say that it was this fact that made of the Birth a manifestation. Polemic against regarding the Birth as a manifestation may be seen in Jerome (on Ezech 1:3 ; PL 25:18) who said scornfully that Christ at His birth was hidden and not manifested.[1] This may well be directed against Jerome's old adversary, Rufinus, who in his translation of the homilies of Gregory Nazianzen had written : ' He was manifested to men by His nativity.' When both feasts, Epiphany and Christmas, were to be kept (*see* CHRISTMAS), it was inevitable that Epiphany should take to itself the idea of a manifestation of Christ to the Magi, but this idea was not at all primitive. A liturgical papyrus of the 4th cent. or early 5th (*Pap. Rainer* 542, in PO 18:438) has the star appearing to the shepherds, even though the account in Lk 2:8–20 has no mention of this.

The evidence of the Canons of Athanasius was

used by Fr Thurston in his discussion of the feast but seems to have been overlooked by other researchers. These Canons (extant in Arabic and Coptic) are of the 4th cent., since they give warnings about the Meletian schism, and may quite probably come from Athanasius himself. What is important here is that they envisage only three feasts in the year : Pasch, Pentecost and Epiphany. This last is called Epiphany (the word has been transliterated in the Coptic) and is described as the Baptism. ' In the month Tubi did Our Saviour appear as God when by a wondrous miracle He made the water wine. . . . In it was the Lord baptized of John ' (Canon 16). In Canon 66 the date is given as 11 Tubi. Another text which Fr Thurston produced was that of the Acts of martyrdom of Philip of Heraclea in Thrace (AA. SS October IX:545) ; the martyrdom was in 304 and the record of it may not be much later, wherein the keeping of Epiphany is mentioned.

The ancient Armenian Lectionary (of which there are now three copies : at Oxford, Paris and Jerusalem) began its liturgical year with Epiphany, and, owing to that fact, none of the copies is quite perfect in what it gives for that feast. When all three are taken together, it appears that the feast was a Birth feast at Jerusalem in the late 4th cent. (for to this place and period must the Lectionary be assigned), but the presence of Ps 2, with 2:7 as a refrain, in the proceedings shows that something survived of the baptismal ideas. The same thing can be seen in the Lectionary of Edessa (published by Burkitt in 1923) which is almost contemporary. Here the gospel for the day has to be either Mt 1:18–2:23, or Lk 3:1–18 or Jn 1:1–28 ; this would suggest that the nativity story has come in to supplant the accounts of John the Baptist. It would seem that the intuition of Brightman in 1924 (JTS 25:268) was correct that it was at Jerusalem in the late 4th cent. that the idea of visiting the scenes of the mysteries of Christ at the correct seasons came into observance. The theological reasons for this may have been quite other than those commonly supposed by liturgical popularizers.

V A doctrinal conclusion may be reached by noting how cautiously the Second Vatican Council dealt with the liturgical year (AAS 56 [1964] 125). It spoke of ' a devout recalling ' of the work of salvation on fixed days in the year and said that in so doing, ' the Church sets before the faithful the wealth of deeds of power and the merits of her Lord, so that on each occasion they are somehow made present to them, that they may grasp them and be filled with saving grace '.[2] The idea of a mystical presence of each mystery of Christ on the day appointed for it (*see* CAUSALITY OF SACRAMENTS V) which some enthusiasts derived from the writings of Dom O. Casel, is here by-passed. It is the merits of Christ that are made present in the liturgy for the faithful to grasp, not the mysteries. The reason for an annual series of feasts of Christ is not even hinted at.

[2] Mysteria redemptionis ita recolens, divitias virtutum atque meritorum Domini sui, adeo ut omni tempore quodammodo praesentia reddantur, fidelibus aperit, qui ea attingant et gratia salutis repleantur.

[1] Tunc enim absconditus est et non apparuit.

'Devout recalling' may be what the church of Jerusalem began in the 4th cent., as stated above, but the true reason for a cycle of feasts has still to be made manifest. When the efforts of Jewish and Christian scholars alike have clarified the process by which the Lectionary cycle was set up in the various provinces of the Church and have shown what borrowings from the Jewish three-year or one-year cycle of readings took place, it will be possible to make theological deductions that are soundly based. One Jewish pioneer in this field, Dr E. Werner, quite justly addressed to Dom Casel the reproach of having gone in every direction but the Jewish for the origin of a simple liturgical idea, 'where a simple reference-book of rabbinics would have yielded many pertinent quotations' (*The Sacred Bridge*, 321). The writings of Qumran may help to determine what cycle of readings would have been used in 1st-cent. Jewry and the lines of evolution may thus become more plain.

The intervention of Pope Siricius (*ep.* 1:2 ; PL 13:1134) in 385 calling for regulation of the feasts (Easter and Pentecost) when baptism should be given may be regarded as the first attempt to legislate officially for a liturgical cycle, and the action of Pope Leo (*ep.* 16:1 ; PL 54:696) a lifetime later reinforced this, but it was singularly ineffective, for one finds Augustine of Canterbury holding a large-scale baptism service for his new converts on the banks of the Medway at Epiphany more than a century later (Gregory, *ep.* 8:30 ; PL 77:932). The term *circulus anni* in a liturgical context appears in the Church orders of the 7th and 8th cents. Later still, in the Middle Ages, Sicard of Cremona gave it mystical overtones, but there is no likelihood that it was the object of Church tradition from the beginning.

Just to outline the kind of problem that remains to be solved before theological conclusions can be drawn, one may consider the feast of the Transfiguration. In the West this has been kept only since 1457, but in the East it has been fixed at 6 August since the 5th cent. The Armenian Lectionary has it between 2 and 6 July. Its gospel (Mt 17:1–9) comes just half-way in Tatian's Diatessaron. Can one say that the fifty-five sections of that work (marked in the medieval Arabic version, which alone survives complete) were meant to cover the space of one year, just as the Jews divided the Law into fifty-four portions for their annual cycle ? Can one go further and say that, as Moses stayed on the mountain of Sinai eighty days from his ascent of it on Pentecost, even so the Transfiguration was kept eighty days from Pentecost by the Christian Church ? Would the 130 days from Pasch to Transfiguration absorb half the lections of the year, leaving the other half to be completed in 235 days ? It is not impossible that progress in ascertaining primitive theological thought may be achieved by means of inquiries on these lines, but each step will need very careful scrutiny.

Bibliography. *A. McArthur, *The Evolution of the Christian Year* (1953) ; the same, *The Christian Year and the Lectionary* (1958) ; *P. Carrington, *The Primitive Christian Calendar* (1952) ; the same,

According to Mark (1960) ; *A. Guilding, *The Fourth Gospel and Jewish Worship* (1960); *J. van Goudoever, *Biblical Calendars* (1959) ; A. Baumstark, *Comparative Liturgy* (1958) ; *I. Elbogen, *Der Judische Gottesdienst* (1962⁴) ; *E. Werner, *The Sacred Bridge* (1959) ; B. Botte OSB, *Les Origines de la Noël et de l'Épiphanie* (1932), with the critical review by O. Casel, *Jahrbuch für Liturgie* XII (1932) 335–8 ; *F. Conybeare, *Rituale Armenorum* (1905), with the collation of the Jerusalem MS. by A. Renoux in *Le Muséon* 74 (1961) 361–85 and 75 (1962) 385–398 ; W. Riedel and W. Crum, *The Canons of Athanasius* (1904) ; *F. C. Burkitt, 'The Early Syriac Lectionary', in *Proceedings of the British Academy* X (1923) 301–38 ; *M. Black, 'The Festival of *Encaenia ecclesiae*', in JEH 5 (1954) 78–85; *W. Frere, *Studies in the Early Roman Liturgy* I (1930); J. Daniélou, 'Les Quatre-Temps de Septembre', in *Maison-Dieu* 46 (1956) 114–36 ; P. de Puniet OSB, 'La Fête de l'Épiphanie', in *Rassegna Gregoriana* 5 (1906) 497–514 ; C. Respighi, 'La Benedizione dell'acqua', in *Rassegna Gregoriana* 10 (1911) 51–8 ; H. Thurston SJ, 'Epiphany', in *Lives of Saints, January* (1926) ; *E. Colwell and D. Riddle, *Studies in the Lectionary Text of the NT* I (1933), II (1944).

J. H. C.

FERMENTUM The consecrated Eucharist, leaven (Mt 13:33) of Church unity, served sometimes as gift of honour from the pope to bishops, as Eusebius disclosed (HE 5:24) ; as bond between bishop and bishop it was not forbidden until the late 4th cent. (Mansi, II:556). As link between pope and priests at Rome, usage there demanded that, before communion, a portion of the pope's consecrated Species was detached, and this, now styled *fermentum*, was dispatched to priests celebrating Mass in the city, who at communion put this *fermentum* into their chalices. Much like the *fermentum* was the *sancta*, a portion of the Eucharist saved from the present mass to be consumed in a subsequent one.

Pope Innocent I wrote to Bishop Decentius of Gubbio, 19 March 416 : 'Concerning the *fermentum*, which we send on Sundays to the title-churches, it is idle to consult us, as all our churches lie within the city. The priests of these churches, who by reason of their flocks, are prevented from assembling with us, receive by acolytes the *fermentum* we have consecrated, lest, that day especially, they feel cut off from us in communion. But I do not think this ought to be done in outlying areas (*per paroecias*), because the "Sacraments" are not to be carried a long distance, nor do we send *fermentum* to the priests stationed at the different cemeteries' (*ep.* 25: 8 ; PL 20:556).[1]

[1] De fermento vero, quod die Dominica per titulos mittimus, superflue nos consulere voluisti, cum omnes ecclesiae nostrae intra civitatem sint constitutae. Quarum presbyteri, quia die ipsa propter plebem sibi creditam nobiscum convenire non possunt, idcirco fermentum a nobis confectum per acolythos accipiunt, ut se a nostra communione, maxime illa die, non iudicent separatos. Quod per paroecias fieri debere non puto ; quia nec longe portanda sunt sacramenta, nec nos per coemeteria diversa constitutis presbyteris destinamus. . . .

This subject was often studied ; in 1952 Professor Jungmann also traced its continuing medieval remnants : details are his.

By about 700 a weekly *fermentum* had been cut down to Holy Week, Easter, Pentecost and Christmas. On Easter especially it was the rule : ' No priest communicates others, before he has been sent part of the pope's oblation '. Gospel-readings, listed for liturgical use about 740, bore the rubric the day before Palm Sunday : ' *Fermentum* in the Lateran consistory '. In that style *fermentum* persisted in Rome until around 1000.

Elsewhere a sort of *fermentum* often attended ordination : when communicating, the new priest received a whole oblation ; from this he put portions into his chalice for seven or even forty masses. A cognate rite associated itself with episcopal consecration, and long endured in the pontificals. More surprising, a type of *fermentum* formerly attached to the profession-Mass of monks and of nuns, in that a portion from the prelate's mass that day served for communion for a varying number of days.

Bibliography. L. Eisenhofer, *Fermentum*, LTK 3 (1930) 1003 ; F. Cabrol, *Fermentum*, DACL 5 (1922) 1371–4 ; A. Fortescue-H. Thurston, *The Mass* (1937) 367–70 ; J. A. Jungmann, *Fermentum*, *Colligere Fragmenta* : *Festschrift . . . Dold* (1952) 185–90.

G. E.

FEUDALISM AND THEOLOGY The word feudalism was hardly used until after the French Revolution, when it became a ' hate-word ' that condemned the past history of France. It is defined by a modern historian as ' a peculiar association of vassalage with fief-holding that was developed in the Carolingian empire and brought into England at the Norman Conquest '. There are many controversies among historians about the extent to which feudalism was truly Germanic or Frankish, and it is not necessary to enter into them here. This article aims at setting out some of the points at which feudalism influenced the development of theology. It had more or less spent its force as an innovation by the time of St Thomas, but his work bears many signs that he thought in its terms. The treatment of apostates (I) is an obvious instance. The idea that ordination was effected by an investiture (II) with the instruments of priestly activity ; the acceptance of single combat as a way of securing justice (III) ; the idea that lordship was lost by sin (IV) ; and finally (V) a note on the blessing of arms and what it involved.

I That apostates were vassals who had turned against their lord was the underlying presumption of St Thomas's treatment of them. A vassal was made by two acts, one pagan and one Christian. He rendered *homagium* to his lord by placing his hands within those of the lord, and he offered *fidelitas* by an oath taken upon holy relics or the book of the gospels. St Thomas (*Summa*, 2–2ae:10:8c), in deciding whether heretics and apostates should be compelled by force to live as Catholics, makes a distinction between those who have been in that

condition all their lives without accepting the faith and those who have once accepted it and then fallen away. These last may be subjected to compulsion, he decides, to make them carry out what they promised and hold to what they undertook.[1] The Gospel parable about the wheat and the tares is set aside as not applying to their case. This is simply a transfer to the Church of the feudal ideas of *homagium* and *fidelitas* ; the heretic has broken the promised fealty to Christ his Lord. A little later (ibid.:11:3c) St Thomas argues that heresy is a spiritual issuing of false coin. That offence was punishable by death in an age when barter was so largely used that monetary exchange was rarer and coinage more precious ; the offence was therefore all the graver. It carried the death penalty, and so by analogy it might be said that heretics might be put to death as spiritual coiners.

II The investiture controversy, as it concerned kings and bishops, is dealt with under CHURCH AND STATE, but there was a theological consequence of more lasting significance. Kings and lords invested bishops or priests, as representative of a particular church, with fiefs that carried the obligation of a service of prayer instead of the usual military commitments ; this investiture had to have its outward sign, *per anulum et baculum* for the bishop (though both of these were of Keltic origin, the ring as wedding him to his diocese and the staff having the name of *cambuta*, a Gaelic word). The legal concept of the benefice is feudal, and it must have seemed obvious, even when the controversy about who does what at a church-investiture was settled, that there had to be an induction of the newly made priest by giving into his hands the chalice with which he would offer the sacrifice of the Mass. This principle was thought by St Thomas to be self-evident : ' The conferring of a power is effected by giving to its subjects something which belongs to the proper exercise of that power ' (*Summa*, *Supplement* 37:5c). From this principle it was easy to establish that the matter of the sacrament of Orders was the *porrectio* in each case of the instrument of that Order, chalice, book, candlestick, key and so on. The fact that the minor Orders were not sacraments did not seem to trouble the theologians of the time. Even the objection (ibid. 34:3@3) that the king was the subject of investiture at his coronation like a bishop, and that therefore he could claim that it was a sacrament, did not trouble St Thomas (*see* CORONATION).

III Justice through single combat was a feudal ideal, and was by some theologians linked with the promise of God (Rom 12:19) that He would avenge injustice. The champion was thought merely to give God the opportunity of doing so in a spectacular way (cf. St Thomas, *lectio* 3 in Rom 12). Champions who fought to decide an issue for a whole city or people were known to the Greeks (who had a chivalry of sorts), and were welcomed at times of stress as effecting an economy in the loss of human life. The story of David and Goliath impressed Christians in

---

[1] Sunt etiam corporaliter compellendi ut impleant quod promiserunt et teneant quod semel susceperunt.

feudal times, as if giving sanction of Scripture to the practice of chivalry. St Thomas (*Summa*, 2–2ae:95: 8@3) cited papal prohibitions of the ordeal (by hot iron or boiling water) and then added : ' The law of single combat seems to fall into the same category, except that it comes closer to the ordinary practice of deciding by lot.' In the same article he had argued that, while there was much superstition involved in the drawing of lots, and while it was wrong to expect God to work miracles, ' if there is urgent necessity, it is lawful to seek the divine judgment with due reverence by the use of the lot '. He remarked that if the single combat was between an ill-matched pair, then God was certainly being asked to work miracles. This remark would imply that in other cases, given urgent necessity, there was no harm in seeking such a decision by combat. In treating of revenge (2–2ae:108:2@2) he says that to avenge the wrongs of God or our neighbour can be an exercise of virtue, since fortitude is needed to overcome the fear of the imminent danger involved, and this would imply that some kind of challenge and combat was contemplated.

Gradually the theologians came to see that duelling, even for a good purpose, was wrong. Local synods had approved the ordeal and there was even a liturgical form (e.g. in the *Lanalet Pontifical*, 116–25) to prepare the one who was to undergo it, but it was not approved by the popes or general councils of the time. The feudal lord who acquired a fief had the right to administer justice within it, and hence St Thomas (*Summa*, 2–2ae:108:1@1) can say that he who takes vengeance of the wicked according to the rank of his estate is not usurping what belongs to God but is using a power that God has given to him.[1] It was not merely kings or dukes who had the right to take vengeance, and this fragmentation of the authority of the state was looked on as something permanent and willed by God. That bishops and ecclesiastics who held church-fiefs should take up arms was held by some to be right, and St Thomas gives four reasons for their view before himself taking up the contrary (*Summa*, 2–2ae:40:2c). The device of a lay protector for such a fief who might do battle or engage in single combat on behalf of the bishop was brought in to meet the objections raised by St Thomas and other theologians, and in time it led to much abuse of church property.

IV Loss of lordship for sin was understood in feudalism, for the vassal was freed from his obligations to a lord if that lord had committed adultery with the wife of the vassal. The German *comitatus* (which goes back to the days of Tacitus's *Germania*) set up mutual obligations between lord and vassal ; it was not a one-way dependence. When one finds among the errors which the Church condemned in Wyclif and Hus the proposition (D 595 and 656) that a temporal lord has no authority if he is in mortal sin, it would seem that some feudal ideas have come down to them from an earlier age. Putting the

---

[1] Ille qui secundum gradum sui ordinis vindictam exercet in malos non usurpat sibi quod est Dei sed utitur potestate sibi divinitus concessa.

question whether an apostate lord lost his lordship, St Thomas (*Summa*, 2–2ae:12:2c) answers that excommunication of their lord releases subjects from their obedience. He cites a decretal of Gregory VII in which this was expressly done and brushes aside a passage in which St Ambrose spoke of Christians obeying Julian the apostate with the remark that in those days the Church was still weak and tolerated such obedience to an apostate for the avoiding of a greater evil. To a modern mind there is a confusion here between the Christian faith and the oath of fealty to a lord, but the fact that the Church had been careful to christianize that oath made the confusion more excusable. The error of Wyclif was to extend this confusion to all mortal sins on the part of the lord, as if his subjects had to become keepers of his conscience.

V The blessing of arms for a knight and the imposition of a vigil was an attempt by the Church to purify chivalry, but it led to some curious consequences. St Thomas (*Summa, Supplement*, 64:6@1) is inclined to agree (*satis probabile est*) with the view that a knight can take the Cross as a Crusader without his wife's consent, ' just as he can join in the war of the lord from whom he holds his fief without the consent of his wife '. The idea that the wife might take a temporary vow, and so deprive her husband of his marriage rights, is rejected, and so some inequality is allowed between husband and wife, in spite of the general doctrine that they were equal in their mutual rights. The fact that the feudal world was so much a man's world tended to arrest the spread of ideas of equality between the sexes which Christianity had first broached. When St Thomas compares (2–2ae:26:8c) the loves that a man has, he lists love of kinsfolk, of fellow-citizens and then of his fellow-soldiers, which last is based on *communicatio bellica*. That was the spirit of feudalism, to find nobility in the hazards of the *comitatus*.

Bibliography. *C. Stephenson, *Medieval Feudalism* (1942) ; *R. Southern, *The Making of the Middle Ages* (1953) ; D. M. Green, *The Carolingian Lord* (1964) ; J. M. Wallace-Hadrill, ' The Bloodfeud of the Franks ', in JRB 41 (1959) 459–87 ; *Sir F. M. Stenton, *The First Century of English Feudalism : 1066–1166* (1932). J. H. C.

FIDEISM is used in Catholic theology to denote a current of thought which denies the validity of human reason at least in the realm of metaphysical, moral and religious truth and attributes knowledge of such truth to faith (which is frequently given qualities with which it is not endowed in the traditional teaching of the Church). Fideism is not without its effects in the realm of the genesis of faith ; since fideists deny the validity of human reason in religious matters, they must provide some means other than reason to defend the prudence of the judgment which leads one to embrace the faith.

The history of fideism, or better, of the tendency to fideism, has never been written in any adequate way. The first faint shadow of it would appear to have been Justin Martyr's doctrine of the *lógos spermatikós* ; Justin's meaning for the expression need not be interpreted as fideistic, though it could easily be understood as such and consequently gave early indication that fideism would be a constant danger in the development of speculation on faith and its characteristics. The same danger was subsequently emphasized when the Fathers came to comment on St John's statement that the Word enlightens every man who comes into the world ; similar tendencies were apparent when some of the Fathers interpreted the Isaian advice to believe in order to understand. Accordingly, not a few statements of the Fathers appear at first sight to be expressions of fideism ; since, however, almost all the writings of the Fathers were occasional ones, it is necessary to place such statements in the total context of their thought ; when this is done—for instance, by noting their treatment of the Pauline teaching that the invisible things of God may be known through the visible things of creation—it becomes apparent that the Fathers, for all their insistence on the importance and necessity of faith, are in no wise prepared to deny the basic validity of human reason.

Fideistic tendencies also appeared during the Middle Ages. Already at the very beginning of the speculative movement of the Middle Ages, John Scotus Erigena advanced the opinion that after the fall of man human reason was capable only of constructing a physics and of proving the existence of God ; in all other matters faith must precede the use of reason. Similar positions, sometimes based on a theological consideration of the effects of Original Sin, sometimes on a philosophical analysis of the limits of the human intellect, continued through the Middle Ages and culminated in the probability philosophy of William of Ockham and in the position of Nicholas of Autrecourt, whose extreme diffidence of the validity of human reason was condemned by Clement VI (D 553–70).

It was, however, in modern times that fideism reached its most developed expression. The Renaissance stress on the unbridled intellect, the Protestant emphasis on private judgment and interpretation, and Kant's rigid dichotomy between the phenomenal and noumenal worlds led many Catholic thinkers to undervalue the validity of human reason and consequently to over-emphasize the role of faith. This tendency was already manifested, though in a fairly muted way, in earlier writers of the modern period such as Montaigne, Pascal, Huet ; but it came to its full expression in the 19th cent. with the work of the traditionalists such as Gerbet, Lamennais, de Bonald and of fideists like the Abbé Louis Bautain. Since the doctrine of the last-named is the fullest as well as the most self-conscious expression of fideism and indeed has come to be almost identified with fideism, it is this that will be considered in the rest of this article.

The Abbé (1796–1867), whose speculative ability easily ranks him first among the Catholic thinkers in France during the first half of the 19th cent., expressed his fideism throughout his writings but especially in his *Philosophie du christianisme*

(Strasbourg, 1835) and his *Psychologie expérimentale* (Strasbourg, 1839). Imbued with a conscious Platonism and convinced by Kant's critique of the limitations of human reason, Bautain stressed the existence of two worlds : the sensible world and the intelligible world. The first of these is made known to us by the senses and by reason ; indeed the validity and usefulness of reason are restricted to this world of sensible reality. The second world—the intelligible one—is perceived only by means of a further human faculty, the intelligence, which is an intuitive faculty, a ' psychic eye '. The fruit of human reason according to Bautain is the ' notion ', an abstraction that gives no entry into the intelligible world. Accordingly Bautain concluded that human reason, when confronted with the question of the existence of God, can say nothing about it ; and if it is rash enough to attempt a proof of His existence, it must necessarily fall into one of two errors : Deism or pantheism.

On the other hand the fruit of what Bautain called the intelligence is the idea, and it is by means of ideas that a human being is able to know intelligible reality. The ideas of life, unity, truth, goodness, being, God and so forth are all to be found in the human intelligence, and it is through them alone and their gradual explicitation in the intelligence that man achieves knowledge (science) of the intelligible world. Thus biology is possible because man has in his intelligence the idea of life ; so too mathematics is possible because of his possession of the idea of unity. It is to be noted that according to Bautain the ideas in man correspond to eternal ' ideals ' in God ; human ideas are but the counterpart of divine ideas.

Given such an explanation of human knowledge, the question of the origin of the ideas immediately arises. The ideas, thought Bautain, do not come from sensible perception nor from rational abstraction, for both the one and the other are limited to the sensible world. Neither is the existence of such ideas to be explained by the postulation of a previous existence or by an appeal to Descartes' theory of innate ideas. Rather, Bautain's explanation of the genesis of the ideas in the human intelligence can be sketched in the following way. In each man there exists the germ of the ideas, a sort of psychological *ratio seminalis* of each idea. These germ-ideas, however, cannot evolve into the full idea unless the intelligence is previously fecundated. The fecundating principle according to Bautain is nothing more than the metaphysical object (the divine ideal) itself ; just as the bodily eye is fecundated by its object, so the human intelligence is fecundated by the presence of its object—goodness, unity, life, as the case may be. This fecundating principle, however, cannot fulfil its role in the origin of ideas unless an intelligible light is also present, just as a sensible object cannot fecundate the human eye unless physical light is present. In the case of the ideas the intelligible light is that ' light which enlightens every man coming into this world ' ; and this light of the Word of God comes to man through interior revelation, immediate or mediate. The former kind of revelation is given only to the geniuses of the intelligible world—mathematicians, biologists, religious prophets and so forth. For the rest of the human race the ideas are generated only by mediate revelation, that is, by the transmission of the divine Word through human tradition. In the final analysis, then, Bautain placed God and divine revelation as the explicative principle of all human knowledge of the intelligible world. His theory, as can be seen from the above, includes a manifest ontologism.

Bautain's position should be distinguished from the traditionalism of such men as de Bonald and Lamennais whose theories he criticized severely. While Bautain admitted the necessity of human tradition for the ordinary generation of ideas, he objected to the role that tradition was given in the traditionalist theory of knowledge. According to Bautain the traditionalists retained human tradition as the cause of human knowledge, thereby interposing a human authority between man and reality. Moreover, Bautain pointed out, the traditionalist theory destroys the possibility of intrinsic evidence as the foundation for human knowledge, for it leaves man only with the common testimony of the human race. Finally, traditionalism substitutes the fallible authority of human tradition for the infallible authority of God. On the contrary Bautain prided himself on having avoided all these pitfalls in his own theory of knowledge. For him human tradition is only a condition (a canal) for the generation of the ideas ; once human tradition has done its work, man's intelligence has immediate commerce with the eternal ideal which fecundates the germs of the intelligence to produce the idea ; by the idea man is capable of testing and feeling the intelligible world so that man's criterion of truth is not the common consent of mankind but evidence given in the experience of the intelligible world.

It is now necessary to see how Bautain inserted faith into his explanation of human knowledge. Since knowledge of the intelligible world comes to man through the channel of the human word, man's first reaction must be that of faith in those who transmit to him human tradition. This faith, however, is a purely human one, not the faith by which the just man lives. This latter kind of faith is the act of submission which man makes when, after the presentation of human tradition, the intelligible light of the Word has manifested the presence of the eternal ideal of which our human ideas are copies. This act of submission to divine reality is also an apprehension, for in his act of faith man secures immediate contact with the intelligible world which is God Himself. It is this apprehension of the divine that gives divine faith its security ; for man is able to taste or touch what he believes in and hence is supremely certain that his faith is secure. In line with the above, Bautain made the following account of the process of conversion : a person accepts on human faith revealed truths, admitting them for the time as working hypotheses for living ; this human faith puts the man into contact with intelligible reality ; man thereby experiences this reality ; and

this experiential contact enables the man to say with all security 'I believe'. Faith then, for Bautain, is an act of apprehension carrying with it experienced evidence and this evidence becomes more and more perceptible as man submits more and more in his acts of faith to the intelligible reality within him.

Bautain's positions, especially his restrictions on the capacities of human reason, soon brought him into conflict with his bishop, and later with Rome. On three occasions (1835, 1840 and 1844) he was obliged to sign a statement of theses contrary to his principal opinions. In each case he signed the document required of him. The text of the three documents can be found in D 1622-7, with the accompanying footnotes. The final and irrevocable condemnation of fideism, at least in its aspect of distrust of the power of human reason, was given by the Vatican Council when it discussed and affirmed the possibility of the human reason achieving a knowledge of God (D 1785).

In conclusion it should be noted that the term fideism is also used in Protestant theology but with a different meaning. In Protestant terminology (and the term is not a frequent one there) fideism is used in the sense given it by the French Protestant theologians, Sabatier and Menegoz. These two theologians employed the word to describe their own basic position : religious doctrines (beliefs), even those of the Bible, have only a symbolic value and are to be distinguished from faith which is the movement of the self towards God accompanied by repentance ; man, therefore, is saved by faith not by belief. The term accordingly is but a modern name for the traditional Protestant doctrine of salvation by fiducial faith.

Bibliography. J.-V. Bainvel in *DAFC* 2:57-63 gives a brief but useful summary of the history of fideism which should be supplemented by the discussion of the various theories of the relation between faith and reason to be found in Étienne Gilson's *History of Christian Philosophy in the Middle Ages* (New York 1955). The best introduction to Bautain's position is E. Baudin's 'La Philosophie de Louis Bautain, "le philosophe de Strasbourg"', in *Revue des sciences religieuses* 1 (1921) 23-61 ; 118-48 ; the most complete treatment of the subject is W. M. Horton's *The Philosophy of Abbé Bautain* (New York 1926) ; this last-named work is especially valuable for tracing the influence of Bautain on (later) French thinkers, especially Blondel. The most recent treatment of Bautain is to be found in 'Le "Cas" Bautain', in Louis Foucher's *La Philosophie catholique en France au xixᵉ siècle* (1955) 71-98, and also in *L'abbé Bautain : un essai de philosophie chrétienne au XIXᵉ siècle*, by Paul Poupard (1961), where the MS. sources on Bautain are catalogued and utilized, many of them for the first time.

R. F. S.

FLORENCE, COUNCIL OF This article will comprise four parts : (I) the Council at Ferrara, (II) the discussion on the *Filioque* clause at Florence,

(III) the other issues at Florence and (IV) the effect of the Council.

I At Ferrara. By the Bulls *Doctoris gentium* of 18 September and *Pridem ex iustis* of 30 December 1437, Pope Eugenius IV transferred the Council of Basle (q.v.) to Ferrara to meet on 8 January 1438 under the presidency of Cardinal Albergati. Eugenius arrived on 24 January. In January and February, during various sessions, the canonical validity of the Council was established, the penalties voted by the Council of Basle were annulled and measures were taken to protect the gathering in Ferrara. The Greeks, who had chosen the papal fleet and Eugenius, instead of the conciliar fleet and Basle, reached Venice on 8 February, after a four months' voyage. The Patriarch of Constantinople, Joseph II, with twenty metropolitans (some also as procurators of the patriarchates of Alexandria, Antioch and Jerusalem, and monks and clerics) the Emperor, John VIII, his brother Demetrius and their suites with three lay philosophers (theological advisers) made up a party of about 700, to be maintained during their stay in Italy and transported back to Constantinople at papal expense. The Orientals hesitated before deciding to go to Ferrara, which they reached on 4–7 March. There was some friction over the reception of the Patriarch, who refused to observe the Latin custom of kissing the papal foot : Eugenius yielded but received him privately.

The Council was solemnly inaugurated on 9 April in the presence of the Pope, the Emperor (the Patriarch was absent, ill), 118 Latin ' mitres ', 20 Eastern bishops and a vast throng of clerics and courtiers, in the cathedral church of St George, but only after some altercation over the position and styles of the thrones. John VIII stipulated for a four months' delay before beginning doctrinal discussions, to allow time for envoys of the Western royal courts to arrive, for one of his principal motives in coming to Italy was to obtain military aid from the West for his capital and empire, always in danger from Turkish aggression. In the event, only two official embassies came, from René of Anjou (1 April 1438) and from Philip of Burgundy (27 November 1438).

Soon the Latins, impatient at the delay in starting conciliar business, persuaded the Greeks to a series of conferences between groups of ten a side. As the Emperor ruled out discussion on the *Filioque* and the Eucharist, the Latins chose as subject Purgatory. Written statements were produced on either side between 4 June and mid-July. The Latins proposed a purgation of punishment, by fire, and the entry to reward or castigation immediately after death. The Greeks, somewhat uncertainly, agreed to the possibility of a cleansing of souls of the departed, denied fire categorically and asserted that souls enter on their final state only at the Last Day. Agreement had not been reached when the conferences were discontinued, possibly because of the plague that visited Ferrara. Meantime the German Electors (17 March) and France, by the Pragmatic Sanction of 7 July 1438, had adopted a policy of neutrality as between Eugenius and Basle, with a bias in favour of the latter. In mid-August, Isidore, Metropolitan of Kiev and All Russia, arrived ; some of his suite fell victims to the plague, though no Greek did. Eugenius thought for a moment of transferring the Council elsewhere but on the advice of the Venetians took no action.

The Greeks too were now anxious to begin the Council proper. On 8 October Bessarion, Metropolitan of Nicaea, gave an inaugural address. Mark Eugenicus, Metropolitan of Ephesus, then opened the discussions on the subject chosen by the Greeks. Between 8 October and 13 December thirteen sessions dealt with the legitimacy of the addition by the Latins of the *Filioque* (*see* TRINITY) to the Creed. There was some friction to start with—the Emperor had a special door made so that he could reach his throne in conformity with Byzantine court etiquette ; the Greeks insisted against Latin opposition on reading in session excerpts from the earlier Councils on the inviolability of the Creed, and the Pope let them have their way.

The Greek case was simple. The Council of Ephesus had forbidden change of the Nicene Creed. This they interpreted, quoting St Cyril, as referring to any change of a word or even a syllable of the Nicene-Constantinopolitan Creed which they said was equivalent to the Nicene. After the Council of Ephesus, they declared, no Council ever did change the Creed ; to meet new needs they made definitions apart from the Creed, for after 431 not even a General Council could legitimately change the Creed, still less the single Church of Rome. Bessarion in one discourse and Mark of Ephesus in all the rest were the speakers. The Latins first alleged that the *Filioque* was not an addition but a clarification of the Creed and then, quoting examples from the Council of Ephesus, interpreted the prohibition of 431 as forbidding not change in expression but only in meaning, i.e. in the doctrine, of the Creed, and Cardinal Cesarini produced a prohibition (actually, falsely) attributed to Nicaea. The discussions, with neither Cesarini nor Eugenicus giving way, went on interminably. The Greeks, already a year away from home, were becoming nostalgic. They were depressed, also, by the ability and determination of the Latins to answer all arguments and were weary of the battle of words. The Latins wanted to leave the question of the addition and to get down to the theological difference that lay behind it, confident that they could prove their case. This optimism added to the Greeks' distress, and they wanted to go home. It was the Emperor who persuaded them to persevere.

They had also another ground of discontent. The Pope, by December 1438, was months behindhand with his maintenance grants to them, which caused no little hardship. Eugenius had engaged himself to pay the Emperor 30 florins, the Patriarch 25, Demetrius 20 and the rest 4 or 3 according as to whether they had been invited personally or not, in all about 1,700 florins monthly. He was, in fact, nearly bankrupt owing to the lessening of his revenue by the competition from Basle, the neutrality of France and Germany, and the upkeep of mercenaries to defend the papal states against Milan and Alfonso of Aragon and Naples ; and by the end of 1438 he was negotiating with Florence to transfer the Council there, because that city offered good terms (he would, nevertheless, have to repay the money that Commune would advance), because Milan's best condottiero, Nicolo Picinnino, was dangerously near Ferrara, and because (this was the reason officially put forward) the plague lingered on and could revive with the spring. The Emperor persuaded the Greeks, first to go to Florence, and then to agree to leave the question of the addition and to discuss the theology of the *Filioque*. On 10 January 1439, in a full session, the Bull of transfer was promulgated and, with all arrears of maintenance paid up and an extra grant given for the journey, though Florence was paying for that in any case, before the end of January the Council moved piecemeal to Florence.

II The Filioque at Florence. There, after a preliminary meeting on 26 February between groups of forty a side to discuss procedure (the Greeks hoped to limit the discussions to committees and to avoid debate in public session), there were eight public sessions, between 2 and 24 March, to be conducted by the method of ' question and answer', i.e. debate, not alternate long speeches as in Ferrara. The subject was the doctrine of the *Filioque*, i.e. whether, as the Latins taught, the Holy Spirit proceeds from the Father and the Son, or, as then held by the Greeks, that He proceeds from the Father only. John of Montenero OP spoke throughout for the Latins and Mark of Ephesus for the Greeks. Very rapidly the discussions deteriorated into continued and repeated arguments about the genuineness of a few texts from the Fathers, chiefly St Basil's *Contra Eunomium* (3:1 ; PG 29:653-6), in the course of which Montenero several times gave explanations of the metaphysics of person, nature, generation, etc., the technical terms for which, unfortunately, had slightly different connotations for Latins and Greeks.

In this way five sessions were held with no progress made. In the sixth, Mark of Ephesus with the Emperor's approval gave a complete exposition of the Greek arguments, from the Scriptures, the Councils and the Fathers : the NT has ' who proceeds from the Father' with no more ; the Creed, though it professes that the Spirit is to be adored and glorified with Father and Son, refrains from saying that He proceeds from Both ; the Fathers wrote of the Father as ' the sole source of divinity'. Montenero answered in the next two sessions under the heads of Scripture, Latin Doctors of the Church acknowledged by the early Councils, Greek Doctors, and a reply to Eugenicus's arguments. The scriptural words, ' to be sent ', ' to receive' in the case of the Blessed Trinity imply origin, as also does the fact that the Spirit makes men ' conformable' to the image of the Son. The Latin Fathers from Leo the Great onwards, and especially St Augustine, teach the double Procession. The Greek

Fathers often speak of the Spirit as from the substance of the Son (Athanasius), as ' flowing forth' from Him (St Cyril of Alexandria). Not the Greek Fathers, but Eugenicus, added the word ' only' to ' proceeds from the Father'. Since the Son receives spirating power from the Father, the Father remains the first source and principle, but Father and Son are one in the Procession of the Holy Spirit.

Montenero ended his exposition in the session of 24 March. The Latins wanted an answer. The Patriarch requested time until after the Easter octave (12 April) to consider. Meantime his illness became acute and he was anointed. The Greeks had several private conferences but could not agree, Eugenicus leading a non-unionistic party (he called the Latins heretics) ; Bessarion, Isidore and Dorotheus of Mitylene favouring union. The Latins insisted that the Greeks either accept their conclusions or refute them in session. To a message from the Pope the answer was given : ' No more interminable discussions : propose a formula of union or else we go home' (11 April). Exhortations from the Pope and the cardinals did not break the Greek determination. Bessarion and Scholarius (one of the lay theological advisers of the Emperor) addressed their compatriots to prove the orthodoxy of the Latin doctrine. To break the impasse, the Emperor proposed conferences between groups of ten. There were four or five meetings with no result. The Greeks asked for a written statement of Catholic faith on the subject. The Latins produced one. The Greeks considered it and amended it so that it became ambiguous and then refused repeated Latin demands for clarification, reiterating their ultimatum of a month before : ' Find a formula of union or we go home' (21 May). As a last resort in the general atmosphere of pessimism, on 27 May, Eugenius addressed the Greeks, praising, blaming, cajoling, exhorting and even warning them. That speech gave the impulse for a fresh start which ended in agreement.

To understand how the Greeks, after months of stubborn resistance to the Latin arguments, could finally accept them, one must consider their theological background. They distrusted syllogistic reasoning in connection with the Blessed Trinity and trusted only in patristics. For all Greeks of that day it was an axiom that the saints, as being inspired by the Holy Spirit that gave them sanctity, must agree in the faith ; if there were differences between them, they were only of expression, not of substance. The Greek Fathers, quoted abundantly by Bessarion, Scholarius and Montenero, spoke of the Spirit as ' coming forth', ' issuing', ' springing forth' from the Father through the Son, from Both, from Father and Son ; the Latin Fathers, quoted by Montenero, stated plainly that He proceeded from Father and Son. The conclusion on the axiom was obvious, so obvious that Mark of Ephesus to avoid it was forced to deny that the Latin saints had ever taught the *Filioque* and to assert therefore that the quotations made by the Latin speaker in the Council were falsified. The whole theological difference on the Procession resolved itself into : ' What did the saints teach ?' and that was the question that the Greeks debated among themselves on 29 May, though such was Eugenicus's prestige that a preliminary question was put : 'Are the quotations from the Latin saints genuine ?'

The Emperor bade them give their decisions in writing. The result was a foregone conclusion. By 3 June the Patriarch, the Emperor, the metropolitans and at least two of the three lay theologians had voted, and all but Ephesus and three others were in favour of union. The Greek formula did not, however, satisfy the Latins and discussions went on until 7 June, when the Greeks at a meeting of the ecclesiastics accepted the Latin formula. The first, and the most formidable, step towards union had been taken. On 10 June the Patriarch died suddenly and was buried in the church of St Maria Novella, a great loss to the spirit of union.

III Other Issues at Florence. The same system was then applied to the other outstanding differences, the primacy of the Roman See, the Eucharist(introduced because Eugenius thought it should be ventilated), Purgatory and the legitimacy of the addition. The Latins prepared a statement, submitted it to the Greeks, discussed and answered difficulties and in the end persuaded. The *cedulae* on the primacy and the Eucharist were explained in session (16 June) and in another session, on 18 June, difficulties were answered. About 24 June it looked as if the Council would break up without any agreement being reached, but, on the part of the Pope, a mixture of firmness (on having 'all his privileges' in respect of the primacy) and of concession (in omitting reference to the *epiklesis* controversy in the definition, in introducing a phrase about different degrees of reward for the blessed, and adding the order of the patriarchates) produced agreement. After some friction about the wording of the decree, on 6 July 1439 union of the Eastern and the Western Churches was proclaimed in the cathedral of Florence, Cesarini and Bessarion reading out the decree in Latin and Greek respectively and the gathered Fathers (Ephesus was not present) approving. It had been signed the day before by the Pope and 116 Latins and by the Emperor and 32 Greeks, four of them acting also as procurators of the Patriarchs of Alexandria, Antioch and Jerusalem.

The decree *Laetentur caeli*, an infallible document, was nothing more than the various *cedulae* with an introduction and a conclusion added. The Holy Spirit was defined as proceeding from Father and Son but as from one principle and spiration, the Latin 'from' and the Greek 'through' being equivalent and causal. The rites in fermented and unfermented bread in the Eucharist were both declared valid. After death some souls are cleansed by purgatorial punishments ; others receive straightway their eternal destiny in Hell or, with different degrees of bliss, in heaven. The Pope is successor of Peter, head and teacher of the whole Church, and successor to the plenitude of power given by Christ to St Peter. The order of precedence of the patriarchates was added.

Soon after the promulgation of the decree, the Greeks began to depart, receiving at the last moment the arrears of their money allowances payable in Florence. On that occasion, not Eugenius, but the Commune of Florence was to blame. Before the last Greeks departed, Armenian delegates arrived on 13 August. Basle meantime had declared Eugenius deposed (25 June 1439). The Pope retaliated by the Bull *Moyses vir Dei* (4 September). The discussions with the Armenians culminated in the Bull *Exultate Deo* (*see* ARMENIAN DECREE) on 22 November 1439. There followed unions with the Copts of Egypt (4 February 1442), with certain Syrians (30 September 1444) and with Chaldeans and Maronites of Cyprus (17 August 1445). The council was moved from Florence to Rome, arriving on 24 September 1443. No extant document records its official closure. Presumably it petered out or ceased with Eugenius's death on 4 February 1447, though the rump-Council of Basle, with its anti-Pope Felix V, elected on 5 November 1439, still continued a tenuous existence.

IV The Effects of Florence. The union of the Latin and the Greek Churches achieved in Florence was short-lived. Mark of Ephesus rallied the conservative elements of Constantinople—the monks, for the most part with no theological training, and the populace—against it and a number of the bishops who had signed the decree in Florence repented in Constantinople. However, all the theologian bishops remained constant—Ephesus in opposition ; Bessarion, Isidore, Dorotheus of Mitylene, Metrophanes of Cyzicus (elected Patriarch to succeed Joseph II) and at least five others with Gregory the monk (Metrophanes's successor) in favour. The reason given for the defections is that the union signed in Florence was not free : the bishops had no freedom of speech, were forced by the Emperor and their own patriotism to obtain material help for their fatherland and were subject to duress from the hardships resulting from the non-payment of their monetary allowances. This is the story started by Silvester Syropoulus, a deacon in the *entourage* of Joseph II who was present throughout the council and signed the decree. His *Memoirs* make it very plausible, but they are inaccurate. Syropoulus is, at least unconsciously, pleading his own defence for having signed. Mark Eugenicus of Ephesus was the only consistent opponent of union, but it was he who was spokesman of the Greeks, with the Emperor's consent obviously, in every session except two in Ferrara and in every single session in Florence. Besides, he said what he liked in all the private Greek conferences, even to calling the Latins heretics. Clearly, freedom of speech was not curtailed. Further, if either patriotism or duress had seriously influenced the Greeks, they would not have wanted to go home with empty hands in December 1438, and after March 1439 they would not have persisted until 29 May in refusing to discuss and to unite, having meantime given the Pope ultimatums on two occasions. On 3 June they accepted from conviction the orthodoxy of the Latin faith without casting doubt on their own, the intellectuals with understanding, the less theologically minded (the majority) by the force of the axiom and the example of their colleagues. It was this majority that recanted at home, influenced this time by the austere Eugenicus, who was almost unopposed, since Isidore had gone to Russia and Bessarion had returned to Rome, and by public opinion. Constantinople was soon divided between unionists and anti-unionists. The Emperor did not use pressure to impose the union, though personally he remained faithful to it. The hopes of military aid connected with the union were dashed when the crusade organized by the Pope was defeated at Varna on 10 November 1444. The decree was promulgated in the church of St Sophia only on 12 December 1452, the eve of the capture of Constantinople by the Turks (29 May 1453). Thereafter the union was certainly dead.

The union with the Greeks was real, even if only ephemeral, and it established the foundation of all sound Church union—tolerance of difference of rite, but identity of faith. One might say that it officially sanctioned even difference of expression in that one faith. Later unions of groups of oriental Christians with Rome were made according to the principles established at Florence.

It produced a more important effect perhaps, but one confined to the Western Church, by its defeat of conciliarism so stoutly and persistently defended at Basle (*see* BASLE, COUNCIL OF). The Council of Florence was an oecumenical council and its definition, *Laetentur caeli*, an infallible pronouncement. That part of it that dealt with the papacy was the assertion of traditional doctrine against the excessive exaltation of Councils and the corresponding diminution of the papacy that began at Pisa, developed at Constance and reached full growth at Basle. Thereafter, though conciliarism was by no means dead, it had lost much of its force owing partly to the extravagances of Basle and more to the implicit condemnation of Florence.

The interest of the Council in Copts, Abyssinians with their monarch, the legendary Prester John, and Indians was responsible for a more remote but worldshaking result. It stimulated the nations of the Iberian peninsula to find their fellow-Christians and help them. In their search they discovered also the Indies, the Spice Islands and America ; and the Cape of Good Hope replaced Venice and the Mediterranean as the gate to the East.

Bibliography. The Acts of the Council were published by the Oriental Institute at Rome, at the instigation of Pius XI, under the general title *Concilium Florentinum : Documenta et Scriptores*. In this enterprise G. Hofmann sJ edited *Epistulae pontificiae ad concilium spectantes* (3 vols., 1940-6) ; also *Acta camerae apostolicae* (1950), *Fragmenta protocolli, diaria et sermones* (1951) and *Acta Latina* (1955) ; J. Gill sJ edited *Quae supersunt actorum Graecorum* (1953) ; E. Candal sJ edited *Ioannis de Torquemada apparatus super decretum Florentinum* (1942) ; *Bessarionis oratio dogmatica* (1958) and *De Spiritus sancti processione* (1961). The *Memoirs* of Syropoulos were published by G. Creyghton (1660) under the title *Vera historia unionis*

non verae. Bessarion's works are in PG 161 and some of those of Mark Eugenicus in PO 15:1-168 and 17:309-524. There is a general study by J. Gill sJ, *The Council of Florence* (1959), which has full bibliography, also *Personalities of the Council of Florence* (1964) ; and many studies of detail concerning the Council were published by those working on the *Acta* in OCP between 1935 and 1964. Earlier treatments of the Council, e.g. by Hefele and von Pastor, are now somewhat outdated.

J. G.

FOREKNOWLEDGE This article does not treat the whole problem of the reconciling of God's foreknowledge with human free will ; various aspects of that problem are considered under FREE WILL, GRACE, CONGRUISM, BANEZ, CALVIN, MOLINA and elsewhere. Here it will be the aim to set out (I) the incidence of the problem with Augustine, (II) the new position of the problem by the Renaissance theologians and (III) the modern attempts to revive the problem.

I Augustine in his *De libero arbitrio*, which he wrote *c.*388-95, as a last fling against the Manichees, was faced with the fact that Cicero and many classical authors had built up a dilemma : either God did not know, or man was not free, for, if He knew, that knowledge must be the cause of the future human choice ; or, if man was free, God could not know what he would do. The classical solution had been generally to leave God in charge and to sacrifice human freedom, which was then explained away as an illusion of greater or less permanence. Augustine (*De libero arbitrio* III:4:10 ; CSEL 74:98) suggested a psychological solution in favour of freedom ; the problem was not simply one of God's foreknowledge but of any foreknowledge. On the human level one can see that A's foreknowing B's act does not force B to do it, and so it should not when God is the foreknower. One might add that the experience of the repentant sinner is pertinent here, for he will sometimes find it difficult to be sincere about a purpose of not sinning again since in his heart he knows he will sin. He has to be instructed that foreknowledge is not the same as determination of will ; he must will, and not bother about prediction of results. A parent, having watched a child grow for some years, will generally know how, in given circumstances, that child will react ; there will be some mistakes and a time may come when the father or mother has to say that the child is becoming quite unpredictable, but there will be for some time quite an abundance of foreknowledge, not all of it firmly held. One may project this situation to the relation between God and His human creatures, removing all unsureness from the foreknowledge as an imperfection that cannot be found in God.

In his later controversies with the Pelagians, Augustine was reminded by them of what he had written in *De libero arbitrio*, and in reply (*De correptione et gratia* 32) he refined on his notion of freedom. ' What is more free than a will that cannot serve sin ? ' This transferred the mystery from God's foreknowledge to the human will, and there it was found by later theologians, some of whom tried to reconcile the two Augustinian positions by what is known of the theory of God's predestination of men *post praevisa merita* (subsequent to His foreknowing their deserts. For this *see* GRACE, PREDESTINATION). Bonaventure (in *I Sent.* 41:1), Henry of Ghent (*quodlibet* 4:19 and 8:5) and Biel (in *I Sent* 41:1) can be cited as sharing this theory. Biel, in fact, allows that God can save men otherwise (and did so with St Paul and Our Lady) but *regulariter* He does not save adults without prevision of their merits. For Biel predestination is foreknowledge. Ockham, Bradwardine and Gregory of Rimini might exalt the omnipotence of God and toss aside the problem of foreknowledge having to be reconciled with freedom, but they did not stand for the whole stream of medieval development of Augustine.

II The new logic of Ramus brought a reassessment of the problem. He criticized (*Animadversiones Aristotelicae*, fol. 26) in 1543 the ideas of Aristotle about knowledge of future contingents (that are expressed in *De interpretatione* 9:18 a 8—19 b 5). As Fr W. J. Ong notes : ' The questions which emerge in the Renaissance disputes over grace and free futuribles . . . find their most elaborate early treatment not in theology but in terminist logic ' (*Ramus, Method and Decay of Dialogue*, [1958] 146). Molina in 1563 (he was born in 1535) commented on this part of Aristotle (see *Neue Molinaschriften*, I:1–5) while lecturing on philosophy at Coimbra. Peter Baro, the French Protestant who was Lady Margaret Professor of Divinity at Cambridge (1574–96), defended a thesis that said : ' God's purpose and decree taketh not away the libertie of man's corrupt will ', and in the course of his argument he claimed that Aristotle, ' saying that these *futuribilia* were neither true nor false is found out and corrected in our own time by Petrus Ramus a philosopher of Paris ' (*Speciall Treatise*, etc., 514). Hence, too, Molina could assert that he was trying to find the answer to a question that differed from the one which had preoccupied Augustine. Molina's new question was this : ' Allowing that man's use of his free will is not the cause of God's predestining him or otherwise helping him, can one say that this use of free will is a condition *sine qua non*, not indeed of God's *giving* or withholding grace, but of God's *knowing* that these and these specific graces will in the one case achieve predestination and in another be no more than providential ? ' It was to answer this question that Molina introduced his famous division of the divine knowledge into three stages, based on the nature of its objects : there was the simple understanding of all that is possible, there was the creative knowledge of all that exists, and between these there was the *scientia media*, a knowledge of what would have been, had human choices been other than they were. One of the main reasons for postulating such a half-way knowledge was that it seemed to have been available to Christ, in such sayings as Mt 11:21 (about Tyre and Sidon) and Jn 15:24. Logically too, there was the idea that future free choices did not lack all reality (even though they should never be made) and therefore did not lack truth, which God could know.

The Thomist reaction to this new theory was based on what was to be found in *Summa*, 1a:83:1, where St Thomas defends the existence of free will in man. God moves other natural unfree causes to act without changing their nature, so why should He not move free causes without changing theirs ? This rather negative treatment of the question left it open to the Thomist contemporaries of Molina to make up explanations of their own to account for the manner of God's moving free causes so as to respect their freedom. They tried to avoid postulating any contingency in God, anything that would somehow determine the divine foreknowledge from man's side, for it was this that constituted their main objection to Molina. The debate was really about the placing of the mystery : did it lie in the knowledge of God or in His will ? Different notions of human freedom were being employed in the debate, the Bannesian (or Thomist) declaring that freedom was the power in the will to direct its attention towards that aspect of an object presented by the reason under which it was lacking in goodness (and all finite objects had this aspect, if it could be seen). The Molinist meant by freedom an active autonomy of will whereby, when all deliberation was complete, the will could yet remain capable of positing or of withholding its choice. Freedom of this kind might seem to imply that God, in knowing such choices, derived His knowledge of them from the creatures themselves, for by hypothesis there could be no prior reason for the choice in God Himself. But it can be said that there is a confusion in this requirement. When it is said that God is not God unless He knows all things in Himself, there is a confusion between the God of the Christians (to whom all things are plain and exposed, as Heb 4:13 says) and the Aristotelian deity who would be degraded by thinking of anything other than Himself.

There can be no doubt that Molina came to his ideas by pondering the results of the definitions of Trent (e.g. D 797 and 814) about justification. He appeals to them often in his writings, to the *Acta* of the Council, to the subsequent writings of those who had been present at Trent and to a living tradition coming to him from Lainez and Salmeron. One of his most important sources was Thomas Stapleton, whose *Universa iustificationis doctrina* (15–82) he cites frequently for its reasoned rejection of Calvinism. The chief Calvinist at Cambridge, William Whitaker, was engaged (1585–95) on a refutation of Stapleton which was never finished ; the notes he had collected were impounded by Archbishop Whitgift and taken to Lambeth. Peter Baro, in his attack on the Cambridge Calvinists, may well have been using Stapleton, for there are complaints at the time about the popish books that were circulating there and his supporter, William Barret, was accused of having set forth ideas ' raked out of the dunghill of poperie and Pelagianisme '. Heylyn, in his history of the episode, recognized that the doctrinal division cut across religious frontiers, for he listed on the one side moderate Lutherans of the school of Melanchthon, Dutch Remonstrants (such as Arminius), Jesuits and Franciscans, while on the other were Calvinists, rigid Lutherans and Dominicans.

The Cambridge explosion of 1595 led Whitgift into the precipitate adoption of the nine so-called Lambeth articles, which, however, Burleigh was able to neutralize. Later at the Hampton Court conference of 1604 the Puritans pressed for their incorporation into the thirty-nine Articles of the English Church, but James I did not like them, and they were allowed to die. Baro lost his professorship in 1596 in consequence of a sermon in which he had propounded his anti-Calvinist views, but his disciples Lancelot Andrewes and John Overall went on to gain commanding positions in the reign of James I, while Benjamin Carier was moved to become a Catholic, starting what might be called a Cambridge movement, which included Crashaw, Vane and Cressy. In fact, the great division of England in the time of Charles I was really begun by the Cambridge disputes. The earlier Puritans such as Cartwright had fought for their ideals of Church government, but in the sequel it was ideas of the extent and availability of salvation and the mechanics of grace that divided English churchmen.

Within the Church the views of Molina were subjected to close scrutiny and to frequent challenge, until Clement VIII took up the dispute with the idea of deciding it. He was in the end to hand it on to his successor Paul V, who in 1607 (D 1090) told both parties to go home and to let the dispute die a natural death. Attempts to revive it in 1654 (D 1097) by means of a forged *Constitutio* of Paul V were quashed, though the same forgery reappeared in 1764, when it was published by those who were seeking the suppression of the Jesuits.

III In modern times there have been a few attempts to restart discussion of the problem of foreknowledge, but these have not registered any great advance. In 1923 M. de la Taille took up the idea of Gregory of Valentia (in his commentary on *Summa*, 1a:14:8) that there were really only two kinds of knowledge in God, the simple understanding of what would never exist and the vision of what would, the latter being distinguishable into three stages according to the status of the object. He appealed to a saying of Augustine (*De Trin.* 15:13 ; PL 42:1076) that God does not know things in any other wise when they are created than when He was to create them.[1] All things would thus be the effect of God's creative knowledge, sin excepted, for sin is a privation of reality, not a positive asset. Amongst them would be even the auto-determination of the human will, with this qualification that sin, or absence of rectitude in our will, being a privation, could not be from God. This denial of any priority as between God's intellect and His will drew a reply from F. de Lanversin, who argued that if succession in God is an impossibility, one might claim that simultaneity is equally a false concept to apply to Him, both ideas

[1] Nec aliter ea scivit creata quam creanda.

being in fact due to the weakness of our apprehension. This would not deny out of hand that both concepts might be useful, in somewhat the same way as the idea of $\sqrt{-1}$ is useful to mathematicians, who realize, while using it, that it is not a reality. He pleaded for a distinction between knowledge and determination in God parallel to that between His attributes of justice and mercy. No one would say that God in His mercy punishes the sinner, and so one should not say that His knowledge is itself creative without regard to the will of God.

Modern developments have been rather in the direction of greater precision of thought, owing to improvements in scriptural exegesis or in historical research, than in the propounding of new and original solutions of the antithesis between foreknowledge and freedom. Thus it is commonly admitted that in Rom 8:28–30 St Paul is not meaning to tell his audience that only some of them are 'foreknown' by God, but regards all those who are Christians as the object of the divine foreknowledge. Again, the researches of Stegmüller (*see* Bibliography) into the gradual growth of Molina's theory have made it possible to understand much better the points at issue in the debate he stirred up. Not long after that debate a history of the whole affair was written by Pierre Poussines SJ but never published, owing to the papal ban on the continuation of the controversy. Copies exist in MS at Rome, Paris and Liège, a copy having been sent to each of the principal Jesuit theological colleges when it was completed in 1659.

A critical edition of Molina's *Concordia* was produced in 1953 by J. Rabeneck SJ, who thereafter in a series of articles went over the ground once more, pointing out how Molina by asking his new question really stands aside from the old dispute about *ante* and *post praevisa merita*, and that he was claimed by Billot (wrongly, in fact) as a supporter of *ante praevisa merita*. Rabeneck's conclusion is that Molina can harmonize his ideas with the theory of *post praevisa merita* but that he is actually concerned with something else, namely the distinction between God's foreknowledge and His will. Ultimately that distinction rests on the analogy of being between ourselves and God. Rabeneck also prints a letter of Molina to a Fr Padilla, a colleague who had asked him to show how his ideas differed from semi-Pelagian views ; the letter was first published by Stegmüller (728) in 1935. In it Molina says that he does not suppose a man must do, or prepare to do, all that in him lies and that then subsequently (at least by nature, if not in time) God should give him grace to make his act of faith supernatural, but that the two moves are simultaneous, from God and from the man. God's act can be called prevenient since He has foreknowledge of the movement of the man's will towards doing what in him lies, whether in view of a natural act or even of an act of faith, and this foreknowledge safeguards human freedom.[2] Molina's

[2] Deus enim sua praescientia servataque arbitrii nostri libertate praevidet quando arbitrium voliturum est facere quod in se est vel ad opus naturale vel ad suam salutem . . . et, quemadmodum illi adest concursu generali ad velle sibi

Concordia was published in 1588, and probably had more effect on England in the long run than had the Armada, which set forth in that year. Certainly it provided a way for the Church to avoid the Calvinist challenge of tidy metaphysics and an unreal human freedom.

Bibliography. The older histories of the 16th-cent. dispute are those of T. de Lemos OP, *Acta omnium congregationum* (1702) ; J. Serry (=A. Le Blanc OP), *Historiae congregationum* (1699) ; L. de Meyere SJ, *Historiae controversiarum* (1745) ; G. Schneemann SJ, *Controversiarum . . . initia et progressus* (1881) ; while the main work, L. Molina SJ, *Concordia liberi arbitrii cum gratiae donis* has been published many times between 1588 and 1953 ; F. Stegmüller, *Neue Molinaschriften* (1935) gathered and edited all the extant letters and memoranda of Molina, as far as then known ; the Cambridge affair is studied by *H. C. Porter, *Reformation and Reaction in Tudor Cambridge* (1958) and more briefly by *P. M. Dawley, *John Whitgift and the Reformation* (1955) ; M. de la Taille and F. de Lanversin published their articles in RSR 13 (1923) 7–23 and 528–42 ; D. J. Hawkins, 'Two Conceptions of Freedom in Theology', in DR 79 (1961) 289–96, had some valuable additions to make to his discussion in *Essentials of Theism* (1949) ; Baro's lecture was printed (in 1600 ?) along with John Ludham's *A Speciall Treatise of God's Providence* ; A. d'Alès SJ, *Providence et libre arbitre* (1927) and R. Garrigou-Lagrange OP, *Providence* (English trans., 1937) are both prior to the publication of the new material ; J. Ternus SJ, 'Neomolinismus', in *Scholastik* 12 (1937) 378–85 and J. Rabeneck SJ, 'Grundzüge der Prädestinationslehre Molinas', in *Scholastik* 31 (1956) 351–69 ; 32 (1957) 27–40 and 33 (1958) 31–62 deals with the new material, as also R. Franco SJ in the *Archivo teologico Granadino* XXIV (1961) 33–42 ; J. Rabeneck also discussed the life of Molina in *Archivum historicum Societatis Iesu* 19 (1950) 75–145 and 24 (1955) 295–326, while the same periodical each year lists in its bibliography all writings concerned with Molina. M. Pontifex OSB edited an English version of Augustine's *De libero arbitrio* (1955) and also has a small work, *Providence and Freedom* (1960). J. H. C.

FRANZELIN, JOHANN BAPTIST (1816–86), Jesuit theologian and cardinal. Franzelin was the most famous Jesuit theologian of the 19th cent., and exercised a very wide influence through his methods and opinions. This influence is here considered (I) in his life and teaching activity and (II) in his theological works.

I Life and Teaching Activity. Franzelin was born at Aldein in the diocese of Trent in the Tyrol, 15 April 1816. He received his early education at a college in Bolzano conducted by the Franciscans, and entered the novitiate of the Austrian province of the Society of Jesus at Graz, 27 July 1834. In 1836 he

was sent to Tarnapol in Galicia to complete his classical studies and to follow the course of philosophy. After six years' teaching at Tarnapol and Lemberg he began his theological studies at the Roman College where he had Perrone and Passaglia as professors of dogma. During this period he assisted Patrizi, the professor of Hebrew. The Roman revolution of 1848 drove the Jesuits from Rome, and Franzelin and some other scholastics moved to England in company with Passaglia and Patrizi. They continued their studies at Ugbrooke Park, Devon, where Lord Clifford had placed his residence at their disposal. After some months Franzelin moved to Louvain, and shortly afterwards to the French Jesuit theologate at Vals near Le Puy where he taught Scripture and Hebrew. He was ordained priest towards the end of 1849. In the following year he returned to the Roman College as assistant to Perrone and lecturer in Oriental languages. After making his tertianship privately he was appointed Prefect of Studies and ' Repetitore ', or tutor, at the German College in Rome, remaining there from 1853–1857. In that year he succeeded to Perrone's chair of dogmatic theology at the Roman College, and occupied that office for nineteen years.

Franzelin was admirably equipped for his work. To a sound theological judgment and great capacity of mind he added immense industry. He had acquired a knowledge of numerous languages, Biblical, classical and modern ; he had a very extensive and detailed grasp of history, and kept abreast of contemporary movements of thought in Germany, France, Italy, England and Russia. His successor, Fr Canastrelli, said of him that ' he had all the scholastic theologians at his finger ends '. At the Roman College his lectures soon won for him a very high reputation by reason of their clarity, allied to solidity, amplitude and religious profundity. They were a good blend of scholastic and positive theology, and were intended to present a view of the faith rather than a metaphysical construction. He explained and proved doctrine by a detailed study of its sources ; this included a careful discussion of scriptural and patristic texts and of the monuments and events of antiquity. This method was very well suited to the needs of the time. It was an age of great advances in historical science and the critical method and of archaeological and textual discoveries which provided fresh material for the theologian. Franzelin was encouraged by Perrone to utilize this material, and Passaglia had already shown how theology could profit from a deeper study of the Fathers. Franzelin was just as well equipped as Passaglia, and was more judicious and exact in the use to which he put his erudition. He adhered more closely to the scholastic method, and this assured his success. Yet he was rather eclectic in his philosophy, owing something to Suarez and Lugo as well as to St Thomas Aquinas.

During his career as a professor at the Roman College, Franzelin was a consultor of several Roman congregations and a qualificator of the Holy Office. One instance will serve to illustrate his influence.

omnino naturale . . ., ita sua infinita misericordia Christi meritis illi adest praeveniente gratia . . . quoties aggredi voluerit facere quod in se est . . . ad finem supernaturalem.

In his book *The Question of Anglican Ordinations Discussed* (London, 1873) Canon E. E. Estcourt had suggested that the Anglican form was not *per se* invalid. Cardinal Manning then ' proposed a *dubium* to the Holy Office', asking whether from the (supposed) decision in the Abyssinian case of 1704 anything could be inferred in favour of the form used for Anglican Orders. The reply was "*Negative*". Franzelin was the theologian consultor, and his *votum* is of considerable interest, as its reasoning . . . is strikingly similar to that later adopted in *Apostolicae Curae*' (Francis Clark SJ, *Anglican Orders and Defect of Intention* [1956], 33 ; cf. 186–8). It was, however, in connection with Vatican Council I that Franzelin's influence notably increased. He was a consultor of the Dogmatic Commission and was chiefly responsible for the first draft of the *schema* of the Decree on Catholic Doctrine. This *schema* was much criticized by the Fathers of the Council on the grounds of the arrangement of the material, its excessively scholastic form and its prolixity. After hearing Franzelin's explanation of the form adopted for the *schema*, the Deputation of the Faith entrusted Mgrs Deschamps, Pie and Martin, assisted by Fr J. Kleutgen SJ, with the task of its revision. In its amended form it retained the greater part of Franzelin's ideas, and in a number of places his expressions. After twenty-two sessions of discussion it was approved unanimously by the 667 prelates present. Although the first Dogmatic Constitution attracted much less attention at the time outside the Council than the definitions of the papal primacy and infallibility, it was a very important document which settled problems on the relation of faith and reason which had agitated the Church from the opening years of the century. In 1876 Pius IX showed his appreciation of Franzelin's services to the Church by creating him a cardinal. It was only with the greatest reluctance that Franzelin was induced to accept this dignity. However, it set the seal of papal approval on his theological authority, which had been growing steadily since the publication of his treatises between 1868 and 1870, and his work at the Vatican Council. Although he ceased to lecture on theology Franzelin continued to lead as austere and laborious a life as before. He was constantly occupied as Prefect of the Congregation of Indulgences and Relics, as a consultor of several other Roman congregations, and with the revision of his published works. More than ever he now turned his attention to the religious problems of the hour. He was particularly interested in the movement for a return to the universal Church inaugurated by Tchadaiev (1794–1856) of which Soloviev (1853–1900) was to be the leading spirit. He foresaw its development, and had followed its phases with the closest attention ever since his sojourn at Tarnapol and Lemberg. He died in Rome, 11 December 1886, leaving a reputation not only for vast theological erudition but also for exceptional holiness of life.

II Theological Works. The list of Franzelin's published works, with the date of the first edition, and the date and number of the last edition, is as follows : *De Sacramentis in Genere*, 1868 (1901⁴) ; *De SS. Eucharistiae Sacramento et Sacrificio*, 1868 (1899⁵) ; *De Deo Trino*, 1869 (1902⁴) ; *De Deo Uno*, 1870 (1883³) ; *De Verbo Incarnato*, 1870 (1903⁵) ; *De Divina Traditione et Scriptura*, 1870 (1896⁴) ; *Examen Doctrinae Macarii Bulgakov . . . de Processione Spiritus Sancti* (1876). This substantial work of 308 pages was published as a supplementary volume to Franzelin's treatise on the Trinity. It was his reply to Bulgakov's attack on the Catholic doctrine which he had not seen at the time when he composed his *De Deo Trino*. *Theses de Ecclesia Christi*, 1887 (1907²) is a posthumous work which he left unfinished. The editor has contributed an account of his life and work in a preface. All the above works were published at Rome. A minor work on the genuineness of the Johannine Comma appeared at Florence in *L'Archivo dell' Ecclesiastico* VI (1866) 358–92. Franzelin's very able explanation and defence of the original *schema* of the Decree on Catholic Doctrine is printed in the Collectio Lacensis, *Acta et Decreta* VII, cols. 1611–28, and in Mansi, *Concilia* 50, cols. 317–40.

The repeated editions of his works ensured that Franzelin's reputation and influence as a theologian went on growing. His ideas, and even his phraseology, are discernible in papal documents issued after his death, such as Leo XIII's encyclicals *Providentissimus Deus* (1893) on the study of Holy Scripture, and *Satis Cognitum* (1896) on the Church. Moreover he had a numerous body of disciples throughout the Church who popularized his ideas in translations and adaptations. Thus in England Fr W. Humphrey SJ acknowledged his indebtedness to the lectures and published work of his former professor in the prefaces to his *The Written Word* (1887) and *His Divine Majesty* (1897). Preachers also found in Franzelin's treatises material admirably suited to their needs. His prestige remained unshaken until with the Thomist revival, inaugurated by Pope Leo XIII, new ideas came into prominence. A more philosophical theology of a strict Thomist inspiration was now in demand. Within a year of Franzelin's death Billot took possession of the chair of dogmatic theology at the Gregorian University which he was to hold uninterruptedly for twenty-three years (*see* BILLOT). He was a strict Thomist with a more brilliant mind than Franzelin, and very critical of a number of the positions defended by his predecessor. But Franzelin was his superior in erudition and in positive theology.

Franzelin's masterpiece is his *De Divina Traditione et Scriptura*. It is a harmonious and strong synthesis of the ideas of the great theologians of the 16th and 17th cents., and is still of the highest value. It does not study the contingent ways in which development has occurred, but solidly establishes the basic theological principle of implication as expounded by Báñez, Suarez and Lugo. To some of the more progressive and liberal theologians and exegetes this principle appeared inadequate, as laying too much emphasis on logical implication, which could not bear the weight of the extensive developments which they postulated. In support of their views they appealed to Newman's ideas on the development of doctrine. In a letter to Franzelin in 1882 in defence of the Abbé Duchesne, Mgr d'Hulst suggested that where the latter's ideas on development differed from those of Franzelin they did not exceed the limits allowed by Newman. Franzelin in his reply categorically asserted that his theory and that of Newman were essentially different. Franzelin's explanation of Biblical inspiration illustrates the rise and decline of his influence. He restricted inspiration in the strict sense to what he called the *formal* element in the sacred books. This comprises the ideas to be expressed, and any particular words or literary forms which are absolutely indispensable for their expression. The remaining verbal and stylistic details constitute the *material* element. This derives from the choice and taste of the individual sacred writers. Yet in order that they should infallibly express all and only the inspired ideas, they are provided with a supernatural divine assistance, distinct from inspiration, but inclusive of the *gratia sermonis*. This theory was dominant for a quarter of a century, and appeared to be definitively established. However from about 1895 it began to be criticized, not always fairly, both by Biblical scholars such as Lagrange and Prat and by metaphysicians like Billot. The result of the discussion was a clarification of the concept of instrumental causality in regard to Biblical inspiration, and the development of new explanations (*see* INSPIRATION).

Franzelin had a talent for rehabilitating older theological opinions and giving them a new lease of life by his theological authority. He thus resuscitated several theories of Lugo, notably on the analysis of the act of faith, on the causality of the sacraments and on the essence of the sacrifice of the Mass. Lugo's analysis of the act of faith was preferred, as more consistent and logical, to that of Suarez, these two being the only explanations generally known at that period. Franzelin's revalidation of the theory of the moral causality of the sacraments was adopted by a number of other theologians of note. Rather surprisingly, when refurbished with Franzelin's patristic erudition, another theory of Lugo, that of the essence of the sacrifice of the Mass, also found widespread acceptance, especially among writers on piety and morality. Here the consecration is regarded as placing Christ in the state of a victim inasmuch as in his sacramental state his humanity is abased to the point of becoming food and drink. As a result of the criticism of Billot, who pointed out that it involves a faulty notion of trans-substantiation, this theory soon became obsolete. Yet Franzelin's reputation does not stand or fall by such isolated opinions as this. There is a richness of doctrine in his works which guarantees their survival. There is also progress in method and substance, notably in his treatise on the Church, unfortunately left incomplete. Here he turns away from the excessively juridical and external treatment of the subject, typical of much post-Reformation controversial theology, and develops a profound dogmatic theology between which

and the encyclical *Mystici Corporis* of Pope Pius XII there are striking resemblances.

Bibliography. N. Walsh SJ, *John Baptist Franzelin* SJ (1895) ; E. Hocedez SJ, *Histoire de la théologie au XIXe siècle* t. II (1952), t. III (1947) ; *Catholicisme* IV, 1564 f. ; DTC VI, 765–7 ; MN 60 (1887) 305–24 ; CE VI, 242 f. ; *Civiltà Cattolica* 8.ser.t. 5 (1872) 194–209 ; A. Merk SJ, ' Kardinal Franzelin u. die Inspiration ', *Scholastik* I (1926) 368–78 ; G. Courtade, ' J. B. Franzelin. Les Formules que le magistère lui a empruntées ', RSR 40 (1952) 317–25.

F. C.

FREEDOM OF THOUGHT

FREEDOM OF THOUGHT The militant movement in the 19th cent. against all revealed religion took as its slogan the words ' freedom of thought ', but in reality it was championing the very opposite, the shut mind and the closed system of the universe where Newtonian physics reigned supreme. The heyday of the movement was from 1880 to 1930 ; in 1880 it became internationally organized with headquarters in Brussels, and in 1930 it was split by the defection of the Communists, who formed their own association, soon to be broken up in Germany by the coming to power of the Nazi government. About the same time the acceptance by scientists of the Heisenberg uncertainty-principle made the Newtonian fabric look less stable and suggested by analogy that the closed system of the universe, in which there was no room for revelation, was unsatisfactory. A pale shadow of the former movement was seen again in Germany in 1952 when the statue of Feuerbach was restored to its place at Nürnberg with its legend : ' Man created God in his own image and likeness.'

The slogan itself comes from the work of Collins the Deist and was first used in 1713 (*see* DEISM). Originally it was a demand for disestablishment of the Anglican Church and may have influenced the famous first amendment to the American Constitution which forbade the making of any establishment of religion (*see* CHURCH AND STATE). When adopted as a slogan in the 19th cent. it connoted the secularization of society ; lay schools, civil marriage and the cremation of the dead. All these were held to be necessary to give man freedom from the shadow of revealed religion. In England the *Hibbert Journal* was founded (largely on a legacy from a West Indian slave-owner) to propagate the new ideas. In later times, as the movement reached more popular levels, the Rationalist Press Association and the Freethinkers' Library spread the same ideas more widely.

Theoretically, the crux of the matter was to determine whether natural man has any duty to envisage the *a priori* possibility of a revelation, for, if he has, then it is clear that to regard the universe as a closed self-explanatory system must be wrong. It should be admitted that the Christian apologetic of the time was slow in answering the rationalist propaganda at its crucial point and was often content to attack the outworks. Not until the later writings of Blondel was a full-scale answer of Christian philosophy provided to the closed-system universe. For this defect the fideism and traditionalism of 19th-cent. France is in part to blame, but it should not be forgotten that there had been for a very long time another current in Christian thought which can be traced back to the *Utopia* of St Thomas More (*see* APOLOGETICS X). Here was provided a sketch of a natural-law republic in which the inhabitants were not content to close their minds to the possibility of a revelation but prayed constantly that, if God had declared more fully His purpose for mankind He would deign to let them know it. Human nature cannot command the advent of the supernatural, but it can ' show willing ' in its regard.

The ultimate analysis of this openness of mind towards the possibility of revelation can be found in the commentaries of St Thomas Aquinas on the *Ethics* of Aristotle. St Thomas takes over the idea that the most pleasurable activity for man is the contemplation of wisdom and distinguishes between the pleasure of search and that of possession (*In libros Ethicorum*, X:10), that of possession being judged greater. Then, going far beyond Aristotle, St Thomas states that the happy contemplative, who is living the life of the intellect and making the good of his intellect his chief care, is also most beloved of God (ibid., *lectio* 13). For Aristotle this would have seemed blasphemy. Whether he or one of his scholars wrote the *Magna Moralia*, the doctrine is his, and there (1208 b 30) it is said : ' Friendship towards God does not admit of love being returned, nor at all of loving. . . . There is, people think, a friendship towards God, but here they are wrong.' Where Aristotle stopped short, St Thomas allowed natural aspiration to continue. ' It is *reasonable* that God should bestow His greatest benefits upon those who love their intellect, do it honour and set its good before all other goods ' (ibid.). Thus did St Thomas create a climate in which revelation might seem not altogether impossible. When (in *Contra Gentiles* 1:4) he shows how convenient revelation is for man in his existential plight, he is going beyond what natural reason might direct, but even so, his language is not unfamiliar to the post-1930 man. In his strictly philosophical treatment of the *Ethics* he is content to use the maxim of St Hilary, that, given the infinite distance between man and God, man will never be able to cover that distance by his own intellectual activity, but it will be good for him to make the attempt and he will ' get somewhere '.[1]

That this attitude towards the natural man was not more widely followed may be due to the sharp attacks upon St Thomas that came at once after his premature death. Roger Marston OFM in 1282 was quite personal in what he said at Oxford : ' There are certain theologians who play the philosopher—and would that they had not fallen into a way of despising the sound simplicity of the saints through the false glamour of human wisdom ! They despise or disregard the wisdom of holy doctors and for their proof of immortality they go to the reasonings

[1] Quamquam nunquam **perveniet**, tamen proficiet prodeundo.

of creatures of Hell ' (*Quaestiones de anima*, 7:360). This outburst is followed by a citation of part of the *Summa* ; there can be no doubt who was intended. Later doubts about proving immortality by reason alone, as expressed by Cajetan in his commentary on Rom 9:21 and Eccles 3:19, made it hard to see how an indefinite progress of the human mind towards God could have been planned by Him, if it was to stop short at death.

Since 1950 the old-fashioned rationalism has changed its name to humanism and continues to proclaim a muted gospel of Progress in spite of the conditions of the time. J. B. Bury's *History of Freedom of Thought* (1913) was issued again in 1952 with an epilogue by the secretary of the Humanist Association, in which *inter alia* the Italian Communist, Togliatti, is praised for having Voltaire's tract on toleration brought out in Rome under the very eyes of the Pope ; but it is at the same time sadly admitted that for Communists toleration is merely a tactical approach in a Catholic country, and not a matter of principle at all. Before 1914 the Rationalist Press found it profitable to re-issue the highly sceptical *Encyclopedia Biblica* in cheap fortnightly parts, since experience showed that to undermine from within was better than to attack Christianity from without. The great failure of the rationalist was in not foreseeing that the real threat to religious liberty was to come from the totalitarian states such as Russia and China (*see further* TOLERATION, ATHEISM).
Bibliography. H. de Lubac SJ, *The Drama of Atheistic Humanism* (1949) ; *J. B. Bury, *History of Freedom of Thought* (1952 [2]) ; *A. Gowans Whyte, *The Story of the Rationalist Press Association* (1949) ; J. H. Crehan SJ, ' Natural Happiness in Theology ', in MN 184 (1947) 278–86 ; J. L. Russell SJ, *Is Humanism enough ?* (1961).   J. H. C.

FREE WILL The article has eight parts, an introduction (I), a definition of free will (II), reason and freedom (III), the moral order and freedom (IV), relation to psychology (V), history of opinions (VI), free will and theology (VII) and freedom in Christ (VIII).

I Basically the term free will suggests that human beings have some measure of power over their own actions. Aristotle attributed such power to human beings in regard to those actions for which we can be praised or blamed ; for such actions we are held *responsible* in so far as they proceed from ourselves and we are masters of them.

It is in attempting to make explicit the meaning of having power over our own actions that difficulties and differences of opinion arise. Generally speaking, it is possible to hold one of two opinions which form the subject of much comment by present-day English philosophers. On the one side are those who hold that when we attribute responsibility to an individual we need in no way contradict a necessary postulate which we apply whenever we attempt to explain any purely physical event in the material universe, namely that it must be *caused* ; that is, it must have as its antecedent some other event or events from which it necessarily follows. Thus actions, of whatever kind, imputed to human beings are in principle capable of explanation in terms, say, of physical, chemical, physiological, psychological, sociological influences. This position is called *determinism*. The other is usually referred to as *indeterminism* or *libertarianism*. It holds that there are some actions of human beings which cannot be fully explained in terms of the sum of these causes, though their influence in all human action must be admitted. It is of these actions, in which a measure of independence of these various forces is present and experienced, that man is master, and the indeterminist calls them *free*. The determinist will use the term *uncaused* in reference to those actions; and he will naturally reject the concept of uncaused action as unintelligible. The libertarian will reply that, though the term *uncaused* may be acceptable in the sense that free actions do not admit of the same type of explanation as others, it is unacceptable if it implies that there is no cause at all. For him the cause will be the *self*—man, the self-conscious agent. To which the determinist will reply that the self (to which he may give the term *character*) is itself the result of forces in the environment. The notion of any other self he finds indefensible. And he may go on to say that the actions of the character, being determined, are in principle predictable; though, because of the complexity of the factors which govern human behaviour, actual prediction is in most cases, and may ever remain, impossible. The libertarian will point out difficulties in the determinist's position here: first that a prediction known to the individual whose behaviour is predicted may well influence him to do the opposite; and that persons are not objects capable of being investigated by a purely objective scientific method; that indeed it may be possible to predict what a person will do and yet know that he does it freely.

It may be thus evident from the foregoing that the question of free will is very closely connected with many other questions, some of them extremely difficult; more especially it is connected with an inquiry into the nature of the *self* said to be responsible for its actions. Can this self be explained as the product of forces within the material universe? Or does it in some sense transcend the material universe; or, to use traditional terminology, must it be regarded as partially spiritual, that is, to have a spiritual soul; and if so, how does a spiritual principle operate within material conditions in such a way that the causal laws which govern bodily events are not interfered with? Thus the whole problem of the mind-matter, soul-body relationship is here involved.

II The meaning of free will: conditions of its operations. It is obviously impossible here to deal with all the themes with which free will is logically connected. It will probably be best to refer to them rather obliquely as occasion arises. Before advancing reasons to justify the assertion that man has free will, it may help first to emphasize somewhat dogmatically the following points:

(*a*) Free will is a *kind* of freedom which must be distinguished from other kinds. Thus, e.g., to distinguish it from one other kind, free will does not mean that man has power over his own actions in the sense of being able to *do* what he wills to do. He may, e.g., very well want to make a speech and yet be prevented from so doing by physical force. Thus the free-will controversy is not primarily concerned with what we may call freedom of *performance*, however highly we value this freedom. This may be called freedom from constraint by *external* forces —the *libertas a coactione* of the Scholastics. Free will means rather freedom from *internal* forces and is sometimes termed *psychological* freedom or freedom of *choice*. It means that man is free in his choices or decisions—though he may often be prevented from carrying them out by external force. Decision may temporarily precede the carrying out of decision, though this is not necessarily always the case. In external activity which we call *voluntary*, it is possible to distinguish the element of conscious decision without which the action is not voluntary and the act regarded in its external bodily aspect. In its aspect of decision the act (say, to go for a walk) is ascribed to will—it is the *actus elicitus voluntatis*, the *volition*; in its aspect of physical activity it is not formally attributed to will but ordered by will— *actus imperatus a voluntate*.

(*b*) Free will does not mean unmotivated action, action for which no reason can be given. Indeed, as we shall emphasize, there is always a reason for action when a man acts freely, and that there should be is a necessary condition for free choice. Choice is possible only when a possible decision is apprehended by the individual concerned to have some value for him, to be in some way satisfying—as useful, or pleasurable, or in accordance with his moral code, etc. From this very fact it is possible to deduce that there may well be limitations in regard to the degree of free will which an individual possesses—for there may be actions in which he may see no value for him at all. There must be some initial attraction for choice to be possible; and this may very well depend on a variety of factors—educational, social, unconscious. The result of this attraction in the subject may be termed inchoate desire (the *complacentia*). It is not to this desire that freedom is attributed but rather to the individual's acceptance or rejection of it, to his act of making it efficacious or not efficacious through the decision which it prompts.

(*c*) Nor does free will imply uncaused action except in the sense in which the term 'uncaused' may be used to exclude a determinist analysis of volition. Free will implies the capacity for self-determination; for determining, i.e. causing, one's own actions, for being master of one's own decisions. A total explanation of a free act will necessarily refer to all the influences in our human environment, but it can never be exhausted by the sum-total of influences or events external to the individual's own choice. If we were to consider the state of an individual antecedent to the moment of choice, we must think of his choice as then being in his power, in the sense that the positing of it, or not positing of it, depends solely on him. In that sense a free choice is one which need not take place ; the individual can choose differently. It is only necessary when it takes place because he wills it to take place. Thus the term *active indifference* has been used to describe the state of an agent who has free will compared with that of an agent who acts in total dependence on causes external to itself.

III Free Will and Reason. The possibility of free choice lies in the nature of the agent himself and in that which distinguishes him from other agents ; this, in man, is *reason*. We use the term here in the very general sense of that aspect of cognitional functioning whereby man differs from the animal. Man is able to reflect on his own actions and, as the result of his experiences, to judge of their possible consequences. He can examine situations in which he is placed in the light of ideals which reason enables him to attain. The possession of ideals is itself indicative of his power of abstracting from particular concrete situations. Thus reason gives him the power to *deliberate* concerning the various impulses, desires or attractions he experiences, in that he is able to examine them in their relation to his ideals and purposes. They are for him possible means to his ends, not just impulses. As long as reason is operative, he has, to use the phrase of St Thomas, power over his *practical judgment*. He is thus free from the various psychological determinations to which the animal is subject.

The difference which reason makes in the practical sphere is perhaps best appreciated in the light of a general theory of appetite or tendency, such as we find in the Aristotelico-Thomist tradition. Of course no attempt to show its validity can be made here and only the merest outline can be given. In that theory material things are regarded as, by their nature, incomplete and as continually tending towards further completion ; that completion consists in the realization of the idea or ' form ' which they embody ; that realization is their own perfection. This tendency, because it belongs to all material things (man is here included), in so far as they are what they are, is called *natural* tendency ; and that towards which tendency is directed is called their *good*. As we ascend the scale of nature we see the element of knowledge enter, first at the animal level (sensory awareness would probably be a better word than knowledge to apply here), and then at the human level. Here tendency becomes experienced or conscious ; and here terms such as desire or appetite (used in this exposition as synonymous with tendency) more strictly apply. Thus the animal has sensory appetite. It experiences its tendency towards its own good. It has *needs*. It is capable of perceiving, e.g. food and drink as that which will give it sensory satisfaction. But man, though he may experience, as does the animal, sensory needs, is able to apprehend them in a different way to the animal. He has reason ; and therefore he has not merely sensory appetite but also rational appetite, the tra-

ditional name for which is *will*. He has thus a tendency towards what will satisfy reason itself, which is a capacity for knowing truth, for knowing other rational creatures as persons entitled to respect and reverence, and for knowing God. He can thus know his sensory tendencies as related to, and subject to, the tendency and end of reason. That end is, as is the end of all tendency, his own perfection ; but his perfection as a rational being, as man. Will is thus conscious tendency which has for its function the realization through use of the means, which are actions in the sensory world, of the ends which man has by virtue of the fact that he is rational. Its causation in the world is not like that of one body moving another ; it is the realization of purpose. Thus will must not be thought of as an isolated power capable of occasional and inexplicable action but as the necessary concomitant of reason, and functioning wherever reason is functioning. Nor must it be thought of as in a realm apart from man's instinctive and sensory life, but as by nature capable of using this for man's own good.

Further, to explore how reason and will are connected would involve long consideration ; but in so far as the problem of free will is concerned, at least the following point can be made. The fact that reason can consider the various attractions which man experiences and compare them with the satisfactions which he is likely to obtain if he yields to or rejects them is possible because it can form a conception of satisfaction, or happiness, which transcends whatever can be gained by any particular action or undertaking restricted to temporal conditions. And, wherever it can compare two alternatives, it can always judge that each has advantages or defects which the other has not ; and therefore it does not find in either a necessary object of choice. Because will, by definition, is a rational tendency, a tendency which is directed by rational appraisal, it would be contradictory to assert that a value apprehended by man as indifferent, i.e. as not capable of giving him complete satisfaction, could necessitate its action. To put this another way, only that good can necessitate the action of will which can fully realize the tendency of will as rational. This in the concrete is the Absolute Good, or God.

IV Free Will and Moral Obligation. Though this approach to the question of free will through a consideration of man's rational nature—sometimes referred to as the *a priori* argument for the existence of free will—is not much discussed today, it does not seem to be out of harmony with the two more popular ways of establishing man's power of self-determination. The first asserts that man's moral experience is unintelligible without free will ; the second that man has experience of determining his own choices which is as immediate and irrefutable as the fact that he exists, or which cannot at least be explained unless we concede that man has free will. Both these approaches are very closely connected ; both link free will with reason, the first because morality belongs to man and not to the brute, precisely because he is rational and able to appreciate moral obligation and moral ideals. The second is linked to reason because the experience of free decision is given when deliberation concerning actions and their consequences is possible ; and such deliberation involves the use of reason—especially in its main feature of being able to reflect on one's self and one's own actions, antecedently to positing them, in positing them and after positing them.

The moral approach may be presented in two ways. The first is to take such notions as praise and blame, duty, right, wrong, justice, obligation, etc. These are all very difficult of analysis either separately or in their interconnection. But when we use them in reference to individuals and to human situations they all seem to imply free will. If we blame X for failing to do something, we do so with the implication that he could have done it, had he the will to, and that he could have willed ; we attribute to him the power, at the moment of not doing it, to do what he did not do. We do not imply, by the way we use praise and blame, that we are using mere psychological stimuli which may influence future action. We judge of actions which took place ; we attribute responsibility to the individual concerned. So also, if we hold that a person is here and now obliged to perform a certain action, that he *ought* to do it, our attitude has meaning only if we are attributing free will to that person. On the one hand we hold that he has it in his power to do it through an act of decision, that is, voluntarily ; on the other hand we hold that he has it in his power to refrain voluntarily from doing it. A man cannot be held to be morally obliged to do what is not in his power; and what, when morally obliged, he has in his power to do, he has in his power to omit.

The discussion of the moral aspect of free will— which would involve examination of such concepts as those of guilt and punishment—is obviously incomplete without a full analysis of the basis of moral imperatives. If these can be fully explained as due to psychological conditioning, or to the intro- jection of parental norms, as in the Freudian Super- ego theory, then the argument would be difficult to sustain. Thus, fully to substantiate it, it would be necessary to show that morality is a fact of human nature which exists in man because of the fact that he is rational ; that reason itself imposes norms (*see* CONSCIENCE). This aspect of the matter is empha- sized in Kant's analysis of the moral factor in man. Man has freedom precisely because he is able to conform his will to imperatives which, in that they are universal and oblige irrespective of the particular immediate sensory well-being of the individual, transcend, and cannot be deduced from, the data of sensory experience. In this analysis, which obviously implies free will in the sense of an ability to obey or disobey the moral law, the attribute of freedom especially stressed is that of man's power to transcend sensory inclinations by obedience to a supreme moral principle for its own sake. Much can be said for and against various aspects of Kant's ideas, but he seems to be quite correct in implying the logical connection between a denial of free will and the assertion that

the only source of moral imperatives is the historical or contemporary environment. No Christian ethic could accept so restricted a source.

V Free Will and Psychology. But if free will be a fact, it must be experienced by the person who possesses it, whose *self*-determination it is. Indeed, in mentioning its connection with reason and morality, we are really referring to man in his *experience* of himself as rational and in his attitude to other persons in his experience of them as rational ; there can be no purely *a priori* approach in this matter. That there is in human beings a conscious- ness of freely determining their own choices in a variety of situations is very difficult to refute. It seems to remain in human beings even when, on philosophical grounds, they uphold a determinist position. An individual may indeed maintain that there is no experience of free will, but rather an illusion of free will based perhaps on ignorance of the various forces which determine our every action. The determinist, however, is in a very difficult position when asked to explain how, within a system which is totally determined in every detail, even the illusion of free will can ever arise. It sounds odd to assert that all normal human beings were pre- determined to think they were capable of acting freely. We are conscious that we can ' make up our own mind ', form ' resolutions ', ' decide for our- selves ', etc., and we speak of ourselves and of others as doing things ' voluntarily ', ' freely ', of ' being ourselves to blame ', etc. ; we are aware, in other words, that when we decide it is not always a case of our character determining us but of ourselves form- ing our character through our own free activity. This type of experience is doubtless more evident at some times than at others, e.g. in cases where we strongly resist a temptation to which we know we could give way, or force ourselves to attend to some problem when we know we could easily refuse to do so.

Analysis of the data of experience raises, of course, many difficult problems. We shall here mention briefly one of them. It has often been alleged that this conviction of the freedom of choice is based on our ignorance of the psychological mechanisms which, unknown to us, are always influencing our behaviour. The real causes of our volitions would then be unconscious impulses, due partially perhaps to past experiences of which we have now but little memory. The reasons we give are really *rationaliza- tions*. Obviously when examining assertions of this kind we should investigate carefully the empirical evidence which can be adduced for it ; that would be outside the scope of this article. All we can note here is that this type of criticism of free will is not so destructive as at first sight it may seem. That the study of the Unconscious, particularly since Freud's great discoveries, has given us new insights into the mind of man there can be no doubt. But when we examine them in relation to our present problem, they should first of all make us emphasize the con- ditions under which free will is claimed for man. A free act is a consciously reasoned decision. Thus when rational reflection is made impossible, as it may well be on many occasions in the life of the normal individual, and doubtless is completely so in many cases of abnormality, there is no such thing as free choice. In these cases the action is not in the strict sense human action ; it is the act of a man (*actus hominis*) but not a human act (*actus humanus*). But the fact that reasoned deliberation is excluded in some cases does not mean that there is never any such thing. (Logically the assertion that all reasons are rationalizations is inherently contradictory, in the sense at least that an individual who affirms this affirms that he has reasonable grounds for holding it and for submitting it to his hearer's rational examination.) The point we have to consider is how the person concerned is able to confront the impulse when it arrives, by whatever devious route, at the level of consciousness. Impulses indeed do arrive in a variety of ways. Man is not a disembodied spirit but a being who needs his sensory nature to be able to have human desires at all. Free will is experienced in the material world in using it to realize within it the ideals which human reason, in its transcendence of the world, possesses. Impulses may be experienced by man because he has taken drugs, or has been subject to suggestion, or had an unfriendly childhood environment, or has an easily aroused imagination. But because impulses are experienced, they are not necessarily determinants of action ; man need not give way to them. No matter what their origin, provided reason can examine them in relation to possible consequences of yielding to them or overcoming them, or in relation to a scheme of moral values, they become matter for rational choice. They are then the subject of rational practical judgment, and thus no longer mere impulses but possible means to the ends of reason.

VI The history of opinions about free will may now be summarily indicated. For the Platonists there was a surd element in reality just as there was in mathematics, and to this corresponded a flaw in human knowledge which led to bad or mistaken choices. The Stoics accepted an overriding determinism and taught (as in the celebrated prayer of Cleanthes) that man should resign himself to the action of its power ; that this resignation must be free was not thought of as an inconsistency within the system. Pantheist philosophies, such as that of Spinoza, where there is no idea of creation, also fail to find room for human freedom. Theological debates about free will at the Reformation (*see* FOREKNOWLEDGE) naturally led to deeper philosophical and psychological reflection on the nature of freedom ; Descartes made will the faculty which assents, allowing it a greater scope (*envergure*) than the intellect, and thus hoping to leave room for error and sin. Kant took up a definition of freedom similar to that left by St Anselm : the power of doing right for rightness' sake.[1] Bergson, reacting somewhat against Kant, held that freedom has to be experienced by the individual in action which is the

[1] Potestas servandi rectitudinem propter ipsam rectitudinem.

full expression of his individuality. This reaction opened the way to the Existentialists who prefer description to logical analysis and who emphasize the commitment of the whole man, emotions and reason together, in human choice. Berdyaev, a forerunner of the Existentialists, maintained that only after a man was committed to Christianity did he become truly free.

British philosophers of the empirical school have been more interested in the analysis of the conceptions used and the words employed for them in speaking of voluntary actions or ethical values. Hume had the quite understandable illusion that he might be able to do for human nature what Newton had done for the physical world and reduce all human activity to a set of laws. Analysis has uncovered some false impressions about the working of free will, but its sphere is limited ; it does not provide a wide prospect of the place of freedom in the universe. The regret of the poet Ovid, that he knew the better way but followed the worse, finds an echo in the heart of man that requires an ulterior explanation, and at this point it becomes imperative to call upon the theologian.

VII Free will for the theologian is a faint imitation of the creative power of God. Its simplest form is the power to choose either to accept or to reject what is presented to it as desirable. A choice between alternative goods is more complex. For God the choice to create rather than to refrain from creating is more fundamental than the choice of the kind of world that will come into being. God is not free in His self-contemplation but is free in creating (*see* CREATION), and hence free will in man can be called a perfection and looked upon as making man more godlike. Owing to the absence of a doctrine of creation in pagan antiquity, the understanding of the freedom of the will was much deepened and transformed by Christian thought. The account of free choice in Aristotle (*Ethica Nicomachea*, 1139a 20–35) has the two elements of ὄρεξις and προαίρεσις (tendency towards an end and choice of means) that were to be taken up by St Thomas as *intentio* and *electio*, but in Aristotle they seem to be little more than aspects of the practical reason and not moments in the operation of a distinct faculty called the will. The ensuing danger of regarding free choice of evil as simply a mistake in knowledge (either ignorance of facts or faulty reasoning) was guarded against in Christian thought by the doctrine of the fall of the angels, for, if they fell when at the height of their power as pure intelligences, this idea of sin being due to ignorance was not really helpful (*see* DEVIL).

The machinery of free will for St Thomas (*Summa*, 1–2ae:1:7c) is that, while all men have the same formal tendency to seek their own perfecting, the choice of means thereto and also the location of this perfecting in this or that object differ widely and account for the phenomena of freedom. It is not difficult to see in this distinction of tendency and choice a likeness of man to God, for in God the internal activity is necessary and the outward-looking activity free. The medieval return to Aristotle meant that there were times when even St Thomas seemed to speak as if the will were a faint copy of the intellect. Thus he can say (*Summa*, 1a:62:8:@3) that the will addresses itself to the problem of choice of means to an end just as the intellect to the drawing out of conclusions. The moral syllogism (for which *see* CONSCIENCE) made this confusion only too pervasive.

The over-simple explanation of the Manichees and Cathars that man's free will was due to his being the battle-ground between two equal powers of good and evil was firmly rejected by Christian thought, for in the *Embassy* of Athenagoras (presented to Marcus Aurelius) it is set down that : 'We apprehend that certain distinct powers exist that are in relation with matter and use it, but that one of these is God's opposite. Not that we consider there is a counterpart to God in the same way as with Empedocles strife is love's counterpart, or night is the counterpart of day among the objects of sense ; for, if anything did stand counter to God it would cease from existence, having the ground of its being dissolved by the power and might of God.' The idea of evil as a privation of some degree of reality sprang from declarations such as this. The Jewish idea of two inclinations, the good and the evil inclination, besetting a man left him still free to adhere to one or the other, but Gnosticism (q.v.) and astrology soon made it appear that he was simply adrift on their tides. With the Christian rejection of this dualism there came the idea that free will was a good thing and godlike, but this brought a difficulty in its train.

Had one to project back into God something that corresponded to the evil choices that men made ? Did God's freedom include ability to sin, and if not, how was freedom a simple good ? In creating free men God permits, though He does not command, the abuse of their freedom by sin. As long as it can be seen that freely-given praise of God is more noble in itself than automatically-delivered praise, this permission need cause no difficulty ; no robot could ever be canonized. It is also necessary to assess the distance of the human creature from his Creator. If human free will were without all tares, man would be on the level of God. Clarity of prevision and alertness of decision must diminish as one goes down the scale of intelligent beings. That in man's case the scales have been tilted towards evil, owing to the sin of Adam, does but heighten a condition that was already present in his nature. To show a positive reason why free will is a perfection, one might urge that man's right use of it bears some analogy with creative activity, for the goal of morality can be presented as the creation by each individual of a personality or the becoming a person (in the sense of a completely integrated human being). Not all men achieve this, but God can permit the shortfall, in the same way and on the same principles as men may reasonably permit (on the principle of the double effect) a secondary evil consequence to issue from their act which is primarily aimed at the good. When this principle is invoked by men, they have to see some just proportion between the evil and the good involved, and it is precisely the mystery of this problem of free will that only God can see the proportion of good and evil arising out of His creation of men endowed with free will.

The blessed in heaven are not free with the freedom of choice. To some this would imply that free will is a transitory gift to man and not a perfection at all. It should, however, be observed that the reason for this is the absorption of their minds and wills in the vision of God. This makes them in some way imitate the internal life of the Trinity, and it is therefore quite to be expected that their creative activity (of making themselves into persons) should now cease, godlike though it was. St Thomas (*Summa*, 2–2ae:88:4:@1) sees in the religious life under vow (where the aim is the absence of sin and the means a certain renunciation of liberty) an anticipation of the state of the blessed ; what the Second Vatican Council (decree on the Church, VI:44) finds in religious life, that it is a sign to the faithful of the kingdom of heaven, would thus be manifested in detail.

VIII In Christ the problem of free will is presented with new dimensions. In the NT His full humanity was declared (Heb 4:15) and His willing obedience (Jn 6:38 and 14:31) to a divine command. The Synoptics (Mt 26:39 ; Lk 22:42 ; Mk 14:36) emphasize the apparent reluctance of the Agony, and there must be freedom in Christ's human nature if there is to be value in the Atonement. Yet where the human intellect is illuminated by divine knowledge, freedom can scarcely be said to linger. The more or less heretical solutions of the problem suggested by Marsilius of Padua, by the Lutheran Thomasius, by Günther and by the school of Bishop Gore will be discussed later (*see* KENOSIS), but it may suffice here to indicate a line of solution. When discussing the conflict of sorrow and joy in the human soul of Christ at the Passion, St Thomas (*Summa*, 3a:46:7c:@4) establishes a distinction between the fine point of the soul, which is permanently in enjoyment of happiness, and the ordinary awareness which is directed upon the senses and what they deliver. He may have been drawing upon some mystical experience of his own for this, and it is strange how few subsequent theologians have attempted to psychologize upon this division of soul in Christ. If at the time of the Passion there were a check imposed on the ordinary overflow (*redundantia*) of happiness arising from the possession of the beatific vision by Christ, then one might be more easily able to explain the division of soul. Those who despaired of a solution even while accepting the duality of nature in Christ became Monothelites or believers in one will for Christ (*see* MONOTHELITES). The psychology of inspiration of the scriptural writers presents a somewhat similar phenomenon. The Holy Spirit possesses the faculties of these men but somehow leaves them to work at their own level when this does not interfere with His essential purposes. In Christ the union of divine and human is immeasurably closer, yet something of this freedom remains.

The sinlessness of Christ, or His inability to sin, did not abate His freedom of will. The fact of sinlessness is clear in the NT (Heb 4:15 ; 2 Cor 5:21 ; 1 Pet 2:22), and as early as Origen one finds (*princ.* II:6:6 ; GCS 22:145) a theological explanation by means of a comparison with the sword in the furnace ; while the sword is there, it remains red-hot ; if it were withdrawn it would become cold steel, but in fact it never is withdrawn. The hypostatic union of natures in Christ means that the holiness of God could not be conjoined with a human sinner. What division was possible in the Passion to allow suffering (*see above*) is not so when sin is involved (*see* TEMPTATION OF CHRIST). The very paradox of a free human will that cannot sin shows that evil must be a privation of reality. Freely-directed effort of will to achieve a harmony of being ever more perfect does not essentially connote a falling short from time to time. If freedom is a creative activity, it must not always happen that the agent stumble or grow weary while at work. St Thomas (*Summa*, 3a:15:2:@2) supposes that in the human nature of Christ there was a yearning of the sensitive appetite, ' for food, drink, sleep and other things which men desire according to right reason ', but that this did not imply any disorderly concupiscence.[1] His immediate

---

[1] Caro Christi concupiscentia appetitus sensitivi naturaliter appetebat escam et potum et somnum et alia quae secundum rectam rationem appetuntur ; ex hoc autem non sequitur quod in Christo fuerit fomes peccati.

followers (such as Hervaeus Natalis) held that in Adam before the fall there was concupiscence, but that the formation of habits of virtue was so easy for him that he would have formed them almost at once, had he not been tempted. In Christ, by reason of the union (which did not come into being gradually) there was a harmony from the beginning of rational life.

Bibliography. Aristotle, *Ethica ad Nicomachum* and the commentary of St Thomas on that book ; also his *Quaestio unica de malo* ; *Summa*, 1a:83c and *Quaestio* 24 *De veritate* ; H. Daudin, *La Liberté de la volonté : signification des doctrines classiques* (1950) ; J. Lebacqz SJ, *Libre arbitre et jugement* (1960) ; A. Kenny, *Action, Emotion and Will* (1963) ; J. Rickaby SJ, *Free Will and Four English Philosophers* (1906) ; *A. Farrer, *The Freedom of the Will* (1957) ; *S. Hampshire, *Thought and Action* (1959) ; *F. Vivian, *Human Freedom and Responsibility* (1964) ; Mary J. Gregor, *Laws of Freedom* : a study of Kant's method of applying the categorical imperative (1963) ; J. Nuttin, *Psycho-analysis and Personality* (1954) ; *M. Cranston, *Freedom, a New Analysis* (1953) ; *N. Berdyaev, *Freedom and the Spirit* (1948) ; *G. N. Vesey, *The Embodied Mind* (1965) ; J. H. Crehan SJ, ' Free Will : the Theological Problem ', in *Encyclopædia Britannica* (1964 printing).

R. M. and J. H. C.

G

GALLICANISM The four Articles of the Gallican clergy, drawn up in 1682, but being based upon manifestos of 1663 and earlier, were declared null and void by Innocent XI and again by Alexander VIII in 1690 (D 1322–6), who released from their oath those who had sworn to maintain them. Pius VI in 1794, in condemning the Synod of Pistoia (D 1598–9), said that the Articles were temerarious, but at that date they could not be called outright heresy. Since the definition of papal infallibility, however, this could be said, for Gallicanism was in reality an attempt to stave off that definition. It grew out of the conciliar movement of the later Middle Ages (*see* CHURCH AND STATE), though its resurgence in the 17th cent. was due to an English occasion, which will be briefly discussed here (I). The parting of the ways between Gallicanism and Jansenism (II) and the renewed influence of the English situation in the time of Archbishop Wake (III) will be shown, while the final rout of Gallicanism in the 19th cent. (IV) will be indicated.

I The affair of the Bishop of Chalcedon, Richard Smith, was the occasion which sparked off the controversy leading to a revival in France of a conciliar movement (*see* BASLE, COUNCIL OF *and* CONSTANCE, COUNCIL OF), which had been dormant in the period of Trent and immediately after it. The Congregation of Propaganda had been set up in 1622, and soon afterwards there was appointed the first Vicar-apostolic for England, William Bishop, who died after a very short time. He was replaced by Richard Smith, who came to England in 1625, and whose flair for organization, in the words of Gordon Albion, 'caused him to overstep his powers as a titular bishop by arrogating to himself ordinary jurisdiction in maintaining a Chapter, Vicars, Archdeacons and Notaries, while he involved himself in a bitter controversy with the Regulars by claiming that their faculties must come from him, otherwise their absolutions would be invalid' (*Charles I and the Court of Rome*, 110). Smith was a graduate of the Sorbonne, as was Matthew Kellison, a professor of Douai, who began the theological controversy by a tract on the hierarchy. A reply to Kellison was produced by Matthew Wilson SJ (alias Edward Knott and also Nicholas Smith), who was a prisoner in the Clink at the time. One of Kellison's arguments had been a proposition taken from Bañez, that it was impossible for the Pope to take away the bishops from the whole Church or from a notable part thereof. Britain in 1629 might or might not be a notable part of the Church, but France was, and the doctors of the Sorbonne were soon engaged heavily on the side of the Bishop of Chalcedon.

The main reply to Wilson and to another tract by John Floyd (published under the name of Daniel a Jesu) was by St Cyran, the future Jansenist, who wrote a large tome under the name of Petrus Aurelius and had his work published at the expense of the French bishops. A passage in Victor Vitensis (2:3 ; CSEL 7:25) was used to show that in North Africa some churches had been content to go for a long time without bishops (*see* BISHOP VI), while on the other side a phrase of Cyprian was urged in which he declared that the (local) church and the bishop were inseparable (*ep. 66 ad Pupianum*). A Brief of Urban VIII to Chalcedon (3 April 1631) ordered a cessation of the controversy and declared valid confessions heard by Regulars in England either in the past or the future, but the French were now caught up in the dispute. An assembly of the bishops and clergy (10 February 1631) gave its approval to the line followed by Kellison and his supporters. The sentence from Dominic de Soto (*De iustitia et iure*, 10:1:4), that it was a matter of divine law that each ecclesiastical region should have its own bishops, was very much to the liking of Gallican bishops, though in the present controversy it was a two-edged tool, for Smith had called himself Bishop of Scotland (where there was no bishop in possession), to say nothing of Wales. Richelieu was Smith's protector and he had designs of his own about England and its queen, Henrietta Maria. Hence the very prompt adoption of the Chalcedon dispute and its transfer to French soil. The Gallican assembly approved the condemnation by the Sorbonne of some eighty propositions, eleven of them taken from Irish sources and sixty-nine from the books of Wilson and Floyd. Some of these concerned the sacrament of confirmation and its necessity, though most of them touched on the kind of society the Church was meant to be. At this point there was an appeal back to the precedents of Constance.

An aristocratic régime for the Church (as advocated by Gallicans) required the frequent calling of councils. The decree *Frequens* passed at Constance on 9 October 1417 (just one month before the election of Martin V as Pope) had ordered this practice, and it is still argued by modern conciliarists that the papacy accepted the decree. Martin may have acquiesced in it through fear of deposition and allowed the convocation of Siena and Basle, but the next pope, Eugenius IV, in two Bulls (*Moyses vir Dei* of 1439 and *Etsi non dubitemus* of 1441), argued that the decree of Constance about its own supremacy had to be construed in the light of Scripture and Tradition which give Peter the supremacy. The bishops and clergy at Basle spent much time composing answers to Eugenius but without winning him over. In the last year of his life (1447) Eugenius was forced by two German Electors to declare : ' We, like our predecessors, from whose footsteps we mean never to deviate, accept, embrace and respect the general Council of Constance, its decree *Frequens* and its other decrees, in the same way as other Councils that represent the Church militant, their power, authority, honour and eminence.' This avowal is remarkable for what it does not say. The word pre-eminence had been urged by the Germans but the Pope would not have it, nor did he express his acceptance of the decree *sancta synodus* in which Constance had set forth its own supremacy. As it was notorious that the limits of that Council's jurisdiction were much contested (*see* CONSTANCE, COUNCIL OF), this omission was most significant.

The debate about Constance had been dormant for many years and now at Richelieu's bidding it flared up again. St Cyran spent some of his time arguing with P. Sirmond about confirmation and devoted some thirty pages to a defence of a misreading of canon 2 of the Council of Orange (*see* CONFIRMATION IV). He had also to deal with the assertion that there was no jurisdiction of French bishops over England, which one of the parties to the controversy had expressed in the maxim : ' Let the Gallican keep to his own dunghill.' [1] He urged that the Gallican church had sent St Patrick on his mission to Ireland. But the main issue was the authority of the Pope in the Church. Was the universal Church so constituted by local churches that these were necessary to it ? Constance had tried to set up such a principle by requiring in the election of Martin V a two-thirds majority in each nation and also a two-thirds majority among the Cardinals. The main principle of Gallicanism, that there had to be an agreement of king and clergy to govern the church of France, thereby holding in check the interference of the Holy See and insisting on the ancient canonical rights of France, was now at risk.

II The appearance of Jansenism did not at first make much difference to the debate. St Cyran had occasionally in his polemic called the English Jesuits ' Molinists ' and had hinted at the effects of their lax moral teaching if they were to be allowed to continue hearing confessions, but the main interest was elsewhere. By the middle of the century things had changed, and it was now the main interest of St Cyran and the Jansenists to present the famous five propositions of Cornelius Jansen as orthodox (D 1092-6) and to counter-attack the Jesuits who opposed them. If in the pursuance of this plan they found it convenient to magnify the bishops of France and to minimize the papal claims, that was accidental. Allegiances changed, too ; thus one of the leading supporters of Jansen was Florence Conry OFM, afterwards Archbishop of Tuam, who was one of the greatest Augustinian scholars of his day. Whereas the Chalcedon affair had divided all religious against the secular clergy, now there began to appear a different distribution of loyalties (*see also* JANSENISM).

The recent study by Canon Martimort of the Gallicanism of Bossuet could not be paralleled by a

[1] Intra suum Gallus sterquilinium dominetur.

similar one on his Jansenism, but at the same time it was the prevalence of Gallican views such as those of Bossuet that made possible the long delay in carrying through the condemnation of the five propositions. The first condemnation by Innocent X in May 1653 had to be repeated several times before the end of the century. Alexander VII renewed the condemnation in a more precise form in 1656 and in the next year the French bishops were on the point of drawing up a statement of the Gallican liberties when Cardinal Mazarin, at the instance of Alexander VII, dissuaded them. Yet the idea lay dormant, and when further trouble between France and the papacy arose in 1681 it was taken up again. Bossuet preached a sermon (9 November 1681), lasting for an hour and three-quarters, before the assembly of the clergy ; he said that heresy had visited the papacy but not to stay.[2] The distinction between the Roman see and its occupant, a distinction that caused much debate at Vatican I, was put forward. The primacy of the Pope was established ' even by the faults of the papacy '. Small wonder that in 1682 the same assembly approved the four Gallican articles (D 1322-6) which were immediately repudiated by Innocent XI. It was not at once obvious at that time that they were heretical, and the Pope had to be content with proscribing books and theses in which they were advocated ; Louis XIV on his side ordered the articles to be taught and upheld in all French universities and seminaries. The first of these articles exempted the king from papal censure ; the second safeguarded a right of appeal from the Pope to a general council ; the third asserted ancient Gallican rights and privileges, while the fourth said that papal decisions were not irrevocable unless they received the consent of the whole Church.

The Jansenists were quite glad to have the dispute with Rome turn on Gallican rights, for it drew attention away from their own heresy and at the same time guarded their position. After the first condemnation of their views in 1653 some of them (e.g. Pascal) wanted to enter an appeal from the Pope to a future council, but Arnaud and others at the time preferred to make the distinction between the propositions which the Pope had condemned and those which were in fact expressive of the mind of Jansenius (*see* DOGMATIC FACTS). Soon afterwards, however, Arnaud wrote a *Mémoire sur l'infaillibilité des papes détruite par la supériorité des conciles generaux* which has never been printed, though some of its material was used by him in 1662 for his *Pernicieuses conséquences des Jésuites*. Even so, he did not admit that a general council could be infallible about dogmatic facts, but he obviously preferred to have the debate about Pope versus council take place before the one about the meaning of Jansenius could arise. The ability with which the Jansenists turned papal attention away from themselves is shown by the letter of Du Vaucel to Arnaud (5 June 1683) boasting that Innocent XI is more afraid of the four Gallican articles than of the five propositions of Jansenius.

[2] Les héresies ont pu y passer, mais non pas y prendre racine.

The Jansenist agency at Rome did all in its power to foster this impression ; it is not really surprising that Père La Chaise should have drawn up a memorandum giving twelve reasons for thinking that Innocent was himself a Jansenist at heart.

III The influence of the English situation was present throughout the development of Gallicanism. Orcibal in his account of the origins of Jansenism (vol. III, appendix 4) goes so far as to say that the Anglican position in the days of Laud was taken as a model by the patriarchal Gallicanism of Richelieu. The collapse of the High Church movement in the civil war may have daunted the Gallicans, but there was a curious group of English Catholic clergy known as Blackloe's Cabal who in 1647 tried to win from the Independents (who were now coming into power with the defeat of Charles I) toleration for Catholics on Gallican lines. Sir Kenelm Digby, in November 1647, wrote to Henry Holden : ' Let not all end in designing and discoursing. . . . Close with the Independents. Make them see their interest to strengthen themselves.' Holden and White (alias Blackloe) were the two chief ecclesiastics in the design and Holden's proposals were printed (by Fr C. Plowden SJ during the dispute with the cis-Alpines in 1794) in a Latin text ; this may have been intended for showing to Cardinals whom it was hoped to enlist in support of the plan. There was to be an oath of allegiance for Catholics. They were to have six or eight bishops (consecrated in France) to rule them : ' These bishops having their authority immediately from Jesus Christ, and consequently independent of all other spiritual authority whatsoever, even that of the Pope. For though all bishops are bound to acknowledge the Pope as their head and first pastor, he cannot lay upon them any precept, of whatsoever kind, unless they and the State in which they dwell judge it to be expedient. This was the former practice in England and is now the practice in France. . . .' Those priests who refused to accept this settlement were to be banished. The modern biographer of Sir Kenelm Digby says that the scheme gradually disintegrated ; that Holden blamed Digby for indiscreet talk about it ; that its promoters judged it impossible to negotiate the scheme with the Cardinals of Propaganda. But it did not die, and it had sympathizers in France. In 1654–5 Digby was to try again, and, with support from Mazarin, managed to win from Cromwell some rather vague promise of leniency to Catholics, but the Holden scheme was not adopted outright.

A more remarkable Gallican project of relations with England began in 1716. Wake, the Archbishop of Canterbury, who had served for three years in Paris (1682–5) as chaplain to the English ambassador, and Dr Du Pin started to discuss the possibility of union between the Anglican and Gallican Churches, both to be independent of the Pope. Louis XIV had died (1 September 1715), and immediately the Jansenists took heart, for in his old age the King had been at one with the Pope in holding them down. Four bishops and a majority of the Sorbonne lodged an appeal to a future general

council against the papal decree *Unigenitus* of 1713 which had condemned the Jansenists (D 1351–1451), and after the issue of the Bull *Pastoralis officii* (28 August 1718) the Archbishop of Paris, Cardinal de Noailles, published his own appeal to a general council. It was against a background of such events that the Anglican negotiation took place. Du Pin produced a *Commonitorium* for Wake in which he set down his opinion of the thirty-nine Articles one by one, being rather less ready to accept them than the Franciscan, Sancta Clara, had been in 1634. It was transubstantiation which he was most anxious to preserve in any future union. On Article 37 about the papacy, Du Pin allowed that the Pope had no temporal nor yet immediate spiritual jurisdiction in France. By virtue of his primacy (' which Anglicans, at least the more moderate, do not contest ') he had the duty of watching that the right faith is everywhere kept and the canons observed and of applying a remedy when they are violated, and that is his sole jurisdiction. The other things which belong to him by human ordinance are not necessary. If the Pope refused to grant letters of appointment to those whom the King nominated to bishoprics, it was right for the metropolitans of France to consecrate them. There was a right of appeal to the Pope according to the canons of the council of Sardica, but the Pope must then name judges to hear the appeal in the country of its origin and not at Rome.

News of the negotiations leaked out in Paris (6 November 1717) and soon all Du Pin's papers were impounded, much to the alarm of Wake. Du Pin fell sick and died (6 June 1719) and afterwards no one of his calibre was found on the French side to carry on the plan. At the same time, in 1718, Wake was devising a scheme of government for the Catholics in the island of Minorca, which with Gibraltar had come under British control. He imposed an oath of allegiance for the clergy (there were six parishes on the island and a vicar-general, but no bishop) and laid it down that these clerics were to be free from all manner of dependence on the Bishop of Majorca or the Archbishop of Valencia and that the convents on the island were to be withdrawn from obedience to foreign Generals or Provincials. When the Pope protested that this was a violation of the Treaty of Utrecht, Wake advised the government to press for the vicar-general of Minorca to be made a bishop ' for his being so long in England, I am persuaded, has removed a good deal of his error and bigotry '. In 1719 a British warship captured a Sicilian bishop and took him to Minorca, so that the inhabitants could receive confirmation, but the experiment in Gallicanism failed soon afterwards. After Canada was conquered search was made by English officials in 1765 for Wake's Minorcan plans, but they could not be found, fortunately for the religious future of the New World.

IV The overthrow of Gallicanism was partly due to the French Revolution, which so weakened the French Church that it could do nothing to support such attempts as that of the Synod of Pistoia in 1786.

It is safe to say that the papal condemnation of this Synod in 1794 would have been impeded by France had there been no revolution. It is also true that the events of 1848, by the reaction they produced among the chief European powers, probably assisted in preparing public opinion for the acceptance of the definition of papal infallibility in 1870. Strong central government in Austria, France and Germany was the order of the day and to many it appeared that the Pope was doing little more than securing the same for the Church. The achievement of this definition will be discussed elsewhere (see VATICAN I, also PRIMACY), and here it may suffice to note that the main opposition came from Gallicans such as Acton and Döllinger.

Acton wrote on Ultramontanism in his *Home and Foreign Review* (July 1863, 162–206) and wrote to Döllinger that he had for the first time traced the doctrine to its source. Acton did not consider himself a Gallican; he preferred to be called a Liberal, though he admitted in his letters (e.g. in the portions omitted by Gasquet from the volume of 1905 and printed in the *Cambridge Historical Journal* of 1951) that his supporters among the English Catholics were largely the descendants of such Gallicans as Berington and Charles Butler. The part reserved in the Gallican scheme for the French king did not please Acton, and he saw that in a new age new models were required. Yet in the crisis of the Vatican Council, when it was becoming clear that the definition of infallibility would go through, he invoked the secular arm. Acton wrote to Gladstone 'on the urgent necessity of assisting the Opposition bishops' and Odo Russell, British agent in Rome, sent a telegram (15 February 1870) to the Foreign Secretary: 'I am requested to ask you to suggest to Count Beust [Austrian Foreign Secretary] to establish a common action with Prussia and Bavaria to support the German bishops in Rome, without which they will be defeated by the court of Rome' (*The Roman Question*, 391). Russell, who all along foresaw that the definition would go through, wrote on the same day that if the French withdrew their troops from Rome the Pope would not be deterred. 'The Pope has not forgotten Mentana and can afford to smile at the threats of his Eldest Son. The only demonstration that could influence the Vatican would be a protest of the 200 opposing bishops against the oecumenicity of the Council, followed by their immediate departure from Rome.' A second telegram on 1 March 1870 was more desperate: 'Lord Acton is anxious the French Government should know that further loss of time will be fatal to the bishops of the opposition' (op. cit., 398).

The First Vatican Council, by defining that the Pope's infallible decisions were not dependent on the consent of the Church (D 1839) and that there was no appeal from him to a general council (D 1830), made Gallicanism heretical in two of its principal tenets. It has been left to the Second Vatican Council to elucidate (*Constitutio de ecclesia*, III:22) how the bishops, as successors of the college of the Apostles in teaching and pastoral rule, are together with the Pope the subject of plenary power in the Church (*see further* HIERARCHY). It was not absolutism which triumphed at the First Vatican Council, but rather a middle party as far removed from Veuillot and W. G. Ward as from the Gallicans. The withdrawal of French troops in 1870 from the papal states was too late to save Gallicanism; it delayed for nearly a century the full elaboration of the teaching of the Church.

Bibliography. V. Martin, *Les Origines du Gallicanisme* (2 vols., 1939) deals with the period down to Trent; H. O. Evennett, *The Cardinal of Lorraine* (1930) has the best account of French policy at Trent; A. Allison, 'Chalcedon, Richelieu and the French Marriage', in *Recusant History* 7 (1964) 148–211; G. Albion, *Charles I and the Court of Rome* (1935); *R. T. Petersson, *Sir Kenelm Digby* (1956) deal with the English interlude and the Chalcedon affair; M. Nédoncelle, 'Un Moine turbulent: John Barnes', in RevSR 24 (1950) 266–300 adds details to this picture; A. Martimort, *Le Gallicanisme de Bossuet* (1953); J. Orcibal, *Les Origines du Jansénisme* (I and II, 1947, and III, 1948); the same, *Louis XIV contre Innocent XI* (1949); with *N. Sykes, *William Wake* (2 vols., 1957); and *G. R. McLean, 'Archbishop Wake and Reunion with the Gallican Church', in *Church Quarterly Review* 131 (1941) 240–52, cover later developments. The decline of Gallicanism has not been much studied, but the efforts of Acton at the time of the First Vatican Council can now be followed in *The Roman Question: Extracts from the Despatches of Odo Russell* (edited by N. Blakiston, 1962); and Döllinger, *Briefwechsel* I:1850–69 (1963), where the letters are almost entirely those of Acton to Döllinger. A modern attempt to revive conciliarist views is examined by J. Gill SJ in *Heythrop Journal* 5 (1964) 131–43; see also J. Leclerc SJ, 'Les Libertés de l'Église gallicane', in RSR 23 (1933) 385–410 and 542–68.

J. H. C.

GELASIAN SACRAMENTARY Sacramentary, *sacramentarium*, *liber sacramentorum*, was a former type of celebrant's manual; for Mass it provided neither Scripture lessons nor choral parts; besides the Canon it needed (chiefly) collects, secrets, prefaces, etc., proper to the day. 'Leonine', 'Gelasian' and 'Gregorian' Sacramentaries are names long in use, but handy as they are, they imply exaggerations. We know that Pope Leo I (440–61) did not compose or impose 'the Leonine', nor Pope Gelasius I (492–6) promulgate 'the Gelasian'; and Gregory's role in editing 'the Gregorian' is now severely limited.

Liber Pontificalis tells that Gelasius I, writing *cauto sermone*, composed prayer-forms; *Fecit etiam sacramentorum praefationes et orationes* (Duchesne, LP I:255). The Carolingians applied the name, 'Gelasian Sacramentary', not merely to prefaces and prayers, but to a whole Mass-manual which was preserved in France, and which Dom Wilmart called 'our foremost liturgical codex'. This ancient *Liber Sacramentorum Romanae Aeclesiae*, thus named 'Gelasian', is the Vatican codex, *Reg. 316*. It was copied by a nun somewhere near Paris c. A.D. 750 (E. Bischoff, E. A. Lowe). Her book provides for priests and for bishops, for monastic and for parish affairs. She drew on sources old and new, with Roman, Frankish (and perhaps English) material mixed in. Schmidt (250) allows the period 500–750 to bridge her materials, the careful study of which engages scholars in many-sided research (Ashworth, Chavasse, Lang, et al).

The three indexed books into which it is divided embody : (1) Christmas and Easter seasons ; (2) Saints' Masses in calendar order ; (3) some Sunday and many Votive Masses. No uniform system of proper parts is found. Most Masses have two prayers before the secret, a proper preface (some with *Hanc-igitur* insert), and end with a prayer over the people.

This 'Old Style Gelasian', in three books, was soon displaced by a single-book 'New Style Gelasian', much favoured by King Pippin (d.768). This survives in many copies : cf. Dom Mohlberg's edition of *MS St-Gall 348*. But Gelasian books passed out ot use, save as lending to the Supplement Alcuin made for the Roman Mass-book, when it was spread by Charlemagne at the end of the 8th cent.

Until 1960 no suitable edition of *Reg. 316* was available, H. A. Wilson's *Gelasian Sacramentary* (1894) being least deficient. Now Mohlberg has given us : *Liber Sacramentorum Romanae Aeclesiae* Ordinis Anni Circuli, *Sacramentarium Gelasianum*. P. Siffrin OSB provides a prayer-by-prayer concordance, as he had also done for 'the Leonine'.

Bibliography. H. Ashworth OSB, 'The Liturgical Prayers of St Gregory the Great', in *Traditio* 15 (1959) 107–61 : B. Bischoff, 'Die Kölner Nonnenhandschriften und das Skriptorium von Chelles', *Karolingische und ottonische Kunst* (1957) 395–411 ; E. Bishop, 'Gelasian Mass Book', in *Liturgica Historica* (1918) 39–61 ; B. Capelle OSB, 'L'Œuvre liturgique de Saint Gélase', in *JTS* (NS) 2 (1951) 129–44 ; A. Chavasse, *Le Sacramentaire gélasien* (1958) ; A. P. Lang SVD, *Leo der Grosse und die Texte des Altgelasianums* (1957) ; E. A. Lowe, *Codices Latini Antiquiores*, I (1934) 105 ; VI (1953) xxii ; VIII (1959) ix–x ; 'The Vatican Manuscript of the Gelasian Sacramentary, and its Supplement at Paris', JTS 27 (1926) 237–73 ; K. Mohlberg OSB, *Das fränkische Sacramentarium Gelasianum in Alamannischer Ueberlieferung : Codex sangall. 348* (1939) ; H. A. Schmidt SJ, *Introduction in Liturgiam Occidentalem* (1959) ; P. Siffrin OSB, *Konkordanztabellen zu den Römischen Sakramentarien, Lib. Sacra. Rom. Aecl.* (1959) ; A. Wilmart OSB, *Codices Reginenses latini*, 2 (1945) 200–4.

G. E.

GIFTS, THE SEVEN This article will attempt the task (I) of situating the Gifts in the supernatural scheme ; (II) examining the sources of the doctrine, which are apparently simple ; and then finding (III) complications in the Scriptural and patristic evidence. There will follow (IV) a positive presentation of modern teaching based upon Leo XIII.

I The Gifts of the Holy Ghost are reckoned as seven, thus forming the renowned *sacrum septenarium*. Four belong to the intellect : wisdom, understanding, counsel and knowledge ; three enrich the will : fortitude, piety and fear of the Lord. The study of them is important for all who want to gain a better understanding of the depths and riches of the grace-life in general, and of the ascetical and mystical ways in particular.

The seven Gifts are a portion of our supernatural inheritance. Normally one receives them first at Baptism, together with the sacramental character, the indwelling of the Holy Ghost, sanctifying grace, the theological and infused moral virtues, actual and sacramental graces. This total supernatural equipment means a new, a deified life, given through a rebirth. In the visible world around us organic life, while it is in itself simple, nevertheless functions through an intricate network of parts : cells and clusters of cells, limbs, organs, bones, nerves, sinews and arteries. So with supernatural life : while ultimately it is a simple reality (the self-communication of the triune God to a human being out of personal love) it nevertheless involves many gifts and fresh capacities ; it includes a new *quasi-nature*, along with its *quasi-faculties*. On top of these come the seven Gifts. This multiplication of entities will not bewilder us if we bear in mind the sober principle enunciated by St Thomas Aquinas : 'God works no less perfectly on the supernatural, than on the natural, plane' (*Summa*, 1–2ae:65:3c).

II Sources: Apparently Simple. At first sight the affair of the seven Gifts looks clear-cut and straightforward. Thus one finds them listed in Is 11:2 f. ; repeated in an edict probably first issued by Pope Damasus (366–84) and echoed by Gelasius (492–6) ; alluded to in the Tridentine decree on Justification from the year 1547 (D 799 : '. . . by a free acceptance of grace and *gifts* . . .') ; and expressly, though succinctly, taught by Leo XIII (*Divinum illud*, ASS 29:645 ff. ; cf. *infra*). Besides, Pius XII singles out three of these Gifts (knowledge, understanding and wisdom) as especially aiding the teachers and pastors of the Church (AAS 35:216).

These references from Scripture and the Magisterium are corroborated by (a) the Liturgy, (b) the Catechisms and (c) the theologians. (a) The rite of Confirmation strongly stresses the seven Gifts, which are further celebrated in the twin Pentecostal hymns : *Veni Sancte Spiritus* (Sequence, Mass) and *Veni Creator Spiritus* (Tierce, Divine Office). (b) As every Catholic child knows, catechisms commonly present the doctrine of the seven Gifts (cf. e.g. Roman Catechism, or those of Sts Peter Canisius, Robert Bellarmine and Cardinal Gasparri). (c) From the 12th cent. onwards theologians, both medieval and modern, treat of the seven Gifts, sometimes at considerable length. Sts Albert the Great, Thomas and Bonaventure are the classical exponents of this theology. They have set the course which later theologians have pursued with only secondary divergencies.

Consequently the case for the seven Gifts *appears*

simple and watertight. When, however, one examines it more closely one perceives chinks and lacunae.

III Complications in the Scriptural and Patristic Evidence. To begin with the Isaian text—foundation of the whole superstructure of doctrine and speculation about Gifts of the Holy Ghost. This text is by no means unencumbered with difficulties.

(*a*) One obvious and superficial difficulty (militating equally against the decree attributed to Damasus) is that Isaias deals directly with the Messias and *his* possession of the seven Gifts, not with *us*, nor *our* possession of them. The prophet foretells the endowment of the Messias with an array of 'spirits' or eminent qualities : he is to enjoy the wisdom and understanding of Solomon, the prudence and bravery of David, the knowledge and fear of Yahweh displayed by the patriarchs and prophets—Abraham, Jacob, Moses.

However this is not a serious difficulty. What is predicated of the individual, 'physical' Christ, or Messias, can be also analogously predicated of the 'total' or mystic Christ—i.e. Christians incorporated into Christ through the sacraments of initiation (cf. Jn 1:16 ; 10:10 ; Gal 3:27 ff. ; Col 2:9-12). The sevenfold Spirit who rests on Christ likewise proportionately descends on those united to Christ through Baptism.

(*b*) A more formidable problem arises out of the original Hebrew text of Is 11:2 ff. Literally translated, this runs : ' on him rests the Spirit of Yahweh; spirit of wisdom and of understanding ; spirit of counsel and courage ; spirit of knowledge and of fear of Yahweh ' (verse 2). ' He is full of the fear of Yahweh ' (verse 3). Verse 2 is a complete period in itself. Verse 3 starts a new sentence that seems to parallel the opening clause of verse 2. Must we then conclude that this passage which provides the scriptural warrant for the later elaborations on the seven Gifts completely fails to yield a sevenfold enumeration ?

Two considerations make one loth to answer this question in the affirmative. First the fact that the Septuagint version, accepted on all hands by the Greek-speaking sector of the Church, counts seven Gifts. The sixth is *eusebeia* or *dutifulness* at the end of verse 2 ; the seventh is *fear* in verse 3. The Vulgate version, universally acknowledged in the Latin-speaking Church, likewise differentiates between *pietas* and *timor*.

Secondly, it is undeniable that the Hebrews invested the number *seven* with a sacred and symbolic significance. Here is our cue to seek a sevenfold enumeration in the original Hebrew text of Isaias. A. Vaccari (*Verbum Domini* 2 [1931] 129-34) suggests how this can be done. The celebrated and never extinguished seven-branched candlestick was the chief religious symbol of ancient Jewry. Instead of its being (as is popularly fancied) a candlestick spreading out into *seven* branches, it was made up of a stem with six arms attached, the stem being counted to make up the sacred quota of seven. Consequently, in the Isaian text we can regard the first

clause, ' On him rests the spirit of Yahweh ', as being the basic or stem gift and add it on to the six that follow. Thus, according to Hebrew calculations, we get a sevenfold spirit.

There is a moral to be drawn from this : one must not press, with rigid mathematical logic, the number *seven*. It has a mystic and sacramental, rather than a strictly arithmetical character. Like the classical cornucopia, it betokens fullness and abundance. Very likely the calling of our Gifts *seven* indicates no more than the principal kinds of impulse or illumination that the Holy Ghost gives men, the chief styles and forms that his bounteous inspirations take. It is not at all clear that they must be rated as seven mutually quite distinct realities abiding in the soul.

(*c*) A third complication in the speciously clear-cut case of the Gifts is the meagreness of patristic witness in their favour. As groundwork for their theology of the Gifts, 12th- and 13th-cent. theologians quote a handful of patristic passages mostly culled from the works of only three Fathers, all of them Latin : Sts Ambrose (*De Spiritu Sancto*, I:16:156-9 ; CSEL 79:81-81), Augustine (*De Doctrina Christiana* 2:7:9-11 ; *De Sermone Domini in Monte* 1:4:11-13 ; 2:11:38 ; PL 34:39-40 ; 1234-5 ; 1286), Gregory the Great (*Moralia in Job* PL 75:544, 547-8).

The merit of this trio of Western writers is the broaching of the subject of the seven Gifts, successfully focusing on it the attention of the medieval theologians. However, one cannot pretend that one has here anything so dignified as a *theology* of the Gifts. Moreover the matter is too scanty, and sometimes even too scrappy, and it arises too late to bear the stamp of being truly traditional. Rather everything about it savours of the personal speculations of freelance writers (cf. J. de Blic SJ, ' Pour l'histoire de la théologie des dons avant Saint-Thomas ', in RAM 22 [1946] 116-79, esp. 152).

This penury of the Western Fathers is doubled in the East. Origen discusses Is 11:2 ff., and, in the footsteps of Justin and Irenaeus, extends its applications beyond Christ to Christians. But he attempts no theology of the Gifts in the medieval and modern sense. St Maximus the Confessor (*c.*580–662), with his elaborations on different gifts (cf. *Quaestiones ad Thalassium*, qq. 54 and 63 ; PG 90:521–4 ; 533 ; 672–81), approximates strikingly to the later Scholastics. Nowhere, however, do the Greek Fathers clearly recognize the seven Gifts as a group apart from other gifts or influences of the Holy Ghost (cf. de Blic, op. cit., 118–21).

The jejuneness, not to say absence, of any consistent and developed patristic teaching on the Gifts will check one from volunteering truculent assertions as to their nature. On the moot point : are the Gifts *really* distinct from the supernatural virtues ? not one iota of cogent patristic support for the affirmative can be alleged. This affirmative position, indeed, is maintained by St Thomas and the Thomists, together with the majority of theologians down to the present day. It is, however, denied by Scotus in the 13th cent., and his followers in the 16th and 17th cents., by Vasquez, by St Francis de Sales and by not a few modern thinkers like Pesch, de Guibert, and especially by Lottin and de Blic, who have completely reassessed the relevant positive data. In favour, then, of a real distinction is the more common, and extrinsically more probable, opinion. But no Catholic can be bound in conscience to accept it.

Christian literature abounds in instances of individual treatment of the seven Gifts as though they were free-standing realities, quite separate not only from the virtues but also from one another. No doubt there is considerable pastoral and ascetical value in such writings, guaranteed as they are by the prestige of some of the authors : Sts Thomas and Bonaventure, John of St Thomas and Lallemant. In general they inculcate the cultivation, under the aegis of the Holy Ghost, of certain very important attitudes of soul and flexibility towards the promptings and tutelage of the Holy Ghost.

However, it would seem unwarranted to affirm categorically that, say, *courage* as one of the seven Gifts must be regarded as an abiding disposition lodged in the soul quite independent of, and different from, the infused moral virtue of the same designation. One's reluctance here is reinforced when one observes, in general, the widely divergent accent, or even interpretation, put by various authors on the same gift, and, in particular, the fact that *wisdom* connotes something different for the Hebrew and the Greek. *Sophia*, for the man of Greek culture, means a gift of contemplation, a capacity belonging to the speculative order, to grasp truth ; for the man of Semitic culture, wisdom spells good management, whether in the private or the public sphere ; it is a gift of the practical order (see J. L. McKenzie SJ : 'The Wisdom of the Hebrews', in *The Two-Edged Sword* [1955] 211–26).

IV Positive Presentation following Leo XIII.
The handiest epitome of the commonly held positive position on the Gifts is given by Leo XIII. His teaching can be articulated in the following propositions :

(i) In addition to the indwelling Spirit and actual graces, the justified man certainly needs those seven Gifts named after the Holy Ghost. (ii) By their aid, his soul is equipped and strengthened to obey more easily and quickly the whispers and promptings of the Holy Ghost. (iii) These Gifts can conduct the justified man to the peaks of holiness. (iv) So excellent are they that they continue to exist in heaven, though more perfectly than on earth. (v) Invigorated by the Gifts, the soul is spurred on and encouraged to reach after and grasp the Gospel-beatitudes which, like springtide blossoms, are heralds and harbingers of everlasting felicity.

In these statements the indebtedness to St Thomas is plain ; indeed the Pope seems to canonize the Thomistic position. However, in the light of the foregoing paragraphs, one will be cautious against urging this point too strongly (cf. de Blic, op. cit., 178–9). It would, for example, seem rash to contend that Leo is, without more ado, condemning and putting out of court the views of Scotus, St Francis de Sales (for whom the Gifts are no more than

appendages or aspects of charity : cf. *Traité de l'Amour de Dieu* XI, 15) and many reputable post-Leonine theologians who disagree with St Thomas. On the contrary it is characteristic of the Magisterium of the Church to cherish to the uttermost freedom of debate for all the great schools of theology within her fold and, as far as possible, for independent thinkers who are loyal Catholics. Under this proviso we comment on each of the above five propositions.

(i) Leo XIII first establishes what is primary about the Gifts : to wit, their *existence* and *necessity*. Alongside sanctifying grace and the infused virtues over and above the Indwelling and actual graces in general, the justified man both *has* and *needs* the seven Gifts of the Holy Ghost. Secondary questions—such as the precise relationship between virtues and Gifts—are not touched. One may, of course, presume that the Pope personally shared the views of St Thomas. Most theologians agree that the Gifts form a cluster of habitual dispositions. But at this point their agreement halts.

(ii) The second clause deals with the *nature* of the Gifts, or with their characteristic formal effect. It describes what is capital about them : they alert the soul, making it responsive to the Holy Ghost ; they are sensitizing principles, giving pliancy in the hands of God, eagerness to heed his whispers, quickness to recognize his knock (cf. Apoc 3:20).

The Gifts would appear to be passive rather than active dispositions, receptive rather than operative capacities. However their precise relationship to the virtues (pigeon-holed by theologians under ' operative habits ') be defined, one must avoid setting up the Gifts as supplanters of the virtues. Thus, the Gifts of understanding, counsel and fortitude do not supersede the virtues of faith, prudence and fortitude respectively : de Guibert rightly insists that such a notion of replacement runs radically counter to the teaching of both Sts Thomas and Bonaventure ('Les Dons du Saint-Espirit', in RAM 14 [1933] 19–21). It would seem that every supernatural act of the man in the state of grace must proceed from one or other of his supernatural virtues. But it will be accomplished more nobly and strongly when that virtue is enhanced by the influence of the appropriate Gift. Whenever a man is responsive to the voice of the Holy Ghost addressing him through the Gifts, he will do supernatural actions without vacillations and shufflings, incomparably more swiftly and surely than would be the case were the virtues ever forced to operate in isolation from the Gifts. Thus . . . 'Counsel takes away the hesitations of prudence ; piety gives a loftier aim to justice . . .' (cf. E. Leen C.S.SP, 'The Gifts, the Fruits and the Beatitudes', in *The Holy Ghost* [1937] ch. XIII).

(iii) The third clause proposes what is the common teaching of theologians : that is to say, the ability of the Gifts to carry the soul to the heights of holiness, to be scaled only with their support (cf. de Guibert, op. cit., 17–18). Saints and mystics best illustrate this efficacy of the Gifts : as truly authentic Christians they attained heroic sanctity because of their openness and tractability to the Holy Ghost or (in other words) because they threw up no barrier to the working of the Gifts in their souls.

The rank-and-file Christian is at many removes from the saint ; for, though he may be free from mortal sin, his selfishness remains active and assertive. Doubtless he will elicit many salutary actions ; the infused virtues will be functioning in him to a greater or lesser extent. Nevertheless his behaviour is tarred with the brush of his selfishness ; the finer touches of the Holy Ghost are hindered ; the Gifts are largely smothered.

The saint or mystic, on the other hand, has not the same dominant and obtrusive egoism : his whole bearing towards God is marked by a docility born not of sloth and servility but of energetic self-conquest. Both virtues and Gifts flourish in him ; his whole conduct is less patently human and more worthy of the deified state to which he is called in Christ.

(iv) The fourth proposition is the logical upshot of the third : the Gifts will endow the elect in heaven. They are thus to be contrasted with the ' wayfarer ' theological virtues of faith and hope, which, once the Beatific Vision is achieved, will cease to have any meaning and likewise, therefore, any existence (cf. D 530 ; Rom 8:24 ; 1 Cor 13:8–13). It is true that, during the vicissitudes of earthly life, the Gifts, like the Eucharist (cf. postcommunion for seventh Sunday after Pentecost) serve a medicinal purpose which, of course, will be superfluous in heaven. That aspect of the Gifts, not the Gifts themselves, will cease hereafter. For, like charity, the Gifts are free from all inherent stain and blemish; moreover, as dispositions keenly sensitizing us to the guidance of the Holy Ghost, they are wholly orientated towards that celestial consummation where God will be all in all (1 Cor 15:28; *Summa*, 1–2ae:68:6c), and where they will shine with their maximum of resplendence.

(v) Leo XIII here matches and juxtaposes Gifts with Beatitudes. He thus follows a tradition which is traceable back beyond St Thomas (cf. *Summa*, 1–2ae:69) and his medieval predecessors to St Augustine (PL 34:39–40 ; 1233–5 ; 39:1525 ff.). The beatitudes, which set out the programme for the citizens of Christ's Kingdom, are the lodestar of Christians. The problem, of course, is one of translating them into the practice of one's daily living. The Pope advises that the solution lies in the seven Gifts. God has designed and destined them to assist our quest of the beatitudes. This they achieve in a twofold direction : (*a*) they give us a personal appreciation of the beatitudes, so fanning into flame our aspiration after them ; and (*b*) they enable us to lead our lives according to their pattern.

Bibliography. J. A. de Aldama SJ, ' De donis Spiritus Sancti ', in *Sacrae Theologiae Summa* (1953) vols. III, IV, cap. III ; L. Billot SJ, ' De donis Spiritus Sancti ', in *de Virtutibus Infusis* (1928) 155–81 ; F. Dander, ' Gaben des Hl. Geistes ', in LTK (1960) 4:478–80 ; J. de Guibert SJ, ' The Gifts of the Holy Ghost ', in *The Theology of the Spiritual Life* (1954)

120–8 ; John of St Thomas, *The Gifts of the Holy Ghost* (1951) ; B. J. Kelly CSSP, *The Seven Gifts* (1941) ; D. Lottin OSB, ' Les Classifications des dons du Saint-Espirit au XIIe et au XIIIe Siècle ', in RAM 2 (1930) 269–86 ; L. M. Martinez, ' The Gifts ', in *The Sanctifier* (1957) 119–99 ; J. A. O'Driscoll SM, *The Holy Spirit and the Art of Living* (1959) ; H. Paissac OP, ' The Gift of the Holy Spirit ', in *Theology Digest* 3 [1955] 85–8 ; M. M. Philipon OP, ' The Gifts of the Holy Spirit ', in *The Sacraments in the Christian Life* (1954) 59–77 ; M. Schmaus, ' Die Gaben des Heiligen Geistes ', in *Katholische Dogmatik* (1951) III:2, 212–19 ; H. Vignon SJ, ' De Donis Spiritus Sancti ', in *De Virtutibus Infusis* (1943) 299–313.   J. P. K.

GLAGOLITHIC LITURGY *Glagol* is a Slavonic word with the meaning ' a word ', and the adjective formed from it is used to designate an alphabet (not the Cyrillic) used formerly in Croatia and also in Moravia. The liturgy that was performed in the Slavonic language and written down or printed in this alphabet was called Glagolithic. The first printed missal of this liturgy dates from 1483, the latest (with Roman script added) from 1927. There has never been a Glagolithic Pontifical, and ordinations were always conducted in Latin, though the consecration of the holy oils has been carried out for some time in the vernacular. The use of the liturgy is confined to some eight dioceses in Croatia, while in Czechoslovakia since 1920 its use has been allowed on some four or five feasts in the year.

A fragmentary Glagolithic missal was found at Kiev in 1872 and portions of three Masses at Vienna in 1889. These date from the 10th and 11th cents., and are based on the *Gregorian Sacramentary*. In 1880 a Slavonic version of the liturgy of St Peter was found at Mt Athos, and in consequence of this a hypothesis was formed (chiefly associated with the names of Mohlberg and Baumstark) to the effect that this *Liturgy of St Peter* must have been put into Slavonic at Thessalonica in the time of Cyril and Methodius (later 9th cent.) and used by them in their mission to the Slavs. As this liturgy was simply the Ordinary and Canon of the Roman Mass within a Byzantine framework, it could have been combined with Gregorian mass-texts for feast-days, as exemplified in the Kiev missal. Since the critical edition of the *Liturgy of St Peter* by Codrington in 1936, however, this hypothesis can no longer be maintained, as he clearly shows that the Liturgy, first arranged in the region of Benevento and put into Greek before it left the Italian shores, could not have reached Macedonia in time to be used by Methodius.

The problem of the vernacular liturgy is illustrated by the chequered existence of the Glagolithic, for it may be considered the first vernacular liturgy in the West. There is little chance that the Arian Goths (who were converted by men from Constantinople) had a full liturgy of their own alongside the Bible of Ulfilas in Gothic. The mission of Methodius to Moravia presented the problem of the vernacular in an acute form. He had been preceded by Scottish or

Irish missionaries from Germany, as recent archaeological discoveries have proved, and they would have used a Latin liturgy. He began to say Mass in Slavonic, and was at first reproved by John VIII in 879 (*ep.* 239 ; PL 126:850). Later, however, John VIII wrote (PL 126:906) that the praise of God was not to be confined to the three tongues, Latin, Greek and Hebrew, for did not the Scripture say : 'Praise the Lord all ye nations'. There was no obstacle to a right faith in the singing of Mass or of the gospel in the Slavonic tongue.[1] These ideas did not prevail for long, as John X wrote to King Tomislav of Croatia that the sacrifical office should be carried out in Latin, and not in a foreign tongue.[2] It has been argued by some Slav historians that the synod of Split (Salona) in 925 (Canon X) again forbade the Slavonic liturgy, but its decree implies the opposite. It orders that no bishop should presume to ordain to any order whatsoever in the Slavonic language ;[3] this would imply that the saying of Mass in Slavonic was not touched by the synod. The anti-vernacular point of view may be seen in the explanation given in *Ordo Romanus XIII* of the practice of having the Creed sung at Mass in Greek as well as Latin : 'If the reason be sought, it is that the singers represent the state of the primitive Church ; there is singing in the three tongues, Latin, Greek and Hebrew'. (The Hebrew was represented by *Hosanna* and *Alleluia*.) Thus there was the idea abroad that the three languages used for the title on the Cross were somehow sacred and alone fit for the worship of God. John VIII repudiated the idea, but it kept coming back, and it may well be that Slavonic historians who are also liturgists will one day be able to trace the vernacular dispute in their lands right down to John Hus and so to the Reformers and to Trent. But hitherto there has rarely been a Slavonic historian who was also a liturgist or a liturgist who was competent in Slavonic history.

The *Liturgy of St Peter* in Slavonic may have been produced at Athos for internal usage only, as Codrington argued. There are Georgian and Armenian versions of it and there is a re-translation back into Latin from the Greek. It seems to have been used in the East by those who wished to assert their link with Rome. It draws its Canon from a non-Gregorian model, having certain affinities with the Irish liturgy (as shown in the *Stowe Missal* and *Bobbio*) and was afterwards (in the late 10th cent.) revised on a Gregorian model. Around the Canon there is a Greek framework, drawn from the *Liturgy of St Mark* (which could not have been known at Thessalonica), with incense-prayer, *proskomide* and intercessions in the Greek style. One Keltic trait in the Slavonic version is in the preface to the *Pater noster* : 'Taught by divine schooling and grounded upon salutary advice ...'. In the *Supplices* : 'Command, Lord, that these divine ministrations be made

[1] Nec sanae fidei obstat . . . sive missas in eadem Sclavinica lingua canere sive evangelium.
[2] Ministerium sacrificii peragant in latina lingua, non autem extranea.
[3] Nullus episcopus nostrae provinciae audeat in quolibet gradu sclavinica lingua promovere.

by the hand of Thy holy angel *at* the altar above ', is also a Keltic touch. The presence of St Cataldus, a Keltic missionary in southern Italy, may account for these, but the suggestion is a shot in the dark and serves to show how little is known of the development of the Roman Canon in the Dark Ages.
Bibliography. S. Smrzik sJ, *The Glagolithic or Roman-Slavonic Liturgy* (1959) ; K. Mohlberg osB, *Il Messale glagolitico di Kiev* (1928) ; H. W. Codrington, *The Liturgy of St Peter* (1936).   J. H. C.

GNOSTICISM To describe Gnosticism, that 2nd-cent. heresy, is to wrestle with the hydra, but the working definition that is found in a statement by one of the disciples of Valentinus (cited in Clement, *excerpta ex Theodoto*, 78 ; GCS 17:131) may serve : 'It is not simply baptism that frees us from being ruled by the stars, but also *Gnosis* (knowledge) of who we were and of what we have become, of where we were and into what we have been cast, whither we are hastening and from what we are being ransomed, of birth and of new birth'. Gnosis was therefore a secret knowledge, a primitive theology that incorporated philosophical ideas, mythology and Christian doctrines in varying proportions. Our acquaintance with Gnosticism has been immeasurably improved by the discoveries of recent years, especially by the Coptic papyri from Nag-Hammadi in Egypt, and it is not yet possible to estimate clearly what effect these discoveries will have on our understanding of theology in the 'tunnel-period' that stretches from the martyrdom of Ignatius to the appearance of the treatise by Irenaeus 'for the scrutiny and overthrow of the falsely-named Gnosis' at the end of the 2nd cent. Not all the papyri have been published, but the appearance of three long documents, the *Gospel of Thomas*, the *Gospel of Philip* and the *Apocryphon of John*, to say nothing of the document which has been entitled by its editors *The Gospel of Truth* and ascribed to Valentinus himself, makes our previous store of Gnostic works seem rather small. Here it will be possible to consider only certain aspects of Gnosticism which offer some help to the study of the beginnings of Christian theology, (I) the Gnostic sacraments, (II) some Gnostic personalities (BARDESANES and BASILIDES have already been treated), (III) Gnosticism in the NT, (IV) some leading ideas, and (V) theological consequences of Gnosticism.
I The Gnostic sacraments are more fully in evidence in the *Gospel of Philip* than in other works ; they include baptism, the eucharist in bread and wine (the wine being mixed with water), a sacrament of anointing with oil (which is called chrism), marriage and perhaps some form of penance. 'The Lord worked everything in a mystery, baptism, and chrism and eucharist, and their ransom and their bride-chamber' (*Gospel of Philip*, lxviii). 'The Father anointed the Son and the Son anointed the Apostles and the Apostles anointed us' (ibid., xcv). 'The cup of prayer, it has wine, it has water, being established as the type of the blood, over which thanks is given ; and it is filled with the Holy

Spirit . . .' (ibid., c: translations by C. J. de Catanzaro). Marriage is spoken of as either earthly or spiritual, and there is much talk of entering the bridal-chamber, which is the Holy of Holies, both in this Gospel and also in that of Thomas (e.g. saying 75). The *Gospel of Philip* knows of the Christian triad of faith, hope and charity ; it has a mention of ' the name of the Father and of the Son and of the Holy Spirit', and says flatly : ' The Eucharist is Jesus, for he is called in Syriac *Pharisatha*, which is, " he who is spread out ". For Jesus came, crucifying the world ' (ibid., liii). Whoever used this work must have been familiar with a religious practice that did not differ outwardly by a great deal from orthodox Christianity of the time. It has been proposed (by E. Segelberg in *Orientalia Suecana* 4 (1959) 3–42) to regard the so-called *Gospel of Truth* as a homily to candidates for confirmation. If there is even the semblance of this—and the case is strongly urged—then one can see how dangerous to the ordinary Christian Gnosticism was. It was not just a matter of erudite philosophizing, but there must have been a pastoral aspect, hitherto concealed from us, but one far more likely to cause trouble to the bishops and clergy of the time.

II Gnostic personalities are coming more into the open, since it is now more certain that the details given by enemies of Gnosticism such as Irenaeus can be trusted. What he and Hippolytus say about the doctrine is borne out by the new material, and therefore it becomes more reasonable to trust these writers for biographical facts too. Irenaeus thinks of three groups as Gnostic, the disciples of Valentinus, the Ophites and the followers of Carpocrates. Basilides he seems to regard as an ultra-Gnostic (*see* BASILIDES) and Marcion as more tolerable (*adv. haer.* III:12:15 H), because no one would be taken in by his open heresy of the two gods, while Valentinus wrapped up his ideas in fair-seeming words. Valentinus had come to Rome from Egypt, probably in the time of Hadrian (i.e. before 138), and, according to Tertullian (*adversus Valentinianos* 4), he became estranged from the Church when he failed to win election as bishop, being passed over in favour of one who had confessed his faith in prison (either Hyginus or Pius, popes of the time). He had had a Greek philosophical training in Alexandria, and the setting up of the school of Justin at Rome soon after the lapse of Valentinus may have been a defensive measure on the part of orthodoxy to counter the new mixture of philosophy and Christian faith which the Gnostics provided. If we had the lost *Syntagma* of Justin, this might be more plainly established. Valentinus showed concern about apostolic tradition, for he claimed to have been the disciple of one Theudas who was himself an immediate follower of St Paul (Clement, *strom.* 7:17:106 ; GCS 17:75).

The Ophites (or Naasenes, for *nahas* is the Hebrew equivalent of the Greek word ὄφις, serpent) claimed to derive from James, brother of the Lord (Hippolytus, *ref. haer.* 5:7 ; GCS 26:79), and this would stamp them as Jewish in origin. The very name they adopted indicates their interest in the creation-story

of Genesis and their desire to champion the serpent rather than to blame it for the Fall. Papias (fragment 7) took the whole story of Paradise as referring to Christ and the Church ; the Johannine circle of Ephesus may thus have unwittingly opened the way for the spread among Christians of another interpretation of the Paradise story, or may even have been reacting against what was already being spread by the Ophites. The *Apocryphon of John* is generally agreed to be one of their productions, and they may have contrived its character (for it purports to be a revelation given by the risen Christ to John the Apostle on the Mount of Olives) in order to win support from orthodox Christians. Most of the book is taken up with the making of Adam and Eve, the Fall, Cain and Abel, the fornicating angels and the Flood. Enlargements upon these episodes are familiar in Jewish apocryphal writing from the 1st cent. and earlier. (Parts of *Jubilees*, *Enoch* and a curious *Genesis Apocryphon* have been found at Qumran.) At what date the first attempts at contamination between these writings and the Christian message took place is very hard to determine, and the question will be briefly examined in the next section below.

Carpocrates was a Platonic philosopher who taught at Alexandria in the early part of the 2nd cent. An associate of his, Marcellina, is said by Irenaeus (*adv. haer.* I:20:4 H) to have come to Rome in the time of Pope Anicetus (*c*.150–60) and to have led many astray. Irenaeus tells of the custom these Gnostics had of honouring the statues of Pythagoras, Plato and Aristotle along with that of Christ. Now at the end of the 2nd cent. some of the catacombs then in use in Rome were of a Gnostic character, with decorative schemes drawn from the gospels and from Homer indifferently (*see* ART AND THE CHURCH, V). It is not too much to suppose that it would be the followers of Carpocrates who frequented these places. In other ways they were indebted to Greek ideas, looking on the soul as imprisoned in the body and on moral laws as due to custom rather than to nature. They added an interpretation of Mt 5:26 about paying the last farthing before being let out of prison, claiming that before the soul could leave the body it must go through the whole gamut of wickedness ; otherwise it would have to migrate to another body and there experience the full tale of sin (Irenaeus, *adv. haer.* I:20:2 H). They believed that because Christ had despised the Jewish teaching in which He had been brought up, He was given power to work miracles, and that those who copied Him in thus ' despising the Archons who made the world ' would have similar powers. One might see here the beginning of Marcion's opposition between the creator-god of the Jews and the true God of the Christians. Carpocrates was probably in full cry when Marcion first came to Rome, but the Marcionite sect (*see* MARCIONITES) was hardly to be compared with the Gnostics.

III Gnosticism in the New Testament has been very differently understood in the recent past. There was a time when the mention in the Pastoral Epistles (esp. 1 Tim 6:20, 'profane bombast and contradictions of the falsely-named Gnosis') of what looked like authentic Gnosticism was used as an argument for taking those Epistles away from Paul and dating them in the 2nd cent. Now the balance has swung unsteadily the other way, and it is proposed by some German critics to regard the Corinth to which 1 Cor was sent as riddled with Gnosticism; the 'party of Christ' there would be the original Gnostics already established within the Church. The change in opinion has come through the realization that the roots of Gnosticism go deep down into Jewish thought, and, although the *Apocryphon of John* does refer to a writing of Zoroaster and thus confirm suspicions that some of the ideas were Oriental, yet the existence of a free-thinking Jewish group at Qumran shows that there was plenty of room for Jewish speculation in the time of Christ and the hitherto little-heeded traces of it are now studied in great detail. The chariot-passage of Ez 1:5–28 with its tetramorph was held by Jews of the time to be wholly mysterious, yet it was used by Christians to account for the four-fold gospel, and this use may go back to Papias. Victorinus of Pettau (on Apoc 4:7; CSEL 49:50) and Irenaeus (*adv. haer.* III:11:11) both have this use of the passage, and their main point of agreement is their common use of the works of Papias. If such speculation was practised in the green wood, what must have been done in the dry?

The Prologue to St John's gospel may be viewed as an exercise in midrashic speculation on Gen 1, wherein the 'beginning' and the creation of light are given Christian counterparts; 'that which has found incorporation in Him is Life, and the Life was the light of men' (Jn 1:3–4) could be taken in a fully orthodox sense, though when the verse was used (with this reading) by Heracleon and other 2nd-cent. Gnostics, it could be made to mean many things. The ending of the Prologue (1:14) with its uncompromising statement of the Incarnation was not so easily adapted to Gnosticism; indeed it has been regarded as intentionally anti-Gnostic.

The change, as between Mt 23:34 and Lk 11:49, from 'I send you' to 'the Wisdom of God sends you' shows that, even while the gospels were being written, the Jewish speculations about Wisdom had been anchored to the Christian doctrine of the Incarnation. 'Christ, the wisdom of God' (1 Cor 1:24), was not to be confused with fleshly wisdom (2 Cor 1:12), though that is precisely what some of the Gnostics proceeded to do. They kept the personification of Wisdom, but used the curious feminine name Prunicus (προύνικος) and made up a saga of the fall and wanderings of Prunicus; from the Hebrew word *hokhma* (wisdom) the name Achamoth was given to this creature and a feminine personality, and to her were annexed some of the rabbinic ideas about Israel as the fallen bride of Jahwe which had been derived from the *Canticle*. None of this found its way into the NT. When Paul says (Gal 3:28) that in Christ there is neither male nor female, he is not proclaiming that there is a new race of Hermaphrodites upon the earth; he is showing

the transcendence of baptism. Sonship of God removes all barriers, that between Jew and Gentile, or between slave and free man, nor is it to be thought that in Christianity the woman has to be saved merely in a secondary way and in dependence on her man; she is baptized and enters the Christian inheritance just as much as her husband. The 2nd-cent. apologists did claim that they were a third race, neither Jew nor Gentile, and this must have given the opportunity for the Gnostic to misappropriate the rest of the text from Paul.

In Col 1:9–23 and 2:18 Paul is guarding a Christian community against Jewish speculations. He may use language ('the Pleroma', 'superior knowledge' and the like) which was already current in such speculation, but his aim is to draw men away from it, not to promote it. When he says that Christ is head of the body, he is not thinking of the later Gnostic fantasy that distributed the letters of the Greek alphabet over the human body, starting with *alpha* for the right side of the head and running down to the right foot, then coming up the left side, so that *omega* was found to designate the left side of the head. One would have to combine Apoc 1:8 with Paul before such speculations could be contemplated.

IV Gnostic leading ideas such as those of Emanation, the Demiurge and the Pleroma are discussed separately under their own names. Here it is possible to say a little about the system of pairings (or syzygies) which was common to most Gnostic writers. F. C. Burkitt did some useful demythologizing of this system when he suggested that it was really meant to give an account of a rather primitive philosophy. *Bythos* and *Ennoia* (the Deep and [a] Thought) were the original pair associated, and they produced Mind and Truth (*Nous* and *Aletheia*). From this pair came *Logos* and *Zoe* (Word and Life) and then *Anthropos* and *Ekklesia* (the Man and the Church) from the last two. This rigmarole could be taken to mean that the subliminal self, when conjoined with a conscious thought, developed both intelligence and truth, which found expression in words and movement. Christ and the Church would then be the completion of a natural process of development. If this is what the Gnostics were trying to say, they would ultimately have come to a theology in which the Incarnation was necessary and not a free gift to men. They did, in fact, hold to predestination when questions of human destiny confronted them. Most men were earthy (chthoic) and would be damned anyhow (Clement, *excerpta ex Theodoto*, 54; GCS 17:124); some were 'psychic' and would have the chance of going to a middle region if they exerted themselves, while the chosen or 'pneumatic' would have Gnosis in this life and would then enter into the Pleroma. Apoc 3:5 and 5:8 show that the orthodox Christian view of the Book of Life was different; it was under the power of Christ, and those who overcame with His aid were then to remain written in it.

Freedom from the law of sin was proclaimed by Paul (Rom 7:25–8:2), and this freedom was claimed by the Gnostics for the 'pneumatics', who were not expected to profess their faith in time of persecution, since all matters of law were indifferent. This freedom was also made an excuse for all manner of immoralities on the part of some of the Gnostics. The Fathers (Justin and Irenaeus among the first) are constantly accusing them of sexual licentiousness, and the history of Simon Magus and his consort, whom he styled Helena, or his ' first conception ' ($\pi\rho\omega\tau\eta$ $\check{\epsilon}\nu\nu o\iota\alpha$), was recounted as a warning. Simon has to be taken more seriously now. When Gnosticism seemed to be a 2nd-cent. creation, it was assumed that the Gnostic Simon could not be the same as Simon Magus of Ac 8:9 ; the discovery of an *Apocalypse* of Dositheus (sub-titled *The Three Stelae of Seth*) at Nag-Hammadi may show us how to go about the problem of identifying the two Simons, for it is agreed that Dositheus was the master of Simon the Gnostic. If it turns out (for the work is not yet published) that a 1st-cent. background for the work is required, then it will be more certain that Gnosticism was already at work in Samaria at the time of Philip's mission there, and may have been originally a small-scale movement like that of Qumran, and pre-Christian at that.

The Fathers had little doubt that Simon and Helena practised a *hieros gamos* for the inspiration of their followers, and Hippolytus (*ref. haer.* 6:19 ; GCS 26:146) professes to quote from their writings an exhortation to promiscuity in the guise of perfect *agape*. Simon and Helena were presented as Jupiter and Minerva, thus bringing in elements of paganism to a cult which began by giving a garbled account of the Christian Trinity and redemption. The (apocryphal but orthodox) *Epistle of the Apostles* warns against Simon and Cerinthus as ' enemies of Christ who pervert the word and the faith and in whom is death and great corruption '. The disciples are there shown asking : ' Is it true, Lord, that the flesh shall be judged, together with the soul and the spirit ? ' One can well understand why they asked.

V Theological consequences of Gnosticism were widespread. One of the most obvious, in the light of what we so far know of the flood of Gnostic treatises, was the need for a Canon of the NT. The earlier the Gnostic danger was felt, the earlier too must have been that need. The *Gospel of Peter* is commonly dated to the first quarter of the 2nd cent., and it already has a monstrous tale of two giants who come down to lead Christ from the Tomb. The unhealthy preoccupation of many Gnostics with a theology of sex must have encouraged the Encratite reaction of the 2nd cent. (*see* CHASTITY). Gnostic hymns and dancing, as described in the *Acts of John* (94-6), may have stimulated Christian worship, but it is matter for great surprise that the recently deciphered Irish liturgical MS of the 7th cent. has a Latin version of an epiklesis-type prayer that is borrowed from the Gnostic *Acts of Thomas* (27) : ' Come, Thou silence that dost make manifest mysteries of great magnitude ; come, Thou dove that hast brought forth twin nestlings . . .'. Augustine says that the Manichees had such a prayer, and Turibius found it among the Priscillians of Spain.

That the Irish should have used it to invoke the Holy Spirit (or possibly the Son of God) shows how long-lived Gnostic ideas could be.

The *recirculatio* of Christ with Adam was common ground to Gnostic and orthodox, for the *Gospel of Truth* (18:12) says : ' He was nailed to a tree. He became the fruit of the knowledge of the Father, but this fruit did not destroy those who ate it.' The seal (of confirmation) as a means of preventing the escape of grace from the soul is spoken of in the *Gospel of Truth* (36:20) : ' When the anointing of a jar shall be destroyed, it leaks ', and Clement is not ashamed to repeat the same idea (*Eclogue propheticae* 12:9 ; GCS 17:140). Borrowing was not, however, all in one direction. The incident manufactured in the *Gospel of Thomas* (saying 12-13) to show that Thomas gave the right answer to Jesus' question about Himself is an obvious counterblast to orthodox insistence on the Petrine position. Many more deductions about 2nd-cent. theology will be possible when the new material has been assimilated.

Bibliography. The best up-to-date survey is *A. D. Nock, Gnosticism, in HTR 57 (1964) 255-79; *F. C. Burkitt, *Church and Gnosis* (1932) is still useful ; J. Doresse, *The Secret Books of the Egyptian Gnostics* (Eng. trans. 1960) is a survey of the Nag-Hammadi finds, published and unpublished ; K. Grobel, *The Gospel of Truth* (1960) overcame the drawbacks of the original publication of that document where the English version of the Coptic was made through a French version ; *R. McL. Wilson, *The Gnostic Problem* (1958) was produced before the publication by the same author of *The Gospel of Philip* (1962) ; another version of this gospel is by C. J. de Catanzaro, in JTS 13 (1962) 35-71 ; E. Peterson, *Frühkirche, Judentum und Gnosis* (1959) is a collection of essays on these three subjects ; *R. M. Grant, *The Secret Sayings of Jesus* (1960) is a version of and commentary on the *Gospel of Thomas*; the same, *Gnosticism and early Christianity* (1959) and an anthology of texts, *Gnosticism* (1961), both useful; A. Orbe sj, *En los Albores de la Exegesis Johannea* (1955) ; *Los primeros Herejes ante la Persecutiòn* (1956); *Hacia la primera Teologia de la Procesion del Verbo* (1958) ; *La Unction del Verbo* (1961) has completed the greater part of a mammoth work on the Gnostics and early theology ; W. Till edited once more the *Pistis Sophia* (1954) ; Charlotte Baynes edited a *Coptic Gnostic Treatise : Bruce MS 96* (1933) ; *A. Böhlig and P. Labib, *Die koptisch-gnostische Schrift ohne Titel aus Codex II* (1962) ; W. Till, *The Gospel of Mary* and other works in *Die gnostischen Schriften des koptischen Papyrus Berolinensis 8502* (1955) ; M. Malinine and others, *De resurrectione, epistula ad Rheginum* (1963) ; M. Krause, *Die drei Versionen des Apokryphon des Johannes* (1962) ; *G. Quispel edited the *Letter of Ptolomaeus to Flora* (1949) for the *Sources chrétiennes*, and at that time it was described by Professor Quasten as the most important Gnostic document known to us. An English version of the *Apokryphon Johannis* has been published by *S. Giversen, as *Acta theologica Danica* V (1963), and A. Böhlig, with P. Labib, has brought out *Koptisch-*

gnostische Apokalypsen aus Codex V von Nag-Hammadi (1963). The spate of studies on the new material is just beginning. One may mention R. M. Grant, 'The mystery of marriage in the Gospel of Philip', in *Vigiliae christianae* 15 (1961) 129–40; H. Ringgren, 'The Gospel of Truth and Valentinian Gnosticism', in *Studia theologica* 18 (1964) 51–65.　　　　J. H. C.

GOD, NATURAL KNOWLEDGE OF. *And see also* ATTRIBUTES. This article deals with the teaching of the Church about that part of our knowledge of God which is possible apart from revelation. The sources and aspects of this teaching will be treated in chronological order : (I) Scripture, (II) the Fathers, (III) the Scholastics, (IV) fideism, traditionalism and ontologism, (V) the Vatican Council of 1870, (VI) the modernist crisis, and (VII) current trends, with (VIII) a corollary on the theological possibility of atheism.

I Scripture. A reading of the OT shows that Jewish monotheism established and developed itself in independence of philosophy. When Jewish tradition came into contact with Greek speculation, it had to face the difficulty that the evidently more subtle Greek thinkers were nevertheless far behind the Jews in their understanding of God. That the Jews did not attribute this defect wholly to the absence of revelation but regarded ignorance of the fundamental truths about God as culpable appears at the end of the OT period in Wis 13.

'All men are vain, in whom there is not the knowledge of God, and who by these good things that are seen could not understand him that is' (Wis 13:1). If they admire the beauty and the force of the elements of this earth or of sun, moon or stars, they should be able to grasp that these were made by a creator of greater majesty and might. 'For by the greatness of the beauty and of the creature the creator of them may be seen, so as to be known thereby' (Wis 13:5). Although the worshippers of natural things and forces can be supposed to be seeking God in his works, they are not to be excused for failing to find him there. Very much less to be excused, however, are those who manufacture idols and worship what they have made themselves (Wis 13:10 ff.).

The teaching of Wisdom is echoed by St Paul. When the people of Lystra want to worship Paul and Barnabas, Paul calls upon them 'to be converted from these vain things to the living God who . . . left not himself without testimony' (Ac 14:14, 16) in the things which he has created and the benefits which he has conferred upon mankind. So also Paul tells the Athenians 'that they should seek God, if haply they may feel after him or find him, although he be not far from every one of us, for in him we live and move and are' (Ac 17:27, 28). More plainly still, St Paul states that 'the invisible things of him from the creation of the world are clearly seen, being understood by the things that are made' (Rom 1:20). Hence those who have failed to acknowledge God or have fallen into idolatry are said to be inexcusable.

Implicitly, therefore, Scripture makes a distinction between what God has specially revealed of himself to the Jews of the OT and finally through Christ and what all men might be expected to know of him. This natural knowledge of a creator is to be obtained by reflection on the visible world and the consequent acknowledgment of a maker in whom the beauty and power which we observe in the world are present in greater fullness.

II The Fathers. The Fathers not only repeat the Scriptural doctrine of the natural knowledge of God, usually in language which shows that they have Wisdom and St Paul in mind, but begin to indicate the lines of thought which lead from the world to God. Among passages which simply affirm that God is known by natural reason the following may be consulted : Irenaeus : *adv. haer.* II:iv:5 H ; Tertullian : *adv. Marc.* 1:10 ; CSEL 48:302 ; Basil : *ep.* 235:1 ; PG 32:872 (ad Amphilochium) ; John Chrysostom : *In ep. ad Rom. hom.* 3:2 ; PG 60:412 ; Augustine : *Sermo* 141:1–2; PL 38:776; Theodoret : *In Rom.* 1:20 ; PG 82:61.

Aristides indicates the argument from change or motion : ' Seeing that the world and all things in it are necessarily in motion, I understand that it was God who moves and conserves it. For the mover is mightier than what is moved, and the conserver mightier than what is conserved. Hence I give the name of God to him who created and conserves all things' (*Apologia* 1). Theophilus (*ad Autolycum* 1:4 sqq ; PG 6:1029), Minucius Felix (*Octavius* 18), Gregory Nazianzen (*orat. theol.* 2:16 ; PG 36:48) and Gregory of Nyssa (*De anima et resurrectione*, PG 46:81–93) suggest the argument from order.

St Augustine frequently appeals to change as the evidence that the world was created. ' Here are heaven and earth ; they cry out that they were made because they change and vary. If anything is not made and yet is, there is nothing in it which was not in it before, which would be to change and vary' (*Confessiones* 11:4 ; CSEL 33:284. Cf. also *De Civitate Dei* 1:8 ; CSEL 40:14). It is especially characteristic of Augustine to see in the eternity of truth an unmistakable reflection of an eternal mind. The Platonic forms or standards, by which we judge what things are, transcend our minds and are timeless ; necessary truths exhibit timeless relations between the forms. This timelessness can be attributed neither to temporal objects of thought nor to our temporal minds ; it can be based only on the eternal mind of God, which illuminates our thinking. Cf. Augustine : *De libero arbitrio* 1:11 ; CSEL 74:6. *De vera religione* 30:31 ; PL 34:146–7.

Finally we may refer to St John Damascene, who offers both the argument from change and the argument from order (*De fide orthodoxa* 1:3 ; PG 94:793). The Fathers, therefore, not only accept the teaching of Wisdom and of St Paul but seek to explain how a knowledge of God is natural to man by reflections which anyone may make who observes the world as it is. In this they partly anticipated the work of the medieval scholastics.

III The Scholastics. The theologians of the Middle Ages developed the formal proofs of the existence of God, of which the classical example is to be found in the Five Ways of St Thomas Aquinas. For details *see* GOD, PROOFS OF THE EXISTENCE OF. Only in the 14th cent., with William of Ockham and his followers, did doubts appear about the validity and certainty of metaphysical argument. In general, however, the Scholastics can be regarded as the typical upholders of the power of philosophy to demonstrate God's existence.

The Scholastic doctrine, then, is that our natural knowledge of God is inferential. This is in accord both with Scripture, which says that it is through the world that the creator comes to be known, and with Aristotelian philosophy, for which the immediate object of human knowledge is the being of material things. Immediate awareness of God is thought of as belonging properly to the Beatific Vision, although there may be some transient foretaste of this in the higher mystical states.

The inference, however, is demonstrative and not merely probable. Philosophical reflection is ideally capable of bringing man to a knowledge of God as a single, absolute, eternal mind of infinite wisdom, goodness and power, but only revelation can tell us of the trinity of persons. Nevertheless St Thomas can say that we know of God *that* he is rather than *what* he is, meaning that the inference from creatures to God is not an instance of univocal thinking but involves an analogical leap into a different order of being. Hence we know God only as imperfectly reflected in his creatures, *per formam alienam* rather than *per formam propriam*. Another classical Scholastic formula for the kind of thinking involved is that it includes the way of *affirmation*, the attribution to God of every genuine perfection that we find in the created world, the way of *negation*, the paring away of the imperfections which limit the perfections of creatures, and the way of *eminence*, the final attribution to God of such perfections not only purified from limitation but positively enhanced in a manner of which we have no proper conception.

Although all this is ideally within the scope of philosophy, St Thomas agrees that men as they are would not attain such a measure of truth by their unaided reflection except with great difficulty, after a long time, and with incidental errors. Hence, for practical purposes, revelation is necessary in order that men should have a sufficient knowledge of God. The Christian philosopher, with revelation to show the way, can develop the rational implications of philosophical principles with a fullness which the pagan thinkers were not in actual fact able to reach. Cf. *Summa*, 1a:1:1c.

IV Fideism, Traditionalism and Ontologism. From the Renaissance onwards man's increasing historical and geographical knowledge made the problem of the diversity of religious beliefs considerably more complicated. There seemed to be almost no absurdity which had not been upheld at some time and place by somebody. The resulting unsettlement is shown in the 16th cent. in the unaggressive scepticism of Montaigne. In the 17th cent. Pascal's tormented genius anticipated much of what continues to be said

on the subject today. Since the *Pensées* are fragmentary, we cannot always be certain what Pascal would have finally said if he had completed and corrected his jottings, but certain points are clear enough. Whatever the logical value of the proofs of the existence of God, Pascal regarded them as inadequate to bear the weight of a genuine religious conviction. We are tempted to put his point in contemporary language and to make him say that an abstract inference is not a sufficient foundation for an existential affirmation. Religious belief, says Pascal, is not in the God of the philosophers but in the God of Abraham, Isaac and Jacob, who is above all the God of Jesus Christ. Again we are tempted to use modern language and to speak of religious faith in terms of an I-Thou relation. Moreover intellectual belief in religion cannot be separated from the quest for salvation. True religious knowledge, as Karl Barth says in our own day, has to be saving knowledge. Hence, Pascal maintains, we must not separate the affirmation of God from the acceptance of Christ. All is matter of one complex and agonizing decision in which the reasons of the heart are more powerful than mere reason. But, Pascal represents God as saying to man : you would not be seeking me if you had not already found me. To seek God is to find him, and to find him is always a seeking of him.

It would be an insult to the profundity of Pascal's thought to put it under some systematic label such as fideism. Nevertheless it may be suggested without impertinence that he is reflecting on the psychological rather than on the logical or metaphysical level, and that his psychological insights do not invalidate what more analytic thinkers have to say on other levels. If we are looking for a systematic fideism, we can find it at the same period as Pascal in the *Traité philosophique de la faiblesse de l'esprit humain* of Pierre Daniel Huet, Bishop of Avranches. For Huet faith is the sole source of certainty ; in philosophy we should select what seems most likely without attaching ourselves exclusively to any school, just as probability has to be our guide in the ordinary affairs of life.

Such points of view occur more frequently in the early 19th cent. among those who sought to recover from the excesses of the French Revolution. When the Goddess of Reason had been enthroned in Notre Dame, her teachings had been very different from those of scholastic philosophy, and what passed for advanced thought was in full retreat from religion. Hence a fear of unbridled reason came very naturally to conservative minds. Fideism, the attribution of all religious certainty to divine revelation, whether a primitive revelation of which the traces were not wholly obliterated or the full Judaeo-Christian revelation, is associated with Bautain (*Philosophie morale*). A slightly wider traditionalism, asserting the absolute need of teaching in passing down the established truths, found supporters in Lamennais (*Essai sur l'indifférence en matière de religion*) during his Catholic period, in the Vicomte de Bonald (*Recherches philosophiques sur les premiers objets des connaissances morales*), and in Bonnetty (*Annales de philosophie chrétienne*).

When we find these systems rejected by the Church we must evidently not suppose that the Church wants us to overlook the practical and psychological importance of divine revelation and human teaching in inculcating even those truths about God which are rationally demonstrable. The Church's intention was to reject their exclusiveness and to uphold the rational character of fundamental religious truths, quite apart from the question of how many men would actually be able to reach them by rational inference alone. That reason is capable of proving with certainty the existence and infinite perfection of God is the first of the propositions to which Bautain was asked to subscribe in 1840 (D 1622–7). Bonnetty subscribed to similar statements in 1855 (D 1649–52).

At the same period Gioberti was seeking a remedy for scepticism in the doctrine known as ontologism, and similar views were advanced in France by Fabre (*Défense de l'ontologisme*) and Branchereau. The characteristic tenet of ontologism is that, since God is pure being, it follows that, in being aware of things as possessing being, we are implicitly aware of God, and that, in affirming the existence of things, we are implicitly affirming the existence of God. Although a certain reflection is needed in order to recognize this, our knowledge of God is not really inferential but immediate. While traditionalism and ontologism might seem to be at opposite extremes, they may be combined if the reflection needed to acknowledge this presence of God in all our thinking is thought to call for the aid of a traditional teaching ; in this way they were combined by the Belgian thinker Ubaghs. Although Rosmini controverted the writings of Gioberti, he was accused by many of going too far in the same direction. In recent years he has had many defenders, so that we cannot with justice say more than that his language was sometimes unguarded. The Church took exception to the doctrine of the ontologists as involving a step towards pantheism. Among propositions listed as dangerous by the Holy Office in 1861 are the immediate knowledge of God and the identification of being in general with the divine being, as understood by these thinkers (D 1659–65). Although Pius IX had given judgment in favour of Rosmini's orthodoxy, some statements, mainly from his posthumous works, were declared unacceptable in 1887 (D 1891 ff.).

V The Vatican Council of 1870. The Vatican Council of 1870 defined that the one true God, our creator and Lord, can be known with certainty by the natural light of human reason through the things that are made. This appears both in the running text and among the canons (D 1785, 1806). The running text goes on to say that in the present condition of the human race it is due to divine revelation that even these natural truths can be known by all speedily, with solid certainty and without incidental error (D 1786). This echoes the language of St Thomas, but the corresponding canon states only that revelation is expedient in order to teach man about God

and the worship due to him (D 1807). The running text continues that this does not make revelation absolutely necessary ; its absolute necessity is due to God's will to raise man to the supernatural order (D 1786).

This definition does not deal with ontologism. When some of the fathers of the Council wished to introduce an emendation excluding any natural immediate knowledge of God, the deputation *de Fide* replied that this was too large a question to be dealt with in an odd phrase or two. It could be treated adequately at a later stage if the Council wished. The premature conclusion of the Council prevented any such treatment.

On the other hand the definition was clearly intended to exclude any radical form of fideism or traditionalism. The deputation *de Fide* rejected suggestions to specify the man capable of a natural knowledge of God as one enjoying the full activity of reason or as an adult living in human society, but also declined to make explicit that the existence of God could be philosophically demonstrated. The Council was anxious not to make its definition unduly complex and considered it sufficient to say that human reason possessed an intrinsic capacity of reaching the knowledge of God without the absolute necessity of tradition or instruction, that this knowledge was attainable by a reflection on created things, and that it was not merely probable but certain.

VI The Modernist Crisis. Although the Thomist revival of the second half of the 19th cent. contributed to the re-establishment of objective metaphysics, the general intellectual climate continued to be strongly anti-metaphysical, as indeed it still is. The modernist movement had many sides, of which only the philosophical comes into question here. But, just as on the biblical and historical side it was a wholesale surrender to the more radical forms of the higher criticism, so on the philosophical side it involved a despair of objective metaphysics and a recourse to a subjective and pragmatic kind of approach to the fundamental truths of religion. Looking back at it now, we can see that what was needed was a critical appraisal of historical criticism and an extension of apologetic method in conjunction with, and not in contradiction to, the older approaches. Thinkers like Blondel and Laberthonnière had something to say about the subjective conditions of religious conviction which, whatever even they themselves may have supposed at the time, did not entail the rejection of that other dimension of thought which is that of objective metaphysics. Blondel at least, in the course of his long life, both became progressively more moderate and was finally recognized by his former opponents as a Christian thinker not to be neglected.

What the Church had to condemn, then, was once again the exclusiveness with which the modernists contemptuously dismissed objective metaphysics in favour of their new ways of approach. Hence the encyclical *Pascendi* (1907) condemned the modernists for rejecting the objective approach as leading only to agnosticism and for relying entirely on the immanent needs and aspirations of the human spirit. The basis of belief was wrongly said to be an innate religious sense which experience showed to be satisfied only by the affirmation of God (D 2072-5, 2077, 2081). The antimodernist oath prescribed to the clergy added to the Vatican definition about the natural knowledge of God that God's existence could be demonstrated by an argument from effect to cause (D 2145).

The purport of the Church's teaching must be neither exaggerated nor underrated. It is clearly a part of Catholic teaching that the affirmation of the existence of God is based on objective reason and that there is no absolute need of revelation or tradition in order to reach this knowledge. But the Church recognizes that men as they are do not readily reach it without the aid of revelation and instruction, and it is certainly not affirmed that every believer is capable of giving a satisfactory metaphysical account of the basis of his belief in God. While the Church upholds the power of metaphysical thinking, there is plenty of room for other approaches to religion if they are put forward as supplementary and not as substitutes for objective reason.

VII Current Trends. More recent Catholic speculation on the natural knowledge of God has moved between the limits established as the result of the conflicts of the 19th cent. On the one hand, it is agreed that there is a genuine natural knowledge of God, so that Catholic thought has no room for an agnosticism on the philosophical plane which would altogether sacrifice reason to faith. On the other hand, it is agreed also that on the level of natural reason there is no fully direct and immediate knowledge of God, as the ontologists wanted to maintain.

Within these limits there has been speculation on the nature of the step from creation to God. The Thomist view is that this is properly described as an inference ; we see that the nature of finite and contingent things entails their having been created by an absolute and infinite being. From the psychological angle, of course, the character of this inference varies from the explicit reasoning of the philosopher to the comparatively vague and implicit process of thought which is all to be expected of the ordinary man, but even the latter kind of thinking deserves to be described as inferential.

Other Catholic thinkers maintain that, just as God is an absolutely unique being, so we reach him by a unique process of thought. Although this is not the immediate apprehension of the ontologist, it is held to be inexactly described as inference ; it is more like an analysis of the finite datum, or a penetration into it in depth, by which we come to see all being as essentially relative to absolute being. Such speculation has been stimulated in this country by the subtle account of the matter given by the Anglican theologian Dr Austin Farrer in his book *Finite and Infinite*, but there are similar tendencies in French Catholic writers like Fr H. de Lubac (*The Discovery of God*) and Fr J. Daniélou (*God and Us*). It may be that these writers take too narrow a view of inference

as being always the application of an established rule to another instance of exactly the same kind, and also that they have not sufficiently appreciated what inference is as a psychological fact in distinction from its explicit logical expression. For a Thomist critic might well say that what they are describing is really an inference, although the description is in psychological rather than logical terms. The movement from finite things to God is indeed a movement to a unique conclusion, but the movement itself may still be placed without impropriety under the heading of inference.

Reflection on the dynamism of the human mind as enforcing the affirmation of God, while by itself it might suggest the subjectivism of the modernists, can be valuably cultivated without prejudice to the more objective approach and as a supplement to it. Our recognition of a scale of value and our striving to fulfil ideals would make no sense without an absolute truth and an absolute goodness. Such considerations are found in the later Blondel (*L'Être et les êtres*), in Louis Lavelle (*La Présence totale*) and René Le Senne (*La Découverte de Dieu*), and from a standpoint nearer to Thomism, in Fr Maréchal and his disciples.

Finally, a number of thinkers have devoted their attention less to the formal proofs of God than to the psychological and ethical conditions under which we come to affirm God's existence. It is those who take this line whom we are accustomed to call the Christian existentialists. The most prominent is Gabriel Marcel (*Being and Having ; the Mystery of Being*). Although the onesidedness of the human mind sometimes leads these thinkers to place less than the proper value on the objective proofs, what they have to say can be positively appreciated on its own level, again without prejudice to the objective metaphysical approach.

VIII The Possibility of Atheism. The teaching of Scripture and Tradition about the natural knowledge of God has led the majority of theologians to assert that an adult human being cannot remain for long in invincible ignorance of God's existence. Evidently he may be a practical atheist ; that is, he may live as if God did not exist. Equally he may assert publicly that God does not exist ; this is called being a positive speculative atheist. Nevertheless the theologians are accustomed to assert that he must really know better ; he cannot be what they call a negative speculative atheist, which is to be without any knowledge of God.

This theological thesis obviously calls for comparison with the facts of history and of contemporary life. The example of contemporary Russia is somewhat ambiguous. The relative ease with which Russian philosophical and scientific thinking has been made officially atheistic counts against the thesis, but the persistence of religion among the people in spite of all the resources of governmental propaganda is plainly in its favour. In countries where the expression of thought is free we find many professed agnostics but very few dogmatic atheists. To what extent does the frequency of contemporary agnosticism count against the traditional thesis? Agnosticism is not complete ignorance of God, for it admits the possibility of God's existence, but it is the absence of the certainty which the natural knowledge of God ought to have.

Perhaps we should ask what ought to rank as an acknowledgment of God. Agnosticism, and even professed atheism, may be a reaction against an unworthy notion of God entertained in a person's environment or against unworthy associations of religion as a person has experienced it. The acceptance of any absolute, whether of truth or of goodness, may be regarded without absurdity as an implicit recognition of God. We might want to say that many agnostics have to be shown not so much the grounds of belief in God as the fact that they really have this belief already.

With simple people some theologians have supposed that, although they may be capable of coping with their ordinary environment, they may never reach the use of reason in any adequate sense in relation to moral and religious questions. This view was advanced by theologians like Molina and Arriaga at a time when the discovery of the Americas seemed to reveal the existence of tribes without religious beliefs or practices. More accurate study seems to show that even the most primitive peoples have such beliefs and practices, although they are often very jealous of betraying them to strangers. In recent times, however, Cardinal Billot, in a series of articles contributed to *Études* between 1919 and 1923, revived this opinion and applied it to people whose moral and religious ideas were so elementary that they hardly seemed a possible basis for the faith, hope and charity which are needed for the salvation even of the unbaptized. By placing the future life of such people in the *limbus puerorum* the problem of the salvation of the unbaptized could be made less acute. This speculation has not found much theological support.

The question of the possibility of atheism remains one of extreme complexity, not only from a theological but from a historical and a psychological point of view. We have to distinguish between what people say and what they think, between what they suppose themselves to think and what they really mean, between the effects of social pressure and a man's more intimate persuasions. But the universal salvific will of God seems to imply that He makes it possible for all developed human beings to recognize Him under some aspect and to some degree.

Bibliography. Apart from the sources mentioned in the text see the relevant sections of the theological treatises *De Deo Uno*. In addition: H. Lennerz, *Natürliche Gotteserkenntnis. Stellungnahme der Kirche in den letzten hundert Jahren* (1926); J. Henry, *Le Traditionalisme et l'ontologisme à l'université de Louvain* (1922); T. Granderath, *Constitutiones Dogmaticae Concilii Vaticani* (1892); Vacant, *Études théologiques sur les constitutions du Concile du Vatican* (1895); E. C. Butler, *The Vatican Council* (1930); J. Rivière, *Le Modernisme dans l'Église* (1929); P. Archambauld, *Initiation à la philosophie blondélienne* (1941); *J. V. Langmead Casserley, *The Christian in Philosophy*

(1949). *See also* bibliography to GOD, PROOFS OF THE EXISTENCE OF.   D. J. B. H.

GODPARENTS The theological importance of the Christian practice of having godparents at the baptism of an infant lies in its implication that it is right to commit the child to the Church long before it can think or choose for itself, since the godparent has the duty of bringing home to the child, when it is able to take notice, the obligation it has incurred. The tradition of having godparents (I) will be briefly outlined and then (II) some justification of the practice given on theological grounds will be shown (*see also* BAPTISM).

I The tradition of having godparents can be traced back to Hippolytus at the end of the 2nd cent., for in his *Traditio apostolica* he directs that in the baptism of little children: 'If they cannot speak, their parents shall answer the word for them, or one of their relatives' (so the Ethiopic version, in Horner's edition, 152). About the same time Tertullian (*De bapt.* 18) gives them the name of *sponsores*. Origen (*c.Cels.* 3:51; GCS 1:247) knew of a practice of having such sponsors for the ordinary adult pagan whose manner of life hitherto might not be quite plain to the Church authorities and who would be required to produce a Christian friend as a guarantor of his fitness. Etheria in her pilgrimage to Jerusalem (about the end of the 4th cent.) found that candidates for baptism had to present themselves accompanied by their 'fathers' (if males) or by their 'mothers' (if females), so that witness could be borne to their lives (CSEL 39:96). Strangers had to have testimonials. As she was describing the Lenten catechesis, she did not mention what was done for infants.

The Greek term for godparents was ἀνάδοχος and its first known use in this sense is found in the works of the pseudo-Dionysius (*Ecclesiastica hierarchia* 2:2; PG 3:396), but as the word is applied to Christ by Marcus Eremita (*Opuscula* 7:15; PG 65:1093) about the time of the Council of Ephesus, it was probably already in use as a technical term even then.

II The theological justification for this assumption of duties on behalf of an infant may be found in the decree of Trent (D 870) which anathematized the idea that infants for whom godparents had spoken should, when they came to years of discretion, be asked whether they wished to accept what had been done on their behalf and, if they did not, should be left to their own devices and not forced to be true to the faith. The immediate source of this idea was Erasmus, but it went back to Tertullian. In writing of baptism (*De bapt.* 18) he had sought to bring into theology some notions of the Roman civil law. 'Shall one to whom earthly wealth is not entrusted be endowed with heavenly?' He may have had in mind the saying in Gaius (*Institutes*, 3:100) that it was not logical for the heir to inherit an obligation which had not affected his father.[1] This would be the case when the child of a pagan father

[1] Inelegans visum est ab heredis persona incipere obligationem.

and Catholic mother was baptized in infancy. That the Church should have persisted with her practice when the spirit and even the letter of Roman law was against her shows that it was taken very seriously. Tertullian shows awareness of arguments in its favour, based on such texts as Mt 19:14. That he felt his case to be weak is shown by the arguments from expediency which he uses. Sponsors may die before they have discharged their obligation; infants may turn out badly and give their sponsors more trouble than they bargained for. These hazards are not to be counted against the Catholic idea that all conditions of mankind, infants along with adults, can take part in the Exodus of Christ which will lead them eventually across the Jordan into a promised land. Those born during the original Exodus were circumcised after the entry into the promised land (Jos 5:5-7), men and boys together, and in Christian typology this act seems to correspond to the conferring of the sacrament of Confirmation (*see* CONFIRMATION I). That babes in arms should have been carried through the Jordan would signify to the early Christian mind that the practice of infant baptism was justified. When it came to be challenged by Pelagius the whole Church rose up to defend it (*see* BAPTISM XIV).

An error in the opposite direction was noted by the Council of Neo-Caesarea in 314 (canon 6; in Turner's *Monumenta Iuris antiqui*, II:1:124): 'There is no community between a pregnant woman and the child she will bear, and hence the intention of each one must be manifested in the baptismal profession of faith.'[1] This was the reply to a doubt whether the baptism of a pregnant mother might count for the child she was carrying at the time. The affirmative opinion could only have arisen where it was commonly held that parents who were Christian could commit their children to the faith they held themselves. J. Jeremias has found a Jewish parallel to this case (TB, *Yebamoth* 78a), where it is decided that the non-Israelite woman who becomes a proselyte while pregnant does not need to have her child purified by proselyte-baptism. The Christian answer to the case was different, but, as the new-born child could not itself profess the faith, it is obvious that some sponsor must have spoken for it.

The words of St Paul (1 Cor 7:14) about the children of Christian parents being holy are not meant to dispense with the baptism of such children, but are spoken rabbinically (as J. Jeremias has quite conclusively shown, *Infant Baptism*, 46). They mean that, just as the unbelieving husband is hallowed through the faith of his Christian wife, or is committed to holiness, even so the children are committed. This prescinds from the question of baptism or the means by which that commitment will be worked out. If the husband were to be converted he would be baptized, and the same is true of the children when they are born. It is this idea of the committing of children to the faith of the believing

[1] Nihil enim commune est parienti et illi qui editur; propter quod seorsum voluntas uniuscuiusque in illa confessione declaretur.

parent that makes the Church so adamant about the education of the children of a mixed marriage in the Catholic faith. God could have chosen another way of having His Church propagated, but in fact He has chosen the way of infant baptism and the trusteeship of the godparent at the font. The nationality of children is something that comes to them at birth, and their citizenship in a heavenly country is very much more valuable than that. The Pelagian looks on faith as his own achievement and wants his children to achieve as much for themselves, but the true Christian knows that it is a gift.

Bibliography. E. Dick, 'Das Pateninstitut im altchristlichen Katechumenat', in ZKT 63 (1939) 1-49; *J. Jeremias, *Infant Baptism in the First Four Centuries* (English trans. 1960); J. Didier, 'A Propos du baptême des enfants', in *Mélanges de science religieuse* 9 (1952) 191-214.   J. H. C.

GOD, PROOFS OF THE EXISTENCE OF

The article on GOD, NATURAL KNOWLEDGE OF, showed that it belonged to Catholic tradition to hold that men are capable of an affirmation of God independent of divine revelation and usually regarded as the conclusion of an inference, whether spontaneous and implicit or philosophical and explicit. Hence Catholic philosophers have sought to work out as clearly as possible the logical paths to the awareness of God's existence. While the proposed proofs are not all of equal force, they will be expounded in a logical order without prejudice to their different value, allowing criticism to emerge from the exposition. They will be divided into (I) arguments from the notion of God, (II) arguments from effect to cause, and (III) arguments from traces of the absolute in the world, followed by (IV) subsidiary considerations and conclusions.

I Arguments from the Notion of God. The characteristic argument from the notion of God is the ontological argument originally advanced by St Anselm (*Proslogion*). Anselm maintains that the being than which nothing greater can be conceived must exist in reality, for, if it only existed as an idea in the mind, it would be less than the same thing existing in reality as well. Hence it would not be the being than which nothing greater can be conceived, and this would be a contradiction in terms. Thus the fact that we think of God as the being than which nothing greater can be conceived implies that He really exists.

In Anselm's lifetime Gaunilo (*Liber pro Insipiente*) ridiculed the argument on the ground that we should equally have to affirm that the most beautiful of all possible islands must really exist, for otherwise it would be less beautiful than a similar island which really existed. Anselm in his reply made clear that his argument applied only to being and not to any particular kind of being. Consequently the proof reduces more properly to the form that the idea of God is the idea of a being which necessarily exists, but it would be contradictory to deny existence to what must be thought of as existing necessarily. St Thomas Aquinas (*Summa*, 1a:2:1c), however, objects that, while we should doubtless see that God necessarily exists if we had a direct knowledge of what God is, our human knowledge of God is too imperfect to enable us to see this. Hence we have to prove that God exists from the facts of experience and not merely from the notion of God. Duns Scotus thought that the argument could be made valid by altering the major premiss into the form that, if God is possible, He exists. Then, by establishing that there can be no contradiction in the notion of infinite being, we can conclude that such a being exists.

In modern times Descartes (*Metaphysical Meditations V*) upholds the argument in its simple form, that it would be contradictory to think of God in any way except as necessarily existent. Leibniz (*Discours de metaphysique* 23 ; *Monadology* 45) modifies the argument in the manner of Scotus ; on the ground that only limitations or negations can be the source of contradiction he maintains that we can see that an infinite being is possible, but, if an infinite and necessary being is possible, it must be realized in fact. Kant (*Critique of Pure Reason*) thinks that all forms of the argument are invalid because they involve the fallacy of supposing existence to be a predicate like other predicates, which can be affirmed or denied without otherwise altering the subject. A man may be tall or short without being different in any other way, and the same is true of all proper predicates. But a man who does not exist is not otherwise the same sort of man as one who does exist ; a non-existent man is nothing at all. Hence existence is not a true predicate, for it cannot be taken away without taking away the whole subject at the same time. Therefore we cannot argue from essence to existence, for prior to existence there is no essence to argue from.

The status of the ontological argument continues to be debated. Perhaps it should be agreed that, as it stands, it is invalid, for what it really amounts to is no more than the entailment proposition that, if God exists, He exists necessarily. Those who have championed it may be thought to have implicitly in their minds the additional premiss that something exists and to be perceiving that, if anything exists, God exists, for God is what being necessarily is. In this form, however, it ceases to be distinct from the causal argument, as we shall see later.

Another argument from the idea of God to his existence is also associated with Descartes (*Metaphysical Meditations III*). Descartes maintains that we could not have an idea of an infinite being unless it had been implanted in us by that being. For the idea of an infinite being contains more than that of any finite being ; hence it cannot be derived from the experience of finite things. It remains that God must Himself produce it in our minds. Therefore God must exist. This argument would work if our notion of infinite being were clear and positive. As it is, it seems to be simply the combination of a negation with the notion of the limited. The elements of this double negation are readily seen to be provided by experience. It is in a similar way

that we first think of the horizon as a limit and then of what is beyond the horizon as negating this limit.

II Arguments from Effect to Cause. Attempts to prove the existence of God with no other basis than the idea of God turn out, we have noticed, to be at least dubious. A majority of thinkers have preferred to start from a solid basis in the world of experience and to argue to God as the source of the world as we know it. The classical proofs of this kind are the first three of the Five Ways of St Thomas Aquinas (*Summa*, 1a:2:3c ; for the first two cf. *Summa Contra Gentiles I:13*). In the First Way St Thomas argues that, since change demands a cause, the fact of change in the world proves the existence of something unchanging which is the source of change. In the Second Way the observation of instances of causal dependence leads us to acknowledge the existence of independent and uncaused being. In the Third Way the observation of contingent and conditionally necessary being makes us affirm the existence of absolutely necessary being as its source.

It should be remarked that these arguments lead formally to the affirmation of uncaused, unchanging and necessary being but that they do not tell us of what sort such being is or even whether there is one such being or there are many such. The dogmatic materialist holds that the primary constituents of matter are uncaused, necessary and intrinsically unchanging ; this view is not yet formally excluded. Therefore we must consider St Thomas's full proof of the existence of God as continuing through a number of the questions of the First Part until he has shown that to be finite entails being caused, so that only the fullness of being can be necessary being, and that this infinite being must be an eternal and omniscient mind. Another point which deserves to be noted about St Thomas's argument is that he does not suppose it to be necessary or possible to offer a philosophical proof that the created world had a beginning ; to his mind it is the fact that this is a world of finite things, whether such have always existed or not, which shows that they are dependent for their existence on an infinite source (*Summa*, 1a:46:2c). The rather disconcertingly expressed Fourth Way may perhaps be taken as a summary statement of St Thomas's conviction that finite being must come from infinite being. For of a finite thing we can always ask why being takes this form or that, and that is to look for a cause ; only infinite being is what being must necessarily be. Next we must notice that a corporeal thing is always of a limited nature ; hence infinite being must realize the character of mind with a fullness beyond human conception. St Thomas's philosophical argument for God may, then, be usefully summarized as consisting in the three steps from caused being to uncaused or necessary being, from necessary being to infinite being, and from infinite being to eternal mind. The first three of the Five Ways state only the first step and prepare the ground for the second and third.

Kant was as well aware as St Thomas that to arrive

at uncaused or necessary being was only a first step, but he thought that it was impossible to take the next step without falling into the fallacy of the ontological argument. Hence he criticized the cosmological or causal proof for being incomplete in itself and incapable of being completed without incurring the mistake of the ontological proof. He argued that the premiss required to complete the cosmological argument, that necessary being is infinite being, was equivalent to the principle of the ontological argument, that infinite being is necessary being. By the ordinary rules of logical conversion the former proposition would yield only the converse that *some* infinite being is necessary being. But, Kant said, there can by definition be only one infinite being. Therefore the restriction to *some* can be removed, and the two unrestricted propositions are seen to be equivalent. Kant's error can be summed up as the supposition that an extensional consideration is relevant to the force of an intensional relation. We are here concerned with entailments, which are connections of meaning or intensional relations. When we express the propositions in appropriate form they become ' if anything is necessary, it is infinite ' and ' if anything is infinite, it is necessary '. Evidently these maxims are logically independent. As a matter of fact they are both true, but only the former enters into a valid proof of God's existence ; the latter would be useful only if we could prove directly that the infinite must exist, which is the mistake of the ontological argument. St Thomas's proof, therefore, does not succumb to Kant's criticism, as later philosophers have too often rashly assumed.

Such is the general and metaphysical causal argument, which is rightly looked upon as the principal philosophical path to God. More specific arguments of a causal sort might be, and have been, advanced from the appearance of new levels of being in the history of the world, for example, the origin of life and intelligence. These cannot be, or are not easily, explained without the intervention of a creative cause. It is not clear, however, that life might not in exceptional circumstances have emerged spontaneously from inorganic matter. The whole conception of the history of the universe as a progressive evolution suggests the dual activity of a material cause and of an efficient and directing cause, but materialists can without absurdity, if not very plausibly, attribute the latter causality to the latent powers of matter itself. The occurrence of the miraculous is another indication of the existence of a power superior to the forces of nature, but, since the miraculous is rare, men in fact accept it more often because they believe in God than they believe in God because they observe the apparently miraculous. The unbeliever can again without logical absurdity, even if somewhat arbitrarily, invoke hidden forces of matter. The argument from finality is an argument to a particular aspect of divine causality, but reason will be given to show that the deepest sense of the teleological argument assigns it to the next section of this article.

III Arguments from Traces of the Absolute in the World.

The absoluteness of truth was an indication of God especially to St Augustine (*De libero arbitrio* 2:9–18 ; CSEL 74:39–41 ; *De Vera religione* 29–31 ; PL 34:145–7). Although things come into being and pass away, their natures are timelessly possible, and necessary truths can be asserted about them. For a Platonist like Augustine it was the timeless necessity of mathematical and ethical truths which produced the most powerful impression. But, he argued, contingent and transitory things cannot be a sufficient foundation for timeless and necessary truths. These truths would not subsist unless they had a basis in an eternal creative mind. Whatever, therefore, of absoluteness can be found in human thinking reveals itself as a reflection of the absolute thought and being of God.

The timeless validity of ethical principles, as we have just seen, impressed St Augustine, but philosophers are on more slippery ground when they point to moral law as demanding a legislator, a cosmic will. For, as Kant would object, is not the moral imperative categorical or unconditional ? Is not duty something which imposes itself in its own right, apart from any legislative will ? St Thomas agrees that God wills the right because He sees it to be right, not that it is right because God wills it to be so. The moral law, therefore, is a reflection of the divine intelligence rather than a fiat of the divine will. Hence Newman's argument from conscience (*Grammar of Assent*) is ambiguous and of doubtful validity.

Kant himself (*Critique of the Practical Reason*) argued from morality to God because he held that the fact of unconditional duty implied a moral governor of the universe who would in the end see that happiness was in proportion to virtue. No doubt moral striving would lose some of its meaning if it were not eventually to be ratified by the course of events, but it is not clear that it could lose all significance. Nor does Kant's assertion that morality demands an eventual harmony of virtue and happiness seem altogether consistent with his first emphasis on the categorical nature of the ethical imperative.

Aesthetic values seem also to offer a road to God, because the experience of beauty shows that value belongs not only to a human sphere of thinking and acting but is an objective feature of the material world itself. Philosophers, however, have more often appealed to the observation of teleology in the material world as evidence for God. This is the Fifth Way of St Thomas. The teleological argument is sometimes put forward as evidence for a benevolent governor of the universe, and appeal is made to the provision of what is required for the survival of species, especially of animals and of the human race. This, however, may be countered by reference to all the apparently purposeless suffering and wastage in nature and, more directly, by the fact that, if the world did not provide what was needed for our survival, we should not be there to lament our extinction. We cannot assume that a different sort of world might not contain equally worthy, or more worthy, species, and we need not go further than the survival of the fittest to explain why those species that actually exist should do so. The argument from specific cases of apparent finality does not seem very helpful. Nevertheless the teleological argument has had a long career and was respected even by Kant ; we should look elsewhere for its deepest sense. For it can be understood not as an argument from particular instances of intelligent order but as a reference to the rule of intelligible order throughout the universe. Things behave in accordance with the laws of their nature ; these are timeless truths embodied in a contingent world. What can they be except reflections of an eternal mind ? Thus the teleological argument acquires its proper significance by merging with the Augustinian argument from eternal truth.

IV Conclusions. Arguments are drawn also from man's need of religion and from the universality of religion among the races of mankind. These can only be supporting considerations, for a need is not a complete guarantee of its possible fulfilment, and the bewildering variety of human conceptions of the divine is just as striking as the universal tendency to recognize divinity in some form. We are left, therefore, with what amounts to one massive line of reflection by which, acknowledging that change needs to be explained by its antecedents and that nothing which changes is completely independent of other things, we find that we cannot be content with the world of history as its own explanation or with its ultimate constituents as completely fundamental and self-existent. We are logically compelled to look for some altogether independent being and recognize this as one which is not impeded by any limitation but is the fullness of being in unity. Superior to the limitations of time and space, the necessary and infinite being is an eternal mind, the creative source of all else that exists. This being we call God.

It was once thought that Kant's criticisms had superseded this line of reflection. Kant's criticisms, however, do not really stand up to countercriticism. Curiously enough, although Kant's reputation has greatly declined among contemporary philosophers, he is still assumed by many to have been successful in his repudiation of a theistic metaphysic. It is time that his failure in this respect should also be admitted. Hence there is nothing to be ashamed of if, in common with the majority of Catholic philosophers, we continue to put forward the classical metaphysical argument which both holds its own on the level of explicit reflection and explains why on the prelogical level an implicit and spontaneous recognition of God comes naturally to the human mind.

Bibliography. Mainly historical : *J. Adam, *Religious Teachers of Greece* (1909) ; *W. Jaeger, *The Theology of the Early Greek Philosophers* (1947) ; *F. Solmsen, *Plato's Theology* (1942) ; E. Gilson, *God and Philosophy* (1941) ; E. Gilson, *Being and Some Philosophers* (1949) ; E. Gilson, *The Philosophy of St Bonaventure* (1938) ; E. Gilson, *The Christian Philosophy of St Thomas Aquinas* (1957) ; E. Gilson, *The Christian Philosophy of St Augustine* (1961) ; E.

Gilson, *Jean Duns Scot* (1952) ; R. Guelluy, *Philosophie et théologie chez Guillaume d'Ockham* (1947) ; G. Grünwald, *Geschichte der Gottesbeweise im Mittelalter* (1907) ; *R. L. Patterson, *The Conception of God in the Philosophy of Aquinas* (1933) ; *C. C. J. Webb, *Studies in the History of Natural Theology* (1915) ; J. Collins, *God in Modern Philosophy* (1960) ; *A. S. Pringle-Pattison, *The Idea of God in the Light of Recent Philosophy* (1917) ; E. A. Sillem, *George Berkeley and the Proofs of the Existence of God* (1957).

Mainly systematic : R. Garrigou-Lagrange, *God, His Existence and Nature* (1935) ; G. H. Joyce, *Principles of Natural Theology* (1923) ; D. J. B. Hawkins, *Essentials of Theism* (1949) ; M. Pontifex, *The Existence of God* (1946) ; I. Trethowan, *The Basis of Belief* (1961) ; E. Sillem, *Ways of Thinking about God* (1961) ; P. Descoqs, *Praelectiones Theologiae Naturalis* (1935) ; G. Rabeau, *Dieu, son existence et sa providence* (1933) ; L. De Raeymaeker, *Philosophie de l'être* (1945) ; R. Jolivet, *Le Dieu des philosophes et des savants* (1956) ; F. Van Steenberghen, *Dieu Caché* (1961) ; *W. R. Sorley, *Moral Values and the Idea of God* (1935) ; *G. Dawes Hicks, *The Philosophical Bases of Theism* (1937) ; *A. Farrer, *Finite and Infinite* (1943) ; *E. L. Mascall, *He Who Is* (1943) ; *E. L. Mascall, *Existence and Analogy* (1949) ; *G. F. Stout, *God and Nature* (1952) ; *H. D. Lewis, *Our Experience of God* (1959) ; *J. V. Langmead Casserley, *Graceful Reason* (1955).   D. J. B. H.

GOOD The matter of this article falls under three main heads : (I) ontological good, (II) moral good, (III) the common good.

I Ontological Good. This term indicates that transcendental property of being whereby it is the object of appetite—*bonum est quod omnia appetunt*, appetite indicating not only the conscious desire of a knowing subject but also the natural tendency of beings bereft of knowledge (cf. St Thomas *in Eth. Nicom.* lib. 1, lectio 1, nn. 9–10). Elaboration of this concept owes much to Plato and Plotinus, echoes of whose teaching have made themselves heard in traditional Christian philosophy and theology, owing mainly to the influence of St Augustine. The latter, however, does not follow them to the extent of so separating *Good* from *Being* that the former alone seems to constitute the Divinity—the One which, according to Plotinus, is utterly incomprehensible but union with which is the ultimate freedom (*Enneads* 2:9:1). For the Christian Doctor goodness in God seems to have a certain priority over being, so that in an oft-quoted phrase we owe our existence rather to the Goodness than to the Being of God— *quia Deus bonus est, nos sumus* (*De doctrina christiana*, 1:xxxii:35 ; *Corpus Christianorum*, 30:26), but God is the Sovereign Being—*summe est* (*De natura Boni* 19; PL 42:551).

Aristotle corrected the exaggerations of Platonic thought, establishing the priority of Being in which Good is immanent ; each individual essence is a determination of Being, which thus realizes itself. Therefore every being is good because everything seeks to be what it is, and all movement tends to a fuller realization of being, but in such a way as to be a response to the attraction of the First Mover, Who is thus the Final Cause of all movement in the universe (*Ethica Nicomachea*, 1:1 ; *Metaphysics* 1072b 1–8). These Aristotelian concepts reappear in the writings of the Angelic Doctor, notably in the *Summa*, where they are most clearly seen in his magnificent synthesis of Christian thought : but they are enriched with Platonic overtones borrowed from St Augustine and, as with the latter, the concept of Good is considered theologically, inasmuch as man in the actual order of Providence must find his ultimate perfection, or goodness or beatitude, in an immediate union with the Supreme Good in the Beatific Vision. Thus in the *Summa*, 1a:5:2:@2 from the Aristotelian notions that Good is founded in Being and that every being is good because the actuation that being implies is a perfection and hence appetible (ibid. 3) he rises to the concept of God as the Sovereign Good, not in the sense apparently imagined by Aristotle as though He were an immensely powerful magnet inert in Himself, but as the Final and Efficient Cause of everything in creation from whom Goodness emanates through a sovereignly free act of His Will and to whom everything created returns (cf. *Summa*, 1a:6:1, 2 ; 19:4, 5; *also I Sent.* 15:4:1). Goodness then in a creature means to be like to God (*Summa*, 1a:4:3) and to become like to Him—*assimilari Deo*—is the law of all created operations (cf. *Contra Gentiles* 3:21, 22, 70).

The Scriptural teaching on the essential goodness of God (cf. Mk 10:18 ; Pss 105, 107, 108) and His creation (Gen 1:10, 12, etc.), and that of the First Vatican Council that God has freely created the spiritual and corporeal universe to manifest His Perfection through the good He imparts to His creatures (D 1783), give a firm dogmatic basis to the above speculations.

II Moral Good. Good, though the object of every appetite, has a special relation to rational appetite or will, and hence to man : for only the will can seek a good which is recognized as such, and thus of corporeal creatures only man can seek consciously his own fulfilment or perfection in loving some person or thing as a good (*Summa*, 1–2ae:1:1 and 2c ; 6:1 and 2c).

This consideration is of prime importance in elucidating the notion of moral good, which for the Angelic Doctor is ontological good in the specifically human context. It can therefore be called *true human good*, that is, the good sought by man from the inner orientation of human reason, in accord with the various needs and urges of his entire nature in its concrete and historical situation. Because he is a being, he experiences and imposes upon himself as a true good his own continuation in being ; because he has animal life he feels the urge and need to propagate himself, from which we have the imperative of marriage and family life ; as a social being he is drawn to, and feels the need of, the co-operation of his fellows, and so life in society is seen as a true human good ; finally, according to his higher

faculties, he is open to values that are spiritual and eternal so that the worship of God and union with Him are sought as goods arising out of the needs of his nature (*Summa*, 1–2ae:94:2c).

St Thomas rarely uses the term 'moral good', but he does identify it with 'honourable good' (*bonum honestum*) and 'useful good' (*bonum utile*) that is, respectively, the good that is of itself the object of a rightly ordered will and the good that is a means whereby to attain that object. He remarks that moral good does not necessarily coincide with his third type of ontological good, 'delectable good' (*bonum delectabile*), because pleasure can be sought in a way out of harmony with human reason (*Summa*, 2–2ae:34:2:@1 ; cf. 1:5:6). Significantly, where he treats *ex professo* of the morality of human actions he does not use the term 'moral good' but underlines its truly ontological character by insisting that a human action is good if it has the fullness of being due to it (*Summa*, 1–2ae:18:1c) ; therefore if in its motive, object and concrete circumstances it is in harmony with reason (ibid., 2 ff. ; 19:3c ; *Quaestio de Malo*, 2:4c). In the supernatural order this fullness of being is had only through the elevation of the reason by faith and the information of the human act by charity (*Summa*, 2–2ae:23:8c ; cf. G. Gilleman, *The Primacy of Charity in Moral Theology*, 1959).

The danger of separating moral good from its ontological basis is seen in the inadequacies of the formal morality of Kant, of the intuitional theories of M. Scheler, E. Hartmann and G. E. Moore (*Principia Ethica*, 1962), of the empirical theories of sociologists such as E. Westermarck (*The Origin and Development of Moral Ideas*, 1906, 1908) and of the views of such linguistic analysts as Professor Ayer, who would reduce moral judgments to exhortations (*Language, Truth and Logic*, 1936). Modern Thomists are engaging in a fruitful dialogue with the intuitionists (J. De Finance, *Essai sur l'agir humaine*, 1962) and the linguistic analysts (E. D'Arcy, *Human Acts : An Essay in their Moral Evaluation*, 1963).

III The Common Good. This is a human, and therefore a moral good, pertaining to man precisely as a member of society. Therefore it has nothing to do with an abstract ideal order as conceived by Hegel or Bosanquet (*The Philosophical Theory of the State*, 1930) nor does it suppose society to be the sole source of human rights after the manner of Hobbes (*The Leviathan*), nor does it subordinate the individual to the good of the race (National Socialism) or to the evolving economic order (the error from opposite points of view of both exaggerated capitalism and Marxism). Equally, it is not the good of the greatest number of citizens according to the formula of Bentham—'the greatest happiness of the greatest number'.

Pius XI aptly describes the good of society as the true temporal prosperity of all, brought about by mutual co-operation (Encyclical *Divini Redemptoris*, 19 March 1937 ; AAS 29 (1937) 79). It includes therefore not only the proper distribution of material goods and social burdens, so that none is excluded, but also a sound juridic order, opportunities for cultural, moral and religious development, and above all the integration of sound moral principles in society itself so far as they pertain to man's social relations and development in any concrete historical situation.

Basic to the Catholic concept of the common good, as expounded in the Christian concept of law developed by the master theologians (St Thomas, *Summa*, 1–2ae:90, Suarez, *De Legibus*, disp. 1) is the truth that society is for man and not man for society, and this can be said to be the keynote of papal social teaching from *Rerum Novarum* of Leo XIII (15 May 1891) to *Pacem in Terris* of John XXIII (11 April 1963 ; AAS 55 (1963) 257–304). Within this framework there is divergence amongst Catholics as to the exact relationship between the citizen and society. Some, with Maritain, place the emphasis on man as a person with a destiny beyond this world, while others, as Fr A. F. Utz OP, insist rather on his essential dependence on society as a part depends on a whole, and consequently in a restricted way admit a certain logical priority of society in the order of finality (*see* Bibliography).

Bibliography (additional). C. Fabro, 'Bene', in *Enciclopedia Cattolica* 3 ; 1215–17 ; A. Gardeil, 'Bien', in DTC 2:825–43 ; G. Vann OP, *Morals and Man* (1960) ; J. de Finance SJ, *Ethica Generalis* (1963); J. Maritain, *The Person and the Common Good* (1952) ; A. Utz, *Éthique sociale* (1958) vol. I, 93–163.

A. R.

GOSPEL KERYGMA The word 'kerygma' is the transliteration of a Greek word meaning 'announcement, proclamation'. It enters into our study of the gospels for both literary and theological reasons. From the point of view of literature, we want to know what exactly a gospel is ; and from the point of view of theology we want to know why they were written. Both questions are clearly connected ; but it will be convenient to begin with the literary point of view.

The gospels are clearly not spontaneous and independent compositions of the individual evangelists ; and in trying to decide their literary *genre*, it is of some importance to see how they came to develop and to trace their prehistory. This leads eventually to an investigation of the most primitive form of Christian preaching, as it is found in the earliest discourses reported in Acts (e.g. 2:14–39 ; 3:12–26 ; 4:8–12 ; 10:34–43), and in St Paul's own references to his earlier preaching (e.g. 1 Cor 15:3–5 ; Gal 3:1 ; 1 Thess 1:9–10).

We find then that this preaching takes the form of a simple proclamation (*kerygma*) of the fact of salvation—that the Scriptures are fulfilled in Jesus ; that he was crucified for our sins ; that God raised him from the dead ; that he sits at the right hand of the Father ; that he is to come as judge.

It must be evident that this kerygma has played a great part in the development of the gospel form. The most striking difference is the expansion of the biographical element in the gospels ; but even this is not absent from the kerygma, in its brief references

to our Lord's ministry (Ac 2:22 ; 10:37–8). And other elements of the kerygma (the Passion, Resurrection, fulfilment of Scripture) are taken over completely by the gospel.

But it is not only their content that they have in common ; their purpose also is the same. Paul can say that the point of his proclaiming Christ to the Galatians was that they should be saved by faith in him (Gal 3:1–2 ; cf. 1 Cor 2:1–5 ; Rom 1:16–17 ; Ac 3:16) ; and the same purpose is stated by the fourth gospel : 'These things are written in order that you may believe' (Jn 20:31). And it is at this point that we come up against the problem of faith and history. Some scholars (Bultmann could be taken as the representative of the school) would hold that what is essential to the Christian religion is the call of God and man's response, which is faith ; that the kerygma is the expression of the call for faith—the simple proclamation of God's intervention, demanding our response ; and that much, at least, of the gospel story is the expression of this intervention in 'mythological' form.

A Catholic theologian would agree that the gospels are very much more an appeal to faith than a simple biography ; that the facts have been selected and arranged in order to bring out the demand of God. But he would also hold that the faith which is demanded is a faith in things which really happened ; they took place 'in the sight of the disciples' (cf. Jn 20:31) ; they were handed down by eye-witnesses and faithful ministers of the word (cf. Lk 1:2). The gospels are the proclamation of the divine intervention ; but that divine intervention took place *historically* in Christ ; and the account of His deeds and words was proclaimed and conserved precisely because the early Church realized that He was himself the Word of God.

The Biblical Commission (21 April 1964) accepts the fact of the kerygma when it distinguishes three stages in the transmission of the facts about Christ : 'The Apostles proclaimed above all the death and resurrection of the Lord as they bore witness to Jesus. They faithfully explained His life and words, while taking into account in their method of preaching the circumstances in which their hearers found themselves. . . . Faith, far from destroying the memory of what had transpired, rather confirmed it . . .'. This Instruction was largely taken over by the Second Vatican Council in its decree (*de revelatione*, 5:17–19).

Bibliography. *La Formation des Évangiles* (Louvain symposium of 1955, edited by J. Heuschen) ; A. Rétif, 'Qu'est-ce que le Kérygme ?', in NRT 71 (1949) 910–22 ; *H. W. Bartsch (editor), *Kerygma and Myth, a Theological Debate* (Eng. trans. 1953) ; *C. H. Dodd, *The Apostolic Preaching and its Developments* (1944²) ; *B. Lindars, *New Testament Apologetic* (1961) ; J. A. Fitzmyer SJ, 'The Biblical Commission's Instruction (21 April 1964) on the Historical Truth of the Gospels', in TS 25 (1964) 386–408 (this article gives an accurate translation of this document with commentary).

L. J.

GOTHIC In the days of the Gothic revival there was a danger that zeal for architectural purity would lead to error or even heresy in theology. In A. W. Pugin's *Contrasts* (1841) the position is taken that pointed architecture is the only fitting style for Christians, and the argument is advanced that as the early Christians stood when they were at worship, so by analogy the arches in a church must be pointed, bolt-upright and not circular or squat. The adequate answer to this could be that Origen had once proposed that, since to the Platonist the sphere was the perfect shape, it was obvious that the risen body that will be given at the Last Day will itself be spherical and the blessed will thereafter circulate as on a billiard-table. Cardinal Newman in his *Letters* (vol. XII ; 220) had to say forcibly what many felt at the time : ' Mr Pugin is . . . a bigot. He sees nothing good in any school of Christian art except that of which he is himself so great an ornament. The canons of Gothic architecture are to him points of faith, and everyone is a heretic who would venture to question them. . . . With only half Christendom on his side, to say nothing of the Greek and Oriental bodies, he rules that the other half is what he calls reproachfully, *pagan*.' To Newman the lack of an uninterrupted tradition of Gothic architecture showed that it could not be bound up with the faith. ' Gothic is now like an old dress, which fitted a man well twenty years back but must be altered to fit him now. It was once the perfect expression of the Church's ritual in those places in which it was in use ; it is not the perfect expression now.' One can see that Newman's concept of living growth and development of doctrine is here being applied to show that Gothic is not a part of the faith. In 1848, when he wrote this letter, it took courage to say as much as he did.

Pugin, who seems to have come from a family background of Swiss Calvinism, had almost fought his way into the Church through his enthusiasm for Gothic, and even before his final breakdown in mind he was prone to identify what had been for himself the occasion with the cause of conversion. He told Newman that he would as soon design a mechanic's institute as an Oratory, and his friend, Ambrose Phillipps, cursed Fr Faber for his Baroque tastes. Newman himself remarked on Pugin's work (ibid. 215) : ' In details Pugin is perfect, but his altars are so small that you can't have a Pontifical High Mass at them, his tabernacles so low that you can scarce have exposition, his East windows so large that everything else is hidden in the glare, and his skreens so heavy that you might as well have the function in the Sacristy, for the seeing it by the congregation.'

The great days of Gothic, from 1093 when there appear at Durham the first signs of what was to be the distinctive feature of Gothic—the transverse stone ribs on the hitherto unbroken surface of a barrel-vault—until the climax of the movement in the 13th cent., there was very little thinking aloud or theorizing about the style and its possible bearing on theology. The very term Gothic is a later creation and in English is first met with in Evelyn's *Diary*,

when in 1641 he goes on a visit to Holland and finds the churches there ' more Gothique ' than at home. In recent times there has been the attempt, based largely on the work of Viollet le Duc, the French architect, to supply a background of theory for Gothic and to relate it to the theological work of St Thomas, on the general grounds that both were permeated by rationality and completely functional. The re-editing by Panofsky of the work of Abbot Suger, who in 1135–40 rebuilt the Carolingian church of St Denis at Paris in the new style, has given some help to these modern theorists, but in reality there is very little to support them. Suger was physically a small man but very full of his own importance. His care to let posterity know what he had done was not due to his consciousness of being a great pioneer of the style that would be named Gothic but to human vanity. Drops of theory can be distilled out of his chronicle of events, but they are not very precious. He was frankly utilitarian in his desire to make the church of which he had the care more easy of access when crowds came to venerate the relics it enshrined ; his description of what the old building was like, with women having to walk on the heads of the men to get to the shrine, sufficiently expresses what moved him to have a triple portal for the West front of his new church. His choice of mosaic (now lost) as the decoration of the tympanum of one of these portals would be curious in one who was consciously wedded to the promotion of a new Gothic style. Suger had some idea of an ascent from the material to the spiritual which had come to him from Plotinus by way of the pseudo-Denys and Scotus Eriugena, but his delight was in brightness and light. He speaks of having torn down a Carolingian screen in the old church ' which as with a dark wall divided the midst of the church ' (in Panovsky's edition, 72), his purpose being to prevent the ' beauty of the spaciousness of the church being darkened by such obstructions '.[1] This act would not have pleased Pugin.

Suger's true mind appears in the account he gives of the small chapel he contrived in the neighbourhood of the shrine within the great church. He calls it (op. cit. 48) : ' the mercy seat, where the constantly-renewed Victim of our redemption might be offered privily without the disturbance of the crowds '.[2] That there could be a place for celebrating mass within the great church where priest and server might be unnoticed by those in the nave was always possible in a Gothic church, and it is this fact that makes the style anathema to many at the present day. Yet it must be said that present-day attacks on the multiplication of ' side-altar masses ' have no good pedigree ; it was Nestorius who began this trend (*see* EPHESUS, COUNCIL OF). Suger would have seen no harm in screening the Mass from the crowds that flocked to the shrines of the saints,

[1] Impedimentum quo medium ecclesiae muro tenebroso secabatur, ne speciositas ecclesiae magnitudinis talibus fuscaretur repagulis.

[2] Divinae propitiationis camera, in qua iugis et frequens redemptionis nostrae hostia absque turbarum molestia secreto immolari debeat.

even though he had torn down a screen himself to make the church look more spacious. People came to church for other reasons besides the hearing of Mass, and he took account of this.

The use of great Gothic churches for the singing of the canonical hours must have led those engaged in the task to appreciate the presence of a screen which gave them some protection from draughts, and in monastic churches this consideration no doubt took precedence over the need of the faithful to see from all angles what was going on at the altar. It may be suggested, too, that the presence in a moderate-sized town of many parish churches along with a cathedral indicates that the cathedral could never have been thronged by those anxious to hear Mass. It may be that on certain days, such as Mid-Lent Sunday, there was the custom that the congregations of the parish churches repaired to the mother-church or cathedral (thus fulfilling the words of the *Introit* of that day), but such gatherings would be rare. It does indeed seem likely that the more recent practice of having family reunions on Mid-Lent Sunday is a distortion (begun by the Reformers, who did not like the notion of a visible Church) from the more ancient practice of gathering the population at the mother-church or 'Jerusalem' of the town. Even in Rome the existence of some of the basilicas alongside the ancient *tituli* has been explained in the same way (cf. R. Vieilliard, *Recherches sur les origines de la Rome chrétienne* [1941]).

Conclusions, therefore, about Gothic as an influence on theology must be negative and sceptical. It cannot be shown to be the product of ideas, mistaken or not theologically, about the nature of the Mass. Nor is it a rationalization of the emotions then considered proper to worship. What St Thomas had to say, out of the pseudo-Denys, about the principles of beauty, and especially about *claritas*, does not seem to have affected the architects, and even Panofsky admits that it is not at all probable that these architects had read a line of St Thomas (so in Panofsky: *Gothic Architecture and Scholasticism*, 23). That the architects should have been 'exposed to the Scholastic point of view in innumerable other ways', as Panofsky there urges, is easily said, but the ways indicated are not very likely to have led to much exchange. They are, briefly, that the architects might have attended public disputations of the *quodlibet* variety, that they listened to sermons and worked alongside those who had charge of the liturgy and pictorial decoration of a church. Now it can be said at once that there is no sign of an original idea expounded in a *quodlibet* being embodied in Gothic building. The sermons of the time may have been more often eschatological than would be true of today, and this may have prompted the choice of the Doom as the subject for the West window of a church (where all would see it as they went out from Mass to resume their ordinary tasks) ; the habit of dividing a topic into three heads (as in the *Summa*) may have had an influence on Gothic decoration, but beyond these *trivia* it does not seem safe to go. That the Greek artists had to follow fixed

laws in their decoration of churches, based in part at least on theological ideas about the sacrifice of the Mass (*see* GREEK LITURGY) seems certain ; that Gothic builders had any such discipline to submit to seems on the other hand far from certain, whatever lights they may have derived from their Scholastic enthusiasms.

Bibliography. A. W. Pugin, *Contrasts* (1841) ; E. Panofsky, *The Abbey Church of St Denis* (1946, an edition with version and commentary of part of the *de administratione* and *de consecratione* of Abbot Suger, whose works are in PL 186) ; *P. Frankl, *Gothic Architecture* (Pelican History of Art, vol. 19, 1962) ; E. Panofsky, *Gothic Architecture and Scholasticism* (1957) ; A. Livermore, The Augustinian origins of Gothic, in DR 267 and 268 (1964) 141–55 and 222–32 (these articles show that Suger was steeped in the writings of Augustine, as were most Abbots of his time, and that this rather than any leaning to Scholasticism ruled his tastes).   J. H. C.

GOVERNMENT, FORMS OF Debate about the best form of government was a practice of the schools of rhetoric ever since they began. Plato, in his *Republic*, had traced a declension of forms from monarchy to oligarchy and finally to democracy, thus showing his own preferences ; the Church never followed Plato in this but kept to a strict neutrality in the debate (*see* CHURCH AND STATE). This neutrality was set forth as the official teaching of the Church by Leo XIII. In his time the question was put with some urgency : 'Does the Church disapprove of a democratic republic ?' Ever since the French Revolution the question had been in men's minds, but the experience of Pius IX in 1848 made it seem unlikely that an answer favourable to democracy would have been given in his time. The letters he exchanged with Franz-Josef of Austria show a fear on both sides that any weakening of the great European monarchies would be followed by revolutionary chaos.

With the advent of Leo XIII in 1878 the problem of France and the Catholic attitude to the republic there became acute. Neither Orléans monarchists nor Napoleonic imperialists could hope to set aside the republic without a disastrous civil war. The part Catholics should play in the affairs of State could be decisive, and Leo instructed his nuncio, Mgr Czacki, on his appointment in 1879, that the Church could live equally well with a republic as with a monarchy; that she did not ally herself with any party in a state and had prejudices against none as long as they left her free to pursue her own ministry. The Napoleonic concordat was still in force, but successive republican governments tried to weaken the teaching authority of the Church by legislating against the religious Orders and by cutting down the financial aid due to the Church under the concordat. There were not wanting even among the French bishops those who considered that the only way to meet these attacks on the Church was to promote a monarchist or an imperialist restoration, but they could not agree which restoration to work for. Leo saw that their disputes were sterile and embarked on the unpopular but theologically correct policy of encouraging French Catholics to rally to the republic as a form of government, but to agitate within its framework for more liberty for the Church. An encyclical, *Nobilissima Gallorum gens* (8 February 1884) tried to heal the divisions among French Catholics and to improve Catholic education, but the new policy was not at first expounded to the French. Prior to that, the general teaching was set out in the encyclical on the Christian constitution of States in 1885 (D 1871 and 1886) ; none of the various forms of government was to be regarded as blameworthy in itself, and any of them wisely administered could provide citizens with very good government. The distinction here suggested between the form of government, or constitution, and the acts of administration by a party governing under that constitution was capital for the French situation, but it was slow in coming to the fore. What papal policy meant for France was not merely acceptance of the republic but something like the formation of a Christian democratic party to hold more radical forces in check. The encyclical *Libertas* of 20 June 1888 repeated this general teaching, adding, however, (D 1934) the important qualification that forms of government were indeed regarded with indifference by the Church, provided always that they were apt for the promotion of the common good of citizens. How vital this qualification was can be seen by comparing the definition of Fascism given by Mussolini (*Enciclopedia Italiana*, s.v. Fascismo) which sets the Fascist State above all consideration of the good of its citizens : ' Fascism is a religious concept, in which man is viewed in his immanent relation to a law higher than himself, to an objective Will that transcends each single individual and elevates him to conscious membership of a spiritual society.'

In 1890, with the encyclical *Sapientiae christianae*, Leo had to elaborate, mainly for French benefit, the distinction between the (democratic) form of government and the unjust laws against the Church which such a government might enact (D 1936 b). In an epigram he concluded : ' It is a sin against democracy when violence is done to religion.'[1] This was the decisive year for his policy. The encyclical was issued on 10 January. On 5 May Cardinal Lavigerie implored Leo to act ' par un coup decisif' to bring Catholics to ' adhere to the republic '. He was encouraged to make a move himself, and on 12 November of the same year Lavigerie, receiving the officers of the French Mediterranean fleet at Algiers, drank to the unity of all citizens and had the Pères Blancs with him break out into the singing of the *Marseillaise*. The sensation was enormous. The dislike of the Austrian emperor for Cardinal Rampolla, who was then Secretary of State, was increased by the episode ; the French hierarchy were deeply divided, and the nuncio in Paris was recalled.

The next step was taken by Leo himself in 1892, when he issued an encyclical in French (*Au milieu des*

[1] Peccatur in rempublicam quidquid in religione delinquitur.

sollicitudes, 16 February 1892) by giving an interview to the editor of *Le Petit Journal* two days before and allowing him an exclusive draft of what it said. This paper, with a circulation of 1,200,000, brought the Pope's message into the homes of most French families. The distinction was again set out that in the speculative order Catholics had the right to prefer one form of government to another, but if one comes to the factual order, then it is clear that each nation has its own proper form of political régime due to manifold circumstances of law and history. ' Inutile de rappeler que tous les individus sont tenus d'accepter ces gouvernements et de ne rien tenter pour les renverser ou pour en changer la forme.' This was said to the monarchists, while it was allowed that gradual change of a constitution was sometimes needed for the common good. The legislation of particular governments was the work of men and not at all permanent ; in fact, some of the French laws were harmful to the Church and therefore to the common good of Frenchmen, and all should unite to have them changed. Separation of Church and State was well enough in some countries, but not in France.

The reply to Leo was not very enthusiastic. The French Catholics remained divided, while the Masonic government brought in a new law to expel or break up the religious Orders, a law which finally achieved its purpose in 1902. When the Jesuits were expelled in that year from France, one of the trustees who took over ownership of one of their colleges was the father of General de Gaulle. The action of Leo had other effects, for the group of Le Sillon begun by Marc Sangnier after Leo's death is still regarded as the origin of the Christian Democratic party of France, the MRP. The affair of the *Action française* and its condemnation in 1926 by Pius XI also owed much to Leo.

It was a paradox that while Pope Leo urged on the French, he held back the Italian Catholics, with the *non expedit*, from forming a political party, going so far as to cause Bishop Bonomelli of Cremona to retract publicly in his own cathedral on Easter Sunday a pastoral letter he had written which suggested the opposite course. To some this holding back implied a Machiavellian desire to ruin the House of Savoy by leaving the Italian parliament without a conservative element. In fact it was rather the legal idea that prevailed, according to which the whole Italian government was a *latrocinium* and should not be acknowledged in any way until a settlement was negotiated. Leo said that whereas in the United States there was a separation of Church and State, with benevolent neutrality on the part of the State, in France there was a similar separation with malevolent neutrality ; he might have added that in Italy there was open war.

Bibliography. E. Soderini, *Il Pontificato di Leone XIII* (1933, 3 vols.) ; A. Dansette, *Histoire religieuse de la France contemporaine* (2 vols., 1948, 1951, English trans. 1958) ; D. Binchy, *Church and State in Fascist Italy* (1941) ; A. Magri, *La Democrazia cristiana in Italia* (1954).   J. H. C.

GRACE The Catholic doctrine on the life of grace is first considered historically and then systematically. The historical part sketches the growth of the doctrine (I) in holy Scripture of the Old and (II) of the New Testament, (III) in the Fathers of the Church of the East and (IV) of the West, (V) in the Scholasticism of the Middle Ages and (VI) of the Tridentine and post-Tridentine times ; it concludes with (VII) a brief survey of the Church documents. The systematic part expounds the theology of grace : (VIII) the relation of grace to Christ and the Church ; (IX) sanctifying grace ; (a) justification, (b) created and Uncreated Grace, (c) formal effects, (d) characteristics ; (X) actual grace ; (a) necessity, (b) nature, (c) effects (systems of grace), (d) distribution ; (XI) growth in grace ; (XII) conclusion ; present-day trends.

I Grace in the OT. The doctrine of grace is in a way proper to the NT. Yet the opposition of the OT to the NT is less that of the law to grace than that of the beginning to the completion or of the promise to the fulfilment.

There may be in the OT no terms exactly equivalent to the Christian term grace, *charis*, in the sense of gratuitous gift sprung from the divine love in Christ and transforming the lives of those who come within His predilection. Hebrew near-equivalents are especially *ḥen* (χάρις in LXX), which expresses the goodwill of the powerful (God) shown in His gratuitous favour for the privileged chosen ones, and also the charm on their part which provokes the favour : and *ḥesed* (ἔλεος), mercy or attachment as exists between kindred or friends, connoting fittingness and reciprocity. Related are also *rahamim*, tenderness (motherly), *'emet* (from root *'mn*), truth or fidelity, and *sedeq*, justice, which makes for peace in the people. The idea expressed in these terms and in their combination when applied to Yahweh in his relation to Israel (cf. Ex 34:6) is that of faithful, generous and forgiving love (cf. Num 14:18 ; Jer 32:18 ; Jl 2:13 ; Ps 86:15 ; 103:8). Its chief manifestation is the alliance between Yahweh and Israel, *the* gift of Yahweh's goodwill (*ḥen*), who is faithful and loyal to His people despite its ever-recurring infidelities (Mich 7:18 ; Jer 4:23 ; 16:5 ; 32:18 ; Is 44:10 ; Os 2:6, 25). Love alone is the clue to this fidelity (Os 2:21 ; Jer 31:20 ; Is 44:6 f.). The alliance entails Yahweh's presence in Israel (*see* INDWELLING). To the people's incurable infidelities, He will answer with a new invention of His love, the coming of the Messias (*see* CHRIST), who will cleanse Jerusalem (Is 1:21–6) and regenerate the hearts of His people (Jer 31:31 ; Os 2:21) by His Spirit (Ez 36:27; 39:29). This is the prophetic announcement of Christian grace.

II Grace in the NT. The term *charis* for beauty, favour, gift, also gratitude, reward, is neither a necessary nor a sufficient clue to the NT doctrine of grace. Two of the synoptics, Matthew and Mark, do not know the word, yet they do have the idea of God's gift to men in Christ (Mt 21:37 ; Mk 12:6), who comes to forgive sin and inaugurate the new alliance (Mt 26:28 ; Mk 14:24), the kingdom of God

(Mt 6:33), where men enter as children of the Father (Mt 5:45 f. ; 6:1, 4, 6, 8) and rise to an interior and filial justice (Mt 5:20). Luke both in his gospel and the Acts makes frequent use of the term, its different meanings centring on the idea of God's favour which picks the chosen ones (Lk 1:28, 30) and admits repentant sinners into the kingdom (the scenes and parables of mercy : 7:36–50 ; 15:11–32 ; 19:1–10). The transforming power of grace is marked especially in the Acts, where χάρις and δύναμις go together (4:33 ; 6:8 ; 20:32 ; cf. also 14:26 ; 15:40 ; 18:27).

St Paul, the convert of Christ's grace (Ac 9:1–19 ; cf. 1 Cor 15:10), is among NT writers the theologian of grace (χάρις 100 times ; only 55 times in remaining NT). Grace is one of his leading ideas. It designates the riches given us in Christ, particularly forgiveness and redemption, for all are sinners and in need of redemption (Rom 3:25). It stands for all that Christ our Saviour brings us, He Himself being the first gift of God to men (Rom 8:32). Grace is at the root of our redemption (Rom 3:23 f.). The gratuity of our salvation through grace is one of Paul's dominant ideas : grace is not due to works (Rom 4:4 ; 11:6), particularly not to the works of the law (Rom 4:16 ; Gal 2:31). Its fruit is our justification in Christ (Rom 5:15, 19). The only condition for justification on our part is faith in Christ (Rom 3:22 f.) whose grace alone can free us from sin (Rom 4:5 ; 5:6 ; Gal 3:22). Justification by grace (Paul knew it from personal experience) is a transformation of man's outlook and being (Rom 5:1–5) ; it is the discovery of Christ and His riches (cf. Eph 3:8 f.), ' communion ' with the Son (1 Cor 1:9), the reception of Christ's Spirit with His gifts (Gal 3:2 f. ; 4:6 ; Rom 5:6), especially charity (Rom 5:6 ; 2 Cor 8:4 f. ; Gal 3:2 f. ; Eph 4:7–15), the adoption of the sons of God (Rom 8:15–17 ; Gal 4:4–7), who do the works of justice (cf. Rom 8:4) or bear the fruits of the Spirit (Gal 5:22) : a new life therefore (Rom 8:14), that of the sons of God led by the Spirit of God (Rom 8:14). Thus grace in St Paul stands for all the divine gifts of the new life bestowed on us in Christ our Saviour.

St John mentions the word *charis* thrice only, in the prologue to his gospel (1:14, 16, 17), in connection with the coming of the Word incarnate, from whose fulness we all receive. What that life of grace, life eternal (17:3), means to us he explains without mentioning the name. It is a life in faith and in knowledge of Christ and the Father (17:3), the initiative of which lies with the Father (6:64 f. ; 10:26 ; 12:39). It is a new birth (3:3), that of the children of God (1:12 ; cf. 1 Jn 3:1 f.). It is possession of the Spirit (3:6 ; 7:39 ; 14:16) and sharing in the unity of the Father and the Son (15:9 f., 16 f.). It is life eternal begun now (3:36) and to be fully revealed in glory (15:8 ; 17:22 f. ; 1 Jn 3:1). Grace, for John also, entails forgiveness of sin (1 Jn 1:7 ; 2:2, 13), though, it is true, he stresses less the redemptive aspect of grace.

St Peter uses the term *charis* rather often, either in the greetings (1 Pet 1:2 ; 2 Pet 1:2 ; 3:18) or in connection with our election (1 Pet 5:10), or charisms

(4:10), or life (3:7) and glory (1:7-10). Particularly noteworthy is the intriguing phrase of 2 Pet 1:4 on our sharing in the divine nature as a result of the divine gifts received in Christ.

To sum up: the NT doctrine on grace presents our new life in Christ, following on our admission into the kingdom or our rebirth in Him and adoption by the Father in the Spirit that is given us, as raising us above sin and flesh to a communion with God or a sharing in the life and love of the Three divine Persons. The gratuitousness of the gifts of grace appears from both its redemptive or healing and its exalting or 'divinizing' aspects. The first of these aspects is prominent in St Paul, the second in St John.

III Grace in the Greek Fathers. Fr Rousselot once wrote (RSR 18 [1928] 87 ff.) that the Greek Fathers continue the Johannine doctrine of grace, while the Latin Fathers, especially St Augustine, follow the Pauline teaching. The remark, as will appear, is correct if it means emphasis only and not exclusiveness. Just as St Paul in no way ignores the 'divinizing' aspect of the grace-life nor St John its sin-forgiving role, so also the Greek Fathers, while centring their teaching on our divinization, do not overlook redemptive grace, nor does Augustine in his insistence on the saving role of divine grace ignore its exalting and divinizing function.

The Greek Fathers' teaching on grace anterior to that of the Doctor of grace, St Augustine, is not only apparent from their frequent use of the term *charis* in various meanings, that of God's benevolence for men and of the gifts which flow from it being the two chief ones (cf. N. N. Glubokowsky, in Whitley, *The Doctrine of Grace*, 87-105); this very use is an indication that grace is central in Christian doctrine. More important and more emphatic is their teaching on our *theopoièsis*, our divinization either by grace or by the Spirit or by the Word. This teaching, in keeping with the Greek approach to God, going out to the Persons rather than to the nature, is trinitarian and brings out the role of each of the Three Persons in our regeneration or 'illumination' by baptism: the Father gives grace through the Son in the Spirit (Irenaeus, *epideixis* 7; in J. P. Smith's translation, 51; Cyril of Alexandria, *dial. VII de Trinitate*, PG 75:1089). The very purpose of the Incarnation is our divinization or adoption as sons of God (Irenaeus, *adv. haer.* 3:19:1; Cyril of Alexandria, *In Ioannem* 1:13; PG 73:156; Athanasius, *adversus Arianos* iv 2:59; PG 26:273). Grace is the divine gift of filial adoption (Irenaeus, *adv. haer.* 3:19:1). By grace we share in the divine nature (Athanasius, *ep. 4 ad Serapionem* 1:24; PG 26:585). Our divinization by the indwelling of the Word (Athanasius, *adv. Arianos* 3:24; PG 26:373) or of the Spirit (Athanasius, *ep. 4 ad Serapionem* 1:24; PG 26:585; Basil, *de Spiritu sancto* 9:22; PG 32:109; Cyril of Alexandria, *In Ioan.* 1:9; PG 73:175) is proof of their divinity. Divinization in fact means both union and assimilation with God; it involves a change in the soul inhabited by the Word or the Spirit or the Trinity (Athanasius, *adv. Arianos* 3:24; PG 26:373; John Chrysostom, *in ep. ad Rom.* 13:8; PG 60:519), after

the manner in which a piece of iron thrown into the fire turns white-hot (Cyril of Jerusalem, *Catecheses* 17:14; PG 33:985), or a crystal is lit up when struck by a ray of the sun (Basil, *de Spiritu sancto* 9:22; PG 32:109). The emphasis of the Greek Fathers, however, is on our union with God rather than on the assimilation, on the 'Uncreated Grace' or the indwelling God rather than on the created gift of grace. But they are aware of the two aspects in our divinization. It is right, no doubt, to sum up their teaching in the phrase of the pseudo-Dionysius (correcting as far as is needed, the neo-platonic connotation of our own active part in this divinization): 'Divinization is assimilation and union with God as far as possible' (*de ecclesiastica hierarchia* 1:3; PG 3:373).[1]

Does divinization involve or presuppose remission of sin? Does the initiative lie with God or with us? The Greek Fathers, generally speaking, are well-nigh silent on these points which Augustine was to emphasize so strongly. They generally relate our divinization less to Christ's redemption than to the Incarnation (cf. above, the purpose of the Incarnation). Yet, St Irenaeus with his doctrine on our recapitulation in Christ (*adv. haer.* 1:3:4; 3:18:7) connects grace with the fall (*adv. haer.* 3:18:2; 23:1), with Christ's death and resurrection (*adv. haer.* 1:10:1) and with the vivifying Spirit (*adv. haer.* 5:9:1) as spirit of adoption (*adv. haer.* 4:1:1). The 'illumination' at baptism appears to them, because of their undeveloped concept of original sin, less as forgiveness than as a positive sanctification; John Chrysostom (*hom. ad Neophytos*, cited by Augustine *c. Iulian.* 1:6, 21; PL 44:654), who says that infants are baptized 'though they have no sin', is the classical difficulty on the point. He also, typical among Greek Fathers, speaks of our initiative in grace in a way which seems to anticipate the semi-Pelagian error: we choose, God leads to fulfilment (*hom. 12 in Hebr.* 3; PG 63:99 f.); yet he knows that God opens the heart to the faith (*in Ac.* 16; PG 60:254), faith is His gift (*hom. in 2 Cor 4:13*; PG 51:276). It remains, then, that the Greek 'theology of grace' is above all concerned with our divinization, less with our liberation from sin and free co-operation with grace.

IV Grace in the Latin Fathers. Among the Latin Fathers, it is particularly the Doctor of grace who emphasized the sin-forgiving role of grace and the problem of our free co-operation; he and they generally stress much less the divinizing function of grace. Before Augustine, there is little explicit teaching on grace. Tertullian does oppose nature and grace (*de anima* 21; PL 2:658) or the image of God through creation to the likeness with Him through the Spirit of baptism (*de baptismo* 5; PL 1:1205). Cyprian, hardly mentioning the term grace, speaks in glowing words of our rebirth in baptism which means forgiveness of sin and a new life (*ad Donatum* 4; PL 4:200), and of our need of God's help to do His will (*de dominica oratione* 14; PL

[1] Ἡ δὲ θέωσίς ἐστιν ἡ πρὸς θεόν ὡς ἐφικτόν ἀφομοίωσίς τε καὶ ἕνωσις.

4:528). But not until Augustine took up the defence of Christ the Redeemer of all men and of the grace we receive from Him as a healing of our fallen nature and an elevation to adoptive sonship of God, do we get a theology of grace.

Pelagius and the Pelagians, who denied Original sin, called grace man's free will, a gift of God, or at most allowed for the external divine helps provided by the preaching of the gospel (see PELAGIANS). Against them Augustine vindicated the Christian doctrine of grace. This setting explains his approach to the problem, a very different one from that of the Greek Fathers. He does have, it is true, an explicit doctrine on our divinization. For him also the purpose of the Incarnation is our sharing in the divine nature (ep. 140:4:10 ; PL 33:542), our divine adoptive filiation (ep. 140:3:9 ; PL 33:541 ; serm. 146:4 ; PL 38:909). Our grace is grace of the members of Christ (de praedestinatione sanctorum 15:31 ; PL 44:982). Grace means a real change of our substance (de Trinitate 15:15:31 ; PL 42:1882), a re-formation or re-creation of God's image in us (de spiritu et littera 22:37 ; PL 44:223). And it entails the indwelling of the Spirit and the Trinity (de Trinitate 15:18:32; PL 42:1082), an indwelling that starts with the illumination at baptism. Augustine, unlike the Greek Fathers, attributes this illumination to the Word rather than to the Three Persons (de Trin. 4:2:4 ; PL 42:889), just as he refers the gift of charity to the Holy Spirit, after Rom 5:5 (de Trin. 15:18:32 ; PL 42:1082). Augustine then is no less definite about our divinization than the Greek Fathers.

Yet his controversies with the Pelagians led him to stress the healing role of Christ's redemptive grace in a manner unknown before. It is mainly to show our need of grace because of the fall that he spent the last twenty years of his life writing against the 'enemies' of Christian grace. Here his teaching on grace is correlative to his doctrine on the fall and its consequences. By Adam's sin mankind has become a mass of perdition, condemned to death of body and soul. Human nature is wounded and subject to concupiscence (de nuptiis et concupiscentia 1:23:25 ; PL 44:428). Man's free will is no longer able to do the good he wishes, his is a wounded liberty inclined to evil rather than to good (contra duas ep. Pelagianorum 1:2:5 ; PL 44:552). His faculty of free choice is not lost but it is not liberated (de correptione et gratia 13:42 ; PL 44:942 [1] ; cf. 11:31 ; PL 44:935). Only the grace of Christ can restore his power to do good (de correptione et gratia 11:31 ; PL 44:935).

Thus Augustine derives the necessity of grace—a help without which we cannot do good—less from the supernaturalness of our goal than from our need of redemption from the fall (de gestis Pelagii 1:3 ; PL 44:321 ; de correptione et gratia 12:34 ; PL 44:936). So also its gratuity (de gestis Pelagii 14:33 ; PL 44:340) which was to be his chief argument against the semi-Pelagians (de praedestinatione sanctorum 2:3 ; PL 44:961) rests mainly on fallen man's inability to do good by himself (de gratia et libero arbitrio 5:12 ; PL 44:889). Grace comes to liberate free will.

[1] Arbitrium, inquam, liberum, non liberatum.

About the 'reconciliation' of grace and free will, Augustine did not attempt a systematic explanation. When he writes his de gratia et libero arbitrio (426–7), it is to affirm the co-existence of both rather than to show how they work together (cf. de peccatorum meritis 2:18:28 ; PL 44:168). There is, however, an evolution in his manner of proposing the problem. In his earlier works he stresses the will's power to consent to grace or refuse its consent (de spiritu et littera 34:60 ; PL 44:240), while in his latest works he emphasizes the power of grace effectively and inescapably guiding the will (de correptione et gratia 12:38 ; PL 44:939). This evolution is dependent on that of his views about the salvific will of God and predestination (see PREDESTINATION). Must we say that Augustine's definitive view on the question may be summed up in his idea of 'triumphant delectation' (delectatio victrix ; cf. In ep. ad Gal. expositio 49 ; PL 40:111 ; de peccatorum meritis 2:19:32 ; PL 44:170) ? The date at which he formulated the principle (393–6), at a time when he explicitly affirmed free will, suggests that this idea does not exclude, but rather includes, free will. A similar explanation should hold good for what he calls the help by which we do good (auxilium quo), a remote forerunner of 'efficacious grace' (de correptione et gratia 12:34 ; PL 44:936).

It remains, however, that Augustine's paradoxical and rigid insistence on the power of grace and on predestination (on the connection of these cf. de praedestinatione sanctorum 10:19 ; PL 44:974) partly explains the protests, if not the error, of those later to be called semi-Pelagians (see SEMI-PELAGIANS). They meant to save free will by withdrawing from 'irresistible' grace the beginning of faith and the fact of perseverance. Augustine would only stiffen his position in his works against them (especially the last two, de praedestinatione sanctorum and de dono perseverantiae). Here also his reason for asserting the all-embracing power of divine grace, from the beginning till the end of man's way to salvation, is drawn from the redemptive or healing function of grace. It is this Augustinian approach to the doctrine of grace (though not suppressing, yet relegating to a second place, his earlier teaching on our divinization) that was to have a definitive influence both on the Fathers of the West, his contemporaries and followers, and on the origin and development of the Scholastic doctrine on grace.

V Grace in medieval scholasticism. The early Scholastic doctrine on grace, in the centuries that mark the transition from patristic to scholastic theology, is thoroughly influenced, even dominated, by St Augustine's ideas. This predominance occasioned in the 9th cent. Gottschalk's predestinationism which hardened Augustine's views into an error, a theory of a twofold predestination, one to glory and another to eternal death, with the inevitable implication that saving grace is not offered and given to all. Predestinational tendencies, even after the condemnation of the error at the council of Quercy (853 ; D 316), were slow in dying and would revive at the time of the Reformation. The father of Scholasticism, St Anselm of Canterbury (d.1109), was Augustinian in his approach to the doctrine of grace seen in the setting of the fall and of predestination, and in his world of ideas. Yet he showed a degree of independence by the stress he laid on free will, partly as a consequence of his relatively new idea of Original sin as privation of original justice ; but he remains Augustinian in attributing all good to grace. His new Augustinism, however, found little immediate following. It is rather the Augustinism of all-powerful grace and predestination that marks the medieval collections of sentences from the Fathers, the first attempts at systematizing the traditional doctrine. At the time when the new 'scholastic' concepts were elaborated which ushered in a new climate in theological thought, many a point of doctrine remains unsatisfactory, as also in the *Summa* of Peter Lombard (d.1160). His identification of charity with the Holy Spirit, and the more or less semi-Pelagian way of some others in explaining man's preparation for grace, would require rectification.

A. Landgraf, in his scholarly research on early Scholasticism [1] has studied the genesis of many a scholastic doctrine on grace. To give one example only, the scholastic idea of sanctifying grace as a permanent created reality in the soul (*habitus*) was arrived at gradually : at first faith and charity were mentioned without specifying whether they were acts or permanent dispositions ; then they were conceived as permanent *habitus* ; and finally distinguished from the permanent disposition that is grace (op. cit., I:219). Both the interest and the importance of early Scholasticism with regard to the doctrine of grace lie not merely in the preservation of the Augustinian inheritance but more in the elaboration of the scholastic method and terminology.

It is the High Scholasticism of the 13th cent., specifically St Thomas Aquinas (d.1274), that was to bring the method and terminology and also the doctrine on grace to a definite, if relative, perfection by the synthesis of Augustinism and Aristotelianism. His adoption and christianization of the Philosopher's metaphysics and his use of it for the conceptual expression of the theology of grace are the adult age of Medieval Scholasticism. The two characteristic features of that theology, its 'realism' based on a confident intellectualism or trust in human reason, and its organic structure in which all elements condition one another, give it a permanent value till our day. By the bold application of the concept of *habitus* to the life of grace and characterizing sanctifying grace as a permanent quality in the soul (*Summa*, 1–2ae:110:2c) St Thomas shifts the centre of gravity from 'actual grace' to 'habitual grace' and thus modifies radically the then current Augustinism. Of the Augustinian approach he keeps the connection between forgiveness of sin and infusion of grace ; but his organic conception of the process that is justification, in which the two condition each other

[1] A. Landgraf, *Dogmengeschichte der Frühscholastik, I–II : Die Gnadenlehre* (1952–3).

and are inseparable as the negative and positive sides of one event (*Summa*, 1–2ae:113:2c) lays the stress on the positive outcome, that is, on the sanctification or divinization of the justified soul which is raised to a certain divine being or shares in the divine nature. Thus he rediscovers, if not the doctrine of the Greek Fathers, at any rate the too-neglected positive part of St Augustine's doctrine on grace, that of our divinization. And by making our free co-operation an intrinsic element, by way of disposition of grace, in the very process of justification (*Summa*, 1–2ae: 113:3c), St Thomas lays down a root principle for the problem of grace and free will. The rediscovery of the divinizing role of grace also led him to connect our state of grace with the divine indwelling ; yet, because in keeping with the plan of his *Summa*, he treated of the divine missions in the tract on the Trinity (*Summa*, 1a:43:3c) and not in that on grace ; the divine indwelling is mentioned there only cursorily (cf. *Summa*, 1–2ae:114:3c, @3), it is not fully integrated in his theology of grace. It remains that St Thomas's remarkable synthesis of the two phases and the two aspects of the Augustinian doctrine on grace, on the one hand, that of the 'elevating' and of the healing functions of grace, and on the other that of habitual grace next and prior to actual grace, is the acme of Scholastic teaching on grace.

St Thomas's synthesis was not the only one in the field. There was also the Franciscan school, which gave the primacy to love rather than to the intellect. In its early days, with St Bonaventure (d.1274), it shared to a large extent the 'realism' of the Angelic Doctor and differed only in more or less secondary points of doctrine, for example, the relation between sanctifying grace and charity which is held for an identity of the two. With Scotus (d.1308), the doctor of subtle distinctions, the organic structure of the theology of grace is loosened, when, for instance, the interconnection between forgiveness of sin and infusion of grace, however necessary, is no longer conceived as flowing from the very nature of things but as the effect of God's disposition. This speculative dissociation between the objective order of things and the divine disposition establishing it—a logical sequel to a voluntarism that lays the ultimate reason of things in God's will rather than in the divine intellect—may not have notably harmed Scotus's own acceptance of the objective reality of grace. It was none the less a natural precursor of Occam's Nominalism. This Franciscan (d.1349) went one step further in the dissociation just mentioned : forgiveness of sin and infusion of grace do not go together of necessity, but only by divine decree ; God could decree otherwise and give grace without removing sin. This 'deviationism' spells the ruin of St Thomas's organic theology of grace. And it announces a theory of 'forensic' justification in which God is not only said to be able to, but in fact does, give grace without removing sin.

VI Grace in Tridentine and post-Tridentine scholasticism. The development of Scholastic teaching on grace after Trent no less than that of the Middle Ages is largely the history of Augustinian ideas, just as the doctrinal errors on grace originated in a misunderstanding of Augustine's doctrine.

Luther's theology of grace, historically prepared by Nominalism, took the further step left open by Occam : God actually bestows His favour, or grace, on a sinner without forgiving his sin (cf. D 742). His three basic ideas on justification (man's radical corruption by Original sin (cf. D 776), extrinsic imputation of Christ's merits (D 821), and justification by faith alone (D 819)) presuppose a Nominalist theology of grace. His theology moves on the psychological rather than the ontological plane. It has, no doubt, its own religious values (cf. Rondet, *Gratia Christi*, 259 f.) but it is basically a misinterpretation of both St Paul and St Augustine.

The reaction at the Council of Trent reasserted the two poles about which the traditional doctrine of grace turns : the objective reality of the sinner's justification (D 799) and the essential role of man's free co-operation (ibid.), both of which were set aside or made void by the Reformers. These are the two essential theses in the Catholic understanding of Augustine's teaching. Tridentine and post-Tridentine Scholastics laboured to uphold these basic truths of the faith. They did so in defence of the teaching of Trent. They even went beyond that teaching by overstressing one-sidedly the point they wished to make ; that was in actual history the case with both the above-mentioned doctrines.

The need for emphasizing the reality of 'created' grace, in the face of Protestant Nominalism, entailed the danger of reifying that grace and overlooking or neglecting its connection with Uncreated Grace. Grace, in fact, is essentially a link with the indwelling God. Trent's stress on the unique formal cause of our justification (D 799), and also the Protestant idea of the imputation of Christ's merits or of God's justice, explain the one-sided emphasis on created grace. All the more so that later in the Catholic camp a legalist and 'extrinsical' concept of the life of grace proposed by Baius (d.1589 ; cf. D 1042) maintained and enhanced the need of stressing the reality of the life of grace (*see* BAIUS). But this 'reification' of grace, considered more as a form or perfection existing in its own right than as a link with Uncreated Grace, could not but lead to an impoverished theology of the life of grace. Besides, subsequent historical events led to a partial neglect of the study of habitual grace.

In fact, the Tridentine emphasis on man's free co-operation with grace in the three stages of the life of grace—the preparation of justification (D 798, 814), the infusion of sanctifying grace (D 799) and the growth in grace by meritorious acts (D 809, 842) —led post-Tridentine theology to give to the problem an importance out of proportion with its real value. While the faith vouches for the fact that free will remains and is perfected in co-operating with grace (D 814), theology raised the problem of how to reconcile divine grace and man's free co-operation. It is at this historical and doctrinal juncture that we witness the birth of the various Catholic systems of grace. Their main intent was to

propose a rational explanation of the collaboration of grace and free will. Their rise was in a way inevitable. It was normal for theology not to rest content with affirming the co-existence of grace and free will but to endeavour to show how they co-exist. Only thus could the Protestant error really be overcome. And with the different schools of theology within the Church that explanation could not but differ in some respects. Again, another historical error within the Catholic fold made the need for an explanation doubly urgent. The Jansenist pseudo-Augustinian doctrine of irresistible grace (cf. D 1093) with its elimination of our free co-operation could be opposed effectively only by a theology of grace which maintained no less the reality of man's free co-operation than the absolute necessity of divine grace (*see* JANSENISM).

The rise of these systems of grace gave occasion to heated controversies. Both Dominicans and Jesuits keenly defended their respective explanations : the first maintaining that divine grace is effective of itself and not from outside, yet does not eliminate man's freedom in co-operating ; the latter emphasizing first of all our free co-operation and thus concluding that grace is effective not of itself but from outside or not without our co-operation. The renowned Congregations *de auxiliis* (1598–1607), which by order of Clement VIII transferred the dispute to the papal court, did not, despite their 85 sessions, lead to any positive result. The final papal decision of Paul V, made in 1607 (D 1090), left the dispute unsettled and allowed both sides to maintain their positions within the Catholic orthodoxy, a decision reiterated fifty years later by Innocent X (1654 ; D 1097). Till today this remains the official Roman judgment on the systems of grace. The practical outcome of these rather sterile controversies was a one-sided stressing of 'actual grace' and a neglect of sanctifying grace, an imbalance which hampered the teaching on grace for three centuries.

Only in the second half of the 19th cent., with the work of M. Scheeben (d.1888) and the revival of positive theology and, later, of Thomism (under Leo XIII), did a reaction set in towards a more balanced theology of grace. This is reaching its maturity in our day. As a consequence, the study of sanctifying grace takes precedence over that of actual grace, and so the disputes over the systems of grace are relegated to a secondary place ; not only created grace but Uncreated Grace also or the divine indwelling is given its proper place.

VII Church documents on grace. The official documents of the Church may be grouped round a few historical occasions. The first is the rise of the Pelagian and semi-Pelagian errors which attributed to man's free will, unaffected by the fall, the whole or at least the beginning and end of salvation. These were set aside (*a*) by the 16th Council of Carthage (418, approved by Pope Zosimus) which taught the necessity of grace, its internal character, its healing function (D 103–5) ; (*b*) by the catalogue (*indiculus*) of Pope Celestine I (between 435–42 ; the work of St Prosper of Aquitaine) which insisted on the necessity of grace for all that is good in man, from beginning to end, and on its liberating effect on free will (D 129–42) ; (c) by the Council of Orange (529, confirmed by Boniface II) which sums up the Catholic doctrine on grace against the semi-Pelagians : universal need for grace for all that is helpful towards eternal life, grace involving infusion and inspiration of the Holy Spirit (D 176–200). In all these documents the main reason for the necessity of grace is Original sin and its consequences, or the healing function of grace.

A second historical occasion for the Church's teaching on grace came ten centuries later, at the time of the Reformation. Against the Protestant errors the Church at Trent opposed her decree on justification (1547). The decree insists on the need of a preparation for justification in which the help of grace takes the initiative and gives effectiveness (D 797 f.), on the reality of our justification, in which not only sin is really forgiven but grace and virtues are infused as a new life of the members of Christ (D 799 f.), and on the free co-operation of man both before, in and after the infusion of sanctifying grace (D 798, 799, 803), its specific outcome in its last stage being our merit of increase in grace and of life eternal (D 809 f.). Though the healing function of grace is not overlooked, it is no longer here the only or decisive reason for the necessity and proper role of grace.

Twenty years later the condemnation of the errors of Baius (1567), particularly those concerning free will, inherent justice and merit as a fruit of grace, reaffirmed by implication the teaching of Trent on the objective reality of our life of grace (D 1025, 35, 40 ; 1042, 63 f., 69 ; 1014 f.).

A third occasion for an official decision on the doctrine on grace (after the already-mentioned conclusion of the de auxiliis controversies) was the condemnation of the Jansenist errors, first in 1653, in the five propositions of Jansenius (D 1092–6), then in 1713 in the errors of Quesnel (D 1351–1451), and again in 1794, in the errors of the synod of Pistoia (D 1501–99). The core of these errors was the false concept of irresistible grace, with the corollary of a restricted dispensation of grace.

To this list of documents should be added the teaching in our own day of Pius XII in his encyclical on the mystical Body of Christ (1943) which explains, with regard to the doctrine of grace, the Christo-centric and 'ecclesial' character of the life of grace (cf. D 2286 and 2288). Faith seeks understanding. The systematic theology of grace, based on revelation as proposed by the Church, seeks to get some insight into the mystery of grace.

VIII Relation of grace to Christ and to the Church. In the present state of fallen and redeemed mankind, our life of grace comes to us through Christ : He offers it to all and grants it to those who accept. As grace comes from Christ, it also incorporates us into Him : it joins us to Him as the branches to the Vine or the members to the Body, and there is a sort of identity of life between Him and us ; we share in His capital grace, the overflow as it were of

His own created grace into His members. Our grace is identical with His, not numerically but specifically, with this difference, however, that His is infinite and absolutely perfect, ours is participated and imperfect.

Because the Church is Christ continued on earth, grace comes to us through the Church and incorporates into the Church. The Church's sanctifying function is the dispensation of graces ; it is in the first place sacramental, working through the Eucharist as sacrifice and sacrament, and the other six sacraments, and further through the sacramentals; it is also intercessional through prayer. This two-fold sanctifying action is world-embracing and reaches beyond the pale of her visible fold to give graces to non-Christians. Grace also incorporates into the Church as the Mystical Body of Christ ; it is of its essence social or communal. Grace of Christians is grace of members.

X Sanctifying grace. This is the permanent, vital principle of the life of grace, an internal, supernatural gift which 'divinizes' us and makes us sharers in the divine life. More commonly it is conceived as distinct from the infused love of God called charity, as supernaturalizing the essence of the soul.

(a) Justification. The starting-point for all men is sin, whether Original only or also personal (see JUSTIFICATION). The passing over from the state of sin to the state of grace is justification. This is not only deletion of sin but also infusion of a new life of union with God. The sinner is made just, he receives sanctifying grace with the virtues and gifts. This renewal is not of itself a psychological event ; it takes place on a level of reality of which we have only an indirect awareness from its signs and causes. The two effects, forgiveness of sin and infusion of grace, are inseparable of their nature ; withdrawal from sin is return to God ; there is no middle state between sin and grace.

Justification takes place in an instant but normally requires a gradual preparation in keeping with our nature. The initiative of it comes from God in two ways : first by the external grace of the Church's preaching (only abnormally can this be dispensed with and supplied for by the prompting of internal grace). This latter is absolutely necessary because of the supernaturalness of the life of grace and because of man's fallen state. Grace is both elevating and healing. The external and internal calls of grace address themselves to man's free consent. Grace respects freedom, which is the expression of our personality. Conversion, therefore, to the faith, or to the life of grace, cannot but be free. There can be no forced conversions (see CONVERSION).

(b) Created and Uncreated Grace. Sanctifying grace is not merely a form or perfection inherent in the soul and transforming it after the divine likeness. It is also of its very essence a link with the indwelling God ; it unites with the Uncreated Grace and initiates a communion of life with the divine Persons. This is, in fact, its chief function. The life of grace, sharing in the divine life, is in the first place God's self-gift to men. Created grace makes that self-gift of God and our union with Him a real fact ;

without a change in us that gift would not be real, since it can mean no change in God.

Grace raises us to a personal encounter and communion with the Triune God. There lies the difference between nature and grace : in the order of nature, or by virtue of our creaturely dependence, we face God as Creator and Lord (His 'function' towards creatures), in the order of grace we face Him as Triune, as Persons, in a triune relationship (*see* INDWELLING OF THE TRINITY).

Created grace and Uncreated Grace are inseparable, they are correlatives. They are two sides of our divinization : assimilation and union with God. This manner of conceiving their connection is more true to reality than the once more or less traditional way of calling the divine indwelling a formal effect of grace. As Fr Galtier has it, 'the opinion is growing ever more common which holds that the special indwelling of God in the soul belongs to the very idea of the formal cause of our justification' (*De SS Trinitate in se et in nobis*, [1933] 288). Created, sanctifying grace, the one formal cause of our justification, is inconceivable without the Uncreated Grace, the quasi-formal cause of our sanctification.

(*c*) *Formal effects*. The riches involved in the mystery of grace are unfolded in its formal effects flowing from the 'form' that is grace. Chief among these is our 'divinization', the transformation following on our union with the Triune God. It affects us as persons and in our nature. Our persons are 'divinized' by our divine adoption. By grace we become sons of God by an adoption which is not purely legal but is a rebirth. Our adoptive filiation is a participation of the natural filiation of Christ who is the only begotten Son of the Father (cf. E. Mersch, 'Filii in Filio', in NRT 65 (1938) 551 f., 681 ff., 809 ff.). Our nature is divinized by a sharing in the divine nature. Our union and assimilation with the Triune God through grace enable us to have a part in the knowledge and love which is the inner life of the Blessed Trinity. In faith, hope and charity we anticipate in a real manner the dynamic transformation of the beatifying vision of God.

There are more manifestations of the riches of grace. Grace makes us just, not merely negatively as being without sin but positively, with a rectitude by which we are as God wishes us to be. Grace makes us holy ; it consecrates us to God in a dedication which is meant to be definitive and all-encompassing. Grace makes us friends of God in the friendship of the sons who seek to please their Father in all things and seek Him rather than His gifts. Grace makes us heirs to eternal life ; as sons of God on pilgrimage to heaven we wait for the moment when the veil will be rent and allow us to enter into the full divine inheritance of which now we possess the pledge and first fruits.

All these glories of divine grace we possess in common as members of the Body of Christ and members of one another. Our life of grace is social; we are helped by helping one another, that mutual help being expressed in prayer and merit of congruity (*see* PRAYER).

(*d*) *Characteristics*. Sanctifying grace with God's self-gift is not of the same degree in all the just. The difference comes from the measure of the divine gift and from each one's disposition, the two commanding each other in a mysterious manner. In all the just, until they reach the end of their pilgrimage, grace can and is meant to grow ; it is but a beginning of glory. Its growth consists in an ever deeper rooting in our souls and a more extensive hold on, and Godward orientation of, our entire being. But grace, according to common teaching, cannot decrease. Its habitual state of perfection is not affected either by venial sin or by remissness in its activity. The fervour of this activity may cool down, but God's gift is without repentance : as He gave it without our merit, so He continues His gift even when it is unappreciated or unexploited. Grace can be lost. Except for those pillars of the Church, such as the Blessed Virgin and the Apostles, of whom it is traditionally held that they were confirmed in grace, sanctifying grace can be lost, and it is lost by grave sin. But lost grace can always be recovered by repentance ; no sin is irremissible in this world. All these characteristics reveal the imperfect state of the grace of pilgrims and of fallen and redeemed men.

The dynamic character of sanctifying grace appears in the gifts that go with it. Being a vital principle of activity, a super-nature, it has its own quasi-potencies through which it acts, namely, the infused virtues : faith, hope and charity, which are principles of a theological life centred in God, and also, according to the more common view, the infused moral virtues which supernaturalize our activity towards created things and persons (*see* VIRTUES). And because the life of grace is the life of the sons of God led by the Spirit of God, they must be receptive to His guidance ; the gifts of the Holy Spirit (*see* GIFTS) make us docile to His inspirations.

XI Actual grace. This is the passing supernatural help which the Holy Spirit grants, in the shape of good thoughts and desires, light for the mind and strength and love for the will, for the just to live their life of grace, and for sinners to come to the state of grace.

1. Necessity. Both sinners and just are in need of actual grace. Sinners need it to prepare for justification by free supernatural acts of faith, hope, repentance, love. The just need it for the meritorious acts by which they must grow in grace.

The basic reason for our need of actual grace is that the activity of the life of grace is supernatural. Herein lies its elevating role. And because of our fallen state, in which even after redemption and baptism we remain with concupiscence (*see* CONCUPISCENCE), we are in need of healing grace. Without this help we are unable to keep free from grave sin for long, given the temptations to which we are inevitably exposed. Even with that help we are liable to sin venially now and then ; only by a special privilege, such as the Church believes was granted to the Blessed Virgin, could we avoid every venial sin. With the help of healing grace, but not without it, we are able to continue in the state of grace even for a lifetime.

2. Nature. Actual grace given to sinners is distinct from sanctifying grace (which they do not have). In the just it may perhaps be conceived as the activation of sanctifying grace ; at any rate, it is a help for supernatural acts, for both mind and will. It normally passes through two stages in its development, in keeping with the psychology of man's moral activity. This activity starts with indeliberate acts, lights of the mind and affections of the will, which are in us without our doing. On these follows a free or deliberate act whether of consent or refusal. So also in our supernatural activity the first stage is that of indeliberate acts ; and the actual grace which arouses and supernaturalizes these is ' awaking grace ' (*gratia excitans*), also called prevenient. When the deliberate act which follows is not a refusal but a consent to grace, then actual grace becomes ' helping grace ' (*gratia adiuvans*), also called concomitant or following. All this is practically common teaching, though at times worded somewhat differently. Differences start when it is asked : what exactly is the divine help of grace ? Some answer that it is the indeliberate acts which God causes in us without ourselves with a view to bringing about our free consent to His invitation. Others say that it is not those acts, which are vital acts of our own faculties, but that it is the supernatural influence of God which causes these acts and makes them supernatural. This difference in concept of the nature of actual grace is linked with the difference of conceiving its effect.

3. Effect : systems of grace. When free consent to the invitation of grace is withheld, then awaking grace fails to develop into helping grace ; then actual grace is purely sufficient (and not efficacious : i.e. through man's fault it fails to lead to the good act for which it was given). When free consent is given, then grace is called efficacious, because it achieves the purpose for which it was offered.

What is the reason why in some cases grace leads to our free consent and in others it does not ? The answer given to this question is what characterizes the various systems of grace, that is, the attempts at explaining the manner of the co-operation of grace and free will. These systems are commanded by different concepts of predestination (*see* PREDESTINATION). They are divided into two main categories : one holds that grace is efficacious of itself or from inside (*ab intrinseco*), the other that it is efficacious from outside (*ab extrinseco*).

To explain the difference between the two, theologians distinguish three moments in the development of actual grace which entails our free consent. At the first it is ' sufficient ' (to bring about our free consent) ; it is potentially efficacious ; at the second, the moment preceding the actual free consent, it is efficacious ' in first act ' (*in actu primo*) or is going to be actually efficacious ; in the third, the moment when the free consent is given, it is efficacious ' in second act ' (*in actu secundo*) or is actually efficacious. Now the difference between the two systems lies in the moment where they place the objective difference

between a grace that is efficacious and one that remains purely sufficient. That moment is not the first, all agree to say ; but the second, so say the systems which hold that grace is efficacious of itself ; or the third, so say the systems which hold that grace is efficacious from outside. The first systems of grace will be explained in the article PREDESTINATION. Here we briefly indicate the setting of the second.

When divine predestination is conceived as taking into account the merits which God foresees will follow upon our free co-operation with grace, the efficacious grace is said to be the one divine help which God gives out of many possible graces and one which He foresees will in fact entail our free consent. Why does that grace entail our free consent ? Here a two-fold answer is given. In pure Molinism (*see* MOLINA) which holds predestination to grace and glory, the only reason is said to be God's prescience of our consent (which is perhaps a way of escaping to answer). In Congruism (*see* CONGRUISM) which rather holds predestination to glory before the prevision of merits, it is said to be that same prescience, but with the additional reason of the congruity or suitableness of the grace picked by God for the situation in which we find ourselves. The point in the two systems is that free consent could not be given but for grace, yet free consent means self-determination and not determination by another. Grace then is not efficacious of itself (at the second moment of its development it contains nothing more than is found in a grace which would remain purely sufficient) ; nor is it made efficacious by our free consent (grace is in no way determined by our consent) ; it is efficacious ' in first act ' by God's favour, who chose the grace He foresaw would be efficacious in preference to another. This divine preference shows also how in these systems efficacious grace ' in first act ' is a greater divine favour than a purely sufficient grace, though it contains nothing more, entitatively ; because it is a sign of greater love of God. The effect of that greater love follows at once when grace is actually efficacious. Then, when the consent is given, actual grace reaches its full development by God's favour and awakening grace becomes helping grace. But the ultimate reason both of the divine preference and of the free self-determination remains a hidden mystery.

4. Distribution. Actual graces are offered to all men, because God wants all men to be saved. All receive at one time or another sufficient grace to lead them to justification, at least remotely if not proximately sufficient ; generally the preparation for justification is a gradual process, fidelity to one grace entails new grace. But because some refuse to co-operate with the grace offered, efficacious grace for actual justification and salvation is not given to all.

The providential ways of this dispensation of graces are mysterious. Normally internal graces require external graces or such a setting of life as suits a Christian. That normal setting is the Catholic fold with its many sacramental and other social means of grace. But God can and does also give grace without these ; He is not bound by His own institutional or sacramental means of grace.

For the building up of this external setting of the Christian life God also dispenses 'communal' or 'gratuitously given' graces (*gratis datae*), namely such graces as are not meant directly for the sanctification of those who receive them but for the common good of the Body of Christ. Such are the charisms of the early Church and of all times (*see* CHARISMS). Such are also the functional graces of state given for the proper discharge of a function within the Church.

XII Growth in grace. According to the Catholic idea of the economy of grace, Christ our Saviour wants us to be the artisans of our own salvation as far as we can with His help. The life of grace is a collaboration between God and men. Besides the reception of the sacraments (*see* SACRAMENTS) which restore or increase grace, the good actions by which we live the life of grace lead to its growth. In these good actions there is a three-fold co-operation with grace, in keeping with the three-fold object or means for growth which it is meant to secure.

First, we merit by them an increase in sanctifying grace by way of condign merit (*see* MERIT). As every vital activity, so also supernatural activity brings about the development of its principle ; there is an intrinsic and immediate link between the two, and this is the basis of strict merit. Secondly, the increase in grace is a call for further growth and for further good actions for which actual graces are needed ; and so we merit by way of 'merit of congruity' sufficient graces for those actions ; there is an intrinsic but mediate link between the two. Finally, the further meritorious actions by which we grow in grace cannot actually be done without the help of efficacious grace ; these we cannot merit in any way (because there is no intrinsic link, whether direct or indirect, between the good actions we do now and these further good actions, our free consent that is needed for these being uncertain) ; we can only obtain these graces in prayer. This shows the place of impetration in the development of the life of grace (*see* PRAYER).

Grace must grow until it blossoms out into glory. It does so by the gift of final perseverance. This also, as the efficacious graces it includes, we cannot merit but only obtain in prayer.

XIII Conclusion: present-day trends. In present-day theology of grace, in contrast with that of the last few centuries, the emphasis is on sanctifying rather than on actual grace. Uncreated Grace is given a central place. The Christo-centric and ecclesial characters of the life of grace are drawn into relief. So is the elevating or divinizing function of grace. All these trends are the outcome of a desire for realism in doctrine and genuineness in life, signs of healthy Catholic doctrine and life.

Bibliography. Latin manuals on Grace by Billot, Lange, Boyer, Van der Meersch. Articles on Grace in EC, DTC, LTK², *Catholicisme*, *Bijbels Woordenboek²* ; H. Rondet, *Gratia Christi : Essai d'histoire du dogme et de théologie dogmatique* (1948) ; ★W. T. Whitley (ed.), *The Doctrine of Grace* (1932) ; G. H.

Joyce, *The Catholic Doctrine of Grace* (1920) ; E. Towers, 'Actual Grace' and 'Sanctifying Grace' in G. D. Smith (ed.), *The Teaching of the Catholic Church* (1948) ; M. Scheeben, *The Glories of Divine Grace* (many editions : latest, in 5 fasc. St Meinrad, Ind., 1949–50) ; the same, *Mysteries of Christianity* (1946), esp. 613–31 ; E. Mersch, *Theology of the Mystical Body* (1951), esp. 594–639 ; J. V. Matthews, *With the Help of Thy Grace* (1944) ; the same, *The Life that is Grace* (1953) ; R. Garrigou-Lagrange, *Grace* (comm. in *Summa*, 1a–2ae:109–14) (1952) ; J. Daujat, *The Theology of Grace* (1959). On contemporary trends, P. de Letter, 'Sanctifying Grace and the Divine Indwelling', in TS 14 (1953) 244–72; the same, 'Contemporary Theology of Grace', in *Clergy Monthly* 20 (1957) 288–97, 326–36.

P. de L.

GRADUALS. *See* MUSIC and THEOLOGY

GREEK LITURGY The liturgies of St Basil and St John Chrysostom have been considered under the headings BASIL, LITURGY OF and BYZANTINE LITURGY respectively, and some of their sources in ANTIOCH, LITURGY OF. It remains here to add something about the later development of the Greek liturgy. It is admitted that by the 11th cent. the liturgy of Basil has given place to that of John Chrysostom almost everywhere and that for the whole year, with a few exceptions, but this more popular liturgy was then undergoing changes which are now hard to interpret. Rubrics were added to the text, and this imposed new interpretations on what was said, these interpretations being often due to treatises on the Mass of which that by Germanos seems to have been the earliest.

Germanos, patriarch of Constantinople (635–733), was the author of a treatise on the Mass (in PG 98) that is sometimes assigned to the second Germanos, patriarch in the 13th cent., but, as some of the details of the treatise are copied by Theodore of Andida in his own treatise (PG 140:417–68), it is hard to accept this transfer of authorship. Most recent opinion makes for the acceptance of the work as by Germanos I. He regards the church-building as 'heaven brought down to earth, where the God of heaven dwells' (PG 98:384) ; the apse (κόγχη) is said to be 'the translation of the Cross', and the holy table, 'instead of the place of burial' (ibid. 388). The altar of sacrifice is the counterpart of the heavenly and spiritual altar where the angels worship. There is still a *bema*, separated by small pillars (κιόνια) from the rest of the nave, and the seats on it are to be understood as representing the preaching of the faith. The idea that the *bema* stood for Jerusalem (whence the preaching began) is thus preserved as it had been in the early Syriac liturgy (*see* EDESSA, LITURGY OF). The place of preparation (σκευοφυλάκιον) of the sacrifice (*proskomide*) was interpreted as 'the place of the Skull' (Jn 19:17), so that the whole area of the sanctuary had assumed its role in symbolizing the places of the Passion. Some of the symbolism of Germanos is poor, as when he takes the closing of the holy doors to be the recalling of the leading of Christ as a prisoner into the house of Annas, while their opening a little later in the liturgy signifies that it is now morning and that Christ is being brought before Pilate. The source of much medieval devotion, to 'the Mass and the Passion' can be recognized here.

Germanos seems, in fact, to have been the pioneer among the Greeks of the whole series of ' explanations of the Mass ', which in Latin start with Walafrid Strabo (d.849) and of which there is an early example in Old Irish in the *Stowe Missal*. Narsai had done the same kind of service for the Syriac Church by his liturgical homilies, and it may be that here, too, the Greek Church was copying the Syriac. In 751 Pope Zachary sent to St Boniface instructions (PL 89:953) about the saying of Mass, detailing exactly at what points the sign of the cross was to be made. It is perhaps significant that Germanos, some fifty years previously, had said that the triple sign of the cross was for the sanctification of the three regions, upper air $(\alpha i\theta\eta\rho)$, air and earth (PG 98:448) ; when the liturgy took place in a church decorated with mosaics on the dome that depicted angels surrounding the heavenly sacrifice and often garbed as deacons, it would not be hard to envisage its action as taking place in three distinct spheres.

The setting for the Greek liturgy became stereotyped in the course of the 10th and 11th cents., and the use of miniatures on the margins of liturgical rolls shows in the choice of these illustrations that thought about the Mass was guided by what could be associated with its various prayers. The words of consecration might have a miniature of the communion of the Apostles set alongside, but when immediately following it there was a representation of the Baptism of Christ, to be followed at the Epiklesis by one of the Palm Sunday entry into Jerusalem, it becomes somewhat difficult to follow the connection that was seen by the artists and users of the liturgy. The descent of the Spirit on Christ at the Baptism could imply that He was always able to send the Spirit upon the offerings, as the Spirit was always with Him (*see* EPIKLESIS). The Entry may have been meant to illustrate the acclamation $\tau\grave{a}$ $\sigma\grave{a}$ $\grave{\epsilon}\kappa$ $\tau\hat{\omega}\nu$ $\sigma\hat{\omega}\nu$, which the people make just before the Epiklesis. The voice from heaven (Jn 12:28) on that occasion might be held to have its earthly counterpart in the acclamation of the faithful. The Jerusalem roll (edited by A. Grabar and dated by him to 1090–1100, *see* BIBLIOGRAPHY) has the resurrection of Christ alongside the Preface and the raising of Lazarus to follow it at the *post-Sanctus*. The one might easily be understood if it had been used with the Anamnesis, but with the Preface it has little in common ; it may be meant to show that the sacrifice about to be carried out is that of the risen Christ. The Lazarus-episode fits in well enough with the wording of the *post-Sanctus* in the Chrysostom liturgy, which speaks of the action of Christ in raising us from our lowly condition. The choice of these same topics for the mosaic decoration of the immediate neighbourhood of the altar in Greek

churches is probably governed by the same set of ideas.

Theodore of Andida (PG 140:441) sees a likeness of Palm Sunday in the offertory-procession. He compares the $\check{\epsilon}\nu\alpha\rho\xi\iota\varsigma$ at the beginning of the Mass with its penitential prayers to the ministry of John the Baptist, and the popularity of this saint in both East and West may have influenced those who introduced these prayers into the Mass. But there is no desire on the part of commentators, miniature-painters or mosaic artists to make the liturgy simply a succession of episodes answering to the sequence of events in the life of Christ. The Ascension is notable by its absence from all three. That there was not an absolute rigidity of interpretation may be seen from the fact that Germanos saw in the gospel entry the likeness of the $\grave{a}\nu\acute{a}\delta\epsilon\iota\xi\iota\varsigma$ or manifestation of Christ at His baptism. By the time of Nicholas Cabasilas (d.1341) the explanation of the liturgy has become something of a polemic against the Western Church (*see* EPIKLESIS). The use of the $\xi\acute{\epsilon}o\nu$ (hot water added to the chalice to represent the fire of the Spirit) goes back at least to the time of the emperor Maurice (582–602), for he had a dispute about it with the Catholicos of Armenia, Moses. A hymn of St John Damascene (cited from manuscripts in DACL VI:1615) proclaims without hesitation that it is Christ the Logos who sends the Spirit ' from His pierced side the divine Logos affixing the seal with the fire of the Spirit '. He is cited for this by a 13th-cent. scholiast of the liturgy who is clearly not alarmed at the doctrine : $\hat{\omega}$ $\Theta\epsilon o\hat{\upsilon}$ $\Lambda\acute{o}\gamma\epsilon$, $\grave{\epsilon}\pi\iota\sigma\phi\rho\alpha\gamma$-$\acute{\iota}\zeta\omega\nu$ $\tau\hat{\eta}$ $\zeta\acute{\epsilon}\sigma\epsilon\iota$ $\tau\grave{o}\nu$ $\pi\nu\epsilon\acute{\upsilon}\mu\alpha\tauo\varsigma$.

Influence on the West was exercised through the Latin version of Germanos made by Anastasius the librarian in 870, through the Italiote Greeks and through the many travellers to the East, before and during the Crusades (*see also* CONSECRATION).

Bibliography. H. J. Schulz, *Die byzantinische Liturgie* (1964) ; P. de Meester OSB in DACL s.v. Grecques (liturgies) ; A. Grabar, 'Un rouleau liturgique constantinopolitain, in *Dumbarton Oaks Papers* 8 (1954) 161–99.   J. H. C.

GREGORIAN SACRAMENTARY Sacramentary, *sacramentarium*, *liber sacramentorum*, a former type of celebrant's manual at Mass : it did not have Scripture lessons or choral parts ; in addition to the Canon it needed only Collects, Secret, Preface, etc., proper to the day. Three such books are widely known as the Leonine, Gelasian and Gregorian Sacramentaries. 'Whatever discussion may arise as to the exact propriety of the names which thus pass current,' says E. Bishop (*Liturgica Historica*, 40), ' they have at least the merit and advantage of clearly indicating three successive stages of liturgical development in the Roman Church.' The stages are : disorderly profusion, initial orderliness, still finer precision.

Gregory's Book of the Sacraments, as of 785, became so mixed with other things that its recovery was effected only in this century. It remains to be seen to what extent the original can be ascertained.

In this connection *Liber Pontificalis* speaks only of the Canon : *Hic augmentavit in praedicationem canonis 'diesque nostros in tua pace dispone' et cetera* (ed. Duchesne, I:312). Gregory's Canon was taken over everywhere in the West ; only verbal traces of the older Canon survive (Bishop).

Egbert of York (735–6) spoke of knowing Gregory's Missal and Antiphonary, both in England and at Rome (PL 89, 441). About 783 Charlemagne asked Rome to furnish an unaltered copy of the Sacramentary, to serve for general use. After much delay the book and letter came : 'Touching the Sacramentary arranged by our inspired predecessor Pope Gregory : as Paul the Grammarian long since asked us on your behalf, that we send you an unaltered copy, according to the tradition of our holy Church, we have sent [it] now . . .'.[1]

This book, styled *Hadrianum* (Duchesne), was for the days of the Pope's stational Mass ; it lacked Sunday Masses and other things needed in parishes. At Charlemagne's request Alcuin compiled a supplement, as long as the work itself, drawn chiefly from Gelasian sources, of things 'needed' in some degree. As published a Preface (*Hucusque*) marked off what came from Rome, and what Alcuin added, so that all could see. The plan was spoiled by copyists moving or soon dropping the Preface-*Hucusque*. Modern scholarship, studying the Preface, has found the true *Hadrianum*.

One codex preserves Hadrianum unaltered, Cambrai's Municipal Library MS. 164, which dates 811, 812. Lietzmann's 1921 edition is the only one based on it alone, *Das Sacramentarium Gregorianum nach dem Aaechener Urexemplar*. Other editions are now preparing.

Bibliography. R. Amiet, 'Les Sac. 88 et 137 . . . de Cologne', in *Scriptorium* 9 (1955) 76–84 ; N. J. Abercrombie, Alcuin and . . . Gregorianum', in *AL* 3 (1953) 99–103 ; E. Bishop, Early Texts of the Roman Canon', in *JTS* 4 (1903) 555–77 ; reprinted, *Liturgica Historica* (1918) 77–115 ; L. Duchesne, *Les Origines du culte chrétien* (1889) ; A. Ebner, *Iter Italicum* (1896) ; T. Klauser, 'Liturgischen Austauschbeziehungen . . .', in *Historisches Jahrbuch* 53 (1953) 169–89 ; G. Morin, '. . . Comes d'Alcuin', in *RB* 29 (1912) 341–9 ; E. Ranke, *Das Kirchliche Perikopensystem . . . der Römischen Liturgie* (1847) ; A. Wilmart, 'Le Lectionnaire d'Alcuin', in *Eph. Lit.* 51 (1937) 136–97 ; H. A. Wilson, *The Gregorian Sacramentary under Charles the Great* (1915).
G. E.

GUARDIAN ANGELS That angels are sent to take care, spiritually and even physically, of each human being in the world is not formally defined as a doctrine of the Church, but the beginnings of the idea in the OT (I) that are here considered and its striking confirmation by the evidence of the NT (II),

[1] De sacramentario vero a sancto disposito predecessori nostro, defluo Gregorio papa : immixtum vobis emitteremus, iam pridem Paulus grammaticus a nobis eum pro vobis petente secundum sanctae nostrae ecclesiae tradicionem, . . . vestrae regali emisimus excellentiae (MGH Epist III, 626).

along with the explanations of the Fathers and the constant devotion of the faithful (III), combine to make it a doctrine that is, if not yet ripe for definition, secure in the plain sense of Scripture and the understanding of the faithful.

I The Old Testament. The idea of a general care for Israel on the part of the angels is expressed in Ps 33:8 : 'The angel of the Lord shall encamp round about them that fear Him', and also in Ps 90:11, in the celebrated passage used by the Devil in the temptation of Christ. The vision of Daniel (7:10), that ten thousand times a hundred thousand stood before the Ancient of Days, was meant to convince him that there were angels in plenty to take care of men, and to assist at their judgment. These passages do not assert a (1:1) correspondence, but in the whole story of Tobias and the angel it is made clear that in some cases at least there could be this companionship. Rabbi Eliezer ben Yose (*Tosepta* on *Shabbat* 18:2) taught that if a just man was to go on a journey, it would be well for others to wait even three days to go with him, as the angels would certainly go with the just man. The Qumran hymns (5:21) say that angels walk at the side of the meek, and the *Manual of Discipline* (3:17) that the angel of God's truth is always there to help the sons of light.

II The NT evidence for guardian angels is quite clear. The words of Christ (Mt 18:10) about 'their angels' are beyond cavil, and the episode of Peter's knocking at the gate after his escape from prison (Ac 12:15), where the whole company tell the serving girl that the knocking must be due to 'his angel', shows what early Christian belief was on the point. The doctrine of Heb 1:14, that the angels are all ministering spirits for the sake of those who are to receive the inheritance of salvation, had thus ample foundation. The words of the angel to John (in Apoc 19:10) 'I am your fellow-slave and that of your brethren who have the witness of Jesus' can be taken as confirmation of the doctrinal statement just cited, while the practice of addressing the seven epistles in Apoc 1–3 to 'the angel of the church' at Sardis, Pergamum, etc., may be a development of the earlier belief. If an angel was concerned with each of the faithful, how much more with the bishop of the city ? It is possible that the bishop himself is being described by analogy as an angel, i.e. one entrusted with the care of Christian souls in a way similar to the charge laid upon the angels.

This doctrine leaves one matter uncertain : are the angels to guard all souls or only the believers ? In the tradition of the Church there are those who took the narrower view. Basil (on Ps 33 ; PG 29:364) and Chrysostom (*hom*. 3 on Col ; PG 62:322) incline to the idea that it is only the faithful who have angels. St Thomas (*Summa*, 1a:113:4c) is much influenced by the comment of Jerome (PL 26:130) on Mt 18:10 in favour of the broader view. The conflict of opinion is shown in the state of the text of that verse. Codex Bezae, the Itala, the Curetonian Syriac and the Sahidic have added to the words 'these little ones' the gloss : 'that believe in Me'. The gloss has come from higher up in Mt 18:6, or Mk 9:42, but it must have served to limit the scope of Christ's statement about 'their angels'.

III The Fathers and the faithful. Origen debated the question when he came to comment on Mt 18:10 (*comm.* 13:27 on Mt ; GCS 40:254-5). In favour of a general guardianship he used Ps 70:6 about God affording protection from the time of gestation in the womb, while on the other side he thought that Jud 2 (τετηρημένοις) implied that only those called by Christ had protection. In his homilies on Numbers he twice (*hom.* 5:3 and 20:3 ; GCS 30:30 and 194) refers to guardian angels as given 'to all the just' or 'to us who are in the Church of God'. It is obvious that a development of the idea of God's salvific will towards all would widen the scope of the term 'the just' in the minds of those who read Origen in later times.

Clement of Alexandria (*eclogae propheticae* 41:GCS 17:149) dabbled in some curious apocryphal writings, citing the *Apocalypse of Peter* for the belief that those infants who were the victims of abortion would have a 'watching angel' (τημελοῦχος ἄγγελος). He later (ibid. 48) amplifies this, describing how, according to this apocryphal work, the watching angel is to win for the victim of criminal abortion that destiny the infant would have had if it had lived on and suffered the ills of a full human life. The popularity of the work is indicated by the fact that for the Ethiopians the word *Tamlach* became the name for 'guardian angel', being derived from the Greek word used uniquely in this passage. While Clement may have influenced the popular imagination and theological debate about unbaptized babies, he did not have any following (apart from a reference in Methodius) in his views about what guardian angels do.

Hermas (36:1 ; GCS 48:32) has a Jewish idea of two guardian spirits for each person, one good and one evil angel. This is an elaboration of the Jewish doctrine of the two ways of life, a doctrine that was held at Qumran as well as by the Christian author of the *Epistle of Barnabas*. The Church has never shown concern about, or imposed belief in, the attachment of a personal devil to each human soul. Bellarmine (*opera*, XII:356) went so far as to say that the idea was an insult to the providence of God.

Tertullian (*de oratione* 16 ; *Corpus christianorum* 1:266) speaks of an angel of prayer who stands in the presence of God and whose function seems to have been to present the prayers of the faithful in a manner similar to what is later envisaged by the *Supplices* in the Canon of the Mass (where St Ambrose certainly had the word *angelorum* in the plural). The Talmud (*TB Berakoth* 61 b) relates how Akiba's last words before his execution were reported to God by the angel of the presence, and therefore the idea that angels perform this service for those on earth must have been common to Jews and Christians in the early centuries.

The feast of the Guardian Angels (2 October) is a much later creation, dating from the 16th or 17th cent. in different lands. The liturgy, with such chants as the *In paradisum* at a funeral, was for long familiar with the idea of angelic ministry on behalf of men, and the votive Mass of the angels (dating from the time of Alcuin, cf. G. Ellard, *Master Alcuin, Liturgist*, 148) with its gospel drawn from Jn 1:47-51 clearly implies that the angels are ministering to men through the mediation of Christ, who is, as it were, another ladder of Jacob by means of whom they ascend and descend.

The medieval doctrine is put firmly by Honorius Augustodunensis (PL 172:1154) and it is worth recalling that he may have been in possession of much earlier Irish traditions if, as is probable, he came from Cashel and not from Autun. St Thomas devoted a whole question of the *Summa* (1a:113:1-8) to the guardian angels, and posed all manner of questions about them. Was there one for Christ, for Adam before the fall, or for Antichrist ? Do they ever desert their charges, and, if not, do they grieve when their charges commit sin ? He judged that, though the text of Heb 1:14 spoke of their ministry to those who are in the way of salvation, even the unbaptized might benefit from their care by being protected from many evils. His idea was (*see* SALVATION OF UNBELIEVERS) that those to whom the gospel had never been preached might have an angel sent to them at the hour of death. In this he seems to have been influenced by the example of Cornelius (Ac 10:3), but he worked out (*Summa*, 1a:111:1@1) general grounds for the illumination of the human mind by angels. For further discussion of angelic powers *see* ANGELS.

Bibliography. E. Peterson, *The Angels in the Liturgy* (1963) ; J. Duhr SJ, in D Sp., s.v. 'anges gardiens' ; C. D. Müller, *Die Engellehre der koptischen Kirche* (1959), important for showing that the Egyptian ideas about angels, which passed through Spain to Ireland, did not come from paganism. *See also* the bibliography for ANGELS.

J. H. C.

GUENTHERIANISM The theological ideas of Anton Guenther (1783-1863) would not be of much importance today if he had not occasioned a considerable part of the dogmatic decisions of the First Vatican Council. He was an independent thinker, ordained priest in 1820, at a time when the teaching of theology was at a low ebb. He was obsessed by fear of Pantheism and, being convinced that the Fathers of the Church had admitted too much pagan thinking into their works, he struck out for himself on entirely new lines. His disciples, of whom there were many in Germany and Austria, spoke of him as *Cartesius correctus*, and indeed, his system had the same introspective beginnings as that of Descartes. By 1850 he had disciples teaching at the universities of Bonn, Tübingen, Breslau and Münster and in the seminaries of Bamberg, Trier, Paderborn and Braunsberg. His works were examined by the Congregation of the Index (1852-7), and all of them condemned (D 1655-8). As the decrees of the Index were held by many reputable theologians not to be operative in Germany, local synods at Cologne and Vienna were active in condemning him, and when the Vatican Council met it had perforce to deal with his views. Many of his disciples passed over to the Old Catholic Church after 1870.

Guenther has been called the Gnostic of the Romantic movement, and his system is difficult to analyse. The recent discovery at Rome of a dossier prepared by J. Schwetz, a Viennese theologian, for the dogmatic commission of the First Vatican Council throws much light on the way in which the condemnations were drawn up and is admirably documented from Guenther's own works. He rejected the distinction between the realm of reason and that of faith ; reason had the right to reach out and explain *why* the mysteries of faith were what they were, even if it could not say *how*, for instance, God was three-in-one. There was an Hegelian dialectic about the Trinity, with thesis, antithesis and synthesis distinguishing the Persons. To this answered an earthly trinity of spirit, nature and man, their synthesis. Just as the supernatural was the necessary complement of nature, so there was a necessity about creation ; the creature was defined as God's non-ego or the counterpoint to God, and this apparent dualism was insisted upon as the one way to escape from Pantheism. The motive of creation was said to be the altruistic sharing-out of

God's blessedness through love. In man there was a trinity of body, sensitive soul and spirit, these last two being hypostatically united to each other. It was this position about the composition of man that caused the Vatican Council (D 1783) to reiterate the teaching of the Council of Vienne on the soul as form of the body. J. Kleutgen SJ, one of the Vatican theologians, had been in sympathy with Guenther as a young man but through his patristic studies came to see that the charge of pagan thinking brought against the Fathers was not justified. He compiled a list of ten heresies in Guenther's work, including a variety of Nestorianism and a denial of the sinlessness of Christ. Much of the discussion of the system went on in pamphlets and periodicals of the day.

Bibliography. J. Kleutgen SJ, *Theologie der Vorzeit* (5 vols., 1867–74) ; A. Guenther, *Vorschule zur spekulative Theologie* (2 vols., 1828–9 and later ; it was his principal work) ; L. Orban, *Theologia guntheriana et concilium Vaticanum* (2 vols., I in 2nd edition 1950 and II, 1949) ; E. Winter, *Die geistliche Entwicklung Anton Guenthers* (1931 ; an attempt to revive the ideas of Guenther, whose whole history is very much that of a pre-Modernist).

J. H. C.

H

HAPPINESS. *See* Beatific Vision

HEART OF CHRIST The Sacred Heart devotion has led in the past three centuries to much theological debate, and the recent Scriptural revival has provided it with much firmer backing than was hitherto thought possible. This Scriptural basis will be studied briefly (I), and then (II) certain other patristic ideas connected with what might be called the typology of the devotion. The medieval justification for the practice (III), the developments subsequent to the time of St John Eudes and St Margaret Mary (IV) and the modern consolidation and definition of the devotion in the papal encyclicals (V) will be considered in turn.

I The capital text for the devotion to the Sacred Heart is Jn 7:37-8. It was not until the lengthy examination of the evidence for the variant reading here ('let him drink that believeth in Me. As the Scripture says: "Out of His belly shall flow streams, of living water"') by H. Rahner in 1941 that the use of the text to support the devotion was seen to be possible. Earlier writers (even A. Hamon, in D Sp., s.v. *Coeur*) ignore it completely. The variant reading was current throughout the West, and it may be that Origen was responsible for ousting it. Irenaeus (*adv. haer.* V:18:1, H and III:38:1, H) certainly knew and accepted the variant, for he speaks of those, 'who partake of the limpid stream that flows from the body of Christ'. Cyprian (*ep.* 63:8 and 73:11, as well as *Testimonia* 1:22, CSEL 3:706, 786 and 58) followed it, and the two works of unknown Western authors (*de rebaptismate*, 14 and *de montibus Sina et Sion*, 9) of the same period also. Some of the MSS. of the Old Latin have kept the reading, though by the time of the Vulgate the rival one had superseded it. One must notice that the reading Rahner ascribed to Origen is now discovered to be that of P 66 (which is said to be, roughly, contemporary with Origen) ; it may be, therefore, that it was not the views of Origen about the fitness of the individual Christian to be a purveyor of living water but the difficulty of finding what OT passage could be referred to in the alternative version that led to a change of reading. In the recent past the search for a suitable passage in the OT has narrowed down somewhat, and the choice seems to be between Ps 78:16 (or 77:16 LXX) with its reference to Moses and the rock and Is 12:3 or Zach 13:1. In any case John was in the habit of citing the OT rather freely, and one cannot expect an exact correspondence. It should also be noticed that on occasion Origen himself can show awareness of the reading that makes Christ Himself the source of living waters (*hom* 2 in Cant; GCS 33:167).

That not only Athanasius and the Alexandrians should have followed Origen in their use of the text, but that Theodore of Mopsuestia and Chrysostom at Antioch should have done so makes it all the more likely that the difference of reading must go back to a time before Origen and even before the making of the *Diatessaron*. This uncertainty, rooted so deep in the past, meant that the doctrinal use of the text as a witness to Christ's dispensing of grace from His wounded side escaped the notice of a large part of the tradition. That the devotion should develop in the West (where the text-form suited to it had once prevailed) and not in the East need not be regarded as surprising.

Behind Irenaeus stand the evidences of the church of Lyons (in the letter cited by Eusebius HE 5:1) and of Justin (*dial.* 34:2 and 69:3) which lead us back to Ephesus and the Johannine circle. Here, according to Papias (fragment 7), it was the practice to interpret the story of creation in terms of Christ and the Church, and the four-fold rivers of Paradise were taken to flow from that body of Christ which is the Church, in fulfilment of what Christ had said in Jn 7:37. This theme was developed by Hippolytus in his commentary on Daniel (1:17 ; GCS 1:29), and also by Cyprian (*ep.* 73:10 ; CSEL 3:785). Thus there is some likelihood that the exegesis which makes of the passage a witness to the spiritual significance of the piercing of the heart of Christ may go back to the circles which first received the gospel of John.

II Augustine, although he was influenced by the reading of Jn 7:37 which had become familiar to his contemporaries and above all to Jerome, yet found his way back to the earlier Western ideas about the piercing of the side of Christ. Twice (*contra Faustum* 12:14 ; CSEL 25:344 and *Civ. Dei* 15:26 ; CSEL 40:117) he takes up an idea that had come to him from Philo about the dimensions of the Ark. Three hundred cubits by fifty by thirty gave proportions which corresponded to those of the human body. The height would be six times the breadth of the body (at the shoulders) and ten times its thickness (from backbone to stomach). This piece of *midrash* was used by Philo (*de plantatione*, 43), and Augustine proceeded to apply it : 'The Church is prefigured by the Ark of Noah, for she is saved by the wood whereon there hung the Mediator between God and men, the man Christ Jesus. The measurements of the length, breadth and depth of the Ark signify the human body, for in such a body the Son of God was foretold as destined to come amongst men, and in fact He came. . . . And as for the fact that there was a door in the side of the Ark, that indeed is the wound where the side of the Crucified was pierced by the lance. By this opening do those who come to Him find entry, for from it there flowed forth the sacraments by which believers are made Christians.' Some twenty years separate this passage from the earlier one (*contra Faustum*, loc. cit.), and one may be assured that Augustine was not yielding to a passing fancy when he took up this *midrash* but expressing the conviction he had reached in his own meditations on Scripture.

Hippolytus in his *Blessings of Moses* (PO 27:189–90) commented on the words of the blessing of Aser: 'He shall dip his foot in oil' (Deut 33:24) thus: 'Moses said this metaphorically and in parable, for those who can understand these words in their highest sense. It means nothing more than what happened at the Passion. The blood which dripped from the side of the Saviour, blood by which His mercy was disclosed to us, bathed His feet. Then was realized the red symbol (of Ex 12:7) and the narrow gate of Life was signified, and the blood of the Lamb, for those who believe, was set as an anointing upon the two posts of the door, and the destroying angel was put to flight by Him. He will dip His foot in oil, that is, in the blood, in order that by this blood He may proclaim in advance that mercy has been done to mankind.' It is at the level of popular devotion that exegesis like this had its effect. The practice the faithful were encouraged to adopt (e.g. by Cyril of Jerusalem, *catech.* 23:22; PG 33:1125) of moistening a finger on their lips after they had received the eucharistic chalice and signing themselves on eyes, ears and breast was a simple application of what Hippolytus had said. Another glimpse of popular devotion is found in the *Physiologus* (30), that Christianized book of moralizing on the facts of natural history, where it is said that the stag attacks its enemy the serpent by shooting out streams of water from its mouth. 'The Lord slew the great dragon with the heavenly waters that He had of virtue and wisdom, as (it is written) in the Divine (i.e. in John the Divine). . . . The Lord poured out from His side blood and water, and thus slew the dragon for us by the water of regeneration.'

This warfare between stag and serpent was alluded to as a Christian allegory by many preachers among the Greek Fathers; Origen twice (*c.Cels.* 2:48; GCS 2:170 and *hom.* 2:11 in Cant; GCS 33:57) speaks of it, though he knew the alternative version of the fable, where the stag drives the serpent out of its hiding-hole by smoke from its nostrils. Basil, Cyril of Alexandria and many others take up the allegory, and by the time the Byzantine version of the *Physiologus* is reached, the allegory has become quite elaborate. The stag drives the serpent out of its hole and so devours it, but must itself find water quickly or it will die. If it find water, it will take on a new lease of life. The tale is now turned into an exhortation to the repentant sinner: 'Drink living water by partaking of the holy Gifts with contrition, and thus renew yourself for the future' (in Sbordone's edition, 174).

That the heart was the seat of the will and affections seemed plain to the Fathers from many passages

of the NT (Ac 11:23; 1 Cor 4:5 and 7:37; 2 Cor 9:7; Lk 21:14 and 24:25, 32). They coined a word to express what had often been said in the OT, that God scrutinized the hearts, i.e. the purposes of men, and it is used (καρδιογνώστης) in the very first Christian prayer on record (Ac 1:24, cf. Ac 15:8). Jerome wrote [1]: 'Feeling is in the heart, and the place of the heart is in the breast. One may enquire what is the location of the highest part of the soul. Plato put it in the head; Christ showed that it was in the heart when He said: "Blessed are the clean of heart." Pleasure and lust are in the liver' (*ep.* 64:1; CSEL 54:587). Augustine (*contra Iulianum* 2:30; PL 44:693) simply identifies heart and will; elsewhere he speaks (*tract.* 18:8 on Jn; PL 35:1540) of the heart first forming the words and then the hand writing them down, when a letter is being written. The Latin Fathers knew their Virgil (Aen. 6:675): *Si fert ita corde voluntas.*

It was natural for the Fathers to interpret the words of Ps 21:15 about the heart melting like wax as a prophecy of the Agony of Christ. Didymus in his commentary on the passage (PG 39:1281) says that this might happen to anyone who had to witness those whom he had begotten undergoing disasters; Christ's heart, being lovingly disposed towards His disciples (ἡ καρδία αὐτοῦ διακειμένη πόρς αὐτοὺς ἀγαπητικῶς) underwent this trial at the Agony. This remarkable passage shows that the assertion of Pius XII in his encyclical *Haurietis* (par. 26) that the Fathers 'never refer these same feelings (of Christ) to His physical heart in such a way as to point to it as a symbol of His boundless love' was somewhat too sweeping. Cyril of Alexandria used another of the 'heart' texts of the OT (Cant. 5:2; in his commentary, PG 69:1289) to refer to Christ: 'He sleeps on the cross, having accepted death for mankind; but His heart watches, for as God He has plundered Hades.' Here it is the divine love of Christ for the patriarchs (*see* DESCENT INTO HELL) that is envisaged, while Didymus saw the heart as symbol of the human love.

Though Origen, by reason of his view of the text of Jn 7:37, was precluded from an easy approach to this understanding of the heart of Christ, he reached it by another way. In the preface to his commentary on John (1:4:23; GCS 4:8) he says: 'It is certain that John may be described as having found rest on the heart which was pre-eminent in Jesus and upon a deep understanding of His doctrines, there seeking and examining the treasures of wisdom and knowledge that are hidden in Christ Jesus.' In commenting on Lev 10:14, where the priests were bidden to eat 'the breast of separation' alone, and in a holy place, he says (*hom.* 7:3 on Lev; GCS 29:380) that Christ and His apostles, the priests of the NT, were to partake of the fullest and most excellent revelation of the godhead. 'What is it that is set apart from all things, . . . save only the substance of the

[1] Sensus in corde est, habitaculum cordis in pectore. Quaeritur ubi sit animae principale. Plato in cerebro, Christus monstrat esse in corde: Beati mundo corde. Voluptas et concupiscentia in iecore.

Trinity ? ' He recurs to the passage in commenting on Cant 1:2 (*hom.* 1:3 on Cant ; GCS 33:32) : ' When one reclines on the breast of Jesus and enjoys some share in His affections, it is . . . His heart that speaks.'

III The medieval Church found it quite natural to continue this devotion, often in terms of the outpouring of grace. Thus Ludolph of Saxony (1295–1378) wrote that Christ received for us the wound of love upon the cross when His heart was pierced through by the shaft of an unconquerable love. The hymn : *Summi regis cor, aveto* (PL 184:1619) was composed at the same period (*c.*1230) by St Herman Joseph, a Premonstratensian canon of Steinfeld, who in another of his hymns speaks thus : ' Grant us the best wine from the bowl of Thy heart ' [1] (*Analecta hymnica*, 50:543). Where the East now differed from the West was in the Eastern reluctance to encourage any language that attributed the sending of the Holy Spirit to Christ. Hence what Lansberger (Lanspurgius) could write for Western readers about the heart of Christ, ' being opened to give us a proof of His infinite love ' and the wound in the heart being ' the gate of Paradise, the entrance to life and the fountain of grace ', could not be repeated in the East. Ambrose (*de spiritu sancto* 1:16:157 ; CSEL 79:81) had spoken of the Holy Spirit as the river proceeding from the side of Christ, as prophesied by Isaias,[2] but no parallel text was there to enlighten the East. St Bernard (PL 183:1072) could follow where Ambrose had led ; William of St Thierry (PL 180:225) could repeat what Augustine had said about the opening in the ark of Noah, but for the East there was no one to revive the ideas of Didymus or of Hippolytus.

The theology of St Bonaventure brought forward the idea that the Incarnation *in carne passibili* (in flesh that could suffer) was the consequence of Adam's sin, but that there would have been an Incarnation even without sin on man's part. From this ground it was easy to reach by speculation the idea that mankind owed a debt of reparation to Christ for His sufferings and for the piercing of His heart. This note of reparation was likewise somewhat foreign to the East, where the teaching of the *Didascalia* (in Connolly's edition, 192) that only the Jews were to weep for the death of Christ, while Christians should rejoice in His Resurrection, had long prevailed, being repeated in the *Apostolic Constitutions* (5:19:6). Bonaventure in the first chapter of the *Stimulus amoris*, to say nothing of the *Vitis mystica* (whether these works be his or another's), makes so much of the wounds of Christ that he establishes a pattern for medieval devotion, and what Gertrude and the two Mechtildes say in their meditations only amplifies and carries out what Bonaventure had expounded. The association of stigmata (*see* STIGMATIZATION) with some of those who meditated on the wounds of

Christ is perhaps not so significant as the fact that such stigmata are apparently lacking in the Eastern churches.

The *devotio moderna* (q.v.) did not diminish the force of the trend established by Bonaventure and the friars in the West but rather augmented it. One may note as significant that the Dominicans celebrated at least from the later Middle Ages a feast of the wound in the side of Christ, and the day fixed for this feast was the Friday after the octave of Corpus Christi. The Charterhouse of Cologne was a centre of the devotion where St Peter Canisius learnt it as a young man.

Theological reflection had been carried forward by St Thomas and others in a way that would make easier the ultimate justification of the devotion. Thus St Thomas (*Summa*, 3a:48:2@3), after showing that the satisfaction for sin rendered by Christ was not merely equal to the offence but superabundant, went on to show that, though sin might be mainly a matter of mind and will, while the satisfaction rendered was in the flesh of Christ, yet this did not disturb the balance, for the flesh of Christ was, by virtue of the hypostatic union, the flesh of God. This appeal to the hypostatic union was made long before there was any question of justifying the cult of the fleshly heart of Christ, and when the challenge *was* made (*see below*) the principle on which to base a reply was at hand. In *Summa*, 3a:15:4c the discussion of the ways in which the human soul of Christ could experience disturbance, both from physical pain and from sensitive appetite, helped towards an understanding of the Passion of Christ and an appreciation of the love He showed therein.

IV The private revelation to St Margaret Mary and the liturgical cult promoted by St John Eudes, though roughly contemporary, are not simply two aspects of one devotion. In 1668 and 1669 Eudes, whose spirituality was of the school of Bérulle (*see* BÉRULLE, INFLUENCE OF), was composing liturgical offices for a feast of the Sacred Heart. In 1671 Margaret Mary entered the Visitation convent at Paray-le-Monial. On 20 October 1672 the Eudist communities with official approval kept the first feast of the Sacred Heart. On 27 December 1673 Margaret Mary experienced her first communication from God. The Eudist devotion, as Bremond has pointed out, gave to the word ' heart ' almost the meaning of person, while for Margaret Mary the heart of Christ was primarily the sign and expression of His love. In Berullian fashion the Eudists turned first to the setting up of a feast of the Heart of Christ, just as Bérulle had planned a feast of Jesus. With the Visitandines the feast came later (in 1685 for the first time). The first publication of the Paray devotion came with the book by Fr Croiset in 1691, the year after the death of St Margaret Mary, and this was followed in 1694 by the work of Dom Le Masson, a compilation for the use of Carthusians, with many passages from their own mystics of earlier times. This work is still in print under the title of *Ancient devotions to the Sacred Heart*.

The reaction of Jansenism to the devotion was not

---

[1] Cordis Tui de catino
   principali da de vino.

[2] Ergo flumen est Spiritus sanctus, et flumen maximum quod secundum Hebraeos de Iesu fluxit internis, ut ore Eseiae accepimus prophetatum.

immediate ; other preoccupations saw to it that the attack on the *Cordicolae* did not come until about the middle of the 18th cent. It was then that the legend was circulated that the whole devotion sprang from an English Puritan, Thomas Goodwin, whose book *The Heart of Christ in heaven towards sinners on earth* (1642) was alleged to have become known to Fr de la Colombière when he was in England (from 13 October 1676 to 4 January 1679) and to have been fed back by him into the mind of a visionary at Paray. This myth did not take an exact account of dates, but more serious was its failure to allow for the immense difference between the two devotions. Goodwin was a stout predestination preacher and he shows it in his book : ' The idea of that beauty is so imprinted on His heart which from everlasting was ordained you, that He will never cease to sanctifie and cleanse you ' (111). ' It is impossible to breake this knot and to take off My heart from you, as My Fathers from Me ' (26). The text that Goodwin most favoured was Jn 13:1, and his whole purpose is shown in his sub-title : *a treatise demonstrating the gracious* disposition and tender affection of Christ in His humane nature now in glory, unto *His members.* . . . It might escape notice that ' members ' is a restrictive term, but the passages cited show that it must be. Goodwin in writing about the heart of Christ may have drawn his inspiration—though not his theology—from Julian of Norwich or some other English medieval source. A priest-prisoner (Blessed Henry Walpole) in the Tower of London had carved a representation of the Heart and nails on the wall of his cell, and a similar ornament was engraved on the wall of the English Jesuit house at Chévremont near Liége in 1653.

Pius XII, in his encyclical *Haurietis* (par. 52), is at some pains to show that it was not the visions of Paray that really caused the devotion to the Sacred Heart. ' They added nothing new to Catholic doctrine.' Their importance was in this, that by them Christ wished to attract men to contemplate the mystery of His love for mankind. It has become a fashion (cf. K. Rahner, *Visions and Prophecies*) to speak of private revelations as commands from God addressed by charismatics to the Church that give new emphasis to old doctrines, but in this case Pius XII does not regard the visions of Paray as a command. He shows that the institution of the feast (1765) was to gratify the faithful and not to obey any private revelation. No doubt the faithful had been responsive to the invitation contained in the revelations, but with that responsiveness went also the operation of the *sensus fidelium*, by which multitudes of those who were led, some more and some less, by the seven gifts of the Holy Ghost were able to judge that this invitation was not a danger to their faith. The action of the Church in dealing with this private revelation might be thought to have exemplified beforehand the rules laid down in the Second Vatican Council for such *charismata* (*constitutio de ecclesia*, II:12).

The condemnation by Pius VI of the Jansenist synod of Pistoia dealt with this devotion in three paragraphs (D 1561–3). It is to be noted that the most grave theological qualification attached to these condemnations was that of *temeraria* (D 1562), a word used to indicate that the opposite doctrine was ' bordering on a matter of faith ' (*fidei proximum*), and here the purpose was to assert that the devotion ' as understood by the Holy See ' was in that category. The Polish bishops who had petitioned the Holy See for the feast which was granted in 1765 had asked for a cult of the Sacred Heart, ' not only as the symbol of all the interior affections of Christ, but as it is in itself '. This is said in their *Memoriale*, 116, whereas the Holy See (cf. the encyclical of Pius XII, 53), then and later, accepted the one (' as the symbol ') without the other (' as it is in itself ').

If one were to wonder why the providence of God should have waited until 1673 before giving this invitation to the faithful to take part in a development of doctrine through devotion, it may be suggested that the function of the heart in the human body was just then coming to be better understood. Goodwin in his book (178) following earlier ideas says : ' The use of blood and spirits is as to nourish so to affect the heart, by their moving to and fro when the soul is affected.' William Harvey's discovery of the circulation of the blood was not really before the public until 1651, and men's views about the heart ' as it is in itself ' were gradually changing at the time of the revelations. The ' animal spirits ' of Cartesian philosophy were being discarded slowly.

V The papal encyclicals of Leo XIII (*Annum sacrum*, 25 May 1899), of Pius XI (*Miserentissimus Redemptor*, 8 May 1928 and *Caritate Christi compulsi*, 3 May 1932) and of Pius XII (*Haurietis aquas*, 15 May 1956) consolidated and clarified the theological argument that had gone on about the devotion in the 19th cent. Leo XIII was mainly concerned with the consecration of the world to the Sacred Heart, and Pius XI with the moral reform that the practice of reparation to the Sacred Heart might bring about. Pius XII stated with authority the theology of the devotion in great detail. The object of the devotion was the heart of Christ as the ' principal token and sign ' (27) of the three-fold love of Christ for men. The three-fold love comprised the divine love ' which He shares with the Father and the Holy Ghost ', the spiritual human love infused into His human soul and the sensitive emotion or affection of human soul and body. This three-fold distinction can be found in the theological treatise of Cardinal Billot (*de Verbo Incarnato*, 7th edition, 1927, 365) and corresponds for two of its members to the distinction psychologists make between sentiment and emotion ; divine love is naturally outside their province. The heart is said (12) to be ' the natural sign or symbol' (*naturalis index seu symbolus*) of love ; it is ' a sharer in and natural and most expressive symbol ' of love (*particeps atque naturale ac significantissimum symbolum*, 42). It is conceded (58) that the heart is not a formal image, i.e. a perfect and adequate sign, of the divine love in Christ, but it is urged that starting from the sensitive level a certain anagogic process can be accomplished which would lead to at least a partial understanding of the high mystery of divine love. The encyclical excludes the Berullian notion of the heart as symbol of the Person of Christ and confines itself to the symbolizing of love.

Since the appearance of the encyclical of 1956 there have been some commentaries upon it and one small controversy. A Spanish theologian, Jose Calveras SJ, took up the position that the true object of the devotion was not the heart of flesh but the pictorial image of that heart surmounted by a cross and marked with the lance-wound. A careful examination of the language of the encyclical by J. Filograssi SJ led him, however, to conclude that Calveras had not made out his case. It seems to have rested on a false historicism which overvalued the earliest representations of the Sacred Heart and not to have recognized that the Church in commending this devotion is insisting on a physical fact, a heart of flesh, just as much as in her witness to the Resurrection she insists on a body of flesh and blood. The anagogic value of the devotion may win support for it in the Eastern churches, while its new-found Scriptural bases may commend it to the evangelical Protestants who themselves in the 18th cent. recovered the true sense of Jn 7:37.

Bibliography. H. Rahner SJ, Flumina de ventre Christi, in Bi 22 (1941) 269–302 and 367–403 ; symposium-volume Le Coeur (1950) in the Études Carmelitaines ; J. Bainvel SJ, Devotion to the Sacred Heart (Eng. trans. 1924) ; J. Filograssi SJ, L'oggetto del culto al Cuore di Gesu, in Gregorianum (40) (1959) 271–96 ; J. Stierli SJ, The Heart of the Saviour (written before the encyclical, but Eng. trans. 1958); I. Le Masson O. Carth, Ancient devotions to the Sacred Heart (4th English edition, 1953) ; the encyclical of Pius XII is published in an English version with numbered paragraphs by the Catholic Truth Society (November 1956) ; F. Courtney SJ, The encyclical Haurietis, in CR 42 (1957) 332–42 (where it is shown that the views of K. Rahner, expressed in Stierli's book, are antiquated by the encyclical) ; M. J. Donnelly SJ, The encyclical on the Sacred Heart, in TS 18 (1957) 17–40 (the fullest commentary on the encyclical) ; *C. H. Turner, On the punctuation of Jn 7:37–38, in JTS 24 (1923) 66–70, where the basic research was done on that text.

J. H. C.

HEAVEN The central experience of heaven is the beatific vision, which has been treated already (see BEATIFIC VISION). This article will discuss (I) the negative and positive approach to the idea of heaven, (II) the nature of the contact with the Infinite, which is (III) immediate and personal, and which involves (IV) love as well as knowledge. The nature of the happiness of heaven (V) and its corporate character (VI) will be considered. The scriptural notion (VII) of the heavenly banquet, the inequalities of heaven (VIII) and its location (IX) will then be briefly examined.

I The negative and positive approach to the idea of heaven need careful attention, for the teaching of the Church, drawn from Scripture and Tradition, has been amplified and even distorted by the popular imagination of many lands in the course of the Christian centuries until some trivial detail (such as the use of harps in heaven) becomes its predominant feature in the popular mind. Much of the abuse directed against the Church's teaching on this matter is really aimed at one or other of these distortions.

Negatively, heaven means release from all those drawbacks and disadvantages that hem us in here, making of this life a valley of tears, where

Our sincerest laughter
With some pain is fraught.

In heaven there will be no more sorrow, suffering, disease and squalor ; no more criticism, treachery, cruelty ; no more sin and enticement to sin ; no more war with its rumour and aftermath ; no more time robbing one of strength, youth, beauty, friends. St Paul is our warrant for thinking of heaven in this fashion : 'This light and momentary affliction brings with it a reward multiplied every way, loading us with everlasting glory ; if only we will fix our eyes on what is unseen, not on what we can see. What we can see lasts but for a moment ; what is unseen is eternal' (2 Cor 4:17 ; Kn : cf. Rom 8:18).

Positively, heaven means everlasting companionship with the most sterling of friends, reunion with loved ones, close association with the angels and saints, with their Queen, Mother of God who is also spiritual mother of men. Above all, it means meeting our 'Comrade-Commander', Christ. This aspect of heaven drew Paul so forcibly that he spoke of his longing to strike camp here and 'be with Christ, a better thing, much more than a better thing' (Phil 1:23 Kn). About the year 100 Paul's aspiration is echoed dramatically by St Ignatius of Antioch, when he pleads to be allowed to shed his blood for Christ : 'Come, fire and cross and battles with wild beasts, crackings of bones, mangling of limbs, grindings of the whole body, foul chastisements of the devil upon me—provided only I gain Jesus Christ' (Rom 5). The boon we beg from Our Lady in the Hail, holy Queen is that after the banishment of this earth she would show us Jesus, the sacred fruit of her womb. The Canon of the Mass prays that God would admit us to the company of the Apostles and martyrs.

II Contact with the Infinite. Though we hesitate to articulate it even to ourselves, we nevertheless fear the everlastingness of heaven. Here on earth much of our time goes in the pursuit of novelties ; we find it hard to sustain over a long period an unbroken interest in the same persons and things. Consequently we tend to dread a contact with God that will run on never-endingly. This unvoiced anxiety is born of our failure to appreciate the infinitude of God. It is because heaven puts us in touch with a peerless Being of boundless perfection that it can never pall on nor weary us.

In the early years of her reign Queen Victoria would summon Lord Melbourne to Buckingham Palace, to pass the evening with her. Many envied

Melbourne his intimacy with Victoria. He, in fact, found those evenings dull and leaden. For Victoria, despite her manifold gifts, was not a being of 'infinite variety' which custom could not stale. So Lord Melbourne would doze on his cushions under the very eyes of his Sovereign.

All created perfection is essentially fragmentary, piecemeal. What is loving is not always truthful ; what is strong is often despotic ; the man of action is seldom the contemplative ; fair is sometimes foul ; might is not necessarily right ; kindliness easily slips into slackness, thrift into avarice, industry and application into a heedless rush to get rich. Male and female differ : one lacks the typical qualities of the other. The creature as such is marked by limitation.

God alone is perfect without flaw or blemish or stint ; the fountain-head of the beauty, truth, wisdom, love, strength that enthrall us in creatures. Consequently, to come into the presence of the Infinite in heaven will be the most absorbing, dynamic, electrifying experience the human mind can possibly enjoy. Before so limitless a Being the mind will be ceaselessly, throughout all eternity, on the quiver with wonder and adoration.

III Immediate and personal contact. This heavenly contact with the Infinite will be immediate and personal. It is easy to assess the difference between an indirect and a personal contact with others. The historian may know much about Englishmen under Edward III ; but such contact, gleaned from records, remains meagre and jejune as against his flesh-and-blood associations with colleagues or students. The discerning reader can gather much about the character of the authors he studies ; but once again his knowledge is inferential, impersonal, less satisfying than the vital, immediate contact he has with his family around the breakfast-table.

On earth our contact with God is always indirect or mediate, never direct and immediate. We can learn about Him from the things He has made : from stars and sunsets, lakes and trees, from life in all its shapes and hues, from human nature in its ideals and virtues. We thus fashion for ourselves a knowledge that, though sound, remains impersonal. This basic contact is enriched a hundred-fold by what God has told us about Himself, speaking through the lips of prophets and especially of His only-begotten Son, Jesus Christ. Yet even this revealed knowledge of God fails to yield direct contact. We seize God only in the twilight of faith, never in the golden sunlight of heaven.

IV Love not only knowledge. The divine encounter of heaven should never be described exclusively in terms of knowing ; for it necessarily involves also a loving possession of God with its sequel of joy : 'Come and share the joy of thy Lord' (Mt 25:21, Kn). It is not just an affair of the mind ; it is also an affair of the heart.

It is indeed of defined faith that the blessed will see the divine *essence* (D 530). Nevertheless we should not beguile ourselves into picturing the life of heaven

as a critical appraisal of a celestial abstraction, as an aloof, dispassionate contemplation of God, as of some almighty museum-piece. The divine essence, as the Council of Florence and Pius XII hint (D 693 and 2290), means the Triune God. Heaven, at its summit, consists in a luminous and loving union with the 'three person'd God'. It entails the immediate self-dedication of the human being to Father, Son and Holy Ghost, each of whom has first loved and given Himself to the near-nothingness of man.

V The happiness of heaven is far above the unaided reach of man. The pagan philosophers of antiquity realized that true happiness involves a marriage between what is highest in man and what is best outside him, i.e. some form of intellectual association with God. But the beatitude brought by Christ is divine and therefore outside man's orbit : 'things no eye has seen, no ear has heard, no human heart conceived, the welcome God has prepared for those who love Him' (I Cor 2:9, Kn). Abbot Vonier has pointed out that the concept of heaven is closely linked with the theology of the Incarnation, with the mystery of the Son of God coming from heaven to dwell upon earth and then returning to His Father. Heaven for a Christian is a participation in the glory of the Son of God (Rom 8:17).

This happiness is so transcendent that it cannot come about in one who is not first divinized by the Spirit of adoption of sons (Gal 4:6–7 ; Rom 8:14–18). Grace as the *inchoatio gloriae* (*Summa*, 1–2ae:69:2c and 114:3@3) or first phase of the life of glory is described by St Paul as the earnest of the final settlement (2 Cor 1:22 and 5:5 ; Eph 1:14 ; Rom 8:14–18). In I Cor 13:11–12 it is suggested that growth from childhood to man's estate is comparable to the passage from this life to heaven. John (3:36) is prepared to say that everlasting life has already begun for the follower of Christ. The Thomistic doctrine was adopted by Leo XIII (encyclical *Divinum illud*, in ASS 29 [1896] 653) and is echoed by Pius XII (D 2290). St Thomas (*Summa*, 2–2ae:24:3@2 ; de Veritate 27:5@6 ; *Summa*, 1–2ae:111:3@2) is concerned to deny that the differences between grace and glory are generic, specific or even numerical. Grace and glory are one and the selfsame reality, seen at two stages of maturation, and even the classifying of the beatific vision as essential happiness and the resurrection of the flesh as accidental somewhat obscures the NT emphasis on the harmony of full beatitude.

A childless sovereign may adopt heirs, and this of his mere bounty. The most unremitting feudal service on the part of one of his barons, while it may earn a man certain proportionate honours, can never entitle him to aspire to a reward wholly beyond the reasonable expectations of vassal—such as royal adoptive sonship, admission into the family-circle of the king.

As mere creatures, if we give God a lifelong loyal service, we may justly claim some reward, some contact with Him beyond the grave, some unfading crown of glory. But it would be effrontery for us to demand a share in that height of intimacy with the Father which is the exclusive natural right of the only-begotten Son. Nevertheless this, in fact, is the heaven thrown open to us by Christ. And we reach it not through any legal fiction (such as is, in last resort, all human adoption), not merely by being reckoned sons of God, but by becoming such in very truth (1 Jn 3:1), through re-birth worked by water and the Holy Ghost.

VI Corporate bliss. Heaven means not only supernatural, but also *corporate*, bliss. In the Doomsday-scene of Mt 25:31–46, one's eternal destiny hinges on one's behaviour towards Christ in others—selfish or unselfish. Those who locked themselves away from others in the dungeon of their own egoism are condemned to hell; those who opened their hearts to others in charity are rewarded with heaven. Hell, then, is solitary confinement; heaven, by contrast, is solidarity with others, communal felicity.

The working out of God's redemptive plan on earth should prepare us for this gregarious character of heaven. In both OT and NT God lodges his mercy first and foremost in the People, the Community as partner to his Alliance. The individual reaps his harvest of graces as a member of this select Society, this *Communio Sanctorum*. The sacramental character of Baptism makes us members of Christ and of His Church, His Mystical Body (*see* COM-MUNION OF SAINTS). But this membership entails precisely and at once fellowship with all others likewise dedicated to Christ. The Church is built out of the fellowship of Christians which has its roots in the unity of each believer with the Father in Christ. The Church Militant is the one Ark of salvation, the authentic way to partake of the Redemption and to be in Christ Jesus; she holds for us the treasures of the Holy Ghost and bridges the gap between earth and heaven. Her *communio sanctorum* leads on to, keeps in touch with, the *communio sanctorum* of the Church Triumphant—a consoling truth put before us by the *Communicantes*-prayer of the Canon of the Mass. And just as grace and sanctification here on earth come in principle through belonging to the 'holy people of God', so joy and glory hereafter come in and through membership of the group of the blessed, the heavenly flock of the elect (Apoc 21:3). The priest, as he stretches his hands over the *oblata* at Mass, begs the Father through Christ to appoint that we be reckoned in the *flock* of his elect: '. . . *in electorum tuorum jubeas GREGE numerari* . . .'

VII Heavenly banquet. Most of the aspects of heaven underlined above can be admirably epito-mized under the imagery of a banquet or wedding-feast—the imagery which Our Lord, in fact, used to convey His great teachings about heaven (Mt 8:11–13; 22:1–4; 25:1–12 and parallels). The appositeness of this figure may be lost on us Westerners with our habits of abstract thought. We need to make an effort at reflection if it is to make the impact on us that Our Lord designed it to make.

Men tend to honour high occasions by a meal eaten in common. There is inevitably the solemn repast when they sign a treaty or gather to celebrate a victory or to plan future policies; when they set out on long journeys or return home. So it is for birthdays and burials, for betrothals, weddings and christenings; or at the conclusion of a ritual sacri-fice. It is the practice of both upper and lower levels of society, of both sophisticated and primitive civilizations. It is a feature of Arab culture today, just as it was one thousand years ago.

The theory behind the meal eaten in company is that it outwardly manifests and strengthens the moral bond uniting the table-companions. Once a man has accepted an invitation to sit down at the same table, in the same spirit, under the same roof and presidency as other men, he must, by that very fact, regard them as his friends and become their ally. He has forged a bond of brotherhood between himself and them. He has knit them to himself by ties of trust and peace. Animosities, treacheries, cruelties are cast out by virtue of the entertainment shared. Or, if they persist, they are double-dyed in malice; they are coloured with sacrilege (cf. Ambrose, *de virginibus* 3:6:26; PL 16:227).

The OT forcefully emphasizes the symbolism of the meal taken in common; so, likewise, does the NT. During His mortal life Our Lord ate and drank with all and sundry. Indeed He made a special point of dining openly with publicans and sinners. The Pharisees were not slow to divine His meaning. They grumbled and protested to His disciples (Mt 9:11). He overheard them and bluntly declared His purpose: 'I did not come to call just, but sinners'. Our Lord made it plain that His dining with sinners was an action fraught with symbolic value. It was a deliberately planned proclamation of an essential feature of His mission. He had come forth from the Father and taken flesh to manifest the mercy of God, casting down the barriers of sin (Lk 15).

By teaching about heaven under the imagery of feasting and entertainment, Our Lord suggests several themes for our meditation: (i) that heaven is not a stiff and frightening audience with God but a warm and friendly union with a most clement and loving Father who wants us to be at our ease with Him, entering into His joy; (ii) that in going to God the individual is not isolated from his fellows, but, on the contrary, his heaven involves, and is enhanced by, the conviviality of companionship; (iii) that heaven is a reward of surpassing munifi-cence, of gratuitous, divine initiative and condescen-sion. If a commoner dines at the royal table in the intimacy of the royal family, it is because the prince has spontaneously manifested, in the most expressive way at his command, his desire for an exchange of familiarity and friendship.

VIII Unequal glory. It is of defined faith that the glory of the elect is unequal, that it is scaled accord-ing to their merits (D 693 and 842). This truth is also, directly or indirectly, attested to in Scripture (1 Cor 3:8; 2 Jn 8; 2 Cor 9:6; Apoc 22:12;

Jn 14:2). It is, besides, what one is led to expect by reflection both on the selective love of God and the more or less generous response it meets with from man. In the whole affair of man's salvation God takes the initiative ; He chooses to love some more, some less. Historically this is realized in the greater or less lavishness with which He distributes His favours, whether visible or invisible : some are actual members of His Church, others are not ; some receive no sacrament or only one ; others, many ; some, even non-Christians, are loaded with precious hidden gifts of faith, hope and charity, others are much less richly endowed. Confronted with God's sovereign overtures, some welcome them with the utmost gladness, while others remain reserved and surly, refusing to co-operate. The graces of adoption (as we have seen) form the bed-rock requirement to qualify for heaven. Our glory in heaven, then, will be fuller or scantier in pro-portion to our energy in cultivating these graces of adoption on earth. To put it another way : through divine adoption one enters into an I-Thou relation-ship with Father, Son and Holy Ghost, each of whom dwells in the grace-endowed soul. This encounter between the individual and the Trinity is eminently personal and, therefore, unique. The self-communi-cation of the Triune God to one creature is never reproduced in exactly the same way elsewhere, precisely because in all cases (and, please God, they are legion) a harmony of personal love and friendship is established. The surrender of person to person in earthly love, and much more the self-communication of a created person to the almighty three-personed Lover is necessarily matchless and never-to-be-repeated. The scale of glory in heaven corresponds in each instance with the eagerness or slackness of this self-communication or grace-relationship on earth. When we affirmed (in VI above) the com-munal character of heaven we were not implying that glory was mass-produced, a sort of celestial 'general issue', that (army-like) would ignore personality. The blessed are indeed joyous together —and this is the inevitable upshot of charity and its expansiveness. Nevertheless each one's joy is his own, issuing from the core of his being and entailing an inimitable I-Thou dialogue with Father, Son and Holy Ghost.

IX Heaven—a place ? Is heaven a place ? First and foremost it is a state or condition. But, at least since Our Lord's Ascension when tangible, physical, though glorified, bodies began to dwell there, heaven is a place. To this notion, Scripture and Tradition have accustomed us especially when they speak about *going up into* heaven (*see* ASCENSION IV). Of course such phrases must be treated with caution. We are earth-bound creatures—a fact reflected in every word of our language. Even if heaven were only a state, we would find it a sheer impossibility to descant upon it for long without being betrayed into some localizing phrase. However, it would be naïve to understand 'going up into heaven' in that crassly materialistic sense in which the shoppers in a city skyscraper hear the liftman's cry of 'going up'. Besides, the earth is round, not flat ; what is for us 'going up' is 'going down' for the dwellers at the antipodes. When *place* is applied to heaven on the one hand and to Sydney or Paris on the other, the sense will be partly the same but also partly different. This happens with many of our concepts. For example, when one speaks of rose-bushes, horses, the Prime Minister, an angel or the Holy Ghost as *living* ; or when one predicates *body* of corruptible and of glorified flesh. Heaven, therefore, is rightly de-scribed as a place, but one at many removes from places on the earth's crust. Its whereabouts cannot be plotted in the reference-terms of military maps ; it is immune from the disabilities attaching to places here : fire, erosion, drought, flooding, war. It is a place of astonishing perfection, beauty and happiness.

Bibliography. St Thomas, *Summa contra Gentiles*, 3:26–41 and 47–64 ; St Augustine, *de civ. Dei*, 22:29 ; *conf.* 9:10 ; J. P. Arendzen, *The Church triumphant* (1928) ; V. de Broglie sj, *de fine ultimo humanae vitae* (1948) ; R. Guardini, *The Last Things* (Eng. trans. 1954) ; G. Panneton, *Le ciel* (1955) ; K. Rahner sj, Zur Hermeneutik eschatologischer Aussagen, in ZKT 82 (1960) 137–58 ; J. P. Kenny sj, Heavenly Banquet, in AER 146 (1962) 47–57 ; J. Daniélou sj, Les répas de la Bible et leur signification, in *Maison Dieu* 18 (1949) 7–34 ; R. Troisfontaines, Le ciel, in NRT 82 (1960) 225–47 ; M. J. Scheeben, *The Mysteries of Christianity* (Eng. trans. 1946), esp. 651–66 on the beatific vision ; M. Schmaus, *Von den letzten Dingen* (1948) ; I. F. Sagues, *De novissimis* (1953) being vol. IV of *Sacrae theologiae summa* ; A. Vonier, Heaven, in Cambridge Summer School symposium *Man and Eternity* (1937).

J. P. K.